Lecture Notes in Computer Science   12248

More information about this series at http://www.springer.com/series/7410

Joseph K. Liu · Hui Cui (Eds.)

Information Security and Privacy

25th Australasian Conference, ACISP 2020
Perth, WA, Australia, November 30 – December 2, 2020
Proceedings

 Springer

Editors
Joseph K. Liu ⓘ
Faculty of Information Technology
Monash University
Clayton, VIC, Australia

Hui Cui
Murdoch University
Perth, WA, Australia

ISSN 0302-9743   ISSN 1611-3349 (electronic)
Lecture Notes in Computer Science
ISBN 978-3-030-55303-6   ISBN 978-3-030-55304-3   (eBook)
https://doi.org/10.1007/978-3-030-55304-3

LNCS Sublibrary: SL4 – Security and Cryptology

This Springer imprint is published by the registered company Springer Nature Switzerland AG
The registered company address is: Gewerbestrasse 11, 6330 Cham, Switzerland

Preface

This volume contains the papers presented at the 25th Australasian Conference on Information Security and Privacy (ACISP 2020), which was held as a virtual online conference, due to COVID-19. ACISP is an annual international forum for worldwide researchers and industry experts to present and discuss the latest research, trends, breakthroughs, and challenges in the domain of information security, privacy, and cybersecurity.

This year we received 151 submissions of excellent quality from around the world. Each paper was reviewed by at least three Program Committee members, and on average 3.7 reviews were received for each paper. Although there are many good papers submitted, in order to maintain the high quality of ACISP we can only select a very small portion of them to be included in the proceeding. After extensive discussion among the Program Committee, we decided to accept 31 full papers and 5 short papers.

We would like to express our thanks to all Program Committee members. Without their hard effort in reviewing papers in such a short time, the conference would not have been successful. We would also like to thank our general co-chairs, Kevin Wong and Jun Zhang, our publication co-chairs, Weizhi Meng and Shi-Feng Sun, and our web chair, Yu Wang. They all devoted a large amount of time for the preparation of this conference.

November 2020

Joseph K. Liu
Hui Cui

Organization

General Co-chairs

Kevin Wong   Murdoch University, Australia
Jun Zhang   Swinburne University of Technology, Australia

Program Co-chairs

Joseph K. Liu   Monash University, Australia
Hui Cui   Murdoch University, Australia

Program Committee

Cristina Alcaraz   Universidad de Málaga, Spain
Rizwan Asghar   The University of Auckland, New Zealand
Elias Athanasopoulos   University of Cyprus, Cyprus
Man Ho Au   The University of Hong Kong, Hong Kong, China
Joonsang Baek   University of Wollongong, Australia
Zubair Baig   Deakin University, Australia
Zhenzhen Bao   Nanyang Technological University, Singapore
Lynn Batten   Deakin University, Australia
Levente Buttyán   Budapest University of Technology and Economics, Hungary
Stefano Calzavara   Università Ca' Foscari Venezia, Italy
Sudipta Chattopadhyay   Singapore University of Technology and Design, Singapore
Chao Chen   Swinburne University of Technology, Australia
Fei Chen   Shenzhen University, China
Jiageng Chen   Central China Normal University, China
Rongmao Chen   National University of Defense Technology, China
Shiping Chen   Data 61, Australia
Ting Chen   University of Electronic Science and Technology of China, China
Xiaofeng Chen   Xidian University, China
Alexander Chepurnoy   IOHK, Hong Kong, China
Vincent Cheval   LORIA, France
Raymond Choo   The University of Texas at San Antonio, USA
Cheng-Kang Chu   Huawei, Singapore
Nicolas Courtois   University College London, UK
Cas Cremers   CISPA, Germany
Hui Cui   Murdoch University, Australia
Jannik Dreier   Université de Lorraine, France

Alex Malozemoff	Galois, Inc., USA
Daniel Masny	Visa Research, USA
Weizhi Meng	Technical University of Denmark, Denmark
Bart Mennink	Radboud University, The Netherlands
Chris Mitchell	Royal Holloway, University of London, UK
Veelasha Moonsamy	Radboud University, The Netherlands
Yi Mu	Fujian Normal University, China
Khoa Nguyen	Nanyang Technological University, Singapore
Josef Pieprzyk	Data 61, Australia
Thomas Plantard	University of Wollongong, Australia
Vidy Potdar	Curtin University, Australia
Fatemeh Rezaeibagha	Murdoch University, Australia
Tamara Rezk	Inria, France
Ruben Rios	Universidad de Málaga, Spain
Na Ruan	Shanghai Jiaotong University, China
Sushmita Ruj	Data 61, Australia
Giovanni Russello	The University of Auckland, New Zealand
Amin Sakzad	Monash University, Australia
Bagus Santoso	The University of Electro-Communications, Japan
Jun Shao	Zhejiang Gongshang University, China
Taeshik Shon	Ajou University, South Korea
Leonie Simpson	Queensland University of Technology, Australia
Jill Slay	La Trobe University, Australia
Chunhua Su	University of Aizu, Japan
Shi-Feng Sun	Monash University, Australia
Shamik Sural	Indian Institute of Technology, Kharagpur, India
Willy Susilo	University of Wollongong, Australia
Davor Svetinovic	Khalifa University of Science and Technology, UAE
Pawel Szalachowski	Singapore University of Technology and Design, Singapore
Qiang Tang	New Jersey Institute of Technology, USA
Haibo Tian	Sun Yat-sen University, China
Damien Vergnaud	Sorbonne Université, France
Petros Wallden	University of Edinburgh, UK
Cong Wang	City University of Hong Kong, Hong Kong, China
Ding Wang	Peking University, China
Guilin Wang	Huawei, Singapore
Jianfeng Wang	Xidian University, China
Yu Wang	Guangzhou University, China
Ziyuan Wang	Swinburne University of Technology, Australia
Ian Welch	Victoria University of Wellington, New Zealand
Sheng Wen	Swinburne University of Technology, Australia
Steffen Wendzel	Hochschule Worms, Germany
Qianhong Wu	Beihang University, China
Jason Minhui Xue	The University of Adelaide, Australia
Toshihiro Yamauchi	Okayama University, Japan

Guomin Yang	University of Wollongong, Australia
Yanjiang Yang	Huawei, Singapore
Wun-she Yap	Universiti Tunku Abdul Rahman, Malaysia
Xun Yi	RMIT, Australia
Jiangshan Yu	Monash University, Australia
Shui Yu	University of Technology Sydney, Australia
Yong Yu	Shaanxi Normal University, China
Xingliang Yuan	Monash University, Australia
Tsz Hon Yuen	The University of Hong Kong, Hong Kong, China
Bingsheng Zhang	ZheJiang University, China
Jun Zhang	Swinburne University of Technology, Australia

Additional Reviewers

Muhammad Shabbir Abbasi	Runchao Han
Isaac Agudo	Shuai Han
Mohammed Alshaboti	Junaid Haseeb
Xinbo Ban	Qinwen Hu
Adam Bobowski	Shabnam Kasra Kermanshahi
Marcus Botacin	Andrei Kelarev
Cailing Cai	Yoonseok Ko
Fabricio Ceschin	Patryk Kozieł
Long Chen	Przemysław Kubiak
Xiao Chen	Andrea Lesavourey
Yijin Chen	Na Li
Yucheng Chen	Shun Li
Haotian Cheng	Xinyu Li
Chengjun Lin	Yannan Li
Chitchanok Chuengsatiansup	Yiming Li
Peter Chvojka	Zengpeng Li
Handong Cui	Chao Lin
Nan Cui	Hsiao-Ying Lin
Dipayan Das	Lin Liu
Gareth T. Davies	Shigang Liu
Jan Peter Drees	Xiangyu Liu
Dung Hoang Duong	Zian Liu
Mohamad El Laz	Xingye Lu
Muhammed Esgin	Junwei Luo
Xuejun Fan	Lin Lyu
Hanwen Feng	Jinhua Ma
Jun Gao	Florette Martinez
Song Gao	Subhra Mazumdar
Jordy Gennissen	Laurens Porzenheim
Jiale Guo	Xianrui Qin
Kevin Guo	Rodrigo Roman

Partha Sarathi Roy
Laltu Sardar
Joshua Scarsbrook
Vishal Sharma
Nasrin Sohrabi
Yongcheng Song
Je Sen Teh
Song Tian
Yangguang Tian
Ming Wan
Haoyang Wang
Jianfeng Wang
Yi Wang
Yunling Wang
Ge Wu
Lei Wu
Shengmin Xu

Liang Xue
Rupeng Yang
S. J. Yang
Zhichao Yang
Wei-Chuen Yau
Zuoxia Yu
Fangguo Zhang
Lei Zhang
Mingyue Zhang
Xiaoyu Zhang
Yanjun Zhang
Raymond Zhao
Yanqi Zhao
Yanwei Zhou
Rahman Ziaur
Vincent Zucca
Cong Zuo

Contents

Post-quantum Cryptography

Lattice Blind Signatures with Forward Security

Huy Quoc Le[1,4]($\boxtimes$), Dung Hoang Duong[1]($\boxtimes$), Willy Susilo[1],
Ha Thanh Nguyen Tran[2], Viet Cuong Trinh[3], Josef Pieprzyk[4,5],
and Thomas Plantard[1]

[1] Institute of Cybersecurity and Cryptology,
School of Computing and Information Technology, University of Wollongong,
Northfields Avenue, Wollongong, NSW 2522, Australia
qhl576@uowmail.edu.au, {hduong,wsusilo,thomaspl}@uow.edu.au
[2] Department of Mathematical and Physical Sciences,
Concordia University of Edmonton,
7128 Ada Blvd NW, Edmonton AB T5B 4E4, Canada
hatran1104@gmail.com
[3] Faculty of Information and Communication Technology, Hong Duc University,
565 Quang Trung, Thanh Hoa, Vietnam
trinhvietcuong@hdu.edu.vn
[4] CSIRO Data61, Sydney, NSW, Australia
Josef.Pieprzyk@data61.csiro.au
[5] Institute of Computer Science, Polish Academy of Sciences, Warsaw, Poland

Abstract. Blind signatures play an important role in both electronic cash and electronic voting systems. Blind signatures should be secure against various attacks (such as signature forgeries). The work puts a special attention to secret key exposure attacks, which totally break digital signatures. Signatures that resist secret key exposure attacks are called forward secure in the sense that disclosure of a current secret key does not compromise past secret keys. This means that forward-secure signatures must include a mechanism for secret-key evolution over time periods. This paper gives a construction of the *first* blind signature that is forward secure. The construction is based on the SIS assumption in the lattice setting. The core techniques applied are the binary tree data structure for the time periods and the trapdoor delegation for the key-evolution mechanism.

Keywords: Key exposure · Forward security · Blind signatures · Lattice-based cryptography · SIS assumption

1 Introduction

Key exposure is one of most serious dangers for both secret and public key cryptography. When secret keys are disclosed, cryptographic systems using them are completely broken. Fortunately, there are some solutions that can be used to

© Springer Nature Switzerland AG 2020
J. K. Liu and H. Cui (Eds.): ACISP 2020, LNCS 12248, pp. 3–22, 2020.
https://doi.org/10.1007/978-3-030-55304-3_1

mitigate secret-key exposure. They are summarized in [6]. Among many possible solutions, forward security seems to be the most promising when trying to minimize a damage caused by secret-key disclosure.

For cryptographic protocols, forward security guarantees that even if the current session key is compromised by an adversary, she gets no information about previous session keys. This means that past sessions are still secure. The notion of *forward security* has been coined by Günther in [15] and later used in [12] to evaluate security of authenticated key-exchange protocols. Note that the authors of [12] and [15] call it *forward secrecy*. Ross Anderson in [5] extends the notion for digital signatures.

Blind signatures, introduced by Chaum [10], allow users to obtain message signatures from a signer without leaking information about message contents. Blind signatures are indispensable in many applications such as electronic cash [23, Section 1] and electronic voting protocols [18]. For such security-critical applications, one would expect blind signatures to be resistant against key disclosure. An obvious solution is to incorporate forward security into blind signatures. There are many works such as [11,13,17] that follow this line of investigation. All solutions published so far rely on number-theoretic assumptions and consequently are insecure against quantum adversaries.

Related Works. Bellare and Milner investigate secret-key exposure of digital signatures in their Crypto99 paper [6]. They formulate a security model and define forward-secure digital signatures. They also design their forward-secure signature assuming intractability of integer factorization. Abdalla and Reyzin [1], and Itkis and Reyzin [16] improve efficiency the Bellare-Miner signature. The work of Duc et al. [13] is the first, which investigates forward security in the context of blind signatures. The authors of [13] adopt the definition and security model from [6] to forward-secure blind signatures. Their blind signature provides forward-secure unforgeability assuming intractability of the strong RSA problem and access to random oracle. Their security proof exploits the forking lemma by Pointcheval and Stern [23]. Later, Chow et al. [11] design forward-secure blind signature using bilinear pairings. Jia et al. [17] describe a forward-secure blind signature that is also based on bilinear pairings. Boyd and Gellert [7] give a comprehensive survey of methods of incorporating forward security to different cryptographic primitives. They also unify different approaches to forward security by generalising the notion and its terminology.

Our Contributions and Approach. Thanks to its quantum resistance, lattice-based cryptography is attracting more and more attention from the research community. However, there is no lattice-based construction of forward-secure blind signatures. Our work fills the gap. We construct *the first forward-secure blind signature in the lattice setting*. Forward security is proven in the random oracle model assuming intractability of the average case of short integer solution (SIS). We also use the rewinding (forking lemma) argument.

Inspired by the works [19,24,25], our signature is designed using the 3-move Fiat-Shamir transformation. To achieve blindness, the rejection sampling technique is applied (see Sect. 2). Thus, an extra move is needed to ensure that a final signature is valid. In order to achieve forward security, we exploit both a binary tree structure for lattice-based schemes introduced in [9] and a trapdoor delegation from [2,9].

To obtain forward-secure signature, we need a mechanism that permits for a secret-key update between two time intervals. For this purpose, we use a binary tree of the depth ℓ, whose leaves are labelled from left to right by consecutive time intervals $t = 0$ up to $t = \tau - 1$, where $\tau = 2^\ell$ is the total number of time intervals. To generate the public key and the initial secret key, we choose random matrices $A_j^{(0)}$, $A_j^{(1)}$ for $j \in [\ell]$ together with a matrix/trapdoor pair (A_0, T_{A_0}). Now, for any node $w^{(i)} = (w_1, \cdots, w_i) \in \{0,1\}^i$, we build up a concatenated matrix of form $F_{w^{(i)}} = [A_0 \| A_1^{(w_1)} \| A_i^{(w_i)}]$. Then, we can compute a trapdoor for $\Lambda_q^\perp(F_{w^{(i)}})$ using T_{A_0}. If the node $w^{(k)}$ is the ancestor of the node $w^{(i)}$, then we can obtain a trapdoor for $\Lambda_q^\perp(F_{w^{(i)}})$ from a trapdoor for $\Lambda_q^\perp(F_{w^{(k)}})$. However, one cannot get a trapdoor for $\Lambda_q^\perp(F_{w^{(k)}})$ from a trapdoor of $\Lambda_q^\perp(F_{w^{(i)}})$. This is the main idea behind the key evolution (key update) mechanism.

2 Preliminaries

For a positive integer ℓ, $[\ell]$ stands for the set $\{1, \cdots, \ell\}$. For a vector $\mathbf{c}$ and a matrix S, $\mathbf{c}[i]$ and $S[i]$ represent the i-th element of $\mathbf{c}$ and the i-th column of S, respectively.

Lattices. Integer lattices are discrete subgroups of $\mathbb{Z}^m$. Formally, a lattice $\mathcal{L}$ in $\mathbb{Z}^m$ is defined as $\mathcal{L} = \mathcal{L}(B) := \{\sum_{i=1}^n \mathbf{b}_i x_i : x_i \in \mathbb{Z}, \forall i = 1, \cdots, n\} \subseteq \mathbb{Z}^m$, where $B = [\mathbf{b}_1, \cdots, \mathbf{b}_n] \in \mathbb{Z}^{m \times n}$ is called a basis of $\mathcal{L}$, and $\mathbf{b}_i$'s are column vectors. We call n the rank of $\mathcal{L}$. We say $\mathcal{L}$ is a full rank lattice if $n = m$.

Given a matrix $A \in \mathbb{Z}^{n \times m}$ and a vector $\mathbf{u} \in \mathbb{Z}_q^n$, we define two lattices:

$$\Lambda_q^\perp(A) := \{\mathbf{e} \in \mathbb{Z}^m \text{ s.t. } A\mathbf{e} = \mathbf{0} \mod q\},$$
$$\Lambda_q^\mathbf{u}(A) := \{\mathbf{e} \in \mathbb{Z}^m \text{ s.t. } A\mathbf{e} = \mathbf{u} \mod q\}.$$

They all are full rank lattices containing $q\mathbb{Z}^m$ and are called q-ary lattices. Note that if $\mathbf{v} \in \Lambda_q^\mathbf{u}(A)$, then $\Lambda_q^\mathbf{u}(A) = \Lambda_q^\perp(A) + \mathbf{v}$.

For a set of vectors $S = \{\mathbf{s}_1, \cdots, \mathbf{s}_k\}$ in $\mathbb{R}^m$, we denote $\|S\| := \max_i \|\mathbf{s}_i\|$. Also, $\widetilde{S} := \{\widetilde{\mathbf{s}}_1, \cdots, \widetilde{\mathbf{s}}_k\}$ stands for the Gram-Schmidt orthogonalization of the vectors $\mathbf{s}_1, \cdots, \mathbf{s}_k$ in that order. The Gram-Schmidt norm of S is denoted by $\|\widetilde{S}\|$. A basis of a lattice is called *short* if its Gram-Schmidt norm is short.

We recall the shortest independent vectors problem (SIVP), which is the worst case of approximation problem on lattices. Note that the i-th minimum of a n-dimensional lattice $\mathcal{L}$ is defined as $\lambda_i(\mathcal{L}) := \min\{r : \dim(\text{span}(\mathcal{L} \cap \mathcal{B}_n(0, r))) \geq i\}$, where $\mathcal{B}_n(0, r) = \{\mathbf{x} \in \mathbb{R}^n : \|\mathbf{x}\| \leq r\}$.

Definition 1 (SIVP). *Given a full-rank basis B of an n-dimensional lattice $\mathcal{L}$. $SIVP_\gamma$ requires to output a set of n linearly independent lattice vectors $S \subset \mathcal{L}(B)$ such that $\|S\| \leq \gamma(n) \cdot \lambda_n(\mathcal{L}(B))$.*

Below we define discrete Gaussian distribution over an integer lattice.

Definition 2 (Gaussian Distribution). *Let $\Lambda \subseteq \mathbb{Z}^m$ be a lattice. For a vector $\mathbf{v} \in \mathbb{R}^m$ and a positive parameter $s \in \mathbb{R}$, define $\rho_{s,\mathbf{v}}(\mathbf{x}) = \exp\left(-\frac{\pi\|\mathbf{x}-\mathbf{v}\|^2}{s^2}\right)$ and $\rho_{s,\mathbf{v}}(\Lambda) = \sum_{\mathbf{x} \in \Lambda} \rho_{s,\mathbf{v}}(\mathbf{x})$. The discrete Gaussian distribution over Λ with center $\mathbf{v}$ and parameter σ is $\forall \mathbf{y} \in \Lambda, \mathcal{D}_{\Lambda,s,\mathbf{v}}(\mathbf{y}) = \frac{\rho_{s,\mathbf{v}}(\mathbf{y})}{\rho_{s,\mathbf{v}}(\Lambda)}$.*

For convenience, ρ_s and $\mathcal{D}_{\Lambda,s}$ denote $\rho_{0,s}$ and $\mathcal{D}_{\Lambda,s,0}$, respectively. When $s = 1$, we will write ρ instead of ρ_1. Also, $\mathcal{D}_{s,\mathbf{v}}^m$ and $\mathcal{D}_s^m$ stand for $\mathcal{D}_{\mathbb{Z}^m,s,\mathbf{v}}$ and $\mathcal{D}_{\mathbb{Z}^m,s}$, respectively.

Lemma 1 ([21, Lemma 4.5]). *For any $\mathbf{v} \in \mathbb{Z}^m$, if $s = \alpha \cdot \|\mathbf{v}\|$, where $\alpha > 0$, we have $\Pr\left[\mathcal{D}_s^m(\mathbf{x})/\mathcal{D}_{s,\mathbf{v}}^m(\mathbf{x}) \le e^{12/\alpha+1/(2\alpha^2)} : \mathbf{x} \leftarrow \mathcal{D}_s^m\right] \ge 1 - 2^{-100}$.*

Remark 1. In Lemma 1, if $\alpha = 12$, i.e., $s = 12\|\mathbf{v}\|$ then $\mathcal{D}_s^m(\mathbf{x})/\mathcal{D}_{s,\mathbf{v}}^m(\mathbf{x}) \le e^{1+1/288}$ with probability not smaller than $1 - 2^{-100}$.

Trapdoors and Trapdoor Delegation. Alwen and Peikert [4] give an algorithm for sampling a uniform matrix $A \in \mathbb{Z}_q^{n \times m}$ together with a short basis T_A for $\Lambda_q^\perp(A)$. It is an improvement of the algorithm published by Ajtai in [3]. We call T_A an *associated trapdoor* for A or for $\Lambda_q^\perp(A)$.

Theorem 1 ([4]). *Let $q \ge 3$ be odd and $m := \lceil 6n \log q \rceil$. There is a probabilistic polynomial-time (PPT) algorithm $\mathsf{TrapGen}(q, n)$ that outputs a pair $(A \in \mathbb{Z}_q^{n \times m}, T_A \in \mathbb{Z}^{m \times m})$ such that A is statistically close to a uniform matrix in $\mathbb{Z}_q^{n \times m}$ and T_A is a basis for $\Lambda_q^\perp(A)$ satisfying $\|\widetilde{T_A}\| \le O(\sqrt{n \log q})$ and $\|T_A\| \le O(n \log q)$ with all but negligible probability in n.*

Regarding Gaussian distribution, q-ary lattices and trapdoors, some useful results are presented in the following lemma and theorem.

Lemma 2 ([14, Corollary 5.4]). *Let m, n, q be positive integers such that q is prime and $m \ge 2n \log q$. Then for all but $2q^{-n}$ fraction of all matrix $A \in \mathbb{Z}_q^{n \times m}$ and for any $s \ge \omega(\sqrt{\log m})$, the distribution of $\mathbf{u} := A\mathbf{e} \pmod q$ is statistically close to uniform over $\mathbb{Z}_q^n$, where $\mathbf{e} \leftarrow \mathcal{D}_{\mathbb{Z}^m,s}$. Furthermore, the conditional distribution of $\mathbf{e} \leftarrow \mathcal{D}_{\mathbb{Z}^m,s}$, given $A\mathbf{e} = \mathbf{u} \pmod q$, is exactly $\mathcal{D}_{\Lambda_q^\mathbf{u}(A),s}$.*

Theorem 2. *Let $q > 2$ and let A, B be a matrix in $\mathbb{Z}_q^{n \times m}$ with $m > n$. Let T_A, T_B be a basis for $\Lambda_q^\perp(A)$ and $\Lambda_q^\perp(B)$, respectively. Then the following statements are true.*

1. *[22, Lemma 4.4]. For $s \ge \|\widetilde{T_A}\| \cdot \omega(\sqrt{\log n})$, we have*

$$\Pr[\mathbf{x} \leftarrow \mathcal{D}_{\Lambda_q^\mathbf{u}(A),s} : \|\mathbf{x}\| > s\sqrt{m}] \le \mathsf{negl}(n).$$

2. *[14, Theorem 4.1]. There is a PPT algorithm* SampleD$(B, s, \mathbf{v})$ *that, given a basis B of an n-dimensional lattice $\Lambda := \mathcal{L}(B)$, a parameters $s \geq \|\widetilde{B}\| \cdot \omega(\sqrt{\log n})$ and a center $\mathbf{v} \in \mathbb{R}^n$, outputs a sample from a distribution statistically close to $\mathcal{D}_{\Lambda,s,\mathbf{v}}$.*

3. *[14, Subsection 5.3.2]. There is a PPT algorithm* SampleISIS$(A, T_A, s, \mathbf{u})$ *that, on input a matrix A, its associated trapdoor T_A, a Gaussian parameter $s \geq \|\widetilde{T_A}\| \cdot \omega(\sqrt{\log n})$ and a given vector $\mathbf{u}$, outputs a vector $\mathbf{e}$ from $\mathcal{D}_{\Lambda_q^{\mathbf{u}}(A),s}$. It performs as follows: first it chooses an arbitrary $\mathbf{t} \in \mathbb{Z}^m$ satisfying that $A\mathbf{t} = \mathbf{u} \pmod{q}$ ($\mathbf{t}$ exists for all but an at most q^{-n} fraction of A). It then samples $\mathbf{w} \leftarrow \mathcal{D}_{\Lambda_q^{\perp}(A),s}$ using* SampleD$(T_A, s, -\mathbf{t})$ *and finally outputs $\mathbf{e} = \mathbf{t} + \mathbf{w}$.*

4. *[19, Section 2]. There is a PPT algorithm* SampleKey(A, T_A, s, K) *that takes as input a matrix $A \in \mathbb{Z}_q^{n \times m}$, its associated trapdoor $T_A \in \mathbb{Z}_q^{m \times m}$, a real number $s \geq \|\widetilde{T_A}\| \cdot \omega(\sqrt{\log n})$ and matrix $K \in \mathbb{Z}_q^{n \times k}$ to output a random (column) matrix $S \in \mathbb{Z}^{m \times k}$ such that the j-th column $S[j] \in$ Dom $:= \{\mathbf{e} \in \mathbb{Z}^m : \|\mathbf{e}\| \leq s\sqrt{m}\}$ for all $j \in [k]$ and that $A \cdot S = K \pmod{q}$ with overwhelming probability. The distribution of S is $\mathcal{D}_{\mathbb{Z}^{m \times k}, s}$ statistically close to the uniform distribution over* Dom^k*. It performs by calling k times the algorithm* SampleISIS$(A, T_A, s, \mathbf{u})$ *in which $\mathbf{u} = K[j]$ for $j \in \{1, \cdots, k\}$.*

In order to securely delegate a basis for an extended lattice, one can call the ExtBasis algorithm described below.

Lemma 3 ([2, Theorem 5]). *Let $A := [A_1 \| A_2 \| A_3]$ be a concatenation of three matrices A_1, A_2, A_3. Suppose that T_{A_2} is a basis of $\Lambda_q^{\perp}(A_2)$. Then, there is a deterministic polynomial time algorithm* ExtBasis(A, T_{A_2}) *that outputs a basis T_A for $\Lambda_q^{\perp}(A)$ such that $\|\widetilde{T_A}\| = \|\widetilde{T}_{A_2}\|$.*

Hardness Assumption. Forward-security of our construction is proven assuming hardness of the SIS problem.

Definition 3 ($l_2 - \mathsf{SIS}_{q,n,m,\beta}$ **problem,** [21, Definition 3.1]). *Given a random matrix $A \leftarrow_{\$} \mathbb{Z}_q^{n \times m}$, find a vector $\mathbf{z} \in \mathbb{Z}^m \setminus \{\mathbf{0}\}$ such that $A\mathbf{z} = \mathbf{0} \pmod{q}$ and $\|\mathbf{z}\| \leq \beta$.*

The hardness of l_2-SIS is stated by the following theorem.

Theorem 3 ([14, Proposition 5.7]). *For any poly-bounded m, $\beta = poly(n)$ and for any prime $q \geq \beta \cdot \omega(\sqrt{n \log n})$, the average case problem $l_2 - \mathsf{SIS}_{q,n,m,\beta}$ is as hard as approximating the SIVP problem (among others) in the worst case for a factor $\gamma = \beta \cdot \tilde{O}(\sqrt{n})$.*

Define the $\mathsf{SIS}_{q,n,m,d}$ distribution by the pair $(A, A\mathbf{s})$, where $A \xleftarrow{\$} \mathbb{Z}_q^{n \times m}$ and $\mathbf{s} \xleftarrow{\$} \{-d, \cdots, 0, \cdots, d\}$ are chosen at random. The distribution is characterised by the following lemma.

Lemma 4 (Discussed in [21]). *For $d \gg q^{m/n}$, the $\mathsf{SIS}_{q,n,m,d}$ distribution is statistically close to uniform over $\mathbb{Z}_q^{n \times m} \times \mathbb{Z}_q^n$. Given $(A, \mathbf{u})$ from the $\mathsf{SIS}_{q,n,m,d}$ distribution, there are many possible solutions $\mathbf{s}$ satisfying $A\mathbf{s} = \mathbf{u}$.*

Rejection Sampling. This is an aborting technique that is frequently used in lattice-based cryptography. The technique plays an important role in guaranteeing the blindness as well as it is used in simulation of the forward-security proof for our signature.

Lemma 5 (Rejection Sampling, [21, Theorem 4.6]). *Let $V = \{\mathbf{v} \in \mathbb{Z}^m :$ $\|\mathbf{v}\| \leq \delta\}$ be a subset of $\mathbb{Z}^m$ and $s = \omega(\delta \log \sqrt{m})$ be a real number. Define a probability distribution $h : V \to \mathbb{R}$. Then there exists a universal $M = O(1)$ satisfying that two algorithms $\mathcal{A}$ and $\mathcal{B}$ defined as:*

1. $(\mathcal{A})$: $\mathbf{v} \leftarrow h$, $\mathbf{z} \leftarrow \mathcal{D}^m_{\mathbf{v},s}$, output $(\mathbf{z}, \mathbf{v})$ with probability $\min(\frac{\mathcal{D}^m_s(\mathbf{z},)}{M\mathcal{D}^m_{\mathbf{v},s}(\mathbf{z})}, 1)$, and
2. $(\mathcal{B})$: $\mathbf{v} \leftarrow h$, $\mathbf{z} \leftarrow \mathcal{D}^m_s$, output $(\mathbf{z}, \mathbf{v})$ with probability $1/M$,

have a negligible statistical distance $\Delta(\mathcal{A}, \mathcal{B}) := 2^{-\omega(\log m)}/M$. Moreover, the probability that $\mathcal{A}$ outputs something is at least $(1 - 2^{-\omega(\log m)})/M$. In particular, if $s = \alpha\delta$ for any $\alpha > 0$, then $M = e^{12/\alpha + 1/(2\alpha^2)}$, $\Delta(\mathcal{A}, \mathcal{B}) = 2^{-100}/M$ and the probability that $\mathcal{A}$ outputs something is at least $(1 - 2^{-100})/M$.

Commitment Functions. A commitment function com maps a pair of two strings $(\mu, \mathbf{d}) \in \{0, 1\}^* \times \{0, 1\}^n$ (called *committed string*) to a *commitment string* $C := \mathsf{com}(\mu, \mathbf{d}) \in \{0, 1\}^n$. We need com that is both *statistically hiding* and *computationally binding*. For more details, see [19, 24].

3   Framework of Forward-Secure Blind Signatures

In this section, we recap the syntax and the security model for forward-secure blind signatures (FSBS). We follow [13], which is in turn adapted from [6].

3.1   Syntax of Forward-Secure Blind Signature Schemes

A forward-secure blind signature (or FSBS for short) consists of the four algorithms Setup, KeyUp, Sign, and Verify. They are described as follows:

- $(pp, pk, sk_0) \xleftarrow{\$} \mathsf{Setup}(1^n)$. The algorithm is a PPT one that takes as input a security parameter n and generates common parameters pp, a public key pk and an initial secret key sk_ϵ.
- $sk_{t+1} \xleftarrow{\$} \mathsf{KeyUp}(sk_t, t)$: The key update algorithm is a PPT one, which derives a secret key sk_{t+1} for the time period $t + 1$ from a secret key sk_t for a time period t. After execution, the algorithm deletes the secret key sk_t.
- $(\mathcal{V}, \Sigma) \xleftarrow{\$} \mathsf{Sign}(pp, pk, sk_t, t, \mu)$: The signing algorithm involves an interaction between a user, say $\mathcal{U}(pp, pk, t, \mu)$ and a signer, say $\mathcal{S}(pp, pk, sk_t, t)$. At a time period t, the user blinds the message μ using the secret key sk_t and sends it to the signer. The signer replies with a signature of the blinded message. After successful interactions, the user obtains a signature Σ of the original message μ at the time t. The signer gets its own view $\mathcal{V}$. If the interaction fails, the user and signer output $\Sigma := \perp$ and $\mathcal{V} := \perp$, respectively.

- $1/0 := \mathsf{Verify}(pp, pk, t, \mu, \Sigma)$: The verification algorithm is a deterministic one that outputs either 1 if Σ is non-$\perp$ and valid or 0, otherwise. As the input, it accepts a parameter pp, a public key pk, a time period t, a message μ and a signature Σ.

The correctness of FSBS is defined as follows. For any $(pp, pk, sk_0) \leftarrow \mathsf{Setup}(1^n)$ and $(\Sigma, \mathcal{V}) \leftarrow \mathsf{Sign}(pp, pk, sk, t, \mu)$, the verification algorithm fails with a negligible probability or

$$\Pr[\mathsf{Verify}(pp, pk, t, \mu, \Sigma) = 1] = 1 - \mathsf{negl}(n).$$

3.2 Security of Forward-Secure Blind Signatures

Two properties required for forward-secure blind signatures are *blindness* and *forward security*. Blindness ensures that it is impossible for the signer to learn any information about messages being signed.

Definition 4 (Blindness). FSBS *is blind if for any efficient algorithm* $\mathcal{S}^*$, *the advantage of* $\mathcal{S}^*$ *in the blindness game* $\mathsf{Blind}_{\mathsf{FSBS}}^{\mathcal{S}^*}$ *is negligible. That is*

$$\mathsf{Adv}_{\mathsf{FSBS}}^{\mathsf{Blind}}(\mathcal{S}^*) := \Pr[\mathsf{Blind}_{\mathsf{FSBS}}^{\mathcal{S}^*} \Rightarrow 1] - 1/2 \leq \mathsf{negl}(n).$$

FSBS *is called perfectly blind if* $\Pr[\mathsf{Blind}_{\mathsf{FSBS}}^{\mathcal{S}^*} \Rightarrow 1]$ *is exactly* $1/2$.

The blindness game $\mathsf{Blind}_{\mathsf{FSBS}}^{\mathcal{S}^*}$ consists of three phases defined below.

1. **Initialization.** The adversary $\mathcal{S}^*$ chooses a security parameter n, then obtains common parameters pp, a public key pk and an initial secret key sk_0 using $\mathsf{Setup}(1^n)$.
2. **Challenge.** $\mathcal{S}^*$ selects and gives the challenger $\mathcal{C}$ two messages μ_0 and μ_1. The challenger $\mathcal{C}$ flips a coin $b \subset \{0,1\}$ and initiates two signing interactions with $\mathcal{S}^*$ on input μ_b and μ_{1-b} (not necessarily in two different time periods). The adversary $\mathcal{S}^*$ acts as the signer in these two interactions and finally attains two corresponding view/signature pairs $(\mathcal{V}_b, \Sigma_b)$ and $(\mathcal{V}_{1-b}, \Sigma_{1-b})$.
3. **Output.** The adversary $\mathcal{S}^*$ outputs $b' \in \{0,1\}$. It wins if $b' = b$.

Following [13], we define forward-security as the *forward-secure unforgeability*. In the $\mathsf{FSUF}_{\mathsf{FSBS}}^{\mathcal{U}^*}$ game, the forger $\mathcal{U}^*$ is a malicious user (adversary).

Definition 5 (Forward-secure Unforgeability). FSBS *is forward-secure unforgeable (FSUF) if for any efficient algorithm* $\mathcal{U}^*$, *the advantage of* $\mathcal{U}^*$ *in the forward-secure unforgeability game* $\mathsf{FSUF}_{\mathsf{FSBS}}^{\mathcal{U}^*}$ *is negligible. That is,*

$$\mathsf{Adv}_{\mathsf{FSBS}}^{\mathsf{FSUF}}(\mathcal{U}^*) := \Pr[\mathsf{FSUF}_{\mathsf{FSBS}}^{\mathcal{U}^*} \Rightarrow 1] \leq \mathsf{negl}(n).$$

In our work, the forward-secure unforgeability game $\mathsf{FSUF}_{\mathsf{FSBS}}^{\mathcal{U}^*}$ in defined in the random oracle model. (We use hashing as an instantiation of random oracle.) We assume that, whenever the adversary wants to make a signing query, it always makes a random oracle query in advance.

1. **Setup.** The forger $\mathcal{U}^*$ gives a security parameter n to the challenger $\mathcal{C}$. The challenger $\mathcal{C}$ generates system parameters pp and outputs the key pair (pk, sk_0) by calling $\mathsf{Setup}(1^n)$. Then $\mathcal{C}$ sends pp and pk to the forger $\mathcal{U}^*$. The key sk_0 is kept secret.

2. **Queries.** At a time period t, the forger $\mathcal{U}^*$ can make a polynomially many random oracle queries as well as a polynomially many signing queries in an adaptive manner. In order to move to the next time period, the forger makes a key update query to get the secret key sk_{t+1} for the time period $t+1$. Note that, once the forger makes a key update query, i.e., it obtains the secret key sk_{t+1}, it cannot issue random oracle and signing queries for past time intervals. Finally, the forger is allowed to make a single break-in query at a time period $\bar{t} \leq T - 1$, when it wants to stop the query phase. The time interval $\bar{t}$ is called the *break-in time*. Once the forger makes the break-in query, it is not able to make further random oracle (or hash) and signing queries. Details of the challenger actions in response to the forger queries are given below.

   - For key update query $KQ(t)$: if $t < T - 1$, then the challenger updates the secret key sk_t to sk_{t+1} and updates t to $t + 1$. If $t = T - 1$ then sk_T is given as an empty string.
   - For each hash queries $HQ(t, \mu)$: the challenger has to reply with a random value.
   - For each signing query $SQ(t, \mu)$: the challenger must send a valid signature back to $\mathcal{U}^*$.
   - For the break-in query $BQ(\bar{t})$ (note that the query is allowed once only): the challenger must send the secret key $sk_{\bar{t}}$ to the adversary and move the game to the output phase.

3. **Output.** $\mathcal{U}^*$ outputs at least one forgery (μ^*, t^*, Σ^*) at time period t^*. He wins the game if $t^* < \bar{t}$, $SQ(t^*, \mu^*)$ has been never queried, and (μ^*, t^*, Σ^*) is valid.

4   Our Construction

4.1   Binary Tree Hierarchy for Time Periods

Our design applies a binary-tree data structure. In the context of encryption, binary trees have been introduced by [8]. For the lattice setting, they have been adapted by Cash et al. in [9]. The tree structure is useful for constructing forward-secure public key encryption schemes [8], HIBE [9] and recently for forward-secure group signature [20]. We need time periods $t \in \{0, \cdots, 2^\ell - 1\}$ to be assigned to leaves of a binary tree of the depth ℓ. The tree leaves are arranged in increasing order from left to right – see Fig. 1. For a time period t, there is a unique path $t = (t_1, \cdots, t_\ell)$ from the root ϵ to the leaf, where for each level $i \in [\ell]$, $t_i = 0$ if this is the left branch or $t_i = 1$ if this is the right branch. Consequently, the i-th level node $w^{(i)}$ in the binary tree can be described by a unique binary bit string $w^{(i)} = (w_1, \cdots, w_i)$ that follows the path from the root to the node. This means that for the node $w^{(i)} = (w_1, \cdots, w_i)$, we can create a corresponding matrix $W_t = [A_0 \| A_1^{(w_1)} \| \cdots \| A_i^{(w_i)}]$ (resp., $F_t = [A_0 \| A_1^{(t_1)} \| \cdots \| A_\ell^{(t_\ell)}])$, where A_0 and its associated trapdoor T_{A_0} are generated by TrapGen and $A_i^{(b)}$ are random matrices for all $i \in [\ell], b \in \{0, 1\}$.

Updating secret keys from time period t to $t + 1$ is done by the trapdoor delegation mechanism using ExtBasis. Each node $w^{(i)} = (w_1, \cdots, w_i)$ is associated with a secret key $T_{w^{(i)}}$, which can be computed from the initial secret key $sk_0 = T_{A_0}$ by evaluating

$$T_{w^{(i)}} \leftarrow \text{ExtBasis}(A_{w^{(i)}}, T_{A_0}), \text{ where } A_{w^{(i)}} = \left[A_0 \| A_1^{(w_1)} \| A_2^{(w_2)} \| \cdots \| A_i^{(w_i)} \right].$$

$T_{w^{(i)}}$ is easily computed if a secret key $T_{w^{(k)}}$ for an ancestor $w^{(k)}$ of $w^{(i)}$ is known. Assume that the binary representation of $w^{(i)}$ is $w^{(i)} = (w_1, \cdots, w_k, w_{k+1}, \cdots, w_i)$, where $k < i$. Then

$$T_{w^{(i)}} \leftarrow \text{ExtBasis}(A_{w^{(i)}}, T_{w^{(k)}}), \text{ where } A_{w^{(i)}} = \left[A_0 \| A_1^{(w_1)} \| \cdots \| A_2^{(w_k)} \| \cdots \| A_i^{(w_i)} \right].$$

Similarly, a secret key for a time period (i.e., a leaf) can be computed if we have any its ancestor's secret key.

4.2 Description of the Proposed Signature

Our lattice-based forward-secure blind signature (FSBS) consists of a setup algorithm Setup, a key update algorithm KeyUp, an interactive signing algorithm Sign and a verification algorithm Verify. They all are described below. Note that, we also use a commitment function com.

Setup($1^n, 1^\ell$): For a security parameter n and a binary tree depth ℓ, the algorithm runs through the following steps.

- Choose $q = poly(n)$ prime, $m = O(n \log q)$, $k, \kappa, \ell, \tau = 2^\ell, \sigma, \sigma_1, \sigma_2, \sigma_3$ (see Sect. 5.4 for details).
- Let $\mathcal{M} = \{0, 1\}^*$ be the message space of the scheme.
- Choose randomly a matrix $K \xleftarrow{\$} \mathbb{Z}_q^{n \times k}$. Similarly, select matrices $A_1^{(0)}, A_1^{(1)}, A_2^{(0)}, A_2^{(1)}, \cdots, A_\ell^{(0)}, A_\ell^{(1)}$ from $\mathbb{Z}_q^{n \times m}$ at random.
- Run TrapGen(q, n) to obtain a pair (A_0, T_{A_0}), where $A_0 \in \mathbb{Z}_q^{n \times m}$ and $T_{A_0} \in \mathbb{Z}^{m \times m}$ are a matrix and its associated trapdoor.
- Let $H : \{0, 1\}^* \to \mathcal{R}_H$ be a collision-resistant and one-way hash function, where $\mathcal{R}_H := \{\mathbf{e}' \in \{-1, 0, 1\}^k : \|\mathbf{e}'\| \leq \kappa\}$.
- Let com : $\{0, 1\}^* \times \{0, 1\}^n \to \{0, 1\}^n$ be a computationally binding and statistically hiding commitment function.
- Output $pp \leftarrow \{n, q, m, \ell, \tau, k, \kappa, \sigma, \sigma_1, \sigma_2, \sigma_3, \mathcal{M}, H, \text{com}\}$, $pk \leftarrow \{A_0, A_1^{(0)}, A_1^{(1)}, \cdots, A_\ell^{(0)}, A_\ell^{(1)}, K\}$, and $sk_\epsilon \leftarrow T_{A_0}$ as common parameters, public key and the initial secret key, respectively.

KeyUp(pp, pk, sk_t, t): We need a key evolution mechanism (KVM) that "forgets" all secret keys of internal nodes that can produce past keys. Additionally, we expect that KVM stores the smallest number of keys necessary for signature to work properly. The key evolution mechanism KVM works as follows.

- For any leaf t, define the minimal cover Node(t) to be the smallest subset of nodes that contains an ancestor of all leaves in $\{t, \cdots, T-1\}$ but does not contain any ancestor of any leaf in $\{0, \cdots, t-1\}$. For example, in Fig. 1, Node(0) = $\{\epsilon\}$, Node(1) = $\{001, 01, 1\}$, Node(2) = $\{01, 1\}$, Node(3) = $\{011, 1\}$ (i.e., two black circles in the tree), Node(4) = $\{1\}$, Node(5) = $\{101, 11\}$, Node(6) = $\{11\}$, Node(7) = $\{111\}$.

- The secret key sk_t at time period t contains secret keys corresponding to all nodes (including leaves) in Node(t). For example, for the tree from Fig. 1, we have $sk_0 = sk_\epsilon = \{T_{A_0}\}$, $sk_1 = \{T_{001}, T_{01}, T_1\}$, where T_{001}, T_{01}, and T_1 are associated trapdoors for $F_{001} = [A_0\|A_1^{(0)}\|A_2^{(0)}\|A_3^{(1)}]$, $F_{01} = [A_0\|A_1^{(0)}\|A_2^{(1)}]$ and $F_1 = [A_0\|A_1^{(1)}]$, respectively.

- To update sk_t to sk_{t+1}, the signer determines the minimal cover Node($t+1$), then derives keys for all nodes in Node($t+1$) \ Node(t) using the keys in sk_t as described in Sect. 4.1. Finally the signer deletes all keys in Node(t) \ Node($t+1$). For example, $sk_2 = \{T_{01}, T_1\}$ (mentioned above), since Node(2) \ Node(1) = $\{01, 1\}$ and Node(1) \ Node(2) = $\{001\}$.

Sign(pp, pk, sk_t, t, μ): The signer interacts with the user in order to produce a signature for a message $\mu \in \mathcal{M}$ at time period t. The interaction consists of five phases. Phases 1, 3 and 5 are done by the signer. Phases 2 and 4 – by the user.

- *Phase 1:* The signer constructs the matrix $F_t = \left[A_0\|A_1^{(t_1)}\|\cdots\|A_\ell^{(t_\ell)}\right] \in \mathbb{Z}_q^{n\times(\ell+1)m}$ for the time $t = (t_1, \cdots, t_\ell)$. Next it computes an ephemeral secret key S_t using SampleKey described in Theorem 2, where $F_t \cdot S_t = K$. Note that S_t can be computed at Phase 3 as well. The signer samples $\mathbf{r} \in \mathbb{Z}^{(\ell+1)m}$ according to the distribution $\mathcal{D}_{\sigma_2}^{(\ell+1)m}$. It finally computes and sends $\mathbf{x} = F_t\mathbf{r} \in \mathbb{Z}_q^n$ to the user.

- *Phase 2:* Upon receiving $\mathbf{x}$, the user samples blind factors $\mathbf{a} \leftarrow \mathcal{D}_{\sigma_3}^{(\ell+1)m}$ and $\mathbf{b} \leftarrow \mathcal{D}_{\sigma_1}^k$, $\mathbf{d}' \xleftarrow{\$} \{0,1\}^n$. It computes $\mathbf{u} = \mathbf{x} + F_t\mathbf{a} + K\mathbf{b}$ and hashes it with $\mathbf{c} := \mathsf{com}(\mu, \mathbf{d}') \in \{0,1\}^n$ using the hash function H to obtain a *real challenge* $\mathbf{e}'$. The rejection sampling technique is called to get the *blinded challenge* $\mathbf{e}$, which is sent back to the user.

- *Phase 3:* The ephemeral secret key S_t and $\mathbf{r}$ are used to compute $\mathbf{z} = \mathbf{r} + S_t\mathbf{e}$. In order to guarantee that no information of S_t is leaked, the rejection sampling is applied, which implies that the distribution of $\mathbf{z}$ and $\mathbf{r}$ are the same. Finally, the *blinded signature* $\mathbf{z}$ is delivered to the user.

- *Phase 4:* The user computes the unblinded signature $\mathbf{z}' = \mathbf{z} + \mathbf{a}$. Again, the rejection sampling is called to make sure that $\mathbf{z}'$ and $\mathbf{z}$ are independent of each other and $\mathbf{z}'$ is bounded in some desired domain. The user returns $(t, \mu, \Sigma = (\mathbf{d}', \mathbf{e}', \mathbf{z}'))$ as the *final signature* if $\|\mathbf{z}'\| \leq \sigma_3\sqrt{(1+\ell)m}$ holds. Otherwise, he outputs "$\perp$". The user is required to confirm validity of the final signature by sending result to the signer: result := accept means the final signature is good, while result := $(\mathbf{a}, \mathbf{b}, \mathbf{e'}, \mathbf{c}))$ requires the user to restart the signing protocol.

- *Phase 5:* Having obtained result, the signer checks whether or not result $\neq$ accept. If not, it returns the *view* $\mathcal{V} = (t, \mathbf{r}, \mathbf{e}, \mathbf{z})$. Otherwise it makes some check-up operations before restarting the signing algorithm. The check-up allows the signer to detect an adversary who controls the user and tries to forge a signature.

Note that the rejection sampling in Phase 2 is not able restart the signing algorithm as it is used locally. In contrast, the rejection sampling in Phase 3 and Phase 4 can make the signing algorithm restart. The reader is referred to Sect. 5 for more details. Figure 2 illustrates the signing algorithm.

Verify(t, pk, μ, Σ): The algorithm accepts a signature Σ on the message μ for the time period $t = (t_1, \cdots, t_\ell)$ and public key pk as its input and performs the following steps:

(i) parse $\Sigma = (\mathbf{d'}, \mathbf{e'}, \mathbf{z'})$;

(ii) form $F_t := \left[A_0 \| A_1^{(t_1)} \| \cdots \| A_\ell^{(t_\ell)} \right] \in \mathbb{Z}^{n \times (1+\ell)m}$;

(iii) compute $\hat{\mathbf{e}} := H(F_t \mathbf{z'} - K\mathbf{e'} \bmod q, \mathrm{com}(\mu, \mathbf{d'}))$;

(iv) if $\|\mathbf{z'}\| \leq \sigma_3 \sqrt{(1+\ell)m}$ and $\hat{\mathbf{e}} = \mathbf{e'}$, then output 1, otherwise return 0.

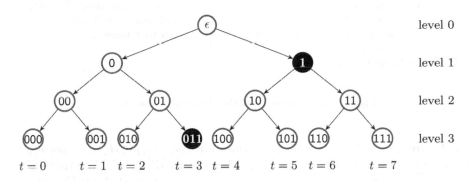

Fig. 1. Binary tree of depth $\ell = 3$, i.e., for $\tau = 8$ time periods. The root is denoted by ϵ. For convenience, we name nodes by their binary representations

5 Correctness, Security and Parameters for FSBS

5.1 Correctness

Theorem 4 (Correctness). *The correctness of* FSBS *scheme holds after at most* e^2 *restarts with probability not smaller than* $1 - 2^{-100}$.

SIGNER $\mathcal{S}(pp, pk, sk_t, t)$:	USER $\mathcal{U}(pp, pk, t, \mu)$:
Phase 1:	**Phase 2:**
01. $F_t := \left[A_0 \| A_1^{(t_1)} \| \cdots \| A_\ell^{(t_\ell)} \right] \in \mathbb{Z}_q^{n \times (\ell+1)m}$	05. $F_t := \left[A_0 \| A_1^{(t_1)} \| \cdots \| A_\ell^{(t_\ell)} \right]$
02. $S_t \in \mathbb{Z}^{(\ell+1)m \times k} \leftarrow \mathsf{SampleKey}(F_t, T_{F_t}, \sigma, K)$	06. $\mathbf{a} \xleftarrow{\$} \mathcal{D}_{\sigma_3}^{(\ell+1)m}$, $\mathbf{b} \xleftarrow{\$} \mathcal{D}_{\sigma_1}^k$
(i.e., $F_t \cdot S_t = K \pmod q$)	07. $\mathbf{d}' \xleftarrow{\$} \{0,1\}^n$, $\mathbf{c} := \mathsf{com}(\mu, \mathbf{d})$,
03. $\mathbf{r} \in \mathbb{Z}^{(\ell+1)m} \xleftarrow{\$} \mathcal{D}_{\sigma_2}^{(\ell+1)m}$, $\mathbf{x} = F_t \mathbf{r} \in \mathbb{Z}_q^n$	$\mathbf{u} = F_t \mathbf{a} + \mathbf{x} + K \mathbf{b} \pmod q$
04. Send $\mathbf{x}$ to the user	08. $\mathbf{e}' = H(\mathbf{u}, \mathbf{c}) \in \mathcal{R}_H^k$, $\mathbf{e} := \mathbf{e}' + \mathbf{b}$
[**Go to Phase 2**]	09. Output $\mathbf{e}$ with probability
Phase 3:	$$\min\left\{ \frac{\mathcal{D}_{\sigma_1}^m(\mathbf{e})}{M_1 \cdot \mathcal{D}_{\sigma_1, \mathbf{e}'}^m(\mathbf{e})}, 1 \right\}$$
11. $\mathbf{z} = \mathbf{r} + S_t \mathbf{e}$	10. Send $\mathbf{e}$ back to the signer.
12. Output $\mathbf{z}$ with probability	[**Go to Phase 3**]
$$\min\left\{ \frac{\mathcal{D}_{\sigma_2}^{(\ell+1)m}(\mathbf{z})}{M_2 \cdot \mathcal{D}_{\sigma_2, S_t \mathbf{e}}^{(\ell+1)m}(\mathbf{z})}, 1 \right\}$$	**Phase 4:**
13. Send $\mathbf{z}$ to the user	14. $\mathbf{z}' = \mathbf{z} + \mathbf{a}$
[**Go to Phase 4**]	15. Output $\mathbf{z}'$ with probability
Phase 5:	$$\min\left\{ \frac{\mathcal{D}_{\sigma_3}^{(\ell+1)m}(\mathbf{z}')}{M_3 \cdot \mathcal{D}_{\sigma_3, \mathbf{z}}^{(\ell+1)m}(\mathbf{z}')}, 1 \right\}$$
18. **if** (result $\neq$ accept):	i.e., **if** ($\|\mathbf{z}'\| < \sigma_3 \sqrt{(\ell+1)m}$) :
19. Parse result $:= (\mathbf{a}, \mathbf{b}, \mathbf{e}', \mathbf{c})$	result $:=$ accept
20. $\mathbf{u} := F_t \mathbf{a} + \mathbf{x} + K \mathbf{b} \pmod q$	**else**: result $:= (\mathbf{a}, \mathbf{b}, \mathbf{e}', \mathbf{c})$
$\hat{\mathbf{u}} := F_t \mathbf{a} + F_t \mathbf{z} - K \mathbf{e}' \pmod q$	16. **Output:** $(t, \mu, \Sigma = (\mathbf{d}', \mathbf{e}', \mathbf{z}'))$
21. **if** $(\mathbf{e} - \mathbf{b} = \mathbf{e}' = H(\mathbf{u}, \mathbf{c})$	or $\perp$ when result $\neq$ accept
and $\mathbf{e}' = H(\hat{\mathbf{u}}, \mathbf{c})$	17. Send result back to the signer.
and $\|\mathbf{z} + \mathbf{a}\| \geq \sigma_3 \sqrt{(\ell+1)m})$:	[**Go to Phase 5**]
restart from Phase 1	
22. **Output:** the view $\mathcal{V} = (t, \mathbf{r}, \mathbf{e}, \mathbf{z})$	

Fig. 2. The signing algorithm $\mathsf{Sign}(pp, pk, sk_t, t, \mu)$

Proof. Given $(t, \mu, \Sigma = (\mathbf{d}', \mathbf{e}', \mathbf{z}'))$ produced by $\mathsf{Sign}(pp, pk, sk_t, \mu)$ – see Fig. 2. It is east to show that $H(F_t \mathbf{z}' - K \mathbf{e}' \pmod q), \mathsf{com}(\mu, \mathbf{d}')) = \mathbf{e}'$. Note that $\|\mathbf{z}'\| \leq \sigma_3 \sqrt{(1+\ell)m}$ with overwhelming probability by Statement 1 of Theorem 2. Remark 1 implies that if $s = 12\|\mathbf{c}\|$, then $\frac{\mathcal{D}_s^m(\mathbf{x})}{M \cdot \mathcal{D}_{s,\mathbf{c}}^m(\mathbf{x})} \leq \frac{e^{1+1/288}}{M}$ with probability at least $1 - 2^{-100}$. The rejection sampling requires that $\mathcal{D}_s^m(\mathbf{x})/(M \cdot \mathcal{D}_{s,\mathbf{c}}^m(\mathbf{x})) \leq 1$, meaning that $M \geq e^{1+1/288}$. It is easy to see that $M \approx e^{1+1/288}$ is the best choice. Applying this observation to the rejection samplings in Phases 3 and 4, we see that a valid signature can be successfully produced after at most $M_2 \cdot M_3 \approx e^2$ repetitions. $\qquad\square$

5.2 Blindness

Theorem 5 (Blindness). *Let* com *be a statistically hiding commitment and H be an one-way and collision-resistant hash function. Then, the proposed forward-secure blind signature* FSBS *is blind.*

Proof. In the blindness game $\text{Blind}_{\text{FSBS}}^{\mathcal{S}^*}$, the adversarial signer $\mathcal{S}^*$ gives the challenger $\mathcal{C}$ two messages μ_0 and μ_1. The challenger $\mathcal{C}$ chooses uniformly at random a bit $b \in \{0,1\}$ and interacts with $\mathcal{S}^*$ in order to sign both messages μ_b and μ_{1-b}. $\mathcal{C}$ acts as two users $\mathcal{U}_b := \mathcal{U}(pp, pk, t, \mu_b)$ and $\mathcal{U}_{1-b} := \mathcal{U}(pp, pk, t, \mu_{1-b})$. Finally, $\mathcal{S}^*$ gets two pairs $(\mathcal{V}_b, \Sigma_b)$ and $(\mathcal{V}_{1-b}, \Sigma_{1-b})$ that correspond to the users $\mathcal{U}_b$ and $\mathcal{U}_{1-b}$, respectively. We argue that the knowledge of $(\mathcal{V}_b, \Sigma_b)$ and $(\mathcal{V}_{1-b}, \Sigma_{1-b})$ is independent of the signed messages. In other words, $\mathcal{S}^*$ cannot distinguish, which user it is communicating with. In other words, it cannot guess b with non-negligible probability.

Indeed, for $\mathcal{V}_b = (t, \mathbf{r}_b, \mathbf{e}_b, \mathbf{z}_b)$ and $\mathcal{V}_{1-b} = (t, \mathbf{r}_{1-b}, \mathbf{e}_{1-b}, \mathbf{z}_{1-b})$, we need to consider the pair $(\mathbf{e}_b, \mathbf{e}_{1-b})$ only, since $\mathbf{z}_b$ and $\mathbf{z}_{1-b}$ are produced by $\mathcal{S}^*$ itself. In Phase 2, the rejection sampling makes sure that the distribution of both $\mathbf{e}_b$ and $\mathbf{e}_{1-b}$ are the same, which is $\mathcal{D}_{\sigma_1}^k$. This means that $\mathbf{e}_b$ and $\mathbf{e}_{1-b}$ are independent of the signed messages. Consider $\Sigma_b = (\mathbf{d}_b', \mathbf{e}_b', \mathbf{z}_b')$ and $\Sigma_{1-b} = (\mathbf{d}_{1-b}', \mathbf{e}_{1-b}', \mathbf{z}_{1-b}')$. As Phase 4 uses the rejection sampling, both $\mathbf{z}_b'$ and $\mathbf{z}_{1-b}'$ have the same distribution, which is $\mathcal{D}_{\sigma_3}^{(1+\ell)m}$. It means that $\mathcal{S}^*$ does not learn anything about the signed messages from the knowledge of $(\mathbf{d}_b', \mathbf{d}_{1-b}')$ and $(\mathbf{e}_b', \mathbf{e}_{1-b}')$. This is true because the former pair are randomly chosen and the latter pair are hash values of the one-way and collision-resistant function H.

Finally, it is easy to see that restarts, which may happen in Phase 5, do not increase advantage of $\mathcal{S}^*$ in the blindness game. In fact, a restart occurs if the user has sent result $:= (\mathbf{a}, \mathbf{b}, \mathbf{e}', \mathbf{c})$ to $\mathcal{S}^*$. The values $\mathbf{d}'$, $\mathbf{a}$ and $\mathbf{b}$ are freshly sampled by the user. Additionally, as com is a statistically hiding commitment, knowing $\mathbf{c}$, $\mathcal{S}^*$ cannot tell apart μ_b from μ_{1-b}. □

5.3 Forward-Secure Unforgeability

We recall the following lemma, which we use to support our witness indistinguishability argument.

Lemma 6 (Adapted from [21, Lemma 5.2]). *Given a matrix* $\mathbf{F} \in \mathbb{Z}_q^{n \times (\ell+1)m}$, *where* $(\ell+1)m > 64 + n\log q / \log(2d+1)$ *and* $\mathbf{s} \xleftarrow{\$} \{-d, \cdots, 0, \cdots, d\}^{(\ell+1)m}$. *Then there exists another* $\mathbf{s}' \xleftarrow{\$} \{-d, \cdots, 0, \cdots, d\}^{(\ell+1)m}$ *such that* $\mathbf{Fs} = \mathbf{Fs}' (\text{mod } q)$ *with probability at least* $1 - 2^{-100}$.

Note that Lemma 4 also gives the same conclusion as Lemma 6 but with the not so clear condition $d \gg q^{(\ell+1)m/n}$.

Theorem 6 (Forward-secure Unforgeability). *Suppose that the commitment function* com *used in* FSBS *is computationally binding and that there exists a forger* $\mathcal{A}$, *who can break the forward-secure unforgeability of* FSBS. *Then, one* can construct a polynomial-time algorithm $\mathcal{B}$ that solves an l_2-$\mathsf{SIS}_{q,n,(1+2\ell)m,\beta}$ problem with $\beta = \max\{(2\sigma_3 + 2\sigma\sqrt{\kappa})\sqrt{(1+\ell)m}, (2\sigma_3 + \sigma_2)\sqrt{(1+\ell)m}\}$.

Proof. The reduction is as follows:

Phase 0 (Instance). Assume that $\mathcal{B}$ wants to solve an instance of the $\mathsf{SIS}_{q,n,(1+2\ell)m,\beta}$ problem

$$F \cdot \mathbf{v} = 0 \quad \mod q, \|\mathbf{v}\| \leq \beta, F \in \mathbb{Z}_q^{n \times (1+2\ell)m}, \tag{1}$$

in which F is parsed as $F = \left[A_0\|U_1^{(0)}\|U_1^{(1)}\|\cdots\|U_\ell^{(0)}\|U_\ell^{(1)}\right]$ with $A_0^{(k)}, U_i^{(b)} \in \mathbb{Z}_q^{n \times m}$ for $\beta = \max\{(2\sigma_3 + 2\sigma\sqrt{\kappa})\sqrt{(1+\ell)m}, (2\sigma_3 + \sigma_2)\sqrt{(1+\ell)m}\}$ and $b \in \{0,1\}$.

Phase 1 (Guessing the target). $\mathcal{B}$ guesses the target time period t^* that $\mathcal{A}$ wants to attack by choosing randomly $t^* = (t_1^*, \cdots, t_\ell^*) \xleftarrow{\$} \{0, \cdots, \tau - 1\}$. The success probability of guessing t^* is $1/\tau$.

Phase 2 (Initialize). $\mathcal{B}$ sets common parameters pp as in the Setup algorithm. However, $\mathcal{B}$ sets the public key pk according to the following steps.

- For $i \in [\ell]$, $\mathcal{B}$ sets $A_i^{(t_i^*)} = U_i^{(t_i^*)}$. For each bit $b \in \{0,1\}$ such that $b \neq t_i^*$, $\mathcal{B}$ invokes TrapGen to generate $A_i^{(b)}$ together with a short basis $T_{A_i^{(b)}}$ of $\Lambda_q^\perp(A_i^{(b)})$.

- $\mathcal{B}$ samples $S^* \leftarrow \mathcal{D}_\sigma^{(1+\ell)m \times k}$ and sets $K := F_{t^*} \cdot S^*$, where $F_{t^*} = \left[A_0\|A_1^{(t_1^*)}\|\cdots\|A_\ell^{(t_\ell^*)}\right] \in \mathbb{Z}_q^{n \times (1+\ell)m}$. Let $d := \sigma\sqrt{(1+\ell)m}$. Then σ should be chosen sufficiently large to satisfy Lemma 2 (i.e., $\sigma \geq \omega(\sqrt{\log((1+\ell)m)})$), Lemma 4 (i.e., $d \gg q^{(1+\ell)m/n}$) and Lemma 6 (i.e., $(1+\ell)m > 64 + n\log q/\log(2d+1)$). Statement 1 of Theorem 2 guarantees that $\|S^*\| \leq d$ with overwhelming probability. According to Lemma 2, K is statistically close to uniform.

- Finally, $\mathcal{B}$ sends pp, and $pk \leftarrow \{A_0, A_1^{(0)}, A_1^{(1)}, \cdots, A_\ell^{(0)}, A_\ell^{(1)}, K\}$ to $\mathcal{A}$ as the common parameters and the public key, while keeping $T_{A_i^{(b)}}$'s and S^* secret.

$\mathcal{B}$ creates and maintains a list $\mathcal{L}_H$ consisting of random oracle queries $(\mathbf{u}, \mathbf{c}) \xleftarrow{\$} \mathbb{Z}_q^n \times \{0,1\}^n$ and their corresponding hash value $\mathbf{e}' \in \mathcal{R}_H$. In other words, $\mathcal{L}_H = \{(\mathbf{u}, \mathbf{c}, \mathbf{e}') \in \mathbb{Z}_q^n \times \{0,1\}^n \times \mathcal{R}_H : \mathbf{e}' = H(\mathbf{u}, \mathbf{c})\}$. In addition, $\mathcal{B}$ also prepares the set of replies for q_H hash queries $\mathcal{R} := \{\mathbf{r}_1, \cdots, \mathbf{r}_{q_H}\}$, where each $\mathbf{r}_i \xleftarrow{\$} \mathcal{R}_H$. It then chooses a random tape ρ and runs $\mathcal{A}$ on (pp, pk, ρ) in a black-box manner.

Phase 3 (Queries). $\mathcal{B}$ plays the role of signer and interacts with $\mathcal{A}$. $\mathcal{B}$ responds to $\mathcal{A}$ queries as follows:

- *Key update queries* $KQ(t), t = (t_1, \cdots, t_\ell)$: If $t \leq t^*$, $\mathcal{B}$ aborts the query. Otherwise, let $k \leq \ell$ be the minimum index such that $t_k \neq t_k^*$. Then, the adversary $\mathcal{B}$ first uses the trapdoor $T_{A_k^{(t_k)}}$ to compute the key T_{t_k} for the node t_k

$$T_{t_k} \leftarrow \mathsf{ExtBasis}(E\|A_k^{(t_k)}, T_{A_k^{(t_k)}}), \text{ where } E = \left[A_0\|A_1^{(t_1)}\|\cdots\|A_{k-1}^{(t_{k-1})}\right],$$

from which $\mathcal{B}$ computes all keys in sk_t as in the real key update algorithm.

- *Hash queries* $HQ(\mathbf{u}, \mathbf{c})$: Having received a hash query $(\mathbf{u}, \mathbf{c})$, $\mathcal{B}$ checks if the list $\mathcal{L}_H$ contains the query. If $\mathcal{B}$ finds out that $(\mathbf{u}, \mathbf{c})$ is in $\mathcal{L}_H$ already, then $\mathcal{B}$ sends the corresponding hash value $\mathbf{e}'$ to the forger $\mathcal{A}$. Otherwise, $\mathcal{B}$ chooses the first unused $\mathbf{r}_i, i \in [q_H]$ from $\mathcal{R}$, takes $\mathbf{e}' := \mathbf{r}_i$ and stores the query-hash value pair $((\mathbf{u}, \mathbf{c}), \mathbf{e}')$ in $\mathcal{L}_H$. Finally, $\mathcal{B}$ sends $\mathbf{e}'$ to the forger $\mathcal{A}$ as the answer.

- *Signing queries* $SQ(t, \mu)$: $\mathcal{B}$ constructs $F_t := \left[A_0^{(k_0)} \| A_1^{(t_1)} \| \cdots \| A_\ell^{(t_\ell)} \right]$ and checks if $t \neq t^*$ or not. If $t \neq t^*$, $\mathcal{B}$ computes $T_{F_t} \leftarrow \mathsf{ExtBasis}(F_t, T_{A_k^{(t_k)}})$, and $S_t \leftarrow \mathsf{SampleKey}(F_t, T_{F_t}, \sigma, K)$, where $k \leq \ell$ is the minimum index such that $t_k \neq t_k^*$. Note that $F_t \cdot S_t = K$. Otherwise, if $t = t^*$, $\mathcal{B}$ simply assigns $S_{t^*} \leftarrow S^*$ since $F_{t^*} \cdot S^* = K$.

- *Break-in queries* $BQ(t)$: Once the adversary $\mathcal{A}$ makes a query $BQ(t)$, if $t \leq t^*$, then $\mathcal{B}$ aborts. Otherwise, i.e., $t > t^*$, $\mathcal{B}$ decides that the break-in time is $\bar{t} \leftarrow t$. $\mathcal{B}$ answers to $\mathcal{A}$ by sending the secret key $sk_{\bar{t}}$ in the same way as replying to the key update queries since $\bar{t} = t > t^*$.

Phase 4 (Forge). Eventually, $\mathcal{A}$ outputs a forgery $(t'_1, \mu^*_1, \Sigma^*_1)$. $\mathcal{B}$ checks if $t'_1 = t^*$ or not. If not, then $\mathcal{B}$ aborts. Otherwise, $\mathcal{B}$ accepts the forgery. For the forgery $(t^*, \mu^*_1, \Sigma^*_1)$, we have: (i) $\Sigma^*_1 = (\mathbf{d}'_1, \mathbf{e}'_1, \mathbf{z}'_1)$; (ii) $\mathbf{e}'_1 := H(F_{t^*}\mathbf{z}'_1 - K\mathbf{e}'_1 \bmod q, \mathsf{com}(\mu^*_1, \mathbf{d}'_1))$, where $F_{t^*} := \left[A_0 \| A_1^{(t_1^*)} \| \cdots \| A_\ell^{(t_\ell^*)} \right] \in \mathbb{Z}^{n \times (1+\ell)m}$; and (iii) $\|\mathbf{z}'_1\| \leq \sigma_3 \sqrt{(1+\ell)m}$.

Analysis. We argue that the simulation of $\mathcal{B}$ is statistically perfect. In other words, the forger $\mathcal{A}$ is not able to distinguish the simulator $\mathcal{B}$ from the real challenger in the FSEU game. Indeed, the simulation proceeds as the real game except the following exceptions.

(i) Some matrices $A_i^{(b)}$ are not really random but is generated by TrapGen. However, Theorem 1 ensures that the distribution of $A_i^{(b)}$ generated by TrapGen is close to uniform.

(ii) The matrix K is not randomly chosen. It is obtained by sampling S^* from $\mathcal{D}_\sigma^{(1+\ell)m \times m}$ and then assigning $K := F \cdot S^*$. Lemma 2 asserts that selection of K is close to uniform. Note that the sufficiently large choice of σ does not affect (iii).

(iii) The matrix S_{t^*} is equal to S^*, which is not computed using SampleKey. The forger $\mathcal{A}$ does not know S_t so consequently does not know S^*. As $\mathbf{z}$ is generated (in Step 12) using the rejection sampling, we always guarantee that $\mathbf{z} \leftarrow \mathcal{D}_{\sigma_2}^{(\ell+1)m}$ and $\mathbf{z}$ is independent of S_t and S^*. Thus the view of $\mathcal{A}$ is independent of S^*.

Now, we show how to obtain the solution to the l_2-SIS problem given by Eq. (1). Let $i \in [q_H]$ be the target forking index, for which $\mathbf{e}'_1 = \mathbf{r}_i$. $\mathcal{B}$ follows the rewinding strategy by keeping $\{\mathbf{r}_1, \cdots, \mathbf{r}_{i-1}\}$ and sampling new fresh answers

$\{\mathbf{r}'_i, \cdots, \mathbf{r}'_{q_H}\} \xleftarrow{\$} \mathcal{R}_H$. Now, $\mathcal{B}$ uses $\mathcal{R}' := \{\mathbf{r}_1, \cdots, \mathbf{r}_{i-1}, \mathbf{r}'_i, \cdots, \mathbf{r}'_{q_H}\}$ to answer to $\mathcal{A}$'s hash queries.

The forking lemma [23, Lemma 4] asserts that $\mathcal{A}$ outputs a new signature $(t'_2, \mu^*_2, \Sigma^*_2)$, where $\Sigma^*_2 = (\mathbf{d}'_2, \mathbf{e}'_2, \mathbf{z}'_2)$ such that $\mathbf{e}'_2 = \mathbf{r}'_i$ using the same hash query as in the first run (i.e., the i-th hash query). Recall that γ is the probability of a restart of FSBS. As before, if $t'_2 \neq t^*$, then $\mathcal{B}$ aborts. If $\mathbf{e}'_2 = \mathbf{e}'_1$, $\mathcal{B}$ aborts and replays $\mathcal{A}(pp, pk, \rho')$ at most q^{qs}_H times using different random tapes ρ' and different hash queries. If $\mathbf{e}'_2 \neq \mathbf{e}'_1$, then $\mathcal{B}$ returns

$$((F_{t^*}\mathbf{z}'_1 - K\mathbf{e}'_1, \mathrm{com}(\mu^*_1, \mathbf{d}'_1)), (F_{t^*}\mathbf{z}'_2 - K\mathbf{e}'_2, \mathrm{com}(\mu^*_2, \mathbf{d}'_2))). \tag{2}$$

Since the pair in Eq. (2) are both coming from the same hash query and com is computationally binding, we have $\mu^*_2 = \mu^*_1$, $\mathbf{d}'_1 = \mathbf{d}'_2$ and

$$F_{t^*}\mathbf{z}'_1 - K\mathbf{e}'_1 = F_{t^*}\mathbf{z}'_2 - K\mathbf{e}'_2 \ (\mathrm{mod}\ q),$$

or equivalently,

$$F_{t^*}(\mathbf{z}'_1 - \mathbf{z}'_2 - S^*(\mathbf{e}'_1 - \mathbf{e}'_2)) = \mathbf{0} \ (\mathrm{mod}\ q).$$

Set $\widehat{\mathbf{v}} := \mathbf{z}'_1 - \mathbf{z}'_2 - S^*(\mathbf{e}'_1 - \mathbf{e}'_2)$. By Lemmas 4 and 6, there is at least one secret key S' such that $F_{t^*}S^* = F_{t^*}S' \ (\mathrm{mod}\ q)$, where S^* and S' have all the same columns except the i-th column. The index i shows the position, where $\mathbf{e}'_1[i] \neq \mathbf{e}'_2[i]$. If $\mathbf{z}'_1 - \mathbf{z}'_2 - S^*(\mathbf{e}'_1 - \mathbf{e}'_2) = \mathbf{0}$, then we can choose $\widehat{v} := \mathbf{z}'_1 - \mathbf{z}'_2 - S'(\mathbf{e}'_1 - \mathbf{e}'_2) \neq \mathbf{0}$. Stress that the view of $\mathcal{A}$ is independent of both S^* and S'. We have shown that $\widehat{\mathbf{v}} \neq \mathbf{0}$ and $F_{t^*} \cdot \widehat{\mathbf{v}} = \mathbf{0} \ (\mathrm{mod}\ q)$. It is easy to see that $\|\widehat{\mathbf{v}}\| \leq 2(\sigma_3 + \sigma\sqrt{\kappa})\sqrt{(1+\ell)m}$, as $\|S^*\| \leq \sigma\sqrt{(1+\ell)m}$, $\|\mathbf{z}'_i\| \leq \sigma_3\sqrt{(\ell+1)m}$, and $\|\mathbf{e}'_i\| \leq \sqrt{\kappa}$ for $i \in \{1, 2\}$.

In particular, we show that if $\mathcal{A}$ can produce a forgery by restarting the signing interaction (with $\mathcal{B}$), then $\mathcal{B}$ is able to find a solution to the l_2-SIS problem given by Eq. (1). Indeed, to restart the signing interaction, $\mathcal{A}$ delivers result$:= (\mathbf{a}, \mathbf{b}, \mathbf{e}', \mathbf{c})$ to $\mathcal{B}$. Now $\mathcal{B}$ with its view $\mathcal{V} = (t, \mathbf{r}, \mathbf{e}, \mathbf{z})$, will check whether all

$$\mathbf{e} - \mathbf{b} = \mathbf{e}' = H(\mathbf{x} + F_{t^*}\mathbf{a} + K\mathbf{b} \ (\mathrm{mod}\ q), \mathbf{c}), \tag{3}$$

$$\mathbf{e}' = H(F_{t^*}\mathbf{a} + F_{t^*}\mathbf{z} - K\mathbf{e}' \ (\mathrm{mod}\ q), \mathbf{c}), \tag{4}$$

$$\|\mathbf{z} + \mathbf{a}\| > \sigma_3\sqrt{(1+\ell)m}. \tag{5}$$

hold or not. If all are satisfied, $\mathcal{B}$ restarts the interaction with $\mathcal{A}$. Let assume that afterwards $\mathcal{A}$ successfully produces a valid signature $\widehat{\Sigma} = (\widehat{\mathbf{d}}', \widehat{\mathbf{e}}', \widehat{\mathbf{z}}')$. Let $\widehat{\mathbf{b}} \in \mathcal{D}^m_{\sigma_1}$ be such that $\mathbf{e} = \widehat{\mathbf{e}}' + \widehat{\mathbf{b}}$. Then, the following relations have to hold

$$\mathbf{e} - \widehat{\mathbf{b}} = \widehat{\mathbf{e}}' = H(\mathbf{x} + F_{t^*}\mathbf{a} + K\widehat{\mathbf{b}} \ (\mathrm{mod}\ q), \mathbf{c}), \tag{6}$$

$$\widehat{\mathbf{e}}' = H(F_{t^*}\widehat{\mathbf{z}} - K\widehat{\mathbf{e}}' \ (\mathrm{mod}\ q), \mathrm{com}(\mu^*, \widehat{\mathbf{d}}')), \tag{7}$$

$$\|\widehat{\mathbf{z}}'\| \leq \sigma_3\sqrt{(1+\ell)m}. \tag{8}$$

Table 1. Choosing parameters for the proposed FSBS scheme

Parameters	Value	Usage
n	–	Security parameter
ℓ	–	Binary tree depth
τ	2^ℓ	# Time points
β	$\beta = \max\{(2\sigma_3 + 2\sigma\sqrt{\kappa})\sqrt{(1+\ell)m},$ $(2\sigma_3 + \sigma_2)\sqrt{(1+\ell)m}\}$	For l_2-SIS$_{q,n,(1+2\ell)m,\beta}$ to be hard, Theorem 3
q	$q \geq \beta \cdot \omega(\sqrt{n \log n})$, prime	
m	$\max\{\frac{1}{1+\ell} \cdot (64 + \frac{n \log q}{\log(2d+1)}), \lceil 6n \log q \rceil\},$ $d = \sigma \cdot \sqrt{(1+\ell)m}$	Lemma 6, TrapGen
σ	$\geq O(\sqrt{n \log q}) \cdot \omega(\sqrt{\log n})$	SampleKey, Theorem 2
M_1, M_2, M_3	$M_1 = M_2 = M_3 = e^{1+1/288}$	Rejection sampling
σ_1	$12\sqrt{\kappa}$	
σ_2	$12\sigma\eta\sigma_1\sqrt{(1+\ell)mk}$	
σ_3	$12\eta\sigma_2\sqrt{m}$	
k, κ	$2^\kappa \cdot \binom{k}{\kappa} \geq 2^\gamma$	Min entropy of the hash function H at least γ

Now, if $\widehat{\mathbf{e}}' \neq \mathbf{e}'$, then $\mathcal{B}$ aborts. Otherwise, Eqs. (4) and (7) give $F_{t^*}\mathbf{a} + F_{t^*}\mathbf{z} \pmod{q} = F_{t^*}\widehat{\mathbf{z}}' \pmod{q}$. Let $\widehat{\mathbf{v}} := \mathbf{a} + \mathbf{z} - \widehat{\mathbf{z}}'$, then $\widehat{\mathbf{v}} \neq 0$. This is true as otherwise $\mathbf{a} + \mathbf{z} = \widehat{\mathbf{z}}'$, which implies that $\|\mathbf{z} + \mathbf{a}\| \leq \eta\sigma_3\sqrt{m}$ (by Eq. (8)). This contradicts Eq. (5). Again, we have $F_{t^*} \cdot \widehat{\mathbf{v}} = 0 \pmod{q}$, $\widehat{\mathbf{v}} \neq \mathbf{0}$ and $\|\widehat{\mathbf{v}}\| \leq \|\mathbf{a}\| + \|\mathbf{z}\| + \|\widehat{\mathbf{z}}'\| \leq (2\sigma_3 + \sigma_2)\sqrt{(1+\ell)m}$.

Note that $F_{t^*} = \left[A_0\|A_1^{(t_1^*)}\|\cdots\|A_\ell^{(t_\ell^*)}\right] = \left[A_0\|U_1^{(t_1^*)}\|\cdots\|U_\ell^{(t_\ell^*)}\right]$. We can get F from F_{t^*} by inserting into the gap between two sub-matrices in F_{t^*} the remaining matrices $\{U_i^{(1-t_i^*)}\}_i$ at relevant positions. We insert zeros into the corresponding position of $\widehat{\mathbf{v}}$ to get the desired solution $\mathbf{v}$ to the problem given by Eq. (1). Obviously, $F \cdot \mathbf{v} = \mathbf{0} \pmod{q}$, and $\|\mathbf{v}\| = \|\widehat{\mathbf{v}}\|$.

To summarise, we have shown that $\mathcal{B}$ can solve the l_2-SIS$_{q,n,(1+2\ell)m,\beta}$ problem, with

$$\beta = \max\{(2\sigma_3 + 2\sigma\sqrt{\kappa})\sqrt{(1+\ell)m}, (2\sigma_3 + \sigma_2)\sqrt{(1+\ell)m}\}.$$

$\square$

Remark 2. In the proof for the forward-secure unforgeability, one may think of the method of programming hash values, instead of using the real signing interaction (with a modification in generating the matrix S_t to compute $\mathbf{z} = \mathbf{r} + S_t\mathbf{e}$) in order to reply signing queries issued by $\mathcal{A}$. We argue that the programming method fails to simulate the perfect environment for the adversary $\mathcal{A}$. Assume that $\mathcal{B}$ does not want to compute S_t in the way we have done in our proof. Then, after replying to a hash query, say $(\mathbf{x} + F_t\mathbf{a} + K\mathbf{b} \pmod{q}, \mathsf{com}(\mu, \mathbf{d}'))$, by giving a hash value, say $\mathbf{e}'$, $\mathcal{B}$ simply chooses $\mathbf{z} \leftarrow \mathcal{D}_{\sigma_2}^{(\ell+1)m}$ and then sends $\mathbf{z}$ to $\mathcal{A}$. In turn,

$\mathcal{A}$ gives $\mathbf{e} := \mathbf{e}' + \mathbf{b}$ to $\mathcal{B}$. After that $\mathcal{B}$ sets $H(F_t\mathbf{a} + F_t\mathbf{z} - K\mathbf{e}', \mathrm{com}(\mu, \mathbf{d}')) := \mathbf{e}'$. However, since the collision resistance of H, the relation $F_t\mathbf{a} + F_t\mathbf{z} - K\mathbf{e}' = \mathbf{x} + F_t\mathbf{a} + K\mathbf{b} \pmod{q}$ has to hold. Thus, $\mathcal{A}$ needs to check whether or not $F_t\mathbf{z} = \mathbf{x} + K\mathbf{e} \pmod{q}$ to distinguish the simulated signing interaction from the real one. One may think that $\mathcal{B}$ can choose $\mathbf{z} \leftarrow \mathcal{D}_{\sigma_2}^{(\ell+1)m}$ such that $F_t\mathbf{z} = \mathbf{x} + K\mathbf{e} \pmod{q}$ before sending $\mathbf{z}$ to $\mathcal{A}$. However, without the knowledge of a trapdoor for F_t, the problem of choosing such a $\mathbf{z}$ is not easy.

5.4 Choosing Parameters

First, we set n as security parameter, ℓ as the highest depth of the binary tree representing time points, $\tau = 2^\ell$ as the number of time points. For TrapGen, we need $m \geq \lceil 6n\log q \rceil$. For SampleKey (Theorem 2) to work, we need $\sigma \geq O(\sqrt{n\log q}) \cdot \omega(\sqrt{\log n})$. Also, let $d := \sigma\sqrt{(1+\ell)m}$ and we set $(\ell+1)m \geq 64 + n\log q / \log(2d+1)$ via Lemma 6. To make sure the min-entropy of H is at least γ, we choose k and κ such that $2^\kappa \cdot \binom{k}{\kappa} \geq 2^\gamma$. Section 5.1 suggests setting $M_i := e^{1+1/288}$ for all $i \in [3]$. We then set $\sigma_1 = 12\|\mathbf{e}'\| = 12\sqrt{\kappa}$, $\sigma_2 = 12\|S^*\mathbf{e}\| = 12\sigma\sigma_1\sqrt{(1+\ell)mk}$ and $\sigma_3 = 12\|\mathbf{z}\| = 12\eta\sigma_2\sqrt{(1+\ell)m}$ (via *Remark* 1). For $l_2\text{-SIS}_{q,n,(1+\ell)m,\beta}$ to be hard by Theorem 3, we set m polybounded, $\beta = poly(n)$ and $q \geq \beta \cdot \omega(\sqrt{n\log n})$, where $\beta = \max\{(2\sigma_3 + 2\sigma\sqrt{\kappa})\sqrt{(1+\ell)m}, (2\sigma_3 + \sigma_2)\sqrt{(1+\ell)m}\}$. The parameter setting is summarized in Table 1.

6 Conclusions and Future Works

In this paper, we propose, for the first time, a forward-secure blind signature based on the hardness of the SIS problem in lattices. Using the rejection sampling technique together with the trapdoor delegation and the binary tree structure for representing of time periods, the proposed signature is blind and forward secure. Forward security is proven in the random oracle setting. Lattice-based forward-secure blind signatures in the standard model should be an interesting topic for future research.

Acknowledgment. We all would like to thank anonymous reviewers for their helpful comments. This work is partially supported by the Australian Research Council Discovery Project DP200100144 and Linkage Project LP190100984. Huy Quoc Le has been sponsored by a Data61 PhD Scholarship. Ha Thanh Nguyen Tran acknowledges the support of the Natural Sciences and Engineering Research Council of Canada (NSERC) (funding RGPIN-2019-04209 and DGECR-2019-00428). Josef Pieprzyk has been supported by the Australian ARC grant DP180102199 and Polish NCN grant 2018/31/B/ST6/03003.

References

1. Abdalla, M., Reyzin, L.: A new forward-secure digital signature scheme. In: Okamoto, T. (ed.) ASIACRYPT 2000. LNCS, vol. 1976, pp. 116–129. Springer, Heidelberg (2000). https://doi.org/10.1007/3-540-44448-3_10

2. Agrawal, S., Boneh, D., Boyen, X.: Efficient lattice (H)IBE in the standard model. In: Gilbert, H. (ed.) EUROCRYPT 2010. LNCS, vol. 6110, pp. 553–572. Springer, Heidelberg (2010). https://doi.org/10.1007/978-3-642-13190-5_28

3. Ajtai, M.: Generating hard instances of the short basis problem. In: Wiedermann, J., van Emde Boas, P., Nielsen, M. (eds.) ICALP 1999. LNCS, vol. 1644, pp. 1–9. Springer, Heidelberg (1999). https://doi.org/10.1007/3-540-48523-6_1

4. Alwen, J., Peikert, C.: Generating shorter bases for hard random lattices. In: Proceedings of the 26th International Symposium on Theoretical Aspects of Computer Science, STACS 2009, Freiburg, Germany, 26–28 February 2009, pp. 75–86 (2009). https://doi.org/10.4230/LIPIcs.STACS.2009.1832

5. Anderson, R.: Two remarks on public key cryptology. Technical report, University of Cambridge, Computer Laboratory (2002). https://www.cl.cam.ac.uk/techreports/UCAM-CL-TR-549.pdf

6. Bellare, M., Miner, S.K.: A forward-secure digital signature scheme. In: Wiener, M. (ed.) CRYPTO 1999. LNCS, vol. 1666, pp. 431–448. Springer, Heidelberg (1999). https://doi.org/10.1007/3-540-48405-1_28

7. Boyd, C., Gellert, K.: A Modern View on Forward Security. Cryptology ePrint Archive, Report 2019/1362 (2019). https://eprint.iacr.org/2019/1362

8. Canetti, R., Halevi, S., Katz, J.: A forward-secure public-key encryption scheme. In: Biham, E. (ed.) EUROCRYPT 2003. LNCS, vol. 2656, pp. 255–271. Springer, Heidelberg (2003). https://doi.org/10.1007/3-540-39200-9_16

9. Cash, D., Hofheinz, D., Kiltz, E., Peikert, C.: Bonsai trees, or how to delegate a lattice basis. In: Gilbert, H. (ed.) EUROCRYPT 2010. LNCS, vol. 6110, pp. 523–552. Springer, Heidelberg (2010). https://doi.org/10.1007/978-3-642-13190-5_27

10. Chaum, D.: Blind signatures for untraceable payments. In: Chaum, D., Rivest, R.L., Sherman, A.T. (eds.) Advances in Cryptology. LNCS, pp. 199–203. Springer, Boston, MA (1983). https://doi.org/10.1007/978-1-4757-0602-4_18

11. Chow, S.S.M., Hui, L.C.K., Yiu, S.M., Chow, K.P.: Forward-secure multisignature and blind signature schemes. Appl. Math. Comput. **168**, 895–908 (2005). https://doi.org/10.1016/j.amc.2004.09.015

12. Diffie, W., Oorschot, P., Wiener, M.: Authentication and authenticated key exchanges. Des. Codes Crypt. **2**, 107–125 (1992). https://doi.org/10.1007/BF00124891

13. Duc, D.N., Cheon, J.H., Kim, K.: A forward-secure blind signature scheme based on the strong RSA assumption. In: Qing, S., Gollmann, D., Zhou, J. (eds.) ICICS 2003. LNCS, vol. 2836, pp. 11–21. Springer, Heidelberg (2003). https://doi.org/10.1007/978-3-540-39927-8_2

14. Gentry, C., Peikert, C., Vaikuntanathan, V.: Trapdoors for hard lattices and new cryptographic constructions. Cryptology ePrint Archive, Report 2007/432 (2008). https://eprint.iacr.org/2007/432

15. Günther, C.G.: An identity-based key-exchange protocol. In: Quisquater, J.-J., Vandewalle, J. (eds.) EUROCRYPT 1989. LNCS, vol. 434, pp. 29–37. Springer, Heidelberg (1990). https://doi.org/10.1007/3-540-46885-4_5

16. Itkis, G., Reyzin, L.: Forward-secure signatures with optimal signing and verifying. In: Kilian, J. (ed.) CRYPTO 2001. LNCS, vol. 2139, pp. 332–354. Springer, Heidelberg (2001). https://doi.org/10.1007/3-540-44647-8_20

17. Jia, Y., et al.: Forward-secure multisignature, threshold signature and blind signature schemes. J. Netw. **5**, 634 (2010). https://doi.org/10.4304/jnw.5.6.634-641

18. Kucharczyk, M.: Blind signatures in electronic voting systems. In: Kwiecień, A., Gaj, P., Stera, P. (eds.) CN 2010. CCIS, vol. 79, pp. 349–358. Springer, Heidelberg (2010). https://doi.org/10.1007/978-3-642-13861-4_37

19. Le, H.Q., Duong, D.H., Susilo, W.: A blind ring signature based on the short integer solution problem. In: You, I. (ed.) WISA 2019. LNCS, vol. 11897, pp. 92–111. Springer, Cham (2020). https://doi.org/10.1007/978-3-030-39303-8_8

20. Ling, S., Nguyen, K., Wang, H., Xu, Y.: Forward-secure group signatures from lattices. In: Ding, J., Steinwandt, R. (eds.) PQCrypto 2019. LNCS, vol. 11505, pp. 44–64. Springer, Cham (2019). https://doi.org/10.1007/978-3-030-25510-7_3

21. Lyubashevsky, V.: Lattice signatures without trapdoors. Cryptology ePrint Archive, Report 2011/537, Full version of paper appearing at Eurocrypt 2012 (2012). https://eprint.iacr.org/2011/537. Accessed 18 Oct 2017

22. Micciancio, D., Regev, O.: Worst-case to average-case reductions based on Gaussian measures. In: Proceedings of 45th Symposium on Foundations of Computer Science (FOCS 2004), Rome, Italy, 17–19 October 2004, pp. 372–381 (2004). https://doi.org/10.1109/FOCS.2004.72

23. Pointcheval, D., Stern, J.: Provably secure blind signature schemes. In: Kim, K., Matsumoto, T. (eds.) ASIACRYPT 1996. LNCS, vol. 1163, pp. 252–265. Springer, Heidelberg (1996). https://doi.org/10.1007/BFb0034852

24. Rückert, M.: Lattice-based blind signatures. In: Abe, M. (ed.) ASIACRYPT 2010. LNCS, vol. 6477, pp. 413–430. Springer, Heidelberg (2010). https://doi.org/10.1007/978-3-642-17373-8_24

25. Zhang, P., Jiang, H., Zheng, Z., Hu, P., Xu, Q.: A new post-quantum blind signature from lattice assumptions. IEEE Access 6, 27251–27258 (2018). https://doi.org/10.1109/ACCESS.2018.2833103

Optimized Arithmetic Operations for Isogeny-Based Cryptography on Huff Curves

Yan Huang[1,2], Fangguo Zhang[1,2(✉)], Zhi Hu[3], and Zhijie Liu[1,2]

[1] School of Data and Computer Science, Sun Yat-sen University,
Guangzhou 510006, China
`isszhfg@mail.sysu.edu.cn`
[2] Guangdong Key Laboratory of Information Security, Guangzhou 510006, China
[3] School of Mathematics and Statistics, Central South University,
Changsha 410083, China

Abstract. Up to now, the state-of-the-art implementations of Super-singular Isogeny Diffie-Hellman (SIDH) work with Montgomery curves or Edwards curves, due to the facts that such curve models provide high efficiency for elliptic curve arithmetic operations. In this work, we propose a new w-coordinate method to optimize the arithmetic operations on Huff curves. Specifically, for the optimal computations of addition operation and doubling operation proposed by Orhon and Hisil on a fixed Huff curve, the costs of these operations can be further improved by about 40%. For the evaluations of odd-degree isogeny and 2-isogeny on variable Huff curves proposed by Moody and Shumow, the costs of evaluating ℓ-isogeny (ℓ is odd) point and ℓ-isogeny curve can be further improved by about 50%. The computations of evaluating 2-isogeny point and 2-isogeny curve can be separately replaced by computing 4-isogeny point and 4-isogeny curve, which need $6M + 2S$ and $4S$, respectively, and avoid square root calculation mentioned in Moody and Shumow's work. Interestingly, the desired computational issues on variable Huff curves have the same computational costs as those on variable Montgomery curves, as well supported by our implementations.

Keywords: Post-quantum cryptography · Huff curves · Isogenies · SIDH

1 Introduction

A recent research area for post-quantum cryptography is from supersingular elliptic curve isogenies. Jao and De Feo [1] first proposed a Diffie-Hellman type key exchange protocol named SIDH, and then led to the development of the key encapsulation mechanisim called Supersingular Isogeny Key Encapsulation (SIKE) [2], which now has become one of Round 2 candidates in the NIST standardization project for post-quantum cryptography (PQC).

© Springer Nature Switzerland AG 2020
J. K. Liu and H. Cui (Eds.): ACISP 2020, LNCS 12248, pp. 23–40, 2020.
https://doi.org/10.1007/978-3-030-55304-3_2

Compared with other candidates such as those based on lattices, error correcting codes, and hash functions, isogeny-based cryptography has the potential of providing significantly smaller key sizes at the same level of security. Nevertheless, its state-of-the-art implementation is slower than other candidates in PQC. Thus, numerous optimized methods for isogeny-based cryptography have been proposed to increase the viability as a PQC candidate. These mainly include two aspects:

a. Optimizing basic field arithmetic operations such as modular multiplication and modular squaring. Bos et al. investigated various arithmetic techniques which can be used to potentially enhance the performance of SIDH, especially regarding arithmetic modulo $2^x p^y \pm 1$ [3]. Seo et al. proposed a faster modular multiplication for SIDH and SIKE resulting in assitional speed improvements on ARM processors [4].
b. Choosing a suitable model of elliptic curve for efficient elliptic curve arithmetic operations. Note that the state-of-the-art implementation works entirely on Montgomery curves, which provides fast point operations and isogeny evaluations [5,23]. Recently, Kim et al. demonstrated the combinational usage of Montgomery curves and Edwards curves could result in better performance [6]. Moreover, Costello utilized the Weil restriction to compute chains of Richelot (2, 2)-isogenies on Kummer surfaces over $\mathbb{F}_p$ instead of computing chains of 2-isogenies on Montgomery curves over $\mathbb{F}_{p^2}$ [7].

On account of the lower computational efficiency and the leakage of additional points [8] compared with other post-quantum cryptography, Castryck et al. proposed a CSIDH [9] which followed the layout of the Couveignes-Rostovtsev-Stolbunov scheme [10]. As they used supersingular elliptic curves over a finite prime field $\mathbb{F}_p$ and the number of $\mathbb{F}_p$-rational points on any supersingular elliptic curve is $p + 1$, these imply that such curves are isogenous. According to [11], when their endomorphism rings are the form $\mathbb{Z}[\pi]$ where π is the Frobenius map, implementing the CSIDH is more efficient than that on ordinary elliptic curves [12] over $\mathbb{F}_p$. Up to now, the optimization of CSIDH mainly focused on choosing a suitable model of elliptic curve. In the light of the birationality between twisted Edwards curves and Montgomery curves [13], Meyer et al. [14] implemented the CSIDH by using Montgomery curves for the computation of scalar multiplications and the evaluation of isogenous points and twisted Edwards curves for the evaluation of the isogenous curves. Because of the w-coordinates proposed by Farashi et al. [15] on Twisted Edwards curves, Kim et al. presented an efficient method to evaluate the isogenous curves with w-coordinates on Edwards curves[16], thus enhancing the efficiency of implementing the CSIDH.

Note that very little information is found in the literature about using Huff curves for isogeny-based cryptography. Although Orhon and Hisil [17] put forward the efficient elliptic curve arithmetic, Moody and Shumow [18] presented isogenous formulae between Huff curves, all these operations were performed with projective coordinates $(X : Y : Z)$ or embedded coordinates $(XT : YZ : TZ)$ [17], which were slower than those on Edwards curves with projective coordinates $(W : Z)$ [16] and those on Montgomery curves with projective coordinates $(X : Z)$ [5].

Our Contributions. This paper aims at exploring efficient arithmetic operations on Huff curves so as to be suitable for isogeny-based cryptography.

- We put forward the w-coordinates on Huff curves for the first time. Applying the coordinates, we present optimized addition and doubling formulae on Huff curves. With the huff curve fixed, our formulae set the new record for operation counts. Concretely speaking, performing a doubling operation and an addition operation need $2M + 2S + C^1$ and $3M + 2S$, respectively, compared with the corresponding latest operations in [17] which need $8M$ and $8M$, respectively. Based on the new results, we present the mixed projective w-coordinate differential addition and doubling formulae to compute scalar multiplications against side-channel attacks.
- We present formulae for computing ℓ-isogeny(where ℓ is odd), 2-isogeny and 4-isogeny points, as well as the corresponding isogenous curves with the w-coordinate in the form of H_c. The computations of evaluating an ℓ-isogeny point and an ℓ-isogeny curve need $4sM + 2S$ and $4sM + 2S$, respectively, where $\ell = 2s + 1$, while using Moody and Shumow's formulae needs $(8s + 3)M + 3S$ and $8sM + 12S$, respectively. The evaluations of a 4-isogeny point and a 4-isogeny curve which use our formulae need $6M + 2S$ and $4S$ on average, while compounding Moody and Shumow's 2-isogeny formulae needs extra square root calculation.
- We present the efficiency analysis of SIDH on Montgomery curves and Huff curves and find that the implementation results on Huff curves are almost the same as those on Montgomery curves.

Organization. This work is organized as follows: The preliminaries are given in Sect. 2. The optimized differential addition and doubling formulae on Huff curves are proposed in Sect. 3, while the optimized isogenous formulae on Huff curves are presented in Sect. 4. In Sect. 5, we provide the computational costs of the optimized arithmetic operations on Huff curves, and present the comparisons of implementing the SIDH between Montgomery curves and Huff curves. Then, we give specific examples and implement the SIDH on Huff curves to confirm the correctness of the above theoretical analyses in Sect. 6. At last, we draw our conclusion and future work in Sect. 7.

2 Preliminaries

This section sets the stage by reviewing some background about Huff curves, including the addition and doubling operations, the isogenous computations and the basic SIDH protocol.

---

[1] The symbols M, S and C mentioned later represent the time needed to multiply two elements, square an element and multiply an element by a constant over a finite field, respectively.

2.1   Huff Curves and Arithmetic Operations

Huff Curves: Huff curves [19] over $\mathbb{K}$ of characteristic $\neq 2$ are defined by the equation

$$E_{\mu,\nu} : \mu x(y^2 - 1) = \nu y(x^2 - 1)$$

where $\mu, \nu \in \mathbb{K}^\times$ and $\mu^2 \neq \nu^2$. $E_{\mu,\nu}/\mathbb{K}$ has the identity element $(0,0)$ and three 2-torsion points $(1 : 0 : 0)$, $(0 : 1 : 0)$ and $(\mu : \nu : 0)$ at infinity. The form $E_{\mu,\nu}$ can also be simplified as

$$H_c : cx(y^2 - 1) = y(x^2 - 1)$$

where $c = \mu/\nu$, which doesn't affect the change in coordinates. Generalized Huff curves proposed by Wu and Feng [20] are defined by the equation

$$H_{a,b}/\mathbb{K} : x(ay^2 - 1) = y(bx^2 - 1). \tag{1}$$

If $a = \mu^2$ and $b = \nu^2$ are squares over $\mathbb{K}$, $H_{a,b}$ is $\mathbb{K}-$isomorphic to the Huff model curve $\mu x'(y'^2 - 1) = \nu y'(x'^2 - 1)$ by the transformation $x' = \nu x$ and $y' = \mu y$.

Unified Addition and Doubling Operations on Huff Curves: For points (x_1, y_1) and (x_2, y_2) on generalized Huff curves $H_{a,b}$, the unified addition of them (i.e., the addition and doubling share the same formulae) is defined as below

$$(x_3, y_3) = \left(\frac{(x_1 + x_2)(1 + ay_1y_2)}{(1 + bx_1x_2)(1 - ay_1y_2)}, \frac{(y_1 + y_2)(1 + bx_1x_2)}{(1 - bx_1x_2)(1 + ay_1y_2)} \right). \tag{2}$$

When points (x_1, y_1) and (x_2, y_2) are on Huff curves H_c, the unified addition of them can be performed as follows:

$$(x_3, y_3) = \left(\frac{(x_1 + x_2)(1 + y_1y_2)}{(1 + x_1x_2)(1 - y_1y_2)}, \frac{(y_1 + y_2)(1 + x_1x_2)}{(1 - x_1x_2)(1 + y_1y_2)} \right). \tag{3}$$

Generally speaking, a projective coordinates $(X : Y : Z) \in \mathbb{P}^2$ where $x = \frac{X}{Z}$ and $y = \frac{Y}{Z}$ is used for the corresponding affine point (x, y) to avoid inversions during elliptic curve arithmetic operations. There are other coordinates system relating to Huff curves such as embedded coordinates $(XT : YZ : TZ)$ which represents the point $((X : Z), (Y : T))$ where $x = \frac{X}{Z}$ and $y = \frac{Y}{T}$ [17].

Odd-Degree Isogenies Between Generalized Huff Curves: Let $F = \{(0,0), (\alpha_i, \beta_i), (-\alpha_i, -\beta_i) : i = 1...s)\}$ be the desired kernel of an isogeny. Let $A = \Pi_{i=1}^s \alpha_i$ and $B = \Pi_{i=1}^s \beta_i$, ψ is an ℓ-isogeny from the curve $H_{a,b}$ to the curve $H_{\widehat{a},\widehat{b}}$ where $\widehat{a} = a^\ell B^4$ and $\widehat{b} = b^\ell A^4$, which is proposed by Moody et al. [18] as follows:

$$\psi(x,y) = \left(x\Pi_{i=1}^s \frac{x^2 - \alpha_i^2}{\alpha_i^2(1 - b^2\alpha_i^2x^2)}, y\Pi_{i=1}^s \frac{y^2 - \beta_i^2}{\beta_i^2(1 - a^2\beta_i^2y^2)} \right). \tag{4}$$

The evaluations of ℓ-isogeny point and ℓ-isogeny curve with projective coordinates $(X : Y : Z)$ need $(8s + 3)M + 3S$ and $8sM + 12S$, respectively, where $\ell = 2s + 1$.

Even-Degree Isogenies Between Generalized Huff Curves: Suppose ψ is a 2-isogeny from the curve $H_{a,b}$ to the curve $H_{\hat{a},\hat{b}}$, where $\hat{a} = -(\sqrt{a}+\sqrt{b})^2$ and $\hat{b} = -(\sqrt{a}-\sqrt{b})^2$. The explicit formula for $\psi(x,y) = (x',y')$ in [18] is given as

$$
\begin{aligned}
x' &= \frac{(bx-ay)((bx-ay)+\sqrt{ab}(x-y))^2}{(b-a)^2(bx^2-ay^2)}, \\
y' &= \frac{(bx-ay)((bx-ay)-\sqrt{ab}(x-y))^2}{(b-a)^2(bx^2-ay^2)}.
\end{aligned}
\tag{5}
$$

Note that the kernel of ψ is $\{(0:0),(a:b:0)\}$, where $(a:b:0)$ is a 2-torsion point at infinity. The evaluations of 2-isogeny point and 2-isogeny curve with projective coordinates $(X:Y:Z)$ need two square root calculations and a few M and S.

2.2 SIDH

We give a brief description of the SIDH as follows, while for a more detailed overview we recommend the lectures of [21].

Let p be a large prime of the form $p = f \cdot \ell_A^{e_A} \cdot \ell_B^{e_B} \pm 1$ for some integer cofactor f, ℓ_A and ℓ_B are small prime numbers, e_A and e_B are positive integers such that $\ell_A^{e_A} \approx \ell_B^{e_B}$. Then we can easily choose a supersingular elliptic curve E_0 over $\mathbb{F}_{p^2}$, with the cardinality $\#E_0 = (f \cdot \ell_A^{e_A} \cdot \ell_B^{e_B})^2$. Thus we have the full ℓ^e- torsion subgroups on E_0 for $\ell \in \{\ell_A, \ell_B\}$ and $e \in \{e_A, e_B\}$. The generation of ℓ^e- torsion subgroup needs to choose two independent points P, Q of orders ℓ^e as the basis.

Suppose Alice and Bob want to exchange a secret key. The system generates a basis $\{P_A, Q_A\}$ for Alice and $\{P_B, Q_B\}$ for Bob. For key generation, Alice selects a random number $m_A \in \{1, 2, ..., \ell_A^{e_A-1}-1\}$ and computes the isogeny $\phi_A : E_0 \to E_A$ with kernel $\langle G_A \rangle = \langle P_A + \ell_A m_A Q_A \rangle$. Then Alice calculates $\phi_A(P_B), \phi_A(Q_B)$ and sends to Bob these points together with her computed curve E_A. Bob repeats the same operation as Alice so that Alice receives $(E_B, \phi_B(P_A), \phi_B(Q_A))$.

For the key establishment, Alice calculates the isogeny $\phi_{A'} : E_B \to E_{AB}$ with kernel $\langle \phi_B(G_A) \rangle = \langle \phi_B(P_A) + \ell_A m_A \phi_B(Q_A) \rangle$, and obtains the curve E_{AB}. Bob repeats the same operation as Alice and calculates the isogeny $\phi_{B'} : E_A \to E_{BA}$ with kernel $\langle \phi_A(G_B) \rangle = \langle \phi_A(P_B) + \ell_B m_B \phi_A(Q_B) \rangle$ and obtains the curve E_{BA}. Finally Alice and Bob obtain the shared secret as the j-invariant of E_{AB}, i.e. $j(E_{AB}) = j(E_{BA})$.

3 Optimized Addition, Doubling and Tripling Operations on Huff Curves

In this section, we provide new differential addition, doubling and tripling formulae on Huff curves H_c with w-coordinates.

Define the rational function w by $w(x,y) = \frac{1}{xy}$ corresponding to the point $P = (x,y)$ on H_c. Suppose $P = (x,y)$, then $-P = (-x,-y)$, thus $w(P) =$

$w(-P)$. The neutral point $(0,0)$ under the action of w-coordinate is $w(0,0) = \infty$. According to the relationship $cx(y^2 - 1) = y(x^2 - 1)$, we can get $w = \frac{1}{xy} = \frac{cy-x}{cx-y}$. Thus

$$x^2 = \frac{c+w}{w(cw+1)},$$
$$y^2 = \frac{1+cw}{w(w+c)}. \tag{6}$$

Let w_P, w_Q, w_{2P}, w_{P-Q} and w_{P+Q} be the corresponding w-coordinates of points P, Q, $2P$, $P-Q$ and $P+Q$, respectively. According to the addition formula Eq. (3), we have

$$x_{2P}y_{2P} = \frac{4x_P y_P}{(1-y_P^2)(1-x_P^2)}, \tag{7}$$

$$x_{P+Q}y_{P+Q} = \frac{(x_P + x_Q)(y_P + y_Q)}{(1 - y_P y_Q)(1 - x_P x_Q)}, \tag{8}$$

and

$$x_{P-Q}y_{P-Q} = \frac{(x_P - x_Q)(y_P - y_Q)}{(1 + y_P y_Q)(1 + x_P x_Q)}. \tag{9}$$

By multiplying Eq. (8) and Eq. (9), it is easy to get

$$x_{P+Q}y_{P+Q}x_{P-Q}y_{P-Q} = \frac{(x_P^2 - x_Q^2)(y_P^2 - y_Q^2)}{(1 - y_P^2 y_Q^2)(1 - x_P^2 x_Q^2)}. \tag{10}$$

According to Eq. (7), Eq. (10) and Eq. (6), the doubling and differential addition formulae are

$$w_{2P} = \frac{(w_P^2 - 1)^2}{4w_P(w_P + c)(w_P + \frac{1}{c})}, \tag{11}$$
$$w_{P+Q} = \frac{(w_P w_Q - 1)^2}{(w_P - w_Q)^2 w_{P-Q}}.$$

A tripling formula can be deduced by a doubling and a differential addition formulae, i.e.,

$$w_{3P} = \frac{((w_P^2 - 1)^2 - 4(w_P + c)(w_P + \frac{1}{c}))^2 w_P}{(4w_P^2(w_P + c)(w_P + \frac{1}{c}) - (w_P^2 - 1)^2)^2}. \tag{12}$$

4   Optimized Isogenies Between Huff Curves

In this section, we exploit the w-coordinates to present new odd-degree isogeny formulae, 2-isogeny formulae as well as 4-isogeny formulae between Huff curves.

4.1   Optimized Odd-Degree Isogeny Formulae Between Huff Curves

We make use of odd-degree isogenous formulae with affine (x, y)-coordinates in the form of $H_{a,b}$ as well as the isomorphism between $H_{a,b}$ and H_c to deduce the odd-degree isogenous formulae with $w-$coordinates in the form of H_c.

Theorem 1. *Let P be a point of odd order $\ell = 2s + 1$ on Huff curve H_c. Let $\langle P \rangle = \{(0,0), (\alpha_i, \beta_i), (-\alpha_i, -\beta_i) : i = 1...s\}$. ϕ is an ℓ-isogeny, with kernel $\langle P \rangle$, from the curve H_c to the curve $H_{\hat{c}}$ where $\hat{c} = c \cdot \Pi_{i=1}^{s}(\frac{1+c \cdot w_i}{c + w_i})^2$. Let $w = \frac{1}{xy}$ where $(x, y) \in H_c$ and $w_i = \frac{1}{\alpha_i \beta_i}$ for $i = 1, ..., s$, the evaluation of w under the map ϕ is given by*

$$\phi(w) = w \cdot \Pi_{i=1}^{s} \left(\frac{w \cdot w_i - 1}{w - w_i} \right)^2. \tag{13}$$

Proof. The desired isogeny ϕ can be derived as

$$\phi : H_c \xrightarrow{\phi_1} H_{a,b} \xrightarrow{\phi_2} H_{\hat{a}, \hat{b}} \xrightarrow{\phi_3} H_{\hat{c}},$$

where the explicit formulae of ϕ_i and related elliptic curves are presented as follows.

– The map

$$\phi_1(x, y) = (x, y/c), \tag{14}$$

sends the H_c to the generalized Huff form $H_{a,b} : x(c^2 \cdot y^2 - 1) = y(x^2 - 1)$ where $a = c^2$ and $b = 1$, together with these kernel points (α_i, β_i) mapped to $(\alpha_i, \beta_i/c)$.
– The map ϕ_2 is the odd-degree isogeny ψ mentioned in Eq. (4) with kernel $\{(0, 0), (\alpha_i, \beta_i/c), (-\alpha_i, -\beta_i/c) : i = 1...s\}$ on $H_{a,b}$. Under the map, we have the image curve $H_{\hat{a}, \hat{b}}$ where $\hat{a} = c^{2\ell} \Pi_{i=1}^{s}(\beta_i/c)^4 = c^2(\Pi_{i=1}^{s}\beta_i)^4$ and $\hat{b} = (\Pi_{i=1}^{s}\alpha_i)^4$.
– The map $\phi_3(x, y) = (\sqrt{\hat{b}}x, \sqrt{\hat{a}}y)$ sends the $H_{\hat{a}, \hat{b}}$ to $H_{\hat{c}}$ where

$$\hat{c} = \frac{\sqrt{\hat{a}}}{\sqrt{\hat{b}}} = \frac{c(\Pi_{i=1}^{s}\beta_i)^2}{(\Pi_{i=1}^{s}\alpha_i)^2}. \tag{15}$$

Let $\phi(x, y) = \phi_3 \circ \phi_2 \circ \phi_1(x, y) = (X, Y)$, then

$$\frac{1}{XY} = \frac{1}{xy} \Pi_{i=1}^{s} \frac{(1 - \alpha_i^2 x^2)(1 - \beta_i^2 y^2)}{(x^2 - \alpha_i^2)(y^2 - \beta_i^2)}.$$

By combining Eq. (6), the above equation can be simplified as

$$\frac{1}{XY} = w \cdot \Pi_{i=1}^{s} \left(\frac{w \cdot w_i - 1}{w - w_i} \right)^2, \tag{16}$$

which gives Eq. (13).

The parameter $\hat{c}$ of the isogenous curve $H_{\hat{c}}$ can be computed as

$$\hat{c} = c \Pi_{i=1}^{s} \left(\frac{1 + cw_i}{c + w_i} \right)^2.$$

$\square$

4.2 Optimized 2-Isogeny Formulae Between Huff Curves

In this subsection, we derive three 2-isogeny formulae with w-coordinates in the form of H_c. We first utilize the corresponding 2-isogeny formulae with kernel $\{(0,0), (a : b : 0)\}$ on $H_{a,b}$ and the isomorphism between $H_{a,b}$ and H_c to deduce the 2-isogeny formulae with kernel $\{(0,0), (c : 1 : 0)\}$ in the form of H_c. Subsequently, we use the similar trick as that on Montgomery curves [21] to derive other 2-isogeny formulae with kernels $\{(0,0), (1 : 0 : 0)\}$ and $\{(0,0), (0 : 1 : 0)\}$, respectively, in the form of H_c.

Theorem 2. *Suppose* $\phi : H_c \to H_{\widehat{c}}$ *is an 2-isogeny with kernel* $\{(0,0), (c : 1 : 0)\}$, *where* $\widehat{c} = |\frac{c+1}{1-c}|$. *Let* $w = \frac{1}{xy}$ *where* $(x, y) \in H_c$, *the evaluation of* w *under* ϕ *is given by*

$$\phi(w) = \frac{(w + c)(cw + 1)}{(c^2 - 1)w}. \tag{17}$$

Proof. The desired isogeny ϕ can be derived as

$$\phi : H_c \xrightarrow{\phi_1} H_{a,b} \xrightarrow{\phi_2} H_{a',b'} \xrightarrow{\phi_3} H_{\widehat{c}},$$

where the explicit formulae of ϕ_i and related elliptic curves are presented as follows.

- Applying the map ϕ_1 in Eq. (14), we can get the image curve with the generalized Huff form $H_{a,b} : x(c^2 \cdot y^2 - 1) = y(x^2 - 1)$ where $a = c^2$ and $b = 1$.
- The map ϕ_2 is the 2-isogeny ψ mentioned in Eq. (5). Under the map, we have the isogenous curve $H_{a',b'}$ where $a' = -(c+1)^2$ and $b' = -(c-1)^2$.
- The map

$$\phi_3(x, y) = (\sqrt{b'}\, x, \sqrt{a'}\, y),$$

sends the curve $H_{a',b'}$ to $H_{\widehat{c}}$ where $\widehat{c} = \frac{\sqrt{a'}}{\sqrt{b'}} = |\frac{c+1}{1-c}|$.

Let $\phi(x, y) = \phi_3 \circ \phi_2 \circ \phi_1(x, y) = (X, Y)$, then

$$\frac{1}{XY} = \frac{(c^2 - 1)^3 (x^2 - y^2)^2}{((x - cy)^2 ((x - cy)^2 - (cx - y)^2)^2}. \tag{18}$$

A combination of Eq. (18) and Eq. (6) yields an equation

$$\frac{1}{XY} = \frac{(w + c)(cw + 1)}{(c^2 - 1)w},$$

which gives Eq. (17).   □

Lemma 1. *Suppose* $\phi : H_c \to H_{\widehat{c}}$ *is an 2-isogeny with kernel* $\{(0,0), (1 : 0 : 0)\}$, *where* $\widehat{c} = \left|\frac{\sqrt{-c^2} + \sqrt{1-c^2}}{\sqrt{-c^2} - \sqrt{1-c^2}}\right|$. *Let* $w = \frac{1}{xy}$ *where* $(x, y) \in H_c$, *the evaluation of* w *under* ϕ *is given by*

$$\phi(w) = \frac{w(1 + cw)}{(c + w)}. \tag{19}$$

Proof. The desired isogeny ϕ can be derived as

$$\phi : H_c \xrightarrow{\phi_1} H_{a,b} \xrightarrow{\phi_2} E_1 \xrightarrow{\phi_3} E_2 \xrightarrow{\phi_4} E_3 \xrightarrow{\phi_5} E_4 \xrightarrow{\phi_6} H_{\widehat{a},\widehat{b}} \xrightarrow{\phi_7} H_{\widehat{c}},$$

where the explicit formula of ϕ_i and related elliptic curves are presented as follows.

- The map $\phi_1 : H_c \to H_{a,b}$ has been given in Eq. (14), where $a = c^2$ and $b = 1$.
- The map

$$\phi_2(x, y) = \left(\frac{bx - ay}{y - x}, \frac{b - a}{y - x} \right)$$

sends the $H_{a,b}$ to the Weierstrass curve $E_1 : y^2 = x^3 + (a + b)x^2 + abx$.
- The map

$$\phi_3(x, y) = (x + a, y)$$

sends the E_1 to the Weierstrass curve $E_2 : y^2 = x(x + b - a)(x - a)$. The 2-isogeny with kernel $\{\mathcal{O}, (0, 0)\}$ on E_2 is

$$\phi_4(x, y) = \left(\frac{x^2 - ab + a^2}{x}, y \frac{x^2 + ab - a^2}{x^2} \right),$$

which sends the curve E_2 to

$$E_3 : y^2 = x^3 + (b - 2a)x^2 + 4a(b - a)x + 4a(b - a)(b - 2a).$$

- The linear transformation

$$\phi_5(x, y) = (x + b - 2a, y), \tag{20}$$

translates the E_3 to $E_4 : y^2 = x^3 - 2(b - 2a)x^2 + b^2x$.
- E_4 can be changed to the Huff curve $H_{\widehat{a},\widehat{b}}$ via the map

$$\phi_6(x, y) = \left(\frac{x - (\sqrt{-c^2} + \sqrt{1 - c^2})^2}{y}, \frac{x - (\sqrt{-c^2} - \sqrt{1 - c^2})^2}{y} \right),$$

where $\widehat{a} = -(\sqrt{-c^2} + \sqrt{1 - c^2})^2$ and $\widehat{b} = -(\sqrt{-c^2} - \sqrt{1 - c^2})^2$.
- Under the rational map

$$\phi_7(x, y) = (\sqrt{\widehat{b}}x, \sqrt{\widehat{a}}y),$$

we convert the $H_{\widehat{a},\widehat{b}}$ back to $H_{\widehat{c}}$, with

$$\widehat{c} = \frac{\sqrt{\widehat{a}}}{\sqrt{\widehat{b}}} = \left| \frac{\sqrt{-c^2} + \sqrt{1 - c^2}}{\sqrt{-c^2} - \sqrt{1 - c^2}} \right|.$$

In sum, the composition of the maps $\phi_i (i = 1, ..., 6)$ leads to the map ϕ, i.e.,

$$\phi(x, y) = \phi_7 \circ \phi_6 \circ \phi_5 \circ \phi_4 \circ \phi_3 \circ \phi_2 \circ \phi_1(x, y).$$

Let $\phi(x, y) = (X, Y)$, then

$$\frac{1}{XY} = \frac{1}{x^2}.$$

Replacing the item x^2 with Eq. (6), we can get Eq. (19).   □

Lemma 2. *Suppose $\phi : H_c \rightarrow H_{\widehat{c}}$ is an 2-isogeny with kernel $\{(0,0), (0 : 1 : 0)$, where $\widehat{c} = \left| \frac{\sqrt{-1}+\sqrt{c^2-1}}{\sqrt{-1}-\sqrt{c^2+1}} \right|$. Let $w = \frac{1}{xy}$ where $(x,y) \in H_c$, the evaluation of w under ϕ is given by*

$$\phi(w) = \frac{c^2 w(w + c)}{1 + cw}.$$

The proof is similar to Lemma 1, here we omit the details.

4.3   4-Isogeny Formulae Between Huff Curves

Note that the points of order 2 are all at infinity, it is not easy to choose an appropriate 2-isogeny formula with w-coordinates for computing 2^e-isogeny when $e \geq 2$. Here we show how to obtain explicit 4-isogeny formulae by exploiting the 4-division polynomial.

By applying the isomorphism between the Huff model and the Weierstrass model of elliptic curves, we can deduce the 4-division polynomial on the H_c with w-coordinate as

$$\psi_4(w) = c(w - 1)(w + 1)\widehat{\psi}_4(w),$$

where $\widehat{\psi}_4(w) = (2cw + w^2 + 1)(cw^2 + c + 2w)$.

For the point w_4 such that $\widehat{\psi}_4(w_4) = 0$, we can composite the 2-isogeny respectively with kernel $\{(0,0), (1 : 0 : 0)\}$ and $\{(0,0), (0 : 1 : 0)\}$ to get the general 4-isogeny formula

$$\phi(w) = \frac{w(ww_4^2 + w - 2w_4)(w^2 w_4^2 - 2ww_4 + 1)}{(w^2 - 2ww_4 + w_4^2)(2ww_4 - w_4^2 - 1)}$$

where $\widehat{c} = \frac{w_4^2 + \sqrt{w_4^4 - 1}}{w_4^2 - \sqrt{w_4^4 - 1}}$.

For $w_4 = \pm 1$, obviously it satisfies $\psi_4(w_4) = 0$, we composite the 2-isogeny with kernel $\{(0,0), (c : 1 : 0)\}$ to get the first 4-isogeny formula as

$$\phi(w) = -\frac{(w + 1)^2 (cw + 1)(w + c)}{(c - 1)^2 w(w - 1)^2},$$

where $\widehat{c} = \frac{c^2 + 4\sqrt{c}(c+1) + 6c + 1}{(c-1)^2}$.

Note that the evaluation of 4-isogeny curve needs square root computation (i.e., to obtain the coefficient $\widehat{c}$), which would remarkably increase the computational cost of SIDH. Fortunately, we only need to compute $\widehat{c} + \frac{1}{c}$ instead of $\widehat{c}$, which could avoid the square root computation. In the following we will see that $\widehat{c} + \frac{1}{c} = \frac{2(2W_4^4 - Z_4^4))}{Z_4^4}$ (in projective coordinates, where (W_4, Z_4) has order 4) for the general 4-isogeny curve, while $\widehat{c} + \frac{1}{\widehat{c}} = \frac{2(c + \frac{1}{c} + 6)}{c + \frac{1}{c} - 2}$ for the first 4-isogeny curve.

5   Efficiency Analysis

In this section, we first analyze the efficiency of arithmetic operations on a fixed Huff curve H_c with projective coordinates $(W : Z)$, and compare them with latest costs in [17]. Then, we present the computational costs for SIDH on Huff curves and compare them on Montgomery curves. In addition, we propose the costs of evaluating ℓ−isogeny points and ℓ−isogeny curves between Huff curves and compare them with the work proposed by Moody and Shumow[18].

5.1   The Costs of Addition and Doubling Operations on a Fixed Huff Curve H_c

Assume the w_P, w_Q, w_{2P}, w_{P-Q} and w_{P+Q} are given as fractions W_P/Z_P, W_Q/Z_Q, W_{2P}/Z_{2P}, W_{P-Q}/Z_{P-Q} and W_{P+Q}/Z_{P+Q}, respectively. From Eq. (11), the explicit projective formulae are given as

$$\frac{W_{2P}}{Z_{2P}} = \frac{(W_P - Z_P)^2 (W_P + Z_P)^2}{4W_P Z_P((W_P + Z_P)^2 + \widehat{C}W_P Z_P)},$$

$$\frac{W_{P+Q}}{Z_{P+Q}} = \frac{(W_P W_Q - Z_P Z_Q)^2 Z_{P-Q}}{(W_P Z_Q - Z_P W_Q)^2 W_{P-Q}}, \tag{21}$$

where $\widehat{C} = (c + \frac{1}{c} - 2)$.

On a fixed curve H_c, the doubling operation takes $2M + 2S + C$ if $\widehat{C} = c + \frac{1}{c} - 2$ is precomputed. The justification of the claimed operation count is given as

$$t_0 = (W_P + Z_P)^2, \quad t_1 = (W_P - Z_P)^2, \quad t_2 = 4 \cdot t_0, \quad W_{2P} = t_2 \cdot t_1,$$

$$t_0 = t_0 - t_1, \quad t_1 = \widehat{C} \cdot t_0, \quad t_2 = t_2 + t_1, \quad Z_{2P} = t_2 \cdot t_0.$$

If we set $Z_{P-Q} = 1$, the addition operation takes $3M + 2S$. The justification of the claimed operation count states as

$$t_0 = (W_P - Z_P)(W_Q + Z_Q), \quad t_1 = (W_P + Z_P)(W_Q - Z_Q), \quad t_2 = t_0 + t_1,$$

$$t_3 = t_0 - t_1, \quad W_{P+Q} = t_2^2, \quad t_1 = t_3^2, \quad Z_{P+Q} = t_1 \cdot W_{P-Q}.$$

To resist against the side-channel attack of scalar multiplications on Huff curves, we adopt the regular scalar multiplication algorithm proposed by

Farashashi et al. [15], which perfectly matches the mixed projective w-coordinate differential addition and doubling formulae as Eq. (21). Such trick is similar to that on Montgomery curves or Edwards curves [15,22]. If we set $Z_{P-Q} = 1$, the mixed projective w-coordinate formulae have the total cost $5M + 4S + 1C$ as follows:

$$t_0 = (W_P + Z_P), \quad s_0 = (W_P - Z_P), \quad t_1 = (W_Q + Z_Q), \quad s_1 = (W_Q - Z_Q),$$
$$t_2 = t_0 \cdot s_1, \quad s_2 = t_1 \cdot s_0, \quad t_3 = t_0^2 - s_0^2, \quad Z_{2P} = t_3 \cdot (4t_0^2 - \widehat{C}t_3), \quad W_{2P} = 4t_0^2 \cdot s_0^2,$$
$$W_{P+Q} = (t_2 + s_2)^2, \quad Z_{P+Q} = (t_2 - s_2)^2 \cdot W_{P-Q}.$$

Table 1 compares the results of arithmetic operations in different Huff forms. Note that all computations for [17] are in projective coordinates $((X : Z), (Y : T))$ and the addition of P, Q (with $T_Q = 1$) is unified, while our work adopts the projective coordinates $(W : Z)$ (with $Z_{P-Q} = 1$) on H_c.

Table 1. Arithmetic operations on fixed Huff forms

The curve equation	Doubling	Addition
$YT(Z^2 + X^2) = cXZ(T^2 + Y^2)$ [17]	$8M$	$8M$
$cx(y^2 - 1) = y(x^2 - 1)$ (This work)	$2M + 2S + C$	$3M + 2S$

5.2   Implementing Considerations for SIDH on Huff Curves

We first provide the computational costs of the optimized doubling, tripling, evaluating 4-isogeny point and 4-isogeny curve, as well as evaluating ℓ-isogeny point and ℓ-isogeny curve (particularly evaluating 3-isogeny point and evaluating 3-isogeny curve) with projective $(W : Z)$-coordinates where ℓ is an odd number. Subsequently, we compare them with those on Montgomery curves in the setting of SIDH. Note that we only need to compute the curve coefficient $\frac{1}{4}(c + \frac{1}{c} - 2)$ instead of computing c, since it has the benefit not only in evaluating the isogenous curve but also in performing the doubling and tripling operations. In the following we denote $\frac{A_1}{A_2} = \frac{1}{4}(c + \frac{1}{c} - 2)$.

Doubling. For $P = (W_P : Z_P)$ on Huff curve H_c, the doubling of P gives $[2]P = (W_{2P} : Z_{2P})$, where W_{2P} and Z_{2P} are defined as follows:

$$W_{2P} = A_2(W_P - Z_P)^2(W_P + Z_P)^2,$$
$$Z_{2P} = 4W_PZ_P(A_2(W_P + Z_P)^2 + A_1 \cdot 4W_PZ_P).$$

The cost of this computation is $4M + 2S$.

Tripling. For $P = (W_P : Z_P)$ on Huff curve H_c represented in projective coordinates, the tripling of P gives $[3]P = (W_{3P} : W_{3P})$, where W_{3P} and Z_{3P}

are defined as

$$W_{3P} = W_P(16A_1W_P Z_P^3 - A_2(W_P - 3Z_P)(W_P + Z_P)^3)^2,$$
$$Z_{3P} = Z_P(16A_1W_P^3 Z_P + A_2(3W_P - Z_P)(W_P + Z_P)^3)^2,$$

which takes $7M + 5S$.

Projective ℓ-isogeny. We use the projective $(W : Z)-$coordinates to evaluate the computational costs of the proposed ℓ-isogeny formulae Eq. (13). Let $w(P_i) = (W_i, Z_i)$ for $i = 1, 2, ..s$ such that P has exact order ℓ on H_c, then any point $(W : Z)$ under the ℓ-isogeny ϕ can be evaluated as $(W' : Z') = \phi(W : Z)$. Specific expressions can be written as

$$W' = W \Pi_{i=1}^s (WW_i - ZZ_i)^2,$$
$$Z' = Z \Pi_{i=1}^s (WZ_i - ZW_i)^2.$$

Thus, evaluating ℓ-isogeny needs $4sM + 2S$.

Let $c = \frac{C_1}{C_2}$. Any curve coefficient $(C_1 : C_2)$ under the ℓ-isogeny ϕ can be evaluated as $(C_1' : C_2') = \phi(C_1 : C_2)$. Specific expressions can be written as

$$C_1' = C_1 \Pi_{i=1}^s (C_2 Z_i + C_1 W_i)^2,$$
$$C_2' = C_2 \Pi_{i=1}^s (C_1 Z_i + C_2 W_i)^2.$$

The evaluation of ℓ-isogeny curve needs $4sM + 2S$.

Particularly, the evaluation of 3-isogeny needs $4M + 2S$, the evaluations of the 3-isogeny curve can also use the way mentioned in [5, Appendix A], where only the coefficient $\frac{1}{4}(c + \frac{1}{c} - 2) = \frac{A_1}{A_2}$ is involved. Let $w(P) = (W_3, Z_3)$ be a point of order 3 on H_c, then specific expressions can be written as

$$A_1' = (W_3 + Z_3)(Z_3 - 3W_3)^3,$$
$$A_2' = 16W_3 Z_3^3,$$

which needs $2M + 3S$.

Projective 4-isogeny. Let $w(P) = (W_4, Z_4)$ such that P has exact order 4 on H_c. For the evaluation of 4-isogeny with projective $(W : Z)$-coordinates, it can be rewritten as

$$W' = W(2W_4 Z_4 Z - W(W_4^2 + Z_4^2))(W_4 W - Z_4 Z)^2,$$
$$Z' = Z(2W_4 Z_4 W - Z(W_4^2 + Z_4^2))(Z_4 W - W_4 Z)^2.$$

The 4-isogeny formula has the same form as that on Montgomery curve, thus needing $6M + 2S$ with one common squaring used to evaluate 4-isogeny curve [5]. Moreover, the coefficients of the image Huff curve can be given as

$$A_1' = W_4^4 - Z_4^4,$$
$$A_2' = Z_4^4,$$

Table 2. The evaluation of isogenous points and isogenous curves on variable Huff forms

	Moody and Shumow [18]	This work
eval_ℓ_isog	$(8s + 3)M + 3S$	$4sM + 2S$
get_ℓ_isog	8sM+12S	$4sM + 2S$
eval_4_isog	Square root calculation	$6M + 2S$
get_4_isog	Square root calculation	$4S$

which needs $4S$.

The Comparisons with Moody and Shumow's Work. Table 2 presents the costs of evaluating ℓ-isogeny point and ℓ-isogeny curve, as well as evaluating 4-isogeny point and 4-isogeny curve on variable Huff curves. The get_ℓ_isog and get_4_isog are functions that compute the coefficients of the isogenous curves, while the eval_ℓ_isog and eval_4_isog are functions that evaluate the isogenies with given input points. As shown in Table 2, the evaluations of ℓ-isogeny point and ℓ-isogeny curve with projective coordinates $(W : Z)$ have great advantage over Moody and Shumow's work with projective coordinates $(X : Y : Z)$ [18]. Besides, the evaluations of 4-isogeny point and 4-isogeny curve with projective coordinates $(W : Z)$ in our wok can avoid square root calculation.

The Comparisons for SIDH Computation. The computation of SIDH includes performing doubling operations and tripling operations, evaluating 4-isogeny points and 4-isogeny curves, as well as evaluating 3-isogeny points and 3-isogeny curves. Table 3 presents the costs of these operations on Montgomery curves [5] and Huff curves. These operations for SIDH on Huff curves share the same computational costs as those on Montgomery curves.

Table 3. Operation costs of SIDH on different curves.

	Montgomery curve [5]	Huff curves
Doubling	4M+2S	4M+2S
Differential addition	4M+2S	4M+2S
get_4_isog	4S	4S
eval_4_isog	6M+2S	6M+2S
Tripling	7M+5S	7M+5S
get_3_isog	2M+3S	2M+3S
eval_3_isog	4M+2S	4M+2S

6   Implementation Results

To evaluate the performance, the algorithms are implemented in C language[2] and on top of the Microsoft SIDH library version 3.0 [24]. All cycle counts were obtained on one core of an Intel Core i7-782x (Skylake-X) at 3.60 GHZ, running Ubuntu 18.04 LTS. For compilation, we used GNU GCC version 7.4.0.

We consider finite field $\mathbb{F}_{p^2}$ where $p = 2^{250}3^{159}-1$ and the initial Huff curve is $c_0x(y^2-1) = y(x^2-1)$ where $c_0 = 4382828174314358768738669361528362374640144022886202834690766438118847939413850683691909151755979923699738866893354958678967660034080196475226251097525$ corresponding to the Montgomery curve $y^2 = x^3 + 6x^2 + x$. We first measure the field operations in Table 4 which summarizes the average cycle counts of field operations over $\mathbb{F}_{p^2}$.

Table 4. Cycle counts of the field operations over $\mathbb{F}_{p^2}$

Field operations	Addition	Multiplication	Squaring	Inversion
Cycle counts	42	454	380	106456

Table 5 compares the cycle counts of point addition and doubling operations on fixed Huff curves. The addition operation and doubling operation on $c_0x(y^2-1) = y(x^2-1)$ with projective $(W:Z)$-coordinates are 43% and 42% faster, respectively, than those operations with projective coordinates $((X:Z),(Y:T))$ on $YT(Z^2+X^2) = cXZ(T^2+Y^2)$.

Table 5. Implementation results of arithmetic operations on the same fixed Huff curves

Huff curves	Addition	Doubling
$YT(Z^2+X^2) = cXZ(T^2+Y^2)$[17]	3632	3632
$c_0x(y^2-1) = y(x^2-1)$ (This work)	2048	2122
Speed-up	43%	42%

Table 6 compares the cycle counts of evaluating different degree isogenous points and curves. These operations with projective $(W:Z)$-coordinates in our work are at least 50% faster than those operations in Moody and Shumow's work [18].

Table 7 compares the cycle counts for implementing the SIDH on Montgomery curves and Huff curves, respectively. For the implementation of SIDH on Huff curves, the parameter c_0 of the initial curve $c_0x(y^2-1) = y(x^2-1)$ needs to

---

[2] See https://github.com/Zhi-Hu-CSU/huzhi/blob/master/Opt-Arith-Operat-isogeny-Huff.zip.

Table 6. Implementation results of evaluating different isogenies

Operation	Moody and Shumow [18]	This work	Speed-up
eval_3_isog	6134	2048	66%
get_3_isog	8192	2576	68%
eval_4_isog	235256	3484	98%
get_4_isog	685846	1520	99%
eval_5_isog	9766	4392	55%
get_5_isog	11824	4392	63%
eval_7_isog	13398	6208	53%
get_7_isog	15456	6208	59%
eval_11_isog	20662	9840	52%
get_11_isog	22720	9840	56%

Table 7. Performance results of SIDH implementation using Huff curves and Montgomery curves.

	Montgomery curve [5]	Huff curves
Alice's keygen	6949582	6910882
Bob's keygen	7672982	7699406
Alice's shared key	5722556	5647278
Bob's shared key	6501746	6522455
Total	26846866	26780021

be transformed into the form $\frac{A_1}{A_2} = \frac{(c_0-1)^2}{4c_0}$, which costs a squaring and 3 addition over $\mathbb{F}_p$. Nevertheless, this can be precomputed. The computational issues listed in Table 3 with the computations of doubling, differential addition, tripling, get_4_isog, eval_4_isog, get_3_isog and eval_3_isog with the curve parameters $\frac{A_1}{A_2}$ have the same costs as those on Montgomery curves. Thus the implementation results on Montgomery curves and Huff curves for SIDH are almost identical.

7   Conclusion

In this work, we exploit the w-coordinates to optimize the elliptic curve group arithmetic formulas as well as the isogenous formulas on Huff curves. On fixed Huff curves, the operations of point addition and doubling both at least have a speedup of 40% compared with the corresponding latest operations proposed by Orhon and Hisil. On variable Huff curves, the operations for evaluating different degree isogenous points and curves both at least have a speedup of 50% compared with the only corresponding work proposed by Moody and Shumow. For the implementation of SIDH, the results show that the desired computational issues on Huff curves provide the same efficiency as those on Montgomery curves, which implies that Huff curves would also serve as an ideal model for isogeny-based cryptography and thus be worth further study.

Acknowledgements. The first and second authors are supported by the National Key R&D Program of China (2017YFB0802500) and the National Natural Science Foundation of China (No. 61672550, No. 61972429) and the Major Program of Guangdong Basic and Applied Research (2019B030302008). The third author is supported by the Natural Science Foundation of China (No. 61972420, No. 61602526) and Hunan Provincial Natural Science Foundation of China (2019JJ50827, 2020JJ3050).

References

1. Jao, D., De Feo, L.: Towards quantum-resistant cryptosystems from supersingular elliptic curve isogenies. In: Yang, B.-Y. (ed.) PQCrypto 2011. LNCS, vol. 7071, pp. 19–34. Springer, Heidelberg (2011). https://doi.org/10.1007/978-3-642-25405-5_2
2. Jao, D., Azarderakhsh, R., Campagna, M., Costello, C., et al.: Supersingular Isogeny Key Encapsulation. NIST Post-Quantum Cryptography (2017). https://csrc.nist.gov/Projects/Post-Quantum-Cryptography/Round-2-Submissions
3. Bos, J., Friedberger, S.: Arithmetic considerations for isogeny based cryptography. IEEE Trans. Comput. **68**(7), 979–990 (2018)
4. Seo, H., Liu, Z., Longa, P., et al.: SIDH on ARM. faster modular multiplications for faster post-quantum supersingular isogeny key exchange. https://eprint.iacr.org/2018/700.pdf
5. Costello, C., Hisil, H.: A simple and compact algorithm for SIDH with arbitrary degree isogenies. In: Takagi, T., Peyrin, T. (eds.) ASIACRYPT 2017. LNCS, vol. 10625, pp. 303–329. Springer, Cham (2017). https://doi.org/10.1007/978-3-319-70697-9_11
6. Kim, S., Yoon, K., Kwon, J., et al.: New hybrid method for isogeny-based cryptosystems using Edwards curves. IEEE Trans. Inf. Theor. **99**, 1 (2019)
7. Costello, C.: Computing supersingular isogenies on kummer surfaces. In: Peyrin, T., Galbraith, S. (eds.) ASIACRYPT 2018. LNCS, vol. 11274, pp. 428–456. Springer, Cham (2018). https://doi.org/10.1007/978-3-030-03332-3_16
8. Petit, C.: Faster algorithms for isogeny problems using torsion point images. In: Takagi, T., Peyrin, T. (eds.) ASIACRYPT 2017. LNCS, vol. 10625, pp. 330–353. Springer, Cham (2017). https://doi.org/10.1007/978-3-319-70697-9_12
9. Castryck, W., Lange, T., Martindale, C., Panny, L., Renes, J.: CSIDH: an efficient post-quantum commutative group action. In: Peyrin, T., Galbraith, S. (eds.) ASIACRYPT 2018. LNCS, vol. 11274, pp. 395–427. Springer, Cham (2018). https://doi.org/10.1007/978-3-030-03332-3_15
10. Rostovtsev, A., Stolbunov, A.: Public-key cryptosystem based on isogenies. https://eprint.iacr.org/2006/145.pdf
11. Delfs, C., Galbraith, S.D.: Computing isogenies between supersingular elliptic curves over $\mathbb{F}_p$. Des. Codes Cryptogr. **78**, 425–440 (2016)
12. De Feo, L., Kieffer, J., Smith, B.: Towards practical key exchange from ordinary isogeny graphs. In: Peyrin, T., Galbraith, S. (eds.) ASIACRYPT 2018. LNCS, vol. 11274, pp. 365–394. Springer, Cham (2018). https://doi.org/10.1007/978-3-030-03332-3_14

13. Bernstein, D.J., Birkner, P., Joye, M., Lange, T., Peters, C.: Twisted edwards curves. In: Vaudenay, S. (ed.) AFRICACRYPT 2008. LNCS, vol. 5023, pp. 389–405. Springer, Heidelberg (2008). https://doi.org/10.1007/978-3-540-68164-9_26
14. Meyer, M., Reith, S.: A faster way to the CSIDH. In: Chakraborty, D., Iwata, T. (eds.) INDOCRYPT 2018. LNCS, vol. 11356, pp. 137–152. Springer, Cham (2018). https://doi.org/10.1007/978-3-030-05378-9_8
15. Farashahi, R.R., Hosseini, S.G.: Differential addition on twisted edwards curves. In: Pieprzyk, J., Suriadi, S. (eds.) ACISP 2017. LNCS, vol. 10343, pp. 366–378. Springer, Cham (2017). https://doi.org/10.1007/978-3-319-59870-3_21
16. Kim, S., Yoon, K., Park, Y.-H., Hong, S.: Optimized method for computing odd-degree isogenies on Edwards curves. In: Galbraith, S.D., Moriai, S. (eds.) ASIACRYPT 2019. LNCS, vol. 11922, pp. 273–292. Springer, Cham (2019). https://doi.org/10.1007/978-3-030-34621-8_10
17. Orhon, N.G., Hisil, H.: Speeding up Huff form of elliptic curves. Des. Codes Crypt. 86(12), 2807–2823 (2018). https://doi.org/10.1007/s10623-018-0475-4
18. Moody, D., Shumow, D.: Analogues of Vélu's formulas for isogenies on alternate models of elliptic curves. Math. Comput. 85, 1929–1951 (2015)
19. Joye, M., Tibouchi, M., Vergnaud, D.: Huff's model for elliptic curves. In: Hanrot, G., Morain, F., Thomé, E. (eds.) ANTS 2010. LNCS, vol. 6197, pp. 234–250. Springer, Heidelberg (2010). https://doi.org/10.1007/978-3-642-14518-6_20
20. Wu, H., Feng, R.: Elliptic curves in Huff's model. Wuhan Univ. J. Nat. Sci. 17, 473–480 (2012)
21. De Feo, L., Jao, D., Plût, J.: Towards quantum-resistant cryptosystems from supersingular elliptic curve isogenies. J. Math. Cryptol. 8, 209–247 (2014)
22. Bernstein, D.J., Lange, T.: Montgomery curves and the montgomery ladder. https://eprint.iacr.org/2017/293.pdf
23. Costello, C., Longa, P., Naehrig, M.: Efficient algorithms for supersingular isogeny Diffie-Hellman. In: Robshaw, M., Katz, J. (eds.) CRYPTO 2016. LNCS, vol. 9814, pp. 572–601. Springer, Heidelberg (2016). https://doi.org/10.1007/978-3-662-53018-4_21
24. Costello, C., Longa, P., Naehrig, M.: SIDH library. https://github.com/microsoft/PQCrypto-SIDH

On Lattice-Based Interactive Protocols:
An Approach with Less or No Aborts

Nabil Alkeilani Alkadri[1(✉)], Rachid El Bansarkhani[2],
and Johannes Buchmann[1]

[1] Technische Universität Darmstadt, Darmstadt, Germany
nabil.alkadri@tu-darmstadt.de, buchmann@cdc.informatik.tu-darmstadt.de
[2] QuantiCor Security GmbH, Darmstadt, Germany
rachid.elbansarkhani@quanticor-security.de

Abstract. A canonical identification (CID) scheme is a 3-move protocol consisting of a commitment, challenge, and response. It constitutes the core design of many cryptographic constructions such as zero-knowledge proof systems and various types of signature schemes. Unlike number-theoretic constructions, CID in the lattice setting usually forces provers to abort and repeat the whole authentication process once the distribution of the computed response does not follow a target distribution independent from the secret key. This concept has been realized by means of rejection sampling, which makes sure that the secrets involved in a protocol are concealed after a certain number of repetitions. This however has a negative impact on the efficiency of interactive protocols because it leads to a number of communication rounds that is multiplicative in the number of aborting participants (or rejection sampling procedures). In this work we show how the CID scheme underlying many lattice-based protocols can be designed with smaller number of aborts or even without aborts. Our new technique exploits (unbalanced) binary hash trees and thus significantly reduces the communication complexity. We show how to apply this new method within interactive zero-knowledge proofs. We also present BLAZE$^+$: a further application of our technique to the recently proposed lattice-based blind signature scheme BLAZE (FC'20). We show that BLAZE$^+$ has an improved performance and communication complexity compared to BLAZE while preserving the size of keys and signatures.

Keywords: Lattice-based cryptography · Aborts · Hash trees

1 Introduction

A canonical identification (CID) scheme allows a prover $\mathcal{P}$ to prove to a verifier $\mathcal{V}$ the possession of a secret key s in the following way: $\mathcal{P}$ sends a commitment to $\mathcal{V}$, who then sends a challenge c back to $\mathcal{P}$. Upon receiving c, $\mathcal{P}$ answers with a response z. This response allows $\mathcal{V}$ to verify $\mathcal{P}$'s authenticity while not leaking any information about the secret key. In number-theoretic constructions like

© Springer Nature Switzerland AG 2020
J. K. Liu and H. Cui (Eds.): ACISP 2020, LNCS 12248, pp. 41–61, 2020.
https://doi.org/10.1007/978-3-030-55304-3_3

Schnorr's CID scheme [34], the response z already hides s, since it is computed by adding a secret masking term y to the term sc, i.e., $z = y + sc$. The term y is chosen uniformly at random from a large distribution and is also used to compute the commitment. This approach has been generalized in [22] to include aborting provers for the lattice setting. In a lattice-based CID scheme y is required to be chosen from a narrow distribution (typically, Gaussian or uniform) and the so called rejection sampling procedure [29] is used to hide the distribution of sc. If the sum z is not accepted, a new masking term is sampled. This procedure is repeated until the sum becomes independently distributed from the secret term sc. Lattice-based CID is a fundamental building block of many cryptographic constructions including zero-knowledge protocols (e.g., [6,9]) as well as signature schemes (e.g., [5,12,23]) and even those with advanced functionalities such as ring signatures (e.g., [7,35]), blind signatures [4,33], and multisignatures [14].

While aborting does not affect the efficiency of constructions with one rejection sampling process like ordinary signatures, it has a significant negative impact on the performance and communication complexity of lattice-based interactive protocols with multiple rejection sampling procedures. For instance, the multisignature scheme proposed in [14] entails a repetition rate that grows exponentially in the number of users participating in the signing protocol. Though it is efficient for a small set of users, one would need to restart the protocol very often when instantiated with a large set because each user has to carry out rejection sampling. Another example is the blind signature scheme BLAZE [4] and its predecessor introduced in [33]. In both constructions not only signers have to carry out rejection sampling and repeat the signing process M_S times until the secret key is concealed, but for maintaining blindness even users have to apply rejection sampling M_U times and request a protocol restart in case of failure. This imposes a multiplicative repetition rate $M_S \cdot M_U$ and an additional communication step due to the possibility of failures causing protocol restarts. In this case, a proof of failure is sent to the signer, i.e., a proof that allows the signer to verify the occurrence of a failure. Although BLAZE has been shown to be practical [4], this additional step increases the time and communication complexity required to generate valid signatures and forces the use of statistically hiding and computationally binding commitments to retain security.

Therefore, masking secrets in lattice-based interactive protocols with multiple rejection sampling procedures such that aborting occurs as little as possible while maintaining efficiency and security remained a very important research question. This would improve the running time and decrease the total amount of communication required to successfully complete the protocol.

Contributions. In this work we show how to reduce the number of repetitions in lattice-based protocols by means of a tool that we call *trees of commitments*. A tree of commitments is an (unbalanced) binary hash tree of height $h \geq 1$, whose leaves are the hash values of $\ell > 1$ commitments computed from masking terms sampled during an instance of a CID-based protocol. The number ℓ is chosen such that rejection sampling succeeds for at least one masking term at a

Table 1. Comparing BLAZE$^+$ (this work) with BLAZE [4] at approximately 128 bits of security. The parameter δ_{abort} denotes the aborting probability by the user, and ℓ denotes the related number of masking terms. Performance is given in cycles and milliseconds (in parentheses), sizes and communication complexity in kilobytes. The corresponding parameters can be found in Table 3. Benchmarking the parameters were carried out on an Intel Core i7-6500U, operating at 2.3 GHz and 8 GB of RAM.

Scheme	δ_{abort}	ℓ	Complexity	BS.KGen	BS.Sign	BS.Verify	sk	pk	Signature
BLAZE$^+$	2^{-128}	71	177.8	222,151 (0.11)	112,540,972 (56.49)	348,724 (0.18)	0.75	3.9	6.7
BLAZE$^+$	2^{-40}	32	189.1	222,151 (0.11)	56,193,762 (28.21)	348,724 (0.18)	0.75	3.9	6.7
BLAZE$^+$	2^{-10}	8	189.2	222,151 (0.11)	24,443,555 (12.27)	348,724 (0.18)	0.75	3.9	6.6
BLAZE	0.38	1	351.6	204,671 (0.10)	35,547,397 (17.85)	276,210 (0.14)	0.8	3.9	6.6

given probability bound. This allows to aggregate ℓ commitments in one tree and send only the root of the tree as a new commitment rather than ℓ commitments. The new response now further includes the authentication path of the leaf with index k ($0 \leq k < \ell$), where at step k rejection sampling accepts for the first time after $k - 1$ trials. Note that by choosing ℓ large enough we can remove aborts completely. Interestingly, only trees with small heights are required to reduce aborts to very small probabilities, e.g., $h = 3$ for a probability of at most 2^{-10}.

We demonstrate the effectiveness of using our method in interactive zero-knowledge proofs and blind signature schemes. More concretely, we show how to reduce the communication complexity of interactive zero-knowledge protocols by using trees of commitments in a lattice-based zero-knowledge proof of knowledge. Furthermore, we utilize trees of commitments in the blind signature scheme BLAZE [4]. We call the new scheme BLAZE$^+$. In the new scheme a user constructs a tree of commitments using ℓ masking terms such that blindness is ensured at a given probability bound. More precisely, given a security level of λ bits we fix an aborting probability δ_{abort} and compute ℓ such that signatures are blind with probability of at least $1 - \delta_{abort}$. For approximately 128 bits of security, our results (summarized in Table 1) show that while preserving the size of keys and signatures, the communication complexity is significantly decreased and the signing speed is improved for $\delta_{abort} = 2^{-10}$. Note that choosing $\delta_{abort} = 2^{-128}$ implies blindness with overwhelming probability. In this case (i.e., when $\delta_{abort} = 2^{-\lambda}$) we can safely remove the last step of the protocol, hence proof of failures and the use of commitment schemes. Thus, we obtain a 3-move version of the protocol similar to the basic structure of CID. We present this version in Sect. 4 and the 4-move scheme in the full version of this paper [3], where aborts at the user side occur with probability of choice. We leave applying trees of commitments to multisignatures [14] as a future work.

Finally, we note that the impossibility results of 3-move blind signature schemes due to [16] do not apply to our 3-move version of BLAZE$^+$. These results show that finding black-box reductions from successful forgers to some non-interactive cryptographic assumption is infeasible in the standard model (i.e., without random oracles) for statistically blind schemes with 3 (or less) moves such that one can verify that an honest user was able to obtain a valid signature from the interaction with the (malicious) signer. In our 3-move protocol, there is no way to check that the user has obtained a valid signature, since he does not reveal the secret information that are involved in generating the signature and are required to check its validity. Furthermore, BLAZE$^+$ is proven secure in the random oracle model rather than the standard model.

Techniques. We show how to reduce the number of repetitions or even remove aborts in CID-based protocols, completely. To this end, we give a brief description of the CID scheme that underlies many lattice-based constructions and was originally introduced in [22]. Let $\mathbf{A}$ be a public matrix selected uniformly at random from $\mathbb{Z}_q^{n \times m}$. The prover $\mathcal{P}$ would like to prove to a verifier $\mathcal{V}$ the possession of a secret matrix $\mathbf{S} \in \mathbb{Z}^{m \times n}$ with small entries such that $\mathbf{B} = \mathbf{AS} \pmod q$. We let χ denote some distribution over $\mathbb{Z}$. Typically, χ is either the discrete Gaussian distribution over $\mathbb{Z}$ or the uniform distribution over a small subset of $\mathbb{Z}$. The challenge space is defined by $\mathcal{C} = \{\mathbf{c} = (c_1, \ldots, c_n) \in \mathbb{Z}^n : c_i \in \{-1, 0, 1\}, \sum_1^n |c_i| = \kappa\}$. We let RejSamp denote an algorithm that carries out rejection sampling. The commitment is a vector $\mathbf{v} = \mathbf{Ay} \pmod q$, where $\mathbf{y}$ is a masking vector chosen from χ^m. For a challenge $\mathbf{c} \in \mathcal{C}$ the response is given by $\mathbf{z} = \mathbf{y} + \mathbf{Sc}$. The verifier accepts if and only if $\mathbf{v} = \mathbf{Az} - \mathbf{Bc} \pmod q$ and $\|\mathbf{z}\|_p \leq B$, where B is a predefined bound and $p \in \{2, \infty\}$ depending on the distribution χ. Aborting occurs if RejSamp$(\mathbf{z})$ does not accept. The protocol is always repeated by sampling a fresh $\mathbf{y}$ until RejSamp accepts such that $\mathbf{z}$ is statistically independent from $\mathbf{Sc}$.

Consider a lattice-based interactive protocol with $N \geq 1$ rejection sampling procedures, where each of them is repeated $x \geq 1$ times on average. The main motivation of this work is the observation that the total average number of repetitions M in such a protocol is multiplicative in N, i.e., $M = x^N$. Thus, the main question is: Can we improve it?

One can use a large enough distribution χ such that RejSamp accepts after a fixed number of repetitions M, e.g., $M \leq 2$. This is already established in previous works as a trade-off between performance and sizes (see, e.g., [5,12,23]), but it does not solve the problem for all interactive protocols as explained above.

Our first attempt is the following. Rather than sampling one masking term $\mathbf{y}$ and repeating this process until RejSamp accepts, $\mathcal{P}$ generates $\ell > 1$ masking vectors $\mathbf{y}_j$ at once and computes the commitment $(\mathbf{v}_0, \ldots, \mathbf{v}_{\ell-1})$, where $\mathbf{v}_j = \mathbf{Ay}_j \pmod q$ and $j = 0, \ldots, \ell - 1$. The response is then $\mathbf{z}_k$, where k $(0 \leq k < \ell)$ is the first index for which RejSamp accepts. This reduces aborts, but the amount of exchanged data grows in ℓ. In particular, any type of lattice-based signature following this approach becomes very large. While this can be decreased by using some cryptographic hash function F and sending $\mathsf{F}(\mathbf{v}_j)$ instead of $\mathbf{v}_j$, this is still not satisfactory. An approach with some similarities has been taken in [30] in a different context for zero-knowledge proofs, where all the hash values of commitments of potential masking terms are sent. We note that no tree structure for commitments has been applied in [30] and furthermore the challenge size increases linearly in the number of masking terms, which is not the case in our attempt. The protocol is then repeated multiple times to achieve negligible soundness error. Thus, such an approach is still inefficient.

Our final solution to this issue is to use a *tree of commitments*: an (unbalanced) binary hash tree of height $h = \lceil \log(\ell) \rceil$, whose leaves are $\mathsf{F}(\mathbf{v}_j)$. The commitment is simply the root of the tree root, and the response is the pair $(\mathbf{z}_k, \mathsf{auth})$, where auth is the authentication path of the leaf with index k. Verification is carried out by checking that $\|\mathbf{z}_k\|_p \leq B$ and root is equal to the root of the tree associated to the leaf $\mathsf{F}(\mathbf{Az}_k - \mathbf{Bc} \pmod{q})$ and its given authentication path auth. Using a tree of commitments obviously reduces the communication complexity. It can also improve the performance of interactive protocols with multiple rejection sampling procedures as we demonstrate in this work. We note that the number of masking terms can be chosen such that the aborting probability is bounded by some given bound. In Sect. 3.3 we show how to optimize this number. We note that our technique may be used in [30] to improve efficiency.

Finally, we briefly explain two further optimizations that can be exploited when using trees of commitments. The first one is to generate trees with randomized hashing similar to the standard of the hash-based signature scheme XMSS [18]. This allows to save space and further reduce the communication complexity, since randomized hashing requires the hash function F to be only second preimage resistant rather than collision resistant. This means the output of F is required to be $\geq \lambda$ rather than $\geq 2\lambda$ bits assuming λ bits of classical security. The second optimization allows to reuse already generated, but not consumed, masking terms in subsequent executions of the protocol. This further improves the performance of the protocol, since complete subtrees of the tree can be reused. This reduces the number of new masking terms to be sampled in addition to the number of multiplications and hash computations.

Related Work. In the context of analyzing the hardness of computational lattice problems, previous works such as [10,11,17] point to techniques called "noise swallowing" or "super-polynomial noise flooding", which use Gaussian masking terms entailing a super-polynomial Gaussian parameter in order to swallow a polynomially large secret term. However, the negative impact on the efficiency is tremendous as the parameters become also super-polynomial. By generating many masking terms at once and capturing them in a tree of commitments, the secret and masking terms remain polynomially bounded while the number of repetitions is reduced. As mentioned above, the approach of sending hashed commitments has been used in [30] for zero-knowledge proofs of small secrets, but without the use of tree structures for commitments and the other efficiency improvements. However, sending commitments in a tree structure has been suggested, e.g., in [20] to reduce the communication complexity of proof systems, but not repetitions of lattice-based protocols. Our work exploits hash trees in the context of lattice-based interactive protocols with aborting participants.

Outline. In Sect. 2 we review the relevant background. In Sect. 3 we define trees of commitments and show how they can be utilized in lattice-based canonical identification schemes and hence, in interactive zero-knowledge protocols. In Sect. 4 we demonstrate the practical relevance of our new technique by introducing a new blind signature scheme that we call BLAZE$^+$.

2   Preliminaries

We let $\mathbb{N}, \mathbb{Z}, \mathbb{R}$ denote the set of natural numbers, integers, and real numbers, respectively. We denote column vectors with bold lower-case letters and matrices with bold upper-case letters. The identity matrix of dimension n is denoted by $\mathbf{I}_n$. For any positive integer q we write $\mathbb{Z}_q$ to denote the set of integers in the range $[-\frac{q}{2}, \frac{q}{2}) \cap \mathbb{Z}$. The Euclidean norm ($\ell_2$-norm) of a vector $\mathbf{v}$ with entries v_i is defined as $\|\mathbf{v}\| = (\sum_i |v_i|^2)^{1/2}$, and its ℓ_∞-norm as $\|\mathbf{v}\|_\infty = \max_i |v_i|$. We define the ring $R = \mathbb{Z}[x]/\langle x^n + 1 \rangle$ and its quotient $R_q = R/qR$, where n is a power of 2. We assume that R is an integral domain. A ring element $a_0 + a_1 x + \ldots + a_{n-1} x^{n-1} \in R_q$ is denoted by $\hat{a}$ and it corresponds to a vector $\mathbf{a} \in \mathbb{Z}_q^n$ via coefficient embedding, hence $\|\hat{a}\| = \|\mathbf{a}\|$ and $\|\hat{a}\|_\infty = \|\mathbf{a}\|_\infty$. We write $\hat{\mathbf{a}} = (\hat{a}_1, \ldots, \hat{a}_k) \in R_q^k$ to denote a vector of ring elements and $\hat{\mathbf{A}}$ for a matrix with entries from R_q. The norms of $\hat{\mathbf{a}}$ are defined by $\|\hat{\mathbf{a}}\| = (\sum_{i=1}^k \|\hat{a}_i\|^2)^{1/2}$ and $\|\hat{\mathbf{a}}\|_\infty = \max_i \|\hat{a}_i\|_\infty$. We let $\mathbb{T}_\kappa^n$ denote the set of all $(n-1)$-degree polynomials with coefficients from $\{-1, 0, 1\}$ and Hamming weight κ. All logarithms in this work are to base 2, i.e., $\log(\cdot) = \log_2(\cdot)$. We always denote the security parameter by $\lambda \in \mathbb{N}$. A function $f : \mathbb{N} \longrightarrow \mathbb{R}$ is called *negligible* if there exists an $n_0 \in \mathbb{N}$ such that for all $n > n_0$, it holds $f(n) < \frac{1}{p(n)}$ for any polynomial p. With $\mathrm{negl}(\lambda)$ we denote a negligible function in λ. A probability is called overwhelming if it is at least $1 - \mathrm{negl}(\lambda)$. The *statistical distance* between two distributions X, Y over a countable domain D is defined by $\Delta(X, Y) = \frac{1}{2}\sum_{n \in D} |X(n) - Y(n)|$. The distributions X, Y are called *statistically close* if $\Delta(X, Y) = \mathrm{negl}(\lambda)$. We write $x \leftarrow D$ to denote that x is sampled according to a distribution D. We let $x \leftarrow_\$ S$ denote choosing x uniformly random from a finite set S.

2.1   Cryptographic Primitives

A canonical identification (CID) scheme is a 3-move interactive protocol of the following form: A prover $\mathcal{P}$ initiates the protocol by sending a commitment message y to a verifier $\mathcal{V}$. Upon receiving y, $\mathcal{V}$ sends a uniform random challenge c to $\mathcal{P}$. Afterwards, a response z is sent from $\mathcal{P}$ back to $\mathcal{V}$, which then allows $\mathcal{V}$ to make a deterministic decision about $\mathcal{P}$'s authenticity. The tuple (y, c, z) represents a protocol transcript. A formal definition follows.

Definition 1 (Canonical Identification Scheme). *A canonical identification scheme with commitment space $\mathcal{Y}$, challenge space $\mathcal{C}$, and response space $\mathcal{Z}$ is defined as a tuple of the following polynomial-time algorithms:*

- $KG(1^\ell)$ is a key generation algorithm that outputs a pair of keys (pk, sk) from some key space $\mathcal{K}$, where pk is a public key and sk is a secret key.
- $P = (P_1(sk), P_2(sk, y, c, st))$ is a prover algorithm consisting of two algorithms: P_1 takes as input a secret key sk and returns a commitment $y \in \mathcal{Y}$ and a state st, whereas P_2 on input sk, y, a challenge $c \in \mathcal{C}$, and st, outputs a response $z \in \mathcal{Z} \cap \{\bot\}$, where the symbol $\bot \notin \mathcal{Z}$ indicates failure.
- $V(pk, y, c, z)$ is a verification algorithm that takes as input a public key pk and a transcript (y, c, z), and outputs 1 if it is valid and 0 otherwise.

The standard security notion of CID schemes is impersonation under the active or passive attack model. In the active attack model, any adversary $\mathcal{A}$ interacting with $\mathcal{P}$ must not be able to extract any useful information. Passive attacks correspond to eavesdropping, i.e., $\mathcal{A}$ is in possession of transcripts generated by interactions between the real prover and verifier. According to [1], impersonation under passive attacks is stronger than the active attack model.

Definition 2 (Blind Signature Scheme). *A blind signature scheme BS is a tuple of polynomial-time algorithms BS = (BS.KGen, BS.Sign, BS.Verify) such that:*

- *BS.KGen(1^λ) is a key generation algorithm that outputs a pair of keys (pk,sk), where pk is a public key and sk is a secret key.*
- *BS.Sign(sk, pk, μ) is an interactive protocol between a signer $\mathcal{S}$ and a user $\mathcal{U}$. The input of $\mathcal{S}$ is a secret key sk, whereas the input of $\mathcal{U}$ is a public key pk and a message $\mu \in \mathcal{M}$, where $\mathcal{M}$ is the message space. The output of $\mathcal{S}$ is a view $\mathcal{V}$ (interpreted as a random variable) and the output of $\mathcal{U}$ is a signature σ, i.e., $(\mathcal{V}, \sigma) \leftarrow \langle \mathcal{S}(sk), \mathcal{U}(pk, \mu) \rangle$. We write $\sigma = \bot$ to denote failure.*
- *BS.Verify(pk, μ, σ) is a verification algorithm that outputs 1 if the signature σ is valid and 0 otherwise.*

Security of blind signatures is captured by two security notions: blindness and one-more unforgeability [19,31]. The former prevents a malicious signer to learn information about user's messages (see [4] for a formal definition). The latter ensures that each completed execution of BS.Sign yields at most one signature.

Definition 3 (One-More Unforgeability). *Let $\mathcal{H}$ be a family of random oracles. A blind signature scheme BS is called $(t, q_{Sign}, q_H, \varepsilon)$-one-more unforgeable in the random oracle model if for any adversarial user $\mathcal{U}^*$ running in time at most t and making at most q_{Sign} signing and q_H hash queries, the game $\mathsf{Forge}_{BS,\mathcal{U}^*}(\lambda)$ depicted in Fig. 1 outputs 1 with probability $\Pr[\mathsf{Forge}_{BS,\mathcal{U}^*}(\lambda) = 1] \leq \varepsilon$. The*

Game $\mathsf{Forge}_{BS,\mathcal{U}^*}(\lambda)$

1: $(pk, sk) \leftarrow \mathsf{BS.KGen}(1^\lambda)$
2: $H \leftarrow \mathcal{H}(1^\lambda)$
3: $((\mu_1, \sigma_1), \ldots, (\mu_l, \sigma_l)) \leftarrow \mathcal{U}^{*H(\cdot), \langle S(sk), \cdot \rangle^\infty}(pk)$
4: $k :=$ number of successful signing invocations
5: **if** $\left(\mu_i \neq \mu_j \text{ for all } 1 \leq i < j \leq l \ \wedge \ \mathsf{BS.Verify}(pk, \mu_i, \sigma_i) = 1, \forall i \in [l] \ \wedge \ k+1 = l \right)$ **then**
6:     **return** 1
7: **return** 0

Fig. 1. The security game of one-more unforgeability of blind signatures.

scheme is strongly $(t, q_{Sign}, q_H, \varepsilon)$-one-more unforgeable if the condition $\mu_i \neq \mu_j$ in the game changes to $(\mu_i, \sigma_i) \neq (\mu_j, \sigma_j)$ for all $1 \leq i < j \leq l$.

2.2   Lattices and Gaussians

Let $\mathbf{B} = \{\mathbf{b}_1, \ldots, \mathbf{b}_k\} \in \mathbb{R}^{m \times k}$ be a set of linearly independent vectors for $k \leq m$. The m-dimensional *lattice* $\mathcal{L}$ of rank k generated by $\mathbf{B}$ is given by $\mathcal{L}(\mathbf{B}) = \{\mathbf{Bx} \mid \mathbf{x} \in \mathbb{Z}^k\} \subset \mathbb{R}^m$. The *discrete Gaussian distribution* $D_{\mathcal{L},\sigma,\mathbf{c}}$ over a lattice $\mathcal{L}$ with standard deviation $\sigma > 0$ and center $\mathbf{c} \in \mathbb{R}^n$ is defined as follows: For every $\mathbf{x} \in \mathcal{L}$ the probability of $\mathbf{x}$ is $D_{\mathcal{L},\sigma,\mathbf{c}}(\mathbf{x}) = \rho_{\sigma,\mathbf{c}}(\mathbf{x})/\rho_{\sigma,\mathbf{c}}(\mathcal{L})$, where $\rho_{\sigma,\mathbf{c}}(\mathbf{x}) = \exp(\frac{-\|\mathbf{x}-\mathbf{c}\|^2}{2\sigma^2})$ and $\rho_{\sigma,\mathbf{c}}(\mathcal{L}) = \sum_{\mathbf{x} \in \mathcal{L}} \rho_{\sigma,\mathbf{c}}(\mathbf{x})$. The subscript $\mathbf{c}$ is taken to be $\mathbf{0}$ when omitted. We recall a lemma that gives a tail bound on discrete Gaussians and a rejection sampling lemma.

Lemma 1 ([23, Lemma 4.4]). *For any $t, \eta > 0$ we have*

1. $\mathrm{Pr}_{x \leftarrow D_{\mathbb{Z},\sigma}}[|x| > t \cdot \sigma] \leq 2\exp(-t^2/2)$.
2. $\mathrm{Pr}_{\mathbf{x} \leftarrow D_{\mathbb{Z}^m,\sigma}}[\|\mathbf{x}\| > \eta\sigma\sqrt{m}] \leq \eta^m \exp(\frac{m}{2}(1 - \eta^2))$.

Lemma 2 ([23, Theorem 4.6, Lemma 4.7]). *Let $V \subseteq \mathbb{Z}^m$ with elements having norms bounded by T, $\sigma = \omega(T\sqrt{\log m})$, and $h : V \to \mathbb{R}$ be a probability distribution. Then there exists a constant $M = O(1)$ such that $\forall \mathbf{v} \in V$: $\mathrm{Pr}[D_{\mathbb{Z}^m,\sigma}(\mathbf{z}) \leq M \cdot D_{\mathbb{Z}^m,\sigma,\mathbf{v}}(\mathbf{z}); \ \mathbf{z} \leftarrow D_{\mathbb{Z}^m,\sigma}] \geq 1 - \varepsilon$, where $\varepsilon = 2^{-\omega(\log m)}$. Furthermore, the following two algorithms are within statistical distance $\delta = \varepsilon/M$.*

1. *$\mathbf{v} \leftarrow h$, $\mathbf{z} \leftarrow D_{\mathbb{Z}^m,\sigma,\mathbf{v}}$, output $(\mathbf{z}, \mathbf{v})$ with probability $\frac{D_{\mathbb{Z}^m,\sigma}(\mathbf{z})}{M \cdot D_{\mathbb{Z}^m,\sigma,\mathbf{v}}(\mathbf{z})}$.*
2. *$\mathbf{v} \leftarrow h$, $\mathbf{z} \leftarrow D_{\mathbb{Z}^m,\sigma}$, output $(\mathbf{z}, \mathbf{v})$ with probability $1/M$.*

Moreover, the probability that the first algorithm outputs something is at least $(1-\varepsilon)/M$. If $\sigma = \alpha T$ for any positive α, then $M = \exp(\frac{12}{\alpha} + \frac{1}{2\alpha^2})$ with $\varepsilon = 2^{-100}$.

We let $\mathsf{RejSamp}(x)$ denote an algorithm that carries out rejection sampling on input x. The algorithm outputs 1 if it accepts and 0 otherwise. Next, we define the lattice problems related to this work.

Definition 4 (Module Short Integer Solution (MSIS) Problem). *Let n, q, k_1, k_2 be positive integers and β a positive real. Given a uniform random matrix $\hat{\mathbf{A}} \in R_q^{k_1 \times k_2}$, the Hermite Normal Form of MSIS asks to find a non-zero vector $\hat{\mathbf{x}} \in R^{k_1+k_2}$ such that $[\mathbf{I}_{k_1} \ \hat{\mathbf{A}}] \cdot \hat{\mathbf{x}} = \mathbf{0} \pmod{q}$, where $\|\hat{\mathbf{x}}\| \leq \beta$.*

Definition 5 (Module Learning With Errors (MLWE) Problem). *Let n, q, k_1, k_2 be positive integers and $\hat{\mathbf{A}}$ be a matrix chosen uniformly at random from $R_q^{k_1 \times k_2}$. Given $(\hat{\mathbf{A}}, \hat{\mathbf{b}})$, the decision MLWE problem asks to distinguish (with non-negligible advantage) whether $\hat{\mathbf{b}}$ were chosen from the uniform distribution over $R_q^{k_1}$ or from the following distribution: Given $\hat{\mathbf{s}} \leftarrow \chi^{k_2}$ and $\hat{\mathbf{e}} \leftarrow \chi^{k_1}$, output the vector $\hat{\mathbf{A}}\hat{\mathbf{s}} + \hat{\mathbf{e}} \pmod{q}$, where χ is an error distribution (typically, either $D_{\mathbb{Z}^n,\sigma}$ or the uniform distribution over a small subset of R_q).*

The MLWE problem [21] generalizes LWE [32] and RLWE [24]. More precisely, by setting $k_1 = 1$ in the definition above we obtain the ring version RLWE, while setting $k_1 > 1$ and $R_q = \mathbb{Z}_q$ yields a definition of the LWE problem. The same applies for MSIS [21] and its special versions SIS [2] and RSIS [27].

3   How to Reduce Aborts in Lattice-Based Protocols

In this section we show how aborting in lattice-based protocols can be reduced or even be removed at all. As stated in Sect. 1, when the number of rejection sampling procedures N in an interactive CID-based protocol grows, the total number of repetitions becomes multiplicative in N, e.g., [4,14,33], and a large amount of communication is required to successfully complete the protocol. Consider the CID protocol sketched in Sect. 1. If rejection sampling fails, a new masking term is sampled, hence a new commitment has to be computed and sent in order to receive a new challenge c. Suppose that c does not change for certain number of masking terms and related commitments, which are sent in an aggregated form while any successfully computed response can be verified and related to the corresponding commitment. In this case repetition does not have to occur often or even not at all. We realize this concept by means of *tree of commitments*: a method by which different commitments belong to one challenge in an aggregated form and only the valid response and its related commitment will be revealed. Masking terms that are rejected or not consumed during rejection sampling remain hidden and will never be revealed.

3.1   Trees of Commitments

In this section we describe trees of commitments. We first define relevant functions and algorithms. For a positive integer $\omega \geq 2\lambda$, we let $\mathsf{F} : \{0,1\}^* \rightarrow \{0,1\}^\omega$ be a collision resistant hash function. We define the algorithms related to binary hash trees in a way that fits to our purposes.

HashTree: An algorithm that computes an (unbalanced) binary hash tree of height $h \geq 1$. Its input consists of $\ell \leq 2^h$ commitments $v_0, \ldots, v_{\ell-1}$ whose hash values are the leaves of the tree, i.e., $(\mathsf{root}, \mathsf{tree}) \leftarrow \mathsf{HashTree}(v_0, \ldots, v_{\ell-1})$, where root is the root of the tree and tree is a sequence of all other nodes.
BuildAuth: An algorithm that on input an index k, a sequence of nodes tree, and a height h outputs the corresponding authentication path auth including the index k, i.e., $\mathsf{auth} \leftarrow \mathsf{BuildAuth}(k, \mathsf{tree}, h)$.
RootCalc: An algorithm that computes the root of a hash tree given a commitment v and its authentication path auth, i.e., $\mathsf{root} \leftarrow \mathsf{RootCalc}(v, \mathsf{auth})$.

In the following we define trees of commitments. The leaves are the hash values of commitments v_j, i.e., $v_0[j] = \mathsf{F}(v_j)$ for $0 \leq j < \ell$. The inner nodes of height i are denoted by $v_i[j]$, where $0 < i \leq h$, $0 \leq j < 2^{h-i}$. They are typically computed as $v_i[j] = \mathsf{F}(v_{i-1}[2j] \parallel v_{i-1}[2j + 1])$. The root is the only node of height h, i.e., $v_h[0] = \mathsf{root}$. A formal definition follows.

Definition 6 (Tree of Commitments). *Let v_j be commitments of $\ell > 1$ secrets y_j, where $0 \leq j < \ell$. A tree of commitments is an (unbalanced) binary hash tree of height $h = \lceil \log(\ell) \rceil$, whose leaves are the hash values of v_j, i.e., $F(v_j)$. The root constitutes an aggregated commitment root, and auth is the authentication path of the commitment v_k generated using the secret y_k, where $0 \leq k < \ell$.*

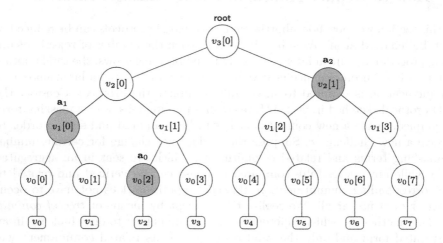

Fig. 2. A tree of commitments of height $h = 3$ and $\ell = 8$ commitments. Assume that the first time RejSamp accepts at step $k = 3$ ($0 \leq k < \ell$), then the gray colored nodes represent the authentication path required to compute the root starting from v_3.

Next we define trees of commitments for lattice-based canonical identification (CID) schemes. Fig. 2 illustrates such a tree of height $h = 3$.

Definition 7 (Tree of Commitments for CID). *Let CID be a lattice-based canonical identification scheme. Let v_j be commitments of CID generated using $\ell > 1$ masking terms y_j ($0 \leq j < \ell$). A tree of commitments for CID is an (unbalanced) binary hash tree of height $h = \lceil \log(\ell) \rceil$, whose leaves are the hash values of v_j, i.e., $F(v_j)$, and its root constitutes an aggregated commitment root to ℓ masking terms for up to ℓ repetitions within CID for the same challenge c. A response is composed of (z_k, auth), where $z_k = y_k + sc$ and y_k is the first masking term for which rejection sampling succeeds (i.e., RejSamp$(z_k) = 1$ for $0 \leq k < \ell$), and auth is the authentication path of the commitment v_k generated by use of the masking term y_k.*

3.2 Canonical Identification Using Trees of Commitments

Figure 3 describes a variant of the CID protocol briefly explained in Sect. 1. The variant shown here is based on MLWE and MSIS and utilizes trees of commitments. Using the Fiat-Shamir transform [15] we obtain a digital signature scheme. In the full version of this paper [3] we give a formal description of this signature scheme and prove its correctness and security. By the equivalence results of [1], we deduce the soundness property of the CID protocol described in this section as well as its security against impersonation under passive attacks. More concretely, the main goal of providing the signature scheme and its security proof in the full version is to show how trees of commitments can also be used in lattice-based Fiat-Shamir signatures, and to establish the security of the CID protocol shown in this section based on the results of [1].

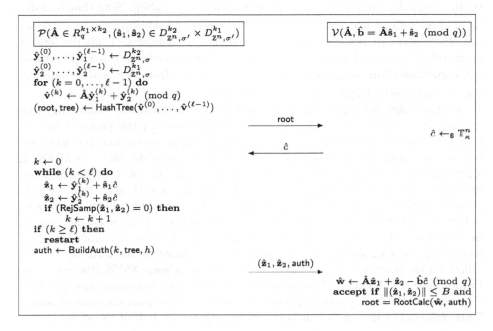

Fig. 3. Canonical identification based on MLWE and MSIS using trees of commitments.

We can choose ℓ such that at least one of the masking pairs $(\hat{\mathbf{y}}_1^{(k)}, \hat{\mathbf{y}}_2^{(k)})$ (see Fig. 3) hides $\hat{\mathbf{S}}\hat{c}$ with probability of at least $1 - \delta_{\text{abort}}$ for a given bound δ_{abort}, where $\hat{\mathbf{S}} = (\hat{\mathbf{s}}_1, \hat{\mathbf{s}}_2)$. This can be established as follows. Since the entries of the masking pairs are chosen from $D_{\mathbb{Z}^n, \sigma}$, the probability of successfully outputting $(\hat{\mathbf{z}}_1, \hat{\mathbf{z}}_2)$ with only one masking pair is $\approx 1/M$, where M is the expected number of repetitions (see Lemma 2). Consequently, one of the ℓ masking pairs conceals the secret key with probability $1 - (1 - 1/M)^{\ell}$. Hence, by choosing ℓ satisfying $(1 - 1/M)^{\ell} \leq \delta_{\text{abort}}$, the protocol aborts with probability at most δ_{abort}. For instance, to obtain a probability negligible in λ we have to select ℓ such that $(1 - 1/M)^{\ell} \leq 2^{-\lambda}$, which allows to completely eliminate aborts.

Let us consider an illustrative example. Suppose that we set $\delta_{\text{abort}} = 2^{-10}$ and use masking pairs with entries sampled from $D_{\mathbb{Z}^n, \sigma}$, where $\sigma = \alpha \|\hat{\mathbf{S}}\hat{c}\|$ and $M = \exp(\frac{12}{\alpha} + \frac{1}{2\alpha^2})$ (Lemma 2). Then, by setting $\alpha = 23$ we need only

$\ell = 8$ masking pairs in order to hide $\hat{\mathbf{S}}\hat{c}$ with probability at least 0.999. This means we need a tree of commitments of height $h = 3$, which is a very small tree. Regarding communication complexity, both the commitment and response consist of only 4 hash values and a pair of Gaussian vectors with $\sigma = 23 \cdot \|\hat{\mathbf{S}}\hat{c}\|$, i.e., $(\mathsf{root}, \hat{\mathbf{z}}_1, \hat{\mathbf{z}}_2, \mathsf{auth} = (\mathbf{a}_0, \mathbf{a}_1, \mathbf{a}_2))$. The choice of $\alpha = 23$ increases σ in this example and hence the size of $(\hat{\mathbf{z}}_1, \hat{\mathbf{z}}_2)$ by at most 1.1 bits per integer entry in comparison to $\alpha = 11$, which is a typical choice (see, e.g., [13]) that induces a repetition rate of $M \approx 3$ and a communication complexity consisting of 3 vectors from $R_q^{k_1}$ and 3 Gaussian vectors with $\sigma = 11 \cdot \|\hat{\mathbf{S}}\hat{c}\|$. Note that in order to hide $\hat{\mathbf{S}}\hat{c}$ with probability $1 - 2^{-10}$ using a single masking pair we need to set $\alpha > 2^{13.6}$, which increases the size of the response to at least 10.1 bits per integer entry when compared with $\alpha = 11$. Hence, a larger modulus q is required and the communication complexity increases to a vector from $R_q^{k_1}$ and a Gaussian vector with a very large σ, i.e., $\sigma > 2^{13.6} \cdot \|\hat{\mathbf{S}}\hat{c}\|$.

Furthermore, we can improve the performance of protocols employing trees of commitments as follows. For subsequent executions of the protocol we can reuse the masking pairs that were sampled in previous executions but were not consumed during rejection sampling. For instance, consider the tree in Fig. 2, where the first time RejSamp accepts at step $k = 3$. For the next protocol run we can simply reuse the whole subtree with root $\mathbf{a}_2 = v_2[1]$ such that we only need to compute a new subtree of height $h - 1$ and combine both subtrees to obtain a new tree of height h. This decreases the number of new masking terms to be sampled and reduces the number of hash computations and multiplications modulo q. We can also lower the security requirement of the hash function F following the standard of the hash-based signature scheme XMSS [18] and using randomized tree hashing. This allows to generate trees of commitments, where F is required to be only second preimage resistant rather than collision resistant. This reduces the size of the authentication path to one half of its original size.

3.3   Optimizing the Number of Masking Terms

The previous section shows how to reduce the overall repetition rate of lattice-based protocols with multiple rejection sampling procedures. In this section we show how to minimize the height of the tree of commitments when using Gaussian distributed masking terms. This improves the performance of interactive protocols significantly. A similar approach can be taken for masking terms sampled from other distributions such as the uniform distribution.

Lemma 3. *Let $\epsilon = 2^{-\omega(\log n)}$ and M be the repetition rate of sampling masking terms from $D_{\mathbb{Z}^n, \sigma}$ such that rejection sampling succeeds. Let δ_{abort} be the desired aborting probability. Then, the number of masking terms ℓ required to conceal a secret-related term with norm bounded by T and with probability at most $1 - \delta_{\mathsf{abort}}$ is minimized by solving the following optimization problem:*

$$\min(\ell) \ \textit{conditioned on} \ (1 - \frac{1 - \epsilon}{M})^\ell \le \delta_{\mathsf{abort}}.$$

Table 2. Values for the required number of Gaussian masking terms ℓ and the bit length of the standard deviation $\sigma = \alpha T = \alpha \cdot 500$ at given aborting probabilities.

Aborting probability δ_{abort}	2^{-128}	2^{-100}	2^{-80}	2^{-40}	2^{-40}	2^{-10}	2^{-10}
Number of masking terms ℓ	64	63	62	31	16	16	8
Height of the binary hash tree h	6	6	6	5	4	4	3
Parameter α	42	30	23	23	62	12	23
Bit length of the standard deviation σ	15	14	14	14	15	13	14

Proof. Given a fixed δ_{abort} we can write ℓ as a function in M using the inequality given above. In particular, if $\sigma = \alpha T$ for $\alpha > 0$, then $M = \exp(\frac{12}{\alpha} + \frac{1}{2\alpha^2})$, $\epsilon = 2^{-100}$, and the probability of aborting using only one masking term is given by $1 - (1-\epsilon)/M$ (see Lemma 2). Hence, ℓ can also be considered as a function in α, i.e., $\ell(\alpha) = \log(\delta_{\mathsf{abort}})/\log\left(1 - \frac{1-2^{-100}}{\exp(\frac{12}{\alpha}+\frac{1}{2\alpha^2})}\right)$. Note that increasing α directly reduces ℓ. Therefore, this problem translates to finding a local minimum of the function $\ell(\alpha)$ within a given range of α, which can be solved using Lagrange optimization.   □

The above lemma shows that reducing the number of masking terms ℓ for a fixed aborting probability δ_{abort} increases σ, hence the size of the responses (or signatures). In Table 2 we exhibit examples for various values of ℓ and $\sigma = \alpha T$ given δ_{abort} and $T = 500$.

4   Applications

As mentioned in Sect. 1, there are various advanced lattice-based constructions that are based on canonical identification (CID) and thus may benefit from using trees of commitments as described in Sect. 3. Our approach can also be applied to interactive zero-knowledge proof systems in a straightforward way. For instance, the scheme depicted in Fig. 3 can be seen as a zero-knowledge proof of knowledge of RLWE secrets with reduced communication complexity.

As a further practical application, we exploit trees of commitments within the blind signature scheme BLAZE [4] resulting in major efficiency gains. The signing protocol of BLAZE consists of 4 moves between a signer $\mathcal{S}$ and a user $\mathcal{U}$. It can be aborted due to 2 rejection sampling procedures; the first one is carried out by $\mathcal{S}$ in order to hide the secret key and the second one by $\mathcal{U}$ to ensure blindness. In case the latter fails, $\mathcal{U}$ must send $\mathcal{S}$ a proof of failure in order to restart the signing protocol. This is why the last move is needed in the protocol as opposed to the standard 3-move structure of the CID scheme underlying BLAZE. Due to the possibility of failures the user must also use a statistically hiding and computationally binding commitment scheme in order to hide the message from the signer.

In the following we redesign BLAZE such that signatures can be generated in 3 moves. We call the new scheme BLAZE$^+$. In particular, we are able to completely remove the rejection sampling procedure carried out by $\mathcal{U}$. This is accomplished by generating enough masking terms at once such that blindness is achieved with overwhelming probability. This allows to safely eliminate the last move in the protocol and hence the need for proof of failures. Consequently, statistically hiding and computationally binding commitments concealing the message from $\mathcal{S}$ are not required anymore. We also describe a 4-move version of BLAZE+ in the full version of this paper [3]. In that version aborts at the user side occur with probability of choice. We note that a similar approach may be applied at the signer side.

In addition to the functions defined in Sect. 3 we need some additional tools. Let $\mathsf{H} : \{0,1\}^* \to \mathbb{T}_\kappa^n$ be a public hash function modeled as a random oracle. Further, let E be a public function that expands given strings to any desired length. Sampling from $D_{\mathbb{Z},s}^n$ using randomness ρ is denoted by $D_{\mathbb{Z},s}^n(\rho)$. We let $\hat{\mathbb{T}} = \{\pm x^i : i \in [n]\} \subset R_q$. Let Compress and Decompress be functions for (de)compressing Gaussian elements (see [4] for description). Next we describe the new blind signature scheme BLAZE+. The respective algorithms are formalized in Fig. 4.

Key Generation. As in BLAZE, the algorithm BS.KGen generates an instance of RSIS (Fig. 4). It's secret vector $\hat{s}$ is sampled from $D_{\mathbb{Z}^n,\sigma}^{m+1}$. However, BLAZE+ employs an additional condition on $\hat{s}$, which can also be used in BLAZE. More concretely, the ℓ_2-norm of $\hat{s}$ is bounded by $\gamma\sigma\sqrt{(m+1)n}$. This condition represents a trade-off between the speed of generating keys and the size of signatures, since the standard deviation s^* of masking terms used by the signer is a multiple of $\|\hat{s}\|$. Therefore, a smaller γ decreases s^*, but reduces the success probability of passing the given condition (see Lemma 1). Note that $\hat{s}$ can also be sampled from the uniform distribution over a subset of R^{m+1}, in which the coefficients of each polynomial from R are in the set $\{-d,\ldots,0,\ldots,d\}$, where $d \in \mathbb{Z}_{>0}$.

Signing. The signing algorithm is similar to that of BLAZE [4]. The difference is that in BLAZE+ the user $\mathcal{U}$ generates $\ell > 1$ masking vectors $\hat{e}^{(0)},\ldots,\hat{e}^{(\ell-1)}$ chosen from $D_{\mathbb{Z}^n,s}^{m+1}$. These vectors are then used to compute $\hat{t}^{(k)} = \hat{a} \cdot \hat{e}^{(k)} + \hat{y}$ (mod q), which are needed to generate a tree of commitments of height $h = \lceil \log(\ell) \rceil$ via the algorithm HashTree. We note that generating $\hat{e}^{(k)}$ and $\hat{a} \cdot \hat{e}^{(k)}$ (mod q), for $k = 0,\ldots,\ell-1$, can be precomputed by $\mathcal{U}$ before starting the protocol with $\mathcal{S}$. The sum $\hat{t}^{(k)}$ containing $\hat{y}$ and the construction of the tree cannot be carried out in advance, since $\hat{y}$ is computed from the commitment sent by $\mathcal{S}$ (see Fig. 4). We also note that $\hat{e}^{(k)}$ can be reused when $\mathcal{S}$ restarts the protocol, since $\hat{e}^{(k)}$ are not revealed and $\hat{c}^*$ is always fresh. After receiving the vector $\hat{z}^*$, $\mathcal{U}$ computes $\hat{z}$ and the authentication path auth associated to the first index $k < \ell$ for which the vector $\hat{e}^{(k)}$ ensures blindness. Note that ℓ is chosen such that this happens with probability at least $1 - 2^{-\lambda}$, i.e., $\mathcal{U}$ outputs a valid signature with overwhelming probability. Also note that for each signature a new root is generated.

Verification. Verifying a signature is straightforward as described in Fig. 4.

BS.KGen(1^λ)

1: seed $\leftarrow_\$ \{0,1\}^\lambda$
2: $\hat{a}' \in R_q^m \leftarrow E(\text{seed})$
3: $\hat{a} \leftarrow [1\ \hat{a}']$
4: $\hat{s} \leftarrow D_{\mathbb{Z}^n,\sigma}^{m+1}$
5: **if** $(\|\hat{s}\| > \gamma\sigma\sqrt{(m+1)n})$ **then**
6:     goto 4
7: $\hat{b} \leftarrow \hat{a} \cdot \hat{s} \pmod{q}$
8: sk := (seed, $\hat{s}$), pk := (seed, $\hat{b}$)
9: **return** (sk, pk)

BS.Verify(pk, μ, ($\hat{z}$, $\hat{c}$, auth))

1: $\hat{a}' \leftarrow E(\text{seed})$
2: $\hat{a} \leftarrow [1\ \hat{a}']$
3: $\hat{z} \leftarrow \text{Decompress}(\hat{z})$
4: $\hat{w} \leftarrow \hat{a} \cdot \hat{z} - \hat{b}\hat{c} \pmod{q}$
5: root $\leftarrow \text{RootCalc}(\hat{w}, \text{auth})$
6: **if** $\left(\|\hat{z}\| \leq B \ \wedge\ \hat{c} = H(\text{root}, \mu) \right)$ **then**
7:     **return** 1
8: **return** 0

BS.Sign(sk, pk, μ)

Signer $\mathcal{S}(\text{sk})$

$\overline{\hat{a}' \leftarrow E(\text{seed})}$, $\hat{a} \leftarrow [1\ \hat{a}']$
$\hat{y}_1^*, \ldots, \hat{y}_\kappa^* \leftarrow D_{\mathbb{Z}^n, s^*}^{m+1}$
for $(j = 1, \ldots, \kappa)$ **do**
    $\hat{y}_j \leftarrow \hat{a} \cdot \hat{y}_j^* \pmod{q}$
$\hat{y} := (\hat{y}_1, \ldots, \hat{y}_\kappa)$

$\xrightarrow{\hspace{3cm}}$

User $\mathcal{U}(\text{pk}, \mu)$

$\hat{a}' \leftarrow E(\text{seed})$, $\hat{a} \leftarrow [1\ \hat{a}']$, $\hat{p}_1, \ldots, \hat{p}_\kappa \leftarrow_\$ \hat{\mathbb{T}}$
$\rho \leftarrow_\$ \{0,1\}^\lambda$, $\hat{e}^{(0)}, \ldots, \hat{e}^{(\ell-1)} \leftarrow D_{\mathbb{Z}^n, s}^{m+1}(\rho)$
$\hat{y} \leftarrow \sum_1^\kappa \hat{p}_j \hat{y}_j \pmod{q}$
for $(k = 0, \ldots, \ell - 1)$ **do**
    $\hat{t}^{(k)} \leftarrow \hat{a} \cdot \hat{e}^{(k)} + \hat{y} \pmod{q}$
(root, tree) $\leftarrow \text{HashTree}(\hat{t}^{(0)}, \ldots, \hat{t}^{(\ell-1)})$
$\hat{c} \leftarrow H(\text{root}, \mu)$, $\hat{c} := \sum_1^\kappa \hat{c}_j$, $\hat{c}_j \in \hat{\mathbb{T}}$
for $(j = 1, \ldots, \kappa)$ **do**
    $\hat{c}_j^* \leftarrow \hat{p}_j^{-1} \cdot \hat{c}_j$
$\hat{c}^* := (\hat{c}_1^*, \ldots, \hat{c}_\kappa^*)$

$\xleftarrow{\hspace{3cm}}$

for $(j = 1, \ldots, \kappa)$ **do**
    $\hat{z}_j^* \leftarrow \hat{y}_j^* + \hat{s}\hat{c}_j^*$
if $(\text{RejSamp}(\hat{z}_1^*, \ldots, \hat{z}_\kappa^*) = 0)$ **then**
    restart
$\hat{z}^* := (\hat{z}_1^*, \ldots, \hat{z}_\kappa^*)$

$\xrightarrow{\hspace{3cm}}$

$\hat{v} \leftarrow \sum_1^\kappa \hat{p}_j \hat{z}_j^*$
if $(\|\hat{v}\| > \eta s^* \sqrt{(m+1)\kappa n})$ **then**
    abort (occurs with probability $2^{-\lambda}$)
$k \leftarrow 0$
while $(k < \ell)$ **do**
    $\hat{z} \leftarrow \hat{e}^{(k)} + \hat{v}$
    if $(\text{RejSamp}(\hat{z}) = 0)$ **then**
        $k \leftarrow k + 1$
if $(k \geq \ell)$ **then**
    abort (occurs with probability $2^{-\lambda}$)
auth $\leftarrow \text{BuildAuth}(k, \text{tree}, h)$
$\hat{z} \leftarrow \text{Compress}(\hat{z})$
return $(\mu, (\hat{z}, \hat{c}, \text{auth}))$

Fig. 4. A formal description of the new blind signature scheme BLAZE$^+$.

In the following we give the main security statements of this section comprising completeness, blindness, and strong one-more unforgeability of BLAZE$^+$. The proofs of both correctness and blindness directly follow from [4] and are hence omitted. In particular, proving blindness requires to show that the exchanged messages during protocol execution together with the user's output does not leak any information about the message being signed. In comparison to BLAZE, the authentication path auth, which is a part of the signature in BLAZE$^+$ is the only additional information exchanged between the signer and the user. Obviously, auth does not give any information about the signed message.

Theorem 1 (Completeness). *Let $\alpha^*, \alpha, \gamma, \eta > 0$, $s^* = \alpha^* \gamma \sigma \sqrt{(m+1)\kappa n}$, $s = \eta \alpha s^* \sqrt{(m+1)\kappa n}$, and $B = \eta s \sqrt{(m+1)n}$. Further, let $(1 - \frac{1-2^{-100}}{U})^\ell \le 2^{-\lambda}$, where $U = \exp(\frac{12}{\alpha} + \frac{1}{2\alpha^2})$. After at most M repetitions, any blind signature produced by BLAZE$^+$ is validated with probability of at least $1 - 2^{-\lambda}$, where $M = \exp(\frac{12}{\alpha^*} + \frac{1}{2\alpha^{*2}})$.*

Theorem 2 (Blindness). *The scheme BLAZE$^+$ is statistically blind. The statistical distance between two executions of its signing protocol is given by $2^{-100}/M$.*

Next, we prove the strong one-more unforgeability of BLAZE$^+$. In the proof we assume that in the unforgeability game (see Definition 3) any forgery output by the adversary $\mathcal{A}$ is considered valid if and only if its associated root was not queried to the signing oracle by $\mathcal{A}$, i.e., a forgery must contain a new root that is distinct from the roots queried to the signing oracle. We note that our 3-move protocol achieves completeness with overwhelming probability, i.e., each completed interaction yields a valid blind signature, where users do not have to request a protocol restart. Therefore, the one-more unforgeability proof does not need to consider aborts at the user side as opposed to BLAZE.

Theorem 3 (Unforgeability). *The scheme BLAZE$^+$ is strongly one-more unforgeable in the random oracle model (ROM) if F is a collision resistant hash function and RSIS is hard. More precisely, suppose that F is collision resistant and it is hard to find a vector $\hat{\mathbf{x}} \ne \mathbf{0}$ satisfying $[1\ \hat{\mathbf{a}}'] \cdot \hat{\mathbf{x}} = 0 \pmod{q}$ and $\|\hat{\mathbf{x}}\| \le \beta$ for $\beta = 2(B + \eta \sigma \sqrt{(m+1)\kappa n})$, then BLAZE$^+$ is strongly one-more unforgeable in the ROM.*

Proof. We assume that there exists a forger $\mathcal{A}$ that wins the one-more unforgeability game given in Definition 3 with probability $\varepsilon_{\mathcal{A}}$. We construct a reduction algorithm $\mathcal{D}$ that finds collisions in the hash function F or computes a vector $\hat{\mathbf{x}} \ne \mathbf{0}$ as described in the theorem statement with probability $\varepsilon_{\mathcal{D}}$ as given below.

Setup. The input of $\mathcal{D}$ is a uniformly random vector $\hat{\mathbf{a}}' \in R_q^m$ and a hash function F. It also has access to an oracle $\mathcal{O}_F$ for F. The reduction $\mathcal{D}$ samples a vector $\hat{\mathbf{s}}$ from $D_{\mathbb{Z}^n, \sigma}^{m+1}$ and randomly selects answers for random oracle queries $\{\hat{h}_1, \ldots, \hat{h}_{q_H}\}$. Then, it runs the forger $\mathcal{A}$ with public key $(\hat{\mathbf{a}}, \hat{b})$, where $\hat{\mathbf{a}} = [1\ \hat{\mathbf{a}}']$ and $\hat{b} = \hat{\mathbf{a}} \cdot \hat{\mathbf{s}} \pmod{q}$.

Random Oracle Query. The reduction $\mathcal{D}$ maintains a list L_H, which includes pairs of random oracle queries and their answers. If H was previously queried on some input, then $\mathcal{D}$ looks up its entry in L_H and returns its answer $\hat{c} \in \mathbb{T}_\kappa^n$. Otherwise, it returns the first unused $\hat{c}$ and updates the list.

Hash Query. Hash queries to F sent by $\mathcal{A}$ are forwarded to the oracle $\mathcal{O}_\mathsf{F}$. The reduction $\mathcal{D}$ also maintains a list L_F, which includes pairs of hash queries to F and their answers as well as the structure of the trees.

Blind Signature Query. Upon receiving signature queries from the forger $\mathcal{A}$ as a user, $\mathcal{D}$ interacts as a signer with $\mathcal{A}$ according to the signing protocol (see Fig. 4).

Output. After $k \leq q_\mathsf{Sign}$ successful executions of the signing protocol, $\mathcal{A}$ outputs $k + 1$ distinct messages and their valid signatures $(\mu_1, \mathsf{sig}_1), \ldots, (\mu_{k+1}, \mathsf{sig}_{k+1})$. Then, one of the following two cases applies.

Case 1. $\mathcal{D}$ finds two signatures of messages $\mu, \mu' \in \{\mu_1, \ldots, \mu_{k+1}\}$ with the same random oracle answer $\hat{c}$. In this case BS.Verify yields $\mathsf{H}(\mathsf{root}, \mu) = \mathsf{H}(\mathsf{root}', \mu')$. If $\mu \neq \mu'$ or $\mathsf{root} \neq \mathsf{root}'$, then a second preimage of $\hat{c}$ has been found by $\mathcal{A}$. If $\mu = \mu'$ and $\mathsf{root} = \mathsf{root}'$, then both signatures were generated using the same hash tree. This does not follow the unforgeability game because the output of $\mathcal{A}$ does not include a valid forgery.

Case 2. If all signatures output by $\mathcal{A}$ have distinct random oracle answers, then $\mathcal{D}$ guesses an index $i \in [k+1]$ such that $\hat{c}_i = \hat{h}_j$ for some $j \in [q_\mathsf{H}]$. Then, it records the pair $(\mu_i, (\hat{\mathbf{z}}_i, \hat{c}_i, \mathsf{auth}_i))$ and invokes $\mathcal{A}$ again with the same random tape and the random oracle queries $\{\hat{h}_1, \ldots, \hat{h}_{j-1}, \hat{h}'_j, \ldots, \hat{h}'_{q_\mathsf{H}}\}$, where $\{\hat{h}'_j, \ldots, \hat{h}'_{q_\mathsf{H}}\}$ are fresh random elements. After the second invocation, the output of $\mathcal{A}$ includes a pair $(\mu'_i, (\hat{\mathbf{z}}'_i, \hat{c}'_i, \mathsf{auth}'_i))$. By the General Forking Lemma [8], $\mathcal{A}$ outputs a forgery containing $\hat{c}'_i$ with probability $\varepsilon_\mathsf{fork}$ (see below), where $\hat{c}_i \neq \hat{c}'_i$ and $\mathsf{root} = \mathsf{root}'$. Let $\hat{w} = \hat{\mathbf{a}} \cdot \hat{\mathbf{z}}_i - \hat{b}\hat{c}_i \pmod q$ and $\hat{w}' = \hat{\mathbf{a}} \cdot \hat{\mathbf{z}}'_i - \hat{b}\hat{c}'_i \pmod q$. Then, one of the following holds:

1. $\hat{\mathbf{z}}_i \neq \hat{\mathbf{z}}'_i$ and $\mathsf{auth}_i = \mathsf{auth}'_i$. If $\hat{w} = \hat{w}'$, then $\hat{\mathbf{a}}(\hat{\mathbf{z}}_i - \hat{\mathbf{z}}'_i) - \hat{b}(\hat{c}_i - \hat{c}'_i) = 0 \pmod q$. Therefore, by setting $\hat{b} = \hat{\mathbf{a}} \cdot \hat{\mathbf{s}} \pmod q$ we obtain $\hat{\mathbf{a}} \cdot \hat{\mathbf{x}} = 0 \pmod q$, where $\hat{\mathbf{x}} = \hat{\mathbf{z}}_i - \hat{\mathbf{z}}'_i - \hat{\mathbf{s}}(\hat{c}_i - \hat{c}'_i)$. Since both signatures are valid, we have $\|\hat{\mathbf{z}}_i\| \leq B$ and $\|\hat{\mathbf{z}}'_i\| \leq B$. Moreover we have $\|\hat{\mathbf{s}}(\hat{c}_i - \hat{c}'_i)\| \leq 2\eta\sigma\sqrt{(m+1)\kappa n}$. Hence, $\|\hat{\mathbf{x}}\| \leq 2(B + \eta\sigma\sqrt{(m+1)\kappa n})$. This constitutes a solution to RSIS with norm bound β. If $\hat{w} \neq \hat{w}'$, then a collision in F has been found in the leaves of the hash tree.

2. $\hat{\mathbf{z}}_i \neq \hat{\mathbf{z}}'_i$ and $\mathsf{auth}_i \neq \mathsf{auth}'_i$. If $\hat{w} = \hat{w}'$, then we have a solution to RSIS (as in **1.**). If $\hat{w} \neq \hat{w}'$, then we consider two cases: If $\hat{w}, \hat{w}'$ belong to different hash trees, then a collision has occurred in F similar to [26], i.e., there exists an index $j \in \{0, \ldots, h-1\}$ such that $\mathbf{a}_j \neq \mathbf{a}'_j$, where $\mathbf{a}_j \in \mathsf{auth}_i$, $\mathbf{a}'_j \in \mathsf{auth}'_i$ and $\mathsf{RootCalc}(\hat{w}, \mathsf{auth}_i) = \mathsf{root} = \mathsf{RootCalc}(\hat{w}', \mathsf{auth}'_i)$. If $\hat{w}, \hat{w}'$ belong to the same hash tree, then $\mathcal{D}$ keeps the pair $(\mu_i, (\hat{\mathbf{z}}_i, \hat{c}_i, \mathsf{auth}_i))$ and invokes $\mathcal{A}$ at most ℓ times with the same random tape and the random oracle queries $\{\hat{h}_1, \ldots, \hat{h}_{j-1}, \hat{h}_j^{(t)}, \ldots, \hat{h}_{q_\mathsf{H}}^{(t)}\}$ (where $t \in \{0, \ldots, \ell - 1\}$) until we obtain two forgeries such that the associated leaves have the same index in the tree and the same hash value. If $\hat{w} = \hat{w}'$, then we have a solution to RSIS (as in **1.**). Otherwise, we have a collision in F.

3. $\hat{\mathbf{z}}_i = \hat{\mathbf{z}}'_i$ and $\mathsf{auth}_i = \mathsf{auth}'_i$. If $\hat{w} = \hat{w}'$, then $\hat{\mathbf{a}} \cdot \hat{\mathbf{s}}(\hat{c}_i - \hat{c}'_i) = \hat{b}(\hat{c}_i - \hat{c}'_i) = 0$ (mod q) and $\|\hat{\mathbf{s}}(\hat{c}_i - \hat{c}'_i)\| \le \beta$. Since $\hat{c}_i \ne \hat{c}'_i$ and R is an integral domain, then $\hat{\mathbf{s}}(\hat{c}_i - \hat{c}'_i) \in R^{m+1} \backslash \{\mathbf{0}\}$. This constitutes a solution to RSIS. Note that if $\hat{b}$ is invertible in R_q, then we obtain $\hat{c}_i - \hat{c}'_i = 0$ (mod q). This contradicts $\hat{c}_i \ne \hat{c}'_i$. Moreover, if $(\hat{c}_i - \hat{c}'_i)$ is invertible in R_q, then $\hat{b} = 0$ (mod q), which is not the case. If $\hat{w} \ne \hat{w}'$, then a collision has occurred in F (in the leaves of the hash tree).

4. $\hat{\mathbf{z}}_i = \hat{\mathbf{z}}'_i$ and $\mathsf{auth}_i \ne \mathsf{auth}'_i$. If $\hat{w} = \hat{w}'$, then we have a solution to RSIS (as in **3.**). If $\hat{w} \ne \hat{w}'$, then one of the cases considered in **2.** (for $\hat{w} \ne \hat{w}'$) applies.

The reduction $\mathcal{D}$ retries at most $q_{\mathsf{H}}^{(k+1)}$ times with different random tape and random oracle queries.

Analysis. First, we note that the environment of $\mathcal{A}$ is perfectly simulated by $\mathcal{D}$ and signatures are generated with the same probability as in the real execution of the signing protocol. Next, one of the $k+1$ pairs output by $\mathcal{A}$ is by assumption not generated during the execution of the signing protocol. The probability of correctly guessing the index i corresponding to this pair is $1/(k+1)$, where there are q_{H}^{k+1} index pairs (i, j) such that $\hat{c}_i = \hat{h}_j$. Therefore, one of the q_{H}^{k+1} reruns of $\mathcal{A}$ yields the correct index pair (i, j). The probability that $\hat{c}_i$ was a random oracle query made by $\mathcal{A}$ is at least $1 - 1/|\mathbb{T}_\kappa^n|$. Thus, the probability that $\hat{c}_i = \hat{h}_j$ is $\varepsilon_{\mathcal{A}} - 1/|\mathbb{T}_\kappa^n|$. By the General Forking Lemma with at most $\ell = O(1)$ rewindings and distinct $\hat{h}_j^{(t)}, \ldots, \hat{h}_{q_{\mathsf{H}}}^{(t)}$, we have $\varepsilon_{\mathsf{fork}} \ge \left(\varepsilon_{\mathcal{A}} - \frac{1}{|\mathbb{T}_\kappa^n|}\right) \cdot \left(\left(\frac{\varepsilon_{\mathcal{A}} - 1/|\mathbb{T}_\kappa^n|}{q_{\mathsf{Sign}} + q_{\mathsf{H}}}\right)^\ell - \tau\right)$, where $\tau = 1 - \prod_{t=1}^{\ell} \frac{|\mathbb{T}_\kappa^n| - t}{|\mathbb{T}_\kappa^n|} \le 1 - \left(\frac{|\mathbb{T}_\kappa^n| - \ell}{|\mathbb{T}_\kappa^n|}\right)^\ell \le \frac{\ell^2}{|\mathbb{T}_\kappa^n|}$. Since $\hat{\mathbf{s}}$ is not uniquely defining $\hat{b}$ when $(m+1)\log(2d) > \log(q)$ (see, e.g., [28]) for a sufficiently large d that is related to the size of the coefficients of $\hat{\mathbf{s}}$, $\mathcal{A}$ does not know which $\hat{\mathbf{s}}$ is being used to construct $\hat{\mathbf{x}}$. Hence, $\hat{\mathbf{x}} \ne \mathbf{0}$ with probability at least $1/2$ (see, e.g., [25,33]). This can be easily shown, e.g., when the coefficients of $\hat{\mathbf{s}}$ are uniformly distributed over $\{-d, \ldots, 0, \ldots, d\}$. The success probability of $\mathcal{D}$ is given by $\varepsilon_{\mathcal{D}} \ge \frac{\varepsilon_{\mathsf{fork}}}{2(k+1)}$, which is non-negligible if $\varepsilon_{\mathcal{A}}$ is non-negligible. $\qquad\square$

Parameters. Table 3 shows our proposed parameters for BLAZE$^+$, which are selected for approximately 128 bits of security. The table also reviews the parameters of BLAZE proposed in [4] for the same security level. Table 1 gives the related communication complexity, performance, and sizes of keys and signatures. For the sake of comparison with BLAZE, we choose $m = 1$ and $m = 3$ for a practical scheme instantiation. Note that the choice of e.g., $m = 1$ implies an instantiation that is based on RLWE rather than RSIS and hence, it is not covered by the security proof as indicated in [4]. This is because the secret key has insufficient entropy or does not satisfy the condition $(m+1)\log(2d) > \log(q)$ (see the proof of Theorem 3). It seems that using RLWE does not reduce the security of the scheme, but rather using RSIS appears to be more an artifact of the proof technique.

Table 3. Parameters for BLAZE$^+$ and BLAZE targeting approximately 128 bits of security. The performance, sizes, and communication complexity corresponding to these parameters are given in Table 1.

Scheme	Parameters															
	δ_{abort}	ℓ	h	n	m	q	σ	γ	κ	α^*	α	s^*	s	$M_{\mathcal{S}}$	$M_{\mathcal{U}}$	M
BLAZE$^+$	2^{-128}	71	7	1024	1	$\approx 2^{31}$	0.5	1.01	16	19	33	1736.9	12450734	1.9	1	1.9
BLAZE$^+$	2^{-40}	32	5	1024	1	$\approx 2^{31}$	0.5	1.01	16	28	22	2559.6	12232099	1.5	1	1.5
BLAZE$^+$	2^{-10}	8	3	1024	1	$\approx 2^{31}$	0.5	1.01	16	28	22	2559.6	12232099	1.5	1	1.5
BLAZE	0.38	1	0	1024	1	$\approx 2^{31}$	0.5	1.2	16	20	25	2172.2	11796306	1.8	1.6	2.9
BLAZE$^+$	2^{-128}	71	7	1024	3	$\approx 2^{31}$	9.6	1.01	16	19	33	47161.3	478102394	1.9	1	1.9
BLAZE$^+$	2^{-40}	32	5	1024	3	$\approx 2^{31}$	9.6	1.01	16	28	22	69500.9	469714882	1.5	1	1.5
BLAZE$^+$	2^{-10}	8	3	1024	3	$\approx 2^{31}$	9.6	1.01	16	28	22	69500.9	469714882	1.5	1	1.5
BLAZE	0.38	1	0	1024	3	$\approx 2^{31}$	9.6	1.2	16	20	25	54067.2	380633088	1.8	1.6	2.9

Acknowledgements. We thank the anonymous reviewers of ACISP'20 for their valuable comments. This work has been partially supported by the Deutsche Forschungsgemeinschaft (DFG, German Research Foundation) – SFB 1119 – 236615297.

References

1. Abdalla, M., An, J.H., Bellare, M., Namprempre, C.: From identification to signatures via the fiat-shamir transform: minimizing assumptions for security and forward-security. In: Knudsen, L.R. (ed.) EUROCRYPT 2002. LNCS, vol. 2332, pp. 418–433. Springer, Heidelberg (2002). https://doi.org/10.1007/3-540-46035-7_28

2. Ajtai, M.: Generating hard instances of lattice problems. In: ACM Symposium on Theory of Computing - STOC 1996, pp. 99–108. ACM (1996)

3. Alkeilani Alkadri, N., El Bansarkhani, R., Buchmann, J.: On lattice-based interactive protocols: an approach with less or no aborts. Cryptology ePrint Archive, Report 2020/007 (2020). http://eprint.iacr.org/2020/007. Full version of this paper

4. Alkeilani Alkadri, N., El Bansarkhani, R., Buchmann, J.: BLAZE: practical lattice-based blind signatures for privacy-preserving applications. In: Financial Cryptography and Data Security - FC 2020. Springer, Cham (2020). http://eprint.iacr.org/2019/1167

5. Bai, S., Galbraith, S.D.: An improved compression technique for signatures based on learning with errors. In: Benaloh, J. (ed.) CT-RSA 2014. LNCS, vol. 8366, pp. 28–47. Springer, Cham (2014). https://doi.org/10.1007/978-3-319-04852-9_2

6. Baum, C., Damgård, I., Lyubashevsky, V., Oechsner, S., Peikert, C.: More efficient commitments from structured lattice assumptions. In: Catalano, D., De Prisco, R. (eds.) SCN 2018. LNCS, vol. 11035, pp. 368–385. Springer, Cham (2018). https://doi.org/10.1007/978-3-319-98113-0_20

7. Baum, C., Lin, H., Oechsner, S.: Towards practical lattice-based one-time linkable ring signatures. In: Naccache, D., Xu, S., Qing, S., Samarati, P., Blanc, G., Lu, R., Zhang, Z., Meddahi, A. (eds.) ICICS 2018. LNCS, vol. 11149, pp. 303–322. Springer, Cham (2018). https://doi.org/10.1007/978-3-030-01950-1_18

8. Bellare, M., Neven, G.: Multi-signatures in the plain public-key model and a general forking lemma. In: ACM Conference on Computer and Communications Security - CCS 2006, pp. 390–399. ACM (2006)

9. Benhamouda, F., Camenisch, J., Krenn, S., Lyubashevsky, V., Neven, G.: Better zero-knowledge proofs for lattice encryption and their application to group signatures. In: Sarkar, P., Iwata, T. (eds.) ASIACRYPT 2014. LNCS, vol. 8873, pp. 551–572. Springer, Heidelberg (2014). https://doi.org/10.1007/978-3-662-45611-8_29

10. Bourse, F., Del Pino, R., Minelli, M., Wee, H.: FHE circuit privacy almost for free. In: Robshaw, M., Katz, J. (eds.) CRYPTO 2016. LNCS, vol. 9815, pp. 62–89. Springer, Heidelberg (2016). https://doi.org/10.1007/978-3-662-53008-5_3

11. Brakerski, Z., Perlman, R.: Order-LWE and the hardness of Ring-LWE with entropic secrets. Cryptology ePrint Archive, Report 2018/494 (2018). https://eprint.iacr.org/2018/494

12. Ducas, L., et al.: CRYSTALS-Dilithium: a lattice-based digital signature scheme. Trans. Cryptogr. Hardware Embed. Syst. TCHES **2018**(1), 238–268 (2018)

13. Ducas, L., Lepoint, T., Lyubashevsky, V., Schwabe, P., Seiler, G., Stehle, D.: CRYSTALS-Dilithium: digital signatures from module lattices. Cryptology ePrint Archive, Report 2017/633 (2017). Version: 20170627:201152. http://eprint.iacr.org/2017/633

14. El Bansarkhani, R., Sturm, J.: An efficient lattice-based multisignature scheme with applications to bitcoins. In: Foresti, S., Persiano, G. (eds.) CANS 2016. LNCS, vol. 10052, pp. 140–155. Springer, Cham (2016). https://doi.org/10.1007/978-3-319-48965-0_9

15. Fiat, A., Shamir, A.: How to prove yourself: practical solutions to identification and signature problems. In: Odlyzko, A.M. (ed.) CRYPTO 1986. LNCS, vol. 263, pp. 186–194. Springer, Heidelberg (1987). https://doi.org/10.1007/3-540-47721-7_12

16. Fischlin, M., Schröder, D.: On the impossibility of three-move blind signature schemes. In: Gilbert, H. (ed.) EUROCRYPT 2010. LNCS, vol. 6110, pp. 197–215. Springer, Heidelberg (2010). https://doi.org/10.1007/978-3-642-13190-5_10

17. Gentry, C.: Fully homomorphic encryption using ideal lattices. In: ACM Symposium on Theory of Computing - STOC 2009, pp. 169–178. ACM (2009)

18. Hülsing, A., Butin, D., Gazdag, S., Rijneveld, J., Mohaisen, A.: XMSS: eXtended Merkle Signature Scheme. RFC 8391, May 2018

19. Juels, A., Luby, M., Ostrovsky, R.: Security of blind digital signatures. In: Kaliski, B.S. (ed.) CRYPTO 1997. LNCS, vol. 1294, pp. 150–164. Springer, Heidelberg (1997). https://doi.org/10.1007/BFb0052233

20. Katz, J., Kolesnikov, V., Wang, X.: Improved non-interactive zero knowledge with applications to post-quantum signatures. In: ACM Conference on Computer and Communications Security - CCS 2018, pp. 525–537. ACM (2018)

21. Langlois, A., Stehlé, D.: Worst-case to average-case reductions for module lattices. Des. Codes Crypt. **75**(3), 565–599 (2014). https://doi.org/10.1007/s10623-014-9938-4

22. Lyubashevsky, V.: Fiat-Shamir with aborts: applications to lattice and factoring-based signatures. In: Matsui, M. (ed.) ASIACRYPT 2009. LNCS, vol. 5912, pp. 598–616. Springer, Heidelberg (2009). https://doi.org/10.1007/978-3-642-10366-7_35

23. Lyubashevsky, V.: Lattice signatures without trapdoors. In: Pointcheval, D., Johansson, T. (eds.) EUROCRYPT 2012. LNCS, vol. 7237, pp. 738–755. Springer, Heidelberg (2012). https://doi.org/10.1007/978-3-642-29011-4_43

24. Lyubashevsky, V., Peikert, C., Regev, O.: On ideal lattices and learning with errors over rings. In: Gilbert, H. (ed.) EUROCRYPT 2010. LNCS, vol. 6110, pp. 1–23. Springer, Heidelberg (2010). https://doi.org/10.1007/978-3-642-13190-5_1

25. Lyubashevsky, V., Peikert, C., Regev, O.: A toolkit for ring-LWE cryptography. In: Johansson, T., Nguyen, P.Q. (eds.) EUROCRYPT 2013. LNCS, vol. 7881, pp. 35–54. Springer, Heidelberg (2013). https://doi.org/10.1007/978-3-642-38348-9_3

26. Merkle, R.C.: A certified digital signature. In: Brassard, G. (ed.) CRYPTO 1989. LNCS, vol. 435, pp. 218–238. Springer, New York (1990). https://doi.org/10.1007/0-387-34805-0_21

27. Micciancio, D.: Generalized compact knapsacks, cyclic lattices, and efficient one-way functions from worst-case complexity assumptions. In: Proceedings of the 43rd Symposium on Foundations of Computer Science FOCS, pp. 356–365. IEEE (2002)

28. Micciancio, D., Regev, O.: Worst-case to average-case reductions based on Gaussian measures. SIAM J. Comput. **37**(1), 267–302 (2007)

29. von Neumann, J.: Various techniques used in connection with random digits. In: Monte Carlo Method. National Bureau of Standards Applied Mathematics Series, vol. 12, pp. 36–38 (1951)

30. del Pino, R., Lyubashevsky, V.: Amortization with fewer equations for proving knowledge of small secrets. In: Katz, J., Shacham, H. (eds.) CRYPTO 2017. LNCS, vol. 10403, pp. 365–394. Springer, Cham (2017). https://doi.org/10.1007/978-3-319-63697-9_13

31. Pointcheval, D., Stern, J.: Security arguments for digital signatures and blind signatures. J. Cryptol. **13**(3), 361–396 (2000)

32. Regev, O.: On lattices, learning with errors, random linear codes, and cryptography. In: ACM Symposium on Theory of Computing, pp. 84–93. ACM (2005)

33. Rückert, M.: Lattice-based blind signatures. In: Abe, M. (ed.) ASIACRYPT 2010. LNCS, vol. 6477, pp. 413–430. Springer, Heidelberg (2010). https://doi.org/10.1007/978-3-642-17373-8_24

34. Schnorr, C.P.: Efficient signature generation by smart cards. J. Cryptol. **4**(3), 161–174 (1991). https://doi.org/10.1007/BF00196725

35. Alberto Torres, W.A., et al.: Post-quantum one-time linkable ring signature and application to ring confidential transactions in blockchain (lattice RingCT v1.0). In: Susilo, W., Yang, G. (eds.) ACISP 2018. LNCS, vol. 10946, pp. 558–576. Springer, Cham (2018). https://doi.org/10.1007/978-3-319-93638-3_32

SKCN: Practical and Flexible Digital Signature from Module Lattice

Boru Gong[1], Leixiao Cheng[2], and Yunlei Zhao[1,3,4(✉)]

[1] School of Computer Science, Fudan University, Shanghai, China
{gongboru,ylzhao}@fudan.edu.cn
[2] School of Mathematical Sciences, Fudan University, Shanghai, China
14110180004@fudan.edu.cn
[3] State Key Laboratory of Integrated Services Networks,
Xidian University, Xi'an, China
[4] State Key Laboratory of Cryptology, P.O. Box 5159, Beijing 100878, China

Abstract. The lattice-based signature scheme Dilithium is one of the most promising signature candidates for the post-quantum era, for its simplicity, efficiency, small public key size, and resistance against side channel attacks. Whether better trade-offs on the already remarkable performance of Dilithium can be made is left in Dilithium as an interesting open question.

In this work, we provide new insights in interpreting the design of Dilithium, in terms of key consensus previously proposed in the literature for key encapsulation mechanisms (KEM) and key exchange (KEX). Based on the deterministic version of the optimal key consensus with noise (OKCN) mechanism originally developed for KEM/KEX, we present *signature from key consensus with noise* (SKCN), which could be viewed as generalization and optimization of Dilithium. The construction of SKCN is generic, modular and flexible, which in particular allows a much broader range of parameters for searching better tradeoffs among security, computational efficiency, and bandwidth. For example, on the recommended parameters, compared with Dilithium our SKCN scheme is more efficient both in computation and in bandwidth, while preserving the same level of post-quantum security. Also, our three sets of parameters are chosen to be as unified as possible, so as to simplify the implementation in practice. Finally, using the same routine of OKCN for both KEM/KEX and digital signature eases (hardware) implementation and deployment in practice, and is useful to simplify the system complexity of lattice-based cryptography in general.

1 Introduction

Over the last decades, lattices have emerged as a very attractive foundation for cryptography. Ever since the seminal work of Ajtai [1] connecting the average-case complexity of lattice problems to their complexity in the worst case, there

---

The full version of this work appears at Cryptology ePrint Archive, 2018/1180.

© Springer Nature Switzerland AG 2020
J. K. Liu and H. Cui (Eds.): ACISP 2020, LNCS 12248, pp. 62–81, 2020.
https://doi.org/10.1007/978-3-030-55304-3_4

has been intriguing and fruitful efforts to base cryptographic schemes on worst-case lattice assumptions. In addition to their unique theoretical properties, lattice-based schemes enjoy many potential advantages: their asymptotic efficiency and conceptual simplicity (usually requiring only linear operations on small integers); their resistance so far to cryptanalysis by *quantum* algorithms; and the guarantee that their random instances are "as hard as possible" [6, 27].

Given the importance of digital signature schemes in modern cryptography, it is natural to consider building practical and provably secure digital signature schemes based on lattice assumptions. Generally speaking, lattice-based signature schemes are designed by either of the following paradigms: hash-and-sign paradigm [8, 14], and Fiat-Shamir heuristic [11, 13, 21]. Nevertheless, given the current research status in lattice-based cryptography, it is commonly suggested that lattice-based signature could be subtler and harder to achieve. For instance, there are more than twenty submissions of lattice-based key encapsulation mechanisms to NIST post-quantum cryptography (NIST-PQC), but only five lattice-based signature submissions. Among them, Falcon [25], and pqNTRUSign [28] follow the hash-and-sign paradigm; Dilithium [12] and qTESLA [5] follow the Fiat-Shamir heuristic. Now, Dilithium [12], qTESLA [5] and Falcon [25] are in the second round submissions of NIST-PQC.

In this work, we focus on the study of Dilithium [12,18]. Dilithium is one of the best lattice-based signature schemes that follow the Fiat-Shamir paradigm, and is one of the most promising lattice-based signature candidates. Some salient features of Dilithium include: simplicity (both for the algorithmic design and for the algebraic structure of the underlying lattice), efficiency, small public key size, and resistance against side channel attacks [4]. Its design is based on a list of pioneering works (e.g., [2, 21, 22] and more), with very careful and comprehensive optimizations in implementation and parameter selection. Whether better trade-offs on the already remarkable performance of Dilithium can be made is left in [9] as an interesting open question.

1.1 Our Contributions

In this work, we present generalization and optimization of Dilithium. This is enabled by new insights in interpreting the design of Dilithium, in terms of symmetric key consensus previously proposed in the literature for achieving key encapsulation mechanisms (KEM) and key exchange (KEX) [3, 10, 15, 19, 24, 27]. Based on the deterministic version of the optimal key consensus with noise (OKCN) mechanism, originally developed in [15, 16] for highly practical KEM/KEX schemes, we present *signature from key consensus with noise* (SKCN). The construction of SKCN is generic, modular and flexible, which in particular allows a much broader range of parameters.

We made efforts to thoroughly search and test a large set of parameters to achieve better trade-offs among security, efficiency, and bandwidth. On the recommended parameters, compared with Dilithium our SKCN scheme is more efficient both in computation and in bandwidth, while preserving the same level of post-quantum security. Also, our three sets of parameters are chosen to be as unified as possible, so as to simplify the implementation in practice. This work also further justifies and highlights the desirability of OKCN, originally developed in [15] for highly practical KEM/KEX, as the same routine can be used for both KEM/KEX and digital signatures, which ease (hardware) implementation and deployment in practice, and is useful to simplify the system complexity of lattice-based cryptography in general.

2   Preliminaries

For any real number $x \in \mathbb{R}$, let $\lfloor x \rfloor$ denote the largest integer that is no more than x, and $\lceil x \rceil := \lfloor x + 1/2 \rfloor$. For any $i, j \in \mathbb{Z}$ such that $i < j$, denote by $[i, j]$ the set of integers $\{i, i+1, \cdots, j-1, j\}$. For the positive integers $r, \alpha > 0$, let $r \bmod \alpha$ denote the unique integer $r' \in [0, \alpha - 1]$ such that $\alpha \mid (r' - r)$, and let $r \bmod^{\pm} \alpha$ denote the unique integer $r'' \in [-\lfloor \frac{\alpha-1}{2} \rfloor, \lfloor \frac{\alpha}{2} \rfloor]$ such that $\alpha \mid (r'' - r)$. For a positive integer q and an element $x \in \mathbb{Z}_q$, we write $\|x\|_{\infty}$ for $|x \bmod^{\pm} q|$. For every $a = \sum_{i=0}^{n-1} a_i \cdot x^i \in \mathcal{R}_q$, $a_i \in \mathbb{Z}_q$, define $\mathsf{Power2Round}_{q,d}(a) \overset{\text{def}}{=} \sum a_i' \cdot x^i$, where $a_i' \overset{\text{def}}{=} \left(a_i - \left(a_i \bmod^{\pm} 2^d \right) \right) / 2^d$.

For a finite set S, $|S|$ denotes its cardinality, and $x \leftarrow S$ denotes the operation of picking an element uniformly at random from the set S. We use standard notations and conventions below for writing probabilistic algorithms, experiments and interactive protocols. For an arbitrary probability distribution $\mathcal{D}$, the notation $x \leftarrow \mathcal{D}$ denotes the operation of picking an element according to the pre-defined distribution $\mathcal{D}$. We say that a positive function $f(\lambda) > 0$ is *negligible* in λ, if for every $c > 0$ there exists a positive $\lambda_c > 0$ such that $f(\lambda) < 1/\lambda^c$ for all $\lambda > \lambda_c$.

Digital Signature Scheme. A digital signature scheme Π consists of three probabilistic polynomial-time algorithms (KeyGen, Sign, Verify). KeyGen is the key generation algorithm that, on input of the security parameter 1^{λ}, outputs (pk, sk). Sign is the signing algorithm that, on input the secret key sk as well as the message $\mu \in \{0,1\}^*$ to be signed, outputs the signature σ. Verify is the *deterministic* verification algorithm that, on input the public key pk as well as the message/signature pair (μ, σ), outputs $b \in \{0,1\}$, indicating whether it accepts the incoming (μ, σ) as a *valid* pair or not. We say a signature scheme $\Pi = $ (KeyGen, Sign, Verify) is *correct*, if for any sufficiently large λ, any (pk, sk) $\leftarrow$ KeyGen(1^{λ}) and any $\mu \in \{0,1\}^*$, we have $\Pr[\mathsf{Verify}(\mathsf{pk}, \mu, \mathsf{Sign}(\mathsf{sk}, \mu)) = 1] = 1$.

(S)EU-CMA. The security for a signature scheme $\Pi=$(KeyGen, Sign, Verify), is defined in the following game between a challenger and an adversary A.

- Setup. Given λ, the challenger runs (pk, sk) $\leftarrow$ KeyGen(1^{λ}). The public key pk is given to adversary A, whereas the secret key sk is kept in private.

- Challenge. The adversary A is given access to the signing oracle. Suppose A makes q_s signature queries. Each signature query consists of the following steps: (1) A adaptively chooses the message $\mu_i \in \{0,1\}^*$, $1 \le i \le q_s$, based upon its entire view, and sends μ_i to the signer; (2) Given the secret key sk as well as the message μ_i to be signed, the challenger generates and sends back the associated signature, denoted σ_i, to A.
- Output. Finally, A outputs a pair of (μ, σ), and wins if (1) Verify(pk, μ, σ) = 1 and (2) $(\mu, \sigma) \notin \{(\mu_1, \sigma_1), \cdots, (\mu_{q_s}, \sigma_{q_s})\}$.

We say the signature scheme Π is *strongly existentially unforgeable under adaptive chosen-message attack*, if the probability that every p.p.t. attacker A wins in the foregoing game is negligible. A weaker model, *i.e.*, the EU-CMA model, could be define by requiring that A wins if and only if (1) Verify(pk, μ, σ) = 1 and (2) $\mu \notin \{\mu_1, \mu_2, \cdots, \mu_{q_s}\}$. Then Π is called *(standard) existentially unforgeable under adaptive chosen-message attack*, if no efficient adversary can win in this weaker game with non-negligible probability.

Module-LWE and Module-SIS. In this work, we always have $n = 256$ and $q = 1952257$. Also, let $\mathcal{R}$ and $\mathcal{R}_q$ denote the rings $\mathbb{Z}[x]/\langle x^n + 1 \rangle$ and $\mathbb{Z}_q[x]/\langle x^n + 1 \rangle$, respectively. For the element $w = \sum_{i=0}^{n-1} w_i x^i \in \mathcal{R}$, its ℓ_∞-norm is defined as $\|w\|_\infty := \max \|w_i\|_\infty$. Likewise, for the element $\mathbf{w} = (w_1, \cdots, w_k) \in \mathcal{R}^k$, its ℓ_∞-norm is defined as $\|\mathbf{w}\|_\infty := \max_i \|w_i\|_\infty$. In particular, when the other parameters are clear from the context, let $S_\eta \subseteq \mathcal{R}$ denote the set of elements $w \in \mathcal{R}$ such that $\|w\|_\infty \le \eta$.

The hard problems underlying the security of our signature scheme are Module-LWE (MLWE), Module-SIS (MSIS) (as well as a variant of the MSIS problem, *i.e.*, the SelfTargetMSIS problem). They were well studied in [20] and could be seen as a natural generalization of the Ring-LWE [19] and Ring-SIS problems [26], respectively. Fix the parameter $\ell \in \mathbb{N}$. The Module-LWE distribution (induced by $\mathbf{s} \in \mathcal{R}_q^\ell$) is the distribution of the random pair $(\mathbf{a}_i, b_i)$ over the support $\mathcal{R}_q^\ell \times \mathcal{R}_q$, where $\mathbf{a}_i \leftarrow \mathcal{R}_q^\ell$ is taken uniformly at random, and $b_i := \mathbf{a}_i^T \mathbf{s} + e_i$ with $e_i \leftarrow S_\eta$ fresh for every sample. Given arbitrarily many samples drawn from the Module-LWE distribution induced by $\mathbf{s} \leftarrow S_\eta^\ell$, the (search) Module-LWE problem asks to recover $\mathbf{s}$. And the associated Module-LWE assumption states that given $\mathbf{A} \leftarrow \mathcal{R}_q^{k \times \ell}$ and $\mathbf{b} := \mathbf{A}\mathbf{s} + \mathbf{e}$ where $k = \text{poly}(\lambda)$ and $(\mathbf{s}, \mathbf{e}) \leftarrow S_\eta^\ell \times S_\eta^k$, no efficient algorithm can succeed in recovering $\mathbf{s}$ with non-negligible probability, provided that the parameters are appropriately chosen.

Fix $p \in [1, \infty]$. Given $\mathbf{A} \leftarrow \mathcal{R}_q^{h \times \ell}$ where $h = \text{poly}(\lambda)$, the Module-SIS problem (in ℓ_p-norm) parameterized by $\beta > 0$ asks to find a "short" yet nonzero pre-image $\mathbf{x} \in \mathcal{R}_q^\ell$ in the lattice determined by $\mathbf{A}$, *i.e.*, $\mathbf{x} \ne \mathbf{0}, \mathbf{A} \cdot \mathbf{x} = \mathbf{0}$ and $\|\mathbf{x}\| \le \beta$. And the associated Module-SIS assumption (in ℓ_p-norm) states that no probabilistic polynomial-time algorithm can find a feasible pre-image $\mathbf{x}$ with non-negligible probability, provided that the parameters are appropriately chosen. In the literature, the module-SIS problem in *Euclidean* norm, *i.e.*, $p = 2$, is well-studied; nevertheless, in this work, we are mostly interested in the Module-SIS problem/assumption *in ℓ_∞-norm, i.e.,* $p = \infty$.

Hashing. As is in [12,18], when the other related parameters are clear from the context, for every positive integer $w > 0$, let $B_w := \{x \in \mathcal{R} \mid \|x\|_\infty = 1, \|x\|_1 = w\}$. In this work, we always have $w = 60$, since the set $B_{60} \subseteq \mathcal{R}$ is of size $2^{60} \cdot \binom{n}{60} \approx 2^{256}$ (recall that $n = 256$ by default). Let $H : \{0,1\}^* \to B_{60}$ be a hash function that is modeled as a random oracle in this work. In practice, to pick a random element in B_{60}, we can use an inside-out version of Fisher-Yates shuffle.

Extendable Output Function. The notion of extendable output function follows that of [12,18]. An *extendable output function* Sam is a function on bit strings in which the output can be extended to any desired length, and the notation $y \in S := \mathsf{Sam}(x)$ represents that the function Sam takes as input x and then produces a value y that is distributed according to the pre-defined distribution S (or according to the uniform distribution over the pre-defined set S). The whole procedure is *deterministic* in the sense that for a given x will always output the same y, *i.e.*, the map $x \mapsto y$ is well-defined. For simplicity we always assume that the output distribution of Sam is perfect, whereas in practice it will be implemented by using some cryptographic hash functions (which are modelled as random oracle in this work) and produce an output that is *statistically close* to the perfect distribution.

3   Building Tools of SKCN

In this section, we first propose the notion of deterministic symmetric key consensus (DKC); then we construct and analyze a concrete DKC instance, *i.e.*, the deterministic symmetric key consensus with noise (DKCN), which is a variant of the optimal key consensus with noise (OKCN) scheme presented in [15]. Based on DKCN, we then define several algorithms/tools, and develop some of their properties. These algorithms will serve as the building tools for our signature scheme to be introduced in Sect. 4.

Roughly speaking, in a two-party game where two players have values $\sigma_1, \sigma_2 \in \mathbb{Z}_q$ respectively, DKCN ensures both party can extract a shared key from σ_1 and σ_2, respectively, *provided that σ_1 and σ_2 are close enough*. Note that although all these algorithms/tools proposed in this section are defined with respect to the finite field $\mathbb{Z}_q$ for some positive rational prime q, they could be naturally generalized to vectors (as well as the ring $\mathcal{R}_q$) in the component-wise manner.

Definition 1. *A DKC scheme* $DKC = (\mathsf{params}, \mathsf{Con}, \mathsf{Rec})$ *is specified as follows.*

- params $= (q, k, g, d, aux)$ *denotes the system parameters, where* q, k, g, d *are positive integers satisfying* $2 \leq k, g \leq q, 0 \leq d \leq \lfloor \frac{q}{2} \rfloor$, *and aux denotes some auxiliary values that are usually determined by* (q, k, g, d) *and could be set to be a special symbol* $\emptyset$ *indicating "empty".*
- $(k_1, v) \leftarrow$ Con$(\sigma_1, $params$)$: *On input* $(\sigma_1 \in \mathbb{Z}_q, $params$)$, *the deterministic polynomial-time conciliation algorithm* Con *outputs* (k_1, v), *where* $k_1 \in \mathbb{Z}_k$ *is the shared-key, and* $v \in \mathbb{Z}_g$ *is a hint signal that will be publicly delivered to the communicating peer to help the two parties reach consensus.*
- $k_2 \leftarrow$ Rec$(\sigma_2, v, $params$)$: *On input* $(\sigma_2 \in \mathbb{Z}_q, v, $params$)$, *the deterministic polynomial-time reconciliation algorithm* Rec *outputs* $k_2 \in \mathbb{Z}_k$.

A DKC scheme is correct, *if* $k_1 = k_2$ *for any* $\sigma_1, \sigma_2 \in \mathbb{Z}_q$ *with* $|\sigma_1 - \sigma_2|_\infty \leq d$.

Next, we develop a concrete instance of DKC, *i.e.*, the rounded symmetric key consensus with noise (DKCN) depicted in Algorithm 1. Note that by Theorem 2, as a concrete DKC, DKCN itself is *correct*, provided that parameters are appropriately set.

Theorem 2. *When* $k \geq 2, g \geq 2$ *and* $2kd < q$, *the DKCN scheme (params,* Con, Rec*) depicted in Algorithm 1 is correct.*

Proof. Suppose $|\sigma_1 - \sigma_2|_\infty \leq d$. Then by Lemma 3, there exist $\theta \in \mathbb{Z}$ and $\delta \in \{-d, \cdots, d\}$ such that $\sigma_2 = \sigma_1 + \theta q + \delta$. From Line 3 to 7 in Algorithm 1, we know that there exists $\theta' \in \mathbb{Z}$ such that $k\sigma_1 = (k_1 + k\theta') \cdot q + v$. Taking these into the formula of k_2 in Rec (Line 12), we have

$$k_2 \equiv \lfloor (k\sigma_2 - v)/q \rceil \equiv \lfloor k(\sigma_1 + \theta q + \delta)/q - v/q \rceil \equiv \lfloor k_1 + k\delta/q \rceil \pmod{k}.$$

It follows from $2kd < q$ that $|k\delta/q| \leq kd/q < 1/2$, making $k_2 = k_1$. ⊔

The following lemma, proposed in [15], is essential for the proof of Theorem 2.

Lemma 3 ([15]). *For any* $x, y, t, l \in \mathbb{Z}$ *where* $t \geq 1$ *and* $l \geq 0$, *if* $|(x - y) \bmod q|_\infty \leq l$, *there exists* $\theta \in \mathbb{Z}$ *and* $\delta \in \{-l, \cdots, l\}$ *such that* $x = y + \theta q + \delta$. □

Algorithm 1. DKCN: Deterministic Symmetric KC with Noise

1: params $:= (q, k, g, d, aux = \emptyset)$
2: **procedure** CON$(\sigma_1, $params$)$ ▷ $\sigma_1 \in \mathbb{Z}_q$
3:     $v := k\sigma_1 \bmod^\pm q$
4:     **if** $k\sigma_1 - v = kq$ **then**
5:         $k_1 := 0$
6:     **else**
7:         $k_1 := (k\sigma_1 - v)/q$
8:     **end if**
9:     **return** (k_1, v)
10: **end procedure**
11: **procedure** REC$(\sigma_2, v, $params$)$ ▷ $\sigma_2 \in \mathbb{Z}_q$
12:     $k_2 := \lfloor (k\sigma_2 - v)/q \rceil \bmod k$
13:     **return** k_2
14: **end procedure**

Based on DKCN, we then present several algorithms and some of their properties, whose proofs are presented in Appendix B. These algorithms would be applied in the design of SKCN. As we shall see in Sect. 4, their properties play an important role in the correctness and security analysis of SKCN.

Proposition 4. *For every $r, z \in \mathbb{Z}_q$ such that $\|z\|_\infty < \lfloor q/(2k) \rfloor$, we have*

$$\mathsf{UseHint}_{q,k}(\mathsf{MakeHint}_{q,k}(z, r), r) = \mathsf{HighBits}_{q,k}(r + z).$$

Proposition 5. *For $r_1' \in \mathbb{Z}_k$, $r \in \mathbb{Z}_q$, $h \in \{0, 1\}$, if $r_1' = \mathsf{UseHint}_{q,k}(h, r)$, then $\|r - \lfloor q \cdot r_1'/k \rceil\|_\infty \leq q/k + 1/2 \leq \lfloor q/k \rceil + 1$.*

Proposition 6. *For $r, z \in \mathbb{Z}_q$ such that $\|z\|_\infty < U < \lfloor q/(2k) \rfloor$. If $\|r_0'\|_\infty < q/2 - kU$ where $(r_1, r_0) \leftarrow \mathsf{Con}(r)$, $(r_1', r_0') \leftarrow \mathsf{Con}(r + z)$, then $r_1 = r_1'$.*

1: **procedure** HIGHBITS$_{q,k}(r)$
2:　　$(r_1, r_0) \leftarrow \mathsf{Con}(r)$
3:　　**return** r_1
4: **end procedure**
5: **procedure** MAKEHINT$_{q,k}(z, r)$
6:　　$r_1 := \mathsf{HighBits}_{q,k}(r)$
7:　　$v_1 := \mathsf{HighBits}_{q,k}(r + z)$
8:　　**if** $r_1 = v_1$ **then**
9:　　　　**return** 0
10:　　**else**
11:　　　　**return** 1
12:　　**end if**
13: **end procedure**

1: **procedure** LOWBITS$_{q,k}(r)$
2:　　$(r_1, r_0) \leftarrow \mathsf{Con}(r)$
3:　　**return** r_0
4: **end procedure**
5: **procedure** USEHINT$_{q,k}(h, r)$
6:　　$(r_1, r_0) := \mathsf{Con}(r)$
7:　　**if** $h = 0$ **then**
8:　　　　**return** r_1
9:　　**else if** $h = 1$ and $r_0 > 0$ **then**
10:　　　　**return** $(r_1 + 1) \bmod k$
11:　　**else**
12:　　　　**return** $(r_1 - 1) \bmod k$
13:　　**end if**
14: **end procedure**

---

4   SKCN: Signature from Key Consensus with Noise

In this section, we propose our signature scheme SKCN, which is defined on a module lattice, and can be proven to be strongly existentially unforgeable under adaptive chosen-message attacks in the quantum random oracle model. SKCN could be seen as a generalization and optimization of Dilithium with the aid of DKCN, and its correctness analysis and security proof roughly follows from that of Dilithium as well.

4.1   Description of SKCN

Our key generation, signing, and verification algorithms are fully described in Algorithms 2, 4 and 3, respectively.

Algorithm 2. Key Generation Algorithm

Input: 1^λ
Output: $(\text{pk} = (\rho, \mathbf{t}_1), \text{sk} = (\rho, \mathbf{s}, \mathbf{e}, \mathbf{t}))$
1: $\rho, \rho' \leftarrow \{0,1\}^{256}$
2: $\mathbf{A} \in \mathcal{R}_q^{h \times \ell} := \text{Sam}(\rho)$
3: $(\mathbf{s}, \mathbf{e}) \in S_\eta^\ell \times S_{\eta'}^h := \text{Sam}(\rho')$
4: $\mathbf{t} := \mathbf{As} + \mathbf{e}$
5: $\mathbf{t}_1 := \text{Power2Round}_{q,d}(\mathbf{t})$
6: **return** $(\text{pk} = (\rho, \mathbf{t}_1), \text{sk} = (\rho, \mathbf{s}, \mathbf{e}, \mathbf{t}))$

Algorithm 3. Verification Algorithm

Input: $\text{pk} = (\rho, \mathbf{t}_1), \mu \in \{0,1\}^*, (\mathbf{z}, c, \mathbf{h})$
Output: $b \in \{0,1\}$
1: $\mathbf{A} \in \mathcal{R}_q^{h \times \ell} := \text{Sam}(\rho)$
2: $\mathbf{w}_1' := \text{UseHint}_{q,k}(\mathbf{h}, \mathbf{Az} - c\mathbf{t}_1 \cdot 2^d)$
3: $c' \leftarrow H(\rho, \mathbf{t}_1, \lfloor q\mathbf{w}_1'/k \rceil, \mu)$
4: **if** $c = c'$ and $\|\mathbf{z}\|_\infty < \lfloor q/k \rfloor - U$ and the number of 1's in $\mathbf{h}$ is $\leq \omega$ **then**
5:     **return** 1
6: **else**
7:     **return** 0
8: **end if**

Algorithm 4. The Signing Algorithm

Input: $\mu \in \{0,1\}^*$, $\text{sk} = (\rho, \mathbf{s}, \mathbf{e}, \mathbf{t})$
Output: $\sigma = (\mathbf{z}, c, \mathbf{h})$
1: $\mathbf{A} \in \mathcal{R}_q^{h \times \ell} := \text{Sam}(\rho)$
2: $\mathbf{t}_1 := \text{Power2Round}_{q,d}(\mathbf{t})$
3: $\mathbf{t}_0 := \mathbf{t} - \mathbf{t}_1 \cdot 2^d$
4: $r \leftarrow \{0,1\}^{256}$
5: $\mathbf{y} \in S_{\lfloor q/k \rfloor - 1}^\ell := \text{Sam}(r)$
6: $\mathbf{w} := \mathbf{Ay}$
7: $\mathbf{w}_1 := \text{HighBits}_{q,k}(\mathbf{w})$
8: $c \leftarrow H(\rho, \mathbf{t}_1, \lfloor q \cdot \mathbf{w}_1/k \rceil, \mu)$
9: $\mathbf{z} := \mathbf{y} + c\mathbf{s}$
10: $(\mathbf{r}_1, \mathbf{r}_0) := \text{Con}(\mathbf{w} - c\mathbf{e})$
11: Restart if $\|\mathbf{z}\|_\infty \geq \lfloor q/k \rfloor - U$ or $\|\mathbf{r}_0\|_\infty \geq q/2 - kU'$ or $\mathbf{r}_1 \neq \mathbf{w}_1$
12: $\mathbf{h} := \text{MakeHint}_{q,k}(-c\mathbf{t}_0, \mathbf{w} - c\mathbf{e} + c\mathbf{t}_0)$
13: Restart if $\|c\mathbf{t}_0\|_\infty \geq \lfloor q/2k \rfloor$ or the number of 1's in $\mathbf{h}$ is greater than ω
14: **return** $(\mathbf{z}, c, \mathbf{h})$

Algorithm 5. The Simulator

Input: $\mu \in \{0,1\}^*$, $\rho, \mathbf{t}_1, \mathbf{t}_0$
Output: $\sigma = (\mathbf{z}, c, \mathbf{h})$
1: $\mathbf{A} \in \mathcal{R}_q^{h \times \ell} := \text{Sam}(\rho)$
2: $(\mathbf{z}, c) \leftarrow S_{\lfloor q/k \rfloor - U} \times B_{60}$
3: $(\mathbf{r}_1, \mathbf{r}_0) := \text{Con}(\mathbf{Az} - c\mathbf{t})$
4: Restart if $\|\mathbf{r}_0\|_\infty \geq q/2 - kU$
5: **if** H has already been defined on $(\rho, \mathbf{t}_1, \lfloor q \cdot \mathbf{r}_1/k \rceil, \mu)$ **then**
6:     Abort
7: **else**
8:     Program $H(\rho, \mathbf{t}_1, \lfloor q \cdot \mathbf{r}_1/k \rceil, \mu) = c$
9: **end if**
10: $\mathbf{h} := \text{MakeHint}_{q,k}(-c\mathbf{t}_0, \mathbf{Az} - c\mathbf{t} + c\mathbf{t}_0)$
11: Restart if $\|c\mathbf{t}_0\|_\infty \geq \lfloor q/2k \rfloor$ or the number of 1's in $\mathbf{h}$ is greater than ω
12: **return** $(\mathbf{z}, c, \mathbf{h})$

Practical Implementation. When we implement SKCN with our recommended parameter set II (cf. Table 3), several improvements that are similar to [12,18] are made, so as to improve its efficiency. Specifically, the sign algorithm in our implementation is *deterministic* in nature which is similar to that of Dilithium [18]. This is achieved by adding some new seeds (tr, key) into the secret key sk; thus, the random nonce $\mathbf{y}$ in the sign algorithm could be obtained via a pseudorandom string, which is obtained by extending the hash value of (tr, key), the message to be signed, and a counter. Thus, the $\mathbf{t}_1$ in sk is no longer necessary, making $\text{sk} = (\rho, \text{tr}, \text{key}, \mathbf{s}, \mathbf{e}, \mathbf{t}_0)$. This minor modification can improve the efficiency of the sign algorithm significantly, and shorten the size of sk.

4.2   Correctness Analysis

In SKCN, the key generation algorithm first chooses a random 256-bit seed ρ and expands it into a matrix $\mathbf{A} \leftarrow \mathcal{R}_q^{h \times \ell}$ by an extendable output function $\mathsf{Sam}(\cdot)$. The crucial component in the secret key is $(\mathbf{s}, \mathbf{e}) \in \mathcal{R}_q^{\ell} \times \mathcal{R}_q^{h}$, and each coefficient of $\mathbf{s}$ (resp., $\mathbf{e}$) is drawn uniformly at random from the set $[-\eta, \eta]$ (resp., $[-\eta', \eta']$). Finally, we compute $\mathbf{t} := \mathbf{A}\mathbf{s} + \mathbf{e} \in \mathcal{R}_q^{h}$. The public key is $\mathrm{pk} = (\rho, \mathbf{t}_1)$ where $\mathbf{t}_1 = \mathsf{Power2Round}_{q,d}(\mathbf{t})$, and the associated secret key is $\mathrm{sk} = (\rho, \mathbf{s}, \mathbf{e}, \mathbf{t})$.

Given the secret key $\mathrm{sk} = (\rho, \mathbf{s}, \mathbf{e}, \mathbf{t})$ as well as the message $\mu \in \{0, 1\}^*$ to be signed, the signing algorithm first recovers the public matrix $\mathbf{A} \in \mathcal{R}_q^{h \times \ell}$ via the random seed ρ in the secret key. After that, the signing algorithm picks a "short" $\mathbf{y}$ from the set $S_{\lfloor q/k \rfloor -1}^{\ell} \subseteq \mathcal{R}_q^{\ell}$ uniformly at random, and computes $\mathbf{w}_1 := \mathsf{HighBits}_{q,k}(\mathbf{w})$, where $\mathbf{w} := \mathbf{A}\mathbf{y}$. Upon input $(\rho, \mathbf{t}_1, \lfloor q \cdot \mathbf{w}_1 / k \rceil, \mu)$, the random oracle $H(\cdot)$ returns a uniform $c \leftarrow B_{60}$. After obtaining c, the signing algorithm conducts a rejection sampling process to check if every coefficient of $\mathbf{z} := \mathbf{y} + c\mathbf{s} \in \mathcal{R}_q^{\ell}$ is "small" enough, if every coefficient of $\mathbf{r}_0$ is "small" enough, and if $\mathbf{r}_1 = \mathbf{w}_1$, where $(\mathbf{r}_1, \mathbf{r}_0) \leftarrow \mathsf{Con}(\mathbf{w} - c\mathbf{e})$; otherwise, the signing algorithm restarts, until all the requirements are satisfied. We should point out that if $\|c\mathbf{e}\|_{\infty} \leq U'$, then by Proposition 6, the requirement $\|\mathbf{r}_0\|_{\infty} < q/2 - kU'$ forces $\mathbf{r}_1 = \mathbf{w}_1$. We hope $\|c\mathbf{e}\|_{\infty} > U'$ occurs with negligible probability, such that the probability that the check $\mathbf{r}_1 = \mathbf{w}_1$ fails is negligible as well. In addition, U is chosen such that $\|c\mathbf{s}\|_{\infty} \leq U$ holds with overwhelming probability. Furthermore, the function $\mathsf{MakeHint}_{q,k}(\cdot)$ is invoked on input $(-c\mathbf{t}_0, \mathbf{w} - c\mathbf{e} + c\mathbf{t}_0)$ to generate the hint $\mathbf{h}$, i.e., a binary vector in $\{0, 1\}^{n \cdot h}$. The signing algorithm concludes by conducting the remaining two checks, i.e., if $\|c\mathbf{t}_0\|_{\infty} < \lfloor q/2k \rfloor$ and if the number of nonzero elements in $\mathbf{h} \in \{0, 1\}^{n \cdot h}$ does not exceed the pre-defined threshold ω; otherwise restart is carried out again. Here, the hint $\mathbf{h}$ corresponds to the fact that it is $\mathbf{t}_1$, not the whole $\mathbf{t} = \mathbf{t}_1 \cdot 2^d + \mathbf{t}_0$ that is contained in the public key. With the hint $\mathbf{h}$, we can still carry out the verification, even without $\mathbf{t}_0$.

Given the public key $\mathrm{pk} = (\rho, \mathbf{t}_1)$, the message $\mu \in \{0, 1\}^*$ and the claimed signature $(\mathbf{z}, c, \mathbf{h})$, the verifying algorithm first recovers $\mathbf{A} \in \mathcal{R}_q^{h \times \ell}$ via the random seed ρ. After that, it computes $\mathbf{w}_1' := \mathsf{UseHint}_{q,k}(\mathbf{h}, \mathbf{A}\mathbf{z} - c\mathbf{t}_1 \cdot 2^d)$. If the given $(\mathbf{z}, c, \mathbf{h})$ is indeed a *honestly generated* signature of the incoming message μ, then it is routine to see that every coefficient of $\mathbf{z}$ is "small" enough, and the number of 1's in $\mathbf{h}$ is no greater than ω; more importantly, we have $\mathsf{HighBits}_{q,k}(\mathbf{A}\mathbf{y}) = \mathsf{HighBits}_{q,k}(\mathbf{A}\mathbf{y} - c\mathbf{e}) = \mathbf{w}_1'$ and therefore $c = c'$, where $c' \leftarrow H(\rho, \mathbf{t}_1, \lfloor q\mathbf{w}_1' / k \rceil, \mu)$. The verifying algorithm would accept the input tuple if and only if the foregoing conditions are all satisfied.

Next, we show that our SKCN signature scheme is always *correct, provided that the involving parameters are appropriately set*. The correctness relies heavily on Proposition 4. When the public/secret key pair $(\mathrm{pk}, \mathrm{sk})$ is fixed, for a *valid* message/signature pair $(\mu, (\mathbf{z}, c, \mathbf{h}))$, it suffices to show that $c = c'$. Since $\|c\mathbf{t}_0\|_{\infty} < q/2k$ and $\mathbf{A}\mathbf{z} - c\mathbf{t}_1 \cdot 2^d = \mathbf{A}\mathbf{y} - c\mathbf{e} + c\mathbf{t}_0$, it follows directly from Proposition 4 that

$$\mathsf{UseHint}_{q,k}(\mathbf{h}, \mathbf{A}\mathbf{z} - c\mathbf{t}_1 \cdot 2^d) = \mathsf{HighBits}_{q,k}(\mathbf{A}\mathbf{y} - c\mathbf{e}).$$

Given that the signing algorithm forces $\mathsf{HighBits}_{q,k}(\mathbf{Ay} - ce) = \mathsf{HighBits}_{q,k}(\mathbf{Ay})$ by rejection sampling, it follows from the following equality that $c = c'$:

$$\mathsf{UseHint}_{q,k}(\mathbf{h}, \mathbf{Az} - ct_1 \cdot 2^d) = \mathsf{HighBits}_{q,k}(\mathbf{Ay} - ce) = \mathsf{HighBits}_{q,k}(\mathbf{Ay}).$$

4.3 Recommended Parameters, and Comparison

To improve the time/space efficiency, our SKCN signature scheme could be set *asymmetrically*, in the sense that as long as the resulting scheme can resist the key-recovery attack, η may not equal to η'. Moreover, the parameter U and U' are carefully chosen such that $\Pr\left[\|cs\|_\infty \geq U\right]$ and $\Pr\left[\|ce\|_\infty \geq U'\right]$ are sufficiently small, say they are both small than 2^{-128}. By default we have $\eta = \eta'$ (and hence $U = U'$).

The efficiency of the signing algorithm is firmly connected to the expected number of repetitions, which depends on the probabilities that the two rejection sampling steps occur. When some assumption is made with respect to the distribution of $\mathbf{w} = \mathbf{Ay} \in \mathcal{R}_q^h$, the probability that the first restart occurs is $\left(\frac{2(\lfloor q/k \rfloor - U) - 1}{2\lfloor q/k \rfloor - 1}\right)^{\ell \cdot n} \cdot \left(\frac{2(\lfloor q/2 \rfloor - kU') - 1}{q}\right)^{h \cdot n}$. In regard to the second restart, experiments are carried to estimate the expected number of repetitions, and parameters are chosen such that in the experiments, the second restarts are carried out with probability no more than 1%. In sum, the average number of repetitions is dominated by the probability that the first restart occurs.

To choose the sets of recommended parameters for SKCN, the following requirements or goals should be taken into account simultaneously: First, the parameters should be appropriately chosen so as to ensure the correctness of our signature scheme; Second, the involved parameters should be well chosen such that it achieves a good security/efficiency tradeoff when achieving 128-bit quantum security; Moreover, the parameters should be chosen such that the expected number of repetitions in the signing algorithm should be as small as possible, so as to ensure the efficiency of the signing algorithm; Finally, the parameters should be chosen such that the sum of the public key size and the signature size should be as minimal as possible.

Under such considerations, we choose three sets of recommended parameters for SKCN depicted in Table 3. It should be stressed that when considering the practical implementation of SKCN, the signing algorithm is made deterministic so as to improve its efficiency, as is done in Dilithium [18]. Note also that for the security issue, the (quantum) security of our recommended parameter set is estimated by following exactly the methodology proposed in [12,18]. Also note that SKCN-II is our recommended parameter set, since it aims at achieving 128-bit quantum security level.

The strength of SKCN is best described by the foregoing quantitative measures (cf. Table 3). Roughly speaking, compared with Dilithium, our parameter sets are as unified as possible, which simplifies the implementation in practice. Also, our parameters are carefully chosen to so that the tradeoff between security and efficiency SKCN-II achieves is as good as possible, since SKCN-II aims at the 128-bit quantum security level, which may be the most important and popular in practice. Finally, compared with Dilithium-III, SKCN-II is *more efficient*: while preserving the same (quantum) security level as Dilithium does, SKCN has shorter public/secret key, has shorter signature, and runs fasters. In particular, we test both the implementations of SKCN-II and that of Dilithium under the same software/hardware environment depicted in Table 1. And the quantitative comparison is summarized in Table 2.

Table 1. The concrete harware/software details for the implementation comparison.

Hardware/Software	Details
Operating system	Ubuntu 18.04.3 LTS system
Computer	Lenovo ThinkPad T480S
CPU	Intel(R) Core(TM) i7-8550U
Memory	16G
Implementation of RO	SHA-3
Compiler	GCC
Hyperthreading option	On

Table 2. Comparison between SKCN-II and Dilithium-III.

	SKCN-II	Dilithium-III
q	1952257	8380417
n	256	256
(h, ℓ)	$(5, 4)$	$(5, 4)$
(η, η')	$(2, 2)$	$(5, 5)$
pk size (in byte)	1312	1472
sk size (in byte)	3056	3504
Sig. size (in byte)	2573	2701
Repetitions	5.7	6.6
KeyGen cycles	177707	198167
Sign cycles	859774	1056305
Verification cycles	191645	201511

Table 3. Recommended parameters for SKCN and Dilithium

	SKCN-I	SKCN-II	SKCN-III	Dilithium-II	Dilithium-III	Dilithium-IV
q	1952257	1952257	1952257	8380417	8380417	8380417
n	256	256	256	256	256	256
k	8	8	8	16	16	16
d	13	13	13	14	14	14
(h, ℓ)	$(4, 3)$	$(5, 4)$	$(6, 5)$	$(4, 3)$	$(5, 4)$	$(6, 5)$
(η, η')	$(2, 2)$	$(2, 2)$	$(2, 2)$	$(6, 6)$	$(5, 5)$	$(3, 3)$
ω	80	96	120	80	96	120
pk size (in byte)	1056	1312	1568	1184	1472	1760
sk size (in byte)	2448	3056	3664	2800	3504	3856
Sig. size (in byte)	1948	2573	3206	2044	2701	3366
Repetitions	3.9	5.7	8.2	5.9	6.6	4.3
Quantum bit-cost against key recovery attack	87	128	169	91	128	158
Quantum bit-cost against forgery attack	93	125	158	94	125	160
NIST security level	1	2	3	1	2	3

5 Security Analysis of SKCN

In this section, we analyze the security of the SKCN signature scheme. Roughly speaking, the security proof consists of two phases: In Phase I, the behavior of the signing oracle is proven to be statistically indistinguishable from that of an efficient simulator; In Phase II, we show that when the underlying hardness assumption holds, no efficient attacker can forge a valid message/signature pair with non-negligible probability, after interacting with the simulator (simulated by the foregoing simulator) polynomially many times.

In the following security proof, we will assume the public key of SKCN is $(\rho, \mathbf{t}_1, \mathbf{t}_0)$ instead of $(\rho, \mathbf{t}_1)$, similar to that of Dilithium [12,18].

5.1 Security Proof in Phase I: The Simulator

The simulation of the signature follows that of [12]. The associated simulator for SKCN is depicted in Algorithm 5. It should be stressed that we assume the public key is $\mathbf{t}$ instead of $\mathbf{t}_1$ as well. It suffices to show that the output of the signing oracle is indistinguishable from that of the simulator. The following two facts play an essential role for the indistinguishability proof. First, in the real signing algorithm, we have $\Pr[\mathbf{z}, c] = \Pr[c] \cdot \Pr[\mathbf{y} = \mathbf{z} - c\mathbf{s} \mid c]$. Since $\|\mathbf{z}\|_{\infty} < \lfloor q/k \rfloor - U$ and $\|c\mathbf{s}\|_{\infty} \le U$ (with overwhelming probability), we know that $\|\mathbf{z} - c\mathbf{s}\|_{\infty} < \lfloor q/k \rfloor$, then $\Pr[\mathbf{z}, c]$ is exactly the same for every such tuple $(\mathbf{z}, c)$. Second, when $\mathbf{z}$ does satisfy $\|\mathsf{LowBits}_{q,k}(\mathbf{w} - c e)\|_{\infty} < q/2 - kU'$, then as long as $\|c e\|_{\infty} < U'$, we have

$$\mathbf{r}_1 = \mathsf{HighBits}_{q,k}(\mathbf{w} - c e) = \mathsf{HighBits}_{q,k}(\mathbf{w}) = \mathbf{w}_1$$

by Proposition 6. Thus the simulator does not need to perform the check whether $\mathbf{r}_1 = \mathbf{w}_1$ or not, and can always assume that it passes.

With the foregoing facts, it is easy to see that the distribution of the pair $(\mathbf{z}, c)$ generated by the simulator is statistically indistinguishable from that of the pair $(\mathbf{z}, c)$ generated by the signing oracle.

After that, the simulator computes $\mathbf{r}_1$ and programs $H(\rho, \mathbf{t}_1, \lfloor q \cdot \mathbf{r}_1/k \rfloor, \mu) = c$. The resulting $(\mathbf{z}, c)$ output by the simulator is indistinguishable from that of the real signing oracle in the security game, *provided that collision occurs with negligible probability.*

It remains to show that for each μ, the probability that $H(\rho, \mathbf{t}_1, \lfloor q \cdot \mathbf{r}_1/k \rfloor, \mu)$ was previously programmed is negligible. This follows directly from the following lemma, whose proof is similar to that of [17] and is presented in Appendix A.

Lemma 7. *For every $\mathbf{A} \leftarrow \mathcal{R}_q^{h \times \ell}$, we have*

$$\Pr\left[\forall \mathbf{w}_1^* : \Pr_{\mathbf{y} \leftarrow S_{\lfloor q/k \rfloor - 1}^{\ell}}\left[\mathsf{HighBits}_{q,k}(\mathbf{A}\mathbf{y}) = \mathbf{w}_1^*\right] \le \left(\frac{q/k + 1}{2 \cdot \lfloor q/k \rfloor - 1}\right)^n\right] > 1 - (n/q)^{h\ell}.$$

It should be stressed that, inequalities $\left(\frac{q/k+1}{2\lfloor q/k \rfloor - 1}\right)^n \ll 2^{-128}, (n/q)^{h\ell} \ll 2^{-128}$ hold for our set of recommended parameters depicted in Table 3.

5.2   Security Proof in Phase II

By applying forking lemma [7], we can show SKCN is strongly existentially unforgeable under adaptive chosen-message attacks in the random oracle model, provided that the parameters are appropriately chosen and the underlying MLWE and MSIS (in ℓ_∞ norm) assumptions hold. However, this proof is not tight, and cannot be directly applied into the quantum setting. In contrast, in this section, we shall develop a quantum reduction of SKCN that is tight in nature by introducing another new underlying hardness assumption for SKCN, as is done in [12,18].

As is observed in [12,18], no counter-examples of schemes whose security is actually affected by the non-tightness of the reduction have been proposed. The main reason for this absence of counter-examples lies in that there is an intermediate problem which is tightly equivalent, to the UF-CMA security of the signature scheme. What is more, this equivalence still holds even under in quantum settings. Compared with classical hardness problems, this problem is essentially a *convolution* of the underlying mathematical problem with a cryptographic hash function $H(\cdot)$. As is justified in [18], as long as there is no relationship between the structure of the math problem and the hash function $H(\cdot)$, solving this intermediate problem is not easier than solving the mathematical problem alone. In our setting, this intermediate problem is called the SelfTargetMSIS problem, which is to be defined later.

5.3   The SelfTargetMSIS Problem, and Quantum Security of SKCN

We follow the definition in [18]. Assume $H : \{0,1\}^* \to B_{60}$ is a cryptographic hash function. For a given adversary A, it is given a random $\mathbf{A} \leftarrow \mathcal{R}_q^{h \times \ell}$ and access to the quantum random oracle $H(\cdot)$, and is asked to output a pair $\left(\mathbf{y} = ([\mathbf{r}, c]^T, \mu)\right)$ such that $0 \leq \|\mathbf{y}\|_\infty \leq \gamma$, $H(\mu, [\mathbf{I}, \mathbf{A}] \cdot \mathbf{y}) = c$. In other words, the adversary A is asked to solve the *SelfTargetMSIS* problem. In this work, let $\mathsf{Adv}_{H,h,\ell,\gamma}^{\mathsf{SelfTargetMSIS}}(A)$ denote the probability that A solves the given SelfTargetM-SIS problem successfully.

Similar to results in [18], given the similarity between SKCN and Dilithium, it follows from [17] that when $H(\cdot)$ is modeled as quantum random oracle, the probability an efficient adversary A breaks the SEU-CMA security of SKCN is

$$\mathsf{Adv}_{\mathsf{SKCN}}^{\mathsf{SUF-CMA}}(A) \leq \mathsf{Adv}_{h,\ell,D}^{\mathsf{MLWE}}(B) + \mathsf{Adv}_{H,h,\ell+1,\zeta}^{\mathsf{SelfTargetMSIS}}(C) + \mathsf{Adv}_{h,\ell,\zeta'}^{\mathsf{MSIS}}(D) + 2^{-254},$$

where D denotes the uniform distribution over S_η, and

$$\zeta = \max(\lfloor q/k \rfloor - U, \lfloor q/k \rfloor + 1 + 60 \cdot 2^{d-1}), \zeta' = \max(2 \cdot (\lfloor q/k \rfloor - U), 2\lfloor q/k \rceil + 2).$$

Similar to Dilithium, SKCN is built upon three underlying hardness assumptions: intuitively, the MLWE assumption is needed to protect against key-recovery attack, the SelfTargetMSIS is the assumption upon which new message forgery is based, and the MSIS assumption is needed for *strong* unforgeability instead of standard unforgeability.

Note that the simulation proof in Sect. 5.1 holds even in quantum setting; equivalently, if an adversary having quantum access to $H(\cdot)$ and classical access to a signing oracle can produce a forgery of a new message, then there is also an adversary who can produce a forgery after interacting with the simulator defined in Sect. 5.1. When MLWE assumption holds with the distribution D, it remains for us to analyze the following experiment: for an efficient adversary A, it is given a random $(\mathbf{A}, \mathbf{t})$, and is asked to output a valid message/signature pair $(\mu, (\mathbf{z}, c, \mathbf{h}))$ such that $\|\mathbf{z}\|_\infty < \lfloor q/k \rfloor - U, \|\mathbf{h}\|_1 \le \omega$, and $H(\mu, \lfloor q \cdot \mathsf{UseHint}_{q,k}(\mathbf{h}, \mathbf{Az} - c\mathbf{t}_1 \cdot 2^d)/k \rceil) = c$.

It follows from the properties presented in Sect. 3 that

$$\lfloor q \cdot \mathsf{UseHint}_{q,k}(\mathbf{h}, \mathbf{Az} - c\mathbf{t}_1 \cdot 2^d)/k \rceil = \mathbf{Az} - c\mathbf{t}_1 \cdot 2^d + \mathbf{u} = \mathbf{Az} - c\mathbf{t} + (c\mathbf{t}_0 + \mathbf{u}),$$

where $\mathbf{u}' \overset{\text{def}}{=} c\mathbf{t}_0 + \mathbf{u}$ satisfies $\|\mathbf{u}'\|_\infty \le \|\mathbf{u}\|_\infty + \|c \cdot \mathbf{t}_0\|_\infty \le 60 \cdot 2^{d-1} + \lfloor q/k \rfloor + 1$. In sum, to forge a valid message/signature pair means to find $\mathbf{z}, c, \mathbf{u}', \mu$ such that

- $\|\mathbf{z}\|_\infty < \lfloor q/k \rfloor - U$; and
- $\|c\|_\infty = 1$; and
- $\|\mathbf{u}'\|_\infty < 60 \cdot 2^{d-1} + \lfloor q/k \rfloor + 1$; and
- $c = H(\mu, \mathbf{Az} + c\mathbf{t} + \mathbf{u}')$.

This is the SelfTargetMSIS problem defined previously.

Note that $\mathbf{u}' = \mathbf{u} + c\mathbf{t}_0$. Here, $60 \cdot 2^{d-1}$ is an upper-bound for $\|c\mathbf{t}_0\|_\infty$; computer experiments show that the probability $\Pr[\|c\mathbf{t}_0\|_\infty \ge 2^{d+4}]$ is smaller than 10^{-6}. This implies that for one random instance, most of the time no more than one coefficient of $c\mathbf{t}_0$ has magnitude greater than 2^{d+4}. Also, note that at most ω coefficients of $\mathbf{u}$ has magnitude greater than $\lfloor q/2k \rfloor$. Thus, in almost all cases, $\|\mathbf{z}\|_\infty < \lfloor q/k \rfloor - U$, and in $\mathbf{u}' = \mathbf{u} + c\mathbf{t}_0$, at most ω coefficients of $\mathbf{u}$ have magnitudes greater than $\lfloor q/2k \rfloor$.

As is analyzed in [18], the only way to solving the SelfTargetMSIS problem appears to be picking some $\mathbf{w} \in \mathcal{R}_q^h$, computing $H(\mu, \mathbf{w}) = c$, and then finding the feasible $\mathbf{z}, \mathbf{u}'$ such that $\mathbf{Az} + \mathbf{u}' = \mathbf{w} + c\mathbf{t}$. And forging a valid forgery in the UF-CMA security of SKCN is finding some $\mathbf{z}, \mathbf{u}'$ such that $\|\mathbf{z}\|_\infty \le \lfloor q/k \rfloor - U, \|\mathbf{u}'\|_\infty \le 60 \cdot 2^{d-1} + \lfloor q/k \rfloor + 1$, and $\mathbf{Az} + \mathbf{u}' = \mathbf{t}'$ for some pre-defined $\mathbf{t}'$.

Finally comes the strong unforgeability of SKCN. In quantum setting, the analysis is similar to that of [12,18]. In addition to the foregoing possible forgery, an extra one needs considering for the strong unforgeability, i.e., when the adversary sees a valid message/signature pair $(\mu, (\mathbf{z}, c, \mathbf{h}))$ and then aims to forge another valid pair $(\mu, (\mathbf{z}', c, \mathbf{h}'))$. In this special case, a successful forgery means the adversary obtains two valid signatures such that

$$\mathsf{UseHint}_{q,k}(\mathbf{h}, \mathbf{Az} - c\mathbf{t}_1 \cdot 2^d) = \mathbf{w}_1 = \mathsf{UseHint}_{q,k}(\mathbf{h}', \mathbf{Az}' - c\mathbf{t}_1 \cdot 2^d).$$

It is routine to see $\mathbf{z} \ne \mathbf{z}'$. Thus, it follows from Proposition 5 that

$$\left\|\mathbf{Az} - c\mathbf{t}_1 \cdot 2^d - \lfloor q/k \cdot \mathbf{w}_1 \rceil\right\|_\infty, \left\|\mathbf{Az}' - c\mathbf{t}_1 \cdot 2^d - \lfloor q/k \cdot \mathbf{w}_1 \rceil\right\|_\infty \le \lfloor q/k \rfloor + 1.$$

It follows from the triangular inequality that we have $\mathbf{A} \cdot \Delta\mathbf{z} + \mathbf{u} = \mathbf{0}$, where $\Delta\mathbf{z} = \mathbf{z} - \mathbf{z}'$ satisfies $\|\Delta\mathbf{z}\|_\infty \le 2(\lfloor q/k \rfloor - U)$, and $\|\mathbf{u}\|_\infty \le 2\lfloor q/k \rfloor + 2$. Careful analysis shows that in $\mathbf{u}$, there are at most 2ω coefficients with magnitudes greater than $\lceil q/k \rceil + 1$, and the magnitudes of the other coefficients is smaller than $\lfloor q/k \rfloor + 1$. The hardness of this reduced problem is thus guaranteed by the hardness of the Module-SIS problem (in the ℓ_∞-norm).

6   The Asymmetric SIS Problem and Its Implications

Recall that in the security proof of SKCN, to forge a signature means to solve a (variant of) SIS problem. For instance, to forge a valid forgery in the UF-CMA security of SKCN is to find some $\mathbf{z}, \mathbf{u}'$ such that in most cases,

- $\|\mathbf{z}\|_\infty < \lfloor q/k \rfloor - U$; and
- In $\mathbf{u}' = \mathbf{u} + c t_0$, at most ω coefficients of $\mathbf{u}$ have magnitudes greater than $\lfloor q/2k \rfloor$. In particular, when instantiated with recommended parameters in Table 3, experiments show that coefficients of $c t_0$ are usually smaller than the theoretical maximum bound $60 \cdot 2^{d-1}$, in the sense that the probability that a random coefficient of $c t_0$ has magnitude greater than 2^{d+4} is smaller than the constant p; thus, the expected number of coefficients in $c t_0$ with magnitude greater than 2^{d+4} is less than 1.
  As a result, most of the time coefficients of $\mathbf{u}'$ can be divided into the following three categories:
    - at most one coefficient of $\mathbf{u}'$ has magnitude between $2^{d+4} + \lfloor q/k \rfloor + 1$ and $60 \cdot 2^{d-1} + \lfloor q/k \rfloor + 1$;
    - at most ω coefficients of $\mathbf{u}'$ have magnitudes between $2^{d+4} + \lfloor q/2k \rfloor$ and $2^{d+4} + \lfloor q/k \rfloor + 1$;
    - the other coefficients of $\mathbf{u}'$ have magnitudes smaller than $2^{d+4} + \lfloor q/2k \rfloor$.

Similarly, in the SEU-CMA security model, to forge a valid forgery is to find some $\mathbf{z}, \mathbf{u}$ such that

- $\|\mathbf{z}\|_\infty \leq 2(\lfloor q/k \rfloor - U)$; and
- At most 2ω coefficients of $\mathbf{u}$ have magnitudes greater than $\lceil q/k \rceil + 1$, and the magnitudes of the other coefficients are between $\lfloor q/k \rfloor + 1$ and $2 \lceil q/k \rceil + 2$.

In Dilithium, a simple upper-bound is chosen so as to estimate the concrete hardness of the given instance. This strategy is rather conservative intuitively.

In fact, these problem could be seen as a variant of the *asymmetric* SIS problem (in ℓ_∞-norm) proposed in [29], where different upper-bound constraints are placed on different coordinates of the desired nonzero solution. To be precise, in ASIS problem (in ℓ_∞-norm) parameterized by $n, q, m_1, m_2, \beta_1, \beta_2$, given a random matrix $\mathbf{A} \leftarrow \mathbb{Z}_q^{n \times (m_1+m_2)}$, we are asked to find a nonzero vector $\mathbf{x} = (\mathbf{x}_1, \mathbf{x}_2) \in \mathbb{Z}^{m_1+m_2}$ such that

$$\mathbf{A} \cdot \mathbf{x} \equiv \mathbf{0} \pmod{q}, \quad \|\mathbf{x}_1\|_\infty \leq \beta_1, \|\mathbf{x}_2\|_\infty \leq \beta_2.$$

Together with the notion of the ASIS as well as its algebraic variants, a concrete hardness estimation strategy was also proposed in [29], which fully utilizes the

Table 4. Other parameter choices for SKCN

q	592897	592897	592897
n	256	256	256
k	5	5	5
d	12	12	12
(h, ℓ)	$(4, 3)$	$(5, 4)$	$(6, 5)$
(η, η')	$(1, 1)$	$(1, 1)$	$(1, 1)$
ω	80	96	120
pk size (in byte)	1056	1312	1568
sk size (in byte)	2096	2608	3120
Sig. size (in byte)	1852	2445	3046
Expected # of repetitions	4.2	6.2	9.1
Quantum bit-cost against key recovery attack	87	128	169
Quantum bit-cost against forgery attack	98	133	169
NIST security level	1	2	3

Table 5. Recommended parameter sets of SKCN'

	SKCN-I'	SKCN-II'	SKCN-III'
q	523777	523777	523777
n	256	256	256
k	4	4	4
d	12	12	12
(h, ℓ)	$(4, 3)$	$(5, 4)$	$(6, 5)$
(η, η')	$(1, 1)$	$(1, 1)$	$(1, 1)$
ω	80	96	120
pk size (in byte)	928	1152	1376
sk size (in byte)	2096	2608	3120
Sig. size (in byte)	1852	2445	3046
Expected # of repetitions	3.7	5.2	7.4
Quantum bit-cost against key recovery attack	89	129	171
Quantum bit-cost against forgery attack	98	133	165
NIST security level	1	2	3

inherent asymmetry of the parameters. Clearly, this hardness estimation strategy could be applied to Dilithium and SKCN, and the result is intuitively more accurate than that of Dilithium [12,18].

With the notion of ASIS and the proposed hardness estimation in [29] we can choose other sets of parameters for SKCN, *e.g.*, those in Table 4. It should be stressed that in Table 4, we have $k \nmid (q - 1)$, and hence these three sets of parameters cannot be applied to Dilithium, which implies the flexibility of

SKCN. Similarly, we can choose another three sets of parameters for SKCN as in Table 4, denoted by SKCN-I', SKCN-II' and SKCN-III', respectively. Compared with Table 3, a better tradeoff between efficiency and security is obtained in Table 4, which implies the efficiency of SKCN (Table 5).

Acknowledgement. This work is supported in part by National Key Research and Development Program of China under Grant No. 2017YFB0802000, National Natural Science Foundation of China under Grant Nos. 61472084 and U1536205, Shanghai Innovation Action Project under Grant No. 16DZ1100200, Shanghai Science and Technology Development Funds under Grant No. 16JC1400801, and Shandong Provincial Key Research and Development Program of China under Grant Nos. 2017CXGC0701 and 2018CXGC0701.

A   Proof of Lemma 7

Lemma 7. For every $\mathbf{A} \leftarrow \mathcal{R}_q^{h \times \ell}$, we have

$$\Pr\left[\forall \mathbf{w}_1^* : \Pr_{\mathbf{y} \leftarrow S_{\lfloor q/k \rfloor - 1}^\ell} \left[\mathsf{HighBits}_{q,k}(\mathbf{Ay}) = \mathbf{w}_1^*\right] \leq \left(\frac{q/k+1}{2 \cdot \lfloor q/k \rfloor - 1}\right)^n\right] > 1 - (n/q)^{h\ell}.$$

Proof. Since the polynomial $x^n + 1$ splits into n linear factors modulo q, the probability that for a uniform $a \leftarrow \mathcal{R}_q$, the probability that a is invertible in $\mathcal{R}_q = \mathbb{Z}_q[x]/\langle x^n + 1 \rangle$ is $(1 - 1/q)^n > 1 - n/q$. Thus the probability that at least one of $h\ell$ polynomials in $\mathbf{A} \leftarrow \mathcal{R}_q^{h \times \ell}$ is invertible is greater than $1 - (n/q)^{h\ell}$.

We shall now prove that for all $\mathbf{A}$ that contain at least one invertible polynomial, we will have that for all $\mathbf{w}_1^*$,

$$\Pr_{\mathbf{y} \leftarrow S_{\lfloor q/k \rfloor - 1}^\ell} \left[\mathsf{HighBits}_{q,k}(\mathbf{Ay}) = \mathbf{w}_1^*\right] \leq \left(\frac{q/k+1}{2 \cdot \lfloor q/k \rfloor - 1}\right)^n,$$

which establishes the correctness of this lemma.

First, let us only consider the row of $\mathbf{A}$ which contains the invertible polynomial. Call the elements in this row $[a_1, \cdots, a_\ell]$ and without loss of generality assume that a_1 is invertible. We want to prove that for all w_1^*,

$$\Pr_{\mathbf{y} \leftarrow S_{\lfloor q/k \rfloor - 1}^\ell} \left[\mathsf{HighBits}_{q,k}(\textstyle\sum a_i y_i) = w_1^*\right] \leq \left(\frac{q/k+1}{2 \cdot \lfloor q/k \rfloor - 1}\right)^n.$$

Define T to be the set containing all the elements w such that $\mathsf{HighBits}_{q,k}(w) = w_1^*$. By the definition of Con in Algorithm 1, the size of T is upper-bounded by $(q/k+1)^n$. Therefore, we can rewrite the above probability as

$$\Pr_{\mathbf{y} \leftarrow S_{\lfloor q/k \rfloor - 1}^\ell} \left[\sum_{i=1}^\ell a_i y_i \in T\right] = \Pr_{\mathbf{y} \leftarrow S_{\lfloor q/k \rfloor - 1}^\ell} \left[y_1 \in a_1^{-1}(T - \sum_{i=2}^\ell a_i y_i)\right] \leq \left(\frac{q/k+1}{2 \cdot \lfloor q/k \rfloor - 1}\right)^n,$$

where the last inequality follows due to the fact that the size of the set $a_1^{-1}(T - \sum_{i=2}^\ell a_i y_i)$ is the same as that of T, and the size of the set $S_{\lfloor q/k \rfloor - 1}^\ell$ is exactly $(2 \cdot \lfloor q/k \rfloor - 1)^n$.   □

B   Properties of Basic Algorithms/Tools

Below, we present properties of the algorithms/tools proposed at the end of Sect. 3. And these properties plays an essential role for us to analyze the correctness and security of our signature schemes developed in Sect. 4.

Proposition 4. For every $r, z \in \mathbb{Z}_q$ such that $\|z\|_\infty < \lfloor q/(2k) \rfloor$, we have

$$\mathsf{UseHint}_{q,k}(\mathsf{MakeHint}_{q,k}(z,r),r) = \mathsf{HighBits}_{q,k}(r+z).$$

Proof. The outputs of $(r_1, r_0) \leftarrow \mathsf{Con}(r)$, $(r_1', r_0') \leftarrow \mathsf{Con}(r+z)$ satisfy $0 \leq r_1, r_1' < k$, and $\|r_0\|_\infty, \|r_0'\|_\infty \leq q/2$. Since $\|z\|_\infty < \lfloor q/(2k) \rfloor$, by Theorem 2, we have $\mathsf{Rec}(r, r_0') = r_1' = \mathsf{HighBits}_{q,k}(r+z)$. Let $h \overset{\text{def}}{=} \mathsf{MakeHint}_{q,k}(z,r)$. Since $r_1' = \mathsf{Rec}(r, r_0') = \lfloor (kr - r_0')/q \rceil \bmod k = \lfloor r_1 + (r_0 - r_0')/q \rceil \bmod k \in \{r_1-1, r_1, r_1+1\}$. When $r_0 > 0$, we have $\mathsf{Rec}(r, r_0') \in \{r_1, r_1+1\}$; when $r_0 < 0$, we have $\mathsf{Rec}(r, r_0') \in \{r_1 - 1, r_1\}$. Recall that by definition, $h = 0$ if and only if $r_1 = r_1'$. The correctness of $\mathsf{HighBits}_{q,k}(r+z) = r_1' = \mathsf{Rec}(r, r_0') = \mathsf{UseHint}_{q,k}(h,r)$ is thus established.   □

Proposition 5. For $r_1' \in \mathbb{Z}_k$, $r \in \mathbb{Z}_q$, $h \in \{0,1\}$, if $r_1' = \mathsf{UseHint}_{q,k}(h,r)$, then $\|r - \lfloor q \cdot r_1'/k \rceil\|_\infty \leq q/k + 1/2 \leq \lfloor q/k \rceil + 1$.

Proof. It is routine to see that for $(r_1, r_0) \leftarrow \mathsf{Con}(r)$, we have $r_1 \in \mathbb{Z}_k, r_0 \in (-q/2, q/2)$, and there exists $\theta \in \{0,1\}$ such that $k \cdot r = (r_1 + k\theta) \cdot q + r_0$. If $h = 0$, then $r_1' = r_1$, and hence $\|r - \lfloor q \cdot r_1'/k \rceil\|_\infty \leq q/(2k) + 1/2$. If $h = 1$ and $r_0 > 0$, then $r_1' = (r_1 + 1) \bmod k$, and hence $\|r - \lfloor q \cdot r_1'/k \rceil\|_\infty \leq q/k + 1/2$. Finally, if $h = 1$ and $r_0 < 0$, then $r_1' = (r_1 - 1) \bmod k$, and therefore $\|r - \lfloor q \cdot r_1'/k \rceil\|_\infty \leq q/k + 1/2 \leq \lfloor q/k \rceil + 1$.   □

Proposition 6. For $r, z \in \mathbb{Z}_q$ such that $\|z\|_\infty < U < \lfloor q/(2k) \rfloor$. If $\|r_0'\|_\infty < q/2 - kU$ where $(r_1, r_0) \leftarrow \mathsf{Con}(r), (r_1', r_0') \leftarrow \mathsf{Con}(r+z)$, then $r_1 = r_1'$.

Proof. Since $k \cdot r = q \cdot (r_1 + k\theta) + r_0$ $(\|r_0\|_\infty < q/2)$ and $k \cdot (r+z) = q \cdot (r_1' + k\theta') + r_0'$ $(\|r_0'\|_\infty < q/2)$ for some integers θ, θ', it is easy to verify $r_1 = \lfloor kr/q \rceil \bmod k = \lfloor k(r+z-z)/q \rceil \bmod k = \lfloor r_1' + (r_0' - kz)/q \rceil \bmod k = r_1'$.   □

References

1. Ajtai, M.: Generating hard instances of lattice problems. Quaderni di Matematica **13**, 1–32 (2004). Preliminary version in STOC 1996
2. Bai, S., Galbraith, S.D.: An improved compression technique for signatures based on learning with errors. In: Benaloh, J. (ed.) CT-RSA 2014. LNCS, vol. 8366, pp. 28–47. Springer, Cham (2014). https://doi.org/10.1007/978-3-319-04852-9_2
3. Bos, J., et al.: Frodo: take off the ring! Practical, quantum-secure key exchange from LWE. In: ACM CCS, pp. 1006–1018 (2016)

4. Groot Bruinderink, L., Hülsing, A., Lange, T., Yarom, Y.: Flush, gauss, and reload – a cache attack on the BLISS lattice-based signature scheme. In: Gierlichs, B., Poschmann, A.Y. (eds.) CHES 2016. LNCS, vol. 9813, pp. 323–345. Springer, Heidelberg (2016). https://doi.org/10.1007/978-3-662-53140-2_16
5. Bindel, N., et al.: qTESLA. Technical report, National Institute of Standards and Technology (2017). https://csrc.nist.gov/projects/post-quantum-cryptography/round-1-submissions
6. Brakerski, Z., Langlois, A., Peikert, C., Regev, O., Stehlé, D.: Classical hardness of learning with errors. In: STOC, pp. 575–584 (2013)
7. Bellare, M., Neven, G.: Multi-signatures in the plain public-key model and a general forking lemma. In: Proceedings of the 13th Association for Computing Machinery (ACM) Conference on Computer and Communications Security (CCS), Alexandria, Virginia, pp. 390–399 (2006)
8. Bellare, M., Rogaway, P.: Random oracles are practical: a paradigm for designing efficient protocols. In: 1st ACM Conference on Computer and Communications Security, pp. 62–73. ACM Press (1993)
9. Presentation of CRYSTALS (Kyber and Dilithium) at 2018 NIST PQC standardizaiton conference. https://csrc.nist.gov/CSRC/media/Presentations/Crystals-Dilithium
10. Ding, J., Xie, X., Lin, X.: A Simple Provably Secure Key Exchange Scheme Based on the Learning with Errors Problem. IACR ePrint:2012/688 (2012)
11. Ducas, L., Durmus, A., Lepoint, T., Lyubashevsky, V.: Lattice signatures and bimodal Gaussians. In: Canetti, R., Garay, J.A. (eds.) CRYPTO 2013, Part I. LNCS, vol. 8042, pp. 40–56. Springer, Heidelberg (2013). https://doi.org/10.1007/978-3-642-40041-4_3
12. Ducas, L., Lepoint, T., Lyubashevsky, V., Schwabe, P., Seiler, G., Stehlé, D.: CRYSTALS - Dilithium: Digital Signatures from Module Lattices. IACR Cryptology ePrint Archive, 2017/633 (2017)
13. Fiat, A., Shamir, A.: How to prove yourself: practical solutions to identification and signature problems. In: Odlyzko, A.M. (ed.) CRYPTO 1986. LNCS, vol. 263, pp. 186–194. Springer, Heidelberg (1987). https://doi.org/10.1007/3-540-47721-7_12
14. Gentry, C., Peikert, C., Vaikuntanathan, V.: Trapdoors for hard lattices and new cryptographic constructions. In: STOC, pp. 197–206 (2008)
15. Jin, Z., Zhao, Y.: Optimal key consensus in presence of noise. In: CoRR, vol. abs/1611.06150 (2016). Extended abstract in ACNS 2019 (Best Student Paper), pp. 302–322. Springer, Cham (2019)
16. Zhao, Y., Jin, Z., Gong, B., Sui, G.: KCL. Technical report, National Institute of Standards and Technology (2017). https://csrc.nist.gov/projects/post-quantum-cryptography/round-1-submissions
17. Kiltz, E., Lyubashevsky, V., Schaffner, C.: A concrete treatment of Fiat-Shamir signatures in the quantum random-oracle model. In: Nielsen, J.B., Rijmen, V. (eds.) EUROCRYPT 2018, Part III. LNCS, vol. 10822, pp. 552–586. Springer, Cham (2018). https://doi.org/10.1007/978-3-319-78372-7_18
18. Lyubashevsky, V., et al.: Crystals-dilithium. Technical report, National Institute of Standards and Technology (2017). https://csrc.nist.gov/projects/post-quantum-cryptography/round-1-submissions
19. Lyubashevsky, V., Peikert, C., Regev, O.: On ideal lattices and learning with errors over rings. In: Gilbert, H. (ed.) EUROCRYPT 2010. LNCS, vol. 6110, pp. 1–23. Springer, Heidelberg (2010). https://doi.org/10.1007/978-3-642-13190-5_1

20. Langlois, A., Stehlé, D.: Worst-case to average-case reductions for module lattices. Des. Codes Crypt. **75**(3), 565–599 (2014). https://doi.org/10.1007/s10623-014-9938-4
21. Lyubashevsky, V.: Fiat-Shamir with aborts: applications to lattice and factoring-based signatures. In: Matsui, M. (ed.) ASIACRYPT 2009. LNCS, vol. 5912, pp. 598–616. Springer, Heidelberg (2009). https://doi.org/10.1007/978-3-642-10366-7_35
22. Lyubashevsky, V.: Lattice signatures without trapdoors. In: Pointcheval, D., Johansson, T. (eds.) EUROCRYPT 2012. LNCS, vol. 7237, pp. 738–755. Springer, Heidelberg (2012). https://doi.org/10.1007/978-3-642-29011-4_43
23. Nguyen, P.Q., Vidick, T.: Sieve algorithms for the shortest vector problem are practical. J. Math. Cryptol. **2**(2), 181–207 (2008)
24. Peikert, C.: Lattice cryptography for the internet. In: Mosca, M. (ed.) PQCrypto 2014. LNCS, vol. 8772, pp. 197–219. Springer, Cham (2014). https://doi.org/10.1007/978-3-319-11659-4_12
25. Prest, T., et al.: Technical report, National Institute of Standards and Technology (2017). https://csrc.nist.gov/projects/post-quantum-cryptography/round-1-submissions
26. Peikert, C., Rosen, A.: Efficient collision-resistant hashing from worst-case assumptions on cyclic lattices. In: Halevi, S., Rabin, T. (eds.) TCC 2006. LNCS, vol. 3876, pp. 145–166. Springer, Heidelberg (2006). https://doi.org/10.1007/11681878_8
27. Regev, O.: On lattices, learning with errors, random linear codes, and cryptography. J. ACM (JACM) **56**(6), 34:1–34:40 (2009)
28. Zhang, Z., Chen, C., Hoffstein, J., Whyte, W.: pqNTRUSign. Technical report, National Institute of Standards and Technology (2017). https://csrc.nist.gov/projects/post-quantum-cryptography/round-1-submissions
29. Zhang, J., Yu, Y., Fan, S., Zhang, Z., Yang, K.: Tweaking the asymmetry of asymmetric-key cryptography on lattices: KEMs and signatures of smaller sizes. In: Kiayias, A., Kohlweiss, M., Wallden, P., Zikas, V. (eds.) PKC 2020. LNCS, vol. 12111, pp. 37–65. Springer, Cham (2020). https://doi.org/10.1007/978-3-030-45388-6_2

Cloud-Assisted Asynchronous Key Transport with Post-Quantum Security

Gareth T. Davies[1] ⓘ, Herman Galteland[2], Kristian Gjøsteen[2],
and Yao Jiang[2](✉)

[1] Bergische Universität Wuppertal, Wuppertal, Germany
[2] Norwegian University of Science and Technology, NTNU, Trondheim, Norway
yao.jiang@ntnu.no

Abstract. In cloud-based outsourced storage systems, many users wish to securely store their files for later retrieval, and additionally to share them with other users. These retrieving users may not be online at the point of the file upload, and in fact they may never come online at all. In this asynchronous environment, key transport appears to be at odds with any demands for forward secrecy. Recently, Boyd et al. (ISC 2018) presented a protocol that allows an initiator to use a modified key encapsulation primitive, denoted a blinded KEM (BKEM), to transport a file encryption key to potentially many recipients via the (untrusted) storage server, in a way that gives some guarantees of forward secrecy. Until now all known constructions of BKEMs are built using RSA and DDH, and thus are only secure in the classical setting.

We further the understanding of the use of blinding in post-quantum cryptography in two aspects. First, we show how to generically build blinded KEMs from homomorphic encryption schemes with certain properties. Second, we construct the first post-quantum secure blinded KEMs, and the security of our constructions are based on hard lattice problems.

Keywords: Lattice-based cryptography · NTRU · Group key exchange · Forward secrecy · Cloud storage · Post-quantum cryptography

1 Introduction

Consider the following scenario: a user of a cloud storage service wishes to encypt and share a file with a number of recipients, who may come online to retrieve the file at some future time. In modern cloud storage environments, access control for files is normally done via the storage provider's interface, and the user is usually tasked with performing any encryption and managing the resulting keys. However the users do not trust the server, and in particular may be concerned that key compromise may occur to any of the involved parties at some point in the future – they thus desire some forward secrecy guarantees.

Recent work by Boyd et al. [8] (hereafter BDGJ) provided a solution that utilized the high availability of the storage provider. The initiator essentially

© Springer Nature Switzerland AG 2020
J. K. Liu and H. Cui (Eds.): ACISP 2020, LNCS 12248, pp. 82–101, 2020.
https://doi.org/10.1007/978-3-030-55304-3_5

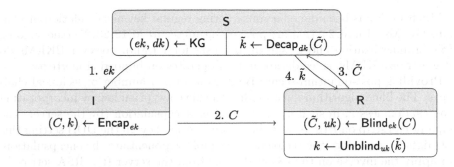

Fig. 1. A simplified overview of an OAGKE protocol [8] between an initiator I, server S and potentially many recipients R (one is given here for ease of exposition), built using a BKEM. File encryption key k is used by I to encrypt one or more files. The numbered arrows indicate the order in which operations occur.

performs key encapsulation, using an (public) encapsulation key belonging to the server, and sends an encapsulated value (out-of-band) to each recipient. Then, each recipient blinds this value in such a way that when it asks the server to decapsulate, the server does not learn anything about the underlying file encryption key, and the homomorphic properties of the scheme enable successful unblinding by the recipient. This encapsulation-and-blinding procedure was named by the authors as a *blinded KEM* (BKEM), and the complete protocol built from this was called offline assisted group key exchange (OAGKE). Forward secrecy is achieved if the recipients delete their ephemeral values after recovering the file encryption key, and if the server deletes its decapsulation key after all recipients have been online and recovered the file.

A conceptual overview of the construction, which can achieve all these security properties, is described in Fig. 1, and we refer to BDGJ [8] for full details. In the protocol, the server runs the key generation algorithm KG and the decapsulation algorithm Decap to help the initiator share file encryption key k. The blinding algorithm Blind, executed by the responder, should prohibit the server from learning any information about the file encryption key. After the server has decapsulated a blinded encapsulation, the responder can use the unblinding algorithm Unblind to retrieve the file encryption key.

While the approach appears promising, their two BKEM constructions built from DDH and RSA, are somewhat ad hoc, and further do not resist attacks in the presence of quantum computers. In this work we focus on one of the components of the OAGKE protocol, namely the BKEM scheme. Our wish is to achieve a post-quantum secure OAGKE protocol, where we need the individual components – a blinded KEM (parameterized by a homomorphic encryption scheme), a collision resistant hash function, a digital signature scheme, and a key derivation function – to all be post-quantum secure. Achieving post-quantum security of all components except for the BKEM has been covered extensively in prior work, and thus we focus on finding post-quantum constructions of BKEMs.

Much work has been done on constructing regular key encapsulation mechanisms (KEMs) [15,16,24] that are post-quantum secure [6,12,23,27] (the ongoing NIST standardization effort[1] specifically asks for KEMs), however BKEMs do not generalize KEMs, since decapsulation operates on blinded ciphertexts.

Providing post-quantum-secure BKEMs invokes a number of technical challenges. The Blind algorithm must modify the file encryption key by incorporating some randomness r, in such a way that after decapsulation (by the server) the recipient can strip off r to recover the file encryption key. In the DDH setting this is straightforward since the recipient can simply exponentiate the encapsulation, and apply the inverse on the received value from the server (the RSA setting is similarly straightforward), and, importantly, the encapsulation (with the underlying file encryption key) *and* multiple blinded samples (each with a value that is derived from the file encryption key) will all look like random group elements. In the security game for BKEMs (as provided by BDGJ), the adversary receives: an encapsulation of a 'real' key, a number of blinded versions of this encapsulation (blinded encapsulations), a number of blinded versions of the 'real' key (blinded keys), and either this 'real' key or a random key, and must decide which it has been given. If the blinded key samples (the $\tilde{k}$s) leak information about the file encryption key then the adversary's task in this game becomes much easier. For example, if the blinding algorithm alters the file encryption key such that the blinded keys are located close to it then exhaustive search becomes possible. We overcome this hurdle by using a large blinding value to hide the file encryption key. Similarly the blinded encapsulation samples (the $\tilde{C}$s) can leak information about the blinding value used to hide the file encryption key, which can be used to recover the file encryption key. For example, if the blinded encapsulation is a linear combination of the original encapsulation, the blinding value, and some small error then the distance between the blinded encapsulation and the original encapsulation could reveal the blinding value, or a small interval containing it, and therefore the file encryption key. By making sure blinded encapsulations look fresh then all blinded encapsulation samples and the encapsulation looks independent of each other. We use these techniques to provide secure BKEMs built from (a variant of) NTRU [22,30] and ideas from Gentry's FHE scheme [20].

The second shortfall of the work of BDGJ lies in the non-generic nature of their constructions. The two provided schemes appear to have similar properties, yet do not immediately indicate how any further BKEM schemes could be constructed. We show how to generically build BKEMs from homomorphic encryption schemes with minimal properties. This allows us to more precisely cast the desirable properties of schemes used to build BKEMs, generalizing the way that the responder alters the content of an encapsulation (ciphertext) by adding an encrypted random value.

---

[1] https://csrc.nist.gov/projects/post-quantum-cryptography/post-quantum-cryptography-standardization.

1.1 Related Work

Boyd et al. [8] formalized OAGKE and BKEMs, and provided BKEM constructions based on Diffie-Hellman and RSA. To our knowledge these are the only
BKEM constructions in the literature.

Gentry introduced the first fully homomorphic encryption (FHE) scheme,
based on lattice problems, and gave a generic framework [20]. Soon after, several
FHE schemes followed this framework [9,14,19,21]: all of these schemes rely on
the learning with errors (LWE) problem. Two FHE schemes based their security
on an overstretched variant of the NTRU problem [7,25], however, subfield lattice
attacks against this variant was subsequently found [1,13], and consequently
these schemes are no longer secure. As a side note, our NTRU based BKEM
construction relies on the hardness of the LWE problem.

To make a BKEM from existing post-quantum secure KEM schemes we
need, for each individual scheme, a method for altering the encapsulations in
a predictable way. Most of the post-quantum secure KEM schemes submitted to
NIST are built from a PKE scheme, where we can use our techniques to make a
BKEM if the PKE scheme supports one homomorphic operation. FrodoKEM is
the only submission that advertises its additive homomorphic properties of its
FrodoPKE scheme [2]. Other submissions based on lattices [26], LWE [3,4,17],
or NTRU [5,11] are potential candidates for a BKEM construction. Note that
the NTRU submission of Chen et al. [11] does not use the Gaussian distribution
to sample their polynomials, and NTRU Prime of Bernstein et al. [5] uses a
large Galois group to construct their polynomial field, instead of a cyclotomic
polynomial. Furthermore, the NTRU construction of Stehlé and Steinfeld [30]
chooses the distribution of the secret keys such that the public key looks uniformly random and they provide a security proof which relies on this.

1.2 Our Contribution

Our aim in this work is to further the understanding of the use of blinding in
cryptography attaining post-quantum security. In particular, we focus on blinded
KEMs and their possible instantiations, in order to deliver secure key transport
protocols in cloud storage environments. Specifically, we provide:

- a generic homomorphic-based BKEM construction, and show that it meets
  the expected indistinguishability-based security property for BKEMs, under
  feasible requirements.
- two instantiations of our homomorphic-based BKEM, built from primitives
  with post-quantum security. The proof chain is as follows.

$$\text{Hard problems} \xrightarrow[\text{or Lyubashevsky et al. [28]}]{\text{Quantum, Gentry [20]}} \text{IND-CPA HE} \xrightarrow{\text{This work}} \begin{array}{c}\text{IND-secure}\\ \text{HE-BKEM}\end{array}$$

As long as the underlying schemes HE (which rely on hard lattice problems) are
post-quantum secure, then our HE-BKEM schemes are post-quantum secure.

2 Notation and Background

Given n linearly independent vectors $\{\mathbf{b}_1, \ldots, \mathbf{b}_n\} \in \mathbb{R}^m$, the m-dimensional *lattice* L generated by the vectors is $L = \{\sum_{i=1}^{n} x_i \mathbf{b}_i \mid x_i \in \mathbb{Z}\}$. If $n = m$ then L is a *full-rank n-dimensional lattice*, we always use full-rank lattices in this paper.

Suppose $\mathbf{B} = \{\mathbf{b}_1, \mathbf{b}_2, \cdots, \mathbf{b}_n\}$ is a basis of I, let $\mathcal{P}(\mathbf{B}) = \{\sum_{i=1}^{n} x_i \mathbf{b}_i \mid x_i \in [-1/2, 1/2), \mathbf{b}_i \in \mathbf{B}\}$ be the half-open parallelepiped associated to the basis $\mathbf{B}$. Let $R = \mathbb{Z}[x]/(f(x))$ be a polynomial ring, where $f(x)$ is a monic polynomial of degree n. Any ideal $I \subseteq R$ yields a corresponding integer sublattice called *ideal lattice* of the polynomial ring. For convenience, we identify all ideals of R with its ideal lattice. Let $\|\mathbf{v}\|$ be the Euclidean norm of a vector $\mathbf{v}$. Define the *norm of a basis* $\mathbf{B}$ to be the Euclidean norm of its longest column vector, that is, $\|\mathbf{B}\| = \max_{1 \le i \le n}(\|\mathbf{b}_i\|)$.

For a full-rank n-dimensional lattice L, let $L^* = \{\mathbf{x} \in \mathbb{R}^n \mid \langle \mathbf{x}, \mathbf{y} \rangle \in \mathbb{Z}, \forall \mathbf{y} \in L\}$ denote its *dual lattice*. If $\mathbf{B}$ is a basis for the full-rank lattice L, then $(\mathbf{B}^{-1})^T$ is a basis of L^*. Let $\gamma_\times(R) = \max_{\mathbf{x}, \mathbf{y} \in R} \frac{\|\mathbf{x} \cdot \mathbf{y}\|}{\|\mathbf{x}\| \cdot \|\mathbf{y}\|}$ be the *multiplicative expansion factor*. For $\mathbf{r} \in R$, define $\mathbf{r} \bmod \mathbf{B}$ to be the unique vector $\mathbf{r}' \in \mathcal{P}(\mathbf{B})$ such that $\mathbf{r} - \mathbf{r}' \in I$. We call $\mathbf{r} \bmod \mathbf{B}$ to be the *distinguished representative* of the coset $\mathbf{r} + I$. Denote $R \bmod \mathbf{B} = \{\mathbf{r} \bmod \mathbf{B} \mid \mathbf{r} \in R\}$ to be the set of all distinguished representatives in R, this set can be chosen to be the same as the half-open parallelepiped $\mathcal{P}(\mathbf{B})$ associated to the basis $\mathbf{B}$. For convenience we treat $R \bmod \mathbf{B}$ and $\mathcal{P}(\mathbf{B})$ as the same set. Let $\mathcal{B}_\mathbf{c}(r)$ denote the closed Euclidean ball centered at $\mathbf{c}$ with radius r, for $\mathbf{c} = \mathbf{0}$ we write $\mathcal{B}(r)$. For any n-dimensional lattice L and $i = 1, \ldots, n$, let the *ith successive minimum* $\lambda_i(L)$ be the smallest radius r such that $\mathcal{B}(r)$ contains i linearly independent lattice vectors.

The *statistical distance* between two discrete distributions D_1 and D_2 over a set S is $\Delta(D_1, D_2) = \frac{1}{2} \sum_{s \in S} |\mathbf{Pr}[D_1 = s] - \mathbf{Pr}[D_2 = s]|$.

2.1 Discrete Gaussian Distributions over Lattices

Let $D_{L,s,\mathbf{c}}$ denote the *discrete Gaussian distribution* over L centered at $\mathbf{c}$ with standard deviation s. The *smoothing parameter* $\eta_\epsilon(L)$ is the smallest s such that $\rho_{1/s}(L^* \setminus \{\mathbf{0}\}) \le \epsilon$, where $\rho_{1/s}(L^* \setminus \{\mathbf{0}\}) = \sum_{\mathbf{x} \in L^* \setminus \{\mathbf{0}\}} \exp(-\pi s^2 \|\mathbf{x} - \mathbf{c}\|^2)$.

If the standard deviation of a discrete Gaussian distribution is larger than the smoothing parameter, then there are known, useful, results of discrete Gaussian distributions that we will use in this paper. Lemma 1 shows that the discrete Gaussian distribution is spherical if its standard deviation is larger than the smoothing parameter. Lemma 2 states that the statistical distance between the original discrete Gaussian distribution and its translated discrete Gaussian distribution is negligible when the distance of the corresponding centers is short.

Lemma 1 (Micciancio and Regev [29]). *Let L be any full-rank n-dimensional lattice. For any $\mathbf{c} \in \mathbb{R}^n$, real $\epsilon \in (0,1)$, and $s \ge \eta_\epsilon(L)$, we have $\mathbf{Pr}[\|\mathbf{x} - \mathbf{c}\| > s \cdot \sqrt{n} \mid \mathbf{x} \leftarrow D_{L,s,\mathbf{c}}] \le \frac{1+\epsilon}{1-\epsilon} \cdot 2^{-n}$.*

Lemma 2 (Brakerski and Vaikuntanathan [10]). *Let L be any full-rank n-dimensional lattice. For any $s \geq \eta_\epsilon(L)$, and any $\mathbf{c} \in \mathbb{R}^n$, we have then the statistical distance between $D_{L,s,\mathbf{0}}$ and $D_{L,s,\mathbf{c}}$ is at most $\|\mathbf{c}\|/s$.*

2.2 Gentry's Homomorphic Encryption Scheme

Let $\mathsf{GHE} = (\mathsf{KG_{GHE}}, \mathsf{Enc_{GHE}}, \mathsf{Dec_{GHE}}, \mathsf{Add_{GHE}})$ be an (additively) Homomorphic encryption scheme derived from ideal lattices, with algorithms as defined in Fig. 2. The scheme is similar to Gentry's somewhat-homomorphic scheme [20]. The parameters of the GHE scheme are chosen as follows:

- Polynomial ring $R = \mathbb{Z}[x]/(f(x))$,
- Basis $\mathbf{B}_I$ of the ideal $I \subseteq R$,
- IdealGen takes $(R, \mathbf{B}_I)$ as input and outputs public and secret bases $\mathbf{B}_J^{pk}$ and $\mathbf{B}_J^{sk}$ of some ideal J, where I and J are relatively prime,
- Samp takes $(\mathbf{B}_I, \mathbf{x} \in R, s)$ as input and outputs a sample from the coset $\mathbf{x} + I$ according to a discrete Gaussian distribution with standard deviation s. In our construction we use the following two distributions.
  - $\mathsf{Samp}_1(\mathbf{B}_I, \mathbf{x}, s) = \mathbf{x} + D_{I,s,-\mathbf{x}}$,
  - $\mathsf{Samp}_2(\mathbf{B}_I, \mathbf{x}, s) = \mathbf{x} + D_{I,s,\mathbf{0}}$.
- Plaintext space $\mathcal{P} = R \mod \mathbf{B}_I$ is the set of distinguished representatives of cosets of I with respect to the basis $\mathbf{B}_I$.

We discuss the correctness of GHE in the full version [18]: the result follows from the correctness analysis in [20].

2.3 The Revised NTRU Encryption Scheme

The NTRU encryption scheme variant by Stehlé and Steinfeld [30], which relies on the LWE problem, has the similar structure as Gentry's homomorphic encryption scheme. We modify the NTRU scheme to use a discrete Gaussian distribution as the noise distribution instead of an elliptic Gaussian. The parameters of the scheme, given in Fig. 3, are as follows:

- $R = \mathbb{Z}[x]/(x^n + 1)$, where $n \geq 8$ is a power of 2,
- q is a prime, $5 \leq q \leq Poly(n)$, $R_q = R/q$,
- $p \in R_q^\times, I - (p)$, the plaintext space $\mathcal{P} = R/p$,
- set the noise distribution to be $D_{\mathbb{Z}^n,s,\mathbf{0}}$.

We discuss the correctness of the revised NTRU encryption scheme in the full version [18]: the result follows from the correctness analysis in [30].

2.4 Quantum Reductions from Prior Work

The following two theorems describe Gentry's reduction from worst-case SIVP (believed to be a hard problem) to the semantic security of the encryption scheme GHE, via the ideal independent vector improvement problem (IVIP).

$\mathsf{KG_{GHE}}(R, \mathbf{B}_I):$

    $(\mathbf{B}_J^{pk}, \mathbf{B}_J^{sk}) \xleftarrow{\$} \mathsf{IdealGen}(R, \mathbf{B}_I)$

    $\mathsf{pk} = (R, \mathbf{B}_I, \mathbf{B}_J^{pk}, \mathsf{Samp}),\ \mathsf{sk} = \mathbf{B}_J^{sk}$

    $\mathbf{return}\ \mathsf{pk}, \mathsf{sk}$

$\mathsf{Dec_{GHE}}(\mathsf{sk}, \psi):$

    $\pi \leftarrow (\psi \mod \mathbf{B}_J^{sk}) \mod \mathbf{B}_I$

    $\mathbf{return}\ \pi$

$\mathsf{Enc_{GHE}}(\mathsf{pk}, s, \pi \in \mathcal{P}):$

    $\psi' \leftarrow \mathsf{Samp}(\mathbf{B}_I, \pi, s)$

    $\psi \leftarrow \psi' \mod \mathbf{B}_J^{pk}$

    $\mathbf{return}\ \psi$

$\mathsf{Add_{GHE}}(\mathsf{pk}, \psi_1, \psi_2):$

    $\psi \leftarrow \psi_1 + \psi_2 \mod \mathbf{B}_J^{pk}$

    $\mathbf{return}\ \psi$

Fig. 2. The algorithms of the GHE homomorphic encryption scheme, which is similar to Gentry's somewhat homomorphic encryption scheme [20].

Theorem 1 (Gentry [20, Corollary 14.7.1], reduce IVIP to semantic security). *Suppose that $s_{\mathsf{IVIP}} < (\sqrt{2}s\epsilon - 4n^2(\max\{\|\mathbf{B}_I\|\})^2)/(n^4\gamma_\times(R)\,\|f\|\,\max\{\|\mathbf{B}_I\|\})$, where s is the Gaussian deviation parameter in the encryption scheme GHE. Also suppose that $s/2$ exceeds the smoothing parameter of I, that IdealGen always outputs an ideal J with $s \cdot \sqrt{n} < \lambda_1(J)$, and that $[R : I]$ is prime. Finally, suppose that there is an algorithm $\mathcal{A}$ that breaks the semantic security of GHE with advantage ϵ. Then there is a quantum algorithm that solves s_{IVIP}-IVIP for an $\epsilon/4$ (up to negligible factors) weight fraction of bases output by IdealGen.*

Theorem 2 (Gentry [20, Theorem 19.2.3 and Corollary 19.2.5], reduce SIVP to IVIP). *Suppose $d_{\mathsf{SIVP}} = (3 \cdot e)^{1/n} \cdot d_{\mathsf{IVIP}}$, where e is Euler's constant. Suppose that there is an algorithm $\mathcal{A}$ that solves s_{IVIP}-IVIP for parameter $s_{\mathsf{IVIP}} > 16 \cdot \gamma_\times(R)^2 \cdot n^5 \cdot \|f\| \cdot g(n)$ for some $g(n)$ that is $\omega(\sqrt{\log n})$, whenever the given ideal has $\det(J) \in [a, b]$, where $[a, b] = [d_{\mathsf{IVIP}}^n, 2 \cdot d_{\mathsf{IVIP}}^n]$. Assume that invertible prime ideals with norms in $[a, b]$ are not negligibly sparse. Then, there is an algorithm $\mathcal{B}$ that solves worst-case d_{SIVP}-SIVP.*

The following theorem and lemma describe the reduction from SIVP or SVP (both are believed to be hard problems) to the IND-CPA security of the encryption scheme NTRU, via the ring learning with errors problem (R-LWE).

$\mathsf{KG_{NTRU}}(n, q \in \mathbb{Z}, p \in R_q^\times, s > 0):$

    $\mathbf{while}\ (f \mod q) \notin R_q^\times \mathbf{do}$

        $f' \leftarrow D_{\mathbb{Z}^n, s, 0}$

        $f = p \cdot f' + 1$

    $\mathbf{while}\ (g \mod q) \notin R_q^\times \mathbf{do}$

        $g \leftarrow D_{\mathbb{Z}^n, s, 0}$

    $h = pg/f \in R_q$

    $(\mathsf{pk}, \mathsf{sk}) \leftarrow (h, f)$

    $\mathbf{return}\ (\mathsf{pk}, \mathsf{sk})$

$\mathsf{Enc_{NTRU}}(\mathsf{pk} = h, s, \pi \in \mathcal{P}):$

    $e_1, e_2 \leftarrow D_{\mathbb{Z}^n, s, 0}$

    $\psi \leftarrow \pi + pe_1 + he_2 \in R_q$

    $\mathbf{return}\ \psi$

$\mathsf{Dec_{NTRU}}(\mathsf{sk} = f, \psi):$

    $\psi' = f \cdot \psi \in R_q$

    $\pi \leftarrow \psi' \mod p$

    $\mathbf{return}\ \pi$

$\mathsf{Add_{NTRU}}(\psi_1, \psi_2):$

    $\psi \leftarrow \psi_1 + \psi_2 \in R_q$

    $\mathbf{return}\ \psi$

Fig. 3. The algorithms of the revised NTRU encryption scheme [30].

Theorem 3 (Lyubashevsky et al. [28]). *Let* $\alpha < \sqrt{\log n / n}$ *and* $q = 1$ mod $2n$ *be a poly(n)-bounded prime such that* $\alpha q \geq \omega(\sqrt{\log n})$. *Then there is a polynomial-time quantum reduction from* $O(\sqrt{n}/\alpha)$-*approximate* SIVP (*or* SVP) *on ideal lattices to* R-LWE$_{q,D_s}$ *given only* $l(\geq 1)$ *samples, where* $s = \alpha \cdot (nl/\log(nl))^{1/4}$.

We consider a different variant of the R-LWE problem, namely R-LWE$^\times_{\mathsf{HNF}}$, which is the same as R-LWE$_{q,\mathcal{D}}$ except for the oracle $\mathcal{O}$ that outputs samples from the distribution $A^\times_{s,D}$ or $U(R^2_q)$, where $A^\times_{s,D}$ outputs $(a, as+e)$ with $a \in R^\times_q, s \in D$. The analysis in the end of Sect. 2 of Stehlé and Steinfeld [30] shows that when $q = \Omega(n)$, R-LWE$^\times_{\mathsf{HNF}}$ remains hard.

The security proof of NTRU encryption scheme is similar to the security proof of Lemma 3.8 of Stehlé and Steinfeld [30]. The proof relies on the uniformity of public key and $p \in R^\times_q$. We chose a slightly different error distribution for our construction in Sect. 5.4, but adaption to our setting is straightforward.

Lemma 3. *Let* $n \geq 8$ *be a power of 2 such that* $\Phi = x^n + 1$ *splits into* n *irreducible factors modulo prime* $q \geq 5$. *Let* $0 < \epsilon < 1/3$, $p \in R^\times_q$ *and* $s \geq 2n\sqrt{\ln(8nq)} \cdot q^{1/2+\epsilon}$. *For any* IND-CPA *adversary* $\mathcal{A}$ *against* NTRU *encryption scheme, there exists an adversary* $\mathcal{B}$ *solving* R-LWE$^\times_{\mathsf{HNF}}$ *such that*

$$\mathbf{Adv}^{\mathsf{IND\text{-}CPA}}_{\mathsf{NTRU}}(\mathcal{A}) \leq \mathbf{Adv}_{\mathsf{R\text{-}LWE}^\times_{\mathsf{HNF}}}(\mathcal{B}) + q^{-\Omega(n)}.$$

3   Blinded KEM

A *blinded KEM* scheme BKEM = (KG, Encap, Blind, Decap, Unblind) is parameterized by a key encapsulation mechanism KEM = (KG, Encap, Decap), a blinding algorithm Blind and an unblinding algorithm Unblind. The *key generation* algorithm KG outputs an encapsulation key $ek \in \mathcal{K}_E$ and a decapsulation key $dk \in \mathcal{K}_D$. The *encapsulation* algorithm Encap takes as input an encapsulation key and outputs a (file encryption) key $k \in \mathcal{K}_F$ together with an encapsulation $C \in \mathcal{C}$ of that key. The *blinding* algorithm takes as input an encapsulation key and an encapsulation and outputs a blinded encapsulation $\tilde{C} \in \mathcal{C}$ and an unblinding key $uk \in \mathcal{K}_U$. The *decapsulation* algorithm Decap takes a decapsulation key and a (blinded) encapsulation as input and outputs a (blinded) key $\tilde{k} \in \mathcal{K}_B$. The *unblinding* algorithm takes as input an unblinding key and a blinded key and outputs a key.

Definition 1 (Correctness of a BKEM). *We say that a blinded KEM scheme* BKEM *has* $(1 - \epsilon)$-*correctness if:*

$$\mathbf{Pr}[\mathsf{Unblind}_{uk}(\tilde{k}) = k] \geq 1 - \epsilon,$$

for $(ek, dk) \leftarrow$ KG, $(C, k) \leftarrow$ Encap$_{ek}$, $(\tilde{C}, uk) \leftarrow$ Blind$_{ek}(C)$ *and* $\tilde{k} \leftarrow$ Decap$_{dk}(\tilde{C})$.

(A KEM scheme KEM has $(1 - \epsilon)$-*correctness* if $\mathbf{Pr}[\mathsf{Decap}_{dk}(C) = k] \geq 1 - \epsilon$, where $(ek, dk) \leftarrow \mathsf{KG}$ and $(C, k) \leftarrow \mathsf{Encap}_{ek}$.)

We parameterize all BKEM schemes by a public key encryption scheme (PKE), since any PKE scheme can trivially be turned into a KEM. We modify the above definition to be a PKE-based BKEM, where the KEM algorithms are described in Fig. 4.

Definition 2 (PKE-based BKEM). *We call BKEM a PKE-based BKEM if the underlying scheme KEM = (KG, Encap, Decap) is parameterized by a PKE scheme PKE = (KG$_{\mathsf{PKE}}$, Enc, Dec) as described in Fig. 4.*

$$\underline{\mathsf{KG}(\lambda):} \qquad\qquad \underline{\mathsf{Encap}_{ek}:} \qquad\qquad \underline{\mathsf{Decap}_{dk}(\tilde{C}):}$$

$$\mathsf{pk}, \mathsf{sk} \leftarrow \mathsf{KG}_{\mathsf{PKE}}(\lambda) \qquad k \xleftarrow{\$} \mathcal{M} \qquad\qquad \tilde{k} \leftarrow \mathsf{Dec}_{dk}(\tilde{C})$$
$$(ek, dk) \leftarrow (\mathsf{pk}, \mathsf{sk}) \qquad C \leftarrow \mathsf{Enc}_{ek}(k) \qquad\qquad \textbf{return } \tilde{k}$$
$$\textbf{return } ek, dk \qquad\qquad \textbf{return } C, k$$

Fig. 4. KEM algorithms parameterized by a PKE scheme PKE = (KG$_{\mathsf{PKE}}$, Enc, Dec).

3.1 Security

We define indistinguishability under chosen-plaintext attack (IND-CPA) for public key encryption and indistinguishability (IND) for blinded KEMs, respectively.

Definition 3. *Let* PKE = (KG$_{\mathsf{PKE}}$, Enc, Dec) *be a public key encryption scheme. The* IND-CPA *advantage of any adversary $\mathcal{A}$ against* PKE *is*

$$\mathbf{Adv}_{\mathsf{PKE}}^{\mathsf{IND\text{-}CPA}}(\mathcal{A}) = 2 \left| \Pr[\mathbf{Exp}_{\mathsf{PKE}}^{\mathsf{IND\text{-}CPA}}(\mathcal{A}) = 1] - 1/2 \right|,$$

where the experiment $\mathbf{Exp}_{\mathsf{PKE}}^{\mathsf{IND\text{-}CPA}}(\mathcal{A})$ *is given in Fig. 5 (left).*

Definition 4. *Let* BKEM = (KG, Encap, Blind, Decap, Unblind) *be a blinded KEM. The* distinguishing advantage *of any adversary $\mathcal{A}$ against* BKEM *getting r blinded encapsulations and their blinded decapsulation tuples is*

$$\mathbf{Adv}_{\mathsf{BKEM}}^{\mathsf{IND}}(\mathcal{A}, r) = 2 \left| \Pr[\mathbf{Exp}_{\mathsf{BKEM}}^{\mathsf{IND}}(\mathcal{A}, r) = 1] - 1/2 \right|,$$

where the experiment $\mathbf{Exp}_{\mathsf{BKEM}}^{\mathsf{IND}}(\mathcal{A}, r)$ *is given in Fig. 5 (right).*

The value r represents the number of recipients in the OAGKE protocol of BDGJ – in practice this will often be fairly small, and certainly bounded by the number of users of the system.

$$\underline{\mathbf{Exp}_{\mathsf{PKE}}^{\mathsf{IND\text{-}CPA}}(\mathcal{A}):}$$
$\quad b \xleftarrow{\$} \{0,1\}$
$\quad (\mathsf{pk},\mathsf{sk}) \leftarrow \mathsf{KG}_{\mathsf{PKE}}$
$\quad (\mathsf{m}_0,\mathsf{m}_1,\mathsf{state}) \xleftarrow{\$} \mathcal{A}(\mathsf{pk})$
$\quad C_b \leftarrow \mathsf{Enc}_{\mathsf{pk}}(\mathsf{m}_b)$
$\quad b' \leftarrow \mathcal{A}(\mathsf{state}, C_b)$
$\quad \mathbf{return}\ b' \stackrel{?}{=} b$

$$\underline{\mathbf{Exp}_{\mathsf{BKEM}}^{\mathsf{IND}}(\mathcal{A},r):}$$
$\quad b \xleftarrow{\$} \{0,1\}$
$\quad (ek, dk) \leftarrow \mathsf{KG}$
$\quad (C, k_1) \leftarrow \mathsf{Encap}_{ek}$
$\quad k_0 \xleftarrow{\$} \mathcal{K}_F$
$\quad \mathbf{for}\ j \in \{1,\ldots,r\}\ \mathbf{do}$
$\qquad (\tilde{C}_j, uk_j) \leftarrow \mathsf{Blind}_{ek}(C)$
$\qquad \tilde{k}_j \leftarrow \mathsf{Decap}_{dk}(\tilde{C}_j)$
$\quad b' \leftarrow \mathcal{A}(ek, C, k_b, \{(\tilde{C}_j, \tilde{k}_j)\}_{1 \le j \le r})$
$\quad \mathbf{return}\ b' \stackrel{?}{=} b$

Fig. 5. IND-CPA experiment $\mathbf{Exp}_{\mathsf{PKE}}^{\mathsf{IND\text{-}CPA}}(\mathcal{A})$ for a PKE scheme PKE (left). Indistinguishability experiment $\mathbf{Exp}_{\mathsf{BKEM}}^{\mathsf{IND}}(\mathcal{A},r)$ for a BKEM scheme BKEM (right).

4 Homomorphic-Based BKEM

We now show how to turn a homomorphic encryption scheme with certain properties into a BKEM, and analyze the security requirements of such a BKEM. We eventually prove that the homomorphic-based BKEM is post-quantum secure as long as the underlying homomorphic encryption scheme is post-quantum secure.

4.1 Generic Homomorphic-Based BKEM

We look for PKE schemes with the following homomorphic property: suppose C and C' are two ciphertexts, then $\mathsf{Dec}_{\mathsf{sk}}(C \oplus_1 C') = \mathsf{Dec}_{\mathsf{sk}}(C) \oplus_2 \mathsf{Dec}_{\mathsf{sk}}(C')$, where $\oplus_1$ and $\oplus_2$ denote two group operations.

We construct blinding and unblinding algorithms using this homomorphic property. Suppose the underlying PKE scheme has $1 - \epsilon$-correctness. To blind an encapsulation C (with corresponding file encryption key k) the Blind algorithm creates a fresh encapsulation C' (with corresponding blinding value k') using the Encap_{ek} algorithm, the blinded encapsulation $\tilde{C}$ is computed as $\tilde{C} \leftarrow C \oplus_1 C'$. The unblinding key uk is the inverse element of k' with respect to $\oplus_2$, that is, $uk \leftarrow k'^{-1}$. The blinding algorithms outputs $\tilde{C}$ and uk. The decapsulation algorithm can evaluate the blinded encapsulation because of the homomorphic property. The blinded key $\tilde{k}$ is the output of this decapsulation algorithm, that is, $\tilde{k} \leftarrow \mathsf{Decap}_{dk}(\tilde{C})$. Hence, $\tilde{k} = k \oplus_2 k'$ with probability $1 - 2\epsilon + \epsilon^2$. To unblind $\tilde{k}$ the unblinding algorithm outputs $\tilde{k} \oplus_2 uk$, which is k except for probability $2\epsilon - \epsilon^2$, and so the BKEM scheme has $(1 - 2\epsilon + \epsilon^2)$-correctness. Formally, we define the BKEM scheme constructed above as follows.

Definition 5 (Homomorphic-based BKEM). *Let BKEM be a PKE-based BKEM, as in Definition 2. Suppose the underlying public key encryption scheme is a homomorphic encryption scheme* $\mathsf{HE} = (\mathsf{KG}_{\mathsf{HE}}, \mathsf{Enc}, \mathsf{Dec})$ *such that for any ciphertexts* $C, C' \in \mathcal{C}$ *and any key pair* $(\mathsf{sk}, \mathsf{pk}) \xleftarrow{\$} \mathsf{KG}_{\mathsf{HE}}$ *it holds that*

$$\mathsf{Dec}_{\mathsf{sk}}(C \oplus_1 C') = \mathsf{Dec}_{\mathsf{sk}}(C) \oplus_2 \mathsf{Dec}_{\mathsf{sk}}(C'),$$

where $(\mathcal{M}, \oplus_2)$ is the plaintext group and $(\mathcal{C}, \oplus_1)$ is the ciphertext group. Furthermore, let the blinding and unblinding algorithms operate as discussed above. We call such a scheme BKEM *a homomorphic-based BKEM.*

We stress that all BKEM schemes we consider in the rest of this paper are homomorphic-based BKEMs.

The homomorphic encryption scheme HE does not need to be fully homomorphic, since we only need one operation in the blinding algorithm: a somewhat group homomorphic encryption scheme is sufficient.

4.2   Security Requirements

In the indistinguishability game IND for BKEMs the adversary $\mathcal{A}$ has r blinded samples. If the decryptions of blinded encapsulations output the correct blinded keys, then these r blinded samples are the following two sets: $\{\tilde{C}_i = C \oplus_1 C_i'\}_{1,\dots,r}$ and $\{\tilde{k}_i = k \oplus_2 k_i'\}_{i=1\dots r}$, where the encapsulation is C and the real file encryption key is k. We want the blinded samples and the encapsulation to be random looking such that the combination of all these values does not reveal any information about the underlying file encryption key k that is being transported.

First, we show how to choose the blinding values k_i' to make the blinded keys $\tilde{k}_i$ look random. Then, we show how to make the blinded encapsulations $\tilde{C}_i$ look random, which is achievable when $\tilde{C}_i$ looks like a fresh output of the encapsulation algorithm: this idea is similar to circuit privacy [20]. Finally, we show how an IND-CPA-secure HE scheme ensures that the encapsulation does not reveal any information about the file encryption key. With these steps in place, we provide the main theorem in this paper stating how to achieve an IND secure BKEM scheme. In particular, if the underlying HE scheme is post-quantum IND-CPA secure then the corresponding homomorphic-based BKEM scheme is post-quantum IND secure.

Random-Looking Blinded Keys. We want the blinded key to look like a random element of the space containing blinded keys. In the IND game the adversary is given several blinded keys of the form $\tilde{k} = k \oplus_2 k'$, where k is the file encryption key and k' is a blinding value, and wishes to gain information about k.

Let k be sampled uniformly at random from the file encryption key set, denoted $\mathcal{K}_F$, and let k' be sampled uniformly at random from the blinding value set, denoted $\mathcal{K}_R$. We would like that the size of $\mathcal{K}_F$ is large enough to prevent a brute force attacker from guessing k, say $|\mathcal{K}_F| = 2^\lambda$ for some security parameter λ. If $\mathcal{K}_R$ is a small set then the value of any blinded key $\tilde{k} = k \oplus_2 k'$ will be located within a short distance around k, so the adversary can successfully guess k with high probability. We always assume that $\mathcal{K}_R$ is at least as large as $\mathcal{K}_F$.

If a given blinded key $\tilde{k}$ can be expressed as a result of any file encryption key k and a blinding value k', with respect to an operation, then our goal is to ensure that the adversary cannot get any information of the true file encryption key hidden in $\tilde{k}$: ideally we wish it to be indistinguishable from a random element.

Definition 6 (ϵ-blinded blinded key). *Let* BKEM *be a blinded KEM with blinded key set* $\mathcal{K}_B$. *Let* k *be sampled uniformly random from the file encryption key set* $\mathcal{K}_F$ *and let* k' *be sampled uniformly random from the blinding value set* $\mathcal{K}_R$. *We define a* ϵ-blinded blinded key set* $\mathsf{S} := \{\tilde{k} \in \mathcal{K}_B \mid \forall k \in \mathcal{K}_F, \exists 1 k' \in \mathcal{K}_R$ *such that* $\tilde{k} = k \oplus_2 k'\}$: *we say that* BKEM *has* ϵ-blinded blinded keys if*

$$\mathbf{Pr}\left[\tilde{k} = k \oplus_2 k' \in \mathsf{S} \mid k \xleftarrow{\$} \mathcal{K}_F, k' \xleftarrow{\$} \mathcal{K}_R\right] = 1 - \epsilon.$$

Suppose the adversary is given any number of ϵ-blinded blinded keys from S with the same underlying file encryption key k. By the definition of the ϵ-blinded blinded set the file encryption key k can be any value in $\mathcal{K}_F$ and all values are equally probable. In other words, guessing k, given ϵ-blinded blinded keys, is the same as guessing a random value from $\mathcal{K}_F$. To prevent giving the adversary a better chance at guessing the key k we wish the blinded keys to be located inside S with high probability, which means we want ϵ to be small.

Fresh-Looking Blinded Encapsulations. In the IND game for BKEMs the adversary $\mathcal{A}$ gets r blinded samples and has knowledge of the set $\{\tilde{C}_i = C \oplus_1 C'_i\}_{1,\ldots,r}$, where C is an encapsulation of a file encryption key k and C'_i is an encapsulation of a blinding value. We cannot guarantee that the set of the blinded encapsulations do not reveal any information about the encapsulation C. However, if each of these blinded encapsulations looks like a fresh output of the encapsulation algorithm then they are independent and random-looking compared to the encapsulation C. Therefore we want this set to be indistinguishable from the output set of the encapsulation algorithm.

Definition 7 (ϵ-blinded blinded encapsulation). *Let* HE-BKEM *be a homomorphic based BKEM. Let* ek *be any encapsulation key and* C_0 *be an encapsulation with the underlying file encryption key* k_0. *We say that* HE-BKEM *has* ϵ-blinded blinded encapsulation if the statistical distance between the following distributions is at most* ϵ:

$$X = \{C_0 \oplus_1 C' \mid k' \xleftarrow{\$} \mathcal{K}_R, C' \leftarrow \mathsf{Enc}_{ek}(k')\},$$

$$Y = \{C \mid k' \xleftarrow{\$} \mathcal{K}_R, C \leftarrow \mathsf{Enc}_{ek}(k_0 \oplus_2 k')\}.$$

This property ensures that the output of the blinding algorithm looks like a fresh encapsulation except for probability ϵ. Note that the BKEM constructions of Boyd et al. [8], DH-BKEM [8, Sect. 4.1] and RSA-BKEM [8, Sect. 4.2], both have 0-blinded blinded encapsulation.

In most fully homomorphic encryption schemes the product of two ciphertexts is much larger in size compared to the sum of two ciphertexts, hence, it is easier to achieve ϵ-blinded blinded encapsulation for one addition compared to one multiplication. In our constructions we use addition.

Indistinguishability of BKEMs. Furthermore, if we want to achieve indistinguishability of blinded KEMs. We require the underlying homomorphic encryption scheme have some kind of semantic security to protect the message (the file encryption key) in the ciphertext (the encapsulation).

Theorem 4 (Main Theorem). *For negligible ϵ_3, let* BKEM *be a homomorphic based BKEM designed as in Definition 5 from a $(1 - \epsilon_3)$-correct homomorphic encryption scheme* HE. *Let the file encryption key k and the blinding value k' be sampled uniformly random from the large sets $\mathcal{K}_F$ and $\mathcal{K}_R$, respectively. Suppose* BKEM *has ϵ_1-blinded blinded encapsulations and ϵ_2-blinded blinded keys. For any adversary $\mathcal{A}$ against* BKEM *getting r blinded encapsulations and their blinded decapsulation samples, there exists an* IND-CPA *adversary $\mathcal{B}$ against* HE *such that*

$$\mathbf{Adv}^{\mathsf{IND}}_{\mathsf{BKEM}}(\mathcal{A}, r) \leq 2(r + 1)(\epsilon_1 + \epsilon_2 + \epsilon_3) + \mathbf{Adv}^{\mathsf{IND\text{-}CPA}}_{\mathsf{HE}}(\mathcal{B})$$

Proof. The proof of the theorem consists of a sequence of games.

Game 0. The first game is the experiment $\mathbf{Exp}^{\mathsf{IND}}_{\mathsf{BKEM}}(\mathcal{A}, r)$, given in Fig. 5 (right). Let E_0 be the event that the adversary's guess b' equals b (and let E_i be the corresponding event for Game i). From Definition 4 we have that

$$\mathbf{Adv}^{\mathsf{IND}}_{\mathsf{BKEM}}(\mathcal{A}, r) = 2 \left| \Pr[E_0] - 1/2 \right|.$$

Game 1. Same as Game 0 except that blinded key given to the adversary is the sum of the file encryption key and the blinding value instead of the decryption of the blinded encapsulation. More precisely, suppose C is the encapsulation with corresponding file encryption key k. For $1 \leq j \leq r$, let $C'_j + C$ is the blinded encapsulation where C'_j is a fresh encapsulation with corresponding blinding value k'_j. When $\mathcal{A}$ queries for the blinded key of user j, the game outputs $k \oplus_2 k'_j$. By the homomorphic property of PKE, if C and $C'_1, \ldots, C'_r$ all decrypt to the correct messages, then the output of blinded keys are the same in both Game 1 and Game 0. Hence the difference between Game 1 and Game 0 is upper bounded by the decryption error of PKE as follows.

$$\left| \Pr[E_1] - \Pr[E_0] \right| \leq 1 - (1 - \epsilon_3)^{r+1} \approx (r + 1)\epsilon_3.$$

Game 2. Same as Game 1 except that blinded encapsulation and blinded key pairs given to the adversary are now independent and random compared to the file encryption key. More precisely, for $1 \leq j \leq r$:

- When $\mathcal{A}$ queries the blinded encapsulation of user j, the game first chooses a random ϵ-blinded blinded key (Definition 6), $\tilde{k}_j \xleftarrow{\$} \mathsf{S}$, and computes an encapsulation of this random key, $\tilde{C}_j \leftarrow \mathsf{Enc}_{ek}(\tilde{k}_j)$, which is given to $\mathcal{A}$.
- When $\mathcal{A}$ queries for the blinded key of user j, the game outputs $\tilde{k}_j$.

Step 1. We first prove that a real pair of blinded key and blinded encapsulation in Game 1 is $(\epsilon_1 + \epsilon_2)$-statistically close to the modified values in Game 2.

Suppose $k_0 \in \mathcal{K}_F$ is the file encryption key and $C_0 \leftarrow \mathsf{Enc}_{ek}(k_0)$ is the encapsulation with k_0, let $X = \{(k_0 \oplus_2 k', C_0 \oplus_1 C') \mid k' \xleftarrow{\$} \mathcal{K}_R, C' \leftarrow \mathsf{Enc}_{ek}(k')\}$ be the statistical distribution of the real pair of blinded key and blinded encapsulation output in Game 1, and $Y = \{(\tilde{k}, \tilde{C}) \mid \tilde{k} \xleftarrow{\$} S, \tilde{C} \leftarrow \mathsf{Enc}_{ek}(\tilde{k})\}$ be the statistical distribution of the modified values output in Game 2. We define a middle distribution $Z = \{(k_0 \oplus_2 k', C) \mid k' \xleftarrow{\$} \mathcal{K}_R, C \leftarrow \mathsf{Enc}_{ek}(k_0 \oplus_2 k')\}$. We compute the statistical distance between X and Y as follows.

$$\Delta(X, Y) \leq \Delta(X, Z) + \Delta(Z, Y)$$

$$= \Delta(X, Z) + \frac{1}{2} (\sum_{\substack{\tilde{k} \in \mathcal{K}_B \\ \tilde{C} \in \mathcal{C}}} \left| \mathbf{Pr}[Z = (\tilde{k}, \tilde{C})] - \mathbf{Pr}[Y = (\tilde{k}, \tilde{C})] \right|)$$

$$\leq \epsilon_1 + \frac{1}{2} (\sum_{\substack{\tilde{k} \in \mathcal{K}_B \\ \tilde{C} \in \mathcal{C}}} \left| \mathbf{Pr}[Z = (\tilde{k}, \tilde{C}) \mid \tilde{k} \in S] \cdot \mathbf{Pr}[\tilde{k} \in S] \right.$$

$$\left. + \mathbf{Pr}[Z = (\tilde{k}, \tilde{C}) \mid \tilde{k} \notin S] \cdot \mathbf{Pr}[\tilde{k} \notin S] - \mathbf{Pr}[Y = (\tilde{k}, \tilde{C})] \right|)$$

$$= \epsilon_1 + \frac{1}{2} (\sum_{\substack{\tilde{k} \in S \\ \tilde{C} \in \mathcal{C}}} \left| \mathbf{Pr}[Z = (\tilde{k}, \tilde{C}) \mid \tilde{k} \in S] \cdot (1 - \epsilon_2) - \mathbf{Pr}[Y = (\tilde{k}, \tilde{C})] \right|$$

$$+ \sum_{\substack{\tilde{k} \notin S \\ \tilde{C} \in \mathcal{C}}} \left| \mathbf{Pr}[Z = (\tilde{k}, \tilde{C}) \mid \tilde{k} \notin S] \cdot \epsilon_2 \right|) \tag{1}$$

$$\leq \epsilon_1 + \frac{1}{2} (\sum_{\substack{\tilde{k} \in S \\ \tilde{C} \in \mathcal{C}}} \left| \epsilon_2 \cdot \mathbf{Pr}[Y = (\tilde{k}, \tilde{C})] \right| + 1 \cdot \epsilon_2) \tag{2}$$

$$\leq \epsilon_1 + \epsilon_2$$

Note that in (1) we split the summation into two parts, namely $\tilde{k} \in S$ and $\tilde{k} \notin S$. For $\tilde{k} \in S$ we have $\mathbf{Pr}[Z = (\tilde{k}, \tilde{C}) \mid \tilde{k} \notin S] \cdot \mathbf{Pr}[\tilde{k} \notin S] = 0$, and for $\tilde{k} \notin S$ we have $\mathbf{Pr}[Z = (\tilde{k}, \tilde{C}) \mid \tilde{k} \in S] \cdot \mathbf{Pr}[\tilde{k} \in S] = 0$ and $\mathbf{Pr}[Y = (\tilde{k}, \tilde{C})] = 0$. Furthermore, (2) holds because distributions Z and Y over set S are equal. For r samples:

$$\left| \mathrm{Pr}[E_2 - \mathrm{Pr}[E_1] \right| \leq r(\epsilon_1 + \epsilon_2).$$

Step 2. Next, we claim that there exists an adversary $\mathcal{B}$ against IND-CPA security of HE such that

$$2 \left| \mathrm{Pr}[E_2] - \frac{1}{2} \right| = \mathbf{Adv}_{\mathsf{HE}}^{\mathsf{IND\text{-}CPA}}(\mathcal{B}).$$

We construct a reduction $\mathcal{B}$ that plays the IND-CPA game by running $\mathcal{A}$, that simulates the responses of Game 2 to $\mathcal{A}$ as follows.

1. $\mathcal{B}$ flips a coin $b \xleftarrow{\$} \{0, 1\}$,
2. $\mathcal{B}$ queries its IND-CPA challenger to get the public key of its IND-CPA game, and forwards this public key as the encapsulation key to $\mathcal{A}$,

3. $\mathcal{B}$ simulates the encapsulation by randomly choosing two group key k_0, k_1, sends challenge query with input (k_0, k_1) to its IND-CPA challenger, and forwards the response C to $\mathcal{A}$,
4. $\mathcal{B}$ simulates the output of Blind and Decap by using the Encap algorithm. $\mathcal{B}$ samples $\tilde{k} \xleftarrow{\$} \mathsf{S}$, computes $\tilde{C} \leftarrow \mathsf{Enc}_{ek}(\tilde{k})$, and outputs $\tilde{C}$ as the blinded encapsulation and $\tilde{k}$ as the decapsulation of the blinded encapsulation,
5. When $\mathcal{A}$ asks for a challenge, $\mathcal{B}$ sends k_b to $\mathcal{A}$,
6. After $\mathcal{A}$ returns b', $\mathcal{B}$ sends $1 \oplus b \oplus b'$ to the challenger.

If the challenge ciphertext $\mathcal{B}$ received in $\mathbf{Exp}_{\mathsf{HE}}^{\mathsf{IND\text{-}CPA}}(\mathcal{B})$ is C_b, then $\mathcal{B}$ perfectly simulates the inputs of $\mathcal{A}$ in Game 2 when the output of the key is a real key. Otherwise (the challenge ciphertext $\mathcal{B}$ received in $\mathbf{Exp}_{\mathsf{HE}}^{\mathsf{IND\text{-}CPA}}(\mathcal{B})$ is $C_{1\text{-}b}$), k_b is a random key to $\mathcal{A}$ and $\mathcal{B}$ perfectly simulate the inputs of $\mathcal{A}$ in Game 2 when the output of the key is a random key.

Remark 1. As a specific case of Theorem 4, the DH-BKEM construction of BDGJ has 0-blinded blinded encapsulations and 0-blinded blinded keys, and the indistinguishibility of DH-BKEM is upper bounded by DDH advantage (defined in the real-or-random sense instead of left-or-right). That is

$$\mathbf{Adv}_{\mathsf{DH\text{-}BKEM}}^{\mathsf{IND}}(\mathcal{A}, r) \le \mathbf{Adv}^{\mathsf{DDH}}(\mathcal{B}).$$

This observation matches with the result of Boyd et al. [8, Theorem 1].

5 Instantiating Homomorphic-Based BKEMs

We provide two homomorphic-based BKEM constructions, based on Gentry's homomorphic encryption scheme (Sect. 2.2) and the NTRU variant by Stehlé and Steinfeld (Sect. 2.3). We show that (for some parameters) our BKEM schemes are post-quantum secure, by Theorem 4, as long as the underlying HE schemes are post-quantum secure [20,28,30]. We only require the HE scheme to support one homomorphic operation, and we have chosen addition. Our HE schemes do not need to support bootstrapping or any multiplicative depth.

5.1 Two Homomorphic-Based BKEM Schemes

Let $\mathsf{HE} = (\mathsf{KG}_{\mathsf{HE}}, \mathsf{Enc}_{\mathsf{HE}}, \mathsf{Dec}_{\mathsf{HE}})$ be a scheme described in Sect. 2.2 or 2.3 with $(1 - \epsilon_3)$-correctness for negligible ϵ_3. Let L be any full-rank n-dimensional lattice, for any $\epsilon \in (0, 1)$, $s \ge \eta_\epsilon(L)$, and $r \ge 2^{\omega(\log(n))} \cdot s$. The abstract construction of HE-BKEM is in Fig. 6.

5.2 Constructions of Random-Looking Blinded Keys

We want the blinded keys to be in the ϵ-blinded blinded key set S with high probability, and we analyze the requirements of the blinding values. We provide two constructions of the ϵ-blinded blinded keys set S as follows.

KG(λ) :
> pk, sk $\leftarrow$ KG$_{HE}$(λ)
> (ek, dk) $\leftarrow$ (pk, sk)
> **return** ek, dk

Encap$_{ek}$:
> $k \xleftarrow{\$} \mathcal{K}_F$
> $C \leftarrow$ Enc$_{HE}$(ek, s, k)
> **return** C, k

Blind$_{ek}$(C) :
> $k' \xleftarrow{\$} \mathcal{K}_R$
> $C' \leftarrow$ Enc$_{HE}$(ek, r, k')
> $\tilde{C} \leftarrow$ Add$_{HE}$(C, C')
> $uk \leftarrow -k'$ mod **B**
> **return** $\tilde{C}$, uk

Decap$_{dk}$($\tilde{C}$) :
> $\tilde{k} \leftarrow$ Dec$_{HE}$(dk, $\tilde{C}$)
> **return** $\tilde{k}$

Unblind$_{uk}$($\tilde{k}$) :
> $k \leftarrow \tilde{k} + uk$ mod **B**
> **return** k

Fig. 6. HE-BKEM, where **B** is the basis of the plaintext space $\mathcal{P}$.

Construction I. A file encryption key of HE-BKEM is a random element located in a subspace of the underlying HE scheme's message space $\mathcal{M}$. We want to take a small file encryption key k and add a large blinding value k' to produce a slightly larger blinded key $\tilde{k}$, hence, the corresponding key sets should satisfy $\mathcal{K}_F \subseteq \mathcal{K}_R \subseteq \mathcal{K}_B \subseteq \mathcal{M}$ Suppose $\mathcal{M}$ is HE scheme's message space with generators $1, x, \ldots, x^{n-1}$ and order q, i.e. $\mathcal{M} = \{d_0 + d_1 x + \cdots + d_{n-1} x^{n-1} \mid d_i \in \mathbb{F}_q\}$. The addition in $\mathcal{M}$ is polynomial addition.

Suppose $\mathcal{K}_F = \{d_0 + d_1 x + \cdots + d_{n-1} x^{n-1} \mid d_i \in \mathbb{Z}_{\lfloor \sqrt{q/2} \rfloor}\}$ and $\mathcal{K}_R = \{d_0 + d_1 x + \cdots + d_{n-1} x^{n-1} \mid d_i \in \mathbb{Z}_{\lfloor q/2 \rfloor}\}$. For any $c_i \in \{\lfloor \sqrt{q/2} \rfloor, \ldots, \lfloor q/2 \rfloor\}$ and any $a_i \in \mathbb{Z}_{\lfloor \sqrt{q/2} \rfloor}$ there exists a unique $b_i = c_i - a_i \in \mathbb{Z}_{\lfloor q/2 \rfloor}$. As such, for these restricted $c_0 + c_1 x + \cdots + c_{n-1} x^{n-1}$ and for any $a_0 + a_1 x + \cdots a_{n-1} x^{n-1} \in \mathcal{K}_F$ there exists a unique $b_0 + b_1 x + \cdots b_{n-1} x^{n-1} \in \mathcal{K}_R$ such that $(a_0 + a_1 x + \cdots a_{n-1} x^{n-1}) + (b_0 + b_1 x + \cdots b_{n-1} x^{n-1}) = c_0 + c_1 x + \cdots + c_{n-1} x^{n-1}$. Then

$$\mathsf{S} = \{d_0 + d_1 x + \cdots + d_{n-1} x^{n-1} \mid d_i \in \{\lfloor \sqrt{q/2} \rfloor, \ldots, \lfloor q/2 \rfloor\}\}$$

Note that for any $i \in \{0, \ldots, n-1\}$,

$$\mathbf{Pr}\left[a_i + b_i \in \{\lfloor \sqrt{q/2} \rfloor, \ldots, \lfloor q/2 \rfloor\} \mid a_i \xleftarrow{\$} \mathbb{Z}_{\lfloor \sqrt{q/2} \rfloor}, b_i \xleftarrow{\$} \mathbb{Z}_{\lfloor q/2 \rfloor}\right] - 1 - \frac{\lfloor \sqrt{q/2} \rfloor - 1}{\lfloor q/2 \rfloor},$$

so the probability that a blinded key is located in the ϵ-blinded blinded set is

$$\mathbf{Pr}\left[\tilde{k} = k + k' \in \mathsf{S} \mid k \xleftarrow{\$} \mathcal{K}_F, k' \xleftarrow{\$} \mathcal{K}_R\right] = \left(1 - \frac{\lfloor \sqrt{q/2} \rfloor - 1}{\lfloor q/2 \rfloor}\right)^n \approx 1 - \frac{n}{\lfloor \sqrt{q/2} \rfloor}.$$

In this construction, HE-BKEM has ϵ-blinded blinded keys with $\epsilon = n/\lfloor \sqrt{q/2} \rfloor$. For suitably large q, the above ϵ can be made negligible.

Construction II. Let the file encryption key k be an element in a subset of $\mathcal{M}$: we want to add a random blinding value k' from the whole message space $\mathcal{M}$ to produce a random-looking blinded key $\tilde{k}$, hence, the corresponding key sets should satisfy $\mathcal{K}_F \subseteq \mathcal{K}_R = \mathcal{K}_B = \mathcal{M}$. For any blinded key $\tilde{k} \in \mathcal{M}$ and any

$k \in \mathcal{K}_F$ there exists a unique random value $k' = \tilde{k} - k \mod \mathbf{B} \in \mathcal{M}$ such that $\tilde{k} = k + k' \mod \mathbf{B}$, thus the ϵ-blinded blinded set S is $\mathcal{M}$ and thus

$$\mathbf{Pr}\left[\tilde{k} = k + k' \mod \mathbf{B} \in \mathsf{S} \mid k \xleftarrow{\$} \mathcal{K}_F, k' \xleftarrow{\$} \mathcal{M}\right] = 1.$$

In this construction, HE-BKEM has ϵ-blinded blinded keys with $\epsilon = 0$.

Remark 2. Both of these constructions can be applied to our HE-BKEM schemes.

5.3   Construction of Fresh-Looking Blinded Encapsulations

We claim that HE-BKEM in Fig. 6 has ϵ-blinded blinded encapsulations with negligible ϵ. The idea is to take the small constant ciphertext and add a ciphertext with large error(s) and the resulting ciphertext should look like a fresh ciphertext with large error(s). The details are given in the following lemma.

Lemma 4. *Let HE-BKEM be a homomorphic based BKEM with the underlying homomorphic encryption scheme described in Sect. 2.2 or 2.3 Let ek be any encapsulation key, and recall that $\mathsf{Enc}_{\mathsf{HE}}(ek, s, \cdot)$ uses the discrete Gaussian distribution $D_{L,s,\mathbf{0}}$ as the error distribution. Suppose $C_0 = \mathsf{Enc}_{\mathsf{HE}}(ek, s, k_0)$ is an encapsulation of k_0. For any $\epsilon \in (0,1)$, let $s \geq \eta_\epsilon(L)$ and $r \geq 2^{\omega(\log(n))} \cdot s$, then the statistical distance between the following distributions is negligible*

$$X = \{C_0 \oplus_1 C' \mid k' \xleftarrow{\$} \mathcal{K}_R, C' \leftarrow \mathsf{Enc}_{\mathsf{HE}}(ek, r, k')\}$$
$$Y = \{C \mid k' \xleftarrow{\$} \mathcal{K}_R, C \leftarrow \mathsf{Enc}_{\mathsf{HE}}(ek, r, k_0 \oplus_2 k')\}.$$

Proof. We prove the result for Gentry's scheme; similar analysis for NTRU follows the same approach. Suppose $C_0 = k_0 + e_0$, where $e_0 \leftarrow D_{L,s,\mathbf{0}}$. Then

$$C_0 \oplus_1 \mathsf{Enc}_{\mathsf{HE}}(ek, r, k') = k_0 + e_0 + k' + D_{L,r,\mathbf{0}} = k_0 + k' + e_0 + D_{L,r,\mathbf{0}}.$$

By Lemma 1, we have $\|e_0\| > s\sqrt{n}$ with negligible probability. For $\|e_0\| \leq s\sqrt{n}$, we have $\frac{\|e_0\|}{r} \leq \frac{\sqrt{n}}{2^{\omega(\log(n))}}$, which is negligible for sufficient large n. By Lemma 2, we have $e_0 + D_{L,r,\mathbf{0}} \stackrel{s}{\approx} D_{L,r,\mathbf{0}}$. Therefore,

$$C_0 \oplus_1 \mathsf{Enc}_{\mathsf{HE}}(ek, r, k') \stackrel{s}{\approx} k_0 + k' + D_{L,r,\mathbf{0}} = \mathsf{Enc}_{\mathsf{HE}}(ek, r, k_0 \oplus_2 k').$$

5.4   Indistinguishability of Our HE-BKEM

The HE-BKEM schemes, defined in Sect. 5.1, have random-looking blinded keys, which follows from the designs discussed in Sect. 5.2. Furthermore, these schemes have fresh-looking blinded encapsulations, which follows from Lemma 4 discussed in Sect. 5.3. The following corollaries show GHE-BKEM and NTRU-BKEM are IND-secure BKEMs with post-quantum security.

Corollary 1. *Let* GHE-BKEM *be a homomorphic-based BKEM described in Sect. 5.1. For negligible ϵ, ϵ_2, choose parameters as in Lemma 4, Theorem 1 and Theorem 2. Suppose* GHE-BKEM *has ϵ_2-blinded blinded keys. If there is an algorithm that breaks the indistinguishability of* GHE-BKEM, *i.e. the distinguishing advantage of this algorithm against* GHE-BKEM *getting r blinded encapsulation and their blinded decapsulation tuples is non-negligible, then there exists a quantum algorithm that solves worst-case* SIVP.

Proof. By Lemma 4 there exists a negligible ϵ_1 such that GHE-BKEM has ϵ_1-blinded blinded encapsulations. Then we can apply Theorem 4, which states that if there is an algorithm that breaks the indistinguishability of GHE-BKEM then there exists an algorithm breaks IND-CPA security of GHE, and by Theorem 1 and 2 we have a quantum algorithm that solves worst-case SIVP.

Corollary 2. *Let* NTRU-BKEM *be a homomorphic-based BKEM described in Sect. 5.1. For negligible ϵ, ϵ_2, choose parameters as in Lemma 4, Lemma 3, and Theorem 3. Suppose* NTRU-BKEM *has ϵ_2-blinded blinded keys. If there is an algorithm that breaks indistinguishability of* NTRU-BKEM *then there exists a quantum algorithm that solves $O(\sqrt{n}/\alpha)$-approximate* SIVP *(or* SVP*) on ideal lattices.*

Proof. Similar to the proof of Corollary 1, from Lemma 4 and Theorem 4 we know that if there is an algorithm that breaks the indistinguishability of NTRU-BKEM then there exists an algorithm that breaks IND-CPA security of NTRU. By Lemma 3 there exists an adversary solving R-LWE$_{HNF}^{\times}$ and by Theorem 3 there exists a quantum algorithm that solves SIVP.

Parameter Settings. For our HE-BKEM schemes, the parameters of the underlying homomorphic encryption schemes are chosen from Gentry [20] or Stehlé and Steinfeld [30], which is required to achieve IND-CPA security. Furthermore, our BKEM schemes require that $r = 2^{\omega(\log(n))} \cdot s$, where s is the standard deviations of a "narrow" Gaussian distributions $D_{L,s,\mathbf{0}}$ and r is the standard deviations of a "wider" Gaussian distributions $D_{L,r,\mathbf{0}}$. We also follows the designs discussed in Sect. 5.2 to construct random-looking blinded keys. We conclude that for these parameter settings our proposed BKEM schemes are post-quantum secure.

Acknowledgements. We would like to thank Liqun Chen and Martijn Stam for a number of useful suggestions for improvement, and anonymous reviewers for valuable comments in improving earlier versions of this work. Gareth T. Davies has been supported by the European Research Council (ERC) under the European Union's Horizon 2020 research and innovation programme, grant agreement 802823.

References

1. Albrecht, M., Bai, S., Ducas, L.: A subfield lattice attack on overstretched NTRU assumptions. In: Robshaw, M., Katz, J. (eds.) CRYPTO 2016. LNCS, vol. 9814, pp. 153–178. Springer, Heidelberg (2016). https://doi.org/10.1007/978-3-662-53018-4_6

2. Alkim, E., et al.: FrodoKEM: Learning With Errors Key Encapsulation. https://frodokem.org/files/FrodoKEM-specification-20190330.pdf. Submission to the NIST Post-Quantum Standardization project, round 2
3. Alkim, E., Ducas, L., Pöppelmann, T., Schwabe, P.: Post-quantum key exchange - a new hope. In: Holz, T., Savage, S. (eds.) USENIX Security Symposium, pp. 327–343. USENIX Association (2016)
4. Avanzi, R., et al.: CRYSTALS-Kyber (version 2.0). https://pq-crystals.org/kyber/data/kyber-specification-round2.pdf. Submission to the NIST Post-Quantum Standardization project, round 2
5. Bernstein, D.J., Chuengsatiansup, C., Lange, T., van Vredendaal, C.: NTRU prime: reducing attack surface at low cost. In: Adams, C., Camenisch, J. (eds.) SAC 2017. LNCS, vol. 10719, pp. 235–260. Springer, Cham (2018). https://doi.org/10.1007/978-3-319-72565-9_12
6. Bos, J.W., et al.: Frodo: take off the ring! Practical, quantum-secure key exchange from LWE. In: Weippl, E.R., Katzenbeisser, S., Kruegel, C., Myers, A.C., Halevi, S. (eds.) ACM Conference on Computer and Communications Security, pp. 1006–1018. ACM (2016). https://doi.org/10.1145/2976749.2978425
7. Bos, J.W., Lauter, K., Loftus, J., Naehrig, M.: Improved security for a ring-based fully homomorphic encryption scheme. In: Stam, M. (ed.) IMACC 2013. LNCS, vol. 8308, pp. 45–64. Springer, Heidelberg (2013). https://doi.org/10.1007/978-3-642-45239-0_4
8. Boyd, C., Davies, G.T., Gjøsteen, K., Jiang, Y.: Offline assisted group key exchange. In: Chen, L., Manulis, M., Schneider, S. (eds.) ISC 2018. LNCS, vol. 11060, pp. 268–285. Springer, Cham (2018). https://doi.org/10.1007/978-3-319-99136-8_15
9. Brakerski, Z., Gentry, C., Vaikuntanathan, V.: (leveled) fully homomorphic encryption without bootstrapping. In: Goldwasser, S. (ed.) ITCS, pp. 309–325. ACM (2012). https://doi.org/10.1145/2090236.2090262
10. Brakerski, Z., Vaikuntanathan, V.: Fully homomorphic encryption from ring-LWE and security for key dependent messages. In: Rogaway, P. (ed.) CRYPTO 2011. LNCS, vol. 6841, pp. 505–524. Springer, Heidelberg (2011). https://doi.org/10.1007/978-3-642-22792-9_29
11. Chen, C., et al.: NTRU. https://ntru.org/f/ntru-20190330.pdf. Submission to the NIST Post-Quantum Standardization project, round 2
12. Cheon, J.H., Han, K., Kim, J., Lee, C., Son, Y.: A practical post-quantum public-key cryptosystem based on spLWE. In: Hong, S., Park, J.H. (eds.) ICISC 2016. LNCS, vol. 10157, pp. 51–74. Springer, Cham (2017). https://doi.org/10.1007/978-3-319-53177-9_3
13. Cheon, J.H., Jeong, J., Lee, C.: An algorithm for NTRU problems and cryptanalysis of the GGH multilinear map without a low-level encoding of zero. LMS J. Comput. Math. 19(A), 255–266 (2016). https://doi.org/10.1112/S1461157016000371
14. Cheon, J.H., Kim, A., Kim, M., Song, Y.: Homomorphic encryption for arithmetic of approximate numbers. In: Takagi, T., Peyrin, T. (eds.) ASIACRYPT 2017. LNCS, vol. 10624, pp. 409–437. Springer, Cham (2017). https://doi.org/10.1007/978-3-319-70694-8_15
15. Cramer, R., Shoup, V.: Design and analysis of practical public-key encryption schemes secure against adaptive chosen ciphertext attack. Cryptology ePrint Archive, Report 2001/108 (2001). https://eprint.iacr.org/2001/108
16. Cramer, R., Shoup, V.: Design and analysis of practical public-key encryption schemes secure against adaptive chosen ciphertext attack. SIAM J. Comput. 33(1), 167–226 (2003). https://doi.org/10.1137/S0097539702403773

17. D'Anvers, J.-P., Karmakar, A., Sinha Roy, S., Vercauteren, F.: Saber: module-LWR based key exchange, CPA-secure encryption and CCA-secure KEM. In: Joux, A., Nitaj, A., Rachidi, T. (eds.) AFRICACRYPT 2018. LNCS, vol. 10831, pp. 282–305. Springer, Cham (2018). https://doi.org/10.1007/978-3-319-89339-6_16

18. Davies, G.T., Galteland, H., Gjsteen, K., Jiang, Y.: Cloud-assisted asynchronous key transport with post-quantum security. Cryptology ePrint Archive, Report 2019/1409 (2019). https://eprint.iacr.org/2019/1409

19. Fan, J., Vercauteren, F.: Somewhat practical fully homomorphic encryption. Cryptology ePrint Archive, Report 2012/144 (2012). https://eprint.iacr.org/2012/144

20. Gentry, C.: A fully homomorphic encryption scheme. Ph.D. thesis, Stanford University, Stanford, CA, USA (2009). aAI3382729

21. Gentry, C., Sahai, A., Waters, B.: Homomorphic encryption from learning with errors: conceptually-simpler, asymptotically-faster, attribute-based. In: Canetti, R., Garay, J.A. (eds.) CRYPTO 2013. LNCS, vol. 8042, pp. 75–92. Springer, Heidelberg (2013). https://doi.org/10.1007/978-3-642-40041-4_5

22. Hoffstein, J., Pipher, J., Silverman, J.H.: NTRU: a ring-based public key cryptosystem. In: Buhler, J.P. (ed.) ANTS 1998. LNCS, vol. 1423, pp. 267–288. Springer, Heidelberg (1998). https://doi.org/10.1007/BFb0054868

23. Hülsing, A., Rijneveld, J., Schanck, J., Schwabe, P.: High-speed key encapsulation from NTRU. In: Fischer, W., Homma, N. (eds.) CHES 2017. LNCS, vol. 10529, pp. 232–252. Springer, Cham (2017). https://doi.org/10.1007/978-3-319-66787-4_12

24. Kurosawa, K., Desmedt, Y.: A new paradigm of hybrid encryption scheme. In: Franklin, M. (ed.) CRYPTO 2004. LNCS, vol. 3152, pp. 426–442. Springer, Heidelberg (2004). https://doi.org/10.1007/978-3-540-28628-8_26

25. López-Alt, A., Tromer, E., Vaikuntanathan, V.: On-the-fly multiparty computation on the cloud via multikey fully homomorphic encryption. In: Karloff, H.J., Pitassi, T. (eds.) STOC, pp. 1219–1234. ACM (2012). https://doi.org/10.1145/2213977.2214086

26. Lu, X., et al.: LAC Lattice-based Cryptosystems, Submission to the NIST Post-Quantum Standardization project, round 2 (2019)

27. Lyubashevsky, V., Peikert, C., Regev, O.: On ideal lattices and learning with errors over rings. In: Gilbert, H. (ed.) EUROCRYPT 2010. LNCS, vol. 6110, pp. 1–23. Springer, Heidelberg (2010). https://doi.org/10.1007/978-3-642-13190-5_1

28. Lyubashevsky, V., Peikert, C., Regev, O.: On ideal lattices and learning with errors over rings. J. ACM 60(6), 43:1–43:35 (2013). https://doi.org/10.1145/2535925

29. Micciancio, D., Regev, O.: Worst-case to average-case reductions based on Gaussian measures. SIAM J. Comput. 37(1), 267–302 (2007). https://doi.org/10.1137/S0097539705447360

30. Stehlé, D., Steinfeld, R.: Making NTRU as secure as worst-case problems over ideal lattices. In: Paterson, K.G. (ed.) EUROCRYPT 2011. LNCS, vol. 6632, pp. 27–47. Springer, Heidelberg (2011). https://doi.org/10.1007/978-3-642-20465-4_4

Symmetric Cipher

Rotational-XOR Cryptanalysis
of Simon-Like Block Ciphers

Jinyu Lu[1], Yunwen Liu[1($\boxtimes$)], Tomer Ashur[2,3], Bing Sun[1], and Chao Li[1]

[1] Department of Mathematics, National University of Defense Technology,
Changsha, China
univerlyw@hotmail.com
[2] imec-COSIC KU Leuven, Leuven, Belgium
[3] TU Eindhoven, Eindhoven, The Netherlands

Abstract. Rotational-XOR cryptanalysis is a cryptanalytic method aimed at finding distinguishable statistical properties in ARX-C ciphers, *i.e.*, ciphers that can be described only by using modular addition, cyclic rotation, XOR, and the injection of constants. In this paper we extend RX-cryptanalysis to AND-RX ciphers, a similar design paradigm where the modular addition is replaced by vectorial bitwise AND; such ciphers include the block cipher families SIMON and SIMECK. We analyze the propagation of RX-differences through AND-RX rounds and develop closed form formula for their expected probability. Finally, we formulate an SMT model for searching RX-characteristics in SIMON and SIMECK.

Evaluating our model we find RX-characteristics of up to 20, 27, and 35 rounds with respective probabilities of $2^{-26}, 2^{-42}$, and 2^{-54} for versions of SIMECK with block sizes of 32, 48, and 64 bits, respectively, for large classes of weak keys in the related-key model. In most cases, these are the longest published distinguishers for the respective variants of SIMECK.

Interestingly, when we apply the model to the block cipher SIMON, the best characteristic we are able to find covers 11 rounds of SIMON32 with probability 2^{-24}. To explain the gap between SIMON and SIMECK in terms of the number of distinguished rounds we study the impact of the key schedule and the specific rotation amounts of the round function on the propagation of RX-characteristics in Simon-like ciphers.

Keywords: RX-cryptanalysis · SIMECK · SIMON · Key schedule

1 Introduction

Rotational-XOR (RX) cryptanalysis is a cryptanalytic technique for ARX ciphers proposed by Ashur and Liu in [1]. RX-cryptanalysis generalizes rotational cryptanalysis by investigating the influence of round constants on the probabilistic propagation of rotational pairs passing through the ARX operations.

© Springer Nature Switzerland AG 2020
J. K. Liu and H. Cui (Eds.): ACISP 2020, LNCS 12248, pp. 105–124, 2020.
https://doi.org/10.1007/978-3-030-55304-3_6

The successful application of RX-cryptanalysis to SPECK [10] reveals that the round constants sometimes interact in a constructive way between the rounds, *i.e.*, that a broken symmetry caused by a round constant in round i may be restored—either fully or partially—by another constant injection in round $j > i$. As a result, new designs such as [8] now show resistance to RX-cryptanalysis as part of their security argument.

AND-RX ciphers, defined as a counterpart of ARX ciphers where the modular addition is replaced by bitwise AND, are of contemporary interest owing to the design of the block cipher SIMON [2] which was followed by other Simon-like ciphers such as SIMECK [22]. Since the AND-RX operations in Simon-like ciphers are bitwise, the resulting statistical properties of individual bits remain independent of the bit-position. We say that such properties are *rotation-invariant*.

To break rotation-invariant properties, round constants are usually injected into the state. In the case of SIMON and SIMECK, the constants are injected to the key schedule and propagate into the round function via the round subkey.

The impact of the key schedule on cryptanalysis is important in particular for lightweight block ciphers as many of them use a simple one. For instance, a study by Kranz *et al.* [9] showed the influence of a linear key schedule on linear cryptanalysis in PRESENT. Yet, information on how to design a good key schedule remains scarce. A folk theorem states that a good key schedule should provide round keys that are independent, which can be interpreted as arguing that a nonlinear key schedule is better than a linear one in such context. The similarity between the round functions of SIMON and SIMECK allows us to compare the two approaches respective to the different key schedules.

Our Contribution. In this paper, we extend the idea of RX-cryptanalysis to AND-RX ciphers with applications to SIMON and SIMECK. The propagation of RX-differences through the AND-RX operations is fully analyzed and a closed algebraic formula is derived for its expected probability. We show that an RX-difference with translation value α passes through the vectorial AND operation with the same probability as that of an α XOR-difference. Due to the different nature of RX-differences and XOR-differences, characteristics of the former type would depend more on the key schedule and choice of round constants than those of the latter type. Using an automated search model we find RX-distinguishers for versions of SIMECK and SIMON; these results are summarised in Table 1.

The RX-characteristics we found for SIMECK variants with block sizes of 32-, 48-, and 64-bit improve previously longest published results by 5, 8, and 10 rounds, respectively, albeit sometimes in a weaker attack model. When comparing for the same number of rounds, our results offer different tradeoffs between the size of the affected key class and the characteristic's probability.

For SIMON32, we found an RX-characteristics covering only 10–11 rounds. For the 10-round case, the probability is slightly better than the previously best one. For 11 rounds, we see that the probability is worse. While the 11-round distinguisher is inferior to previous work, it highlights the interesting observation that RX-cryptanalysis works better in the case of SIMECK than it does in the

Table 1. Comparison of RX-characteristics for rotation offset $\gamma = 1$ with the longest published (related-key) differentials for SIMECK32, SIMECK48, SIMECK64, and SIMON32, and with integral distinguishers for SIMECK32, SIMECK48, SIMECK64. The distinguisher types are denoted by DC for differential characteristics, RKDC for related-key differential characteristics, ID for integral distinguishers, and RX for RX characteristics. All attacks require chosen plaintexts.

Cipher	Number of attacked rounds	Data complexity	Size of weak key class	Type	Reference
SIMECK32	13	2^{32}	Full	DC	[12]
	15	2^{31}	Full	ID	[19]
		2^{24}	2^{54}	RKDC	[20]
		2^{18}	2^{44}	RX	Sect. 5.1
	19	2^{24}	2^{30}	RX	Sect. 5.1
	20	2^{26}	2^{30}	RX	Sect. 5.1
SIMECK48	16	2^{24}	2^{80}	RKDC	[20]
		2^{18}	2^{68}	RX	Sect. 5.1
	18	2^{47}	Full	ID	[19]
		2^{22}	2^{66}	RX	Sect. 5.1
	19	2^{48}	Full	DC	[12]
		2^{24}	2^{62}	RX	Sect. 5.1
	27	2^{42}	2^{44}	RX	Sect. 5.1
SIMECK64	21	2^{63}	Full	ID	[19]
	25	2^{64}	Full	DC	[12]
		2^{34}	2^{80}	RX	Sect. 5.1
	35	2^{54}	2^{56}	RX	Sect. 5.1
SIMON32	10	2^{16}	Full	RKDC	[20]
		2^{14}	Full	RX	Sect. 5.2

case of SIMON. We conjecture that the difference is due to the key schedule. To test this conjecture, we define three toy ciphers:

- SIM-1 which uses the round function of SIMON and the key schedule of SIMECK,
- SIM-2 which uses the round function of SIMECK with the key schedule of SIMON, and
- SIM-3 which uses a Simon-like round function but with yet another set of rotation amounts and the key schedule of SIMON.

We observe that the RX-characteristics found for SIM-1 have a higher probability compared to those found for SIMON. For SIM-2 and SIM-3 we see that the number of distinguished rounds is comparable to that of SIMON. We conclude that resistance to RX-cryptanalysis in Simon-like ciphers is heavily influenced by the key schedule.

Organization. We recall Simon-like ciphers and RX-cryptanalysis in Sect. 2. In Sect. 3, we generalize RX-cryptanalysis to Simon-like ciphers, and give a closed form algebraic formula for probabilistic propagation of an RX-difference. In Sect. 4 we provide an automated search model for finding good RX-characteristics. This model is evaluated in Sect. 5. In Sect. 6 we test how the choice of the key schedule affects the resistance of Simon-like ciphers to RX-cryptanalysis. Sect. 7 concludes this paper.

2   Preliminaries

In this section, we give a brief overview of the structure of Simon-like ciphers and recall the general idea of Rotational-XOR cryptanalysis. Table 2 presents the notation we use.

2.1   Simon-Like Ciphers

SIMON is a family of block ciphers following the AND-RX design paradigm, *i.e.*, members of the family can be described using only the bitwise operations AND ($\odot$), XOR ($\oplus$), and cyclic rotation by γ bits (S^γ). Simon-like ciphers generalize the structure of SIMON's round function with different parameters than the original ones.

The Round Function
SIMON is a family of lightweight block ciphers designed by the US NSA [2]. A member of the family is denoted by SIMON$2n/mn$, to specify a block size of

Table 2. The notations used throughout the paper

Notation	Description
$x = (x_{n-1}, \ldots, x_1, x_0)$	Binary vector of n bits; x_i is the bit in position i with x_0 the least significant one
$x \odot y$	Vectorial bitwise AND between x and y
$x_i \odot y_i$	Bitwise AND between x_i and y_i
$x \oplus y$	Vectorial bitwise XOR between x and y
$x_i \oplus y_i$	Bitwise XOR between x_i and y_i
$x \| y$	Concatenation of x and y
$x	y$	Vectorial bitwise OR between x and y
$wt(x)$	Hamming weight of x
$x \lll \gamma, S^\gamma(x)$	Circular left shift of x by γ bits
$x \ggg \gamma, S^{-\gamma}(x)$	Circular right shift of x by γ bits
$(I \oplus S^\gamma)(x)$	$x \oplus S^\gamma(x)$
$\overline{x}$	Bitwise negation

$2n$ for $n \in \{16, 24, 32, 48, 64\}$, and key size of mn for $m = \{2, 3, 4\}$. The round function of SIMON is defined as

$$f(x) = \left(S^8\left(x\right) \odot S^1\left(x\right)\right) \oplus S^2(x).$$

Simon-like ciphers are ciphers that share the same round structure as SIMON, but generalize it to arbitrary rotation amounts (a, b, c) such that the round function becomes

$$f_{a,b,c}(x) = \left(S^a\left(x\right) \odot S^b\left(x\right)\right) \oplus S^c(x).$$

Of particular interest in this paper is the SIMECK family of lightweight block ciphers designed by Yang et al. [22], aiming at improving the hardware implementation cost of SIMON. SIMECK$2n/4n$ denotes an instance with a $4n$-bit key and a $2n$-bit block, where $n \in \{16, 24, 32\}$. Since the key length of SIMECK is always $4n$ we use lazy writing in the sequel and simply write SIMECK$2n$ throughout the paper. The rotation amounts for all SIMECK versions are $(a, b, c) = (5, 0, 1)$.

The Key Schedule
The nonlinear key schedule of SIMECK reuses the cipher's round function to generate the round keys. Let $K = (t_2, t_1, t_0, k_0)$ be the master key for SIMECK$2n$, where $t_i, k_0 \in \mathbb{F}_2^n$. The registers of the key schedule are loaded with

$$K = k_3 || k_2 || k_1 || k_0$$

for K the master key, and the sequence of round keys $(k_0, \ldots, k_{T-1})$ is generated with

$$k_{i+1} = t_i$$

where

$$t_{i+3} = k_i \oplus f_{5,0,1}(t_i) \oplus c \oplus (z_j)_i,$$

and $c \oplus (z_j)_i \in \{\texttt{0xfffc}, \texttt{0xfffd}\}$ a round constant. A single round of SIMECK is depicted in Fig. 1a.

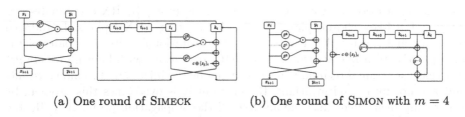

(a) One round of SIMECK   (b) One round of SIMON with $m = 4$

Fig. 1. Illustration of the SIMECK and SIMON ciphers

SIMON, conversely, uses a linear key schedule to generate the round keys. Let $K = (k_{m-1}, \ldots, k_1, k_0)$ be a master key for SIMON$2n$, where $k_i \in \mathbb{F}_2^n$. The sequence of round keys k_i is generated by

$$K_{i+m} = \begin{cases} k_i \oplus (I \oplus S^{-1})S^{-3}k_{i+1} \oplus c \oplus (z_j)_i, & \text{if } m = 2 \\ k_i \oplus (I \oplus S^{-1})S^{-3}k_{i+2} \oplus c \oplus (z_j)_i, & \text{if } m = 3 \\ k_i \oplus (I \oplus S^{-1})(S^{-3}k_{i+3} \oplus k_{i+1}) \oplus c \oplus (z_j)_i, & \text{if } m = 4 \end{cases}$$

for $0 \leq i \leq (T-1)$, and $c \oplus (z_j)_i$ is the round constant. A single round of SIMON with $m = 4$ is depicted in Fig. 1b.

2.2 Previous Work

The security of Simon-like ciphers has been widely explored over the last few years and a large number of cryptanalytic techniques were applied to it. To name just a few: linear cryptanalysis [5,13], differential cryptanalysis [3,5,12], related-key differential cryptanalysis [20], integral cryptanalysis and the division property [7,17,18,23]. For a comparison of our results with relevant previous work see Table 1.

Due to the unclear design rationale of SIMON, much attention was focused on understanding the rotation amounts. Kölbl et al. studied in [5] different sets of rotation amounts for Simon-like ciphers and found parameters, other than the specified $(8, 1, 2)$, which are optimal with respect to differential and linear cryptanalysis. Then, Kondo et al. further evaluated these parameter sets in terms of resistance to integral distinguishers in [7]. As they have shown, the parameter set $(12, 5, 3)$ is optimal with respect to differential cryptanalysis, linear cryptanalysis, and integral cryptanalysis. Also the SIMECK parameter set $(5, 0, 1)$ belongs to the same optimal class respective to several attack techniques. SIMON and SIMECK were also compared by Kölbl et al. in [6] by considering the differential effect.

2.3 Rotational-XOR Cryptanalysis

As a generalization of rotational cryptanalysis (see [4]), RX-cryptanalysis is also a related-key chosen plaintext attack targeting ARX ciphers. Introduced by Ashur and Liu in [1] it uses the fact that rotational pairs, i.e., pairs of the form $(x, S^\gamma(x))$ propagate through the ARX operations with known probability. Whereas the original technique was thwarted by the injection of round constants that are not rotational-invariant, RX-cryptanalysis overcomes this problem by integrating their effect into the analysis of the propagation probability. Rather than considering just a rotational pair as in the case of rotational cryptanalysis, RX-cryptanalysis considers an RX-pair of the form $(x, S^\gamma(x) \oplus \alpha)$ where α is called the *translation*. The technique was successfully applied to ARX-based primitives, including the block cipher SPECK [10] and the hash function SIPHASH [21].

3 Rotational-XOR Cryptanalysis of AND-RX Constructions

AND-RX constructions are similar in concept to ARX constructions where the non-linear operation (*i.e.*, modular addition) is replaced with a vectorial bit-wise AND. Since all operations are now bit oriented, such constructions are always rotation-invariant. More generally, they are structurally invariant under any affine transformation of the bit-indices as was shown in [5]. Superficially, it is believed that this invariance cannot be preserved over a large number of rounds if non-invariant constants are injected into the state since they will break the symmetry between bits in different positions. Despite their close relation to ARX constructions, the security of Simon-like ciphers against RX-cryptanalysis has not received much attention. We now set to rectify this omission in this section.

3.1 The Expected Probability of an RX-transition

In [1] an RX-pair was defined to be a rotational pair with rotational offset γ under translations δ_1 and δ_2, *i.e.*, it is the pair $(x \oplus \delta_1, (x \lll \gamma) \oplus \delta_2)$. We opt for a slightly different notation with x and $x' = (x \lll \gamma) \oplus \delta$, or $(x, (x \lll \gamma) \oplus \delta)$ as an RX-pair.

Definition 1 ([1] (adapted)). *The RX-difference of x and $x' = (x \lll \gamma) \oplus \delta$ with rotational offset γ, and translation δ is denoted by*

$$\Delta_\gamma(x, x') = x' \oplus (x \lll \gamma).$$

The propagation of an RX-difference $\Delta_\gamma(x, x') = x' \oplus (x \lll \gamma)$ through linear operations of the AND-RX structure is deterministic and follows these rules:

- **XOR.** For two input RX-pairs $(x, (x \lll \gamma) \oplus \delta_1)$ and $(y, (y \lll \gamma) \oplus \delta_2)$, their XOR is the RX-pair $(z, z') = (x \oplus y, ((x \oplus y) \lll \gamma) \oplus \delta_1 \oplus \delta_2)$;
- **Cyclic rotation by η bits.** The cyclic rotation of each of the values in $(x, (x \lll \gamma) \oplus \delta)$ by η bits is the RX-pair $(z, z') = (x \lll \eta, (x \lll (\gamma + \eta)) \oplus (\delta \lll \eta))$;
- **XOR with a constant c.** The XOR of a constant c to each of the values in the RX-pair $(x, (x \lll \gamma) \oplus \delta)$ is the RX-pair $(z, z') = (x \oplus c, (x \lll \gamma)) \oplus \delta \oplus c)$, the corresponding RX-difference is denoted by $\Delta_\gamma c = c \oplus (c \lll \gamma)$

all with probability 1.

Intuitively, the bitwise nature of the AND operation restricts the propagation of an RX-difference compared to modular addition. When two rotational pairs enter into the vectorial AND operation, the rotational relation is preserved with probability 1 due to the localized nature of bit-oriented operations. If the inputs form an RX-pair with translation $\delta \neq 0$, as is the case of SIMON and SIMECK, the propagation of the RX-difference through the vectorial AND is probabilistic and its probability is given by the following theorem.

Theorem 1. *Let $(x, (x \lll \gamma) \oplus \alpha)$ and $(y, (y \lll \gamma) \oplus \beta)$ be two RX-pairs where γ is the rotation offset and (α, β) the translations, respectively. Then, for an output translation Δ it holds that:*

$$\Pr[((x \odot y) \lll \gamma) \oplus \Delta = ((x \lll \gamma) \oplus \alpha) \odot ((y \lll \gamma) \oplus \beta)] = \tag{1}$$

$$\Pr[(x \odot y) \oplus \Delta = (x \oplus \alpha) \odot (y \oplus \beta)] \tag{2}$$

i.e., the propagation probability of an RX-difference with translations (α, β) through $\odot$ is the same as that of a normal XOR-difference through the same operation when the translations are considered as input XOR-differences.

Proof. To prove the theorem, we rewrite the right hand side of (1) as

$$((x \lll \gamma) \oplus \alpha) \odot ((y \lll \gamma) \oplus \beta) = ((x \odot y) \lll \gamma) \oplus ((x \lll \gamma) \odot \beta) \oplus$$
$$((y \lll \gamma) \odot \alpha) \oplus (\alpha \odot \beta)$$

Similarly, distributing the right hand side of (2) we get

$$(x \oplus \alpha) \odot (y \oplus \beta) = (x \odot y) \oplus (x \odot \beta) \oplus$$
$$(y \odot \alpha) \oplus (\alpha \odot \beta)$$

Rewriting Theorem 1 as

$$\Pr[((x \odot y) \lll \gamma) \oplus \Delta = ((x \odot y) \lll \gamma) \oplus ((x \lll \gamma) \odot \beta) \oplus$$
$$((y \lll \gamma) \odot \alpha) \oplus (\alpha \odot \beta)] = \tag{3}$$
$$\Pr[(x \odot y) \oplus \Delta = (x \odot y) \oplus (x \odot \beta) \oplus$$
$$(y \odot \alpha) \oplus (\alpha \odot \beta)], \tag{4}$$

the proof is completed by observing that $(x \odot y) \lll \gamma, x \lll \gamma$, and $y \lll \gamma$ have the same probability distribution as $x \odot y, x$, and y, respectively, due to the rotation-invariance of bit-oriented operations. $\qquad \square$

Kölbl *et al.* showed in [5] that in the special case of Simon-like ciphers (*e.g.*, SIMON and SIMECK) where $y = S^{a-b}(x)$, the difference propagation distribution (and thus, the RX-propagation distribution) is given by the following proposition.

Proposition 1. *For $S^a(x) \odot S^b(x)$ where $\gcd(n, a - b) = 1$, n is even, $a > b$ and $x = (x_{n-1}, \ldots, x_1, x_0) \in \mathbb{F}_2^n$, the difference propagation distribution table and RX propagation distribution are given by*

$$P(\alpha \to \beta) = \begin{cases} 2^{-n+1} & \text{if } \alpha = \mathtt{0xf} \cdots \mathtt{f} \\ & wt(\beta) \equiv 0 \bmod 2; \\ 2^{-wt((S^a(\alpha)|S^b(\alpha)) \oplus (\overline{S^a(\alpha)} \odot S^{2a-b}(\alpha) \odot S^b(\alpha)))} & \text{if } \alpha \neq \mathtt{0xf} \cdots \mathtt{f}, \\ & \beta \odot (\overline{S^a(\alpha) \mid S^b(\alpha)}) = 0, \\ & (\beta \oplus S^{a-b}(\beta)) \odot \\ & (\overline{S^a(\alpha)} \odot S^{2a-b}(\alpha) \\ & \odot S^b(\alpha)) = 0; \\ 0 & \text{otherwise} \end{cases}$$

Proof. The proof for the difference propagation distribution was given in [5]. The case for RX-propagation follows then from Theorem 1.   □

3.2   Discussion

Based on Theorem 1, it can be seen that the RX-difference passes through the vectorial AND component of a cipher with the same probability as an XOR-difference. However, resulting RX-characteristics are in general different from the corresponding (related-key) differential characteristics, due to the XOR of constants in the round function which affects the propagation.

It is interesting to see that in ARX ciphers, the probability for the rotational-transition part of the RX-transition is maximized with $2^{-1.415}$ when $\gamma \in \{1, n - 1\}$ and decreases for other γ. Conversely, the same transition passes with probability 1 through the vectorial AND in AND-RX ciphers. In other words, a rotational pair would propagate with probability 1 through all AND-RX operations, but only with some probability $p < 1$ through the ARX operations. We conclude that in general, AND-RX constructions are more susceptible to RX-cryptanalysis than ARX constructions.

4   Automated Search of RX-Characteristics in Simon-Like Ciphers

Similar to other statistical attacks, RX-cryptanalysis works in two phases: offline and online. In the offline phase, the adversary is searching for a distinguishable property respective to the algorithm's structure. Having found such a property, the adversary tries to detect it from data collected in the online phase.

Automated search methods are a common way to assist finding such a property (*i.e.*, Phase 1). The idea behind these tools is to model the search problem as a set of constraints and solve it using one of the available constraint solvers. For ciphers using Boolean and arithmetic operations, the search problem can be converted into a Boolean Satisfiability Problem (SAT) or a Satisfiability Module Problem (SMT). The respective solver then returns an answer on whether all constraints can be satisfied simultaneously, and if the answer is positive it also returns a valid assignment. A number of ARX and AND-RX ciphers were studied using automatic search tools, in the context of differential cryptanalysis, linear cryptanalysis, division property, and RX-cryptanalysis [10,11,14–16].

In this section, we give a detailed description of an automatic search model for RX-characteristics in Simon-like ciphers.

4.1   The Common Round Function

From Theorem 1 we learn that the propagation of RX-differences through the AND operation follows a probabilistic rule, with a probability distribution as in Proposition 1. We use $\Delta_1 a^r$ and $\Delta_1 b^r$ to denote the two n-bit vectors representing RX-differences at the beginning of round r, and $\Delta_1 d^r$ the n-bit vector

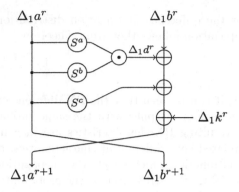

Fig. 2. Notation of the RX-differences in the encryption function.

representing the RX-difference at the output of the vectorial AND at the same round. A schematic view of this notation is depicted in Fig. 2.

Then, the following two Boolean equations should be satisfied simultaneously for the propagation of RX-differences through the vectorial AND to be valid

$$0 = \Delta_1 d^r \odot (\overline{S^a(\Delta_1 a^r) \mid S^b(\Delta_1 a^r)}); \tag{5}$$

$$0 = (\Delta_1 d^r \oplus S^{a-b}(\Delta_1 d^r)) \odot (\overline{S^a(\Delta_1 a^r)} \odot S^{2a-b}(\Delta_1 a^r) \odot S^b(\Delta_1 a^r)). \tag{6}$$

In simple words, (5) ensures that any active bit in $\Delta_1 d^r$ results from at least one active bit in the corresponding position of $\Delta_1 a^r$. If a bit $\Delta_1 d^r$ was activated by exactly one bit from $\Delta_1 a^r$, (6) ensures that either a second bit in $\Delta_1 d^r$ is active, or that another active bit in $\Delta_1 a^r$ had deactivated said bit. This encodes the implicit expansion function, *i.e.*, the dependency between the bit in position i and that in position $i + a - b$ before they enter the vectorial AND.

If the propagation is valid, the probability in round r is given by $2^{-w_d^r}$, where

$$w_d^r = wt((S^a(\Delta_1 a^r) \mid S^b(\Delta_1 a^r)) \oplus (\overline{S^a(\Delta_1 a^r)} \odot \\ S^{2a-b}(\Delta_1 a^r) \odot S^b(\Delta_1 a^r))), \tag{7}$$

is said to be the weight of the non-linear transition in round r.

In addition, the propagation of an RX-difference through the linear operations is described by the following expressions:

$$\Delta_1 b^{r+1} = \Delta_1 a^r; \tag{8}$$

$$\Delta_1 a^{r+1} = \Delta_1 d^r \oplus \Delta_1 b^r \oplus S^c(\Delta_1 a^r) \oplus \Delta_1 k^r. \tag{9}$$

4.2   The Key Schedule of SIMECK

The key schedule of SIMECK is modeled analogously to the round function. Let $\Delta_1 ka^r$, $\Delta_1 kb^r$, and $\Delta_1 kd^r$ be n-bit variables in round r which denote the left input RX-difference, the right input RX-difference, and the output RX-difference of the vectorial AND (see Fig. 3a). As before, the following two Boolean equations should be satisfied simultaneously for the propagation of RX-differences through the non-linear part of SIMECK's key schedule to be valid:

$$0 = \Delta_1 kd^r \odot \overline{S^a(\Delta_1 ka^r) \mid S^b(\Delta_1 ka^r)}; \tag{10}$$

$$0 = (\Delta_1 kd^r \oplus S^{a-b}(\Delta_1 kd^r)) \odot (\overline{S^a(\Delta_1 ka^r)} \odot$$
$$S^{2a-b}(\Delta_1 ka^r) \odot S^b(\Delta_1 ka^r)), \tag{11}$$

with weight w_k^r set as

$$w_k^r = wt((S^a(\Delta_1 ka^r) \mid S^b(\Delta_1 ka^r)) \oplus (\overline{S^a(\Delta_1 ka^r)} \odot$$
$$S^{2a-b}(\Delta_1 ka^r) \odot S^b(\Delta_1 ka^r))). \tag{12}$$

The propagation of RX-difference through the linear operations of the key schedule is modeled by the following constraints:

$$\Delta_1 kb^{r+1} = \Delta_1 ka^r; \tag{13}$$

$$\Delta_1 ka^{r+3} = \Delta_1 kd^r \oplus \Delta_1 kb^r \oplus S^c(\Delta_1 ka^r) \oplus \Delta_1 c^r. \tag{14}$$

Finally, the key schedule and the round function are linked via the following expression:

$$\Delta_1 k^r = \Delta_1 kb^r. \tag{15}$$

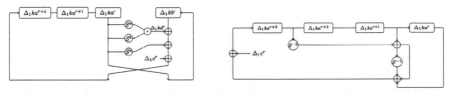

(a) Notation of the RX-differences with a nonlinear key schedule.

(b) Notation of the RX-differences with a linear key schedule.

Fig. 3. Notations of the RX-differences.

4.3 The Key Schedule of SIMON

In the key schedule of SIMON $2n/4n$, let $\Delta_1 ka^r$, $\Delta_1 ka^{r+1}$, and $\Delta_1 ka^{r+3}$ be n-bit variables denoting the input RX-differences to the key schedule at round r, and let $\Delta_1 ka^{r+4}$ denote the output RX-difference fed back to the leftmost register in the key schedule and injected into the round (see Fig. 3b); then, the propagation of RX-differences is modeled as

$$\Delta_1 ka^{r+4} = S^{-3}(\Delta_1 ka^{r+3}) \oplus \Delta_1 ka^{r+1} \oplus S^{-1}(S^{-3}(\Delta_1 ka^{r+3}) \oplus$$
$$\Delta_1 ka^{r+1}) \oplus \Delta_1 ka^r \oplus \Delta_1 c^r \tag{16}$$

and the injection of the subkey the state in round r as

$$\Delta_1 k^r = \Delta_1 k a^r. \tag{17}$$

4.4   The Objective Function

To evaluate the model, we define an objective function, *i.e.*, a quantity that the model is trying to optimize and which can be used to compare the "quality" of different solutions. The original model in [10], which was the first model to search for RX-differences in ciphers with a non-linear key schedule, operated in two steps. First, a good key RX-characteristic was sought. Then, a good RX-characteristic was sought for the state with respect to the selected key RX-characteristic.

In this paper we take a different approach. Rather than considering the two search problems separately, we generate good RX-characteristics "on-the-fly" without a-priori fixing the key characteristic. We start by searching for an RX-characteristics minimizing the total weight in both the data and key parts, namely $w_d + w_k$. Then, conditioned on the total weight $w_d + w_k$ fixed to the minimum found, we further minimize the weight in the data part w_d in order to improve the data complexity of the attack.

For SIMON our strategy would yield the same results as the strategy in [10] since $w_k^r = 0$ for all r due to the linear key schedule. The objective function for the R-round SIMON model is expressed as

$$\min(w) \text{ s.t.}$$
$$\max(R) \text{ s.t.}$$
$$(w = (\sum_{r=1}^{R} w_d^r)) \wedge (w \le 2n) \tag{18}$$

For SIMECK we first observe that the key difference injected in round r is actually generated in round $r - 4$ where its cost is "paid". As a result, the total probability of an R-round characteristic in the key schedule part only needs to take into account the cost of rounds 1 to $R - 4$. Hence, we set the objective function as follows:

$$\min(w_d) \text{ s.t.}$$
$$\min(w) \text{ s.t.}$$
$$\max(R) \text{ s.t.}$$
$$(w = (\sum_{r=1}^{R} w_d^r + \sum_{r=1}^{R-4} w_k^r)) \wedge (w \le 4n) \wedge (w_d = \sum_{r=1}^{R} w_d^r) \wedge (w_d \le 2n)$$
$$\tag{19}$$

Table 3. The weights of the best found RX-characteristic in round-reduced SIMECK32, SIMECK48 and SIMECK64 with $\gamma = 1$. For each of the ciphers we report the results in three rows: number of distinguished rounds, weight of the round function part, and weight of the key schedule part. For instance, the best found RX-characteristic covering 20-round SIMECK32 has a data probability of 2^{-26} for a weak key class of size $2^{64-34} = 2^{30}$.

SIMECK32												
Rounds	10	11	12	13	14	15	16	17	18	19	20	
Data	6	10	12	12	16	18	18	18	22	24	26	
Key	8	12	12	18	18	20	28	32	30	34	34	
SIMECK48												
Rounds	15	16	17	18	19	20	21	22	23	24	25	26	27
Data	18	18	18	22	24	26	30	30	32	36	36	40	42
Key	20	28	32	30	34	34	36	40	44	46	48	48	52
SIMECK64												
Rounds	23	24	25	26	27	28	29	30	31	32	33	34	35
Data	30	32	34	38	38	40	42	44	46	48	50	52	54
Key	44	46	48	50	54	58	60	62	64	66	68	70	72

5 Results

Now that we have a model for finding RX-characteristics in AND-RX constructions, we can use one of the existing solvers to evaluate it. We describe the model using the SMTLIB language and apply the Boolector solver with several parameter settings. Our experiments were carried out on a laptop having an Intel Core i7-7700HQ CPU running at 2.80 GHz and having 8 GB of RAM.[1]

5.1 SIMECK

Using the above model, we found RX-characteristics which cover up to 20, 27, and 35 rounds for variants of SIMECK with block size of 32, 48, and 64 bits, respectively. These results are presented in Table 3. We further proved that there exists no RX-characteristic with $w_d + w_k \leq 64$ for more than 20 rounds of SIMECK32; therefore, our 20-round RX-characteristic gives a tight bound on the number of rounds that can be distinguished using RX-cryptanalysis.

Recalling the previous results in Table 1 we see that previously published distinguishers cover up to 15, 19, and 25 rounds of SIMECK32, SIMECK48, and SIMECK64, respectively, whereas our RX-characteristics improve the number of distinguished rounds by 5, 8, and 10 rounds, albeit for a smaller key class than previous results. Benchmarking for the same number of rounds, detecting our distinguishers requires fewer data.

---

[1] Our source code is available on Github at https://github.com/JIN-smile/Simon32-and-Simeck32.

Table 4. A 15-round RX-characteristics in SIMECK 32/64

Round	RX-difference in key	RX-difference in data
0	0014	(0000||0010)
1	0008	(0004||0000)
2	0004	(0000||0004)
3	0001	(0000||0000)
4	0002	(0001||0000)
5	0002	(0001||0001)
6	0000	(0000||0001)
7	0003	(0001||0000)
8	0002	(0000||0001)
9	0007	(0003||0000)
10	0001	(0000||0003)
11	0002	(0002||0000)
12	0008	(0004||0002)
13	0002	(0002||0004)
14	0000	(0000||0002)
15		(0002||0000)
Prob.	2^{-26}	2^{-18}

Experimental Verification. To empirically validate our results we implemented the 15-round RX-characteristic presented in Table 4. We first sample a random 64-bit master key K and obtain its respective matching key $K' = S^1(K) \oplus (0001\|\|0004\|\|0008\|\|0014)$. We then check if the resulting sub-keys satisfy the required RX-difference. If not, a new K is picked and the above process is repeated until a good pair (K, K') is found. This pair of related keys is used to encrypt 2^{32} plaintext pairs. For each encrypted plaintext pair, we check if the intermediate RX-differences match those of the RX-characteristic.

We sampled about $2^{33.6} = 2^{26.6+7}$ keys, out of which 2^7 satisfied the requested key RX-difference. For these keys, the average probability that a randomly selected plaintext satisfies the RX-characteristic was around $2^{-18.005}$. These figures confirm our claims.

5.2 SIMON

Interestingly, despite their similar structure, finding good RX-characteristics for SIMON seems to be much harder than for SIMECK. For the smallest version SIMON32/64, the solver does not produce solutions (SAT or UNSAT) for more than 11 rounds given reasonable resources and time. We conjecture that the reason for this is the key schedule which forces all key RX-transitions to be deterministic in the key part. In the case of SIMECK the non-deterministic key

RX-transitions offered more freedom for backtracking steps in search for cancellation effects in the data part; similar freedom is not afforded for SIMON due to the linear key schedule.

The complexity of our RX-distinguishers against SIMON32/64 with 10 rounds are presented in Table 1. For 11 rounds of SIMON32/64 we find a characteristic with probability 2^{-24} which is inferior to previous results. We do not expect RX-cryptanalysis to be able to improve the distinguishing cost for more than 11 rounds. In Sect. 6 we discuss the distinctive behaviors of RX-characteristics in SIMON and SIMECK.

6   Comparing the Resistance to RX-cryptanalysis of SIMON and SIMECK

In Sect. 5 we saw that SIMECK appears to be more vulnerable to RX-cryptanalysis than its counterpart SIMON. The two main differences between these ciphers are the key schedule (linear in SIMON vs. non-linear in SIMECK) and the rotation amounts ((8, 1, 2) in SIMON vs. (5, 0, 1) in SIMECK). To understand how each of these decisions affects the resistance of the resulting cipher to RX-cryptanalysis, we define three additional variants:

- SIM-1 which uses the round function of SIMON for and the key schedule of SIMECK,
- SIM-2 which uses the round function of SIMECK and the key schedule of SIMON ($m = 4$), and
- SIM-3 which uses a Simon-like round function with rotation amounts $(12, 5, 3)$ and the key schedule of SIMON ($m = 4$).[2]

To determine the effect of the key schedule and rotation amounts on the resistance of a Simon-like cipher to RX-cryptanalysis we take the same approach as in Sect. 5, this time searching RX-characteristics for SIM-1, SIM-2, and SIM-3. We present in Table 5 the RX-distinguishers we found and compare them to those found for SIMON and SIMECK.

The results show that, for some optimal parameters of the Simon-like round function, the rotation amounts have no effect on the probability of the RX-characteristics. However, the difference between the linear key schedule of SIMON and the non-linear one of SIMECK plays a significant role in the resistance to RX-cryptanalysis. In other words, the key schedule of SIMECK makes it more vulnerable to RX-cryptanalysis.

It would be interesting to consider two more experiments, one where the key schedule is yet another non-linear function (e.g., the key schedule of SPECK) and one where the rotation amounts are suboptimal. This is left for future work.

---

[2] This set of rotation amounts was determined in [7] to be optimal against certain attacks.

Table 5. A comparison of the optimal probability in RX-characteristics found in Simon-like ciphers: SIM-1, SIM-2, SIM-3, SIMECK and SIMON.

Rounds	SIM-1	SIM-2	SIM-3	SIMECK32	SIMON32
5	1	1	1	1	1
6	1	1	1	1	1
7	2^{-2}	2^{-4}	2^{-4}	2^{-2}	2^{-4}
8	2^{-4}	2^{-6}	2^{-4}	2^{-4}	2^{-6}
9	2^{-6}	2^{-10}	2^{-10}	2^{-4}	2^{-10}
10	2^{-8}	2^{-14}	2^{-14}	2^{-6}	2^{-14}
11	2^{-12}	2^{-24}	2^{-24}	2^{-8}	2^{-24}

7   Conclusion

In this paper, we generalized the idea of Rotational-XOR cryptanalysis to AND-RX ciphers by showing that an RX-difference has the same propagation probability as a corresponding XOR-difference through the same function. We formulated a SAT/SMT model for RX-cryptanalysis in AND-RX constructions and applied it to reduced-round versions of SIMON and SIMECK. We found distinguishers covering up to 20, 27, and 35 rounds of SIMECK32, SIMECK48, SIMECK64, respectively. These are the longest distinguishers for this cipher family.

Moreover, we noticed that finding good RX-characteristics in SIMON is more difficult than in SIMECK. By applying our SAT/SMT model to toy examples we were able to conclude that it is the different key schedule which makes SIMECK more vulnerable to RX-cryptanalysis than SIMON. We conjectured that the gap between the two ciphers is due to the (non-)linearity of the key schedule and left this for future work.

Acknowledgement. This paper was supported by National Natural Science Foundation of China (NSFC) under grants 61672530, 61902414 and 61772545. Tomer Ashur is an FWO post-doctoral fellow under Grant Number 12ZH420N.

A   Reported RX-Characteristics for SIMECK32/48/64

See Tables 6 and 7.

Table 6. A 20-round RX-characteristic for SIMECK32/64 and a 27-round RX-characteristics for SIMECK48/96

Round	SIMECK32/64		SIMECK48/96	
	Key	Data	Key	Data
	RX-difference	RX-difference	RX-difference	RX-difference
0	0004	(0000||0004)	000004	(000001||000006)
1	0000	(0000||0000)	000000	(000000||000001)
2	0001	(0000||0000)	000002	(000001||000000)
3	0002	(0001||0000)	000003	(000001||000001)
4	0002	(0000||0001)	000002	(000001||000001)
5	0005	(0003||0000)	000000	(000000||000001)
6	0001	(0000||0003)	000003	(000001||000000)
7	0002	(0002||0000)	000003	(000000||000001)
8	000a	(0004||0002)	000004	(000002||000000)
9	0002	(0000||0004)	000000	(000000||000002)
10	0000	(0006||0000)	000002	(000002||000000)
11	0013	(000a||0006)	00000e	(000004||000002)
12	000a	(0001||000a)	000002	(000000||000004)
13	0004	(0002||0001)	000000	(000006||000000)
14	0000	(0001||0002)	000013	(00000c||000006)
15	0001	(0000||0001)	00000c	(000001||00000c)
16	0000	(0000||0000)	000004	(000002||000001)
17	0002	(0000||0000)	000000	(000001||000002)
18	0006	(0002||0000)	000002	(000001||000001)
19	0007	(0000||0002)	000002	(000001||000001)
20		(0005||0000)	000001	(000000||000001)
21			000000	(000000||000000)
22			000003	(000000||000000)
23			000004	(000003||000000)
24			000004	(000002||000003)
25			000000	(000001||000002)
26			00000d	(000000||000001)
27				(00000c||000000)
Prob.	2^{-34}	2^{-26}	2^{-52}	2^{-42}

Table 7. A 35-round RX-characteristics for SIMECK64/128

Round	Key RX-difference	Data RX-difference
0	00000006	(00000001‖00000004)
1	00000000	(00000000‖00000001)
2	00000003	(00000001‖00000000)
3	00000002	(00000001‖00000001)
4	00000000	(00000000‖00000001)
5	00000002	(00000001‖00000000)
6	00000003	(00000000‖00000001)
7	00000004	(00000002‖00000000)
8	00000000	(00000000‖00000002)
9	00000002	(00000002‖00000000)
10	0000000a	(00000004‖00000002)
11	00000001	(00000000‖00000004)
12	00000001	(00000005‖00000000)
13	00000013	(0000000a‖00000005)
14	0000000c	(00000002‖0000000a)
15	00000005	(00000002‖00000002)
16	00000001	(00000001‖00000002)
17	00000002	(00000001‖00000001)
18	00000002	(00000001‖00000001)
19	00000002	(00000001‖00000001)
20	00000003	(00000001‖00000001)
21	00000002	(00000001‖00000001)
22	00000003	(00000001‖00000001)
23	00000000	(00000000‖00000001)
24	00000002	(00000001‖00000000)
25	00000003	(00000000‖00000001)
26	00000006	(00000002‖00000000)
27	00000000	(00000000‖00000002)
28	00000002	(00000002‖00000000)
29	0000000a	(00000004‖00000002)
30	00000000	(00000000‖00000004)
31	00000000	(00000004‖00000000)
32	00000010	(0000000c‖00000004)
33	0000000c	(00000000‖0000000c)
34	00000005	(00000000‖00000000)
35		(00000005‖00000000)
Prob.	2^{-72}	2^{-54}

References

1. Ashur, T., Liu, Y.: Rotational cryptanalysis in the presence of constants. IACR Trans. Symmetric Cryptol. **2016**(1), 57–70 (2016)
2. Beaulieu, R., Shors, D., Smith, J., Treatman-Clark, S., Weeks, B., Wingers, L.: The SIMON and SPECK lightweight block ciphers. In: DAC. Lecture Notes in Computer Science, vol. 2013, pp. 175:1–175:6. ACM (2015)
3. Beierle, C.: Pen and paper arguments for SIMON and SIMON-like designs. In: Zikas, V., De Prisco, R. (eds.) SCN 2016. LNCS, vol. 9841, pp. 431–446. Springer, Cham (2016). https://doi.org/10.1007/978-3-319-44618-9_23
4. Khovratovich, D., Nikolić, I.: Rotational cryptanalysis of ARX. In: Hong, S., Iwata, T. (eds.) FSE 2010. LNCS, vol. 6147, pp. 333–346. Springer, Heidelberg (2010). https://doi.org/10.1007/978-3-642-13858-4_19
5. Kölbl, S., Leander, G., Tiessen, T.: Observations on the SIMON block cipher family. In: Gennaro, R., Robshaw, M. (eds.) CRYPTO 2015. LNCS, vol. 9215, pp. 161–185. Springer, Heidelberg (2015). https://doi.org/10.1007/978-3-662-47989-6_8
6. Kölbl, S., Roy, A.: A brief comparison of SIMON and SIMECK. In: Bogdanov, A. (ed.) LightSec 2016. LNCS, vol. 10098, pp. 69–88. Springer, Cham (2017). https://doi.org/10.1007/978-3-319-55714-4_6
7. Kondo, K., Sasaki, Y., Todo, Y., Iwata, T.: On the design rationale of SIMON block cipher: integral attacks and impossible differential attacks against SIMON variants. IEICE Trans. **101-A**(1), 88–98 (2018)
8. Koo, B., Roh, D., Kim, H., Jung, Y., Lee, D.-G., Kwon, D.: CHAM: a family of lightweight block ciphers for resource-constrained devices. In: Kim, H., Kim, D.-C. (eds.) ICISC 2017. LNCS, vol. 10779, pp. 3–25. Springer, Cham (2018). https://doi.org/10.1007/978-3-319-78556-1_1
9. Kranz, T., Leander, G., Wiemer, F.: Linear cryptanalysis: key schedules and tweakable block ciphers. IACR Trans. Symmetric Cryptol. **2017**(1), 474–505 (2017)
10. Liu, Y., De Witte, G., Ranea, A., Ashur, T.: Rotational-xor cryptanalysis of reduced-round SPECK. IACR Trans. Symmetric Cryptol. **2017**(3), 24–36 (2017)
11. Liu, Y., Wang, Q., Rijmen, V.: Automatic search of linear trails in ARX with applications to SPECK and chaskey. In: Manulis, M., Sadeghi, A.-R., Schneider, S. (eds.) ACNS 2016. LNCS, vol. 9696, pp. 485–499. Springer, Cham (2016). https://doi.org/10.1007/978-3-319-39555-5_26
12. Liu, Z., Li, Y., Wang, M.: Optimal differential trails in SIMON-like ciphers. IACR Trans. Symmetric Cryptol. **2017**(1), 358–379 (2017)
13. Liu, Z., Li, Y., Wang, M.: The security of SIMON-like ciphers against linear cryptanalysis. IACR Cryptology ePrint Archive **2017**, 576 (2017)
14. Sun, L., Wang, W., Liu, R., Wang, M.: Milp-aided bit-based division property for ARX-based block cipher. IACR Cryptology ePrint Archive **2016**, 1101 (2016)
15. Sun, L., Wang, W., Liu, R., Wang, M.: Milp-aided bit-based division property for ARX ciphers. SCIENCE CHINA Inf. Sci. **61**(11), 118102:1–118102:3 (2018)
16. Sun, L., Wang, W., Wang, M.: Automatic search of bit-based division property for ARX ciphers and word-based division property. In: Takagi, T., Peyrin, T. (eds.) ASIACRYPT 2017. LNCS, vol. 10624, pp. 128–157. Springer, Cham (2017). https://doi.org/10.1007/978-3-319-70694-8_5
17. Todo, Y., Morii, M.: Bit-based division property and application to SIMON family. In: Peyrin, T. (ed.) FSE 2016. LNCS, vol. 9783, pp. 357–377. Springer, Heidelberg (2016). https://doi.org/10.1007/978-3-662-52993-5_18

18. Wang, Q., Liu, Z., Varıcı, K., Sasaki, Y., Rijmen, V., Todo, Y.: Cryptanalysis of reduced-round SIMON32 and SIMON48. In: Meier, W., Mukhopadhyay, D. (eds.) INDOCRYPT 2014. LNCS, vol. 8885, pp. 143–160. Springer, Cham (2014). https://doi.org/10.1007/978-3-319-13039-2_9

19. Wang, S., Hu, B., Guan, J., Zhang, K., Shi, T.: MILP-aided method of searching division property using three subsets and applications. In: Galbraith, S.D., Moriai, S. (eds.) ASIACRYPT 2019. LNCS, vol. 11923, pp. 398–427. Springer, Cham (2019). https://doi.org/10.1007/978-3-030-34618-8_14

20. Wang, X., Wu, B., Hou, L., Lin, D.: Automatic search for related-key differential trails in SIMON-like block ciphers based on MILP. In: Chen, L., Manulis, M., Schneider, S. (eds.) ISC 2018. LNCS, vol. 11060, pp. 116–131. Springer, Cham (2018). https://doi.org/10.1007/978-3-319-99136-8_7

21. Xin, W., Liu, Y., Sun, B., Li, C.: Improved cryptanalysis on SipHash. In: Mu, Y., Deng, R.H., Huang, X. (eds.) CANS 2019. LNCS, vol. 11829, pp. 61–79. Springer, Cham (2019). https://doi.org/10.1007/978-3-030-31578-8_4

22. Yang, G., Zhu, B., Suder, V., Aagaard, M.D., Gong, G.: The Simeck family of lightweight block ciphers. In: Güneysu, T., Handschuh, H. (eds.) CHES 2015. LNCS, vol. 9293, pp. 307–329. Springer, Heidelberg (2015). https://doi.org/10.1007/978-3-662-48324-4_16

23. Zhang, H., Wu, W.: Structural evaluation for simon-like designs against integral attack. In: Bao, F., Chen, L., Deng, R.H., Wang, G. (eds.) ISPEC 2016. LNCS, vol. 10060, pp. 194–208. Springer, Cham (2016). https://doi.org/10.1007/978-3-319-49151-6_14

A New Improved AES S-box with Enhanced Properties

Abderrahmane Nitaj[1]([✉]), Willy Susilo[2], and Joseph Tonien[2]

[1] LMNO, University of Caen Normandie, Caen, France
abderrahmane.nitaj@unicaen.fr
[2] Institute of Cybersecurity and Cryptology,
School of Computing and Information Technology,
University of Wollongong, Wollongong, Australia
{willy.susilo,joseph.tonien}@uow.edu.au

Abstract. The Advanced Encryption Standard (AES) is the most widely used symmetric encryption algorithm. Its security is mainly based on the structure of the S-box. In this paper, we present a new way to create S-boxes for AES and exhibit an S-box with improved cryptographic properties such as Bit Independence Criterion (BIC), periodicity, algebraic complexity, Strict Avalanche Criterion (SAC) and Distance to SAC.

1 Introduction

The Advanced Encryption Standard (AES) [13] is the main and widely used symmetric cryptosystem. It was standardized by NIST in 2000 in replacement of DES [7]. AES is a Substitution Permutation Network (SPN) which is based on a non-linear substitution layer and a linear diffusion layer. The non-linear layer is represented by a 16×16 S-box which is a permutation of the Galois finite field $\mathbb{F}_{2^8}$. The design of the S-box is a challenging task since the security of AES is mainly based on its structure. A strong S-box should satisfy several cryptographic criteria to resist the known cryptanalytic attacks, such as linear cryptanalysis [12] and differential cryptanalysis [1]. Although AES is resistant to linear and differential attacks, it presents some weaknesses in regards with a variety of cryptanalytic criteria. A typical example is that an S-box should have high algebraic degree when expressed as a polynomial. The AES S-box has algebraic degree 254 with only 9 monomials which is very simple [11]. Another weak criterion for the AES S-box is that some elements of $\mathbb{F}_{2^8}$ have short iterative periods as it is the case with $S^2(0x73) = 0x73$, $S^{27}(0xfa) = 0xfa$, $S^{59}(0x00) = 0x00$, $S^{81}(0x01) = 0x01$, and $S^{87}(0x04) = 0x04$ (see [5]). One more weak criterion for the AES S-box is the distance to SAC (Strict Avalanche Criterion) which is evaluated to 432 [5] while it should be as small as possible. Yet another example of the weakness of the AES S-box is its affine transformation period [5,16]. It is equal to 4 which is very low in comparison with the optimal value 16.

In the literature, various techniques and tools have been proposed to create strong S-boxes for AES (see [5,9,10,15,17,20,21] for various constructions of

© Springer Nature Switzerland AG 2020
J. K. Liu and H. Cui (Eds.): ACISP 2020, LNCS 12248, pp. 125–141, 2020.
https://doi.org/10.1007/978-3-030-55304-3_7

S-boxes). In most cases, the proposed S-box is based on a bijective function on $\mathbb{F}_{2^8}$ with an explicit formulae. In AES [13], the S-box is a 16×16 table of bytes obtained by a function of the form $f(x) = Ax^{-1} + b$ where, for $x \neq 0$, x^{-1} is the inverse of x in $\mathbb{F}_{2^8}$, and $0^{-1} = 0$, and where A is a 8×8 a circular matrix of bits and $b = 0x63$. In [5], the proposed S-box is obtained by a function of the form $f(x) = A'(A'x + b')^{-1} + b'$ where A' is a 8×8 circular matrix of bits obtained by $0x5b$ and $b' = 0x5d$. The proposed S-box in [5] has better values for some cryptographic criteria. Typically, the distance to SAC is reduced to 372, the iterative period is increased to 256, the affine transformation period is increased to 16, and the number of terms in the algebraic expression is increased to 255.

In this paper, we propose a new function over $\mathbb{F}_{2^8}$ to construct 16×16 S-boxes of bytes with good cryptographic properties. The function is defined for a byte x by

$$S(x) = \begin{cases} \frac{Ax+\alpha}{Ax+\beta}, & \text{if } x \neq A^{-1}\beta \\ 0x01 & \text{if } x = A^{-1}\beta, \end{cases}$$

where A is an 8×8 invertible matrix of bits and α and β are two fixed different bytes. The cryptographic properties of the new S-boxes depend on the choice of A, α and β and there are approximately 5.3×10^{18} of possible values. In this paper, we consider the parameters

$$A = \begin{pmatrix} 1 & 0 & 0 & 0 & 1 & 1 & 0 & 1 \\ 1 & 1 & 0 & 0 & 1 & 0 & 0 & 1 \\ 0 & 1 & 1 & 1 & 0 & 0 & 0 & 1 \\ 0 & 0 & 0 & 0 & 1 & 1 & 0 & 1 \\ 0 & 0 & 1 & 0 & 0 & 0 & 1 & 0 \\ 1 & 0 & 0 & 0 & 1 & 0 & 1 & 1 \\ 0 & 1 & 1 & 1 & 0 & 0 & 0 & 0 \\ 1 & 1 & 0 & 1 & 0 & 1 & 1 & 0 \end{pmatrix}, \quad \alpha = 0xfe, \quad \beta = 0x3f.$$

With the former values, some of the cryptographic criteria are improved. The distance to SAC is reduced to 328, the iterative period is increased to 256, and the number of terms in the algebraic expression is increased to 255. We notice that our construction ovoids any affine structure while in AES and in [5], there are induced affine transformations of the form $f(x) = A'x + b$ where the 8×8 bit-matrix A' and the byte b are constant.

The rest of the paper is organized as follows. In Sect. 2, we present some known facts related to AES, in Sect. 3, we present the new S-box and, in Sect. 4, we study the cryptographic criteria of the proposed S-box. In Sect. 5, we give a comparison of the new S-box with the AES S-box and other existing S-boxes. We conclude the paper in Sect. 6.

2   Preliminaries

In this section, we present the main mathematical properties that will be used in this paper.

2.1 Description of an S-box

An S-box of a block cipher is a $n \times n$ matrix defined by a multivariate Boolean function $S : \mathbb{F}_{2^n} \to \mathbb{F}_{2^n}$ such that for $x \in \mathbb{F}_{2^n}$,

$$S(x) = (S_{n-1}(x), \ldots, S_0(x)),$$

where S_i, $0 \leq i \leq n - 1$ is a component Boolean function. An S-box should be bijective with no fixed point and should guarantee nonlinearity to the cryptosystem and strengthen its cryptographic security. Moreover, it should satisfy several criteria such as balancedness [14], strict avalanche criterion (SAC) [18], distance to SAC [18], bit independence criterion (BIC) [8], algebraic complexity and algebraic degree [2].

2.2 Description of AES

AES is a block cipher with 128-bits blocks. It operates on blocks, called states which are 4×4 arrays of bytes. Each state is indexed $0, \ldots, 15$. The rows are in the form $(i, i + 4, i + 8, i + 12)$ while the columns are in the form $(4i, 4i + 1, 4i + 2, 4i + 3)$ for $0 \leq i \leq 3$. AES has $N_r \in \{10, 12, 14\}$ rounds, formed by the transformations AddRoundKey, SubBytes, ShiftRows, and MixColumns as follows.

1. The first round is preceded by a transformation denoted AddRoundKey.
2. The first $N_r - 1$ rounds are composed by 4 transformations:
   (a) SubBytes Transformation: it is a non linear transformation of the state and is represented by the S-box;
   (b) ShiftRows Transformation: it is a circular shift on the rows of the state;
   (c) MixColumns Transformation: it is a linear transformation of the state;
   (d) AddRoundKey Transformation: it is a transformation of the state by xoring a 128 bit key.
3. The final round is composed by the three transformations:
   (a) SubBytes Transformation;
   (b) ShiftRows Transformation;
   (c) AddRoundKey Transformation.

SubBytes is the transformation that is based on the S-box. The security of AES depends mainly on the structure of the S-box.

2.3 Structure of the AES S-box

AES uses the Galois field $\mathbb{F}_{2^8}$, defined by

$$\mathbb{F}_{2^8} = \mathbb{F}_2[t]/(t^8 + t^4 + t^3 + t + 1),$$

where each byte $b = (b_7, b_6, b_5, b_4, b_3, b_2, b_1, b_0) \in \mathbb{F}_2^8$ is mapped to the element

$$b_7 t^7 + b_6 t^6 + b_5 t^5 + b_4 t^4 + b_3 t^3 + b_2 t^2 + b_1 t + b_0$$

of the Galois field $\mathbb{F}_{2^8}$. For example, the byte $0x53 = (0, 1, 0, 1, 0, 0, 1, 1)$ is identified with the field element $t^6 + t^4 + t + 1$.

The AES S-box S is constructed by combining two transformations f and g for $x \in \mathbb{F}_{2^8}$ by $S(x) = g \circ f(x)$ where

1. The first transformation is the nonlinear function f defined by

$$f(x) = \begin{cases} 0 & \text{if } x = 0, \\ x^{-1} & \text{if } x \neq 0. \end{cases}$$

   Hence, the function f maps zero to zero, and for a non-zero field element x, it maps the element to its multiplicative inverse x^{-1} in $\mathbb{F}_{2^8}$.

2. The second transformation g is the affine function defined by $g(x) = Ax + b$ where A is 8×8 bit-matrix and b is a constant. Namely, for a field element $x = (x_7, x_6, x_5, x_4, x_3, x_2, x_1, x_0)$, $y = Ax + b$ with

$$\begin{pmatrix} y_0 \\ y_1 \\ y_2 \\ y_3 \\ y_4 \\ y_5 \\ y_6 \\ y_7 \end{pmatrix} = \begin{pmatrix} 1\,0\,0\,0\,1\,1\,1\,1 \\ 1\,1\,0\,0\,0\,1\,1\,1 \\ 1\,1\,1\,0\,0\,0\,1\,1 \\ 1\,1\,1\,1\,0\,0\,0\,1 \\ 1\,1\,1\,1\,1\,0\,0\,0 \\ 0\,1\,1\,1\,1\,1\,0\,0 \\ 0\,0\,1\,1\,1\,1\,1\,0 \\ 0\,0\,0\,1\,1\,1\,1\,1 \end{pmatrix} \begin{pmatrix} x_0 \\ x_1 \\ x_2 \\ x_3 \\ x_4 \\ x_5 \\ x_6 \\ x_7 \end{pmatrix} + \begin{pmatrix} 1 \\ 1 \\ 0 \\ 0 \\ 0 \\ 1 \\ 1 \\ 0 \end{pmatrix}$$

Here is an example showing $S(0x53) = 0xed$:

- $0x53 = (0, 1, 0, 1, 0, 0, 1, 1)$ is mapped to $t^6 + t^4 + t + 1$;
- the inverse of $t^6 + t^4 + t + 1$ modulo $t^8 + t^4 + t^3 + t + 1$ is $t^7 + t^6 + t^3 + t$ so

$$f(t^6 + t^4 + t + 1) = t^7 + t^6 + t^3 + t,$$

  which is $(1, 1, 0, 0, 1, 0, 1, 0)$ in binary form;
- apply the affine transformation g

$$\begin{pmatrix} 1\,0\,0\,0\,1\,1\,1\,1 \\ 1\,1\,0\,0\,0\,1\,1\,1 \\ 1\,1\,1\,0\,0\,0\,1\,1 \\ 1\,1\,1\,1\,0\,0\,0\,1 \\ 1\,1\,1\,1\,1\,0\,0\,0 \\ 0\,1\,1\,1\,1\,1\,0\,0 \\ 0\,0\,1\,1\,1\,1\,1\,0 \\ 0\,0\,0\,1\,1\,1\,1\,1 \end{pmatrix} \begin{pmatrix} 0 \\ 1 \\ 0 \\ 1 \\ 0 \\ 0 \\ 1 \\ 1 \end{pmatrix} + \begin{pmatrix} 1 \\ 1 \\ 0 \\ 0 \\ 0 \\ 1 \\ 1 \\ 0 \end{pmatrix} = \begin{pmatrix} 1 \\ 0 \\ 1 \\ 1 \\ 0 \\ 1 \\ 1 \\ 1 \end{pmatrix};$$

- the S-box output is then $(1, 1, 1, 0, 1, 1, 0, 1)$, that is $0xed$.

2.4   Algebraic Complexity of AES S-box

The algebraic complexity of an S-box S is measured by the number of non trivial monomials in the representation of S by a polynomial such that

$$S(x) = a_{255}x^{255} + a_{254}x^{254} + \cdots + a_1 x + a_0.$$

The AES S-box is constructed using the function $S(x) = g \circ f(x)$ where $f(x) = x^{-1} = x^{254}$ and $g(x) = Ax + B$. Hence f is a power function and g is an affine function. For a combination of such kind of functions, the following result fixes the algebraic complexity (see [4]).

Theorem 1. *Let $S = g \circ f$ be the function of an S-box on $\mathbb{F}_2^n$ with a power function f and an affine function g. Then the algebraic complexity of S is at most $n + 1$.*

The former result partially explains why the algebraic complexity of AES is 9 [4].

3   The Proposed S-box

In this section, we present the new S-box. We first define a 8×8 invertible matrix A with components in $\mathbb{F}_2$ and two constants $\alpha, \beta \in \mathbb{F}_{2^8}$. The following result gives the number of invertible matrices with entries in $\mathbb{F}_2$ (see [19], Section 3.3).

Lemma 1. *Let $\mathbb{F}_q$ be a finite field with q elements. For $n \geq 2$, let $GL(n, \mathbb{F}_q)$ be the group of invertible $n \times n$ matrices with entries in $\mathbb{F}_q$. The order of $GL(n, \mathbb{F}_q)$ is*

$$|GL(n, \mathbb{F}_q)| = \prod_{k=0}^{n-1} \left(q^n - q^k\right).$$

For $n = 8$ and $q = 2$, the group $GL(8, \mathbb{F}_2)$ of invertible 8×8 matrices A with entries in $\mathbb{F}_2$, the order is

$$|GL(8, \mathbb{F}_2)| = 5\ 348\ 063\ 769\ 211\ 699\ 200 \approx 5.3 \times 10^{18}.$$

Let

$$A = \begin{pmatrix} 1 & 0 & 0 & 0 & 1 & 1 & 0 & 1 \\ 1 & 1 & 0 & 0 & 1 & 0 & 0 & 1 \\ 0 & 1 & 1 & 1 & 0 & 0 & 0 & 1 \\ 0 & 0 & 0 & 0 & 1 & 1 & 0 & 1 \\ 0 & 0 & 1 & 0 & 0 & 0 & 1 & 0 \\ 1 & 0 & 0 & 0 & 1 & 0 & 1 & 1 \\ 0 & 1 & 1 & 1 & 0 & 0 & 0 & 0 \\ 1 & 1 & 0 & 1 & 0 & 1 & 1 & 0 \end{pmatrix}$$

and

$$\alpha = 0xfe = (1,1,1,1,1,1,1,0), \quad \beta = 0x3f = (0,0,1,1,1,1,1,1).$$

The new S-box is generated by the multivariate Boolean function S_N defined for $x \in \mathbb{F}_{2^8}$ by

$$S_N(x) = \begin{cases} \frac{Ax+\alpha}{Ax+\beta}, & \text{if } Ax + \beta \neq 0 \\ 0x01 & \text{if } Ax + \beta = 0, \end{cases} \tag{1}$$

Here are two examples showing $S_N(0xdd) = 0xed$ and $S_N(0xfa) = 0x01$.

Example 1: $S_N(0xdd) = 0xed$

- $0xdd = (1, 1, 0, 1, 1, 1, 0, 1) = (x_7, x_6, x_5, x_4, x_3, x_2, x_1, x_0)$
- apply the affine transformation $Ax + \beta$

$$
\begin{pmatrix}
1 & 0 & 0 & 0 & 1 & 1 & 0 & 1 \\
1 & 1 & 0 & 0 & 1 & 0 & 0 & 1 \\
0 & 1 & 1 & 1 & 0 & 0 & 0 & 1 \\
0 & 0 & 0 & 0 & 1 & 1 & 0 & 1 \\
0 & 0 & 1 & 0 & 0 & 0 & 1 & 0 \\
1 & 0 & 0 & 0 & 1 & 0 & 1 & 1 \\
0 & 1 & 1 & 1 & 0 & 0 & 0 & 0 \\
1 & 1 & 0 & 1 & 0 & 1 & 1 & 0
\end{pmatrix}
\begin{pmatrix} 1 \\ 0 \\ 1 \\ 1 \\ 1 \\ 0 \\ 1 \\ 1 \end{pmatrix}
+
\begin{pmatrix} 1 \\ 1 \\ 1 \\ 1 \\ 1 \\ 1 \\ 0 \\ 0 \end{pmatrix}
=
\begin{pmatrix} 0 \\ 0 \\ 0 \\ 1 \\ 1 \\ 1 \\ 0 \\ 1 \end{pmatrix}
$$

so $Ax + \beta = (1, 0, 1, 1, 1, 0, 0, 0) = 0xb8$

- apply the affine transformation $Ax + \alpha$

$$
\begin{pmatrix}
1 & 0 & 0 & 0 & 1 & 1 & 0 & 1 \\
1 & 1 & 0 & 0 & 1 & 0 & 0 & 1 \\
0 & 1 & 1 & 1 & 0 & 0 & 0 & 1 \\
0 & 0 & 0 & 0 & 1 & 1 & 0 & 1 \\
0 & 0 & 1 & 0 & 0 & 0 & 1 & 0 \\
1 & 0 & 0 & 0 & 1 & 0 & 1 & 1 \\
0 & 1 & 1 & 1 & 0 & 0 & 0 & 0 \\
1 & 1 & 0 & 1 & 0 & 1 & 1 & 0
\end{pmatrix}
\begin{pmatrix} 1 \\ 0 \\ 1 \\ 1 \\ 1 \\ 0 \\ 1 \\ 1 \end{pmatrix}
+
\begin{pmatrix} 0 \\ 1 \\ 1 \\ 1 \\ 1 \\ 1 \\ 1 \\ 1 \end{pmatrix}
=
\begin{pmatrix} 1 \\ 0 \\ 0 \\ 1 \\ 1 \\ 1 \\ 1 \\ 0 \end{pmatrix}
$$

so $Ax + \alpha = (0, 1, 1, 1, 1, 0, 0, 1) = 0x79$

- Calculate the S-box value

$$
\begin{aligned}
S_N(0xdd) &= \frac{Ax + \alpha}{Ax + \beta} \\
&= \frac{0x79}{0xb8} \\
&= \frac{t^6 + t^5 + t^4 + t^3 + 1}{t^7 + t^5 + t^4 + t^3} \\
&= t^7 + t^6 + t^5 + t^3 + t^2 + 1 \quad (\bmod \ t^8 + t^4 + t^3 + t + 1) \\
&= (1, 1, 1, 0, 1, 1, 0, 1) \\
&= 0xed.
\end{aligned}
$$

Example 2: $S_N(0xfa) = 0x01$

- $0xfa = (1, 1, 1, 1, 1, 0, 1, 0) = (x_7, x_6, x_5, x_4, x_3, x_2, x_1, x_0)$
- apply the affine transformation $Ax + \beta$

$$
\begin{pmatrix}
1 & 0 & 0 & 0 & 1 & 1 & 0 & 1 \\
1 & 1 & 0 & 0 & 1 & 0 & 0 & 1 \\
0 & 1 & 1 & 1 & 0 & 0 & 0 & 1 \\
0 & 0 & 0 & 0 & 1 & 1 & 0 & 1 \\
0 & 0 & 1 & 0 & 0 & 0 & 1 & 0 \\
1 & 0 & 0 & 0 & 1 & 0 & 1 & 1 \\
0 & 1 & 1 & 1 & 0 & 0 & 0 & 0 \\
1 & 1 & 0 & 1 & 0 & 1 & 1 & 0
\end{pmatrix}
\begin{pmatrix} 0 \\ 1 \\ 0 \\ 1 \\ 1 \\ 1 \\ 1 \\ 1 \end{pmatrix}
+
\begin{pmatrix} 1 \\ 1 \\ 1 \\ 1 \\ 1 \\ 1 \\ 0 \\ 0 \end{pmatrix}
=
\begin{pmatrix} 0 \\ 0 \\ 0 \\ 0 \\ 0 \\ 0 \\ 0 \\ 0 \end{pmatrix}
$$

so $Ax + \beta = (0,0,0,0,0,0,0,0) = 0x00$

- Therefore, using the definition of S_N in (1), we get

$$S_N(0xfa) = 0x01.$$

Applying the function S_N to $\mathbb{F}_{2^8}$, we get the new S-box presented in Table 1.

Table 1. The new S-box

	0	1	2	3	4	5	6	7	8	9	a	b	c	d	e	f
0	36	94	89	cb	77	96	d2	4b	05	f7	ab	c5	6d	a1	d6	5b
1	61	91	e7	d0	1f	a9	43	1d	9b	be	f4	b8	42	63	87	bb
2	02	58	c3	ac	e4	e5	eb	b3	83	70	64	20	57	08	60	85
3	2f	90	07	ee	23	33	81	12	14	ea	39	21	62	cd	28	2e
4	2c	f6	dd	25	bc	11	a7	e6	fd	53	98	9c	38	1b	5c	54
5	75	95	26	00	09	3b	44	9d	15	5d	1c	9a	5f	c9	a4	78
6	5a	f3	0b	0c	c9	0a	06	3c	71	e1	fa	f5	7f	65	19	df
7	8e	32	fb	74	50	d9	72	24	45	0f	69	76	da	41	b1	db
8	79	80	3a	49	e8	bf	73	16	18	8d	ce	a3	0e	c6	ef	e3
9	d7	99	6e	35	fc	af	a2	c1	de	c2	1e	d1	6c	f1	aa	7e
a	8c	52	d4	4a	7c	93	f0	e2	d8	66	04	9e	84	3c	13	ae
b	86	88	a5	68	d3	37	3d	56	6a	5e	7a	ad	c8	b2	40	67
c	0d	b7	46	7d	a6	82	6b	3f	34	22	b0	c0	29	4e	59	7b
d	c7	31	ba	47	fe	c4	d5	e0	92	b9	10	a0	8b	ed	55	97
e	ca	1a	f9	2a	cc	f2	4c	51	03	30	4d	f8	b4	bd	cf	48
f	ec	2b	9f	ff	27	17	b6	8f	8a	b5	01	a8	6f	4f	dc	2d

The inverse function of S_N is S_N^{-1} and is defined for a byte y by

$$S_N^{-1}(y) = \begin{cases} A^{-1}\left(\frac{\beta y + \alpha}{y + 1}\right), & \text{if } y \neq 0x01 \\ A^{-1}\beta & \text{if } y = 0x01. \end{cases}$$

The new inverse S-box is presented in Table 2.

4 Cryptographic Criteria of the New S-box

4.1 Linear Cryptanalysis of the New S-box

The resistance against linear cryptanalysis of a block cipher with an S-box function S over $\mathbb{F}_{2^n}$ is measured by the non-linearity parameter $NL(S)$, defined as (see [2], Section 3)

$$NL(S) = 2^{n-1} - \frac{1}{2} \max_{a \in \mathbb{F}_2^{n*}, b \in \mathbb{F}_2^n} \left| \sum_{x \in \mathbb{F}_{2^n}} (-1)^{a \cdot S(x) \oplus b \cdot x} \right|,$$

Table 2. The new inverse S-box

	0	1	2	3	4	5	6	7	8	9	a	b	c	d	e	f
0	53	fa	20	e8	aa	08	66	32	2d	54	65	62	63	c0	8c	79
1	da	45	37	ae	38	58	87	f5	88	6e	e1	4d	5a	17	9a	14
2	2b	3b	c9	34	77	43	52	f4	3e	cc	e3	f1	40	ff	3f	30
3	e9	d1	71	35	c8	93	00	b5	4c	3a	82	55	ad	b6	67	c7
4	be	7d	1c	16	56	78	c2	d3	ef	83	a3	07	e6	ea	cd	fd
5	74	e7	a1	49	4f	de	b7	2c	21	ce	60	0f	4e	59	b9	5c
6	2e	10	3c	1d	2a	6d	a9	bf	b3	7a	b8	c6	9c	0c	92	fc
7	29	68	76	86	73	50	7b	04	5f	80	ba	cf	a4	c3	9f	6c
8	81	36	c5	28	ac	2f	b0	1e	b1	02	f8	dc	a0	89	70	f7
9	31	11	d8	a5	01	51	05	df	4a	91	5b	18	4b	57	ab	f2
a	db	0d	96	8b	5e	b2	c4	46	fb	15	9e	0a	23	bb	af	95
b	ca	7e	bd	27	ec	f9	f6	c1	1b	d9	d2	1f	44	ed	19	85
c	cb	97	99	22	d5	0b	8d	d0	bc	5d	e0	03	e4	3d	8a	ee
d	13	9b	06	b4	a2	d6	0e	90	a8	75	7c	7f	fe	42	98	6f
e	d7	69	a7	8f	24	25	47	12	84	64	39	26	f0	dd	33	8e
f	a6	9d	e5	61	1a	6b	41	09	eb	e2	6a	72	94	48	d4	f3

where $u \cdot v$ is the dot product of u and v, defined by

$$u \cdot v = (u_{n-1}, \cdots, u_0) \cdot (v_{n-1}, \cdots, v_0) = u_{n-1}v_{n-1} \oplus \cdots \oplus u_0 v_0.$$

The non-linearity parameter $NL(S)$ is upper bounded by $2^{n-1} - 2^{\frac{n}{2}-1}$ (see [6]). For $n = 8$, the upper bound becomes $2^7 - 2^3 = 120$ while the non-linearity value $NL(S)$ is 112 for both AES S-box and the new S-box, which is very close to the maximal value of perfect nonlinear function.

4.2   Differential Cryptanalysis of the New S-box

The resistance against differential cryptanalysis of a block cipher with S-box function S over $\mathbb{F}_{2^n}$ is measured by the differential uniformity parameter $\delta(S)$, defined as

$$\delta(S) = \max_{(a,b) \in \mathbb{F}_{2^n}^* \times \mathbb{F}_{2^m}} D(a,b),$$

where, for $(a, b) \in \mathbb{F}_{2^n}^2$,

$$D(a,b) = |\{x \in \mathbb{F}_{2^n} \mid S(x) + S(x + a) = b\}|,$$

is the differential distribution of the S-box. For the new S-box, we have the following properties which are similar than the AES S-box:

- $D(0,0) = 256$.
- For all $a \neq 0$, $D(a,0) = 0$.
- For all $b \neq 0$, $D(0,b) = 0$.
- For all $a \neq 0$, $|\{b \in \mathbb{F}_{2^n} | D(a,b) = 0\}| = 129$.
- For all $b \neq 0$, $|\{a \in \mathbb{F}_{2^n} | D(a,b) = 0\}| = 129$.
- For all $a \neq 0$, $|\{b \in \mathbb{F}_{2^n} | D(a,b) = 2\}| = 126$.
- For all $b \neq 0$, $|\{a \in \mathbb{F}_{2^n} | D(a,b) = 2\}| = 126$.
- For all $a \neq 0$, $|\{b \in \mathbb{F}_{2^n} | D(a,b) = 4\}| = 1$.
- For all $b \neq 0$, $|\{a \in \mathbb{F}_{2^n} | D(a,b) = 4\}| = 1$.
- For all $\delta \notin \{0, 2, 4\}$, $\left|\{(a,b) \in \mathbb{F}_{2^n}^2 | D(a,b) = \delta\}\right| = 0$.

The lower bound of the differential uniformity for an S-box defined over $\mathbb{F}_{2^n}$ is 2 [3]. The maximal differential uniformity for the new S-box is 4, which is similar than the AES S-box (see [3,4]).

4.3 Bit Independence Criterion (BIC) of the New S-box

The bit independence criterion (BIC) was introduced by Webster and Tavares in [18]. It states that, if any input bit i is inverted in x, this changes any output bits j and k without any dependence on each other. This is useful to avoid any statistical pattern or statistical dependencies between output bits of the output vectors. Hence, for a strong S-box, the dependence between output bits should be as small as possible.

Definition 1. *Let* $S : \mathbb{F}_{2^n} \to \mathbb{F}_{2^n}$ *be a multivariate Boolean function defining an S-box. Let* $\alpha_i = (\delta_{i,n-1}, \ldots, \delta_{i,0})$ *where* $\delta_{i,i} = 1$ *and* $\delta_{i,j} = 0$ *if* $i \neq j$. *For all* $x \in \mathbb{F}_{2^n}$, *the corresponding vector to* $S(x) \oplus S(x \oplus \alpha_i)$ *is*

$$v(i,x) = (a_{i,n-1}(x), \ldots, a_{i,0}(x))).$$

The list $(a_{i,j}(x))$ *of all* $x \in \mathbb{F}_{2^n}$ *is denoted* $a_{i,j}$.

The correlation coefficient of $(a_{i,j}, a_{i,k})$ is defined as

$$\text{corr}(a_{i,j}, a_{i,k}) = \frac{\frac{1}{2^n}\left(\sum_{x \in \mathbb{F}_{2^n}} a_{i,j}(x)a_{i,k}(x)\right) - E(a_{i,j})E(a_{i,k})}{\sqrt{E\left(a_{i,j}^2\right) - (E(a_{i,j}))^2} \cdot \sqrt{E\left(a_{i,k}^2\right) - (E(a_{i,k}))^2}},$$

where $E(t)$ is the expected value of the list t.

A bit independence parameter corresponding to the independence of the output bits j and k under the effect of the change of the input bit i is defined as

$$BIC(j,k) = \max_{0 \leq i \leq n-1} \text{corr}(a_{i,j}, a_{i,k}).$$

The table of $BIC(i,j)$, $0 \leq i,j \leq 7$, for the new S-box is listed in Table 3. For comparison, the table of $BIC(i,j)$, $0 \leq i,j \leq 7$, for the AES S-box is listed in Table 4.

Table 3. Table of $BIC(a_j, a_k)$ for the New S-box

	$k=0$	$k=1$	$k=2$	$k=3$	$k=4$	$k=5$	$k=6$	$k=7$
$j=0$	1	0.090	0.097	0.12	0.097	0.067	0.12	0.090
$j=1$	0.090	1	0.12	0.093	0.098	0.094	0.12	0.097
$j=2$	0.097	0.12	1	0.095	0.12	0.095	0.10	0.12
$j=3$	0.12	0.093	0.095	1	0.064	0.12	0.12	0.12
$j=4$	0.097	0.098	0.12	0.064	1	0.12	0.064	0.072
$j=5$	0.067	0.094	0.095	0.12	0.12	1	0.093	0.093
$j=6$	0.12	0.12	0.10	0.12	0.064	0.093	1	0.059
$j=7$	0.090	0.097	0.12	0.12	0.072	0.093	0.059	1

Table 4. Table of $BIC(a_j, a_k)$ for the AES S-box

	$k=0$	$k=1$	$k=2$	$k=3$	$k=4$	$k=5$	$k=6$	$k=7$
$j=0$	1	0.098	0.12	0.12	0.12	0.13	0.066	0.095
$j=1$	0.098	1	0.098	0.13	0.067	0.12	0.098	0.12
$j=2$	0.12	0.098	1	0.12	0.097	0.067	0.098	0.12
$j=3$	0.12	0.13	0.12	1	0.12	0.13	0.066	0.096
$j=4$	0.12	0.067	0.097	0.12	1	0.097	0.12	0.066
$j=5$	0.13	0.12	0.067	0.13	0.097	1	0.10	0.071
$j=6$	0.066	0.098	0.098	0.066	0.12	0.10	1	0.098
$j=7$	0.095	0.12	0.12	0.096	0.066	0.071	0.098	1

For the whole S-box, defined by the function S, the bit independence criterion parameter is defined as

$$BIC(S) = \max_{0 \leq j < k \leq n-1} BIC(j, k).$$

For the new S-box, the BIC value is 0.12. This is better than the BIC of the AES S-box which is 0.13.

4.4   Periodicity of the New S-box

The periodicity of an S-box is related to the number of minimum compositions to get the identity function (see [5,16]).

Definition 2. *Let $S : \mathbb{F}_{2^n} \to \mathbb{F}_{2^n}$ be the function defining an S-box. For $x \in \mathbb{F}_{2^n}$, the period of x under S is the smallest positive integer n such that $S^n(x) = x$.*

It is shown in Table 5 that in AES, there are 5 possible periods, namely 2, 27, 59, 81 and 87 containing respectively 2, 27, 59, 81 and 87 different elements of $\mathbb{F}_{2^8}$.

For the new S-box, as shown in Table 6, 256 is the unique period so that the distribution of elements of $\mathbb{F}_{2^8}$ is more balanced for the periodicity criterion.

Table 5. Periodicity of the AES S-box

	0	1	2	3	4	5	6	7	8	9	a	b	c	d	e	f
0	59	81	59	59	87	59	59	59	87	81	87	27	81	81	81	59
1	81	81	81	81	27	87	81	81	87	59	81	87	87	87	81	87
2	59	59	87	27	59	59	27	81	87	59	87	27	87	27	59	87
3	87	59	27	59	87	87	59	87	59	81	81	87	81	81	87	59
4	81	81	87	81	87	27	87	81	59	87	87	81	59	81	87	81
5	87	87	59	87	59	87	27	81	59	87	87	81	87	59	59	81
6	87	27	81	59	81	81	59	87	27	87	59	59	87	81	27	59
7	87	87	81	2	81	59	59	59	81	87	81	59	81	81	81	59
8	81	81	81	81	81	87	87	81	87	87	81	81	81	59	59	2
9	87	81	81	87	87	87	87	87	87	87	87	27	87	59	27	27
a	81	27	81	87	87	59	59	87	59	59	81	81	81	87	87	87
b	87	27	87	81	59	59	87	59	87	27	87	81	81	81	87	87
c	87	81	59	59	87	59	59	59	27	81	81	87	81	81	81	81
d	87	87	59	59	59	59	87	81	27	87	81	27	87	81	87	27
e	81	81	87	81	87	87	59	87	27	81	81	81	81	87	87	27
f	81	27	87	81	87	59	87	27	81	87	27	59	87	59	81	81

4.5 Fixed and Opposite Points

Definition 3. *The opposite of $x \in \mathbb{F}_{2^8}$ is the field element $\bar{x} \in \mathbb{F}_{2^8}$ such that $x + \bar{x} = 0xff$.*

The AES S-box has no fixed point, that is $S(x) \neq x$ and no opposite fixed points, that is $S(x) \neq \bar{x}$) for all $x \in \mathbb{F}_{2^8}$ (see [6]). Similarly, the new S-box has no fixed points and no opposite fixed points.

4.6 Algebraic Complexity of the New S-box

Let S be an S-box over $\mathbb{F}_{2^n}$. Then S is completely defined by the set $\{(x_i, y_i) \mid x_i \in \mathbb{F}_{2^n}, \ y_i = S(x_i)\}$. A polynomial expression for S is determined by Lagrange's interpolation polynomial

$$P(x) = \sum_{i=1}^{n} y_i L_i(x), \quad L_i(x) = \frac{\prod_{j \neq i}(x - x_j)}{\prod_{j \neq i}(x_i - x_j)}.$$

The polynomial $P(x)$ is of degree of at most $2^n - 1$ and the number of its non-zero monomials is called the *algebraic complexity*. For AES, the polynomial is [4]

$$P(x) = 05x^{254} + 09x^{253} + f9x^{251} + 25x^{247} + f4x^{239} + 01x^{223} + b5x^{191}$$
$$+ 8fx^{127} + 63,$$

Table 6. Periodicity of the new S-box

	0	1	2	3	4	5	6	7	8	9	a	b	c	d	e	f
0	256	256	256	256	256	256	256	256	256	256	256	256	256	256	256	256
1	256	256	256	256	256	256	256	256	256	256	256	256	256	256	256	256
2	256	256	256	256	256	256	256	256	256	256	256	256	256	256	256	256
3	256	256	256	256	256	256	256	256	256	256	256	256	256	256	256	256
4	256	256	256	256	256	256	256	256	256	256	256	256	256	256	256	256
5	256	256	256	256	256	256	256	256	256	256	256	256	256	256	256	256
6	256	256	256	256	256	256	256	256	256	256	256	256	256	256	256	256
7	256	256	256	256	256	256	256	256	256	256	256	256	256	256	256	256
8	256	256	256	256	256	256	256	256	256	256	256	256	256	256	256	256
9	256	256	256	256	256	256	256	256	256	256	256	256	256	256	256	256
a	256	256	256	256	256	256	256	256	256	256	256	256	256	256	256	256
b	256	256	256	256	256	256	256	256	256	256	256	256	256	256	256	256
c	256	256	256	256	256	256	256	256	256	256	256	256	256	256	256	256
d	256	256	256	256	256	256	256	256	256	256	256	256	256	256	256	256
e	256	256	256	256	256	256	256	256	256	256	256	256	256	256	256	256
f	256	256	256	256	256	256	256	256	256	256	256	256	256	256	256	256

which shows that the algebraic complexity for AES is 9. For the new S-box, the polynomial is of the form

$$P(x) = \sum_{i=0}^{255} a_i x^i,$$

where the list of the coefficients a_i is listed in Table 7. From this table, we see that the algebraic complexity of the new S-box is 255, which is optimal and makes it more resistant to possible algebraic attacks than the AES S-box.

Similarly, the algebraic expression of the inverse of the new S-box is presented in Table 8 and has 254 monomials which is almost optimal.

4.7 Strict Avalanche Criterion (SAC) of the New S-box

In [18], Webster and Tavares introduced an important criterion for strong S-boxes, called strict avalanche criterion (SAC). This criterion states that a single bit change in the input of a strong S-box should change the output bit with probability approaching $\frac{1}{2}$.

Definition 4. *A vectorial Boolean function* $S : \mathbb{F}_{2^n} \to \mathbb{F}_{2^n}$ *satisfies SAC if and only if for all* i, $0 \leq i \leq n-1$,

$$\sum_{x \in \mathbb{F}_{2^n}} f(x) \oplus S(x \oplus \alpha_i) = \left(2^{n-1}, \ldots, 2^{n-1}\right),$$

Table 7. Algebraic expression of the new S-box

	f	e	d	c	b	a	9	8	7	6	5	4	3	2	1	0
f	00	b6	6c	30	3e	32	e5	06	68	b2	9c	8e	54	b9	0d	c8
e	01	c0	6d	aa	3a	0c	1a	7e	eb	52	48	4e	b5	cf	8a	5c
d	56	5b	1d	0b	42	43	4d	06	5c	15	37	49	02	ea	e9	d6
c	c4	35	b7	f2	ca	d0	0c	9a	28	ba	1c	8a	d7	ef	31	be
b	2e	ac	b5	6e	b1	6c	18	61	a3	06	8f	c4	10	0e	3b	c1
a	ff	55	f8	60	99	0c	b8	3a	88	90	ad	c6	61	83	a7	16
9	a4	48	5a	1b	a4	1f	b8	c4	3c	af	d5	33	4d	90	7d	60
8	cf	65	7e	5d	bb	43	b4	41	95	6c	0c	86	e0	02	b2	93
7	a2	6f	c6	e1	1d	71	6a	93	9d	12	c6	9f	d4	5e	c7	84
6	c3	84	1f	38	6e	a9	52	ea	98	97	ec	1f	bd	12	c4	32
5	49	ae	1a	63	b4	fe	7b	b4	e7	f4	04	2b	f8	e4	f2	47
4	fa	e3	04	c6	72	f8	fb	2c	bf	c8	e6	e1	0c	2a	2d	4a
3	e5	c3	73	0c	99	8a	8d	a9	25	39	16	c1	1b	3f	c0	19
2	5d	fd	9b	5d	fb	1d	f9	c7	a8	c4	03	48	63	63	15	83
1	f6	50	18	50	3c	57	96	0b	dc	dd	41	a0	fd	05	e7	50
0	13	66	d8	f8	fa	ea	93	72	a7	1d	5b	5e	0b	75	45	36

where the binary representation of $\alpha_i \in \mathbb{F}_{2^n}$ is a vector of length n with a 1 in the ith position and 0 elsewhere.

Consequently, an S-box having a value of SAC closer to $(2^{n-1}, \ldots, 2^{n-1})$ has a good SAC property. Table 9 gives the SAC values of the new S-box and Table 10 gives the Sac values of the AES S-box.

From Table 9 and Table 10, we see that the mean value for SAC for the new S-box is 128.625 while it is 129.25 for the AES S-box.

4.8   Distance to SAC of the New S-box

In general, the SAC criterion is not absolutely performed by an S-box. A practical way to measure the deviation of the SAC the S-box is to compute the distance to sac.

Definition 5. *Let $S : \mathbb{F}_{2^n} \to \mathbb{F}_{2^n}$ be the function defining an S-box such that*

$$S(x_{n-1}, \ldots, x_0) = (f_{n-1}(x), \ldots, f_0(x_0)).$$

The distance to SAC of S is the value

$$DSAC(S) = \sum_{j=0}^{n-1} \sum_{i=0}^{n-1} \left| \sum_{x \in \mathbb{F}_{2^n}} f_i(x \oplus \alpha_j) \oplus f_i(x) - 2^{n-1} \right|.$$

Table 8. Algebraic expression of the inverse of the new S-box

	f	e	d	c	b	a	9	8	7	6	5	4	3	2	1	0
f	00	b6	f2	44	37	81	c5	73	49	ff	bb	0d	7e	c8	8c	3a
e	01	b7	f3	45	36	80	c4	72	48	fe	ba	0c	7f	c9	8d	3b
d	d7	61	25	93	e0	56	12	a4	9e	28	6c	da	a9	1f	5b	ed
c	d6	60	24	92	e1	57	13	a5	9f	29	6d	db	a8	1e	5a	ec
b	65	d3	97	21	52	e4	a0	16	2c	9a	de	68	1b	ad	e9	5f
a	64	d2	96	20	53	e5	a1	17	2d	9b	df	69	1a	ac	e8	5e
9	b2	04	40	f6	85	33	77	c1	fb	4d	09	bf	cc	7a	3e	88
8	b3	05	41	f7	84	32	76	c0	fa	4c	08	be	cd	7b	3f	89
7	20	96	d2	64	17	a1	e5	53	69	df	9b	2d	5e	e8	ac	1a
6	21	97	d3	65	16	a0	e4	52	68	de	9a	2c	5f	e9	ad	1b
5	f7	41	05	b3	c0	76	32	84	be	08	4c	fa	89	3f	7b	cd
4	f6	40	04	b2	c1	77	33	85	bf	09	4d	fb	88	3e	7a	cc
3	45	f3	b7	01	72	c4	80	36	0c	ba	fe	48	3b	8d	c9	7f
2	44	f2	b6	00	73	c5	81	37	0d	bb	ff	49	3a	8c	c8	7e
1	92	24	60	d6	a5	13	57	e1	db	6d	29	9f	ec	5a	1e	a8
0	93	25	61	d7	a4	12	56	e0	da	6c	28	9e	ed	5b	1f	53

Table 9. SAC of the new S-box

α_i	Bit 7	Bit 6	Bit 5	Bit 4	Bit 3	Bit 2	Bit 2	Bit 1
00000001	120	120	132	136	132	132	136	120
00000010	136	140	132	128	124	124	132	140
00000100	128	120	136	128	136	132	116	124
00001000	136	128	132	132	132	120	128	120
00010000	128	140	124	124	116	128	128	116
00100000	136	120	128	132	132	132	128	132
01000000	128	128	144	124	128	116	120	120
10000000	124	132	132	124	128	132	124	128

where the binary representation of $\alpha_j \in \mathbb{F}_{2^n}$ is a vector of length n with a 1 in the jth position and 0 elsewhere.

A strong S-box should have a small DSAC. From Table 10, we find that DSAC for the AES S-box is 432 (see [5]) while Table 9 shows that DSAC for the new S-box 328.

Table 10. SAC of the AES S-box

α_i	Bit 7	Bit 6	Bit 5	Bit 4	Bit 3	Bit 2	Bit 2	Bit 1
00000001	128	116	124	116	144	116	132	132
00000010	136	128	116	124	128	144	124	120
00000100	128	136	128	124	120	128	132	132
00001000	140	128	136	128	116	120	136	136
00010000	136	140	128	128	132	116	128	116
00100000	136	136	140	120	120	132	132	116
01000000	124	136	136	120	132	120	136	136
10000000	132	124	136	124	136	132	144	132

5   Comparison with Existing S-boxes

In Table 11, we listed the performance of the AES S box, the S-box proposed by Cui et al. [5] and the new S-box. The table shows that, for all cryptographic criteria, the performance of the new S-box is equal or better than the former ones and they are closer to the performances of an optimal S-box. This implies that the new S-box has better security than the former ones and is suitable for use in AES.

Table 11. Comparison of the new S-box with two former S-boxes

Criterion	AES S-box	Cui et al. S-box [5]	New S-box	Optimal value
Linear cryptanalysis	112	112	**112**	120
Differential cryptanalysis	4	4	**4**	4
Periodicity	Less than 87	256	**256**	256
Algebraic complexity	9	255	**255**	255
Inverse algebraic complexity	255	253	**254**	255
Mean of SAC	129.25	127.9375	**128.25**	128
Distance to SAC	432	372	**328**	0
Maximal BIC	0.13	0.13	**0.12**	0

6   Conclusion

In this paper, we presented a new S-box for the AES encryption scheme and analyzed its security by studying the main cryptographic criteria. For all the criteria, the performances of the new S-box are at least as good as the performances of the existing S-boxes. More specifically, the new S-box has better distance to SAC, better BIC and better algebraic complexity.

References

1. Biham, E., Shamir, A.: Differential cryptanalysis of DES-like cryptosystems. J. Cryptol. **4**(1), 3–72 (1991). https://doi.org/10.1007/BF00630563
2. Carlet, C.: Vectorial boolean functions for cryptography. In: Crama, Y., Hammer, P. (eds.) Boolean Models and Methods in Mathematics, Computer Science, and Engineering. Encyclopedia of Mathematics and its Applications, pp. 398–470. Cambridge University Press, Cambridge (2010)
3. Canteaut, A.: Lecture Notes on Cryptographic Boolean Functions, 10 March 2016. https://www.rocq.inria.fr/secret/Anne.Canteaut/poly.pdf
4. Cui, L., Cao, Y.: A new S-box structure named affine-power-affine. Int. J. Innov. Comput. Inf. Control **3**(3), 751–759 (2007)
5. Cui, J., Huang, L., Zhong, H., Chang, C., Yang, W.: An improved AES S-box and its performance analysis. Int. J. Innov. Comput. Inf. Control **75**(A), 2291–2302 (2011)
6. Daemen J., Rijmen V.: AES Proposal: Rijndael (1999). https://csrc.nist.gov/csrc/media/projects/cryptographic-standards-and-guidelines/documents/aes-development/rijndael-ammended.pdf
7. Data Encryption Standard, National Bureau of Standards, NBS FIPS PUB 46. U.S. Department of Commerce (1977)
8. Detombe, J., Tavares, S.: Constructing large cryptographically strong S-boxes. In: Seberry, J., Zheng, Y. (eds.) AUSCRYPT 1992. LNCS, vol. 718, pp. 165–181. Springer, Heidelberg (1993). https://doi.org/10.1007/3-540-57220-1_60
9. Dragomir, I.R., Lazar, M.: Generating and testing the components of a block cipher. In: 8th International Conference on Electronics, Computers and Artificial Intelligence (ECAI), Ploiesti, pp. 1–4 (2016)
10. Juremi, J., Mahmod, R., Sulaiman, S.: A proposal for improving AES S-box with rotation and key-dependent. In: Proceedings of the International Conference on Digital Cyber Security, CyberWarfare and Digital Forensic, Kuala Lumpur, Malaysia, pp. 26–28 (2012)
11. Ma, H., Liu, L.: Algebraic expression for AES S-box and InvS-box. Comput. Eng. **32**(18), 149–151 (2006)
12. Matsui, M.: Linear cryptanalysis method for DES cipher. In: Helleseth, T. (ed.) EUROCRYPT 1993. LNCS, vol. 765, pp. 386–397. Springer, Heidelberg (1994). https://doi.org/10.1007/3-540-48285-7_33
13. National Institute of Standards and Technology: Federal Information Processing Standards Publication 197: Announcing the Advanced Encryption Standard (AES). http://csrc.nist.gov/publications/fips/fips197/fips-197.pdf. Accessed 09 June 2019
14. Prouff, E.: DPA attacks and S-boxes. In: Gilbert, H., Handschuh, H. (eds.) FSE 2005. LNCS, vol. 3557, pp. 424–441. Springer, Heidelberg (2005). https://doi.org/10.1007/11502760_29
15. Sahoo, O.B., Kole, D.K., Rahaman, H.: An optimized S-box for advanced encryption standard (AES) design. In: Proceedings of the International Conference on Advanced Computer Communication, Chennai, India, pp. 3–5 (2012)
16. Wang, Y.B.: Analysis of structure of AES and its S-box. J. PLA Univ. Sci. Technol. **3**(3), 13–17 (2002)
17. Wang, H., Zheng, H., Hu, B., Tang, H.: Improved lightweight encryption algorithm based on optimized S-box. In: 2013 International Conference on Computational and Information Sciences, Shiyang, pp. 734–737 (2013)

18. Webster, A.F., Tavares, S.E.: On the design of S-boxes. In: Williams, H.C. (ed.) CRYPTO 1985. LNCS, vol. 218, pp. 523–534. Springer, Heidelberg (1986). https:// doi.org/10.1007/3-540-39799-X_41
19. Wilson, R.A.: The Finite Simple Groups. Graduate Texts in Mathematics, vol. 251. Springer, London (2009). https://doi.org/10.1007/978-1-84800-988-2
20. Zahid, A.H., Arshad, M.J.: An innovative design of substitution-boxes using cubic polynomial mapping. Math. Comput. Sci. Symmetry **11**(3), 437 (2019)
21. Zahid, A.H., Arshad, M.J., Ahmad, M.: A novel construction of efficient substitution-boxes using cubic fractional transformation. Entropy **21**(3), 245 (2019)

Galaxy: A Family of Stream-Cipher-Based Space-Hard Ciphers

Yuji Koike[1]([✉]), Kosei Sakamoto[1], Takuya Hayashi[2], and Takanori Isobe[1,3]

[1] University of Hyogo, Hyogo, Japan
{aa19s503,takanori.isobe}@ai.u-hyogo.ac.jp, k.sakamoto0728@gmail.com
[2] Digital Garage, Inc., Tokyo, Japan
contact@tak884.jp
[3] National Institute of Information and Communications Technology, Tokyo, Japan

Abstract. Whitebox cryptography seeks to ensure the security of cryptographic algorithms against adversaries who have unlimited access to the environments for their implementation. At ACM CCS 2015, Bogdanov and Isobe proposed a security notion called space hardness and a secure block cipher named SPACE in the whitebox setting. SPACE is a table-based cryptographic primitive whose table comprises the pairs of inputs to a block cipher such as AES and the corresponding outputs. In line with SPACE, other whitebox cryptographic schemes were proposed and offer sufficient security as SPACE does. However, there is still room for improvement in the performance of their encryption and table generation. In this paper, we propose a new family of whitebox cryptographic primitives called Galaxy to enhance the performance of the encryption and table generation. Galaxy employs a stream cipher to generate the table instead of a block cipher. The security of Galaxy against key-extraction attacks in the whitebox setting is reduced to the key-extraction problem for the stream cipher in the blackbox setting. Additionally, we utilize type-2 generalized Feistel network with optimal shuffle layers for the algorithm of Galaxy to improve the encryption performance. Type-2 generalized Feistel network enables parallel table lookups in the algorithm of Galaxy. As a result, we successfully increase the speed of encryption by 1.3–15 times. Besides, when we use chacha for table generation of Galaxy and AES for other existing block-cipher-based whitebox schemes, we can create the table of Galaxy 1.5–10 times faster than that of other existing whitebox schemes.

Keywords: Whitebox cryptography · Space hardness · Code lifting · Decomposition · Key extraction · Block cipher · Stream cipher

1 Introduction

Whitebox cryptography, first introduced by Chow et al. in 2002 [6], aims to protect cryptographic implementation in software under the circumstances where

This study was done while the third author was working at the National Institute of Information and Communications Technology, Japan.

© Springer Nature Switzerland AG 2020
J. K. Liu and H. Cui (Eds.): ACISP 2020, LNCS 12248, pp. 142–159, 2020.
https://doi.org/10.1007/978-3-030-55304-3_8

adversaries have unlimited access to the environments for their implementation. This situation is called whitebox setting, where adversaries are assumed to have control over the execution environment and allowed to observe and modify internal values of the cryptographic algorithm, in contrast to the standard setting called the blackbox setting where it is assumed that the adversaries can only observe the input and output of cryptographic algorithms. Whitebox cryptography draws more attention from application vendors, considering the immense demand for security solutions in electronic devices without hardware support such as hardware security module and secure enclave.

Whitebox cryptography, precisely the implementation of DES and AES in the whitebox context, was first introduced by Chow et al. [6,7] in 2002. Their method is to represent algorithms of DES and AES in the form of continual lookups in the tables which are created by secret key and components of cryptographic operation (i.e. DES or AES). After these pioneering works, several derived whitebox implementations were proposed, but all of them up to date were broken by key extraction and table-decomposition attacks.

At ACM CCS 2015, Bogdanov and Isobe proposed a security notion called space hardness and a secure block cipher named SPACE in the whitebox setting [2]. SPACE is a table-based block cipher whose table is composed of some pairs of the input to an underlying block cipher such as AES and the corresponding output. SPACE uses the table as a large secret key. In SPACE, the difficulty to extract the master key used to generate the table in the whitebox setting is reduced to the difficulty to recover the secret key of the underlying block cipher such as AES in the blackbox setting. Space hardness is a security notion which shows the relationship between the amount of stolen table data and the corresponding security level. SPACE provides $(T/4, 128)$-space hardness. This means even if the adversary successfully steals one fourth of the table for SPACE, the probability that (s)he, with knowledge of the partial table, can correctly encrypt (decrypt) a plaintext (ciphertext) is 2^{-128}. There also exist other symmetric cryptographic schemes which are secure in the whitebox setting, such as White-Block [9], and WEM [5]. WhiteBlock alternates with table lookups and a call to a block cipher (e.g. AES) as a permutation in each round. The way to generate the table in WhiteBlock is quite similar to the way in SPACE with the slight difference of which bits to discard. Thus, just like SPACE, the security of WhiteBlock against key extraction in the whitebox setting is reduced to the key recovery problem for the underlying block cipher such as AES. Similar to WhiteBlock, WEM looks up values in tables and calls a round-reduced block cipher (e.g. five-round AES) interchangeably. Different from other whitebox-friendly block ciphers, WEM uses the Fisher-Yates algorithm seeded by outputs of a block cipher (e.g. AES) to create a table. All the existing dedicated block ciphers for the whitebox setting offer sufficient security both in the whitebox context and the standard blackbox context.

However, there is still room for enhancement in the performance of their encryption and table generation. For those ciphers, generating their tables costs too much computational resources. For example, SPACE and WhiteBlock require many calls to a block cipher such as AES to generate a table, i.e., they require encryption of a long message for their table generation. WEM takes another strategy for table generation: it employs the Fisher-Yates algorithm seeded by outputs of a block cipher such as AES, but this algorithm itself is inefficient. As a consequence, they are not applicable to the protocols which require frequent updates of the secret key, such as SSL/TLS, QUIC transport protocol [12], and Signal protocol [13]. Regarding the encryption performance, SPACE is a target heavy generalized Feistel network, which prevents it from parallel table lookups in each round. As a result, SPACE requires at least 128 rounds for the encryption (decryption) to ensure sufficient security. Although the algorithm of WhiteBlock and WEM enables parallel table lookups, they call a full-round block cipher or round-reduced block cipher as a permutation, which has a negative influence on the encryption performance.

To improve the performance of encryption and table generation, we propose Galaxy, a new family of whitebox secure block ciphers. In Galaxy, we employ a stream cipher as an underlying cipher to generate the table. Stream ciphers generally facilitate faster encryption of a long message than block ciphers do in software, which enables faster table generation. In addition, utilizing a stream cipher to generate a table for Galaxy makes it possible to reduce the security of Galaxy against key extraction in the whitebox setting to the difficulty of key recovery attacks on the stream cipher in the standard blackbox setting.

However, utilizing a stream cipher as an underlying cipher for Galaxy brings a single disadvantage: a table made out of output from the stream cipher is not a bijective mapping, which prevents us from choosing SPN as a structure of algorithm for Galaxy. Therefore, we employ the Feistel structure for Galaxy to deal with this problem. Specifically, we use type-2 Generalized Feistel Network (abbreviated as GFN-2) for the algorithm of Galaxy. To optimize the encryption speed, we exploit optimal permutations for GFN-2 found in previous works [4,8,15,16]. We introduce three instances of Galaxy: Galaxy-8, Galaxy-16, and Galaxy-32, and present security evaluations of them both in the blackbox context and the whitebox context. In the blackbox context, we evaluate the security against the differential attack, linear attack, impossible differential attack, and integral attack by Mix Integer Linear Programming (abbreviated as MILP) [14]. In the whitebox context, we evaluate the security against key extraction attacks and the code lifting attack. In addition, we give experimental measurements of these implementations whose total numbers of rounds are based on the security evaluation results. It is shown that while keeping the same security level, Galaxy achieves speed-ups of approximately 1.3–15 times in encryption and 1.8–10 times in table generation, compared with SPACE, WhiteBlock, and WEM.

Note that taking advantage of a stream cipher as an underlying cipher may reduce the performance of encryption (decryption) in the blackbox setting i.e., with non-table-based implementation. However, in a lot of real world applications such as Digital Rights Management (abbreviated as DRM) or Host Card Emulation (abbreviated as HCE), whitebox ciphers are used in the whitebox context and implemented with the table. Therefore, the implementation of Galaxy in the blackbox context is out of our focus.

2 Preliminaries

In this section, we introduce a security notion used to evaluate the security of Galaxy, and give a brief description of other existing space-hard ciphers.

2.1 Space Hardness

At ACM CCS 2015, Bogdanov and Isobe introduced a new security notion called space hardness to evaluate the difficulty for compression of cryptographic implementations while keeping the same functionality. The definition of space hardness is given as follows.

Definition 1 ((M, Z)-space hardness [2]). *Block cipher E_K is an (M, Z)-space hard cipher if it is computationally difficult to encrypt (decrypt) randomly chosen plaintext (ciphertext) with the probability of more than 2^{-Z} in the situation where the adversary is given code (table) size of less than M.*

Space hardness aims at measuring the security against the code lifting attack where the adversary copies the implementation code and uses it as an effective large secret key in a stand-alone way. For instance, $(T/4, 128)$-space hard cipher E_K denotes that even if the adversary obtains one fourth of T, the (s)he can not correctly encrypt (decrypt) the randomly drawn plaintext (ciphertext) with the probability of more than 2^{-128}, where T is the code size (table size) of block cipher E_K.

2.2 Space-Hard Block Cipher SPACE

Bogdanov and Isobe proposed SPACE, which is a block cipher with the property of space hardness [2]. SPACE is an l-line target-heavy generalized Feistel network (shown in Fig. 1) which encrypts an n-bit plaintext with a secret key K into an n-bit ciphertext where the size of each line is n_a ($= n/l$) bits.

Let the state in r-th round of total rounds R be $X^r = \{x_0^r, x_1^r, ..., x_{l-1}^r\}$, $x_i^r \in \{0,1\}^{n_a}$. Then, it is updated as:

$$X^{r+1} = (F_{n_a}^r(x_0^r) \oplus (x_1^r \parallel x_2^r \parallel ... \parallel x_{l-1}^r)) \parallel x_0^r,$$

where $\parallel$ denotes concatenation, and $F_{n_a}^r$ is a following n_a bit to $n_b (= n - n_a)$ bit function (shown in Fig. 2):

$$F_{n_a}^r(x) = (msb_{n_b}(E_K(C_0 \parallel x))) \oplus r,$$

where E_K is a block cipher which takes an n-bit input and a k-bit secret key K, $msb_{n_b}(x)$ takes the most significant n_b bits of x, and C_0 denotes n_b-bit zero.

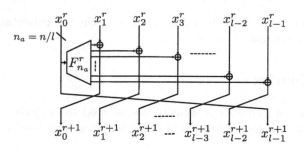

Fig. 1. Round function of SPACE

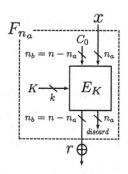

Fig. 2. F function of SPACE: $F_{n_a}^r(x) = (msb_{n_b}(E_K(C_0 \parallel x))) \oplus r$

Let $F_{n_a}(x) = (msb_{n_b}(E_K(C_0 \parallel x)))$. Then, F_{n_a} is implemented in the whitebox setting as F'_{n_a} which is a table comprising 2^{n_a} entries of n_a-bit inputs x and the corresponding n_b-bit outputs $F_{n_a}(x)$, i.e., each of the 2^{n_a} entries for F'_{n_a} is $(x, F_{n_a}(x)) : x \in \{0,1\}^{n_a}, F_{n_a}(x) \in \{0,1\}^{n_b}$. In the whitebox setting, SPACE uses the only F'_{n_a} as the secret key.

Variants of SPACE. SPACE has following four variants of SPACE-(n_a, R) with different table size where R is the total number of round.

- SPACE-(8, 300): $n = 128$, $l = 16$, $n_a = 8$, $F_8^r : \{0,1\}^8 \to \{0,1\}^{120}$
- SPACE-(16, 128): $n = 128$, $l = 8$, $n_a = 16$, $F_{16}^r : \{0,1\}^{16} \to \{0,1\}^{112}$
- SPACE-(24, 128): $n = 128$, $l = 16$, $n_a = 24$, $F_{24}^r : \{0,1\}^{24} \to \{0,1\}^{104}$
- SPACE-(32, 128): $n = 128$, $l = 4$, $n_a = 32$, $F_{32}^r : \{0,1\}^{32} \to \{0,1\}^{96}$

In the whitebox setting in order to generate table F'_{n_a} of each variant, the underlying cipher E_K such as AES is called 2^8 times 2^{16} times 2^{24} times, and 2^{32} times for SPACE-(8, 300), SPACE-(16, 128), SPACE-(24, 128), and SPACE-(32, 128), respectively.

Security of SPACE. The security of SPACE against key recovery attacks in the whitebox setting is reduced to the key-extraction security of the underlying block cipher E_K in the blackbox setting. Therefore, as long as E_K is secure against key recovery attacks in the blackbox setting, it is computationally difficult to mount such attacks on SPACE in the whitebox setting. Moreover, each variant of SPACE provides $(T/4, 128)$-space hardness where T denotes the size of table F'_{n_a}. This means even if the adversary successfully obtains one fourth of the table of SPACE, the probability that (s)he can correctly encrypt (decrypt) a plaintext (ciphertext) is 2^{-128}. For a better understanding, let me give the decryption phase in SPACE as an instance. The decryption in SPACE is based on continual table lookups, and each table lookup is independent. (the encryption in SPACE is same as the decryption). If the adversary successfully extracts the entire table, the probability that (s)he can produce a correct intermediate value in each round by a table lookup with the stolen table is 1, and (s)he can always decrypt arbitrary ciphertexts. However, in the case of $(T/4, 128)$-space hardness, (s)he has only one fourth of the table. Assuming that the adversary has to look up a value in the stolen table based on the pseudo random input each round, the probability that (s)he can produce a correct intermediate value in each round by querying the value in the stolen table is $1/4(=2^{-2})$. Hence, the probability that (s)he can produce all the correct intermediate values and successfully decrypt arbitrary ciphertexts of SPACE is $(1/4)^R(=(2^{-2})^R)$, where R denotes total rounds of cryptographic operation for SPACE, and SPACE has enough rounds R to ensure $(T/4, 128)$-space hardness.

2.3   Other Existing Space-Hard Ciphers Based on Block Cihper

WhiteBlock. At ASIACRYPT 2016, Fouque et al. proposed another secure block cipher in whitebox setting WhiteBlock [9]. It is one of Feistel ciphers which encrypts a 128-bit plaintext with multiple secret keys into a 128-bit ciphertext where the size of each secret key is 128 bits. The structure of WhiteBlock is made up of two components: it alternates with table lookups and a call to a block cipher (such as AES) as a permutation in each round. The way to generate a table in WhiteBlock is quite similar to the one as in SPACE with a slight difference of which bits to truncate. However different from SPACE, it generates several tables with different secret keys and uses them as large secret keys.

WEM. At CT-RSA 2017, Cho et al. proposed an Even-Mansour-based whitebox block cipher called WEM [5]. It is an Even-Mansour-like cipher which encrypts a 128-bit plaintext with a secret key into a 128-bit ciphertext where the size of the secret key is 128 bits. The difference between the Even-Mansour structure and WEM is that WEM replaces key addition operation in the Even-Mansour structure with table lookups and employs a round-reduced block cipher (e.g. five-round AES as in their original paper) as a public permutation. The value of the secret key for the round-reduced block cipher which is the public permutation is 128-bit zero. The several tables in WEM are created by the Fisher-Yates algorithm seeded by the outputs of an underlying block cipher in counter mode (e.g. AES-CTR).

SPNbox. At ASIACRYPT 2016, Bogdanov, Isobe, and Tischhauser proposed another dedicated block cipher called SPNbox for the whitebox setting [3]. It is an AES-based block cipher which encrypts a 128-bit plaintext with a secret key into a 128-bit ciphertext where the size of the secret key is 128 bits. The algorithm of SPNbox is composed of three layers: a nonlinear substitution layer, a linear diffusion layer, and an affine layer. In the nonlinear substitution layer, several values are queried in a single table which is generated from the combination of AES S-box, a diffusion operation based on MixColumns operation of AES, and the secret key.

SPNbox is not a generic whitebox cipher in the sense that it can not deploy any well-studied block ciphers (e.g. AES) as an underlying cipher for table generation. This is because SPNbox employs a dedicated cipher as an underlying cipher for table generation which has gone through a bare minimum of security evaluation so far. As a consequence, in contrast to the other existing whitebox ciphers, the key extraction security of SPNbox in the whitebox context is reduced to the key extraction problem not for well-studied block ciphers such as AES, but for the "poorly-studied" block cipher.

Therefore, SPNbox is out of our focus when we compare the performance of Galaxy with other whitebox ciphers.

2.4   Downside of Existing Block-Cipher-Based Space-Hard Ciphers

Existing block-cipher-based space-hard ciphers offer sufficient security both in the whitebox setting and blackbox setting. However, they have the following downsides.

1. Inefficiency of generating a table.
2. Inefficiency of encryption/decryption.

Regarding the first one, assuming AES is the underlying block cipher E_K, SPACE-32 requires 2^{32} times of AES encryption calls to generate a table. Even worse, WhiteBlock-32 requires 2^{33} times of AES encryption calls, as it generates two tables. When it comes to WEM, it uses the Fisher-Yates algorithm seeded by outputs of the block cipher such as AES, and the Fisher-Yates algorithm itself is inefficient. Due to this downside, they are not applicable to the protocols which require frequent key updates, such as SSL/TLS, QUIC transport protocol [12], and Signal protocol [13].

Regarding the second one, since SPACE is a target heavy generalized Feistel network, it requires at least 128 rounds for encryption (decryption) to ensure sufficient security, which is inefficient. The other two whitebox ciphers have much fewer rounds than SPACE does, but they use a block cipher (full rounds or five rounds of AES in their original paper) as a permutation, which has a negative impact on the performance of the cryptographic algorithm. Note that FPL, which was published very recently at CT-RSA 2020 [11] has the same downsides

3   Design Goal

In this paper, we propose a new family of space-hard ciphers called Galaxy, which addresses the issues mentioned in Sect. 2.4.

First of all, in order to cope with the 1st issue, we utilize the **stream cipher** rather than the block cipher as the underlying cipher. While WEM uses outputs of the block cipher as seeds to generate the random permutation (WEM indirectly uses outputs of the block cipher for table generation), Galaxy directly utilizes the output of a stream cipher for table generation. It enables that the security of Galaxy against key extraction from the table in the whitebox setting is reduced to the problem of key recovery for stream ciphers in the blackbox setting. In addition, as opposed to block ciphers, stream ciphers can output a sequence of key stream with flexible stream size, which enables us to generate the table for a cryptographic algorithm without truncation of any bits of output. Besides, especially for software, stream ciphers generally enable faster encryption of a long message than block ciphers do.

Note that utilizing a stream cipher as the underlying cipher may reduce the performance of encryption (decryption) in the blackbox setting i.e., with non-table-based implementation, but in a lot of real world applications such as DRM or HCE, whitebox ciphers are used in the whitebox context and implemented with the table. Therefore, the implementation of Galaxy in the blackbox setting is out of our focus.

Moreover, in order to address the 2nd issue, we employ **Type-2 Generalized Feistel Network** for the cryptographic algorithm, instead of target heavy generalized Feistel network. The rationale behind this change is that a table based on stream cipher is not a bijective mapping, which limits our choices for the cryptographic algorithm of Galaxy to Feistel structure. Especially, it is well known that type-2 generalized Feistel network ensures sufficient security in fewer rounds [4,8,15]. Besides, to optimize the encryption performance, we exploit the optimal permutations for 4-, 8-, and 16-line type-2 generalized Feistel network found in previous works [4,8,15,16].

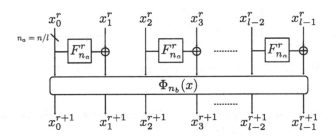

Fig. 3. Round function of Galaxy

4   Specification of Galaxy

Galaxy is an l-line type-2 generalized Feistel network (shown in Fig. 3) which encrypts an n-bit plaintext with secret key K into an n-bit ciphertext where the size of each line is n_a $(=n/l)$. Let the state in r-th round be $X^r = \{x_0^r, x_1^r, ..., x_{l-1}^r\}$, $x_i^r \in \{0,1\}^{n_a}$. Then, it is updated as:

$$X^{r+1} = \Phi(F_{n_a}^r(x_0^r) \oplus x_1^r \parallel F_{n_a}^r(x_2^r) \oplus x_3^r \parallel ... \parallel F_{n_a}^r(x_{n-1}^r) \oplus x_n^r),$$

where $\Phi_{n_b}(x)$ denotes n_b $(=n_a/8)$ byte-wise permutation of x, and $\parallel$ denotes concatenation. $F_{n_a}^r$ is a n_a bit to n_a bit function that derives from a stream cipher, and it is defined (and shown in Fig. 4) as:

$$F_{n_a}^r(x) = F_{n_a}(x) \oplus r,$$
$$F_{n_a}(x) = \phi_{n_a}(keygen(K), x), \tag{1}$$

where $keygen(K)$ denotes a sequence of key stream that derives from an underlying stream cipher with k-bit secret key K, and $\phi_{n_a}(S, x)$ takes n_a-bit starting from the $(x \cdot n_a)$-th bit in S (which is expressed as $S[x \cdot n_a : (x+1) \cdot n_a]$ in Algorithm 2). In Galaxy, $F_{n_a}(x)$ is implemented as a table.

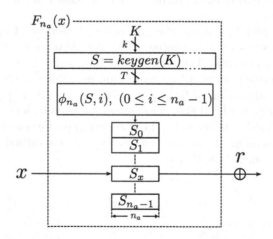

Fig. 4. Table generation function: $F_{n_a}^r(x) = F_{n_a}(x) \oplus r$

The algorithms of encryption and table generation for Galaxy are given in Algorithm 1 and Algorithm 2 below.

4.1   Variants of Galaxy

Galaxy has the following variants with different table size, and the algorithm of each variant is shown in Fig. 5.

Algorithm 1. Galaxy Algorithm

$X^0 \Leftarrow$ INPUT
$i, j \Leftarrow 0$
$\{x_0^0, x_1^0, ..., x_{l-1}^0\} \Leftarrow$ SPLIT(X^0) //divide input into l elements
while $i < R$ **do**
    while $j < l/2$ **do**
        $x_{2 \cdot j+1}^i \Leftarrow x_{2 \cdot j+1}^i \oplus (F_{n_a}'(x_{2 \cdot j}^i) \oplus i)$
        $j \Leftarrow j + 1$
    end while
    $(x_0^i, x_1^i, ..., x_{l-1}^i) \Leftarrow \Phi(x_0^i, x_1^i, ..., x_{l-1}^i)$ //permute the elements
    $\{x_0^{i+1}, x_1^{i+1}, ..., x_{l-1}^{i+1}\} \Leftarrow (x_0^i, x_1^i, ..., x_{l-1}^0)$ //copy to the state of next round
    $i \Leftarrow i + 1$
end while
$X^R \Leftarrow$ COMBINE$(\{x_0^R, x_1^R, ..., x_{l-1}^R\})$ //combine the elements
OUTPUT $\Leftarrow X^R$

Algorithm 2. Table Generation

$S \Leftarrow keygen(K, s)$ //generate s-bit key stream
$i \Leftarrow 0$
while $i \leq 2^{n_a} - 1$ **do**
    $F_{n_a}'(i) \Leftarrow S[i \cdot n_a : (i+1) \cdot n_a]$ // $= \phi_{n_a}(S, i)$ defined in formula (1)
    $i \Leftarrow i + 1$
end while

- Galaxy-$(8, R) : n = 128, l = 16, n_a = 8, n_b = 1, F_8^r : \{0,1\}^8 \to \{0,1\}^8$,
  $\Phi_{n_b}(x) = \{5, 0, 1, 4, 7, 12, 3, 8, 13, 6, 9, 2, 15, 10, 11, 14\}$
- Galaxy-$(16, R) : n = 128, l = 8, n_a = 16, n_b = 2, F_{16}^r : \{0,1\}^{16} \to \{0,1\}^{16}$,
  $\Phi_{n_b}(x) = \{3, 0, 1, 4, 7, 2, 5, 6\}$
- Galaxy-$(32, R) : n = 128, l = 4, n_a = 32, n_b = 4, F_{32}^r : \{0,1\}^{32} \to \{0,1\}^{32}$,
  $\Phi_{n_b}(x) = \{3, 0, 1, 2\}$

The table size T for each variant is estimated as $(2^{n_a} \cdot n_a)$ bits. Thus, the size of table $F_{n_a}'(x)$ for Galaxy-8, Galaxy-16, and Galaxy-32 is 256 B, 128 KB, and 16 GB, respectively. Additionally, we employ the optimal permutations $\Phi_{n_b}(x)$ for Galaxy-8 [16], Galaxy-16 [15], and Galaxy-32. Regarding the permutation $\Phi_{n_b}(x)$ in Galaxy-32, we search for optimal one by MILP [14]. The previous works [15,16] and our search for the optimal permutation by MILP [14] show that Galaxy-8, Galaxy-16, and Galaxy-32 ensure the full diffusion in 8, 6, and 4 rounds.

5 Security Evaluation

In this section, we discuss the security of Galaxy both in the whitebox context and the blackbox context.

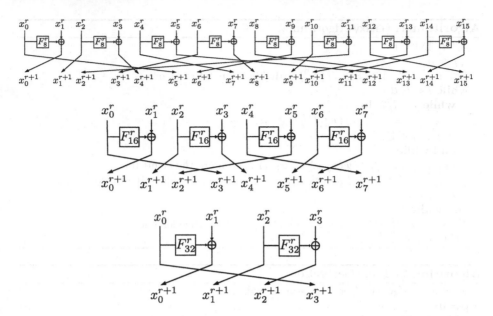

Fig. 5. Round function of Galaxy-8, Galaxy-16, and Galaxy-32

5.1   Security in the Whitebox Setting

Key Recovery Attack. In the whitebox setting, the adversary has access to internal values in the cryptographic algorithm. Thus, (s)he can obtain some pairs of inputs and the corresponding outputs in the table. In order to extract the secret key K from the table $F_{n_a}(x) = \phi_{n_a}(keygen(K), x)$, (s)he has to recover the secret key K from $keygen(K)$ in the blackbox setting. Therefore, the security of Galaxy against key recovery attacks in the whitebox setting is reduced to the problem of key recovery for the stream cipher in the blackbox setting. As a corollary, provided that the underlying stream cipher used to generate the table is secure against key recovery attacks in the blackbox setting, it is computationally difficult to extract the secret key K from the table of Galaxy in the whitebox setting.

Code Lifting Attack. Suppose a part of the table is leaked to the adversary, i.e., (s)he successfully obtains $i \leq 2^{n_a}$ entries of the table. Then, the probability that each entry of the table is among the leaked entries is $i/2^{n_a}$. Thus, the probability that the adversary can obtain the correct intermediate value by looking up leaked entries in any round is estimated as $(i/2^{n_a})^{l/2}$, and after R rounds, the correct output can be computed from randomly given input with the probability of $(i/2^{n_a})^{(l/2)\cdot R}$.

This estimation quantifies the security against code lifting attack and should be considered as an upper bound of space hardness. Hence, (M, Z)-space hardness for Galaxy-8, Galaxy-16, and Galaxy-32 are $(i, (i/2^{n_a})^{8R})$, $(i, (i/2^{n_a})^{4R})$, and $(i, (i/2^{n_a})^{2R})$-space hardness, respectively. As a corollary, in order to ensure

$(T/4, 128)$-space hardness just like SPACE, required numbers of R are 8, 16, 32 for Galaxy-8, Galaxy-16, and Galaxy-32, respectively.

5.2 Security in the Blackbox Setting

Key Recovery Attacks. In the blackbox setting, the adversary has only access to input and the corresponding output of a cryptographic algorithm, and (s)he is unable to collect any pairs of inputs and outputs in the table $F_{n_a}(x) = \phi_{n_a}(keygen(K), x)$. Thus, it is more computationally difficult to mount key recovery attacks on Galaxy in the blackbox setting than to recover the secret key from the underlying stream cipher.

Differential Cryptanalysis. We analyze the security of function $F_{n_a}(x)$ for each variant of Galaxy against differential attacks. In differential cryptanalysis, the adversary derives multiple differential probabilities DP_f for one round transition from input differences Δx_i and output differences Δy_j. The maximum of the differential probability DP_f is used as maximum differential probability DP_{fmax} to evaluate the security of the cryptographic algorithm against differential attacks. Multiplication of DP_{fmax} results in differential characteristic probability DCP, and DCP is exploited to mount differential cryptanalysis. Suppose the size of the input is n-bit. Then, if DCP of cipher E_K is less than 2^n, i.e., $DCP \leq 2^n$, E_K will be indistinguishable from a random permutation. The security against differential attacks is estimated as $(DP_{fmax})^m$, where m is the number of functions $F_{n_a}(x)$ that take different inputs, and we define the function $F_{n_a}(x)$ taking different inputs as differentially active function $F_{n_a}(x)$ just as the definition of active S-box. In the analysis of Galaxy, we cite the maximum differential probability DP_{fmax} from [2]. It shows that DP_{fmax} for Galaxy-8, Galaxy-16, and Galaxy-32 are 2^{-7}, 2^{-15}, and $2^{-30.4}$, respectively.

Our analysis for the number of differentially active functions $F_{n_a}(x)$ by Mixed Integer Linear Programming (MILP) [14] shows that Galaxy-8, Galaxy-16, and Galaxy-32 require 11, 8, and 6 rounds in order to have 17, 11, and 6 active functions $F_{n_a}(x)$, respectively.

Linear Cryptanalysis. We analyze the security of function $F_{n_a}(x)$ for each variant of Galaxy against linear attacks. In linear cryptanalysis, the adversary derives linear probability LP that a non-linear cryptographic algorithm can approximate to linear function by a vector called linear mask. The maximum of the linear probability LP that corresponds to the linear mask is used as maximum linear probability LP_{max} to evaluate the security of the cryptographic algorithm against linear attacks. The security against linear cryptanalysis is estimated as $(LP_{max})^m$ where m is the number of functions $F_{n_a}(x)$ that take non-zero value deriving from the linear mask. If $(LP_{max})^m \leq 2^n$ holds for cipher E_K, E_K will be indistinguishable from a random permutation. In the analysis of Galaxy, we cite the maximum linear probability LP_{max} from [2]. It shows that LP_{max} for Galaxy-8, Galaxy-16, and Galaxy-32 are 2^{-4}, 2^{-12}, and 2^{-28}, respectively.

Our analysis for the number of linearly active functions $F_{n_a}(x)$ by MILP [14] shows that Galaxy-8, Galaxy-16, and Galaxy-32 require 15, 8, and 6 rounds in order to have 32, 11, and 5 active functions $F_{n_a}(x)$, respectively.

Other Attacks. Apart from the differential cryptanalysis and linear cryptanalysis, we also consider impossible differential cryptanalysis and integral cryptanalysis with MILP [14]. Table 1 shows a summary of the required rounds to achieve full diffusion and ensure sufficient security against each attack.

Table 1. Summary of security evaluation for Galaxy: round numbers required for the security against attacks

	F	D	L	ID	I
Galaxy-(8, R)	8	11	15	14	14
Galaxy-(16, R)	6	8	8	10	11
Galaxy-(32, R)	4	6	6	7	7

F: Full diffusion, D: Differential attack, L: Linear attack, ID: Impossible differential attack, I: Integral attack

Recommended Rounds. We conservatively recommend the round number R ensuring the security level of $(T/4, 128)$-space hardness mentioned in Sect. 5.1 or the round number with enough margin which provides the security against best blackbox distinguisher of Sect. 5.2, whichever is higher. As a result, recommended numbers of rounds R for Galaxy-8, Galaxy-16, and Galaxy-32 are 25, 20, and 32, respectively. Such parameters provide sufficient security both in the whitebox setting and the blackbox setting.

We use these parameters in experimental measurements of performance for each variant.

6   Implementation

In this section, we present experimental measurements of performance for Galaxy, SPACE [2], WhiteBlock [9], and WEM [5]. We evaluate implementations of Galaxy, SPACE [2], WhiteBlock [9], and WEM [5] in the whitebox context (i.e. table-based implementations), and compare Galaxy with the others in the aspects of the performance for encryption and table generation. The basis of our comparison is the input space. Specifically, Galaxy-8 is compared with SPACE-8, and Galaxy-16 is compared with SPACE-16, WhiteBlock-16, and WEM, and Galaxy-32 is compared with SPACE-32 and WhiteBlock-32. We conduct all the experiments with the machine that has Intel Core i9-9900K 3.60 GHz and 128 GB DDR4 RAM. The processor on the machine has 512 KB L1 cache, 2 MB L2 cache, and 16 MB L3 cache, respectively. Moreover, it supports the AES instruction set [10] and the SSE instructions up to AVX2.

For the underlying stream cipher used to generate the table of Galaxy, we use chacha[1] [1] which is implemented with AVX2. In addition, we use AES which is implemented with the AES-NI [10] as the underlying block cipher for table generation of SPACE [2], WhiteBlock [9], and WEM [5]. Concerning the permutation in the encryption algorithm of WhiteBlock and WEM, we use full-round AES for WhiteBlock and five-round AES for WEM (as in their original paper) which are implemented with AES-NI [10]. We compile the source codes with GCC 4.8.5 in O3 optimization level.

Note that the comparison of Galaxy with other whitebox block ciphers in the blackbox context (i.e. comparison of non-table-based implementations) is out of our focus, as whitebox ciphers are generally implemented and used in the whitebox context.

Performance of Encryption. We evaluate the encryption performance for Galaxy, SPACE [2], WhiteBlock [9], and WEM [5], respectively. The evaluation results are summarized in Table 2 and Fig. 6 (numbers in the "Encryption" column are given in cycle per byte). It shows that encryption performance for Galaxy-8 is about 10 times as efficient as that for SPACE-8 and encryption by Galaxy-16 is roughly 15, 6.5, and 11 times faster than that by SPACE-16, WhiteBlock-16, and WEM, respectively. Galaxy-32 is roughly 3.5 and 1.3 times faster in encryption than SPACE-32 and WhiteBlock-32, respectively. We are convinced that two factors contribute to the encryption performance of Galaxy: simplicity of the permutation and exploitation of pipelining capability.

Regarding the exploitation of pipelining capability, Galaxy can query values in the table with pipelining ability, which facilitates faster table lookups. On the other hand, SPACE does not allow for parallel table lookups, as it is target heavy generalized Feistel network. Although, WhiteBlock and WEM can look up values in their tables in a parallel way as Galaxy can, Galaxy has an advantage over WhiteBlock and WEM: simplicity of permutation. The permutation in Galaxy is just a byte-wise permutation, and it can be implemented with vpshufb instruction which costs few cycles. Yet, the permutation in WhiteBlock is full-round AES, and the one in WEM is five-round AES (as in their original paper). Their permutations cost much more cycles than the simple byte-wise permutations in Galaxy do.

Performance of Table Generation. We evaluate the performance for table generation in Galaxy and compare it with that in equivalent instances of SPACE [2] and other whitebox ciphers including WhiteBlock [9] and WEM [5]. Note that we ignore the computational cost to store data to the entries of the table. This is because the performance of storing outputs of the underlying algorithms to the entries of the table is highly dependent on the platform, and the

---

[1] https://github.com/floodyberry/chacha-opt

Table 2. Evaluation of encryption performance and comparison with existing algorithms

Algorithm	Round R	Table size T	Encryption (cycle/byte)
Galaxy-8	25	256 B	23.45
Galaxy-16	20	128 KB	21.78
Galaxy-32	32	16 GB	725.14
SPACE-8 [2]	300	3.75 KB	235.86
SPACE-16 [2]	128	896 KB	325.14
SPACE-32 [2]	128	48 GB	2489.94
WhiteBlock-16 [9]	18	2 MB	141.65
WhiteBlock-20 [9]	23	24 MB	451.05
WhiteBlock-24 [9]	34	256 MB	849.69
WhiteBlock-28 [9]	34	4 GB	872.31
WhiteBlock-32 [9]	34	64 GB	952.06
WEM [5]	12	13 MB	253.58

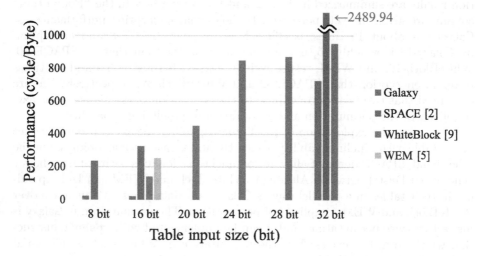

Fig. 6. Encryption performance

underlying algorithms such as chacha, AES, and the Fisher-Yates algorithm take the most computational resources (i.e. storing outputs to the table takes negligible computational resources). The evaluation results are summarized in Table 3.

It reveals that the table generation for Galaxy-8 is roughly 1.5 times faster than that for SPACE-8, that for Galaxy-16 is roughly 2.2 times, 2.2 times, and 10 times faster than that for SPACE-16, WhiteBlock-16, and WEM, and that for Galaxy-32 is 2.3 times and 2.3 times faster than that for SPACE-32 and

WhiteBlock-32, respectively. We believe that this improvement of efficiency in table generation comes from a single factor: the nature of stream ciphers.

Generally, the encryption speed of block ciphers is consistent, i.e., whether the message size for the encryption is small or large, the encryption performance of block ciphers does not change. On the other hand, the encryption speed of stream ciphers is inconsistent, i.e., as the message size is larger, the encryption performance of stream ciphers increases. When it comes to the Fisher-Yates algorithm, the algorithm itself is far less efficient than stream ciphers and even block ciphers.

Table 3. Evaluation of table generation and comparison with existing algorithms

Algorithm	Table size T	Table generation (cycle)	Table generation (cycle/byte)
Galaxy-8	256 B	313.11	1.222
Galaxy-16	128 KB	112.95×10^3	0.861
Galaxy-32	16 GB	14.76×10^9	0.859
SPACE-8 [2]	3.75 KB	7.84×10^3	1.914
SPACE-16 [2]	896 KB	2.01×10^6	1.917
SPACE-32 [2]	48 GB	131.57×10^9	1.914
WhiteBlock-16 [9]	2 MB	2.01×10^6	1.917
WhiteBlock-20 [9]	24 MB	32.12×10^6	1.914
WhiteBlock-24 [9]	256 MB	514.14×10^6	1.915
WhiteBlock-28 [9]	4 GB	8.22×10^9	1.915
WhiteBlock-32 [9]	64 GB	131.57×10^9	1.914
WEM [5]	13 MB	117.93×10^6	8.596

7 Conclusion

In this work, we proposed Galaxy, which ameliorates the efficiency of encryption and table generation. Galaxy is a type-2 generalized Feistel network and employs a stream cipher as the underlying cipher for its table generation. This leads to the improvement on the performance of encryption and table generation. Compared with other existing whitebox ciphers, we successfully increased the speed of encryption by 1.3–15 times. Besides, when we used chacha for table generation of Galaxy and AES for other existing block-cipher-based whitebox schemes, we successfully created the table of Galaxy 1.8–10 times faster than that of other existing whitebox schemes.

Acknowledgments. This work is supported by Grant-in-Aid for and Technology (DST) for Japan Society for the Promotion of Science (JPJSBP 120197735) and SECOM science and technology foundation.

References

1. Bernstein, D.J.: ChaCha, a variant of Salsa20. In: Workshop Record of SASC 2008: The State of the Art of Stream Ciphers (2008), January 2008
2. Bogdanov, A., Isobe, T.: White-box cryptography revisited: space-hard ciphers. In: Proceedings of the 22nd ACM SIGSAC Conference on Computer and Communications Security, Denver, CO, USA, 12–16 October 2015, pp. 1058–1069 (2015)
3. Bogdanov, A., Isobe, T., Tischhauser, E.: Towards practical whitebox cryptography: optimizing efficiency and space hardness. In: Cheon, J.H., Takagi, T. (eds.) ASIACRYPT 2016. LNCS, vol. 10031, pp. 126–158. Springer, Heidelberg (2016). https://doi.org/10.1007/978-3-662-53887-6_5
4. Cauchois, V., Gomez, C., Thomas, G.: General diffusion analysis: how to find optimal permutations for generalized type-II feistel schemes. IACR Trans. Symmetric Cryptol. **2019**(1), 264–301 (2019)
5. Cho, J., et al.: WEM: a new family of white-box block ciphers based on the even-mansour construction. In: Handschuh, H. (ed.) CT-RSA 2017. LNCS, vol. 10159, pp. 293–308. Springer, Cham (2017). https://doi.org/10.1007/978-3-319-52153-4_17
6. Chow, S., Eisen, P., Johnson, H., van Oorschot, P.C.: A white-box DES implementation for DRM applications. In: Feigenbaum, J. (ed.) DRM 2002. LNCS, vol. 2696, pp. 1–15. Springer, Heidelberg (2003). https://doi.org/10.1007/978-3-540-44993-5_1
7. Chow, S., Eisen, P., Johnson, H., Van Oorschot, P.C.: White-box cryptography and an AES implementation. In: Nyberg, K., Heys, H. (eds.) SAC 2002. LNCS, vol. 2595, pp. 250–270. Springer, Heidelberg (2003). https://doi.org/10.1007/3-540-36492-7_17
8. Derbez, P., Fouque, P.-A., Lambin, B., Mollimard, V.: Efficient search for optimal diffusion layers of generalized feistel networks. IACR Trans. Symmetric Cryptol. **2019**(2), 218–240 (2019)
9. Fouque, P.-A., Karpman, P., Kirchner, P., Minaud, B.: Efficient and provable white-box primitives. In: Cheon, J.H., Takagi, T. (eds.) ASIACRYPT 2016. LNCS, vol. 10031, pp. 159–188. Springer, Heidelberg (2016). https://doi.org/10.1007/978-3-662-53887-6_6
10. Gueron, S.: Intel Advanced Encryption Standard (AES) New Instructions Set, May 2010. https://www.intel.com/content/dam/doc/white-paper/advanced-encryption-standard-new-instructions-set-paper.pdf
11. Kwon, J., Lee, B., Lee, J., Moon, D.: FPL: white-box secure block cipher using parallel table look-ups. In: Jarecki, S. (ed.) CT-RSA 2020. LNCS, vol. 12006, pp. 106–128. Springer, Cham (2020). https://doi.org/10.1007/978-3-030-40186-3_6
12. Langley, A., et al.: The QUIC transport protocol: design and internet-scale deployment. In: Proceedings of the Conference of the ACM Special Interest Group on Data Communication, SIGCOMM 2017, Los Angeles, CA, USA, 21–25 August 2017, pp. 183–196. ACM (2017)
13. Marlinspike, M., Perrin, T.: The Double Ratchet Algorithm, November 2016. https://signal.org/docs/specifications/doubleratchet/doubleratchet.pdf
14. Mouha, N., Wang, Q., Gu, D., Preneel, B.: Differential and linear cryptanalysis using mixed-integer linear programming. In: Wu, C.-K., Yung, M., Lin, D. (eds.) Inscrypt 2011. LNCS, vol. 7537, pp. 57–76. Springer, Heidelberg (2012). https://doi.org/10.1007/978-3-642-34704-7_5

15. Suzaki, T., Minematsu, K.: Improving the generalized feistel. In: Hong, S., Iwata, T. (eds.) FSE 2010. LNCS, vol. 6147, pp. 19–39. Springer, Heidelberg (2010). https://doi.org/10.1007/978-3-642-13858-4_2
16. Suzaki, T., Minematsu, K., Morioka, S., Kobayashi, E.: *TWINE*: a lightweight block cipher for multiple platforms. In: Knudsen, L.R., Wu, H. (eds.) SAC 2012. LNCS, vol. 7707, pp. 339–354. Springer, Heidelberg (2013). https://doi.org/10.1007/978-3-642-35999-6_22

Automated Search for Block Cipher Differentials: A GPU-Accelerated Branch-and-Bound Algorithm

Wei-Zhu Yeoh[1], Je Sen Teh[1(✉)], and Jiageng Chen[2]

[1] Universiti Sains Malaysia, Penang, Malaysia
yeohweizhu@gmail.com, jesen_teh@usm.my
[2] Central China Normal University, Wuhan, China
chinkako@gmail.com

Abstract. In this paper, we propose a GPU-accelerated branch-and-bound algorithm. The proposed approach substantially increases the performance of the differential cluster search. We were able to derive a branch enumeration and evaluation kernel that is 5.95 times faster than its CPU counterpart. To showcase its practicality, the proposed algorithm is applied on TRIFLE-BC, a 128-bit block cipher. By incorporating a meet-in-the-middle approach with the proposed GPU kernel, we were able to improve the search efficiency (on 20 rounds of TRIFLE-BC) by approximately 58 times as compared to the CPU-based approach. Differentials consisting of up to 50 million individual characteristics can be constructed for 20 rounds of TRIFLE, leading to slight improvements to the overall differential probabilities. Even for larger rounds (43 rounds), the proposed algorithm is still able to construct large clusters of over 500 thousand characteristics. This result depicts the practicality of the proposed algorithm in constructing large differentials even for a 128-bit block cipher, which could be used to improve cryptanalytic findings against other block ciphers in the future.

Keywords: Automated search · Block cipher · Branch-and-bound · Cryptanalysis · Differential characteristic · Differential cluster · GPU

1 Introduction

Differential cryptanalysis is one of the most widely-known cryptanalytical methods, resistance to which has become a basic requirement for modern block ciphers [1,9]. The success of differential cryptanalysis relies on identifying differential characteristics that occur with high probability. The search for these characteristics is a non-trivial task especially for block ciphers with large block sizes and number of rounds. In addition, differential cryptanalysis also takes into consideration differentials (clusters of single characteristics) for a more accurate estimate of the overall differential probability[1] [10].

---

[1] We use the term differential *cluster* interchangeably with differentials to ensure that there is a clear distinction between differentials and individual characteristics.

© Springer Nature Switzerland AG 2020
J. K. Liu and H. Cui (Eds.): ACISP 2020, LNCS 12248, pp. 160–179, 2020.
https://doi.org/10.1007/978-3-030-55304-3_9

Recently automated search for differential characteristics has been used instead of manual searching. Matsui [12] proposed a branch-and-bound technique to search for differential characteristics and linear trails. This technique was used at that time to study DES. Since then, there were numerous improvements that have been made to the branch-and-bound algorithm. In [3] an ARX version of the branch-and-bound searching algorithm was proposed and the algorithm was also subsequently improved in [6] by the introduction of a sorted partial differential distribution table. In addition, [5] incorporated a meet-in-the-middle approach to the differential cluster search, and updated the pruning rules to bound the number of active of s-boxes to further improve upon the search efficiency.

In [14], a mixed-integer linear programming (MILP) approach was proposed as an alternative to the branch-and-bound algorithm. The MILP model requires identifying relevant linear inequalities which are then fed into a MILP solver which produces the minimal number of active s-boxes for a particular block cipher. The MILP framework had been extended by [23] to be applicable to bit-oriented block ciphers. [21] demonstrated the capability of MILP to enumerate differential characteristics to form differential clusters or linear hulls. However, the aforementioned method is impractical for identifying differential clusters for block ciphers with large block sizes and rounds. In addition, none of the related-works attempt to utilize specialized hardware acceleration to perform the search.

General purpose graphical processing unit (GPGPU) technology that utilizes specialized GPU hardware could be used to improve the efficiency of the branch-and-bound search. This would alleviate some of the computational load needed to identify differential clusters for large block ciphers. However, the GPU requires tasks to be divided into smaller tasks so that the subdivided tasks could be processed across a large number of processing units simultaneously. The GPU architecture also has its own array of optimization problems such as memory limitations, work divergence, low number of available subdivided tasks, and many more. Therefore, any GPU-accelerated searching algorithm needs to be optimized with respect to the architecture of the GPU to obtain a reasonable performance boost. Although GPU-accelerated branch-and-bound algorithm had been studied in [11] for knapsack, [13] for flow-shop scheduling, and [4] for multiproduct batch plants optimization sub-problems, there exists no prior work that uses GPU to accelerate the branch-and-bound search for differential cryptanalysis.

Our Contributions. The proposed work is a novel approach leveraging GPU hardware acceleration for the specific sub-problem of differential cluster search. It also incorporates the meet-in-the-middle (MITM) technique [5] to further improve its efficiency. The proposed algorithm can achieve a substantial speedup, up to a factor of approximately 5.95. A comparison based on cloud computing also indicates that the GPU-based algorithm can save costs by up to 85% as compared to its CPU-based counterpart in enumerating high number of branches.

To showcase the practicality and feasibility of the proposed GPU-accelerated algorithm, we investigate the differential clustering properties of the 128-bit block cipher, TRIFLE-BC [16] as a proof-of-concept. By applying the proposed

GPU-accelerated automatic search for differential clusters, the computational time needed to construct differential clusters for a large number of rounds of 128-bit TRIFLE-BC was significantly shortened. This effectively allowed us to identify differentials with the highest probability to date, thus making this work one of the first successful attempts in implementing an automated differential search for a block cipher with 128-bit block size at a very large number of rounds (43 rounds). Previous automated search attempts have focused on block ciphers with block sizes of 64 bits or less [5,21]. For literature that involve 128-bit block ciphers, the number of rounds searched were noticeably lower (typically $<= 20$), and are only capable of identifying singular differential characteristics [2,7]. Although the framework proposed in [22] was able to identify clusters for SPECK128 and LEA-128, it is not applicable to most ARX ciphers due to its reliance on the independent addition assumption. Also, it could be noted that all prior findings could be potentially improved by applying the proposed GPU framework. All source codes are available for download at https://github.com/leon5905/GPU-bnb-differential-cluster.

Outline. The rest of this paper is organized as follows: Sect. 2 introduces the GPU architecture and CUDA technology, followed by TRIFLE and its cryptanalytic results. Section 3 describes the conventional branch-and-bound differential search and its improved version that serves as the basis for this work. The GPU-accelerated algorithm is detailed in Sect. 4, the performance of which is compared with its CPU-counterpart. Capabilities and limitations of the proposed algorithm are also discussed. Section 5 investigates the differential cluster effect of TRIFLE-BC. Section 6 concludes the paper.

2   Preliminaries

In this section, background information on GPU architecture, CUDA and TRIFLE are provided to aid readers' understanding of the remaining sections of this paper.

2.1   GPU Architecture and CUDA

A graphics processing unit (GPU) is specialized hardware designed for highly multithreaded and parallelized data processing workflow. The primary function of a GPU is to manipulate computer graphics and perform image processing. However, the massively parallel processing architecture of GPUs has also enabled them to outperform central processing units (CPUs) in other non-graphical processing algorithms that involve a massive amount of data. With the introduction of the Compute Unified Device Architecture (CUDA) in 2006 by NVIDIA, the parallel processing power of GPUs becomes readily available for solving many other computationally complex problems.

CUDA is a general-purpose parallel computing platform and application programming interface (API) designed by NVIDIA for NVIDIA GPU cards.

GPUs are based on the single instruction, multiple threads (SIMT) execution model whereby multiple distinct threads perform the same operation on multiple data concurrently. By dedicating more transistors to data processing (arithmetic logic unit, ALU) and consequently de-emphasizing data caching and flow control, parallel computation becomes more efficient. The aforementioned structure is schematically illustrated in Fig. 1. This unique property of GPUs allows them to efficiently solve data-parallel computational problems that are arithmetic-heavy but with lower memory access frequency.

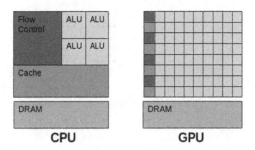

Fig. 1. Structural differences between CPU and GPU.

CUDA threads run on a separate physical **device** (GPU) to accelerate parallel tasks given by the co-running **host** program (CPU) as illustrated by Fig. 2. The host and device analogy will be used throughout the paper. A kernel is a CUDA device function that will be executed in parallel by different CUDA threads on the device. A single kernel consists of a single grid that may hold a maximum of $2^{31} - 1$ number of blocks, whereas each block can contain a maximum of 2^{10} threads. When a kernel is launched, the blocks that reside within the kernel are assigned to idle streaming multiprocessors (SM). The multiprocessors execute parallel threads within the assigned block in groups of 32 called warps. A warp executes one common instruction at a time. If threads of a warp diverge due to conditional instruction, each branch path will be executed in different warp cycles. Therefore, the use of conditional branches should be minimized to maximize the multiprocessors' efficiency. Since an SM executes a warp of 32 threads at a time, it is advisable to choose the number of threads per block to be a multiple of 32 to optimize GPU utilization.

CUDA threads are able to read data from multiple types of memory during their execution. Each thread has its own local memory. Threads reside within the same thread block can access a shared memory space called the shared memory. There are three types of memory visible to all threads namely global memory, read-only constant memory, and read-only texture memory. Global memory is the slowest memory and requires read/write to be coalesced in 32, 64, or 128-byte memory to achieve maximum efficiency. Constant memory is optimized for broadcasting, whereby the maximum efficiency is reached when all threads of the same warp request the same memory address. Texture memory is optimized

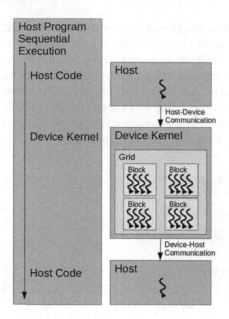

Fig. 2. Heterogeneous programming architecture of a typical GPU-accelerated algorithm. (Note that serial host code executes on the CPU while parallel device code executes on the GPU)

for 2D spatial locality [20], whereby threads of the same warp reading memory locations that are close to each other will lead to maximum efficiency. Since the different memory types are better suited for different tasks, the memory access pattern of a CUDA program should also be optimized accordingly to maximize efficiency.

The CUDA model maintains separate memory spaces for host and device memory. To alleviate the complexity of memory management, unified memory may be used to unify the host and device memory spaces. Unified managed memory provides a single coherent memory address visible to both CPU and GPU. If a large amount of memory transfer is needed and the transfer happens often, it is advised to pin down the memory to avoid the cost of the transfer between page-able and pinned memory. Pinned memory also enables the asynchronous (non-blocking) execution of kernel and data transfer.

This section has only covered information that are relevant to the proposed work. There are a lot more features left unexplored such as concurrent kernel launches, asynchronous execution, and multi-device execution. For a more detailed guide and reference in optimizing for CUDA, refer to [19].

2.2   TRIFLE

Notation. The following mathematical notations will be used throughout the paper:

- $\{0,1\}^*$ denotes the set of all strings.
- $\{0,1\}^n$ denotes the set of strings of length n.
- $|M|$ denotes the length (number of bits) in string M.
- $M_1 \| M_2$ denotes concatenation of string M_1 and string M_2.
- $\oplus$ denotes field addition and $\otimes$ field multiplication.
- $\mathrm{OZP}(X)$ applies an optional 10^* padding on n bits. If $|X| < n$, then $\mathrm{OZP}(X)$ $= 0^{n-|X|-1}\|1\|X$. If $|X| = n$, then $\mathrm{OZP}(X) = X$.
- $\lfloor X \rfloor$ is an integer floor function that produces an integer i closest to X such that $i \leq X$.
- $>>>$ denotes bitwise right rotations.
- $W_{bit}(X)$ denotes the number of 1 bits in a given binary string X while $W_{nibble}(X)$ denotes the number of non-zero 4-bit values in a binary string X.
- AS is used to represent the number of active s-boxes.
- P_c represents the probability of a differential cluster and P_t is the probability of a single differential trail.
- ΔX is an XOR difference, ΔU_i is the ith nibble value inside ΔX, and $\Delta A U_i$ is the ith active nibble value (non-zero difference) inside ΔX.

Description. TRIFLE is a round-1 candidate of the lightweight encryption standardization effort by NIST [17]. It is a 128-bit block cipher-based authenticated encryption scheme. It receives an encryption key $K \in \{0,1\}^{128}$, nonce $N \in \{0,1\}^{128}$, associated data $A \in \{0,1\}^*$ and message $M \in \{0,1\}^*$ as inputs, and produces an encrypted ciphertext $C \in \{0,1\}^{|M|}$ and an authentication tag $T \in \{0,1\}^{128}$ as outputs. The corresponding verification and decryption scheme receives a key, nonce, associated data, ciphertext and a tag as inputs, and produces the decrypted plaintext if the authentication tag is valid. The underlying block cipher, TRIFLE-BC is a 50-round 128-bit SPN block cipher. Each round of TRIFLE-BC consists of four consecutive functions namely SubNibbles, BitPermutation, AddRoundKey, and AddRoundConstant. For a more detailed TRIFLE specification, refer to [16].

Differential Properties of TRIFLE-BC. By analyzing the differential distribution table of TRIFLE's s-box, it was found that each ΔU that has a hamming weight of a single bit ($W_{bit} = 1$) can be differentially mapped back to ΔV with $W_{bit} = 1$. These 1-bit to 1-bit differential relationships ($1 \rightarrow 8, 2 \rightarrow 1, 4 \rightarrow 2,$ and $8 \rightarrow 4$) hold with a probability of 2^{-3}. The 1-bit ΔV will be permuted and propagated to the next round to become yet another ΔU with $W_{bit} = 1$ due to the nature of bitwise permutation that shuffles bits without affecting the total number of active bits in the block cipher.

Therefore, for any n arbitrary rounds of TRIFLE, there exists a differential characteristic $\Delta X(X_0, X_1, ..., X_{31}) \to \Delta Y(Y_0, Y_1, ..., Y_{31})$ such that $W_{bit}(X_i^j) = 1$ where $0 \le i < 32, 0 \le j < n$ and $P(\Delta X \to \Delta Y) = 2^{-3n}$. Moreover, there exist 4 differentials $\Delta U \to \Delta V$ ($7 \to 4, B \to 2, D \to 1,$ and $E \to 8$) where $W_{bit}(\Delta U) > 1$, $W_{bit}(\Delta V) = 1$ and $P(\Delta U \to \Delta V) = 2^{-2}$. This set of differentials can be used to improve the first round of the aforementioned single-bit differential characteristics to increase the probability to 2^{-3n+1} for any n arbitrary rounds. Since there also exists a ΔV for every ΔU with $W_{bit}(\Delta U) = 1$ such that $P(\Delta U \to \Delta V) = 2^{-2}$, these differential relationships can be used at the final round. Thus, the single-bit differential characteristics with improved first and final rounds that have a probability of 2^{-3n+2} exist for any n arbitrary rounds of TRIFLE provided that $n \ge 3$. In fact, there are exactly 128 (128 different starting bit position) such characteristics for every round. These observations have also been discussed in [8] and [18].

Based on the aforementioned improved single-bit differential characteristics, a key recovery strategy had been discussed in [8] that recovers the key for 11 rounds of TRIFLE with a time complexity and data complexity of 2^{104} and 2^{63} respectively. The authors proposed using a 42-round improved single-bit differential in their key recovery strategy on TRIFLE-BC. However, the authors made an error of using the 41-round ($2^{-3(41)+2} = 2^{-121}$) differential probability in their calculation instead of 42 ($2^{-3(42)+2} = 2^{-124}$). Therefore, the differential attack of TRIFLE-BC in [8] should able to recover the secret key of a 43-round TRIFLE-BC (instead of 44 rounds) with the time and data complexity of 2^{126}.

The differential discussed in this subsection only considers the probability of a single characteristic. The differential probability can be potentially improved by incorporating probability gains from the clustering effect (also referred to as the differential effect) shown in [15], whereby multiple differential characteristics with the same $\Delta X \to \Delta Y$ are considered for the probability of a given differential.

3   Automatic Search for Differential

Matsui proposed a branch-and-bound algorithm [12] for searching linear paths and differential characteristics. The algorithm had been used on DES to find the best characteristic at the time. The algorithm relied on pruning *bad* branches that have lower probability than the best one found so far, $\overline{B_n}$. The initial value of $\overline{B_n}$ also helps break off bad branches in the early parts of the algorithm. Thus, when $\overline{B_n}$ approaches the real value of the best probability, B_n where $\overline{B_n} \le B_n$, the search speed is improved as well. The algorithm also used the knowledge of $\overline{B_{n-i}}$ computed from round 0 to round i to estimate the probability of the current branch being searched. It will effectively cut off branches with probabilities that are estimated to be worse than $\overline{B_n}$.

Since then, several improvements have been made to Matsui's algorithm. A cluster search algorithm such as [5] improved upon Matsui's algorithm by searching for differential clusters after identifying a main differential characteristic.

The differential cluster search includes all differential characteristics that share the same input ΔX and output ΔY differences but with different intermediary differences. This led to differentials with improved probability for block ciphers such as LBlock and TWINE [5]. It is also worth noting that [5] used the number of active s-boxes as part of the pruning rules to eliminate bad branches. There were also other researchers [3,6] that use a type of automatic search known as the threshold search for ARX ciphers.

A combination of the number of active s-boxes and the differential probability threshold will be used as the pruning rules for the proposed GPU-based automatic search. The combination of both allows for greater flexibility during the search, and also effectively filters branches quickly if configured correctly. This CPU-based recursive algorithm is described in Algorithm 1[2].

4   GPU-Accelerated Automatic Search for Differential Characteristics and Their Clusters

To facilitate the differential search for block ciphers with a large block size and number of rounds, the processing power of GPUs can be leveraged to provide a substantial performance boost to the conventional branch-and-bound searching algorithm. The proposed GPU-accelerated algorithm is a variant of a depth-first search whereby the algorithm will first visit nodes (possible branches) in successive rounds before backtracking to visit other nodes. The difference is that once a node is visited, all of its corresponding child branches are enumerated. This enables the task of enumeration for the relevant child branches, and subsequently the evaluation of the pruning rules to be parallelized and solved by the GPU. All this can be performed while keeping the memory footprint to a manageable range by enumerating one branch at a time rather than all possible branches of a particular depth at once (breadth-first search). The exception exists for the final round of the search whereby all of the branches are visited and evaluated simultaneously. The behaviour of the modified depth-first search algorithm is illustrated in Fig. 3.

However, if the total number of possible child branches for a particular difference pattern is too low, then it will cause the GPU kernel to have low efficiency due to low occupancy (insufficient tasks to be distributed across multiprocessors). In the proposed algorithm for TRIFLE, this scenario occurs when the number of active s-boxes for a particular difference is <4. To alleviate this problem, differences with a low number of possible branches are instead enumerated and evaluated by the CPU-variant procedure. The GPU kernel and its CPU-variant are discussed in Subsect. 4.1. The complete algorithm for the proposed GPU-accelerated branch-and-bound differential cluster search without enumeration kernels and method details is provided in Algorithm 2. Note that the correctness of the proposed algorithm has been verified by comparing the results of Algorithms 1 and 2.

---

[2] All algorithms are described in Appendix A.

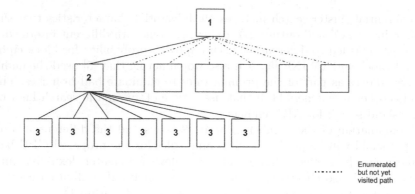

Fig. 3. The searching strategy for the proposed algorithm.

4.1 Enumeration Using GPU Kernel and CPU

The GPU kernel has been optimized for TRIFLE's structure which has a constant branching number of 7 for ΔV. This means that $\forall \Delta U$ that goes through the TRIFLE's s-box, there are precisely 7 possible choices of ΔV. Despite this specific customization used, the kernel can be generalized to any SPN block cipher while still retaining a similar efficiency by estimating the correct number of branches and assigning workload among the threads accordingly.

The configuration of the proposed GPU architecture will utilize 1D blocks for each kernel launch. Since each block within a grid contains its own block threads, each thread is assigned a unique thread ID based on its position in a given grid. This thread ID assignment facilitates the process of work distribution and reduction. For TRIFLE, the number of possible branches of ΔX_i is 7^{AS_i}. When $AS_i = 4$, there are 2401 tasks to be distributed. 19 blocks (>9 SMs in NVIDIA GTX-1060) are declared for a grid and each block contains 128 threads (32|128) totalling up to 2432 threads (excess threads are terminated during runtime immediately).

Let NB_1, NB_2, NB_3, NB_4 be the number of possible branches, and $I_1, I_2, I_3,$ I_4 be the nth numbered branches in the four active ΔU branches respectively. Thread ID, T_i can also be computed as

$$ID(I_1, I_2, I_3, I_4) = (I_1 \times NB_0) + (I_2 \times \prod_{i=0}^{1} NB_i) + (I_3 \times \prod_{i=0}^{2} NB_i) + (I_4 \times \prod_{i=0}^{3} NB_i), \quad (1)$$

where $NB_0 = 1$. The work assignment (the branch taken by each individual thread) is done by computing $ID^{-1}(T_i)$. For $AS_i > 4$, the work assignment will still occur for the first four active ΔU branches, but the remaining active ΔU branches are exhaustively enumerated by each working thread individually. The last round follows the same logic of Algorithm 1 whereby after a branch (now a trail) is enumerated, $\Delta Y_n == \Delta Y$ is checked, then P_i is incremented accordingly. To avoid race conditions, each thread has its own probability accumulator, P_i.

The final cluster probability, $P_c = \sum_{i=1}^{T_{total}} P_i + P_h$ is computed in the host procedure where P_h is the host probability accumulator.

Special attention needs to be given to memory management. All of the necessary device memory allocation and host memory pinning are done during program initialization. Both the allocated memory and pinned memory are reused whenever possible since allocation and de-allocation of the memory are expensive and will impact the overall efficiency of the proposed algorithm. DDT and permutation lookup tables are specifically loaded into the shared memory each time the kernel is launched because the improved latency of the shared memory will ease the frequent access of the DDT and permutation table. The complete algorithm for the kernel is summarized in Algorithm 4.

The GPU kernel can only be used when there is a large number of branches to maintain high GPU utilization. For $AS \leq 3$, a CPU-version of enumeration method is used instead. The CPU-version follows the general logic of the GPU kernel without parallelized processing. The complete CPU enumeration method is shown in Algorithm 3.

4.2   Meet-in-the-Middle Searching Approach

The meet-in-the-middle (MITM) approach described in [5] is used to further improve the efficiency of the search. Since the number of branches grows exponentially as the number of rounds increases, the search for large number of rounds could be completed much quicker if the number of rounds to search is split between α rounds and β rounds instead of searching directly for $(\alpha + \beta)$ rounds.

The steps involved in the MITM approach starts off by dividing the search into forward α rounds and backward β rounds. For the forward search, the proposed algorithm mentioned in Algorithm 2 is used. The difference is that during the αth (final) round, instead of evaluating ΔY_α, the ΔY_α and its probability is accumulated in an array for matching purposes. Since the amount of information needed to store all of the possible permutations of 128-bit data far exceeds the practical memory storage option currently available, an encoding method is used to index into the array. The encoding is computed by using the format of $[Pos_{\Delta AV_i}, \Delta AV_i, Pos_{\Delta AV_{i+1}}, \Delta AV_{i+1}, Pos_{\Delta AV_{i+2}}, \Delta AV_{i+2}]$. The total number of nibbles to be stored is currently limited to a maximum of 3 (12 bits). Since each nibble requires 5 bits to represent its nibble position, thus the total number of bits needed to represent 3 nibbles among 32 possible nibble positions is 27 bits. This amounts to an array size of 134217728 that requires 1.07 GB of memory when using a 64-bit double-precision floating point format to store the probability.

Meanwhile, the backward search requires the computation of a reversed DDT and the corresponding reversed permutation table. During the βth (final) round, ΔY_β is encoded using the same method described earlier to index into the storage array to check for matching trails. Matching trails contribute toward the final cluster probability P_c. The MITM approach detailed in this section is illustrated in Fig. 4.

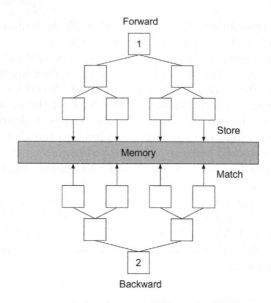

Fig. 4. Meet-in-the-middle approach.

4.3 Performance Comparison of GPU and CPU-Based Automatic Search for Differential Algorithms

The CPU and GPU algorithms are implemented using C++ and CUDA/C respectively. The performance results are obtained by running the implementations on a single Linux desktop computer with Intel 6th generation Skylake Core i5-6600K CPU clocked at 3.5 GHz, NVIDIA Pascal GeForce GTX-1060 with 3 GB memory, and 16 GB of RAM.

A fixed problem set which satisfies a specific $W_{nibble}(\Delta X)$ criteria has been computed on both the GPU-accelerated kernel and CPU-enumeration method. The results obtained (including the time spent on memory transfer) are recorded in Table 1 and is an average of a hundred instances. These results show the potential of the performance improvement of the GPU-accelerated functions which can be up to a factor of 5.95 over the CPU-enumeration method. Also, if the GPU possesses higher on-chip memory whereby the necessary computing differential caches are able to fit, it is possible for the proposed algorithm to reach a speedup of up to 27.07 as shown in Table 2. A similar experiment is performed for a series of Google VM Cloud-based CPU and GPU. The performance results indicate that for $AS = 8$, the cost reduction is estimated to be around 16% to 85% of the original cost compared to the reference XEON CPU (Table 3). These results depict the potential of the proposed algorithm in terms of cost-saving for large numbers of active s-boxes.

A series of practical tests of the proposed algorithm is performed on various rounds of TRIFLE-BC. The results are recorded in Table 4 and these results are bounded by $PROB\_BOUND = P_t \times 2^{-21}$ and are an average of ten instances.

It can be seen that although the algorithm depict a speed-up of 5.95, as the number of rounds increases, the performance also increases and stabilizes at approximately 2.5. This result is obtained because the computation is not GPU-accelerated when the number of active s-boxes is between 1 and 3. It can also be noted that the MITM approach greatly increases the performance of the searching algorithm over the traditional recursive method for up to a factor of approximately 58 at round 20.

Table 1. Search time (μs) comparison of CPU and GPU kernel enumeration.

$W_{nibble}(\Delta X)$	GPU-Accel	CPU-Enum	Speedup
4	35.5	173.7	4.89
5	141.2	716.6	5.08
6	861.4	4589.0	5.33
7	5974.9	32 200.4	5.39
8	41 561.5	247 393.0	5.95

Table 2. Search time (μs) comparison of CPU and GPU kernel enumeration (without output memory synchronization).

$W_{nibble}(\Delta X)$	GPU-Accel	CPU-Enum	Speedup
4	34.2	173.7	5.08
5	70.3	716.6	10.19
6	286.9	4589.0	16.00
7	1656.7	32 200.4	19.44
8	9140.1	247 393.0	27.07

4.4 Limitations and Capabilities of the Proposed Algorithm

The proposed algorithm presented in this paper is not without its limitations. Firstly, the kernel is only utilized when AS of ΔX is ≥ 4. It should be theoretically possible to bundle several small work units into a large compiled work unit to be sent to kernel for processing. The added benefit of this is the higher performance gains for cases of $AS\_BOUND < 8$, which could achieve a speedup equivalent to using $AS\_BOUND = 8$. Doing so will definitely incur more overhead. Thus, the feasibility of such an idea may be studied in future work.

This method also requires a large amount of memory especially as compared to a recursive version of the algorithm shown in Algorithm 1. The dependency on the GPU hardware requires some tweaking on the number of blocks and the number of threads per block so that the GPU utilization could be maximized. Currently, the proposed algorithm requires some customization to be applicable to other SPN block ciphers. Its feasibility for other types of block ciphers such

Table 3. Cloud computing cost (USD) comparison without memory synchronization for $\Delta X_i \rightarrow \Delta X_{i+1}$ for $W_{nibble}(\Delta X) = 8$.

Device	Time (μs)	Cost/Month	Core equivalent	Cost%
Xeon Skylake 2.0 GHz*	506 703.0	27.46	1	100
Tesla T4	8531.6	255.50	60	16
Tesla P100	8080.4	1065.80	63	62
Tesla V100	6528.0	1810.40	78	85

Table 4. Search time (ms) of various rounds of TRIFLE-BC.

Round(s)	MITM-GPU-Accel	GPU-Accel	CPU-Enum
5	1135.9	661.5	787.2
10	2197.3	8644.5	19 564.6
15	8795.6	62 928.7	156 725.0
20	15 675.2	363 274.2	908 978.1

as ARX and Feistel will be investigated in future work. Further work is also needed to generalize the proposed algorithm for SPN block ciphers with minimal modifications.

With that said, the proposed algorithm is able to use GPU hardware to shorten the searching runtime drastically. This enables the automated search to be conducted for block ciphers with large block sizes (128-bit) for a large number of rounds (≥ 30). This has yet to be attempted in previous works. The possibility of distributing the workload of the proposed algorithm across a grid or grids of CPU-GPU computing nodes makes it possible to enhance the efficiency of the search even further. For example, by enumerating all the second or third level branches in a breadth-first manner, these branches can be divided into individual work items that can be distributed across CPU-GPU computing nodes. This also requires the modification of the proposed algorithm to be able to utilize more CPU cores to better utilize the available computing resources. In addition, the algorithm can be easily adapted to search for linear hulls.

5   Differential Clustering Effect of TRIFLE-BC

The proposed algorithm has been used to study the differential cluster effect in TRIFLE-BC. The 128 improved single-bit differences propagation trails described in Subsect. 2.2 are clustered using the proposed algorithm. The cluster search was conducted for 43-round TRIFLE-BC using $AS\_BOUND = 4$ and $PROB\_BOUND = P_t \times 2^{-21}$. A equivalent search is conducted for 20-round TRIFLE-BC using $AS\_BOUND = 4$ and $PROB\_BOUND = P_t \times 2^{-31}$. A slightly higher bound is used here in an attempt to cluster more differential trails. The time required to complete the search is two days using the desktop computer described in Subsect. 4.3.

Table 5. Differential for 20-round TRIFLE-BC

ΔX	ΔY	P_t	P_c	# of Trails
0000 0000 0000 0000 00b0 0000 0000 0000	0000 0000 0000 0000 0000 0001 0000 0001	2^{-58}	$2^{-57.97}$	50901814
0000 0000 0000 0000 0000 d000 0000 0000	0000 0100 0000 0100 0000 0000 0000 0000	2^{-58}	$2^{-57.97}$	39432495
0000 0000 0000 0000 0000 0000 0700 0000	0000 0000 0000 0000 0000 0002 0000 0002	2^{-58}	$2^{-57.97}$	51377914
0000 0000 0000 0000 0000 0b00 0000 0000	0000 0000 0000 0000 0000 0400 0000 0400	2^{-58}	$2^{-57.996}$	30372009

Since the differential probabilities are similar, we select only 4 differentials with 3 being the best probability and 1 differential being the differential described in [8] to show in Table 5 and Table 6. We found that the effect of clustering these paths do not significantly improve the probability. However, large differential clusters could be enumerated, consisting of up to 51 and 0.5 million trails for 20-round and 43-round TRIFLE-BC respectively. The differential used in [8] for a key recovery attack against TRIFLE can be improved slightly from 2^{-58} to $2^{-57.996}$.

Table 6. Differential for 43-round TRIFLE-BC

ΔX	ΔY	P_t	P_c	# of Trails
0000 0000 0000 b000 0000 0000 0000 0000	0000 0000 0010 0000 0010 0000 0000 0000	2^{-127}	$2^{-126.931}$	544352
0000 0000 0000 0000 b000 0000 0000 0000	0000 0002 0000 0002 0000 0000 0000 0000	2^{-127}	$2^{-126.931}$	564220
0000 0000 0000 0000 0007 0000 0000 0000	0020 0000 0020 0000 0000 0000 0000 0000	2^{-127}	$2^{-126.931}$	584356
0000 0000 0000 0000 0000 0b00 0000 0000	0000 0000 0000 0000 0000 0400 0000 0400	2^{-127}	$2^{-126.995}$	381035

The improved efficiency of the searching algorithm allows for practical identification of large clusters. Although the large clusters found in TRIFLE did not contribute to significant improvements in terms of differential probability, this may not be the case for other block ciphers, especially block ciphers with smaller block size. When the block size is larger, the differential probability is distributed into more trails, whereby the number of possible trails is a factor of 2^{64} more than lightweight block ciphers. Meanwhile, when the block size is smaller, the probability of each trail is, by comparison, much larger. Thus, the proposed searching algorithm can be used to more accurately determine the security margin of these ciphers, and also provide a detailed look at their clustering effects.

6   Conclusion

In this work, a new GPU-accelerated branch-and-bound algorithm for differential cluster search of block ciphers has been proposed. Rather than just a direct application of GPUs to the problem, we implicitly partitioned the difference branches into chunk sizes which corresponds to a individual thread in the GPU kernel. The implicit partitioning allows the thread to acquire its work unit in a fixed amount of step without thread divergence and synchronization mechanisms to maximize the GPU core utilization. The proposed algorithm can achieve a tremendous speedup especially when enumerating large amount of branches. The speedup enables the search for large differential clusters for block ciphers with a large block size over a large number of rounds. Aided by the proposed GPU framework, we provide a detailed look at the clustering effect of the authenticated cipher TRIFLE, which also served to showcase the practically of the proposed framework. We were able to construct large clusters consisting of hundreds of thousands to millions of individual differential characteristics, even for a large number of rounds of TRIFLE's underlying 128-bit block cipher. The GPU-accelerated algorithm can be adapted to suit other SPN block ciphers by changing the permutation and differential distribution table, and customizing the kernel thread number based on the GPU hardware capability. However for other block cipher structures such as Feistel and ARX, more work still has to be done with respect to the feasibility of the proposed approach. The proposed approach can also be extended to utilize a grid of CPU-GPU computing nodes in a real-world environment for an even higher efficiency gains. In addition, it can be easily adapted to search for linear hulls. Last but not least, the GPU framework described in this paper can be used to provide a more accurate security bound on differential cryptanalysis for block ciphers.

Acknowledgement. This work is supported in part by the Ministry of Education Malaysia under the Fundamental Research Grant Scheme project no. FRGS/1/2019/ICT05/USM/02/1, the National Natural Science Foundation of China under grant no. 61702212, and the Fundamental Research Funds for the Central Universities under grant no. CCNU19TS017.

Appendix

A   CPU and GPU-Accelerated Algorithms for Differential Cluster Search

Algorithm 1. Differential characteristics (cluster) searching algorithm with constraints on probability and number of active s-boxes.

Input: Input difference ΔX and output difference ΔY.
Output: Probability P_c of $\Delta X \to \Delta Y$ cluster.
Adjustable Parameters:
1. AS_BOUND : Maximum of number of active sboxes for ΔY.
2. $PROB\_BOUND$: Maximum probability of $\Delta X \to \Delta Y$.
3. P_{AS} : Estimated probability of a nibble $\Delta U \to \Delta V$.

procedure CLUSTER_SEARCH_ROUND_i $(1 \le i < n)$
    for each candidate ΔY_i **do**
        $p_i \leftarrow \Pr(\Delta X_i, \Delta Y_i)$
        $AS_{i+1} \leftarrow W_{nibble}(\Delta Y_i)$
        if $AS_{i+1} \le AS\_BOUND$ **then**
            $p_{i+1} \leftarrow (P_{AS})^{AS_{i+1}}$
            $p_r \leftarrow (P_{AS})^{n-i-1}$
            if $[p_1, ..., p_i, p_{i+1}, p_r] \ge PROB\_BOUND$ **then**
                call procedure CLUSTER_SEARCH_ROUND_$(i + 1)$
            end if
        end if
    end for
end procedure

procedure CLUSTER_SEARCH_ROUND_n
    for each candidate ΔY_n **do**
        if $\Delta Y_n == \Delta Y$ **then**
            $p_n \leftarrow \Pr(\Delta X_n, \Delta Y_n)$
            $P_c \leftarrow P_c + [p_1, ..., p_n]$
        end if
    end for
end procedure

Algorithm 2. GPU-accelerated differential (cluster) searching algorithm.

---

procedure CLUSTER_SEARCH
    call procedure CLUSTER_SEARCH_ROUND_0
    $P_c \leftarrow (\sum_{i=1}^{T_{total}} P_i) + P_h$
end procedure

procedure CLUSTER_SEARCH_ROUND_i $(1 \leq i < n)$
    $AS_i \leftarrow W_{nibble}(\Delta X_i)$
    if $AS_i > 3$ **then**
        call procedure ENUMERATION_DEVICE_i
    else
        call procedure ENUMERATION_HOST_i
    end if
    for each computed ΔY_i^j **do**
        if $(\Delta Y_{condition})_i^j ==$ TRUE **then**
            if $i+1 < N$ **then**
                call procedure CLUSTER_SEARCH_ROUND_$(i+1)$
            else
                if $AS_{i+1} > 3$ and $AS_i > 3$ **then**
                    call procedure ENUMERATION_DEVICE_n
                else
                    call procedure ENUMERATION_HOST_n
                end if
            end if
        end if
    end for
end procedure

Algorithm 3. Host (CPU) enumeration and evaluation method.

---

procedure ENUMERATION_HOST_i $(1 \leq i \leq n)$
    for each candidate $(\Delta AV_1, \Delta AV_2, ..., \Delta AV_{AS\_BOUND})$ **do**
        if $i \neq n$ **then**
            $(\Delta Y_{condition})_i^{candidate\_index} \leftarrow FALSE$
            $p_i \leftarrow \Pr(\Delta X_i, \Delta Y_i)$
            $AS_{i+1} \leftarrow W_{nibble}(\Delta Y_i)$
            if $AS_{i+1} \leq AS\_BOUND$ **then**
                $p_{i+1} \leftarrow (P_{AS})^{AS_{i+1}}$
                $p_r \leftarrow (P_{AS})^{n-i-1}$
                if $[p_1, ..., p_i, p_{i+1}, p_r] \geq PROB\_BOUND$ **then**
                    $(\Delta Y_{condition})_i^{candidate\_index} \leftarrow TRUE$
                end if
            end if
        else if $\Delta Y_i == \Delta Y$ **then**
            $P_i \leftarrow P_i + p_i$
        end if
    end for
end procedure

Algorithm 4. Device (GPU) enumeration and evaluation method.

Input: Input Difference ΔX.

Output: Enumerated branches, its evaluation result and probabilities P_i.

Adjustable Parameters:

1. AS_BOUND : Maximum of number of active s-boxes for ΔY.
2. $PROB\_BOUND$: Maximum probability of $\Delta X \to \Delta Y$.
3. P_{AS} : Estimated probability of a nibble $\Delta U \to \Delta V$.

Assumption:

1. Non-active nibble (s-boxes) will have a difference value of zero. Thus, an attempt to differentially substitute it will yield $0 \to 0$ with a probability of 1.

procedure ENUMERATION_DEVICE_i $(1 \leq i \leq n)$

    synchronize necessary information with device memory (asynchronously)

    call $KERNEL\_i$ (asynchronously)

    synchronize device information with host memory (asynchronously)

    cuda stream synchronized (wait for device to complete its computation)

end procedure

procedure KERNEL_i $(1 \leq i \leq n)$

    copy permutation table, sorted DDT (Descending Frequency), and branch size table

    to shared memory

    $T_i \leftarrow (blockIdx.x \times blockDim.x + threadIdx.x)$

    //Work assignment

    $Value \leftarrow T_i,\ Divide\_Value \leftarrow 1$

    for each active nibble values,ΔAU_i where $1 \leq i \leq 4$ **do**

        $I_i \leftarrow \lfloor Value/Divide\_Value \rfloor \bmod NB_i$

        $\Delta AV_i \leftarrow$ sorted DDT$[\Delta AU_i][I_i]$

        update p_i

        $Divide\_Value \leftarrow Divide\_Value \times NB_i$

    end for

    //Enumerating all remaining branches if $AS\_BOUND > 4$

    //Note that the for loop will still be entered even if $AU_5 = 0$

    for each candidate $(\Delta AV_5, \Delta AV_6, ..., \Delta AV_{AS\_BOUND})$ **do**

        if $i \neq n$ **then**

            $global\_offset \leftarrow (\prod_{j=1}^{AS\_BOUND} NB_j \times T_i + candidate\_index)$

            $(\Delta Y_{condition})_i^{global\_offset} \leftarrow FALSE$

            $p_i \leftarrow \Pr(\Delta X_i, \Delta Y_i)$

            $AS_{i+1} \leftarrow W_{nibble}(\Delta Y_i)$

            if $AS_{i+1} \leq AS\_BOUND$ **then**

                $p_{i+1} \leftarrow (P_{AS})^{AS_{i+1}}$

                $p_r \leftarrow (P_{AS})^{n-i-1}$

                if $[p_1, ..., p_i, p_{i+1}, p_r] \geq PROB\_BOUND$ **then**

                    $(\Delta Y_{condition})_i^{global\_offset} \leftarrow TRUE$

                end if

            end if

        else if $\Delta Y_i == \Delta Y$ **then**

            $P_i \leftarrow P_i + p_i$

        end if

    end for

end procedure

References

1. Banik, S., et al.: GIFT: a small present. In: Fischer, W., Homma, N. (eds.) CHES 2017. LNCS, vol. 10529, pp. 321–345. Springer, Cham (2017). https://doi.org/10. 1007/978-3-319-66787-4_16
2. Biryukov, A., Nikolić, I.: Automatic search for related-key differential characteristics in byte-oriented block ciphers: application to AES, Camellia, Khazad and others. In: Gilbert, H. (ed.) EUROCRYPT 2010. LNCS, vol. 6110, pp. 322–344. Springer, Heidelberg (2010). https://doi.org/10.1007/978-3-642-13190-5_17
3. Biryukov, A., Velichkov, V.: Automatic search for differential trails in ARX ciphers. In: Benaloh, J. (ed.) CT-RSA 2014. LNCS, vol. 8366, pp. 227–250. Springer, Cham (2014). https://doi.org/10.1007/978-3-319-04852-9_12
4. Borisenko, A., Haidl, M., Gorlatch, S.: A GPU parallelization of branch-and-bound for multiproduct batch plants optimization. J. Supercomput. **73**(2), 639–651 (2016). https://doi.org/10.1007/s11227-016-1784-x
5. Chen, J., Miyaji, A., Su, C., Teh, J.: Improved differential characteristic searching methods. In: 2015 IEEE 2nd International Conference on Cyber Security and Cloud Computing, pp. 500–508. IEEE, New York, November 2015. https://doi.org/10. 1109/CSCloud.2015.42, http://ieeexplore.ieee.org/document/7371529/
6. Chen, K., et al.: An improved automatic search method for diffiierential trails in TEA cipher. Int. J. Netw. Secur. **18**(4), 644–649 (2016). https://doi.org/10.6633/ IJNS.201607.18(4).05
7. ElSheikh, M., Abdelkhalek, A., Youssef, A.M.: On MILP-based automatic search for differential trails through modular additions with application to Bel-T. In: Buchmann, J., Nitaj, A., Rachidi, T. (eds.) AFRICACRYPT 2019. LNCS, vol. 11627, pp. 273–296. Springer, Cham (2019). https://doi.org/10.1007/978-3-030-23696-0_14
8. Fukang, L., Takanori, I.: Iterative Differential Characteristic of TRIFLE-BC (2019). https://eprint.iacr.org/2019/727.pdf
9. Guo, J., Peyrin, T., Poschmann, A., Robshaw, M.: The LED block cipher. In: Preneel, B., Takagi, T. (eds.) CHES 2011. LNCS, vol. 6917, pp. 326–341. Springer, Heidelberg (2011). https://doi.org/10.1007/978-3-642-23951-9_22
10. Lai, X., Massey, J.L., Murphy, S.: Markov ciphers and differential cryptanalysis. In: Davies, D.W. (ed.) EUROCRYPT 1991. LNCS, vol. 547, pp. 17–38. Springer, Heidelberg (1991). https://doi.org/10.1007/3-540-46416-6_2
11. Lalami, M.E., El-Baz, D.: GPU implementation of the branch and bound method for knapsack problems. In: 2012 IEEE 26th International Parallel and Distributed Processing Symposium Workshops & PhD Forum, pp. 1769–1777. IEEE, Shanghai, May 2012. https://doi.org/10.1109/IPDPSW.2012.219, http://ieeexplore.ieee.org/ document/6270853/
12. Matsui, M.: On correlation between the order of S-boxes and the strength of DES. In: De Santis, A. (ed.) EUROCRYPT 1994. LNCS, vol. 950, pp. 366–375. Springer, Heidelberg (1995). https://doi.org/10.1007/BFb0053451
13. Melab, N., Chakroun, I., Mezmaz, M., Tuyttens, D.: A GPU-accelerated branch-and-bound algorithm for the flow-shop scheduling problem. In: 2012 IEEE International Conference on Cluster Computing, pp. 10–17. IEEE, Beijing, September 2012. https://doi.org/10.1109/CLUSTER.2012.18, http://ieeexplore.ieee.org/ document/6337851/

14. Mouha, N., Wang, Q., Gu, D., Preneel, B.: Differential and linear cryptanalysis using mixed-integer linear programming. In: Wu, C.-K., Yung, M., Lin, D. (eds.) Inscrypt 2011. LNCS, vol. 7537, pp. 57–76. Springer, Heidelberg (2012). https://doi.org/10.1007/978-3-642-34704-7_5

15. Nicky, M., Bart, P.: Towards Finding Optimal Differential Characteristics for ARX: Application to Salsa20. Cryptology ePrint Archive, Report 2013/328 (2013). https://eprint.iacr.org/2013/328

16. Nilanjan, D., Ashrujit, G., Debdeep, M., Sikhar, P., Stjepan, P., Rajat, S.: TRIFLE, March 2019. https://csrc.nist.gov/CSRC/media/Projects/Lightweight-Cryptography/documents/round-1/spec-doc/trifle-spec.pdf

17. NIST: Lightweight Cryptography, Round-1 Candidates, April 2019. https://csrc.nist.gov/projects/lightweight-cryptography/round-1-candidates

18. NIST: Round 1 Lightweight Cryptography — Official Comments - TRIFLE (2019). https://csrc.nist.gov/CSRC/media/Projects/Lightweight-Cryptography/documents/round-1/official-comments/TRIFLE-official-comment.pdf

19. NVIDIA: CUDA C Programming Guide Version 9.0, October 2019. https://docs.nvidia.com/cuda/cuda-c-programming-guide/

20. Padua, D. (ed.): Encyclopedia of Parallel Computing. Springer, Boston (2011). https://doi.org/10.1007/978-0-387-09766-4

21. Siwei, S., et al.: Towards Finding the Best Characteristics of Some Bit-oriented Block Ciphers and Automatic Enumeration of (Related-key) Differential and Linear Characteristics with Predefined Properties (2014)

22. Song, L., Huang, Z., Yang, Q.: Automatic differential analysis of ARX block ciphers with application to SPECK and LEA. In: Liu, J.K., Steinfeld, R. (eds.) ACISP 2016. LNCS, vol. 9723, pp. 379–394. Springer, Cham (2016). https://doi.org/10.1007/978-3-319-40367-0_24

23. Sun, S., Hu, L., Song, L., Xie, Y., Wang, P.: Automatic security evaluation of block ciphers with S-bP Structures against related-key differential attacks. In: Lin, D., Xu, S., Yung, M. (eds.) Inscrypt 2013. LNCS, vol. 8567, pp. 39–51. Springer, Cham (2014). https://doi.org/10.1007/978-3-319-12087-4_3

Signature

From Rerandomizability to Sequential Aggregation: Efficient Signature Schemes Based on SXDH Assumption

Sanjit Chatterjee and R. Kabaleeshwaran[✉]

Department of Computer Science and Automation, Indian Institute of Science,
Bangalore, India
{sanjit,kabaleeshwar}@iisc.ac.in

Abstract. An aggregate signature allows one to generate a short aggregate of signatures from different signers on different messages. A sequential aggregate signature (SeqAS) scheme allows the signers to aggregate their individual signatures in a sequential manner. All existing SeqAS schemes that do not use the random oracle assumption either require a large public key or the security depends upon some non-standard interactive/static assumptions. In this paper, we present an efficient SeqAS scheme with constant-size public key under the SXDH assumption. In the process, we first obtain an optimized (and more efficient) variant of Libert et al.'s randomizable signature scheme. While both the schemes are more efficient than the currently best ones that rely on some static assumption, they are only slightly costlier than the most efficient ones based on some interactive assumption.

Keywords: Rerandomizable signature · Sequential aggregate signature · Dual-form signature technique · Standard assumption

1 Introduction

The notion of rerandomizable signature (RRS) was introduced by Camenisch and Lysyanskaya [4]. Rerandomizability guarantees that given a signature σ on some message m under the public key PK, anybody can compute another valid signature on the same message which is indistinguishable from the original signature. The above feature makes RRS a very useful tool in building privacy-preserving protocols.

The notion of aggregate signature was introduced by Boneh et al. [3]. As the name suggests, aggregation allows one to generate a (compressed) aggregate of a collection of individual signatures on different messages generated by different signers. This notion is inspired by several applications such as certificate chains of public-key infrastructure and secure routing in the context of border gateway protocol [3]. Sequential aggregate signature (SeqAS), introduced in [22], is a special type of aggregate signature. In SeqAS each signer sequentially adds his/her signature on the aggregated-so-far signature. Lu et al. [21] presented the

© Springer Nature Switzerland AG 2020
J. K. Liu and H. Cui (Eds.): ACISP 2020, LNCS 12248, pp. 183–203, 2020.
https://doi.org/10.1007/978-3-030-55304-3_10

first SeqAS scheme without random oracle based on the Waters signature [28] under the CDH assumption. However, their construction requires a large public key (linear in the security parameter).

In 2011, Schröder [26], showed how to construct a SeqAS scheme with constant-size public key based on the Camenisch-Lysyanskaya rerandomizable signature (CL-RRS). However, like the original CL-RRS scheme, security of Schröder's construction is based on a non-standard interactive assumption, called LRSW [23]. [26] relies upon the *randomness re-use* technique of [21], which makes use of the randomness of the so-far aggregated signature to construct the aggregate signature. Lee et al. [14] improved Schröder's construction further by introducing *public key sharing* technique, in which one of the elements from the public key of the underlying signature scheme (in this case, CL-RRS) is placed in the public parameter. Due to this new technique, they have achieved efficient verification and optimized public key size.

In 2013, Lee et al. [16] presented a SeqAS scheme with constant-size public key. Their SeqAS scheme is built on a signature scheme that supports multi-user setting and is publicly rerandomizable. In particular, the signature scheme is obtained by introducing suitable components to the signature derived from Lewko-Waters IBE [18] through Naor transformation. They have also used Gerbush et al.'s [8] dual-form signature technique to prove unforgeability under a previously introduced static assumption [18] along with some standard assumptions. Their follow-up work [15] improved upon the previous SeqAS in terms of signature size as well as signing/verification at the cost of a slightly larger public key under the same standard assumption along with two previously introduced static assumptions [18].

Apart from the reliance on non-standard assumption, another limitation of the CL-RRS scheme is that the signature size is linear in the number of message blocks signed. In 2016, Pointcheval and Sanders [24] presented another rerandomizable signature scheme (called, PS-RRS) where the signature size is independent of the message block length. However, unforgeability of PS-RRS scheme is proved under a new interactive assumption. Following the idea of [14], they have also presented an efficient SeqAS scheme based on the PS-RRS scheme.

In 2016, Libert et al. [19] presented a randomizable signature scheme (denoted as LMPY-RS). They suitably combined a previously proposed signature scheme [20] with a quasi-adaptive NIZK (QA-NIZK) argument [12] to obtain a constant size randomizable signature for multiple message blocks. Using the dual-form signature technique [8], they argue unforgeability of their construction under the SXDH assumption.

1.1   Our Contribution

Our first contribution is to propose an efficient rerandomizable signature scheme under the SXDH assumption. We then use the proposed RRS to realize a sequential aggregate signature scheme with constant-size public key under the SXDH assumption. The performance of the proposed schemes is very close to that of previous proposals based on some *non-standard interactive assumption*. For detailed comparison, see Table 2 (resp. Table 4) for RRS (resp. SeqAS).

For the randomizable signature, compared to Libert et al. [19], our main novelty lies in the application of the QA-NIZK proof system of Kiltz and Wee [12]. In particular, instead of the real QA-NIZK proof component, we use the simulated one. Hence we first generate the secret exponent of the signature scheme and then define the trapdoor keys with respect to the linear subspace relation of the proof system. Then, using the dual-form signature technique [8] we argue unforgeability based on the SXDH assumption while full rerandomizability [9] is shown to follow unconditionally. See Sect. 3 for the detail.

Next, our RRS serves as a building block to construct a sequential aggregate signature (SeqAS) scheme in Sect. 4. Our construction employs both 'randomness re-use' and 'public key sharing' techniques [14]. Since the original LMPY-RS is not directly amenable to signature aggregation, we tweak the signature scheme to realize the desired functionality. As can be seen from Table 4, existing schemes in a similar setting have one of the following limitations. To have security based on a standard assumption, the scheme suffers from large public key size [21]. When public key size is constant, security relies on some non-standard assumption [17]. In contrast, we obtain an efficient construction with constant size public key (and signature) where security is argued based on the well-known SXDH assumption.

2 Preliminaries

For a prime p, $\mathbb{Z}_p^*$ denotes the set of all non-zero elements from $\mathbb{Z}_p$. We denote $a \overset{\$}{\leftarrow} A$ to be an element chosen uniformly at random from the non-empty set A. We define the bilinear group generator as follows.

Definition 1. *A bilinear group generator $\mathcal{P}$ is a probabilistic polynomial time (PPT) algorithm which takes the security parameter λ as input and outputs $\Theta = (p, \mathbb{G}, \mathbb{H}, \mathbb{G}_T, e, g, h)$, where p is prime, $\mathbb{G}$, $\mathbb{H}$ and $\mathbb{G}_T$ are the prime p order groups and g (resp. h) is an arbitrary generator of $\mathbb{G}$ (resp. $\mathbb{H}$) and $e : \mathbb{G} \times \mathbb{H} \longrightarrow \mathbb{G}_T$ is a bilinear map that satisfies, (i)* **Bilinearity:** *For all $g, g' \in \mathbb{G}$ and $h, h' \in \mathbb{H}$, one has $e(g \cdot g', h \cdot h') = e(g, h) \cdot e(g, h') \cdot e(g', h) \cdot e(g', h')$, (ii)* **Non degeneracy:** *If a fixed $g \in \mathbb{G}$ satisfies $e(g, h) = 1$ for all $h \in \mathbb{H}$, then $g = 1$ and similarly for elements of $\mathbb{H}$ and (iii)* **Computability:** *The map e is efficiently computable.*

We recall the decisional Diffie-Hellman assumption (DDH) in $\mathbb{G}$ (denoted as $\text{DDH}_\mathbb{G}$) as follows.

Assumption 1. *Given $(\Theta = (p, \mathbb{G}, \mathbb{H}, \mathbb{G}_T, e, g, h), g^a, g^b)$ and $T = g^{ab+\theta}$, it is hard to decide whether $\theta = 0$ or not, for $a, b \overset{\$}{\leftarrow} \mathbb{Z}_p$.*

In the same way, we can define the DDH assumption in $\mathbb{H}$ (denoted as $\text{DDH}_\mathbb{H}$). When $\mathcal{P}$ satisfies the DDH assumption in both $\mathbb{G}$ and $\mathbb{H}$, then we say that $\mathcal{P}$ satisfies the symmetric external Diffie-Hellman (SXDH) assumption.

We recall from [10] the double pairing assumption (DBP) in $\mathbb{H}$ (denoted as $\text{DBP}_\mathbb{H}$) as follows.

Assumption 2. *Given* $(\Theta = (p, \mathbb{G}, \mathbb{H}, \mathbb{G}_T, e, g, h), h_r, h_s)$, *it is hard to compute* $(R, S) \neq (1, 1)$ *from* $\mathbb{G}^2$ *such that* $e(R, h_r)e(S, h_s) = 1$.

In the same way, we can define the DBP assumption in $\mathbb{G}$ (denoted as $\mathrm{DBP}_{\mathbb{G}}$). From [1, Lemma 2], it is clear that, $\mathrm{DBP}_{\mathbb{G}}$ is reducible to $\mathrm{DDH}_{\mathbb{G}}$ and $\mathrm{DBP}_{\mathbb{H}}$ is reducible to $\mathrm{DDH}_{\mathbb{H}}$. The formal definition of digital signature, rerandomizable signature and sequential aggregate signature schemes can be found in the full version [6].

3   Rerandomizable Signature

In this section, we describe an efficient rerandomizable signature scheme, whose security is proved under the SXDH assumption. Our construction is inspired from [19]. In [19], one requires to know the public key components to randomize the signature, whereas in our scheme one needs to know only the underlying group order. This feature will later play an important role in the construction of aggregate signature of Sect. 4.

3.1   Construction

Libert et al. [19] presented a randomizable signature scheme (denoted as LMPY-RS) based on QA-NIZK proof system. In particular, to prove that a vector of group elements belongs to some linear subspace, [11,12] showed that the argument size will be independent of the subspace dimension. [19] exploited this property to obtain a randomizable signature scheme for multiple block messages with a constant size signature. In order to prove unforgeability, they have used Gerbush et al.'s [8] dual-form signature technique.

In LMPY-RS scheme the secret key SK consists of ω from $\mathbb{Z}_p$ and the public key PK consists of $(g, g_0, h, U_1 = g^{u_1}, \{V_{1j} = g^{v_{1j}}\}_{j=1}^{\ell}, \Omega = g_0^{\omega}, \mathrm{CRS})$ with CRS consisting of $(z, U_2, \{V_{2j}\}_{j=1}^{\ell}, h_z, h_0 = h_z^{\delta_0}, h_{\ell+1} = h_z^{\delta_{\ell+1}}, h_{10} = h_z^{\delta_{10}}, h_{20} = h_z^{\delta_{20}}, \{h_{1j} = h_z^{\delta_{1j}}, h_{2j} = h_z^{\delta_{2j}}\}_{j=1}^{\ell})$, where $g, z, g_0, U_1, U_2, V_{1j}, V_{2j}$ are from $\mathbb{G}$ and $h, h_z, h_0, h_{\ell+1}, h_{10}, h_{20}, h_{1j}, h_{2j}$ are from $\mathbb{H}$. Note that the trapdoor information $(\delta_0, \delta_{\ell+1}, \delta_{10}, \delta_{20}, \{\delta_{1j}, \delta_{2j}\}_{j=1}^{\ell})$ are generated in such a way that $z = g^{\delta_0} g_0^{\delta_{\ell+1}}$, $U_2 = U_1^{\delta_0} g^{\delta_{10}} g_0^{\delta_{20}}$ and $V_{2j} = V_{1j}^{\delta_0} g^{\delta_{1j}} g_0^{\delta_{2j}}$ holds. Hence one can write $U_2 = g^{u_2}, \{V_{2j} = g^{v_{2j}}\}_{j=1}^{\ell}$, where $u_2 = \delta_0 u_1 + \delta_{10} + a\delta_{20}$, $v_{2j} = \delta_0 v_{1j} + \delta_{1j} + a\delta_{2j}$ and $g_0 = g^a$. The randomizable signature on the message $\boldsymbol{m} = (m_1, \ldots, m_\ell)$ consists of $\sigma = (\sigma_1, \sigma_2, \sigma_3, \pi)$, where

$$\sigma_1 = g^{\omega}\Big(U_1 \prod_{j=1}^{\ell} V_{1j}^{m_j}\Big)^s, \ \sigma_2 = g^s, \ \sigma_3 = g_0^s, \ \pi = z^{\omega}\Big(U_2 \prod_{j=1}^{\ell} V_{2j}^{m_j}\Big)^s.$$

Note that the signature component π corresponds to the QA-NIZK proof that the statement $(\sigma_1, \sigma_2^{m_1}, \ldots, \sigma_2^{m_\ell}, \sigma_2, \sigma_3^{m_1}, \ldots, \sigma_3^{m_\ell}, \sigma_3, \Omega)$ belongs to a linear subspace generated by the matrix $M \in \mathbb{Z}_p^{(\ell+2) \times (2\ell+4)}$ as defined in Eq. 1. Our RRS scheme is obtained from LMPY-RS scheme by removing the first row and the last $\ell + 2$ columns of the matrix M, which results in the matrix N as defined in Eq. 1.

$$
M = \begin{pmatrix}
g & \begin{array}{ccccc} 1 & 1 & \dots & 1 & 1 \end{array} & \begin{array}{ccccc} 1 & 1 & \dots & 1 & 1 \end{array} & g_0 \\
V_{11} & \begin{array}{ccccc} g & 1 & \dots & 1 & 1 \end{array} & \begin{array}{ccccc} g_0 & 1 & \dots & 1 & 1 \end{array} & 1 \\
V_{12} & \begin{array}{ccccc} 1 & g & \dots & 1 & 1 \end{array} & \begin{array}{ccccc} 1 & g_0 & \dots & 1 & 1 \end{array} & 1 \\
\vdots & \begin{array}{ccccc} \vdots & \vdots & \ddots & \vdots & \vdots \end{array} & \begin{array}{ccccc} \vdots & \vdots & \ddots & \vdots & \vdots \end{array} & \vdots \\
V_{1\ell} & \begin{array}{ccccc} 1 & 1 & \dots & g & 1 \end{array} & \begin{array}{ccccc} 1 & 1 & \dots & g_0 & 1 \end{array} & 1 \\
U_1 & \begin{array}{ccccc} 1 & 1 & \dots & 1 & g \end{array} & \begin{array}{ccccc} 1 & 1 & \dots & 1 & g_0 \end{array} & 1
\end{pmatrix}, \quad N = \begin{pmatrix}
V_{11} & \begin{array}{cccc} g & 1 & \dots & 1 & 1 \end{array} \\
V_{12} & \begin{array}{cccc} 1 & g & \dots & 1 & 1 \end{array} \\
\vdots & \begin{array}{cccc} \vdots & \vdots & \ddots & \vdots & \vdots \end{array} \\
V_{1\ell} & \begin{array}{cccc} 1 & 1 & \dots & g & 1 \end{array} \\
U_1 & \begin{array}{cccc} 1 & 1 & \dots & 1 & g \end{array}
\end{pmatrix}. \tag{1}
$$

Notice that the removal of the first row of M corresponds to putting $\omega = 0 \bmod p$ which amounts to removing g^ω (resp. z^ω) from σ_1 (resp. π) and Ω from PK. The last $\ell + 2$ columns of M correspond to the second generator g_0 and $\{\{h_{2j}\}_{j=1}^\ell, h_{20}, h_{\ell+1}\}$ in PK of LMPY-RS. In the signature generation, we directly use the simulated proof component instead of the real QA-NIZK proof component. This allows to set SK containing the trapdoor dependent information $u_2, \{v_{2j}\}_{j=1}^\ell$ along with $g, u_1, \{v_{1j}\}_{j=1}^\ell$.

Table 1. RRS scheme in the prime-order setting.

Setup(λ)

Run $\mathcal{P}(\lambda) \to (p, \mathbb{G}, \mathbb{H}, \mathbb{G}_T, e, g, h)$, where $g \xleftarrow{\$} \mathbb{G}, h \xleftarrow{\$} \mathbb{H}$,
Return $PP = (p, \mathbb{G}, \mathbb{H}, \mathbb{G}_T, e, g, h)$.

KeyGen(PP)

Choose $\delta_0, u_1, u_2, \{v_{1j}, v_{2j}\}_{j=1}^\ell \xleftarrow{\$} \mathbb{Z}_p, h_z \xleftarrow{\$} \mathbb{H}$ and set $h_0 := h_z^{\delta_0}$,
$\delta_{10} := u_2 - \delta_0 u_1, \delta_j := v_{2j} - \delta_0 v_{1j}$, for all $j \in [1, \ell]$.
Set $SK := \{g, u_1, u_2, \{v_{1j}, v_{2j}\}_{j=1}^\ell\}, PK := \{h_z, h_0, h_{10} := h_z^{\delta_{10}}, \{h_j := h_z^{\delta_j}\}_{j=1}^\ell\}$.
Return (SK, PK).

Sign($SK, \boldsymbol{m} = (m_1, \dots, m_\ell)$)

Choose $r \xleftarrow{\$} \mathbb{Z}_p$ and set $A := g^{r(u_1 + \sum_{j=1}^\ell v_{1j} m_j)}, B := g^r, C := g^{r(u_2 + \sum_{j=1}^\ell v_{2j} m_j)}$.
Return $(\boldsymbol{m}, \sigma = (A, B, C))$.

Ver($PK, \boldsymbol{m} = (m_1, \dots, m_\ell), \sigma = (A, B, C)$)

Accept if $B \neq 1$ and

$$
e(A, h_0) e(B, h_{10} \prod_{j=1}^\ell h_j^{m_j}) = e(C, h_z). \tag{2}
$$

Rand($PK, \boldsymbol{m} = (m_1, \dots, m_\ell), \sigma = (A, B, C)$)

If Ver($PK, \boldsymbol{m}, \sigma$)=1, then choose $s \xleftarrow{\$} \mathbb{Z}_p$ and compute $A' := A^s, B' := B^s, C' := C^s$.
Return $\sigma' = (A', B', C')$.
Else Return $\perp$.

The RRS scheme consists of four PPT algorithms, which are defined in Table 1. Notice that, we avoid the trivial forgery attack by checking $B \neq 1$. Suppose, we do not check the above condition, then anyone can output $\sigma = (1, 1, 1)$ as a (trivial) forgery on any message $\boldsymbol{m} \in \mathbb{Z}_p^\ell$. Correctness of the scheme can be verified using the following derivation,

$$e(A, h_0)e(B, h_{10} \prod_{j=1}^{\ell} h_j^{m_j}) = e(g^{r(u_1 + \sum_j v_{1j} m_j)}, h_z^{\delta_0})e(g^r, h_z^{\delta_{10} + \sum_j \delta_j m_j})$$

$$= e(g^{r(\delta_0 u_1 + \delta_{10}) + r \sum_j (\delta_0 v_{1j} + \delta_j) m_j}, h_z)$$

$$= e(g^{r(u_2 + \sum_j v_{2j} m_j)}, h_z) = e(C, h_z).$$

The first equality is obtained by substituting the values of the signature and public key components. Second equality is obtained using the bilinearity of the pairing map. The third equality is obtained by substituting the value of u_2 and v_{2j} components from Table 1.

Notice that, it is sufficient to consider the elements $U_1 = g^{u_1}, U_2 = g^{u_2}$ and $\{V_{1j} = g^{v_{1j}}, V_{2j} = g^{v_{2j}}\}_{j=1}^{\ell}$, as part of the SK. However, for better efficiency, we consider the respective exponents of U_1, U_2, V_{1j} and V_{2j} as part of the SK, which saves 2ℓ many exponentiation and multiplication in the group $\mathbb{G}$.

3.2   Randomizability

The main feature of a rerandomizable signature scheme is the so-called *randomizability property*. This feature has been utilized effectively in the construction of several other protocols, such as group signature [2] and anonymous credential scheme [4].

Theorem 1. *The RRS scheme satisfies perfect randomizability.*

Proof. We argue that our RRS scheme satisfies perfect randomizability. To establish that, it is sufficient to prove that the signature returned by Rand and Sign are identically distributed. First, we consider the signature $\sigma = (A, B, C)$ returned by the adversary $\mathcal{A}$ using Sign on the message $\boldsymbol{m} = (m_1, \ldots, m_\ell)$. In particular, we write

$$A = g^{r(u_1 + \sum_j v_{1j} m_j)}, B = g^r, C = g^{r(u_2 + \sum_j v_{2j} m_j)},$$

for some randomness r from $\mathbb{Z}_p$. Then we consider the signature $\sigma_1 = (A_1, B_1, C_1)$ returned by Rand on the message and signature pair $(\boldsymbol{m}, \sigma)$, where $A_1 = A^s = g^{sr(u_1 + \sum_j v_{1j} m_j)}$, $B_1 = B^s = g^{rs}$ and $C_1 = C^s = g^{sr(u_2 + \sum_j v_{2j} m_j)}$, for some randomness s from $\mathbb{Z}_p$. Now we consider the signature $\sigma_0 = (A_0, B_0, C_0)$ returned by Sign on the same message $\boldsymbol{m}$, where

$$A_0 = g^{z(u_1 + \sum_j v_{1j} m_j)}, B_0 = g^z, C_0 = g^{z(u_2 + \sum_j v_{2j} m_j)}$$

for some randomness z from $\mathbb{Z}_p$. Notice that, in the signature σ_1, the exponent s is the source of randomness whereas in the signature σ_0, the exponent z is the source of randomness. Thus it is clear that both the signatures σ_0 and σ_1 are identically distributed, as rs and z are independent and identically distributed. $\qquad\square$

3.3   Unforgeability

We use the Gerbush et al.'s [8] dual-form signature technique and prove unforgeability under the SXDH assumption. Note that, unlike [19], we argue unforgeability without appealing to the security of the underlying QA-NIZK proof system.

Partition of Forgery Space: Let $\mathcal{V}$ be the set of all message and signature pairs such that they verify under the public key PK. We partition the forgery class $\mathcal{V}$ into two disjoint sets $\mathcal{V}_I$ and $\mathcal{V}_{II}$ which are defined as follows.

Type-I: $\mathcal{V}_I = \{(m^*, \sigma^*) \in \mathcal{V} : S_1^* = 1 \text{ and } S_2^* = 1\}$,
Type-II: $\mathcal{V}_{II} = \{(m^*, \sigma^*) \in \mathcal{V} : S_1^* \neq 1 \text{ and } S_2^* \neq 1\}$,

where $S_1^* := A^*(B^*)^{-u_1 - \sum_{j=1}^{\ell} v_{1j} m_j^*}$ and $S_2^* := (C^*)^{-1}(B^*)^{u_2 + \sum_{j=1}^{\ell} v_{2j} m_j^*}$. Now we argue that the Type-II forgery class is same as the complement of Type-I forgery class with respect to the forgery space $\mathcal{V}$, i.e., $\mathcal{V}_{II} = \mathcal{V} - \mathcal{V}_I$. Notice that from the verification Eq. 2, we can simplify as follows.

$$
\begin{aligned}
1 &= e(A^*, h_0)e(B^*, h_{10} \prod_{j=1}^{\ell} h_j^{m_j^*})e(C^*, h_z)^{-1} \\
&= e(A^*, h_z^{\delta_0})e(B^*, h_z^{(u_2 - \delta_0 u_1) + \sum_{j=1}^{\ell}(v_{2j} - \delta_0 v_{1j})m_j^*})e(C^*, h_z)^{-1} \\
&= e(A^*(B^*)^{-u_1 - \sum_{j=1}^{\ell} v_{1j} m_j^*}, h_z^{\delta_0})e((C^*)^{-1}(B^*)^{u_2 + \sum_{j=1}^{\ell} v_{2j} m_j^*}, h_z) \\
&= e(S_1^*, h_0)e(S_2^*, h_z)
\end{aligned}
$$

In the above derivation, the second equality is obtained by the values of h_{10} and h_j and then substituting the values of δ_{10} and δ_j. The third equality is obtained by using the bilinearity of the pairing map and the last equality is obtained by the definition of S_1^* and S_2^*. Suppose $S_1^* = 1$, then the above equation can be simplified as $e(S_2^*, h_z) = 1$. Then from the non-degeneracy of the pairing, we have S_2^* must be 1. In the same way, suppose $S_2^* = 1$, then S_1^* must be 1. Hence there is no valid forgery such that (i) $S_1^* = 1$ and $S_2^* \neq 1$ hold or (ii) $S_1^* \neq 1$ and $S_2^* = 1$ hold.

Structure of Forged Signature: Consider the message and signature pair (m^*, σ^*) satisfying the verification Eq. 2, where $m^* = (m_1^*, \ldots, m_\ell^*) \in \mathbb{Z}_p^\ell$ and $\sigma^* = (A^*, B^*, C^*) \in \mathbb{G}^3$. Suppose the forgery is Type-II, then we explain, how the signature components are written explicitly in terms of the secret exponents. Since $B^* \in \mathbb{G}$, $B^* \neq 1$ and g is the generator of $\mathbb{G}$, we can write $B^* = g^r$, for some $r \in \mathbb{Z}_p^*$. For the Type-II forgery, the condition $S_1^* \neq 1$ holds, we can write $S_1^* = g^{s_1}$, for some $s_1 \in \mathbb{Z}_p^*$. Then substituting B^* value in S_1^* we obtain that $A^* = g^{r(u_1 + \sum_{j=1}^{\ell} v_{1j} m_j^*) + s_1}$. The condition $S_2^* \neq 1$ holds for a Type-II forgery. Then we can write $S_2^* = g^{-s}$, for some $s \in \mathbb{Z}_p^*$. By substituting the value of B^* in S_2^*, we obtain that $C^* = g^{r(u_2 + \sum_{j=1}^{\ell} v_{2j} m_j^*) + s}$. Now from the verification Eq. 2, the additional terms g^{s_1} and g^s must satisfy the condition $e(g^{s_1}, h_0) = e(g^s, h_z)$, so that the Type-II forgery is valid. From the above condition, we can derive that $s_1 = s/\delta_0$. Hence a Type-II forgery can be written as,

$$A^* = g^{r(u_1 + \sum_{j=1}^{\ell} v_{1j} m_j^*) + s/\delta_0}, \quad B^* = g^r, \quad C^* = g^{r(u_2 + \sum_{j=1}^{\ell} v_{2j} m_j^*) + s}, \quad (3)$$

for some $r, s \in \mathbb{Z}_p$.

Suppose the forgery is Type-I, then we see that both conditions, $S_1^* = 1$ and $S_2^* = 1$ hold. From the above explanation for the Type-II forgery case and the above conditions, it is clear that s has to be zero modulo p for a Type-I forgery. Hence by substituting $s = 0$ in Eq. 3, we obtain the desired form of Type-I forgery as defined in Table 1.

Two Signing Algorithms: Let Sign_A be same as the Sign algorithm defined in Table 1. Next we define the following Sign_B algorithm, which is used by the simulator in the unforgeability proof. The Sign_B algorithm takes the secret key SK along with element δ_0 from $\mathbb{Z}_p$ and the message $\boldsymbol{m} \in \mathbb{Z}_p^{\ell}$ and outputs a message-signature pair.

Sign_B $(SK \cup \{\delta_0\}, \boldsymbol{m} = (m_1, \ldots, m_\ell))$: Choose $r, s \xleftarrow{\$} \mathbb{Z}_p$ and compute $A := g^{r(u_1 + \sum_{j=1}^{\ell} v_{1j} m_j) + s/\delta_0}, B := g^r \ C := g^{r(u_2 + \sum_{j=1}^{\ell} v_{2j} m_j) + s}$. Return $(\boldsymbol{m}, \sigma := (A, B, C))$.

From the verification Eq. 2, the additional element g^{s/δ_0} in A paired with $h_z^{\delta_0}$ is same as the additional element g^s in C paired with h_z. Hence, the signature returned by Sign_B also verifies under PK.

Proof Intuition: We prove unforgeability of our RRS scheme using a hybrid argument. Let Game_R be the real EUF-CMA security game, i.e., given the public key, adversary $\mathcal{A}$ makes q many signing oracle queries which are answered using Sign_A and returns a forgery (from $\mathcal{V}$) on a new message. Next, we define a new game Game_0 which is similar to Game_R except that $\mathcal{A}$ returns a Type-I forgery. The only difference between Game_R and Game_0 is that of $\mathcal{A}$ producing a Type-II forgery. Then we prove that under the $\mathsf{DBP}_{\mathbb{H}}$ assumption, $\mathcal{A}$ cannot return a Type-II forgery, which ensures that Game_R and Game_0 are indistinguishable. In this reduction, simulator $\mathcal{B}$ embeds the DBP instance to generate the public key terms h_z and $h_z^{\delta_0}$. Then by choosing all the other secret exponents, $\mathcal{B}$ can answer for Sign_A queries. Finally, from the Type-II forgery returned by $\mathcal{A}$, $\mathcal{B}$ computes the solution for the $\mathsf{DBP}_{\mathbb{H}}$ instance.

Next, we define another game Game_k which is similar to Game_0, except that the first k signing queries are answered using Sign_B algorithm. Then we prove that Game_{k-1} and Game_k are indistinguishable under the $\mathsf{DDH}_{\mathbb{G}}$ assumption. In this reduction, simulator $\mathcal{B}$ embeds one of the terms (say g^b) from the DDH instance to define u_1 and u_2. In particular, $\mathcal{B}$ defines $u_1 = \tilde{u}_1 + tb/\delta_0$ and $u_2 = \tilde{u}_2 + tb$, for random exponents $\tilde{u}_1, \tilde{u}_2, \delta_0, t$. Then $\mathcal{B}$ uses the other term (say g^a) from the DDH instance for the k-th signature and embeds g^a and $g^{ab+\theta}$ to answer for the k-th signing query. For a given DDH tuple with $\theta = 0$ we are simulating Game_{k-1}, otherwise we are simulating Game_k.

Finally, we argue that the advantage of Game_q is negligible under the $\mathsf{DBP}_{\mathbb{H}}$ assumption. In this reduction, simulator $\mathcal{B}$ embeds the DBP instance to simulate the public key components h_z and $h_z^{\delta_0}$. Then $\mathcal{B}$ defines the exponents u_1 and

u_2 in such a way that $\mathcal{B}$ can answer for Sign_B oracle queries. In particular, $\mathcal{B}$ defines $u_1 = \tilde{u}_1 - t/\delta_0$ and $u_2 = \tilde{u}_2 - t$, for random exponents $t, \tilde{u}_1, \tilde{u}_2$. Once the adversary returns a Type-I forgery, then $\mathcal{B}$ could extract the solution for the DBP problem.

Theorem 2. *If SXDH assumption holds in $\mathcal{P}$, then the RRS scheme is EUF-CMA secure.*

Proof. First we define the following games.

Game_R: This is the original EUF-CMA game. Recall that, after receiving the PK from the challenger, the adversary $\mathcal{A}$ makes q many signing oracle queries adaptively and then returns a forgery on a new message.

Game_0: Same as Game_R except that $\mathcal{A}$ returns a forgery from $\mathcal{V}_I$. Let E be the event that $\mathcal{A}$ returns a forgery from $\mathcal{V}_{II}$ in Game_0. In Lemma 3, we prove that the event E happens with negligible probability under $\mathrm{DBP}_{\mathbb{H}}$ assumption. Thus we deduce that Game_R and Game_0 are computationally indistinguishable under $\mathrm{DBP}_{\mathbb{H}}$ assumption. In particular we have,

$$|Adv_{\mathcal{A}}^{\mathsf{Game}_R} - Adv_{\mathcal{A}}^{\mathsf{Game}_0}| \leq Pr[E] \leq Adv_{\mathcal{B}}^{DBP_{\mathbb{H}}}.$$

Game_k: Same as Game_0 except that the first k signing queries are answered using Sign_B, for $k \in [1, q]$, whereas the last $q - k$ queries are answered using Sign_A. For $k \in [1, q]$, in Lemma 4, we prove that Game_{k-1} and Game_k are computationally indistinguishable under $\mathrm{DDH}_{\mathbb{G}}$ assumption. In particular we have,

$$|Adv_{\mathcal{A}}^{\mathsf{Game}_{k-1}} - Adv_{\mathcal{A}}^{\mathsf{Game}_k}| \leq Adv_{\mathcal{B}}^{DDH_{\mathbb{G}}}.$$

Finally in Lemma 5, we prove that $Adv_{\mathcal{A}}^{\mathsf{Game}_q}$ is negligible under $\mathrm{DBP}_{\mathbb{H}}$ assumption. In particular we have,

$$Adv_{\mathcal{A}}^{\mathsf{Game}_q} \leq Adv_{\mathcal{B}}^{DBP_{\mathbb{H}}}.$$

Hence by the hybrid argument and from Eqs. 4, 5 and 6, described below, we have,

$$\begin{aligned} Adv_{\mathcal{A}}^{UF} = Adv_{\mathcal{A}}^{\mathsf{Game}_R} &= |Adv_{\mathcal{A}}^{\mathsf{Game}_R} - Adv_{\mathcal{A}}^{\mathsf{Game}_0} + Adv_{\mathcal{A}}^{\mathsf{Game}_0} - Adv_{\mathcal{A}}^{\mathsf{Game}_1} + \ldots + \\ & Adv_{\mathcal{A}}^{\mathsf{Game}_{k-1}} - Adv_{\mathcal{A}}^{\mathsf{Game}_k} + \ldots - Adv_{\mathcal{A}}^{\mathsf{Game}_q} + Adv_{\mathcal{A}}^{\mathsf{Game}_q}| \\ &\leq |Adv_{\mathcal{A}}^{\mathsf{Game}_R} - Adv_{\mathcal{A}}^{\mathsf{Game}_0}| + \sum_{k=1}^{q} |Adv_{\mathcal{A}}^{\mathsf{Game}_{k-1}} - Adv_{\mathcal{A}}^{\mathsf{Game}_k}| + |Adv_{\mathcal{A}}^{\mathsf{Game}_q}| \\ &\leq Adv_{\mathcal{B}}^{DBP_{\mathbb{H}}} + q\, Adv_{\mathcal{B}}^{DDH_{\mathbb{G}}} + Adv_{\mathcal{B}}^{DBP_{\mathbb{H}}} \\ &\leq (q+2)\, Adv_{\mathcal{B}}^{SXDH}. \end{aligned}$$

$\square$

Lemma 3. *If $DBP_{\mathbb{H}}$ assumption holds in $\mathcal{P}$, then $Pr[E]$ is negligible.*

Proof. Assume that the event E happens with some non-negligible probability. Then we construct a simulator $\mathcal{B}$ to break the $DBP_{\mathbb{H}}$ assumption as follows. $\mathcal{B}$ is given Θ and h_r, h_s from $\mathbb{H}$ and his goal is to compute $(R, S) \neq (1, 1)$ from $\mathbb{G}^2$ such that $e(R, h_r)e(S, h_s) = 1$. Now $\mathcal{B}$ chooses $u_1, u_2, \{v_{1j}, v_{2j}\}_{j=1}^{\ell}$ uniformly at random from $\mathbb{Z}_p$. First $\mathcal{B}$ implicitly sets $\delta_{10} = u_2 - \delta_0 u_1$ and $\delta_j = v_{2j} - \delta_0 v_{1j}$, for $j \in [1, \ell]$. Then $\mathcal{B}$ defines the public key as,

$$PK := \left\{ h_z := h_r, h_0 := h_s, h_{10} := h_r^{u_2} h_s^{-u_1}, \{h_j := h_r^{v_{2j}} h_s^{-v_{1j}}\}_{j=1}^{\ell} \right\}.$$

Once PK is given to $\mathcal{A}$, he makes q many signing oracle queries to $\mathcal{B}$. Since $\mathcal{B}$ knows all the SK components such as $g, u_1, u_2, \{v_{1j}, v_{2j}\}_{j=1}^{\ell}$, he can answer all the signing queries using Sign_A algorithm.

Finally, $\mathcal{A}$ returns a forgery $(\boldsymbol{m}^*, \sigma^*)$, where $\boldsymbol{m}^* = (m_1^*, \ldots, m_{\ell}^*) \in \mathbb{Z}_p^{\ell}$ and $\sigma^* = (A^*, B^*, C^*) \in \mathbb{G}^3$. Then $\mathcal{B}$ checks (i) the forgery $(\boldsymbol{m}^*, \sigma^*)$ is valid and (ii) the message $\boldsymbol{m}^*$ is not queried earlier. If any of these checks fail to hold, then $\mathcal{B}$ aborts. Otherwise, $\mathcal{B}$ tries to solve the $DBP_{\mathbb{H}}$ assumption as follows. First $\mathcal{B}$ computes $S = A^*(B^*)^{-u_1 - \sum_{j=1}^{\ell} v_{1j} m_j^*}$ and $R = (C^*)^{-1}(B^*)^{u_2 + \sum_{j=1}^{\ell} v_{2j} m_j^*}$. Since the forgery is valid, hence it satisfies the verification Eq. 2 which can be re-written and then simplified as follows.

$$1 = e(C^*, h_z)^{-1} \cdot e(A^*, h_0) \cdot e(B^*, h_{10} \prod_j h_{1j}^{m_j^*})$$

$$= e(C^*, h_r)^{-1} e(A^*, h_s) \cdot e(B^*, h_r^{u_2} h_s^{-u_1} \prod_j (h_r^{v_{2j}} h_s^{-v_{1j}})^{m_j^*})$$

$$= e((C^*)^{-1}(B^*)^{u_2 + \sum_j v_{2j} m_j^*}, h_r) e(A^*(B^*)^{-u_1 - \sum_j v_{1j} m_j^*}, h_s)$$

$$= e(R, h_r) e(S, h_s).$$

In the above derivation, the second equality follows from the structure of public key components and the third equality follows from the bilinearity of the pairing map. The last equality follows from the definition of R and S.

In order to break the $DBP_{\mathbb{H}}$ problem, it is sufficient to argue that $(R, S) \neq (1, 1)$. From our contradiction assumption, $\mathcal{A}$ returns a Type-II forgery, then it must satisfy $S = A^* (B^*)^{-u_1 - \sum_j v_{1j} m_j^*} \neq 1$ and $R = (C^*)^{-1}(B^*)^{u_2 + \sum_j v_{2j} m_j^*} \neq 1$. Then $\mathcal{B}$ returns (R, S) as a non-trivial solution for the $DBP_{\mathbb{H}}$ instance. Thus we have,

$$Pr[E] \leq Adv_{\mathcal{B}}^{DBP_{\mathbb{H}}}. \tag{4}$$

$\square$

Lemma 4. *If $DDH_{\mathbb{G}}$ assumption holds in $\mathcal{P}$, then $\mathsf{Game}_{k-1} \approx_c \mathsf{Game}_k$, for $k \in [1, q]$.*

Proof. Suppose there exists a PPT adversary $\mathcal{A}$, who distinguishes Game_{k-1} from Game_k with some non-negligible probability under the condition that $\mathcal{A}$ returns a Type-I forgery. Then we construct a simulator $\mathcal{B}$ to break the $DDH_{\mathbb{G}}$

assumption as follows. $\mathcal{B}$ is given Θ, g^a, g^b, $g^{ab+\theta}$ and his goal is to decide whether $\theta = 0 \mod p$ or not. Now $\mathcal{B}$ chooses $\delta_0, \tilde{u}_1, \tilde{u}_2, t$ uniformly at random from $\mathbb{Z}_p$ and implicitly sets $u_1 = \tilde{u}_1 + tb/\delta_0$ and $u_2 = \tilde{u}_2 + tb$. $\mathcal{B}$ also chooses h_z uniformly at random from $\mathbb{H}$ and defines $h_0 = h_z^{\delta_0}$. Then $\mathcal{B}$ defines $\delta_{10} := u_2 - \delta_0 u_1 = \tilde{u}_2 - \delta_0 \tilde{u}_1$ and hence s/he simulates h_{10} as $h_z^{\tilde{u}_2 - \delta_0 \tilde{u}_1}$. $\mathcal{B}$ also chooses v_{1j}, v_{2j} uniformly at random from $\mathbb{Z}_p$ and defines h_j as $h_z^{v_{2j} - \delta_0 v_{1j}}$. Here PK consists of $\{h_z, h_0, h_{10}, \{h_j\}_{j=1}^{\ell}\}$, which is then sent to $\mathcal{A}$. Notice that $\mathcal{B}$ can simulate the SK components $g, \{v_{1j}, v_{2j}\}_{j=1}^{\ell}$ along with δ_0. However, $\mathcal{B}$ can simulate $U_1 := g^{\tilde{u}_1}(g^b)^{t/\delta_0}$ and $U_2 = g^{\tilde{u}_2}(g^b)^t$, so that he can answer for the signing queries. $\mathcal{B}$ computes $V_{1j} := g^{v_{1j}}, V_{2j} := g^{v_{2j}}$, for $j \in [1, \ell]$.

After receiving PK, $\mathcal{A}$ makes signing queries on some message $\boldsymbol{m}_i = (m_{i1}, \ldots, m_{i\ell})$. For the first $k - 1$ (resp. last $q - k$) queries, $\mathcal{B}$ uses $\mathsf{Sign}_{\mathcal{B}}$ (resp. $\mathsf{Sign}_{\mathcal{A}}$) algorithm to answer for signing queries, as he knows the components $g, U_1, U_2, \{V_{1j}, V_{2j}\}_{j=1}^{\ell}$ as well as δ_0. In particular, $\mathsf{Sign}_{\mathcal{B}}$ queries are answered by computing $\sigma_i = (A_i, B_i, C_i)$, where

$$A_i = (U_1 \prod_j V_{1j}^{m_{ij}})^r g^{s/\delta_0}, \quad B_i = g^r, \quad C_i = (U_2 \prod_j V_{2j}^{m_{ij}})^r g^s$$

and r, s are chosen uniformly at random from $\mathbb{Z}_p$. However, $\mathsf{Sign}_{\mathcal{A}}$ queries are answered by letting $s = 0$ in the above signature obtained using $\mathsf{Sign}_{\mathcal{B}}$ algorithm. For the k-th query, $\mathcal{B}$ embeds the DDH instance to construct the signature $\sigma_k = (A_k, B_k, C_k)$, where $B_k := g^a$ and

$$A_k := (g^a)^{\tilde{u}_1}(g^{ab+\theta})^{t/\delta_0}(g^a)^{\sum_j v_{1j} m_{kj}} = g^{a\left((\tilde{u}_1 + tb/\delta_0) + \sum_j v_{1j} m_{kj}\right)} g^{t\theta/\delta_0}$$
$$= g^{a(u_1 + \sum_j v_{1j} m_{kj}) + t\theta/\delta_0},$$

$$C_k := (g^a)^{\tilde{u}_2}(g^{ab+\theta})^t(g^a)^{\sum_j v_{2j} m_{kj}} = g^{a\left((\tilde{u}_2 + tb) + \sum_j v_{2j} m_{kj}\right)} g^{t\theta},$$
$$= g^{a(u_2 + \sum_j v_{2j} m_{kj}) + t\theta}.$$

In the above derivation, we re-arrange the terms appropriately and use the definition of u_1 and u_2. Note that the exponent a from the DDH instance is used to simulate the signature randomness whereas $s = t\theta \mod p$. Suppose $\theta = 0 \mod p$, then $s = 0 \mod p$, i.e., the signature σ_k is distributed as an output of $\mathsf{Sign}_{\mathcal{A}}$. If $\theta \neq 0 \mod p$, then $s \neq 0 \mod p$, i.e., the signature σ_k is distributed as an output of $\mathsf{Sign}_{\mathcal{B}}$ with non-zero exponent $s = t\theta \mod p$.

Finally, $\mathcal{A}$ returns a forgery $(\boldsymbol{m}^*, \sigma^*)$. As before, $\mathcal{B}$ checks (i) the forgery is valid and (ii) the message $\boldsymbol{m}^* = (m_1^*, \ldots, m_\ell^*)$ is not queried earlier. Note that σ_k is generated using the DDH instance. Since $\mathcal{B}$ knows δ_0, U_1, U_2 and all the other secret key components, $\mathcal{B}$ can generate the k-th signature of any type properly. However, $\mathcal{B}$ cannot on her/his own decide the type of the signatures generated using the problem instance, as s/he cannot compute S_1^* and S_2^* which uses the exponents u_1 and u_2. In other words, $\mathcal{B}$ needs to rely on the advantage of $\mathcal{A}$.

From Lemma 3, under DBP assumption, $\mathcal{A}$ only returns a Type-I forgery. Also from our initial contradiction assumption, $\mathcal{A}$ distinguishes between

Game_{k-1} and Game_k with some non-negligible probability. So $\mathcal{B}$ leverages $\mathcal{A}$ to break the DDH assumption. Thus we have,

$$\left| Adv_{\mathcal{A}}^{\mathsf{Game}_{k-1}} - Adv_{\mathcal{A}}^{\mathsf{Game}_k} \right| \leq Adv_{\mathcal{B}}^{DDH_{\mathbb{G}}}. \tag{5}$$

$\square$

Lemma 5. *If* $DBP_{\mathbb{H}}$ *assumption holds in* $\mathcal{P}$, *then* Adv^{Game_q} *is negligible.*

Proof. Suppose there exists a PPT adversary $\mathcal{A}$, who wins in Game_q and produces a Type-I forgery with some non-negligible probability. Then we construct a simulator $\mathcal{B}$ to break the $DBP_{\mathbb{H}}$ assumption as follows. $\mathcal{B}$ is given Θ and h_r, h_s from $\mathbb{H}$ and his goal is to compute $(R, S) \neq (1, 1)$ from $\mathbb{G}^2$ such that $e(R, h_r)e(S, h_s) = 1$. Now $\mathcal{B}$ sets $h_z := h_r$, $h_z^{\delta_0} := h_s$ and implicitly sets $u_1 := \tilde{u}_1 - t/\delta_0$ and $u_2 := \tilde{u}_2 - t$, for randomly chosen $\tilde{u}_1, \tilde{u}_2, t$ from $\mathbb{Z}_p$. Thus $\mathcal{B}$ can simulate $U_1' := g^{\tilde{u}_1} = g^{u_1 + t/\delta_0}$ and $U_2' := g^{\tilde{u}_2} = g^{u_2 + t}$. Next $\mathcal{B}$ chooses $\{v_{1j}, v_{2j}\}_{j=1}^{\ell}$ uniformly at random from $\mathbb{Z}_p$ and implicitly sets $\delta_{10} := u_2 - \delta_0 u_1 = \tilde{u}_2 - \delta_0 \tilde{u}_1$ and $\delta_j := v_{2j} - \delta_0 v_{1j}$, for $j \in [1, \ell]$. Then $\mathcal{B}$ computes $h_{10} = h_z^{\delta_{10}} = h_r^{\tilde{u}_2} h_s^{-\tilde{u}_1}$ and $h_j = h_z^{\delta_j} = h_r^{v_{2j}} h_s^{-v_{1j}}$, for $j \in [1, \ell]$. Now $\mathcal{B}$ defines the PK as $\left(h_z, h_0, h_{10}, \{h_j\}_{j=1}^{\ell} \right)$. Notice that $\mathcal{B}$ knows the secret exponents $\{v_{1j}, v_{2j}\}_{j=1}^{\ell}$. Hence $\mathcal{B}$ computes $V_{1j} = g^{v_{1j}}, V_{2j} = g^{v_{1j}}$, for $j \in [1, \ell]$.

After receiving PK, $\mathcal{A}$ makes signing oracle queries on the message $\boldsymbol{m}_i = (m_{i1}, \ldots, m_{i\ell})$. Then $\mathcal{B}$ answers the Sign_B queries by computing $\sigma_i = (A_i, B_i, C_i)$, where $B_i := g^r$ and

$$A_i := \left(U_1' \prod_j V_{1j}^{m_{ij}} \right)^r = \left(g^{u_1 + t/\delta_0} \prod_j (g^{v_{1j}})^{m_{ij}} \right)^r = g^{r(u_1 + \sum_j v_{1j} m_{ij}) + rt/\delta_0},$$

$$C_i := \left(U_2' \prod_j V_{2j}^{m_{ij}} \right)^r = \left(g^{u_2 + t} \prod_j (g^{v_{2j}})^{m_{ij}} \right)^r = g^{r(u_2 + \sum_j v_{2j} m_{ij}) + rt},$$

for r randomly chosen from $\mathbb{Z}_p$. From the above derivation, it is clear that signature σ_i is properly distributed as an output of Sign_B with $s = rt$ modulo p. Finally $\mathcal{A}$ returns a forgery $(\boldsymbol{m}^*, \sigma^*)$, where $\boldsymbol{m}^* = (m_1^*, \ldots, m_{\ell}^*)$ and $\sigma^* = (A^*, B^*, C^*)$. As before, $\mathcal{B}$ checks (i) the forgery is valid and (ii) $\boldsymbol{m}^*$ is not queried earlier. If any of these checks fail to hold then $\mathcal{B}$ aborts. Otherwise, $\mathcal{B}$ breaks the DBP assumption as follows.

From the contradiction assumption, $\mathcal{A}$ returns a Type-I forgery with some non-negligible probability. Then, $\mathcal{B}$ can write the Type-I forgery components as, $A^* = g^{r(u_1 + \sum_{j=1}^{\ell} v_{1j} m_j^*)}$, $B^* = g^r$ and $C^* = g^{r(u_2 + \sum_{j=1}^{\ell} v_{2j} m_j^*)}$, for some $r \in \mathbb{Z}_p$. Now $\mathcal{B}$ computes

$$S = A^*(B^*)^{-\tilde{u}_1 - \sum_{j=1}^{\ell} v_{1j} m_j^*} = g^{r(\tilde{u}_1 - t/\delta_0) - r\tilde{u}_1} = g^{-rt/\delta_0},$$

$$R = (C^*)^{-1}(B^*)^{\tilde{u}_2 + \sum_{j=1}^{\ell} v_{2j} m_j^*} = g^{-r(\tilde{u}_2 - t) + r\tilde{u}_2} = g^{rt}.$$

In the above derivation, we have used the definition of $u_1 = \tilde{u}_1 - t/\delta_0$ and $u_2 = \tilde{u}_2 - t$. Then one can verify that $e(R, h_r)e(S, h_s) = e(g^{rt}, h_z)e(g^{-rt/\delta_0}, h_z^{\delta_0}) = 1$, here we have used the values of h_r and h_s. From the verification Eq. 2, $B^* \neq 1$ holds and hence $R \neq 1$ holds. In other words, (R, S) is a non-trivial solution of $DBP_{\mathbb{H}}$ problem instance. Thus we have,

$$Adv_A^{\mathsf{Game}_q} \leq Adv_B^{DBP_{\mathbb{H}}}. \tag{6}$$

$\square$

3.4 Comparison

In Table 2, we compare our rerandomizable signature scheme with some existing schemes in the prime-order pairing setting. We use the following metrics: public key size (denoted as $|PK|$), signature size (denoted as $|\sigma|$), signing cost, verification cost and the computational assumption required to prove unforgeability.

Table 2. Comparing rerandomizable signatures for multiple block messages.

	$|PK|$	$|\sigma|$	Signing cost	Verification cost	Assum.
PS-RRS	$(\ell + 2)|\mathbb{H}|$	$2|\mathbb{G}|$	$2E_{\mathbb{G}}$	$2\mathbb{P} + \ell(E_{\mathbb{H}} + M_{\mathbb{H}})$	PS
LMPY-RS	$(2\ell + 5)|\mathbb{G}| + (2\ell + 6)|\mathbb{H}|$	$4|\mathbb{G}|$	$6E_{\mathbb{G}} + (2\ell + 2)M_{\mathbb{G}}$	$5\mathbb{P} + 3M_{\mathbb{G}_T} + 2\ell M_{\mathbb{H}}$	SXDH
RRS Sect. 3.1	$(\ell + 3)|\mathbb{H}|$	$3|\mathbb{G}|$	$3E_{\mathbb{G}}$	$3\mathbb{P} + M_{\mathbb{G}_T} + \ell(E_{\mathbb{H}} + M_{\mathbb{H}})$	SXDH

For any group $X \in \{\mathbb{G}, \mathbb{H}, \mathbb{G}_T\}$, E_X, M_X respectively denote the cost of exponentiation, multiplication in X and $|X|$ is the bit size of X whereas $\mathbb{P}$ denotes pairing computation cost. PS denote the interactive assumption used in [24].

We denote PS-RRS to be the rerandomizable signature scheme described in [24]. As we can see, PS-RRS is an efficient scheme in terms of the size of the public key and signature as well as the running time of signing and verification algorithms. However, unforgeability of the PS-RRS scheme is proved under an interactive assumption [24, Assumption 1].

Libert et al.'s [19] randomizable signature scheme (LMPY-RS) is currently the most efficient one under the SXDH assumption. Here the size of the public key and running time of the signing algorithm are at least three times that of the PS-RRS scheme whereas, the signature size is double and the verification time is two and a half times that of the PS-RRS scheme.

The performance of the RRS scheme proposed in this paper is roughly two times better than that of LMPY-RS scheme, in terms of public key size and running time of the signing and verification algorithms, whereas our scheme has three signature components instead of four in LMPY-RS. Compared to the PS-RRS scheme, our scheme requires just one additional group element $\mathbb{H}$ in the public key and only one additional exponentiation in $\mathbb{G}$ for signing and one additional pairing plus a single multiplication in $\mathbb{G}_T$ for signature verification. However, in contrast to the interactive assumption used in [24], security of our scheme requires only the SXDH assumption.

4   Sequential Aggregate Signature

In this section, we present a sequential aggregate signature (SeqAS) scheme with constant-size public key and signature and prove its unforgeability under the SXDH assumption. Like [14], our construction uses both 'randomness re-use' and 'public key sharing' techniques.

4.1   Construction

The starting point of the SeqAS is our RRS scheme. We observe that the LMPY-RS scheme does not allow signature aggregation. For that, it seems necessary to make one element of the trapdoor key of the underlying knowledge system, namely δ_0, publicly available. However, in that case, the security reduction no longer works. We resolve this issue, by first letting the setup authority choose u_1, u_2, δ_0 from $\mathbb{Z}_p$ and define $\delta_{10} = u_2 - \delta_0 u_1$. Then the j-th signer chooses v_{1j}, v_{2j} from $\mathbb{Z}_p$ and implicitly defines $\delta_j = v_{2j} - \delta_0 v_{1j}$. Note that the above changes are possible as, unlike [19], our scheme uses simulated QA-NIZK proof component.

To construct the SeqAS scheme, we thus extend the RRS structure to the multi-user setting. Recall that our RRS signature is of the form $g^{r(u_1 + \sum_j v_{1j} m_j)}, g^r$ and $g^{r(u_2 + \sum_j v_{2j} m_j)}$. As mentioned above we treat v_{1j} and v_{2j} as the j-th signer's secret key. However, to apply the 'public key sharing' technique [14], g, g^{u_1} and g^{u_2} need to be made public for aggregation and h_z, h_0, h_{10} are also needed for verification. This implies that the public parameter $AS.PP$ of the SeqAS scheme consists of $\{g, U_1 = g^{u_1}, U_2 = g^{u_2}, h_z, h_0 = h_z^{\delta_0}, h_{10} = h_z^{u_2} h_0^{-u_1}\}$. Then, the j-th signer implicitly sets $\delta_j = v_{2j} - \delta_0 v_{1j}$, where the corresponding secret key SK_j contains $\{v_{1j}, v_{2j}\}$ and the verification key PK_j contains $\{h_j = h_z^{\delta_j} = h_z^{v_{2j}} h_0^{-v_{1j}}\}$.

Now we explain, how to aggregate the signature using 'randomness re-use' technique. Consider a message m_1 which is signed by the first user using $SK_1 = \{v_{11}, v_{21}\}$ by computing $\sigma_1 = (A_1, B_1, C_1)$, where $A_1 = (U_1 g^{v_{11} m_1})^{t_1}$, $B_1 = g^{t_1}, C_1 = (U_2 g^{v_{21} m_1})^{t_1}$, for some t_1 randomly chosen from $\mathbb{Z}_p$. Then, given (m_1, σ_1), the second user uses $SK_2 = \{v_{12}, v_{22}\}$ to compute the aggregate signature $\sigma_2 = (A_2, B_2, C_2)$ on the message m_2, where $A_2 = (A_1 B_1^{v_{12} m_2})^{t_2}, B_2 = B_1^{t_2}, C_2 = (C_1 B_1^{v_{22} m_2})^{t_2}$, for t_2 randomly chosen from $\mathbb{Z}_p$. In the same way, we can extend the above procedure for polynomial many aggregation. We present our SeqAS construction in Table 3.

Correctness. Note that the verification Eq. 7 of the SeqAS scheme is same as the verification Eq. 2 of our RRS scheme. Hence, it is sufficient to ensure the resulting aggregate signature can be written explicitly as in the RRS scheme. This will guarantee the correctness of the SeqAS scheme. Now we establish the structure of the signature returned by AS.Sign using mathematical induction. If $s = 0$, then AS.Sign sets $\sigma = (A, B, C) = (g^{u_1}, g, g^{u_2})$ and computes the

Table 3. SeqAS scheme in the prime-order setting.

AS.Setup(λ)

Run $\mathcal{P}(\lambda) \to (p, \mathbb{G}, \mathbb{H}, \mathbb{G}_T, e, g, h)$, where $g \xleftarrow{\$} \mathbb{G}, h \xleftarrow{\$} \mathbb{H}$.

Choose $u_1, u_2, \delta_0 \xleftarrow{\$} \mathbb{Z}_p, h_z \xleftarrow{\$} \mathbb{H}$, define $\delta_{10} := u_2 - \delta_0 u_1$ and
  compute $U_1 = g^{u_1}, U_2 = g^{u_2}, h_0 = h_z^{\delta_0}, h_{10} = h_z^{\delta_{10}}$.

Return $AS.PP := \{p, \mathbb{G}, \mathbb{H}, \mathbb{G}_T, e, g, h, U_1, U_2, h_z, h_0, h_{10}\}$.

AS.KeyGen($AS.PP$)

Choose $v_{1j}, v_{2j} \xleftarrow{\$} \mathbb{Z}_p$ and compute $h_j := h_z^{v_{2j}} h_0^{-v_{1j}}$.

Return $(SK_j := \{v_{1j}, v_{2j}\}, PK_j := \{h_j\})$.

AS.Sign($SK, m = (m_1, \ldots, m_s), \sigma, (PK_1, \ldots, PK_s), m$)

Check the following,
  If $s = 0$, then set $\sigma = (U_1, g, U_2)$,
  If $s > 0$ and AS.Ver$((PK_1, \ldots, PK_s), (m_1, \ldots, m_s), \sigma) = 0$, then it halts,
  If $m = 0$ or any of $m_i = 0$, then it halts,
  If for some $j \in [1, s]$ such that $PK_j = PK$, then it halts,
Suppose the algorithm did not halt, then
  parse SK as $\{v_{1\tau}, v_{2\tau}\}$, PK as $\{h_\tau\}$, σ as (A, B, C).
  Select $t \xleftarrow{\$} \mathbb{Z}_p$ and compute $A' = (AB^{v_{1\tau}m})^t, B' = B^t$ and $C' = (CB^{v_{2\tau}m})^t$.
Return $((m_1, \ldots, m_s, m), \sigma' = (A', B', C'))$.

AS.Ver($AS.PP, (PK_1, \ldots, PK_s), (m_1, \ldots, m_s), \sigma = (A, B, C)$)

Parse $PK_j = \{h_j\}$, for all $j \in [1, s]$ and continue only if the followings hold: $m_i = 0$
or $PK_i = PK_j$, for any $i \neq j, i, j \in [1, s]$. Accept if

$$B \neq 1 \text{ and } e(A, h_0)e(B, h_{10} \prod_{j=1}^{s} h_j^{m_j}) = e(C, h_z). \tag{7}$$

---

signature $\sigma_1 = (A_1, B_1, C_1)$ on the message m_1, where $A_1 = (AB^{v_{11}m_1})^t = g^{t(u_1 + v_{11}m_1)}, B_1 = B^t = g^t$ and $C_1 = (CB^{v_{12}m_1})^t = g^{t(u_2 + v_{12}m_1)}$. Let's assume that after k many aggregation, the aggregate signature $\sigma_k = (A_k, B_k, C_k)$ on the messages $(m_1, \ldots, m_k)$ under the public keys $(PK_1, \ldots, PK_k)$ can be written as $A_k = g^{r(u_1 + \sum_{j=1}^{k} v_{1j}m_j)}, B_k = g^r, C_k = g^{r(u_2 + \sum_{j=1}^{k} v_{2j}m_j)}$, for some $r \in \mathbb{Z}_p$. Now we prove that the aggregate signature $\sigma_{k+1} = (A_{k+1}, B_{k+1}, C_{k+1})$ of the messages $(m_1, \ldots, m_k, m_{k+1})$ under $(PK_1, \ldots, PK_k, PK_{k+1})$ can be written explicitly as in Table 3. Observe that from the definition of AS.Sign, we can write $A_{k+1} = (A_k B_k^{v_{1k+1}m_{k+1}})^t = g^{rt(u_1 + \sum_{j=1}^{k+1} v_{1j}m_j)}, B_{k+1} = B_k^t = g^{rt}$ and $C_{k+1} = (C_k B_k^{v_{2k+1}m_{k+1}})^t = g^{rt(u_2 + \sum_{j=1}^{k+1} v_{2j}m_j)}$, for $t \xleftarrow{\$} \mathbb{Z}_p$. Thus the resulting signature σ_{k+1} is distributed as similar to the RRS scheme of Sect. 3.1. Hence correctness of the SeqAS scheme follows from that of RRS scheme.

4.2   Security

We argue the unforgeability of SeqAS scheme in the certified public key setting [21], see our full version [6] for the formal security definition. Informally, given the public key and access to join and signing oracle queries, the adversary cannot produce a valid forgery.

We give a reduction from the security of our RRS scheme. In the certified public key model, the adversary gives both public and secret keys to the simulator. Hence simulator knows all the secret keys except the secret key of the underlying RRS scheme (for single message). The simulator responds to an aggregate signature query by first obtaining a signature of the underlying RRS from its challenger and then constructing the aggregate signature. From the aggregate signature structure, which can be viewed as a linear function of the secret exponents, the aggregation is oblivious to the order in which the messages are signed. Once the adversary returns a non-trivial forgery, the simulator extracts the forgery for the underlying RRS scheme by using the secret keys of all the other signers.

Theorem 6. *If RRS scheme is EUF-CMA secure, then SeqAS scheme is EUF-CMA secure in the certified public key setting.*

Proof. Suppose there exists a PPT adversary $\mathcal{A}$ who breaks the EUF-CMA security of SeqAS scheme in the certified public key setting, with some non-negligible probability. Then we construct a simulator $\mathcal{B}$ that breaks the EUF-CMA security of the RRS scheme as follows.

Setup: First, $\mathcal{B}$ initializes the key list KeyList as empty. Next $\mathcal{B}$ obtains the public parameter PP as $(p, \mathbb{G}, \mathbb{H}, \mathbb{G}_T, e, \tilde{g}, h)$ along with the public-key PK as $\{h_z, h_0, h_{10}, h_\tau\}$, from his challenger $\mathcal{C}$. Then $\mathcal{B}$ sets $PK^* = h_\tau$. Now $\mathcal{B}$ requests a signature query on zero message to $\mathcal{C}$. Then $\mathcal{C}$ returns $\sigma_0 = (A_0, B_0, C_0) = (\tilde{g}^{ru_1}, \tilde{g}^r, \tilde{g}^{ru_2})$, for some $r \in \mathbb{Z}_p$. Now $\mathcal{B}$ assigns $g := B_0, U_1 := A_0, U_2 := C_0$ and computes the public parameter for our SeqAS scheme as, $AS.PP := \{g, h, U_1, U_2, h_z, h_0, h_{10}\}$. Then $\mathcal{B}$ forwards $AS.PP$ and PK^* to $\mathcal{A}$.

Join Query: $\mathcal{A}$ makes the join queries by sending the key pair $SK_j = \{v_{1j}, v_{2j}\}$ and $PK_j = \{h_j\}$ to $\mathcal{B}$. $\mathcal{B}$ checks whether (SK_j, PK_j) are generated correctly by checking

$$h_j \overset{?}{=} h_z^{v_{2j}} h_0^{-v_{1j}}. \tag{8}$$

For correctly generated key pair (SK_j, PK_j), $\mathcal{B}$ adds it in the KeyList.

Signing Query: $\mathcal{A}$ makes a sequential aggregate signature query on the message m_i to $\mathcal{B}$ by sending an aggregate signature σ_i on the messages $(m_{i1}, \ldots m_{is_i})$ under the public keys $(PK_{i1}, \ldots, PK_{is_i})$. $\mathcal{B}$ aborts, if any of the following condition holds, (i) if $s_i > 0$ and the aggregate signature σ_i is invalid, (ii) if there exists $j \in [1, s_i]$ such that PK_{ij} does not belong to KeyList, (iii) if there exists some $j \in [1, s_i]$ such that $PK_{ij} = PK^*$. Otherwise, $\mathcal{B}$ requests a signature query on m_i to his challenger $\mathcal{C}$, which returns $\sigma = (A, B, C)$. Note that, all the public keys PK_{ij} involved in the signing queries are certified before. Hence, $\mathcal{B}$ knows the associated key pairs (SK_{ij}, PK_{ij}), for all $j \in [1, s_i]$. Then, $\mathcal{B}$ parses SK_{ij} as $\{v_{1ij}, v_{2ij}\}$. Next, $\mathcal{B}$ chooses t uniformly at random from $\mathbb{Z}_p$ and computes the aggregate signature $\sigma_i' = (A_i', B_i', C_i')$, where $A_i' = \left(AB^{\sum_{j=1}^{s_i} v_{1ij}m_{ij}}\right)^t, B_i' = B^t, C_i' = \left(CB^{\sum_{j=1}^{s_i} v_{2ij}m_{ij}}\right)^t$. It is easy to see that the signature generated above is properly distributed. From the linear structure of the signature exponents, the order of aggregation does not matter. Hence, σ_i' is a valid aggregate signature on $(m_{i1}, \ldots, m_{is_i}, m_i)$ under the public keys $(PK_{i1}, \ldots, PK_{is_i}, PK^*)$.

Output: After q many number of aggregate signature queries, $\mathcal{A}$ returns a forgery $\sigma^* = (A^*, B^*, C^*)$ on the messages $(m_1^*, \ldots, m_s^*)$ under the public keys $(PK_1, \ldots, PK_s)$. Now $\mathcal{B}$ ensures the validity of the forgery, if the following conditions are satisfied,

 i. AS.Ver$((PK_1, \ldots, PK_s), \sigma^*, (m_1^*, \ldots, m_s^*)) = 1$,
 ii. For all $PK_j \neq PK^*$, $PK_j \in$ KeyList,
 iii. There exists one $j^* \in [1, s]$, $PK^* = PK_{j^*}$ and $m_{j^*}^* \neq m_i$, for all $i \in [1, q]$.

Condition (i) ensures that the forgery σ^* satisfies the verification Eq. 7. Whereas, the condition (ii) ensures that $\mathcal{B}$ knows all the secret key SK_j components such that Eq. 8 holds, for the associated keys $PK_j \neq PK^*$. Recall that the public keys are generated independently by each of signer. Also the condition (iii) ensures that the aggregate signature forgery includes the challenge public key PK^* as part of the aggregation. Now $\mathcal{B}$ computes the rerandomizable signature forgery $\sigma_m^* = (A_m^*, B_m^*, C_m^*)$, where $A_m^* = A^*(B^*)^{-\sum_{j \neq j^*} v_{1j}m_j^*}$, $B_m^* = B^*$ and $C_m^* = C^*(B^*)^{-\sum_{j \neq j^*} v_{2j}m_j^*}$. Next we prove that the above constructed rerandomizable signature σ_m^* satisfies the verification Eq. 2 as follows,

$$e(C_m^*, h_z) = e(C^*(B^*)^{-\sum_{j \neq j^*} v_{2j}m_j^*}, h_z) = e(C^*, h_z)e((B^*)^{-\sum_{j \neq j^*} v_{2j}m_j^*}, h_z)$$

$$= \left(e(A^*, h_0)e(B^*, h_{10}h_\tau^{m_{j^*}^*} \prod_{j \neq j^*} h_j^{m_j^*})\right)e((B^*)^{-\sum_{j \neq j^*} v_{2j}m_j^*}, h_z)$$

$$= e(A^*(B^*)^{-\sum_{j \neq j^*} v_{1j}m_j^*}, h_0)e(B^*, h_{10}h_\tau^{m_{j^*}^*})$$

$$= e(A_m^*, h_0)e(B_m^*, h_{10}h_\tau^{m_{j^*}^*})$$

The first equality is obtained by using the value of C_m^* and the second equality is obtained by using the bilinearity of the pairing. Third equality is obtained from the verification Eq. 7. The fourth equality is obtained by canceling the v_{2j} terms. The final equality is obtained using the values of A_m^* and B_m^*.

The condition (iii) of aggregate signature forgery ensures the non-trivial forgery with respect to the queried messages. Hence, the resulted forgery σ_m^* on the message $m_{j^*}^*$ under PK^* is clearly a valid forgery for the RRS scheme. □

4.3   Comparison

We compare our SeqAS scheme with the existing schemes in Table 4. We consider all the sequential aggregate signature schemes in asymmetric pairing setting [7] whose unforgeability is proved in the certified public key setting in the standard model. Here we use the following metrics: public key size (denoted as $|PK|$), aggregate signature size (denoted as $|AS|$), signing and verification cost and the computational assumption required to prove unforgeability of the aggregate signature scheme.

Table 4. Comparing sequential aggregate signature schemes using certified public key setting in the standard model.

Scheme	$|PK|$	$|AS|$	Signing cost	Verification cost	Assumption
LOSSW-3a	$\lambda|\mathbb{G}| + \lambda|\mathbb{H}|$ $+ 1|\mathbb{G}_T|$	$2|\mathbb{G}|$	$2\mathbb{P} + \ell M_{\mathbb{G}_T} + (\ell-1)\lambda M_{\mathbb{H}}$ $+ 6E_{\mathbb{G}} + (2\ell\lambda + 6)M_{\mathbb{G}}$	$2\mathbb{P} + \ell M_{\mathbb{G}_T}$ $+ \ell\lambda M_{\mathbb{H}}$	CDH
SAS1	$2|\mathbb{G}| + 8|\mathbb{H}|$ $+ 1|\mathbb{G}_T|$	$8|\mathbb{G}|$	$8\mathbb{P}\ (4\ell + 14)E_{\mathbb{H}}$ $+ 10E_{\mathbb{G}} + 1E_{\mathbb{G}_T}$	$8\mathbb{P} + 1E_{\mathbb{G}_T}$ $+ (4\ell + 14)E_{\mathbb{H}}$	SXDH, DBDH LW2
SAS2	$6|\mathbb{G}| + 6|\mathbb{H}|$ $+ 1|\mathbb{G}_T|$	$6|\mathbb{G}|$	$6\mathbb{P} + (3\ell + 6)E_{\mathbb{H}}$ $+ (3\ell + 18)E_{\mathbb{G}} + 1E_{\mathbb{G}_T}$	$6\mathbb{P} + 1E_{\mathbb{G}_T}$ $+ (3\ell + 6)E_{\mathbb{H}}$	LW1, DBDH LW2
LLY-SeqAS	$1|\mathbb{H}|$	$3|\mathbb{G}|$	$5\mathbb{P} + M_{\mathbb{G}_T} + \ell E_{\mathbb{H}}$ $+ 2\ell M_{\mathbb{H}} + 5E_{\mathbb{G}} + 2M_{\mathbb{G}}$	$5\mathbb{P} + M_{\mathbb{G}_T} + \ell E_{\mathbb{H}}$ $+ 2\ell M_{\mathbb{H}}$	LRSW
PS-SeqAS	$1|\mathbb{H}|$	$2|\mathbb{G}|$	$2\mathbb{P} + \ell(E_{\mathbb{H}} + M_{\mathbb{H}})$ $+ 3E_{\mathbb{G}} + 1M_{\mathbb{G}}$	$2\mathbb{P} + \ell(E_{\mathbb{H}} + M_{\mathbb{H}})$	PS
SeqAS	$1|\mathbb{H}|$	$3|\mathbb{G}|$	$3\mathbb{P} + M_{\mathbb{G}_T} + \ell(E_{\mathbb{H}} + M_{\mathbb{H}})$ $+ 5E_{\mathbb{G}} + 2M_{\mathbb{G}}$	$3\mathbb{P} + M_{\mathbb{G}_T}$ $+ \ell(E_{\mathbb{H}} + M_{\mathbb{H}})$	SXDH

For any group $X \in \{\mathbb{G}, \mathbb{H}, \mathbb{G}_T\}$, we denote E_X, M_X and $|X|$ be the exponentiation, multiplication in X and bit size of X and $\mathbb{P}$ denotes asymmetric pairing computation time. λ denotes the security parameter and ℓ denotes the number of signature aggregated so far. PS and LRSW denote the interactive assumptions in [24] and [23].

Chatterjee et al. [5] presented aggregate signature variants of [21] denoted as LOSSW-3a, whose security is proved under the CDH assumption. However, the size of the public key is some multiple of the security parameter λ, where λ takes 256 for the 128 bit-level security. This results in a sequential aggregate signature with a large public key size.

In 2012, Lee et al. [13, Section 3.5] extended the idea from [26] and presented a sequential aggregate signature scheme based on the Camenisch-Lysyanskaya (CL) signature in the asymmetric pairing setting. The resulted scheme is denoted as LLY-SeqAS and it has a constant size public key. The security of the LLY-SeqAS scheme is based on the security of the CL-signature scheme, which is proved under an interactive assumption. In 2015, Lee et al. [17] presented two SeqAS schemes, namely SAS1 and SAS2 schemes. The security of SAS1 is proved under SXDH, DBDH and LW2 assumptions and SAS2 is proved under DBDH, LW1 and LW2 assumptions described in [18]. Note that, both LW1 and LW2 assumptions are non-standard static assumptions whose hardness is established in the generic group model, which provides only the lower bound [27]. They have used the dual system encryption technique to prove the security of their schemes. However, their public key size (resp. aggregate signature size) increases by a factor of 9 (resp. 2) with respect to the LLY-SeqAS construction.

In 2016, [24] presented a sequential aggregate signature (denoted as PS-SeqAS) scheme based on their rerandomizable signature construction. One can see that PS-SeqAS is the most efficient scheme among all the SeqAS schemes presented in Table 4. However, the security of the PS-SeqAS scheme is proved under an interactive assumption. The performance of our **SeqAS** scheme is very close to PS-SeqAS even though we argue security under the SXDH assumption. In particular, public key size remains the same in both schemes, whereas signature size increases by one group element in our scheme as compared to the PS-SeqAS scheme. Also, we require one additional pairing and one target group multiplication to verify the signature.

5 Concluding Remark

We proposed the first construction of a sequential aggregate signature scheme with constant-size public key in the standard model based on the SXDH assumption in the prime order bilinear pairing setting. This is achieved by suitably modifying a randomizable signature scheme from [19]. The performance of both the rerandomizable signature scheme and sequential aggregate signature scheme comes quite close to prior proposals where security is based on some interactive assumption.

References

1. Abe, M., Fuchsbauer, G., Groth, J., Haralambiev, K., Ohkubo, M.: Structure-preserving signatures and commitments to group elements. J. Cryptology **29**(2), 363–421 (2016)
2. Bichsel, P., Camenisch, J., Neven, G., Smart, N.P., Warinschi, B.: Get shorty via group signatures without encryption. In: Garay, J.A., De Prisco, R. (eds.) SCN 2010. LNCS, vol. 6280, pp. 381–398. Springer, Heidelberg (2010). https://doi.org/10.1007/978-3-642-15317-4_24
3. Boneh, D., Gentry, C., Lynn, B., Shacham, H.: Aggregate and verifiably encrypted signatures from bilinear maps. In: Biham, E. (ed.) EUROCRYPT 2003. LNCS, vol. 2656, pp. 416–432. Springer, Heidelberg (2003). https://doi.org/10.1007/3-540-39200-9_26
4. Camenisch, J., Lysyanskaya, A.: Signature schemes and anonymous credentials from bilinear maps. In: Franklin, M. (ed.) CRYPTO 2004. LNCS, vol. 3152, pp. 56–72. Springer, Heidelberg (2004). https://doi.org/10.1007/978-3-540-28628-8_4
5. Chatterjee, S., Hankerson, D., Knapp, E., Menezes, A.: Comparing two pairing-based aggregate signature schemes. Des. Codes Cryptogr. **55**(2–3), 141–167 (2010)
6. Chatterjee, S., Kabaleeshwaran, R.: From rerandomizability to sequential aggregation: efficient signature schemes based on SXDH assumption. IACR Cryptology ePrint Archive, 2020:575 (2020)
7. Galbraith, S.D., Paterson, K.G., Smart, N.P.: Pairings for cryptographers. Discrete Appl. Math. **156**(16), 3113–3121 (2008)
8. Gerbush, M., Lewko, A., O'Neill, A., Waters, B.: Dual form signatures: an approach for proving security from static assumptions. In: Wang, X., Sako, K. (eds.) ASIACRYPT 2012. LNCS, vol. 7658, pp. 25–42. Springer, Heidelberg (2012). https://doi.org/10.1007/978-3-642-34961-4_4
9. Ghadafi, E.: Short structure-preserving signatures. In: Sako [25], pp. 305–321 (2016)

10. Groth, J.: Homomorphic Trapdoor Commitments to Group Elements. IACR Cryptology ePrint Archive 2009:007 (2009)
11. Jutla, C.S., Roy, A.: Switching lemma for bilinear tests and constant-size NIZK proofs for linear subspaces. In: Garay, J.A., Gennaro, R. (eds.) CRYPTO 2014. LNCS, vol. 8617, pp. 295–312. Springer, Heidelberg (2014). https://doi.org/10. 1007/978-3-662-44381-1_17
12. Kiltz, E., Wee, H.: Quasi-adaptive NIZK for linear subspaces revisited. In: Oswald, E., Fischlin, M. (eds.) EUROCRYPT 2015. LNCS, vol. 9057, pp. 101–128. Springer, Heidelberg (2015). https://doi.org/10.1007/978-3-662-46803-6_4
13. Lee, K., Lee, D.H., Yung, M.: Aggregating cl-signatures revisited: extended functionality and better efficiency. IACR Cryptology ePrint Archive, 2012:562 (2012)
14. Lee, K., Lee, D.H., Yung, M.: Aggregating CL-signatures revisited: extended functionality and better efficiency. In: Sadeghi, A.-R. (ed.) FC 2013. LNCS, vol. 7859, pp. 171–188. Springer, Heidelberg (2013). https://doi.org/10.1007/978-3-642-39884-1_14
15. Lee, K., Lee, D.H., Yung, M.: Sequential aggregate signatures made shorter. In: Jacobson, M., Locasto, M., Mohassel, P., Safavi-Naini, R. (eds.) ACNS 2013. LNCS, vol. 7954, pp. 202–217. Springer, Heidelberg (2013). https://doi.org/10. 1007/978-3-642-38980-1_13
16. Lee, K., Lee, D.H., Yung, M.: Sequential aggregate signatures with short public keys: design, analysis and implementation studies. In: Kurosawa, K., Hanaoka, G. (eds.) PKC 2013. LNCS, vol. 7778, pp. 423–442. Springer, Heidelberg (2013). https://doi.org/10.1007/978-3-642-36362-7_26
17. Lee, K., Lee, D.H., Yung, M.: Sequential aggregate signatures with short public keys without random oracles. Theor. Comput. Sci. **579**, 100–125 (2015)
18. Lewko, A., Waters, B.: New techniques for dual system encryption and fully secure HIBE with short ciphertexts. In: Micciancio, D. (ed.) TCC 2010. LNCS, vol. 5978, pp. 455–479. Springer, Heidelberg (2010). https://doi.org/10.1007/978-3-642-11799-2_27
19. Libert, B., Mouhartem, F., Peters, T., Yung, M.: Practical "signatures with efficient protocols" from simple assumptions. In: Chen, X., Wang, X., Huang, X. (eds.) AsiaCCS, pp. 511–522. ACM, New York (2016)
20. Libert, B., Peters, T., Yung, M.: Short group signatures via structure-preserving signatures: standard model security from simple assumptions. In: Gennaro, R., Robshaw, M. (eds.) CRYPTO 2015. LNCS, vol. 9216, pp. 296–316. Springer, Heidelberg (2015). https://doi.org/10.1007/978-3-662-48000-7_15
21. Lu, S., Ostrovsky, R., Sahai, A., Shacham, H., Waters, B.: Sequential aggregate signatures and multisignatures without random oracles. In: Vaudenay, S. (ed.) EUROCRYPT 2006. LNCS, vol. 4004, pp. 465–485. Springer, Heidelberg (2006). https://doi.org/10.1007/11761679_28
22. Lysyanskaya, A., Micali, S., Reyzin, L., Shacham, H.: Sequential aggregate signatures from trapdoor permutations. In: Cachin, C., Camenisch, J.L. (eds.) EUROCRYPT 2004. LNCS, vol. 3027, pp. 74–90. Springer, Heidelberg (2004). https://doi.org/10.1007/978-3-540-24676-3_5
23. Lysyanskaya, A., Rivest, R.L., Sahai, A., Wolf, S.: Pseudonym systems. In: Heys, H., Adams, C. (eds.) SAC 1999. LNCS, vol. 1758, pp. 184–199. Springer, Heidelberg (2000). https://doi.org/10.1007/3-540-46513-8_14
24. Pointcheval, D., Sanders, O.: Short randomizable signatures. In: Sako [25], pp. 111–126 (2016)
25. Sako, K. (ed.): CT-RSA, vol. 9610. Springer, Heidelberg (2016)

26. Schröder, D.: How to aggregate the CL signature scheme. In: Atluri, V., Diaz, C. (eds.) ESORICS 2011. LNCS, vol. 6879, pp. 298–314. Springer, Heidelberg (2011). https://doi.org/10.1007/978-3-642-23822-2_17

27. Shoup, V.: Lower bounds for discrete logarithms and related problems. In: Fumy, W. (ed.) EUROCRYPT 1997. LNCS, vol. 1233, pp. 256–266. Springer, Heidelberg (1997). https://doi.org/10.1007/3-540-69053-0_18

28. Waters, B.: Efficient identity-based encryption without random oracles. In: Cramer, R. (ed.) EUROCRYPT 2005. LNCS, vol. 3494, pp. 114–127. Springer, Heidelberg (2005). https://doi.org/10.1007/11426639_7

Parallel Implementation of SM2 Elliptic Curve Cryptography on Intel Processors with AVX2

Junhao Huang[1], Zhe Liu[1,2(✉)], Zhi Hu[3], and Johann Großschädl[4]

[1] College of Computer Science and Technology,
Nanjing University of Aeronautics and Astronautics, Nanjing, China
jhhuang_nuaa@126.com
[2] State Key Laboratory of Cryptology, P.O. Box 5159, Beijing 100878, China
sduliuzhe@gmail.com
[3] Central South University, Hunan, China
huzhi_math@csu.edu.cn
[4] University of Luxembourg, Esch-sur-Alzette, Luxembourg
johann.groszschaedl@uni.lu

Abstract. This paper presents an efficient and secure implementation of SM2, the Chinese elliptic curve cryptography standard that has been adopted by the International Organization of Standardization (ISO) as ISO/IEC 14888-3:2018. Our SM2 implementation uses Intel's Advanced Vector Extensions version 2.0 (AVX2), a family of three-operand SIMD instructions operating on vectors of 8, 16, 32, or 64-bit data elements in 256-bit registers, and is resistant against timing attacks. To exploit the parallel processing capabilities of AVX2, we studied the execution flows of Co-Z Jacobian point arithmetic operations and introduce a parallel 2-way Co-Z addition, Co-Z conjugate addition, and Co-Z ladder algorithm, which allow for fast Co-Z scalar multiplication. Furthermore, we developed an efficient 2-way prime-field arithmetic library using AVX2 to support our Co-Z Jacobian point operations. Both the field and the point operations utilize branch-free (i.e. constant-time) implementation techniques, which increase their ability to resist Simple Power Analysis (SPA) and timing attacks. Our software for scalar multiplication on the SM2 curve is, to our knowledge, the first constant-time implementation of the Co-Z based ladder that leverages the parallelism of AVX2.

1 Introduction

Roughly 35 years ago, Koblitz and Miller proposed to use the group of points on an elliptic curve defined over a finite field for the implementation of discrete logarithm cryptosystems [17,19]. Today, *Elliptic Curve Cryptography (ECC)* is enjoying wide acceptance in the embedded/mobile domain due to the benefits of smaller key size, faster computation time, and reduced memory requirements compared to classic public-key cryptosystems [30]. Furthermore, ECC becomes increasingly popular in application domains where high data transmission rates

© Springer Nature Switzerland AG 2020
J. K. Liu and H. Cui (Eds.): ACISP 2020, LNCS 12248, pp. 204–224, 2020.
https://doi.org/10.1007/978-3-030-55304-3_11

(i.e. high throughput) are important, e.g. networking, web services, and cloud computing. The 64-bit Intel architecture plays a major role in the latter two domains, which makes a good case to optimize ECC software with respect to the computing capabilities of modern Intel processors, especially their parallel processing capabilities. In 2011, Intel presented a new set of SIMD instructions called *Advanced Vector Extensions 2 (AVX2)* that was first integrated into the Haswell microarchitecture. AVX2 instructions support integer operations with 256-bit vectors, which allows one to do calculations on e.g. four 64-bit integers in parallel, and have a "non-destructive" three-operand format, i.e. two source registers and one destination register. Even though AVX2 was mainly designed to accelerate graphics and video processing, it can also be leveraged to speed up cryptographic workloads like ECC computations.

The security of elliptic curve cryptosystems relies on the (presumed) hardness of the *Elliptic Curve Discrete Logarithm Problem (ECDLP)*, which asks to find the scalar k given two points P and $Q = kP$ on an elliptic curve [12]. An operation of the form kP, called *scalar multiplication*, is an integral part of all ECC schemes and, in general, their most computation-intensive component. In addition, the scalar multiplication can be vulnerable to side-channel attacks, in particular timing analysis or Simple Power Analysis (SPA), when implemented carelessly [4,28]. Therefore, an efficient and secure (in the sense of side-channel resistant) implementation of the scalar multiplication is crucial for any elliptic curve cryptosystem. The Montgomery ladder algorithm, originally proposed in [20], has a very regular execution profile, which lends itself to implementations with constant execution time, provided the underlying field arithmetic satisfies certain requirements. This algorithm is not only suitable for Montgomery curves like Curve25519 [1], but has also been generalized to Weierstrass elliptic curves [4,16]. The present paper focusses on a parallel constant-time implementation of the Montgomery ladder for Weierstrass curves (like SM2) using AVX2. An AVX2 implementation of Curve25519 can be found in e.g. [7].

SM2 was introduced by the State Cryptography Administration of China in 2010 [26] and is supposed to replace RSA and other public-key cryptographic algorithms for electronic authentication systems, key management systems, and application systems. In addition, SM2 was standardized by ISO/IEC in 2018 as ISO/IEC 14888-3:2018 [15]. Hence, in the next couple of years, SM2 will have excellent application prospects in both Chinese and international commercial electronic products. For all these reasons, it makes sense to investigate how the prime-field arithmetic, elliptic curve operations, and protocols using SM2 can be implemented efficiently, e.g. by utilizing the parallel computing capabilities of AVX2. It should be noted that many of the optimizations we present in this paper can also be applied to NIST P-256 or other Weierstrass curves by simply providing a parallel 2-way implementation of the field arithmetic.

1.1 Overview of Related Work and Motivation for Our Work

Currently, there exist only a few papers about implementing SM2 starting from the basic prime-field arithmetic up to the protocol level. Most implementations of SM2 are based on the field arithmetic and elliptic curve operations provided by the open-source software OpenSSL [21]; typical examples are GmSSL[1] and TASSL[2]. However, implementation details of the prime-field arithmetic and the point (i.e. group) operations of SM2 are, to our knowledge, not documented in any form, which makes it difficult to reason about their efficiency.

To improve the execution time of public-key cryptographic algorithms like RSA and ECC on Intel processors, the SIMD-level parallelism of AVX2 can be exploited. Vector implementations of Montgomery modular multiplication and efficient modular exponentiation for RSA were introduced in [10,29]. Gueron and Krasnov presented in [11] a highly-optimized AVX2 software for fixed-base scalar multiplication on NIST's P-256 curve that executes four point additions in parallel. Taking advantage of AVX2 instructions, Faz-Hernández and López [7] developed an optimized Montgomery ladder for Curve25519, which performs two field-operations (e.g. two field-multiplications) simultaneously. In order to further reduce the latency, each field-multiplication (resp. squaring) multiplies two pairs of 25 or 26-bit limbs in parallel, whereby two limbs belonging to one operand are stored in a 128-bit lane of an AVX2 register. In a recent follow-up work, Faz-Hernández et al. [8] presented fast 2-way and 4-way implementations of the field-arithmetic and point operations using both the Montgomery model and the Edwards model of Curve25519. There are various other studies exploring the optimization of ECC for different vector instruction sets, such as Intel SSE2, Intel AVX-512, and ARM NEON, see e.g. [2,24].

Parallel implementations of the Montgomery ladder for GPUs and FPGAs have also been reported, some of which use Meloni's Co-Z Jacobian arithmetic from [18]. Bos [3] introduced a low-latency 7-way GPU implementation of an (X, Z)-only Co-Z ladder for the NIST curve P-224. Peng et al. [22] presented an optimized multi-core FPGA implementation of the X-only Co-Z ladder from [13] for a set of Weierstrass curves, whereby they combined a number of Montgomery modular multipliers to work in parallel. They concluded that a 3-core implementation achieves the best throughput-resource ratio.

1.2 Our Contributions

The contribution of this paper is twofold and can be summarized as follows:

1. We present novel parallel 2-way Co-Z Jacobian point arithmetic algorithms that utilize the parallel processing capabilities of Intel's AVX2 instruction set. Our parallel Co-Z addition, Co-Z conjugate addition, and combination thereof (i.e. the Co-Z ladder step) outperform their sequential counterparts by factors of about 1.26, 1.60, and 1.33, respectively. By pre-computing two values, we managed to resolve data dependencies in the parallel execution of the Co-Z ladder algorithm and minimize its execution time. Thanks to these parallel Co-Z point operations, our Co-Z based Montgomery ladder is 1.31 times faster than a sequential Co-Z Montgomery ladder.

---

[1] See http://gmssl.org (accessed on 2020–05–24).
[2] See http://github.com/jntass/TASSL (accessed on 2020–05–24).

2. To speed up the field arithmetic, we developed a fast 2-way implementation of modular reduction and carry propagation for the SM2 prime using the AVX2 instruction set. Both are integrated into our modular multiplication and modular squaring functions, which employ a radix-2^{26} representation of the operands. We aimed for resistance against timing/SPA attacks and avoided conditional statements like branch instructions to ensure the field arithmetic (and also point arithmetic) has operand-independent execution time. To achieve this, we utilized constant-time techniques such as operand masking, Fermat-based inversion, and a highly regular ladder algorithm.

The rest of this paper is structured as follows. In Sect. 2, we firstly provide a brief introduction to AVX2, the representation of operands, and the notation used throughout this paper. Section 3 presents the new parallel Co-Z Jacobian arithmetic and the Co-Z based Montgomery ladder algorithm. Thereafter, in Sect. 4, we introduce our implementation of the 2-way field-arithmetic for SM2 using AVX2 instructions. The results of our implementation are summarized in Sect. 5 and compared with the results from some previous papers. Finally, we give concluding remarks in Sect. 6.

2   Preliminaries

Overview of AVX2. Starting with the Haswell microarchitecture (released in 2013), modern 64-bit Intel processors support AVX2, which is, in essence, an extension of AVX to include 256-bit integer operations (classical AVX provides 256-bit floating-point instructions, but only 128-bit integer instructions). There are various AVX2 integer instructions that can be used to speed up prime-field arithmetic; the most important is VPMULUDQ (in the following abbreviated as MUL), which executes four (32×32)-bit multiplications in parallel and places the four 64-bit products in a 256-bit AVX2 register. Similarly, AVX2 contains instructions for parallel addition and subtraction of four packed 64-bit integers (abbreviated as ADD and SUB) [14]. Other members of the AVX2 instruction set with relevance for ECC include instructions to combine data elements from two AVX2 registers into a single one (BLEND), to shuffle data elements within a register (SHUF), to permute elements (PERM), to left/right shift elements by the same or different distances (SHL, SHR, SHLV, SHRV), to concatenate 128-bit lanes from two registers (ALIGN), and to carry out bit-wise operations (e.g. AND, XOR). We refer to [14] for a detailed description these instructions and to [9] for information about their latency and throughput.

Representation of Field Elements. It is common practice to represent the elements of a prime field $\mathbb{F}_p$ as integers in the range of $[0, p-1]$, which means they have a length of up to $m = \lceil \log_2(p) \rceil$ bits. An m-bit integer can be stored in an array of words ("limbs") whose bitlength equals the register size n of the target platform, e.g. $n = 64$. Arithmetic algorithms for addition, multiplication (and other operations) in $\mathbb{F}_p$ process these words using the instructions of the processor, e.g. $(n \times n)$-bit multiply, n-bit add, n-bit add-with-carry, etc. While such a canonical radix-2^n representation of integers has the advantage that the total number of words $k = \lceil m/n \rceil$ is minimal for the target platform, it entails a lot of carry propagation and, as a consequence, sub-optimal performance on modern 64-bit processors [1,7]. Fortunately, it is possible to avoid most of the carry propagations by using a *reduced-radix representation* (also referred to as redundant representation [8]), which means the number of bits per limb n' is slightly less than the bitlength n of the processor's registers, e.g. $n' = 51$ when implementing Curve25519 for a 64-bit processor. In this way, several limbs can be added up in a 64-bit register without causing overflow and the result of the field-addition (and other arithmetic operations) does not necessarily need to be fully reduced, i.e. can be larger than p. Only at the very end of a cryptographic operation (e.g. scalar multiplication), a full reduction to the least non-negative residue and conversion to canonical form has to be carried out.

Formally, when using a reduced radix of $2^{n'}$ (i.e. $n' < n$ bits per limb), an m-bit integer A is represented via a sequence of limbs $(a_{k'-1}, a_{k'-2}, \ldots, a_0)$ so that $A = \sum_{i=0}^{k'-1} a_i 2^{in'}$, whereby a limb a_i does not necessarily need to be less than $2^{n'}$ but can (temporarily) become as big as $2^n - 1$. Although a reduced-radix representation may increase the number of limbs $k' = \lceil m/n' \rceil$ versus the full-radix setting (i.e. $k' > k$), there is typically still a net-gain in performance when taking advantage of "lazy carrying" and "lazy reduction" [8]. We will use uppercase letters to denote field elements and indexed lowercase letters for the individual limbs they consist of. As is usual practice, we analyze and compare the efficiency of point operations (i.e. addition and doubling) by counting the number of multiplications (M), squarings (S), additions/subtractions (A), and inversions (I) in the underlying finite field.

SM2 Elliptic Curve. The specific elliptic curve used for the implementation described in the following sections is SM2 [27], which is defined by a simplified Weierstrass equation $E : y^2 = x^3 + ax + b$ over a prime field $\mathbb{F}_p$. This field is given by the pseudo-Mersenne prime $p = 2^{256} - 2^{224} - 2^{96} + 2^{64} - 1$ and allows for a special modular reduction method [25]. The curve parameter a is fixed to -3 to reduce the cost of the point arithmetic when using Jacobian projective coordinates [12]. A Jacobian projective point $(X : Y : Z)$, $Z \neq 0$ corresponds to the affine point $(x, y) = (X/Z^2, Y/Z^3)$. The projective form of the Weierstrass equation is

$$E : Y^2 = X^3 - 3XZ^4 + bZ^6. \tag{1}$$

Like other standardized Weierstrass curves, the cardinality $\#E(\mathbb{F}_p)$ of the SM2 curve is prime, i.e. it has a co-factor of $h = 1$. The full specification of the SM2 curve can be found in [27].

Co-Z Jacobian Arithmetic. First proposed by Meloni [18], Co-Z Jacobian arithmetic is based on the observation that the addition of two distinct points in projective coordinates can be accelerated when they are represented with the same Z-coordinate. As specified by Eq. (2), the sum $R = P + Q$ of the points

$P = (X_P, Y_P, Z)$ and $Q = (X_Q, Y_Q, Z)$ can computed at an overall cost of five multiplications (5M), two squarings (2S) and seven additions/subtractions (7A) in $\mathbb{F}_p$, which is significantly less than the cost of a conventional point addition using Jacobian projective coordinates (12M+4S+7A, see [6, Sect. 2.3]) and lies even below the 8M+3S+7A for a "mixed" Jacobian-affine addition [6,12]. This Co-Z point-addition technique was applied by Rivain [23] to develop a fast and regular Montgomery ladder algorithm that is suitable for scalar multiplication on Weierstrass curves and does not require the order to be divisible by 4.

$$A = (X_Q - X_P)^2,\ B = X_P A,\ C = X_Q A,\ D = (Y_Q - Y_P)^2,\ E = Y_P(C - B)$$
$$X_R = D - (B + C),\ Y_R = (Y_Q - Y_P)(B - X_R) - E,\ Z_R = Z(X_Q - X_P) \quad (2)$$

Note that the Co-Z addition formula also yields a new representation of the point $P = (X_P, Y_P, Z)$ because $B = X_P(X_Q - X_P)^2$, $E = Y_P(X_Q - X_P)^3$, and $Z_R = Z(X_Q - X_P)$ [23]. Consequently, $(X_P, Y_P, Z) \sim (B, E, Z_R)$, which means this new representation of the point P and the sum $R = P + Q$ have the same Z-coordinate. According to Eq. (3) the difference $R' = P - Q = (X'_R, Y'_R, Z_R)$ can be computed with very little extra cost and has the same Z-coordinate as $R = P + Q$. In total, 6M+3S+11A are needed to obtain $P + Q$ and $P - Q$.

$$A, B, C, D,\text{ and } E \text{ as in Eq. (2)},\ F = (Y_P + Y_Q)^2$$
$$X'_R = F - (B + C),\ Y'_R = (Y_P + Y_Q)(X'_R - B) - E \quad (3)$$

Venelli and Dassance [28] presented a further optimization of Co-Z arithmetic by eliminating the computation of the Z-coordinate from the formulae for the Co-Z addition and Co-Z conjugate addition. Concretely, they proposed a novel Co-Z Montgomery ladder algorithm based on addition formulae that compute only the X and Y-coordinate of the intermediate points (we refer to this kind of operation as "(X, Y)-only addition"). The Z-coordinate can be recovered at the end of the ladder at little extra cost. Omitting the Z-coordinates reduces the computational cost of the Co-Z addition and the Co-Z conjugate addition by 1M to 4M+2S+7A and 5M+3S+11A, respectively. The implementation we present in this paper is based on (X, Y)-only Co-Z operations.

3   Parallel Co-Z Jacobian Arithmetic for SM2

In this section we first demonstrate that most of the field-arithmetic operations of Co-Z addition and Co-Z conjugate addition can be executed in parallel and then we present a ladder that exploits the processing capabilities of AVX2.

3.1   Parallel Co-Z Jacobian Point Addition

In order to utilize the parallelism of AVX2, we carefully analyzed the execution flow of the (X, Y)-only Co-Z Jacobian arithmetic and found that many of the field operations have no sequential dependency and can, therefore, be executed

---

Algorithm 1. SIMD_XYCZ_ADD: Parallel (X,Y)-only Co-Z addition

Input: $P = (X_P, Y_P)$, $Q = (X_Q, Y_Q)$.
Output: $(R, P') = (P + Q, P)$ where $P' \sim P$ has the same Z-coordinate as $P + Q$.

1:	$T_1 = X_P - X_Q$	$T_2 = Y_Q - Y_P$	{sub}
2:	$A = T_1^2$	$D = T_2^2$	{sqr}
3:	$B = X_P A$	$C = X_Q A$	{mul}
4:	$T_1 = B + C$		{add}
5:	$X_R = D - T_1$	$T_3 = C - B$	{sub}
6:	$T_1 = B - X_R$		{sub}
7:	$T_1 = T_1 T_2$	$E = Y_P T_3$	{mul}
8:	$Y_R = T_1 - E$		{sub}
9:	**return** $((X_R, Y_R), (B, E))$		

Algorithm 2. SIMD_XYCZ_ADDC: Parallel (X,Y)-only Co-Z conjugate addition

Input: $P = (X_P, Y_P)$, $Q = (X_Q, Y_Q)$, $A' = (X_Q - X_P)^2$, $T' = (X_Q - X_P)A' = C' - B'$
Output: $(R, R') = (P + Q, P - Q)$

1:	$C = X_Q A'$	$E = Y_P T'$	{mul}
2:	$B = C - T'$	$T_1 = Y_Q - Y_P$	{sub}
3:	$T_2 = B + C$	$T_3 = Y_P + Y_Q$	{add}
4:	$D = T_1^2$	$F = T_3^2$	{sqr}
5:	$X_R = D - T_2$	$X'_R = F - T_2$	{sub}
6:	$T_2 = B - X_R$	$T_4 = X'_R - B$	{sub}
7:	$T_2 = T_1 T_2$	$T_3 = T_3 T_4$	{mul}
8:	$Y_R = T_2 - E$	$Y'_R = T_3 - E$	{sub}
9:	**return** $((X_R, Y_R), (X'_R, Y'_R))$		

---

in parallel. This applies, for example, to the temporary values B and C of the formulae for the Co-Z addition given in Eq. (2), which means it is possible to obtain them simultaneously with a 2-way parallel field-multiplication. Also the computation of A and D can be "paired" and performed simultaneously if the used field-arithmetic library supports 2-way parallel squaring. Algorithm 1 and Algorithm 2 are optimized implementations of the (X,Y)-only Co-Z addition and Co-Z conjugate addition, respectively, whereby the prime-field operations are scheduled to facilitate a 2-way parallel execution. Each line performs two times the same operation in parallel using two sets of operands (the operation being carried out is commented on the right). Unfortunately, some operations of Algorithm 1 could not be paired (line 4, 6, and 8), but those operations are relatively cheap additions and subtractions. On the other hand, all operations of Algorithm 2 are performed pair-wise, but this became only possible because of the pre-computation of A' and T' (we will discuss further details of this pre-computation below). Without pre-computation of A' and T', the latency of the (X,Y)-only Co-Z conjugate addition would be significantly worse.

The 2-way parallel execution of the Co-Z point addition almost halves the latency compared to the straightforward (i.e. sequential) scheduling of the field operations. More concretely, the latency of the (X,Y)-only Co-Z addition

---

Algorithm 3. SIMD_XYCZ_ADDC_ADD: Parallel Co-Z ladder step

Input: $P = (X_P, Y_P) = R_a$, $Q = (X_Q, Y_Q) = R_{1-a}$, $A = (X_Q - X_P)^2$, $T' = (X_Q - X_P)A' = C' - B'$ where $a \in \{0,1\}$ and R_a, R_{1-a} are two Co-Z Jacobian points that are intermediate results of the Montgomery ladder algorithm.

Output: $(R_a, R_{1-a}) = (2R_a, R_a + R_{1-a})$ and update of $A' = (X_{R_a} - X_{R_{1-a}})^2$ and $T' = (X_{R_{1-a}} - X_{R_a})A'$.

1: $C' = X_Q A'$	$E' = Y_P T'$	{mul}
2: $B' = C' - T'$	$T_1 = Y_Q - Y_P$	{sub}
3: $T_2 = B' + C'$	$T_3 = Y_P + Y_Q$	{add}
4: $D' = T_1^2$	$F' = T_3^2$	{sqr}
5: $X_R = D' - T_2$	$X_R' = F' - T_2$	{sub}
6: $T_2 = B' - X_R$	$T_4 = X_R' - B'$	{sub}
7: $T_2 = T_1 T_2$	$T_4 = T_3 T_4$	{mul}
8: $Y_R = T_2 - E'$	$Y_R' = T_4 - E'$	{sub}
9: $T_1 = X_R' - X_R$	$T_2 = Y_R' - Y_R$	{sub}
10: $A = T_1^2$	$D = T_2^2$	{sqr}
11: $X_P = B = X_R A$	$C = X_R' A$	{mul}
12: $T_3 = T_2 + B$	$T_4 = B + C$	{add}
13: $X_Q = D - T_4$	$T_1 = C - B$	{sub}
14: $T_4 = X_Q - X_P$	$T_3 = T_3 - X_Q$	{sub}
15: $A' = T_4^2$	$T_3 = T_3^2$	{sqr}
16: $T' = T_4 A'$	$X_P = E = Y_R T_1$	{mul}
17: $T_1 = D + A'$	$T_2 = E + E$	{add}
18: $T_3 = T_3 - T_1$		{sub}
19: $Y_Q = \frac{1}{2}(T_3 - T_2)$		{sub}
20: **return** $((X_Q, Y_Q), (X_P, Y_P))$		

---

decreases from 4M+2S+7A to 2M̈+1S̈+5Ä, i.e. the delay due to multiplications and squarings is reduced by 50% (assuming that 2-way parallel field-operations have the same delay as single field-operations). We abbreviate a 2-way parallel multiplication, squaring, and addition (resp. subtraction) in $\mathbb{F}_p$ by M̈, S̈, and Ä, respectively, to distinguish them from the corresponding simple 1-way field operations. The 2-way parallel scheduling of the field-arithmetic decreases the latency of the (X, Y)-only Co-Z conjugate addition from 5M+3S+11A for the sequential variant given by Eq. (3) to 3M̈+1S̈+6Ä (this latency includes the pre-computation of A' and T', which will be discussed below).

As shown in [28] is is possible to convert the basic Montgomery ladder into a Co-Z based ladder algorithm by simply replacing the operations in the main loop by a (X, Y)-only Co-Z conjugate addition followed by a (X, Y)-only Co-Z addition as shown in Eq. (4). Algorithm 3 combines these two operations into a single "ladder step," which we optimized for an arithmetic library that is capable to execute the field operations in a 2-way parallel fashion. We designed Algorithm 3 by firstly analyzing the sequential versions of the Co-Z addition and CoZ conjugate addition. Their combined latency is 9M+5S+18A, but an optimization described in [23, Sect. A.2] (which replaces a field-multiplication by one squaring and four additions) makes it possible to reduce the latency to

---

Algorithm 4. Co-Z based Montgomery ladder algorithm

Input: A point $P \neq \mathcal{O}$, a scalar $k \in \mathbb{F}_p$ satisfying $k_{n-1} = 1$.
Output: The result of the scalar multiplication $R = k \cdot P$.
1: $(R_1, R_0) = \text{XYCZ\_IDBL}(P)$
2: $a = k_{n-2}$
3: $A' = (X_{R_{1-a}} - X_{R_a})^2$, $T' = (X_{R_{1-a}} - X_{R_a})A'$
4: **for** i from $n - 2$ by 1 down to 1 **do**
5:     $a = (k_i + k_{i+1}) \bmod 2$
6:     $(R_a, R_{1-a}, A', T') = \text{SIMD\_XYCZ\_ADDC\_ADD}(R_a, R_{1-a}, A', T')$
7: **end for**
8: $a = (k_0 + k_1) \bmod 2$
9: $(R_{1-a}, R_a) = \text{SIMD\_XYCZ\_ADDC}(R_a, R_{1-a}, A', T')$
10: $\frac{\lambda}{Z} = \text{FinalInvZ}(R_{1-a}, R_a, P, a)$
11: $(R_0, R_1) = \text{SIMD\_XYCZ\_ADD}(R_0, R_1)$
12: **return** $((\frac{\lambda}{Z})^2 X_{R_0}, (\frac{\lambda}{Z})^3 Y_{R_0})$

8M+6M+22A. This indicates that, in theory, a parallel implementation of the ladder step using 2-way parallel field operations could have a latency as low as 4M̈+3S̈+11Ä. However, the latency of a parallel Co-Z addition (Algorithm 1) together with the parallel Co-Z conjugate addition (Algorithm 2) amounts to 5M̈+2S̈+11Ä and does not reach this (theoretical) lower bound. We then tried to reschedule the field operations of the sequential 8M+6M+22A ladder step in order to optimize it for 2-way parallel execution, but some data dependencies did not allow us to reach the best possible latency of 4M̈+3S̈+11Ä.

In order to obtain the minimal latency, we propose to pre-compute the two terms $A' = (X_Q - X_P)^2$ and $T' = (X_Q - X_P)A'$ before entering the main loop of the ladder algorithm and update A' and T' in each iteration (as part of the ladder step, see Algorithm 3). In this way, we managed to perfectly resolve the data dependencies and achieve a latency of 4M̈+3S̈+13Ä, which is close to the minimum (all field operations except two subtractions at the very end could be properly paired, which makes Algorithm 3 very well suited for a 2-way parallel execution of field operations). Compared to the combination of Co-Z addition and Co-Z conjugate addition, the proposed ladder step trades 1M̈ for 1S̈ and 2Ä, which reduces the latency in our case (see Sect. 5).

3.2 Parallel Co-Z Based Montgomery Ladder

The Montgomery ladder can not only be used for Montgomery curves, but also for general Weierstrass curves [4,16], which includes the SM2 curve. Venelli and Dassance [28] proposed (X, Y)-only Co-Z arithmetic and further optimized the Co-Z based Montgomery ladder algorithm by avoiding the computation of the Z-coordinate during the main loop of the scalar multiplication.

Algorithm 4 shows our (X, Y)-only Co-Z Montgomery ladder based on the parallel ladder step described before. It starts by computing the initial points $(R_1, R_0) = (2P, P)$ for the ladder using a doubling operation with Co-Z update (called XYCZ_IDBL, see [23, Sect. C] for details). Thereafter, the two values A' and T' are pre-computed, which is necessary to minimize the latency of the parallel Co-Z ladder step as discussed before. During the execution of the main loop, our parallel Co-Z ladder algorithm with minimum latency maintains the following relationship between the ladder points:

$$(R_{1-a}, R_a) = (R_a + R_{1-a}, R_a - R_{1-a})$$
$$R_a = R_{1-a} + R_a \tag{4}$$

where $a = (k_i + k_{i+1}) \bmod 2$. As Algorithm 4 shows, our parallel Co-Z based Montgomery ladder executes a parallel Co-Z ladder step in each iteration, and has therefore a regular execution profile and constant execution time. The two constants A', T' get updated with each call of the ladder-step function. At the end of the ladder, a conversion from Co-Z Jacobian coordinates to affine coordinates needs to be carried out. We perform this conversion with the function FinalInvZ, which computes $Z = X_P Y_{R_a}(X_{R_0} - X_{R_1})$, $\lambda = y_P X_{R_a}$ and outputs $\frac{\lambda}{Z}$ at a cost of 1I+3M+1A, i.e. this conversion requires an inversion in $\mathbb{F}_p$.

Due to the parallel (X, Y)-only Co-Z Jacobian arithmetic, our Co-Z based ladder outperforms the sequential Co-Z ladder by a factor of roughly 1.31. To the best of our knowledge, the parallel Co-Z Montgomery ladder we presented in this section is the first attempt of minimizing the latency of a variable-base scalar multiplication by combining (X, Y)-only Co-Z Jacobian point arithmetic with a 2-way parallel implementation of the prime-field arithmetic.

4   2-Way Parallel Prime-Field Arithmetic for SM2

The Co-Z based Montgomery ladder presented in the previous section requires a 2-way parallel implementation of the arithmetic operations in the underlying prime field $\mathbb{F}_p$. As explained in Sect. 2, the prime field used by SM2 is defined by the 256-bit generalized-Mersenne prime $p = 2^{256} - 2^{224} - 2^{96} + 2^{64} - 1$. The special form of p allows one to speed up the modular reduction [25].

We explained in Sect. 2 that, in order to reduce carry propagation, it makes sense to use a reduced-radix representation on modern 64-bit processors. This is also the case when implementing multi-precision integer arithmetic for SIMD engines like AVX2 since they do not offer an add-with-carry instruction. The implementation we introduce in this section adopts a radix-2^{26} representation for the field elements, i.e. a 256-bit integer consists of $k' = \lceil 256/26 \rceil = 10$ limbs and each limb is $n' = 26$ bits long (but can temporarily become longer). When putting four limbs into an AVX2 register, it is possible to perform four limb-multiplications in parallel, each producing a 52-bit result. However, each of the 10 limbs can become as long as 29 bits without causing an overflow during the multiplication of field elements since the sum of 10 limb-products still fits into 64 bits: $10 \times 2^{29} \times 2^{29} < 2^{62}$. In addition, since 10 is a multiple of two, we can split a field element evenly into five limb-pairs for 2-way parallel execution.

The AVX2 implementation of the $\mathbb{F}_p$-arithmetic we describe below performs an arithmetic operation in a 2-way parallel fashion, which two times the same operation is executed, but with different operands. Each of the two operations uses pairs of limbs instead of a single limb as "smallest unit" of processing. We put a limb-pair of operand A into the higher 128-bit lane of a 256-bit AVX2 register and a limb-pair of operand B into the lower 128-bit lane, i.e. there are four limbs altogether in an AVX2 register. Consequently, we need five registers to store all limbs of A and B. Similar to [7], we use a set of *interleaved tuples* $\langle A, B \rangle_i$ for $i \in [0, 5)$ to denote such five AVX2 registers, whereby the i-th tuple $\langle A, B \rangle_i$ contains the four limbs $[a_{2i+1}, a_{2i}, b_{2i+1}, b_{2i}]$.

4.1   Addition and Subtraction

Due to the redundant representation, the 2-way addition/subtraction over two sets of interleaved tuples $\langle A, B \rangle_i \pm \langle C, D \rangle_i = \langle A \pm C, B \pm D \rangle_i$ can be performed by executing five AVX2 add (ADD)/subtract (SUB) instructions that operate on 64-bit data elements in parallel. To avoid overflow during the addition, we assert that the length of each limb of the operands must not exceed 63 bits. On the other hand, to avoid underflow during subtraction, we add an appropriate multiple of the SM2 prime p to $\langle A, B \rangle_i$ and then perform the subtraction. We do not reduce the result modulo p unless the next operation would overflow.

4.2   Modular Multiplication and Squaring

Multiplication/Squaring. Our implementation of the 2-way parallel multiplication using AVX2 instructions was inspired by the work of Faz-Hernández and López for Curve25519 [7] (with some modifications for the SM2 prime). As shown in Algorithm 5, the outer loop (starting at line 4) traverses through the set of interleaved tuples $\langle A, B \rangle_i$. Since there are two limbs of each A and B in an interleaved tuple, we have two inner loops and use the SHUF instruction to separate the two limbs of A and B. Each of the inner loops traverses through the set $\langle C, D \rangle_j$, multiplies the tuple $\langle C, D \rangle$ (or $\langle C', D' \rangle$) by the shuffled tuple $\langle A, B \rangle$, and adds the obtained partial-product to Z_{i+j} (or Z_{i+j+1}). Due to the radix-2^{26} representation, we can assure that this multiply-accumulate process does not overflow the 64-bit data element in which the sum is kept. When the multiplication is finished, we call the function FastRed (Algorithm 6) to get the final result $\langle E, F \rangle_i = \langle A \cdot C \bmod p, B \cdot D \bmod p \rangle_i$. Squaring is quite similar to the multiplication, except that a number of MUL instructions can be replaced by left-shift (i.e. SHL) instructions, see e.g. [7, Algorithm 4].

Fast Reduction. There exist some well-known modular reduction techniques for arbitrary primes, such as the algorithms of Barrett or Montgomery [12]. The 2-way modular reduction we implemented takes advantage of the generalized-Mersenne form of the SM2 prime, which allows for a special reduction method with linear complexity [25]. However, we had to re-design the fast reduction to make it compatible with our radix-2^{26} representation, see Algorithm 6. We use the congruence relations specified by Eq. (5) to "fold" the upper half of the

Algorithm 5. 2-way parallel multiplication using AVX2 instructions

Input: Two sets of interleaved tuples $\langle A, B \rangle_i$, $\langle C, D \rangle_i$ with $A, B, C, D \in \mathbb{F}_p$.
Output: Modular product $\langle E, F \rangle_i = \langle AC \bmod p, BD \bmod p \rangle_i$.

1:   $Z_i = 0$ for $i \in [0, 10)$
2: **for** i from 0 by 1 up to 4 **do**
3:     $\langle C', D' \rangle_i = \mathrm{ALIGN}(\langle C, D \rangle_{i+1 \bmod 5}, \langle C, D \rangle_i)$ $\{[c_{2i+2}, c_{2i+1}, d_{2i+2}, d_{2i+1}]\}$
4: **end for**
5: **for** i from 0 by 1 up to 4 **do**
6:     $U = \mathrm{SHUF}(\langle A, B \rangle_i, \langle A, B \rangle_i, \mathtt{0x44})$ $\{[a_{2i}, a_{2i}, b_{2i}, b_{2i}]\}$
7:     **for** j from 0 by 1 up to 4 **do**
8:        $Z_{i+j} = \mathrm{ADD}(Z_{i+j}, \mathrm{MUL}(U, \langle C, D \rangle_j))$ $\{[a_{2i}c_{2j+1}, a_{2i}c_{2j}, b_{2i}d_{2j+1}, b_{2i}d_{2j}]\}$
9:     **end for**
10:   $V = \mathrm{SHUF}(\langle A, B \rangle_i, \langle A, B \rangle_i, \mathtt{0xEE})$ $\{[a_{2i+1}, a_{2i+1}, b_{2i+1}, b_{2i+1}]\}$
11:    **for** j from 0 by 1 up to 3 **do**
12:      $Z_{i+j+1} = \mathrm{ADD}(Z_{i+j+1}, \mathrm{MUL}(V, \langle C', D' \rangle_j))$
                        $\{[a_{2i+1}c_{2j+2}, a_{2i+1}c_{2j+1}, b_{2i+1}d_{2j+2}, b_{2i+1}d_{2j+1}]\}$
13:    **end for**
14:   $W = \mathrm{MUL}(V, \langle C, D \rangle_4)$ $\{[a_{2i+1}c_0, a_{2i+1}c_9, b_{2i+1}d_0, b_{2i+1}d_9]\}$
15:   $Z_i = \mathrm{ADD}(Z_i, \mathrm{BLEND}(W, [0,0,0,0], \mathtt{0x33}))$ $\{[a_{2i+1}c_0, 0, b_{2i+1}d_0, 0]\}$
16:   $Z_{i+5} = \mathrm{ADD}(Z_{i+5}, \mathrm{BLEND}(W, [0,0,0,0], \mathtt{0xCC}))$ $\{[0, a_{2i+1}c_9, 0, b_{2i+1}d_9]\}$
17: **end for**
18: $\langle E, F \rangle_i = \mathrm{FastRed}(Z)$ $\{\text{Algorithm 6}\}$
19: **return** $\langle E, F \rangle_i$

20-limb product Z, i.e. the 10 limbs z_{10} to z_{19}, which have a weight of between 2^{260} and 2^{494}), into the lower half of Z. Our fast modular reduction technique replaces the large powers of two on the left side of Eq. (5), which all exceed 2^{260}, by sums of smaller powers of two (i.e. less than 2^{260}) based on the special form of $p = 2^{256} - 2^{224} - 2^{96} + 2^{64} - 1$. Consequently, the modular reduction boils down to basic shifts, additions, and subtractions of limbs. However, note that Eq. (5) assumes the limbs of the product Z to be 26 bits long.

$$z_{10}2^{260} \equiv z_{10}(2^{228} + 2^{100} - 2^{68} + 2^4) \bmod p$$
$$z_{11}2^{286} \equiv z_{11}(2^{254} + 2^{126} - 2^{94} + 2^{30}) \bmod p$$
$$z_{12}2^{312} \equiv z_{12}(2^{248} + 2^{152} - 2^{88} + 2^{56} + 2^{24}) \bmod p$$
$$z_{13}2^{338} \equiv z_{13}(2^{242} + 2^{178} + 2^{50} + 2^{18}) \bmod p$$
$$z_{14}2^{364} \equiv z_{14}(2^{236} + 2^{204} + 2^{108} + 2^{44} + 2^{12}) \bmod p$$
$$z_{15}2^{390} \equiv z_{15}(2^{231} + 2^{134} + 2^{102} + 2^{38} + 2^6) \bmod p \qquad (5)$$
$$z_{16}2^{416} \equiv z_{16}(2^{257} + 2^{160} + 2^{128} + 2^{64} + 2^{32}) \bmod p$$
$$z_{17}2^{442} \equiv z_{17}(2^{251} + 2^{186} + 2^{154} + 2^{123} - 2^{90} + 2^{58} + 2^{27}) \bmod p$$
$$z_{18}2^{468} \equiv z_{18}(2^{245} + 2^{212} + 2^{180} + 2^{149} + 2^{116} - 2^{84} + 2^{53} + 2^{21}) \bmod p$$
$$z_{19}2^{494} \equiv z_{19}(3 \cdot 2^{238} + 2^{206} + 2^{175} + 2^{142} + 2^{110} + 2^{47} + 2^{15}) \bmod p$$

The modular reduction function specified in Algorithm 6 first converts the limbs in the upper half of the AVX2 registers into a radix-2^{28} form, i.e. 28 bits

Algorithm 6. 2-way parallel modular reduction using AVX2 instructions

Input: A set of interleaved tuples Z consisting of 20 limbs.

Output: Modular-reduced set of interleaved tuples $\langle E, F \rangle_i$ consisting of 10 limbs.

1: **for** i from 4 by 1 up to 8 **do**
2:     $L_i = \text{AND}(Z_i, [2^{n'} - 1, 2^{n'} - 1, 2^{n'} - 1, 2^{n'} - 1])$
3:     $M_i = \text{SHR}(Z_i, [n', n', n', n'])$
4:     $M_i = \text{AND}(M_i, [2^{n'} - 1, 2^{n'} - 1, 2^{n'} - 1, 2^{n'} - 1])$
5:     $H_i = \text{SHR}(Z_i, [2n', 2n', 2n', 2n'])$
6: **end for**
7: $L_9 = \text{AND}(Z_9, [2^{n'} - 1, 2^{n'} - 1, 2^{n'} - 1, 2^{n'} - 1])$
8: $M_9 = \text{SHR}(Z_9, [n', n', n', n'])$
9: **for** i from 5 by 1 up to 9 **do**
10:     $M_i' = \text{ALIGN}(M_i, M_{i-1})$
11:     $Z_i = \text{ADD}(\text{ADD}(L_i, M_i'), H_{i-1})$
12: **end for**
13: $Z_9 = \text{ALIGN}(Z_9, M_9)$
14: $\langle E, F \rangle_i = \text{SimpleRed}(Z)$
15: **return** $\langle E, F \rangle_i$

per limb. Since the reduction is carried out immediately after a multiplication or squaring, the maximum limb-length can be 60 bits. In order to reduce the length of the upper limbs to 28 bits, we first split them into three parts of up to $n' = 26$ bits: a lower part containing the 26 least significant bits, a middle part consisting of the next 26 bits, and a higher part with the rest. Each of the parts has a certain weight, and parts of the same weight (which can be up to three) are added together, yielding limbs of a length of at most 28 bits. This conversion is performed by the two loops of Algorithm 6 (i.e. line 1–12). At the end of these loops, we have an intermediate result Z of which the lower limbs are less than 60 bits long, while the upper limbs can have a length of up to 28 bits (with exception of the limbs in Z_9, which can be up to 30 bits long). The actual modular reduction based on the congruence relations of Eq. (5) is then carried out in line 14 by the SimpleRed operation (explained in Sect. A). Note that SimpleRed produces a result consisting of 10 limbs, whereby each limb is less than $2^4 \cdot 2^{28} \cdot 2^{24} + 2^{60} < 2^{61}$ and easily fits in a 64-bit data element (this remains correct when the maximum limb-length is 30 instead of 28 bits).

4.3   Carry Propagation (Conversion to 28-Bit Limbs)

The result of the SimpleRed operation consists of 10 limbs (which are stored in five AVX2 registers), whereby each limb is smaller than 2^{61}, i.e. no more than 60 bits long. However, a result given in such a form needs to be converted into a representation with limbs of a length of $n' = 26$ bits (or a little longer). This conversion requires a method to "carry" the excess bits of a limb over to the next-higher limb, and to reduce the excess bits of the highest limb modulo the prime p). To achieve this, each 60-bit limb has to be split into three parts as follows: $a_i = h_i \| m_i \| l_i$ where $|l_i| = |m_i| = n'$ and $|h_i| = 60 - 2n'$ (similar as

---

Algorithm 7. 2-way parallel carry propagation using AVX2 instructions

---

Input: A set of interleaved tuples $\langle A, B \rangle_i$.
Output: A set of interleaved tuples $\langle A, B \rangle_i$ with $|a_i|, |b_i| \leq n' + 1$ for $i \in [0, 10)$.

1: $H_4 = \text{SHRV}(\langle A, B \rangle_4, [n', 2n', n', 2n'])$
2: $\langle A, B \rangle_4 = \text{AND}(\langle A, B \rangle_4, [2^{n'} - 1, 2^{2n'} - 1, 2^{n'} - 1, 2^{2n'} - 1])$
3: $Q = \text{ADD}(H_4, \text{SHUF}(H_4, H_4, 0\text{x}4\text{E}))$
4: $Q' = \text{SUB}([0,0,0,0], Q)$
5: $\langle A, B \rangle_0 = \text{ADD}(\langle A, B \rangle_0, \text{SHLV}(\text{BLEND}(Q, [0,0,0,0], 0\text{xCC}), [0,4,0,4]))$
6: $\langle A, B \rangle_1 = \text{ADD}(\langle A, B \rangle_1, \text{SHLV}(\text{BLEND}(Q, Q', 0\text{x}33), [22,16,22,16]))$
7: $\langle A, B \rangle_4 = \text{ADD}(\langle A, B \rangle_4, \text{SHLV}(\text{BLEND}(Q, [0,0,0,0], 0\text{xCC}), [0,20,0,20]))$
8: **for** i from 0 by 1 up to 4 **do**
9:     $L_i = \text{AND}(\langle A, B \rangle_i, [2^{n'} - 1, 2^{n'} - 1, 2^{n'} - 1, 2^{n'} - 1])$
10:    $M_i = \text{SHR}(\langle A, B \rangle_i, [n', n', n', n'])$
11:    $M_i = \text{AND}(M_i, [2^{n'} - 1, 2^{n'} - 1, 2^{n'} - 1, 2^{n'} - 1])$
12:    $H_i = \text{SHR}(\langle A, B \rangle_i, [2n', 2n', 2n', 2n'])$
13: **end for**
14: **for** i from 0 by 1 up to 4 **do**
15:    $M_i' = \text{ALIGN}(M_i, M_{i-1 \bmod 5})$
16:    $\langle A, B \rangle_i = \text{ADD}(\text{ADD}(L_i, M_i'), H_{i-1 \bmod 5})$
17: **end for**
18: **return** $\langle A, B \rangle$

---

in the previous subsection). Algorithm 7 specifies the conversion. In line 1–7 we estimate the excess bits of the highest limb, which means we estimate a value q of weight 2^{260} by computing $q = (h_{k'-1} || m_{k'-1} + h_{k'-2})$. Then, we reduce the value q via the congruence $q \cdot 2^{260} \equiv q \cdot (2^{228} + 2^{100} - 2^{68} + 2^4) \bmod p$, i.e. we add q to (or subtract it from) limbs with the corresponding terms. The code in line 8–17 reduces the bit-length of the remaining limbs based on the equations $a_0' = l_0$, $a_1' = l_1 + m_0$, and $a_i' = l_i + m_{i-1} + h_{i-2}$ for $i \in [2, 10)$. This algorithm ensures $|a_i'| <= 28$ for $i \in [0, k' - 1]$, which means the limbs are within a safe range so that they can serve as operand in any of our field operations.

4.4   Modular Inversion

Modular inversion is the most costly among the prime-field operations needed in ECC. Using Jacobian projective coordinates, we only need one inversion to convert the result from projective to affine coordinates. The Binary Extended Euclidean Algorithm (BEEA) is a well-known algorithm for inversion, but has an irregular execution flow and operand-dependent execution time, which can enable timing and SPA attacks [5]. Therefore, we chose Fermat's little theorem and perform the inversion through an exponentiation: $a^{-1} \equiv a^{p-2} \bmod p$. When utilizing an addition chain as in e.g. [30], the modular inversion can be carried out at an overall cost of 15M+255S.

5   Performance Evaluation

We benchmarked the described implementation on a 64-bit Intel Cascade Lake processor clocked at 2.5 GHz. The execution times we present in this section were obtained by measuring the cycles for 10^6 iterations of the field-operations and 10^4 iterations of the point operations, on a single core and single thread.

Table 1. Comparison of the execution time of the 1-way and 2-way implementation of the prime-field operations (in clock cycles)

Implementation	Add/sub	Mul	Sqr	Inv	Carry prop.
1-way (1 op)	5	75	65	18,459	23
2-way (2 ops)	8	99	81	–	30
Speed-up ratio	1.25	1.52	1.60	–	1.53

Table 1 provides the timings of a standard (i.e. 1-way) and a 2-way parallel implementation of the prime-field operations. The results show that, when one and the same operation has to be performed on two sets of field-elements, the 2-way parallel implementation is much faster than two subsequent executions of the basic 1-way version; the speed-up factors range from 1.25 to 1.60. Since our 2-way field arithmetic is based on techniques from [7], the execution times of the operations are similar. However, the reduction modulo the SM2 prime is more complicated (and thus slower) than the reduction for Curve25519.

Table 2. Execution time (in clock cycles) of Co-Z addition, Co-Z conjugate addition, Co-Z ladder step, and Co-Z based Montgomery ladder algorithm.

Implementation	Co-Z ADD	Co-Z ADDC	Co-Z L-Step	Co-Z Ladder
Sequential	555	786	1,334	359,868
2-way parallel	439	489	1,001	274,908
Speed-up ratio	1.26	1.60	1.33	1.31

Table 2 shows the execution times of the sequential and the 2-way parallel version of the Co-Z addition, Co-Z conjugate addition, Co-Z ladder step, and Co-Z based full Montgomery ladder algorithm. Similarly as above, the parallel versions clearly outperform their sequential counterparts. The 2-way parallel CoZ Montgomery ladder has an execution time of 275k clock cycles, which is 1.31 times faster than the sequential ladder. To the best of our knowledge, this paper is the first to present a Co-Z based Montgomery ladder utilizing AVX2 instructions and to demonstrate the ability of a 2-way parallel implementation of the field arithmetic to speed up Co-Z based Jacobian point operations. Table 3 compares our parallel Co-Z Montgomery ladder with similar AVX2 implementations of variable-base scalar multiplication on Curve25519 and the

Table 3. Comparison of the computational cost and execution time (in clock cycles on a Cascade Lake or Haswell processor) of our Co-Z based Montgomery ladder and other AVX2 implementations of variable-base scalar multiplication.

Implementation	Cost per bit	Additional cost	Execution time
SM2 (this work)	$4\ddot{\text{M}}+3\ddot{\text{S}}+13\ddot{\text{A}}$	$1\text{I}+8\text{M}+7\text{S}+12\text{A}$	274,908 (CL)
Curve25519 [7]	$3\ddot{\text{M}}+2\ddot{\text{S}}+1\ddot{\text{C}}+4\ddot{\text{A}}$	$1\text{I}+1\text{M}$	156,500 (H)
Curve25519 [8]	$3\ddot{\text{M}}+2\ddot{\text{S}}+1\ddot{\text{C}}+4\ddot{\text{A}}$	$1\text{I}+1\text{M}$	121,000 (H)
NIST P-256 [11]	n/a	n/a	312,000 (H)

NIST curve P-256. Since Curve25519 is Montgomery curve [20], it supports an efficient "X-coordinate-only" algorithm for variable-base scalar multiplication that costs only $5\text{M}+4\text{S}+1\text{C}+8\text{A}$ per scalar-bit ("C" stands for a multiplication of a field-element by a curve constant, which is normally much faster than an ordinary field-multiplication). Furthermore, as already mentioned, a reduction modulo the 255-bit pseudo-Mersenne prime used by Curve25519 can be carried out more efficiently than a reduction modulo the SM2 prime. Faz-Hernández and López reported in [7] an execution time of roughly 156,500 Haswell cycles for their AVX2 implementation of Curve25519, which is significantly better than our 274,908 clock cycles for SM2 on a more recent Cascade Lake CPU. There are three main reasons for this difference in execution time. First, as shown in Table 3, the parallel version of the Co-Z based ladder-step for the SM2 curve is $1\ddot{\text{M}}+1\ddot{\text{S}}+9\ddot{\text{A}}$ more costly than the parallel ladder-step for Montgomery curves (i.e. [7, Algorithm 1]). The second reason is the higher additional cost outside the ladder loop for such tasks like the initial point doubling, the computation of the values A' and T', and the recovery of the Z-coordinate at the end of the ladder. Finally, the reduction modulo the SM2 prime is more complicated, and therefore slower, than the reduction modulo $p - 2^{255} - 19$.

Table 4. Comparison of the execution time of ECDH key exchange and ECDSA signature generation/verification using the SM2 curve on a 2.5 GHz Cascade Lake processor and the NIST curve P-256 on a 3.4 GHz Haswell processor.

Implementation	Processor	ECDH key ex.	ECDSA sign	ECDSA verify
SM2 (this work)	Cascade Lake	148 µs	24 µs	98 µs
NIST P-256 [11]	Haswell	93 µs	41 µs	122 µs

Gueron and Krasnov presented in [11] optimized implementations of fixed-base and variable-base scalar multiplication, both specifically optimized for the NIST curve P-256. Their paper includes benchmarking results generated on an Intel Haswell processor clocked at 3.4 GHz; some of these results can be found in Table 3 and Table 4 (taken from the operations/second in [11, Fig. 7]). The fixed-base scalar multiplication uses a windowing method with a window size of 7 and performs four point additions in parallel in the AVX2 engine. On the other hand, the variable-base scalar multiplication has smaller windows of size

5 and executes the point operations sequentially (the prime-field arithmetic is written in x86_64 assembly and does not exploit the parallelism of AVX2). The execution time in the variable-base case is 312,000 Haswell cycles (about 92 μs when the clock frequency is 3.4 GHz). Gueron and Krasnov also benchmarked ECDH key exchange (computation of the shared key only), ECDSA signature generation (mainly fixed-base scalar multiplication) and the verification of an ECDSA signature; the corresponding timings are listed in Table 4.

Also given in Table 4 are the execution times of our AVX2 implementation of SM2-based ECDH key exchange, and the generation and verification of an ECDSA signature, which we measured on a 2.5 GHz Cascade Lake CPU. We implemented the fixed-base scalar multiplication (for signature generation) in the same way as [11], i.e. by means of a windowing method with a window size of 7. The execution time of our fixed-base scalar multiplication is about 64,000 Cascade Lake cycles. Note that the SM2 key exchange protocol authenticates the involved parties and, therefore, the computation of the shared key requires two scalar multiplications. This explains why SM2 key exchange is slower than a basic static ECDH key exchange. Unfortunately, a comparison of the results of our implementation with that of [11] is difficult since the micro-architectural properties and features of Haswell and Cascade Lake differ significantly.

6   Conclusions

We introduced a 2-way parallel implementation of SM2 prime-field arithmetic and Co-Z Jacobian point operations that leverage the processing capabilities of AVX2. Due to a careful rescheduling of the field arithmetic along with the pre-computation of two values outside the main loop, we managed to minimize the execution time of the parallel Co-Z ladder algorithm. More concretely, the 2-way parallel field arithmetic and Co-Z Jacobian point operations reduce the execution time of the ladder algorithm for variable-base scalar multiplication by a factor of 1.31 compared to sequential execution. Furthermore, our parallel ladder has a highly regular execution profile, which helps to achieve resistance against timing and SPA attacks. The main take-away message of this paper is that SIMD-level parallelism helps to narrow the performance gap between the classical Montgomery ladder on Montgomery curves and the Co-Z ladder on Weierstrass curves. When executed sequentially, the difference between these two scalar multiplication methods is 3M+2S (i.e. 5M+4S vs. 8M+6S), but this difference shrinks to 1$\ddot{\text{M}}$+1$\ddot{\text{S}}$ (3$\ddot{\text{M}}$+2$\ddot{\text{S}}$ vs. 4$\ddot{\text{M}}$+3$\ddot{\text{S}}$) in the case of 2-way parallel execution. Finally, we remark that all optimization techniques proposed in this paper can also be applied to the NIST curves.

Acknowledgments. Zhe Liu is supported by the National Natural Science Foundation of China (grant no. 61802180), the Natural Science Foundation of Jiangsu Province (grant no. BK20180421), the National Cryptography Development Fund (grant no. MM-JJ20180105) and the Fundamental Research Funds for the Central Universities (grant no. NE2018106). Zhi Hu is supported by the Natural Science Foundation of China (grants no. 61972420, 61602526) and the Hunan Provincial Natural Science Foundation of China (grants no. 2019JJ50827 and 2020JJ3050).

A   SimpleRed Operation

Based on the congruence relations in Eq. (5), we add or subtract each of the upper limbs z_i with $i \in [10, 20)$ to the corresponding lower limbs in Z to obtain the residue $\langle E, F \rangle_i$ from the intermediate result Z. For example, all the terms with weight $2^0 \sim 2^{26}$ and $2^{26} \sim 2^{52}$ will be added to or subtracted from Z_0 to obtain $\langle E, F \rangle_0$. Similarly to Z_0, the terms with other weights will be added to or subtracted from the corresponding terms of the intermediate result Z. The details are fully specified in Algorithm 8, which executes only simple additions (resp. subtractions), shifts, and permutation instructions.

Algorithm 8. 2-way parallel SimpleRed operation using AVX2 instructions

---

Input: An intermediate result Z consisting of 20 limbs.
Output: A modular residue $\langle E, F \rangle_i$ consisting of ten 28-bit limbs.

1: $\langle E, F \rangle_0 = \text{ADD}(Z_0, \text{SHL}(Z_5, 4))$
2: $\langle E, F \rangle_0 = \text{ADD}(\langle E, F \rangle_0, \text{SHL}(Z_6, 24))$
3: $\langle E, F \rangle_0 = \text{ADD}(\langle E, F \rangle_0, \text{SHL}(\text{SHUF}(Z_6, Z_7, 0x5), 18))$
4: $\langle E, F \rangle_0 = \text{ADD}(\langle E, F \rangle_0, \text{SHL}(Z_7, 12))$
5: $\langle E, F \rangle_0 = \text{ADD}(\langle E, F \rangle_0, \text{SHL}(\text{SHUF}(Z_7, Z_8, 0x5), 6))$
6: $\langle E, F \rangle_0 = \text{ADD}(\langle E, F \rangle_0, \text{SHL}(Z_9, 21))$
7: $\langle E, F \rangle_0 = \text{ADD}(\langle E, F \rangle_0, \text{SHLV}(\text{BLEND}(\text{PERM64}(Z_9, 0xB1), Z_8, 0xCC), [1, 15, 1, 15]))$
8: $Z'_8 = \text{SUB}([0,0,0,0], Z_8)$, $Z'_9 = \text{SUB}([0,0,0,0], Z_9)$
9: $\langle E, F \rangle_1 = \text{SUB}(Z_1, \text{SHL}(Z_5, 16))$
10: $\langle E, F \rangle_1 = \text{ADD}(\langle E, F \rangle_1, \text{SHLV}(\text{BLEND}(Z_6, \text{PERM64}(Z_5, 0xB1), 0xCC), [22, 4, 22, 4]))$
11: $\langle E, F \rangle_1 = \text{SUB}(\langle E, F \rangle_1, \text{SHLV}(\text{SHUF}([0,0,0,0], Z_6, 0x5), [10, 0, 10, 0]))$
12: $\langle E, F \rangle_1 = \text{ADD}(\langle E, F \rangle_1, \text{SHL}(\text{BLEND}(Z_8, Z'_8, 0xCC), 12))$
13: $\langle E, F \rangle_1 = \text{ADD}(\langle E, F \rangle_1, \text{SHL}(\text{SHUF}(Z_8, Z'_9, 0x5), 6))$
14: $\langle E, F \rangle_1 = \text{ADD}(\langle E, F \rangle_1, \text{SHLV}(\text{BLEND}(Z_9, Z_7, 0xCC), [24, 1, 24, 1]))$
15: $\langle E, F \rangle_2 = \text{ADD}(Z_2, \text{SHL}(\text{SHUF}(Z_5, Z_6, 0x5), 22))$
16: $\langle E, F \rangle_2 = \text{ADD}(\langle E, F \rangle_2, \text{SHL}(Z_7, 4))$
17: $\langle E, F \rangle_2 = \text{ADD}(\langle E, F \rangle_2, \text{SHL}(Z_8, 24))$
18: $\langle E, F \rangle_2 = \text{ADD}(\langle E, F \rangle_2, \text{SHL}(\text{SHUF}(Z_8, Z_9, 0x5), 19))$
19: $\langle E, F \rangle_2 = \text{ADD}(\langle E, F \rangle_2, \text{SHL}(Z_9, 12))$
20: $\langle E, F \rangle_2 = \text{ADD}(\langle E, F \rangle_2, \text{SHL}(\text{SHUF}(Z_9, [0,0,0,0], 0x5), 6))$
21: $\langle E, F \rangle_3 = \text{ADD}(Z_3, \text{SHL}(\text{SHUF}(Z_6, Z_7, 0x5), 22))$
22: $\langle E, F \rangle_3 = \text{ADD}(\langle E, F \rangle_3, \text{SHL}(Z_8, 4))$
23: $\langle E, F \rangle_3 = \text{ADD}(\langle E, F \rangle_3, \text{SHL}(Z_9, 24))$
24: $\langle E, F \rangle_3 = \text{ADD}(\langle E, F \rangle_3, \text{SHL}(\text{SHUF}(Z_9, [0,0,0,0], 0x5), 19))$
25: $\langle E, F \rangle_4 = \text{ADD}(Z_4, \text{SHL}(Z_5, 20))$
26: $\langle E, F \rangle_4 = \text{ADD}(\langle E, F \rangle_4, \text{SHLV}(\text{SHUF}(Z_7, Z_7, 0x5), [2, 23, 2, 23]))$
27: $\langle E, F \rangle_4 = \text{ADD}(\langle E, F \rangle_4, \text{SHL}(Z_9, 4))$
28: $T = \text{ADD}(\text{SHLV}(Z_6, [8, 14, 8, 14]), \text{SHLV}(Z_8, [17, 23, 17, 23]))$
29: $T = \text{ADD}(T, \text{SHLV}(Z_9, [5, 11, 5, 11]))$
30: $\langle E, F \rangle_4 = \text{ADD}(\langle E, F \rangle_4, \text{ADD}(\text{SHUF}([0,0,0,0], T, 0x5), \text{BLEND}([0,0,0,0], T, 0xCC)))$
31: **return** $\langle E, F \rangle_{0...4}$

References

1. Bernstein, D.J.: Curve25519: new Diffie-Hellman speed records. In: Yung, M., Dodis, Y., Kiayias, A., Malkin, T. (eds.) PKC 2006. LNCS, vol. 3958, pp. 207–228. Springer, Heidelberg (2006). https://doi.org/10.1007/11745853_14
2. Bernstein, D.J., Schwabe, P.: NEON crypto. In: Prouff, E., Schaumont, P. (eds.) CHES 2012. LNCS, vol. 7428, pp. 320–339. Springer, Heidelberg (2012). https://doi.org/10.1007/978-3-642-33027-8_19
3. Bos, J.W.: Low-latency elliptic curve scalar multiplication. Int. J. Parallel Prog. **40**(5), 532–550 (2012). https://doi.org/10.1007/s10766-012-0198-5
4. Brier, É., Joye, M.: Weierstraß elliptic curves and side-channel attacks. In: Naccache, D., Paillier, P. (eds.) PKC 2002. LNCS, vol. 2274, pp. 335–345. Springer, Heidelberg (2002). https://doi.org/10.1007/3-540-45664-3_24
5. Cabrera Aldaya, A., Cabrera Sarmiento, A.J., Sánchez-Solano, S.: SPA vulnerabilities of the binary extended Euclidean algorithm. J. Cryptogr. Eng. **7**(4), 273–285 (2017). https://doi.org/10.1007/s13389-016-0135-4
6. Cohen, H., Miyaji, A., Ono, T.: Efficient elliptic curve exponentiation using mixed coordinates. In: Ohta, K., Pei, D. (eds.) ASIACRYPT 1998. LNCS, vol. 1514, pp. 51–65. Springer, Heidelberg (1998). https://doi.org/10.1007/3-540-49649-1_6
7. Faz-Hernández, A., López, J.: Fast implementation of curve25519 using AVX2. In: Lauter, K., Rodríguez-Henríquez, F. (eds.) LATINCRYPT 2015. LNCS, vol. 9230, pp. 329–345. Springer, Cham (2015). https://doi.org/10.1007/978-3-319-22174-8_18
8. Faz-Hernández, A., López, J., Dahab, R.: High-performance implementation of elliptic curve cryptography using vector instructions. ACM Trans. Math. Softw. **45**(3), 1–35 (2019)
9. Fog, A.: Instruction tables: lists of instruction latencies, throughputs and microoperation breakdowns for Intel, AMD, and VIA CPUs. Manual (2019). http://www.agner.org/optimize/instruction_tables.pdf
10. Gueron, S., Krasnov, V.: Software implementation of modular exponentiation, using advanced vector instructions architectures. In: Özbudak, F., Rodríguez-Henríquez, F. (eds.) WAIFI 2012. LNCS, vol. 7369, pp. 119–135. Springer, Heidelberg (2012). https://doi.org/10.1007/978-3-642-31662-3_9
11. Gueron, S., Krasnov, V.: Fast prime field elliptic-curve cryptography with 256-bit primes. J. Cryptogr. Eng. **5**(2), 141–151 (2015). https://doi.org/10.1007/s13389-014-0090-x
12. Hankerson, D.R., Menezes, A.J., Vanstone, S.A.: Guide to Elliptic Curve Cryptography. Springer, New York (2004). https://doi.org/10.1007/b97644
13. Hutter, M., Joye, M., Sierra, Y.: Memory-constrained implementations of elliptic curve cryptography in co-Z coordinate representation. In: Nitaj, A., Pointcheval, D. (eds.) AFRICACRYPT 2011. LNCS, vol. 6737, pp. 170–187. Springer, Heidelberg (2011). https://doi.org/10.1007/978-3-642-21969-6_11
14. Intel Corporation: Intel instruction set architecture extensions. Documentation (2013). http://software.intel.com/en-us/isa-extensions

15. International Organization for Standardization: ISO/IEC 14888–3:2018 - IT security techniques - Digital signatures with appendix - Part 3: Discrete logarithm based mechanisms (2018)
16. Izu, T., Takagi, T.: A fast parallel elliptic curve multiplication resistant against side channel attacks. In: Naccache, D., Paillier, P. (eds.) PKC 2002. LNCS, vol. 2274, pp. 280–296. Springer, Heidelberg (2002). https://doi.org/10.1007/3-540-45664-3_20
17. Koblitz, N.I.: Elliptic curve cryptosystems. Math. Comput. **48**(177), 203–209 (1987)
18. Meloni, N.: New point addition formulae for ECC applications. In: Carlet, C., Sunar, B. (eds.) WAIFI 2007. LNCS, vol. 4547, pp. 189–201. Springer, Heidelberg (2007). https://doi.org/10.1007/978-3-540-73074-3_15
19. Miller, V.S.: Use of elliptic curves in cryptography. In: Williams, H.C. (ed.) CRYPTO 1985. LNCS, vol. 218, pp. 417–426. Springer, Heidelberg (1986). https://doi.org/10.1007/3-540-39799-X_31
20. Montgomery, P.L.: Speeding the Pollard and elliptic curve methods of factorization. Math. Comput. **48**(177), 243–264 (1987)
21. OpenSSL Software Foundation: OpenSSL. Software (2019). http://www.openssl.org
22. Peng, B.-Y., Hsu, Y.-C., Chen, Y.-J., Chueh, D.-C., Cheng, C.-M., Yang, B.-Y.: Multi-core FPGA implementation of ECC with homogeneous Co-Z coordinate representation. In: Foresti, S., Persiano, G. (eds.) CANS 2016. LNCS, vol. 10052, pp. 637–647. Springer, Cham (2016). https://doi.org/10.1007/978-3-319-48965-0_42
23. Rivain, M.: Fast and regular algorithms for scalar multiplication over elliptic curves. Cryptology ePrint Archive, Report 2011/338 (2011)
24. Seo, H., Liu, Z., Großschädl, J., Choi, J., Kim, H.: Montgomery modular multiplication on ARM-NEON revisited. In: Lee, J., Kim, J. (eds.) ICISC 2014. LNCS, vol. 8949, pp. 328–342. Springer, Cham (2015). https://doi.org/10.1007/978-3-319-15943-0_20
25. Solinas, J.A.: Generalized Mersenne numbers. Technical report CORR-99-39, University of Waterloo, Waterloo, Canada (1999)
26. State Cryptography Administration of China: Public key cryptographic algorithm SM2 based on elliptic curves. Specification (2010). http://www.sca.gov.cn/sca/xwdt/2010-12/17/content_1002386.shtml
27. State Cryptography Administration of China: Recommended curve parameters of public key cryptographic algorithm SM2 based on elliptic curves. Specification (2010). http://www.sca.gov.cn/sca/xwdt/2010-12/17/content_1002386.shtml
28. Venelli, A., Dassance, F.: Faster side-channel resistant elliptic curve scalar multiplication. In: Kohel, D., Rolland, R. (eds.) Contemporary Mathematics, vol. 512, pp. 29–40. American Mathematical Society (2010)

29. Zhao, Y., Pan, W., Lin, J., Liu, P., Xue, C., Zheng, F.: PhiRSA: exploiting the computing power of vector instructions on Intel Xeon Phi for RSA. In: Avanzi, R., Heys, H. (eds.) SAC 2016. LNCS, vol. 10532, pp. 482–500. Springer, Cham (2017). https://doi.org/10.1007/978-3-319-69453-5_26
30. Zhou, L., Su, C., Hu, Z., Lee, S., Seo, H.: Lightweight implementations of NIST P-256 and SM2 ECC on 8-bit resource-constraint embedded device. ACM Trans. Embed. Comput. Syst. **18**(3), 1–13 (2019)

Improved Security Proof for the Camenisch-Lysyanskaya Signature-Based Synchronized Aggregate Signature Scheme

Masayuki Tezuka[✉] and Keisuke Tanaka

Tokyo Institute of Technology, Tokyo, Japan
tezuka.m.ac@m.titech.ac.jp

Abstract. The Camenisch-Lysyanskaya signature scheme in CRYPTO 2004 is a useful building block to construct privacy-preserving schemes such as anonymous credentials, group signatures or ring signatures. However, the security of this signature scheme relies on the interactive assumption called the LRSW assumption. Even if the interactive assumptions are proven in the generic group model or bilinear group model, the concerns about these assumptions arise in a cryptographic community. This fact caused a barrier to the use of cryptographic schemes whose security relies on these assumptions.

Recently, Pointcheval and Sanders proposed the modified Camenisch-Lysyanskaya signature scheme in CT-RSA 2018. This scheme satisfies the EUF-CMA security under the new q-type assumption called the Modified-q-Strong Diffie-Hellman-2 (q-MSDH-2) assumption. However, the size of a q-type assumptions grows dynamically and this fact leads to inefficiency of schemes.

In this work, we revisit the Camenisch-Lysyanskaya signature-based synchronized aggregate signature scheme in FC 2013. This scheme is one of the most efficient synchronized aggregate signature schemes with bilinear groups. However, the security of this synchronized aggregate scheme was proven under the one-time LRSW assumption in the random oracle model. We give the new security proof for this synchronized aggregate scheme under the 1-MSDH-2 (static) assumption in the random oracle model with little loss of efficiency.

Keywords: Synchronized aggregate signature · Camenisch-Lysyanskaya signature · Static assumption

Supported in part by Input Output Hong Kong, Nomura Research Institute, NTT Secure Platform Laboratories, Mitsubishi Electric, I-System, JST CREST JPMJCR14D6, JST OPERA and JSPS KAKENHI 16H01705, 17H01695.

J. K. Liu and H. Cui (Eds.): ACISP 2020, LNCS 12248, pp. 225–243, 2020.
https://doi.org/10.1007/978-3-030-55304-3_12

1   Introduction

1.1   Background

Aggregate Signature Schemes. Aggregate signature schemes originally introduced by Boneh, Gentry, Lynn, and Shacham [8] allow anyone to convert n individual signatures $(\sigma_1, \ldots, \sigma_n)$ produced by different n signers on different messages into the aggregate signature Σ whose size is much smaller than a concatenation of the individual signatures. This feature leads significant reductions of bandwidth and storage space in BGP (Border Gateway Protocol) routing [5,8,20], bundling software updates [1], sensor network data [1], authentication [23], and blockchain protocol [18,25,27]. After the introduction of aggregate signature schemes, various aggregate signature schemes have been proposed: sequential aggregate signature schemes [21], identity-based aggregate signature schemes [12], synchronized aggregate signature schemes [1,12], and fault-tolerant aggregate signature schemes [14].

Synchronized Aggregate Signature Schemes. Synchronized aggregate signature schemes are a special type of aggregate signature schemes. The concept of the synchronized setting aggregate signature scheme was introduced by Gentry and Ramzan [12]. Ahn, Green, and Hohenberger [1] revisited the Gentry-Ramzan model and formalized the synchronized aggregate signature scheme. In this scheme, all of the signers have a synchronized time period t and each signer can sign a message at most once for each period t. A set of signatures that are all generated for the same period t can be aggregated into a short signature.

It is useful to adopt synchronized aggregate signature schemes to systems which have a natural reporting period, such as log or sensor data. As mentioned in [18], synchronized aggregate signature schemes are also useful for blockchain protocols. For instance, we consider a blockchain protocol that records several signed transactions in each new block creation. The creation of an additional block is a natural synchronization event. These signed transactions could use a synchronized aggregate signature scheme with a block number as a time period number. This reduces the signature overhead from one per transaction to just one synchronized signature per block iteration.

Several provable secure synchronized aggregate signature schemes with bilinear groups have been proposed (see Fig. 1). Ahn, Green, and Hohenberger [12] constructed two synchronized aggregate signature schemes based on the Hohenberger-Waters [17] short signature scheme. One is constructed in the random oracle model and the other is constructed in the standard model. The security of both schemes relies on the computational Diffie-Hellman (CDH) assumption. Lee, Lee, and Yung [19] proposed a synchronized aggregate signature scheme based on the Camenisch-Lysyanskaya signature (CL) scheme [10]. This is the most efficient synchronized aggregate signature scheme with bilinear groups in that the number of pairing operations in the verification of an aggregate signature and the number of group elements in an aggregate signature is smaller than those of [12,17]. The security of this scheme relies on the one-time Lysyanskaya-Rivest-Sahai-Wolf (OT-LRSW) assumption [22] in the random oracle model.

As the provable secure synchronized aggregate signature schemes without bilinear groups, Hohenberger and Waters [18] proposed the synchronized aggregate signature scheme based on the RSA assumption.

Scheme	Assumption	Security	pp size	vk size	Agg size	Agg Ver (in Pairings)
GR [12]	CDH + ROM	EUF-CMA*	$O(1)$	ID	3	3
AGH [1] §4	CDH	EUF-CMA in CK	$O(k)$	1	3	$k+3$
AGH [1] §A	CDH + ROM	EUF-CMA in CK	$O(1)$	1	3	4
LLY [19]	OT-LRSW + ROM (interactive assumption)	EUF-CMA in CK	$O(1)$	1	2	3
LLY [19] (New proof)	1-MSDH-2 + ROM (static assumption)	EUF-CMA in CK	$O(1)$	1	2	3

In our work, we prove that the scheme LLY [19] satisfies the EUF-CMA security in the certified-key model under the 1-MSDH-2 assumption in the random oracle model.

Fig. 1. Summary of synchronized aggregate signature schemes with bilinear groups. In the column of "Assumption", "ROM" means the random oracle model. In the column of "Security", "CK" means the certified-key model. "pp size", "vk size", "Agg size", "Agg Ver" mean the number of group elements in a public parameter pp, a verification key vk, an aggregate signature, and the number of pairing operations in aggregate signatures verification respectively. The scheme GR [12] is an identity-based scheme that has a verification key size of "ID". In the scheme AGH [1], k is a special security parameter. As mentioned in [1], k could be five in practice. * Note that Gentry and Ramzan [12] only provided heuristic security arguments.

Camenisch-Lysyanskaya Signature Scheme. Camenisch and Lysyanskaya [10] proposed the CL scheme which has a useful feature called randomizability. This property allows anyone to randomize a valid signature σ to σ' where σ and σ' are valid signatures on the same message. The CL scheme is widely used to construct various schemes: anonymous credentials [10], anonymous attestation [3], divisible E-cash [11], batch verification [9], group signatures [4], ring signatures [2], and aggregate signatures [26]. The security of the CL scheme relies on the Lysyanskaya-Rivest-Sahai-Wolf (LRSW) assumption which is an interactive assumption. An interactive assumption allows us to design an efficient scheme, however, these are not preferable.

Modified Camenisch-Lysyanskaya Signature Scheme. Pointcheval and Sanders [24] proposed the Modified q-Strong Diffie-Hellman-2 (q-MSDH-2) assumption which is defined on a type 1 bilinear group. This assumption is a q-type assumption [6] where the number of input elements depends on the number of adversarial queries. They proved that the q-MSDH-2 assumption holds in the generic bilinear group model [7] and the CL scheme satisfies the weak-existentially unforgeable under chosen message attacks (weak-EUF-CMA) security under the q-MSDH-2 assumption. Moreover, they proposed the modified Camenisch-Lysyanskaya signature (MCL) scheme which has randomizability. Then, they showed that the MCL scheme satisfies the existentially unforgeable under chosen message attacks (EUF-CMA) security under the q-MSDH-2 assumption. Their modification from the CL scheme to the MCL scheme incurs a slight increase in the complexity.[1]

1.2   Our Results

To our knowledge, the most efficient synchronized aggregate signature scheme with bilinear groups is Lee et al.'s [19] scheme. However, the security of this scheme relies on the interactive assumption (the OT-LRSW assumption). Even if interactive assumptions hold in the generic group model or bilinear group model, the concerns about these assumptions arise in a cryptographic community. This fact causes a barrier to the use of this scheme. Also, it is not desired that the security of the scheme depends on q-type assumptions. Because the size of these assumptions grows dynamically and this fact leads to inefficiency of the scheme. Hence, it is desirable to prove the security of this scheme under the non-q-type (static) assumptions or construct another efficient synchronized aggregate signature scheme whose security does not rely on interactive assumptions or q-type assumptions.

Security Proof Under the Static Assumption. In this paper, we give a new security proof for Lee et al.'s synchronized aggregate scheme under the static assumption in the random oracle model. More specifically, we convert from the MCL scheme to Lee et al.'s [19] synchronized aggregate signature scheme. Then, we reduce the security of Lee et al.'s scheme to the one-time EUF-CMA (OT-EUF-CMA) security of the MCL scheme in the random oracle model. We refer the reader to Sect. 4 for details about these techniques. Since the EUF-CMA security of the MCL scheme is implied by the 1-MSDH-2 assumption, the security of Lee et al.'s scheme can be proven under the 1-MSDH-2 assumption. We can regard the 1-MSDH-2 assumption as the static assumption. Therefore, we can see that the security of Lee et al.'s scheme relies on the static assumption. Notably, while the EUF-CMA security of the MCL scheme is proved under the q-type assumption, the security of Lee et al.'s synchronized aggregate signature scheme can be proven under the static assumption in the random oracle model.

Trade-offs with Little Loss of Efficiency. In general, there is a trade-off that efficiency is reduced when we design a scheme based on weaker computational assumptions. Surprisingly, we can change the assumptions underlying the security of Lee et al.'s [19] scheme from the interactive assumption (OT-LRSW) to the static assumption (1-MSDH-2) with little loss in the efficiency of the scheme. Specifically, the size of verification key vk, the size of aggregate signature Σ, and the number of pairing operations in an aggregate signature verification do not increase at all.

---

[1] Their modification from the CL scheme to the MCL scheme increases the number of group elements in a signature and an aggregate signature from 2 to 3.

1.3   Related Works

Boneh et al.'s [8] proposed the first full aggregate signature scheme which allows any user to aggregate signatures of different signers. Furthermore, this scheme allows us to aggregate individual signatures as well as already aggregated signatures in any order. They constructed a full aggregate signature scheme in the random oracle model. Hohenberger, Sahai, and Waters [16] firstly constructed a full aggregate signature scheme in the standard model by using multilinear maps. Hohenberger, Koppula, and Waters [15] constructed a full aggregate signature scheme in the standard model by using the indistinguishability obfuscation.

Several variants of aggregate signature schemes have been proposed. One major variant is a sequential aggregate signature scheme which was firstly proposed by Lysyanskaya, Micali, Reyzin, and Shacham [21]. In this scheme, an aggregate signature is constructed sequentially, with each signer modifying the aggregate signature in turn. They constructed a sequential aggregate signature scheme in the random oracle model by using families of trapdoor permutations. Lu, Rafail Ostrovsky, Sahai, Shacham, and Waters [20] firstly constructed the sequential aggregate signature scheme in the standard model based on the Waters signature scheme. Another major variant of aggregate signature schemes is a synchronized aggregate signature scheme explained in Sect. 1.1. Furthermore, Lee et al. [19] proposed a combined aggregate signature scheme. In this scheme, a signer can use two modes of aggregation (sequential aggregation or synchronized aggregation) dynamically. They constructed a combined aggregate signature scheme in the random oracle model based on the CL scheme.

1.4   Road Map

In Sect. 2, we recall bilinear groups, the 1-MSDH-2 assumption, and a digital signature scheme. In Sect. 3, we review the definition of a synchronized aggregate signature scheme and its security notion. In Sect. 4, we review the MCL scheme. Next, we explain the relationship between the MCL scheme and Lee et al.'s aggregate signature scheme. In particular, we explain how to convert from the MCL to Lee et al.'s aggregate signature scheme. Then, we describe Lee et al.'s aggregate signature scheme construction and newly give a security proof under the 1-MSDH-2 assumption in the random oracle model.

2   Preliminaries

Let 1^λ be the security parameter. A function $f(\lambda)$ is negligible in λ if $f(\lambda)$ tends to 0 faster than $\frac{1}{\lambda^c}$ for every constant $c > 0$. PPT stands for probabilistic polynomial time. For an integer n, $[n]$ denotes the set $\{1, \ldots, n\}$. For a finite set S, $s \xleftarrow{\$} S$ denotes choosing an element s from S uniformly at random. For a group $\mathbb{G}$, we define $\mathbb{G}^* := \mathbb{G}\backslash\{1_\mathbb{G}\}$. For an algorithm A, $y \leftarrow A(x)$ denotes that the algorithm A outputs y on input x.

2.1 Bilinear Groups

In this work, we use type 1 pairings and introduce a bilinear group generator. Let G be a bilinear group generator that takes as an input a security parameter 1^λ and outputs the descriptions of multiplicative groups $\mathcal{G} = (p, \mathbb{G}, \mathbb{G}_T, e)$ where $\mathbb{G}$ and $\mathbb{G}_T$ are groups of prime order p and e is an efficient computable, non-degenerating bilinear map $e : \mathbb{G} \times \mathbb{G} \to \mathbb{G}_T$.

1. Bilinear: for all $u \in \mathbb{G}$, $v \in \mathbb{G}$ and $a, b \in \mathbb{Z}_p$, then $e(u^a, v^b) = e(u, v)^{ab}$.
2. Non-degenerate: for any $g \in \mathbb{G}^*$ and $\tilde{g} \in \mathbb{G}^*$, $e(g, \tilde{g}) \neq 1_{\mathbb{G}_T}$.

2.2 Computational Assumption

Pointcheval and Sanders [24] introduced the new q-type assumption which is called the Modified q-Strong Diffie-Hellman-2 (q-MSDH-2) assumption. This is a variant of the q-Strong Diffie-Hellman (q-SDH) assumption and defined on a type 1 bilinear group. The q-MSDH-2 assumption holds in the generic bilinear group model [7]. In this work, we fix the value to $q = 1$ and only use 1-MSDH-2 assumption in a static way. We can regard 1-MSDH-2 as a static assumption.

Assumption 1 (Modified 1-Strong Diffie-Hellman-2 Assumption [24]).
Let G *be a type-1 pairing-group generator. The Modified 1-Strong Diffie-Hellman-2 (1-MSDH-2) assumption over* G *is that for all* $\lambda \in \mathbb{N}$, *for all* $\mathcal{G} = (p, \mathbb{G}, \mathbb{G}_T, e) \leftarrow \mathsf{G}(1^\lambda)$, *given* $(\mathcal{G}, g, g^x, g^{x^2}, g^b, g^{bx}, g^{bx^2}, g^a, g^{abx})$ *where* $g \leftarrow \mathbb{G}^*$ *and* $a, b, x \xleftarrow{\$} \mathbb{Z}_p^*$ *as an input, no PPT adversary can, without non-negligible probability, output a tuple* $(w, P, h^{\frac{1}{x+w}}, h^{\frac{a}{x \cdot P(x)}})$ *with* $h \in \mathbb{G}$, P *a polynomial in* $\mathbb{Z}_p[X]$ *of degree at most 1, and* $w \in \mathbb{Z}_p^*$ *such that* $X + w$ *and* $P(X)$ *are relatively prime.*[2]

2.3 Digital Signature Schemes

We review the definition of a digital signature scheme and its security notion.

Definition 1 (Digital Signature Scheme). *A digital signature scheme* DS *consists of following four algorithms* (Setup, KeyGen, Sign, Verify).

- Setup(1^λ) : *Given a security parameter* λ, *return the public parameter pp. We assume that pp defines the message space* $\mathcal{M}_{pp}$.
- KeyGen(pp) : *Given a public parameter pp, return a verification key* vk *and a signing key* sk.
- Sign(pp, sk, m) : *Given a public parameter pp, a signing key sk, and a message* $m \in \mathcal{M}_{pp}$, *return a signature* σ.
- Verify(pp, vk, m, σ) : *Given a public parameter pp, a verification key vk, a message* $m \in \mathcal{M}_{pp}$, *and a signature* σ, *return either* 1 *(Accept) or* 0 *(Reject)*.

---

[2] In the q-MSDH-2 assumption, an input is changed to $(\mathcal{G}, g, g^x, \ldots, g^{x^{q+1}}, g^b, g^{bx}, \ldots, g^{bx^{q+1}}, g^a, g^{abx})$ and the condition of the order of $P(x)$ is changed to at most q.

Correctness: Correctness is satisfied if for all $\lambda \in \mathbb{N}$, $pp \leftarrow \mathsf{Setup}(1^\lambda)$ *for all* $m \in \mathcal{M}_{pp}$, $(\mathsf{vk}, \mathsf{sk}) \leftarrow \mathsf{KeyGen}(pp)$, *and* $\sigma \leftarrow \mathsf{Sign}(pp, \mathsf{sk}, m)$, $\mathsf{Verify}(pp, \mathsf{vk}, m, \sigma) = 1$ *holds.*

The EUF-CMA security [13] is the standard security notion for digital signature schemes.

Definition 2 (EUF-CMA Security [13]). *The EUF-CMA security of a digital signature scheme* DS *is defined by the following unforgeability game between a challenger* C *and a PPT adversary* A.

- C *runs* $pp \leftarrow \mathsf{Setup}(1^\lambda)$, $(\mathsf{vk}, \mathsf{sk}) \leftarrow \mathsf{KeyGen}(pp)$, *sets* $Q \leftarrow \{\}$, *and gives* (pp, vk) *to* A.
- A *is given access (throughout the entire game) to a sign oracle* $\mathcal{O}^{\mathsf{Sign}}(\cdot)$. *Given an input* m, $\mathcal{O}^{\mathsf{Sign}}$ *sets* $Q \leftarrow Q \cup \{m\}$ *and returns* $\sigma \leftarrow \mathsf{Sign}(pp, \mathsf{sk}, m)$.
- A *outputs a forgery* (m^*, σ^*).

A digital signature scheme DS *satisfies the* EUF-CMA *security if for all PPT adversaries* A, *the following advantage*

$$\mathsf{Adv}^{\mathsf{EUF\text{-}CMA}}_{\mathsf{DS},\mathsf{A}} := \Pr[\mathsf{Verify}(pp, \mathsf{vk}, m^*, \sigma^*) = 1 \wedge m^* \notin Q]$$

is negligible in λ.

If the number of signing oracle $\mathcal{O}^{\mathsf{Sign}}$ query is restricted to the one-time in the unforgeability security game, we call DS satisfies the one-time EUF-CMA (OT-EUF-CMA) security.

3 Synchronized Aggregate Signature Schemes

In this section, we review the definition of a synchronized aggregate signature scheme and its security notion.

3.1 Synchronized Aggregate Signature Schemes

Synchronized aggregate signature schemes [1,12] are a special type of aggregate signature schemes. In this scheme, all of the signers have a synchronized time period t and each signer can sign a message at most once for each period t. A set of signatures that are all generated for the same period t can be aggregated into a short signature. The size of an aggregate signature is the same size as an individual signature. Now, we review the definition of synchronized aggregate signature schemes.

Definition 3 (Synchronized Aggregate Signature Schemes [1,12]). *A synchronized aggregate signature scheme* SAS *for a bounded number of periods is a tuple of algorithms* (SAS.Setup, SAS.KeyGen, SAS.Sign, SAS.Verify, SAS.Aggregate, SAS.AggVerify).

- SAS.Setup($1^\lambda, 1^T$) : *Given a security parameter λ and the time period bound T, return the public parameter pp. We assume that pp defines the message space $\mathcal{M}_{pp}$.*
- SAS.KeyGen(pp) : *Given a public parameter pp, return a verification key* vk *and a signing key* sk.
- SAS.Sign(pp, sk, t, m) : *Given a public parameter pp, a signing key* sk, *a time period $t \leq T$, and a message $m \in \mathcal{M}_{pp}$, return the signature σ.*
- SAS.Verify(pp, vk, m, σ) : *Given a public parameter pp, a verification key* vk, *a message $m \in \mathcal{M}_{pp}$, and a signature σ, return either 1 (Accept) or 0 (Reject).*
- SAS.Aggregate(pp, (vk$_1, \ldots,$ vk$_r$), ($m_1, \ldots, m_r$), ($\sigma_1, \ldots, \sigma_r$)) : *Given a public parameter pp, a list of verification keys* (vk$_1, \ldots,$ vk$_r$), *a list of messages $(m_1, \ldots, m_r)$, and a list of signatures $(\sigma_1, \ldots, \sigma_r)$, return either the aggregate signature Σ or $\bot$.*
- SAS.AggVerify(pp, (vk$_1, \ldots,$ vk$_r$), ($m_1, \ldots, m_r$), Σ) : *Given a public parameter pp, a list of verification keys* (vk$_1, \ldots,$ vk$_r$), *a list of messages $(m_1, \ldots, m_r)$, and an aggregate signature, return either 1 (Accept) or 0 (Reject).*

Correctness: Correctness is satisfied if for all $\lambda \in \mathbb{N}$, $T \in \mathbb{N}$, pp $\leftarrow$ SAS.Setup($1^\lambda, 1^T$), *for any finite sequence of key pairs* (vk$_1,$ sk$_1), \ldots$ (vk$_r,$ sk$_r$) $\leftarrow$ SAS.KeyGen(pp) *where* vk$_i$ *are all distinct, for any time period $t \leq T$, for any sequence of messages $(m_1, \ldots m_r) \in \mathcal{M}_{pp}$, $\sigma_i \leftarrow$* SAS.Sign(pp, sk$_i, t, m_i$) *for $i \in [r]$, $\Sigma \leftarrow$* SAS.Aggregate(pp, (vk$_1, \ldots,$ vk$_r$), ($m_1, \ldots, m_r$), ($\sigma_1, \ldots, \sigma_r$)), *we have*

$$\text{SAS.Verify}(pp, \text{vk}_i, m_i, \sigma_i) = 1 \text{ for all } i \in [r]$$
$$\wedge \text{ SAS.AggVerify}(pp, (\text{vk}_1, \ldots, \text{vk}_r), (m_1, \ldots, m_r), \Sigma) = 1.$$

In a signature aggregation, it is desirable to confirm that each signature is valid. This is because if there is at least one invalid signature, the generated aggregate signature will be invalid.[3] In this work, before aggregating signatures, SAS.Aggregate checks the validity of each signature.

3.2 Security of Synchronized Aggregate Signature Schemes

We introduce the security notion of synchronized aggregate signature schemes. The EUF-CMA security of synchronized aggregate signature schemes proposed by Gentry and Ramzan [12] captures that it is hard for adversaries to forge an aggregate signature without signing key sk*. However, they only provided heuristic security arguments in their synchronized aggregate signature scheme.

Ahn, Green, and Hohrnberger [1] introduced the certified-key model for the EUF-CMA security of synchronized aggregate signature schemes. In this model, signers must certify their verification key vk by proving knowledge of their signing

---

[3] Fault-tolerant aggregate signature schemes [14] allow us to determine the subset of all messages belonging to an aggregate signature that were signed correctly. However, this scheme has a drawback that the aggregate signature size depends on the number of signatures to be aggregated into it.

key sk. In other words, no verification key vk is allowed except those correctly generated by the SAS.KeyGen algorithm. In certified-key model, to ensure the correct generation of a verification key $vk_i \neq vk^*$, EUF-CMA adversaries must submit (vk_i, sk_i) to the certification oracle $\mathcal{O}^{Cert}$. As in [1,19], we consider the EUF-CMA security in the certified-key model.

Definition 4 (EUF-CMA Security in the Certified-Key Model [1,19]). *The EUF-CMA security of a sequential aggregate signature scheme SAS in the certified-key model is defined by the following unforgeability game between a challenger C and a PPT adversary A.*

- C *runs* $pp^* \leftarrow$ SAS.Setup$(1^\lambda, 1^T)$, $(vk^*, sk^*) \leftarrow$ SAS.KeyGen(pp^*), *sets* $Q \leftarrow$ $\{\}$, $L \leftarrow \{\}$, $t_{ctr} \leftarrow 1$, *and gives* (pp, vk^*) *to* A.
- A *is given access (throughout the entire game) to a certification oracle* $\mathcal{O}^{Cert}(\cdot, \cdot)$. *Given an input* (vk, sk), $\mathcal{O}^{Cert}$ *performs the following procedure.*
  - *If the key pair* (vk, sk) *is valid,* $L \leftarrow L \cup \{vk\}$ *and return* "accept".
  - *Otherwise return* "reject".
  (A *must submit key pair* (vk, sk) *to* $\mathcal{O}^{Cert}$ *and get* "accept" *before using* vk.)
- A *is given access (throughout the entire game) to a sign oracle* $\mathcal{O}^{Sign}(\cdot, \cdot)$. *Given an input* ("inst", m), $\mathcal{O}^{Sign}$ *performs the following procedure.* ("inst" $\in$ { "skip", "sign"} *represent the instruction for* $\mathcal{O}^{Sign}$ *where* "skip" *implies that* A *skips the concurrent period* t_{ctr} *and* "sign" *implies that* A *require the signature on message* m.)
  - *If* $t_{ctr} \notin [T]$, *return* $\perp$.
  - *If* "inst" $=$ "skip", $t_{ctr} \leftarrow t_{ctr} + 1$.
  - *If* "inst" $=$ "sign", $Q \leftarrow Q \cup \{m\}$, $\sigma \leftarrow$ SAS.Sign(pp^*, sk^*, t, m), $t_{ctr} \leftarrow$ $t_{ctr} + 1$, *return* σ.
- A *outputs a forgery* $((vk_1^*, \ldots, vk_{r^*}^*), (m_1^*, \ldots, m_{r^*}^*), \Sigma^*)$.

A sequential aggregate signature scheme SAS satisfies the EUF-CMA security in the certified-key model if for all PPT adversaries A, the following advantage

$$\text{Adv}_{SAS,A}^{EUF\text{-}CMA} := \Pr \begin{bmatrix} \text{SAS.AggVerify}(pp^*, (vk_1^*, \ldots, vk_{r^*}^*), (m_1^*, \ldots, m_{r^*}^*), \Sigma^*) = 1 \\ \wedge \text{ For all } j \in [r^*] \text{ such that } vk_j^* \neq vk^*, vk_j^* \in L \\ \wedge \text{ For some } j^* \in [r^*] \text{ such that } vk_{j^*}^* = vk^*, m_{j^*}^* \notin Q \end{bmatrix}$$

is negligible in λ.

4   Lee et al.'s Aggregate Signature Scheme

In this section, first, we review the MCL scheme proposed by Pointcheval and Sanders [24]. Next, we explain an intuition that there is a relationship between the MCL scheme and Lee et al.'s aggregate signature scheme. Concretely, we explain that there is a conversion from the MCL scheme to Lee et al.'s aggregate signature scheme. Then, we describe Lee et al.'s aggregate signature scheme construction. Finally, we give a new security proof for Lee et al.'s scheme under the 1-MSDH-2 assumption in the random oracle model.

4.1   Modified Camenisch-Lysyanskaya Signature Scheme

Pointcheval and Sanders [24] proposed the modified Camenisch-Lysyanskaya signature scheme which supports a multi-message (vector message) signing. In this work, we only need a single-message signing scheme. Here, we review the single-message modified Camenisch-Lysyanskaya signature scheme MCL = (MCL.Setup, MCL.KeyGen, MCL.Sign, MCL.Verify) as follows.

- MCL.Setup(1^λ) :
  $\mathcal{G} = (p, \mathbb{G}, \mathbb{G}_T, e) \leftarrow \mathsf{G}(1^\lambda)$.
  Return $pp \leftarrow \mathcal{G}$.
- MCL.KeyGen(pp) :
  $g \overset{\$}{\leftarrow} \mathbb{G}^*, x \overset{\$}{\leftarrow} \mathbb{Z}_p^*, y \overset{\$}{\leftarrow} \mathbb{Z}_p^*, z \overset{\$}{\leftarrow} \mathbb{Z}_p^*, X \leftarrow g^x, Y \leftarrow g^y, Z \leftarrow g^z$.
  Return $(\mathsf{vk}, \mathsf{sk}) \leftarrow ((g, X, Y, Z), (x, y, z))$.
- MCL.Sign(pp, sk, m) :
  Parse sk as (x, y, z)
  $w \overset{\$}{\leftarrow} \mathbb{Z}_p, A \overset{\$}{\leftarrow} \mathbb{G}^*, B \leftarrow A^y, C \leftarrow A^z, D \leftarrow C^y, E \leftarrow A^x B^{mx} D^{wx}$.
  Return $\sigma \leftarrow (w, A, B, C, D, E)$.
- MCL.Verify($pp, \mathsf{vk}, m, \sigma$) :
  Parse vk as (g, X, Y, Z), σ as (w, A, B, C, D, E).
  If $(e(A, Y) \neq e(B, g)) \vee (e(A, Z) \neq e(C, g)) \vee (e(C, Y) \neq e(D, g))$, return 0.
  If $e(AB^m D^w, X) = e(E, g)$, return 1.
  Otherwise return 0.

Pointcheval and Sanders [24] proved that if the q-MSDH-2 assumption holds, then the MCL scheme satisfies the EUF-CMA security where q is a bound on the number of adaptive signing queries. In this work, we only need the OT-EUF-CMA security for the MCL scheme.

Theorem 1 ([24]). *If the* 1-MSDH-2 *assumption holds, then the* MCL *scheme satisfies the* OT-EUF-CMA *security.*

4.2   Conversion to Lee et al.'s Aggregate Signature Scheme

We explain that the MCL scheme can be converted into Lee et al.'s aggregate signature scheme. Our idea of conversion is a similar technique in [19] which converts the Camenisch-Lysyanskaya signature CL scheme to the synchronized aggregate signature scheme.

Now, we explain an intuition of our conversion. We start from the MCL scheme in Sect. 4.1. A signature of the MCL scheme on a message m is formed as

$$\sigma = (w, A, B = A^y, C = A^z, D = C^y, E = A^x B^{mx} D^{wx}).$$

where $w \overset{\$}{\leftarrow} \mathbb{Z}_p$ and $A \overset{\$}{\leftarrow} \mathbb{G}_1^*$. If we can force signers to use same w, A, $B = A^y$, $C = A^z$, and $D = C^y$, we can obtain an aggregate signature

$$\Sigma = \left(w, A, B, C, D, E' = \prod_{i=1}^{r} E_i = A^{\sum_{i=1}^{r} x_i} B^{\sum_{i=1}^{r} m_i x_i} D^{\sum_{i=1}^{r} w x_i}\right)$$

on a message list $(m_1, \ldots, m_r)$ from valid signatures $(\sigma_1, \ldots \sigma_r)$ where $\sigma_i = (w, A, B, C, D, E_i)$ is a signature on a message m_i generated by each signer. If we regard E' as $E' = (AD^w)^{\sum_{i=1}^{r} x_i} B^{\sum_{i=1}^{r} m_i x_i}$, verification of the aggregate signature Σ on the message list $(m_1, \ldots, m_r)$ can be done by checking the following equation.

$$e(E', g) = e\left(AD^w, \prod_{i=1}^{r} \mathsf{vk}_i\right) \cdot e\left(B, \prod_{i=1}^{r} \mathsf{vk}_i^{m_i}\right)$$

Then, required elements to verify the aggregate signature Σ are $F = AD^w$, B, and E'. Similar to Lee et al.'s conversion, the three verification equations $e(A, Y) = e(B, g)$, $e(A, Z) = e(C, g)$, $e(C, Y) = e(D, g)$ in MCL.Verify is discarded in this conversion. This does not affect the security proof in Sect. 4.4. We use hash functions to force signers to use the same F and B for each period t. We choose hash functions H_1 and H_2 and set $F \leftarrow H_1(t)$ and $B \leftarrow H_2(t)$. Then, we can derive Lee et al.'s aggregate signature scheme. In this derived aggregate signature scheme, a signature on a message m and period t is formed as

$$\sigma = (E = H_1(t)^x H_2(t)^{mx}, t).$$

An aggregate signature Σ' on a message list $(m_1, \ldots, m_r)$ and period t is formed as

$$\Sigma = \left(E' = \prod_{i=1}^{r} E_i = H_1(t)^{\sum_{i=1}^{r} x_i} H_2(t)^{\sum_{i=1}^{r} m_i x_i}, t\right)$$

where $\sigma_i = (E_i = H_1(t)^{x_i} H_2(t)^{m_i x_i}, t)$ is a signature on a message m_i generated by each signer. In our conversion, we need to hash a message with a time period for the security proof. This conversion is used for the reduction algorithm B in Sect. 4.4.

4.3 Lee et al.'s Synchronized Aggregate Signature Scheme

We describe Lee et al.'s synchronized aggregate signature scheme obtained by adapting the conversion in Sect. 4.2 to the MCL scheme. Let T be a bounded number of periods which is a polynomial in λ. The Lee et al.'s synchronized aggregate signature scheme $\mathsf{SAS_{LLY}} = (\mathsf{SAS_{LLY}.Setup}, \mathsf{SAS_{LLY}.KeyGen}, \mathsf{SAS_{LLY}.Sign}, \mathsf{SAS_{LLY}.Verify}, \mathsf{SAS_{LLY}.Aggregate}, \mathsf{SAS_{LLY}.AggVerify})$ [19] is given as follows.[4]

- $\mathsf{SAS_{LLY}.Setup}(1^\lambda, 1^T)$:
    1. $\mathcal{G} = (p, \mathbb{G}, \mathbb{G}_T, e) \leftarrow \mathsf{G}(1^\lambda)$, $g \xleftarrow{\$} \mathbb{G}^*$.
    2. Choose hash functions:
        $H_1 : [T] \rightarrow \mathbb{G}$, $H_2 : [T] \rightarrow \mathbb{G}^*$, $H_3 : [T] \times \{0, 1\}^* \rightarrow \mathbb{Z}_p$.
    3. Return $pp \leftarrow (\mathcal{G}, g, H_1, H_2, H_3)$.
- $\mathsf{SAS_{LLY}.KeyGen}(pp)$:

---

[4] The $\mathsf{SAS_{LLY}}$ scheme described here is slightly different from the original ones [19] in that the range of H_2 is changed from $\mathbb{G}$ to $\mathbb{G}^*$.

1. $x \xleftarrow{\$} \mathbb{Z}_p^*$, $X \leftarrow g^x$.
2. Return $(\mathsf{vk}, \mathsf{sk}) \leftarrow (X, x)$.

- $\mathsf{SAS_{LLY}.Sign}(pp, \mathsf{sk}, t, m)$:
  1. $m' \leftarrow H_3(t, m)$, $E \leftarrow H_1(t)^{\mathsf{sk}} H_2(t)^{m'\mathsf{sk}}$.
  2. Return (E, t).

- $\mathsf{SAS_{LLY}.Verify}(pp, \mathsf{vk}, m, \sigma)$:
  1. $m' \leftarrow H_3(t, m)$, parse σ as (E, t),.
  2. If $e(E, g) = e(H_1(t)H_2(t)^{m'}, \mathsf{vk})$, return 1.
  3. Otherwise return 0.

- $\mathsf{SAS_{LLY}.Aggregate}(pp, (\mathsf{vk}_1, \ldots, \mathsf{vk}_r), (m_1, \ldots, m_r), (\sigma_1, \ldots, \sigma_r))$:
  1. For $i = 1$ to r, parse σ_i as (E_i, t_i).
  2. If there exists $i \in \{2, \ldots, r\}$ such that $t_i \neq t_1$, return $\perp$.
  3. If there exists $(i, j) \in [r] \times [r]$ such that $i \neq j \wedge \mathsf{vk}_i = \mathsf{vk}_j$, return $\perp$.
  4. If there exists $i \in [r]$ suth that $\mathsf{SAS_{LLY}.Verify}(pp, \mathsf{vk}_i, m_i, \sigma_i) \neq 0$, return $\perp$.
  5. $E' \leftarrow \prod_{i=1}^r E_i$.
  6. Return $\Sigma \leftarrow (E', w)$.

- $\mathsf{SAS_{LLY}.AggVerify}(pp, (\mathsf{vk}_1, \ldots, \mathsf{vk}_r), (m_1, \ldots, m_r), \Sigma)$:
  1. There exists $(i, j) \in [r] \times [r]$ such that $i \neq j \wedge \mathsf{vk}_i = \mathsf{vk}_j$, return 0.
  2. For $i = 1$ to r, $m_i' \leftarrow H_3(t, m_i)$.
  3. Parse Σ as (E', w).
  4. If $e(E', g) = e\left(H_1(t), \prod_{i=1}^r \mathsf{vk}_i\right) \cdot e\left(H_2(t), \prod_{i=1}^r \mathsf{vk}_i^{m_i'}\right)$, return 1.
  5. Otherwise, return 0.

Now, we confirm the correctness. Let $(\mathsf{vk}_i, \mathsf{sk}_i) \leftarrow \mathsf{SAS_{LLY}.KeyGen}(pp)$ and $\sigma_i \leftarrow \mathsf{SAS_{LLY}.Sign}(pp, \mathsf{sk}_i, t, m_i)$ for $i \in [r]$ where vk_i are all distinct. Then, for all $i \in [r]$, $E_i \leftarrow H_1(t)^{\mathsf{sk}_i} H_2(t)^{m_i'\mathsf{sk}_i}$ holds where $m_i' \leftarrow H_3(t, m_i)$ and $\sigma_i = (E_i, t)$. This fact implies that $\mathsf{SAS_{LLY}.Verify}(pp, \mathsf{vk}_i, m_i, \sigma_i) = 1$. Furthermore, let $\Sigma \leftarrow \mathsf{SAS_{LLY}.Aggregate}(pp, (\mathsf{vk}_1, \ldots, \mathsf{vk}_r), (m_1, \ldots, m_r), (\sigma_1, \ldots, \sigma_r))$. Then,

$$E' = \prod_{i=1}^r E_i = H_1(t)^{\sum_{i=1}^n \mathsf{sk}_i} H_2(t)^{\sum_{i=1}^n m_i'\mathsf{sk}_i}$$

holds where $\Sigma = (E', t)$ and $m_i' \leftarrow H_3(t, m_i)$ for all $i \in [r]$. This fact implies that $\mathsf{SAS_{LLY}.AggVerify}(pp, (\mathsf{vk}_1, \ldots, \mathsf{vk}_r), (m_1, \ldots, m_r), \Sigma) = 1$.

4.4 New Security Proof Under the Static Assumption

We reassess the EUF-CMA security of the $\mathsf{SAS_{LLY}}$ scheme. In particular, we newly prove the EUF-CMA security of the $\mathsf{SAS_{LLY}}$ scheme under the 1-MSDH-2 assumption.

Theorem 2. *If the MCL scheme satisfies the OT-EUF-CMA security, then, in the random oracle model, the $\mathsf{SAS_{LLY}}$ scheme satisfies the EUF-CMA security in the certified-key model.*

Proof. We give an overview of our security proof. Similar to the work in [19], we reduce the EUF-CMA security of the $\mathsf{SAS_{LLY}}$ scheme to the OT-EUF-CMA security of the MCL scheme. We construct a reduction algorithm according to the following strategy. First, the reduction algorithm chooses a message m_{MCL} at random, make signing query on m_{MCL}, and obtains its signature $\sigma_{\mathsf{MCL}} = (w_{\mathsf{MCL}}, A_{\mathsf{MCL}}, B_{\mathsf{MCL}}, C_{\mathsf{MCL}}, D_{\mathsf{MCL}}, E_{\mathsf{MCL}})$ of the MCL scheme. Then, the reduction algorithm guesses the time period t' of a forged aggregate signature and an index $k' \in [q_{H_3}]$ at random where q_{H_3} be the maximum number of H_3 hash queries. Then reduction algorithm programs hash values as $H_1(t') = A_{\mathsf{MCL}} D_{\mathsf{MCL}}^{w_{\mathsf{MCL}}}$, $H_2(t') = B_{\mathsf{MCL}}$, and $H_3(t', m_{k'}) = m_{\mathsf{MCL}}$. For a signing query on period $t \neq t'$, the reduction algorithm generate the signature by programmability of hash functions H_1, H_2, and H_3. For a signing query on period $t \neq t'$, if the query index j of H_3 is equal to the index k', the reduction algorithm can compute a valid signature by using σ_{MCL} (This can be done by using the conversion technique in Sect. 4.2.). Otherwise, the algorithm should abort the simulation. Finally, the reduction algorithm extracts valid forgery of the MCL scheme from a forged aggregate signature on time period t' of the $\mathsf{SAS_{LLY}}$ scheme.

Now, we give the security proof. Let A be an EUF-CMA adversary of the $\mathsf{SAS_{LLY}}$ scheme, C be the OT-EUF-CMA game challenger of the MCL scheme, and q_{H_3} be the maximum number of H_3 hash queries. We construct the algorithm B against the OT-EUF-CMA game of the MCL scheme. The construction of B is given as follow.

- **Initial setup:** Given an input $pp = \mathcal{G}_{\mathsf{MCL}}$ and $\mathsf{vk} = (g_{\mathsf{MCL}}, X_{\mathsf{MCL}}, Y_{\mathsf{MCL}}, Z_{\mathsf{MCL}})$ from C, B performs the following procedure.
  - $\mathcal{G} \leftarrow \mathcal{G}_{\mathsf{MCL}}$, $g \leftarrow g_{\mathsf{MCL}}$, $pp^* \leftarrow (\mathcal{G}, g)$, $\mathsf{vk}^* \leftarrow X_{\mathsf{MCL}}$. $t' \overset{\$}{\leftarrow} [T]$, $k' \overset{\$}{\leftarrow} [q_{H_3}]$, $t_{ctr} \leftarrow 1$, $L \leftarrow \{\}$, $\mathbb{T}_1 \leftarrow \{\}$, $\mathbb{T}_2 \leftarrow \{\}$, $\mathbb{T}_3 \leftarrow \{\}$, $Q \leftarrow \{\}$.
  - $m_{\mathsf{MCL}} \overset{\$}{\leftarrow} \mathbb{Z}_p$, query C for the signature on the message m_{MCL} and get its signature $\sigma_{\mathsf{MCL}} = (w_{\mathsf{MCL}}, A_{\mathsf{MCL}}, B_{\mathsf{MCL}}, C_{\mathsf{MCL}}, D_{\mathsf{MCL}}, E_{\mathsf{MCL}})$,
  - Give (pp^*, vk^*) to A as an input.
- $\mathcal{O}^{\mathsf{Cert}}(\mathsf{vk}, \mathsf{sk})$: If $\mathsf{vk} = g^{\mathsf{sk}}$, update a list $L \leftarrow L \cup \{\mathsf{vk}\}$ and return "accept" to A. Otherwise return "reject" to A.
- $\mathcal{O}^{H_1}(t_i)$: Given an input t_i, B responds as follows.
  - If there is an entry $(t_i, \cdot, F_i)$ ('·' represents an arbitrary value or $\bot$) for some $F_i \in \mathbb{G}_1$ in $\mathbb{T}_1$, return F_i.
  - If $t_i \neq t'$, $r_{(1,i)} \overset{\$}{\leftarrow} \mathbb{Z}_p$, $F_i \leftarrow g^{r_{(1,i)}}$, $\mathbb{T}_1 \leftarrow \mathbb{T}_1 \cup \{(t_i, r_{(1,i)}, F_i)\}$, return F_i.
  - If $t_i = t'$, $\mathbb{T}_1 \leftarrow \mathbb{T}_1 \cup \{(t_i, \bot, A_{\mathsf{MCL}} D_{\mathsf{MCL}}^{w_{\mathsf{MCL}}})\}$, return $A_{\mathsf{MCL}} D_{\mathsf{MCL}}^{w_{\mathsf{MCL}}}$.
- $\mathcal{O}^{H_2}(t_i)$: Given an input t_i, B responds as follows.
  - If there is an entry $(t_i, \cdot, B_i)$ ('·' represents an arbitrary value or $\bot$) for some $B_i \in \mathbb{G}_1^*$ in $\mathbb{T}_3$, return B_i.
  - If $t_i \neq t'$, $r_{(2,i)} \overset{\$}{\leftarrow} \mathbb{Z}_p^*$, $B_i \leftarrow g^{r_{(2,i)}}$, $\mathbb{T}_2 \leftarrow \mathbb{T}_2 \cup \{(t_i, r_{(2,i)}, B_i)\}$, return D_i.
  - If $t_i = t'$, $\mathbb{T}_2 \leftarrow \mathbb{T}_2 \cup \{(t_i, \bot, B_{\mathsf{MCL}})\}$, return B_{MCL}.
- $\mathcal{O}^{H_3}(t_i, m_j)$: Given an input (t_i, m_j), B responds as follows.

- If there is an entry $(t_i, m_j, m'_{(i,j)})$ for some $m'_{(i,j)} \in \mathbb{Z}_p$ in $\mathbb{T}_3$, return $m'_{(i,j)}$.
- If $t_i \neq t' \lor j \neq k'$, $m'_{(i,j)} \overset{\$}{\leftarrow} \mathbb{Z}_p$, $\mathbb{T}_3 \leftarrow \mathbb{T}_3 \cup \{(t_i, m_j, m'_{(i,j)})\}$, return $m'_{(i,j)}$.
- If $t_i = t' \land j = k'$, $\mathbb{T}_3 \leftarrow \mathbb{T}_3 \cup \{(t_i, m_j, m_{\mathsf{MCL}})\}$, return m_{MCL}.

- $\mathcal{O}^{\mathsf{Sign}}(\text{``inst''}, m_j)$ : Given an input $(\text{``inst''}, m_j)$, B performs the following procedure.
  - If $t_{ctr} \notin [T]$, return $\perp$.
  - If ``inst''} = \text{``skip'', $t_{ctr} \leftarrow t_{ctr} + 1$.
  - If ``inst''} = \text{``sign'',
    * If $t_{ctr} \neq t'$, $E \leftarrow X_{\mathsf{MCL}}^{r_{(1,ctr)}} X_{\mathsf{MCL}}^{r_{(2,ctr)} m'_{(ctr,j)}}$ where $r_{(1,i)}$, $r_{(2,i)}$, and $m'_{(i,j)}$ are retreived from $(t_{ctr}, r_{(1,ctr)}, F_{ctr}) \in \mathbb{T}_1$, $(t_{ctr}, r_{(2,ctr)}, B_{ctr}) \in \mathbb{T}_2$, and $(t_{ctr}, m_j, m'_{(ctr,j)}) \in \mathbb{T}_3$ respectively. $Q \leftarrow Q \cup \{m_j\}$, return $\sigma_{ctr,j} \leftarrow (E, t_{ctr})$, then update $t_{ctr} \leftarrow t_{ctr} + 1$.
    * If $t_{ctr} = t' \land j = k'$, $Q \leftarrow Q \cup \{m_j\}$, return $\sigma_{ctr,j} \leftarrow (E_{\mathsf{MCL}}, t_i)$, then update $t_{ctr} \leftarrow t_{ctr} + 1$
    * If $t_{ctr} = t' \land j \neq k'$, abort the simulation.
- **Output procedure:** B receives a forgery $((\mathsf{vk}_1^*, \ldots, \mathsf{vk}_{r^*}^*), (m_1^*, \ldots, m_{r^*}^*), \Sigma^*)$ outputted by A. Then B proceeds as follows.
1. If $\mathsf{SAS}_{\mathsf{LLY}}.\mathsf{AggVerify}(pp^*, (\mathsf{vk}_1^*, \ldots, \mathsf{vk}_{r^*}^*), (m_1^*, \ldots, m_{r^*}^*), \Sigma^*) \neq 1$, then abort.
2. If there exists $j \in [r^*]$ such that $\mathsf{vk}_j^* \neq \mathsf{vk}^* \land \mathsf{vk}_j^* \notin L$, then abort.
3. If there is no $j^* \in [r^*]$ such that $\mathsf{vk}_{j^*}^* = \mathsf{vk}^* \land m_{j^*}^* \notin Q$, then abort.
4. Set $j^* \in [r^*]$ such that $\mathsf{vk}_{j^*}^* = \mathsf{vk}^* \land m_{j^*}^* \notin Q$.
5. Parse Σ^* as $(E^{*\prime}, t^*)$.
6. If $t^* \neq t'$, then abort.
7. $m_{j^*}^{*\prime} \leftarrow H_3(t^*, m_{j^*}^*)$
8. If $m_{j^*}^{*\prime} = m_{\mathsf{MCL}}$, then abort.
9. For $i \in [r^*] \backslash \{j^*\}$, retrieve $x_i \leftarrow \mathsf{sk}_i^*$ of vk_i^* from L.
10. $F' \leftarrow H_1(t^*)$, $B' \leftarrow H_2(t^*)$, $m_i' \leftarrow H_3(t^*, m_i^*)$ for $i \in [r^*] \backslash \{j^*\}$,
$$E' \leftarrow E^{*\prime} \cdot \left(F'^{\sum_{i \in [r^*] \backslash \{j^*\}} x_i} B'^{\sum_{i \in [r^*] \backslash \{j^*\}} x_i m_i'} \right)^{-1}.$$
11. Return $(m_{\mathsf{MCL}}^*, \sigma_{\mathsf{MCL}}^*) \leftarrow (m_{j^*}^*, (w_{\mathsf{MCL}}, A_{\mathsf{MCL}}, B', C_{\mathsf{MCL}}, D_{\mathsf{MCL}}, E'))$.

We confirm that if B does not abort, B can simulate the EUF-CMA game of the $\mathsf{SAS}_{\mathsf{LLY}}$ scheme.

- **Initial setup:** First, we discuss the distribution of pp^*. In the original EUF-CMA game of the $\mathsf{SAS}_{\mathsf{LLY}}$ scheme, $pp^* = (\mathcal{G}, g)$ is constructed by $\mathcal{G} = (p, \mathbb{G}, \mathbb{G}_T, e) \leftarrow \mathbb{G}(1^\lambda)$ and $g \overset{\$}{\leftarrow} \mathbb{G}^*$. In the simulation of B, pp^* is a tuple $(\mathcal{G}_{\mathsf{MCL}}, g_{\mathsf{MCL}})$. This tuple is constructed by C as $\mathcal{G}_{\mathsf{MCL}} = (p, \mathbb{G}, \mathbb{G}_T, e) \leftarrow \mathbb{G}(1^\lambda)$ and $g_{\mathsf{MCL}} \overset{\$}{\leftarrow} \mathbb{G}^*$. Therefore, B simulates pp^* perfectly. Next, we discuss the distribution of vk^*. In the original EUF-CMA game of the $\mathsf{SAS}_{\mathsf{LLY}}$ scheme, vk is computed by $x \overset{\$}{\leftarrow} \mathbb{Z}_p^*$ and $\mathsf{vk}^* \leftarrow g^x$. In the simulation of B, vk^* is set by X_{MCL}. Since X_{MCL} is computed by C as $x_{\mathsf{MCL}} \overset{\$}{\leftarrow} \mathbb{Z}_p$ and $X_{\mathsf{MCL}} \leftarrow g^{x_{\mathsf{MCL}}}$, distributions of vk between the original game and simulation of B are identical. Hence, the distributions of (pp^*, vk^*) are identical.

- **Output of $\mathcal{O}^{\mathsf{Cert}}$:** This is clearly that B can simulate the original EUF-CMA game of the $\mathsf{SAS}_{\mathsf{LLY}}$ scheme perfectly.
- **Output of $\mathcal{O}^{H_1}$:** In the original game, hash values of H_1 is chosen from $\mathbb{G}$ uniformly at random. In the simulation of B, if $t_i \neq t'$, the hash value $H(t_i)$ is set by $g^{r_{(1,i)}}$ where $r_{(1,i)} \xleftarrow{\$} \mathbb{Z}_p$. Obviously, in this case, B can simulate $\mathcal{O}^{H_1}$ perfectly. If $t_i = t'$, the hash value $H(t_i)$ is set by $F = A_{\mathsf{MCL}} D_{\mathsf{MCL}}^{w_{\mathsf{MCL}}} = A_{\mathsf{MCL}}^{1 + y_{\mathsf{MCL}} z_{\mathsf{MCL}} w_{\mathsf{MCL}}}$ where $Y_{\mathsf{MCL}} = g_{\mathsf{MCL}}^{y_{\mathsf{MCL}}}$, $Z_{\mathsf{MCL}} = g_{\mathsf{MCL}}^{z_{\mathsf{MCL}}}$, and w_{MCL} is chosen by C as $w_{\mathsf{MCL}} \leftarrow \mathbb{Z}_p$. For fixed $y_{\mathsf{MCL}} \in \mathbb{Z}_p^*$ and $z_{\mathsf{MCL}} \in \mathbb{Z}_p^*$, the distribution α where $\alpha \xleftarrow{\$} \mathbb{Z}_p$ and $w_{\mathsf{MCL}} \xleftarrow{\$} \mathbb{Z}_p$, $\alpha \leftarrow 1 + y_{\mathsf{MCL}} z_{\mathsf{MCL}} w_{\mathsf{MCL}}$ are identical. This fact implies that B also simulate $\mathcal{O}^{H_1}$ perfectly in the case of $t_i = t'$. Therefore, B simulates $\mathcal{O}^{H_1}$ perfectly.
- **Output of $\mathcal{O}^{H_2}$:** As the same argument of $\mathcal{O}^{H_1}$, if $t_i \neq t'$, B can simulate hash values $H(t_i)$ perfectly. In the case of $t_i = t'$, the hash value $H(t_i)$ is set by $B_{\mathsf{MCL}} = A^{y_{\mathsf{MCL}}} = g^{x_{\mathsf{MCL}} y_{\mathsf{MCL}}}$. For fixed $x_{\mathsf{MCL}} \in \mathbb{Z}_p^*$, the distributions of B where $y_{\mathsf{MCL}} \xleftarrow{\$} \mathbb{Z}_p^*$, $B \leftarrow g^{x_{\mathsf{MCL}} y_{\mathsf{MCL}}}$ and $B \xleftarrow{\$} \mathbb{G}^*$ are identical. Therefore, B simulates $\mathcal{O}^{H_2}$ perfectly.
- **Output of $\mathcal{O}^{H_3}$:** If $t_i \neq t' \vee j \neq k'$, clearly B can simulate $\mathcal{O}^{H_3}$ perfectly. If $t_i = t' \wedge j = k'$, the hash value $H_3(t_i, m_j)$ is set by m_{MCL}. Since m_{MCL} is chosen by B as $m_{\mathsf{MCL}} \xleftarrow{\$} \mathbb{Z}_p$, B simulates $\mathcal{O}^{H_3}$ perfectly.
- **Output of $\mathcal{O}^{\mathsf{Sign}}$:** For the sake of argument, we denote $X_{\mathsf{MCL}} = g_{\mathsf{MCL}}^{x_{\mathsf{MCL}}}$ ($x_{\mathsf{MCL}} \in \mathbb{Z}_p^*$). If $t_i \neq t'$, B sets $E \leftarrow X_{\mathsf{MCL}}^{r_{(1,i)}} X_{\mathsf{MCL}}^{r_{(2,i)} m'_{(i,j)}}$ and output the signature $\sigma = (E, t_i)$. Now we confirm that σ is a valid signature on the message m_j. The following equation

$$E = X_{\mathsf{MCL}}^{r_{(1,i)}} X_{\mathsf{MCL}}^{r_{(2,i)} m'_{(i,j)}} = (g_{\mathsf{MCL}}^{x_{\mathsf{MCL}}})^{r_{(1,i)}} (g_{\mathsf{MCL}}^{x_{\mathsf{MCL}}})^{r_{(2,i)} m'_{(i,j)}}$$
$$= H_1(t_i)^{x_{\mathsf{MCL}}} H_2(t_i)^{x_{\mathsf{MCL}} m'_{(i,j)}}$$

holds where $m'_{(i,j)} = H_3(t_i, m_j)$. This fact implies that

$$e(E, g) = e(H_1(t_i) H_2(t_i)^{m'_{(i,j)}}, \mathsf{vk}^*)$$

holds. Therefore, σ is valid signature on the message m_j.
If $t_i \neq t' \wedge j = k'$, B sets $E \leftarrow E_{\mathsf{MCL}}$, return $\sigma_{i,j} \leftarrow (E, t_i)$ to A. We also confirm that σ is a valid signature on the message m_j. In the case, $H_1(t_i) = A_{\mathsf{MCL}} D_{\mathsf{MCL}}^{w_{\mathsf{MCL}}}$, $H_2(t_i) = B_{\mathsf{MCL}}$, and $H_3(t_i, m_j) = m'_{(i,j)} = m_{\mathsf{MCL}}$ hold. Since E_{MCL} is the valid signature of the MCL scheme on message m_{MCL},

$$e(E_{\mathsf{MCL}}, g) = e(A_{\mathsf{MCL}} B_{\mathsf{MCL}}^{m_{\mathsf{MCL}}} D_{\mathsf{MCL}}^{w_{\mathsf{MCL}}}, X_{\mathsf{MCL}})$$
$$= e((A_{\mathsf{MCL}} D_{\mathsf{MCL}}^{w_{\mathsf{MCL}}}) B_{\mathsf{MCL}}^{m_{\mathsf{MCL}}}, X_{\mathsf{MCL}})$$

holds. This implies that $e(E, g) = e(H_1(t_i) H_2(t_i)^{m'_{(i,j)}}, \mathsf{vk}^*)$ where $m'_{(i,j)} = H_3(t_i, m_j)$.

By the above discussion, we can see that B does not abort, B can simulate the EUF-CMA game of the $\mathsf{SAS}_{\mathsf{LLY}}$ scheme.

Second, we confirm that when A successfully output a valid forgery $(\mathsf{vk}_1^*, \ldots,$ $\mathsf{vk}_{r^*}^*), (m_1^*, \ldots, m_{r^*}^*), \Sigma^*)$ of the $\mathsf{SAS_{LLY}}$ scheme, B can forge a signature of the MCL scheme. Let $(\mathsf{vk}_1^*, \ldots, \mathsf{vk}_{r^*}^*), (m_1^*, \ldots, m_{r^*}^*), \Sigma^*)$ be a valid forgery output by A. Then there exists $j^* \in [r^*]$ such that $\mathsf{vk}_{j^*}^* = \mathsf{vk}^*$. By the verification equation of $\mathsf{SAS_{LLY}.Verify}$,

$$e(E^{*\prime}, g) = e\left(H_1(t^*), \prod_{i=1}^{r^*} \mathsf{vk}_i^*\right) \cdot e\left(H_2(t^*), \prod_{i=1}^{r^*} (\mathsf{vk}_i^*)^{m_i^*}\right)$$

holds where $\Sigma^* = (E^{*\prime}, t^*)$ and $H_3(t^*, m_i^*) = m_i^{*\prime}$ for $i \in [r^*]$. If B does not abort in Step 6 of **Output procedure**, $t^* = t'$ holds. This means that $H_1(t^*) = A_{\mathsf{MCL}} D_{\mathsf{MCL}}^{w_{\mathsf{MCL}}}$ and $H_2(t^*) = B_{\mathsf{MCL}}$ hold. These facts imply that

$$E^{*\prime} = H_1(t^*)^{\sum_{i=1}^{r^*} \mathsf{sk}_i^*} H_2(t^*)^{\sum_{i=1}^{r^*} m_i^{*\prime} \mathsf{sk}_i^*}$$

$$= (A_{\mathsf{MCL}} D_{\mathsf{MCL}}^{w_{\mathsf{MCL}}})^{\sum_{i=1}^{r^*} x_i^*} B_{\mathsf{MCL}}^{\sum_{i=1}^{r^*} m_i^{*\prime} x_i^*}$$

holds where $\mathsf{sk}_i^* = x_i^*$ is a secret key corresponding to vk_i^*.

By setting $F' \leftarrow A_{\mathsf{MCL}} D_{\mathsf{MCL}}^{w_{\mathsf{MCL}}}$ and $B' \leftarrow B_{\mathsf{MCL}}$,

$$E' = E^{*\prime} \cdot \left(F'^{\sum_{i \in [r^*] \setminus \{j^*\}} x_i} B'^{\sum_{i \in [r^*] \setminus \{j^*\}} x_i m_i'}\right)^{-1}$$

$$= (A_{\mathsf{MCL}} D_{\mathsf{MCL}}^{w_{\mathsf{MCL}}})^{x_{j^*}^*} B_{\mathsf{MCL}}^{m_{j^*}^{*\prime} x_{j^*}^*}$$

Moreover, $e(A_{\mathsf{MCL}}, Y_{\mathsf{MCL}}) = e(B_{\mathsf{MCL}}, g_{\mathsf{MCL}})$, $e(A_{\mathsf{MCL}}, Z_{\mathsf{MCL}}) = e(C_{\mathsf{MCL}}, g_{\mathsf{MCL}})$, and $e(C_{\mathsf{MCL}}, Y_{\mathsf{MCL}}) = e(D_{\mathsf{MCL}}, g_{\mathsf{MCL}})$ holds. If B does not abort in Step 8 of **Output procedure**, $m_{j^*}^*$ is a not queried message for the signing of the OT-EUF-CMA game of the MCL scheme. Therefore, if B does not abort and outputs $(m_{\mathsf{MCL}}^*, \sigma_{\mathsf{MCL}}^*) \leftarrow (m_{j^*}^*, (w_{\mathsf{MCL}}, A_{\mathsf{MCL}}, B', C_{\mathsf{MCL}}, D_{\mathsf{MCL}}, E'))$, B can forge a signature of the MCL scheme.

Finally, we analyze the probability that B succeeds in forging a signature of the MCL scheme. First, we consider the probability that B does not abort at the simulation of signatures. B aborts the simulation of $\mathcal{O}^{\mathsf{Sign}}$ if $t_{ctr} = t' \wedge j \neq k'$. The probability that B succeeds in simulating $\mathcal{O}^{\mathsf{Sign}}$ is at least $1/q_{H_3}$. Next, we consider the probability that B aborts in Step 6 of **Output procedure**. Since B chooses the target period $t' \leftarrow [T]$, the probability $t^* \neq t'$ is $1/[T]$. Finally, the probability that B aborts in Step 8 of **Output procedure** is $1/p$. Let $\mathsf{Adv}_{\mathsf{SAS_{LLY}},A}^{\mathsf{EUF\text{-}CMA}}$ be the advantage of the EUF-CMA game for the $\mathsf{SAS_{LLY}}$ scheme of A. The advantage of the OT-EUF-CMA game for the MCL scheme of B is

$$\mathsf{Adv}_{\mathsf{MCL},B}^{\mathsf{OT\text{-}EUF\text{-}CMA}} \geq \frac{\mathsf{Adv}_{\mathsf{SAS_{LLY}},A}^{\mathsf{EUF\text{-}CMA}}}{T \times q_{H_3}} \left(1 - \frac{1}{p}\right).$$

Therefore, we can conclude the proof of Theorem 2.   □

By combining Theorem 1 and Theorem 2, we have the following corollary.

Corollary 1. *If the* 1-MSDH-2 *assumption holds, then, in the random oracle model, the* SAS$_{LLY}$ *scheme satisfies the* EUF-CMA *security in the certified-key model.*

Acknowledgement. We would like to thank anonymous referees for their constructive comments.

References

1. Ahn, J.H., Green, M., Hohenberger, S.: Synchronized aggregate signatures: new definitions, constructions and applications. In: Proceedings of the 17th ACM Conference on Computer and Communications Security, CCS 2010, Chicago, Illinois, USA, 4–8 October 2010, pp. 473–484 (2010)
2. Bender, A., Katz, J., Morselli, R.: Ring signatures: stronger definitions, and constructions without random oracles. In: Halevi, S., Rabin, T. (eds.) TCC 2006. LNCS, vol. 3876, pp. 60–79. Springer, Heidelberg (2006). https://doi.org/10.1007/11681878_4
3. Bernhard, D., Fuchsbauer, G., Ghadafi, E., Smart, N.P., Warinschi, B.: Anonymous attestation with user-controlled linkability. Int. J. Inf. Secur. **12**(3), 219–249 (2013)
4. Bichsel, P., Camenisch, J., Neven, G., Smart, N.P., Warinschi, B.: Get shorty via group signatures without encryption. In: Garay, J.A., De Prisco, R. (eds.) SCN 2010. LNCS, vol. 6280, pp. 381–398. Springer, Heidelberg (2010). https://doi.org/10.1007/978-3-642-15317-4_24
5. Boldyreva, A., Gentry, C., O'Neill, A., Yum, D.H.: Ordered multisignatures and identity-based sequential aggregate signatures, with applications to secure routing. In: Proceedings of the 2007 ACM Conference on Computer and Communications Security, CCS 2007, Alexandria, Virginia, USA, 28–31 October 2007, pp. 276–285 (2007)
6. Boneh, D., Boyen, X.: Short signatures without random oracles. In: Cachin, C., Camenisch, J.L. (eds.) EUROCRYPT 2004. LNCS, vol. 3027, pp. 56–73. Springer, Heidelberg (2004). https://doi.org/10.1007/978-3-540-24676-3_4
7. Boneh, D., Boyen, X., Goh, E.-J.: Hierarchical identity based encryption with constant size ciphertext. In: Cramer, R. (ed.) EUROCRYPT 2005. LNCS, vol. 3494, pp. 440–456. Springer, Heidelberg (2005). https://doi.org/10.1007/11426639_26
8. Boneh, D., Gentry, C., Lynn, B., Shacham, H.: Aggregate and verifiably encrypted signatures from bilinear maps. In: Biham, E. (ed.) EUROCRYPT 2003. LNCS, vol. 2656, pp. 416–432. Springer, Heidelberg (2003). https://doi.org/10.1007/3-540-39200-9_26
9. Camenisch, J., Hohenberger, S., Pedersen, M.Ø.: Batch verification of short signatures. In: Naor, M. (ed.) EUROCRYPT 2007. LNCS, vol. 4515, pp. 246–263. Springer, Heidelberg (2007). https://doi.org/10.1007/978-3-540-72540-4_14
10. Camenisch, J., Lysyanskaya, A.: Signature schemes and anonymous credentials from bilinear maps. In: Franklin, M. (ed.) CRYPTO 2004. LNCS, vol. 3152, pp. 56–72. Springer, Heidelberg (2004). https://doi.org/10.1007/978-3-540-28628-8_4
11. Canard, S., Pointcheval, D., Sanders, O., Traoré, J.: Divisible e-cash made practical. In: Katz, J. (ed.) PKC 2015. LNCS, vol. 9020, pp. 77–100. Springer, Heidelberg (2015). https://doi.org/10.1007/978-3-662-46447-2_4

12. Gentry, C., Ramzan, Z.: Identity-based aggregate signatures. In: Yung, M., Dodis, Y., Kiayias, A., Malkin, T. (eds.) PKC 2006. LNCS, vol. 3958, pp. 257–273. Springer, Heidelberg (2006). https://doi.org/10.1007/11745853_17

13. Goldwasser, S., Micali, S., Rivest, R.L.: A digital signature scheme secure against adaptive chosen-message attacks. SIAM J. Comput. **17**(2), 281–308 (1988)

14. Hartung, G., Kaidel, B., Koch, A., Koch, J., Rupp, A.: Fault-tolerant aggregate signatures. In: Cheng, C.-M., Chung, K.-M., Persiano, G., Yang, B.-Y. (eds.) PKC 2016, Part I. LNCS, vol. 9614, pp. 331–356. Springer, Heidelberg (2016). https://doi.org/10.1007/978-3-662-49384-7_13

15. Hohenberger, S., Koppula, V., Waters, B.: Universal signature aggregators. In: Oswald, E., Fischlin, M. (eds.) EUROCRYPT 2015, Part II. LNCS, vol. 9057, pp. 3–34. Springer, Heidelberg (2015). https://doi.org/10.1007/978-3-662-46803-6_1

16. Hohenberger, S., Sahai, A., Waters, B.: Full domain hash from (leveled) multilinear maps and identity-based aggregate signatures. In: Canetti, R., Garay, J.A. (eds.) CRYPTO 2013, Part I. LNCS, vol. 8042, pp. 494–512. Springer, Heidelberg (2013). https://doi.org/10.1007/978-3-642-40041-4_27

17. Hohenberger, S., Waters, B.: Short and stateless signatures from the RSA assumption. In: Halevi, S. (ed.) CRYPTO 2009. LNCS, vol. 5677, pp. 654–670. Springer, Heidelberg (2009). https://doi.org/10.1007/978-3-642-03356-8_38

18. Hohenberger, S., Waters, B.: Synchronized aggregate signatures from the RSA assumption. In: Nielsen, J.B., Rijmen, V. (eds.) EUROCRYPT 2018, Part II. LNCS, vol. 10821, pp. 197–229. Springer, Cham (2018). https://doi.org/10.1007/978-3-319-78375-8_7

19. Lee, K., Lee, D.H., Yung, M.: Aggregating CL-signatures revisited: extended functionality and better efficiency. In: Sadeghi, A.-R. (ed.) FC 2013. LNCS, vol. 7859, pp. 171–188. Springer, Heidelberg (2013). https://doi.org/10.1007/978-3-642-39884-1_14

20. Lu, S., Ostrovsky, R., Sahai, A., Shacham, H., Waters, B.: Sequential aggregate signatures and multisignatures without random oracles. In: Vaudenay, S. (ed.) EUROCRYPT 2006. LNCS, vol. 4004, pp. 465–485. Springer, Heidelberg (2006). https://doi.org/10.1007/11761679_28

21. Lysyanskaya, A., Micali, S., Reyzin, L., Shacham, H.: Sequential aggregate signatures from trapdoor permutations. In: Cachin, C., Camenisch, J.L. (eds.) EUROCRYPT 2004. LNCS, vol. 3027, pp. 74–90. Springer, Heidelberg (2004). https://doi.org/10.1007/978-3-540-24676-3_5

22. Lysyanskaya, A., Rivest, R.L., Sahai, A., Wolf, S.: Pseudonym systems. In: Heys, H., Adams, C. (eds.) SAC 1999. LNCS, vol. 1758, pp. 184–199. Springer, Heidelberg (2000). https://doi.org/10.1007/3-540-46513-8_14

23. Ozmen, M.O., Behnia, R., Yavuz, A.A.: Fast authentication from aggregate signatures with improved security. In: Goldberg, I., Moore, T. (eds.) FC 2019. LNCS, vol. 11598, pp. 686–705. Springer, Cham (2019). https://doi.org/10.1007/978-3-030-32101-7_39

24. Pointcheval, D., Sanders, O.: Reassessing security of randomizable signatures. In: Smart, N.P. (ed.) CT-RSA 2018. LNCS, vol. 10808, pp. 319–338. Springer, Cham (2018). https://doi.org/10.1007/978-3-319-76953-0_17

25. Saxena, A., Misra, J., Dhar, A.: Increasing anonymity in bitcoin. In: Böhme, R., Brenner, M., Moore, T., Smith, M. (eds.) FC 2014. LNCS, vol. 8438, pp. 122–139. Springer, Heidelberg (2014). https://doi.org/10.1007/978-3-662-44774-1_9

26. Schröder, D.: How to aggregate the CL signature scheme. In: Atluri, V., Diaz, C. (eds.) ESORICS 2011. LNCS, vol. 6879, pp. 298–314. Springer, Heidelberg (2011). https://doi.org/10.1007/978-3-642-23822-2_17

27. Zhao, Y.: Practical aggregate signature from general elliptic curves, and applications to blockchain. In: Proceedings of the 2019 ACM Asia Conference on Computer and Communications Security, AsiaCCS 2019, Auckland, New Zealand, July 09–12, 2019, pp. 529–538 (2019)

Network Security and Blockchain

DCONST: Detection of Multiple-Mix-Attack Malicious Nodes Using Consensus-Based Trust in IoT Networks

Zuchao Ma[1], Liang Liu[1], and Weizhi Meng[2](✉)

[1] College of Computer Science and Technology,
Nanjing University of Aeronautics and Astronautics, Nanjing, China
[2] Department of Applied Mathematics and Computer Science,
Technical University of Denmark, Lyngby, Denmark
weme@dtu.dk

Abstract. The Internet of Things (IoT) is growing rapidly, which allows many smart devices to connect and cooperate with each other. While for the sake of distributed architecture, an IoT environment is known to be vulnerable to insider attacks. In this work, we focus on this challenge and consider an advanced insider threat, called multiple-mix attack, which typically combines three sub-attacks: tamper attack, drop attack and replay attack. For protection, we develop a Distributed Consensus based Trust Model (DCONST), which can build the nodes' reputation by sharing particular information, called *cognition*. In particular, DCONST can detect malicious nodes by using the K-Means clustering, without disturbing the normal operations of a network. In the evaluation, as compared with some similar models, DCONST can overall provide a better detection rate by increasing around 10% to 40%.

Keywords: IoT network · Malicious node · Trust management · Consensus · K-means method

1 Introduction

The Internet of Things (IoT) is becoming an increasingly popular infrastructure to support many modern applications or services, like smart homes, smart healthcare, public security, industrial monitoring and environmental protection [14]. These IoT devices could be used to collect information from surroundings or control units to help gather information and make suitable strategies. Also, these devices can use various IoT protocols [20], with the aim of transferring their data including ZigBee, WiFi, Bluetooth, etc.

The IoT topology is flexible (e.g., multihop network), but it also suffers from many insider threats, where an attacker can launch an intrusion inside a network. For example, attackers can compromise some devices in an IoT network and then

© Springer Nature Switzerland AG 2020
J. K. Liu and H. Cui (Eds.): ACISP 2020, LNCS 12248, pp. 247–267, 2020.
https://doi.org/10.1007/978-3-030-55304-3_13

use these devices to infer sensitive information and tamper data. Therefore, it is very essential to design an effective security mechanism to identify malicious nodes in IoT networks.

Motivation. Most existing studies often focus on a single attack scenario in an IoT, but an advanced attacker may choose to perform several attacks simultaneously. Hence a stronger and more advanced attacker should be considered - who can control some internal nodes in IoT networks and perform a multiple-mix-attack. For example, Liu et al. [8] discussed a scenario of multiple-mix-attack by combining data tampering, packet dropping and duplication. They proposed a perceptron-based trust to help detect malicious nodes, but their method has to inject many packets to analyze the nodes' reputation, resulting in a disturbance of network operations. In addition, their detection accuracy depends heavily on network diversity and attack probability, i.e., the low network diversity and the high attack probability may cause low detection accuracy.

Contributions. Motivated by the literature, our work develops a Distributed Consensus based Trust Model (DCONST), which can achieve the self-detection via consensus among IoT nodes. It can work without disturbing the normal network operations and build the nodes' trust by sharing a kind of particular information called *cognition* among nodes. To mitigate the impact caused by the low network diversity and the high attack probability, DCONST makes a strategy that malicious nodes should receive more punishment while benign nodes should obtain more award. The contributions can be summarized as below.

- In this work, we formalize system models and propose DCONST by using consensus of nodes to improve the detection performance. In particular, our DCONST can generate punishment evidence to reduce the trust values of potential malicious nodes, and provide award evidence to improve the reputation of benign nodes. A base station can collect all cognitions of nodes to complete a final trust evaluation.
- We use the K-Means method to cluster nodes into benign group and malicious group. For the performance analysis, we compare our approach with two similar approaches: Perceptron Detection with Enhancement (PDE) [8] and Hard Detection (HD) [9]. The experimental results demonstrate that DCONST could achieve better detection performance.

Organization. The remaining parts are organized as follows. Section 2 introduces related work on trust-based detection in IoT networks. Section 3 formalizes the network model and message model. Section 4 describes DCONST in detail. Section 5 discusses our experimental environment and analyzes evaluation results. Finally, Sect. 6 concludes our work with future directions.

2   Related Work

The Internet of Things (IoT) is beneficial for its wide adoption and sustainable development, which can be divided into four layers including perception layer, network layer, middle-ware layer and application layer. Due to the distributed architecture, insider attacks are one big challenge in IoT networks.

Trust-Based Detection. Building a proper trust mechanism is a promising solution to discover insider attacks [13]. For instance, Cho et al. [2] proposed a provenance-based trust model, called PROVEST, for delay tolerant networks to handle the trust evaluation of nodes by using both direct and indirect trust information. Dinesh et al. [1] developed a detection scheme, named BAN-Trust for identifying malicious nodes in body area networks according to the nature acquired through the nodes by their own as well as partner nodes. BAN-Trust could conceive the common behavior among nodes and gather the information to measure the trust. Liu et al. [8] proposed a perceptron-based detection using machine learning in the multiple-mix-attack environment. The trust is evaluated according to the reputation of paths, but the detection accuracy depends heavily on the network diversity. Some other related studies can refer but not limited to [3,7,15,21].

Consensus-Based Trust. In this work, our goal is to detect malicious nodes based on the knowledge of all network nodes, which is a typical group decision making (GDM) problem. Consensus-based trust models are widely used in solving this problem with two typical steps: 1) *trust estimation* that evaluates the trust from a single group member, and *trust aggregation* that predicts the trust based on the aggregated knowledge from trust estimation. For example, Rathore et al. [17] presented a consensus-aware sociopsychological model for detecting fraudulent nodes in WSNs. They used three factors for trust computation, such as ability, benevolence, and integrity. Sharma et al. [18] proposed a consensus framework for mitigating zero-day attacks in IoT networks. Their approach uses the context behavior of IoT devices as a detection mechanism, working with an alert message protocol and a critical data sharing protocol. Mazdin et al. [12] analyzed the application of a binary trust-consensus protocol in multi-agent systems with switching communication topology. The trust in their work represents a belief of one agent that another one is capable of executing a specific task. Some other related studies can refer to [4,5,22].

Advanced Attack. In this work, similar to former work [8], we consider a multiple-mix attack in which an insider can perform three typical attacks: tamper attack, drop attack and replay attack. More specifically, *tamper attack* is one of the most harmful internal threats, where malicious nodes along a multihop path can modify the received packets (randomly or with specific goals) before they reach the destination [6]. Under a *drop attack*, malicious nodes can drop received packets (randomly or with specific goals) to prevent these packets from reaching the destination [19]. The third attack is *replay attack*, where malicious nodes can send the received packets repeatedly to cause overhanded data flow, aiming to consume the link bandwidth and mislead network functions [11].

Most existing research studies focus mainly on a single/separate attack, but in fact an advanced attacker can handle multiple types of attacks at the same time. In such case, it is more difficult to identify malicious nodes precisely. Thus, in this work, we consider an advanced attacker who can launch a multiple-mix-attack by combining these three attacks with a probability.

3 System Model

In this work, we adopt the same attack model in [8], called multiple-mix-attack, which consists of tamper attack, drop attack and replay attack. This section formalizes our network model and message model.

3.1 Network Model

Node Model. In this work, we consider that malicious nodes can make a tamper attack, a drop attack and a replay attack at the same time or choose combining some of them intentionally. We assume that a node can be represented by using the following equation:

$$Node = <id, T, pu, pr, cogl, p_{TA}, p_{DA}, p_{RA}> \tag{1}$$

where, id represents the unique identifier of the node; T represents the trust of the node; pu and pr represent a public-private key pair of the node to be used for encryption and decryption when network nodes transfer data and cognitions; $cogl$ is the list of cognitions that includes all cognitions of the nodes about others. p_{TA} is the probability of node N making a tamper attack, p_{DA} is the probability of node N making a drop attack, and p_{RA} is the probability of node N making a reply attack. For a benign node, the probability of node's p_{TA}, p_{DA} and p_{RA} should be all zero, whereas a malicious node's p_{TA}, p_{DA} and p_{RA} should be a positive number.

Path Model. The path of a packet can be represented as:

$$Path = <node_1, node_2, node_3...node_n> \tag{2}$$

where, if packet A arrives at destination with a $Path = <node_1, node_2, node_3 ... node_n>$, then it means packet A is delivered through $node_1$, $node_2$, $node_3$, ... $node_n$ in a sequence.

3.2 Message Model

We assume that the IoT network contains a trusted authority (TA) that can distribute keys to provide IoT nodes with a shield to defeat both external attacks and insider attacks. The key management method can refer to [2]. Distributed keys can be divided into two types:

1. A symmetric key K for encryption to defend external attackers;
2. Asymmetric key pairs $<pu, pr>$ used for encryption and signing to defeat insider attackers, referred in Eq. (1).

Message can be formalized as

$$M = [(D)_{pu_R}, Si_D, Cog_{x_1,y_1}, Si_{x_1,y_1}, ..., Cog_{x_m,y_m}, Si_{x_m,y_m}]_K \qquad (3)$$

where, D represents the original data that need to be transferred, pu_R represents using the public key of the receiver to encrypt the data, and Si_D is the signature. Cog_{x_i,y_i} represents the cognition of node x_i about node y_i. Si_{x_i,y_i} represents the signature of Cog_{x_i,y_i} that is generated by node x_i. Cognition will be introduced in Sect. 4.3, which is the assessment about the node trust. K means the symmetric key and K is used to encrypt the whole message.

To defend against insider attacks, the sender of the communication uses the public key of the receiver to encrypt the data-part of transferred packets. The cognition-part of packets do not need to be encrypted, because relay nodes in the transferred path may need to access the cognition. Besides, it is important to protect data and cognitions from being tampered and there should be a notification if tampered behavior is detected. Hence the data owner and the cognition should provide their signatures.

4   DCONST

This section introduces our proposed DCONST, including core workflow, trust model, cognition, cognition aggregation, cognition sharing, punishment and award, trust evaluation, and the K-means based detection.

4.1   Core Workflow

Figure 1 shows the core workflow of DCONST, mainly consisting of trust evaluation and detection of malicious nodes. For trust evaluation, nodes have to measure the reputation of others within the network by sharing particular information, called *cognition* (refer to Sect. 4.3). To identify malicious nodes, the base station in the IoT network has to collect all cognitions from nodes and create the Cognition-Matrix, where Cog_{xy} represents the cognition of node x about node y. The base station should perform a central trust evaluation and obtain the trustworthiness of each node. For detection of malicious nodes, nodes' trust should be forwarded to the K-means clustering module. The output includes *Tamper-malicious set* - malicious nodes that launch tamper attacks; *Drop-malicious set* - malicious nodes that launch drop attacks; and *Replay-malicious set* - malicious nodes that launch replay attacks; and Benign set - benign nodes.

4.2   Trust Model

To evaluate the reputation of nodes by considering three attack types, we design the trust model with three dimensions accordingly - honesty, volume and straight. **Honesty** is the dimension that demonstrates whether a node tampers the received data or not. An evidence about tamper behavior can reduce

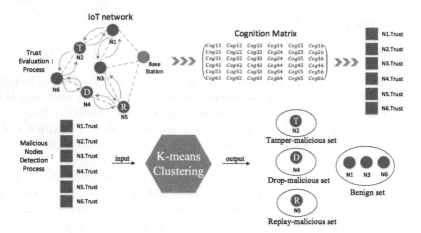

Fig. 1. Core workflow

the honesty of the node. **Volume** illustrates whether a node drops the received data or not. An evidence about drop behavior can reduce the volume of the node. **Straight** validates whether a node replays the received data or not. An evidence about replay behavior can reduce the straight of the node. Hence the trust of a node can be formalized as follow:

$$Node.T = <H, V, S>$$ (4)

where, H represents the honesty; V represents the volume; S represents the straight. All of them range from 0 to 100; the negative side is 0 and the positive side is 100. The higher value reached by the H, V, S of a node, the better trust it possesses. Note that H, V, S are all integers rather than decimals, which can be space-saving in the data communication.

4.3 Cognition

Cognition is the assessment about the reputation of nodes in the view of the cognition owner (a type of node). In DCONST, nodes obtain the trust of others by exchanging their cognitions. We formalize the cognition as

$$Cog = <Sub, Obj, H, V, S, isNei>$$ (5)

where, Sub represents the subject of the cognition and Obj represents the object of the cognition. Cog means the cognition of Sub about Obj. The parameters of H, V, S are the same in Eq. (4). $isNei$ represents whether Sub is the neighbor of Obj. For example, if node X and node Y are neighbors, and we set the honesty, the volume and the straight of node Y as 100, 100 and 50 respectively, then there is a cognition $<X, Y, 100, 100, 50, 1>$ of node X.

4.4   Cognition Aggregation

When a node receives a new cognition from other nodes, it updates its own cognition via cognition aggregation. Essentially, cognition aggregation is the process about mixing own cognition (old cognition) with the new cognition in a specific ratio. This ratio depends on the credibility of the new cognition, which can be evaluated from two aspects: Reliability and Fluctuation.

Reliability. If the new-cognition provider is reliable in the old-cognition of the receiver, it makes sense to believe the new-cognition more. This is because the precision of cognition of a node could be affected by its malicious behavior. For example, assume there is a packet passing a path that contains a malicious node N. If this packet is attacked by node N, then there will be a punishment evidence created, which we will discuss in Sect. 4.6. As this punishment evidence is negative, the cognition of node N would lack persuasion. To evaluate the reliability of a node n, we can have the following:

$$r(n) = \frac{c.H + c.V + c.S}{H_{max} + V_{max} + S_{max}} \tag{6}$$

where, c is the cognition about the node n; parameters of H, V and S are the same in Eq. (5); H_{max}, V_{max} and S_{max} are the maximum of H, V and S. In our system, H_{max}, V_{max} and S_{max} are set as 100.

Fluctuation. If the new-cognition differs from the old-cognition greatly, the new-cognition provider may be suspicious as the persuasion of the new-cognition is poor. The apparent difference may be caused by a wrong cognition or some negative evidence, and therefore we can reduce its weight in the aggregation.

To evaluate the fluctuation of a new-cognition compared to the old-cognition, we can have the following:

$$f(ncog) = \frac{|ncog.H + ncog.V + ncog.S - ocog.H - ocog.V - ocog.S|}{H_{max} + V_{max} + S_{max}} \tag{7}$$

where, $ncog$ is the new-cognition; $ocog$ is the old-cognition of the receiver; H_{max}, V_{max} and S_{max} are the maximum of H, V and S.

Thus, the credibility of the new-cognition can be evaluated as

$$cred(ncog) = \begin{cases} \rho_d * (1 - f(ncog)) * r(ncog.Sub) & \text{if } ncog.Obj \text{ is a} \\ & \text{neighbor of } ncog.Sub \\ \rho_i * (1 - f(ncog)) * r(ncog.Sub) & otherwise \end{cases} \tag{8}$$

where, $ncog$ is the new-cognition; $ncog.Sub$ is the provider of the cognition that can be referred in Eq. (5); whether $ncog.Obj$ is a neighbor of $ncog.Sub$ can be concluded according to $ncog.isNei$ in Eq. (5). ρ_d and ρ_i are the maximum of the credibility with $\rho_d > \rho_i$. The setting of ρ_d and ρ_i is mainly based on the common sense that a cognition from a node's neighbor about the node can be more objective and accurate.

Based on the credibility of the new-cognition, we update the old-cognition of the receiver by aggregating the new-cognition as follows:

$$[ucog.H, ucog.V, ucog.S] =$$
$$[\log_2(1 + \frac{ncog.H * cred(ncog) + ocog.H * (1 - cred(ncog))}{H_{max}}) * H_{max},$$
$$\log_2(1 + \frac{ncog.V * cred(ncog) + ocog.V * (1 - cred(ncog))}{V_{max}}) * V_{max}, \qquad (9)$$
$$\log_2(1 + \frac{ncog.S * cred(ncog) + ocog.S * (1 - cred(ncog))}{S_{max}}) * S_{max}]$$

where, $ucog$ is the cognition of the receiver updated after the cognition aggregation. The motivation of using the log function is due to that it needs more positive cognitions if any H, V or S improves. On the contrary, H, V or S of a node could decrease fast when there are negative cognitions.

4.5   Cognition Sharing

The cognition sharing of DCONST can be defined with two operations - Cognition Extraction and Cognition Spread. *Cognition Extraction* is the process to determine which cognition should be sent with the packet when the packet passes a node. Considering the bandwidth of a network, it is not an efficient way to send all cognitions, so that a wise strategy should balance both performance and cost. *Cognition Spread* aims to check whether a cognition can be aggregated by other nodes, as the aggregation process will bring some cost when the node calculates the credibility of a new cognition.

- **Cognition Extraction.** When a packet is transferred by a node, the node can create a new packet by adding three cognitions to the end of the packet. As the new packet is sent by the node, the cognition of the node is spread. For implementation, there are three prior queues, negative queue (NQ), reduction queue (RQ) and improvement queue (IQ) in the memory of each node. NQ sorts cognitions by their sum of honesty, volume and straight (the head of queue is the cognition having the smallest sum of honesty, volume and straight); RQ sorts cognitions by their reduction (the head of queue is the cognition that reduces the most and is updated recently); and IQ sorts cognitions by their improvement (the head of queue is the cognition that improves the most and is updated recently). A cognition exists in three queues, and if it is removed from a queue then it will be also removed by other two queues. DCONST selects the heads of these queues to spread including the most negative cognition, the cognition with the latest and the largest reduction, and the cognition with the latest and the largest improvement that has not been sent. That is, DCONST attempts to spread negative cognitions and cognitions whose fluctuation is evident promptly.
- **Cognition Spread.** Cognition transferred with packets can be aggregated by both relay nodes and destination node. The relay nodes can update their

cognitions when they receive packets. They also need to add their extracted cognitions to the transferred packet and forward them to the next node. During idle time, nodes can send their extracted cognitions to their neighbors aiming to accelerate the process of updating cognitions.

The whole process of Cognition Sharing is shown in Fig. 2. Green blocks with Cog_{i1}, Cog_{i2} and Cog_{i3} represent the cognition selected from node n_i. Green full-line-arrow means the cognition can be aggregated by the pointed node. Green dotted-line-arrow shows that nodes can send the extracted cognitions to their neighbors during idle time.

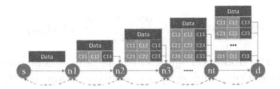

Fig. 2. DCONST cognition sharing

4.6   Punishment and Award

To identify malicious nodes in IoT networks, it is important to create the trust gap between benign nodes and malicious nodes, through punishing malicious nodes and awarding benign nodes. Essentially, award is the reverse process of punishment, which aims to recover the correct cognition about those nodes that are misunderstood by some wrong punishment evidence. The trigger of punishment is different from the trigger of award - one malicious transmission can trigger one punishment while accumulating enough successful transmission may only bring one award. This is because few successful transmission cannot prove that there are no malicious nodes existing in the path. To analyze different attack types, we design corresponding punishment and award as below.

Punishment of Tamper Attack. The evidence of punishment about tamper attack is called Indirect Tamper Punishment Evidence (ITPE). Note that relay nodes only check whether the cognition in the packet is tampered because they do not have the key to decrypt the data part in the packet. Only the last node (with the key) can check both the cognitions and the data. ITPE could be generated in the following two cases:

Case A (Destination Punishment). Assume there is a packet transferred via a path $p = <s, n_1, n_2, n_3, ..., n_t, d>$ and node d checks whether the original data or cognition is tampered with their signature. If a tamper attack is detected, an ITPE will be created by node d. Then node d can use ITPE to update its cognitions about n_1, n_2, n_3, ..., n_t. If the data part of a packet is tampered, n_1,

$n_2, n_3, ..., n_t$ will be pointed by ITPE. While if Cog_{n_x,n_y} (refer to Eq. (3)) is tampered, $n_i(i > x)$ will be pointed by ITPE. This is because only latter nodes can tamper the cognitions in the packet from previous nodes.

Case B (Middle Punishment). Assume there is a packet transferred via a path $p = <s, n_1, n_2, n_3, ..., n_t, d>$ and node n_k checks whether the cognition is tampered with their signature. If a tamper attack is detected, an ITPE can be created by node n_k. While if Cog_{n_x,n_y} (refer to Eq. (3)) is tampered, $n_i(i > x)$ will be pointed by ITPE. In this case, node n_k can use ITPE to update the cognition about $n_{x+1}, n_{x+2}, ..., n_{k-1}$. To evaluate the punishment of tamper attack, when an ITPE is created, the cognition about all nodes pointed by ITPE will be updated by the producer of ITPE (the punishment provider) as below:

$$ucog.H = \log_2(1 + \frac{ocog.H - \theta_{hi}}{H_{max}}) * H_{max} \tag{10}$$

where, $ucog$ is the updated cognition of the punishment provider (i.e., relay nodes and the destination node), $ocog$ is the old cognition, and θ_{hi} is a parameter that determines the reduction of the honesty with ITPE.

Award About No Tamper. Award about No Tamper is the reverse process of Punishment of Tamper Attack. Cnt_{hi} is a counter in each node to record the positive behavior of relay nodes. When the value of a node in this counter meets the threshold σ_{hi}, an indirect honesty award evidence (IHAE) can be created to increase the node's honesty. We use $Cnt_{hi}.n.val$ to represent the value of node n in Cnt_{hi}. If a packet is successfully transmitted, all nodes related to the packet will be awarded. Taking the above Case A as an example, if the tamper attack does not exist, the value of each relay node in Cnt_{hi} can be increased by 1, i.e., $Cnt_{hi}.n_1.val = Cnt_{hi}.n_1.val + 1$, $Cnt_{hi}.n_2.val = Cnt_{hi}.n_2.val + 1$, ..., $Cnt_{hi}.n_t.val = Cnt_{hi}.n_t.val + 1$. Finally, if we have $Cnt_{hi}.n.val = \sigma_{hi}$, then an IHAE about node n will be created. If an IHAE or an ITPE about node n is created, $Cnt_{hi}.n.val$ will be set as zero.

To evaluate the award of no tamper attack, when an IHAE is created, the cognition about all nodes pointed by IHAE will be updated by the producer of IHAE (the award provider) as below:

$$ucog.H = \log_2(1 + \frac{ocog.H + \theta_{hi}}{H_{max}}) * H_{max} \tag{11}$$

where, $ucog$ is the updated cognition of the award provider and $ocog$ is the old cognition. θ_{hi} is a parameter that determines the improvement of the honesty with IHAE and its value is equal to that in Eq. (10).

Punishment of Drop Attack. The evidence of punishment about drop attack is called Indirect Drop Punishment Evidence (IDPE). Suppose there is a packet transferred via a path $p = <n_0, n_1, n_2, n_3, ..., n_t, d>$ and if node d receives the packet, it has to send an acknowledgement (ack) to node n_0 with the path

$rp = <d, n_t, ..., n_3, n_2, n_1, n_0>$. If we assume the ack cannot be faked and the node does not receive the ack after transferred the packet, then a drop attack can be detected and an IDPE can be created. Node n_i can use IDPE to update the cognition of n_{i+1}. For example, if node n_3 is a malicious node that drops the packet and node n_0, n_1, n_2 cannot get the ack from node d, then node n_0 can create an IDPE about node n_1; node n_1 can create an IDPE about node n_2; and node n_2 can create an IDPE about node n_3. Thus, IDPE can be regarded as a chain to connect all potential drop-malicious nodes.

To evaluate the punishment of drop attack, when an IDPE is created, the cognition about the node pointed by IDPE will be updated by the producer of IDPE (the punishment provider) as below:

$$ucog.V = \log_2(1 + \frac{ocog.V - \theta_{vi}}{V_{max}}) * V_{max} \tag{12}$$

where, $ucog$ is the updated cognition of the punishment provider, $ocog$ is the old cognition, and θ_{vi} is a parameter that determines the reduction of the volume with IDPE.

Award About No Drop. Award about No Drop is the reverse process of Punishment of Drop Attack. Cnt_{vi} is the counter to record the positive behavior with the acknowledgement from the destination node. When the value of a node in this counter meets the threshold σ_{vi}, an indirect volume award evidence (IVAE) can be created to increase the volume of the node. Similar to the *award about no tamper*, if a packet successfully arrives at its destination, the value in Cnt_{vi} of all nodes related to the packet can be increased by 1.

When an IVAE is created, the cognition about the node pointed by the IVAE will be updated by the producer of IVAE (the award provider) as below:

$$ucog.V = \log_2(1 + \frac{ocog.V + \theta_{vi}}{V_{max}}) * V_{max} \tag{13}$$

where, $ucog$ is the updated cognition of the award provider and $ocog$ is the old cognition. θ_{vi} is a parameter that determines the improvement of the volume with IVAE and its value is equal to that in Eq. (12).

Punishment of Replay Attack. The evidence of punishment about replay attack is called Indirect Replay Punishment Evidence (IRPE). Assume there is a packet transferred via a path $p = <n_0, n_1, n_2, n_3, ..., n_t, d>$ and if node d receives the packet, it has to send an acknowledgement (ack) to node s with the path $rp = <d, n_t, ..., n_3, n_2, n_1, n_0>$. If any nodes in the path receive redundant acks, a replay attack can be detected. For example, when node n_0 sends the packet to node d, it should receive one ack about this packet from node d instead of two acks or more. Once a replayed attack happens, node d will receive two or more identical packets and return identical acks. In this case, node $s, n_1, n_2, ...n_t$ can realize there is a replay attack, and create an IRPE. Then node n_i can use IRPE to update the cognition of node n_{i+1} except for node d. For example, if node n_3 is a malicious node that replays the packet once, then node d can get two identical packets and return two identical acks to node s. Thus node s can create an IRPE about node n_1; node n_1 can create an IRPE about node n_2; and node n_2 can create an IRPE about node n_3. Basically, IRPE can be regarded as a chain to connect all potential replay-malicious nodes.

To evaluate the punishment of replay attack, when an IRPE is created, the cognition about the node pointed by the IRPE will be updated by the producer of IRPE (the punishment provider) as below:

$$ucog.S = \log_2(1 + \frac{ocog.S - \theta_{si}}{V_{max}}) * V_{max} \tag{14}$$

where, $ucog$ is the updated cognition of the punishment provider and $ocog$ is the old cognition. θ_{si} is a parameter that determines the reduction of the straight with IRPE.

Award About No Replay. Award about No Replay is the reverse process of Punishment of Replay Attack. Cnt_{si} is a counter to record the positive behavior with the acknowledgement from the destination node. When the value of a node in this counter meets the threshold σ_{si}, an indirect straight award evidence (ISAE) can be created to increase the straight of the node. If a packet successfully arrives at its destination and no redundant acks are found, the value in Cnt_{si} of all nodes related to the packet can be increased by 1.

When an ISAE is created, the cognition about the node pointed by the ISAE will be updated by the producer of ISAE (the award provider) as below:

$$ucog.S = \log_2(1 + \frac{ocog.S + \tau_{si}}{S_{max}}) * S_{max} \tag{15}$$

where, $ucog$ is the updated cognition of the award provider and $ocog$ is the old cognition. τ_{si} is a parameter that determines the improvement of the straight with ISAE and its value is smaller than θ_{si} in Eq. (14). Here is the explanation about $\tau_{si} < \theta_{si}$: when a node receives the supposed ack, it increases the Cnt_{si} without considering whether it will receive a duplicated ack in the future. So if the node receives the duplicated ack later (a replay attack is detected), it will create an IRPE to reduce the straight of its next node, and $\tau_{si} < \theta_{si}$ can guarantee the reduction of the straight could be larger than the increase. Otherwise, the reduction and the increase of the straight will counteract each other, i.e., making the punishment about the replay attack invalid.

4.7   Trust Evaluation

Trust evaluation has to be executed in the base station of an IoT network, when there is a need to analyze the security situation. The base station can collect all cognitions of every node and perform a centralized process. The final trust of a node should be evaluated based on the consensus (cognition) of all members.

In the base station, after all cognitions are collected, a Cognition Matrix can be created and defined as below:

$$CogMat = \begin{pmatrix} Cog_{1,1} & Cog_{1,2} & Cog_{1,3} & \dots & Cog_{1,n} \\ \dots & \dots & \dots & \dots & \dots \\ Cog_{n-1,1} & Cog_{n-1,2} & Cog_{n-1,3} & \dots & Cog_{n-1,n} \\ Cog_{n,1} & Cog_{n,2} & Cog_{n,3} & \dots & Cog_{n,n} \end{pmatrix} \tag{16}$$

where, $Cog_{x,y}$ represents the cognition of node x about node y. Note that we set $Cog_{x,x}$ as $<x,x,0,0,0>$, indicating that the recognition of a node about itself will be ignored.

Then we denote Re_{ix} as the reputation of node x according to node i. Re_{ix} can be regarded as the weight on the cognition of node i in all nodes' cognitions (except node x), when evaluating the trust of node x. The reputation of a node is based on the similarity with the cognition from their neighbors. It is believed that the cognition from a node's neighbors can help evaluate the reputation more persuasively. This is because most evidence of punishment and award comes from neighbors directly. The higher the similarity is, the better the reputation can be. We define Re_{ix} as below:

$$Re_{ix} = \frac{w_{ix}}{\sum_{k=1}^{n} w_{kx}} \tag{17}$$

where, w_{kx} means the weight of the cognition when node k evaluates node x. w_{kx} can be defined as below:

$$w_{kx} = \begin{cases} 0 & \text{if } k = x \\ \frac{1}{n-1} + (1 - \frac{Distance(Cog_{k,x}, Aver(x))}{H_{max}+V_{max}+S_{max}}) * \frac{1}{n-1} & \text{otherwise} \end{cases} \tag{18}$$

$$Distance(Cog_{k,x}, Aver(x)) = |Cog_{k,x}.H - Aver(x).H| + |Cog_{k,x}.V \\ - Aver(x).V| + |Cog_{k,x}.S - Aver(x).S| \tag{19}$$

where, $Distance(Cog_{k,x}, Aver(x))$ is the function to evaluate the similarity between $Cog_{k,x}$ and the cognition from neighbors of node x. $Aver(x)$ is the average of the cognition from neighbors of node x. $Cog_{j,x}.H$ represents the honesty of $Cog_{j,x}$, $Cog_{j,x}.V$ represents the volume of $Cog_{j,x}$, and $Cog_{j,x}.S$ represents the straight of $Cog_{j,x}$. In particular, $Aver(x)$ can be defined as:

$$[Aver(x).H, Aver(x).V, Aver(x).S] = \\ \frac{[\sum Cog_{nei(x),x}.H, \sum Cog_{nei(x),x}.V, \sum Cog_{nei(x),x}.S]}{\text{the count of the neighbors of node } x} \tag{20}$$

where, $nei(x)$ represents the neighbor of node x. Finally, we can evaluate the trust of node i.

$$[Node_i.T.H, Node_i.T.V, Node_i.T.S] = \\ [\sum_{j=1}^{n} [Cog_{j,i}.H * Re_{ji}], \sum_{j=1}^{n} [Cog_{j,i}.V * Re_{ji}], \sum_{j=1}^{n} [Cog_{j,i}.S * Re_{ji}]] \tag{21}$$

4.8   Detection Based on K-Means Method

When obtaining the trust of all nodes, an intuitive way is to identify malicious nodes by selecting a trust threshold: if the trust value of a node is higher than the threshold, then this node is benign; otherwise, the node is malicious. Here comes a question that how to choose a proper threshold in our scenario - when there is a mix-attack, it is very hard to analyze the threshold, since all types of attacks may influence the threshold selection. In this work, we advocate using the clustering method to classify groups and then identify malicious nodes. The adoption of K-means method in this work aims to facilitate the comparison with similar studies like [9, 10].

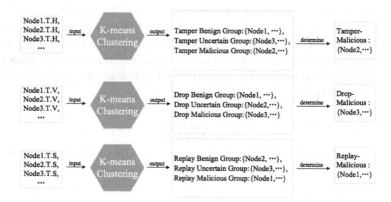

Fig. 3. K-means based malicious node detection

K-means method has been widely adopted in practice, which is a typical clustering method with unsupervised learning and the main argument is the count of clusters [16]. To identify malicious nodes, we use K-means method to cluster nodes in terms of honesty, volume and straight individually. **That is, K-means method will be executed three times to detect malicious nodes with three attack types and the input of K-means will be changed each time.** The three different inputs of K-means method are the tuple of honesty, the tuple of volume and the tuple of straight. In each cluster, we set the count of clusters to be three, then we can classify all nodes into three clusters - benign group, uncertain group and malicious group. **Only the nodes in the malicious group can be determined as malicious**, and this strategy aims to reduce the false positive rate. If the center of benign group and the center of malicious group are very close (i.e., a distance less than 10 in our evaluation), all nodes can be determined as benign. For example, when we input the tuple of honesty to detect tamper-malicious nodes, all nodes can be classified to benign group, uncertain group and malicious group. Those nodes in malicious group can be identified as tamper-malicious nodes. **It is vital to highlight** that, a node can be classified into different malicious groups at the same time (e.g., tamper-malicious group and drop-malicious group) if it launches multiple attacks.

The K-means based detection is described in Fig. 3. That is, malicious nodes include all nodes in the tamper-malicious group, the drop-malicious group, and the replay-malicious group. In this work, our main focus is to identify malicious nodes (without distinguishing the attack types), while the detection performance of different attack types will be addressed in our future work.

5   Evaluation

In the evaluation, we compare our DCONST with two similar approaches called Hard Detection (HD) [9] and Perceptron Detection with enhancement (PDE) [8]. In more detail, **HD** is a mathematical method to detect malicious nodes that can perform a tamper attack. As the focus of HD is not fully the same in this work, we tune HD to make it workable in a multiple-mix attack environment. In particular, we added a module to help detect duplicated packets corresponding to replay attack, and enabled HD to search replay-attack malicious nodes. **PDE** is a detection scheme that uses both perceptron and K-means method to compute IoT nodes' trust values and detect malicious nodes accordingly. It also adopts an enhanced perceptron learning process to reduce the false alarm rate.

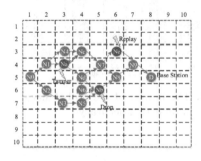

Fig. 4. A distribution of IoT nodes

Table 1. Environmental settings

Item	Description
CPU	Intel Core i7-4700MQ, 2.4 GHz, 4 Core (8 Threads)
Memory	Kingston DDR3L 8 GB * 2
OS	Ubuntu 18.04 LTS
Python	3.6.8
Scikit-learn	0.20

We use the accuracy as the main metric to evaluate the performance. When a malicious node is identified as malicious (even the attack type is labeled wrongly), it will be a True Positive (TP). When a benign node is identified as benign, it will be a True Negative (TN). Thus, if the total number of predictions is S, we can define $accuracy = (TP + TN)/S$.

5.1   Experimental Setup

In our environment, all IoT nodes are deployed in a $100 \times 100\,\mathrm{m}^2$ rectangle area discretely, and each node's communication range is $10\,\mathrm{m}$–$15\,\mathrm{m}$. Our IoT network is generated randomly but it has a feature - for each node, there is at least one path from the node to the base station, enabling IoT devices to be connected. Figure 4 shows an example of the distribution, where the green node is the base station, blue nodes are normal and red nodes are malicious - N_a is tamper-malicious, N_b is drop-malicious, N_e is replay-malicious.

To avoid result bias, we ran our simulation for each experiment in 10 rounds with 10 different networks. We then selected the average value to represent the final experimental result. In particular, we used Python to realize all algorithms, and used the scikit-learn, which is a famous machine learning tool library, to help cluster nodes according to their trust values via the K-means method. Our detection was deployed at the base station. Table 1 shows the detailed experimental settings. Besides, we set ρ_d in Eq. (8) as 0.4; ρ_i in Eq. (8) as 0.1; σ_{hi} in Sect. 4.6 as 3; σ_{vi} in Sect. 4.6 as 3; σ_{si} in Sect. 4.6 as 3; θ_{hi} in Eq. (10) as 40; θvi in Eq. (12) as 40 and θ_{si} in Eq. (14) as 40; and τ_{si} in Eq. (15) as 10, accordingly.

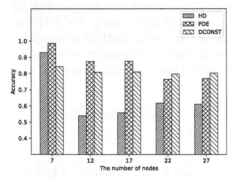

Fig. 5. The impact of the number of nodes on detection accuracy

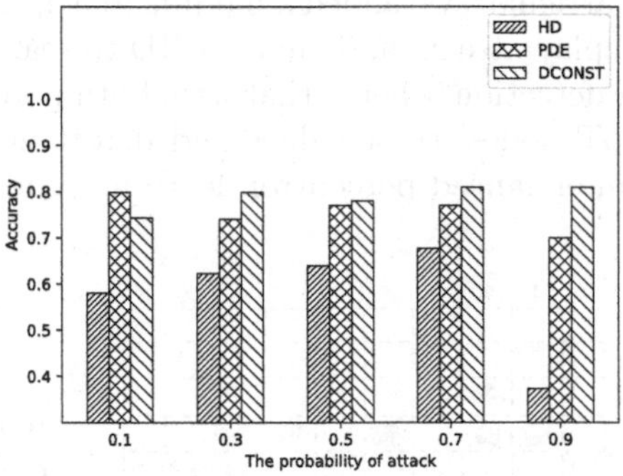

Fig. 6. The impact of the probability of attack on detection accuracy

5.2   Impact of the Number of Nodes

This variable means the scale of the topology, which can affect the detection performance of malicious nodes. To explore the performance, we consider a typical IoT network and a multiple-mix-attack, with the number of nodes as 7, 12, 17, 22 and 27, respectively. In this experiment, we set the number of passing packets as 20000; the probability of attack is 0.5; the percentage of malicious nodes as 0.3; and the diversity of network is all-type (use all paths).

Figure 5 shows that when the IoT network is small-scale, all schemes can reach a high accuracy rate in which PDE performed the best. With the increase of nodes, the accuracy of HD and PDE has an obvious decrease. By contrast, DCONST can maintain stable and outperform HD and PDE when the network scale becomes large. This is because when the network scale is too small, numerous passing packets may cause too many redundant cognitions and make the cognitions of all nodes similar to each other, resulting in a worse case for DCONST.

A small network scale indicates few paths available in the network, in which malicious nodes can be easily identified by HD and PDE. On the other hand, Fig. 5 shows that when the number of nodes reaches 17 or more, the network topology may become more complicated and it is more difficult for HD and PDE to identify all malicious nodes. In such scenario, our DCONST can outperform the other two schemes. As PDE can reduce the false alarm rate by applying perceptron, it can perform much better than HD.

5.3   Impact of Attack Probability

In practice, insider attackers (malicious nodes) can choose a strategy to launch attacks with a certain probability, which would influence the detection performance. To explore this variable, we set the probability of multiple-mix-attack to be 0.1,0.3,0.5,0.7 and 0.9, respectively. In this experiment, we set the number of nodes as 27; the number of passing packets as 2000; the percentage of malicious nodes as 0.3; and the diversity of network is all-type (use all path).

Figure 6 shows that our DCONST could outperform HD in all cases, and the accuracy of HD had a significant decrease when the probability of attack reaches 0.9. When the attack probability is very low (like 0.1), PDE could outperform DCONST, while with the increase of attack probability, DCONST could work better than PDE. The main reasons are analyzed as below.

- It is more beneficial for DCONST to detect malicious nodes with the high attack probability than with the low attack probability. This is because high attack probability can trigger numerous punishment evidence and few award evidence to malicious nodes. However, when the attack probability is low, the most accurate cognitions are often owned by neighbors of the malicious node. Cognitions owned by other nodes of the network are not accurate and the cognition aggregation from those non-neighbor nodes may cause a negative impact on detection accuracy. With the increase of attack probability, there is a better chance to obtain accurate cognitions.
- On the other hand, it is difficult for HD and PDE to handle high attack probability like 0.9. This is because the detection accuracy of HD and PDE depends on the reputation of paths. If there is a node with a high attack probability along a path, then the path reputation might become very low, making it hard to analyze the trust of all nodes within this path.

5.4   Impact of the Percentage of Malicious Nodes

The percentage here means the number of malicious nodes in the IoT network, which may have an impact on the detection accuracy. In the experiment, we set the percentage of malicious nodes under multiple-mix-attack to be 0.1, 0.2, 0.3, 0.4 and 0.5, respectively. In this experiment, we set the number of nodes as 27;

the number of injected packets as 2000; the probability of attack as 0.5; and the diversity of network is all-type (use all paths). Figure 7 shows the detection performance, and below are the main observations.

– It is found that DCONST could outperform HD and PDE in all cases. When the percentage of malicious nodes is small, there is a very obvious gap between DCONST and HD, i.e., DCONST could perform the best while HD only achieved the lowest accuracy. This is because when the percentage is small, only limited nodes can be pointed by punishment evidence while most nodes should be pointed by award evidence, making it more accurate for DCONST to identify malicious nodes from the whole network. By contrast, for HD and PDE, a small percentage may result in a high false positive since there are fewer malicious nodes in a path. Again, PDE can achieve better performance than HD by reducing the false rates via perceptron.
– When the percentage of malicious nodes increases, the performance of both PDE and DCONST could decrease gradually. This is because with more malicious nodes, the fewer award evidence can be obtained pointing to benign nodes, which may cause more errors. While DCONST could still outperform the other two schemes under such scenario.

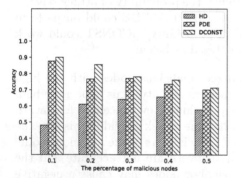 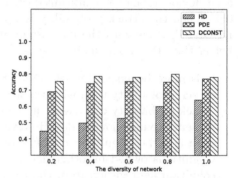

Fig. 7. The impact of the percentage of malicious nodes on detection accuracy

Fig. 8. The impact of the diversity of network on detection accuracy

5.5   Impact of Network Diversity

The diversity presents the type of paths through which packets can be delivered. To explore the detection performance under the multiple-mix-attack, we set the rate of valid paths to be 0.2, 0.4, 0.6, 0.8 and 1, respectively. In this experiment, we consider the number of nodes as 27; the number of injected packets as 2000; the probability of attack as 0.5, and the percentage of malicious nodes as 0.3.

Figure 8 shows that when the network diversity is very low like 0.2, the detection accuracy of HD and PDE could not work well. This is because the detection of malicious nodes depends on analyzing the same nodes in different paths. As an example, assume that a path includes node A and node B. If there is an attack detected, either node A or node B could be malicious. We can only know node B is benign based on the other paths that include node B as well. If node B is determined, then it is easy to determine node A. This is why the detection accuracy could be increased with more valid paths.

As a comparison, the network diversity does not have a significant impact on the accuracy of DCONST. This is because DCONST relies on the strategy that enabling malicious nodes to receive more punishment and providing benign nodes with more award. In such case, even when the network diversity is low, DCONST can work well as long as there is an extra communication channel among benign nodes. For example, suppose there is a path $p = <n_1, n_2, n_3, n_4>$ where n_2 is a malicious node. If n_3 and n_4 have another data communication channel, then they can award each other and improve their trust during the detection. This self-healing feature is a special merit of DCONST.

Discussion. Based on the above results, our proposed DCONST could outperform the similar schemes of HD and PDE in most cases. In particular, the low network diversity and the high attack probability would cause a big impact on HD and PDE, while DCONST could still maintain the detection accuracy. Hence we consider that the performance of DCONST is overall better than HD and PDE, and in practice, PDE and DCONST can complement each other.

6   Conclusion and Future Work

Due to the distributed nature of IoT networks, there is a significant need to design proper security mechanisms to defeat insider attacks. Most existing studies mainly consider a single attack, but we notice that an advanced intruder may perform several attacks simultaneously to make a more harmful impact. In this work, we target on this issue and focus on a multiple-mix attack including three typical sub-attacks: tamper attack, drop attack and replay attack. We develop DCONST that uses both the consensus of nodes and the K-means method to help measure nodes' trust and detect malicious nodes. Our experimental results demonstrate that DCONST can provide a better detection rate by around 10% to 40% as compared with two similar methods of Hard Detection (HD) and Perceptron Detection with Enhancement (PDE).

As our work is an early study in applying consensus, there are some open challenges that can be considered in our future work. First, DCONST is a method based on consensus of distributed nodes and the detection could be affected by each node. Thus, it is hard to provide a sufficient strategy to control the whole detection process. Then, the parameters of DCONST could be further optimized to deal with different network settings (i.e., improving accuracy and stability). Also, our future work can further investigate the impact of attack types and the number of passing packets on the detection performance.

Acknowledgments. This work is supported by the National Natural Science Foundation of China under Grant No. 61402225 and the Science and Technology Funds from National State Grid Ltd. (The Research on Key Technologies of Distributed Parallel Database Storage and Processing based on Big Data).

References

1. Anguraj, D.K., Smys, S.: Trust-based intrusion detection and clustering approach for wireless body area networks. Wireless Pers. Commun. **104**(1), 1–20 (2019)
2. Cho, J.H., Chen, R.: PROVEST: provenance-based trust model for delay tolerant networks. IEEE Trans. Dependable Secure Comput. **15**(1), 151–165 (2016)
3. Cho, J., Swami, A., Chen, I.: A survey on trust management for mobile ad hoc networks. IEEE Commun. Surv. Tutor. **13**(4), 562–583 (2011)
4. Hongning, L., Xianjun, L., Leilei, X.: Analysis of distributed consensus-based spectrum sensing algorithm in cognitive radio networks. In: 2014 Tenth International Conference on Computational Intelligence and Security, pp. 593–597. IEEE (2014)
5. Kaveri, A., Geetha, K., Kaveri, A., Geetha, K.: Enhanced secure data transmission in manet networks using consensus based and trust aware protocol. Int. J. **4**, 14–25 (2018)
6. Komninos, N., Philippou, E., Pitsillides, A.: Survey in smart grid and smart home security: issues, challenges and countermeasures. IEEE Commun. Surv. Tutor. **16**(4), 1933–1954 (2014)
7. Li, W., Meng, W., Kwok, L., Ip, H.H.: Enhancing collaborative intrusion detection networks against insider attacks using supervised intrusion sensitivity-based trust management model. J. Netw. Comput. Appl. **77**, 135–145 (2017)
8. Liu, L., Ma, Z., Meng, W.: Detection of multiple-mix-attack malicious nodes using perceptron-based trust in IoT networks. Future Gener. Comput. Syst. **101**, 865–879 (2019)
9. Liu, X., Abdelhakim, M., Krishnamurthy, P., Tipper, D.: Identifying malicious nodes in multihop IoT networks using diversity and unsupervised learning. In: 2018 IEEE International Conference on Communications (ICC), pp. 1–6. IEEE (2018)
10. Liu, X., Abdelhakim, M., Krishnamurthy, P., Tipper, D.: Identifying malicious nodes in multihop IoT networks using dual link technologies and unsupervised learning. Open J. Internet Things (OJIOT) **4**(1), 109–125 (2018)
11. Mahmoud, R., Yousuf, T., Aloul, F., Zualkernan, I.: Internet of things (IoT) security: current status, challenges and prospective measures. In: 2015 10th International Conference for Internet Technology and Secured Transactions (ICITST), pp. 336–341. IEEE (2015)
12. Mazdin, P., Arbanas, B., Haus, T., Bogdan, S., Petrovic, T., Miskovic, N.: Trust consensus protocol for heterogeneous underwater robotic systems. IFAC-PapersOnLine **49**(23), 341–346 (2016)
13. Meng, W.: Intrusion detection in the era of IoT: building trust via traffic filtering and sampling. Computer **51**(7), 36–43 (2018)
14. Meng, W., Choo, K.R., Furnell, S., Vasilakos, A.V., Probst, C.W.: Towards Bayesian-based trust management for insider attacks in healthcare software-defined networks. IEEE Trans. Netw. Serv. Manag. **15**(2), 761–773 (2018)
15. Meng, W., Li, W., Xiang, Y., Choo, K.K.R.: A Bayesian inference-based detection mechanism to defend medical smartphone networks against insider attacks. J. Netw. Comput. Appl. **78**, 162–169 (2017)

16. Nahiyan, K., Kaiser, S., Ferens, K., McLeod, R.: A multi-agent based cognitive approach to unsupervised feature extraction and classification for network intrusion detection. In: International Conference on Advances on Applied Cognitive Computing (ACC), pp. 25–30 (2017)

17. Rathore, H., Badarla, V., Shit, S.: Consensus-aware sociopsychological trust model for wireless sensor networks. ACM Trans. Sens. Netw. (TOSN) **12**(3), 21 (2016)

18. Sharma, V., Lee, K., Kwon, S., Kim, J., Park, H., Yim, K., Lee, S.Y.: A consensus framework for reliability and mitigation of zero-day attacks in IoT. Secur. Commun. Netw. **2017**, 1–24 (2017). Article ID 4749085

19. Wang, C., Feng, T., Kim, J., Wang, G., Zhang, W.: Catching packet droppers and modifiers in wireless sensor networks. In: 2009 6th Annual IEEE Communications Society Conference on Sensor, Mesh and Ad Hoc Communications and Networks, pp. 1–9. IEEE (2009)

20. Withanage, C., Ashok, R., Yuen, C., Otto, K.: A comparison of the popular home automation technologies. In: 2014 IEEE Innovative Smart Grid Technologies-Asia (ISGT Asia), pp. 600–605. IEEE (2014)

21. Yun, J., Seo, S., Chung, J.: Centralized trust-based secure routing in wireless networks. IEEE Wirel. Commun. Letters **7**(6), 1066–1069 (2018)

22. Zou, J., Ye, B., Qu, L., Wang, Y., Orgun, M.A., Li, L.: A proof-of-trust consensus protocol for enhancing accountability in crowdsourcing services. IEEE Trans. Serv. Comput. **12**, 429–445 (2018)

A Black-Box Attack on Neural Networks Based on Swarm Evolutionary Algorithm

Xiaolei Liu[1(✉)], Teng Hu[1,2], Kangyi Ding[2], Yang Bai[2,3], Weina Niu[2], and Jiazhong Lu[4]

[1] Institute of Computer Application, China Academy of Engineering Physics, Mianyang, China
luxaole@gmail.com, mailhuteng@gmail.com
[2] University of Electronic Science and Technology of China, Chengdu, China
kangyiding@gmail.com, alicepub@163.com, niuweina1@126.com
[3] China Electronic Technology Cyber Security Co., Ltd., Chengdu, China
[4] Chengdu University of Information Technology, Chengdu, China
ljz@cuit.edu.cn

Abstract. Neural networks play an increasingly important role in the field of machine learning and are included in many applications in society. Unfortunately, neural networks suffer from adversarial examples generated to attack them. However, most of the generation approaches either assume that the attacker has full knowledge of the neural network model or are limited by the type of attacked model. In this paper, we propose a new approach that generates a black-box attack to neural networks based on the swarm evolutionary algorithm. Benefiting from the improvements in the technology and theoretical characteristics of evolutionary algorithms, our approach has the advantages of effectiveness, black-box attack, generality, and randomness. Our experimental results show that both the MNIST images and the CIFAR-10 images can be perturbed to successful generate a black-box attack with 100% probability on average. In addition, the proposed attack, which is successful on distilled neural networks with almost 100% probability, is resistant to defensive distillation. The experimental results also indicate that the robustness of the artificial intelligence algorithm is related to the complexity of the model and the data set. In addition, we find that the adversarial examples to some extent reproduce the characteristics of the sample data learned by the neural network model.

Keywords: Adversarial examples · Neural networks · Deep learning · Swarm evolutionary algorithm

1 Introduction

In recent years, neural network models have been widely applied in various fields, especially in the field of image recognition, such as image classification [11,31]

X. Liu—This research was supported by Director of Computer Application Research Institute Foundation (SJ2020A08, SJ2019A05).

J. K. Liu and H. Cui (Eds.): ACISP 2020, LNCS 12248, pp. 268–284, 2020.
https://doi.org/10.1007/978-3-030-55304-3_14

and face recognition [4]. However, users of such model are more concerned about the performance of the model and largely ignore the vulnerability and robustness of the model. In fact, most existing models are easily misled by adversarial examples deliberately designed by attackers and enable the attackers to achieve the purpose of bypassing the detection [20,30]. For example, in an image classification system, by adding the disturbance information to the original image, attackers can achieve the goal of changing image classification results with high probability [21]. The generated adversarial examples can even be classified with an arbitrary label according to the purpose of an attacker, making this type of attack a tremendous threat to the image classification system [6]. More seriously, printing the generated images of adversarial examples and then photographing them with a camera, the captured images are still misclassified, confirming the presence of adversarial examples in the real world [15]. These vulnerability problems make people raise the question on whether neural networks can be applied to security-critical areas.

Several papers have studied related security issues [16,17,19]. Unfortunately, in most previous generation approaches of adversarial examples, when ϵ is fixed, the similarity of the sample is fixed: in the algorithm's calculation, it won' change dynamically. This may cause the image to be disturbed so much that it can be visually distinguishable [22]. Moreover, the existing approaches mainly use gradient information to transform the original samples into the required adversarial examples. If the parameters of the model are unknown, the attackers cannot generate effective adversarial examples [7,12]. Others also proposed some black-box attack approaches [24,25]. However, Papernot [25] takes the transferability assumption. If transferability of the model to be attacked is reduced, the effectiveness of the attack will be reduced. LSA [24] cannot simply modify the required distance metrics, such as L_0, L_2, L_{max}. In most cases, it is only guaranteed that the disturbance is successful at Lmax, but not guaranteed that the disturbance can be kept minimum under other distance functions.

In this paper, we propose a new approach that generates a *black-box attack* to deep neural networks. Our approach is named BANA, denoting A (B)lack-box (A)ttack on (N)eural Networks Based on Swarm Evolutionary (A)lgorithm. Compared with the previous approaches [2,8,26,30], our approach has the following main advantages:

Effectiveness. The adversarial examples generated by our approach can misclassify the neural networks with 100% probability both on non-targeted attacks and targeted attacks. The L_2 distance between adversarial examples and original images is less than 10 on average, indicating that images can be disturbed with so small changes that are not to be undetectable. If we continue to increase the number of iterations of our proposed algorithm, we expect to achieve even better results.

Black-Box Attack. adversarial examples can be generated without the knowledge of the internal parameters of the target network, such as gradients and structures. Existing attacks such as Carlini and Wagner's attacks [2] usually require such information.

Generality. Our proposed attack is a general attack to neural networks. For the attack, we can generate effective adversarial examples of DNNs, CNNs, etc. We have even tested our proposed attack in a wider range of machine learning algorithms and it still misleads the model with 100% probability.

Randomness. Benefiting from the characteristics of evolutionary algorithms, the adversarial examples generated each time are different for the same input image, so they are able to resist defensive mechanisms such as defensive distillation.

In particular, our proposed attack is based on the swarm evolutionary algorithm [1]. The swarm evolutionary algorithm is a population-based optimization algorithm for solving complex multi-modal optimization problems. It can transform the optimization problems into the individual fitness function and has a mechanism to gradually improve individual fitness. Evolutionary algorithms do not require the use of gradient information for optimization and do not require that the objective function be differentiable or deterministic. Different from another approach also based on an evolutionary algorithm [29], our approach focuses on the optimization of results rather than the number of disturbed pixels. Therefore, we have completely different optimization function and iterative processes from the one pixel attack. Without knowing the parameters of the model, our proposed approach uses the original sample as the input to apply to generate an adversarial example of the specific label. The used information is only the probability of the various labels produced by the model.

Our attack also addresses technical challenges when applying the swarm evolutionary algorithm to generate the adversarial examples. The improvements made in our approach include the optimization of calculation results and convergence speed (see more details in Sect. 3).

The rest of the paper is organized as follows. Section 2 introduces the related work of adversarial examples. Section 3 presents SEAA (Swarm Evolutionary Algorithm For Black-box Attacks to Deep Neural Networks. Section 4 presents and discusses our experimental results. Section 5 concludes.

2   Related Work

The adversarial examples of deep neural networks have drawn the attention of many researchers in recent years. [30] used a constrained L-BFGS algorithm to generate adversarial examples. L-BFGS requires that the gradient of the model can be solved, limiting the diversity of the model and the objective function, and making this approach computationally expensive to generate adversarial examples. [8] proposed the fast gradient sign method (FGSM). However, this approach is designed without considering the similarity of the adversarial examples: the similarity of the generated adversarial samples may be low. The consequence is that the generated adversarial samples may be detected by defensive approaches or directly visually distinguished. An adversarial example attack named the Jacobian-based Saliency Map Attack (JSMA) was proposed by [26]. JSMA also requires the gradient of the model to be solved, and the approach is limited to the L_0 distance, and cannot be generated using other distance algorithms [2]. These approaches all assume that the attackers have full access to the parameters of the model. [23] proposed a non-targeted attack approach named Deepfool. This approach assumes that the neural network is linear and makes a contribution to the generation of adversarial examples, while actually neural networks may be not linear. Besides, this approach also does not apply to nonneural network model. Some previous research focused on generating adversarial examples to the malware detection models [3,18,32]. These adversarial examples also successfully disrupted the model's discriminant results, showing that the common models of machine learning are vulnerable to attacks.

Some recent research aimed to defend against the attack of adversarial examples and proposed approaches such as defensive distillatione [5,10,27]. However, experiment results show that these approaches do not perform well in particular situations due to not being able to defend against adversarial examples of high quality [9].

3 Methodology

3.1 Problem Description

The generation of adversarial examples can be considered as a constrained optimization problem. We use L_p distance (which is L_p norm) to describe the similarity between the original images and the adversarial images. Let f be the m-class classifier that receives n-dimensional inputs and gives m-dimensional outputs. Different from L-BFGS [30], FGS [8], JSMA [26], Deepfool [23] and Carlini and Wagner's attack [2], our approach is a black-box attack without using the gradient information. This optimization problem is formalized as follows:

$$F = D(x, x') + M \times loss(x') \tag{1}$$

where for a non-targeted attack (whose purpose is to mislead the classifier to classify the adversarial examples as any of the error categories), $loss(x')$ is defined as

$$loss(x') = max([f(x')]_r - max([f(x')]_{i \neq r}), 0) \tag{2}$$

and for a targeted attack (whose purpose is to mislead the classifier to classify the adversarial examples as a specified category), $loss(x')$ is defined as

$$loss(x') = max(max([f(x')]_{i \neq t}) - [f(x')]_t, 0) \tag{3}$$

and $x = (x_1, ..., x_n)$ is the original image, $x' = (x'_1, ..., x'_n)$ is the adversarial example to be produced and $D(x, x')$ is the L_p distance. M is a positive number much larger than $D(x, x')$, r is the real label, and t is the target label. The output of $[f(x)]_r$ is the probability that the sample x is recognized as the label r and the output of $[f(x)]_{i \neq r}$ is the probability set that the sample x is separately recognized as other labels. Since $loss(x') \geq 0$, we discuss the case of $loss(x') > 0$ and $loss(x') = 0$ for the targeted attacks, respectively. The non-targeted attacks are the same.

(1) When $loss(x') > 0$, the $[f(x')]_t$ is not the maximum in Eq. 3, indicating that the adversarial example x' is not classified as the targeted label at this time. Since M is much larger than $D(x, x')$, the objective function in Eq. 1 is approximately equal to the latter half. In this case, it is equivalent to optimizing x' to minimize Q, i.e., increasing the probability that the classifier identifies the sample x' as being a class t.

$$minimize \; loss(x') \qquad (4)$$

(2) When $loss(x) = 0$, the adversarial example has been classified as the target label at this time. In this case, it is equivalent to optimizing x' to minimize the value of $D(x, x')$, i.e., to improve the similarity between the adversarial example and the original sample as much as possible.

$$minimize \; D(x, x') \qquad (5)$$

Through the preceding objective function, the population is actually divided into two sections, as shown in Fig. 1. The whole optimization process can be divided into three steps.

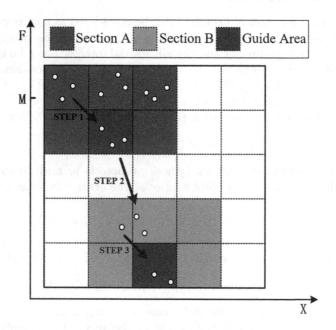

Fig. 1. Individuals distribution diagram

Step 1. At this time the adversarial example cannot successfully mislead the classifier. Individuals at the top of section A gradually approach the bottom through crossover and mutation operators.

Step 2. The individuals move from Section A to Section B, indicating that $loss(x') = 0$, i.e., the adversarial examples generated at this time can successfully mislead the classifier.

Step 3. Individuals at the top of Section B gradually approach the bottom, indicating the improvement of the similarity between the adversarial image and the original image.

Eventually, the bottom individual of Section B becomes the optimal individual in the population, and the information that it carries is the adversarial example being sought out.

3.2 Our BANA Approach

As the generation of adversarial examples has been considered as an optimization problem formalized as Eq. 1, we solve this optimization problem by the swarm evolution algorithm. In this algorithm, fitness value is the result of F, population is a collection of x' and many individuals make up the population. By constantly simulating the process of biological evolution, the adaptive individuals which have small fitness value in the population are selected to form the subpopulation, and then the subpopulation is repeated for similar evolutionary processes until the optimal solution to the problem is found or the algorithm reaches the maximum number of iterations. After the iterations, the optimal individual obtained is the adversarial example x'. As a widely applied swarm evolutionary algorithm, such genetic algorithm is flexible in coding, solving fitness, selection, crossover, and mutation. Therefore, in the algorithm design and simulation experiments, we use the following improved genetic algorithm as an example to demonstrate the effectiveness of our BANA approach. The advantages of this approach are not limited to the genetic algorithm. We leave as the future work the investigation of the effects of different types of swarm evolutionary algorithms on our approach.

Algorithm Workflow. The whole algorithm workflow is shown in Fig. 2. Classifiers can be logistic regression, deep neural networks, and other classification models. We do not need to know the model parameters and just set the input and output interfaces. Each individual is transformed into an adversarial example and then sent to the classifier to get the classification result. After that, the individual fitness value is obtained through solving the objective function. The individuals in the population are optimized by the genetic algorithm to solve the feasible solution of the objective function (i.e., the adversarial example of the image).

The workflow of our BANA approach is as follows:

Step 1. Population Initialization. One gene corresponds to one pixel, and for the grayscale images of (28, 28), there are a total of 784 genes, and there are $32 \times 32 \times 3 = 3072$ genes for the color image of (32, 32).

Step 2. Calculate the Fitness Value. Calculate the value of the fitness function according to the approach described in Sect. 3.1 and take this value as the fitness

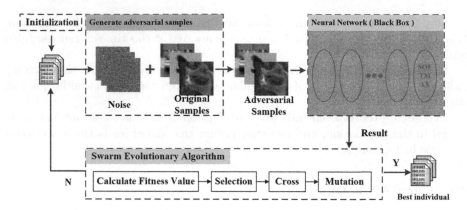

Fig. 2. Algorithm workflow of our BANA approach

of the individual. Since this problem is a minimization problem, the smaller the value, the better the individual's fitness. After that, the best individual with the minimum fitness value in the current population is saved as the optimal solution.

Step 3. Select Operation. According to the fitness of individuals in the population, through the tournament algorithm, individuals with higher fitness are selected from the current population.

Step 4. Cross Operation. Common crossover operators include single-point crossover, multi-point crossover, and uniform crossover. Our algorithm uses uniform crossover. That is, for two random individuals, each gene crosses each independently according to the probability p. Due to the large number of genes that each individual carries, uniform crossover allows for a greater probability of generating new combinations of genes and is expected to combine more beneficial genes to improve the searching ability of genetic algorithms.

Step 5. Mutation Operation. In order to speed up the search ability of genetic algorithms, combining with the characteristics of the problem to be solved, the operator adopts a self-defined Gaussian mutation algorithm. In the process of mutation, Gaussian noise $gauss(m, s)$ is randomly added to the individual (shown in Eq. 6 below), where m is the mean of Gaussian noise and s is the standard deviation of Gaussian noise:

$$x_{mutation} = x_{origin} \pm gauss(m, s) \tag{6}$$

The reason for adopting this mutation operation is that the resulting adversarial example inevitably has a high degree of similarity with the input sample, and a feasible solution to the problem to be solved must also be in the vicinity. This technique can effectively reduce the number of iterations required to solve the problem.

Step 6. Terminate the Judgment. The algorithm terminates if the exit condition is satisfied, and otherwise returns to Step 2.

Improvements. There are two major technical improvements made in our approach.

Improvements of Result. In order to improve the optimization effect of BANA, we adopt a new initialization technique. Considering the problem to be solved requires the highest possible degree of similarity, this technique does not use random numbers while using the numerical values related to the original pixel values. Let x be the original image, and x' be the initialized adversarial image. Then $x' = x + \epsilon$, where ϵ is a very small value.

Improvements of Speed. In order to speed up the convergence of BANA, on one hand, we constrain the variation step of each iteration in the mutation stage. On the other hand, we try to keep the point that has the pixel value of 0, because it is more likely that such a point is at the background of the picture. These improvements help the algorithm converge faster to the optimal solution.

4   Experiments

The datasets used in this paper include MNIST [14], CIFAR-10 [13] and ImageNet [28]. 80% of the data are used as a training set and the remaining 20% as a test set. In order to assess the effectiveness of the adversarial examples, we attack a number of different classifier models. The used classifiers include logistic regression (LR), fully connected deep neural network (DNN), and convolutional neural network (CNN). We evaluate our BANA approach by generating adversarial examples from the MNIST and CIFAR10 test sets.

The parameters used by BANA are shown in Table 1. The experimental results show that different parameters affect the convergence rate of BANA. However, with the increase of the iterations, the results would eventually be close. The parameters listed in Table 1 are our empirical values.

Table 1. The parameters of BANA

Database	MNIST	CIFAR-10	ImageNet
Population	100	200	300
Genes number	$28 \times 28 \times 1 = 784$	$32 \times 32 \times 3 = 3072$	$200 \times 200 \times 3 = 120000$
Cross probability	0.5	0.5	0.5
Mutation probability	0/05	0/05	0/05
Iterations	200	200	100
Gaussian mean	0	0	0
Gaussian variance	30	20	40

4.1   Adversarial Example Generation on MNIST

In the first experiment, the used dataset is MNIST. The used classification models are LR, DNN, and CNN. We train each of these models separately and then

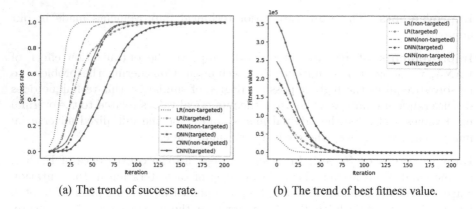

(a) The trend of success rate.   (b) The trend of best fitness value.

Fig. 3. The results of targeted attacks and non-targeted attacks for each undistilled model on MNIST.

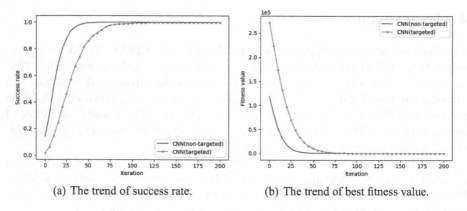

(a) The trend of success rate.   (b) The trend of best fitness value.

Fig. 4. The results of targeted attacks and non-targeted attacks for each undistilled model on CIFAR-10.

test the accuracy of each model on the test set. Logistic Regression (LR), DNN, and CNN achieve the accuracy of 92.46%, 98.49%, and 99.40% respectively. In the generation of adversarial examples, we set the number of iterations of the genetic algorithm is 200, and the sample with the smallest objective function value generated in each iteration is selected as the optimal sample. For a targeted attack, we select first 100 samples initially correctly classified from the test set to attack. Each of the samples generates adversarial examples from 9 different target labels, resulting in 100 * 9 = 900 corresponding target adversarial examples. For non-targeted attacks, we select the first 900 samples initially correctly classified from the test set to attack. Each sample generates a corresponding adversarial example, resulting in 900 non-target adversarial examples.

The results are shown in Table 2 and Fig. 3. For each model, our attacks find adversarial examples with less than 10 in the L_2 distance, and succeed with

Table 2. Comparison of our attacks with previous work for a number of MNIST models.

MNIST		Models							
		LR		DNN		CNN		CNN**	
		UD(Undistilled)	D(Distilled*)	UD	D*	UD	D*	UD	D*
Non-targeted attack	Mean	0.82	–	2.48	2.91	3.90	3.99	1.76	2.20
	SD	0.62	–	1.67	2.34	2.46	2.70	–	–
	Prob	100%	–	100%	99.89%	100%	100%	100%	100%
Targeted attack	Mean	3.65	–	5.04	7.93	7.60	8.33	–	–
	SD	3.80	–	2.88	5.95	4.12	5.34	–	–
	Prob	100%	–	100%	99.78%	100%	100%	–	–

(* The details of distilled model are shown in Sect. 4.3. There is no distilled LR model.
*** This model is attacked by the approach proposed by Carlini and Wagner [2].)

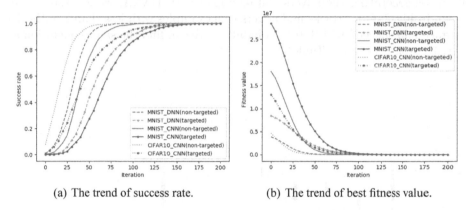

(a) The trend of success rate.   (b) The trend of best fitness value.

Fig. 5. The results of targeted attacks and non-targeted attacks for each distilled model on MNIST and CIFAR-10. Compare to Fig. 3 and Fig. 4 for undistilled models.

100% probability. Compared with the results generated by Carlini and Wagner's attack [2], our perturbations are slightly larger than their results. However, both of our attacks succeed with 100% probability and our BANA is a black-box attack. Besides, there is no visual difference between the adversarial examples. Figure 3(a) and Fig. 3(b) show that as the model becomes more complex, the number of iterations required to produce an effective adversarial example increases. The distribution of the 900 best fitness values after 200 iterations is shown in Fig. 6(a). The figure indicates that the more complex the model, the larger the mean and standard deviation. The reason is that simple classification models do not have good decision boundaries. For the same classification model, non-targeted attacks require fewer iterations than targeted attacks, resulting in about 2× lower distortion and stability. Such result indicates that for the attacker the targeted adversarial example is generated at a higher cost. However, with the increasing of iterations, all the best fitness values tend to be 0. The difficulty caused by the targeted attack can be overcome by increasing the number of iterations. Overall, BANA is able to generate effective adversarial examples for LR, DNN, and CNN on MNIST.

By comparing the trend of success rate and best fitness values for targeted attack and non-targeted attack, respectively, it can be seen that the robustness of the classification model against adversarial examples is related to the complexity of the model, and the more complex the model, the better the robustness of the corresponding classification model.

4.2   Adversarial Example Generation on CIFAR-10 and ImageNet

In the second experiment, the used dataset is CIFAR-10. Our purpose is to find whether BANA is able to generate effective adversarial examples on CIFAR-10. Considering the conclusion in Sect. 4.1, we choose CNN as the classification model to be attacked. Our CNN achieves an accuracy of 77.82% on CIFAR-10. After generating the adversarial examples with BANA, we get the results shown in Fig. 3. Our attacks find adversarial examples with less than 2 in the L_2 distance and succeed with 100% probability. We can find the same conclusion as Sect. 4.1 from Fig. 4 and Table 3.

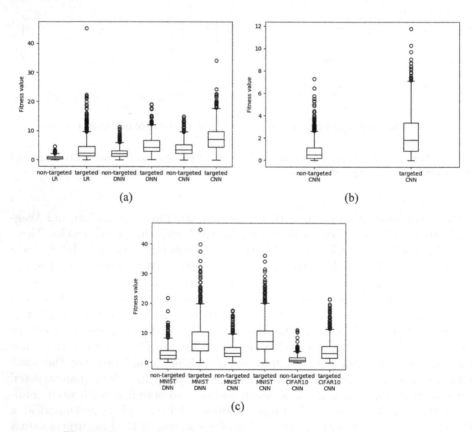

Fig. 6. The distribution of best fitness in Fig. 3, Fig. 4 and Fig. 5.

Figure 7 shows a case study of our BANA on ImageNet. As shown in Fig. 7, there is no visual difference between the original images and the perturbed images. Figure 7 shows that our attack is able to generate adversarial examples with small visually invisible perturbations even on complex datasat.

More importantly, by comparing the experimental results for CNN on MNIST and CIFAR, it can be seen that the average best fitness value and the standard deviation on CIFAR are smaller than them on MNIST, indicating that the adversarial examples generated on CIFAR dataset are more likely to be misleading and more similar to the original data. We find that the robustness of the classification model against adversarial examples is not only related to the complexity of the model but also to the trained data set; however, not the more complex the data set, the better the robustness of the generated classification model.

4.3 Defensive Distillation

We train the distilled DNN and CNN, using *softmax* at temperature $T = 10$. The experimental results are shown in Tables 2 and 3. The observation is that the average fitness value and standard deviation of undistilled models are smaller than those of distilled model both on targeted attacks and non-targeted attacks. However, the attack success rate of the adversarial examples produced by BABA on the distilled model is still 100% or close to 100%. Our attack is able to break defensive distillation. The reason may be related to the randomness of the swarm evolutionary algorithm. Even with the same model and data, BANA produces a different adversarial example each time, making it effective against defensive distillation.

Table 3. Comparison of our attacks with previous work for a number of CIFAR models.

Models		CIFAR-10					
		Non-targeted attack			Targeted attack		
		Mean	SD	Prob	Mean	SD	Prob
CNN	Undistilled model	0.82	0.93	100%	2.33	1.89	100%
	Distilled model*	1.26	1.29	100%	4.18	3.57	99.89%
CNN**	Undistilled model	0.33	–	100%	–	–	–
	Distilled model*	0.60	–	100%	–	–	–

(* The details of distilled model are shown in Sect. 4.3.
*** This model is attacked by the approach proposed by Carlini and Wagner [2].)

Fig. 7. A case study of our BANA on ImageNet. The top row shows the original images and the bottom row shows the perturbed images attacked by our approach.

5   Conclusions

In this paper, we have presented a new approach that generates a black-box attack to neural networks based on the swarm evolutionary algorithm. Our experimental results show that our approach generates high-quality adversarial examples for LR, DNN, and CNN, and our approach is resistant to defensive distillation. Finally, our results indicate that the robustness of the artificial intelligence algorithm is related to the complexity of the model and the complexity of the data set. Our future work includes designing an effective defense approach against our proposed attack.

Appendix

Here we give some case studies of our experiment results to let you have a more intuitive visual experience, which are shown from Fig. 8, 9, 10, and 11. For reproducibility, all of these adversarial examples are generated by our method with the parameters shown in Table 1.

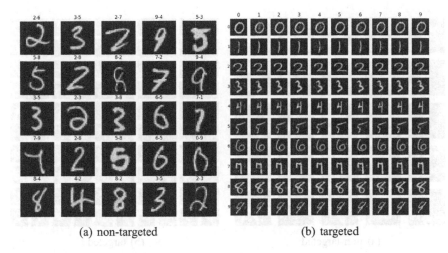

(a) non-targeted   (b) targeted

Fig. 8. A case study of targeted attacks and non-targeted attacks for LR model on MNIST.

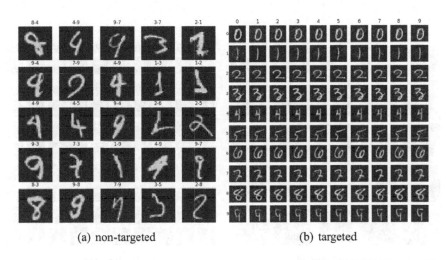

(a) non-targeted   (b) targeted

Fig. 9. A case study of targeted attacks and non-targeted attacks for DNN model on MNIST.

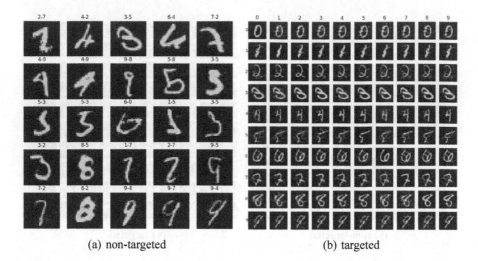

(a) non-targeted   (b) targeted

Fig. 10. A case study of targeted attacks and non-targeted attacks for CNN model on MNIST.

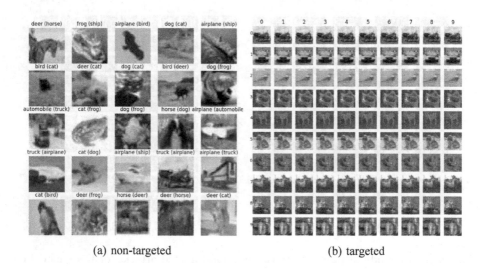

(a) non-targeted   (b) targeted

Fig. 11. A case study of targeted attacks and non-targeted attacks for CNN model on CIFAR-10.

References

1. Bansal, J.C., Singh, P.K., Pal, N.R. (eds.): Evolutionary and Swarm Intelligence Algorithms. SCI, vol. 779. Springer, Cham (2019). https://doi.org/10.1007/978-3-319-91341-4
2. Carlini, N., Wagner, D.: Towards evaluating the robustness of neural networks. In: 2017 IEEE Symposium on Security and Privacy (SP), pp. 39–57 (2017)

3. Demontis, A., et al.: Yes, machine learning can be more secure! a case study on android malware detection. IEEE Trans. Dependable Secure Comput. **16**, 711–724 (2017)
4. Deng, J., Guo, J., Xue, N., Zafeiriou, S.: ArcFace: additive angular margin loss for deep face recognition. In: Proceedings of the IEEE Conference on Computer Vision and Pattern Recognition, pp. 4690–4699 (2019)
5. Dong, Y., Pang, T., Su, H., Zhu, J.: Evading defenses to transferable adversarial examples by translation-invariant attacks. In: Proceedings of the IEEE Conference on Computer Vision and Pattern Recognition, pp. 4312–4321 (2019)
6. Eykholt, K., et al.: Robust physical-world attacks on deep learning visual classification. In: Proceedings of the IEEE Conference on Computer Vision and Pattern Recognition, pp. 1625–1634 (2018)
7. Goodfellow, I., et al.: Generative adversarial nets. In: Advances in Neural Information Processing Systems, pp. 2672–2680 (2014)
8. Goodfellow, I.J., Shlens, J., Szegedy, C.: Explaining and harnessing adversarial examples (2014). arXiv preprint arXiv:1412.6572
9. He, W., Wei, J., Chen, X., Carlini, N., Song, D.: Adversarial example defense: ensembles of weak defenses are not strong. In: 11th USENIX Workshop on Offensive Technologies WOOT 2017 (2017)
10. Hendrycks, D., Gimpel, K.: Early methods for detecting adversarial images. arXiv preprint arXiv:1608.00530 (2016)
11. Hossain, M.Z., Sohel, F., Shiratuddin, M.F., Laga, H.: A comprehensive survey of deep learning for image captioning. ACM Comput. Surv. (CSUR) **51**(6), 1–36 (2019)
12. Hu, W., Tan, Y.: Generating adversarial malware examples for black-box attacks based on GAN. arXiv preprint arXiv:1702.05983 (2017)
13. Krizhevsky, A., Hinton, G.: Learning multiple layers of features from tiny images. Technical report (2009)
14. LeCun, Y., Bottou, L., Bengio, Y., Haffner, P.: Gradient-based learning applied to document recognition. Proc. IEEE **86**(11), 2278–2324 (1998)
15. Lecuyer, M., Atlidakis, V., Geambasu, R., Hsu, D., Jana, S.: Certified robustness to adversarial examples with differential privacy. In: 2019 IEEE Symposium on Security and Privacy (SP), pp. 656–672. IEEE (2019)
16. Li, T., Ruan, D., Geert, W., Song, J., Xu, Y.: A rough sets based characteristic relation approach for dynamic attribute generalization in data mining. Knowl. Based Syst. **20**(5), 485–494 (2007)
17. Liu, W., Luo, Z., Li, S.: Improving deep ensemble vehicle classification by using selected adversarial samples. Knowl. Based Syst. **160**, 167–175 (2018)
18. Liu, X., Du, X., Zhang, X., Zhu, Q., Wang, H., Guizani, M.: Adversarial samples on android malware detection systems for IoT systems. Sensors **19**(4), 974 (2019)
19. Liu, X., et al.: TLTD: a testing framework for learning-based IoT traffic detection systems. Sensors **18**(8), 2630 (2018)
20. Liu, X., Zhang, X., Wan, K., Zhu, Q., Ding, Y.: Towards weighted-sampling audio adversarial example attack. arXiv preprint arXiv:1901.10300 (2019)
21. Moosavi-Dezfooli, S.M., Fawzi, A., Fawzi, O., Frossard, P.: Universal adversarial perturbations. arXiv preprint (2017)
22. Moosavi-Dezfooli, S.M., Fawzi, A., Fawzi, O., Frossard, P., Soatto, S.: Analysis of universal adversarial perturbations. arXiv preprint arXiv:1705.09554 (2017)
23. Moosavi-Dezfooli, S.M., Fawzi, A., Frossard, P.: Deepfool: a simple and accurate method to fool deep neural networks. In: Proceedings of the IEEE Conference on Computer Vision and Pattern Recognition, pp. 2574–2582 (2016)

24. Narodytska, N., Kasiviswanathan, S.P.: Simple black-box adversarial attacks on deep neural networks. In: CVPR Workshops, pp. 1310–1318 (2017)
25. Papernot, N., et al.: Practical black-box attacks against machine learning. In: Proceedings of the 2017 ACM on Asia Conference on Computer and Communications Security, pp. 506–519 (2017)
26. Papernot, N., et al.: The limitations of deep learning in adversarial settings. In: IEEE European Symposium on Security and Privacy (EuroS&P) 2016, pp. 372–387 (2016)
27. Papernot, N., McDaniel, P., Wu, X., Jha, S., Swami, A.: Distillation as a defense to adversarial perturbations against deep neural networks. In: 2016 IEEE Symposium on Security and Privacy (SP), pp. 582–597 (2016)
28. Russakovsky, O., et al.: Imagenet large scale visual recognition challenge. Int. J. Comput. Vis. **115**(3), 211–252 (2015)
29. Su, J., Vargas, D.V., Sakurai, K.: One pixel attack for fooling deep neural networks. IEEE Trans. Evol. Comput. **23**(5), 828–841 (2019)
30. Szegedy, C., et al.: Intriguing properties of neural networks. arXiv preprint arXiv:1312.6199 (2013)
31. de Vos, B.D., et al.: A deep learning framework for unsupervised affine and deformable image registration. Med. Image Anal. **52**, 128–143 (2019)
32. Yang, W., Kong, D., Xie, T., Gunter, C.A.: Malware detection in adversarial settings: exploiting feature evolutions and confusions in android apps. In: Proceedings of the 33rd Annual Computer Security Applications Conference, pp. 288–302 (2017)

A Blockchain-Based Resource Supervision Scheme for Edge Devices Under Cloud-Fog-End Computing Models

Tongchen Wang[1,2], Jianwei Liu[1], Dawei Li[1(✉)], and Qianhong Wu[1]

[1] School of Cyber Science and Technology, Beihang University, Beijing, China
lidawei@buaa.edu.cn
[2] School of Electronic and Information Engineering, Beihang University, Beijing, China

Abstract. As a combination of cloud computing and edge computing, cloud-fog-end computing models are gradually replacing traditional centralized cloud computing models due to their high controllability and low latency. However, this model has certain shortcomings in terms of resource awareness of edge devices. Two problems are the most prominent. One is that it is difficult to measure the resources of the edge device fairly, and the other is that it is challenging to monitor the resource status in real-time. This circumstance significantly limits the future application of this model. In this paper, we propose a blockchain-based resource supervision scheme for edge devices under the framework of the cloud-fog-end computing model. The scheme uses the data openness and verifiability of the public chain to measure and record the resource status of the edge devices through the smart contract. Besides, it uses the high controllability and designability of the consortium chain to supervise the resource status of the edge devices in the fog computing network in real-time. In addition, based on the structure of the scheme, we demonstrate the feasibility and security from multiple perspectives and carry out simulation experiments in the model of TensorFlow-federated. Experimental results show that the scheme can effectively monitor the resources of edge devices in real-time, and this scheme can be used to implement federated machine learning in fog computing networks.

Keywords: Blockchain · Edge computing · Resource supervision

1 Introduction

With the rapid development of the Internet of Things (IoT) technology and the popularization of 4G/5G wireless network technology, the era of the Internet of Everything has arrived. With the emergence of business models such as Internet of Vehicles, smart homes, and smart cities, the amount of data generated by various types of equipment has shown a blowout growth. Faced with such a massive amount of data, the difficulties faced by cloud computing in terms of data latency and network bandwidth have become increasingly severe [1]. Cloud servers are increasingly challenging to meet the needs of certain delay-sensitive services in the Internet of Things, such as real-time, mobility, and

© Springer Nature Switzerland AG 2020
J. K. Liu and H. Cui (Eds.): ACISP 2020, LNCS 12248, pp. 285–305, 2020.
https://doi.org/10.1007/978-3-030-55304-3_15

location awareness [2]. As an emerging technology, edge computing [3] has the characteristics of high real-time performance and light network dependence. It can effectively alleviate the difficulties faced by cloud computing through the computing resources of edge devices [4, 5] deployed at the edge of the network. As a combination of cloud computing and edge computing, cloud-fog-end computing models are gradually replacing traditional centralized cloud computing models due to their high controllability and low latency. Therefore, more and more scholars have begun to focus on how to make full use of the computing resources owned by edge devices under this model, to efficiently support various services and application businesses based on the Internet of Everything.

However, with the further development of edge computing technology in the field of the IoT, researchers have found that the shortcomings of edge computing technology in resource perception limits its future application prospects. Different from traditional cloud computing resource supervision, the resource supervisor in edge computing cannot directly obtain the software and hardware information of the resource provider to complete the resource estimation and prediction. They often need additional communications to realize the acquisition of resource data. In the open IoT, different edge devices often come from different operators, with different device models and computing resources, and lack of trust between each other. It is difficult for the traditional resource supervision scheme to break the trust barrier between the cloud server and the edge device group and realize the effective perception of computing resources. Therefore, there is an urgent need for a publicly verifiable technology to publicly measure and store the computing resources of edge devices and supervise the resources of edge devices in real-time.

Blockchain [6], as a decentralized distributed ledger technology, has been widely used in various industries (such as Software-Defined Networking [7], Product traceability, Intrusion Detection [8]) in recent years. The public blockchain can effectively solve the trust problem among multiple nodes in the open network through the consistency protocol. In 2014, Ethereum [9] appeared, enabling people to purposefully operate the data on the blockchain through a program called smart contract, and selectively display some processed data publicly. In addition, the consortium chain, as a form of blockchain, is capable of deciding the degree of openness to the public according to the application scenarios. To sum up, both the blockchain technology and the IoT technology are based on the technology of distributed resource management. The combination of the two seems to be a natural fit.

In this paper, we propose a blockchain-based resource supervision scheme for edge devices in the cloud-fog-end computing model. Any edge device that tries to provide its computing resources needs to accept public verification of its computing capabilities on Ethereum and face real-time monitoring of computing resources in the consortium chain. Some previous studies have shown that it is feasible and inexpensive to use smart contracts [10] to process data from edge devices. Therefore, in this solution, we design and develop a smart contract on Ethereum using the Solidity language to verify the computing capabilities of edge computing devices. The miners on the public chain run smart contracts to publicly verify and document the computing power provided by edge devices. In the fog computing network, edge devices receive computing tasks from the cloud server. As a tool for measuring the completion of these tasks, a token, called ResourceCoin (RCoin), indirectly reflects the resource status of edge devices in the prior period. Any user of edge resources, including cloud servers, can sense the resource status of edge devices in real-time through the RCoin value. Finally, based on the structure of the scheme, we carry out simulation experiments in the model of TensorFlow-federated. Experimental results show that the scheme can effectively monitor the resources of edge devices in the application scenario of federated machine learning. It makes full use of the data openness and public verifiability of the public chain and the high controllability of the consortium chain.

2 Related Work

In this section, we analyze the existing resource monitoring strategy and IoT-Blockchain architecture.

2.1 Resource Monitoring

Pan [11] proposed a resource management strategy based on blockchain. In this strategy, once an IoT device requires additional resources, it can initiate a request to edge servers through smart contracts deployed on the blockchain. The smart contract then verifies that the resource status of the edge server meets the requirements. Once verified, the smart contract containing the resource allocation algorithm will provide the required resources to the IoT device.

Based on the combination of the IoT and the blockchain, Uddin et al. [12] proposed a framework with a miner selection consensus protocol for smart home devices. In this framework, the Smart Gateway will select a node with the best resource status to become a miner through the Miner Selection Algorithm, which take into account three metrics of the nodes: Network Latency (NL), Energy Consumption (EC), and Availability of all miners (AV). This protocol focuses on the design of resource verification algorithms without considering the public verifiability and real-time nature of the resources.

Park [13] proposed a resource monitoring scheme based on the Markov chain model, which analyzes and predicts the resource status of mobile devices. The cloud system can model the past resource conditions of the mobile device and effectively predict the future status of the resource, making it possible to resist the instability caused by the volatility of the mobile device. Although it achieves near real-time resource monitoring by the Markov chain model, the resource status still cannot be publicly verified by a third party because data is transmitted point-to-point between the cloud system and the mobile device and is finally stored in the cloud.

Hikvision's AI Cloud architecture enables the monitoring of resources by embedding resource monitoring modules into edge devices. The edge device sends its resource status to the cloud periodically. The scheme sets the time interval of adjacent messages on a smaller level, which can be evaluated as close to real-time. Nowadays, this resource supervision method has been well applied in various architectures such as the Internet of Vehicles (IoV) and Smart City. However, the debate on the authenticity of data between consumers and service providers still exist.

Jalali [14] proposes a new platform: DEFT, which automatically senses the idle resources of cloud servers or surrounding edge devices, and then assigns tasks to the right place through a machine learning-based task allocation algorithm. In this scenario, the edge device node periodically broadcasts its available resources to surrounding nodes and the cloud. Moreover, once the node's resource changes exceed the specified range, the node must repeatedly broadcast its device status to surrounding nodes (including task initiators and handlers) to ensure that its changes can be detected and recorded by the system. This platform enables public validation of resource monitoring and achieves near real-time by setting short-interval of messages.

In this paper, we propose a blockchain-based resource supervision scheme. Relying on the blockchain's public ledger, it can realize the real-time monitoring of resources while realizing the public verification of resources.

2.2 IoT-Blockchain Framework

Uddin et al. [12] proposed a smart home supervision system that deploys blockchain on Smart Gateways. In this system, the gateway collects data from IoT devices. It transmits the data block to the miner, who is elected by the Smart Gateways with performing an efficient selective Miner consensus protocol. This architecture separates data producers from data processors, fully considering the data processing capabilities of IoT devices. However, due to the high energy consumption PoW protocol used in the solution, a new blockchain network must be applied for data verification, thus creating unnecessary data communication overhead.

Ali [15] first optimized the blockchain to make it suitable for smart homes. The optimization scheme is based on a three-tier structure, including cloud storage, overlay, and smart home. In this structure, the IoT device transmits data to the miner in the form of multiple transactions according to the purpose, and the miner stores the data in the storage in the form of a blockchain. Although this solution effectively solves the problem that IoT devices are not compatible with PoW, the processing and storage of data by a single node bring about the possibility of DoS attacks.

Stanciu [16] advanced a Blockchain-based distributed control system for Edge Computing. The consortium chain Fabric was utilized to achieve cloud edge collaboration in the system, which inspires us to use the consortium chain on the IoT.

Huh [17] proposed using Ethereum as a computing platform for managing IoT devices, enabling data storage for smartphones and meters through smart contracts. The most significant contribution of this paper is the realization of the scheme, which makes the feasibility of deploying Ethereum in IoT equipment verified.

Pan [11] proposed and implemented an IoT-edge framework based on Ethereum: Edgechain, which aims to solve the resource management problem of IoT devices in edge computing. In the scenario, the internal credit-based token is used to measure the difficulty of IoT devices to obtain edge server resources. IoT devices with a higher token get more resources in the edge server more quickly. Also, depending on the capabilities of IoT devices, the scenario separates devices into two categories: legacy and nonlegacy. A legacy device can participate in the Edgechain network by executing a proxy on a nonlegacy device, which solves the problem that resource-constrained devices are incapable of deploying a blockchain.

Xiong [18] first introduced a new concept of edge computing for mobile blockchain. Based on the analysis of the obstacles that occurred during the combination of mobile devices and blockchain technology, they proposed that edge computing technology can be used as an effective solution to solve the application of mobile blockchain. They also propose a game-based economic maximization scheme for resource allocation of edge equipment and prove its theoretical feasibility through experimental data.

Based on the investigation of previous work, we thoroughly considered the possibility of combining edge computing with blockchain and proposed an IoT-Blockchain framework combining public chain and consortium chain.

3 Framework of Scheme

A blockchain-based resource monitoring framework for edge computing is shown in Fig. 1. This framework includes cloud servers, the Ethereum platform, several fog computing networks that deploy the consortium chain, and four kinds of blockchain nodes: Consortium administrator Node, Fog Node, Ethereum Node, New-Device Node. Each fog is a collection of edge devices for edge computing. Edge devices with considerable computing power (such as PC, UAV, smart gateways, edge servers, ITS cameras) as new nodes will accept the public resource verification by the Ethereum nodes on the Ethereum platform and be authorized by the cloud server to join the appropriate fog. In the fog, the edge devices, as the fog nodes, participate in maintaining the blockchain network while undertaking the calculation tasks, and accept the supervision of the Consortium administrator Nodes. The performance analysis of the proposed scheme is shown in Sect. 6, including structural feasibility analysis and security analysis.

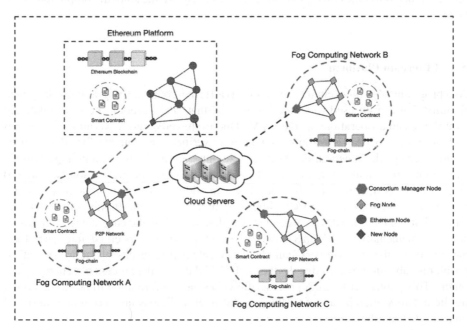

Fig. 1. A blockchain-based resource monitoring framework for edge computing.

3.1 Cloud Server

In this framework, the cloud server mainly plays the following two roles:

Deployer of Resource Verification Tasks. The resource verification tasks refer to the mathematical problem used to investigate the authenticity of device resources when the edge device first joins the network. In this scenario, this mathematical problem is deployed in the public Ethereum network in the form of a smart contract. As the deployer of the resource verification tasks, the cloud servers deploy Ethereum full nodes on the local server to complete the deployment of smart contracts. After receiving the resource registration information of the edge device, the cloud server must reasonably design the mathematical problem in the smart contract, to thoroughly investigate the resource status of the edge device.

The Administrator of the Fog Computing Network. The cloud server participates in the supervision of each fog resource as the administrator of fog computing network. First, when an edge device passes the resource verification on the Ethereum, the cloud server needs to generate an access license and send it to the edge device for completing the authentication. Secondly, the cloud server needs to issue computing tasks to the edge devices based on the resource status and computing capabilities of the edge devices. These tasks are deployed in the consortium chain in the form of smart contracts. Finally, the cloud needs to monitor the data recorded on the blockchain in real-time to achieve real-time monitoring of device resources. Once the resource status of the device changes, the cloud needs to take corresponding measures to ensure the smooth completion of the tasks.

3.2 Ethereum Platform

As a programmable blockchain, Ethereum has a Turing-complete programming language Solidity that can be used to create "contracts" that allow users to perform relatively complex custom operations in the EVM. Due to this advantage, we utilize Ethereum and its miners to form a resource authenticity verification platform for edge devices in this framework. When an edge device attempts to join the fog computing network, Ethereum is responsible for verifying the authenticity of the device's resources through smart contracts deployed on its blockchain. In addition to programmability, another reason we chose Ethereum is the public verifiability of its data. In this framework, the authenticity of the edge device's resources is determined by the edge device's ability to solve the mathematical problems in the smart contract within a specified time. Therefore, any miner on the P2P network can check the calculation results of the mathematical problems submitted by the edge device on the EVM during the process of generating the block. This public verification process allows resource information to be stored on the public network, thereby avoiding the possibility of malicious tampering of data stored on a single centralized server.

3.3 Fog Computing Network

The fog computing network (FCN), as a collection of edge devices with an amount of computing power, is responsible for pre-processing data at the edge of the network. In this framework, we apply the decentralized distributed ledger technology of the consortium chain to the FCN, aiming to achieve publicly verifiable data and real-time supervision of resource status. Figure 2 shows the specific structure of the FCN we designed. In this structure, there are three types of entities: IoT devices, edge devices, and cloud servers. Among them, IoT devices are producers of data. The cloud server is the administrator of the FCN, being responsible for delivering the computing task to edge devices. Edge devices act as data processors, pulling data from IoT devices, and processing the data according to task requirements. By refining and combining the functions of these entities, we can classify three blockchain nodes in the network: data processing node, endorsement node, and cloud node.

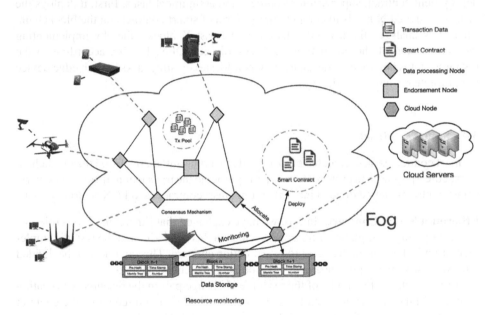

Fig. 2. The specially designed structure of the FCN.

Data Processing Node. Data processing node (DPN) is an edge device with an amount of computing power, e.g., light PC which accounts for the most substantial proportion of all nodes in an FCN. Each DPN pulls data from some IoT devices that affiliated to it and processed the data according to the task requirements delivered by the cloud node. These tasks are deployed on the blockchain through smart contracts, and those processed data are stored in the transaction pool of the blockchain. In the current (cloud-fog-end computing model) application scenario, we believe that the consensus protocol should be non-competitive. A low-power consensus protocol (such as PBFT) runs between the DPNs to elect endorsement nodes to package the processed data into blocks and record them on the blockchain. In future work, we will explore more practical hybrid consensus protocols based on specific application scenarios and specific needs.

Endorsement Node. Under the specific election mechanism, some DPNs are elected as endorsement nodes (ENs) with an amount of tokens locked. These nodes are responsible for verifying the correctness of the data in the transaction pool and serializing the correct data into blocks according to specific rules, and finally extending the newly generated blocks after the existing blockchain with an amount of tokens paid as incentives. The election mechanism stipulates the life cycle of the ENs so that the ENs are rotated after the X blocks (defined as system parameter) generated.

Cloud Node. As mentioned above, the cloud server is the administrator of the fog consortium chain so that it plays a role as a cloud node (CN) in the FCN. CN does not participate in the block generation process. Its primary function consists of three parts: deployment contract, supervision resources, and assignment tasks. First, it deploys the tasks that the DPN needs to compute in the form of smart contracts on the blockchain. Then, CN analyzes the task completion in the past X blocks, thereby implementing the supervision of the computing resources of each DPN. Finally, according to the resource status obtained by the analysis, CN allocates existing tasks to each edge device to complete resource scheduling.

3.4 Smart Contract

A smart contract is an executable piece of code that runs automatically on the blockchain to execute a pre-defined protocol between the parties to the transaction. In this framework, smart contracts can be divided into Ethereum smart contracts and FCN smart contracts.

Ethereum Smart Contract. In 2-B, we have explained that Ethereum plays a role as a resource verification platform for edge devices in this scenario, and the specific implementation is done through a resource-verification contract. This contract can be divided into two parts: margin management part and resource challenge part.

Figure 3 shows the model of the resource challenge part in the resource-verification contract. In this model, the smart contract can be divided into three parts: the contract body, the verification function, and the time control function. The contracting body is the core component of the entire contract and will be specifically designed according to the resource conditions provided by the edge device. In the contract body, the challenge algorithm is an ordered combination of mathematical problems that require the consumption of device resources for operations. To fully verify the resources of the device, these mathematical problems should include the following three types: memory-dependent problems, storage-dependent problems, and time-dependent problems. Also, to prevent the edge device from calculating the answer to the question in advance based on the previous information recorded in the block, the combination of mathematical problems should fully consider the randomness of the mathematical problem and the randomness of the operation sequence. In the current scheme, the challenge algorithm adopts a hash collision method, and its logical expression is:

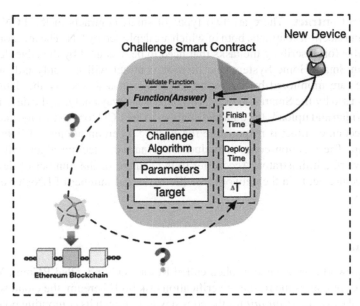

Fig. 3. The model of the resource challenge part in the resource-verification contract.

$$f_{challenge}(N) = A$$

where $f_{challenge}$ is the challenge algorithm mentioned above, N is a random number given by task deployer, and A is the target value to be displayed to the edge device.

Some parameters of N (such as length, type) and A are given in the contract body. Based on this information, the edge device needs to calculate the N and pass it to the smart contract within the specified time ΔT. The miners of Ethereum will verify the correctness and time validity of the calculation results through the verification function and time control function in the smart contract.

Definition 1. The correctness of the results:

$$S_{N'} = S_N, f_{challenge}(N') = A$$

where N' is the answer calculated by edge device, S is the parameter set of random number N and N'.

Definition 2. The time validity of results:

$$\Delta T > T_{finish} - T_{deploy}$$

FCN Smart Contract. There are two types of smart contracts in the FCN: mission contracts and election contracts, both of which are deployed by CN. The mission contract is responsible for describing the tasks that need to be executed by the edge device. For example, in Smart Home System, the mission contract will not only indicate which IoT devices are monitored by the Smart Gateway but also specify the data analysis algorithms used by the Smart Gateway. The Smart Gateway analyzes the data according to the algorithm and uploads the data and analysis to the FCN for verification and storage.

The election contract is responsible for electing a certain number of ENs from the DPN group. The election contract includes a dynamic selection algorithm designed by the network administrator. According to the change of the number of devices and resource requirements in the network, the life cycle and number of ENs have adjusted accordingly.

3.5 Token

In this framework, we created a token called ResourceCoin (called RCoin). When the edge device completes the resource verification task on Ethereum, the cloud server sets the initial token value *RCoinInit* for the edge device to match its computing power. After completing the cloud-delivered tasks in the FCN, the edge device will receive RCoin as an incentive. The amount of Rcoin included in the task will be proportional to the computing resources required to complete the task. The token mechanism in different FCNs is the same, but there will be differences in *RCoinInit* and the degree of incentives.

We need to make additional explanations about the real-time in the article. We believe that under the cloud-fog-edge computing model, as long as the interval of the information queue containing the device resource status is short enough, it can ensure that the device can not change its resource status within the interval To fake their own computing power. Therefore, in our scheme, we can increase the tps so that the time interval for producing blocks containing resource status is small, thereby achieving near real-time. Time cost and calculation cost will be carried out in future research.

In addition, FCN will run a blockchain data monitor to monitor the RCoin value of each node. This monitoring mechanism consists of two parts. First, the monitor will count the RCoin value of each edge device in the last X blocks to reflect the task completion of the device over a period of time. Secondly, the monitor will monitor the total amount of Rcoin in the X blocks of the edge device in a cumulative manner to reflect the resource stability of the device (see Chapter 5 for a detailed explanation). Based on the above design ideas, we believe that RCoin can directly reflect the task completion status of the edge device during the past X block generation, and indirectly reflect the resource status of the edge device during the same period, thereby monitoring the resource status of each edge device.

4   Workflow of Scheme

In this section, we introduce the specific workflow of the resource monitoring program. The program is divided into two phases, the first phase is the resource-verification phase, and the second phase is the resource real-time monitoring phase.

4.1   Parameter Notations

We have defined some parameter notations for this section below.

Table 1. The parameter notations.

Symbol	Definition
Pn	An edge device trying to join the FCN
Px	An edge device performed as a DPN in a FCN
Request-Tx	A transaction for submitting margin and device's information
Info	The specific information of edge device
Task-Set	Set of resource verification contracts containing the mathematical problems
Answer-Set	The calculation result set of Task-Set
License	Access license file obtained by Pn after resource verification
Record	The record of information during resource verification
Period	The cycle in which an EN generates X blocks
RCoinP	RCoin value of Pn obtained in Period
H()	Sha256 hash algorithm
Data	Data collected by edge devices from IoT devices
Mission-Set	Set of mission contracts deployed by FCN administrator

4.2   Resource Verification Phase

When an edge device attempts to join an FCN to contribute its computing power and get a corresponding return, it first needs to accept the authenticity test of the computing resources proposed by the cloud. The cloud server sends a challenge to the new device in the form of a smart contract based on the device resource information provided by the new device. If the node can calculate the result of the challenge within the specified time and the miner verifies the result, the cloud server will recognize the device's resources and then add it to the appropriate fog. The specific workflow of resource verification is shown in Fig. 4.

1. *Pn* initiates a transaction *Request-Tx* to the margin contract. The margin contract will process the *Request-Tx*, transfer the margin to the contract wallet for temporary storage, and publicize Info. The *Info* includes four parameters, where C is the CPU model of *Pn*, S is the storage of *Pn*, M is the RAM of *Pn*, A is *Pn's* MAC address for unique identification.
2. The cloud server designs mathematical problems within a reasonable range according to *Info* of *Pn* and deploys *Task-Set = {T1, T2...Ti}* on the Ethereum. The deployment time of the contract is an essential parameter of the time control function mentioned in Sect. 3-D.

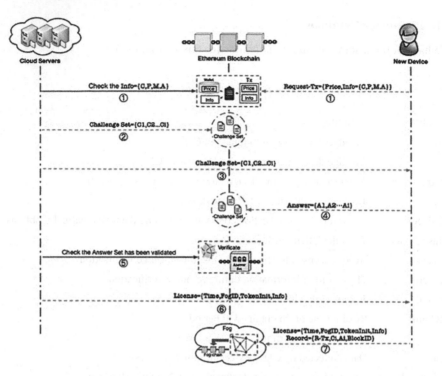

Fig. 4. The specific workflow of resource verification.

3. The cloud servers send the addresses of tasks in *Task-Set* = *{T1, T2...Ti}* to *Pn* in the form of transaction, thereby ensuring that the challenge distribution process is retained on the public network to prevent man-in-the-middle attacks against the challenged content.

4. *Pn* calculates the mathematical problem in *Task-Set* = *{T1, T2...Ti}* locally within the specified time *ΔT*, and sends *Answer-Set* = *{A1, A2...Ai}* to *Task-Set* = *{T1, T2...Ti}* in the form of transaction for late verification.

5. All miners working on the Ethereum can verify the correctness of the results and the validity of the time. The results of the verification are recorded by the miners on the Ethereum public chain. Once the result is recorded, it means that the new device has passed the challenge initiated by the cloud, and the resources it provided are authentic.

6. According to the *Info* of *Pn*, the cloud servers send *Pn* the *License* of the FCN, which is suitable for the resource of *Pn*. The *License* includes four parameters, where Time is the time difference between contract deployment time and contract finish time, *FogID* is the ID of FCN that Pn is being added to, *TokenInit* is the initial Token value of *Pn* (mentioned in Sect. 3-E)

7. *Pn* provides the administrator of the FCN with its access authentication file *License* and participates in the FCN. At the same time, *Pn* integrates the above transaction information to *Record* and publishes it on the FCN as publicity. The *Record* includes four parameters, where R-Tx is the *Request-Tx* mentioned in step 1, and TS is the

Task-Set mentioned in step 2, AS is the *Answer-Set* mentioned in step 4, BlockID is the height of the block where the result is located.

Although in the current solution, the license issuer in step 6 and the administrator in step 7 are the same entity: the cloud server, we still think that the process of forwarding license described in steps 6 and 7 is meaningful. The specific reasons are as follows:

First, the license issuer and the administrator of the FCN are in two architectures and play different roles. Therefore, by adding one step to the scheme description, the two are separated to make the scheme clearer and easier to understand.

Second, such a logical setting is beneficial to optimize the solution. In the future, we can divide the two roles into different clouds and further divide the roles, responsibilities, and tasks to improve the robustness of the system.

4.3 Resource Real-Time Monitoring Phase

As an FCN administrator, the cloud server realizes real-time monitoring of resources through *RCoin* Monitoring Software running locally. This monitoring activity is always ongoing as long as the FCN is working.

Since *RCoinP* has a positive correlation with the number of tasks that *Pn* completes in *Period*, *RCoinP* can reflect the stability of node resources within *Period*. When a DPN joins the FCN and usually runs, the RCoin of the node will increase linearly within *Period*. After *Period*, the *RCoin* monitoring software will remove the *RCoin* from the earliest block and count the *RCoin* in the latest block. Based on the above operation, the *RCoin* of the normally operating node should exhibit a relatively stable state of fluctuation. Once a node maintains such a statistical model, the cloud server will consider that the DPN has proper resource utilization in the prior period, and the device resource status is stable. Besides, since the EN does not undertake data processing tasks for a certain period, the *RCoin* of the EN should be locked and updated after being re-established as a DPN and motivated.

The specific workflow of real-time resource monitoring is shown in Fig. 5.

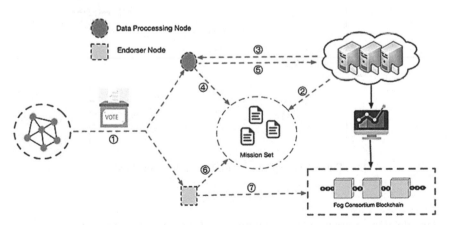

Fig. 5. The specific workflow of real-time resource monitoring.

1. The FCN elects a certain number of ENs from the DPNs through an election contract.
2. As an administrator, the CN deploys the *Mission set = {M1, M2...Mi}* on the fog consortium blockchain.
3. CN obtains the *RCoin* of *Px* through the *RCoin* Monitoring Software. According to the stability of *RCoin* and the initial resource information Info of the *Px*, CN sends *Px* the address of *Mi*, which is suitable for its resource status.
4. *Px* pulls Data from the IoT device according to the demand of *Mi* and calculates it locally. Then, *Px* sends the result of *Mi* and the *H(Data)* to the mission contract *Mi* in the form of transaction *Tx*.
5. *Px* uploads Data to the cloud server for storage.
6. The EN pulls the Data from the cloud server and calculates *H'(Data)*. If

$$H'(Data) == H(Data)$$

the EN will acknowledge that Data has not tampered. Then, the EN checks the result according to the requirements of the mission contract *Mi*.
7. If the result is verified, the EN will package the *Tx* mentioned in step 4 with other validated transactions into a block and extends it into the blockchain.

4.4 Endorsement Phase

During the endorsement phase, the election contracts and endorsement nodes will follow an endorsement agreement called a "vote box" to ensure the orderliness and reliability of the endorsement process. The specific workflow of "vote box" is shown in the Fig. 6:

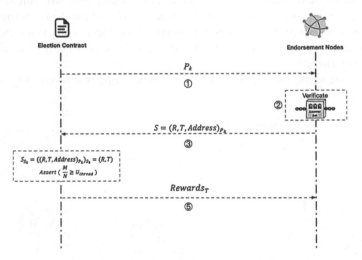

Fig. 6. The specific workflow of the "vote box".

1. The election contract sends the public key P_k to the endorsement nodes.

2. ENs checks the calculation result G of a specific task (see the workflow of 4-B for details).
3. ENs adds the timestamp as the salt to the verification result R and encrypts it with P_k to obtain a vote S and send it to the election contract.

$$S = (R, T, Address)_{P_k}$$

4. After the election contract receives all R within the specified time T_{limit} (overdue invalid), it decrypts S with the private key S_k and publicizes the R.

$$S_{S_k} = \left((R, T, Address)_{P_k}\right)_{S_k} = (R, T)$$

We measure the effectiveness of G by introducing a vote pass rate:

Definition 3. The vote pass rate:

$$U = M / N$$

Where M is the number of votes supporting G, and N is the number of endorsement nodes. If the vote pass rate reaches U_{limit}, G is considered correct.

$$Assert(U \geq U_{limit})$$

5. According to the timestamp T of voting S, rewards are issued to the nodes in descending order, thereby inspiring endorsing nodes to improve the checking efficiency.

Based on the above process, we can effectively prevent nodes from acting lazily or maliciously. Since multiple miners submit verification results at a time, even if a malicious EN intentionally submits its own incorrect data, several other ENs will find this problem and reject the wrong data. The number of ENs is a very important parameter in this protocol. Too much EN will cause the protocol to be inefficient and the verification cost will be too high. Too little EN will make the protocol less secure. Therefore, we believe that the number of ENs will be planned according to specific application scenarios. In FCNs with more reliable nodes, the number of ENs can be reduced to improve efficiency and reduce costs, and vice versa.

5 Experimental Results

In the application scenario of federated machine learning, we use the TensorFlow federated model as an example to simulate the real-time supervision of resources in the proposed scheme. We deploy three computers as edge devices in the FCN and performed distributed machine learning on the MNIST dataset several times (hundreds of rounds at a time). Details of the devices are shown in Table 2.

In this scenario, two critical indicators of machine learning: Loss and Accuracy, together with other parameters such as the number of calculation rounds, execution time, and learning rate, determine the RCoin value, which measures the resource status of each device. The specific formula is:

$$RCoin_i = \frac{A * R_i}{L * t * S}$$

where A is the accuracy of the result, R_i is the number of rounds of the i-th machine learning, L is the loss of the result, t represents the operation time, and S is the learning rate of the device. In this formula, the independent variables are S and R_i and the remaining parameters are the output of machine learning.

Figure 7 shows the RCoin value of device A when it performs distributed machine learning 11 times. Figure 8 shows the average frequency of device A's CPU during operation where the learning rate is set to 0.02 and the execution rounds is 100. During the first 7 executions, we did not make any restrictions on the resources of the device, and the device was running in the best-performing state. Starting from the eighth execution process, we have limited the resources of the device to halve its computing power. As can be seen from the figure, RCoin was at a high level and stable during the first seven executions. From the eighth time, it has experienced a significant decline and subsequently maintained a low and stable operation. This trend is very close to the average frequency of the actual CPU operation.

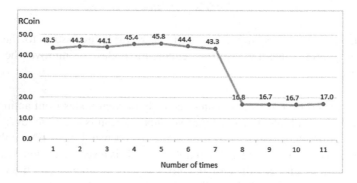

Fig. 7. Trend of *RCoin* value of device A.

This result shows that RCoin can adequately reflect the actual resources of the device. Once the device is subject to resource requirements from outside the task, which affects the task's execution resources, RCoin can reflect the resource status of the device through the trend. If we set the time interval of a single task small enough or subdivide the task so that the execution time of a single task is short, it can reflect the resource status of the device in near real-time.

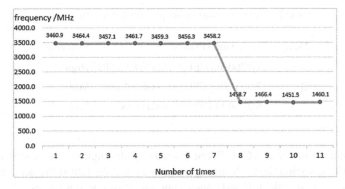

Fig. 8. Trend of CPU frequency of device A.

In this simulation, we set the cumulative round number X to 5 (see in Sect. 5), that is, the RCoin obtained from the past 5 tasks reflects the resource stability of the device in the past period:

$$RCoinP_i = \begin{cases} \sum_{i-4}^{i} RCoin_j, & 5 \leq i \\ \sum_{0}^{i} RCoin_j, & 0 \leq i \leq 4 \end{cases}$$

where $RCoin_j$ is the $Rcoin$ value obtained by the j-th task.

As described in Sect. 3, the device will be added to different FCNs to contribute computing power according to its computing resources. Figure 9 compares the $RCoinP$ of the three devices in the experiment. When performing machine learning tasks with the same parameters, the $RCoinP$ of device A is significantly higher than the other two devices. As can be seen from the information in Table 1, the computing resources of device A are indeed better than those of device B and device C.

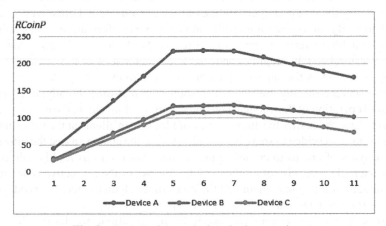

Fig. 9. *RcoinP* of three devices in the experiment.

Table 2. Devices information in simulation experiments.

Device	Device information	Resource
A	i7-7700HQ CPU@2.8 GHz 16 GB	High
B	i7-4710HQ CPU@2.5 GHz 4 GB	Mid
C	i5-3360 M CPU@2.6 GHz 6 GB	Low

This result shows that *RCoinP* can effectively distinguish the resource status of different devices, so that the FCN manager can dynamically adjust the network to which the device belongs to make full and appropriate use of its computing resources. Besides, although Table 1 shows that the computing resources of the two devices are different, the *RCoinP* of devices B and C are very close.

This result shows that the computational tasks of distributed machine learning TensorFlow federated run on devices with weak computing capabilities and have small differences. Based on this conclusion, FCN managers can perform task-based clustering of devices with different computing capabilities based on the similarity of *RCoinP*, thereby improving the matching between computing tasks and edge devices.

For more details of the experiment code and the smart contracts mentioned in Sect. 3, see [19].

6 Performance Analysis

6.1 Feasibility Analysis

As described in Sect. 4, a complete resource management solution for edge devices should ensure public resource verification and real-time monitoring of resources within the FCN and realize the coordinated operation of the two. In response to the above requirements, we have adopted a system structure combining the public chain and consortium chain. In the public chain, we fully utilize the resources of the entire network of miners to verify the computing capabilities of the equipment and effectively use smart contracts to verify the verification results and equipment information, which solves the difficulty of publicly verifying and storing resources. Also, we take advantage of the partially decentralized and highly controllable characteristics of the consortium chain to deploy the cloud as the supervisor of the consortium chain to perform the tasks of dispatching and monitoring the status of resources in real-time. Finally, to achieve the coordinated operation of the public chain and the consortium chain, the nodes in the system need to have the ability to run two types of blockchain clients at the same time. The cloud performs as a bridge to share information across the chain to assist the information in the two types of chains to complete interaction. Based on this multi-chain collaborative structure design, this solution can make full use of the respective characteristics and advantages of the public chain and the consortium chain to meet the needs of open resource verification and real-time supervision of resources.

Besides, based on meeting the needs of the solution, we have fully considered the adaptability and convenience of the combination of various consortium chains and Ethereum, and compared the four mature consortium chains from five aspects: Programming language, underlying architecture, TPS, number of peers, storage consumption.

According to the comparison in the Table 3, the Fisco Bcos consortium chain will be the best choice for this solution. First, the same underlying architecture and medium-level storage consumption as Ethereum can effectively reduce unnecessary resource consumption. Secondly, the same smart contract programming language is conducive to achieving the linkage and collaboration between the consortium chain and the public chain. Finally, the infinite number of nodes and the high TPS brings excellent scalability to the system. Based on the above reasons, we finally chose the Fisco consortium chain to implement our solution.

Table 3. The comparison of current mainstream consortium chains.

Consortium chain	Programming language	Underlying architecture	Transaction per second (TPS)	Number of peers	Storage consumption
Fabric	Goland	Fabric	300–500	Limited	Much high
Quorum	Solidity	Ethereum	400–800	Unlimited	High
Corda	Java	Corda	–	Unlimited	Low
Fisco Bcos	Solidity	Ethereum	1000	Unlimited	Low

6.2 Security Analysis

Impersonation Attack. In the framework of this solution, different nodes have different identities and work content. As the deployer of the resource verification task and the manager of the FCN, the cloud server has some special powers in the resource monitoring system. This inequality leads to the possibility of malicious nodes impersonating cloud servers to do evil. To prevent malicious nodes from impersonating cloud nodes to perform malicious actions such as deploying unreasonable tasks, changing internal parameters of smart contracts, and tampering with endorsed node lists, we have added an identity verification module to smart contracts. Based on the uniqueness of the node's address in the blockchain, the transaction initiator is authenticated to prevent impersonation attacks by malicious nodes.

Sybil Attack. The cloud server will formulate a particular resource verification task for the edge device when it tries to join the network. This process needs to bring workload to the cloud server. If an adversary initiates a large number of join requests for this link, it will cause the workload of the cloud server to become excessive or even paralyzed. Therefore, to prevent this malicious behavior, we have added a margin module to the smart contract, requiring each edge device to add a certain margin as a credential in the application for joining the network. Since smart contracts can be used as wallets, we use margin management part to temporarily store margins paid by edge devices and return the margin to the edge device after the resource verification.

Plagiarism Attack. The edge device elected as the endorsement node will verify the calculation results in the FCN. This verification process consumes the resources of the endorsing node, so there is a possibility of malicious behavior: to saving its computing power, the endorsing node copies the previous verification results of other endorsing nodes. To prevent this, we designed a ballot box protocol in the smart contract. The agreement stipulates that the verification result will be transmitted in the form of ciphertext before contract receiving the entire verification result, the smart contract will save the received verification result in the form of a black box to prevent malicious endorsement nodes from forging their results. Besides, the agreement also stipulates that the rewards brought by the endorsement process will decrease according to the order of completion of the verification work, thereby urging endorsement nodes to complete the task more actively.

7   Conclusion and Future Works

This paper proposes a blockchain-based resource supervision scheme for edge devices under the framework of the cloud-fog-end computing model. It makes full use of the data openness and public verifiability of the public chain and the high controllability of the consortium chain to achieve real-time supervision of the edge devices. In addition, a simulation experiment was implemented in the model of TensorFlow-federated. The experimental results show that this scheme can effectively monitor the resource status of edge devices in real-time so that managers can more efficiently schedule device resources in the fog computing network. This positive result laid the foundation for the combination of fog computing and federal computing in the future.

For future work, we will investigate the possibility of using smart contracts to implement resource scheduling on the chain under this framework. We will also optimize the scheme to handle more complex applications of federated machine learning.

References

1. Pan, J., McElhannon, J.: Future edge cloud and edge computing for IoT applications. IEEE Internet Things J. **5**(1), 439–449 (2018). https://doi.org/10.1109/JIOT.2017.2767608
2. Li, G., Liu, Y., Junhua, W., Lin, D., Zhao, S.: Methods of resource scheduling based on optimized fuzzy clustering in fog computing. Sensors **19**(9), 2122 (2019)
3. Bonomi, F., Milito, R., Zhu, J., Addepalli, S.: Fog computing and its role in the IoT. In: Proceedings of the 1st Edition of the ACM MCC Workshop Mobile Cloud Computing, pp. 13–16 (2012)
4. Shi, W., Cao, J., Zhang, Q., Li, Y., Xu, L.: Edge computing: vision and challenges. IEEE Internet Things J. **3**(5), 637–646 (2016)
5. Mobile-Edge Computing Initiative, European Telecommunications *Standards* Institute, Sophia Antipolis, France (2016). http://www.etsi.org/technologies-clusters/technologies/mobile-edge-computing

6. Nakamoto, S.: Bitcoin: A Peer-to-Peer Electronic Cash System (2008)
7. Li, W., Meng, W., Liu, Z., Au, M.H.: Towards blockchain-based software-defined networking: security challenges and solutions. IEICE Trans. Inf. Syst. **103**(2), 196–203 (2020)
8. Li, W., Tug, S., Meng, W., Wang, Y.: Designing collaborative blockchained signature-based intrusion detection in IoT environments. Future Gener. Comput. Syst. **96**, 481–489 (2019)
9. Buterin, V., et al.: A next-generation smart contract and decentralized application platform, white paper (2014)
10. Lo, S.K., Liu, Y., Chia, S.Y.: Analysis of blockchain solutions for IoT: a systematic literature review. IEEE Access **7**, 58822–58835 (2019)
11. Pan, J., Wang, J., Hester, A.: EdgeChain: an edge-IoT framework and prototype based on blockchain and smart contracts. IEEE Internet Things J. **6**(3), 4719–4732 (2019)
12. Uddin, Md. A., Stranieri, A., Gondal, I.: An efficient selective miner consensus protocol in blockchain oriented IoT smart monitoring. In: ICIT pp. 1135–1142 (2019)
13. Park, J.S., Yu, H.-C., Chung, K.-S.: Markov chain based monitoring service for fault tolerance in mobile cloud computing. In: AINA Workshops 520–525 (2011)
14. Jalali, F., Lynar, T., Smith, O.J.: Dynamic edge fabric environment: seamless and automatic switching among resources at the edge of IoT network and cloud. In: EDGE, 77–86 (2019)
15. Dorri, A., Kanhere, S.S., Jurdak, R., Gauravaram, P.: Blockchain for IoT security and privacy: the case study of a smart home. In: PerCom Workshops, pp. 618–623 (2017)
16. Stanciu, A.: Blockchain based distributed control system for edge computing. In: CSCS, pp. 667–671 (2017)
17. Huh, S., Cho, S., Kim, S.: Managing IoT devices using blockchain platform. In: 19th International Conference on Advanced Communication Technology (ICACT) (2017)
18. Xiong, Z., Zhang, Y., Niyato, D., Wang, P., Han, Z.: When mobile blockchain meets edge computing. IEEE Commun. Mag. **56**(8), 33–39 (2018)
19. Project webpage. https://github.com/kingtongBUAA/Blockchain-based_RSS

Cryptographic Primitives

SHOSVD: Secure Outsourcing of High-Order Singular Value Decomposition

Jinrong Chen, Lin Liu$^{(\boxtimes)}$, Rongmao Chen$^{(\boxtimes)}$, and Wei Peng

School of Computer, National University of Defense Technology, Changsha, China
chenjr001@126.com, {liulin16,chromao,wpeng}@nudt.edu.cn

Abstract. Tensor decomposition is a popular tool for multi-dimensional data analysis. In particular, High-Order Singular Value Decomposition (HOSVD) is one of the most useful decomposition methods and has been adopted in many applications. Unfortunately, the computational cost of HOSVD is very high on large-scale tensor, and the desirable solution nowadays is to outsource the data to the clouds which perform the computation on behalf of the users. However, how to protect the data privacy against the possibly untrusted clouds is still a wide concern for users. In this paper, we design a new scheme called SHOSVD in the two-cloud model for secure outsourcing of tensor decomposition. At the core of our technique is the adoption of additive secret sharing. Our SHOSVD could guarantee the outsourced data privacy for users assuming no collusion between the two clouds. Moreover, it supports off-line users which means that no interaction between users and clouds is required during the computation process. We prove that our scheme is secure in the semi-honest model, and conduct the theoretical analyses regarding its computational and communicational overhead. The experiment results demonstrate that our scheme is of desirable accuracy.

Keywords: Tensor decomposition · Privacy preservation · High-Order Singular Value Decomposition · Additive secret sharing

1 Introduction

Nowadays, due to the development of the information technology, the size of data is growing rapidly towards petabyte level [13]. Conducting analysis on such large-scale data consumes lots of computation resources [6,13,30], which is particularly unacceptable for users who are usually with limited computation resources. Fortunately, outsourcing extensive computations to the clouds turns to be a desirable solution for users as clouds could offer considerable computation and storage resources. Nevertheless, it is a common concern for users that their data privacy could be possibly revealed to the clouds which perform the computation tasks on behalf of them [6,22]. To the end, users would prefer to

© Springer Nature Switzerland AG 2020
J. K. Liu and H. Cui (Eds.): ACISP 2020, LNCS 12248, pp. 309–329, 2020.
https://doi.org/10.1007/978-3-030-55304-3_16

encrypt their data before outsourcing them to the clouds for computation, and this has been widely adopted in the literature [6,13,14,22].

In this work, we investigate the study of secure outsourcing of High-Order Singular Value Decomposition (HOSVD) which is well-known as a powerful tool for conducting tensor analysis [2,31]. A tensor could be viewed as the expansion of vector or matrix in multi-dimensional space [30], and it has been widely used to model a variety of heterogeneous and multi-aspect data such as social tagging systems [9,31] and color images [2]. By performing HOSVD, one can conveniently derive possible associations underlying the noisy and redundant data. To realize the secure outsourcing of HOSVD to the clouds, several methods in the literature have been proposed for privacy-preserving tensor decomposition. Particularly, Kuang et al. [13,14] proposed schemes based on homomorphic encryption which, however, requires users to remain on-line during the computation process by the clouds. To further release the burden of users, based on Paillier encryption [26], Feng et al. [6] proposed a privacy-preserving tensor decomposition scheme to support off-line users. Unfortunately, as we will shown in Sect. 5.5, their scheme has some subtle problems of correctness.

Our Contributions. In this work, we propose a Secure High-Order Singular Value Decomposition (SHOSVD) scheme in the two-cloud model based on additive secret sharing [29]. The contributions of our work are three-fold.

- Based on additive secret sharing, we first propose a protocol for secure integer division with public divisor (SDP) and secure integer square root (SSR). Compared with the existing protocol [21], the newly designed is more efficient. Moreover, we propose a method for additive secret sharing of signed integers, and extend the basic protocols to deal with signed integers.
- We then design a secure scheme for outsourcing HOSVD based on additive secret sharing. Our scheme supports off-line users and thus significantly reduces the computation and communication costs for users. We also analyze the security of our scheme and conduct experimental evaluation to demonstrate its accuracy.
- We also investigate the correctness of Feng et al.'s scheme [6] and show that their designed secure integer division protocol could not be used for building secure Lanzcos method and secure QR decomposition protocol. Concretely, the protocol would return incorrect division results after several iterations.

Related Work. The privacy-preserving tensor decomposition on clouds has received wide attention recent years. Roughly, the tensor decomposition methods can be divided into two categories [12], i.e., CP decomposition and HOSVD. Luo et al. [22] proposed a scheme for privacy-preserving CP decomposition by multiplying a sparse pseudorandom matrix before outsourcing the original tensor to the clouds. Their method turns out to be efficient regarding the computation cost but is not applicable for HOSVD. Feng et al. proposed a privacy-preserving SVD scheme [5], and late improved it [4]. These works are inspiring while the orthogonal tensor SVD in their schemes is different from HOSVD. Kuang et al. [13] first proposed a complete secure scheme for HOSVD in single cloud model, and they also proposed a similar scheme in [14], both of which require users to cooperate with the clouds during the tensor decomposition process. To support off-line users, Feng *et al.* [6] proposed a privacy-preserving tensor decomposition scheme based on Paillier homomorphic encryption. Unfortunately, some correctness problems exist in their scheme, which will be discussed in Subsect. 5.5.

Organizations. The reminder of this paper is organized as follows. We review some preliminary concepts in Sect. 2. We formulate the considered problem in Sect. 3. Section 4 presents several building blocks that are cornerstones of our SHOSVD scheme. We propose our SHOSVD scheme in Sect. 5. Section 6 analyzes the security of the proposed protocols and scheme. Section 7 provides performance analyses, which include thorough theoretical analyses and the experiment results. Section 8 concludes this paper.

2   Preliminaries

Notations. In this paper, we use the notations presented in Table 1 to describe our scheme, which tackles both unsigned operations and signed operations. We use a mark "m" to distinguish them (e.g., Add denotes Secure Unsigned Addition, while mAdd denotes Secure Signed Addition). Note that the operations involved in matrices and vectors are all signed operations.

Table 1. Notation table

Notations	Definition
$\langle x \rangle$	Additive secret sharing of unsigned integer x
$[x]$	Additive secret sharing of signed integer x
v_x, s_x	The absolute value and sign of signed integer x
$[x]_v, [x]_s$	Additive secret sharing of v_x and s_x
$\langle x \rangle^A, [x]^A$	Party A's additive secret sharing of x
$\mathbb{Z}_n, \mathbb{R}$	Ring of integers modulo n, field of rational numbers
Rec/mRec	Recover the shares
Add/mAdd	Secure addition
Mul/mMul	Secure multiplication
SD/mSD	Secure integer division
SDP/mSDP	Secure integer division with public divisor
SC	Secur comparison
SSR	Secure integer square root
mSMM/mSMV/mSMS	Secure matrix-matrix/matrix-vector/matrix-scalar multiplication
mSVV/mSVS	Secure vector-vector/vector-scalar multiplication
mSSV	Secure subtraction of vectors
mSMSD/mSVSD	Secure matrix-scalar/vector-scalar division
mST	Secure transposition

2.1   Additive Secret Sharing

Additive secret sharing was proposed by Shamir [29]. This scheme requires a large prime n. In this work, we use $\langle x \rangle$ to denote the sharing of the unsigned

---

Algorithm 1. Lanczos Method

Input: Symmetric matrix $M \in \mathbb{R}^{n \times n}$.
Output: Tridiagonal matrix L and orthogonal matrix W.
1: Randomly choose a vector $\boldsymbol{w}_1 \in \mathbb{R}^n$, so that $\|\boldsymbol{w}_1\| = 1$.
2: $\boldsymbol{u}_1 = M\boldsymbol{w}_1$, $j = 1$.
3: $\alpha_j = \boldsymbol{w}_j^T \boldsymbol{u}_j$.
4: $\boldsymbol{\gamma}_j = \boldsymbol{u}_j - \alpha_j \boldsymbol{w}_j$.
5: $\beta_j = \|\boldsymbol{\gamma}_j\|$.
6: **if** $\beta_j = 0$ **then**
7:      **break.**
8: **else**
9:      $\boldsymbol{w}_{j+1} = \boldsymbol{\gamma}_j / \beta_j$.
10:     $\boldsymbol{u}_{j+1} = M\boldsymbol{w}_{j+1} - \beta_j \boldsymbol{w}_j$.
11:     $j = j + 1$.
12:     goto 3.
13: **end if**

---

integer x, i.e., $x = \langle x \rangle^A + \langle x \rangle^B \mod n$, where $\langle x \rangle^A, \langle x \rangle^B \in \mathbb{Z}_n$ are only known by A and B respectively. To recover x, A and B send $\langle x \rangle^A$ and $\langle x \rangle^B$ to each other, and calculate the sum of the shares locally. We use Rec to denote this procedure, i.e, $x \leftarrow \text{Rec}(\langle x \rangle^A, \langle x \rangle^B) = \langle x \rangle^A + \langle x \rangle^B \mod n$.

2.2 Tensor Decomposition

We use $\mathcal{T} \in \mathbb{R}^{J_1 \times J_2 \times \cdots \times J_N}$ to denote an N−th order tensor, and $t_{j_1 j_2 \cdots j_N}$ to denote the element of $\mathcal{T}$. We also use $M \in \mathbb{R}^{J_1 \times J_2}$ to represent a matrix and $m_{j_1 j_2}$ to denote the element of M. High-Order Singular Value Decomposition (HOSVD) is a kind of tensor decomposition method, which can decompose a tensor to a core tensor and several truncated orthogonal bases [12]. The decomposition of a tensor $\mathcal{T}$ is defined as

$$\mathcal{T} \cong \mathcal{S} \times_1 U_1 \times_2 U_2 \times_3 U_3 \cdots \times_N U_N, \tag{1}$$

where $\mathcal{S}$ and U_i ($i = 1, 2, \cdots, N$) denote the core tensor and the truncated orthogonal matrices respectively. The core tensor $\mathcal{S}$ is usually regarded as the compression of $\mathcal{T}$.

2.3 Lanczos Method

Lanczos method is an efficient algorithm to transform an symmetric matrix M into a symmetric tridiagonal matrix L, which is usually used in HOSVD [6,13]. Suppose the input is a symmetric matrix $M = [\boldsymbol{m}_1, \boldsymbol{m}_2, \cdots, \boldsymbol{m}_k]$, then the output consists of a symmetric tridiagonal matrix

$$L = \begin{bmatrix} \alpha_1 & \beta_1 & & & \\ \beta_1 & \alpha_2 & \ddots & & \\ & \ddots & \ddots & \beta_{k-1} \\ & & \beta_{k-1} & \alpha_k \end{bmatrix}, \tag{2}$$

and an orthogonal matrix denoted as $W = [w_1, w_2, \cdots, w_k]$. The details of Lanczos can be found in Algorithm 1. With Lanzcos method, one can transform the eigen decomposition problem for M into the eigendecomposition problem for a tridiagonal matrix L. With L, we can easily get the QR algorithm [7] to solve the eigendecomposition problem of a tridiagonal matrix.

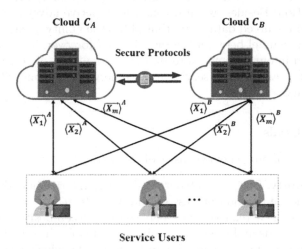

Fig. 1. System model

3 System Model and Design Goals

3.1 System Model

As illustrated in Fig. 1, our SHOSVD scheme is built in a two-cloud model consisting of several service users and two clouds. i.e. cloud C_A and cloud C_B.

1. **Service User.** The service users split the tensor data into two shares, and then outsource them to the cloud C_A and C_B respectively. Moreover, a modulus n should be sent to all the parties involved, which is used for the data splitting and reconstruction.

2. **Cloud** $C_A \& C_B$. The two non-colluding clouds maintain a dataset outsourced from service users. These two clouds cooperate with each other to decompose the tensors and return the service users the decomposition results in a privacy-preserving manner.

We stress that such a non-colluding two-cloud model is reasonable in the real-world. For example, the cloud C_A and C_B may belong to different companies, i.e., Google and Amazon. Note that in the literature, many privacy-preserving schemes also adopt this model to realize desirable properties [6,10,11,18,20,24].

3.2   Threat Model

All the parties in our scheme are semi-honest, which means that they will execute the protocol correctly but are curious about data and query privacy during the protocol execution. Besides, we also consider an active adversary $\mathcal{A}$, who aims to recover the outsourced data. Note that $\mathcal{A}$ has the ability of eavesdropping the communication channel between the two clouds. Moreover, it can also comprise one of the cloud in our scheme. Note that such an adversary $\mathcal{A}$ cannot comprise both C_A and C_B and all the service users otherwise it is infeasible to achieve desirable security.

3.3   Design Goals

The design goals of our scheme consist of follows.

1. **Confidentiality.** Both the outsourced data and intermediate data calculated during the decomposition process should be protected.
2. **Correctness.** The relative error between the decomposition results calculated by the clouds and the decomposition results obtained by the traditional non-privacy-preserving scheme should be negligible, which is the main target of our SHOSVD.
3. **Off-line Service User.** The service users with limited computational and communicational abilities should be off-line during the decomposition execution process.

4   Building Blocks

In this section, we introduce several protocols that are cornerstones to our SHOSVD scheme. All these protocols will be given in the form of algorithms run between cloud C_A and C_B. The unsigned integers are all in the integer ring $\mathbb{Z}_n$, where n is a l−bit prime. For simplicity, we omit the "mod n" hereafter.

4.1 The Existing Protocols

We first describe some existing protocols used for building our scheme.

- **Secure Addition (Add):** C_A and C_B with input $\langle x \rangle$ and $\langle y \rangle$ securely compute the sum $\langle z \rangle$, where $z = x + y$. C_A and C_B only know $\langle z \rangle^A$ and $\langle z \rangle^B$ respectively. The details of Add are available in [19]. We use $\langle z \rangle \leftarrow \langle x \rangle + \langle y \rangle$ to denote this protocol.
- **Secure Multiplication (Mul):** C_A and C_B with input $\langle x \rangle$ and $\langle y \rangle$ securely compute the product $\langle z \rangle$, where $z = x \cdot y$. C_A and C_B only know $\langle z \rangle^A$ and $\langle z \rangle^B$ respectively. Note that a precomputed arithmetic multiplication Beaver triple $(\langle a \rangle, \langle b \rangle, \langle c \rangle)$ is needed in this operation, where $a \cdot b = c$. There are usually two ways to obtain such a triple. The first is use Oblivious Transfer protocol [28], while the other is to use a trusted third party [27]. The details of Mul are available in [19]. We use $\langle z \rangle \leftarrow \langle x \rangle \cdot \langle y \rangle$ to denote this protocol.
- **Secure Integer Division (SD):** C_A and C_B with input dividend $\langle x \rangle$ and divisor $\langle y \rangle$ securely compute the integer quotient $\langle z \rangle$, where $z = \lfloor x/y \rfloor$. C_A and C_B only know $\langle z \rangle^A$ and $\langle z \rangle^B$ respectively. The details of SD are available in [21]. We use $\langle z \rangle \leftarrow \text{SD}(\langle x \rangle, \langle y \rangle)$ to denote this protocol.
- **Secure Comparison (SC):** C_A and C_B with input $\langle x \rangle$ and $\langle y \rangle$ securely to compute the comparison result $\langle t \rangle$. C_A and C_B only know $\langle t \rangle^A$ and $\langle t \rangle^B$ respectively. If $x \leqslant y$, $t = 1$; otherwise, $t = 0$. The details of SC are available in [3,10]. We use $\langle z \rangle \leftarrow \text{SC}(\langle x \rangle, \langle y \rangle)$ to denote this protocol.

Note that if one of the input is a public constant number c, we only need C_A sets $\langle c \rangle^A \leftarrow c$ and C_B sets $\langle c \rangle^B \leftarrow 0$, and the above protocols can be also run.

4.2 Our Proposed Protocols

We then describe our proposed protocols which serve as building blocks of our whole SHOSVD scheme.

Secure Integer Division with Public Divisor (SDP). The first protocol is *Secure Integer Division with Public Divisor* (SDP). In this protocol, cloud C_A and C_B have shared an integer $\langle x \rangle$ and a public divisor d. At the end of the algorithm, C_A and C_B get the additive share $\langle \lfloor x/d \rfloor \rangle$. First, cloud C_A and C_B calculate $\langle z \rangle = \langle x \rangle + r$, where r is a random number in $\mathbb{Z}_n$. Then C_B runs Rec on $\langle z \rangle$ to recover z. Note that if $x + r < n$, $x + r = z$; otherwise, $x + r = z + n$. Since $x < n$, if $z > r$, a carry over has not occurred, i.e, $z = x + r$; otherwise, a carry over has occurred, i.e, $x + r = z + n$. For simplicity, in the following, we use z' to denote $x + r$, where $z' = z$ or $z' = z + n$. Note that, if $(x \mod d) + (r \mod d) < d$, $\lfloor z'/d \rfloor = \lfloor x/d \rfloor + \lfloor r/d \rfloor$; otherwise, $\lfloor z'/d \rfloor = \lfloor x/d \rfloor + \lfloor r/d \rfloor + 1$. Moreover, the condition $(x \mod d) + (r \mod d) < d$ is equivalent to $(z' \mod d) = (x \mod d) + (r \mod d) \geqslant (r \mod d)$. Following such an idea, we let C_A and C_B first make three comparisons on r and z, $(r \mod d)$ and $(z \mod d)$, and also $(r \mod d)$ and $(z + n \mod d)$. The final division result

---

Algorithm 2. Standard Integer Division with Public Divisor (SDP)

Input: A dividend $\langle x \rangle$ that is shared by C_A and C_B. A divisor d that is public known by C_A and C_B. Note that integer $x, d \in \mathbb{Z}_n$ and n is a l−bit prime.

Output: $\langle q \rangle$ shared by C_A and C_B, where $q = \lfloor x/d \rfloor$.

1: C_A: Pick a random number $r \in \mathbb{Z}_n$, set $\langle z \rangle^A \leftarrow \langle x \rangle^A + r$, and send $\langle z \rangle^A$ to C_B.
2: C_B: Set $\langle z \rangle^B \leftarrow \langle x \rangle^B$, and recover $z \leftarrow \text{Rec}(\langle z \rangle^A, \langle z \rangle^B)$.
3: $C_A \& C_B$: $\langle t \rangle \leftarrow \text{SC}(r, z)$, $\langle t_1 \rangle \leftarrow \text{SC}((r \mod d), (z \mod d))$, and $\langle t_2 \rangle \leftarrow \text{SC}((r \mod d), ((z + n) \mod d))$.
4: C_A: $\langle a \rangle^A \leftarrow -\lfloor r/d \rfloor + \langle t_1 \rangle^A - 1$, $\langle b \rangle^A \leftarrow -\lfloor r/d \rfloor + \langle t_2 \rangle^A - 1$.
5: C_B: $\langle a \rangle^B \leftarrow \lfloor z/d \rfloor + \langle t_1 \rangle^B$, $\langle b \rangle^B \leftarrow \lfloor (z + n)/d \rfloor + \langle t_2 \rangle^B$.
6: $C_A \& C_B$: $\langle \alpha \rangle \leftarrow \langle t \rangle \cdot \langle a \rangle$, $\langle \beta \rangle \leftarrow \langle 1 - t \rangle \cdot \langle b \rangle$.
7: C_A: $\langle q \rangle^A \leftarrow \langle \alpha \rangle^A + \langle \beta \rangle^A$.
8: C_B: $\langle q \rangle^B \leftarrow \langle \alpha \rangle^B + \langle \beta \rangle^B$.

---

is $\langle q \rangle \leftarrow \langle t(\lfloor z/d \rfloor - \lfloor r/d \rfloor - t_1) \rangle + \langle (1-t)(\lfloor (z+N)/d \rfloor - \lfloor r/d \rfloor - t_2) \rangle$. We show the details of our SDP in Algorithm 2.

Discussion. Apart from the SDP algorithm, there is also a *Secure Division* (SD) algorithm proposed in [21]. In SD, the two integers $\langle x \rangle$ and $\langle y \rangle$ are all additively shared by cloud C_A and C_B. After running SD, the two clouds get a shared division result, i.e., $\langle \lfloor x/y \rfloor \rangle$. We use T_{SC} to denote the runtime of SC. We note that the computational overhead of Liu *et al.*'s SD [21] is more than $\mathcal{O}(n^2) T_{\text{SC}}$, while the overhead of our SDP is just $\mathcal{O}(1) T_{\text{SC}}$.

Secure Integer Square Root (SRR). We also design a *Secure Integer Square Root* (SSR) algorithm. Suppose that $\langle x \rangle$ is shared by cloud C_A and C_B. After running this SSR algorithm, C_A and C_B obtain the additive share of $\langle \lfloor \sqrt{x} \rfloor \rangle$. Note that there exists a secure square root protocol proposed by Lidel [16]. Their protocol needs to normalize the radicand to the interval $[1/2, 1]$, but additive secret sharing works in a integer ring [15, 17], which implies that their protocol is not for our scheme. Our SSR is designed based on the *Standard Integer Square Root Method* [6] as algorithm 3, where operator $\ll$ denotes the left shift while operator $\gg$ denotes the right shift.

Algorithm 3. Standard Integer Square Root

Input: An integer x whose bit-length is less than l-bit.

Output: Integer $r = \lfloor \sqrt{x} \rfloor$.

1: $r = 0$, $\alpha = 2^{l/2 - 1}$.
2: **for each** $i = 0$ to $l/2 - 1$ **do**
3: $\quad \beta = (((r \ll 1) + \alpha) \ll (l/2 - 1 - i))$.
4: $\quad$ **if** $x \geq \beta$ **then**
5: $\quad\quad r = r + \alpha$, $x = x - \beta$,
6: $\quad$ **end if**
7: $\quad \alpha = \alpha \gg 1$.
8: **end for**
9: **return** r.

In our SSR, cloud C_A and C_B first share $\langle r \rangle$, where $r = 0$. As the method is bit-by-bit, the following loops will run $l/2$ times. First, C_A and C_B compute $\langle \beta \rangle \leftarrow \langle (2 \cdot r + 2^{l/2-1-i}) \cdot 2^{l/2-1-i} \rangle$. Then, C_A and C_B run SC on $\langle x \rangle$ and $\langle \beta \rangle$. Let $\langle c \rangle = \text{SC}(\langle \beta \rangle, \langle x \rangle)$. C_A and C_B compute $\langle r \rangle \leftarrow \langle 2^{l/2-1-i} \cdot c + r \rangle$. Finally, they calculate $\langle x \rangle \leftarrow \langle x - c \cdot \beta \rangle$. After running these loops, C_A and C_B output $\langle r \rangle$ as the result.

Algorithm 4. Secure Integer Square Root (SSR)

Input: A radicand $\langle x \rangle$ shared by C_A and C_B. Note that $0 \leqslant x < 2^l$.
Output: The root $\langle r \rangle$, where $r = \lfloor \sqrt{x} \rfloor$.
1: C_A: Pick a random $\langle r \rangle^A \in \mathbb{Z}_n$, compute $\langle r \rangle^B \leftarrow n - \langle r \rangle^A$, and send $\langle r \rangle^B$ to C_B, so that $\langle r \rangle = \langle 0 \rangle$.
2: **for each** $i = 0$ to $l/2 - 1$ **do**
3:     C_A: $\langle \beta \rangle^A \leftarrow (2 \cdot \langle r \rangle^A + 2^{l/2-1-i}) \cdot 2^{l/2-1-i}$.
4:     C_B: $\langle \beta \rangle^B \leftarrow (2 \cdot \langle r \rangle^B) \cdot 2^{l/2-1-i}$.
5:     $C_A \& C_B$: $\langle c \rangle \leftarrow \text{SC}(\langle \beta \rangle, \langle x \rangle)$.
6:     C_A: $\langle r \rangle^A \leftarrow 2^{l/2-1-i} \cdot \langle c \rangle^A + \langle r \rangle^A$.
7:     C_B: $\langle r \rangle^B \leftarrow 2^{l/2-1-i} \cdot \langle c \rangle^B + \langle r \rangle^B$.
8:     $C_A \& C_B$: $\langle u \rangle \leftarrow \langle c \rangle \cdot \langle \beta \rangle$.
9:     C_A: $\langle x \rangle^A \leftarrow \langle x \rangle^A - \langle u \rangle^A$.
10:    C_B: $\langle x \rangle^B \leftarrow \langle x \rangle^B - \langle u \rangle^B$.
11: **end for**
12: **return** $\langle r \rangle$.

4.3 Extensions for Signed Integers

Note that the aforementioned protocols are all dealing with unsigned integers. However, in the actual situation, both the data users outsource to the cloud and the values generated during calculation may be negative. This motivates us to extend our protocols to support additive secret sharing of signed integers.

Assume that x is a signed integer in an open interval $(-n, n)$, where n is a large prime. Then we use a tuple (v_x, s_x) to denote x, where v_x is the absolute value of x and s_x is the sign of x. If $x < 0$, $s_x = 1$; otherwise, $s_x = 0$. Note that $v_x, s_x \in \mathbb{Z}_n$ are unsigned integer, so that v_x and s_x can be additively shared by A and B as $(\langle v_x \rangle^A, \langle s_x \rangle^A)$ and $(\langle v_x \rangle^B, \langle s_x \rangle^B)$. Then we use $[x]$ to denote the sharing of signed integer x, where $[x]^A = (\langle v_x \rangle^A, \langle s_x \rangle^A)$ and $[x]^B = (\langle v_x \rangle^A, \langle s_x \rangle^A)$. To recover x, A and B run Rec on $\langle v_x \rangle$ and $\langle s_x \rangle$, and then they reconstruct the value by obtaining $x \leftarrow (-1)^{s_x} \cdot v_x$. We use $x \leftarrow \text{mRec}([x]^A, [x]^B)$ to denote this procedure. For simplicity, we use $[x]_v$ and $[x]_s$ to denote the sharing of absolute value and the sign of x respectively.

With this method for additive secret sharing of signed integers, we can extend the aforementioned protocols to deal with signed integers as follows.

1. **Secure Addition (mAdd):** If $s_x = s_y$, then set $v_z = v_x + v_y$ and $s_z = s_x$. Otherwise, v_x and v_y are compared. If $v_x \leqslant v_y$, set $v_z = v_y - v_x$ and $s_z = s_y$; if $v_x > v_y$, set $v_z = v_x - v_y$ and $s_z = s_x$. See Algorithm 5 for more details.

Algorithm 5. Secure Addition (mAdd)

Input: $[x]$ and $[y]$ shared by C_A and C_B.
Output: $[z]$, where $z = x + y$.
1: $\langle p \rangle \leftarrow [x]_s - [y]_s$.
2: $\langle q \rangle \leftarrow \langle p \rangle \cdot \langle p \rangle$.
3: $\langle t \rangle \leftarrow \mathtt{SC}([x]_v, [y]_v)$.
4: $\langle \alpha \rangle \leftarrow (1 - \langle q \rangle) \cdot ([x]_v + [y]_v)$.
5: $\langle a \rangle \leftarrow (1 - \langle t \rangle) \cdot ([x]_v - [y]_v)$, $\langle b \rangle \leftarrow \langle t \rangle \cdot ([y]_v - [x]_v)$.
6: $\langle \beta \rangle \leftarrow \langle q \rangle \cdot (\langle a \rangle + \langle b \rangle)$.
7: $[z]_v \leftarrow \langle \alpha \rangle + \langle \beta \rangle$.
8: $\langle \gamma \rangle \leftarrow (1 - \langle q \rangle) \cdot [x]_s$.
9: $\langle a \rangle \leftarrow (1 - \langle t \rangle) \cdot [x]_s$, $\langle b \rangle \leftarrow \langle t \rangle \cdot [y]_s$.
10: $\langle \zeta \rangle \leftarrow \langle q \rangle \cdot (\langle a \rangle + \langle b \rangle)$.
11: $[z]_s \leftarrow \langle \gamma \rangle + \langle \zeta \rangle$.
12: **return** $[z] \leftarrow ([z]_v, [z]_s)$.

---

2. **Secure Multiplication (mMul):** If $s_x = s_y$, $s_z = 0$; otherwise, $s_z = 1$. Note one could easily get the absolute value v_z of z by $v_z = v_x \cdot v_y$. More details are depicted in Algorithm 6.

Algorithm 6. Secure Multiplication (mMul)

Input: $[x]$ and $[y]$ shared by C_A and C_B.
Output: $[z]$, where $z = x \cdot y$.
1: $\langle p \rangle \leftarrow [x]_s - [y]_s$, $[z]_s \leftarrow \langle p \rangle \cdot \langle p \rangle$.
2: $[z]_v \leftarrow [x]_v \cdot [y]_v$.
3: **return** $[z] \leftarrow ([z]_v, [z]_s)$.

---

3. **Secure Integer Division (mSD):** If $s_x = s_y$, $s_z = 0$; otherwise, $s_z = 1$. And it's easy to get the absolute value v_z of z by $v_z = \lfloor v_x / v_y \rfloor$. More details are depicted in Algorithm 7.

Algorithm 7. Secure Integer Division (mSD)

Input: $[x]$ and $[y]$ shared by C_A and C_B.
Output: $[z]$, where $z = \lfloor x/y \rfloor$.
1: $\langle p \rangle \leftarrow [x]_s - [y]_s$, $[z]_s \leftarrow \langle p \rangle \cdot \langle p \rangle$.
2: $[z]_v \leftarrow \mathtt{SD}([x]_v, [y]_v)$.
3: **return** $[z] \leftarrow ([z]_v, [z]_s)$.

---

4. **Secure Integer Division with Public Divisor (mSDP):** If d is a positive integer, z and x have same sign; otherwise, z and x have opposite signs. The C_A and C_B get the absolute value v_z of z by $v_z = \lfloor v_x/v_d \rfloor$. More details are depicted in Algorithm 8.

Algorithm 8. Secure Integer Division with Public Divisor (mSDP)

Input: $[x]$ shared by C_A and C_B, and a public signed divisor d.
Output: $[z]$, where $z = \lfloor x/d \rfloor$.
1: **if** $s_d == 0$ **then**
2:   $[z]_s \leftarrow [x]_s$.
3: **else**
4:   $[z]_s \leftarrow 1 - [x]_s$.
5: **end if**
6: $[z]_v \leftarrow \text{SDP}([x]_v, s_d)$.
7: **return** $[z] \leftarrow ([z]_v, [z]_s)$.

4.4 The Case of Matrices and Vectors

Since the sharing of a matrix or a vector could be viewed as the sharing of each element individually, our protocols could be also easily extended to realize Secure Matrix-Scalar Division (mSMSD), Secure Vector-Scalar Division (mSVSD) and Secure Transposition (mST).

1. **Secure Matrix-Scalar Division (mSMSD):** C_A and C_B with input $[A]$ and a public scalar b securely compute $[C]$, where A, C are matrices and for each element $a_{i,j}, c_{i,j}$ in A, C there are $c_{i,j} = \lfloor a_{i,j}/b \rfloor$. C_A and C_B only know $[C]^A$ and $[C]^B$ respectively. For each $[c_{i,j}]$, C_A and C_B compute $[c_{i,j}] \leftarrow \text{mSDP}([a_{i,j}], b)$. We use $[c] \leftarrow \text{mSMSD}([a], [b])$ to denote this protocol.
2. **Secure Vector-Scalar Division (mSVSD):** C_A and C_B with input $[a]$ and a public scalar b securely compute $[c]$, where a, c are vectors and for each element a_i, c_i in a, c there are $c_i = \lfloor a_i/b \rfloor$. C_A and C_B only know $[c]^A$ and $[c]^B$ respectively. For each $[c_i]$, C_A and C_B compute $[c_i] \leftarrow \text{mSDP}([a_i], b)$. We use $[c] \leftarrow \text{mSVSD}([a], b)$ to denote this protocol.
3. **Secure Transposition (mST):** C_A and C_B with input $[A]$ securely compute $[B]$, where A, B are matrices and $B = A^T$. C_A and C_B only know $[B]^A$ and $[B]^B$ respectively. C_A just need to set $[B]^A \leftarrow ([A]^A)^T$, while C_B sets $[B]^B \leftarrow ([A]^B)^T$. We use $[B] \leftarrow [A]^T$ to denote this protocol.

The other matrices/vectors protocols, e.g., mSMM, can be extended from the vectorization protocols proposed by Mohassel *et al.* [23], which is based on additive secret sharing of unsigned integers, by substituting Add and Mul in these protocols with mAdd and mMul respectively.

5   Secure High-Order Singular Value Decomposition

We are now ready to describe our designed SHOSVD scheme in full. Using the full scheme, the clouds could finally decompose the shared tensor to several additively shared truncated bases and core tensor.

5.1   The Basic Idea

The basic idea of our SHOSVD is as follows. First, the tensor data are split into additive shares before outsourcing to the two clouds. Receiving shares of the tensor $[\mathcal{T}]$, the two clouds unfold them into additively shared matrices $[T_{(1)}], [T_{(2)}], \cdots , [T_{(H)}]$, where H is the order of $\mathcal{T}$ and $T_{(i)}$ is the mode$-i$ matricization of $\mathcal{T}$. Since the tensor elements and the matrix elements are one-to-one mapping relationship [12], the two clouds just need to unfold their own shared tensor to get the corresponding shared matrices. Then, for each $1 \leqslant i \leqslant H$, cloud C_A and C_B calculate $[M_i] \leftarrow \mathtt{mSMM}([T_{(i)}] \cdot [T_{(i)}]^T)$. For each $[M_i]$, C_A and C_B securely compute its corresponding truncated matrix $[U_i]$. Finaly, they can use $[U_1], [U_2], \cdots , [U_H]$ to calculate the core tensor $[\mathcal{S}]$. Note that the users do not need to interact with the clouds during the tensor decomposition process, except outsourcing tensor data at the beginning and receiving the decomposition results at the end.

5.2   Data Outsourcing

The outsourced data may be float numbers in practice. One straightforward method is to round the float numbers to the nearest integers before outsourcing them. To improve the accuracy, the data owners are suggested to scale the variables with a positive integer ρ. Specifically, let ρx_i denote a scaled integer. The data owner chooses random $p_i, q_i \in \mathbb{Z}_n$, sets $[\rho x_i]^A \leftarrow (p_i, q_i)$, and sets $[\rho x_i]^B \leftarrow ((|\rho x_i| - p_i) \mod n, (s_{x_i} - q_i) \mod n)$, where s_{x_i} denotes the sign of x_i - if x_i is a negative number, $s_{x_i} = 1$, otherwise $s_{x_i} = 0$. After that, $[\rho x_i]^A$ and $[\rho x_i]^B$ are sent to cloud C_A and C_B respectively through secure communication channels. After all data are outsourced, C_A and C_B hold the joint tensor $[\rho \mathcal{T}]$.

5.3   Secure Lanczos Method

For a specific matricization $[\rho T]$ of shared tensor $[\rho \mathcal{T}]$, cloud C_A and C_B securely calculate $[\rho^2 M] \leftarrow \mathtt{mSMM}([\rho T], [\rho T]^T)$. Note that $\rho^2 M$ is a symmetric matrix. We design a *Secure Lanczos* (mSL) method based on Algorithm 1. By mSL, the clouds can get an additively shared tridiagonal matrix $[\rho^2 \sigma B]$ and an additively shared orthogonal matrix $[\sigma W]$, where σ is also a public positive integer used to improve the accuracy. To facilitate the narrative, we suppose that the order of $\rho^2 M$ is k, and assume that

$$
\rho^2 \sigma B = \begin{bmatrix} \rho^2 \sigma \alpha_1 & \rho^2 \sigma \beta_1 & & \\ \rho^2 \sigma \beta_1 & \rho^2 \sigma \alpha_2 & \ddots & \\ & \ddots & \ddots & \rho^2 \sigma \beta_{k-1} \\ & & \rho^2 \sigma \beta_{k-1} & \rho^2 \sigma \alpha_k \end{bmatrix}, \tag{3}
$$

and

$$
\sigma W = [\sigma w_1, \sigma w_2, \cdots, \sigma w_k]. \tag{4}
$$

The details of our mSL are shown in Algorithm 9.

Algorithm 9. Secure Lanczos (mSL)

Input: A symmetric matrix $[\rho^2 M]$ shared by C_A and C_B.
Output: $[\rho^2 \sigma B]$ and $[\sigma W]$ shared by C_A and C_B.
1: C_A: Pick a random $w_1 \in \mathbb{R}^k$, where $\|w_1\| = 1$, and send $[\sigma w_1]^B$ to C_B. Set $j = 1$.
2: $[\rho^2 \sigma^2 u_1] \leftarrow$ mSVS(mSMV($[\rho^2 M], [\sigma w_i]), [\sigma]$), where $[\sigma]^A = (\sigma, 0)$ and $[\sigma]^B = (0,0)$.
3: $[\rho^2 \sigma \alpha_j] \leftarrow$ mSDP(mSVV($[\sigma w_i]^T, [\rho^2 \sigma^2 u_i]), \sigma^2$).
4: $[\rho^2 \sigma^2 \gamma_j] \leftarrow$ mSSV($[\rho^2 \sigma^2 u_j]$, mSVS($[\sigma w_j]), [\rho^2 \sigma \alpha_j]$).
5: **for each** $i = 1$ to $j - 1$ **do**
6:     $[\rho^2 \sigma a] \leftarrow$ mSDP(mSVV($[\rho^2 \sigma^2 \gamma_j]^T, [\sigma w_i]), \sigma^2$).
7:     $[\rho^2 \sigma^2 a w_i] \leftarrow$ mSVS($[\sigma w_i], [\rho^2 \sigma a]$).
8:     $[\rho^2 \sigma^2 \gamma_j] \leftarrow$ mSSV($[\rho^2 \sigma^2 \gamma_j], [\rho^2 \sigma^2 a w_i]$).
9: **end for**
10: $[\rho^2 \sigma^2 \beta_j]_v \leftarrow$ SSR($\sum_{i=1}^k [\rho^2 \sigma^2 \gamma_{ji}]_v \cdot [\rho^2 \sigma^2 \gamma_{ji}]_v$), γ_{ji} denotes the $i-$th element of γ_j.
11: **if** SC($\langle \rho^2 \sigma^2 \beta_i \rangle, \rho^2 \sigma^2) == 0$ **then**
12:     **break**.
13: **else**
14:     $[\rho^2 \sigma \beta_j]_v \leftarrow$ SDP($[\rho^2 \sigma^2 \beta_j]_v, \sigma$).
15:     $[\rho^2 \sigma \beta_j] \leftarrow ([\rho^2 \sigma \beta_j]_v, 0)$.
16:     $[\sigma w_{j+1}] \leftarrow$ mSVSD($[\rho^2 \sigma^2 \gamma_j], [\rho^2 \sigma \beta_j]$).
17:     $[\rho^2 \sigma^2 u_{j+1}] \leftarrow$ mSSV(mSVS(mSMV($[\rho^2 M], [\sigma w_{j+1}]), [\sigma]$), mSVS($[\sigma w_j], [\rho^2 \sigma \beta_j]$)).
18:     $j = j + 1$.
19:     goto 3.
20: **end if**
21: **return** $[\rho^2 \sigma B], [\sigma W]$.

REMARK. Since there exist rounding errors in Algorithm 9, the column vectors in σW obtained will lose orthogonality quicky [25]. To avoid getting wrong answer, we use Gram-Schmidt method to make sure that these vectors are mutually orthogonal, which are from line 5 to line 9. From line 10 to line 14, in order to improve efficiency, we don't consider the signs of the variables since they must be positive. In line 15, we restart to consider the sharing of the sign.

5.4   Secure Core Tensor Construction

With an additively shared tridiagonal matrix $[\rho^2 \sigma B]$ and an additively shared orthogonal matrix $[\sigma W]$, C_A and C_B can employ the QR method [7] to compute the shared truncated orthogonal bases $[\sigma U]$. In particular, C_A and C_B first compute $[\sigma Q]$, whose column vectors are the eigenvectors of $[\rho^2 \sigma B]$, and then obtain $[\sigma U] \leftarrow \mathtt{mSMSD}(\mathtt{mSMM}([\sigma Q], [\sigma W]), \sigma)$. Using the building blocks in Sect. 4, we can obtain Secure QR method ($\mathtt{mSQR}$) in a similar way as $\mathtt{mSL}$.

For all the matricization $[\rho T_{(i)}]$ of shared tensor $[\rho \mathcal{T}]$, C_A and C_B can get all the truncated orthogonal bases, i.e., $[\sigma U_1], [\sigma U_2], \cdots, [\sigma U_H]$. Note that the secure $i-$mode product $[\mathcal{T}] \times_i [U]$ can be calculated as $\mathtt{mSMM}([U], [T_{(i)}])$ [12], so that clouds can employ Eq. 1 to obtain the core tensor as Algorithm 10.

Algorithm 10. Secure Core Tensor Construction ($\mathtt{mSCT}$)

Input: A tensor $[\rho \mathcal{T}]$ and truncated orthogonal bases $[\sigma U_1], [\sigma U_2], \cdots, [\sigma U_H]$ shared
  by C_A and C_B.
Output: An additively shared core tensor $[\rho \sigma^H \mathcal{S}]$.
1: Set $[\mathcal{S}_0] \leftarrow [\rho \mathcal{T}]$.
2: **for** each $i = 1$ to H **do**
3:   $[\mathcal{S}_i] \leftarrow [\mathcal{S}_{i-1}] \times_i [\sigma U_i]^T$.
4: **end for**
5: **return** $\langle \rho \sigma^H \mathcal{S} \rangle$, where $\langle \rho \sigma^H \mathcal{S} \rangle \leftarrow \langle \mathcal{S}_H \rangle$.

5.5   On the Correctness of Feng *et al.*' Scheme [6]

Most recently, Feng *et al.* [6] have proposed a similar Privacy-Preserving Tensor Decomposition (PPTD) scheme in the two-cloud model based on Paillier homomorphic encryption [26]. They designed a secure division protocol in this scheme, which is based on the standard integer division method, and the exact bit length of dividend (*divid*) and divisor (*diviv*) is known by cloud C_A. However, C_A only has the ciphertext of *divid* and *diviv*, which could cause some problems. Below we give more details. In the line 11 of the secure Lanczos method ($\mathtt{SLM}$) in their scheme, this protocol calculates the division of $[\![\rho^2 \sigma^2 \beta_j]\!]$, $[\![\sigma]\!]$. Note that C_A knows the bit length of σ which is a public scalar integer. However, β_j is an intermediate data calculated from previous computations on the ciphertext in $\mathtt{SLM}$. Since C_A cannot infer the bit length of the original outsourced data, it's unable to know the bit length of β_j either. The only way to solve such a problem is assuming that the $[\![\rho^2 \sigma^2 \beta_j]\!]$ has a maximum bit length. Therefore, the first several bits of computation result may be 0 under such an assumption. However, it may lead to an incorrect computation result. Note that the division result $[\![\rho^2 \sigma \beta_j]\!]$ of the line 11 is used as a divisor to obtain $[\![\sigma w_{j+1}]\!]$ in the line 12, with a dividend $[\![\rho^2 \sigma^2 \gamma_j]\!]$. Here, we give an example to illustrate this point. In the line 11, we suppose that the bit length of σ is 3, the maximum bit length of Paillier plaintext domain is 16, and the real bit length of $\rho^2\sigma^2\beta_j$ is 10. Therefore, the real bit length of $\rho^2\sigma\beta_j$ is 7, while the bit length of the calculated result is 13. In the line 12, we assume the bit length of $\rho^2\sigma^2\gamma_j$ is 16, so that the bit length of the calculated result in $\sigma\boldsymbol{\omega}_{j+1}$ is 3, while the correct bit length of the data in $\sigma\boldsymbol{\omega}_{j+1}$ is 9. Therefore, we can conclude that the SLM in [6] is incorrect. As we know, SLM is an important building block for tensor decomposition in Feng *et al.*'s scheme. Thus, such a scheme cannot get the correct tensor decomposition result. Since our SDP/mSDP is not designed in such bit-by-bit way, our protocols will not suffer such a issue. We also note that the aforementioned secure division algorithm is also used in the secure QR decomposition in Feng *et al.*'s scheme and a similar problem may also exist in their secure QR decomposition.

6   Security Analysis

In this section, we analyze the security of each building block which contributes to the security of our full SHOSVD scheme. We first give the security definition of protocol in the semi-honest model [8].

Definition 1. *A protocol is secure in the semi-honest model if and only if there exists a probabilistic polynomial-time simulator Sim that can generate a view, which is computationally indistinguishable from its real view, for the adversary $\mathcal{A}$ in the real world.*

The security of our proposed protocols essentially relay on the following two lemmas of which the analysis are available in [10].

Lemma 1. *If r is an integer uniformly chosen from $\mathbb{Z}_n$ and independent from any variable $x \in \mathbb{Z}_n$, $r + x$ is also uniformly random and independent from x.*

Lemma 2. *A protocol is perfectly simulatable if all its sub-protocols are perfectly simulatable.*

We now analyse the security of our proposed protocols.

Theorem 1. *The proposed SDP and SSR are secure in the semi-honest model.*

Proof. On one hand, the execution image of cloud C_B for the SDP can be denoted as $\Pi_{C_B}(\text{SDP}) - \{\langle z\rangle^B, z, \langle t\rangle^B, \langle t_1\rangle^B, \langle t_2\rangle^B, \langle a\rangle^B, \langle b\rangle^B, \langle \alpha\rangle^B, \langle \beta\rangle^B, \langle q\rangle^B\}$. We also represent the simulated image of cloud C_B for the SDP as $\Pi_{C_B}^S(\text{SDP})$, which is $\Pi_{C_B}^S(\text{SDP}) = \{z_1, z_2, t', t_1', t_2', a', b', \alpha', \beta', q'\}$, where all the elements in $\Pi_{C_B}^S(\text{SDP})$ are randomly chosen from $\mathbb{Z}_n$. $\langle x\rangle^B$ is a part of x's share which is random in $\mathbb{Z}_n$, and $\langle x\rangle^B$ is equal to $\langle x\rangle^B$, so that $\langle z\rangle^B$ is indistinguishable from z_1. $z, \langle t\rangle^B, \langle t_1\rangle^B, \langle t_2\rangle^B, \langle a\rangle^B, \langle \beta\rangle^B$ are computation result of Rec, SC, Mul, which means they are computationally indistinguishable from $z_2, t', t_1', t_2', a', b', \alpha', \beta'$, for the security of Rec, SC and Mul[1]. $\langle a\rangle^B, \langle b\rangle^B$ are the addition results of an

---

[1] The proof of the security of Rec, SC and Mul can be found in [29], [10] and [1] respectively.

integer with a random number which are random according to Lemma 1. Therefore, we can draw a conclusion that the execution image of cloud C_B for SDP is computationally indistinguishable from the simulated image.

Similarly, we can also prove that $\Pi_{C_A}(\text{SDP})$ is computationally indistinguishable from $\Pi^S_{C_A}(\text{SDP})$. Combining the above, we can conclude that the proposed SDP is secure in the semi-honest model. Note that the security analysis of SSR is similar and thus we omit it here due to the page limitation. $\qquad \square$

Theorem 2. *Our proposed protocol for additive secret sharing of signed integers is secure in the semi-honest model.*

Proof. Let x denote the signed integer to be shared. The shares of x is just the shares of the absolute value v_x and its sign s_x, where v_x and s_x are unsigned integers. By the result in [29], the protocol for additively secret sharing for the unsigned integer is secure in the semi-honest model, so that we can conclude that our protocol for the case of signed integer is also secure by Lemma 2. $\qquad \square$

Theorem 3. *The extended protocols for signed integers are secure in the semi-honest model.*

Proof. The extended protocols we propose include mAdd, mMul, mSC, mSDP. Due to the page limitation, here we only prove the security of the comparatively complicated one, i.e., mAdd. Proofs of others can be conducted similarly.

The execution image of mAdd for C_B can be denoted by $\Pi_{C_B}(\text{mAdd}) = \{\langle p \rangle^B, \ \langle q \rangle^B, \langle t \rangle^B, \langle a \rangle^B, \langle b \rangle^B, \langle \alpha \rangle^B, \langle \beta \rangle^B, \ \langle \gamma \rangle^B, \langle \zeta \rangle^B, [z]^B_v, [z]^B_s\}$. Moreover, we can denote the simulated image of mAdd as $\Pi^S_{C_B}(\text{mAdd}) = \{p', q', t', a', b', \alpha', \beta', \gamma', \zeta', v'_z, s'_z\}$, which are randomly chosen from $\mathbb{Z}_n$. Since $\langle p \rangle^B$ and $\langle q \rangle^B$ are computation results of Add and Mul that have been proved in [29] and [1], $\langle p \rangle^A$ and $\langle q \rangle^B$ are random. $\langle t \rangle^B$ is the comparison result obtained by SC, which is random due to the proof in [10]. The computations of $\langle a \rangle^B, \langle b \rangle^B, \langle \alpha \rangle^B, \langle \beta \rangle^B, \langle \gamma \rangle^B, \langle \zeta \rangle^B, [z]^B_v, [z]^B_s$ are combined by Add and Mul. By Lemma 2, they are all random. Thus, we can conclude $\Pi_{C_B}(\text{mAdd})$ is computationally indistinguishable from $\Pi^S_{C_B}(\text{mAdd})$.

Similarly, we can also prove that $\Pi_{C_A}(\text{mAdd})$ is computationally indistinguishable from $\Pi^S_{C_A}(\text{mAdd})$. Therefore, the proposed mAdd is secure in the semi-honest model. $\qquad \square$

Theorem 4. *The proposed protocols for matrices and vectors are secure in the semi-honest model.*

Proof. The protocols involved in matrices and vectors we propose include mSMM, mSMV, mSMS, mSVV, mSVS, mSSV, mSMSD, mSVSD, mST. Note mSMM, mSMV, mSMS, mSVV, mSVS, mSSV are based on the vectorization protocols whose security has been proved in [23], and we just use mAdd and mMul to substitute Add and Mul respectively in them. According to Lemma 2, mSMM, mSMV, mSMS, mSVV, mSVS, mSSV are secure in the semi-honest model. The mSMSD and mSVSD are just the combination of several mSDPs which have been proved to secure. According to Lemma 2, we can conclude that they are secure. mST is just the simple substitution for coordinates of elements in respective sharing matrices for C_A and C_B. There is not any numerical calculations. What's more, C_A and C_B don't communicate to each other. It's easy to see that mST is also secure. □

Based on the above results, one could have the following theorem.

Theorem 5. *Our SHOSVD scheme is secure in the semi-honest model.*

Proof. From the description shown in Algorithm 9, we can see that our mSL is the combination of mSMV, mSVS, mSVV, mSDP, Mul, SSR, Rec, SDP, mSVSD and mSSV which are secure. According to Lemma 2, we can draw a conclusion that our mSL is secure in the semi-honest model. The security of mSQR and mSCT can be proved in a similar way. Therefor, our SHOSVD is secure. □

7 Performance Analysis

In this section, we evaluate the performance of our SHOSVD scheme. Experiments are conducted on two computers (PC) with 2.30 GHz Intel(R) Core(TM) i5-8300H CPU, 8 GB RAM and 8 Cores. Note that we mainly focus on the on-line computational and communicational overheads in our scheme.

7.1 Theoretical Analysis

Computational Overhead. For a tensor $\mathcal{T} \in \mathbb{R}^{I_1 \times I_2 \times \cdots \times I_H}$. Let m be the size of $\mathcal{T}$, so that $m = I_1 I_2 \cdots I_H$. According to our SHOSVD, before uploading the tensor, the user needs to separate all the elements into two parts by additive secret sharing scheme. Hence, the computational complexity of user is $\mathcal{O}(m)$.

Let T_{mat}, T_{sym}, T_{mSL}, T_{mSQR} and T_{mSCT} be the runtime of tensor matricization, matrix symmetrization, secure Lanczos method, secure QR method and secure core tensor construction protocol respectively, so that the computational overhead T_{clouds} of clouds can be expressed as

$$T_{\mathrm{clouds}} = T_{\mathrm{mat}} + T_{\mathrm{sym}} + T_{\mathrm{mSL}} + T_{\mathrm{mSQR}} + T_{\mathrm{mSCT}}. \tag{5}$$

Tensor matricization needs to unfold the whole tensor H times, so that $T_{\mathrm{mat}} = \mathcal{O}(H I_1 I_2 \cdots I_H)$. Since matrix symmetrization requires $\mathcal{O}(I_i^2 I_1 I_2 \cdots I_{i-1} I_{i+1} \cdots I_H)$ computational complexity for each $i = 1, 2, \cdots H$, $T_{\mathrm{sym}} = \Sigma_{i=1}^{H} \mathcal{O}(I_i^2 I_1 I_2 \cdots I_{i-1} I_{i+1} \cdots I_H)$. For each $i = 1, 2, \cdots H$, the computational complexity of secure Lanczos method and secure QR method are $\mathcal{O}(I_i^3)$ and $\mathcal{O}(t I_i^3)$ respectively, where t is the maximum iteration number in QR method. Therefore, $T_{\mathrm{mSL}} = \Sigma_{i=1}^{H} \mathcal{O}(I_i^3)$ and $T_{\mathrm{mSQR}} = \Sigma_{i=1}^{H} \mathcal{O}(t I_i^3)$. For each truncated orthogonal bases, there is a mode product in the secure core tensor construction protocol, so that $T_{\mathrm{mSCT}} = \Sigma_{i=1}^{H} \mathcal{O}(I_i^2 I_1 I_2 \cdots I_{i-1} I_{i+1} \cdots I_H)$. In conclusion, the computational cost of clouds is $\Sigma_{i=1}^{H} (\mathcal{O}(I_i m) + \mathcal{O}(t I_i^3))$, where m is the size of $\mathcal{T}$.

Communicational Overhead. Let m be the size of the tensor $\mathcal{T} \in \mathbb{R}^{I_1 \times I_2 \times \cdots \times I_H}$. Users only need to communicate with the clouds twice, i.e., outsourcing tensor data and receiving the decomposition results, so that the communicational overhead between users and clouds is $\mathcal{O}(m)$. There are $\mathcal{O}(1)$ round communications in Rec. According to [10], there are $\mathcal{O}(l)$ rounds communications in SC, so that there exist $\mathcal{O}(l)$ rounds communications in SDP and mSDP. Moreover, there are $\mathcal{O}(l^2)$ rounds communications in SSR, where l denotes the bit length of the element of the tensor. mSMSD and mSVSD contain mSDP, therefore their communicational rounds depends on the times of mSDP used. Since there are $\mathcal{O}(I_i)$ Rec, $\mathcal{O}(I_i^2)$ SDP/mSDP and $\mathcal{O}(I_i)$ SSR in mSL for each $i = 1, 2, \cdots H$, the communicational cost of mSL is $\Sigma_{i=1}^{H} \mathcal{O}(I_i + lI_i^2 + l^2 I_i)$. Similarly, the communicational cost of mSQR is $\Sigma_{i=1}^{H} \mathcal{O}(t(lI_i^2 + l^2 I_i))$. There is no communication in mSCT. So that the total communicational overhead between clouds is $\Sigma_{i=1}^{H} \mathcal{O}(I_i + t(lI_i^2 + l^2 I_i))$.

7.2 Simulated Dataset Experiment

To evaluate the overall performance of our SHOSVD, we randomly generate several tensors from $\mathbb{Z}^{I_1 \times I2 \times \cdots \times I_H}$, where $3 \leqslant H \leqslant 5$, and for each $1 \leqslant i \leqslant H$, the size of I_i is random as shown in Table 2.

Table 2. Simulated dataset

Dataset	$\mathcal{T}_1$	$\mathcal{T}_2$	$\mathcal{T}_3$	$\mathcal{T}_4$
H	3	3	4	5
I_1	100–1000	100–1000	100–1000	100–1000
I_2	100–1000	100–1000	100–1000	10–100
I_3	10–100	100–1000	10–100	10–100
I_4	–	–	10–100	10–100
I_5	–	–	–	5

Note that there are two scaling factors ρ and σ in our scheme to improve the accuracy as mentioned in Sect. 5. To evaluate their effects on the results, we set different scaling factors in different simulated tensors to compare our SHOSVD with the traditional HOSVD scheme, and qualify the relative errors as

$$RelativeError = \|\mathcal{S} - \mathcal{S}'\| / \|\mathcal{S}'\|, \tag{6}$$

where $\mathcal{S}$ is the core tensor generated by our SHOSVD, $\mathcal{S}'$ is the core tensor generated by the traditional method without any encryption, and $\|\mathcal{S}\|$ denotes the norm of tensor $\mathcal{S}$. Because ρ only impacts on the outsourced tensor, we set $\rho = 1$ for simplicity, and set σ to 10^3, 10^4, 10^5, 10^6, 10^7 and 10^8. For each certain scale factor, we set the size N of the elements of the tensor to 10^1, 10^2, 10^3 and 10^4 to simulate different sized tensors.

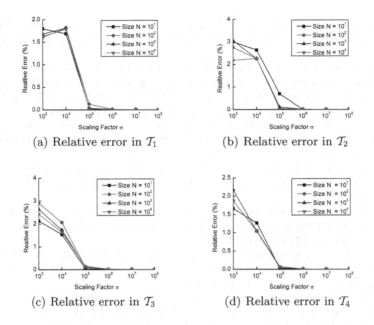

Fig. 2. Relative error of SHOSVD for varying σ using simulated dataset

From Fig. 2, it's clearly to see that the scaling factors are of vital importance in reducing the relative errors, and the relative errors converge to zero rapidly with the growth of σ. When the value of σ is more than 10^6, the rounding errors can be neglected. In addition, the optimum σ has little relation with the tensor's order or the elements' size. With proper scaling factors, our scheme has promising accuracy.

8 Conclusion

In this paper, we designed a secure integer division protocol with public divisor and a secure integer square root protocol in a two-cloud model based on additive secret sharing. And based on them, we proposed a Secure High-Order Singular Value (SHOSVD) scheme that supports off-line users. We also analyzed the correctness problem in the privacy-preserving tensor decomposition scheme proposed by Feng *et al.* [6]. Security analyses of our scheme are made and the experimental results show the accuracy of our scheme.

References

1. Beaver, D.: Efficient multiparty protocols using circuit randomization. In: Feigenbaum, J. (ed.) CRYPTO 1991. LNCS, vol. 576, pp. 420–432. Springer, Heidelberg (1992). https://doi.org/10.1007/3-540-46766-1_34

2. Chang, L., Zhou, J., He, K.: Image compression based on truncated HOSVD. In: International Conference on Information Engineering and Computer Science, 2009. ICIECS 2009 (2010)
3. Damgård, I., Fitzi, M., Kiltz, E., Nielsen, J.B., Toft, T.: Unconditionally secure constant-rounds multi-party computation for equality, comparison, bits and exponentiation. In: Halevi, S., Rabin, T. (eds.) TCC 2006. LNCS, vol. 3876, pp. 285–304. Springer, Heidelberg (2006). https://doi.org/10.1007/11681878_15
4. Feng, J., Yang, L.T., Dai, G., Chen, J., Yan, Z.: An improved secure high-order-lanczos based orthogonal tensor SVD for outsourced cyber-physical-social big data reduction (2018)
5. Feng, J., Yang, L.T., Dai, G., Wang, W., Zou, D.: A secure higher-order lanczos-based orthogonal tensor SVD for big data reduction. IEEE Trans. Big Data 5(3), 355–367 (2018)
6. Feng, J., Yang, L.T., Zhu, Q., Choo, K.K.R.: Privacy-preserving tensor decomposition over encrypted data in a federated cloud environment. IEEETrans. Dependable Secure Comput. 17, 857–868 (2018)
7. Francis, J.G.F.: The QR transformation. Comput. J. 4(4), 332–345 (1962)
8. Goldreich, O.: Foundations of Cryptography: Volume 2 Basic Applications. Cambridge University Press, New York (2009)
9. Lim, H., Kim, H.J.: Tensor-based tag emotion aware recommendation with probabilistic ranking. KSII Trans. Internet Inf. Syst. (TIIS) 13(12), 5826–5841 (2019)
10. Huang, K., Liu, X., Fu, S., Guo, D., Xu, M.: A lightweight privacy-preservingcnn feature extraction framework for mobile sensing. IEEE Trans. Dependable Secure Comput. (2019). https://doi.org/10.1109/TDSC.2019.2913362
11. Kim, J., Koo, D., Kim, Y., Yoon, H., Shin, J., Kim, S.: Efficient privacy-preserving matrix factorization for recommendation via fully homomorphic encryption. ACM Trans. Privacy Security (TOPS) 21(4), 17 (2018)
12. Kolda, T.G., Bader, B.W.: Tensor decompositions and applications. SIAM Rev. 51(3), 455–500 (2009)
13. Kuang, L., Yang, L., Feng, J., Dong, M.: Secure tensor decomposition using fully homomorphic encryption scheme. IEEE Trans. Cloud Comput. 6(3), 868–878 (2015)
14. Kuang, L., Yang, L.T., Zhu, Q., Chen, J.: Secure tensor decomposition for big data using transparent computing paradigm. IEEE Trans. Comput. 68(4), 585–596 (2019)
15. Li, Q., Cascudo, I., Christensen, M.G.: Privacy-preserving distributed average consensus based on additive secret sharing. In: 27th European Signal Processing Conference (EUSIPCO), pp. 1–5 (2019)
16. Liedel, M.: Secure distributed computation of the square root and applications. In: Ryan, M.D., Smyth, B., Wang, G. (eds.) ISPEC 2012. LNCS, vol. 7232, pp. 277–288. Springer, Heidelberg (2012). https://doi.org/10.1007/978-3-642-29101-2_19
17. Liu, L., Chen, R., Liu, X., Su, J., Qiao, L.: Towards practical privacy-preserving decision tree training and evaluation in the cloud. IEEE Trans. Inf. Forensics and Secur. 15, 2914–2929 (2020)
18. Liu, L., et al.: Privacy-preserving mining of association rule on outsourced cloud data from multiple parties. In: Susilo, W., Yang, G. (eds.) ACISP 2018. LNCS, vol. 10946, pp. 431–451. Springer, Cham (2018). https://doi.org/10.1007/978-3-319-93638-3_25
19. Liu, L., et al.: Toward highly secure yet efficient KNN classification scheme on outsourced cloud data. IEEE Internet Things J. 6(6), 9841–9852 (2019)

20. Liu, X., Deng, R.H., Choo, K.K.R., Weng, J.: An efficient privacy-preserving outsourced calculation toolkit with multiple keys. IEEE Trans. Inf. Forensics Secur. **11**(11), 2401–2414 (2016)

21. Liu, Y., Ma, Z., Liu, X., Ma, S., Ren, K.: Privacy-preserving object detection for medical images with faster R-CNN. IEEE Trans. Inf. Forensics Secur. 1 (2019). https://doi.org/10.1109/TIFS.2019.2946476

22. Luo, C., Salinas, S., Li, P.: Efficient privacy-preserving large-scale CP tensor decompositions, pp. 1–6 (2018)

23. Mohassel, P., Zhang, Y.: Secureml: A system for scalable privacy-preserving machine learning. In: IEEE Symposium on Security and Privacy (SP), pp. 19–38. IEEE (2017)

24. Nikolaenko, V., Weinsberg, U., Ioannidis, S., Joye, M., Boneh, D., Taft, N.: Privacy-preserving ridge regression on hundreds of millions of records. In: IEEE Symposium on Security and Privacy (SP), pp. 334–348. IEEE (2013)

25. Paige, C.C.: The computation of eigenvalues and eigenvectors of very large sparse matrices. University of Landon. Ph.D. thesis, vol. 17(1), pp. 87–94 (1975)

26. Paillier, P.: Public-key cryptosystems based on composite degree residuosity classes. In: Stern, J. (ed.) EUROCRYPT 1999. LNCS, vol. 1592, pp. 223–238. Springer, Heidelberg (1999). https://doi.org/10.1007/3-540-48910-X_16

27. Riazi, M.S., Weinert, C., Tkachenko, O., Songhori, E.M., Schneider, T., Koushanfar, F.: Chameleon: a hybrid secure computation framework for machine learning applications. In: Proceedings of the 2018 on Asia Conference on Computer and Communications Security, pp. 707–721. ACM (2018)

28. Schneider, T., Zohner, M.: GMW vs. Yao? Efficient secure two-party computation with low depth circuits. In: Sadeghi, A.-R. (ed.) FC 2013. LNCS, vol. 7859, pp. 275–292. Springer, Heidelberg (2013). https://doi.org/10.1007/978-3-642-39884-1_23

29. Shamir, A.: How to share a secret. Commun. ACM **22**(11), 612–613 (1979)

30. Sidiropoulos, N.D., Sidiropoulos, N.D., Sidiropoulos, N.D.: Tensors for data mining and data fusion: models, applications, and scalable algorithms (2016)

31. Symeonidis, P.: ClustHOSVD: item recommendation by combining semantically enhanced tag clustering with tensor HOSVD. IEEE Trans. Syst. Man Cybern. Syst. **46**(9), 1240–1251 (2016)

Efficient Forward-Secure Threshold
Public Key Encryption

Rafael Kurek[✉]

Group of IT Security and Cryptography,
University of Wuppertal, Wuppertal, Germany
kurek@uni-wuppertal.de

Abstract. The purpose of forward-secure threshold public key encryption schemes is to mitigate the damage of secret key exposure. We construct the first CCA forward-secure threshold public key encryption scheme based on bilinear pairings with groups of prime order that is secure against adaptive and malicious adversaries in the standard model. Our scheme is very efficient since it has a non-interactive key update and decryption procedure. Additionally, our scheme does not require a trusted dealer and has optimal resilience as well as small ciphertexts of constant size. It is the first scheme which achieves all of these and that can also be implemented on standardized elliptic curves.

1 Preliminaries

In a standard public key encryption scheme (PKE), once an adversary gets access to the secret key the adversary is able to decrypt all ciphertexts. There are different approaches to mitigate the damage due to secret key exposure. Two of these approaches are so-called *forward-secure* public key encryption schemes and *threshold* public key encryption schemes. Forward-secure schemes allow to evolve the secret key in regular time periods, while the public key remains fixed. Thus, every adversary with an outdated secret key cannot decrypt ciphers for time periods in the past. In a (n, k)-*threshold* PKE the secret key is split into n shares and at least $k + 1$ shares are required to decrypt a ciphertext, whereas any subset of k shares is insufficient. Due to the fact that forward security and thresholds improve security guarantees against secret key exposure in a different manner, their combination can even reinforce these guarantees. For digital signature schemes their combination was first proposed by Abdalla et al. [1] and Tzeng and Tzeng [18] and later revisited [8,16,20]. For PKE, the combination of forward-secure and threshold mechanisms to a *forward-secure threshold PKE* (fst-PKE) was proposed by Libert and Yung [15]: an adversary that wants to decrypt a ciphertext which was encrypted with a fst-PKE for time period t, needs not only to gain $k + 1$

R. Kurek—Supported by the European Research Council (ERC) under the European Union's Horizon 2020 research and innovation programme, grant agreement 802823, and by the German Research Foundation (DFG) within the Collaborative Research Center "On-The-Fly Computing" (SFB 901/3).

J. K. Liu and H. Cui (Eds.): ACISP 2020, LNCS 12248, pp. 330–349, 2020.
https://doi.org/10.1007/978-3-030-55304-3_17

of the stored secret key shares but it also needs to gain these key shares before time period t expires. It follows that for an adversary with restricted capacities, the combination of forward-security and threshold mechanism provides additional security. To the best of our knowledge the only existing fst-PKE scheme that is CCA forward-secure against adaptive adversaries is due to Libert and Yung.[1] It is highly efficient in terms of communication rounds: the key update procedure as well as the decryption procedure are both non-interactive. For the key update this means that there is no communication at all between the key storage hosts. Besides efficiency, this is also desirable because some of these hosts might be offline or temporarily unavailable. In the case of an interactive key update their unavailability could halt the update procedure entirely or exclude these hosts from further decryption procedures because of outdated key shares. For decryption, the non-interactive procedure means that if a decryption is requested each host can either deny the decryption or provide a valid decryption share without interacting with the other hosts.

Furthermore, the scheme by Libert and Yung is robust against malicious adversaries, which means that invalid decryption shares can be detected and do not manipulate the decrypted message. Their scheme requires bilinear pairings with groups of composite order. To guarantee security, these groups must be very large which results in very expensive computation and much larger keys as well as ciphers when compared to bilinear pairings with groups of prime order. Furthermore the scheme requires a trusted dealer that delivers the initial secret key shares to all participating parties. The only fst-PKE based on pairings with groups of prime order is due to Zhang et al. [21]. It is proven CCA forward secure against adaptive adversaries in the Random Oracle Model and requires a trusted dealer. It requires T elements in the public key, where T is the maximum number of time periods. Moreover, the public key needs to be stored for updating the secret key, which leads to secret keys of size T as well. Although the prime order groups enable fast computation the big key sizes restrict the usage for many applications.

Our Contribution. We present a highly efficient *forward-secure threshold* public key encryption scheme based on bilinear pairings, which can be implemented on *standardized pairing-friendly curves* with groups of prime order. This scheme provides a *non-interactive key update and decryption procedure* and requires *no trusted dealer*. In addition, this scheme provides *ciphertexts of constant size*: one bit string of length $\log T$, where T is the maximum number of supported time periods, and three group elements from prime order groups. The public key is of size $\log T$ and the secret keys have size at most $\log^2 T$. The scheme has *optimal resilience*, i.e., it can tolerate $(n-1)/2$ maliciously compromised parties and is proved CCA forward secure against adaptive adversaries in the *standard model*. Furthermore, it is possible to add pro-active security to our scheme. This enables security against mobile adversaries, i.e. against adversaries which can switch between the parties they corrupt. We discuss this concept and our techniques in Sect. 4.

---

[1] Adaptive adversaries can corrupt parties at any time. Static adversaries need to corrupt the parties before the protocol execution begins. For a proper overview see [1].

2 Forward-Secure Threshold Public Key Encryption (fst-PKE)

Definition 1. *We adapt the definition of fst-PKE and its security from Libert and Yung [15]. A **Forward-secure threshold public key encryption scheme**. (fst-PKE) (T, n, k)-Π_{fst} is defined via the following components:*

FST.KeyGen(n, k, T) $\rightarrow$ $(pk, (pk_i)_{i \in [n]}, (sk_{0,i})_{i \in [n]})$. *On input the maximum number of time periods T, the maximum number of parties n, and a threshold k, it outputs a common public key pk, user public keys $(pk_i)_{i \in [n]}$, and initial secret key shares, $(sk_{0,i})_{i \in [n]}$.*

FST.KeyUpdate$(sk_{t,i})$ $\rightarrow$ $sk_{t+1,i}$. *On input a secret key share for a time period $t < T-1$, it outputs a secret key share for the next time period $t+1$ and deletes the input from its storage. Else it outputs $\perp$.*

FST.Enc(t, pk, M) $\rightarrow$ C. *On input a time period t, a common public key pk, and a message M, it outputs a ciphertext C.*

FST.Dec(t, C) $\rightarrow$ M. *If run by at least $k+1$ honest and uncompromised parties on input a time period t and a ciphertext C, it outputs a message M.*

The key generation procedure can be either a protocol between all parties or executed by a trusted dealer. The key update procedure is assumed to be non-interactive. The decryption procedure is a protocol and contains of various steps: ciphertext-verify, share-decrypt, share-verify, and combine. For simplicity we defined the input only as a time period and a ciphertext and omit the key material held by all participating parties.

Definition 2. Correctness. *Let $(pk, (pk_{0,i})_{i \in [n]}, (sk_{0,i})_{i \in [n]})$ $\leftarrow$**FST.KeyGen** and $(sk_{t,i})$ $\leftarrow$ **FST.KeyUpdate**$(sk_{j-1,i})$ for $j = 1, \ldots, t$ and $i \in [n]$. We call Π_{fst} correct if for all messages M, all time periods $t \in \{0, \ldots, T-1\}$, and all subsets $\mathcal{U} \subseteq \{sk_{t,1}, \ldots sk_{t,n}\}$ of size at least $k+1$ held by uncorrupted parties it holds that*

$$\Pr[\textbf{FST.Dec}(t, \textbf{FST.Enc}(t, pk, M)) = M] = 1.$$

*Note that the secret keys are an implicit input to **FST.Dec**.*

We adapt the robustness notion of threshold signature schemes by Gennaro et al.[10] to forward-secure threshold public key encryption schemes.

Definition 3. Robustness. *A forward-secure threshold PKE Π_{fst} is (n, k_1, k_2)-robust if in a group of n parties, even in the presence of an adversary who halts up to k_1 and corrupts maliciously k_2 parties, **FST.Keygen** and **FST.Dec** complete successfully.*

Note that malicious adversaries can either deviate from the protocol in any way and especially halt some parties. Hence, they are stronger than halting adversaries, see [1].

CCA Forward Security. Chosen ciphertext attack (CCA) forward security against adaptive (static)[1] adversaries is defined by the following game between a challenger and an adversary $\mathcal{A}$. Let $\mathcal{B}$ and $\mathcal{G}$ be the sets of indices, which denote the corrupted and uncorrupted parties, respectively. Initially $\mathcal{B}$ is empty and $\mathcal{G} = \{1, \ldots, n\}$. The challenger (on behalf of the uncorrupted parties) and the adversary (on behalf of the corrupted parties) run **FST.KeyGen**(n, k, T). The adversary receives the common public key pk, all user public keys $(pk_i)_{i \in [n]}$ and the initial user secret key shares $(sk_{i,0})_{i \in \mathcal{B}}$. The adversary has access to the following oracles:

Break-In*(t',j)*. On input time period t' and index $j \in \mathcal{G}$, the challenger checks if $|\mathcal{B}| < k$. If this holds, the challenger removes j out of $\mathcal{G}$ and adds it to $\mathcal{B}$. If $sk_{t,j}$ is already defined, i.e. after **FST.KeyGen** had finished, it is delivered to $\mathcal{A}$. If $|\mathcal{B}| = k$, the challenger outputs $sk_{t,j}$ for all $j \in \mathcal{G}$.[2]

Challenge(t^*, M_0, M_1). The adversary submits a time period t^* and two messages M_0, M_1. The challenger picks a bit b uniformly at random and responds with a challenge ciphertext $C^* =$**FST.Enc**(t^*, pk, m_b).

Dec*(t, C)*. On input time period t and ciphertext C, the challenger (on behalf of the uncorrupted parties) and the adversary $\mathcal{A}$ (on behalf of the corrupted parties) run the decryption protocol **FST.Dec**(t, C). The output of this execution is delivered to $\mathcal{A}$. If **Challenge**(t^*, M_0, M_1) has already been queried and C^* is the response to this query then query **Dec**(t^*, C^*) is disallowed.

Guess*(b')*. The adversary outputs its guess $b' \in \{0, 1\}$. The challenger outputs 1 if $b = b'$, else 0. The game stops.

The adversary is allowed to make $k + 1$ queries **Break-In**(t', j) one query **Challenge**(t^*, m_0, m_1), and multiple queries **Dec**(t, C), in any order, subject to $0 \le t^* < t'_{k+1} < T$, where t'_{k+1} is the time period of the $k + 1$-th query to **Break-In**. After **Break-In**(t'_{k+1}, j), **Dec**(t, C) cannot be queried anymore. **Guess**(b') can only be queried after **Challenge**(t^*, M_0, M_1). For all queries the time periods must be in $[0, \ldots, T-1]$.

Definition 4. *Let $\mathcal{A}$ be an adaptive (static) adversary playing the CCA forward-security game for a fst-PKE (T, n, k) Π_{fst}. It $(t_{\mathcal{A}}, \varepsilon_{\mathcal{A}})$ breaks the CCA forward security of (T, n, k)-Π_{fst}, if it runs in time $t_{\mathcal{A}}$ and*

$$|\Pr[\textbf{Guess}(b') = 1] - 1/2| \ge \varepsilon_{\mathcal{A}}.$$

The only difference between the CPA and CCA security game is that the adversary has no access to the decryption oracle in the former game.

---

[1] In the static security model the adversary has to submit its choice of k parties it wants to corrupt before receiving the public key. In the adaptive model it can corrupt the parties at any time. For a proper overview see [1].

[2] Note that this case can only occur for time periods $t > 0$, i.e. after **FST.KeyGen** had finished. Otherwise the adversary would have no possibility to win the security game.

Definition 5. *Let* $\mathbb{G}_1$, $\mathbb{G}_2$, *and* $\mathbb{G}_T$ *be cyclic groups of prime order* q *with generators* g_1, g_2, g_T. *We call* $e : \mathbb{G}_1 \times \mathbb{G}_2 \rightarrow \mathbb{G}_T$ *a bilinear pairing if: i.* $e(g_1^a, g_2^b) = e(g_1, g_2)^{ab}$ *for all* $a, b \in \mathbb{Z}_q$, *ii.* $e(g_1, g_2) \neq 1_T$, *and iii.* e *can be efficiently computed. If there is no efficiently computable isomorphism from* $\mathbb{G}_2$ *to* $\mathbb{G}_1$ *we call it a Type-3 pairing. For more information we refer to [5, 7].*

The following definition of hierarchical identity-based encryption schemes (HIBE)is reproduced from [6].

Definition 6. *A hierarchical identity-based encryption scheme (HIBE)* Π_{HIBE} *is defined via the following algorithms:* **HIBE.Setup**$(\ell) \rightarrow (pk, sk_0)$, **HIBE.Key Derive**$(id, sk_{id'}) \rightarrow sk_{id'}$, *where* id *is a prefix of* id', **HIBE.Enc**$(id, pk, M) \rightarrow C$. **HIBE.Dec**$(id, sk_{id}, C) \rightarrow M$.

The CPA (CCA) security can be defined analogously to forward-security, see [6].

Definition 7. *A digital signature scheme* Σ *is defined via the following algorithms:* **Sig.Keygen**$\rightarrow$ $(vk, signk)$, **Sig.Sign**$(signk, M)$ $\rightarrow$ σ, **Sig.Verify**$(vk, M, \sigma) \rightarrow b$, *where* $b \in \{0, 1\}$.

Strong Existential Unforgeability Under a One Chosen Message Attack (sEUF-1CMA). In the sEUF-1CMA security game the adversary is allowed to query one signature and has to forge a signature for any message. The only restriction is that it cannot output the same pair of message *and* signature as for the query. If the message is the same then the signature must differ.

3   Our CCA Forward-Secure Threshold PKE

The key generation phase our fst-PKE uses the distributed key generation protocol **DKG** by Gennaro et al. [10]. This protocol is instantiated with the group $\mathbb{G}_2$ from the bilinear pairing we use in our fst-PKE. It outputs a common public key $pk = g_2^x \in \mathbb{G}_2$ as well as user public keys $pk_i = g_2^{x_i} \in \mathbb{G}_2$ for all parties $P_i, i \in [n]$. The user public keys are required to check the decryption shares for validity and hence provide robustness against malicious adversaries in our fst-PKE. Moreover, this protocol provides to each party P_i a secret share $h^{x_i} \in \mathbb{G}_1$ of $h^x \in \mathbb{G}_1$.[3] We apply the secret shares to our fst-PKE by updating them to the first time period. We want to emphasize that for forward security it is crucial to erase the plain values x_i, h^{x_i} for all $i \in [n]$ from every storage. Our fst-PKE scheme $(T, n, k)\text{-}\Pi_{fst}$ is defined as follows.

Common Parameters. The common parameters consist of a the description of a cryptographic Type-3 pairing group with groups of order q, the description

---

[3] Note that in [10] the secret value is set as x instead of h^x. This modification happens only internally and has no impact on the adversary's view or security.

of a cryptographic hash function $H : \{0,1\}^* \to \mathbb{Z}_q$, a value ℓ s.t. $T = 2^\ell$ is the number of time periods, random group elements $h, h_0, \ldots, h_{\ell+1} \leftarrow \mathbb{G}_1$, and random generators $g_2, \tilde{h} \leftarrow \mathbb{G}_2$.

FST.KeyGen. The n parties run the **DKG**(n, k) protocol from Fig. 1. Subsequently, each party P_i holds the common public key $pk = g_2^x \in \mathbb{G}_2$, all user public keys $(g_2^{x_j})_{j \in [n]}$ as well as its own secret share $h^{x_i} \in \mathbb{G}_1$. Each party computes its initial secret key share $sk_{0,i}$ as

$$\left(g_2^{r_i}, h^{x_i} h_0^{r_i}, h_1^{r_i}, \ldots, h_{\ell+1}^{r_i}\right) \in \mathbb{G}_2 \times \mathbb{G}_1^{\ell+2},$$

where $r_i \leftarrow \mathbb{Z}_q$ is picked uniformly at random. The value h^{x_i} is erased from the storage. The common public key pk is published.[4]

FST.KeyUpdate$(sk_{t,i})$. We assume the T time periods $0, \ldots, 2^\ell - 1$ as being organized as leaves of a binary tree of depth ℓ and sorted in increasing order from left to right. This means, $00 \ldots 0$ is the first and $11 \ldots 1$ is the last time period. The path from the root of the tree to a leaf node t equals the bit representation $t_1 \ldots t_\ell$, where we take the left branch for $t_z = 0$ and the right one for $t_z = 1$. Prefixes of time periods correspond to internal nodes $\omega = \omega_1, \ldots, \omega_s$, where $s < \ell$. Let $r_i' \leftarrow \mathbb{Z}_q$ be picked uniformly at random. Then, we associate to each party $P_i, i \in [n]$ and each node ω a secret key:

$$(c_i, d_i, e_{i,s+1}, \ldots, e_{i,\ell+1}) = \left(g_2^{r_i'}, h^{x_i}(h_0 \prod_{v=1}^{s} h_v^{\omega_v})^{r_i'}, h_{s+1}^{r_i'}, \ldots, h_{\ell+1}^{r_i'}\right). \quad (3)$$

Given such a secret key, we derive a secret key for a descendant node $\omega' = \omega_1 \ldots \omega_{s'}$, where $s' > s$ as

$$(c_i', d_i', e_{i,s'+1}', \ldots, e_{i,\ell+1}')$$
$$= \left(c_i \cdot g_2^{r_i''}, d_i \cdot \prod_{v=s+1}^{s'} e_{i,v}^{\omega_v}(h_0 \prod_{v=1}^{s'} h_v^{\omega_v})^{r_i''}, e_{i,s'+1} \cdot h_{s'+1}^{r_i''}, \ldots, e_{i,\ell+1} \cdot h_{\ell+1}^{r_i''}\right),$$

where $r_i'' \leftarrow \mathbb{Z}_q$ is picked uniformly at random.

We define C_t as the smallest subset of nodes that contains an ancestor or leaf for each time period $t, \ldots, T - 1$, but no nodes of ancestors or leafs for time periods $0, \ldots, t - 1$. For time period t, we define the secret key $sk_{i,t}$ of party P_i as the set of secret keys associated to all nodes in C_t. To update the secret key

---

[4] Note that the secret share x_i is computed commonly by all parties and the randomness r_i is computed locally by party P_i and is not a share of another random value. This approach is more efficient than computing random values commonly, especially to different bases.

Protocol DKG(n, k)**:**

   Generation of shared secret x**:**

1. (a) Each Party $P_i, i \in [n]$ picks two random polynomials $a_i(z)$ and $b_i(z)$ over $\mathbb{Z}_q$ of degree k:

$$a_i(z) = a_{i0} + a_{i1}z + \cdots + a_{ik}z^k \text{ and}$$
$$b_i(z) = b_{i0} + b_{i1}z + \cdots + b_{ik}z^k.$$

   (b) Each party P_i computes and broadcasts $C_{is} = g_2^{a_{is}}\tilde{h}^{b_{is}} \in \mathbb{G}_2$ for $s = 0, \ldots, k$.

   (c) Each party P_i computes $s_{ij} = a_i(j)$ and $s'_{ij} = b_i(j) \mod q$ for $j = 1, \ldots, n$. It sends s_{ij}, s'_{ij} secretly to P_j.

   (d) For $i = 1, \ldots, n$ each party P_j checks if

$$g_2^{s_{ij}}\tilde{h}^{s'_{ij}} = \prod_{s=0}^{k}(C_{is})^{j^s}. \tag{1}$$

   If there is an index $i \in [n]$ such that the check fails, P_j broadcasts a *complaint* against P_i.

   (e) If a dealer P_i receives a complaint from P_j then it broadcasts the values s_{ij} and s'_{ij} satisfying Equation 1.

   (f) Each party disqualifies any player that either received more than k *complaints* or answered to a complaint with values that does not satisfy Equation 1.

2. Each party P_i defines the set $QUAL$, which indicates all non-disqualified parties.

3. The shared secret is defined as $h^x = h^{\sum_{i \in QUAL} a_{i0}} \in \mathbb{G}_1$. Each party P_i sets its share of this secret as $h^{x_i} = h^{\sum_{j \in QUAL} s_{ij}} \in \mathbb{G}_1$.

   Extracting $y := g_2^x \in \mathbb{G}_2$**:**

4. (a) Each party $P_i, i \in QUAL$ computes and broadcasts $A_{is} = g_2^{a_{is}} \in \mathbb{G}_2$ for all $s = 0, \ldots, k$.

   (b) For each $i \in QUAL$, each party P_j checks if

$$g_2^{s_{ij}} = \prod_{s=0}^{k}(A_{is})^{j^s}. \tag{2}$$

   If there is an index $i \in QUAL$ such that the check fails, P_j *complaints* about P_i by broadcasting s_{ij} and s'_{ij} that satisfy Eq. 1 but not Eq. 2.

   (c) For all parties P_i who received at least one valid complaint in the extraction phase, the other parties run a reconstruction of $a_i(z)$ and A_{is} for $s = 0, \ldots, k$ in the clear, using the values s_{ij}.

   (d) Each party P_i computes the common public key as $y = \prod_{i \in QUAL} A_{i0} \in \mathbb{G}_2$ and the user public keys pk_j as $g_2^{x_j} = \prod_{i \in QUAL} \prod_{k=0}^{t}(A_{ik})^{j^k}$ for all $j \in [n]$.

Fig. 1. The **DKG** protocol due to Gennaro et al.

to time period $t+1$, determine C_{t+1} and compute the secret keys for all nodes in $C_{t+1}\backslash C_t$. Afterwards, delete $sk_{i,t}$ and all used re-randomization exponents r_i''.[5]

FST.Encrypt(pk, t, M). Let $M \in \mathbb{G}_3$ be the message and $t_1 \ldots t_\ell$ the bit representation of time period t. First, run **Sig.KeyGen**$\rightarrow (vk, signk)$ and compute $H(vk) =: VK$. Then, pick a uniformly random $r \leftarrow \mathbb{Z}_q$ and compute (C_1, C_2, C_3) as

$$\left(e(h, pk)^r \cdot M, \; g_2^r, \; (h_0 \prod_{v=1}^{\ell} h_v^{t_v} \cdot h_{\ell+1}^{VK})^r \right) \in \mathbb{G}_3 \times \mathbb{G}_2 \times \mathbb{G}_1$$

and **Sig.Sign**$(signk, (C_1, C_2, C_3),) \rightarrow \sigma$. Output the ciphertext

$$C = (C_1, C_2, C_3), vk, \sigma).$$

FST.Decrypt $(t, (C_1, C_2, C_3), vk, \sigma)$. Let $\mathcal{W}$ be the set of indices of all participating parties. W.l.o.g. we assume that $\mathcal{W}$ contains at least $k+1$ distinct indices. The participating parties run the decryption protocol from Fig. 2.[6]

Remark 1. Note that the subset $\mathcal{V} \subseteq \mathcal{W}$ from the decryption protocol (Fig. 2) might be of size greater than $k + 1$, while $k + 1$ partial decryption shares are sufficient to decrypt the ciphertext. For this reason aggregating only $k + 1$ decryption shares avoids computational overhead.

Remark 2. The secret keys in our fst-PKE have a binary tree structure in the sense of [6], except for the lowest level. In Theorem 4 from [6], it is shown that encryption schemes, which have a binary tree structure on all levels, imply forward security. Although it is possible to remove the lowest level and the strong one-time signature scheme in our construction, doing so would result in a scheme which is only forward secure against CPA instead of CCA.

Proof of Correctness. We have to prove that (c', d') is a valid decryption key for ciphertext $C = (C_1, C_2, C_3, vk, \sigma)$ under t, VK and the common public key

---

[5] Example: Let $T = 2^3$. Then $t_0 = 000$, $t_1 = 100$, $t_2 = 010$,... . Given a substring xy, we can compute $xy0$ and $xy1$. Hence, for time period t_2 the set C_{t_2} consists of the node keys for 01 and 1. From 01 it can compute the secret key for $t_2 = 010$ and $t_3 = 011$. From 1 it can compute the secret key for all time periods greater t_3: 100, 101, 110, 111. The keys for time periods $t_0 = 000$ and $t_1 = 001$ cannot be computed from this set. If we update to time period t_3, we need to compute 011 and erase the node key for 01. Thus C_{t_3} consists of the key for 011 and the node key 1. Then, also the key for 010 cannot be computed anymore.

[6] Note that decryption happens with respect to a time period. Since time periods are encoded in full bit length (even if they start with zero) they are low in the binary tree. Hence, they only have left $e_{i,\ell+1}$ as going down one level in depth erases one value $e_{i,x}, x \in [\ell]$.

$pk = g_2^x$. To that end we show first that set $\mathcal{V}$, which indicates the correct decryption shares, can be determined. That is, we show that we can check whether the decryption shares (c'_i, d'_i), $i \in \mathcal{W}$ are correct. Let (c'_i, d'_i) be an honestly generated decryption in Step 2 of the protocol. Then d'_i is equal to

$$d_i e_{i,\ell+1}^{VK}(h_0 \prod_{v=1}^{\ell} h_v^{t_v} h_{\ell+1}^{VK})^{v_i} = h^{x_i}(h_0 \prod_{v=1}^{\ell} h_v^{t_v})^{r_i} e_{i,\ell+1}^{VK}(h_0 \prod_{v=1}^{\ell} h_v^{t_v} h_{\ell+1}^{VK})^{v_i}$$

$$= h^{x_i}(h_0 \prod_{v=1}^{\ell} h_v^{t_v} h_{\ell+1}^{VK})^{r_i+v_i}, \tag{5}$$

$\underline{\textbf{Dec}(t, (C_1, C_2, C_3), vk, \sigma, P_1, ..., P_n)}$**:**

1. **Ciphertext-Verify.** At decryption request of $((C_1, C_2, C_3), vk, \sigma)$ at time $t = t_1 \ldots t_\ell$, each party $P_i, i \in \mathcal{W}$ checks whether **Sig.Verify**$(vk, (C_1, C_2, C_3), \sigma) = 1$ and whether the ciphertext is valid for time period t and for the hashed verification key $VK = H(vk)$. That is, it checks whether the following equation holds.

$$e((h_0 \prod_{v=1}^{s} h_v^{t_v} \cdot h_{\ell+1}^{VK}), C_2) = e(C_3, g_2).$$

   If one or both checks fail it aborts.
2. **Share-Decrypt.** Else each party picks a uniformly random $v_i \leftarrow \mathbb{Z}_q$ and uses its secret key $sk_{i,t} = (c_i, d_i, e_{i,\ell+1})$ to compute a decryption share (c'_i, d'_i), where

$$d'_i := d_i \cdot e_{i,\ell+1}^{VK}(h_0 \prod_{v=1}^{\ell} h_v^{t_v} \cdot h_{\ell+1}^{VK})^{v_i} \quad \text{and} \quad c'_i := c_i \cdot g_2^{v_i}.$$

   Afterwards, each party $P_i, \in \mathcal{W}$ sends (c'_i, d'_i) secretly to all other parties.
3. **Share-Verify.** All parties in $\mathcal{W}$ use the public keys $pk_j, j \in \mathcal{W}$ to check if the contributed decryption shares are valid. That is, if

$$e(d'_j, g_2) = e(h, pk_j) \cdot e(h_0 \prod_{v=1}^{\ell} h_v^{t_v} \cdot h_{\ell+1}^{VK}, c'_j).$$

4. **Combine.** Let $\mathcal{V} \subseteq \mathcal{W}$ indicate a set of parties sending valid decryption shares. If $\mathcal{V}$ contains at least $k+1$ distinct indices then the decryption key (c', d') is computed as

$$c' = \prod_{i \in \mathcal{V}} c_i'^{L_i} \quad \text{and} \quad d' = \prod_{i \in \mathcal{V}} d_i'^{L_i},$$

   where $L_i = \prod_{j \in \mathcal{V}, j \neq i}(-i)/(j-i)$ are the Lagrange coefficients.
5. Finally, the plaintext is computed as

$$C_1 \cdot e(C_3, c')/e(d', C_2) = M. \tag{4}$$

Fig. 2. The **decryption** protocol of our fst PKE.

where we used the fact that $e_{i,\ell+1} = h_{i,\ell+1}^{r_i}$. Furthermore, $c_i' = g_2^{r_i+v_i}$. If a decryption share (c_i', d_i') satisfies (5) and $c_i' = g_2^{r_i+v_i}$ then the validity check in Step 3 is correct, because

$$e(d_i', g_2) = e(h^{x_i}(h_0 \prod_{v=1}^{\ell} h_v^{t_v} h_{\ell+1}^{VK})^{r_i+v_i}, g_2)$$

$$= e(h^{x_i}, g_2)e((h_0 \prod_{v=1}^{\ell} h_v^{t_v} h_{\ell+1}^{VK})^{r_i+v_i}, g_2) = e(h, pk_i)e(h_0 \prod_{v=1}^{\ell} h_v^{t_v} h_{\ell+1}^{VK}, c_i').$$

For this reason, we can indeed check whether a decryption share (c_i', d_i') for message C under t, VK and user public key $g_2^{x_i}$ is correct and thus include i into set $\mathcal{V}$. It remains to show that all decryption shares (c_i', d_i'), $i \in \mathcal{V}$ interpolate to a valid decryption key under the common public key g_2^x. For this purpose, we set $R := \sum_{i \in \mathcal{V}} L_i(r_i + v_i)$. Then, d' is equal to

$$\prod_{i \in \mathcal{V}} d_i'^{L_i} = h^{\sum_{i \in \mathcal{V}} L_i x_i}(h_0 \prod_{v=1}^{\ell} h_v^{t_v} h_{\ell+1}^{VK})^{\sum_{i \in \mathcal{V}} L_i(r_i+v_i)} = h^x(h_0 \prod_{v=1}^{\ell} h_v^{t_v} h_{\ell+1}^{VK})^R,$$

where $\sum_{i \in \mathcal{V}} L_i x_i = x$. Furthermore, $c' = \prod_{i \in \mathcal{V}} c_i'^{L_i} = g_2^{\sum_{i \in \mathcal{V}} L_i(r_i+v_i)} = g_2^R$. Overall, we have for a valid ciphertext

$$C_1 e(C_3, c')/e(d', C_2)$$

$$= Me(h, g_2^x)^r e((h_0 \prod_{v=1}^{\ell} h_v^{t_v} \cdot h_{\ell+1}^{VK})^r, g_2^R)/e(h^x(h_0 \prod_{v=1}^{\ell} h_v^{t_v} \cdot h_{\ell+1}^{VK})^R, g_2^r) = M.$$

Proof of Security. As preparation for the security proof we describe in Fig. 3 how the reduction simulates the **DKG** protocol. The simulation in Fig. 3 is also due to Gennaro et al. Additionally, Fig. 4 describes how the reduction simulates.

FST.Decrypt. According to Definition 4, the adversary is allowed to control up to k parties during the key generation and decryption procedure. First, we assume a static adversary as in the proof in [10]. In the proof of Theorem 3, it is shown how to achieve security against adaptive adversaries. In Sect. 4, it is explained why this approach gives a more efficient scheme than the use of composite order groups as in [15]. W.l.o.g. we assume the corrupted parties to be $P_1, \ldots, P_k$. Let $\mathcal{B} := \{1, \ldots, k\}$ indicate the set of corrupted parties, controlled by the adversary $\mathcal{A}$, and let $\mathcal{G} := \{k+1, \ldots, n\}$ indicate the set of uncorrupted parties, run by the simulator.

Note that during the simulation of the decryption procedure the simulator already executed **DKGSim** (Fig. 3). Therefore, it is in possession of the secret shares $x_1, \ldots, x_k$ and the polynomials $a_i(z), b_i(z)$ for all $i \in [n]$.

Protocol DKGSim$(y = g_2^x, n, k)$:

1. The simulator performs Steps 1a–1f and 2 on behalf of the uncorrupted parties exactly as in the **DKG**(n, k) protocol. Additionally, it reconstructs the polynomials $a_i(z), b_i(z)$ for $i \in \mathcal{B}$. Then:
   - The set $QUAL$ is well-defined and $\mathcal{G} \subseteq QUAL$ and all polynomials are random for all $i \in \mathcal{G}$.
   - The adversary sees $a_i(z), b_i(z)$ for $i \in \mathcal{B}$, the shares $(s_{ij}, s'_{ij}) = (a_i(j), b_i(j))$ for $i \in QUAL, j \in \mathcal{B}$ and C_{is} for $i \in QUAL, s = 0, \ldots, k$.
   - The simulator knows all polynomials $a_i(z), b_i(z)$ for $i \in QUAL$ as well as all shares s_{ij}, s'_{ij}, all coefficients a_{is}, b_{is} and the public values C_{is}.
2. The simulator performs as folllows:
   - Computes $A_{is} = g_2^{a_{is}} \in \mathbb{G}_2$ for $i \in QUAL \setminus \{n\}, s = 0, \ldots, k$.
   - Sets $A_{n0}^* = y \cdot \prod_{i \in QUAL \setminus \{n\}} (A_{i0}^{-1})$.
   - Sets $s_{nj}^* = s_{nj} = a_n(j)$ for $j = 1, \ldots, k$.
   - Computes $A_{ns}^* = (A_{n0}^*)^{\lambda_{s0}} \cdot \prod_{i=1}^k (g_2^{s_{ni}^*})^{\lambda_{si}} \in \mathbb{G}_2$ for $s = 1, \ldots, k$, where the λ_{is}s are the Lagrange interpolation coefficients.
   (a) The simulator broadcasts A_{is} for $i \in \mathcal{G} \setminus \{n\}$ and A_{ns}^* for $s = 0, \ldots, k$.
   (b) It performs for all uncorrupted parties the verification of (2) on the values A_{ij} for $i \in \mathcal{B}$. In case of a fail it broadcasts a complaint (s_{ij}, s'_{ij}). Since the adversary controls at most k parties and the simulator behaves honestly, only secret shares of corrupted parties can be reconstructed.
   (c) Afterwards it performs the Steps 4c and 4d of the **DKG**(n, k) protocol.

Fig. 3. The simulation of the **DKG** protocol due to Gennaro et al.

In the **DKG** protocol (Fig. 1) the secret shares for all parties $P_j, j \in [n]$ are defined as $x_j := \sum_{i \in QUAL} s_{ij} \mod q$. In **DKGSim** however, the shares are defines as $x_j := \sum_{i \in QUAL \setminus \{n\}} s_{ij} + s_{nj}^* \mod q$, where the values s_{nj}^* for $j = k + 1, \ldots, n$, i.e. for $j \in \mathcal{G}$, are not explicitly known. Moreover, in **DKGSim** the public key of user $P_j, j \in [n]$ is $g_2^{x_j} = \prod_{i \in QUAL \setminus \{n\}} g_2^{s_{ij}} g_2^{s_{nj}^*} = \prod_{i \in QUAL \setminus \{n\}} \prod_{s=0}^k (A_{is})^{j^s} \prod_{s=0}^k (A_{ns}^*)^{j^s}$, where the values A_{ns}^* include the common public key $y = g_2^x$. Hence, in order to compute the secret share h^{x_j} for $j \in \mathcal{G}$ either the corresponding value h^x or s_{nj}^* is required. Although these values are not known to the simulator it is still able to simulate the role of the uncompromised parties during the decryption of a valid ciphertext $(t, C_1, C_2, C_3, vk, \sigma)$. In order to do so it requires a valid secret key (c, d) for time t together with the hashed verification key $VK = H(vk)$, i.e. for the string t, VK. If the simulator is an adversary breaking the CPA security of the HIBE scheme from [2] this key can be requested in its own security experiment. Let $t = t_1 \ldots t_\ell$ and $(c, d) = \left(g_2^r, h^x (h_0 \prod_{v=1}^\ell h_v^{t_v} \cdot h_{\ell+1}^{VK})^r \right)$. Define consistently with **DKGSim**:

- $H_{is} := h^{a_{is}}$ for all $i \in QUAL \setminus \{n\}, s = 0, \ldots, k$
- $H_{n0}^* := \prod_{i \in QUAL \setminus \{n\}} (H_{i0}^{-1}) h^x$

- $s_{nj}^* := s_{nj} = a_n(j)$ for $j = 1, \ldots, k$
- $H_{ns}^* := (H_{n0}^*)^{\lambda_{s0}} \prod_{i=1}^{k} (h^{s_{ni}^*})^{\lambda_{si}}$ for $s = 1, \ldots, k$
- $\hat{H}_{n0} := \prod_{i \in QUAL\setminus\{n\}} (H_{i0}^{-1} d)$.

Thus, $pk_j = h^{x_j}, j \in \mathcal{G}$ are defined as $\prod_{i \in QUAL\setminus\{n\}} \prod_{s=0}^{k} (H_{is})^{j^s} \prod_{s=0}^{k} (H_{ns}^*)^{j^s}$. To obtain a valid decryption share for $P_j, j \in \mathcal{G}$ compute an intermediate d_j'' as

$$\prod_{i \in QUAL\setminus\{n\}} \prod_{s=0}^{k} (H_{is})^{j^s} (\hat{H}_{n0}) \prod_{s=1}^{k} \left((\hat{H}_{n0})^{\lambda_{s0}} \prod_{i=1}^{k} (h^{s_{ni}^*})^{\lambda_{si}} \right)^{j^s}$$

$$= \prod_{i \in QUAL\setminus\{n\}} \prod_{s=0}^{k} (H_{is})^{j^s} \left(\prod_{i \in QUAL\setminus\{n\}} (H_{i0}^{-1}) h^x (h_0 \prod_{v=1}^{\ell} h_v^{t_v} h_{\ell+1}^{VK})^r \right)$$

$$\prod_{s=1}^{k} \left(\left(\prod_{i \in QUAL\setminus\{n\}} (H_{i0}^{-1}) h^x (h_0 \prod_{v=1}^{\ell} h_v^{t_v} h_{\ell+1}^{VK})^r \right)^{\lambda_{s0}} \prod_{i=1}^{k} (h^{s_{ni}^*})^{\lambda_{si}} \right)^{j^s}$$

$$= \prod_{i \in QUAL\setminus\{n\}} \prod_{s=0}^{k} (H_{is})^{j^s} \left(\prod_{i \in QUAL\setminus\{n\}} (H_{i0}^{-1}) h^x \right) (h_0 \prod_{v=1}^{\ell} h_v^{t_v} h_{\ell+1}^{VK})^r$$

$$\prod_{s=1}^{k} \left(\left(\prod_{i \in QUAL\setminus\{n\}} (H_{i0}^{-1}) h^x \right)^{\lambda_{s0}} \prod_{i=1}^{k} (h^{s_{ni}^*})^{\lambda_{si}} \right)^{j^s} \prod_{s=1}^{k} \left((h_0 \prod_{v=1}^{\ell} h_v^{t_v} h_{\ell+1}^{VK})^{r\lambda_{s0}} \right)^{j^s}$$

$$= \prod_{i \in QUAL\setminus\{n\}} \prod_{s=0}^{k} (H_{is})^{j^s} (\prod_{s=0}^{k} (H_{ns}^*)^{j^s}) (h_0 \prod_{v=1}^{\ell} h_v^{t_v} h_{\ell+1}^{VK})^{r \sum_{s=1}^{k} \lambda_{s0} j^s + r}$$

$$- h^{x_j} (h_0 \prod_{v=1}^{\ell} h_v^{t_v} h_{\ell+1}^{VK})^{r \sum_{s=1}^{k} \lambda_{s0} j^s + r}.$$

To re-randomize, pick a uniformly random $w_j \leftarrow \mathbb{Z}_p$ and compute d_j' and c_j' as

$$d_j''(h_0 \prod_{v=1}^{\ell} h_v^{t_v} h_{\ell+1}^{VK})^{w_j} \text{ and } c^{\sum_{s=1}^{k} \lambda_{s0} j^s + 1} g_2^{w_j}. \tag{6}$$

Lemma 1. *The protocols **DKG** and **DKGSim** as well as **Dec** and **DecSim** are indistinguishable.*

Proof. For **DKG** and **DKGSim** the proof can be found in Theorem 2 of [10]. In the same fashion it can be easily verified that the adversary has the same view **Dec** and **DecSim**. □

Theorem 1. *The scheme (T, n, k)-Π_{fst} from Sect. 3 is (n, k_1, k_2)-robust if $k_1 + k_2 \leq k$ and $n \geq 2k + 1$. In particular, the scheme is $(n, 0, k)$-robust, i.e. robust against malicious adversaries.*

DecSim$(t, (C_1, C_2, C_3), vk, \sigma), (c, d))$

1. The decryption is requested. Let $t = t_1 \ldots t_\ell$. The simulator performs the validity checks from Step 1 of protocol **Dec**. If one of these checks fail it aborts.
2. Else, the simulator uses the polynomials $a_i(z), b_i(z)$ for all $i \in [n]$ and the decryption key (c, d) for t, VK to compute valid decryption shares on behalf of all uncorrupted parties: for $j = k + 1, \ldots, n$ it computes d_j'' as

$$\prod_{i \in QUAL \setminus \{n\}} \prod_{s=0}^{k} (H_{is})^{j^s} \cdot (\hat{H}_{n0}) \cdot \prod_{s=1}^{k} ((\hat{H}_{n0})^{\lambda_{s0}} \cdot \prod_{i=1}^{k} (h^{s_{ni}^*})^{\lambda_{si}})^{j^s}.$$

Then, it picks $w_j \leftarrow \mathbb{Z}_q$ uniformly at random and computes d_j' as

$$d_j'' \cdot (h_0 \prod_{v=1}^{\ell} h_v^{t_v} \cdot h_{\ell+1}^{VK})^{w_j}.$$

Afterwards, it computes c_j' as:

$$c^{\sum_{s=1}^{k} \lambda_{s0} \cdot j^s + 1} \cdot g_2^{w_j}.$$

Then, the simulator sends (c_j', d_j') for all $j = k + 1, \ldots, n$ to the corrupted parties $P_1, \ldots, P_k$. The simulator might receive decryption shares on behalf of the corrupted parties.
3. The simulator does nothing.
4. The adversary can use any set $\mathcal{V}$ of at least $k + 1$ partial decryption shares to construct the final decryption key:

$$(c', d') = (\prod_{i \in \mathcal{V}} c_i'^{L_i}, \prod_{i \in \mathcal{V}} d_i'^{L_i}),$$

where $L_i = \prod_{j \in \mathcal{V}, j \neq i} (-i)/(j - i)$ are Lagrange coefficients. The simulator does nothing.
5. The adversary can use the decryption key (c, d) to decrypt the ciphertext. The simulator does nothing.

Fig. 4. The simulation of the **decryption** protocol.

Proof. We argue for the strongest case, i.e. $(n, 0, k)$. To show that Π_{fst} is $(n, 0, k)$-robust we analyze all protocols where the adversary on behalf of the uncompromised parties may interact with the honest ones, i.e. **FST.KeyGen** and **FST.Decrypt**. More precisely, we show that the adversary is incapable to prevent the honest parties from executing these protocols successfully. The **FST.KeyGen** protocol is instantiated with the **DKG** protocol from [10], which was shown to be robust against malicious adversaries. The reason for this is that a party which deviates from the protocol specification is either disqualified or its secret share is reconstructed by the honest parties. In the case of the

FST.Decrypt protocol the adversary has two options to attempt cheating. One option is to try manipulating the ciphertext. This however, is prevented in Step 1 of the decryption protocol by checking the ciphertext for validity. The second option is to try manipulating or denying decryption shares. This is prevented in Step 3 by using the user public keys $g^{x_i}, i \in [n]$ to check if the decryption shares are valid. Hence only valid decryption shares are aggregated and the message is decrypted correctly. Moreover, the adversary is allowed to control or halt at most k parties. Thus, a valid decryption share can still be computed as long as $n \geq 2k + 1$. □

Theorem 2. *Let $n \geq 2k + 1$ and let $\mathcal{A}$ be a static adversary that $(t_{\mathcal{A}}, \varepsilon_{\mathcal{A}})$- breaks the CCA forward security of (T, n, k)-Π_{fst} from Sect. 3. Given $\mathcal{A}$, we can build an adversary $\mathcal{A}'$ that $(t_{\mathcal{A}'}, \varepsilon_{\mathcal{A}'})$-breaks the CPA security of HIBE Π_{HIBE} from [2], an adversary $\mathcal{A}''$ that $(t_{\mathcal{A}''}, \varepsilon_{\mathcal{A}''})$-breaks the sEUF-1CMA security of a signature scheme Σ, and an adversary $\mathcal{A}'''$ that $(t_{\mathcal{A}'''}, \varepsilon_{\mathcal{A}'''})$-breaks the collision resistance of hash function H, such that*

$$t_{\mathcal{A}'''} \approx t_{\mathcal{A}''} \approx t_{\mathcal{A}'} \approx t_{\mathcal{A}} \text{ and } \varepsilon_{\mathcal{A}'''} + \varepsilon_{\mathcal{A}''} + \varepsilon_{\mathcal{A}'} \geqslant \varepsilon_{\mathcal{A}}.$$

□

Proof. Conceptually, we follow the proofs from Sections. 4 and 6 in [4], which were also reproduced in Section 4.1 in [3]. In [4], a CPA-secure HIBE with $\ell + 1$ levels and identities of length $n + 1$ bits is turned into a CCA-secure HIBE with ℓ levels and identities of length n bits. The reason for the shorter identities in the CCA-secure scheme is that this framework uses one bit of the identity as a padding. This padding guarantees that decryption queries do not correspond to prefixes of the challenge identity. In our scheme however, the first ℓ levels are single bits and the deepest level has elements in $\mathbb{Z}_q$, which makes it impossible to spend one bit of each identity for the padding. However, in our scheme the adversary is only allowed to make decryption queries with respect to time periods (plus a value in $\mathbb{Z}_q$). Since time periods are always encoded with full length they cannot correspond to prefixes of each other. Thus a padding is not necessary.

We start with describing an adversary $\mathcal{A}'$ playing the CPA security game for HIBE Π_{HIBE} and simulating the CCA forward security game for a static adversary $\mathcal{A}$.

At the beginning, $\mathcal{A}$ sends its choice of the k parties it wants to corrupt to $\mathcal{A}'$. Let $\mathcal{B}$ denote the set of the indices of these parties and $\mathcal{G} := \{1, \ldots, n\} \setminus \mathcal{B}$. Adversary $\mathcal{A}'$ runs **Sig.KeyGen** to obtain $(vk^*, signk^*)$. Then it computes $H(vk^*) := VK^*$. Moreover, it receives a master public key $mpk := g_2^x \in \mathbb{G}_2$ from its own security experiment. In order to simulate the **FST.KeyGen** procedure adversary $\mathcal{A}'$ (on behalf of the uncompromised parties) runs the **DKGSim** protocol on input (g_2^x, n, k). Both adversaries receive all information to compute the secret key shares of all compromised parties and the user public keys pk_i for all $i \in [n]$ as well as the common public key $pk = g_2^x$. Afterwards, $\mathcal{A}$ has access to the following procedures, which are simulated by $\mathcal{A}'$ as follows.

Break-In(t',j). On input a time period $t' = t_1 \ldots t_\ell$ adversary $\mathcal{A}'$ queries **Key-Query** on all nodes from the set $C_{t'}$, which was defined in the **KeyUpdate** procedure in 3. According to the definition of $C_{t'}$ these are all the nodes which allow the computation of the secret keys for all time periods $t \geqslant t'$ but for no time period $t < t'$. As a response it obtains tuples of the form

$$(c, d, e_{s+1}, \ldots, e_{\ell+1}) = \left(g_2^r, h^x (h_0 \prod_{v=1}^{s} h_v^{w_v})^r, h_{s+1}^r, \ldots, h_{\ell+1}^r \right),$$

which correspond to internal nodes $\omega = \omega_1 \ldots \omega_s$, where $s \leq \ell$. In order to compute the secret keys $sk_{t',j}$ for all $j \in \mathcal{G}$ it proceeds as follows. It defines equivalently to **DecSim**:

- $H_{is} := h^{a_{is}}$ for all $i \in QUAL \setminus \{n\}, s = 0, \ldots, k$
- $H_{n0}^* := \prod_{i \in QUAL \setminus \{n\}} (H_{i0}^{-1}) \cdot h^x$
- $s_{nj}^* := s_{nj} = a_n(j)$ for $j = 1, \ldots, k$
- $H_{ns}^* := (H_{n0}^*)^{\lambda_{s0}} \cdot \prod_{i=1}^{k} (h^{s_{ni}^*})^{\lambda_{si}}$ for $s = 1, \ldots, k$
- $\bar{H}_{n0} := \prod_{i \in QUAL \setminus \{n\}} (H_{i0}^{-1} \cdot d)$ for each tuple $(c, d, \ldots)$ separately.

It computes for all tuples a corresponding value d_j as:

$$\prod_{i \in QUAL \setminus \{n\}} \prod_{s=0}^{k} (H_{is})^{j^s} \cdot (\bar{H}_{n0}) \cdot \prod_{s=1}^{k} \left((\bar{H}_{n0})^{\lambda_{s0}} \cdot \prod_{i=1}^{k} (h^{s_{ni}^*})^{\lambda_{si}} \right)^{j^s}$$

and for all values $\tilde{x}$ from $\{c, e_{i+1}, \ldots, e_{\ell+1}\}$ it computes $\tilde{x}_j$ as $\tilde{x}^{\sum_{s=1}^{k} \lambda_{s0} \cdot j^s + 1}$.

In order to guarantee a perfect simulation $\mathcal{A}'$ re-randomizes the secret keys of all parties in the same fashion as the decryption shares in (6). Finally, it outputs $sk_{t',j}$ for all $j \in \mathcal{G}$ as the stack of tuples of the form $(c_j, d_j, e_{j,i+1}, \ldots, e_{j,\ell+1})$.

Analogously to the decryption in **DecSim** it holds that

$$d_j = h^{x_j} \cdot (h_0 \prod_{v=1}^{s} h_v^{w_v})^{r' \cdot \sum_{s=1}^{k} \lambda_{k0} \cdot j^s + r'}.$$

Overall, these stacks form valid secret keys $sk_{t',j}$ for all $j \in \mathcal{G}$ and their simulation is perfect. If **Challenge**(t^*, M_0, M_1) was already queried then all break-in queries with $t' \leqslant t^*$ are invalid.

Challenge(t^*, M_0, M_1). Adversary $\mathcal{A}$ submits two messages M_0, M_1 and challenge time period t^*. Adversary $\mathcal{A}'$ forwards $(t^*.VK^*, M_0, M_1)$ to **Challenge** in its own security game and receives a ciphertext (C_1, C_2, C_3) which equals

$$\left(e(h, pk)^r \cdot M_b, \ g_2^r, \ (h_0 \prod_{v=1}^{\ell} h_v^{t_v} \cdot h_{\ell+1}^{VK^*})^r \right) \in \mathbb{G}_3 \times \mathbb{G}_2 \times \mathbb{G}_1,$$

where b is a uniformly random bit. Afterwards, it computes a signature $\sigma^* \leftarrow$ **Sig.Sign**$(signk^*, (C_1, C_2, C_3))$ and outputs the challenge ciphertext $C^* = (C_1,$

C_2, C_3, vk^*, σ^*). If **Break-In** on input $t' \leqslant t^*$ was previously queried then the challenge query is invalid.

$\underline{\textbf{Dec}(t, C_1, C_2, C_3, vk, \sigma)}$. Whenever $\mathcal{A}$ asks for a decryption then $\mathcal{A}'$ proceeds as follows. First, it checks if $vk = vk^*$ and **Sig.Verify**$(vk, (C_1, C_2, C_3), \sigma) = 1$ or if $vk \neq vk^*$ and $H(vk) = VK^*$. If one of these conditions is true then $\mathcal{A}'$ aborts and outputs a uniformly random bit to **Guess** in its own security game. Else it queries **KeyQuery**(t, VK) to obtain the decryption key $sk_{t,VK} = (c, d)$. Then, it simulates the decryption procedure by running **DecSim**$(t, (C_1, C_2, C_3), vk, \sigma, (c, d))$. Since t, VK is unequal to and no prefix of $t^*.VK^*$ the query to **KeyQuery** is valid. **Dec** cannot be queried on input (t^*, C^*).

$\underline{\textbf{Guess}(b')}$. Adversary $\mathcal{A}$ outputs its guess $b' \in \{0, 1\}$, which $\mathcal{A}'$ forwards to **Guess** in its own experiment.

We denote **Forge** the event that $\mathcal{A}'$ aborts during a decryption query because of the first condition and **Coll** that it aborts because of the second condition. Together with Lemma 1 it can be seen that adversary $\mathcal{A}'$ provides a perfect simulation to $\mathcal{A}$ as long as any of these two events do *not* happen. Thus,

$$|\varepsilon_{\mathcal{A}} - \varepsilon_{\mathcal{A}'}| \leqslant \Pr[\textbf{Forge} \cup \textbf{Coll}] = \Pr[\textbf{Forge}] + \Pr[\textbf{Coll}]. \tag{7}$$

In order to determine $\Pr[\textbf{Forge}]$ note that if **Forge** occurs then $\mathcal{A}$ has submitted a valid ciphertext $(C_1, C_2, C_3, vk^*, \sigma^*)$, which means that σ^* is a valid signature for message (C_1, C_2, C_3) under verification key vk^*. We show how to build an adversary $\mathcal{A}''$ that breaks the sEUF-1CMA security of Σ using $\mathcal{A}$.

Adversary $\mathcal{A}''$ plays the sEUF-1CMA security game with respect to Σ. At the beginning, it receives a verification key vk^* from its challenger. After $\mathcal{A}$ has submitted its choice of corrupted parties adversary $\mathcal{A}''$ picks a uniformly random $x \leftarrow \mathbb{Z}_q$ and executes **DKGSim**(g_2^x, n, k) on behalf of the uncorrupted parties. Since $\mathcal{A}''$ is in possession of x it is able to simulate all secret keys queried to **Break-In**. If $\mathcal{A}$ makes a valid query **Dec**$(t, C_1, C_2, C_3, vk^*, \sigma^*)$ then $\mathcal{A}''$ outputs $(C_1, C_2, C_3, \sigma^*)$ as a forgery to its own security experiment. If $\mathcal{A}$ makes a query **Challenge**(t^*, M_0, M_1) then $\mathcal{A}''$ picks a bit b uniformly at random and computes **FST.Encrypt**$(pk, t^*, M_b) \rightarrow (C_1, C_2, C_3)$. Afterwards, it queries the signing oracle in its own security experiment on input (C_1, C_2, C_3). It receives a signature σ and returns $(t^*, C_1, C_2, C_3, vk^*, \sigma)$ to $\mathcal{A}$. If $\mathcal{A}$ happens to query **Dec**$(C_1, C_2, C_3, vk^*, \sigma^*)$ then, $\mathcal{A}''$ submits $((C_1, C_2, C_3), \sigma^*)$ as its forgery. Note that if the challenge oracle was already queried we still have $((C_1, C_2, C_3), \sigma) \neq ((C_1, C_2, C_3), \sigma^*)$. It follows that

$$\Pr[\textbf{Forge}] = \varepsilon_{\mathcal{A}''}. \tag{8}$$

It remains to determine $\Pr[\textbf{Coll}]$ for H by building an adversary $\mathcal{A}'''$ that breaks the collision resistance of H. It is easy to see that adversary $\mathcal{A}'''$ can simulate the CCA forward security game for $\mathcal{A}$ perfectly by running **FST.KeyGen** and **Sig.KeyGen**. Whenever a collision occurs it forwards the corresponding inputs to H to its own challenger. It follows that

$$\Pr[\textbf{Coll}] = \varepsilon_{\mathcal{A}'''}. \tag{9}$$

Putting (8) and (9) in (7) gives us $\varepsilon_{\mathcal{A}} \leqslant \varepsilon_{\mathcal{A}'} + \varepsilon_{\mathcal{A}''} + \varepsilon_{\mathcal{A}'''}$.

It is easy to see that all algorithms run in approximately the same time. This completes the proof.   □

Theorem 3. *Let $n \geq 2k + 1$ and let $\mathcal{A}$ be an adaptive adversary that $(t_{\mathcal{A}}, \varepsilon_{\mathcal{A}})$-breaks the CCA forward security of (T, n, k)-Π_{fst} from Sect. 3. Given $\mathcal{A}$ we can build an adversary $\mathcal{A}'$ that $(t_{\mathcal{A}'}, \varepsilon_{\mathcal{A}'})$-breaks the CPA security of HIBE Π_{HIBE} from [2], an adversary $\mathcal{A}''$ that $(t_{\mathcal{A}''}, \varepsilon_{\mathcal{A}''})$-breaks the sEUF-1CMA security of a signature scheme Σ, and an adversary $\mathcal{A}'''$ that $(t_{\mathcal{A}''}, \varepsilon_{\mathcal{A}'''})$-breaks the collision resistance of hash function H, such that*

$$t_{\mathcal{A}'''} \approx t_{\mathcal{A}''} \approx t_{\mathcal{A}'} \approx t_{\mathcal{A}} \ and \ \varepsilon_{\mathcal{A}'''} + \varepsilon_{\mathcal{A}''} + \binom{n}{k} \cdot \varepsilon_{\mathcal{A}'} \geqslant \varepsilon_{\mathcal{A}}.$$

Proof. Adversary $\mathcal{A}'$ proceeds as in the proof of Theorem 2. The only difference is that it guesses in advance of step 1 of **DKGSim** which parties the adversary is going to corrupt. Whenever the adversary corrupts a party P_j, $j \in \mathcal{B}$ then it takes over the role of this party and receives all values computed and stored on behalf of this party by $\mathcal{A}'$. If at the end $\mathcal{A}$ outputs a bit but has not corrupted at least k parties then $\mathcal{A}'$ adds some artificial corruptions to the set $\mathcal{B}$ uniformly at random such that it has exactly k corrupted parties. Adversary $\mathcal{A}'$ aborts the simulation and outputs uniformly random bit if a guess was wrong (either of $\mathcal{A}$ or $\mathcal{A}'$). The simulation is successful with probability $1/\binom{n}{k}$.

Adversary $\mathcal{A}''$ also proceeds as in the proof of Theorem 2. Since it is in possession of the common secret x it can compute the secret values h^{x_i} for all $i \in [n]$ directly. Hence, it has no additional loss in its success probability. Guessing the corrupted parties has also no effect on breaking collision resistance and thus its probability remains unchanged as well.

4   Discussions

Tolerating Mobile Adversaries. A mobile adversary is able to switch between the parties it corrupts. It holds in general that it is not possible to tolerate such adversaries while having a non-interactive key update procedure. The reason is that a mobile adversary could gain all secret key shares successively without ever exceeding the threshold in any time period. Then, by updating all the shares to the latest time period it would be able to reconstruct the secret key. However, in our fst-PKE prevention against mobile adversaries is possible by adding a proactive security mechanism [11,12,17]. Proactive security allows to refresh the secret key shares in a way such that all shares which were *not* refreshed cannot be used to reconstruct the secret key anymore (except for the case that the amount of not refreshed shares is bigger than the threshold). Although the proactive security mechanism is *interactive*, the secret share holders can decide how often or when they are willing to execute it. For instance, this could happen with a different level of granularity than the non-interactive key update mechanism or only when necessary. In order to proactivize the key material in our scheme it does not even require an additional protocol. Indeed, it suffices that the users execute the **DKG** protocol where each party P_i sets the constant term of polynomial a_i to 0. Then, the final share held by all parties is multiplied to all terms d_i' in their secret key shares.

From Static to Adaptive Adversaries. To protect against adaptive adversaries we used complexity leveraging. This approach results in an additional security loss of $\binom{n}{k}$, where n is the number of parties and k the threshold. Although, this loss seems to be quite big, in practice n is relatively small. For instance for a threshold scheme with $10, 20$ or 30 parties the maximum loss is $2^8, 2^{18}$ and 2^{28}, respectively. Libert and Yung [15] also achieve security against adaptive adversaries but circumvent complexity leveraging by using bilinear pairings of composite order. This approach is known as the dual system approach and prior to their work it was only used to achieve full security for (Hierarchical-)IBE and attribute-based encryption schemes [13,14,19]. Although the dual system approach is a very powerful tool to obtain full security or security against adaptive adversaries it lacks efficiency when implemented. The reason for this is that groups of composite order require a much bigger modulus to guarantee the same level of security than elliptic curves on groups of prime order.[7] It can be seen that the security loss in our scheme can be compensated by a slightly bigger modulus. This modulus remains much smaller compared to one of composite order and thus results in a much more efficient scheme.

Finally, it should be mentioned that there exist several techniques to transfer the dual system approach to prime order groups [9,14,19]. However, they result in larger ciphertexts and seem also to be less efficient in terms of communication rounds for decryption. Moreover, it is not clear whether they can be instantiated without a trusted dealer. We leave it as an open problem to use these techniques to achieve the same efficiency and advantages as our fst-PKE, i.e. a *non-interactive* key update and decryption procedure, *no trusted dealer*, and the possibility to implement the scheme on *standardized elliptic curves*.

References

1. Abdalla, M., Miner, S., Namprempre, C.: Forward-Secure threshold signature schemes. In: Naccache, D. (ed.) CT-RSA 2001. LNCS, vol. 2020, pp. 441–456. Springer, Heidelberg (2001). https://doi.org/10.1007/3-540-45353-9_32
2. Boneh, D., Boyen, X., Goh, E.-J.: Hierarchical identity based encryption with constant size ciphertext. In: Cramer, R. (ed.) EUROCRYPT 2005. LNCS, vol. 3494, pp. 440–456. Springer, Heidelberg (2005). https://doi.org/10.1007/11426639_26
3. Boneh, D., Boyen, X., Halevi, S.: Chosen ciphertext secure public key threshold encryption without random oracles. In: Pointcheval, D. (ed.) CT-RSA 2006. LNCS, vol. 3860, pp. 226–243. Springer, Heidelberg (2006). https://doi.org/10.1007/11605805_15

---

[7] For comparison of concrete sizes see the common recommendations: https://www.keylength.com/.

4. Boneh, D., Canetti, R., Halevi, S., Katz, J.: Chosen-ciphertext security from identity-based encryption. SIAM J. Comput. **36**(5), 1301–1328 (2007)
5. Boneh, D., Lynn, B., Shacham, H.: Short signatures from the weil pairing. In: Boyd, C. (ed.) ASIACRYPT 2001. LNCS, vol. 2248, pp. 514–532. Springer, Heidelberg (2001). https://doi.org/10.1007/3-540-45682-1_30
6. Canetti, R., Halevi, S., Katz, J.: A forward-secure public-key encryption scheme. In: Biham, E. (ed.) EUROCRYPT 2003. LNCS, vol. 2656, pp. 255–271. Springer, Heidelberg (2003). https://doi.org/10.1007/3-540-39200-9_16
7. Chatterjee, S., Hankerson, D., Menezes, A.: On the efficiency and security of pairing-based protocols in the type 1 and type 4 settings. In: Hasan, M.A., Helleseth, T. (eds.) WAIFI 2010. LNCS, vol. 6087, pp. 114–134. Springer, Heidelberg (2010). https://doi.org/10.1007/978-3-642-13797-6_9
8. Chow, S.S.M., Go, H.W., Hui, L.C.K., Yiu, S.-M.: Multiplicative forward-secure threshold signature scheme. Int. J. Netw. Secur. **7**, 397–403 (2008)
9. Freeman, D.M.: Converting pairing-based cryptosystems from composite-order groups to prime-order groups. In: Gilbert, H. (ed.) EUROCRYPT 2010. LNCS, vol. 6110, pp. 44–61. Springer, Heidelberg (2010). https://doi.org/10.1007/978-3-642-13190-5_3
10. Gennaro, R., Jarecki, S., Krawczyk, H., Rabin, T.: Secure distributed key generation for discrete-log based cryptosystems. J. Cryptology **20**(1), 51–83 (2006). https://doi.org/10.1007/s00145-006-0347-3
11. Herzberg, A., Jakobsson, M., Jarecki, S., Krawczyk, H., Yung, M.: Proactive public key and signature systems. In: Proceedings of the ACM Conference on Computer and Communications Security, January 1997
12. Herzberg, A., Jarecki, S., Krawczyk, H., Yung, M.: Proactive secret sharing or: how to cope with perpetual leakage. In: Coppersmith, D. (ed.) CRYPTO 1995. LNCS, vol. 963, pp. 339–352. Springer, Heidelberg (1995). https://doi.org/10.1007/3-540-44750-4_27
13. Lewko, A., Okamoto, T., Sahai, A., Takashima, K., Waters, B.: Fully secure functional encryption: attribute-based encryption and (Hierarchical) inner product encryption. In: Gilbert, H. (ed.) EUROCRYPT 2010. LNCS, vol. 6110, pp. 62–91. Springer, Heidelberg (2010). https://doi.org/10.1007/978-3-642-13190-5_4
14. Lewko, A., Waters, B.: New techniques for dual system encryption and fully secure HIBE with short ciphertexts. In: Micciancio, D. (ed.) TCC 2010. LNCS, vol. 5978, pp. 455–479. Springer, Heidelberg (2010). https://doi.org/10.1007/978-3-642-11799-2_27
15. Libert, B., Yung, M.: Adaptively secure non-interactive threshold cryptosystems. Theoret. Comput. Sci. **478**, 76–100 (2013)
16. Liu, L.-S., Chu, C.-K., Tzeng, W.-G.: A threshold GQ signature scheme. In: Zhou, J., Yung, M., Han, Y. (eds.) ACNS 2003. LNCS, vol. 2846, pp. 137–150. Springer, Heidelberg (2003). https://doi.org/10.1007/978-3-540-45203-4_11
17. Ostrovsky, R., Yung, M.: How to withstand mobile virus attacks (extended abstract). In: Proceedings of the Tenth Annual ACM Symposium on Principles of Distributed Computing, PODC 1991, pp. 51–59. ACM, New York (1991)
18. Tzeng, W.-G., Tzeng, Z.-J.: Robust forward-secure signature schemes with proactive security. In: Kim, K. (ed.) PKC 2001. LNCS, vol. 1992, pp. 264–276. Springer, Heidelberg (2001). https://doi.org/10.1007/3-540-44586-2_19
19. Waters, B.: Dual system encryption: realizing fully secure IBE and HIBE under simple assumptions. In: Halevi, S. (ed.) CRYPTO 2009. LNCS, vol. 5677, pp. 619–636. Springer, Heidelberg (2009). https://doi.org/10.1007/978-3-642-03356-8_36

20. Yu, J., Kong, F.: Forward secure threshold signature scheme from bilinear pairings. In: Wang, Y., Cheung, Y., Liu, H. (eds.) CIS 2006. LNCS (LNAI), vol. 4456, pp. 587–597. Springer, Heidelberg (2007). https://doi.org/10.1007/978-3-540-74377-4_61

21. Zhang, X., Xu, C., Zhang, W.: Efficient chosen ciphertext secure threshold public-key encryption with forward security. In: Proceedings of the 2013 Fourth International Conference on Emerging Intelligent Data and Web Technologies, EIDWT 2013, USA, pp. 407–413. IEEE Computer Society (2013)

A New Targeted Password Guessing Model

Zhijie Xie[1], Min Zhang[1(✉)], Anqi Yin[2], and Zhenhan Li[1]

[1] College of Electronic Engineering, National University of Defense Technology, Hefei 230037, China
{xzj9510,zhangmindy,lizhenhan17}@nudt.edu.cn
[2] Institute of Information Science and Technology, Zhengzhou 450001, China
yinaq0222@foxmail.com

Abstract. TarGuess-I is a leading targeted password guessing model using users' personally identifiable information (PII) proposed at ACM CCS 2016 by Wang et al. Owing to its superior guessing performance, TarGuess-I has attracted widespread attention in password security. Yet, TarGuess-I fails to capture popular passwords and special strings in passwords correctly. Thus we propose TarGuess-I$^+$: an improved password guessing model, which is capable of identifying popular passwords by generating top-300 most popular passwords from similar websites and grasping special strings by extracting continuous characters from user-generated PII. We conduct a series of experiments on 6 real-world leaked datasets and the results show that our improved model outperforms TarGuess-I by 9.07% on average with 1000 guesses, which proves the effectiveness of our improvements.

Keywords: TarGuess · Targeted password guessing · Probabilistic Context-Free Grammar (PCFG) · Personally Identifiable Information (PII)

1 Introduction

Password-based authentication is still an essential method in cybersecurity [1]. To understand password security, people have gone through several stages, from the initial heuristic methods with no theoretical basis, to the scientific probabilistic algorithms [2]. Since the emergence of Markov-based [3,4] and PCFG-based [5,6] probabilistic password guessing models, trawling password guessing has been intensively studied [7–10]. Recently, several large-scale personal information database leakage events have caused widespread concern in the field of password security [11–14]. With the development of related researches, it has been found that a large part of net-users tend to create passwords with their PII and the targeted password guessing models based on users' PII have emerged [15–17].

Das et al. [15] have studied the threat posed by password reuse and proposed a cross-site password guessing algorithm for the first time. However, due to the

© Springer Nature Switzerland AG 2020
J. K. Liu and H. Cui (Eds.): ACISP 2020, LNCS 12248, pp. 350–368, 2020.
https://doi.org/10.1007/978-3-030-55304-3_18

lack of popular password recognition, this algorithm is not optimal. Li et al. [16] studied what extent a user's PII can affect password security, and they proposed a targeted password guessing model, personal-PCFG, which adopts a length-based PII matching and substitution. But it could not accurately capture users' PII usage, which greatly hinders the efficiency of password guessing. As a milestone work on password guessing, Wang et al. [17] put forward a targeted password guessing framework, TarGuess, which contains the password reuse behavior analysis and type-based PII semantic recognition, significantly improving the efficiency of the password guessing. Wang et al.'s [17] remarkable achievements have motivated successive new studies on password security [18–21] and even led the revision of the NIST SP800-63-3 [22,23].

TarGuess framework is proposed after an in-depth analysis of users' vulnerable behaviors such as password construction using PII and password reuse, including four password guessing models for four attacking Scenarios #1 ∼ #4. TarGuess-I caters for Scenario #1 where the attacker is equipped with the victim user's PII information such as name, birthday, phone number, which can be easily obtained from the Internet [24]. And the rest three models required user information such as PII attributes that play an implicit role in passwords (e.g., gender and profession) and/or sister passwords that were leaked from the user's other accounts. This work mainly focuses on Scenario #1. As more users' PII is being leaked these days, Scenario #1 becomes more practical.

Wang et al. [17] showed that their TarGuess-I model is more efficient than previous models using users' PII to crack users' passwords, which can gain success rates over 20% with just 100 guesses. However, we find that there is still room for improvement in the analysis of users' vulnerable behaviors after using this model to analyze the real data. Therefore, based on TarGuess-I, we put forward two improvements and proposed an improved model, TarGuess-I$^+$, to make it more consistent with users' vulnerable behavior characteristics and improve the performance of guessing.

Our Contributions. In this work, we make the following key contributions:

(1) **An Improved Password Guessing Model.** After analyses of users' vulnerable behaviors based on a total of 147,877,128 public leaked data and TarGuess-I, we find that the effectiveness of some semantic tags has not been testified and employed in the experiments of Wang et al. [17]. To fill the gap, we make use of the adaptiveness of TarGuess-I PII tags and define two new tags: the Popular Password tag P_1 and the Special String tag X_n. This gives rise to a variant of TarGuess-I, we call it TarGuess-I$^+$.

(2) **An Extensive Evaluation.** To demonstrate the feasibility of the improvements, we perform a series of experiments on the real-world leaked datasets. The experimental results show that the success rate of the improved model TarGuess-I$^+$ outperforms the original model TarGuess-I by 9.07% on average with 1000 guesses, which proves the feasibility of the improvements.

(3) **A Novel Method.** We introduce a novel method to the password guessing: parsing the password segments into special strings, such as anniversary days

and someone's name, that appeared in user-generated PII, such as e-mail addresses and user names.

2 Preliminaries

This section explicates what kinds of users' vulnerable behaviors are considered in this work and gives a brief introduction to the models.

2.1 Explication of Users' Vulnerable Behaviors

Users' vulnerable behaviors are the key influence factor of password crackability [25]. A series of related studies have been conducted since the pioneering work of Morris and Thompson in 1979 [26]. Part of the studies are based on data analyses, such as [3,12,14,27–30], the others are based on user surveys, such as [15,31–34]. In summary, the discovered users' vulnerable behaviors can be classified into the following three categories:

1. **Popular Passwords.** A large number of studies (such as [3,14,29]) have shown that users often choose simple words as passwords or make simple transformed strings to meet the requirements of the website password setting strategy, such as "123456a" meeting the "alphanumeric" strategy. These strings, which are frequently used by users, are called popular passwords. Furthermore, Wang et al. [35] have found that the Zipf distribution is the main cause of the aggregation of popular passwords.
2. **Password Reuse.** After a series of interviews to investigate how users cope with keeping track of many accounts and passwords, Stobert et al. [31] point out that users have more than 20 accounts on average and it is fairly impossible for them to create a unique password for each account, so reusing passwords is a rational approach. At the same time, password-reuse is a vulnerable behavior, the key is how to reuse.
3. **Password Containing Personal Information.** Wang et al. [36] note that Chinese users tend to construct passwords with their pinyin name and relevant digits, such as phone number and birthdate, which is quite different from English users. They revealed a new insight into what extent users' native languages influence their passwords and what extent users' personal information plays a role in their passwords.

Considering the scenario on which TarGuess-I is based, we only analyze the users' vulnerable behaviors of using popular passwords and making use of personal information.

2.2 The PCFG-Based Password Guessing Model [5]

TarGuess-I model is built on Weir et al.'s PCFG-based model, which has shown great success in dealing with trawling guessing scenarios [17]. The Context-free grammar in [17] is defined as $\mathcal{G} = (\mathcal{V}, \Sigma, \mathcal{S}, \mathcal{R})$, where:

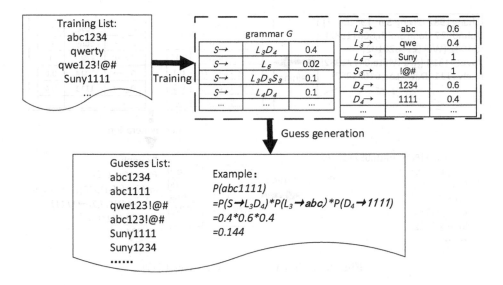

Fig. 1. An illustration of PCFG-based model

- $\mathcal{V}$ is a finite set of variables;
- Σ is a finite set disjoint from $\mathcal{V}$ and contains all the terminals of $\mathcal{G}$;
- $\mathcal{S}$ is the start symbol and $\mathcal{S} \in \mathcal{V}$;
- $\mathcal{R}$ is a finite set of productions of the form: $\alpha \rightarrow \beta$, where α & $\beta \in \mathcal{V} \cup \Sigma$.

The core assumption of the model is the segments of letters, numbers, and symbols in a password were independent of each other, so in the $\mathcal{V}$ except for the $\mathcal{S}$ start symbol, only to join L_n letters, D_n digits and S_n symbols tag sets, where n represents the segment length, such as L_3 represents 3-letter segments, D_4 represents 4-digit segments.

There are two phases in the model, the training phase and the guess generation phase, as shown in Fig. 1. In the training phase, the password is parsed into the LDS segments based on the length and the type to generate the corresponding password base structure (the start symbol $\mathcal{S}$). Then, it counts the segments frequency table in each tag set, and it outputs the context-free grammar $\mathcal{G}$. In the guess generation phase, passwords are derived by the grammar $\mathcal{G}$ and the segments frequency table. The final output set is arranged based on the probability multiplied by all the frequency of segments in the password.

2.3 The Targeted Password Guessing Model TarGuess-I [17]

TarGuess-I adds 6 PII tags (N_n name, U_n username, B_n birthday, T_n phone number, I_n id card, E_n mailbox) to the three basic tags of LDS in the PCFG-based model. For each PII tag, its index number n is different from the LDS tag, which represents the type of generation rule for this PII. For example, N stands for name usage, while N_1 stands for the full name, and N_2 stands for

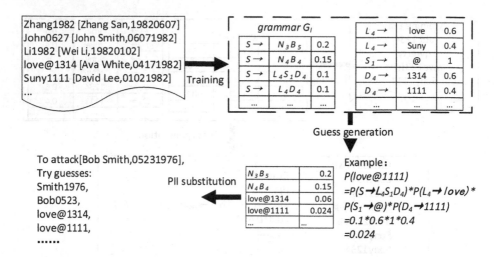

Fig. 2. An illustration of TarGuess-I [17]

the abbreviation of the full name (such as "Zhang San" abbreviated as "zs"). B stands for birthday usage, while B_1 stands for the use of birthday in the format of month/year (e.g., 19820607), B_2 stands for the use of birthday in the format of month/day/year. For a specific description, see Fig. 4.

Figure 2 shows an illustration of the model. For each user, the element set of each PII tag is first generated through the user's PII to match with the password, and the rest of the segments are parsed into LDS segments. Then the frequency of the elements of each set will be calculated as with PCFG. Finally, the context-free grammar $\mathcal{G}_\mathcal{I}$ containing the PII tags will be output.

3 Analysis of Real Password Data and TarGuess-I Model

This section analyzes the real-world leaked password data and TarGuess-I to provide the basis for the improvement of the model. We dissect 146,570,537 leaked user passwords from 6 websites (see Table 1) to find out the disadvantages of TarGuess-I.

Table 1. Basic information about our personal-info datasets

Dataset	Web service	When leaked	Total	With PII
Duduniu	E-commerce	2011	16,258,891	
Tianya	Social forum	2011	29,020,808	
CSDN	Programmer	2011	6,428,277	
renren	Social forum	2011	2,185,997	
12306	Train ticketing	2014	129,303	✓
youku	Video entertainment	2016	92,547,261	

Table 2. Ranking and proportion of top-10 popular passwords

Rank	Duduniu	Tianya	CSDN	Renren	12306	Youku
1	123456	123456	123456789	123456	123456	123456
2	111111	111111	12345678	123456789	a123456	123456789
3	123456789	000000	11111111	111111	123456a	xuanchuan
4	a123456	123456789	dearbook	12345	woaini1314	111111
5	123123	123123	00000000	5201314	5201314	123123
6	5201314	121212	123123123	123123	111111	000000
7	12345	123321	1234567890	12345678	qq123456	5201314
8	aaaaaa	111222TIANYA	88888888	1314520	1qaz2wsx	1234
9	12345678	12345678	111111111	123321	1q2w3e4r	a123456
10	123456a	5201314	147258369	7758521	123qwe	123321
%	5.27%	1.17%	3.34%	4.91%	1.10%	3.89%

3.1 Analysis of Popular Passwords

According to the frequency of occurrence, the top-10 popular passwords in 6
password databases with the proportion of them were calculated, and the results
are shown in Table 2. Table 2 shows that 1.10% to 5.27% of users' passwords could
be guessed successfully by just using top-10 popular passwords. Chinese users
prefer simple combinations of numbers, such as "123456", "111111", "000000",
and the strings with the meaning of love, such as "5201314" and "woaini1314".

There are also some unique passwords in the top-10 list, such as
"111222TIANYA" in Tianya, "dearbook" and "147258369" in CSDN, "7758521"
in Renren and "xuanchuan" in Youku. These passwords may come from the
name or the culture of the website, or they maybe come from a large number of
"ghost accounts" held by a particular user of the website. Besides, "1qaz2wsx"
and "1q2w3e4r" in the top-10 of 12306 is the password constructed with the
QWERTY keyboard pattern.

By analyzing the list of popular passwords, we find that there is one
missing item in the password recognition of the TarGuess-I model: the popular
passwords.

Popular Password. The statistical results of the distribution of base structures
analyzed by the PCFG-based model for top-10000 popular passwords are shown
in Table 3.

Table 3 illustrates that the majority of popular passwords are pure numbers.
Besides, composite passwords (that is, the structure includes multiple types of
character) also account for a considerable part, especially 63.15% in the 12306
data set. Since the grammar $\mathcal{G}_{II}$ of TarGuess-I does not contain tags related to
the popular passwords, while TarGuess-I is based on data-driven probabilistic
statistical PCFG algorithm, which generates passwords based on the existing
base structures in the data and the set of elements in various tags. Therefore, in
the training phase, the model parses the password into *LDS* segments, an illusion

Table 3. Form distribution of the top-10000 popular passwords

Form	Duduniu	Tianya	CSDN	Renren	12306	Youku
Letter	11.47%	10.93%	15.56%	10.67%	4.56%	12.46%
Digit	39.18%	63.37%	65.66%	66.27%	32.29%	63.77%
Symbol	0.02%	0.03%	0.04%	0.02%	0.00%	0.08%
Composite	49.34%	25.67%	18.74%	23.05%	63.15%	23.69%

is shown in Fig. 1. Due to the guess generation phase of the PCFG algorithm, it might generate many invalid outputs at last.

For example, "adbc1234" is the 28th most popular password in 12306, which is divided into L_4D_4 syntax using PCFG algorithm. In the element set of L_4, "love" ranks the first, while "1234" ranks the first in D_4. Therefore, in the guessing stage, the first output password with the base structure L_4D_4 is "love1234". This password occupies a relatively small proportion in the actual password distribution but ranks much higher in the model guessing list due to the high probability, thus reducing the overall password guessing success rate.

3.2 Analysis of Passwords Containing Personal Information

We adopt the improved TarGuess-I^+P model, which contains the popular password tag P_1, to analyze the passwords. The results of the top-10 password base structures and the proportion of the password containing PII have been shown in Table 4. Due to the lack of datasets containing users' PII, we choose the unique PII (such as e-mail, phone, ID number) in 12306 to match passwords in other datasets. The sizes of the password sets are shown in Table 5.

The results indicate that nearly 50% of users generally construct passwords using PII or choose popular passwords. And we find that the top-10 password base structures contain several base structures with base tags that are not relevant to users' PII. Based on the above analysis of the users' behavior in constructing the password, we can speculate that the top-10 base structures of passwords should be related to the strings which are accessible for the user to memorize.

The strings which are accessible to memorize include users' PII conversions and popular passwords. They also include user-generated strings (hereinafter referred to as the special strings) that have special meaning for the user but are of no equal importance to other users. For $\mathcal{A}$ user, for example, "080405" is $\mathcal{A}$'s particular date, but for another user $\mathcal{B}$, "080405" is just a very ordinary day, then the probability of $\mathcal{A}$'s password containing this string is different from that of $\mathcal{B}$'s. Meanwhile, we can not find the string "080405" in $\mathcal{A}$'s and $\mathcal{B}$'s demographic information (such as name, ID number, telephone number, etc.). The special string cannot be extracted from the user's demographic information but may appear in strings which are generated by the user, such as e-mail address and

Table 4. Ranking of top-10 base structure, proportion of the passwords containing PII and proportion of popular passwords

Rank	Duduniu	Tianya	CSDN	Renren	12306	Youku
1	E_1	D_6	P_1	D_7	P_1	P_1
2	D_7	D_7	D_8	D_6	D_6	D_6
3	P_1	P_1	E_1	P_1	D_7	D_7
4	D_6	D_8	B_1	D_8	N_2D_6	D_8
5	D_8	E_1	D_9	E_1	U_1	N_2D_6
6	N_2D_6	D_{10}	N_2D_6	U_3	D_8	U_1
7	A_1D_7	B_1	U_1	D_9	E_1	U_3
8	N_2D_7	B_8	D_{11}	B_1	N_2D_7	E_1
9	U_1	D_9	N_2D_7	B_8	U_3	B_1
10	A_2D_6	N_2D_6	D_{10}	D_{11}	A_2D_6	N_1D_3
% of PII	41.54%	35.43%	39.64%	36.85%	42.78%	40.65%
% of P_1	3.99%	5.91%	8.91%	6.27%	4.14%	5.58%

user name, or it may appear in passwords on other servers of the user. Therefore, we found another lack of recognition in TarGuess-I: the special string.

The Special String. The analyses of the user data in TarGuess-I also include the user-generated strings, such as e-mail address E_n and user name U_n. However, the analyses of these 2 user-generated strings are not accurate enough. Only three parse type (Entire $E_1\&U_1$, the first letter segments $E_2\&U_2$ and the first digit segments $E_3\&U_3$) are proposed.

The probability distribution of special strings for each user is different. If we use the original TarGuess-I model for password recognition, because of the lack of recognition of the special string, most of these segments will be parsed into typical LDS segments, merging the users' behavior characteristics, thus they hinder the effectiveness of the model. Therefore, we consider adding the special string tags X_n to the set $\mathcal{V}$ of TarGuess-I.

Considering that only two user-generated PII are needed in TarGuess-I, the e-mail address and the user name, we employ the sliding window algorithm to analyze the coverage of consecutive substrings of the e-mail address and user name in the password to verify the validity of the special string improvement. The result is shown in Fig. 3. Note that, to differ from TarGuess-I, we only consider substrings with $len \geq 2$, and we ignore the full strings of e-mail address prefix and user name.

Figure 3 shows that a significant number of user passwords do overlap user-created strings. It gives us a new hint that when an attacker obtains information about a user that is not public or very useful, they may turn that information into a special string to participate in password guessing.

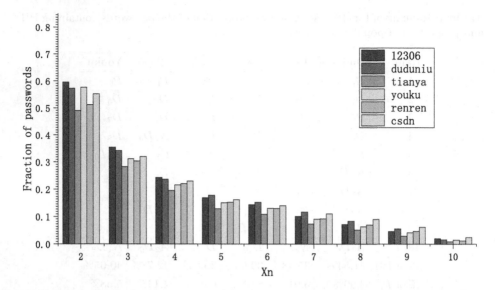

Fig. 3. The probability of the occurrence of the special string X_n in the password

3.3 Brief Summary

We find two improvements of TarGuess-I model in this section:

- Add the popular password tag P_1 to the set $\mathcal{V}$ of probability context $\mathcal{G}_{II}$ and apply the popular password list generated from a data set similar to the target website or server type.
- Add the special string tag X_n to the set $\mathcal{V}$ of probability context $\mathcal{G}_{II}$, and add the special string associated with the user for password guessing.

4   The Improved Model TarGuess-I⁺

We now propose TarGuess-I⁺, which is capable of identifying the popular passwords and the special strings. The context-free grammar $\mathcal{G}_{II} = (\mathcal{V}, \Sigma, \mathcal{S}, \mathcal{R})$ in the model is described as below:

1. $\mathcal{S} \in \mathcal{V}$ is the start symbol;
2. $\mathcal{V} = \{\mathcal{S}; L_n, D_n, S_n; N_n, B_n, U_n, E_n, I_n, T_n; P_1, X_n\}$ is a finite set of variables, where:
   (a) Letters (L_n), Digits (D_n), Symbols (S_n) are the basic tag of the PCFG algorithm, we rename them in case to differ from other improvement tags;
   (b) Name (N_n), Birthday (B_n), User name (U_n), E-mail address (E_n), ID number (I_n), and Phone number (T_n) are the PII tags created in TarGuess-I model, see Fig. 4 for an example of generation;
   (c) Popular password (P_1) and Special string (X_n) are proposed in this paper, the implementation detail have been shown in Subsect. 4.1.

3. $\Sigma = \{95$ printable ASCII codes, $Null\}$ is a finite set disjoint from $\mathcal{V}$ and contains all the terminals of $\mathcal{G}_{\mathcal{II}}$;
4. $\mathcal{R}$ is a finite set of rules of the form $A \to \alpha$, with $A \in \mathcal{V}$ and $\alpha \in \mathcal{V} \cup \Sigma$.

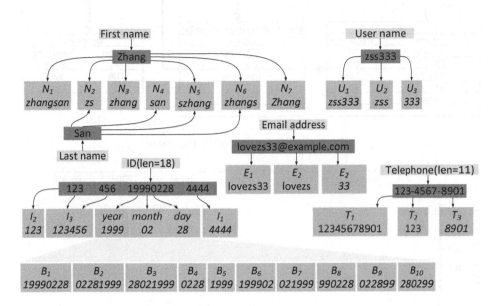

Fig. 4. An illustration of PII tags generation

4.1   Model Implementation

Popular Password P_1. Add the popular password tag P_1 to $\mathcal{V}$ set of the grammar $\mathcal{G}_{\mathcal{T}}$, and the element set in P_1 tag is a top-N popular password list based on the data statistics of relevant websites. The index 1 in P_1 has no meaning just to conform to the overall format. The parse of P_1 tag is shown in Fig. 5.

In the training phase, the top-N list is matched with the password data by a regular expression. If the match occurs, the occurrence of the corresponding password in P_1 set is increased by 1. In the guess generation phase, the probability of containing P_1 password structures is multiplied by the frequency of the corresponding password in the element set of P_1 as the final probability of output password.

Figure 6 shows the similarity between the top-k list of the popular passwords compiled by six websites and the top-k list of the popular passwords of each website (k represents the first k pieces of password ranking). It can be seen from the figure that when k value is around 300, the similarity tends to a stable peak, and then the similarity continues to decrease. Therefore, the size of the popular

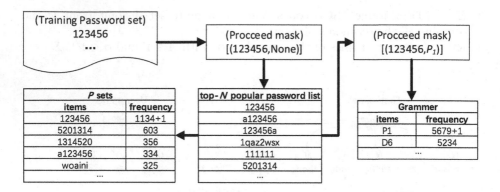

Fig. 5. An illustration of P_1 tag parse

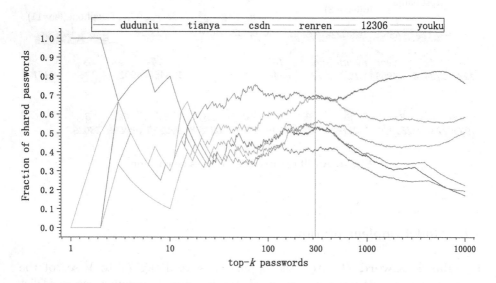

Fig. 6. The similarity of the popular passwords

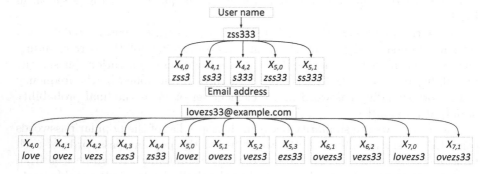

Fig. 7. An illustration of X_n tags parse

password list should be limited to about $N = 300$ to improve the success rate of cross-site guessing.

Special String X_n. The element sets of the special string X_n tag are generated from the e-mail address prefix and user name. Since there are various and different ways for each user to generate special strings, it is difficult to categorize the generation methods of special strings uniformly and may cause sparse data. Therefore, n is only classified according to the length of the string. To avoid generating too many conventional strings with excessive extraction granularity, which results in invalid recognition, we only consider strings with $len \geq 4$. An illustration of special string X_n parse is shown in Fig. 7. The second number in $X_{n,m}$ tags represents the generation type in the element sets, which means the starting position of the substrings.

5   Experiments

TarGuess-I is mainly used in online guessing scenarios, where the guess number allowed is the most scarce resource, while computational power and bandwidth are not essential [17]. Therefore, we mainly evaluate the availability of the model by guess-number graphs.

5.1   Experiment Setup

Our experiments need various types of users' PII. Because of the limited experimental resources and the lack of original datasets associated with PII, we only employed 10^5 pieces of 12306 data containing users' PII to match the rest of datasets using e-mail addresses, and the obtained data size is shown in Table 5.

Table 5. The size of experiment datasets

	Duduniu	Tianya	CSDN	Renren	12306	Youku	Total
Training set	–	–	–	–	25,372	11,554	36,926
Testing set	7,539	6,792	2,998	1,062	74,516	27,278	120,185
Total	7,539	6,792	2,998	1,062	99,888	38,832	157,091

Note that, to make our experiments as scientific as possible, we follow 4 rules:

1. Training sets and testing sets are strictly separated;
2. The comparison experiments of the two models are based on the same training sets and testing sets;
3. The base structures of password sets for the experiments are evenly distributed;
4. The training sets and testing sets shall be as large as possible.

To follow the rules 3 and 4, we first filtrate the password data by analyzing the base structure of the passwords using TarGuess-I. We store the passwords which have their base structure with more than 10 occurrences. And we choose the **12306** set and **Youku** set as training sets and testing sets at a ratio of 7:3, the other data sets have been entirely used for testing.

5.2   Experiment 1: Validation of the Improvements

We adopted two improvement methods to generate two models: TarGuess-I+P with popular password tag P_1, and TarGuess-I+X with special string tag X_n, then we chose **12306** training data and **Youku** training data to generate the context-free grammars $\mathcal{G}_I$ and $\mathcal{G}_{II}$. At last, we implemented comparison experiments with the corresponding testing data. The results are shown in Fig. 8 and Table 6.

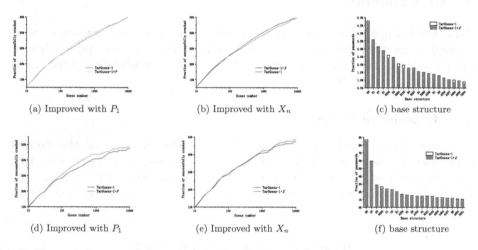

(a) Improved with P_1	(b) Improved with X_n	(c) base structure
(d) Improved with P_1	(e) Improved with X_n	(f) base structure

Fig. 8. Figs. 8(a), (b) and (c) are the results of experiments based on **12306** data set; Figs. (d), (e) and (f) are the results of experiments based on **Youku** data set.

Popular Password. Figure 8(a) shows that the success rate of TarGuess-I+P is slightly lower than that of TarGuess-I within 100 guesses, but grows higher than the latter from 100 to 10^4 guesses. This maybe due to the largest part of passwords with pure-digits base structures in **12306** set. These types of passwords will be generated more at first by TarGuess-I's grammar $\mathcal{G}_I$, but a few by TarGuess-I+P's grammar $\mathcal{G}_{II}$. Figure 8(d) and Table 6 show that TarGuess-I+P significantly outperforms TarGuess-I by 0.28%–6.35% in the **Youku**-based experiment, which proves the effectiveness of the improvement of popular passwords.

Special String. Figures. 8(b) and 8(e) show that TarGuess-I+X is close to TarGuess-I with a slightly lower success rate within 1000 guesses, but gradually

Table 6. The statistics of Fig. 8

Setup	Model	10	10^2	10^3	10^4
12306-train	TarGuess-I	12.655	22.808	29.354	35.085
↓	TarGuess-I+P	12.651	22.954	29.898	35.187
12306-test	TarGuess-I+X	12.643	23.028	32.003	35.668
Youku-train	TarGuess-I	14.877	24.223	30.394	33.795
↓	TarGuess-I+P	15.102	25.392	31.891	34.366
Youku-test	TarGuess-I+X	14.634	24.613	31.008	34.305

Table 7. The top-5 rank of password base structure with the special string X_n tags

12306			Youku		
Structure	Proportion	Rank	Structure	Proportion	Rank
X_8	0.2449%	89	X_6	0.2749%	75
X_9	0.2335%	92	X_8	0.2456%	86
X_6	0.1803%	115	X_7	0.2383%	91
X_{10}	0.1718%	122	X_9	0.2236%	96
$X_4 D_6$	0.1601%	127	$X_5 D_3$	0.1833%	108

outperforms TarGuess-I with the increasing number of guesses. The main reason is that the passwords containing the special strings account for a relatively small proportion of the entire password data, seeing Table 7. And some higher-ranked base structures will be reduced, seeing Figs. 8(c) and 8(f), because some of the passwords, which were originally parsed into these base structures, will be parsed into which contains X_n.

5.3 Experiment 2: Evaluation of TarGuess-I$^+$

We add 2 new tags to the variable set $\mathcal{V}$ of TarGuess-I to generate a new improved model TarGuess-I$^+$, and choose the large datasets **12306** and **Youku** for training to generate the context-free grammar $\mathcal{G}_{II}$. Then, we perform a series of comparison experiments using the 6 password datasets mentioned at subsect. 5.1. Figure 9 gives 6 graphs for the experiment results, and Table 8 displays the detailed statistics of the 6 graphs.

From the results, we can see that there is an obvious difference in Fig. 9(c) of the **CSDN**-based experiment. The success rate of TarGuess-I$^+$ based on **12306** data is significantly higher than that of TarGuess-I, but the same comparison based on **Youku** data is not so clear like the former. We conjecture that this difference maybe because the grammar $\mathcal{G}_{II}$ generated by TarGuess-I$^+$ based on **12306** data is more suitable for **CSDN** data. Table 9 shows that the **12306**-based grammar $\mathcal{G}_{II}$ generated by TarGuess-I$^+$ has the largest proportion of base structures with PII tags, and the pure-digits base structures rank lower than others, which may satisfy the distribution of **CSDN** data.

Table 8. The statistics of Fig. 9

Training set	Testing set	Model	10	10^2	10^3	10^4
12306-train	12306-test	TarGuess-I	12.655	22.808	29.354	35.085
		TarGuess-I$^+$	12.643	23.028	30.182	35.668
	Youku-test	TarGuess-I	15.119	25.002	31.614	37.161
		TarGuess-I$^+$	15.145	25.444	32.505	37.810
	Duduniu	TarGuess-I	10.639	17.957	23.892	29.671
		TarGuess-I$^+$	10.203	19.109	28.383	34.008
	Tianya	TarGuess-I	12.832	19.173	23.814	30.134
		TarGuess-I$^+$	12.812	19.678	26.666	32.743
	CSDN	TarGuess-I	12.341	19.902	26.308	33.222
		TarGuess-I$^+$	15.808	23.291	29.598	34.417
	Renren	TarGuess-I	15.873	22.607	27.754	36.027
		TarGuess-I$^+$	15.873	23.665	34.151	41.751
Youku-train	12306-test	TarGuess-I	12.032	21.558	27.013	30.067
		TarGuess-I$^+$	12.438	22.366	29.015	31.691
	Youku-test	TarGuess-I	14.877	24.223	30.394	33.795
		TarGuess-I$^+$	15.076	25.469	32.488	35.05
	Duduniu	TarGuess-I	10.223	17.028	21.985	26.254
		TarGuess-I$^+$	10.484	18.287	24.105	27.996
	Tianya	TarGuess-I	12.509	18.829	22.571	28.041
		TarGuess-I$^+$	12.731	19.355	23.996	29.133
	CSDN	TarGuess-I	11.890	21.136	25.994	29.422
		TarGuess-I$^+$	12.204	20.979	26.543	29.481
	Renren	TarGuess-I	15.200	22.222	26.070	31.890
		TarGuess-I$^+$	15.584	22.799	27.706	32.949

It is interesting to find that the success rates of TarGuess-I$^+$ grow dramatically during a short period of the growing guess number. One is based on **Youku**-train data in **Duduniu**-based experiment, and two are based on **12306**-train data in **Renren**-based and **Tianya**-based experiments. We attribute this to the contribution of popular password tag P_1, which outputs the popular passwords concentrated in a certain period of the guess number.

Table 10 calculates the percentage of improvements of TarGuess-I$^+$ in the password guessing success rate compared to TarGuess-I with 1000 guesses based on 6 test datasets. The results show that TarGuess-I$^+$ outperforms TarGuess-I by 2.11%-23.05% and 9.07% on average. Though the effectiveness of each improvement fluctuates wildly because of the suitableness of grammar $\mathcal{G}_{II}$ for each data set, it does prove that our improvements are effective. The results of this paper also show the necessity of multi-factor authentication in critical information systems (e.g., military systems, medical systems) [37,38].

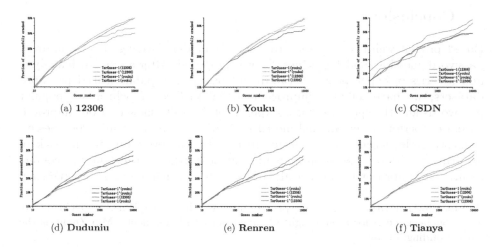

(a) 12306   (b) Youku   (c) CSDN

(d) Duduniu   (e) Renren   (f) Tianya

Fig. 9. Experiment results for comparison with TarGuess-I$^+$ and TarGuess-I based on 6 datasets.

Table 9. The top-10 rank of base structures and proportion of that with additional tags (PII tags and popular password tag)

Rank	12306-train				Youku-train			
	TarGuess-I		TarGuess-I$^+$		TarGuess-I		TarGuess-I$^+$	
1	D_6	4.70235	P_1	5.46191	D_6	8.50502	P_1	8.15309
2	U_1	3.5697	U_1	3.57776	D_7	5.8582	D_6	6.2028
3	D_7	3.08793	D_6	3.32009	D_8	2.83745	D_7	5.40362
4	E_1	2.90005	E_1	2.90005	N_2D_6	2.4342	D_8	2.68715
5	U_3	2.42767	D_7	2.75646	U_1	2.39387	U_1	2.36088
6	N_2D_6	2.42767	U_3	2.3807	U_3	2.31689	U_3	2.23623
7	N_2B_1	1.88013	N_2B_1	1.89087	E_1	2.04194	E_1	2.03461
8	N_1D_3	1.78217	N_1D_3	1.78217	L_2D_6	1.63135	N_2D_6	1.8843
9	D_8	1.75801	N_2D_6	1.71373	B_1	1.5617	B_1	1.55803
10	N_2D_7	1.68823	D_8	1.66944	N_1	1.47249	N_1	1.45905
% of additional tag	63.51863		70.12532		49.49045		60.6011	

Table 10. The improvements of TarGuess-I$^+$ compared with TarGuess-I within 1000 guesses

Training set	Testing set						
	Duduniu	**Tianya**	**CSDN**	**Renren**	**12306**	**Youku**	**Average**
12306	18.80%	11.98%	12.51%	23.05%	2.82%	2.82%	11.69%
Youku	9.64%	6.31%	2.11%	6.28%	7.41%	6.89%	6.44%

6   Conclusion

Based on the well-known password guessing model TarGuess-I, an improved password guessing model TarGuess-I$^+$ was proposed. After an in-depth analysis and a series of experiments of TarGuess-I based on 6 public leaked password datasets, we have found 2 improvements in TarGuess-I, which are popular passwords and the special strings. Experimental results show that our improved model outperforms the original model by 9.07% on average with 1000 guesses, suggesting the feasibility of our improvements. However, due to the lack of experimental data, the improvements will be further verified in the coming future. Our improvement of special strings sheds new light on password guessing.

Acknowledgments. We give our special thanks to Chenxi Xu, Hui Guo, Weinan Cao, and Youcheng Zhen for their insightful suggestions and comments. Min Zhang is the corresponding author.

References

1. Bonneau, J., Herley, C., Van Oorschot, P.C., Stajano, F.: Passwords and the evolution of imperfect authentication. Commun. ACM **58**(7), 78–87 (2015)
2. Wang, D.: Research on key issues in password security. PhD Dissertation, Peking University (2017). http://wangdingg.weebly.com/uploads/2/0/3/6/20366987/phd_thesis0103.pdf
3. Ma, J., Yang, W., Luo, M. and Li, N.: A study of probabilistic password models. In: 2014 IEEE Symposium on Security and Privacy, pp. 689–704. IEEE (2014)
4. Narayanan, A., Shmatikov, V.: Fast dictionary attacks on passwords using time-space tradeoff. In: Proceedings of the 12th ACM conference on Computer and communications security, pp. 364–372 (2005)
5. Weir, M., Aggarwal, S., De Medeiros, B., Glodek, B.: Password cracking using probabilistic context-free grammars. In: 2009 30th IEEE Symposium on Security and Privacy, pp. 391–405. IEEE (2009)
6. Veras, R., Collins, C., Thorpe, J.: On semantic patterns of passwords and their security impact. In: NDSS (2014)
7. Melicher, W., et al.: Fast, lean, and accurate: modeling password guessability using neural networks. In: 25th USENIX Security Symposium (USENIX Security 16), pp. 175–191 (2016)
8. Aggarwal, S., Houshmand, S., Weir, M.: New technologies in password cracking techniques. In: Lehto, M., Neittaanmäki, P. (eds.) Cyber Security: Power and Technology. ISCASE, vol. 93, pp. 179–198. Springer, Cham (2018). https://doi.org/10.1007/978-3-319-75307-2_11
9. Tirado, E., Turpin, B., Beltz, C., Roshon, P., Judge, R., Gagneja, K.: A new distributed brute-force password cracking technique. In: Doss, R., Piramuthu, S., Zhou, W. (eds.) FNSS 2018. CCIS, vol. 878, pp. 117–127. Springer, Cham (2018). https://doi.org/10.1007/978-3-319-94421-0_9
10. Hitaj, B., Gasti, P., Ateniese, G., Perez-Cruz, F.: PassGAN: a deep learning approach for password guessing. In: Deng, R.H., Gauthier-Umaña, V., Ochoa, M., Yung, M. (eds.) ACNS 2019. LNCS, vol. 11464, pp. 217–237. Springer, Cham (2019). https://doi.org/10.1007/978-3-030-21568-2_11

11. Ji, S., Yang, S., Xin, H., Han, W., Li, Z., Beyah, R.: Zero-sum password cracking game: a large-scale empirical study on the crackability, correlation, and security of passwords. IEEE Trans. Dependable Secure Comput. **14**(5), 550–564 (2015)
12. Li, Z., Han, W., Xu, W.: A large-scale empirical analysis of Chinese web passwords. In: 23rd USENIX Security Symposium (USENIX Security 14), pp. 559–574 (2014)
13. Yampolskiy, R.V.: Analyzing user password selection behavior for reduction of password space. In: Proceedings 40th Annual 2006 International Carnahan Conference on Security Technology, pp. 109–115. IEEE (2006)
14. Gong-Shen, M.K.L., Wei-Dong, Q., Jian-Hua, L.: Password vulnerability assessment and recovery based on rules mined from large-scale real data. Chin. J. Comput. **39**(3), 454–467 (2016)
15. Das, A., Bonneau, J., Caesar, M., Borisov, N., Wang, X.: The tangled web of password reuse. In: NDSS Symposium 2014, p. 7 (2014)
16. Li, Y., Wang, H., Sun, K.: A study of personal information in human-chosen passwords and its security implications. In: IEEE INFOCOM 2016-The 35th Annual IEEE International Conference on Computer Communications, pp. 1–9. IEEE (2016)
17. Wang, D., Zhang, Z., Wang, P., Yan, J., Huang, X.: Targeted online password guessing: an underestimated threat. In: Proceedings of the 2016 ACM SIGSAC conference on computer and communications security, pp. 1242–1254 (2016)
18. Merhav, N., Cohen, A.: Universal randomized guessing with application to asynchronous decentralized brute-force attacks. IEEE Trans. Inf. Theory **66**(1), 114–129 (2020)
19. Coby Wang, K., Reiter, M.K.: How to end password reuse on the web. In: Proceedings ACM CCS (2019)
20. Lu, B., Zhang, X., Ling, Z., Zhang, Y., Lin, Z.: A measurement study of authentication rate-limiting mechanisms of modern websites. In: Proceedings of the 34th Annual Computer Security Applications Conference, pp. 89–100 (2018)
21. Pal, B., Daniel, T., Chatterjee, R., Ristenpart, T.: Beyond credential stuffing: Password similarity models using neural networks. In: 2019 IEEE Symposium on Security and Privacy, SP, pp. 417–434. IEEE (2019)
22. Grassi, P.A., et al.: Nist special publication 800–63b: digital identity guidelines. enrollment and identity proofing requirements (2017). https://pages.nist.gov/800-63-3/sp800-63b.html
23. Jaggard, A.D., Syverson, P.: Oft target. In: Proceedings of the PET (2018)
24. Guri, M., Shemer, E., Shirtz, D., Elovici, Y.: Personal information leakage during password recovery of internet services. In: 2016 European Intelligence and Security Informatics Conference, EISIC, pp. 136–139. IEEE (2016)
25. Adams, A., Sasse, M.A.: Users are not the enemy. Commun. ACM **42**(12), 40–46 (1999)
26. Morris, R., Thompson, K.: Password security: a case history. Commun. ACM **22**(11), 594–597 (1979)
27. Bonneau, J.: The science of guessing: analyzing an anonymized corpus of 70 million passwords. In: 2012 IEEE Symposium on Security and Privacy, pp. 538–552. IEEE (2012)
28. Mazurek, M.L.: Measuring password guessability for an entire university. In: Proceedings of the 2013 ACM SIGSAC conference on Computer & communications security, pp. 173–186 (2013)

29. Bailey, D.V., Dürmuth, M., Paar, C.: Statistics on password re-use and adaptive strength for financial accounts. In: Abdalla, M., De Prisco, R. (eds.) SCN 2014. LNCS, vol. 8642, pp. 218–235. Springer, Cham (2014). https://doi.org/10.1007/978-3-319-10879-7_13
30. Tatlı, E.I.: Cracking more password hashes with patterns. IEEE Trans. Inf. Forensics Secur. **10**(8), 1656–1665 (2015)
31. Stobert, E., Biddle, R.: The password life cycle: user behaviour in managing passwords. In: 10th Symposium on Usable Privacy and Security, SOUPS 2014, pp. 243–255 (2014)
32. Kelley, P.G.: Guess again (and again and again): measuring password strength by simulating password-cracking algorithms. In: 2012 IEEE symposium on security and privacy, pp. 523–537. IEEE (2012)
33. Ur, B.: "i added '!' at the end to make it secure": observing password creation in the lab. In: Eleventh Symposium On Usable Privacy and Security, SOUPS 2015, pp. 123–140 (2015)
34. Shay, R.: A spoonful of sugar? The impact of guidance and feedback on password-creation behavior. In: Proceedings of the 33rd Annual ACM Conference on Human Factors in Computing Systems, pp. 2903–2912 (2015)
35. Wang, D., Cheng, H., Wang, P., Huang, X., Jian, G.: Zipf's law in passwords. IEEE Trans. Inf. Forensics Secur. **12**(11), 2776–2791 (2017)
36. Wang, D., Wang, P., He, D., Tian, Y.: Birthday, name and bifacial-security: understanding passwords of Chinese web users. In: 28th USENIX Security Symposium (USENIX Security 19), pp. 1537–1555 (2019)
37. Karapanos, N., Marforio, C., Soriente, C., Capkun, S.: Sound-proof: usable two-factor authentication based on ambient sound. In: 24th {USENIX} Security Symposium ({USENIX} Security 15), pp. 483–498 (2015)
38. Wang, D., Wang, P.: Two birds with one stone: two-factor authentication with security beyond conventional bound. IEEE Trans. Dependable Secure Comput. **15**(4), 708–722 (2016)

Multi-input Laconic Function Evaluation

Bo Pang[1,2,3], Long Chen[3], Xiong Fan[4], and Qiang Tang[3(✉)]

[1] State Key Laboratory of Information Security, Institute of Information
Engineering, Chinese Academy of Sciences, Beijing, China
pangbo@iie.ac.cn
[2] School of Cyber Security, University of Chinese Academy of Sciences,
Beijing, China
[3] New Jersey Institute of Technology, Newark, USA
{longchen,qiang}@njit.edu
[4] University of Maryland, College Park, USA
xfan@cs.umd.edu

Abstract. Recently, Quach, Wee and Wichs (FOCS 2018) proposed a new powerful cryptographic primitive called *laconic function evaluation* (LFE). Using an LFE scheme, Alice can compress a large circuit f into a small digest. Bob can encrypt some data x under this digest in a way that enables Alice to recover $f(x)$ without learning anything else about Bob's data. The laconic property requires that the size of the digest, the runtime of the encryption algorithm and the size of the ciphertext should be much smaller than the circuit-size of f. This new tool is motivated by an interesting application of "Bob-optimized" two-round secure two-party computation (2PC). In such a 2PC, Alice will get the final result thus the workload of Bob will be minimized.

In this paper, we consider a "client-optimized" two-round secure multiparty computation, in which multiple clients provide inputs and enable a server to obtain final outputs while protecting privacy of each individual input. More importantly, we would also minimize the cost of each client. For this purpose, we propose multi-input laconic function evaluation (MI-LFE), and give a systematic study of it.

It turns out that MI-LFE for general circuit is not easy. Specifically, we first show that the directly generalized version, i.e., the public-key MI-LFE implies virtual black-box obfuscation. Hence the public-key MI-LFE (for general circuits) is infeasible. This forces us to turn to secret key version of MI-LFE, in which encryption now needs to take a secret key. Next we show that secret-key MI-LFE also implies heavy cryptographic primitives including witness encryption for NP language and the indistinguishability obfuscation. On the positive side, we show that the secret-key MI-LFE can be constructed assuming indistinguishability obfuscation and learning with errors assumption. Our theoretical results suggest that we may have to explore relaxed versions of MI-LFE for meaningful new applications of "client-optimized" MPC and others.

Keywords: Multi-party computation · Laconic function evaluation · Indistinguishability obfuscation

© Springer Nature Switzerland AG 2020
J. K. Liu and H. Cui (Eds.): ACISP 2020, LNCS 12248, pp. 369–388, 2020.
https://doi.org/10.1007/978-3-030-55304-3_19

1   Introduction

In a recent paper [31], Quach, Wee and Wichs described an interesting secure two-round two-party computation (2PC) protocol which is "Bob-optimized". In such a protocol, Alice and Bob who have inputs x_A and x_B respectively want to jointly compute $f(x_A, x_B)$, and Alice initiates the first round message, and learns the output $f(x_A, x_B)$ in the second round. More interestingly, Alice does all the work while Bob's computation and communication during the protocol execution are both smaller than the size of the circuit f or even Alices input x_A, (concretely, the computational cost of Bob is only $(|x_B| + |f(x_A, x_B)|) \cdot \mathsf{poly}(d)$, where d is the depth of the circuit f). Such kind of "Bob-optimized" secure 2PC was considered more natural as it is Alice who obtains the output should do the work [31]. This is in contrast to prior solutions based on fully homomorphic encryption [12,13,21,23] which optimized the work of Alice.

To construct such kind of two-round "Bob-optimized" secure 2PC, a new cryptographic primitive *laconic function evaluation* (LFE) was formulated in [31]. In an LFE scheme, Alice can compress a potentially large circuit f into a small digest. Bob then can encrypt some data x under this digest s.t. Alice can recover $f(x)$ without learning anything else about the original data x. The size of the digest, the run-time of the encryption algorithm and the size of the ciphertext should all be much smaller than the size of circuit f, In this way, Bob's workload in the 2PC is minimized. In [31], they provided the first construction of LFE for general circuits under the learning with errors (LWE) assumption.

"Client-Optimized" 2-Round MPC. The "Bob-optimized" two-round 2PC is useful in many applications such as privacy preserving data analytics, especially when the client device (Bob in the above setting) is resource restrained (e.g., mobile devices), while the circuit representing the analytic function is substantially complex (e.g., some complicated data mining or machine learning algorithms). However, in many relevant scenarios, the data of "Bob" may not be generated all at once, or even come from multiple clients. Consider the following scenarios:

Privacy Preserving Data Analytic System. Many data analytic applications running in a server solicit input data via multiple data collectors. For instance, many surveillance cameras are now deployed on the roads to monitor traffic conditions by local governments, and the videos are collected and submitted to a central server to analyze the road condition.

It is not hard to see that those individual inputs may be sensitive, e.g., the videos could contain confidential geographic information regarding the cars traveling on the roads, thus they should not be directly submitted to the server in the plain. However, there are multiple clients (the cameras) to provide inputs, we need now to deploy a multiparty computation protocol. On the other hand, similar as before, those clients (cameras) are not powerful computing devices, thus the computation and communication cost on the cameras (as data collectors) have to be minimized. And it is not realistic to ask all the cameras to coordinate other than directly communicating with a server.

Privacy Preserving Call Records Surveillance. It is known that several major telephone companies were cooperating with the intelligent service to monitor the phone records of U.S. citizens, and store them in a large database known [1,2]. Though it is a constant debate that sometimes surveillance may be needed for law enforcement to do investigations, it is obviously unacceptable that personal call records are uploaded and stored in the clear. It would be necessary to design a privacy preserving call records surveillance system.

In such a setting, each client continuously uploads obfuscated call records, and the mobile phones are mostly not so powerful devices that would demand the optimization on the client side workload for a privacy preserving protocol. Moreover, since investigation may apply complex data mining algorithms on multiple pieces of call records from each targeted individual, similar as above, we would need to design a 2-round client-optimized multiparty (depending how many pieces of records needed) computation.[1]

"Client-Optimized" 2-Round MPC. To capture above two exemplary application scenarios, we need a 2-round "client-optimized" secure multi-party computation protocol in which there might be multiple inputs from multiple clients. [2] In particular, we wish to have a 2-round protocol, that the server initializes the protocol with a first round message, then each client (the same client in different time period sending a different input would be viewed as a different client) sends out a message and then the server obtains the final output $f(x_1, \ldots, x_n)$, where f is the analytic function and $x_1, \ldots, x_n$ are all the inputs. More importantly, the "client-optimized" property here refers to (1) the computation and communication of each client is as efficient as that of Bob in the "Bob-optimized" 2PC; and (2) there is no communication among each clients.

Insufficiencies of Existing Tools. There are several possible paths to proceed, unfortunately none of them reaches a satisfying solution. Let us analyze one by one. (1) The second property above disallowing communication among clients already excludes straightforward solutions such as the general multiparty computation protocol [4,6,30,32], let alone it is not clear how to ensure the low client costs. (2) Laconic functional evaluation [31] was also shown to be applicable to MPC with small online computation. However, in our setting, the similar idea letting the server first compress the function to obtain a digest, then all clients and the server run an MPC protocol for the encryption function of the laconic function evaluation scheme (with the server input of the digest) is not satisfying. Although there exist 2-round MPC protocol [20], the communications among clients could be potentially large, let alone in some of the scenarios,

---

[1] One may suggest to let the client wait and upload a bunch of call records all at once, however, each individual has no incentive to do so and this is not how call records stored nowadays.

[2] In this paper, we only consider semi-honest security for our MPC application, which is analogous to the Bob-optimized 2PC in the LFE paper. In this setting, we assume the server will only choose a proper function permitted by clients. Furthermore, a semi-honest security protocol can be easily upgraded to adaptively secure by standard techniques such as adding NIZK.

the clients may not be able to talk to each other. (3) Another related notion is functional encryption [10,18,26], especially multi-input functional encryption (MIFE) [9,24]. Straightforward application of MIFE requires an extra trusted party to generate the decryption key for the server (which is already a huge overload that is proportional to the size of f), while we cannot let the server to do this, otherwise no security of the inputs can be present. (4) Last but not least, similar as in [31], multi-key fully homomorphic encryption [15,30] cannot enable the server to learn the output in two rounds.

Formalizing Multi-input Laconic Function Evaluation. Motivated by the client-optimized 2-round MPC application and the deficiencies of existing tools, we generalize the notion of LFE to *multi-input laconic function evaluation* (MI-LFE). In a MI-LFE scheme, the server has a large circuit f defined over n inputs, which can be deterministically compressed into a short digest $\mathsf{digest}_f = \mathsf{Compress}(f)$. Then each client i can encrypt his input data x_i under this digest, resulting in a ciphertext $\mathsf{ct}_i \leftarrow \mathsf{Enc}(\mathsf{digest}_f, x_i)$, respectively. After receiving n ciphertexts, the server is then able to decrypt using her knowledge of f to recover the output $f(x_1, \ldots, x_n) = \mathsf{Dec}(f, \mathsf{ct}_1, \ldots, \mathsf{ct}_n)$. Security ensures that the server does not learn anything else about the n inputs $x_1, \ldots, x_n$ beyond the output $f(x_1, \ldots, x_n)$, as formalized via the simulation paradigm. Similar to LFE, the laconic property of MI-LFE requires that each client's computation and communication complexity is small, and in particular, the size of the digest digest_f, the run-time of the encryption algorithm $\mathsf{Enc}(\mathsf{digest}_f, x_i)$ and the size of the ciphertext ct_i should be much smaller than the circuit-size of f.

With the new primitive at hand, the client-optimized 2-round MPC protocol can be easy: the server compresses the function and broadcasts the digest to all clients. Each client then uses the encryption algorithm to obfuscate his input and sends it to the server. The server then pools all ciphertext and evaluate. The laconic property guarantees that the workload of each client is small compared to the complex function f, and no communication is needed among clients.

The Difficulty of Constructing MI-LFE. We then systematically study the concept of MI-LFE. It turns out that such a notion is quite difficult to obtain. In particular, the most nature model for MI-LFE is in the public-key setting which generalizes LFE in [31] in a straightforward fashion. The only difference is that the function here is evaluated on multiple inputs, so the different inputs x_i for $i = 1, \ldots, n$ are encrypted into different ciphertexts ct_i for $i = 1, \ldots, n$, and the decryption procedure involves multiple ciphertexts. In Sect. 4, we show that public key MI-LFE actually implies virtual black-box obfuscation. Since VBB obfuscation is known to be impossible for general circuits [5], this yields us impossibility results for (general) MI-LFE in the public setting.

To circumvent such an impossibility but still enabling the client-optimized MPC, we turn to MI-LFE in the private-key setting. It follows the syntax of the version of the public-key setting, but an additional key generation procedure is involved and the encryption procedure will always take the private key as input.[3] Restricting encryption procedure allows us to bypass the implication to VBB that essentially compresses a universal circuit and uses MI-LFE encryption algorithm to encrypt the function and input as different ciphertext to evaluate.

Then we find that even in the private key setting, constructing MI-LFE from standard assumptions is not an easy task. We show that the private-key MI-LFE with reasonable security definition implies the witness encryption (WE) for NP language [3,7,11,17,22] and the indistinguishability obfuscation (iO) for general circuits [14,16,28,29], respectively. Since these two advanced primitives have no constructions from the standard assumptions so far, leveraging some heavy tools in the construction of MI-LFE seems inevitable. As a byproduct, we notice that MI-LFE also implies MIFE, thus MI-LFE could be applicable in multiple advanced scenarios, if it ever exists. But the reverse implication is not straightforward, since MIFE do not have the compression property.

Constructing Private-Key MI-LFE. Next we show that the private-key MI-LFE can indeed be constructed from indistinguishability obfuscation and learning with errors (LWE) assumption. Our construction of MI-LFE is inspired by the techniques developed in the context of multi-input functional encryption [25] and laconic function evaluation [31]. Intuitively, the message x_i for i-th coordinate of circuit C in MI-LFE is encrypted using public key encryption and equipped with a proof showing that this encryption is done correctly. The other part of the i-th ciphertext is an indistinguishability obfuscation of a circuit that first checks the legitimacy of the input ciphertexts and then transforms public key encryptions of messages $\{x_i\}$ into an LFE ciphertext of the message $x_1, \ldots, x_n$. A decryptor in MI-LFE that has all ciphertexts of messages $\{x_i\}$ for a pre-compressed circuit C first obtains LFE encryption of messages for each coordinate of circuit C after evaluating the obfuscated program, and then the actual result $C(\{x_i\})$ by evaluating the decryption algorithm in LFE.

The laconic property of our scheme follows from the laconic property of LFE encryption algorithm. Only the LFE encryption procedure in the indistinguishable obfuscation is corresponding to the circuit C, and other parts in our encryption procedure is independent with the circuit C, we know that LFE encryption only scales with the circuit depth, much smaller than the circuit size. Even after been obfuscated, should still much smaller than the circuit size.[4]

The security definition of MI-LFE requires to simulate the challenge ciphertexts. Recall that there are two parts in a ciphertext: (1) two independent semantically secure public key encryption of the actual message and a proof showing the correctness and legitimacy of the encryption; (2) an obfuscation of a circuit

---

[3] We remark here that a secret key MI-LFE is enough for many of our applications of client-optimized 2-round MPC: if for one client generating inputs overtime, the client's device may have a pre-installed secret key by the device manufacturer; while for data analytics via multiple data collectors such as cameras, a secret key maybe installed by the government who deploy them.

[4] we consider an unbounded-size circuit class $\mathcal{C}$, meaning that there exists a large size circuit $C \in \mathcal{C}$. We refer to Lemma 3 for the details of laconic property of our construction.

that contains proofs verification and encryption transformation. Specifically, the simulation of first part relies on semantic security of the public-key encryption and special property of the proof system, i.e. witness indistinguishability. The circuit to be obfuscated can be changed according to changes happened in the first part of challenge ciphertext. We also would like to remark that in our construction, we simply rely on a common random string, rather than a common reference string used previously in MIFE.

1.1 Additional Related Works

Multi-input Functional Encryption. MI-LFE also appears to be related to multi-input functional encryption (MIFE) [9,24]. In MIFE, multiple ciphertexts are also encrypted independently by different parties, while the one holding the decryption key sk_f can only recover $f(x_1, \ldots, x_n)$ without learning anything else about $x_1, \ldots, x_n$. Despite of the similarities, a MIFE scheme involves a master authority whose duty is to derive a decryption key sk_f respect to a function f from the master key msk. More importantly, the complexity of the decryption key generation procedure may be proportion to the size of the function f. Note that in some application scenario like the one mention above, there are no parties that can be both trustworthy and capable to afford such workload.

Fully Homomorphic Encryption. FHE [12,13,21,23] can be viewed as the dual version of the LFE. In FHE, one party, say Alice, can encrypt different values x_i, resulting in a ciphertext $ct_i \leftarrow Enc(pk, x_i)$, respectively. Then another party, say Bob, can homomorphically evaluate a function f on these ciphertexts. When Alice sees the evaluation, she can decrypt and recover the message $f(x_1, \ldots, x_n)$. In contrast with MI-LFE and LFE, here it is the encryptor to get the final result.

General MPC. Since our application is a special case of secure multi party computation, theoretically it can be realized in two round by the general MPC technique [4,6,32]. However, here we additionally require that the computation complexity for each surveillance to be cheap, and they only need to communicate with the data center but not with each other. Considering all these additional requirements, this application is hard to be directly achievable via general MPC. There exist 2-round MPC protocol [20,30], the communications cost among clients could be potentially large, i.e. an multiplicative overhead of the depth of circuit and size of input.

2   Preliminaries

In this section, we give background on two classical cryptographic primitives used in paper: non-interactive witness-indistinguishable proofs and perfectly binding commitments.

Non-interactive Proof Systems. Here, we recall the syntax and property of non-interactive witness-indistinguishable proofs.

Syntax. Let R be an efficiently computable binary relation. For pairs $(x, w) \in R$, we call x the statement and w the witness. Let L be the language consisting of statements in R. A non-interactive proof system [8,27] for a language L, consists of a CRS generation algorithm CRSGen, a proving algorithm Prove and a verification algorithm Verify, defined as follows:

- CRSGen(1^λ): On input the security parameter λ, it outputs a common reference string crs.
- Prove(crs, x, w): On input the common reference string crs, and a statement x along with a witness w. If $(x, w) \in R$, it produces a proof string π, otherwise it outputs **fail**.
- Verify(crs, x, π): On input the common reference string crs, and a statement x along with a proof string π, it outputs 1 if the proof is valid, and 0 otherwise.

Definition 1 (Non-interactive Proof System). *A non-interactive proof system for a language L with a PPT relation R is a tuple of algorithms (CRSGen, Prove, Verify) such that the following properties hold:*

> ***Perfect Completeness.*** *A proof system is complete if an honest prover with a valid witness can convince an honest verifier. More formally, for all $x \in [L]$ and every w such that $(x, w) \in R$, it holds that*
>
> $$\Pr[\mathsf{Verify}(\mathsf{crs}, x, \mathsf{Prove}(\mathsf{crs}, x, w)) = 1] = 1$$
>
> *where* crs $\leftarrow$ CRSGen(1^λ) *and the probability is taken over the coins of* CRSGen, Prove *and* Verify.
>
> - ***Statistical Soundness.*** *A proof system is sound if it is infeasible to convince an honest verifier when the statement is false. More formally, for all adversary (even unbounded) $\mathcal{A}$, it holds that*
>
> $$\Pr[\mathsf{Verify}(\mathsf{crs}, x.\pi) = 1 \wedge x \notin L | \mathsf{crs} \leftarrow \mathsf{CRSGen}(1^\lambda), (x, \pi) \leftarrow \mathcal{A}(\mathsf{crs})] = \mathsf{negl}(\lambda)$$

Definition 2 (NIWI). *A non-interactive proof system (CRSGen, Prove, Verify) for a language L with a PPT relation R is witness indistinguishable if for any triplet (x, w_0, w_1) such that $(x, w_0) \in R$ and $(x, w_1) \in R$, the distributions $\{\mathsf{crs}, \mathsf{Prove}(\mathsf{crs}, x, w_0)\}$ and $\{\mathsf{crs}, \mathsf{Prove}(\mathsf{crs}, x, w_1)\}$ are computationally indistinguishable, where* crs $\leftarrow$ CRSGen(1^λ).

Non-interactive and Perfectly Binding Commitment Schemes. We let Com($\cdot; \cdot$) denote the commitment function of a non-interactive commitment scheme. Com is a PPT algorithm that takes as input a string x and randomness r, and outputs $c \leftarrow$ Com($x; r$). A perfectly binding commitment scheme must satisfy the following properties:

- **Perfectly Binding.** This property states that the two different strings cannot have the same commitment. More formally, $\forall x_1 \neq x_2$, Com(x_1) $\neq$ Com(x_2).
- **Computationally Hiding.** For all strings x_0 and x_1 (of the same length), and all PPT adversaries $\mathcal{A}$, we have that:

$$|\Pr[\mathcal{A}(\mathsf{Com}(x_0)) = 1] - \Pr[\mathcal{A}(\mathsf{Com}(x_1)) = 1]| \leq \mathsf{negl}(\lambda)$$

3   Multi-input LFE: Syntax and Security Definition

In this section, we define the notion of multi-input laconic function evaluation (MI-LFE) for a class of n-ary circuits $\mathcal{C}$. We assume that every circuit $C \in \mathcal{C}$ is associated with some circuit parameters C.params. By default we consider $\mathcal{C}$ to be the class of all circuits with C.params $= (1^n, 1^k, 1^d)$, which take as input n bit-strings $(x_1, \ldots, x_n)$, where $x_i \in \{0,1\}^k$, and d denotes the circuit depth.

Definition 3 (MI-LFE). *A private-key multi-input laconic function evaluation for circuits class $\mathcal{C}$ consists of five algorithms* (crsGen, KeyGen, Compress, Enc, Dec) *with details as follows:*

- crsGen$(1^\lambda, C$.params$)$ *takes as input the security parameter 1^λ and circuit parameters C.params, and outputs a uniformly random common random string* crs *of appropriate length.*
- KeyGen$(1^\lambda,$ crs$)$ *takes as input the security parameter 1^λ and the common random string* crs, *and outputs a private key* SK.
- Compress$($crs$, C)$ *is a deterministic algorithm that takes as input the common random string* crs *and a circuit $C \in \mathcal{C}$, and outputs a digest* digest$_C$.
- Enc$($crs$,$ digest$_C,$ SK$, i, x_i)$ *takes as input the common random string* crs, *a digest* digest$_C$, *a private key* SK, *an index i, and a message x_i, and outputs a ciphertext* ct$_i$.
- Dec$($crs$, C,$ ct$_1, \ldots,$ ct$_n)$ *takes as input the common random string* crs, *a circuit $C \in \mathcal{C}$, and n ciphertexts* ct$_1, \ldots,$ ct$_n$, *and outputs a message y.*

Correctness. For correctness, we require that for all λ and $C \in \mathcal{C}$ with C.params, it holds that

$$
\Pr\left[y = C(x_1, \ldots, x_n) \,\middle|\, \begin{array}{l} \text{crs} \leftarrow \text{crsGen}(1^\lambda, C.\text{params}), \\ \text{SK} \leftarrow \text{KeyGen}(1^\lambda, \text{crs}), \\ \text{digest}_C \leftarrow \text{Compress}(\text{crs}, C), \\ \text{ct}_i \leftarrow \text{Enc}(\text{crs}, \text{digest}_C, \text{SK}, i, x_i), \\ y \leftarrow \text{Dec}(\text{crs}, C, \text{ct}_1, \ldots, \text{ct}_n), \end{array} \right] = 1
$$

Definition 4 (SIM-Based Security). *For security, we say a private-key MI-LFE is (n, q)-SIM-secure, where n denotes the number of input strings for a circuit C, and q is number of challenge message tuples, if there exists a* PPT *simulator* SIM *such that for all stateful* PPT *adversary $\mathcal{A}$, it holds:*

$$
\left| \Pr[\text{Expt}_{\text{MI-LFE}}^{\text{Real}}(1^\lambda) = 1] - \Pr[\text{Expt}_{\text{MI-LFE}}^{\text{Ideal}}(1^\lambda) = 1] \right| \leq \text{negl}(\lambda)
$$

where the experiments $\text{Expt}_{\text{MI-LFE}}^{\text{Real}}(1^\lambda)$ *and* $\text{Expt}_{\text{MI-LFE}}^{\text{Ideal}}(1^\lambda)$ *are defined in Fig. 1.*

   In Fig. 1, oracle $O(C, \cdot)$ denotes the trusted party. It accepts queries of the form $(j_1, \ldots, j_n)$, where $j_1, \ldots, j_n \in \{1, \ldots, q\}$. On input such a query, $O(C, \cdot)$ outputs the $C(x_1^{j_1}, \ldots, x_n^{j_n})$; otherwise outputs $\perp$. We refer to the above as adaptive security.

(a) $\mathsf{Expt}^{\mathsf{Real}}_{\mathsf{MI\text{-}LFE}}(1^\lambda)$	(b) $\mathsf{Expt}^{\mathsf{Ideal}}_{\mathsf{MI\text{-}LFE}}(1^\lambda)$
1. $C.\mathsf{params} \leftarrow \mathcal{A}(1^\lambda)$ 2. $\mathsf{crs} \leftarrow \mathsf{crsGen}(1^\lambda, C.\mathsf{params})$ 3. $\mathsf{SK} \leftarrow \mathsf{KeyGen}(1^\lambda, \mathsf{crs})$ 4. $((x_1^j, \ldots, x_n^j)_{j=1}^q, C) \leftarrow \mathcal{A}(\mathsf{crs}) : C \in \mathcal{C}$ 5. $\mathsf{digest}_C \leftarrow \mathsf{Compress}(\mathsf{crs}, C)$ 6. $\mathsf{ct}_i^j \leftarrow \mathsf{Enc}(\mathsf{crs}, \mathsf{digest}_C, \mathsf{SK}, i, x_i^j),$ $\quad \forall i \in [n], j \in [q]$ 7. output $\mathcal{A}\left(\{\mathsf{ct}_i^j\}_{i \in [n], j \in [q]}\right).$	1. $C.\mathsf{params} \leftarrow \mathcal{A}(1^\lambda)$ 2. $\mathsf{crs} \leftarrow \mathsf{crsGen}(1^\lambda, C.\mathsf{params})$ 3. $((x_1^j, \ldots, x_n^j)_{j=1}^q, C) \leftarrow \mathcal{A}(\mathsf{crs}) : C \in \mathcal{C}$ 4. $\mathsf{digest}_C \leftarrow \mathsf{Compress}(\mathsf{crs}, C)$ 5. $\mathsf{ct}_i^j \leftarrow \mathsf{SIM}^{O(C, \cdot)}(\mathsf{crs}, C, \mathsf{digest}_C, i),$ $\quad \forall i \in [n], j \in [q]$ 6. output $\mathcal{A}\left(\{\mathsf{ct}_i^j\}_{i \in [n], j \in [q]}\right).$

Fig. 1. SIM-based Security Experiments for MI-LFE

Definition 5 (IND-Based Security). *We say a private-key* MI-LFE *is* (n, q)-*IND-secure, where* n *denotes the number of inputs for a circuit* C, *and* q *is the number of* n-*ary challenge message tuples, if for any* PPT *adversary* $\mathcal{A}$,

$$\mathsf{Adv}^{\mathsf{IND}}_{\mathcal{A}, \mathsf{MI\text{-}LFE}}(1^\lambda) = \left| \Pr[\mathsf{Expt}^{\mathsf{IND}}_{\mathcal{A}, \mathsf{MI\text{-}LFE}}(1^\lambda) = 1] - \frac{1}{2} \right|$$

is $\mathsf{negl}(\lambda)$, *where the experiments* $\mathsf{Expt}^{\mathsf{IND}}_{\mathcal{A}, \mathsf{MI\text{-}LFE}}(1^\lambda)$ *is defined in Fig. 2.*

$\mathsf{Expt}^{\mathsf{IND}}_{\mathcal{A}, \mathsf{MI\text{-}LFE}}(1^\lambda)$
1. $C.\mathsf{params} \leftarrow \mathcal{A}(1^\lambda)$ 2. $\mathsf{crs} \leftarrow \mathsf{crsGen}(1^\lambda, C.\mathsf{params}), \mathsf{SK} \leftarrow \mathsf{KeyGen}(1^\lambda, \mathsf{crs})$ 3. $(\boldsymbol{X}^0, \boldsymbol{X}^1, C) \leftarrow \mathcal{A}(\mathsf{crs})$: where $C \in \mathcal{C}$, $\boldsymbol{X}^b = ((x_1^{j, b}, \ldots, x_n^{j, b})_{j \in [q]})$, $\quad$ such that $C(x_1^{j_1, 0}, \ldots, x_n^{j_n, 0}) = C(x_1^{j_1, 1}, \ldots, x_n^{j_n, 1}), \forall i \in [n], j_i \in [q]$ 4. $\mathsf{digest}_C \leftarrow \mathsf{Compress}(\mathsf{crs}, C),$ 5. $b \xleftarrow{\$} \{0, 1\}, \mathsf{ct}_i^j \leftarrow \mathsf{Enc}(\mathsf{crs}, \mathsf{digest}_C, \mathsf{SK}, i, x_i^{j, b}), \forall i \in [n], j \in [q]$ 6. $b' \leftarrow \mathcal{A}\left(\{\mathsf{ct}_i^j\}_{i \in [n], j \in [q]}\right).$ 7. Output 1 if $b = b'$ and 0 otherwise.

Fig. 2. IND-based Security Experiment For MI-LFE

Remark 1 (Selective Security). A weaker notion, called selective security, in both SIM-based and IND-based security, can be defines as: adversary $\mathcal{A}$ has to choose challenge plaintext at the very beginning of the experiments (as described in Fig. 1 and Fig. 2) before seeing crs.

Lemma 1. *If a MI-LFE scheme* Π *is SIM secure, then* Π *is also IND secure.*

Proof (Proof Sketch). We note that if a MI-LFE scheme Π satisfies SIM-based security, then we show that it also satisfies IND-based security. Now, for challenge message queries $(\boldsymbol{X}^0, \boldsymbol{X}^1)$, where $\boldsymbol{X}^b = \{(x_1^{j,b}, \ldots, x_n^{j,b})\}_{j \in [q]}$, the challenger in the IND-based security experiment chooses a random bit b, then invokes the simulator in SIM-based security game to compute

$$\mathsf{ct}_i^j \leftarrow \mathsf{SIM}^{O(C,\cdot)}(\mathsf{crs}, C, \mathsf{digest}_C, i), \quad \forall i \in [n], j \in [q]$$

where $O(C, \cdot)$ accepts the queries of the form $(j_1, \ldots, j_n)$ and outputs $C(x_1^{j_1,b}, \ldots, x_n^{j_n,b})$. Hence, by the SIM-based security, for all $i \in [n], j \in [q]$, each respond $\mathsf{ct}_i^j \leftarrow \mathsf{SIM}^{O(C,\cdot)}(\mathsf{crs}, C, \mathsf{digest}_C, i)$ is computationally indistinguishable from real execution $\mathsf{ct}_i^j \leftarrow \mathsf{Enc}(\mathsf{crs}, \mathsf{digest}_C, \mathsf{SK}, i, x_i^{j,b})$. And the bit b is chosen from random, this completes the IND-based security experiment for MI-LFE. Since $(\boldsymbol{X}^0, \boldsymbol{X}^1)$ satisfies $C(x_1^{j_1,0}, \ldots, x_n^{j_n,0}) = C(x_1^{j_1,1}, \ldots, x_n^{j_n,1}), \forall i \in [n], j_i \in [q]$, we have that $\{ct_i^j\}$, output by the challenger, is independent with the bit b.

Laconic property. Same as LFE, we insist that the size of $(\mathsf{crs}, \mathsf{digest}_C, \mathsf{SK}, \mathsf{ct}_i)$ and the running time of Enc are at most sublinear of the size of circuit C.

4   Hardness of MI-LFE

In this section, we show the difficulty of MI-LFE schemes. In particular, we show public-key MI-LFE for general circuits is impossible by constructing a virtual black-box obfuscator from it. Moreover, even the private-key MI-LFE implies witness encryption and indistinguishability obfuscation.

Public-Key MI-LFE. We first discuss the syntax and security definition of public key MI-LFE. Then, we show that a MI-LFE scheme for all circuits implies virtual black-box obfuscation for all circuits, which is proved impossible by Barak et al. [5]. The main difference between MI-LFE in public-key setting and that in private-key setting (c.f. Sect. 3) is that algorithm $\mathsf{KeyGen}(1^\lambda, \mathsf{crs})$ does not exist in public-key setting, meaning that encryption algorithm can be performed by anyone who knows common reference string and the digest of circuit.

Security Definition. In this part, we discuss the intuition of simulation-based public key MI-LFE security. To illustrate the difference between public-key and private-key setting, it suffices to consider the case of 2-ary functions and *one* challenge message tuple (x_1, x_2). In this example, the simulation-based security in the private-key setting guarantees that for one function f, an adversary cannot learn anything more than $f(x_1, x_2)$ where (x_1, x_2) is the challenge message pair. However, its counterpart in the public-key setting cannot guarantee this property. The reason is that an adversary who knows the public key can create its own chiphertexts, thus can learn additional information $\{f(x_1, \cdot)\}$ and $\{f(\cdot, x_2)\}$ given ciphertexts for (x_1, x_2). This additional information must be taken into account for the simulator (adversary in ideal world) in the ideal world. We refer to the full version for the formal SIM-based security game.

VBB Obfuscation from Public-Key MI-LFE. Here we show that a virtual black-box obfuscator [5], can be derived from a two party public-key MI-LFE. The basic idea is to let the compressed function of the MI-LFE be a universal circuit U. The input of the first party is the function f which we wish to obfuscate, and the input of the second party is the input value x of the function f. So the obfuscator should output the first party's ciphertext $\mathsf{Enc}(\mathsf{crs}, \mathsf{digest}_U, 1, f)$.

Specifically, for a universal circuit U, the obfuscator **VBB** works as follow:

1. **Obfuscation:** Run the crsGen and $\mathsf{Compress}$ algorithm to generate crs and digest_U, compute $\mathsf{ct}_1 \leftarrow \mathsf{Enc}(\mathsf{crs}, \mathsf{digest}_U, 1, f)$, and output the obfuscated circuit **VBB**$(f) = (\mathsf{crs}, \mathsf{digest}_U, U, \mathsf{ct}_1)$.
2. **Evaluation:** To evaluate the obfuscated circuit **VBB**(f) on an input x, one just needs to compute $\mathsf{ct}_2 \leftarrow \mathsf{Enc}(\mathsf{crs}, \mathsf{digest}_U, 2, x)$ and run $\mathsf{Dec}(\mathsf{crs}, U, \mathsf{ct}_1, \mathsf{ct}_2)$.

According to the correctness of MI-LFE, the decryption result should be $U(f, x) = f(x)$. The virtual black-box property of this obfuscator follows from the simulation security of the MI-LFE, hence we have the following theorem.

Theorem 1. *A $(2, 1)$-SIM-secure MI-LFE in public-encryption setting for general 2-ary functions implies virtual black-box obfuscation for all circuits.*

Given an VBB adversary $\mathcal{A}$, we use A to construct an MI-LFE adversary $\mathcal{B}$, the full proof is given in full version.

Witness Encryption from Private-Key MI-LFE. Since public key MI-LFE for general circuits does not exist, we have to turn our attention to private key MI-LFE. We firstly introduce MI-ABLFE (a variant of private-key MI-LFE). Then, we construct witness encryption for NP language, for general circuits. Since MI-LFE trivially implies an MI-ABLFE, thus we conclude the implication of private key MI-LFE to witness encryption, introduced by Garg et al. [19].

MI-ABLFE. We start from LFE for a restricted class of functionalities, which call attribute-based LFE (AB-LFE) in analogy to attribute-based encryption [31]. We formalize the definition and security requirement of MI-ABLFE as follow:

Definition 6 (MI-ABLFE). *Let $C : (\{0, 1\}^k)^n \to \{0, 1\}$ be a circuit. We define the Conditional Disclosure Functionality (CDF) of C as the function*

$$\mathsf{CDF}[C]((x_1, u), \ldots, (x_n, u)) = \begin{cases} (x_1, \ldots, x_n, u) & \text{if } C(x_1, \ldots, x_n) = 1 \\ (x_1, \ldots, x_n, \perp) & \text{if } C(x_1, \ldots, x_n) = 0 \end{cases}$$

where $x_i \in \{0, 1\}^k$, and $u \in \{0, 1\}$.

A MI-ABLFE scheme for a circuit family $\mathcal{C}$ is a MI-LFE scheme that supports circuits $CDF[C]$ defined as above, for all $C \in \mathcal{C}$. We define $CDF[C].params = C.params = (1^n, 1^k, 1^d)$, where d is the depth of C.

Remark 2 (Security of MI-ABLFE). The IND-based security notion of MI-ABLFE can be defined similarly as MI-LFE, except for the difference that the payload u remains private if for any message queries (x_i, u), it holds that $C(x_1, \ldots, x_n) = 0$.

Witness Encryption from MI-ABLFE. Intuitively, the witness encryption [19] can use the MI-ABLFE in the following way: the general circuit C is used as the NP verifier such that the decryptor of MI-ABLFE can recover the message u if he has the witness w for the statement x satisfying $C(x, w) = 1$. More specifically, given an NP language L, the construction of $\Pi = (\mathsf{Enc}, \mathsf{Dec})$ for L is as follows:

- $\mathsf{Enc}(1^\lambda, x, u)$: On input a statement $x \in \{0,1\}^n$ (whose witness has length bounded by m), and a message $u \in \{0,1\}$, the executes the following:
  1. Set $C : \{0,1\}^n \times \{0,1\}^m \to \{0,1\}$ to be the NP verifier for language L that takes as the input $x \in \{0,1\}^n$, $w \in \{0,1\}^m$, and outputs 1 iff $(x, w) \in L$. Compute $\mathsf{MI\text{-}ABLFE.crsGen}(1^\lambda, C.\mathsf{params})$ to generate CRS string crs.
  2. Then it runs $\mathsf{MI\text{-}ABLFE.Compress}(\mathsf{crs}, C)$ to generate digest_C, and $\mathsf{MI\text{-}ABLFE.KeyGen}(\mathsf{crs})$ to get SK.
  3. For $i \in [n]$, compute $\mathsf{MI\text{-}ABLFE.Enc}(\mathsf{crs}, \mathsf{digest}_C, \mathsf{SK}, i, x_i, u)$, where x_i is the i-th bit of x.
  4. For $b \in \{0,1\}, j \in [m]$, compute $\mathsf{MI\text{-}ABLFE.Enc}(\mathsf{crs}, \mathsf{digest}_C, \mathsf{SK}, j, b, u), \forall b \in \{0,1\}, j \in [m]$.
  Output $\mathsf{ct} = \big(\mathsf{crs}, C, x, \{\mathsf{ct}_i\}_{i\in[n]}, \{\mathsf{ct}_{j,b}\}_{j\in[m], b\in\{0,1\}}\big)$.
- $\mathsf{Dec}(\mathsf{ct}, w)$: On input a witness $w \in \{0,1\}^m$ for the statement $x \in \{0,1\}^n$, and a ciphertext ct for x, the decryption algorithm computes and outputs

$$\mathsf{MI\text{-}ABLFE.Dec}\big(\mathsf{crs}, C, \{\mathsf{ct}_i\}_{i\in[n]}, \{\mathsf{ct}_{j,w_j}\}_{j\in[m]}\big)$$

where w_j is the j-th bit of witness w.

The correctness of the witness encryption follows from the correctness of the MI-ABLFE.

Theorem 2. *Assuming the $(n + m, 2)$-IND-based selective security of MI-ABLFE scheme* MI-ABLFE *for general circuits, then the witness encryption scheme Π described above is secure.*

Given an witness encryption adversary $\mathcal{A}$, we describe an MI-LFE adversary $\mathcal{B}$ invoke A as a subroutine to attack the security of MI-LFE. The proof is completed in full version.

Indistinguishable Obfuscation from Private-Key MI-LFE. We can derive an indistinguishability obfuscator for all circuits [16], with k-bit inputs from a $(k + 1)$-party MI-LFE in private-key setting. This, in particular, means that the use of indistinguishable obfuscation is inevitable for the private-key MI-LFE.

Now, we describe how to construct an indistinguishable obfuscator for a circuit class $\mathcal{C}$, where for every $C \in \mathcal{C}$, $C : \{0,1\}^k \to \{0,1\}^{k'}$ and $|C| = \ell$. Assuming there is a $(k + 1, 2)$-IND-secure MI-LFE scheme MI-LFE $=$ $(\mathsf{crsGen}, \mathsf{KeyGen}, \mathsf{Compress}, \mathsf{Enc}, \mathsf{Dec})$, where $k + 1$ denotes the number of party and 2 denotes the number of challenge message tuples. The intuition here is to let the actual function to be evaluated in MI-LFE to be a universal circuit U, defined as following:

$$U(x_1, \ldots, x_k, C) = C(x_1, \ldots, x_k), \quad \forall i \in [k], x_i \in \{0,1\}, C \in \{0,1\}^\ell$$

For each party $i \in [k]$, the input is random bit $b \in \{0, 1\}$. And the input of the final party is the description of circuit C, the circuit to be obfuscated. The indistinguishable obfuscation of circuit C is MI-LFE encryption of all possible inputs bit plus description of circuit C.

Specifically, the construction of $i\mathcal{O}$ is as follows:

- **Obfuscation:** On input circuit C, Run the crsGen(U.params) to generate crs, KeyGen(crs) to generate SK and Compress(crs, U) to generate digest$_U$. Then for $i \in [k], b \in \{0, 1\}$, compute: $\mathsf{ct}_i^b \leftarrow \mathsf{Enc}(\mathsf{crs}, \mathsf{digest}_U, \mathsf{SK}, i, b)$ and next compute

$$\mathsf{ct}_{k+1} \leftarrow \mathsf{Enc}(\mathsf{crs}, \mathsf{digest}_U, \mathsf{SK}, k+1, C)$$

Finally, output the obfuscated circuit as $i\mathcal{O}(C) = \big(\{\mathsf{ct}_i^b\}_{i \in [k], b \in \{0,1\}}, \mathsf{ct}_{k+1},$ crs, $U\big)$.
- **Evaluation:** On input $x \in \{0, 1\}^k$, evaluate the obfuscated circuit $i\mathcal{O}(C)$ as computing $\mathsf{Dec}(\mathsf{crs}, U, \mathsf{ct}_1^{x_1}, \ldots, \mathsf{ct}_k^{x_k}, \mathsf{ct}_{k+1})$.

The correctness of our $i\mathcal{O}$ construction directly follows that of MI-LFE scheme. By the correctness of MI-LFE, the decryption result should be $U(x_1, \ldots, x_k, C) = C(x_1, \ldots, x_k)$.

Theorem 3. *Assuming MI-LFE is $(k+1, 2)$-IND-secure (c.f. Definition 5), then the above construction is a secure indistinguishability obfuscator for all circuits.*

Given an $i\mathcal{O}$ adversary $\mathcal{A}$, we use it to construct an MI-LFE adversary $\mathcal{B}$, the full proof is completed in full version.

MIFE from MI-LFE. We have shown that private-key MI-LFE implies iO. Since Goldwasser et al. have proved that MIFE can be constructed from the indistinguishable obfuscation and one-way function, the detour inspires us that MI-LFE can imply MIFE. However, one can imagine a more directly reduction from $n+1$ inputs private-key MI-LFE to n inputs private-key MIFE. Here we present the intuition. One can fix the circuit of MI-LFE as a universal circuit U. Given the description of a function f, we should have $U(f, x_1, \ldots, x_n) = f(x_1, \ldots, x_n)$. The master secret key and the encryption key of MIFE are both the secret key of the MI-LFE scheme. The decryption key for function f of the MIFE is a MI-LFE ciphertext c_0 of the description of the function f respect to digest$_U$. The encryption of MIFE of message $x_1, \ldots, x_n$ are the MI-LFE ciphertexts $c_1, \ldots, c_n$ of the same messages respect to digest$_U$. The decryption of the MIFE is just the MI-LFE evaluation on the ciphetexts c_0 and $c_1, \ldots, c_n$. Such an implication alone is trivial, but as a byproduct, MI-LFE could be used for all the applications of MIFE, which might provide a new route for the special cases.

5   Constructing Private-Key MI-LFE

The components we use in the construction include: (1) an indistinguishable obfuscator $i\mathcal{O}$ [16](of polynomial p of its input size), (2) a NIWI proof system (NIWI.crsGen, NIWI.Prove, NIWI.Verify), (3) a perfectly binding commitment scheme Com, (4) a semantically secure public-key encryption scheme

PKE = (PKE.Setup, PKE.Enc, PKE.Dec) and (5) a secure laconic function evaluation LFE = (LFE.crsGen, LFE.Compress, LFE.Enc, LFE.Dec) [31].

We denote the length of ciphertext in PKE by ℓ_{ct}. In particular, for a circuit $C : (\{0,1\}^k)^n \rightarrow \{0,1\}^\ell$ of circuit size $|C| = \omega(p(n,k,\lambda))$ and depth d, the description of our MI-LFE construction is as follows:

- crsGen(1^λ, C.params $= (1^n, 1^k, 1^d)$): The CRS generation algorithm first computes a common random string $crs_1 \leftarrow$ NIWI.crsGen(1^λ) for the NIWI proof system. Next, it computes a common random string $crs_2 \leftarrow$ LFE.crsGen(1^λ, $(1^{n \times k}, 1^d)$). The algorithm outputs $crs = (crs_1, crs_2)$.
- KeyGen(1^λ, crs): The key generation algorithm first computes two key pairs $(pk_1, sk_1) \leftarrow$ PKE.Setup(1^λ) and $(pk_2, sk_2) \leftarrow$ PKE.Setup. Then it computes the following commitments:

$$z_{1,i}^j \leftarrow \mathsf{Com}(0^{2\ell_{ct}}), \forall i \in [n], j \in [q], \quad z_2 \leftarrow \mathsf{Com}(0; r_0)$$

It outputs SK $= (pk_1, pk_2, sk_1, \{z_{1,i}^j\}, z_2, r_0)$, where r_0 is the randomness used to compute the commitment z_2.
- Compress(crs, C): The deterministic algorithm compression runs and outputs $digest_C \leftarrow$ LFE.Compress(crs_2, C).
- Enc(crs, $digest_C$, SK, i, x_i): On input crs, digest $digest_C$, secret key SK, index i and input x_i, the encryption algorithm.
  1. Choose two random strings $r_{i,1}, r_{i,2}$, and compute $c_{i,1} =$ PKE.Enc(pk_1, $x_i; r_{i,1}$) and $c_{i,2} =$ PKE.Enc($pk_2, x_i; r_{i,2}$).
  2. Generate proof $\pi \leftarrow$ NIWI.Prove(crs_1, y, w) for statement $y = (c_{i,1}, c_{i,2}, pk_1, pk_2, \{z_{1,i}^j\}_{i \in [n], j \in [q]}, z_2)$:
     • Either $c_{i,1}$ and $c_{i,2}$ are encryptions of the same message and z_2 is a commitment to 0;
     • Or there exists $j \in \{1, \ldots, q\}$, such that $z_{1,i}^j$ is a commitment to $c_{i,1} \parallel c_{i,2}$.
     A witness $w_{real} = (m, r_{i,1}, r_{i,2}, r_0)$ for the first part of the statement, referred as the real witness, includes the message m, and the randomness $r_{i,1}$ and $r_{i,2}$ used to compute the ciphertexts $c_{i,1}$ and $c_{i,2}$, respectively, and the randomness r_0 used to compute z_2. A witness $w_{td} = (j, r_{1,i}^j)$ for the second part of the statement, referred as the trapdoor witness, includes an index j and the randomness $r_{1,i}^j$ used to compute $z_{1,i}^j$.
  3. Compute $iO(G_{digest_C})$, defined in Fig. 3.
  Output ciphertext $CT_i = (c_{i,1}, c_{i,2}, \pi_i, iO(G_{digest_C}))$.
- Dec(crs, C, $CT_1, \ldots, CT_n$): The decryption algorithm first runs

$$ct \leftarrow iO(G_{digest_C})((c_{1,1}, c_{1,2}, \pi_1), \ldots, (c_{n,1}, c_{n,2}, \pi_n))$$

Then it computes and outputs $y =$ LFE.Dec(crs_2, C, ct').

Lemma 2 (Correctness). *Assuming the correctness of the underlying semantically secure* PKE, *laconic function evaluation* LFE *and indistinguishability obfuscation* iO, *the completeness property of* NIWI, *then the construction above is correct.*

$G_{\mathsf{digest}_C}[\mathsf{SK}, \mathsf{digest}_C]((c_{1,1}, c_{1,2}, \pi_1), \ldots, (c_{n,1}, c_{n,2}, \pi_n))$

Input: PKE ciphertexts and proof pairs $(c_{i,1}, c_{i,2}, \pi_i)$, for $i \in [n]$.
Hardcoded: secret key SK and digest digest_C.

(a) For $i = 1$ to n, let $y_i = (c_{i,1}, c_{i,2}, \mathsf{pk}_1, \mathsf{pk}_2, \{z_{1,i}^j\}, z_2)$ be the statement associate with the proof string π_i. If $\mathsf{NIWI.Verify}(\mathsf{crs}_1, y_i, \pi_i) = 0$, then stop and output $\bot$; Otherwise continue to $i + 1$.
(b) Compute $x_i = \mathsf{PKE.Dec}(\mathsf{sk}_1, c_{i,1})$.
(c) Outputs $\mathsf{ct} \leftarrow \mathsf{LFE.Enc}(\mathsf{crs}_2, \mathsf{digest}_C, (x_1, \ldots, x_n))$.

Fig. 3. Description of circuit G_{digest_C}

Proof. Now, by the perfect completeness of NIWI, the honest encryption algorithm can use the real witness $w_{\mathsf{real}} = (m, r_{i,1}, r_{i,2}, r_0)$ to generate the proof string π_i, such that $\mathsf{NIWI.Verify}(\mathsf{crs}_1, y_i, \pi_i) = 1$, for every $i \in [n]$. Then, by the property of $i\mathcal{O}$ and the correctness of the underlying PKE and LFE, we have:

$$y = \mathsf{LFE.Dec}(\mathsf{crs}_2, C, \mathsf{ct}')$$
$$= \mathsf{LFE.Dec}(\mathsf{crs}_2, C, i\mathcal{O}(G_{\mathsf{digset}_C})((c_{1,1}, c_{1,2}, \pi_1), \ldots, (c_{n,1}, c_{n,2}, \pi_n)))$$
$$= \mathsf{LFE.Dec}(\mathsf{crs}_2, C, \mathsf{LFE.Enc}(\mathsf{crs}_2, \mathsf{digest}_C, x_1 \| \ldots \| x_n)) = C(x_1, \ldots, x_n)$$

Lemma 3. (Laconic Property). *According to the efficiency of underlying PKE, NIWI, $i\mathcal{O}$ (assume $i\mathcal{O}$ is of polynomial p to its input size), and LWE-based LFE [31], our construction above is laconic for unbounded-size circuit class $\mathcal{C}$.*

Proof. Now, for a circuit $C \in \mathcal{C} : (\{0,1\}^k)^n \rightarrow \{0,1\}^\ell$ of circuit size $|C| = \omega(p(n, k, \lambda))$ and depth d, and security parameter λ, according to the parameters of LWE-based LFE, we analysis the parameters in our construction as follows:

- The crs consists of crs_1 for NIWI, and crs_2 of size $(n \times k) \cdot \mathsf{poly}(\lambda, d)$ for LWE-based LFE. Hence, the size of crs is much smaller than the circuit size of C.
- The digest is of size $\mathsf{poly}(\lambda)$ for LWE-based LFE. The SK consists of $(\mathsf{pk}_1, \mathsf{pk}_2, \mathsf{sk}_1)$ for PKE encryption scheme, commitments $\{z_{1,i}^j\}$ and z_2, and randomness r_0. Then, both the size of the digest and SK is independent with $|C|$.
- The encryption algorithm consists of generating two PKE encryptions, a NIWI proof string and an indistinguishable obfuscation for a circuit. The generation of two PKE encryptions and the corresponding proof string is independent with the circuit size of C. And, the main size of the circuit been obfuscated is the size of LWE-based LFE.Enc, about $\tilde{O}(n \times k + \ell) \cdot \mathsf{poly}(\lambda, d)$. Then, the obfuscation of the circuit should be around $p(\lambda, n, k, \ell, d)$. Therefore, both the run-time of the encryption algorithm and the size of the ciphertext are much smaller than the circuit size $|C| = \omega(p(n, k, \lambda))$ of circuit C.

As the discussion above, we conclude that our construction is laconic.

Theorem 4. (Security Proof). *Let $q = q(\lambda)$ be such that $q^n = \mathsf{poly}(\lambda)$, Then assume indistinguishability obfuscator for all polynomial-size computable* *circuits, one-way functions and selectively (adaptively) secure laconic function evaluation, the above construction is (n,q)-SIM selectively (adaptively) secure.*

Proof. (Proof Sketch). To prove the above theorem, we first construct an ideal world simulator S.

Simulator S Recall the security definition in Fig. 1, the simulator is given the common reference string crs, circuit C, digest digest$_C$, and values $\{C(x_1^{j_1}, \ldots, x_n^{j_n})\}$ for $j_1, \ldots, j_n \in [q]$. The simulator S works as follows:

Simulate PKE Encryptions of Challenge Message:
- For all $i \in [n]$ and $j \in [q]$, S computes $c_{i,1}^j \leftarrow$ PKE.Enc($pk_1, 0$) and $c_{i,2}^j \leftarrow$ PKE.Enc($pk_2, 0$).
- S computes $z_2 \leftarrow$ Com(1).

Simulate NIWI proof for PKE Encryptions of Challenge Message:
- For every $i \in [n]$, $j \in [q]$, S computes $z_{1,i}^j \leftarrow$ Com($c_{i,1}^j \parallel c_{i,2}^j$). Let $r_{1,i}^j$ denote the randomness used to compute $z_{1,i}^j$.
- Let $y_i^j = (c_{i,1}^j, c_{i,2}^j, pk_1, pk_2, \{z_{1,i}^j\}, z_2)$. S computes the proof string $\pi_i^j \leftarrow$ NIWI.Prove(crs$_1, y_i^j, \omega_i^j$), where the witness ω_i^j corresponds to the trapdoor witness $(j, r_{1,i}^j)$. That is, ω_i^j establishes that $z_{1,i}^j$ is a commitment to $c_{i,1}^j \parallel c_{i,2}^j$.

Simulate Indistinguishable Obfuscation: S computes indistinguishable obfuscation of the circuit SIM.G_{digest_C}, where SIM.G_{digest_C} is defined in Fig. 4

Then we describe a sequence of hybrid experiments $\mathbf{H}_0, \ldots, \mathbf{H}_7$, where $\mathbf{H}_0$ corresponds to the real world experiment and $\mathbf{H}_7$ corresponds to the ideal world experiment. For every i, we will prove that the output of $\mathbf{H}_i$ is computationally indistinguishable from the output of $\mathbf{H}_{i+1}$.

Hyb $\mathbf{H}_0$: This is the real world experiment.

Hyb $\mathbf{H}_1$: This experiment is the same as $\mathbf{H}_0$ except that in every challenge ciphertext $\mathsf{CT}_i^j = (c_{i,1}^j, c_{i,2}^j, \pi_i^j, i\mathcal{O}(G_{\text{digest}_C}))$, the indistinguishable obfuscation of G_{digest_C} is replaced by the indistinguishable obfuscation of G', G' is defined in Fig. 5.

The indistinguishability between hybrids $\mathbf{H}_0$ and $\mathbf{H}_1$ follows from the property of indistinguishable obfuscator and security of laconic function evaluation. We refer to the full version for more details.

Hyb $\mathbf{H}_2$: This experiment is the same as $\mathbf{H}_1$ except that we start generating $z_{1,i}^j$ as a commitment to $c_{i,1}^j \parallel c_{i,2}^j$ rather than $0^{2\ell_{ct}}$, for all $i \in [n], j \in [q]$.

The indistinguishability between hybrids $\mathbf{H}_1$ and $\mathbf{H}_2$ follows directly from the computational hiding property of the commitment scheme, since that there is nothing else corresponding to the commitments $\{z_{1,i}^j\}$ in these two experiments.

Hyb $\mathbf{H}_3$: This experiment is the same as $\mathbf{H}_2$ except that in every challenge ciphertext $\mathsf{CT}_i^j = (c_{i,1}^j, c_{i,2}^j, \pi_i^j, i\mathcal{O}(G'))$, the corresponding proof string π_i^j is computed using a trapdoor witness $(j, r_{1,i}^j)$, where $r_{1,i}^j$ be the randomness to generate $z_{1,i}^j \leftarrow$ Com($c_{i,1}^j \parallel c_{i,2}^j$), for all $i \in [n], j \in [q]$.

$\mathsf{SIM}.G_{\mathsf{digest}_C}[\{(c_{i,1}^j, c_{i,2}^j)\}, \{z_{1,i}^j\}, z_2, \{C(x_1^{j_1}, \dots, x_n^{j_n})\}]((c_{1,1}, c_{1,2}, \pi_1), \dots, (c_{n,1}, c_{n,2}, \pi_n))$

Input: PKE ciphertext and proof pairs $(c_{i,1}, c_{i,2}, \pi_i)$, for $i \in [n]$.
Hardcoded: statements of challenge ciphertext $(c_{i,1}^j, c_{i,2}^j, \mathsf{pk}_1, \mathsf{pk}_2, \{z_{1,i}^j\}, z_2)$ for $i \in [n], j \in [q]$, and values $\{C(x_1^{j_1}, \dots, x_n^{j_n})\}$ for $j_1, \dots, j_n \in [q]$.

1. For every $i = 1, \dots, n$, let $y_i = (c_{i,1}, c_{i,2}, \mathsf{pk}_1, \mathsf{pk}_2, \{z_{1,i}^j\}, z_2)$ be the statement corresponding to the proof string π_i. If $\mathsf{NIWI.Verify}(\mathsf{crs}_1, y_i, \pi_i) = 0$, then stop and output $\bot$; Otherwise continue to $i + 1$.
2. If $\exists (j_1, \dots, j_n), s.t$ for every $i \in [n]$: $c_{i,1} = c_{i,1}^{j_i}$, and $c_{i,2} = c_{i,2}^{j_i}$, then stop and output $\mathsf{LFE.SIM}(\mathsf{crs}, \mathsf{digest}_C, C, C(x_1^{j_1}, \dots, x_n^{j_n}))$; Otherwise output $\bot$.

Fig. 4. Description of the Circuit $\mathsf{SIM}.G_{\mathsf{digest}_C}$

The indistinguishability between hybrids $\mathbf{H}_2$ and $\mathbf{H}_3$ follows directly from the witness indistinguishable property of NIWI proof system.

Hyb $\mathbf{H}_4$: This experiment is the same as $\mathbf{H}_3$ except that we start generating z_2 as a commitment to 1 instead of 0.

The indistinguishability between hybrids $\mathbf{H}_3$ and $\mathbf{H}_4$ follows directly from the computational hiding property of the commitment scheme.

Hyb $\mathbf{H}_5$: This experiment is the same as $\mathbf{H}_4$ except that in the ciphertexts of PKE encryption for challenge message pairs, the second ciphertext $c_{i,2}^j$ is an encryption of zeros, i.e., $c_{i,2}^j \leftarrow \mathsf{PKE.Enc}(\mathsf{pk}_2, 0)$.

The indistinguishability between hybrids $\mathbf{H}_4$ and $\mathbf{H}_5$ follows immediately from the semantic security of PKE encryption scheme.

Hyb $\mathbf{H}_6$: This experiment is the same as $\mathbf{H}_5$ except that in each challenge ciphertext $\mathsf{CT}_i^j = (c_{i,1}^j, c_{i,2}^j, \pi_i^j, i\mathcal{O}(G'))$, the indistinguishable obfuscation of G' is replaced by the indistinguishable obfuscation of $\mathsf{SIM}.G_{\mathsf{digest}_C}$.

The indistinguishability between hybrids $\mathbf{H}_5$ and $\mathbf{H}_6$ follows from the property of indistinguishable obfuscator, the perfectly binding property of the commitment scheme, and the statistical soundness property of NIWI proof system. We refer to the full version for formal proof.

Hyb $\mathbf{H}_7$: This experiment is the same as $\mathbf{H}_6$ except that in the ciphertexts of PKE encryption for challenge message pairs, the first ciphertext $c_{i,1}^j$ is an encryption of zeros, i.e., $c_{i,1}^j \leftarrow \mathsf{PKE.Enc}(\mathsf{pk}_1, 0)$. Note that this is the ideal world experiment.

The indistinguishability between hybrids $\mathbf{H}_6$ and $\mathbf{H}_7$ follows immediately from the semantic security of PKE encryption scheme.

This completes the security proof of our construction.

$G'[\mathsf{SK}, \mathsf{digest}_C, \{(c_{i,1}^j, c_{i,2}^j)\}, \{C(x_1^{j1}, \ldots, x_n^{jn})\}]((c_{1,1}, c_{1,2}, \pi_1), \ldots, (c_{n,1}, c_{n,2}, \pi_n))$

Input: PKE ciphertext and proof pairs $(c_{i,1}, c_{i,2}, \pi_i)$, for $i \in [n]$.
Hardcoded: secret key SK, digest digest_C, PKE encryptions for challenge message $\{(c_{i,1}^j, c_{i,2}^j)\}$ and values $\{C(x_1^{j1}, \ldots, x_n^{jn})\}$.

1. For every $i = 1, \ldots, n$, let $y_i = (c_{i,1}, c_{i,2}, \mathsf{pk}_1, \mathsf{pk}_2, \{z_{1,i}^j\}, z_2)$ be the statement corresponding to the proof string π_i. If $\mathsf{NIWI.Verify}(\mathsf{crs}_1, y_i, \pi_i) = 0$, then stop and output $\perp$; Otherwise continue to $i + 1$.
2. If $\exists (j_1, \ldots, j_n), s.t$ for every $i \in [n]$: $c_{i,1} = c_{i,1}^{ji}$, and $c_{i,2} = c_{i,2}^{ji}$, then stop and output $\mathsf{LFE.SIM}(\mathsf{crs}, \mathsf{digest}_C, C, C(x_1^{j1}, \ldots, x_n^{jn}))$; Otherwise continue to the next step.
3. Compute $x_i = \mathsf{PKE.Dec}(\mathsf{sk}_1, c_{i,1})$.
4. Outputs $\mathsf{ct}' \leftarrow \mathsf{LFE.Enc}(\mathsf{crs}_2, \mathsf{digest}_C, (x_1, \ldots, x_n))$.

Fig. 5. Description of the circuit G'

6   Conclusion

The client-optimized MPC is the main motivation for this work, which yields the first study regarding multi-input laconic function evaluation. We propose definitions of variant multi-input laconic function evaluation and then explore construction and impossibility result of variants of it. Specifically, We show that public-key MI-LFE implies VBB obfuscation for all circuits, a primitive that is impossible to achieve. Then we build private-key MI-LFE from $i\mathcal{O}$. The use of $i\mathcal{O}$ is inevitable here as private-key MI-LFE can be used to construct witness encryption or $i\mathcal{O}$, which do not have constructions based on standard assumptions yet. Therefore, an interesting open problem is to explore MI-LFE for some special function families, such as inner product, or weaken the security requirement of MI-LFE to make it plausible to have a construction based on standard assumptions.

Acknowledgement. The authors thank anonymous reviewers for valuable comments. Qiang is supported by NSF CNS #1801492, and a Google Faculty Award. Bo Pang is supported by National Key R&D Program of China-2017YFB0802202 NSFC61772516.

References

1. Hemisphere project. https://en.wikipedia.org/wiki/Hemisphere_Project
2. Official words on surveillance. https://www.usatoday.com/news/washington/2006-05-10-nsa_x.htm
3. Ananth, P., Jain, A., Naor, M., Sahai, A., Yogev, E.: Universal constructions and robust combiners for indistinguishability obfuscation and witness encryption. In: Robshaw, M., Katz, J. (eds.) CRYPTO 2016. LNCS, vol. 9815, pp. 491–520. Springer, Heidelberg (2016). https://doi.org/10.1007/978-3-662-53008-5_17

4. Applebaum, B., Brakerski, Z., Tsabary, R.: Perfect secure computation in two rounds. In: Beimel, A., Dziembowski, S. (eds.) TCC 2018. LNCS, vol. 11239, pp. 152–174. Springer, Cham (2018). https://doi.org/10.1007/978-3-030-03807-6_6
5. Barak, B., et al.: On the (Im)possibility of obfuscating programs. In: Kilian, J. (ed.) CRYPTO 2001. LNCS, vol. 2139, pp. 1–18. Springer, Heidelberg (2001). https://doi.org/10.1007/3-540-44647-8_1
6. Beaver, D.: Foundations of secure interactive computing. In: Feigenbaum, J. (ed.) CRYPTO 1991. LNCS, vol. 576, pp. 377–391. Springer, Heidelberg (1992). https://doi.org/10.1007/3-540-46766-1_31
7. Bellare, M., Hoang, V.T.: Adaptive witness encryption and asymmetric password-based cryptography. In: Katz, J. (ed.) PKC 2015. LNCS, vol. 9020, pp. 308–331. Springer, Heidelberg (2015). https://doi.org/10.1007/978-3-662-46447-2_14
8. Blum, M., Feldman, P., Micali, S.: Non-interactive zero-knowledge and its applications (extended abstract). In: 20th ACM STOC, pp. 103–112. ACM Press, May 1988
9. Boneh, D., Lewi, K., Raykova, M., Sahai, A., Zhandry, M., Zimmerman, J.: Semantically secure order-revealing encryption: multi-input functional encryption without obfuscation. In: Oswald, E., Fischlin, M. (eds.) EUROCRYPT 2015. LNCS, vol. 9057, pp. 563–594. Springer, Heidelberg (2015). https://doi.org/10.1007/978-3-662-46803-6_19
10. Boneh, D., Sahai, A., Waters, B.: Functional encryption: definitions and challenges. In: Ishai, Y. (ed.) TCC 2011. LNCS, vol. 6597, pp. 253–273. Springer, Heidelberg (2011). https://doi.org/10.1007/978-3-642-19571-6_16
11. Brakerski, Z., Jain, A., Komargodski, I., Passelègue, A., Wichs, D.: Non-trivial witness encryption and null-io from standard assumptions. In: Catalano, D., De Prisco, R. (eds.) SCN 2018. LNCS, vol. 11035, pp. 425–441. Springer, Cham (2018). https://doi.org/10.1007/978-3-319-98113-0_23
12. Brakerski, Z., Vaikuntanathan, V.: Fully homomorphic encryption from ring-LWE and security for key dependent messages. In: Rogaway, P. (ed.) CRYPTO 2011. LNCS, vol. 6841, pp. 505–524. Springer, Heidelberg (2011). https://doi.org/10.1007/978-3-642-22792-9_29
13. Brakerski, Z., Vaikuntanathan, V.: Lattice-based FHE as secure as PKE. In: Naor, M., (ed.) ITCS 2014, pp. 1–12. ACM, January 2014
14. Canetti, R., Holmgren, J., Jain, A., Vaikuntanathan, V.: Succinct garbling and indistinguishability obfuscation for RAM programs. In: Servedio, R.A., Rubinfeld, R., (eds.) 47th ACM STOC, pp. 429–437. ACM Press, June 2015
15. Clear, M., McGoldrick, C.: Multi-identity and multi-key leveled FHE from learning with errors. In: Gennaro, R., Robshaw, M. (eds.) CRYPTO 2015. LNCS, vol. 9216, pp. 630–656. Springer, Heidelberg (2015). https://doi.org/10.1007/978-3-662-48000-7_31
16. Garg, S., Gentry, C., Halevi, S., Raykova, M., Sahai, A., Waters, B.: Candidate indistinguishability obfuscation and functional encryption for all circuits. In: 54th FOCS, pp. 40–49. IEEE Computer Society Press, October 2013
17. Garg, S., Gentry, C., Halevi, S., Wichs, D.: On the implausibility of differing-inputs obfuscation and extractable witness encryption with auxiliary input. In: Garay, J.A., Gennaro, R. (eds.) CRYPTO 2014. LNCS, vol. 8616, pp. 518–535. Springer, Heidelberg (2014). https://doi.org/10.1007/978-3-662-44371-2_29
18. Garg, S., Gentry, C., Halevi, S., Zhandry, M.: Functional encryption without obfuscation. In: Kushilevitz, E., Malkin, T. (eds.) TCC 2016. LNCS, vol. 9563, pp. 480–511. Springer, Heidelberg (2016). https://doi.org/10.1007/978-3-662-49099-0_18

19. Garg, S., Gentry, C., Sahai, A., Waters, B.: Witness encryption and its applications. In: Boneh, D., Roughgarden, T., Feigenbaum, J., (eds.) 45th ACM STOC, pp. 467–476. ACM Press, June 2013

20. Garg, S., Srinivasan, A.: Two-round multiparty secure computation from minimal assumptions. In: Nielsen, J.B., Rijmen, V. (eds.) EUROCRYPT 2018. LNCS, vol. 10821, pp. 468–499. Springer, Cham (2018). https://doi.org/10.1007/978-3-319-78375-8_16

21. Gentry, C.: Fully homomorphic encryption using ideal lattices. In: Mitzenmacher, M. (ed.) 41st ACM STOC, pp. 169–178. ACM Press, May/June 2009

22. Gentry, C., Lewko, A., Waters, B.: Witness encryption from instance independent assumptions. In: Garay, J.A., Gennaro, R. (eds.) CRYPTO 2014. LNCS, vol. 8616, pp. 426–443. Springer, Heidelberg (2014). https://doi.org/10.1007/978-3-662-44371-2_24

23. Gentry, C., Sahai, A., Waters, B.: Homomorphic encryption from learning with errors: conceptually-simpler, asymptotically-faster, attribute-based. In: Canetti, R., Garay, J.A. (eds.) CRYPTO 2013. LNCS, vol. 8042, pp. 75–92. Springer, Heidelberg (2013). https://doi.org/10.1007/978-3-642-40041-4_5

24. Goldwasser, S., et al.: Multi-input functional encryption. In: Nguyen, P.Q., Oswald, E. (eds.) EUROCRYPT 2014. LNCS, vol. 8441, pp. 578–602. Springer, Heidelberg (2014). https://doi.org/10.1007/978-3-642-55220-5_32

25. Goldwasser, S., Goyal, V., Jain, A., Sahai, A.: Multi-input functional encryption. Cryptology ePrint Archive, Report 2013/727 (2013). http://eprint.iacr.org/2013/727

26. Goldwasser, S., Kalai, Y., Popa, R.A., Vaikuntanathan, V., Zeldovich, N.: Reusable garbled circuits and succinct functional encryption. In: Boneh, D., Roughgarden, T., Feigenbaum, J., (eds.) 45th ACM STOC, pp. 555–564. ACM Press, June 2013

27. Groth, J., Ostrovsky, R., Sahai, A.: Perfect non-interactive zero knowledge for NP. In: Vaudenay, S. (ed.) EUROCRYPT 2006. LNCS, vol. 4004, pp. 339–358. Springer, Heidelberg (2006). https://doi.org/10.1007/11761679_21

28. Koppula, V., Lewko, A.B., Waters, B.: Indistinguishability obfuscation for turing machines with unbounded memory. In: Servedio, R.A., Rubinfeld, R., (eds.) 47th ACM STOC, pp. 419–428. ACM Press, June 2015

29. Lin, H., Pass, R., Seth, K., Telang, S.: Indistinguishability obfuscation with nontrivial efficiency. In: Cheng, C.-M., Chung, K.-M., Persiano, G., Yang, B.-Y. (eds.) PKC 2016. LNCS, vol. 9615, pp. 447–462. Springer, Heidelberg (2016). https://doi.org/10.1007/978-3-662-49387-8_17

30. Mukherjee, P., Wichs, D.: Two round multiparty computation via multi-key FHE. In: Fischlin, M., Coron, J.-S. (eds.) EUROCRYPT 2016. LNCS, vol. 9666, pp. 735–763. Springer, Heidelberg (2016). https://doi.org/10.1007/978-3-662-49896-5_26

31. Quach, W., Wee, H., Wichs, D.: Laconic function evaluation and applications. In: Thorup, M. (ed.) 59th FOCS, pp. 859–870. IEEE Computer Society Press, October (2018)

32. Yao, A.C.C.: How to generate and exchange secrets (extended abstract). In: 27th FOCS, pp. 162–167. IEEE Computer Society Press, October 1986

Mathematical Foundation

Arbitrary-Centered Discrete Gaussian Sampling over the Integers

Yusong Du[1,2(✉)], Baoying Fan[1], and Baodian Wei[1,2]

[1] School of Data and Computer Science, Sun Yat-sen University,
Guangzhou 510006, China
duyusong@mail.sysu.edu.cn, weibd@mail.sysu.edu.cn
[2] Guangdong Key Laboratory of Information Security Technology,
Guangzhou 510006, China

Abstract. Discrete Gaussian sampling over the integers, which is to sample from a discrete Gaussian distribution $\mathcal{D}_{\mathbb{Z},\sigma,\mu}$ over the integers $\mathbb{Z}$ with parameter $\sigma > 0$ and center $\mu \in \mathbb{R}$, is one of fundamental operations in lattice-based cryptography. The sampling algorithm should support a varying center μ and even a varying parameter σ, when it is used as one of the subroutines in an algorithm for sampling trapdoor lattices, or sampling from Gaussian distributions over a general n-dimensional lattice Λ. In this paper, combining the techniques in Karney's algorithm for exactly sampling the standard normal distribution, we present an exact sampling algorithm for $\mathcal{D}_{\mathbb{Z},\sigma,\mu}$ with an integer-valued parameter σ. This algorithm requires no pre-computation storage, uses no floating-point arithmetic, supports centers of arbitrary precision, and does not have any statistical discrepancy. Applying the convolution-like property of discrete Gaussian distributions, we also present an approximated sampling algorithm for $\mathcal{D}_{\mathbb{Z},\sigma,\mu}$ with a real-valued parameter σ. It also supports centers of arbitrary precision, and we show that the distribution it produces has a smaller max-log distance to the ideal distribution, as compared to Micciancio-Walter sampling algorithm, which was introduced by Micciancio et al. in Crypto 2017 for discrete Gaussian distributions with varying σ and μ over the integers.

Keywords: Lattice-based cryptography · Discrete Gaussian distribution · Rejection sampling · Exact sampling · Max-log distance

1 Introduction

Lattice-based cryptography has been accepted as a promising candidate for public key cryptography in the age of quantum computing. Discrete Gaussian sampling, which is to sample from a discrete Gaussian distribution $\mathcal{D}_{\Lambda,\sigma,\mathbf{c}}$ with

This work was supported by National Key R&D Program of China (2017YFB0802500), National Natural Science Foundations of China (Grant Nos. 61672550, 61972431), Guangdong Major Project of Basic and Applied Research (2019B030302008), Guangdong Basic and Applied Basic Research Foundation (No. 2020A1515010687) and the Fundamental Research Funds for the Central Universities (Grant No. 19lgpy217).

© Springer Nature Switzerland AG 2020
J. K. Liu and H. Cui (Eds.): ACISP 2020, LNCS 12248, pp. 391–407, 2020.
https://doi.org/10.1007/978-3-030-55304-3_20

parameter $\sigma > 0$ and center $\mathbf{c} \in \mathbb{R}^n$ over an n-dimensional lattice Λ, plays a fundamental role in lattice-based cryptography. Discrete Gaussian sampling is not only one of the fundamental operations in many lattice-based cryptosystems but is also at the core of security proofs of these cryptosystems [10,18,21]. It has been considered by the cryptography research community as one of the fundamental building blocks of lattice-based cryptography [19,20,22,24].

An important sub-problem of discrete Gaussian sampling, which is denoted by SampleℤZ, is to sample from a discrete Gaussian distribution $\mathcal{D}_{\mathbb{Z},\sigma,\mu}$ over the integers $\mathbb{Z}$ with parameter $\sigma > 0$ and center $\mu \in \mathbb{R}$. Since SampleℤZ is much more efficient and simpler than sampling from discrete Gaussian sampling over a general lattice, the operations involving discrete Gaussian sampling in some lattice-based cryptosystems such as [6,23,27] are nothing but SampleℤZ. A good sampling algorithm for a discrete Gaussian distribution (not necessarily over the integers $\mathbb{Z}$) should not only be efficient, but also have a negligible statistical discrepancy with the target distribution. Therefore, how to design and implement good sampling algorithms for discrete Gaussian distributions over the integers has received a lot of attentions in recent years.

The commonly used methods (techniques) for SampleℤZ are the inversion sampling (using a cumulative distribution table, CDT) [24], the Knuth-Yao method (using a discrete distribution generating (DDG) tree) [7,28], the rejection sampling [6,10,16], and the convolution technique [22,25] (based on the convolution-like properties of discrete Gaussian distributions developed by Peikert in [24]).

The first SampleℤZ algorithm, which was given by Gentry et al. in [10], uses rejection sampling. Although this algorithm supports varying parameters (including μ and σ), it is not very efficient, since it requires about 10 trials on average before outputting an integer in order to get a negligible statistical distance to the target discrete Gaussian distribution.[1]

Most of improved SampleℤZ algorithms are designed only for the case where center μ is fixed in advance, such as [6,11,14,15,28,29]. It is necessary to consider generic SampleℤZ algorithms that support varying parameters. Sampling from discrete Gaussian distributions over the integers is also usually one of the subroutines in discrete Gaussian sampling algorithms for distributions over a general n-dimensional lattice Λ. Examples include the SampleD algorithm [10] for distributions over an n-dimensional lattice of a basis $\mathbf{B} \in \mathbb{R}^n$, Peikert's algorithm for distributions over a q-ary integer lattice $\Lambda \subseteq \mathbb{Z}^n$ [24], and Gaussian sampling algorithms for trapdoor lattices [9,20]. A SampleℤZ algorithm should support a varying center μ, and even a varying parameter σ, if it is used in these cases.

1.1   Related Work

In 2016, Karney proposed an algorithm for sampling exactly (without statistical discrepancy) from a discrete Gaussian distribution over the integers $\mathbb{Z}$ [16].

---

[1] The number of trials could be decreased by using more cryptographically efficient measures, like Rényi divergence [2,26].

This algorithm uses no floating-point arithmetic and does not need any precomputation storage. It allows the parameters (including σ and μ) to be arbitrary rational numbers of finite precision. This may be the second generic SampleZ algorithm since the one given by Gentry et al. in [10].

In 2017, Micciancio and Walter developed a new SampleZ algorithm [22]. We call this algorithm Micciancio-Walter sampling algorithm. It extends and generalizes the techniques that were used in the sampler proposed by Pöeppelmann et al. [25]. Micciancio-Walter algorithm is also generic, i.e., it can be used to sample from discrete Gaussian distributions with arbitrary and varying parameters of specified (finite) precision. Moreover, Aguilar-Melchor et al. also designed a non-centered CDT algorithm with reduced size of precomputation tables [1].

More recently, it was suggested that the Bernoulli sampling, introduced by Ducas et al. in [6] for centered discrete Gaussian distributions over the integers, could be improved by using the polynomial approximation technique. Specifically, the rejection operation in the Bernoulli sampling can be performed very efficiently by using an approximated polynomial [3,32]. The polynomial (its coefficients) can be determined in advance, and it also allows us to sample from Gaussian distributions with a varying center $\mu \in [0,1)$. Combining the convolution-like property of discrete Gaussian distributions [22,24,25], a non-centered Bernoulli sampling could be further extended to a generic sampling algorithm for any discrete Gaussian distribution over the integers. Howe et al. further presented a modular framework [12] for generating discrete Gaussians with arbitrary and varying parameters, which incorporates rejection sampling, the polynomial approximation technique, and the sampling technique used in Falcon signature [27].

Another alternative method of discrete Gaussian sampling over the integers is to sample from the (continuous) standard normal distribution, and then obtain the samples of discrete Gaussian distributions by rejection sampling [31]. This method is very efficient and supports discrete Gaussian distributions with arbitrary and varying parameters, although it relies on floating-point arithmetic (even involving logarithmic function and trigonometric function due to sampling from the standard normal distribution). In fact, a more simple and efficient method is to replace discrete Gaussians with rounded Gaussians [13], which are the nearest integers of sample values from the continuous normal distribution, but the security analysis of rounded Gaussians is only confined to the cryptosystems like Bliss signature.

Except Karney's sampling algorithm, the existing algorithms for sampling from $\mathcal{D}_{\mathbb{Z},\sigma,\mu}$ with varying parameters, either rely on floating-point arithmetic, such as the algorithms in [10,32], or require a large amount of precomputation storage, such as Micciancio-Walter sampling algorithm [22] and the one given by Aguilar-Melchor et al. [1]. The sampler presented by Barthe et al. in [3] supports a varying $\mu \in \mathbb{R}$ but not a varying parameters σ. It needs to perform another polynomial approximation procedure for the new σ.

Furthermore, except Karney's sampling algorithm, those algorithms mentioned above are all the approximated algorithms, which only produce samples approximately from the target distribution. They usually involve complicated and careful security analysis based on statistical measures (e.g. Rényi divergence [2,26], max-log distance [22], relative error [30]), since attaining a negligible statistical measure to the ideal Gaussian distribution may be crucial for lattice-based cryptography, especially for signatures [17] and lattice trapdoors [10], to provide zero-knowledgeness. Therefore, it is interesting to consider exact sampling algorithms in lattice-based cryptography. The security analysis based on statistical measures for exact algorithms can be simplified or even be omitted.

1.2 Our Contribution

On one hand, we note that Karney's sampling algorithm [16] is exact sampling algorithm, but it allows only the case where σ and μ are rational numbers of specified (finite) precision. In this paper, for an integer-valued parameter σ, we present an exact sampling algorithm for $\mathcal{D}_{\mathbb{Z},\sigma,\mu}$. This algorithm requires no pre-computation storage, uses no floating-point arithmetic and supports a varying μ of arbitrary precision. On the other hand, although Micciancio-Walter sampling algorithm [22] supports varying parameters (including μ and σ) with specified (finite) precision, its base sampler requires a large amount of precomputation storage. Based on our proposed exact algorithm, applying the convolution-like property of discrete Gaussian distributions we give an approximated sampling algorithm for $\mathcal{D}_{\mathbb{Z},\sigma,\mu}$ with a real-valued parameter σ. It requires no pre-computation storage, and supports a varying μ of arbitrary precision. We show that the distribution it produces has a smaller max-log distance to the ideal distribution $\mathcal{D}_{\mathbb{Z},\sigma,\mu}$, as compared to the distribution produced by Micciancio-Walter sampling algorithm.

1.3 Techniques

Let σ be a positive integer, $\mu \in [0,1)$ be a real number of arbitrary precision, and x be a non-negative integer. We give an algorithm for exactly generating a Bernoulli random value which is true with probability

$$\exp\left(-t\frac{2x+t}{2x+2}\right),$$

where t is in the form of $(y - s\mu)/\sigma$, $s \in \{-1, 1\}$, and y is an integer taken uniformly from $[(1 + s)/2, \sigma + (1 + s)/2)$. In our exact sampling algorithm for discrete Gaussian distributions, which is based on the rejection sampling, we show that the rejection operation can be performed by repeatedly using this algorithm of generating the Bernoulli random value.

In fact, this algorithm is adapted from Karney's algorithm for exactly generating the Bernoulli random value (see Algorithm B in [16]). Karney also used it as the rejection operation in his algorithm for standard normal distribution as well as discrete Gaussian distributions over the integers. However, t is only regarded as a random deviate from $[0, 1)$ in Karney's algorithm. The value of t

corresponds exactly to the fraction part of the prospective output and can be obtained directly as a random number in case of standard normal distribution, while the determination of the value of t in the case of discrete Gaussian distributions needs the computation with respect to the parameters σ and μ. In order to maintain the exactness, μ is only allowed to be a rational number for sampling from discrete Gaussian distributions, which limits the functionality of Karney's algorithm.

2   Preliminaries

2.1   Notation

We denote the set of real numbers by $\mathbb{R}$, the set of integers by $\mathbb{Z}$, and the set of non-negative integers by $\mathbb{Z}^+$. We extend any real function $f(\cdot)$ to a countable set A by defining $f(A) = \sum_{x \in A} f(x)$ if it exists. The Gaussian function on $\mathbb{R}$ with parameter $\sigma > 0$ and $\mu \in \mathbb{R}$ evaluated at $x \in \mathbb{R}$ can be defined by $\rho_{\sigma,\mu}(x) = \exp\left(-\frac{(x-\mu)^2}{2\sigma^2}\right)$. For real $\sigma > 0$ and $\mu \in \mathbb{R}$, the discrete Gaussian distribution over $\mathbb{Z}$ is defined by $\mathcal{D}_{\mathbb{Z},\sigma,\mu}(x) = \rho_{\sigma,\mu}(x)/\rho_{\sigma,\mu}(\mathbb{Z})$ for $x \in \mathbb{Z}$. Similarly, a discrete Gaussian distribution over $\mathbb{Z}^+$ is defined by $\mathcal{D}_{\mathbb{Z}^+,\sigma}(x) = \rho_{\sigma,\mu}(x)/\rho_{\sigma,\mu}(\mathbb{Z}^+)$. By convention, the subscript μ is omitted when it is taken to be 0.

2.2   Rejection Sampling

Rejection sampling is a basic method (technique) used to generate observations from a distribution [5]. It generates sampling values from a target distribution X with arbitrary probability density function $f(x)$ by using a proposal distribution Y with probability density function $g(x)$. The basic idea is that one generates a sample value from X by instead sampling from Y and accepting the sample from Y with probability

$$f(x)/Mg(x),$$

repeating the draws from Y until a value is accepted, where M is a constant such that $f(x) \le Mg(x)$ for all values of x in the support of X. If $f(x) \le Mg(x)$ for all x then the rejection sampling procedure produces exactly, with enough replicates, the distribution of X. In fact, $f(x)$ is allowed to be only a relative probability density function. Rejection sampling can be used to sample from a distribution X whose normalizing constant is unknown as long as the support of Y includes the support of x.

2.3   Karney's Algorithm

Karney's exact sampling algorithm for discrete Gaussian distributions, which is described as Algorithm 1, uses rejection sampling, and it is a discretization of his algorithm for sampling exactly from the normal distribution. Here, parameter σ and μ are in the set of rational numbers $\mathbb{Q}$.

Algorithm 1. [16] Sampling $\mathcal{D}_{\mathbb{Z},\sigma,\mu}$ for $\sigma, \mu \in \mathbb{Q}$ and $\sigma > 0$

Input: rational number σ and μ
Output: an integer z according to $\mathcal{D}_{\mathbb{Z},\sigma,\mu}$
1: select $k \in \mathbb{Z}^+$ with probability $\exp(-k/2) \cdot (1 - \exp(-1/2))$.
2: accept k with probability $\exp\left(-\frac{1}{2}k(k-1)\right)$, otherwise, **goto** step 1.
3: set $s \leftarrow \pm 1$ with equal probabilities.
4: set $i_0 \leftarrow \lceil k\sigma + s\mu \rceil$ and set $x_0 \leftarrow (i_0 - (k\sigma + s\mu))/\sigma$.
5: sample $j \in \mathbb{Z}$ uniformly in $\{0, 1, 2, \cdots, \lceil \sigma \rceil - 1\}$.
6: set $x \leftarrow x_0 + j/\sigma$ and **goto** step 1 if $x \geq 1$.
7: **goto** step 1 if $k = 0$ and $x = 0$ and $s < 0$.
8: accept x with probability $\exp\left(-\frac{1}{2}x(2k+x)\right)$, otherwise **goto** step 1.
9: **return** $s(i_0 + j)$

From the perspective of rejection sampling, in Algorithm 1, we can see that step 1 and step 2 together form a rejection sampling procedure, which generates $k \in \mathbb{Z}^+$ according to

$$\mathcal{D}_{\mathbb{Z}^+,1}(k) = \rho_1(k)/\rho_1(\mathbb{Z}^+),$$

which is a discrete Gaussian distribution over the set of non-negative integers $\mathbb{Z}^+$. Then, the proposal distribution for the whole algorithm can be written as

$$g(z) = g(s(\lceil k\sigma + s\mu \rceil + j)) = \rho_1(k)/(2\lceil \sigma \rceil \rho_1(\mathbb{Z}^+))$$

with $z = s(\lceil k\sigma + s\mu \rceil + j)$. The algorithm accepts z as the returned value with probability $e^{-\frac{1}{2}x(2k+x)}$, where $x = (\lceil k\sigma + s\mu \rceil - (k\sigma + s\mu) + j)/\sigma < 1$. It is not hard to see that

$$\rho_1(k) \cdot \exp(-\frac{1}{2}x(2k+x)) = \exp(-\frac{(\lceil k\sigma + s\mu \rceil + j - s\mu)^2}{2\sigma^2}) = \rho_{\sigma,\mu}(z),$$

which guarantees the correctness of Algorithm 1.

In Algorithm 1, in order to exactly sample $k \in \mathbb{Z}^+$ with (relative) probability density $\rho_1(k) = \exp(-k^2/2)$, Karney also gave an algorithm for exactly generating a Bernoulli random value which is true with probability $1/\sqrt{e}$. Specifically, one needs $(k+1)$ Bernoulli random values from $\mathcal{B}_{1/\sqrt{e}}$ to select an integer $k \geq 0$ with probability $\exp(-k/2) \cdot (1 - \exp(-1/2))$ (step 1), then continues to generate $k(k-1)$ Bernoulli random values from $\mathcal{B}_{1/\sqrt{e}}$ to accept k with probability $\exp\left(-\frac{1}{2}k(k-1)\right)$ (step 2). Karney's algorithm for exactly generating a Bernoulli random value which is true with probability $1/\sqrt{e}$ is adapted from Von Neumann's algorithm for exactly sampling from the exponential distribution e^{-x} for real $x > 0$ (see Algorithm V and Algorihtm H in [16]).

In Algorithm 1, step 8 is implemented by using a specifically designed algorithm so that it produces no any statistical discrepancy, and we will discuss this algorithm in Sect. 3.

3   Sampling from Arbitrary-Centered Discrete Gaussians

Algorithm 2 is our proposed algorithm for sampling from arbitrary-centered discrete Gaussian distributions. We give the proof of its correctness.

Algorithm 2. Sampling from $\mathcal{D}_{\mathbb{Z},\sigma,\mu}$ with an integer-valued σ and a real-valued μ of arbitrary precision

---

Input: positive integer σ and $\mu \in [0, 1)$
Output: an integer z according to $\mathcal{D}_{\mathbb{Z},\sigma,\mu}$
1: select $x \in \mathbb{Z}^+$ with probability $\exp(-x/2) \cdot (1 - \exp(-1/2))$.
2: accept x with probability $\exp\left(-\frac{1}{2}x(x-1)\right)$, otherwise, **goto** step 1.
3: set $s \leftarrow \pm 1$ with equal probabilities.
4: sample $y \in \mathbb{Z}$ uniformly in $\{0, 1, 2, \cdots, \sigma - 1\}$ and set $y \leftarrow y + 1$ if $s = 1$.
5: **return** $z = s(\sigma \cdot x + y)$ with probability $\exp\left(-((y - s\mu)^2 + 2\sigma x(y - s\mu))/(2\sigma^2)\right)$, otherwise **goto** step 1.

Theorem 1. *The integer $z \in \mathbb{Z}$ output by Algorithm 2 is exactly from the discrete Gaussian distribution $\mathcal{D}_{\mathbb{Z},\sigma,\mu}$ with an integer-valued σ and a real-valued μ of arbitrary precision, if the probability*

$$\exp\left(-\frac{(y - s\mu)^2 + 2\sigma x(y - s\mu)}{2\sigma^2}\right)$$

can be calculated exactly.

Proof. From the perspective of rejection sampling, following Karney's approach (step 1 and 2 in Algorithm 1), we generate an integer x exactly from $\mathcal{D}_{\mathbb{Z}^+,1}(x) = \rho_1(x)/\rho_1(\mathbb{Z}^+)$, and use $\mathcal{D}_{\mathbb{Z}^+,1}$ as the proposal distribution. For a given positive integer σ, any $z \in \mathbb{Z}$ can be uniquely written as

$$z = s\left(\sigma x + y + \frac{1+s}{2}\right),$$

where $s \in \{-1, 1\}$, and x, y are integers such that $x \geq 0$ and $y \in [0, \sigma)$. This guarantees that the support of the distribution produced by Algorithm 2 is the set of all the integers. For simplicity, we set $y \leftarrow y+1$ if $s = 1$. Then, $z = s(\sigma x + y)$ and the target distribution density function $f(z)$ for $z \in \mathbb{Z}$ can be written as

$$f(z) = f(s(\sigma x + y)) = \frac{\rho_{\sigma,\mu}(s(\sigma x + y))}{\rho_{\sigma,\mu}(\mathbb{Z})}.$$

In Algorithm 2, for a given integer x exactly from $\mathcal{D}_{\mathbb{Z}^+,1}$, we sample $s \leftarrow \pm 1$ with equal probabilities, take $z = s(\sigma x + y)$, and then accept the value of z as the returned value with probability $\exp\left(-((y - s\mu)^2 + 2\sigma x(y - s\mu))/(2\sigma^2)\right)$. It is not hard to see that

$$\rho_1(x) \cdot \exp\left(-\frac{(y - s\mu)^2 + 2\sigma x(y - s\mu)}{2\sigma^2}\right) = \exp\left(-\frac{(\sigma x + y - s\mu)^2}{2\sigma^2}\right)$$

$$= \exp\left(-\frac{(s(\sigma x + y) - \mu)^2}{2\sigma^2}\right)$$

$$= \rho_{\sigma,\mu}(s(\sigma x + y)),$$

which is proportional to the desired (relative) probability density. This implies that the probability of Algorithm 2 going back to step 1 is equal to a constant,

$$1 - (1 - \exp(-1/2)) \sum_{z=-\infty}^{+\infty} \rho_{\sigma,\mu}(z) = 1 - (1 - \exp(-1/2)) \rho_{\sigma,\mu}(\mathbb{Z}).$$

We denote by Q_∞ this constant and let $q(z) = (1 - \exp(-1/2)) \cdot \rho_{\sigma,\mu}(z)$. Then, the probability that Algorithm 2 outputs an integer $z \in \mathbb{Z}$ can be given by

$$q(z) + q(z)Q_\infty + \ldots + q(z)Q_\infty^i + \ldots = q(z) \cdot \sum_{i=0}^{\infty} Q_\infty^i = \frac{\rho_{\sigma,\mu}(z)}{\rho_{\sigma,\mu}(\mathbb{Z})},$$

which shows the correctness of Algorithm 2. Since all the operations, including computing the value of probability

$$\exp\left(-\frac{(y - s\mu)^2 + 2\sigma x(y - s\mu)}{2\sigma^2}\right),$$

can be performed without any statistical discrepancy, and thus Algorithm 2 produces exactly the discrete Gaussian distribution $\mathcal{D}_{\mathbb{Z},\sigma,\mu}$. □

The most important problem of Algorithm 2 is to compute exaclty the value of the exponential function for a real-valued μ of arbitrary precision, and get a Bernoulli random value which is true with probability of this value. Addressing this problem is based on the following observation.

$$\exp\left(-\frac{(y - s\mu)^2 + 2\sigma x(y - s\mu)}{2\sigma^2}\right)$$

$$= \exp\left(-\frac{1}{2}\left(\frac{y - s\mu}{\sigma}\right)\left(2x + \frac{y - s\mu}{\sigma}\right)\right)$$

$$= \left(\exp\left(-\frac{1}{2}\left(\frac{y - s\mu}{\sigma}\right)\left(\frac{2x + (y - s\mu)/\sigma}{x + 1}\right)\right)\right)^{x+1}$$

$$= \left(\exp\left(-\left(\frac{y - s\mu}{\sigma}\right)\left(\frac{2x + (y - s\mu)/\sigma}{2x + 2}\right)\right)\right)^{x+1}$$

$$= \left(\exp\left(-\tilde{y}\left(\frac{2x + \tilde{y}}{2x + 2}\right)\right)\right)^{x+1},$$

where $\tilde{y} = (y - s\mu)/\sigma$ and $0 \leq \tilde{y} < 1$. Therefore, we can repeatedly sample from the Bernoulli distribution $\mathcal{B}_p$ a total of $x + 1$ times to obtain a Bernoulli random value which is true with our desired probability, where

$$p = \exp\left(-\tilde{y}\left(\frac{2x + \tilde{y}}{2x + 2}\right)\right).$$

Sampling the Bernoulli distribution $\mathcal{B}_p$ can be accomplished by using Algorithm 3, which was proposed by Karney in [16]. The function $C(m)$ with $m = 2x + 2$ in Algorithm 3 is a random selector that outputs -1, 0 and 1 with probability $1/m$, $1/m$ and $1 - 2/m$ respectively.

Algorithm 3. [16] Generating a Bernoulli random value which is true with probability $\exp(-t(2x + t)/(2x + 2))$ with integer $x \geq 0$ and real $t \in [0, 1)$

Output: a Boolean value according to $\exp(-t\frac{2x+t}{2x+2})$
1: set $u \leftarrow t$, $n \leftarrow 0$.
2: sample a uniform deviate v with $v \in [0, 1)$; **goto** step 6 unless $v < u$.
3: set $f \leftarrow C(2x + 2)$; if $f < 0$ **goto** step 6.
4: sample a uniform deviate $w \in [0, 1)$ if $f = 0$, and **goto** step 6 unless $w < t$.
5: set $u \leftarrow v$, $n \leftarrow n + 1$; **goto** step 2.
6: **return true** if n is even, otherwise **return false**.

The main idea is to sample two sets of uniform deviates $v_1, v_2, \ldots$ and $w_1, w_2, \ldots$ from $[0, 1)$, and to determine the maximum value $n \geq 0$ such that

$$t > v_1 > v_2 > \ldots > v_n \quad \text{and} \quad w_i < (2x + t)/(2x + 2) \quad \text{for } i = 1, 2, \ldots, n.$$

If n is even, it returns **true**, and the probability is exactly equal to

$$1 - t\left(\frac{2x + t}{2x + 2}\right) + \frac{t^2}{2!}\left(\frac{2x + t}{2x + 2}\right)^2 - \frac{t^3}{3!}\left(\frac{2x + t}{2x + 2}\right)^3 + \ldots = \exp\left(-t\frac{2x + t}{2x + 2}\right).$$

This follows from the Taylor expansion of the exponential function. Then, applying this procedure at most $k + 1$ times, one can obtain a Bernoulli random value which is true with probability $\exp\left(-\frac{1}{2}t(2x + t)\right)$ for given x and t. Taking

$$t = \tilde{y} = \frac{y - s\mu}{\sigma}$$

and applying Algorithm 3, we can sample from the Bernoulli distribution $\mathcal{B}_p$ with $p = \exp\left(-\tilde{y}\left((2x + \tilde{y})/(2x + 2)\right)\right)$.

The remaining issue is that we need to compare $\tilde{y}$ with a randomly generated deviate in $[0, 1)$, but do not use floating-point arithmetic. This can guarantee the exactness. We observe that any real $u \in [0, 1)$ of arbitrary precision can be represented by

$$u = \frac{j - sr}{\sigma}$$

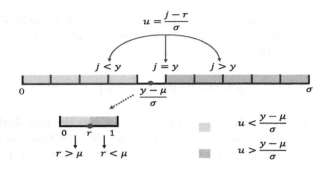

Fig. 1. Comparing $u = (j - r)/\sigma$ with $(y - \mu)/\sigma$

with given σ and s, where j is an integer from $[(1 + s)/2, \sigma + (1 + s)/2)$ and $r \in [0, 1)$ is a real number of arbitrary precision. Then, we can do the comparison as follows.

To obtain a randomly generated deviate in the form of $u = (j - sr)/\sigma \in [0, 1)$, we sample j uniformly in $\{0, 1, 2, \cdots, \sigma - 1\}$, sample a uniform deviate $r \in [0, 1)$ and set $j = j + 1$ if $s = 1$. To compare a randomly generated deviate $u = (j - sr)/\sigma$ with a given $(y - s\mu)/\sigma$, we compare j with y firstly and return the result if they are not equal. Otherwise, we compare r with μ to complete the whole procedure. Figure 1 shows the above idea in the case of $s = 1$. We summarize the whole procedure of comparison in Algorithm 4.

Algorithm 4. Compare $(y - s\mu)/\sigma$ with a randomly generated deviate $u \in [0, 1)$

Input: integers $\sigma > 0$, $s \in \{-1, 1\}$, $y \in [(1 + s)/2, \sigma + (1 + s)/2)$, and real $\mu \in [0, 1)$
Output: true if $u < (y - s\mu)/\sigma$ or **false** if otherwise
1: sample j uniformly in $\{0, 1, 2, \cdots, \sigma - 1\}$ and set $j \leftarrow j + 1$ if $s = 1$
2: **return true** if $j < y$, or **false** if $j > y$
3: sample a uniform deviate $r \in [0, 1)$
4: **return** the value of Boolean expression '$r < \mu$' if $s = -1$
5: **return** the value of Boolean expression '$r > \mu$' if $s = 1$

Note that comparing r with μ can be realized without floating-point arithmetic through bitwise operations. This implies that Algorithm 4 allows μ to be a real number of arbitrary precision and there is no case where $r = \mu$. Specifically, following the implementation of Karney's algorithm for random numbers of arbitrary precision, the comparison of two deviates is realized digit-by-digit, and each digit of a deviate is generated online according to the actual needs. To determine the relation between r and μ, we take the first digit of r and μ, respectively, denoted by r_1 and μ_1. If r_1 or μ_1 does not exist, then we generate it uniformly online. If r_1 and μ_1 are equal, then we take the second digit of r and μ, namely r_2 and μ_2, and continue to compare them. In fact, one digit could consist of only one bit or a small number of bits, such as 4 bits, 8 bits or 16 bits.

We call the number of bits in each digit the digit size, which can be specified in the source code in advance.

Finally, if each random deviate in $[0,1)$ used in Algorithm 3 is handled in the form of $u = (j - sr)/\sigma$, then Algorithm 3 allows μ to be a real number of arbitrary precision, and we can implement it without floating-point arithmetic.

4   Applying the Convolution-Like Property

In this section, we try to extend Algorithm 2 to the case of discrete Gaussian distributions with arbitrary parameters (including σ and μ) by using the convolution-like property of discrete Gaussian distributions.

Informally, for a Gaussian distribution with a relatively large standard deviation σ, we compute two samples x_1 and x_2 with smaller variances σ_1^2 and σ_2^2. We hope that their combination $x_1 + c \cdot x_2$ with a constant c is Gaussian with variance $\sigma_1^2 + c \cdot \sigma_2^2$. Although this is not generally the case for discrete Gaussian distributions, Peikert showed that the distribution of $x_1 + c \cdot x_2$ is statistically close to discrete Gaussian distribution with variance $\sigma_1^2 + c \cdot \sigma_2^2$ under certain conditions with respect to the smoothing parameter of lattices [24]. This observation was called by Peikert the convolution-like property of discrete Gaussian distributions.

Definition 1 (a special case of [21], Definition 3.1). *Let $\epsilon > 0$ be a positive real. The smoothing parameter of lattice $\mathbb{Z}$, denoted by $\eta_\epsilon(\mathbb{Z})$, is defined to be the smallest real s such that $\rho_{1/s}(\mathbb{Z} \setminus \{0\}) \leq \epsilon$.*

Lemma 1 (Adapted from Lemma 3.3 [21]). *For any real $\epsilon > 0$, the smoothing parameter of lattice $\mathbb{Z}$ satisfies[2] $\eta_\epsilon(\mathbb{Z}) \leq \sqrt{\ln(2(1 + 1/\epsilon))/2/\pi}$.*

Here, we apply the conclusion described by Micciancio and Walter in [22] about the convolution-like property, since it deals with non-centered discrete Gaussian over the integers $\mathbb{Z}$ and uses a more cryptographically efficient measure of closeness between probability distributions, named the max-log distance.

Definition 2 [22]. *The max-log distance between two distributions $\mathcal{P}$ and $\mathcal{Q}$ over the same support S is $\Delta_{\mathrm{ML}}(\mathcal{P}, \mathcal{Q}) = \max_{x \in S} |\ln \mathcal{P}(x) - \ln \mathcal{Q}(x)|$.*

Lemma 2 (Corollary 4.2 in [22]). *Let $\sigma_1, \sigma_2 > 0$, $\sigma^2 = \sigma_1^2 + \sigma_2^2$ and $\sigma_3^{-2} = \sigma_1^{-2} + \sigma_2^{-2}$. Let $\Lambda = h \cdot \mathbb{Z}$ be a copy of the integer lattice $\mathbb{Z}$ scaled by a constant h. For any μ_1 and $\mu_2 \in \mathbb{R}$, we denote by $\tilde{\mathcal{D}}_{\mu_1 + \mathbb{Z}, \sigma}$ the distribution of*

$$x_1 \leftarrow x_2 + \tilde{\mathcal{D}}_{\mu_1 - x_2 + \mathbb{Z}, \sigma_1} \quad \text{with} \quad x_2 \leftarrow \tilde{\mathcal{D}}_{\mu_2 + \Lambda, \sigma_2}.$$

If $\sigma_1 \geq \eta_\epsilon(\mathbb{Z})$, $\sigma_3 \geq \eta_\epsilon(\Lambda) = h \cdot \eta_\epsilon(\mathbb{Z})$, $\Delta_{\mathrm{ML}}(\mathcal{D}_{\mu_2 + \Lambda, \sigma_2}, \tilde{\mathcal{D}}_{\mu_2 + \Lambda, \sigma_2}) \leq \epsilon_2$ and $\Delta_{\mathrm{ML}}(\mathcal{D}_{\mu + \mathbb{Z}, \sigma_1}, \tilde{\mathcal{D}}_{\mu + \mathbb{Z}, \sigma_1}) \leq \epsilon_1$ for any $\mu \in \mathbb{R}$, then

$$\Delta_{\mathrm{ML}}(\mathcal{D}_{\mu_1 + \mathbb{Z}, \sigma}, \tilde{\mathcal{D}}_{\mu_1 + \mathbb{Z}, \sigma}) \leq 4\epsilon + \epsilon_1 + \epsilon_2,$$

where ϵ_1 and ϵ_2 are positive real numbers.

---

[2] It allows to decrease the smoothing condition by a factor of $\sqrt{2\pi}$ since the Gaussian function is defined to be $\exp(-\frac{(x-\mu)^2}{2\sigma^2})$ but not $\exp(-\pi \frac{(x-\mu)^2}{\sigma^2})$.

Definition 3 (Randomized rounding operator $\lfloor \cdot \rceil_\lambda$ **[22]).** *For* $\mu \in [0, 1)$ *and a positive integer* λ*, the randomized rounding operator* $\lfloor \mu \rceil_\lambda$ *is defined by*

$$\lfloor \mu \rceil_\lambda = \lfloor 2^\lambda \mu \rfloor / 2^\lambda + B_\alpha / 2^\lambda$$

with a Bernoulli random variable B_α *of parameter* $\alpha = 2^\lambda \mu - \lfloor 2^\lambda \mu \rfloor$*. In particular, if* $\mu > 1$ *then*

$$\mu' \leftarrow \lfloor \mu \rfloor + \lfloor \{\mu\} \rceil_\lambda,$$

where $\lfloor \mu \rfloor$ *and* $\{\mu\}$ *is the integer part and the fractional part of* μ *respectively.*

Lemma 3 (Adapted from Lemma 5.3 in [22]). *Let* $\lambda > \log_2 4\pi$ *be a positive integer and* $b = 2^\lambda$*. If* $\sigma \geq \eta_\epsilon(\mathbb{Z})$*, then*

$$\Delta_{\mathrm{ML}}(\mathcal{D}_{\mathbb{Z},\sigma,\mu}, \tilde{\mathcal{D}}_{\mathbb{Z},\sigma,\lfloor \mu \rceil_\lambda}) \leq (\pi/b)^2 + 2\epsilon,$$

where $\lfloor \cdot \rceil_\lambda$ *is the randomized rounding operator as defined above.*

Combining our proposed exact algorithm (Algorithm 2), and applying the convolution-like property, namely Lemma 2, we give Algorithm 5.

Algorithm 5. Sampling $\mathcal{D}_{\mathbb{Z},\sigma,\mu}$ with $\sigma > \eta_\epsilon(\mathbb{Z})$ and $\mu \in [0, 1)$

Input: $\sigma > 1$ and $\mu \in [0, 1)$
Output: an integer z
1: sample $x \in \mathbb{Z}$ from $\mathcal{D}_{\mathbb{Z}, 2\eta_\epsilon(\mathbb{Z})}$
2: set $h = \sqrt{\sigma^2 - \lfloor \sigma \rfloor^2} / (2\eta_\epsilon(\mathbb{Z}))$
3: set $\mu' \leftarrow \lfloor \mu + hx \rceil_\lambda$
4: sample z from $\mathcal{D}_{\mathbb{Z}, \lfloor \sigma \rfloor, \mu'}$ and **return** z

---

Theorem 2 gives the correctness of Algorithm 5 and estimates the (theoretical) max-log distance between the distribution $\tilde{\mathcal{D}}_{\mathbb{Z},\sigma,\mu}$ produced by Algorithm 5 and the ideal distribution $\mathcal{D}_{\mathbb{Z},\sigma,\mu}$. The equation that

$$\mu + \mathcal{D}_{-\mu+\mathbb{Z},\sigma} = \mathcal{D}_{\mathbb{Z},\sigma,\mu}$$

for any $\sigma > 0$ and $\mu \in \mathbb{R}$ will be repeatedly used in the proof.

Theorem 2. *Let* $\lambda > \log_2 4\pi$ *be a positive integer and* $b = 2^\lambda$*. Denote by* $\tilde{\mathcal{D}}_{\mathbb{Z},\sigma,\mu}$ *the probability distribution of integers that are output by Algorithm 5. If* $\lfloor \sigma \rfloor > \eta_\epsilon(\mathbb{Z})$ *and* $\eta_\epsilon(\mathbb{Z})$ *is taken to be a rational number, then we have*

$$\Delta_{\mathrm{ML}}(\mathcal{D}_{\mathbb{Z},\sigma,\mu}, \tilde{\mathcal{D}}_{\mathbb{Z},\sigma,\mu}) \leq (\pi/b)^2 + 6\epsilon,$$

by using Algorithm 1 in step 1, and using Algorithm 2 in step 4.

Proof. Let $\sigma_1 = \lfloor \sigma \rfloor$ and $\sigma_2 = 2h\eta_\epsilon(\mathbb{Z})$. Then, we have $\sigma^2 = \sigma_1^2 + \sigma_2^2$ and

$$\sigma_3 = \left(\sigma_1^{-2} + (2h\eta_\epsilon(\mathbb{Z}))^{-2}\right)^{-1/2} = \frac{\sigma_1}{\sigma} \cdot \sqrt{\sigma^2 - \sigma_1^2} \geq \sqrt{\sigma^2 - \sigma_1^2} \cdot \frac{\eta_\epsilon(\mathbb{Z})}{2\eta_\epsilon(\mathbb{Z})} = \eta_\epsilon(h\mathbb{Z}).$$

This is due to the fact that $\sigma_1/\sigma = \lfloor \sigma \rfloor/\sigma \geq 1/2$ for $\sigma > 1$. With the notation of Lemma 2, taking $\mu_1 = -\mu$, $\mu_2 = 0$, $\Lambda = h\mathbb{Z}$, $x_2 = hx$ and $x_1 \leftarrow x_2 + \tilde{\mathcal{D}}_{\mu_1 - x_2 + \mathbb{Z}, \sigma_1}$, we have $x_2 = hx \leftarrow \tilde{\mathcal{D}}_{\mu_2 + \Lambda, \sigma_2} = \tilde{\mathcal{D}}_{h\mathbb{Z}, h(2\eta_\epsilon(\mathbb{Z}))} = h \cdot \tilde{\mathcal{D}}_{\mathbb{Z}, 2\eta_\epsilon(\mathbb{Z})}$ and

$$\mu + x_1 \leftarrow \mu + (x_2 + \tilde{\mathcal{D}}_{\mu_1 - x_2 + \mathbb{Z}, \sigma_1}) = \mu + hx + \tilde{\mathcal{D}}_{-\mu - hx + \mathbb{Z}, \lfloor \sigma \rfloor} = \tilde{\mathcal{D}}_{\mathbb{Z}, \lfloor \sigma \rfloor, \mu + hx}.$$

Since $\eta_\epsilon(\mathbb{Z})$ is a rational number, in Algorithm 5, $\tilde{\mathcal{D}}_{\mathbb{Z}, 2\eta_\epsilon(\mathbb{Z})}$ can be exactly sampled (without any statistical discrepancy) via Algorithm 1, which implies that

$$\Delta_{\mathrm{ML}}(\mathcal{D}_{\mathbb{Z}, 2\eta_\epsilon(\mathbb{Z})}, \tilde{\mathcal{D}}_{\mathbb{Z}, 2\eta_\epsilon(\mathbb{Z})}) = 0.$$

In contrast, $\tilde{\mathcal{D}}_{\mathbb{Z}, \lfloor \sigma \rfloor, \mu + hx}$ can be only realized by sampling from $\mathcal{D}_{\mathbb{Z}, \lfloor \sigma \rfloor, \lfloor \mu + hx \rceil_\lambda}$ with max-log distance $\Delta_{\mathrm{ML}} \leq (\pi/b)^2 + 2\epsilon$. Applying Lemma 2, we obtain that

$$\mu + x_1 \leftarrow \mu + (x_2 + \tilde{\mathcal{D}}_{\mu_1 - x_2 + \mathbb{Z}, \sigma_1}) = \mu + (hx + \tilde{\mathcal{D}}_{-\mu - hx + \mathbb{Z}, \lfloor \sigma \rfloor})$$
$$\approx \mu + \mathcal{D}_{-\mu + \mathbb{Z}, \sigma} = \mathcal{D}_{\mathbb{Z}, \sigma, \mu},$$

where '$\approx$' means that $\Delta_{\mathrm{ML}}(hx + \mathcal{D}_{-\mu - hx + \mathbb{Z}, \lfloor \sigma \rfloor}, \mathcal{D}_{-\mu + \mathbb{Z}, \sigma})$ is not more than

$$4\epsilon + \Delta_{\mathrm{ML}}(\mathcal{D}_{-\mu - hx + \mathbb{Z}, \lfloor \sigma \rfloor}, \tilde{\mathcal{D}}_{-\mu - hx + \mathbb{Z}, \lfloor \sigma \rfloor}) + \Delta_{\mathrm{ML}}(\mathcal{D}_{h\mathbb{Z}, h(2\eta_\epsilon(\mathbb{Z}))}, \tilde{\mathcal{D}}_{h\mathbb{Z}, h(2\eta_\epsilon(\mathbb{Z}))})$$
$$= 4\epsilon + \Delta_{\mathrm{ML}}(\mathcal{D}_{\mathbb{Z}, 2\eta_\epsilon(\mathbb{Z})}, \tilde{\mathcal{D}}_{\mathbb{Z}, 2\eta_\epsilon(\mathbb{Z})})$$
$$+ \Delta_{\mathrm{ML}}(\mu + hx + \mathcal{D}_{-\mu - hx + \mathbb{Z}, \lfloor \sigma \rfloor}, \mu + hx + \tilde{\mathcal{D}}_{-\mu - hx + \mathbb{Z}, \lfloor \sigma \rfloor})$$
$$\leq 4\epsilon + \Delta_{\mathrm{ML}}(\mathcal{D}_{\mathbb{Z}, 2\eta_\epsilon(\mathbb{Z})}, \tilde{\mathcal{D}}_{\mathbb{Z}, 2\eta_\epsilon(\mathbb{Z})}) + \Delta_{\mathrm{ML}}(\mathcal{D}_{\mathbb{Z}, \lfloor \sigma \rfloor, \mu + hx}, \tilde{\mathcal{D}}_{\mathbb{Z}, \lfloor \sigma \rfloor, \mu + hx})$$
$$\leq 4\epsilon + ((\pi/b)^2 + 2\epsilon).$$
$$= 6\epsilon + (\pi/b)^2.$$

This completes the proof.   ⊓⊔

The distribution produced by Algorithm 5 has a smaller max-log distance to the ideal distribution, as compared to one produced by Micciancio-Walter sampling algorithm, since both step 1 and step 4 can be implemented exactly, and do not lead to any statistical discrepancy. In contrast, the two corresponding steps in Micciancio-Walter algorithm are approximated ones (see Sect. 5 in [22]). The statistical discrepancy they produce must be counted in the total statistical discrepancy.

For instance, we take $\epsilon = 2^{-112}$ and $\eta_\epsilon(\mathbb{Z}) = 2$, as $\sqrt{\ln(2(1 + 1/\epsilon))/2}/\pi \leq 2$ when $\epsilon = 2^{-112}$. We take $\lambda = 30$ and $b = 2^{30}$, which results in $(\pi/b)^2 \leq 2^{-56}$. Then, we have $\Delta_{\mathrm{ML}}(\mathcal{D}_{\mathbb{Z}, \sigma, \mu}, \tilde{\mathcal{D}}_{\mathbb{Z}, \sigma, \mu}) \leq 2^{-56} + 6 \cdot 2^{-112}$. The practical max-log distance should also include the statistical discrepancy due to the floating-point operations in step 2. One can just follow the argument at the end of Sect. 5.3 in [22].

Moreover, the first step in Micciancio-Walter algorithm requires sampling from a centered discrete Gaussian distribution $\mathcal{D}_{\mathbb{Z},\sigma_{\max}}$ with a possible varying parameter $\sigma_{\max}$, which should be determined before sampling according to the desired distribution. In Algorithm 5, however, step 1 is just to sample from a centered discrete Gaussian distribution with a fixed parameter $2\eta_\epsilon(\mathbb{Z}) = 4$. This means that Algorithm 5 has a simpler form than Micciancio-Walter algorithm.

5   Experimental Results

Karney's sampling algorithm for discrete Gaussian distributions over the integers $\mathbb{Z}$ can be realized by using C++ library 'RandomLib'[3], in which the source code of his algorithm is encapsulated as a .hpp file named "DiscreteNormal.hpp". "RandomLib" also supports the generation and some basic operations of random numbers of arbitrary precision.

On a laptop computer (Intel i7-6820 hq, 8 GB RAM), using the g++ compiler and enabling -O3 optimization option, we tested our Algorithm 2. The source code was based on the adaptation of 'DiscreteNormal.hpp' as well as the runtime environment provided by 'RandomLib'. For discrete Gaussian distribution $\mathcal{D}_{\mathbb{Z},\sigma,\mu}$ with σ from 4 to 2^{20} and μ uniformly from $[0,1)$ of precision 128 bits, combining Algorithms 3 and 4, one could get about 5.0×10^6 samples per second by using Algorithm 2. It has almost the same performance as Karney's algorithm.

We also tested the performance of the Micciancio-Walter algorithm with the same parameters. Using this algorithm, one could get about 1.3×10^6 integers per second. We implemented its base sampler with the CDT-based method, which required an amount of extra memory, and took $\lambda = 8$ and $b = 16$. This guarantees the max-log distance to the ideal distribution is not more than 2^{-52}.

We note that Micciancio-Walter algorithm has a constant execution time for given parameters if its base sampler is a constant-time algorithm. However, our Algorithm 2 as well as Algorithm 5 is not a constant-time one, and it seems to be inherently costly to turn into a constant-time one due to the fact that Algorithm 2 is always probabilistically rejecting samples. Therefore, an open question is how to make Algorithm 2 constant-time and be protected against side-channel attacks [4,8].

6   Conclusion

For an integer-valued parameter σ, there exists an exact sampling algorithm for $\mathcal{D}_{\mathbb{Z},\sigma,\mu}$. It requires no precomputation storage, uses no floating-point arithmetic, supports a varying μ of arbitrary precision, and does not have any statistical discrepancy. Applying the convolution-like property of discrete Gaussian distributions, it can be further extended to an approximated sampling algorithm for $\mathcal{D}_{\mathbb{Z},\sigma,\mu}$ with a real-valued parameter σ. The extended algorithm also supports centers of arbitrary precision and it produces a distribution with a smaller max-log distance to the ideal distribution, as compared to Micciancio-Walter sampling algorithm.

---

[3] 'RandomLib' is available at http://randomlib.sourceforge.net/.

References

1. Aguilar-Melchor, C., Albrecht, M.R., Ricosset, T.: Sampling from arbitrary centered discrete Gaussians for lattice-based cryptography. In: Gollmann, D., Miyaji, A., Kikuchi, H. (eds.) ACNS 2017. LNCS, vol. 10355, pp. 3–19. Springer, Cham (2017). https://doi.org/10.1007/978-3-319-61204-1_1
2. Bai, S., Lepoint, T., Roux-Langlois, A., Sakzad, A., Stehlé, D., Steinfeld, R.: Improved security proofs in lattice-based cryptography: using the rényi divergence rather than the statistical distance. J. Cryptol. **31**(2), 610–640 (2018)
3. Barthe, G., Belaïd, S., Espitau, T., Fouque, P., Rossi, M., Tibouchi, M.: GALACTICS: Gaussian sampling for lattice-based constant- time implementation of cryptographic signatures, revisited. In: Cavallaro, L., Kinder, J., Wang, X., Katz, J. (eds.) Proceedings of the 2019 ACM SIGSAC CCS, pp. 2147–2164. ACM, New York (2019)
4. Groot Bruinderink, L., Hülsing, A., Lange, T., Yarom, Y.: Flush, gauss, and reload – a cache attack on the BLISS lattice-based signature scheme. In: Gierlichs, B., Poschmann, A.Y. (eds.) CHES 2016. LNCS, vol. 9813, pp. 323–345. Springer, Heidelberg (2016). https://doi.org/10.1007/978-3-662-53140-2_16
5. Devroye, L.: Non-Uniform Random Variate Generation. Springer, New York (1986)
6. Ducas, L., Durmus, A., Lepoint, T., Lyubashevsky, V.: Lattice signatures and bimodal Gaussians. In: Canetti, R., Garay, J.A. (eds.) CRYPTO 2013. LNCS, vol. 8042, pp. 40–56. Springer, Heidelberg (2013). https://doi.org/10.1007/978-3-642-40041-4_3
7. Dwarakanath, N.C., Galbraith, S.D.: Sampling from discrete Gaussians for lattice-based cryptography on a constrained device. Appl. Algebra Eng. Commun. Comput **25**(3), 159–180 (2014)
8. Espitau, T., Fouque, P.A., Gérard, B., Tibouchi, M.: Side-channel attacks on bliss lattice-based signatures: exploiting branch tracing against strongswan and electromagnetic emanations in microcontrollers. In: Thuraisingham, B., Evans, D., Malkin, T., Xu, D. (eds.) Proceedings of the 2017 ACM SIGSAC CCS, pp. 1857–1874. ACM, New York (2017)
9. Genise, N., Micciancio, D.: Faster Gaussian sampling for trapdoor lattices with arbitrary modulus. In: Nielsen, J.B., Rijmen, V. (eds.) EUROCRYPT 2018. LNCS, vol. 10820, pp. 174–203. Springer, Cham (2018). https://doi.org/10.1007/978-3-319-78381-9_7
10. Gentry, C., Peikert, C., Vaikuntanathan, V.: Trapdoors for hard lattices and new cryptographic constructions. In: Ladner, R., Dwork, C. (eds.) Proceedings of the 2008 ACM SIGACT STOC, pp. 197–206. ACM, New York (2008)
11. Howe, J., Khalid, A., Rafferty, C., Regazzoni, F., O'Neill, M.: On practical discrete Gaussian samplers for lattice-based cryptography. IEEE Trans. Comput. **67**(3), 322–334 (2018)
12. Howe, J., Prest, T., Ricosset, T., Rossi, M.: Isochronous Gaussian sampling: from inception to implementation. In: Ding, J., Tillich, J.-P. (eds.) PQCrypto 2020. LNCS, vol. 12100, pp. 53–71. Springer, Cham (2020). https://doi.org/10.1007/978-3-030-44223-1_4
13. Hülsing, A., Lange, T., Smeets, K.: Rounded Gaussians. In: Abdalla, M., Dahab, R. (eds.) PKC 2018. LNCS, vol. 10770, pp. 728–757. Springer, Cham (2018). https://doi.org/10.1007/978-3-319-76581-5_25
14. Karmakar, A., Roy, S.S., Reparaz, O., Vercauteren, F., Verbauwhede, I.: Constant-time discrete Gaussian sampling. IEEE Trans. Comput. **67**(11), 1561–1571 (2018)

15. Karmakar, A., Roy, S.S., Vercauteren, F., Verbauwhede, I.: Pushing the speed limit of constant-time discrete Gaussian sampling. A case study on the falcon signature scheme. In: Aitken, R. (ed.) Proceedings of the 56th DAC, pp. 1–6. ACM, New York (2019)

16. Karney, C.F.: Sampling exactly from the normal distribution. ACM Trans. Math. Softw. **42**(1), 3:1–3:14 (2016)

17. Lyubashevsky, V.: Lattice signatures without trapdoors. In: Pointcheval, D., Johansson, T. (eds.) EUROCRYPT 2012. LNCS, vol. 7237, pp. 738–755. Springer, Heidelberg (2012). https://doi.org/10.1007/978-3-642-29011-4_43

18. Lyubashevsky, V., Peikert, C., Regev, O.: On ideal lattices and learning with errors over rings. J. ACM **60**(6), 43:1–43:35 (2013)

19. Lyubashevsky, V., Prest, T.: Quadratic time, linear space algorithms for Gram-Schmidt orthogonalization and gaussian sampling in structured lattices. In: Oswald, E., Fischlin, M. (eds.) EUROCRYPT 2015. LNCS, vol. 9056, pp. 789–815. Springer, Heidelberg (2015). https://doi.org/10.1007/978-3-662-46800-5_30

20. Micciancio, D., Peikert, C.: Trapdoors for lattices: simpler, tighter, faster, smaller. In: Pointcheval, D., Johansson, T. (eds.) EUROCRYPT 2012. LNCS, vol. 7237, pp. 700–718. Springer, Heidelberg (2012). https://doi.org/10.1007/978-3-642-29011-4_41

21. Micciancio, D., Regev, O.: Worst-case to average-case reductions based on Gaussian measures. SIAM J. Comput. **37**(1), 267–302 (2007)

22. Micciancio, D., Walter, M.: Gaussian sampling over the integers: efficient, generic, constant-time. In: Katz, J., Shacham, H. (eds.) CRYPTO 2017. LNCS, vol. 10402, pp. 455–485. Springer, Cham (2017). https://doi.org/10.1007/978-3-319-63715-0_16

23. Naehrig, M., et al.: Frodokem learning with errors key encapsulation. https://frodokem.org/files/FrodoKEM-specification-20171130.pdf. Accessed 28 Feb 2020

24. Peikert, C.: An efficient and parallel Gaussian sampler for lattices. In: Rabin, T. (ed.) CRYPTO 2010. LNCS, vol. 6223, pp. 80–97. Springer, Heidelberg (2010). https://doi.org/10.1007/978-3-642-14623-7_5

25. Pöppelmann, T., Ducas, L., Güneysu, T.: Enhanced lattice-based signatures on reconfigurable hardware. In: Batina, L., Robshaw, M. (eds.) CHES 2014. LNCS, vol. 8731, pp. 353–370. Springer, Heidelberg (2014). https://doi.org/10.1007/978-3-662-44709-3_20

26. Prest, T.: Sharper bounds in lattice-based cryptography using the Rényi divergence. In: Takagi, T., Peyrin, T. (eds.) ASIACRYPT 2017. LNCS, vol. 10624, pp. 347–374. Springer, Cham (2017). https://doi.org/10.1007/978-3-319-70694-8_13

27. Prest, T., et al.: Falcon: fast-fourier lattice-based compact signatures over NTRU. https://falcon-sign.info/. Accessed 20 Feb 2020

28. Sinha Roy, S., Vercauteren, F., Verbauwhede, I.: High precision discrete Gaussian sampling on FPGAs. In: Lange, T., Lauter, K., Lisoněk, P. (eds.) SAC 2013. LNCS, vol. 8282, pp. 383–401. Springer, Heidelberg (2014). https://doi.org/10.1007/978-3-662-43414-7_19

29. Saarinen, M.J.O.: Arithmetic coding and blinding countermeasures for lattice signatures. J. Cryptogr. Eng. **8**, 71–84 (2018)

30. Walter, M.: Sampling the integers with low relative error. In: Buchmann, J., Nitaj, A., Rachidi, T. (eds.) AFRICACRYPT 2019. LNCS, vol. 11627, pp. 157–180. Springer, Cham (2019). https://doi.org/10.1007/978-3-030-23696-0_9

31. Zhao, R.K., Steinfeld, R., Sakzad, A.: COSAC: COmpact and Scalable Arbitrary-Centered discrete Gaussian sampling over integers. In: Ding, J., Tillich, J.-P. (eds.) PQCrypto 2020. LNCS, vol. 12100, pp. 284–303. Springer, Cham (2020). https://doi.org/10.1007/978-3-030-44223-1_16
32. Zhao, R.K., Steinfeld, R., Sakzad, A.: FACCT: fast, compact, and constant-time discrete Gaussian sampler over integers. IEEE Trans. Comput. **69**(1), 126–137 (2020)

New Assumptions and Efficient Cryptosystems from the e-th Power Residue Symbol

Xiaopeng Zhao[1], Zhenfu Cao[1,2]($\boxtimes$), Xiaolei Dong[1], Jun Shao[3], Licheng Wang[4], and Zhusen Liu[1]

[1] Shanghai Key Laboratory of Trustworthy Computing,
East China Normal University, Shanghai, China
{52164500025,52184501023}@stu.ecnu.edu.cn,
{zfcao,dongxiaolei}@sei.ecnu.edu.cn

[2] Cyberspace Security Research Center, Peng Cheng Laboratory, Shenzhen and Shanghai Institute of Intelligent Science and Technology, Tongji University, Shanghai, China

[3] School of Computer and Information Engineering, Zhejiang Gongshang University, Hangzhou, China
chn.junshao@gmail.com

[4] State Key Laboratory of Networking and Switching Technology,
Beijing University of Posts and Telecommunications, Beijing 100876, China
wanglc@bupt.edu.cn

Abstract. The e-th power residue symbol $\left(\frac{\alpha}{\mathfrak{p}}\right)_e$ is a useful mathematical tool in cryptography, where α is an integer, $\mathfrak{p}$ is a prime ideal in the prime factorization of $p\mathbb{Z}[\zeta_e]$ with a large prime p satisfying $e|p-1$, and ζ_e is an e-th primitive root of unity. One famous case of the e-th power symbol is the first semantic secure public key cryptosystem due to Goldwasser and Micali (at STOC 1982). In this paper, we revisit the e-th power residue symbol and its applications. In particular, we prove that computing the e-th power residue symbol is equivalent to solving the discrete logarithm problem. By this result, we give a natural extension of the Goldwasser-Micali cryptosystem, where e is an integer only containing small prime factors. Compared to another extension of the Goldwasser-Micali cryptosystem due to Joye and Libert (at EUROCRYPT 2013), our proposal is more efficient in terms of bandwidth utilization and decryption cost. With a new hardness assumption naturally extended from the one used in the Goldwasser-Micali cryptosystem, our proposal is provable IND-CPA secure. Furthermore, we show that our results on the e-th power residue symbol can also be used to construct lossy trapdoor functions and circular and leakage resilient public key encryptions with more efficiency and better bandwidth utilization.

Keywords: Power residue symbol · Goldwasser-Micali cryptosystem · Joye-Libert cryptosystem · Lossy trapdoor function · Leakage resilient public key encryption

© Springer Nature Switzerland AG 2020
J. K. Liu and H. Cui (Eds.): ACISP 2020, LNCS 12248, pp. 408–424, 2020.
https://doi.org/10.1007/978-3-030-55304-3_21

1 Introduction

We have witnessed the critical role of the power residue symbol in the history of public key encryption. Based on the quadratic residuosity assumption, Goldwasser and Micali [18] proposed the first public key encryption (named GM) scheme with semantic security and additive homomorphism. This scheme is revolutionary but inefficient in terms of bandwidth, which hinders its use in practice. Following the light of the GM scheme, many attempts [2–5,11–13,15,24,26,27] have been made to address this issue.

Recall the encryption in the GM scheme. A message $m \in \{0,1\}$ in the GM scheme is encrypted by $c = y^m r^2 \bmod N$, where $N = p \cdot q$, p and q are large primes, $\left(\frac{y}{N}\right) = \left(\frac{y}{p}\right) \times \left(\frac{y}{q}\right) = -1 \times -1 = 1$ and r is an element picked at random from $\mathbb{Z}_N$. It is easy to see that the value of $\log_r(r^2 \bmod N)$ determines the message space. Hence, one intuitive approach to improve the bandwidth utilization in the GM scheme is to enlarge $\log_r(r^e \bmod N)$. At STOC 1994, Benaloh and Tuinstra [2,15] set e as a special prime instead of 2. In particular, e is a prime, $e|p-1$, $e^2 \nmid p-1$, and $e \nmid q-1$. The corresponding decryption requires to locate m in $[0,e)$ by a brute-force method. Hence, e is limited to 40 bits. At ACM CCS 1998, Naccache and Stern [24] improved Benaloh and Tuinstra's method by setting e as a smooth and square-free integer $e = \prod p_i$ such that $p_i|\varphi(N)$ but $p_i^2 \nmid \varphi(N)$ for each prime p_i. The message m in this scheme is recovered from $m \equiv m_i \pmod{p_i}$ using the Chinese Remainder Theorem where each m_i is computed by a brute-force method. Nevertheless, the constraint $p_i^2 \nmid \varphi(N)$ limits the possibility for enlarging the message space dramatically. At EUROCRYPT 2013, based on the 2^k-th power residue symbol, Joye and Libert [3] enlarged e to 2^k to obtain a nice and natural extension (named JL) of the GM scheme with better bandwidth utilization than previous schemes. Later on, Cao et al. [13] demonstrated that the JL scheme could be further improved by setting e as a product of small primes. As shown in [13], the resulting scheme (named CDWS) is more efficient than the JL scheme in terms of bandwidth utilization and decryption cost. Nonetheless, the corresponding security proof is complicated and hard to follow.

By virtue of the fruitful use in cryptography, algorithms for computing the e-th power residue symbol have also attracted many researchers [6,8,9,14,20,21,31]. Several efficient algorithms for the cases of $e \in \{2,3,4,5,7,8,11,13\}$ have been proposed. However, as we know, these algorithms cannot be used for improving the GM-type schemes in [3,13] owing to the small value of e. The general case of computing the e-th power residue symbol was tackled by Squirrel [31] and Boer [6], but the resulting algorithms are probabilistic and inefficient. Hence, their results may not be applied in improving the GM scheme either. Although Freeman et al. [17] conducted that a "compatibility" identity can be used to compute the e-th power residue symbol, this identity could be useless in the case of a prime power e. As a result, we cannot use Freeman et al.'s algorithm to improve the GM scheme.

In order to solve the above problems, in this paper, we revisit the problem of computing the e-th power residue symbol, and obtain an efficient algorithm that can be applied in the GM-type scheme and other cryptographic primitives. Our contributions in this paper can be summarized as follows.

- **New algorithm for computing e-th power residue symbol:** We prove that computing the e-th power residue symbol is equivalent to solving the discrete logarithm problem, if the parameters in the e-th power residue symbol $\left(\frac{\alpha}{\mathfrak{p}}\right)_e$ satisfy the following properties.
  - α is an integer.
  - p is a prime number satisfying $e|p-1$.
  - $\mathfrak{p}$ is a prime ideal in the prime factorization of $p\mathbb{Z}[\zeta_e]$, and ζ_e is an e-th primitive root of unity.

  As we know, there exist several efficient algorithms for solving the discrete logarithm problem when the corresponding order is a product of small primes. Hence, we obtain an efficient algorithm for computing e-th power residue symbol when the above conditions are satisfied.
- **New extension of the GM scheme:** We demonstrate that we can obtain a natural extension of the GM scheme based on the e-th power residue symbol. Compared to the JL scheme, our extension enjoys better bandwidth utilization and higher decryption speed. While compared to the CDWS scheme, our extension has a simpler security proof.
- **New lossy trapdoor function:** As in [3,13], our GM extension can also be used to construct an efficient lossy trapdoor function, which inherits the advantages of our GM extension.
- **New circular and leakage resilient encryption:** We also give an instantiation of the subgroup indistinguishability (SG) assumption by using the e-th power residue symbol. At CRYPTO 2010, Brakerski and Goldwasser [7] gave a generic construction of circular and leakage resilient public key encryption based on the SG assumption. Hence, we obtain a new circular and leakage resilient encryption scheme. Compared to the scheme in [7], our scheme is more efficient in terms of bandwidth utilization, due to the use of the e-th power residue symbol instead of the Jacobi symbol.

The rest of this paper is organized as follows. In Sect. 2, we introduce some definitions and preliminaries about the e-th power residue symbol. In what follows, we show how to compute the e-th power residue symbol defined in Sect. 2 efficiently. Some properties and a hardness assumption related to the e-th power residue symbol are also analyzed and discussed in this section. After that, we give our extension of the GM scheme and its security and performance analysis in Sect. 4. In Sect. 5, we give two applications of our results on the e-th power residue symbol following the methods described in [3,7].

2 Notations and Basic Definitions

2.1 Notations

For simplicity, we would like to introduce the notations used in this paper in Table 1.

Table 1. Notations used in this paper.

Notation	Description
K	A number field
$\mathcal{O}_K$	The ring of integers in a number field K
Letters in $\mathfrak{mathfrak}$	Ideals in $\mathcal{O}_K$
$a = b \pmod{\mathfrak{D}}$	The relation $a - b \in \mathfrak{D}$, where elements $a, b \in \mathcal{O}_K$
$\#X$	The cardinality of a set X
X^n	The Cartesian product $\prod_{i=1}^{n} X$
$\langle X \rangle$	The group generated by a set X
$x \overset{R}{\leftarrow} X$	x is sampled from the uniform distribution over a set X
$\otimes$	The direct product of two algebraic structures
φ	The Euler's totient function
$\gcd(x, y)$	The greatest common divisor of x and y
$\mathrm{lcm}(x, y)$	The least common multiple of x and y
$\log$	The binary logarithm
ζ_e	An e-th primitive root of unity, i.e., $\zeta_e = \exp(2\pi i / e)$
$\mathbb{Z}_n$	The ring $\{0, 1, \ldots, n - 1\}$ of integers mod n
$\mathbb{Z}_n^*$	The multiplicative group $\{x \in \mathbb{Z}_n \mid \gcd(x, n) = 1\}$ mod n
p, q	Large prime numbers
N	$N = p \cdot q$
e_p, e_q	$e_p \mid p - 1$ and $e_q \mid q - 1$

2.2 Power Residue Symbols

We say a prime ideal $\mathfrak{A}$ in $\mathcal{O}_K$ is prime to an integer $e \geq 1$ if $\mathfrak{A} \nmid e\mathcal{O}_K$. It is easy to deduce that the corresponding necessary and sufficient condition is $\gcd(\mathrm{Norm}(\mathfrak{A}), e) = 1$, where $\mathrm{Norm}(\mathfrak{A}) = \#(\mathcal{O}_K / \mathfrak{A})$. Then, we have

$$\alpha^{\mathrm{Norm}(\mathfrak{A})-1} = 1 \pmod{\mathfrak{A}} \quad (\text{for } \alpha \in \mathcal{O}_K, \alpha \notin \mathfrak{A}).$$

Furthermore, if we have an additional condition that $\zeta_e \in K$, then we have that the order of group $\langle \zeta_e / \mathfrak{A} \rangle$ generated in $(\mathcal{O}_K / \mathfrak{A})^\times$ is e, and hence $e \mid \mathrm{Norm}(\mathfrak{A}) - 1$. Now, we can define the e-th *power residue symbol* $\left(\frac{\alpha}{\mathfrak{A}}\right)_e$ as follows: if $\alpha \in \mathfrak{A}$, then $\left(\frac{\alpha}{\mathfrak{A}}\right)_e = 0$; otherwise, $\left(\frac{\alpha}{\mathfrak{A}}\right)_e$ is the unique e-th root of unity such that

$$\left(\frac{\alpha}{\mathfrak{A}}\right)_e = \alpha^{\frac{\mathrm{Norm}(\mathfrak{A})-1}{e}} \pmod{\mathfrak{A}}.$$

The definition can be naturally extended to the case that $\mathfrak{A}$ is not a prime ideal, such that $\mathfrak{A} = \prod_i \mathfrak{B}_i$ and $\gcd(\mathtt{Norm}(\mathfrak{B}_i), e) = 1$. In particular, we define

$$\left(\frac{\alpha}{\mathfrak{A}}\right)_e = \prod_i \left(\frac{\alpha}{\mathfrak{B}_i}\right)_e.$$

In the rest of this paper, we simply consider the case of $K = \mathbb{Q}(\zeta_e)$, since we have $\mathcal{O}_K = \mathbb{Z}[\zeta_e]$ in this case. We suggest interested readers to refer to [19,23,25] for more details about the power residue symbol.

2.3   Security Definition

A public key encryption is composed of three algorithms: the key generation algorithm KeyGen, the encryption algorithm Enc, and the decryption algorithm Dec. The IND-CPA security for a public key encryption is defined as follows:

Definition 1 (IND-CPA Security). *The public key encryption scheme PKE = (KeyGen, Enc, Dec) is said to be IND-CPA secure if for any probabilistic polynomial time (PPT) distinguisher, given the public key* pk *generated by KeyGen, and any pair of messages* m_0, m_1 *of equal length, the non-negative advantage function* $\epsilon(\kappa)$ *in the security parameter* κ *for distinguishing* $c_0 = $ Enc (pk, m_0) *and* $c_1 = $ Enc (pk, m_1) *is* negligible, *i.e., we have* $\lim_{\kappa \to \infty} P(\kappa) \cdot \epsilon(\kappa) = 0$ *for every polynomial P.*

3   Computation and Properties of the Power Residue Symbol

In this section, we show how to compute the power residue symbol in some circumstance and investigate some relative properties that we will employ in this paper later.

3.1   Computing Power Residue Symbols

In this subsection, we show that computing the power residue symbol is equivalent to solving the discrete logarithm problem if some specific conditions are satisfied.

Before giving the proof, we would like to introduce the concept of *non-degenerate primitive* (e_p, e_q)-th root of unity modulo N. Let μ_p and μ_q be primitive roots modulo p and q respectively. We say an integer μ is a non-degenerate primitive (e_p, e_q)-th root of unity modulo N if both the following two congruences hold.

$$\mu = \mu_p^{\frac{p-1}{e_p}\alpha} \pmod{p} \quad \text{for some } \alpha \in \mathbb{Z}_{e_p}^*, \text{ and}$$

$$\mu = \mu_q^{\frac{q-1}{e_q}\beta} \pmod{q} \quad \text{for some } \beta \in \mathbb{Z}_{e_q}^*.$$

According to the result in [25, Proposition I.8.3], we have

$$p\mathbb{Z}[\zeta_{e_p}] = \prod_{i \in \mathbb{Z}_{e_p}^*} \mathfrak{p}_i, \ \text{Norm}(\mathfrak{p}_i) = p \ (i \in \mathbb{Z}_{e_p}^*), \text{ and}$$

$$q\mathbb{Z}[\zeta_{e_q}] = \prod_{j \in \mathbb{Z}_{e_q}^*} \mathfrak{q}_j, \ \text{Norm}(\mathfrak{q}_j) = q \ (j \in \mathbb{Z}_{e_q}^*),$$

where $\mathfrak{p}_i = p\mathbb{Z}[\zeta_{e_p}] + (\zeta_{e_p} - \mu^i)\mathbb{Z}[\zeta_{e_p}]$ and $\mathfrak{q}_j = q\mathbb{Z}[\zeta_{e_q}] + (\zeta_{e_q} - \mu^j)\mathbb{Z}[\zeta_{e_q}]$. We will write $\mathfrak{p} = \mathfrak{p}_1$ and $\mathfrak{q} = \mathfrak{q}_1$ for brevity.

With the notation μ and some integer α, we can establish Theorem 1 which shows that computing $\left(\frac{\alpha}{\mathfrak{p}}\right)_{e_p}$ is equivalent to solving the discrete logarithm in the cyclic subgroup $\langle \mu \rangle \subset \mathbb{Z}_p^*$ of order e_p. We can obtain a similar result for the case of $\left(\frac{\alpha}{\mathfrak{q}}\right)_{e_q}$ by analogy with Theorem 1.

Theorem 1. $\left(\frac{\alpha}{\mathfrak{p}}\right)_{e_p} = \zeta_{e_p}^x \iff \mu^x = \alpha^{\frac{p-1}{e_p}} \pmod{p}$.

Proof. We give the proof in two parts as follows.

$\Longrightarrow$ From the definition of the power residue symbol and $\text{Norm}(\mathfrak{p}) = p$, we have that $\left(\frac{\alpha}{\mathfrak{p}}\right)_{e_p} = \alpha^{\frac{\text{Norm}(\mathfrak{p})-1}{e_p}} = \alpha^{\frac{p-1}{e_p}} \pmod{\mathfrak{p}}$. Together with $\left(\frac{\alpha}{\mathfrak{p}}\right)_{e_p} = \zeta_{e_p}^x$, we obtain that $\zeta_{e_p}^x = \alpha^{\frac{p-1}{e_p}} \pmod{\mathfrak{p}}$. Furthermore, from the definition of $\mathfrak{p}$, we have $\mu = \zeta_{e_p} \pmod{\mathfrak{p}}$. Then, $\mu^x = \zeta_{e_p}^x = \alpha^{\frac{p-1}{e_p}} \pmod{\mathfrak{p}}$ is deduced. At last, due to $\mu^x = \alpha^{\frac{p-1}{e_p}} \pmod{\mathfrak{p}}$ and $(\mu^x, \alpha^{\frac{p-1}{e_p}}) \in \mathbb{Z}^2$, we can finally get $\mu^x = \alpha^{\frac{p-1}{e_p}} \pmod{p}$.

$\Longleftarrow$ From $\mu^x = \alpha^{\frac{p-1}{e_p}} \pmod{p}$, we have that $\mu^x = \alpha^{\frac{p-1}{e_p}} \pmod{\mathfrak{p}}$. Furthermore, we have that $\left(\frac{\alpha}{\mathfrak{p}}\right)_{e_p} = \alpha^{\frac{p-1}{e_p}} \pmod{\mathfrak{p}}$ and $\zeta_{e_p} = \mu \pmod{\mathfrak{p}}$ as in the previous case. Hence, we have that $\left(\frac{\alpha}{\mathfrak{p}}\right)_{e_p} = \alpha^{\frac{p-1}{e_p}} = \mu^x = \zeta_{e_p}^x \pmod{\mathfrak{p}}$ and $\left(\frac{\alpha}{\mathfrak{p}}\right)_{e_p} = \zeta_{e_p}^x$.

This completes the proof. □

It is well-known that the discrete logarithm problem is intractable in general but quite easy in some special cases. For instance, when the order of the underlying finite cyclic group is *smooth*, i.e., it only contains small prime factors, the discrete logarithm problem can be easily solved by virtue of the Pohlig-Hellman algorithm [29]. In our case, if e_p is chosen with appropriate prime factors, the e_p-th power residue symbol can be efficiently computed by virtue of the Pohlig-Hellman algorithm. For the completeness, we describe the Pohlig-Hellman algorithm for prime powers in Algorithm 1.

Algorithm 1. Pohlig-Hellman algorithm for prime powers

Input: (g, y, p, s^k), where p and s are primes, $s^k | p - 1$, and the order of g in $\mathbb{Z}_p^*$ is s^k.
Output: $x = (x_{k-1}, \ldots, x_0)_s$, where $g^x = y \pmod{p}$, $x = \sum_{i=0}^{k-1} x_i s^i$, and $x_i \in [0, s-1]$ for $i \in [0, k-1]$.

1: $y_0 \leftarrow y$
2: Find $x_0 \in \mathbb{Z}_s$ such that $\left(g^{s^{k-1}}\right)^{x_0} = y_0^{s^{k-1}} \pmod{p}$.
3: **for** $1 \le i \le k - 1$ **do**
4: $\quad y_i \longleftarrow y_{i-1}\left(g^{-s^{i-1}}\right)^{x_{i-1}} \mod p$
5: $\quad$ Find $x_i \in \mathbb{Z}_s$ such that $\left(g^{s^{k-1}}\right)^{x_i} = y_i^{s^{k-i-1}} \pmod{p}$.
6: **end for**
7: **return** $\mathbf{x} = (x_{k-1}, \ldots, x_0)_s$

Remark 1 (Hints for Optimization). From line 2 and line 5 in Algorithm 1, we can see that values of $\left(g^{s^{k-1}}\right)^i \mod p$ for each $i \in [0, s-1]$ are used repeatedly. Hence, we can save the computational cost by pre-computing and storing these values. Similar method can be also applied to $g^{-s^i} \mod p$ for each $i \in [0, k-1]$ to save more computational cost.

Furthermore, according to line 4 in Algorithm 1, we have that

$$y_i^{s^{k-i-1}} = \left(y_{i-1}\left(g^{-s^{i-1}}\right)^{x_{i-1}}\right)^{s^{k-i-1}} = y_{i-1}^{s^{k-i-1}}\left(g^{-s^{k-2}}\right)^{x_{i-1}} \pmod{p}.$$

We can save the cost of computing $y_i^{s^{k-i-1}}$ if we have known the value of $y_{i-1}^{s^{k-i-1}}$, which can be recorded during the computing process of $y_{i-1}^{s^{k-(i-1)-1}}$. However, this optimization cannot be applied for every y_i ($i \in [0, k-1]$). It is because that once the computation of $y_i^{s^{k-i-1}}$ is based on the value of $y_{i-1}^{s^{k-(i-1)-1}}$, there is no $y_i^{s^{k-i-2}}$ for computing $y_{i+1}^{s^{k-i-2}}$. As a result, this optimization can only be applied on the odd indices.

3.2 A New Assumption from Power Residue Symbols

In this subsection, we would like to give a new assumption named (e_p, e_q)-th power residue (denoted as (e_p, e_q)-PR) assumption which will be used in our proposed public key encryption in Sect. 4 and lossy trapdoor functions in Sect. 5.1. We set that $\mathbb{ER}_N^e = \{x | \exists y \in \mathbb{Z}_N^*, y^e = x \pmod{N}\}$ and

$$\mathbb{NR}_N^{(e_p, e_q)} = \left\{ x \;\middle|\; x \in \mathbb{Z}_N^*, \left(\frac{x}{\mathfrak{a}}\right)_t = 1, \left(\frac{x}{\mathfrak{p}}\right)_{e_p} \text{ and } \left(\frac{x}{\mathfrak{q}}\right)_{e_q} \text{ are primitive} \right\},$$

where N, e_p, e_q, $\mathfrak{p}$, and $\mathfrak{q}$ are the same as those in Sect. 3.1, $\mathfrak{a} = \mathfrak{p}\mathfrak{q}$, and $t = \gcd(p-1, q-1)$. We define the (e_p, e_q)-PR assumption as follows.

Definition 2 ((e_p, e_q)-th Power Residue Assumption). *Given a security parameter κ and $N, (e_p, e_q), \mu, x$, it is intractable to decide whether x is in* $\mathrm{ER}_N^{\mathrm{lcm}(e_p,e_q)}$ *or* $\mathrm{NR}_N^{(e_p,e_q)}$ *if x is chosen at random from* $\mathrm{ER}_N^{\mathrm{lcm}(e_p,e_q)}$ *and* $\mathrm{NR}_N^{(e_p,e_q)}$. *Formally, the advantage* $\mathrm{Adv}_{\mathcal{A}}^{(e_p,e_q)\text{-PR}}(\kappa)$ *defined as*

$$\left| \mathrm{Prob}\left[\mathcal{A}\left(N, \mathrm{lcm}(e_p, e_q), \mu, x\right) = 1 \;\middle|\; x \xleftarrow{R} \mathrm{ER}_N^{\mathrm{lcm}(e_p,e_q)} \right] - \right.$$
$$\left. \mathrm{Prob}\left[\mathcal{A}\left(N, \mathrm{lcm}(e_p, e_q), \mu, x\right) = 1 \;\middle|\; x \xleftarrow{R} \mathrm{NR}_N^{(e_p,e_q)} \right] \right|$$

is negligible for any PPT *adversary $\mathcal{A}$; the probabilities are taken over the experiment of generating $(N, (e_p, e_q), \mu)$ with respect to the security parameter κ and choosing at random x from* $\mathrm{ER}_N^{\mathrm{lcm}(e_p,e_q)}$ *and* $\mathrm{NR}_N^{(e_p,e_q)}$.

Remark 2. It is easy to see that if we set $t = 2$, $e_p = 2$ and $e_q = 1$, the (e_p, e_q)-PR assumption becomes the standard quadratic residuosity (QR) assumption with $\gcd(p-1, q-1) = 2$. Furthermore, if we set $t = 2$, $e_p = 2^k$ and $e_q = 1$, the (e_p, e_q)-PR assumption becomes the Gap-2^k-Res assumption with $q = 3 \pmod 4$ which has been used in [1] and [3]. From [3, Theorem 2], we note that the Gap-2^k-Res assumption with $q = 3 \pmod 4$ solely relies on a QR-based assumption, namely, the k-QR assumption.

3.3 Some Properties of Power Residue Symbols

In this subsection, we present some properties of the power residue symbol that will be used in the design of circular and leakage resilient public key encryption (especially for the instantiation of *subgroup indistinguishability assumption*) in Sect. 5.2. Note that only in this subsection and Sect. 5.1, we require that $e_q = e_p = e$.

If $e_q = e_p = e$, according to the result in [17], we have

$$\mathfrak{a}_i = \mathfrak{p}_i \mathfrak{q}_i, \quad \mathrm{Norm}(\mathfrak{a}_i) = N, \quad \text{and} \quad N\mathbb{Z}[\zeta_e] = \prod_{i \in \mathbb{Z}_e^*} \mathfrak{a}_i,$$

where $p\mathbb{Z}[\zeta_e] = \prod_{i \in \mathbb{Z}_e^*} \mathfrak{p}_i$, $\mathrm{Norm}(\mathfrak{p}_i) = p$, $q\mathbb{Z}[\zeta_e] = \prod_{i \in \mathbb{Z}_e^*} \mathfrak{q}_i$, $\mathrm{Norm}(\mathfrak{q}_i) = q$, and $\mathfrak{a}_i = N\mathbb{Z}[\zeta_e] + (\zeta_e - \mu^i)\mathbb{Z}[\zeta_e]$ for each $i \in \mathbb{Z}_e^*$. Let $\mathfrak{a} = \mathfrak{a}_1$.

Let $\mathrm{ER}_\Delta = \{x \in \mathbb{Z}_N^* \mid \exists y, y^e = x \pmod \Delta\}$, $\mathbb{J}_N^e = \{x \in \mathbb{Z}_N^* \mid \left(\frac{x}{\mathfrak{a}}\right)_e = 1\}$, and $\mathcal{U} = \{\zeta_e^i \mid i \in [0, e-1]\}$, where $\Delta \in \{p, q, N\}$. We have the following theorems.

Theorem 2. $\mathbb{Z}_p^* / \mathrm{ER}_p^e \cong \mathcal{U} \cong \mathbb{Z}_q^* / \mathrm{ER}_q^e$.

Proof. We would like to prove $\mathbb{Z}_p^* / \mathrm{ER}_p^e \cong \mathcal{U}$ at first. Consider the homomorphism $\theta : \mathbb{Z}_p^* \mapsto \mathcal{U}$ defined by $x \mapsto \left(\frac{x}{\mathfrak{p}}\right)_e$. Since the number of the distinct roots of the polynomial $f(x) = x^{(p-1)/e} - 1$ over the field $\mathbb{Z}[\zeta_e]/\mathfrak{p}$ is at most $(p-1)/e$ and the cardinality of ER_p^e is exactly $(p-1)/e$, we know that an element $z \in \mathbb{Z}_p^*$

satisfying $\left(\frac{z}{p}\right)_e = 1$ must lie in $\mathbf{ER}_p^e$. Hence, we have that the kernel of θ is $\mathbf{ER}_p^e$, i.e., the homomorphism $\tau : \mathbb{Z}_p^*/\mathbf{ER}_p^e \mapsto \mathcal{U}$ induced by θ is a monomorphism. Furthermore, we know the cardinality of $\mathbb{Z}_p^*/\mathbf{ER}_p^e$ equals to e, which is also the value of the cardinality of $\mathcal{U}$. As a result, $\mathbb{Z}_p^*/\mathbf{ER}_p^e \cong \mathcal{U}$.

Similarly, we can get $\mathbb{Z}_q^*/\mathbf{ER}_q^e \cong \mathcal{U}$. Hence, we accomplish the proof.   □

Theorem 3. *If the condition* $\gcd((p-1)/e, e) = \gcd((q-1)/e, e) = 1$ *holds, then there exists an integer* ν *satisfying the following properties.*

- ν *is a non-degenerate primitive* (e, e)-*th root of unity modulo* N.
- $\left(\frac{\nu}{a_i}\right)_e = 1$ *for every* $i \in \mathbb{Z}_e^*$.
- $\mathbf{J}_N^e = \langle \nu \rangle \otimes \mathbf{ER}_N^e$.

Proof. The proof is given one by one.

- The condition $\gcd((p-1)/e, e) = \gcd((q-1)/e, e) = 1$ implies that there exist integers $s_p \in \mathbb{Z}_e^*$, $t_p, s_q \in \mathbb{Z}_e^*$, t_q such that $s_p\frac{p-1}{e} + t_p e = s_q\frac{q-1}{e} + t_q e = 1$. Let $\mu_p = \mu \pmod{p}$ and $\mu_q = \mu \pmod{q}$. We can get a non-degenerate primitive (e, e)-th root of unity modulo N by the following congruences.

$$\nu = \mu_p^{s_p} \pmod{p}$$
$$\nu = \mu_q^{-s_q} \pmod{q}$$

- When ν is generated as above, we have

$$\left(\frac{\nu}{p}\right)_e = \left(\frac{\mu_p^{s_p}}{p}\right)_e = \left(\frac{\zeta_e^{s_p}}{p}\right)_e = \zeta_e^{\frac{p-1}{e}s_p},$$
$$\left(\frac{\nu}{q}\right)_e = \left(\frac{\mu_q^{-s_q}}{q}\right)_e = \left(\frac{\zeta_e^{-s_q}}{q}\right)_e = \zeta_e^{-\frac{q-1}{e}s_q}.$$

Consequently,

$$\left(\frac{\nu}{a}\right)_e = \left(\frac{\nu}{p}\right)_e \left(\frac{\nu}{q}\right)_e = 1.$$

Since $\nu \in \mathbb{Z}$, the result $\left(\frac{\nu}{a_i}\right)_e = 1$ for each $i \in \mathbb{Z}_e^*$ follows immediately from Galois theory.

- To prove the last property we only need to prove that every element of $\mathbf{J}_N^e$ can be written as a product of two elements in $\langle \nu \rangle$ and $\mathbf{ER}_N^e$ respectively since $\langle \nu \rangle \cap \mathbf{ER}_N^e = \{1\}$. For any $x \in \mathbf{J}_N^e$, since there exists $j \in \mathbb{Z}_e$ such that $\left(\frac{\nu^j}{p}\right)_e = \left(\frac{x}{p}\right)_e$ and $\left(\frac{\nu^j}{q}\right)_e = \left(\frac{x}{q}\right)_e$, we have $x = \nu^j y^e \pmod{p}$ and $x = \nu^j z^e \pmod{q}$ for some $x \in \mathbb{Z}_p^*$ and $y \in \mathbb{Z}_q^*$ from Theorem 2. Take $w = y \pmod{p}$ and $w = z \pmod{q}$; then we have $x = \nu^j w^e \pmod{N}$, as desired.

As a result, we obtain this theorem.   □

Remark 3. From Theorem 3, when $e = 2$, we derive the well-known result: $\mathbf{J}_N \cong \{-1, +1\} \otimes \mathbf{QR}_N$, where N is a *Blum integer*, $\mathbf{J}_N = \{x \in \mathbb{Z}_N^* \mid \left(\frac{x}{N}\right)_2 = 1\}$, and $\mathbf{QR}_N = \{x \mid \exists y \in \mathbb{Z}_N^*, x = y^2 \pmod{N}\}$.

4   A New Homomorphic Public Key Cryptosystem

In this section, we present a natural extension of the GM scheme [18] by virtue of the power residue symbol.

4.1   Description

KeyGen (1^κ): Given a security parameter κ, KeyGen outputs the public and private key pair as follows:

$$\mathtt{pk} = \{N, \mathrm{lcm}(e_p, e_q), y\}, \quad \mathtt{sk} = \{p, q, e_p, e_q, \mu\},$$

where $N = pq$, $e_p | p-1$, $e_q | q-1$, p and q are large primes, e_p and e_q are smooth integers, y is chosen randomly from $\mathbb{NR}_N^{(e_p,e_q)}$, and μ is a non-degenerate primitive (e_p, e_q)-th root of unity modulo N. Note that μ is generated by definition.

Enc $(\mathtt{pk}, m)$: To encrypt a message $m \in \mathbb{Z}_{\mathrm{lcm}(e_p,e_q)}$, Enc picks a random $r \in \mathbb{Z}_N$ and returns the ciphertext

$$c = y^m r^{\mathrm{lcm}(e_p,e_q)} \mod N.$$

Dec $(\mathtt{sk}, c)$: Given the ciphertext c and the private key $\mathtt{sk} = \{p, q, e_p, e_q, \mu\}$, Dec first computes z_p and z_q satisfying $\left(\frac{c}{\mathfrak{p}}\right)_{e_p} = \zeta_{e_p}^{z_p}$ and $\left(\frac{c}{\mathfrak{q}}\right)_{e_q} = \zeta_{e_q}^{z_q}$ by means of Theorem 1. Then, Dec recovers the message $m \in \mathbb{Z}_{\mathrm{lcm}(e_p,e_q)}$ from

$$m = z_p k_p^{-1} \pmod{e_p} \quad \text{and} \quad m = z_q k_q^{-1} \pmod{e_q} \tag{1}$$

via the Chinese Remainder Theorem with non-pairwise coprime moduli, where k_p, k_q satisfying $\left(\frac{y}{\mathfrak{p}}\right)_{e_p} = \zeta_{e_p}^{k_p}$ and $\left(\frac{y}{\mathfrak{q}}\right)_{e_q} = \zeta_{e_q}^{k_q}$ respectively, can be pre-computed.

CORRECTNESS. The correctness and the additive homomorphism property of the above public key encryption can be easily obtained by the following arguments:

$$\zeta_{e_p}^{z_p} = \left(\frac{c}{\mathfrak{p}}\right)_{e_p} = \left(\frac{y^m r^{\mathrm{lcm}(e_p,e_q)}}{\mathfrak{p}}\right)_{e_p} = \left(\frac{y}{\mathfrak{p}}\right)_{e_p}^m = \zeta_{e_p}^{mk_p}, \text{ and}$$

$$\zeta_{e_q}^{z_q} = \left(\frac{c}{\mathfrak{q}}\right)_{e_q} = \left(\frac{y^m r^{\mathrm{lcm}(e_p,e_q)}}{\mathfrak{q}}\right)_{e_q} = \left(\frac{y}{\mathfrak{q}}\right)_{e_q}^m = \zeta_{e_q}^{mk_q}$$

Thus, we derive the formula (1). Since every message $m \in \mathbb{Z}_{\mathrm{lcm}(e_p,e_q)}$ corresponds to the unique pair $(\alpha, \beta) \in \mathbb{Z}_{e_p} \times \mathbb{Z}_{e_q}$ such that $m = \alpha \pmod{e_p}$ and $m = \beta \pmod{e_q}$, the decryption algorithm recovers the unique $m \in \mathbb{Z}_{\mathrm{lcm}(e_p,e_q)}$ from the formula (1). Furthermore, the scheme is homomorphic for the addition modulo $\ell = \mathrm{lcm}(e_p, e_q)$: if $c_0 = y^{m_0} r_0^\ell \pmod{N}$ and $c_1 = y^{m_1} r_1^\ell \pmod{N}$ are the ciphertexts of two messages m_0 and m_1 respectively, then $c_0 \cdot c_1 = y^{m_0+m_1}(r_0 r_1)^\ell$ $\pmod{N}$ is a valid ciphertext of $(m_0 + m_1) \mod \ell$.

4.2 Security Analysis

The security of the above public key encryption scheme can be obtained by the similar security analysis as for the GM scheme.

Theorem 4. *Our proposed public key encryption is* IND-CPA *secure under the* (e_p, e_q)*-*PR *assumption.*

Proof. Consider changing the distribution of the public key. Under the (e_p, e_q)-PR assumption, we may choose y uniformly in $\mathbb{ER}_N^{\text{lcm}(e_p, e_q)}$ instead of choosing it from $\mathbb{NR}_N^{(e_p, e_q)}$, while this is done without noticing the adversary. In this case, the ciphertext carries no information about the message and hence our proposed public key encrypiton is IND-CPA secure. □

4.3 Parameter Selection

As described in the algorithm KeyGen, p and q are large primes, $p = 1 \pmod{e_p}$, $q = 1 \pmod{e_q}$, and both e_p and e_q only contain small prime factors. In practice, it would be preferable to choose p, q, e_p, e_q such that $0 \leq \log e_p < \frac{\log p}{2}$, $0 \leq \log e_q < \frac{\log q}{2}$, where p and q are efficiently generated in a similar way as in [3, Sect. 5.1]. The major difference is that the size of $\log e_p + \log e_q$ is bounded by $\frac{\log N}{2}$. The reason is provided by the following proposition related to Coppersmith's method for finding small roots of bivariate modular equations.

Proposition 1 [32, Lemma 8]. *Let p and q be equally sized primes and $N = pq$. Let* d *be a divisor of $\varphi(N) = (p-1)(q-1)$. If there exists a positive constant* c *such that* d $> N^{\frac{1}{2}+c}$ *holds, then there exists a* PPT *algorithm that given N and* d*, it factorizes N.*

Note that taking $\frac{\log N}{4} < \log e_p + \log e_q < \frac{\log N}{2}$ does not contradict the setting of Φ-*Hiding Assumption* [10] as the prime factors of $\varphi(N)$ known to the public are very small. However, $\log e_p + \log e_q$ shall not be close to $\frac{\log N}{2}$ because we don't know whether there exists an attack of mixing together Coppersmith's attack and exhaustive searches. In particular, if we take $e_p = 2^k$, $e_q = 1$ and $k > \frac{\log N}{4}$, the low-order $\frac{\log N}{4}$ bits of p is revealed to an adversary, and hence it can factorize N by implementing Coppersmith's attack [16]. Therefore, if we choose e_p and e_q not to be a power of 2 and to be coprime, we may handle messages at least twice as long as the JL scheme does. The key generation algorithm also requires a random integer $y \in \mathbb{Z}_N^*$ sampled from $\mathbb{NR}_N^{(e_p, e_q)}$. We can use Theorem 2 and the following fact for uniformly sampling integers in $\mathbb{NR}_N^{(e_p, e_q)}$. Note that a random integer in $\mathbb{Z}_N^*$ has a probability of exactly $\frac{\varphi(e_p)\varphi(e_q)}{e_p e_q}$ of being in the set containing all $x \in \mathbb{Z}_N^*$ whose symbols $\left(\frac{x}{p}\right)_{e_p}$ and $\left(\frac{x}{q}\right)_{e_q}$ are primitive. Let $t = \gcd(p-1, q-1)$. We first choose at random an element $x \in \mathbb{Z}_N^*$ such that $\left(\frac{x}{p}\right)_t = \zeta_t^\alpha$ and $\left(\frac{x}{q}\right)_t = \zeta_t^\beta$ are primitive after several trials. Then, we can obtain a suitable element

$y \in \{\gamma \in \mathbb{Z}_N^* \mid \left(\frac{\gamma}{a}\right)_t = 1\}$ from the relations $y = x^{-(\alpha^{-1} \bmod t)} \beta z^t \pmod{p}$ and $y = x \pmod{q}$, where $z \xleftarrow{R} \mathbb{Z}_p^*$. If $y \in \mathbb{NR}_N^{(e_p, e_q)}$, we have done; otherwise, we repeat the above steps until y is in $\mathbb{NR}_N^{(e_p, e_q)}$.

4.4 Performance and Comparisons

The prominent operation in the JL scheme and our proposal is the modular multiplications over $\mathbb{Z}_p^*$, if the time for searching an item in a look-up table is negligible. For decrypting a 128-bit message, the JL scheme, according to the remark following [3, Algorithm 1], roughly needs

$$\log p - 128 + \frac{128(128-1)}{4} + \frac{128}{2} = \log p + 4000$$

modular multiplications on average. On the contrary, our proposal (specially Algorithm 1 with optimization) only needs about

$$\log p - 128 + \sum_{\substack{k=0 \\ k \text{ is even}}}^{12} \log(929^k) + 128 \approx \log p + 414$$

modular multiplications on average, when we set $e_p = 929^{13} > 2^{128}$ and $e_q = 1$. If N is taken as 2048 bits, the decryption of our proposal is approximately 3.5 times faster than that of the JL scheme. We note that both JL scheme and our proposal can be used to encrypt a 128- or 256-bit symmetric key in a KEM/DEM construction [30].

On the other hand, our proposal has the similar computational cost with the CDWS scheme in algorithms Enc and Dec. The main difference between these two schemes is the choice of y. In particular, in the setting of CDWS scheme, y is from $\left\{y \in \mathbb{Z}_N^* \mid \exists (x, x'), y^{\frac{p-1}{e_p}} = x \pmod{p}, y^{\frac{q-1}{e_q}} = x' \pmod{q}\right\}$, which is contained by $\mathbb{NR}_N^{(e_p, e_q)}$. This means that we can obtain y more efficiently than the CDWS scheme does. Furthermore, our security proof is much easier to follow due to the choice of y.

5 More Cryptographic Designs Based on the Power Residue Symbols

5.1 Lossy Trapdoor Functions

Lossy trapdoor functions (LTDFs) [28] were introduced by Peikert and Waters and since then numerous applications emerge in cryptography. Informally speaking, the LTDFs consist of two families of functions. The functions in one family are injective trapdoor functions, while functions in the other family are lossy, that is, the image size is smaller than the domain size. It also requires that the functions sampled from the first and the second family are computationally indistinguishable. Using the constructions in [28], one can obtain IND-CCA secure public key encryptions. So far, the LTDFs are mainly constructed from assumptions such as DDH [28], LWE [28], QR [17], DCR [17], and Φ-Hiding. [22].

Joye and Libert constructed LTDFs with short outputs and keys based on the k-QR, k-SJS and DDH assumptions in [3]. Of course, it is an easy matter to generalize their constructions, using our techniques based on the power residue symbols. Hence, we only propose a new generic construction of the LTDFs and the corresponding conclusions. We follow the definition of the LTDFs in [3] and omit the security analysis since it proceeds in exactly the same way in [3].

InjGen(1^κ): Given a security parameter κ, let ℓ_N, k and n (n is a multiple of k) be parameters determined by κ. InjGen defines $m = n/k$ and performs the following steps.
1. Select smooth integers e_p and e_q such that $k < \log(\text{lcm}(e_p, e_q)) < \ell_N/2$. Generate an ℓ_N-bit RSA modulus $N = pq$ such that $p - 1 = e_p p'$ and $q - 1 = e_q q'$ for large primes p, q, p', q'. Pick at random μ a non-degenerate primitive (e_p, e_q)-th root of unity modulo N and $y \overset{R}{\leftarrow} \mathbb{NR}_N^{(e_p,e_q)}$.
2. For each $i \in \{1, \ldots, m\}$, pick h_i in $\mathbb{ER}_N^{\text{lcm}(e_p,e_q)}$ at random.
3. Choose $r_1, \ldots, r_m \overset{R}{\leftarrow} \mathbb{Z}_{p'q'}$ and compute a $m \times m$ matrix $(Z_{i,j})_{i,j \in \{1,\ldots,m\}}$ with
$$Z_{i,j} = \begin{cases} y \cdot h_j^{r_i} \bmod N, & \text{if } i = j; \\ h_j^{r_i} \bmod N, & \text{otherwise.} \end{cases}$$

Output the evaluation key and the secret key as follows:
$$\text{ek} = \{N, Z\}, \quad \text{sk} = \{p, q, e_p, e_q, \mu, y\}.$$

LossyGen(1^κ): The process of LossyGen is identical to the process of InjGen, except that
  – Set $Z_{i,j} = h_j^{r_i} \bmod N$ for each $1 \le i, j \le m$.
  – LossyGen does not output the secret key sk.
Evaluation(ek, x): Given ek $= \{N, Z = (Z_{i,j})_{i,j \in \{1,\ldots,m\}}\}$ and a message $x \in \{0,1\}^n$, Evaluation parses x as a k-adic string $\boldsymbol{x} = (x_1, \ldots, x_m)$ with $x_i \in \mathbb{Z}_{2^k}$ for each i. Then, Evaluation computes and returns $\boldsymbol{y} = (y_1, \ldots, y_m) \in (\mathbb{Z}_N^*)^m$ with $y_j = \prod_{i=1}^m Z_{i,j}^{x_i} \pmod{N}$.
Inversion(sk, $\boldsymbol{y}$): Given sk $= \{p, q, e_p, e_q, \mu, y\}$ and $\boldsymbol{y} = (y_1, \ldots, y_m) \in (\mathbb{Z}_N^*)^m$, Inversion applies the decryption algorithm Dec(sk, y_j) of the cryptosystem in Sect. 4 for each y_j to recover x_j for $j = 1$ to m. Inversion recovers and outputs the input $x \in \{0,1\}^n$ from the resulting vector $\boldsymbol{x} = (x_1, \ldots, x_m) \in \mathbb{Z}_{2^k}^m$.

Proposition 2. *Let $\ell = n - \log(p'q')$. The above construction is a (n, ℓ)-LTDF if the (e_p, e_q)-th power residue assumption holds and the DDH assumption holds in the subgroup $\mathbb{ER}_N^{\text{lcm}(e_p,e_q)}$.*

Clearly, our new proposed LTDFs outperform those in [3] in terms of the decryption cost and the bandwidth exploitation. Specifically, our LTDFs have $\ell = n - \log(p'q') > (n - \ell_N) + \log e_p + \log e_q$ bits of lossiness. Therefore, the lossiness may also be improved since there are no known attacks against the factorization of N when $\ell_N/4 < \log e_p + \log e_q < \ell_N/2$ and $0 \le \log e_p < \frac{\log p}{2}, 0 \le \log e_q < \frac{\log q}{2}$.

5.2   Circular and Leakage Resilient Public Key Encryption

Brakerski and Goldwasser introduced the notion of *subgroup indistinguishability* (SG) **assumption** in [7, Sect. 3.1]. They instantiated the SG assumption based on the QR and the DCR assumptions and proposed a generic construction of schemes which achieve *key-dependent security* and *auxiliary-input security* based on the SG assumption. However, the scheme based on the QR assumption can only encrypt a 1-bit message at a time. In this subsection, we will show how to instantiate the SG assumption under another new hardness assumption named *e-th power residue assumption*. In this way, the scheme becomes much more efficient in bandwidth exploitation.

Definition 3 (Subgroup Indistinguishability Assumption [7]). *Given a security parameter κ, and three commutative multiplicative groups (indexed by κ) $\mathbb{G}_U$, $\mathbb{G}_M$ and $\mathbb{G}_L$ such that $\mathbb{G}_U$ is a direct product of $\mathbb{G}_M$ (of order M) and $\mathbb{G}_L$ (of order L) where $\mathbb{G}_M$ is cyclic and $\gcd(M, L) = 1$. We require that the generator h for $\mathbb{G}_M$ is efficiently computable from the description of $\mathbb{G}_U$. We further require that there exists a PPT algorithm that outputs $I_{\mathbb{G}_U} = (OP_{\mathbb{G}_U}, S_{\mathbb{G}_M}, S_{\mathbb{G}_L}, h, T)$ an instance of $\mathbb{G}_U$, where $OP_{\mathbb{G}_U}$ is an efficient algorithm performs group operations in $\mathbb{G}_U$, $S_{\mathbb{G}_M}, S_{\mathbb{G}_L}$ are efficient algorithms sample a random element from $\mathbb{G}_M, \mathbb{G}_L$ respectively and T is a known upper bound such that $T \ge M \cdot L$. For any adversary $\mathcal{A}$ we denote the subgroup distinguishing advantage of $\mathcal{A}$ by*

$$SGAdv[\mathcal{A}] = \left| \text{Prob}\left[\mathcal{A}(1^\kappa, x) \mid x \xleftarrow{R} \mathbb{G}_U\right] - \text{Prob}\left[\mathcal{A}(1^\kappa, x) \mid x \xleftarrow{R} \mathbb{G}_L\right]\right|$$

The subgroup indistinguishability assumption is that for any PPT adversary $\mathcal{A}$ it holds that for a properly sampled instance $I_{\mathbb{G}_U}$, we have that $SGAdv[\mathcal{A}]$ is negligible.

Now, we instantiate the SG assumption from the e-th power residue symbol. Let e be a smooth integer. We sample a random RSA modulus $N = pq$ such that $e = \gcd(p-1, q-1)$ and $\gcd((p-1)/e, e) = \gcd((q-1)/e, e) = 1$. Let $\mathbb{ER}_N^e$ and $\mathbb{J}_N^e$ be described as in Sect. 3.3. Then, there exists a $\nu \in \mathbb{J}_N^e \setminus \mathbb{ER}_N^e$ such that $\mathbb{J}_N^e = \langle \nu \rangle \otimes \mathbb{ER}_N^e$ from Theorem 3. The groups $\mathbb{J}_N^e$, $\langle \nu \rangle$ and $\mathbb{ER}_N^e$ are of orders $\varphi(N)/e$, e and $\varphi(N)/e^2$ respectively. We denote $\varphi(N)/e$ by N'. The condition $\gcd((p-1)/e, e) = \gcd((q-1)/e, e) = 1$ implicates that $\gcd(e, \varphi(N)/e^2) = 1$. We define as follows the e-th power residue (e-PR) assumption which is similar to the (e_p, e_q)-PR assumption defined previously.

Definition 4 (e-th Power Residue Assumption). *Given a security param-
eter κ. A* PPT *algorithm* RSAgen (κ) *generates a smooth integer e and a random*
RSA *modulus $N = pq$ such that $e = \gcd(p-1, q-1)$ and $\gcd((p-1)/e, e) = \gcd((q-1)/e, e) = 1$, and chooses at random μ a non-degenerate primitive (e, e)-th root of unity modulo N. The e-th Power Residue $(e\text{-PR})$ assumption* with
respect to RSAgen (κ) *asserts that the advantage* $\text{Adv}^{e\text{-PR}}_{\mathcal{A},\text{RSAgen}}(\kappa)$ *defined as*

$$\left| \text{Prob}\left[\mathcal{A}(N, x, e) = 1 \mid x \xleftarrow{R} \mathbb{ER}^e_N \right] - \text{Prob}\left[\mathcal{A}(N, x, e) = 1 \mid x \xleftarrow{R} \mathbb{J}^e_N \right] \right|$$

is negligible for any PPT *adversary $\mathcal{A}$; the probabilities are taken over the experiment of running $(N, e, \mu) \leftarrow$ RSAgen (κ) and choosing at random $x \in \mathbb{ER}^e_N$ and
$x \in \mathbb{J}^e_N$.*

Since there exist efficient sampling algorithms that sample a random element
from $\mathbb{ER}^e_N$ and $\mathbb{J}^e_N$ according to Theorems 2 and 3, the e-PR assumption leads
immediately to the instantiation of the SG assumption by setting $\mathbb{G}_U = \mathbb{J}^e_N$,
$\mathbb{G}_M = \langle \nu \rangle$, $\mathbb{G}_L = \mathbb{ER}^e_N$, $h = \nu$, and $T = N \geq eN'$. The corresponding encryption
scheme is presented as follows:

KeyGen (1^κ): Given a security parameter κ, KeyGen selects a smooth integer e
and samples a random RSA modulus $N = pq$ such that $e = \gcd(p-1, q-1)$
and $\gcd((p-1)/e, e) = \gcd((q-1)/e, e) = 1$. KeyGen selects an integer ν as
in Theorem 3, and an $\ell \in \mathbb{N}$ which is polynomial in κ. KeyGen also samples
$s \xleftarrow{R} (\mathbb{Z}_e)^\ell$ and sets the secret key $\text{sk} = s$. KeyGen then samples $g \xleftarrow{R} (\mathbb{ER}^e_N)^\ell$
and sets

$$g_0 = \left(\prod_{1 \leq i \leq \ell} g_i^{s_i} \right)^{-1} \mod N.$$

The public key is set to be $\text{pk} = \{N, g_0, g\}$.

Enc (pk, m): On inputting a public key $\text{pk} = \{N, g_0, g\}$ and a message $m \in \langle \nu \rangle$,
Enc samples $r \xleftarrow{R} \{1, 2, \ldots, N^2\}$ and computes $c = g^r \mod N$ and $c_0 = m \cdot g_0^r$
$(\mod N)$. Enc returns the ciphertext (c_0, c).

Dec (sk, c): On inputting the secret key $\text{sk} = s$ and a ciphertext $\{c_0, c\}$, Dec
computes and returns $m = c_0 \cdot \prod_{1 \leq i \leq \ell} c_i^{s_i} \mod N$.

6   Conclusion

In this paper, we have made natural extension on the GM cryptosystem by using
the e-th power residue symbol, where e is merely required to be smooth in practice. Our proposals are proved to be secure under new well-defined assumptions.
Furthermore, they inherit all advantages from the JL cryptosystem and LTDFs,
also enhance the decryption speed as well as the efficiency of the bandwidth
utilization.

When applied to the Brakerski-Goldwasser framework for building circular
and leakage resilient public key encryptions, our scheme takes advantages of
the e-th power residue symbol rather than the Jacobi symbol, thereby is more
efficient in bandwidth utilization.

Acknowledgements. This work was supported in part by the National Natural Science Foundation of China (Grant No.61632012 and 61672239), in part by the Peng Cheng Laboratory Project of Guangdong Province (Grant No. PCL2018KP004), and in part by "the Fundamental Research Funds for the Central Universities".

References

1. Brakerski, Z., Gentry, C., Halevi, S.: Packed ciphertexts in LWE-based homomorphic encryption. In: Kurosawa, K., Hanaoka, G. (eds.) PKC 2013. LNCS, vol. 7778, pp. 1–13. Springer, Heidelberg (2013). https://doi.org/10.1007/978-3-642-36362-7_1

2. Benaloh, J.D.C.: Verifiable secret-ballot elections. Ph.D. thesis. Yale University, New Haven, CT, USA (1987)

3. Benhamouda, F., Herranz, J., Joye, M., Libert, B.: Efficient cryptosystems from 2^k-th power residue symbols. J. Cryptol. **30**(2), 519–549 (2016). https://doi.org/10.1007/s00145-016-9229-5

4. Blum, L., Blum, M., Shub, M.: A simple unpredictable pseudo-random number generator. SIAM J. Comput. **15**(2), 364–383 (1986)

5. Blum, M., Goldwasser, S.: An *efficient* probabilistic public-key encryption scheme which hides all partial information. In: Blakley, G.R., Chaum, D. (eds.) CRYPTO 1984. LNCS, vol. 196, pp. 289–299. Springer, Heidelberg (1985). https://doi.org/10.1007/3-540-39568-7_23

6. de Boer, K.: Computing the power residue symbol. Master's thesis. Nijmegen, Radboud University (2016). www.koendeboer.com

7. Brakerski, Z., Goldwasser, S.: Circular and leakage resilient public-key encryption under subgroup indistinguishability. In: Rabin, T. (ed.) CRYPTO 2010. LNCS, vol. 6223, pp. 1–20. Springer, Heidelberg (2010). https://doi.org/10.1007/978-3-642-14623-7_1

8. Brier, E., Ferradi, H., Joye, M., Naccache, D.: New number-theoretic cryptographic primitives. IACR Cryptology ePrint Archive 2019, 484 (2019). https://eprint.iacr.org/2019/484

9. Brier, E., Naccache, D.: The thirteenth power residue symbol. IACR Cryptology ePrint Archive 2019, 1176 (2019). https://eprint.iacr.org/2019/1176

10. Cachin, C., Micali, S., Stadler, M.: Computationally private information retrieval with polylogarithmic communication. In: Stern, J. (ed.) EUROCRYPT 1999. LNCS, vol. 1592, pp. 402–414. Springer, Heidelberg (1999). https://doi.org/10.1007/3-540-48910-X_28

11. Cao, Z.: A type of public key cryptosystem based on Eisenstein ring $\mathbb{Z}[\omega]$. In: Proceedings of the 3rd Chinese Conference of Source Coding, Channel Coding and Cryptography, pp. 178–186 (1988)

12. Cao, Z.: A new public-key cryptosystem based on k^{th}-power residues (full version). J. China Inst. Commun. **11**(2), 80–83 (1990)

13. Cao, Z., Dong, X., Wang, L., Shao, J.: More efficient cryptosystems from k-th power residues. IACR Cryptology ePrint Archive 2013, 569 (2013)

14. Caranay, P.C., Scheidler, R.: An efficient seventh power residue symbol algorithm. Int. J. Number Theor. **6**(08), 1831–1853 (2010)

15. Cohen, J.D., Fischer, M.J.: A robust and verifiable cryptographically secure election scheme (extended abstract). In: 26th Annual Symposium on Foundations of Computer Science, pp. 372–382. IEEE Computer Society (1985). https://doi.org/10.1109/SFCS.1985.2

16. Coppersmith, D.: Small solutions to polynomial equations, and low exponent RSA vulnerabilities. J. Cryptol. **10**(4), 233–260 (1997)
17. Freeman, D.M., Goldreich, O., Kiltz, E., Rosen, A., Segev, G.: More constructions of lossy and correlation-secure trapdoor functions. J. Cryptol. **26**(1), 39–74 (2013)
18. Goldwasser, S., Micali, S.: Probabilistic encryption. J. Comput. Syst. Sci. **28**(2), 270–299 (1984)
19. Ireland, K., Rosen, M.: A Classical Introduction to Modern Number Theory, vol. 84. Springer, New York (2013)
20. Joye, M.: Evaluating octic residue symbols. IACR Cryptology ePrint Archive 2019, 1196 (2019). https://eprint.iacr.org/2019/1196
21. Joye, M., Lapiha, O., Nguyen, K., Naccache, D.: The eleventh power residue symbol. IACR Cryptology ePrint Archive 2019, 870 (2019). https://eprint.iacr.org/2019/870
22. Kiltz, E., O'Neill, A., Smith, A.: Instantiability of RSA-OAEP under chosen-plaintext attack. J. Cryptol. **30**(3), 889–919 (2017)
23. Lemmermeyer, F.: Reciprocity Laws: From Euler to Eisenstein. Springer, Heidelberg (2013)
24. Naccache, D., Stern, J.: A new public key cryptosystem based on higher residues. In: CCS 1998, pp. 59–66. ACM (1998). https://doi.org/10.1145/288090.288106
25. Neukirch, J.: Algebraic Number Theory, vol. 322. Springer, Heidelberg (2013)
26. Okamoto, T., Uchiyama, S.: A new public-key cryptosystem as secure as factoring. In: Nyberg, K. (ed.) EUROCRYPT 1998. LNCS, vol. 1403, pp. 308–318. Springer, Heidelberg (1998). https://doi.org/10.1007/BFb0054135
27. Paillier, P.: Public-key cryptosystems based on composite degree residuosity classes. In: Stern, J. (ed.) EUROCRYPT 1999. LNCS, vol. 1592, pp. 223–238. Springer, Heidelberg (1999). https://doi.org/10.1007/3-540-48910-X_16
28. Peikert, C., Waters, B.: Lossy trapdoor functions and their applications. SIAM J. Comput. **40**(6), 1803–1844 (2011)
29. Pohlig, S.C., Hellman, M.E.: An improved algorithm for computing logarithms over GF(p) and its cryptographic significance. IEEE Trans. Information Theory **24**(1), 106–110 (1978). https://doi.org/10.1109/TIT.1978.1055817
30. Shoup, V.: Using hash functions as a hedge against chosen ciphertext attack. In: Preneel, B. (ed.) EUROCRYPT 2000. LNCS, vol. 1807, pp. 275–288. Springer, Heidelberg (2000). https://doi.org/10.1007/3-540-45539-6_19
31. Squirrel, D.: Computing reciprocity symbols in number fields. Undergraduate thesis, Reed College (1997)
32. Yamakawa, T., Yamada, S., Hanaoka, G., Kunihiro, N.: Adversary-dependent lossy trapdoor function from hardness of factoring semi-smooth RSA subgroup moduli. In: Robshaw, M., Katz, J. (eds.) CRYPTO 2016. LNCS, vol. 9815, pp. 3–32. Springer, Heidelberg (2016). https://doi.org/10.1007/978-3-662-53008-5_1

Revisiting the Hardness of Binary Error LWE

Chao Sun[1(✉)], Mehdi Tibouchi[1,2], and Masayuki Abe[1,2]

[1] Kyoto University, Kyoto, Japan
sun.chao.46s@st.kyoto-u.ac.jp
[2] NTT Secure Platform Laboratories, Tokyo, Japan
{mehdi.tibouchi.br,masayuki.abe.cp}@hco.ntt.co.jp

Abstract. Binary error LWE is the particular case of the learning with errors (LWE) problem in which errors are chosen in $\{0, 1\}$. It has various cryptographic applications, and in particular, has been used to construct efficient encryption schemes for use in constrained devices. Arora and Ge showed that the problem can be solved in polynomial time given a number of samples quadratic in the dimension n. On the other hand, the problem is known to be as hard as standard LWE given only slightly more than n samples.

In this paper, we first examine more generally how the hardness of the problem varies with the number of available samples. Under standard heuristics on the Arora–Ge polynomial system, we show that, for any $\epsilon > 0$, binary error LWE can be solved in polynomial time $n^{O(1/\epsilon)}$ given $\epsilon \cdot n^2$ samples. Similarly, it can be solved in subexponential time $2^{\tilde{O}(n^{1-\alpha})}$ given $n^{1+\alpha}$ samples, for $0 < \alpha < 1$.

As a second contribution, we also generalize the binary error LWE to problem the case of a non-uniform error probability, and analyze the hardness of the non-uniform binary error LWE with respect to the error rate and the number of available samples. We show that, for any error rate $0 < p < 1$, non-uniform binary error LWE is also as hard as worst-case lattice problems provided that the number of samples is suitably restricted. This is a generalization of Micciancio and Peikert's hardness proof for uniform binary error LWE. Furthermore, we also discuss attacks on the problem when the number of available samples is linear but significantly larger than n, and show that for sufficiently low error rates, subexponential or even polynomial time attacks are possible.

Keywords: Binary Error LWE · Algebraic attacks · Macaulay matrix · Sample complexity · Complexity tradeoffs · Lossy function family

1 Introduction

Most of the public-key cryptography deployed today, such as the RSA cryptosystem [15] and Diffie–Hellman key exchange [6], relies on the conjectured hardness of integer factoring or the discrete logarithm problem, both of which are known to be broken by sufficiently large quantum computers [16]. As the advent of such

© Springer Nature Switzerland AG 2020
J. K. Liu and H. Cui (Eds.): ACISP 2020, LNCS 12248, pp. 425–444, 2020.
https://doi.org/10.1007/978-3-030-55304-3_22

quantum computers becomes increasingly plausible, it is important to prepare the transition towards *postquantum cryptography*, based on problems that are believed to be hard even against quantum adversaries.

One such problem particularly worthy of attention is the learning with errors problem (LWE), introduced by Regev in 2005 [14]. LWE and its variants are at the core of lattice-based cryptography, which offers attractive constructions for a wide range of cryptographic primitives in the postquantum setting from encryption and signatures all the way to fully homomorphic encryption, combining good efficiency with strong security guarantees. From a security perspective, the nice feature of LWE is that, while it is in essence an *average-case problem* (and hence easy to generate instances for), it is nevertheless as hard as *worst-case* lattice problems, for suitable parameter choices.

In terms of efficiency, standard LWE itself has relatively large keys, but a number of variants have been proposed with excellent performance in an asymptotic sense or for concrete security levels. These include structured versions of LWE, like Ring-LWE [10], and instantiations in more aggressive ranges of parameters than those for which Regev's worst-case to average-case reduction holds.

An important example is *binary error LWE*, where the error term is sampled from $\{0,1\}$ (instead of a wider discrete Gaussian distribution). Binary error LWE is a particularly simple problem with various interesting cryptographic applications, such as Buchmann et al.'s efficient lattice-based encryption scheme for IoT and lightweight devices [5] (based on the ring version of binary error LWE, with the additional constraint that the secret is binary as well). However, the problem is not hard given arbitrarily many samples: in fact, an algebraic attack due to Arora and Ge [3] solves uniform Binary-Error LWE in polynomial time given around $n^2/2$ samples. The same approach can also be combined by Gröbner basis techniques to reduce the number of required samples [2]. On the other hand, Micciancio and Peikert [13] showed that the uniform binary error LWE problem reduces to standard LWE (and thus is believed to be exponentially hard) when the number of samples is restricted to $n + O(n/\log n)$. Thus, the hardness of binary error LWE crucially depends on the number of samples released to the adversary.

1.1   Our Results

In this paper, we show that a simple extension of the Arora-Ge attack (based on similar ideas as the Gröbner basis approach, but simpler and at least as fast) provides a smooth time-sample trade-off for binary error LWE: the attack can tackle any number of samples, with increasing complexity as the number of samples decreases. In particular, for binary error LWE with $\epsilon \cdot n^2$ samples ($\epsilon > 0$ constant), we obtain an attack in polynomial time $n^{O(1/\epsilon)}$, assuming standard heuristics on the polynomial system arising from the Arora-Ge approach (namely, that it is *semi-regular*, a technical condition that is in particular known to be satisfied with overwhelming probability by random polynomial systems). Similarly, for $n^{1+\alpha}$ samples ($0 < \alpha < 1$), we obtain an attack in subexponential time $2^{\tilde{O}(n^{1-\alpha})}$ (again assuming semi-regularity). The precise complexity for any concrete number of samples is also easy to compute, which makes it possible to precisely set parameters for cryptographic schemes based on binary error LWE.

In public-key encryption schemes, however, the number of samples given out to the adversary (as part of the public key) is typically of the form $c \cdot n$ for some constant $c > 1$. Therefore, it is neither captured by the Micciancio–Peikert security proof, nor within reach of our subexponential algebraic attack. In order to understand what additional results can be obtained with algebraic means in that range of parameters, we also generalize the binary error LWE to the non-uniform case, in which the error is chosen from $\{0, 1\}$ and the error is 1 with some probability p not necessarily equal to $1/2$.

We analyze this problem from two perspectives. On the one hand, we show that for any error rate $p \leq 1/2$, non-uniform binary error LWE is as hard as worst-case lattice problems given $n + O(pn/\log n)$ samples. This is a direct generalization of the hardness proof given by Micciancio and Peikert to the non-uniform case. On the other hand, we show that when the error rate is $p = 1/n^{\alpha}$ ($\alpha > 0$), there is a subexponential attack using only $O(n)$ samples (which is even polynomial time if $\alpha \geq 1$).

In order to show a clear view of our result, the hardness result for binary error LWE is depicted in Fig. 1. When the number of available samples is quadratic in dimension n, Arora-Ge algorithm gives a polynomial time attack. When the number of available samples is $n^{1+\alpha}(0 < \alpha < 1)$, we show a subexponential algebraic attack. Besides, on the one hand, the blue line corresponds to the Micciancio-Peikert hardness proof, where we generalize to the whole trapezoid. On the other hand, the red line corresponds to our attack against non-uniform binary error LWE.

1.2   Techniques

Macaulay Matrices. The basic Arora–Ge attack can be described as follows. Each binary error LWE sample provides a *quadratic equation* in the coefficients $s_1, \ldots, s_n$ of the secret key:

$$f(s_1, \ldots, s_n) = 0, \tag{1}$$

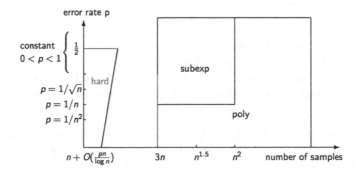

Fig. 1. Hardness Result for Binary Error LWE

obtained by observing that the corresponding error value is equal to either 0 or 1, and hence one of the two linear equations corresponding to these error values holds, so their product vanishes. Arora and Ge form a polynomial system with these equations and *linearize* it, replacing each of the monomials of degree ≤ 2 appearing in the system by a new variable, and solving that linear system. This is of course only possible if the number of equations is sufficiently large: one needs at least as many equations as there are monomials of degree ≤ 2 in $s_1, \ldots, s_n$, namely $\binom{n+2}{2} \approx n^2/2$.

To go beyond that bound, one can try and increase the degree of the system. Instead of deducing a single Eq. (1) from the binary LWE sample, one can derive $\binom{n+d}{d}$ equations by multiplying by all possible monomials of degree up to d, for some degree bound d to be chosen later:

$$
\begin{cases}
f(s_1, \ldots, s_n) = 0 \\
s_1 f(s_1, \ldots, s_n) = 0 \\
\quad \vdots \\
s_1 s_2 f(s_1, \ldots, s_n) = 0 \\
\quad \vdots \\
s_n^d f(s_1, \ldots, s_n) = 0
\end{cases}
$$

When linearizing, we get more variables since the degree of the system is larger and there are thus more monomials, but we also get many more equations, and on balance, the minimal number of samples to start with in order for the resulting system to be solvable decreases (although a naive bound obtained by comparing the number of equations and the number of variables is insufficient, since the equations are no longer necessarily linearly independent with high probability).

The matrix of that linear system is called the *Macaulay matrix* of degree d. The basic idea of the extended attack is basically to start with the Arora–Ge polynomial system, and find the minimal d such that the Macaulay matrix becomes full-rank. This is difficult to estimate in full generality, but assuming that the Arora–Ge system is semi-regular, this can be done using techniques from complex analysis.

From Uniform to Non-uniform. For the hardness proof for non-uniform binary error LWE, we follow the outline of Micciancio and Peikert's proof, but have to adapt the various parts of the proof that rely on the input distribution being uniform. For instance, their proof of uninvertibility uses the following lemma:

Lemma 1. *Let $\mathcal{L}$ be a family of functions on the common domain X, and let $\chi = \mathcal{U}(X)$ be the uniform input distribution over X. Then $(\mathcal{L}, \mathcal{X})$ is ϵ-uninvertible statistically, for $\epsilon = \mathbb{E}_{f \leftarrow \mathcal{L}}[|f(X)|]/|X|$.*

In the proof for this lemma, the uniform property of the input distribution serves as a key factor to bound the success probability of the adversary. Suppose that f is a function and the domain, range of f is denoted as X, Y respectively. If $y \in Y$ has several preimages, since the input distribution is uniform, the adversary can not do better than randomly guessing one preimage, even with unbounded computation power. However, this is not the case for a non-uniform input distribution. Suppose that the domain of f is $\{0, 1, 2, 3\}$ with probability $\{1/2, 1/6, 1/6, 1/6\}$ respectively and $f(0) = 0, f(1) = 0, f(2) = 0, f(3) = 1$. If the adversary is given $y = 0$, instead of randomly guessing, the adversary can get some advantage by guessing the preimage with the highest conditional probability, so the adversary can always output 0. If guessing randomly, the adversary only has $1/3$ probability of correctness, but if always guessing 0, the success probability becomes $(1/2)/(1/2 + 1/6 + 1/6) = 3/5$. Therefore, we need to prove new lemmas for non-uniform error distributions.

Our Algorithm to Attack Non-uniform Binary Error LWE. Our algorithm comes from a simple idea: Suppose that we have n samples from non-uniform binary error LWE with error rate $p = 1/n$, the probability that n samples are all error free is $(1 - 1/n)^n$. Since

$$\lim_{n \to \infty} (1 - 1/n)^n = 1/e$$

the probability is asymptotically a constant. Intuitively, we can have the following simple algorithm:

- Step 1: Get n samples from the LWE oracle.
- Step 2: By assuming that the n samples are error free, solve the linear system.
- Step 3: If this fails, go back to step 1.

Since the success probability is a constant asymptotically, this algorithm is supposed to end in polynomial time. However, this algorithm has some slight issues. The first issue is that the n samples may not guarantee that LWE is well defined. The second issue is that this algorithm runs in *expected* polynomial time and uses $O(n)$ samples *on average*, but these are not absolute bounds. To obtain a satisfactory algorithm, we need to modify the approach somewhat, and rely on careful tail bounds to analyze the resulting attacks.

2 Preliminaries

2.1 Learning with Errors

Definition 1 (LWE). *The (search) LWE problem, defined with respect to a dimension n, a modulus q and an error distribution χ over $\mathbb{Z}_q$, asks to recover a secret vector $\mathbf{s} \in \mathbb{Z}_q^n$ given polynomially many samples of the form*

$$(\mathbf{a}, \langle \mathbf{a}, \mathbf{s} \rangle + e \bmod q) \in \mathbb{Z}_q^n \times \mathbb{Z}_q \tag{2}$$

where $\mathbf{a}$ is uniformly random in $\mathbb{Z}_q^n$, and e is sampled according to χ. One can optionally specify the number of available samples as an additional parameter.

2.2 Arora-Ge Algorithm

Arora and Ge proposed an algebraic approach to the LWE problem, which essentially amounts to expressing LWE as a system of polynomial equations, and then solving that system by unique linearization techniques. More precisely, solving an instance $(\mathbf{A}, \mathbf{b})$ of the binary error LWE problem amounts to finding a vector $\mathbf{s} \in \mathbb{Z}_q^n$ (which is uniquely determined) such that for $i = 1, \ldots, m$, we have:

$$b_i - \langle \mathbf{a}_i, \mathbf{s} \rangle \in \{0, 1\},$$

where the vectors $\mathbf{a}_i$ are the rows of $\mathbf{A}$, and the scalars b_i the coefficients of $\mathbf{b}$. The idea of Arora and Ge is to rewrite that condition as:

$$\big(b_i - \langle \mathbf{a}_i, \mathbf{s} \rangle\big) \cdot \big(b_i - \langle \mathbf{a}_i, \mathbf{s} \rangle - 1\big) = 0,$$

which is a quadratic equation in the coefficients $s_1, \ldots, s_n$ of $\mathbf{s}$.

   In general, solving a multivariate quadratic system is hard. However, it becomes easy when many equations are available. Arora and Ge propose to solve this system using a simple linearization technique: replace all the monomials appearing in the system by a new variable.

   There are $\binom{n+2}{2} = (n+2)(n+1)/2$ monomials of degree at most 2. Therefore, if the number of samples m is at least $(n+2)(n+1)/2$, linearizing the quadratic system should yield a full rank linear system with high probability, and the secret $\mathbf{s}$ can be recovered by solving this linear system. This takes time $O\left(\binom{n+2}{2}^\omega\right) = O(n^{2\omega})$, and therefore shows that Binary-Error LWE can be solved in polynomial time given $m \approx n^2/2$ samples.

2.3 Function Family

A function family is a probability distribution $\mathcal{F}$ over a set of functions $\mathcal{F} \subset (X \to Y)$ with common domain X and range Y. Let $\mathcal{X}$ be a probability distribution over the domain X of a function family $\mathcal{F}$. We recall the following standard security notions:

One Wayness: $(\mathcal{F}, \mathcal{X})$ is (t, ϵ)-one-way if for all probabilistic algorithms $\mathcal{A}$ running in time at most t,

$$\Pr\left[f \leftarrow \mathcal{F}, x \leftarrow \mathcal{X} : \mathcal{A}(f, f(x)) \in f^{-1}(f(x))\right] \leq \epsilon$$

Uninvertibility: $(\mathcal{F}, \mathcal{X})$ is (t, ϵ)-uninvertible if for all probabilistic algorithms $\mathcal{A}$ running in time at most t,

$$\Pr[f \leftarrow \mathcal{F}, x \leftarrow \mathcal{X} : \mathcal{A}(f, f(x)) = x] \leq \epsilon$$

Second Preimage Resistance: $(\mathcal{F}, \mathcal{X})$ is (t, ϵ)-second preimage resistant if for all probabilistic algorithms $\mathcal{A}$ running in time at most t,

$$\Pr\left[f \leftarrow \mathcal{F}, x \leftarrow \mathcal{X}, x' \leftarrow \mathcal{A}(f, x) : f(x) = f(x') \wedge x \neq x'\right] \leq \epsilon$$

Pseudorandomness: $(\mathcal{F}, \mathcal{X})$ is (t, ϵ)-pseudorandom if the distributions $\{f \leftarrow \mathcal{F}, x \leftarrow \mathcal{X} : (f, f(x))\}$ and $\{f \leftarrow \mathcal{F}, y \leftarrow \mathcal{U}(Y) : (f, y)\}$ are (t, ϵ)-indistinguishable, where $\mathcal{U}(Y)$ denotes the uniform distribution over Y.

2.4 Lossy Function Families

Lossy function family is a concept introduced by Micciancio and Peikert, which is a general framework to prove the one-wayness of some functions.

Definition 2 (Lossy Function Families [13]). *Let $(\mathcal{L}, \mathcal{F})$ be two probability distributions(with possibly different supports) over the same set of (efficiently computable) functions $\mathcal{F} \subset X \to Y$, and let $\mathcal{X}$ be an efficiently sampleable distribution over the domain X. We say that $(\mathcal{L}, \mathcal{F}, \mathcal{X})$ is a lossy function family if the following properties are satisfied:*

- *the distributions $\mathcal{L}$ and $\mathcal{F}$ are indistinguishable.*
- *$(\mathcal{L}, \mathcal{X})$ is uninvertible.*
- *$(\mathcal{F}, \mathcal{X})$ is second preimage resistant.*

The following two lemmas are some properties of lossy function family.

Lemma 2 ([13]). *Let $\mathcal{F}$ be a family of functions computable in time t'. If $(\mathcal{F}, \mathcal{X})$ is both (t, ϵ)-uninvertible and $(t + t', \epsilon')$-second preimage resistant, then it is also $(t, \epsilon + \epsilon')$-one-way.*

Lemma 3 ([13]). *Let $\mathcal{F}$ and $\mathcal{F}'$ be any two indistinguishable, efficiently computable function families, and let $\mathcal{X}$ be an efficiently sampleable input distribution. Then if $(\mathcal{F}, \mathcal{X})$ is uninvertible(respectively, second-preimage resistant), then $(\mathcal{F}', \mathcal{X})$ is also uninvertible(resp., second preimage resistant). In particular, if $(\mathcal{L}, \mathcal{F}, \mathcal{X})$ is a lossy function family, then $(\mathcal{L}, \mathcal{X})$ and $(\mathcal{F}, \mathcal{X})$ are both one-way.*

2.5 SIS and LWE Function Family

The Short Integer Solution function family $\mathrm{SIS}(m, n, q, X)$ is the set of all functions f_A indexed by $\mathbf{A} \in \mathbb{Z}_q^{n \times m}$ with domain $X \subseteq \mathbb{Z}^m$ and range $Y = \mathbb{Z}_q^n$ defined as $f_\mathbf{A}(\mathbf{x}) = \mathbf{Ax} \bmod q$. The Learning With Errors function family $\mathrm{LWE}(m, n, q, X)$ is the set of all functions g_A indexed by $\mathbf{A} \in \mathbb{Z}_q^{n \times m}$ with domain $\mathbb{Z}_q^n \times X$ and range $Y = \mathbb{Z}_q^m$, defined as $g_\mathbf{A}(\mathbf{s}, \mathbf{x}) = \mathbf{A}^T \mathbf{s} + \mathbf{x} \bmod q$. The following theorems are needed in our proof.

Theorem 1 ([11,12]). *For any $n, m \geq n + \omega(log n), q$, and distribution $\mathcal{X}$ over $\mathbb{Z}^m$, the $LWE(m, n, q)$ function family is one-way (resp. pseudorandom, or uninvertible) with respect to input distribution $U(\mathbb{Z}_q^n) \times \mathcal{X}$ if and only if the $SIS(m, m - n, q)$ function family is one-way (resp. pseudorandom, or uninvertible) with respect to the input distribution $\mathcal{X}$.*

Theorem 2 ([13]). *For any positive* m, n, δ, q *such that* $\omega(\log n) \leq m - n \leq n^{O(1)}$ *and* $2\sqrt{n} < \delta < q < n^{O(1)}$, *if* q *has no divisors in the range* $((\delta/\omega_n)^{1+n/k}, \delta \cdot \omega_n)$, *then the* $SIS(m, m - n, q)$ *function family is pseudorandom with respect to input distribution* $D_{\mathbb{Z},\delta}^m$, *under the assumption that no (quantum) algorithm can efficiently sample(up to negligible statistical errors)* $D_{\wedge,\sqrt{2n}q/\delta}$. *In particular, assuming the worst-case (quantum) hardness of* $SIVP_{n\omega_n q/\delta}$ *on* n-*dimensional lattices, the* $SIS(m, m - n, q)$ *function family is pseudorandom with respect to input distribution* $D_{\mathbb{Z},\delta}^m$.

3   Sample-Time Trade-Off for Binary Error LWE

In this section, we use the Macaulay matrix approach to get a sample-time trade-off for the binary error LWE.

3.1   Hilbert's Nullstellensatz for Arora–Ge

Slightly informally, Hilbert's Nullstellensatz essentially states that the ideal generated by a family of polynomials $f_1, \ldots, f_m \in \mathbb{Z}_q[x_1, \ldots, x_n]$ coincides with the ideal of polynomials that vanish on the set $V(f_1, \ldots, f_m)$ of solutions of the polynomial system:

$$f_1(x_1, \ldots, x_n) = \cdots = f_m(x_1, \ldots, x_n) = 0$$

Now consider the application of Hilbert's Nullstellensatz to the polynomial system arising from Arora and Ge's approach to Binary-Error LWE. That system is of the form:

$$\begin{cases} f_1(x_1, \ldots, x_n) = 0 \\ \qquad \vdots \\ f_m(x_1, \ldots, x_n) = 0 \end{cases}$$

where $f_1, \ldots, f_m \in \mathbb{Z}_q[x_1, \ldots, x_n]$ are known quadratic polynomials. By the uniqueness of LWE solution, the set $V(f_1, \ldots, f_m)$ of solutions of that system is reduced to a single point:

$$V(f_1, \ldots, f_m) = \{(s_1, \ldots, s_n)\} = \{\mathbf{s}\},$$

namely, the unique solution of the Binary-Error LWE problem. It follows that the ideal $I = (f_1, \ldots, f_m) \subset \mathbb{Z}_q[x_1, \ldots, x_n]$ generated by the polynomials f_i coincides with the ideal of polynomial functions vanishing on $\{\mathbf{s}\}$, which is just $(x_1 - s_1, \ldots, x_n - s_n)$.

As a consequence, for $j = 1, \cdots, n$, there exists polynomials $g_{1j}, \cdots, g_{mj} \in \mathbb{Z}_q[x_1 \cdots x_n]$ such that:

$$g_{1j} \cdot f_1 + \cdots + g_{mj} \cdot f_m = x_j - s_j.$$

3.2   The Macaulay Matrix

Now consider the Arora-Ge approach of linearizing the polynomial system, except that we do not apply it to the quadratic system directly, but instead to an equivalent, expanded polynomial system. This expanded system is obtained by multiplying each equation $f_i = 0$ by all possible monomials of degree up to d, for some fixed $d \geq 0$. The d-th Macaulay linear system is then the linear system obtained by taking this expanded polynomial system and linearizing it, i.e., replacing each monomial appearing in the system by a new variable. Since the maximum degree is $d + 2$, the resulting linear system consists of $m\binom{n+d}{d}$ equations in $\binom{n+d+2}{d+2}$ unknowns. The matrix of the system is called Macaulay matrix.

Consider then the polynomials g_{ij} introduced above and let d be the maximum of their total degrees. Clearly, the polynomial $g_{1j} \cdot f_1 + \cdots + g_{mj} \cdot f_m$ is a linear combination of the polynomials appearing in the expanded system. But by definition, this polynomial is equal to $x_j - s_j$. Therefore, any solution of the d-th Macaulay linear system must assign the variable associated to x_j to s_j, the j-th coefficient of the actual solution s.

3.3   Semi-regularity

We can completely determine the cost of the approach above provided that we can determine the minimal value D sufficient to recover s, starting from a given number m of samples. This value D is called the degree of regularity of the system.

In general, the degree of regularity is difficult to compute, but has a tractable expression for a certain subclass of polynomial systems called semi-regular polynomial systems. It is believed that random polynomial systems are semi-regular with overwhelming probability,[1] and therefore assuming semi-regularity is a standard heuristic assumption.

We omit the formal definition of a semi-regular system here. For our purpose, it suffices to explain how the degree of regularity of a semi-regular system can be computed. Consider a polynomial system of m equations in n unknowns with $m > n$, defined by polynomials $f_1, \cdots, f_m$ of total degree $d_1, \cdots, d_m$ respectively, and introduce

$$H(z) = \frac{\prod_{i=1}^{m}(1 - z^{d_i})}{(1 - z)^{n+1}}$$

Note that this function H is a polynomial $1 + H_1 z + H_2 z^2 + \cdots$ with integer coefficients since $1 - z$ divides $1 - z^{d_i}$ for all i, and $m \geq n + 1$. If the polynomial system is semi-regular, then its degree of regularity D is the smallest j such that the coefficient H_j of degree j of H satisfies $H_j \leq 0$.

---

[1] More precisely, it is known that among of systems of m equations of prescribed degrees in n unknowns, non-semi-regular systems form a Zariski closed subset. It is believed that this subset has relatively large codimension, so that only a negligible fractions of possible systems fail to be semi-regular. This is related to a conjecture of Fröberg [9]. See e.g. [1, Sect. 1] for an extended discussion.

3.4   Application to Binary Error LWE

The Arora-Ge polynomial system arising from binary error LWE is a polynomial system as above with $d_1 = \cdots = d_m = 2$. Therefore, we can sum up the results of this section as the following theorem.

Theorem 3. *Under the standard heuristic assumption that the Arora-Ge polynomial system is semi-regular, one can solve Binary Error LWE in time $O(\binom{n+D}{D}^{\omega})$, where D is the smallest j such that the coefficient of degree j of the following polynomial*

$$H(z) = \frac{(1 - z^2)^m}{(1 - z)^{n+1}}$$

is non-positive.

One can apply this result for concrete instances of the binary error LWE problems. For instance, the first two parameter sets proposed for the scheme of Buchmann et al. [5] correspond to the case when $n = 256$ and $m = 2n = 512$. One can easily check that the first non-positive coefficient of $(1 - z^2)^{512}/(1 - z)^{257}$ is the coefficient of degree 30. Therefore, this algebraic attack reduces to solving a polynomial system in $\binom{256+30}{30} \approx 2^{135}$ unknowns.

The attack can in fact be improved due to the fact that the secret in that scheme is also binary, which provides n more quadratic equations of the form $s_i(s_i - 1) = 0$, for a total of 768. The first non-positive coefficient of $(1 - z^2)^{768}/(1-z)^{257}$ is the coefficient of degree 20, reducing the number of unknowns to $\binom{256+20}{20} \approx 2^{100}$. The resulting attack is better than the naive attack by guessing the error vector, but is worse than what can be achieved by lattice reduction techniques against the same parameters.

To estimate the complexity of the attack in more general cases, we simply need to find asymptotic estimates for the degree of the first non-positive coefficient of the polynomial H.

Remark 1. One can ask how this approach compares to simply applying Gröbner basis computation algorithm to the Arora–Ge polynomial system. The answer is that the two approaches are essentially equivalent (and in fact, some Gröbner basis algorithms such as Matrix-F4 for a suitable monomial ordering can be expressed in terms of Macaulay matrix [8]), but knowing the degree D in advance avoids the difficulties related to the iterative nature of Gröbner basis algorithms, and hence saves some polynomial factors in terms of asymptotic complexity. It also makes it clear that the problem reduces to solving a relatively sparse linear system (since the rows of the Macaulay matrix have only $O(n^2)$ nonzero coefficients among $O(n^D)$), which can yield to various algorithmic optimizations.

Nevertheless, our results can be regarded as closely related to the Gröbner-based analysis presented in [1]. The main difference is that we are interested in a wider range of asymptotic regimes in order to obtain a full, smooth time-sample trade-off.

3.5 Sample-Time Trade-Off

As discussed above, estimating the asymptotic complexity of our algebraic attack reduces to computing the degree of regularity D of the Arora-Ge polynomial system, which is equivalent to finding the degree of the smallest non-positive coefficient of $H_z = \frac{(1-z^2)^m}{(1-z)^{n+1}}$.

We consider two distinct asymptotic regimes: $m \sim \epsilon \cdot n^2$ for $\epsilon > 0$ and $m \sim n^{1+\alpha}$ for some $\alpha \in (0,1)$. The analysis in the first case can be done combinatorially in a way that is essentially fully explicit, and shows that the attack is polynomial time for any $\epsilon > 0$. The second case is more similar to previous cases considered in the literature, and can be dealt with using techniques from complex analysis as demonstrated by Bardet et al. [4]; the attack in that case is subexponential.

Attack with Quadratically Many Samples. Consider first the case $m \sim \epsilon \cdot n^2$ for some $\epsilon > 0$. We claim that the attack is then polynomial: this means in particular that the degree of regularity is constant. In other words, there exists a fixed d depending on ϵ such that for all large enough n, the d-th coefficient h_d of the Hilbert polynomial:

$$H_{m,n}(z) = \frac{(1-z^2)^m}{(1-z)^{n+1}} = (1-z)^{m-n-1}(1+z)^m = \sum_{d \geq 0} h_d z^d \qquad (3)$$

is non positive. To find this d, we can write down h_d explicitly, and try to estimate its sign for $n \to +\infty$. After some combinatorial computations (left to the full version of this paper), we find that the sign of h_d is related to the sequence $(P_d)_{d \geq 0}$ of polynomials with rational coefficients uniquely defined as follows:

$$P_0 = P_1 = 1 \qquad P'_k = -P_{k-2} \quad \text{(for all } k \geq 2) \qquad P_k(0) = \frac{1}{k!}.$$

The relationship between those polynomials and the problem at hand is as follows.

Lemma 4. *Suppose $m \sim \epsilon \cdot n^2$ for some $\epsilon > 0$, and fix $d \geq 0$. Then we have, for $n \to +\infty$:*

$$h_d = P_d(\epsilon) \cdot n^d + O(n^{d-1}).$$

In particular, the sign of h_d for sufficiently large n is the same as the sign of $P_d(\epsilon)$ as long as $P_d(\epsilon) \neq 0$.

Furthermore, the polynomials P_k can be expressed in terms of the well-known Hermite polynomials, and hence their roots are well-understood.

Lemma 5. *Let $H_k(x) = (-1)^k e^{x^2} \frac{d^k}{dx^k} e^{-x^k}$ be the k-th Hermite polynomial. Then we have:*

$$P_k(x^2) = \frac{x^k}{k!} H_k\left(\frac{1}{2x}\right)$$

for all $k \geq 0$. In particular, for $k \geq 2$, the roots of P_k are all real, positive, and simple. Denote by $x_k > 0$ the smallest root of P_k. The sequence $(x_k)_{k \geq 2}$ decreases towards 0, and we have $x_k \sim_{k \to +\infty} 1/(8k)$.

Combining the lemmas above, we obtain:

Theorem 4. *Suppose $m \sim \epsilon \cdot n^2$ (ϵ a positive constant), and let $(x_k)_{k \geq 1}$ be the decreasing sequence defined in Lemma 5, with the convention that $x_1 = +\infty$. Then the degree of regularity d_{reg} of a semi-regular system of m quadratic equations in n variables satisfies that $d_{\text{reg}} \leq d$ as soon as $\epsilon > x_d$. In particular, d_{reg} is always bounded, and if $\epsilon \notin \{x_2, x_3, \dots\}$, it is exactly equal to the unique d such that $x_d < \epsilon < x_{d-1}$. Furthermore, as ϵ approaches 0, it behaves as $d_{\text{reg}} \sim 1/(8\epsilon)$. The time complexity $O\left(\binom{n + d_{\text{reg}}}{d_{\text{reg}}}^{\omega}\right)$ of the attack on binary error LWE is always polynomial in this setting.*

Attack with Subquadratically Many Samples. We now turn to the case when $m \sim n^{1+\alpha}$ for some $\alpha \in (0, 1)$. As mentioned earlier, the attack in this case is subexponential.

Theorem 5. *For $m = n^{1+\alpha} + o(n)$ (α a constant in $(0, 1)$) quadratic equations in n variables, the degree of regularity d_{reg} of a semi-regular system behaves asymptotically as $d_{\text{reg}} \sim \frac{1}{8} n^{1-\alpha}$. The time complexity $O\left(\binom{n + d_{\text{reg}}}{d_{\text{reg}}}^{\omega}\right)$ of the attack on binary error LWE is then subexponential.*

The proof essentially follows [1, Appendix A.1].

Proof. Denote again by h_d the d-th coefficient of the Hilbert series.

$$H_{m,n}(z) = \frac{(1 - z^2)^m}{(1 - z)^{n+1}} = \sum_{d=0}^{\infty} h_d z^d \tag{4}$$

Since our goal is to determine the first index d such that h_d is non-positive, we try to estimate the behavior of h_d asymptotically as d increases. To do so, we write h_d as an integral using Cauchy's integral formula:

$$h_d = \frac{1}{2i\pi} \oint H_{m,n}(z) \frac{dz}{z^{d+1}}$$

where the integration path encloses the origin and no other singularity of $H_{m,n}(z)$. Since we are looking for the smallest value d such that h_d crosses from positive to negative, this amounts to solving for real $d > 0$ such that the integral vanishes. To do so, we estimate the integral using Laplace's method. Write:

$$h_d = \frac{1}{2i\pi} \oint e^{nf(z)} dz$$

for some function f. By identification, we have:

$$e^{nf(z)} = \frac{(1 - z)^{m-n-1}(1 + z)^m}{z^{d+1}},$$

which gives:

$$nf(z) = (m - n - 1)\log(1 - z) + m\log(1 + z) - (d + 1)\log z.$$

Laplace's method shows that the behavior is determined by the point z_0 where f vanishes (or the points in the case of multiple roots). Since we have:

$$nf'(z) = \frac{n - m + 1}{1 - z} + \frac{m}{1 + z} - \frac{d + 1}{z},$$

z_0 is a root of the quadratic equation:

$$(n - 2m + d + 2)z^2 + (n + 1)z - (d + 1) = 0.$$

If the discriminant Δ of this equation is not zero, it means that there are two distinct saddle points. The contribution of these two saddle points to the integral are conjugate values whose sum does not vanish. Hence the two saddle points must be identical, which means that $\Delta = 0$. Now:

$$\Delta = 4(d + 1)^2 + 4(n - 2m + 1)(d + 1) + (n + 1)^2 = 0.$$

Solving this equation, we get

$$d + 1 = m - \frac{n + 1}{2} - \sqrt{m(m - n)}.$$

Substituting $m = n^{1+\alpha}$, it follows that:

$$d + 1 = n^{1+\alpha} - \frac{n + 1}{2} - n^{1+\alpha}\sqrt{1 - \frac{1}{n^\alpha}}$$

$$= n^{1+\alpha} - \frac{n + 1}{2} - n^{1+\alpha}\left[1 - \frac{1}{2n^\alpha} - \frac{1}{8n^{2\alpha}} + o(n^{-2\alpha})\right]$$

$$= n^{1+\alpha} - \frac{n + 1}{2} - n^{1+\alpha} + \frac{n}{2} + \frac{1}{8}n^{1-\alpha} + o(n^{1-\alpha})$$

$$= \left(\frac{1}{8} + o(1)\right)n^{1-\alpha}$$

as required. One easily checks that the same estimate still holds for $m = n^{1+\alpha} + o(n)$, i.e., $m = (1 + t)n^{1+\alpha}$ for some $t = o(n^{-\alpha})$.

4   Hardness of LWE with Non-uniform Binary Error

In this section we analyze the hardness of non-uniform binary error LWE.

4.1   Hardness of Non-uniform Binary Error LWE with Limited Samples

First, we show that non-uniform binary error LWE is as hard as worst-case lattice problems when the number of available samples is restricted. We follow the outline of Micciancio-Peikert proof [13] (for some other similar work, see [7]), by constructing a lossy function family with respect to the non-uniform input distribution χ. As previously stated, we overcome the difficulty of transforming from uniform to non-uniform, hence adapting the various parts of proof that relies on the distribution being uniform. In order to prove $(\mathcal{L}, \mathcal{F}, \mathcal{X})$ is a lossy function family, we will prove:

- $\mathcal{L}$ is uninvertible with respect to $\mathcal{X}$.
- $\mathcal{F}$ is second preimage resistant with respect to $\mathcal{X}$.
- $(\mathcal{L}, \mathcal{F})$ are indistinguishable.

where $\mathcal{F} = \mathrm{SIS}(m, m-n, q)$ and $\mathcal{L} = \mathrm{SIS}(l, m-n, q) \circ \mathcal{I}(m, l, \mathcal{Y})$, where $\circ$ means the composition of two functions and $\mathcal{I}(m, l, \mathcal{Y})$ is defined in Definition 3.

Statistical Uninvertibility

Lemma 6. *Let m be a positive integer, $\mathcal{L}$ be a family of functions on the common domain $X = \{0, 1\}^m$, we define a non-uniform distribution χ over $\{0, 1\}^m$ such that each coefficient $x_i (i = 1, \cdots, m)$ is 1 with probability $p (0 < p < 1)$, and set $p' = \max(p, 1 - p)$. Then $\mathcal{L}$ is ϵ-uninvertible statistically w.r.t χ for $\epsilon = \mathbb{E}_{f \leftarrow \mathcal{L}}(p')^m \cdot |f(X)|$, where $|f(X)|$ means the number of elements in the range and $\mathbb{E}$ means taking the expectation over the choice of f.*

Proof. Fix any $f \leftarrow \mathcal{L}$ and choose a input x from the distribution χ. Denote $y = f(x)$. The best attack that the adversary can achieve is to choose the element with the highest conditional probability.

$$\Pr[\text{adversary can invert}] = \sum_x \Pr[x] \cdot \Pr[\text{adversary can invert given } f(x)]$$

$$= \sum_x \Pr[x] \cdot \Pr[\text{x is the preimage with highest conditional probability in } f^{-1}(f(x))]$$

$$= \sum_{y \in f(X)} \frac{\max_{x \in f^{-1}(y)} \Pr(x)}{\sum_{x \in f^{-1}(y)} \Pr(x)} \cdot \sum_{x \in f^{-1}(y)} \Pr(x) = \sum_{y \in f(X)} \max_{x \in f^{-1}(y)} \Pr(x)$$

All the possible probability for sampling x from χ is $p^k \cdot (1 - p)^{m-k}$ $(k = 0, 1, 2 \cdots m)$, we know that the maximum probability is $(\max(p, 1 - p))^m$. Then let $p' = \max(p, 1 - p)$, the result follows.

In order to establish a connection with standard LWE, the following definition is needed.

Definition 3 ([13]). *For any probability distribution $\mathcal{Y}$ over $\mathbb{Z}^l$ and integer $m \geq l$, let $\mathcal{I}(m, l, \mathcal{Y})$ be the probability distribution over linear functions $[I \mid Y] : \mathbb{Z}^m \rightarrow \mathbb{Z}^l$ where I is $l \times l$ identity matrix, and $Y \in \mathbb{Z}^{l \times (m-l)}$ is obtained choosing each column of Y independently at random from $\mathcal{Y}$.*

The following lemma shows that, for the Gaussian distribution, the function family $\mathcal{I}(m, l, \mathcal{Y})$ is statistically uninvertible.

Lemma 7. *Let m be a positive integer, χ be a not necessarily uniform distribution over $\{0,1\}^m$ such that each coefficient x_i $(i = 1, \cdots, m)$ is 1 with probability p $(0 < p < 1)$, $\mathcal{Y} = D^l_{\mathbb{Z},\delta}$ be the discrete Gaussian distribution with parameter $\delta > 0$, $p' = max(p, 1 - p)$. Then $\mathcal{I}(m, l, \mathcal{Y})$ is ϵ-uninvertible with respect to the non-uniform distribution χ, for $\epsilon = O(\delta m/\sqrt{l})^l \cdot (p')^m + 2^{-\Omega(m)}$.*

Proof. In order to use Lemma 6, we only need to bound the size of the range $f(X)$. Recall that $f = [I \mid Y]$ where $Y \leftarrow D^{l \times (m-l)}_{\mathbb{Z},\delta}$. Since the entries of $Y \in \mathbb{R}^{l \times (m-l)}$ are independent mena-zero subgaussians with parameter δ, by a standard bound from the theory of random matrices, the largest singular value $s_1(Y) = max_{0 \neq \mathbf{x} \in \mathbb{R}^m} ||Y x||/||\mathbf{x}||$ of Y is at most $\delta \cdot O(\sqrt{l} + \sqrt{m-l}) = \delta \cdot O(\sqrt{m})$, except with probability $2^{-\Omega(m)}$. We now bound the l_2 norm of all vectors in the image $f(X)$. Let $\mathbf{u} = (\mathbf{u_1}, \mathbf{u_2}) \in X$, with $u_1 \in \mathbb{Z}^l$ and $u_2 \in \mathbb{Z}^{m-l}$. Then

$$||f(\mathbf{u})|| \leq ||\mathbf{u_1} + Y\mathbf{u_2}|| \leq ||\mathbf{u_1}|| + ||Y\mathbf{u_2}|| \leq (\sqrt{l} + s_1(Y)\sqrt{m - l})$$
$$\leq (\sqrt{l} + \delta \cdot O(\sqrt{m})\sqrt{m - l}) = O(\delta m)$$

The number of integer points in the l-dimensional zero-centered ball of radius $R = O(\delta m)$ can be bounded by a simple volume argument, as $|f(X)| \leq (R + \sqrt{l}/2)^n V_l = O(\delta m/\sqrt{l})^l$, where $V_l = \pi^{l/2}/(l/2)!$ is the volume of the l-dimensional unit ball. From Lemma 6, and considering the event that $s_1(Y)$ is not bounded as above, we get that $\mathcal{I}(m, l, \mathcal{Y})$ is ϵ-uninvertible for $\epsilon = O(\delta m/\sqrt{l})^l \cdot (p')^m + 2^{-\Omega(m)}$.

Second Preimage Resistance

Lemma 8. *Let χ be a not necessarily uniform distribution over $\{0,1\}^m$ such that each coefficient x_i $(i = 1, \cdots, m)$ is 1 with probability p $(0 < p < 1)$. For any positive integers m, k, any prime q, the function family $SIS(m, k, q)$ is (statistically) ϵ-second preimage resistant with respect to the non-uniform distribution χ for $\epsilon = 2^m/q^k$.*

Proof. Let $\mathbf{x} \leftarrow \chi$ and $A \leftarrow SIS(m, k, q)$ be chosen at random. We want to evaluate the probability that there exists an $\mathbf{x}' \in \{0,1\}^m \backslash \{\mathbf{x}\}$ such that $A\mathbf{x} = A\mathbf{x}'(\text{mod } q)$, or equivalently, $A(\mathbf{x} - \mathbf{x}') = \mathbf{0}(\text{mod } q)$. Fix two distinct vectors $\mathbf{x}, \mathbf{x}' \in \{0,1\}^m$ and let $\mathbf{z} = \mathbf{x} - \mathbf{x}'$. Then considering taking the random choice of A, since all coordinates of $\mathbf{z}$ are in the range $z_i \in \{-1, 0, 1\}$ and at least one of them is nonzero, the vectors $A\mathbf{z}(\text{mod } q)$ is distributed uniformly at random in $(\mathbb{Z}_q)^k$, the probability of $A\mathbf{z} = \mathbf{0}$ (mod q) is $1/q^k$. Therefore, by using union bound(over $\mathbf{x}' \in X \backslash \{\mathbf{x}\}$) for any $\mathbf{x}$, the probability that there is a second preimage $\mathbf{x}'$ is at most $(2^m - 1)/q^k < 2^m/q^k$.

Indistinguishability of $\mathcal{L}$ and $\mathcal{F}$

Lemma 9. *Let $\mathcal{F} = SIS(m, m - n, q)$ and $\mathcal{L} = SIS(l, m - n, q) \circ \mathcal{I}(m, l, \mathcal{Y})$, where $\mathcal{I}(m, l, \mathcal{Y})$ is defined in Definition 3. If $SIS(l, m - n, q)$ is pseudorandom with respect to the distribution $\mathcal{Y}$, then $\mathcal{L}$ and $\mathcal{F}$ are indistinguishable.*

Proof. Choose a random input $\mathbf{x} \in \mathbb{Z}^m$. According to the definition of $\mathcal{F}$ and $\mathcal{L}$

$$\mathcal{L} : \mathbf{x} \to A[I|Y]\mathbf{x} \bmod q$$
$$\mathcal{F} : \mathbf{x} \to [A'_1, A'_2]\mathbf{x} \bmod q$$

With the property of block matrix multiplication, A can be divided into two blocks: A_1 is a $l \times l$ matrix, A_2 is a $(m - n - l) \times l$ matrix, so we have

$$\mathcal{L} : \mathbf{x} \to [A_1, A_2 Y]\mathbf{x} \bmod q$$
$$\mathcal{F} : \mathbf{x} \to [A'_1, A'_2]\mathbf{x} \bmod q$$

Since A_1 and A'_1 are uniformly random chosen, $A_1\mathbf{x}$ and $A'_1\mathbf{x}$ are indistinguishable. Recall that $\mathrm{SIS}(l, m-n, q)$ is pseudorandom with respect to the distribution $\mathcal{Y}$, thus $A_2 Y$ is indistinguishable from A'_2. Then we can conclude that $\mathcal{L}$ and $\mathcal{F}$ are indistinguishable.

One-Wayness

Theorem 6. *Let m, n, k ($0 < k \le n \le m$) be some positive integer, q be a prime modulus and let χ be a not necessarily uniform distribution over $\{0, 1\}^m$ such that each coefficient x_i ($i = 1, \cdots, m$) is 1 with probability p ($0 < p < 1$), $p' = max(p, 1 - p)$, and $\mathcal{Y}$ be the discrete Gaussian distribution $\mathcal{Y} = D^l_{\mathbb{Z}, \delta}$ over $\mathbb{Z}^l$, where $l = m - n + k$. If $\mathrm{SIS}(l, m - n, q)$ is pseudorandom with respect to the discrete Gaussian distribution $\mathcal{Y} = D^l_{\mathbb{Z}, \delta}$, then $\mathrm{SIS}(m, m - n, q)$ is $(2\epsilon + 2^{-\Omega(m)})$-one-way with respect to the input distribution χ if*

$$(C'\delta m/\sqrt{l})^l/\epsilon \le 1/(p')^m \text{ and } 2^m \le \epsilon \cdot (q)^{m-n}$$

where C' is universal constant in big O notation in Lemma 7.

Proof. We will prove that $(\mathcal{L}, \mathcal{F}, \mathcal{X})$ is a lossy function family, where $\mathcal{F} = \mathrm{SIS}(m, m - n, q)$ and $\mathcal{L} = \mathrm{SIS}(l, m - n, q) \circ \mathcal{I}(m, l, \mathcal{Y})$. It follows from Lemma 8 that $\mathcal{F}$ is second-preimage resistant with respect to χ. The indistinguishability of $\mathcal{L}$ and $\mathcal{F}$ follows from Lemma 9. By Lemma 7, we have the uninvertibility of $\mathcal{I}(m, l, \mathcal{Y})$, since $\mathcal{L} = \mathrm{SIS}(l, m - n, q) \circ \mathcal{I}(m, l, \mathcal{Y})$, the uninvertibility of $\mathcal{L}$ follows. With the three properties of lossy function family, we conclude that $(\mathcal{L}, \mathcal{F}, \mathcal{X})$ is a lossy function family. Then from the property of lossy function family with Lemma 3, this theorem is proved.

Instantiation for the LWE Parameter. After getting the hardness result for SIS function, the one-wayness of LWE function can be established.

Theorem 7 (LWE Parameter). *Let $0 < k \le n \le m$, $0 < p < 1$, $p' = max(p, 1 - p)$, $l = m - n + k$, $1/p' \ge (Cm)^{l/m}$ for a large enough universal constant C, and q be a prime such that $max(3\sqrt{k}, 8^{m/(m-n)}) \le q \le k^{O(1)}$. Let χ be a non-uniform distribution over $\{0, 1\}^m$ such that each coefficient x_i ($i = 1, \cdots, m$) is 1 with probability p, the $\mathrm{LWE}(m, n, q)$ function family is one-way* *with respect to the distribution $U_{\mathbb{Z}_q^n} \times \chi$. In particular, these conditions can be satisfied by setting $k = n/(c_2 \log_{1/p'} n)$, $m = n(1 + 1/(c_1 \log_{1/p'} n))$, where $c_1 > 1$ is any constant, and c_2 such that $1/c_1 + 1/c_2 < 1$.*

Proof. In order to prove the one-wayness of $\text{LWE}(m, n, q)$(SIS and LWE are equivalent according to Theorem 1) using Theorem 6, we need to satisfy the two requirements:

$$(C'\delta m/\sqrt{l})^l/\epsilon \leq 1/(p')^m \text{ and } 2^m \leq \epsilon \cdot (q)^{m-n}$$

Set $\delta = 3\sqrt{k}$, and with $l \geq k$, the first requirement can be simplified to $\frac{(3C'm)^l}{(1/p')^m} < \epsilon$. Since we have $1/p' \geq (Cm)^{l/m}$, so $(1/p')^m \geq (Cm)^l$. Let $C = 4C'$, we get that $\frac{(3C'm)^l}{(1/p)^m} \leq (3/4)^{-l} \leq (3/4)^{-k}$ is exponentially small in k, so the first inequality is satisfied. Since $q > 8^{m/(m-n)}$, the second inequality is also satisfied.

Besides, we also need to prove the pseudorandomness of $\text{SIS}(l, m-n, q)$ with respect to discrete Gaussian distribution $\mathcal{Y} = D_{\mathbb{Z},\delta}^l$, which can be based on the hardness of SIVP on k-dimensional lattice using Theorem 2. After properly renaming the variables, and using $\delta = 3\sqrt{k}$, the requirement becomes $\omega(\log k) \leq m - n \leq k^{O(1)}, 3\sqrt{k} < q < k^{O(1)}$. The corresponding assumption is the worst-case hardness of SIVP_γ on k-dimensional lattices, for $\gamma = \tilde{O}(\sqrt{k}q)$.

For the particular instantiation, let $m = n(1 + 1/(c_1 \log_{\frac{1}{p'}} n))(c_1 > 1)$, $k = n/(c_2 \log_{\frac{1}{p'}} n)$($c_2$ is a positive constant such that $1/c_1 + 1/c_2 < 1$). The requirement $1/p' \geq (Cm)^{l/m}$ is equivalent to $m \geq l \log_{1/p'} Cm$. Since we can do a asymptotic analysis:

$$l = m - n + k = (1/c_1 + 1/c_2)n/\log_{1/p'} n$$

and

$$\log_{1/p'} Cm = \log_{1/p'} Cn(1 + 1/log_{1/p'}n) \approx \log_{1/p'} n + \log_{1/p'} C$$

So we have

$$l \log_{1/p'} Cm \approx (1/c_1 + 1/c_2)n(1 + \log_{1/p'} C/\log_{1/p'} n)$$

When $(1/c_1 + 1/c_2) < 1$, $m \geq l\log_{1/p'} Cm$ asymptotically(we only need to consider the dominant term). This concludes the proof.

4.2   Attacks Against Non-uniform Binary Error LWE

Now we consider the case where the number of available samples is not so strongly restricted and the error rate is a function of n such that $p = 1/n^\alpha(\alpha > 0)$. We show an attack against LWE with non-uniform binary error given $O(n)$ samples. The idea behind our attack is quite simple:

- Step 1: Get n samples from the LWE oracle.
- Step 2: By assuming the n samples are all error free, solve the linear equation system.
- Step 3: If failed, go back to step1.

For instance, when the error rate $p = 1/n$, the probability that all samples are error free is:

$$\lim_{n \to \infty} (1 - 1/n)^n = 1/e$$

This means that our algorithm is expected to stop after polynomial times of trials. However, the number of total samples used is not bounded. Therefore, we slightly modified the algorithm as follows:

- Step 1: Get $3n$ samples from the LWE oracle.
- Step 2: Choose $2n$ samples randomly from the 3n samples got in step1.
- Step 3: By assuming the $2n$ samples are all error free, solve the linear equation system.
- Step 4: If failed, go back to step2.

We analyze the following two cases respectively:

- $p = 1/n^\alpha$ for any constant $\alpha \geq 1$.
- $p = 1/n^\alpha$ for any constant $0 < \alpha < 1$.

and have the following results:

Theorem 8. *By applying the above algorithm, for any positive constant $\alpha \geq 1$, non-uniform binary error LWE with error rate $p = 1/n^\alpha$ can be attacked in polynomial time with $O(n)$ samples, and for any positive constant $0 < \alpha < 1$, non-uniform binary error LWE with error rate $p = 1/n^\alpha$ can be attacked in subexponential time with $O(n)$ samples.*

Proof. Suppose that there are m errors within the $3n$ samples. The probability that $2n$ samples are all error free is

$$\Pr\,(\text{success}) = \frac{\binom{3n-m}{2n}}{\binom{3n}{2n}} = \frac{(3n-m)!}{(n-m)!(2n)!} \cdot \frac{(2n)!(n!)}{(3n)!} = \frac{(3n-m)!}{(n-m)!} \cdot \frac{(n!)}{(3n)!}$$

$$= \frac{n \cdots (n-m+1)}{3n \cdots (3n-m+1)} \geq \left(\frac{n-m}{3n}\right)^m \geq \left(\frac{1}{3} - o(1)\right)^m$$

provided that $m = o(n)$. With tail bound for binomial distribution,

$$\Pr(m \geq k) \leq \exp(-nD(\frac{k}{n}||p)) \text{ if } p < \frac{k}{n} < 1$$

where $D(a||p)$ is the relative entropy between an a-coin and a p-coin($0 < a < 1$ and $0 < p < 1$).

$$D(a||p) = a \log \frac{a}{p} + (1-a) \log \frac{1-a}{1-p}$$

We consider the cases $\alpha \geq 1$ and $0 < \alpha < 1$ separately.

Case 1: $\alpha \geq 1$ For this case, we set $k = \log n$.

$$D(\frac{k}{n}||p) = D(\frac{\log n}{n}||\frac{1}{n^{\alpha}}) = \frac{\log n}{n} \cdot \log(n^{\alpha-1}\log n) + (1 - \frac{\log n}{n})\log \frac{1 - \frac{\log n}{n}}{1 - \frac{1}{n^{\alpha}}}$$

$$= (\alpha - 1)\frac{(\log n)^2}{n} + \frac{\log n}{n}\log\log n + O\left(\frac{\log n}{n}\right).$$

Since $(\alpha - 1)\frac{(\log n)^2}{n}$ is the dominant term (or $\frac{1}{n}\log n \cdot \log\log n$ if $\alpha = 1$), we have that

$$\Pr(m \geq \log n) \leq \exp(-nD(\frac{k}{n}||p))$$

is negligible. Thus, with overwhelming probability on the choice of the initial $3n$ samples, there are $m \leq \log n$ erroneous samples. Thus, the probability that the $2n$ samples chosen in Step 2 are all error-free is bounded as:

$$\Pr(\text{success}) \geq (1/3 - o(1))^{\log n} = 1/\text{poly}(n)$$

and hence the secret key is recovered with overwhelming probability after polynomially many iterations of Steps 2–3 as required.

Note that it can never happen in that case that the algorithm returns an incorrect secret key: indeed, the linear system solved in Step 3 consists of $3n$ equations in n unknowns, $3n - m > 2n$ of which are error-free. Thus, it must either be rank-deficient (in which case it is not solvable) or contain at least n linearly independent equations with the correct solution, and thus if it is solvable, the correct secret key is the only possible solution.

Case 2: $0 < \alpha < 1$ For this case, we set $k = n^{1-\alpha}\log n$

$$D(\frac{k}{n}||p) = D(\frac{n^{1-\alpha}\log n}{n}||\frac{1}{n^{\alpha}}) = D(\frac{\log n}{n^{\alpha}}||\frac{1}{n^{\alpha}})$$

$$= \frac{\log n}{n^{\alpha}}\log\log n + (1 - \frac{\log n}{n^{\alpha}})\log\frac{1 - \frac{\log n}{n^{\alpha}}}{1 - \frac{1}{n^{\alpha}}} = \frac{\log n}{n^{\alpha}}\log\log n + O\left(\frac{\log n}{n^{\alpha}}\right).$$

The dominant term is $\frac{\log n}{n^{\alpha}}\log\log n$, so

$$\Pr(m \geq n^{1-\alpha}\log n) \leq \exp(-nD(\frac{k}{n}||p))$$

$$\leq \exp(-n^{1-\alpha}\log n \log\log n)$$

This probability is again negligible. Thus, as before, with overwhelming probability on the choice of the initial $3n$ samples, there are $m \leq n^{1-\alpha}\log n$ erroneous samples. As a result, the success probability at Steps 2–3 satisfies:

$$\Pr(\text{success}) \geq (1/3 - o(1))^{n^{1-\alpha}\log n} = 1/\text{subexp}(n)$$

This means that after repeating Steps 2–3 subexponentially times, we can recover the secret key with overwhelming probability.

References

1. Albrecht, M.R., Cid, C., Faugère, J., Fitzpatrick, R., Perret, L.: Algebraic algorithms for LWE problems. ACM Commun. Comput. Algebra **49**(2), 62 (2015)
2. Albrecht, M.R., Player, R., Scott, S.: On the concrete hardness of learning with errors. J. Math. Cryptol. **9**(3), 169–203 (2015)
3. Arora, S., Ge, R.: New algorithms for learning in presence of errors. In: Aceto, L., Henzinger, M., Sgall, J. (eds.) ICALP 2011. LNCS, vol. 6755, pp. 403–415. Springer, Heidelberg (2011). https://doi.org/10.1007/978-3-642-22006-7_34
4. Bardet, M., Faugere, J.C., Salvy, B., Yang, B.Y.: Asymptotic behaviour of the index of regularity of quadratic semi-regular polynomial systems. In: Gianni, P. (ed.) The Effective Methods in Algebraic Geometry Conference (MEGA 2005), pp. 1–14. Citeseer (2005)
5. Buchmann, J., Göpfert, F., Güneysu, T., Oder, T., Pöppelmann, T.: High-performance and lightweight lattice-based public-key encryption. In: Proceedings of the 2nd ACM International Workshop on IoT Privacy, Trust, and Security, pp. 2–9. ACM (2016)
6. Diffie, W., Hellman, M.: New directions in cryptography. IEEE Trans. Inf. Theory **22**(6), 644–654 (1976)
7. Döttling, N., Müller-Quade, J.: Lossy codes and a new variant of the learning-with-errors problem. In: Johansson, T., Nguyen, P.Q. (eds.) EUROCRYPT 2013. LNCS, vol. 7881, pp. 18–34. Springer, Heidelberg (2013). https://doi.org/10.1007/978-3-642-38348-9_2
8. Faugere, J.C.: A new efficient algorithm for computing gröbner bases (f4). J. Pure Appl. Algebra **139**(1–3), 61–88 (1999)
9. Fröberg, R.: An inequality for Hilbert series of graded algebras. Math. Scand. **56**, 117–144 (1985)
10. Lyubashevsky, V., Peikert, C., Regev, O.: On ideal lattices and learning with errors over rings. In: Gilbert, H. (ed.) EUROCRYPT 2010. LNCS, vol. 6110, pp. 1–23. Springer, Heidelberg (2010). https://doi.org/10.1007/978-3-642-13190-5_1
11. Micciancio, D.: Duality in lattice cryptography. In: Public Key Cryptography. p. 2 (2010)
12. Micciancio, D., Mol, P.: Pseudorandom knapsacks and the sample complexity of LWE search-to-decision reductions. In: Rogaway, P. (ed.) CRYPTO 2011. LNCS, vol. 6841, pp. 465–484. Springer, Heidelberg (2011). https://doi.org/10.1007/978-3-642-22792-9_26
13. Micciancio, D., Peikert, C.: Hardness of SIS and LWE with small parameters. In: Canetti, R., Garay, J.A. (eds.) CRYPTO 2013. LNCS, vol. 8042, pp. 21–39. Springer, Heidelberg (2013). https://doi.org/10.1007/978-3-642-40041-4_2
14. Regev, O.: The learning with errors problem. Invited Surv. CCC **7** (2010)
15. Rivest, R.L., Shamir, A., Adleman, L.: A method for obtaining digital signatures and public-key cryptosystems. Commun. ACM **21**(2), 120–126 (1978)
16. Shor, P.W.: Polynomial-time algorithms for prime factorization and discrete logarithms on a quantum computer. SIAM Rev. **41**(2), 303–332 (1999)

Machine Learning Security

PALOR: Poisoning Attacks Against Logistic Regression

Jialin Wen[1], Benjamin Zi Hao Zhao[2], Minhui Xue[3], and Haifeng Qian[1(✉)]

[1] East China Normal University, Shanghai, China
hfqian@cs.ecnu.edu.cn
[2] The University of New South Wales and Data61 CSIRO, Eveleigh, Australia
[3] The University of Adelaide, Adelaide, Australia

Abstract. With Google, Amazon, Microsoft, and other entities establishing "Machine Learning as a Service" (MLaaS), ensuring the security of the resulting machine learning models has become an increasingly important topic. The security community has demonstrated that MLaaS contains many potential security risks, with new risks constantly being discovered. In this paper, we focus on one of these security risks – *data poisoning attacks*. Specifically, we analyze how attackers interfere with the results of logistic regression by poisoning the training datasets. To this end, we analyze and propose an alternative formulation for the optimization of poisoning training points capable of poisoning the logistic regression classifier, a model that has previously not been susceptible to poisoning attacks. We evaluate the performance of our proposed attack algorithm on the three real-world datasets of wine cultivars, adult census information, and breast cancer diagnostics. The success of our proposed formulation is evident in decreasing testing accuracy of logistic regression models exposed to an increasing number of poisoned training samples.

Keywords: Data poisoning · Logistic regression · Machine learning

1 Introduction

With the widespread adoption of Machine Learning (ML) algorithms, it has been elevated out of the exclusive use of high-tech companies. Many services, such as "Machine Learning as a Service" (MLaaS) [21], can assist companies without domain expertise in ML to solve business problems with ML. However, in the MLaaS setting, there exists the potential for data poisoning attacks, in which malicious MLaaS providers can manipulate the integrity of the training data supplied by the company and compromise the training process.

In such a poisoning attack, the attacker's objective may be to indiscriminately alter prediction results, create a denial of service, or cause specific targeted mis-predictions during test time. The attacker seeks to create these negative effects while preserving correct predictions on the remaining test samples to evade detection. An inconspicuous attack that may produce dire consequences,

© Springer Nature Switzerland AG 2020
J. K. Liu and H. Cui (Eds.): ACISP 2020, LNCS 12248, pp. 447–460, 2020.
https://doi.org/10.1007/978-3-030-55304-3_23

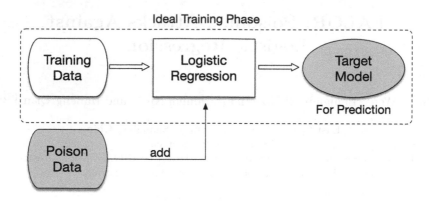

Fig. 1. The poisoning attack on logistic regression

and thus the necessity to study poisoning attacks on ML. A conceptual example of poisoning attacks is illustrated in Fig. 1.

Many poisoning attacks have been proposed and demonstrated against different ML architectures. Biggio et al. [4] propose a black-box poisoning attack on Support Vector Machines (SVM), and Muñoz-Gonzàlez et al. [17] propose a black-box poisoning attack on Deep Neural Networks (DNNs). Both works seek to indiscriminately alter prediction results, or cause specific mis-predictions at test time. Additional works [2,4,12,17] have shown that poisoning attacks are very effective in interfering with the accuracy of classification tasks. Alfeld et al. [1] demonstrated the effectiveness of data poisoning against Autoregressive Models. For regression learning, Ma et al. [16] were the first to propose a white-box poisoning attack against linear regression, aimed at manipulating the trained model by adversarially modifying the training set. Additionally, Jagielski et al. [12] propose a black-box poisoning attack against linear regression, which aims to increase the loss function on the original training set.

Logistic regression is not only a generalized linear regression model, but also a binary prediction model. To date, there has been no study on the effectiveness of a poisoning attack against the logistic regression model. As such, it is of upmost importance to study the severity of the attack against this popular model.

Our contributions of this work are as follows:

- We are the first to consider the problem of poisoning logistic regression in an adversarial training setting. Without a study on the effectiveness of a poisoning attack against this widely used model, one cannot evaluate the risk they are exposed to when being serviced by a malicious MLaaS.
- We extensively evaluate our attack on three types of logistic regression models (Logistic, Ridge, and LASSO). As it is understood that the different logistic regression models are used for their own disadvantages and advantages, but are still vulnerable to the poisoning attack via the same learning framework.

– We perform our evaluation on multiple datasets from different real-world domains, including datasets about wine cultivars, adult census information, and breast cancer diagnostics.

2 Preliminaries

2.1 Logistic Regression

Logistic regression is a statistical model that in its basic form uses a logistic function to model a binary dependent variable. Although many additional extensions exist; for example in the context of multi-class classification, logistic regression at its core is a binary classifier that creates a single boundary, separating the input feature space into two classes. Mathematically, a logistic regression model maps the dependence of an input variable with two possible output classes, for example, a positive and negative class. These outputs represent our indicator variable.

When solving the dichotomy between the two classes, we introduce a binary variable $y = \{0, 1\}$, where 1 represents the positive class and 0 represents the negative class. The logistic regression model finds a function $h_\theta(x) = g(\theta^T x)$ to map the actual value between 0 and 1 based on the actual predicted value from the linear function $\theta^T x$. If $h_\theta(x) \geq 0.5$, then label $y = 1$; if $h_\theta(x) < 0.5$, then label $y = 0$.

In logistic regression, the logit function is selected as $h_\theta(x)$. The logit function is part of the greater family of Sigmoid functions. The mathematical expression of the prediction function in logistic regression is shown in Eq. (1):

$$h_\theta(x) = g(\theta^T x) = \frac{1}{1 + e^{-\theta^T x}}. \tag{1}$$

The loss function of logistic regression is shown in Equation (2):

$$\text{Cost}(h_\theta(x), y) = \begin{cases} -\log(h_\theta(x)), & \text{if } y = 1 \\ -\log(1 - h_\theta(x)), & \text{if } y = 0 \end{cases} \tag{2}$$

We assume the logistic regression has been trained on a dataset $D_{tr} = \{x_i, y_i\}_{i=1}^n$, $x_i \in \mathbb{R}^d$. Then we add the regularization term to the logistic regression loss function to have Eq. (3).

$$L(D_{tr}, \theta) = -\frac{1}{m} \sum_{i=1}^m [y_i \log h_\theta(x_i) + (1 - y_i) \log(1 - h_\theta(x_i))] + \lambda \Omega(\omega), \tag{3}$$

where $\Omega(w)$ is a regularization term penalizing large weight values, and λ is the regularization parameter used to prevent overfitting.

The primary distinction between popular types of logistic regression methods is in the choice of the regularization term. In this paper, we study logistic regression with the following three regularization terms:

- **Ordinary logistic regression**, in which $\Omega(w) = 0$ (i.e., no regularization).
- **Ridge**, which uses l_2−norm regularization $\Omega(w) = \frac{1}{2} \|w\|_2^2$.
- **LASSO**, which uses l_1−norm regularization $\Omega(w) = \|w\|_1$.

2.2 Threat Model

Adversary's Goal. The goal of the adversary is to corrupt the learning model generated from the training phase, such that predictions on unseen data will greatly differ to the expected behaviour in the testing phase. If the attacker's objective is to indiscriminately alter prediction results, and/or create a denial of service, the attack is considered a poisoning availability attack. Alternatively, if the objective is to cause specific mis-predictions at test time, while preserving correct predictions on the remaining test samples, the attack is known as a poisoning integrity attack. These categorizations of the poisoning attack is similar to those used for backdoor poisoning attacks emerging in the classification setting [5,11]. In this work we focus on the *poisoning availability attack*.

Adversary's Knowledge. Poisoning attacks can be executed in two distinct attack scenarios, either as a *white-box attack* or a *black-box attack*. For *white-box attacks*, the attacker is assumed to have knowledge of the training data D_{tr}, the feature values x, the learning algorithm L, and the trained parameters θ. These attacks have been studied in previous works, although primarily on classification algorithms [2,4]. In the *black-box attack* setting, the attacker has no knowledge of the training set D_{tr} but can collect a substitute dataset D'_{tr}. The feature set x and learning algorithm L are known; however, the trained parameters θ are not. An attacker, however, can estimate θ' by optimizing L on the substitute dataset D'_{tr}. This setting is useful for evaluating the transferability of poisoning attacks across different training sets, as discussed in [2,4]. However in this work, we focus on the *white-box attack* setting.

Adversary's Capability. In poisoning attacks, the attacker will inject poisoning datapoints into the training set before the machine learning model is trained. The attacker's capability is normally limited by an upper bound on the number of poisoning points p that can be injected into the training data. The poisoning of feature values and response variables are arbitrarily set by the attacker within a specified range (Typically the range is bounded by the training data, for example $[0, 1]$, when features are normalized.) [2,4]. The total number of points in the poisoning training set is therefore $N = n + p$, with n being the number of pristine training samples, and p the number of poisoning points. We then define the ratio $\alpha = p/n$, as the poisoning rate, the actual fraction of the training set controlled by the attacker, i.e., $\frac{n}{N} = \frac{n}{n+p} = \frac{1}{1+p/n} = \frac{1}{1+\alpha}$. Prior works rarely consider poisoning rates larger than 20%, as the attacker is assumed to be able to control only a small fraction of the training data. This restriction is motivated by practical scenarios, such as data crowdsourcing or network traffic analysis, in which attackers can only practically influence a small fraction of the contributed data and network packets, respectively. Moreover, learning a sufficiently-accurate regression function in the presence of higher poisoning rates would be an ill-posed task, if not infeasible at all [2,4]. In this paper, we perform evaluations up to a maximum poisoning rate of $\alpha = 0.2$.

2.3 Attack Performance Metrics

The objective of our attack is to induce incorrect predictions on unseen data. Therefore, to measure the rate of success for the attack, and thus effectiveness of the poisoning attack on the machine learning model; we compare the testing accuracy of the poisoned model with the testing accuracy of the non-poisoned model trained on the same dataset.

3 Poisoning Attacks on Logistic Regression

3.1 Attack Strategy

We assume that the attacker is not aiming to cause specific errors, but only generic misclassifications. Consequently, this poisoning attack (as with any other poisoning attack) requires solving a bilevel optimization, where the inner problem is the learning problem and the outer problem is to find the most suitable poisoning points through optimization.

Logistic regression is a statistical model that in its foundation uses a logit function to model a binary variable dependent on inputs. In order to interfere with the classification accuracy, we add poisoning points to optimize the attack. Half of the poisoning points are to be labeled as $y = 0$, whilst the other half of the poisoning points are labeled as $y = 1$. The choice of poisoning points follows Eq. (4). While we optimize our poisoning points with an even number in both classes, however, we note that it is feasible additional optimizations can be engaged for the unbalanced placement of poisoning points into a class label that is more difficult to influence.

$$\arg \max_{D_p} L(D_{tr} \cup D_p, \theta^{(p)})$$
$$\text{s.t.} \quad \theta^{(p)} \in \arg \min_{\theta} L(D_{tr} \cup D_p, \theta), \tag{4}$$

where D_{tr} is a training dataset and D_p is a poisoning dataset. Through enforcing the bilevel optimization, we find the poisoning point that maximizes the logistic regression loss function. Only one poisoning point is found for each iteration, with the specific algorithm shown in Algorithm 1.

3.2 Gradient Computation

The aforementioned algorithm is essentially a standard gradient-ascent algorithm with line search. The challenging component is to understand how to compute

---

Algorithm 1: Poisoning attacks against logistic regression.

Input: $D = D_{tr}$ (white-box) or $D = D'_{tr}$ (black-box), L, the initial poisoning attack
    samples $D_p^{(0)} = (x_c, y_c)_{c=1}^p$, a small positive constant ε.
1: $i \leftarrow 0$ (iteration counter);
2: $\theta^{(i)} \leftarrow \arg\min_\theta L(D \cup D_p^{(i)})$;
3: **repeat**
4:     $l^{(i)} \leftarrow L(\theta^{(i)})$;
5:     $\theta^{(i+1)} \leftarrow \theta^{(i)}$;
6:     **for** $c = 1, \ldots, p$ **do**
7:         $x_c^{(i+1)} \leftarrow$ linesearch $(x_c^{(i)}, \nabla_{x_c} L(\theta^{(i+1)}))$;
8:         $\theta^{(i+1)} \leftarrow \arg\min_\theta L(D_{tr} \cup D_p^{(i+1)})$;
9:         $l^{(i+1)} \leftarrow L(\theta^{(i+1)})$;
10:    **end for**
11:    $i \leftarrow i + 1$;
12: **until** $\left| l^{(i)} - l^{(i+1)} \right| < \varepsilon$

Output: The final poisoning attack sample $D_p \leftarrow D_p^{(i)}$.

---

the required gradient $\nabla_{x_c} L(\theta^{(p)})$, as this has to capture the implicit dependency of the parameters θ of the inner problem on the poisoning point x_c. We can compute $\nabla_{x_c} L(\theta^{(p)})$ by using the chain rule:

$$\nabla_{x_c} L = \nabla_{x_c} \theta(x_c)^T \cdot \nabla_\theta L, \tag{5}$$

where we have made explicitly that θ depends on x_c. While the second term is simply the derivative of the outer objective with respect to the regression parameters, the first one captures the dependency of the solution θ of the learning problem on x_c.

We now focus on the computation of the term $\nabla_{x_c} \theta(x_c)$. For bi-level optimization problems, in which the inner problem is not convex (e.g., when the learning algorithm is a neural network), this requires efficient numerical approximations; however, when the inner learning problem is convex, the gradient of interest can be computed in a closed form expression. The underlying trick is to replace the inner learning problem with its Karush-Kuhn-Tucker (KKT) equilibrium conditions, i.e., $\nabla_\theta L(D_{tr} \cup D_p, \theta) = 0$, and require such conditions to remain valid while updating x_c. To this end, we simply obtain that the derivative with respect to x_c remains at equilibrium, i.e., $\nabla_{x_c} \nabla_\theta L(D_{tr} \cup D_p, \theta) = 0$. Now, it is clear that the function L depends explicitly on x_c in its first argument, and implicitly through the regression parameters θ. Thus, when differentiating again with the chain rule, one yields the following linear system:

$$\nabla_{x_c} \nabla_\theta L + \nabla_{x_c} \theta^T \cdot \nabla_\theta^2 L = 0. \tag{6}$$

For the specific form of L given in Eq. (6), it is easy to calculate the derivative:

$$(\nabla_{x_c} \theta) A = B + \alpha I_n, \tag{7}$$

where,

$$A_{ij} = \sum_k^c x_{ki}x_{kj}\left(\frac{y_k e^{-\theta^T x_k}}{(1+e^{-\theta^T x_k})^2} - \frac{1-y_k}{e^{-2\theta^T x_k}(1+e^{-\theta^T x_k})^2}(e^{-\theta^T x_k} + 2e^{-2\theta^T x_k})\right),$$

$$B_{ij} = \theta_j x_{ci}\left(\frac{(1-y_c)}{e^{-2\theta^T x_c}(1+e^{-\theta^T x_c})^2}(e^{-\theta^T x_c} + 2e^{-2\theta^T x_c}) - \frac{e^{-\theta^T x_c}y_c}{(1+e^{-\theta^T x_c})^2}\right),$$

I_n is the Identity matrix, and

$$\alpha = \frac{1-y_c}{e^{-\theta^T x_c}(1+e^{-\theta^T x_c})} - \frac{y_c}{1+e^{-\theta^T x_c}}.$$

As logistic regression is a binary classification algorithm, the response variable y_c of x_c can only take two values of 0 and 1, so we can simply set $y_c = 1$ in the case of poisoning attack.

4 Experiment

We implemented our attack algorithm in Python 3.7, leveraging the numpy and sklearn libraries. We ran our experiments on an i5-4200M equipped laptop running at 2.50 GHz with 12 GB of RAM. We parallelize our optimization-based attack implementations to take advantage of multi-core capabilities. We use a standard cross-validation method to split the datasets into 1/3 for training, 1/3 for validation, and 1/3 for testing, and report results as averages over 5 independent runs. We use one key metric to evaluate the effectiveness of our poisoning attack: testing accuracy.

The remainder of this section is laid out as follows. We describe the datasets used in our experiments in Sect. 4.1. Followed by Sect. 4.2, where we show results from our poisoning optimization algorithm on the datasets we have obtained, and across three different types of regression models.

4.1 Datasets

Wine Cultivars Dataset [6]. The wine cultivars dataset contains a total of 178 records from wines of a chemical analysis of wines grown in the same region in Italy, originating from 3 different cultivars. The 13 chemical properties are the quantities of 13 constituents found in each of the three wine cultivars. The cultivars can be inferred from chemical analysis. Hence, there are 3 class labels in the Wine dataset; however, We only perform a binary classification algorithm on this dataset, to determine whether the wine belongs to cultivar "1" or not.

Adult Census Dataset [7]. The adult census dataset was extracted from the database of the 1994 U.S. census and is used to predict a residents' income. The binary variable class label of this dataset is whether an individual's annual income exceeds \$50k or not. The input attributes contain personal information such as age, job, education, occupation, and race. The adult dataset contains 48,842 records.

Breast Cancer Wisconsin Dataset [8]. This is a dataset about the diagnosis of breast cancer, whereby the output of the diagnosis has 2 class labels: malignant or benign. The dataset contains 32 input attributes, computed from a digitized image of a fine needle aspirate (FNA) of a breast mass. This dataset has a total of 569 entries. We use this data for a binary classification task to predict the diagnosis of breast cancer.

4.2 Poisoning Attacks

We now perform experiments on our three selected datasets to evaluate our newly proposed attack on logistic regression models. To enable the evaluation of this attack, we provide comparisons between the accuracy of a model trained in the presence of our poisoning training samples and the model trained on an unpoisoned dataset. We use testing accuracy as the metric for assessing the effectiveness of an attack. We note that if the testing accuracy is observed to decrease with an increasing amount of poisoned data, the attack is effective. We vary the poisoning rate between 4% and 20% at intervals of 4% with the goal of inferring the trend in attack success. Figures 2, 3, and 4 show the testing accuracy of each attack on the original logistic regression, Ridge and LASSO, respectively.

We plot results for the unpoisoned dataset called "Unpoison", and our optimization attack as termed "PALOR". The x-axis describes the poisoning rate, that is, the proportion of pollution data in the original data, and the y-axis is the testing accuracy measured from the resulting logistic regression modes trained on either the poisoned or unpoisoned dataset. It is evident from the figures that generating poisoning samples in our optimization attack (PALOR) can effectively cause mis-predictions on logistic regression modes irrespective of the type of regularization used.

We detail the specific testing accuracies of our optimization attack (PALOR) in Table 1. It can be seen from the table, when the poisoning rate is $\alpha = 0.2$, our attack (PALOR) on average across all datasets and types of logistic regression produces an 8.19% reduction in the testing accuracy. A formidable decrease in the testing accuracy and demonstration in the effectiveness of the poisoning attack.

As such, our results confirm that the optimization framework we design demonstrates increased effectiveness when poisoning both different logistic regression models and across datasets.

5 Related Work

Machine learning algorithms can be easily attacked by slight perturbations, such as *data poisoning attacks* and *Trojan backdoor attacks*. In data poisoning attacks, the attacker can either breach the integrity of the system without preventing the regular users to use the system, or make the system unavailable for all users by manipulating the training data. Backdoor attacks are one type of attack aimed at fooling the model with premeditated inputs. An attacker can train the model with poisoned data to obtain a model that performs well on a service test set but behaves erroneously with crafted triggers. In Trojan backdoor attacks, neural

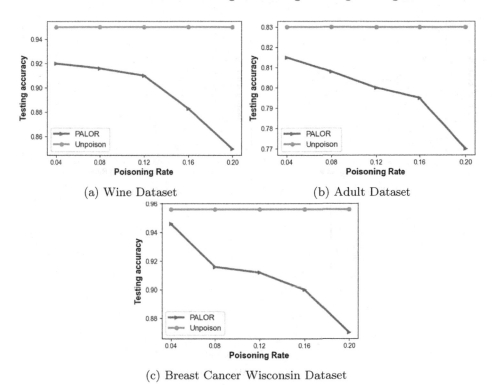

(a) Wine Dataset   (b) Adult Dataset

(c) Breast Cancer Wisconsin Dataset

Fig. 2. Testing accuracy of poisoning attacks on logistic regression on the three datasets

Table 1. Comparison of testing accuracy between unpoisoned data and our PALOR poisoning algorithms.

Dataset	Regression	Testing accuracy	
		Unpoison	PALOR ($\alpha = 0.2$)
Wine cultivars	Logistic	0.95	0.85
	Ridge	0.90	0.855
	LASSO	0.958	0.86
Adult census	Logistic	0.83	0.77
	Ridge	0.835	0.76
	LASSO	0.84	0.765
Breast cancer diagnostic	Logistic	0.956	0.87
	Ridge	0.96	0.9
	LASSO	0.958	0.88

Trojans, surfaced with a trigger pattern, can be embedded in the neural networks when the networks are trained with a compromised dataset. This process typically involves the encoding of malicious functionality and normal behavior

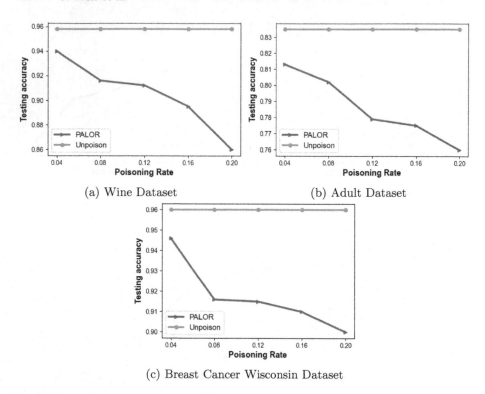

(a) Wine Dataset   (b) Adult Dataset

(c) Breast Cancer Wisconsin Dataset

Fig. 3. Testing accuracy of poisoning attacks on ridge regression on the three datasets

within the weights of the deep network. We therefore survey both attacks as follows.

Data Poisoning Attacks. Data poisoning attacks are generally referred to attacks that manipulate the training data of a machine-learning or data-mining system such that the learnt model makes predictions as an attacker desires. For instance, existing studies have demonstrated that effective data poisoning attacks can be launched against different applications, such as anomaly detection [19] and spam filters [18]. Data poisoning attacks also have a good attack impact on many different types of machine learning algorithms, such as SVMs [4,23], regression [2,12], graph-based approaches [22,25], neural networks [11], and federated learning [9]. Many of the applications above are targeted at classification tasks; however, there is also work focusing on attacking specific types of recommender systems [10,13,24]. For example, Fang et al. [10] proposed efficient poisoning attacks on graph-based recommender systems, where they inject fake users with carefully crafted rating scores into the recommender system to promote a specific target item. They modeled the attack as an optimization problem to decide the rating scores for the fake users. Li et al. [13] proposed poisoning attacks against matrix-factorization-based recommender systems. Instead of attacking

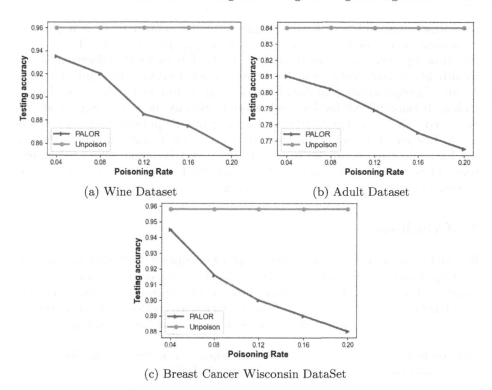

(a) Wine Dataset   (b) Adult Dataset

(c) Breast Cancer Wisconsin DataSet

Fig. 4. Testing accuracy of poisoning attacks on LASSO regression on the three datasets

the top-N recommendation lists, their goal was to manipulate the predictions for all missing entries of the rating matrix.

Trojan Backdoor Attacks. Although most Trojan insertion techniques use a predetermined pattern, it is desirable to make these patterns indistinguishable when mixed with legitimate data in order to evade human inspection. Barni et al. [3] propose a Trojan insertion methodology where the label of the poisoned data remains untampered. The advantage of this approach is that upon inspection, the poisoned samples would not be detected merely on the basis of an accompanying poisoned label, as a clear mismatch between the sample and the label would be evident. To perform the attack, a target class t is chosen and a fraction of training data samples belonging to a target class is poisoned by adding a backdoor trigger. After the neural network is trained on the training set which is contaminated with poisoned samples of a target class, test samples not belonging to the target class but corrupted with the trigger end up being classified as the target class, without any impact on the original samples belonging to the target class. Thus, the network learns that the presence of the trigger in a sample is an indicator of the sample belonging to the target class. Liao et al. [15] designed static and adaptive Trojan insertion techniques. In their work, the indistinguishability of Trojan trigger examples is attained by a magnitude constraint on the perturbations to craft such examples. Li et al. [14] generalized this approach and demonstrated the trade-off between the effectiveness and stealth of Trojans. They also developed an optimization algorithm involving L_2 and L_0 regularization to distribute the trigger throughout the victim image, making it more difficult for Trojan defenses to identify the attack. Saha et al. [20] proposed to hide the Trojan triggers by not using the poisoned data in training at all. Instead, they took a fine-tune approach in the training process, whereby the backdoor trigger samples are given the correct label and only used at test time. These samples are visually indistinguishable from legitimate data but bear certain features that will trigger the Trojan.

6   Conclusion

In conclusion, we have demonstrated a proof-of-concept work that extends the existing data poisoning attack framework to also function on logistic regression classification models. We have shown through experimentation on different real-world datasets and various types of logistic regression models that this poisoning attack is still effective in causing mis-predictions of previously unseen data.

Acknowledgment. This work was, in part, supported by the National Natural Science Foundation of China under Grant No. 61961146004.

References

1. Alfeld, S., Zhu, X., Barford, P.: Data poisoning attacks against autoregressive models. In: Schuurmans, D., Wellman, M.P. (eds.) Proceedings of the Thirtieth AAAI Conference on Artificial Intelligence, 12–17 February 2016, Phoenix, Arizona, USA, pp. 1452–1458. AAAI Press (2016). http://www.aaai.org/ocs/index.php/AAAI/AAAI16/paper/view/12049
2. Bach, F.R., Blei, D.M. (eds.): Proceedings of the 32nd International Conference on Machine Learning, ICML 2015, Lille, France, 6–11 July 2015, JMLR Workshop and Conference Proceedings, vol. 37. JMLR.org (2015). http://proceedings.mlr.press/v37/
3. Barni, M., Kallas, K., Tondi, B.: A new backdoor attack in CNNS by training set corruption without label poisoning. In: 2019 IEEE International Conference on Image Processing, ICIP 2019, Taipei, Taiwan, 22–25 September 2019, pp. 101–105. IEEE (2019). https://doi.org/10.1109/ICIP.2019.8802997
4. Biggio, B., Nelson, B., Laskov, P.: Poisoning attacks against support vector machines. In: Proceedings of the 29th International Conference on Machine Learning, ICML 2012, Edinburgh, Scotland, UK, 26 June–1 July 2012 (2012). http://icml.cc/2012/papers/880.pdf
5. Chen, X., Liu, C., Li, B., Lu, K., Song, D.: Targeted backdoor attacks on deep learning systems using data poisoning. CoRR abs/1712.05526 (2017). http://arxiv.org/abs/1712.05526
6. Dua, D., Graff, C.: UCI machine learning repository (2017). http://archive.ics.uci.edu/ml/datasets/Wine

7. Dua, D., Graff, C.: UCI machine learning repository (2017). http://archive.ics.uci. edu/ml/datasets/Adult
8. Dua, D., Graff, C.: UCI machine learning repository (2017).http://archive.ics.uci. edu/ml/datasets/Breast+Cancer+Wisconsin+%28Diagnostic%29
9. Fang, M., Cao, X., Jia, J., Gong, N.Z.: Local model poisoning attacks to byzantine-robust federated learning. CoRR abs/1911.11815 (2019). http://arxiv.org/abs/ 1911.11815
10. Fang, M., Yang, G., Gong, N.Z., Liu, J.: Poisoning attacks to graph-based recommender systems. In: Proceedings of the 34th Annual Computer Security Applications Conference, ACSAC 2018, San Juan, PR, USA, 03–07 December 2018, pp. 381–392. ACM (2018). https://doi.org/10.1145/3274694.3274706
11. Gu, T., Dolan-Gavitt, B., Garg, S.: BadNets: identifying vulnerabilities in the machine learning model supply chain. CoRR abs/1708.06733 (2017). http://arxiv. org/abs/1708.06733
12. Jagielski, M., Oprea, A., Biggio, B., Liu, C., Nita-Rotaru, C., Li, B.: Manipulating machine learning: Poisoning attacks and countermeasures for regression learning. In: Proceedings of 2018 IEEE Symposium on Security and Privacy, SP 2018, 21–23 May 2018, San Francisco, California, USA, pp. 19–35 (2018). https://doi.org/10. 1109/SP.2018.00057
13. Li, B., Wang, Y., Singh, A., Vorobeychik, Y.: Data poisoning attacks on factorization-based collaborative filtering. In: Lee, D.D., Sugiyama, M., von Luxburg, U., Guyon, I., Garnett, R. (eds.) Advances in Neural Information Processing Systems 29: Annual Conference on Neural Information Processing Systems 2016, 5–10 December 2016, Barcelona, Spain, pp. 1885–1893 (2016)
14. Li, S., Zhao, B.Z.H., Xue, M., Kaafar, D., Zhu, H.: Invisible backdoor attacks against deep neural networks. CoRR abs/1909.02742 (2019). http://arxiv.org/abs/ 1909.02742
15. Liao, C., Zhong, H., Squicciarini, A.C., Zhu, S., Miller, D.J.: Backdoor embedding in convolutional neural network models via invisible perturbation. CoRR abs/1808.10307 (2018). http://arxiv.org/abs/1808.10307
16. Ma, Y., Zhu, X., Hsu, J.: Data poisoning against differentially-private learners: attacks and defenses. In: Proceedings of the Twenty-Eighth International Joint Conference on Artificial Intelligence, IJCAI 2019, Macao, China, 10–16 August 2019, pp. 4732–4738 (2019). https://doi.org/10.24963/ijcai.2019/657
17. Muñoz-González, L., et al.: Towards poisoning of deep learning algorithms with back-gradient optimization. In: Proceedings of the 10th ACM Workshop on Artificial Intelligence and Security, pp. 27–38 (2017)
18. Nelson, B., et al.: Exploiting machine learning to subvert your spam filter. In: Monrose, F. (ed.) Proceedings of First USENIX Workshop on Large-Scale Exploits and Emergent Threats, LEET 2008, San Francisco, CA, USA, 15 April 2008. USENIX Association (2008). http://www.usenix.org/events/leet08/tech/ full_papers/nelson/nelson.pdf
19. Rubinstein, B.I.P., et al.: ANTIDOTE: understanding and defending against poisoning of anomaly detectors. In: Feldmann, A., Mathy, L. (eds.) Proceedings of the 9th ACM SIGCOMM Internet Measurement Conference, IMC 2009, Chicago, Illinois, USA, 4–6 November 2009, pp. 1–14. ACM (2009). https://doi.org/10.1145/ 1644893.1644895
20. Saha, A., Subramanya, A., Pirsiavash, H.: Hidden trigger backdoor attacks. CoRR abs/1910.00033 (2019). http://arxiv.org/abs/1910.00033

21. Shokri, R., Stronati, M., Song, C., Shmatikov, V.: Membership inference attacks against machine learning models. In: 2017 IEEE Symposium on Security and Privacy, SP 2017, San Jose, CA, USA, 22–26 May 2017, pp. 3–18 (2017). https://doi.org/10.1109/SP.2017.41
22. Wang, B., Gong, N.Z.: Attacking graph-based classification via manipulating the graph structure. In: Cavallaro, L., Kinder, J., Wang, X., Katz, J. (eds.) Proceedings of the 2019 ACM SIGSAC Conference on Computer and Communications Security, CCS 2019, London, UK, 11–15 November 2019, pp. 2023–2040. ACM (2019). https://doi.org/10.1145/3319535.3354206
23. Xiao, H., Xiao, H., Eckert, C.: Adversarial label flips attack on support vector machines. In: Raedt, L.D., et al. (eds.) ECAI 2012–20th European Conference on Artificial Intelligence. Including Prestigious Applications of Artificial Intelligence (PAIS-2012) System Demonstrations Track, Montpellier, France, 27–31 August 2012. Frontiers in Artificial Intelligence and Applications, vol. 242, pp. 870–875. IOS Press (2012). https://doi.org/10.3233/978-1-61499-098-7-870
24. Yang, G., Gong, N.Z., Cai, Y.: Fake co-visitation injection attacks to recommender systems. In: 24th Annual Network and Distributed System Security Symposium, NDSS 2017, San Diego, California, USA, 26 February–1 March 2017. The Internet Society (2017). https://www.ndss-symposium.org/ndss2017/ndss-2017-programme/fake-co-visitation-injection-attacks-recommender-systems/
25. Zügner, D., Akbarnejad, A., Günnemann, S.: Adversarial attacks on neural networks for graph data. In: Kraus, S. (ed.) Proceedings of the Twenty-Eighth International Joint Conference on Artificial Intelligence, IJCAI 2019, Macao, China, 10–16 August 2019, pp. 6246–6250. ijcai.org (2019). https://doi.org/10.24963/ijcai.2019/872

DeepCapture: Image Spam Detection Using Deep Learning and Data Augmentation

Bedeuro Kim[1,2], Sharif Abuadbba[2,3], and Hyoungshick Kim[1,2(✉)]

[1] Sungkyunkwan University, Suwon, Republic of Korea
{kimbdr,hyoung}@skku.edu
[2] Data61, CSIRO, Sydney, Australia
{Bedeuro.Kim,Sharif.Abuadbba,Hyoung.Kim}@data61.csiro.au
[3] Cyber Security Cooperative Research Centre, Joondalup, Australia

Abstract. Image spam emails are often used to evade text-based spam filters that detect spam emails with their frequently used keywords. In this paper, we propose a new image spam email detection tool called DeepCapture using a convolutional neural network (CNN) model. There have been many efforts to detect image spam emails, but there is a significant performance degrade against entirely new and unseen image spam emails due to overfitting during the training phase. To address this challenging issue, we mainly focus on developing a more robust model to address the overfitting problem. Our key idea is to build a CNN-XGBoost framework consisting of eight layers only with a large number of training samples using data augmentation techniques tailored towards the image spam detection task. To show the feasibility of DeepCapture, we evaluate its performance with publicly available datasets consisting of 6,000 spam and 2,313 non-spam image samples. The experimental results show that DeepCapture is capable of achieving an F1-score of 88%, which has a 6% improvement over the best existing spam detection model CNN-SVM [19] with an F1-score of 82%. Moreover, DeepCapture outperformed existing image spam detection solutions against new and unseen image datasets.

Keywords: Image spam · Convolutional neural networks · XGBoost · Spam filter · Data augmentation

1 Introduction

Image-based spam emails (also referred to as "image spam emails") are designed to evade traditional text-based spam detection methods by replacing sentences or words contained in a spam email with images for expressing the same meaning [11]. As image spam emails become popular [16], several spam detection methods [9,12,15] have been proposed to detect image spam emails with statistical properties of image spam emails (e.g., the ratio of text contents in an

© Springer Nature Switzerland AG 2020
J. K. Liu and H. Cui (Eds.): ACISP 2020, LNCS 12248, pp. 461–475, 2020.
https://doi.org/10.1007/978-3-030-55304-3_24

email sample). However, these countermeasures have disadvantages due to a high processing cost for text recognition in images [2]. Recently, a convolutional neural network (CNN) model-based detection [19] was presented to address this processing cost issue and improve the detection accuracy. The recent advance of deep learning technologies in the image domain would bring a new angle or approach to security applications. CNN has the potential to process raw data inputs (e.g., the input image itself) by extracting important (low-level) features in an automated manner [14]. However, we found that the detection accuracy of the existing CNN based image spam detection model [19] could be degraded significantly against new and unseen image spam emails.

To overcome the limitation of existing image spam detectors against new and unseen datasets, we propose a new image spam email detection tool called DeepCapture. DeepCapture consists of two phases: (1) data augmentation to introduce new training samples and (2) classification using a CNN-XGBoost model. In this paper, we focus on developing new data augmentation techniques tailored for image spam training dataset and designing an effective CNN architecture capable of detecting images used for spam emails with the optimized configuration for number of layers, number of filters, filter size, activation function, a number of epochs and batch size.

To examine the feasibility of DeepCapture, we evaluate the performance of DeepCapture compared with existing image spam email detectors such as RSVM based detector [1] and CNN-SVM based detector [19]. In our experiments, we use a dataset consisting of 6,000 spam and 2,313 non-spam (hereinafter referred to as ham) image samples collected from real-world user emails. We also use our data augmentation techniques to balance the distribution of ham and spam samples and avoid performance degradation against new and unseen datasets. We evaluate the performance of the DeepCapture in two ways. First, we evaluate the performance of DeepCapture with/without data augmentation. Second, we also evaluate the performance of DeepCapture via cross data training scenarios with/without data augmentation. Our experimental results demonstrate that DeepCapture produced the best classification results in F1-score (88%) compared with existing solutions. Moreover, for two cross data training scenarios against unseen datasets, DeepCapture also produced the best F1-score results compared with other classifiers. The use of data augmentation techniques would be necessary for processing new and unseen datasets. In the cross data training scenarios, F1-scores of all classifiers are less than 40% without applying our data augmentation techniques.

This paper is constructed as follows: Sect. 2 describes the background of image spam email, convolutional neural network and data augmentation. Section 3 describes the model architecture of DeepCapture. Section 4 describes experiment setups and evaluation results of DeepCapture. Section 5 describes the related work for image spam detection and we conclude in Sect. 6.

2   Background

This section first presents the definition of the image spam email and then briefly provides the concept of a convolutional neural network. Finally, we present the description of data augmentation that is a widely used technique [14] for improving the robustness of deep learning models. It increases the size of labeled training samples by leveraging task-specific data transformations that preserve class labels.

2.1   Image Spam Email

Since image spam emails appeared in 2004, several studies were conducted to formally define image spam emails and construct models to detect image spam emails in academia. Klangpraphan et al. [13] observed that image spam emails contain an image-based link to a website, which looks like a text. Soranamageswari et al. [21] introduced the definition of image spam email as spam email having at least one image containing spam content.

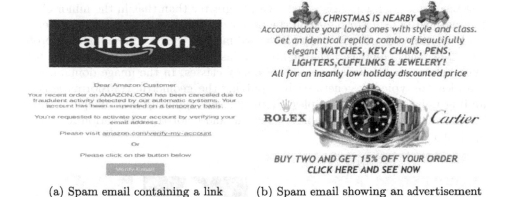

(a) Spam email containing a link   (b) Spam email showing an advertisement

Fig. 1. Examples of image spam emails.

Figure 1 shows two examples of image spam emails. In Fig. 1(a), if a user clicks the "Verify Email" button, it tries to visit an attacker's website or download malware. In Fig. 1(b), the spam image shows unwanted advertisement information to email recipients. Basically, the goal of image spam emails is to hide the attacker's message into an image for circumventing text-based spam filters. Based on this observation, in this paper, we define the image spam email as spam email with images displaying unwanted text information.

2.2   Convolutional Neural Network (CNN)

Convolutional neural network (CNN) is a kind of deep learning methods. Recently, in many classification tasks, CNN outperformed traditional machine learning methods. Therefore, it is widely believed that CNN has the potential to be used for security applications.

CNN can automatically extract features of target objects from lower to higher levels by using convolutional and pooling layers. Convolutional layers play a role in extracting the features of the input. A convolutional layer consists of a set of filters and activation functions. A filter is a function to emphasize key features that are used to recognize target objects. The raw input data is converted into feature maps with filters, which becomes more clear after processing the activation functions. A pooling layer (or sub-sampling) reduces the number of features, which prevents overfitting caused by a high number of features and improve the learning rate. Finally, feature map layers are used as the input layer for the fully connected classifier. These are popularly applied to computer vision tasks such as object recognition [3].

2.3   Data Augmentation

In a classification problem, it is widely known that the performance of classifiers deteriorates when an imbalanced training dataset is used. If the number of instances in the major class is significantly greater than that in the minor class, the classification performance on the major class will be higher, and vice versa.

Data augmentation is a popularly used method to solve the imbalance problem [20], which increases the number of instances in minority classes to balance between majority classes and minority classes. In the image domain, new samples are typically generated by applying the geometric transformations or adding noise to training samples. Figure 2 shows typically used image manipulation techniques such as flipping, rotation, and color transformation for image applications.

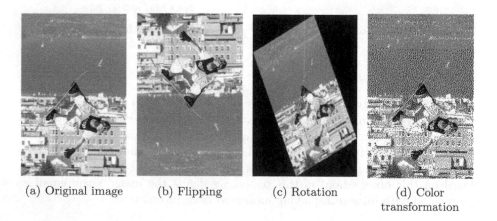

(a) Original image   (b) Flipping   (c) Rotation   (d) Color
                                                                    transformation

Fig. 2. Examples of the image manipulation techniques.

In the image spam detection problem, however, the effects of such general data augmentation techniques would be limited because the typical ham and spam images are different from the samples generated from such augmentation techniques. Therefore, in this paper, we focus on developing data augmentation for image ham and spam emails.

3   Overview of DeepCapture

We designed DeepCapture using data augmentation and CNN to make it robust against new and unseen datasets. Figure 3 shows an overview of DeepCapture architecture.

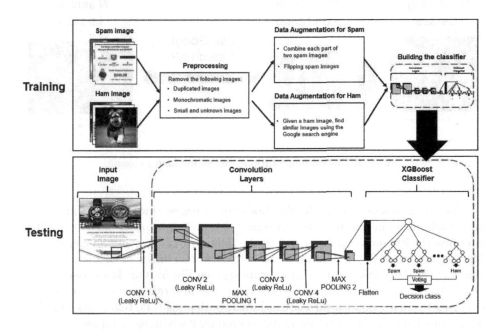

Fig. 3. Overview of DeepCapture.

DeepCapture consists of two phases: (1) data augmentation to introduce new training samples and (2) classification using a CNN model.

3.1   Data Augmentation in DeepCapture

To address the class imbalance problem in image spam datasets and generalize the detection model, we introduce a new data augmentation method to create new ham and spam samples for training. The goal of data augmentation is to make augmented samples that are similar to real data.

For both ham and spam images, we commonly remove unnecessary images such as duplicate images, solid color background images, small and unknown images that cannot be recognized by human users. After removing unnecessary images, we apply different data augmentation methods to ham and spam images, respectively.

For ham images, we randomly choose an image among ham images and use an API to search images that are similar to the given image. For example, the Google Image Search API can be used to crawl the images similar to the ones we uploaded. For each uploaded image, N (e.g., $N = 100$) similar images can be obtained as ham-like images for training (see Fig. 4). Those images would be regarded as additional ham images because those are also actually used images on other websites.

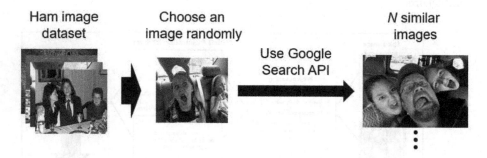

Fig. 4. Data augmentation process for ham images.

For spam images, we randomly choose two images among spam images and split each image in half from left to right ("left and right parts"). Next, we then combine the left part of an image with the right part of the other image. To combine parts from different images, we resize a part of an image so that its size is the same as the size of the part of another image (see Fig. 5). Our key observation is that a spam image typically consists of the image and text parts. Therefore, it is essential to create augmented samples having both image and text parts. Our data augmentation techniques are designed to produce such image samples.

3.2   CNN-XGBoost Classification in DeepCapture

As shown in Fig. 3, the architecture of DeepCapture is composed of eight layers. Given an input image, the input image is resized to 32 × 32 pixels. The first six layers are convolutional layers, and the remaining two layers are used for the XGBoost classifier to determine whether a given image is spam or not.

All convolutional layers use 3 × 3 kernel size and the Leaky ReLU function [17], which is used as the activation function. The Leaky ReLU function has the advantage to solve the gradient saturation problem and improve convergence speed. Unlike ReLU, in which the negative value is totally dropped, Leaky ReLU assigns a relatively small positive gradient for negative inputs. We also apply the 2 × 2 max pooling to the 3rd and 6th layers, which selects the maximum value

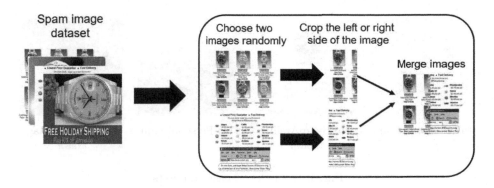

Fig. 5. Data augmentation process for spam images.

from the prior feature map. The use of max pooling reduces the dimension of feature parameters and can help extract key features from the feature map. We also use regularization techniques to prevent the overfitting problem. We specifically use both L2 regularization [18] and the dropout method [22] as regularization techniques for DeepCapture.

After extracting features from the input image through the convolutional layers, we use the XGBoost [6] classifier, which is a decision-tree-based ensemble machine learning algorithm that uses a gradient boosting framework. XGBoost builds a series of gradient boosted decision trees in a parallel manner and makes the final decision using a majority vote over those decision trees. In many situations, a CNN model typically uses the fully connected layers. However, for the image spam detection problem, we found that we can improve the detection accuracy if we replace the fully connected layers with a classifier such as XGBoost. We use the random search [4] method for optimizing hyperparameters used in the XGBoost classifier.

4   Evaluation

This section presents the performance evaluation results of DeepCapture (presented in Sect. 3) compared with state-of-the-art classification methods: SVM [1], RSVM [1] and CNN-SVM [19].

4.1   Dataset

To evaluate the performance of image spam email detection models, we use publicly available mixed datasets with two spam ("Personal spam" and "SpamArchive spam") and two ham ("Personal ham" and "Normal image ham") image datasets. Figure 6 shows examples of those datasets.

In the "Personal spam" dataset, spam images were collected from 10 email accounts for one month, and ham images were collected from two email accounts for two years. The "SpamArchive spam" dataset [7] was constructed with many

(a) Personal spam   (b) SpamArchive   (c) Personal ham   (d) Normal image
                        spam   ham

Fig. 6. Examples of image datasets.

anonymous users. "Normal image ham" dataset [10] was collected from a photo-sharing website called "Flickr" (https://www.flickr.com/) and 20 scanned documents. From those datasets, we removed unnecessary image samples such as duplicated images, solid color background images, small and unknown images. In particular, since the "SpamArchive spam" dataset contains a lot of duplicated images such as the advertisement for a watch or corporate logo, we need to remove such duplicated images. After eliminating image samples that cannot be categorized as either normal ham or spam images, we were left with a dataset of 8,313 samples for experiments. The details of the dataset are presented in Table 1. In the final dataset, the number of spam images is 6,000, while the number of ham images is 2,313. The ratio of ham to spam is around 1:3.

Table 1. Description of the datasets.

Category	Corpus	Total count
Spam	Personal spam	786
	SpamArchive spam	5,214
	Total	6,000
Ham	Personal ham	1,503
	Normal image ham	810
	Total	2,313

4.2 Experiment Setup

Our experiments were conducted using the Google Colab environment (https://colab.research.google.com/). It supports a GPU Nvidia Tesla K80 with 13 GB of memory and an Intel(R) Xeon(R) CPU at 2.30 GHz. We use Keras framework with the scikit-learn library in Python 3 to implement DeepCapture.

For classification, we randomly divided 8,313 samples into a training set (60%) and a testing set (40%) with similar class distributions.

To address the data imbalance issue and make the classifier more robust against new and unseen image datasets, we use the data augmentation (DA) techniques presented in Sect. 3.1 to create additional image samples. Finally, we obtained 5,214 ham-like and 4,497 spam-like image samples with the images in the training set through our data augmentation techniques. Those image samples are used for training only.

4.3   Classification Results

To evaluate the performance of classifiers, we use the four following metrics:

- **Accuracy (Acc.):** the proportion of correctly classified images;
- **Precision (Pre.):** the proportion of images classified as spam that actually are spam;
- **Recall (Rec.):** the proportion of spam images that were accurately classified;
- **F1-score (F1.):** the harmonic mean of *precision* and *recall*.

Because the dataset used in our experiments is imbalanced, accuracy is not the best measure to evaluate the performance of classifiers. F1-score would be a more effective measure since it considers both precision and recall measures. Table 2 shows the performance of classifiers with/without data augmentation techniques used for DeepCapture. DeepCapture produced the best results in all metrics except precision (accuracy: 85%, precision: 91%, recall: 85%, F1-score: 88%). The existing solutions (SVM [1] with DA, RSVM [1] with DA, and CNN-SVM [19]) achieved high precision, but their recall was poor. Interestingly, traditional machine learning-based solutions (SVM [1] and RSVM [1]) failed to achieve a very low F1-score, less than 20%, without the training samples generated by the proposed data augmentation method. In contrast with those existing techniques, deep learning-based solutions (DeepCapture and CNN-SVM [19]), achieved an F1-score of 85% and 82%, respectively, without data augmentation.

Table 2. Performance of classifiers (DA represents "Data Augmentation").

Model	Acc.	Pre.	Rec.	F1.
DeepCapture	**85%**	**91%**	**85%**	**88%**
DeepCapture without DA	81%	90%	81%	85%
SVM [1]	51%	50%	09%	15%
SVM [1] with DA	71%	96%	36%	52%
RSVM [1]	53%	52%	11%	18%
RSVM [1] with DA	73%	98%	42%	59%
CNN-SVM [19]	76%	99%	71%	82%
CNN-SVM [19] with DA	84%	90%	83%	86%

We compare DeepCapture against existing solutions (SVM [1], RSVM [1] and CNN-SVM [19]) with respect to the training and testing times. Training time refers to the time taken to train a model with training samples. Testing time refers to the time taken to perform classification with all testing samples. Table 3 shows the training and testing times of all classifiers. DeepCapture took 300.27 s for training and 5.79 s for testing. CNN-based solutions such as DeepCapture and CNN-SVM outperformed SVM and RSVM with respect to the training time. However, DeepCapture produced the worst result with respect to the training time. We surmise that the testing time of XGBoost is relatively slower than other classifiers such as SVM and RSVM because XGBoost is an ensemble of multiple regression trees. For a single image, however, the average testing time of DeepCapture was only 0.0017 s. Hence, we believe that the testing time of DeepCapture would be practically acceptable.

Table 3. Training and testing times (sec.) of classifiers.

Model	Training time	Testing time
DeepCapture	**300.27**	**5.79**
SVM (Annadatha et al. [1])	2000.00	0.01
RSVM (Annadatha et al. [1])	2000.00	0.01
CNN-SVM (Shang et al. [19])	320.24	0.03

To test the robustness of classifiers against new and unseen image spam emails, we evaluate the performance of DeepCapture with cross data training. For cross data training, we trained classifiers on ham and spam images collected from one specific source, and evaluated the performance of classifiers against a different unseen dataset.

For training, we used 6,024 samples collected from "SpamArchive spam" and "Normal image ham" datasets, while for testing, we used 2,289 samples collected from "Personal spam" and "Personal ham" datasets. To make classifiers more robust against the unseen dataset, we additionally created 5,190 ham-like and 786 spam-like image samples with the images in the training set through our data augmentation techniques. Those image samples are used for training only. Table 4 shows the evaluation results for the first cross data training scenario. DeepCapture achieved an F1-score of 72% and outperformed the other classifiers. Surprisingly, F1-scores of all classifiers, including DeepCapture itself, are less than 35% without the training samples created by data augmentation, indicating that our data augmentation techniques are necessary to process unseen and unexpected image samples.

As another cross data training scenario, we used 2,289 samples collected from "Personal spam" and "Personal ham" datasets for training while we used 6,024 samples collected from "SpamArchive spam" and "Normal image ham" datasets for testing. Again, to make classifiers more robust against the unseen dataset,

Table 4. Performance of classifiers with a cross data training scenario (training dataset: "SpamArchive spam" and "Normal image ham" datasets; and testing dataset: "Personal spam" and "Personal ham" datasets).

Model	Acc.	Pre.	Rec.	F1.
DeepCapture	**71%**	**81%**	**71%**	**72%**
DeepCapture without DA	36%	37%	34%	35%
SVM [1]	89%	14%	10%	12%
SVM [1] with DA	65%	45%	22%	29%
RSVM [1]	90%	12%	11%	13%
RSVM [1] with DA	69%	58%	27%	30%
CNN-SVM [19]	35%	35%	34%	35%
CNN-SVM [19] with DA	68%	73%	45%	55%

we additionally created 4,497 ham-like and 5,214 spam-like image samples with the images in the training set through our data augmentation techniques. Those image samples are used for training only. Table 5 shows the evaluation results for the second cross data training scenario. DeepCapture and RSVM [1] with DA achieved an F1-score of 76% and outperformed the other classifiers. F1-scores of all classifiers, including DeepCapture, are less than 40% without the training samples created by data augmentation.

We note that in the second cross data training scenario, RSVM [1] with DA also produced the best classification results comparable with DeepCapture. We surmise that underlying dataset differences may explain this. In the "Personal spam" dataset, the ratio of spam to ham image samples is approximately 1.9:1 while in the "SpamArchive spam" dataset, the ratio of spam to ham image samples is approximately 6.4:1. These results demonstrate that the performance of RSVM [1] with DA can significantly be affected by the class distribution of samples. In contrast, DeepCapture overall works well regardless of the imbalanced class distribution of samples.

5   Related Work

To avoid spam analysis and detection, spammers introduced the image spam technique to replace text spam messages with images. This strategy would be an effective technique to circumvent the text analysis of emails, which are commonly used in spam filters [5]. To detect image spam emails, several classification methods have been proposed [1,8,9,12,15,19]. However, the solutions offered so far exhibit several critical weaknesses. Existing detection techniques can be categorized into two approaches: (1) keyword-based analysis and (2) image classification.

Table 5. Performance of classifiers with a cross data training scenario (training dataset: "Personal spam" and "Personal ham" datasets; and testing dataset: "SpamArchive spam" and "Normal image ham" datasets).

Model	Acc.	Pre.	Rec.	F1.
DeepCapture	**73%**	**82%**	**72%**	**76%**
DeepCapture without DA	31%	47%	32%	38%
SVM [1]	74%	61%	14%	22%
SVM [1] with DA	60%	84%	52%	64%
RSVM [1]	82%	71%	22%	34%
RSVM [1] with DA	62%	94%	67%	76%
CNN-SVM [19]	24%	42%	23%	30%
CNN-SVM [19] with DA	64%	69%	47%	56%

5.1   Keyword-Based Analysis

Keyword-based analysis is to extract texts from a given image and analyze them using a text-based spam filter. Several techniques [9,12,15] using keyword analysis were introduced. Also, this approach was deployed in real-world spam filters such as SpamAssassin (https://spamassassin.apache.org/). Unsurprisingly, the performance of this approach depends on the performance of optical character recognition (OCR). Sophisticated spammers can intentionally embed abnormal text characters into an image, which cannot be recognized by typical OCR programs but can still be interpreted by human victims. The performance of keyword-based spam detection methods could be degraded significantly against such image spam emails. Moreover, a high processing cost of OCR is always required for analyzing images. Therefore, in this paper, we propose an image spam detection method in the direction of establishing an image classifier to distinguish spam images from ham images.

5.2   Image Classification

To address the high processing cost issue of keyword-based analysis, some researchers have tried to develop image spam detection methods using low-level features that are directly extracted from images. Annadatha et al. [1] demonstrated that image spam emails could be detected with high accuracy using either Principal Component Analysis (PCA) or Support Vector Machines (SVM). To build a classifier, they manually selected 21 features (e.g., image color, object edges) that can be extracted from spam and ham images. Shang et al. [19] proposed an alternative image classification method using a CNN model and an SVM classifier together, which is composed of 13 layers. The CNN model proceeds classification in the last fully connected layer. However, they use the output from the last fully connected layer as the input for the SVM classifier. In this paper, we develop a more compact CNN-XGBoost model consisting of

8 layers. Our evaluation results show that DeepCapture outperforms Shang et al.'s architecture in terms of detection accuracy. Fatichah et al. [8] also discussed the possibility of CNN models to detect image spam. Unlike other previous studies, they focused on building CNN models to detect the image spam on Instagram (https://www.instagram.com/), a social photo-sharing service. They evaluated the performance of four pre-trained CNN models (3-layer, 5-layer, AlexNet, and VGG16) with 8,000 images collected from Instagram. They found that the VGG16 architecture achieves the best accuracy (about 0.84) compared with the other models. Since VGG16 is a pre-trained network and its performance is not advantageous, we do not directly compare DeepCapture with VGG16.

We note that the performances of previous methods have been evaluated on different data sets with different configurations. Therefore, we cannot directly compare their reported performances. In this paper, we needed to reimplement their models and used the publicly available datasets to compare the performance of DeepCature with those of the best existing models (SVM [1], RSVM [1] and CNN-SVM [19]).

6   Conclusion

In this paper, we proposed a new image spam email detection tool called DeepCapture. To overcome the performance degrade of existing models against entirely new and unseen datasets, we developed a classifier using CNN-XGBoost and data augmentation techniques tailored towards the image spam detection task. To show the feasibility of DeepCapture, we evaluate its performance with three publicly available datasets consisting of spam and non-spam image samples. The experimental results demonstrated that DeepCapture is capable of achieving 88% F1-score, which has 6% improvement over the best existing spam detection model, CNN-SVM [19], with an F1-score of 82%. Furthermore, Deep-Capture outperforms other classifiers in cross data training scenarios to evaluate the performance of classifiers with the new and unseen dataset.

For future work, we plan to develop more sophisticated data augmentation methods to add a more real-like synthetic dataset effectively. In addition, we will increase the size of the dataset and examine any changes in detection accuracy. It would also be interesting to add the functionality of DeepCapture to an open-source project such as SpamAssassin.

Acknowledgement. Hyoungshick Kim is the corresponding author. This work has been supported in part by the Cyber Security Research Centre Limited whose activities are partially funded by the Australian Government's Cooperative Research Centres Programme and the NRF grant (No. 2017H1D8A2031628) and the ITRC Support Program (IITP-2019- 2015-0-00403) funded by the Korea government. The authors would like to thank all the anonymous reviewers for their valuable feedback.

References

1. Annadatha, A., Stamp, M.: Image spam analysis and detection. J. Comput. Virol. Hacking Tech. **14**(1), 39–52 (2016). https://doi.org/10.1007/s11416-016-0287-x

2. Attar, A., Rad, R.M., Atani, R.E.: A survey of image spamming and filtering techniques. Artif. Intell. Rev. **40**(1), 71–105 (2013)
3. Bappy, J.H., Roy-Chowdhury, A.K.: CNN based region proposals for efficient object detection. In: Proceeding of the 23rd International Conference on Image Processing, pp. 3658–3662 (2016)
4. Bergstra, J., Bengio, Y.: Random search for hyper-parameter optimization. J. Mach. Learn. Res. **13**(10), 281–305 (2012)
5. Biggio, B., Fumera, G., Pillai, I., Roli, F.: A survey and experimental evaluation of image spam filtering techniques. Pattern Recognit. Lett. **32**(10), 1436–1446 (2011)
6. Chen, T., Guestrin, C.: Xgboost: A scalable tree boosting system. In: Proceedings of the 22nd ACM International Conference on Knowledge Discovery and Data Mining, pp. 785–794 (2016)
7. Dredze, M., Gevaryahu, R., Elias-Bachrach, A.: Learning fast classifiers for image spam. In: Proceedings of the 4th Conference on Email and Anti-Spam, pp. 487–493 (2007)
8. Fatichah, C., Lazuardi, W.F., Navastara, D.A., Suciati, N., Munif, A.: Image spam detection on instagram using convolutional neural network. In: Proceedings of the 3rd Conference on Intelligent and Interactive Computing, pp. 295–303 (2019)
9. Fumera, G., Pillai, I., Roli, F.: Spam filtering based on the analysis of text information embedded into images. J. Mach. Learn. Res. **7**, 2699–2720 (2006)
10. Gao, Y., et al.: Image spam hunter. In: Proceeding of the 32nd International Conference on Acoustics, Speech and Signal Processing, pp. 1765–1768 (2008)
11. Ismail, A., Khawandi, S., Abdallah, F.: Image spam detection: problem and existing solution. Int. Res. J. Eng. Technol. **6**(2), 1696–1710 (2019)
12. Kim, J., Kim, H., Lee, J.H.: Analysis and comparison of fax spam detection algorithms. In: Proceedings of the 11th International Conference on Ubiquitous Information Management and Communication, pp. 1–4 (2017)
13. Klangpraphant, P., Bhattarakosol, P.: PIMSI: a partial image SPAM inspector. In: Proceedings of the 5th International Conference on Future Information Technology, pp. 1–6 (2010)
14. Krizhevsky, A., Sutskever, I., Hinton, G.E.: ImageNet classification with deep convolutional neural networks. Commun. ACM **60**(6), 84–90 (2017)
15. Kumar, P., Biswas, M.: SVM with Gaussian kernel-based image spam detection on textual features. In: Proceedings of the 3rd International Conference on Computational Intelligence and Communication Technology, pp. 1–6 (2017)
16. Leszczynski, M.: Emails going to spam? 12 reasons why that happens and what you can do about it (2019). https://www.getresponse.com/blog/why-emails-go-to-spam
17. Maas, A.L., Hannun, A.Y., Ng, A.Y.: Rectifier nonlinearities improve neural network acoustic models. In: Proceedings of the 30th International Conference on Machine Learning, pp. 1–6 (2013)
18. Ng, A.Y.: Feature selection, L 1 vs. L 2 regularization, and rotational invariance. In: Proceedings of the 21st International Conference on Machine learning, pp. 1–8 (2004)
19. Shang, E.X., Zhang, H.G.: Image spam classification based on convolutional neural network. In: Proceedings of the 15th International Conference on Machine Learning and Cybernetics, pp. 398–403 (2016)
20. Shorten, C., Khoshgoftaar, T.M.: A survey on image data augmentation for deep learning. J. Big Data **6**(1), 60 (2019)

21. Soranamageswari, M., Meena, C.: Statistical feature extraction for classification of image spam using artificial neural networks. In: Proceedings of the 2nd International Conference on Machine Learning and Computing, pp. 101–105 (2010)
22. Srivastava, N., Hinton, G., Krizhevsky, A., Sutskever, I., Salakhutdinov, R.: Dropout: a simple way to prevent neural networks from overfitting. J. Mach. Learn. Res. **15**(1), 1929–1958 (2014)

Attack

Rolling Attack: An Efficient Way to Reduce Armors of Office Automation Devices

Linyu Li[1,2], Lei Yu[1,2(✉)], Can Yang[1,2], Jie Gou[1,2], Jiawei Yin[1,2],
and Xiaorui Gong[1,2]

[1] Institute of Information Engineering, Chinese Academy of Sciences,
Beijing 100093, China
{lilinyu,yulei,yangcan,goujie,yinjiawei,gongxiaorui}@iie.ac.cn
[2] School of Cyber Security, University of Chinese Academy of Sciences,
Beijing 100029, China

Abstract. Firmware security is always a focus of IoT security in recent years. The security of office automation device's firmware also attracts widespread attention. Previous work on attacking office automation devices mainly focused on code flaws in firmware. However, we noticed that to find these vulnerabilities and apply them in office automation devices requires rich experience and long-term research of specific devices, which is a big cost. In this work, we designed an easy but efficient attack, Rolling Attack, which rolls back firmware to perform attacks on the office automation device, even if the firmware is up-to-date. By rolling back firmware, attackers can use Rolling Attack to exploit vulnerabilities that have been fixed by the latest firmware on office automation devices covering personal computers, network printers, network projectors and servers. We also proposed a system called Rolling Attack Pentest System to test the device by Rolling Attack. By crawling the firmware on the Internet, we have collected 99,120 models of devices' firmware packages in the past 2 years. We also collected firmware's vulnerabilities. We verified Rolling Attack on popular office automation devices covering 45 vendors, including Lenovo, HP, Samsung, Canon, Brother, Sony, Dell and so on. We performed Rolling Attack on 104 different office automation devices covering 4 types (personal computer, network printer, network projector, server) with the collected historical versions of firmware. 50.00% of the total models of devices we tested can be rolled back. 88.46% of the devices that have been rolled back are vulnerable to public vulnerabilities. We concluded that 44.23% of the devices we tested were affected by the Rolling Attack. Finally, we give some suggestions on how to mitigate Rolling Attack.

Keywords: Firmware · Downgrade · Rolling Attack · Vulnerability · Office automation devices · IoT security

L. Li and L. Yu contributed equally to this work.

© Springer Nature Switzerland AG 2020
J. K. Liu and H. Cui (Eds.): ACISP 2020, LNCS 12248, pp. 479–504, 2020.
https://doi.org/10.1007/978-3-030-55304-3_25

1   Introduction

Office automation devices [27] refer to devices such as personal computers, network printers, network projectors, servers, etc, which are used to create, collect, store, manipulate, relay office information needed for completing basic tasks. Firmware is an important part of office automation devices. In the previous research, researchers mainly focused on exploiting firmware vulnerabilities to attack office automation devices.

Previous Research on Security of Office Automation Devices. Cui et al. [6] injected malicious firmware into the HP printer in 2013. Zaddach et al. [34] discovered code flaws in the embedded systems' firmwares through dynamic analysis in 2014. In 2017, FoxGlove Security [22] exploited a certain HP printer by modifying solution packages. Müller et al. [17] focused on flows in network printer protocols, thus discovered a series of vulnerabilities. In 2018, Check Point [20] used a public vulnerability to exploit a certain HP printer, and then they discovered multiple remote code execution vulnerabilities.

Existing Gaps. During our research we found that these methods have some limitations.

- Vulnerability discovery on firmware of office automation devices requires researchers with excellent reverse engineering skills and vulnerability analysis capabilities to spend a lot of time developing attack tools.
- The firmware of some devices is difficult to extract and analyze because many firmware packages are encrypted.
- Attacks are poorly scalable and difficult to form a universal and effective tool for that different vendors have different firmware specifications.

Considering the above limitations, we proposed a general method called Rolling Attack to attack office automation devices. Rolling Attack mainly leverages the weak check of firmware to attack devices. By downgrading the firmware version to an older version, Rolling Attack uses some public vulnerabilities to exploit the device. This method does not require special professional skills, nor does it take too much time, so it could be easily used. This is a universal method for office automation firmware attacks.

For research, we selected 4 types of office automation devices, including personal computer, network printer, network projector and server. Here are the reasons why we chose these four types of office automation devices:

- Personal computer. Personal computer is often used to create office information in office environment. Attackers could obtain important information directly from personal computers.
- Network printer. Network printer is a commonly used device in the office environment, which is used for printing, scanning, and copying documents. On May 3, 2020, 3,542,240 network printers were connected to the Internet according to the statistics of zoomeye's [35]. Many research groups have revealed many printer vulnerabilities [17]. Attackers could obtain important information on the network printer by leveraging these vulnerabilities.
- Network projector. In recent years, the network projector has played an important role in office presentations. Attackers may steal meeting information by a vulnerable network projector.
- Server. Server is commonly used for information sharing and business services in office. Attackers may take full control of the vulnerable server by exploiting server vulnerabilities.

As shown in the Table 1, we tested 104 different models of devices. Covering 4 types.

Table 1. Office automation devices we tested.

Device type	Number of vendors	Number of devices
Personal computer	5	15
Network printer	18	50
Network projector	15	25
Server	7	14

Our main contributions are as follows:

- We proposed Rolling Attack and tested it on a total of 104 models of devices. Rolling Attack can leverage the flaw of firmware version checking mechanism to attack office automation devices, even if the firmware has been updated.
- We implemented a Rolling Attack Pentest System. This system could automatically perform Rolling Attack test on the target device.

- We systematically evaluated the impact of Rolling Attack on four types of devices by using the Rolling Attack Pentest System. **50.00%** of the total models we tested could be rolled back. **88.46%** of models that had been rolled back were vulnerable to public vulnerabilities after firmware rollback. **44.23%** of the models we tested were affected by Rolling Attack, which could lead to elevation of privilege, denial of service, disclosure of information, remote code execution, etc.

2   Foundations

We need to prepare the historical firmware before Rolling Attack. So we implemented a system to download firmware automatically based on scrapy [21] and selenium [18]. We spent 2 years to download all available versions of firmware of 99,120 models of devices. The details of obtaining firmware are as follows.

Personal Computer. The personal computer's firmware is usually called BIOS (Basic Input/Output System [32]) or UEFI (Unified Extensible Firmware Interface [8]). BIOS/UEFI is a small piece of software used to set up the hardware and boot the operating system at boot time. BIOS/UEFI firmware can be obtained directly from vendors' official websites.

Network Printer. Firmware of the network printer is usually provided by vendors' official websites. Müller et al. [16] collected websites for users to download firmware. We also collected websites like firmware center [9] to download firmware. However, some vendors' official websites did not provide firmware. For example, Brother's official websites only provided an update program. After analysis, we could use oh-brother [13] to obtain old version firmware.

Network Projector. Acquisition of the network projector's firmware is similar to that of the network printer. Firmware of the network projector could be downloaded directly from the vendors' official websites. Besides, firmware center [9] also provided firmware of network projectors.

Server. BMC (Baseboard Management Controller [30]) firmware is usually used in the server. Common functions of BMC firmware are powering off the server, restarting the fan, monitoring fan speed and so on. The acquisition of BMC firmware is similar to the personal computer's firmware acquisition. BMC firmware could be obtained from the vendor's official website. Périgaud [19] also listed some websites for downloading BMC firmware.

3   Rolling Attack

This section details Rolling Attack. Rolling Attack is divided into two steps. First, we roll back the firmware. Second, we exploit public vulnerabilities on the device. We explain the details of this attack in this section.

3.1   Personal Computer

Compared to spending a lot of time finding vulnerabilities like SMM (System Management Mode [10]) callback attacks [7,15] in BIOS/UEFI, our Rolling Attack is easier.

Rolling Back Vectors. Rolling back vector indicates the path or means by which the attacker downgrades the target device. There are three vectors to roll back firmware in personal computers.

– Network rolling back vector through automatic update service. Attackers need to replace the firmware of the target device during the automatic update process.
– Local rolling back vector through manual update service. Attackers could download the firmware to the target device's operating system and run update program to downgrade BIOS/UEFI firmware.
– Physical rolling back vector through USB. Attackers could downgrade the BIOS/UEFI firmware using a USB flash drive.

Roll Back Firmware. The version checking mechanism of BIOS/UEFI firmware version is divided into three categories:

– Without version checking mechanism. Many personal computers do not have version checking mechanism during the BIOS/UEFI firmware update process. Taking the ThinkPad L440 as an example, we could roll back to specific version of BIOS/UEFI firmware by running the specific version of firmware update program.
– Weak version checking mechanism. The version checking mechanism is not in the BIOS/UEFI firmware, but in the firmware update program. We could easily bypass it. Take Lenovo L470 as an example, the update program will detect the current firmware version. If the firmware version to be updated is lower than the current firmware version, the update will be stopped. We bypassed this check by patching the logic of the firmware update program.
– Strong version checking mechanism. The version checking mechanism is in the BIOS/UEFI firmware. Take the MSI B450 motherboard as an example. Downgrading it directly would fail. However, after some analysis, we found that there is a problem with the version check in the BIOS/UEFI firmware, which is similar to the bypass method mentioned in [4]. Finally, it could be bypassed by modifying the firmware.

Partial results of rolling back BIOS/UEFI firmware are shown in Table 2. The detailed results are shown in Table 7 in Appendix A. All vendors of personal computers we tested could be downgraded. It could be found that the BIOS/UEFI could be downgraded successfully on all personal computers we tested. The possible reason is that the firmware update of the personal computer may bring instability. For stability, the vendor may allows the personal computer to be downgraded.

Table 2. Partial results of rolling back firmware test on personal computers.

Vendor	Model	Factory version	Oldest version	Latest version	C2V[a]	L2V[b]
Lenovo	ThinkPad E431	1.16	1.12	1.33	√	√
ASUS	453UJ	308	305	308	√	√
HP	TowerWorkstation Z240	01.78	01.63	01.78	√	√
MSI	B450	7C02v18	7C02v10	7C02v1D	√	√

[a]Roll back from the factory version to the oldest version.
[b]Roll back from the latest version to the oldest version.

Exploit Public Vulnerabilities. We tested 64 public vulnerabilities of BIOS/UEFI. For example, according to Lenovo's vulnerability report, ThinkPad L470 contains multiple vulnerabilities [12]. These vulnerabilities could allow an attacker to achieve elevation of privilege [3] on the ThinkPad L470. We could successfully exploit the computer. The attack result is shown in the Fig. 1.

Fig. 1. Lenovo L470 was exploited after the firmware was rolled back successfully.

Vulnerabilities test results are shown in Table 10 in Appendix A. Since most publicly disclosed authentication bypass attacks are not targeted at the models we tested, the number of successful attacks is 1. Elevation of privilege attacks and disclosure of information attacks are more effective, because most vulnerabilities we tested in the BIOS/UEFI were belong to these types.

3.2   Network Printer

Rolling Back Vectors. There are 4 vectors to roll back firmware in network printers.

– Network rolling back vector through automatic update service. Attackers could replace the firmware of target device during the automatic update process.
– Network rolling back vector through BOOTP [31]/TFTP update service. Attackers could update firmware by uploading firmware to BOOTP/TFTP update service.
– Network rolling back vector through port 9100. Vendors' firmware update programs usually update printer through port 9100. Attackers could roll back firmware by sending firmware to port 9100 directly.
– Network rolling back vector through FTP service. Attackers may forge an ftp server to provide older firmware to the network printer.
– Physical rolling back vector through the USB. Attackers could downgrade the firmware through a USB flash drive.

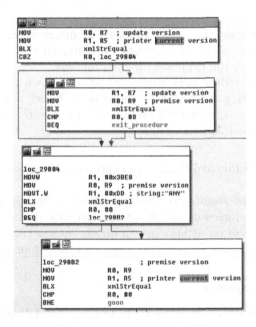

Fig. 2. Version check in a network printer firmware update program.

Roll Back Firmware. Most network printers' firmware can be updated through a firmware update program on client computer. The firmware update program would first detect whether there is a printer of the corresponding model in the local area network, and then check that whether the firmware version is

Table 3. Partial results of rolling back firmware test on network printers.

Vendor	Model	Factory version	Oldest version	Latest version	C2V[a]	L2V[b]
HP	OfficeJet Pro 8210	1937C	1709A	1937C	√	√
Canon	LBP 252dw	1.16	1.16	5.01	×	√
Konica Minolta	PagePro 1550DN	3.17	–	–	×	×
Brother	DCP 7180DN	3.17	3.13	–	√	×
Epson	L551 C463A	GM01I7	GM00I6	–	√	×
Panasonic	KX MB2128CN	–	–	–	×	×
OKI	B840	1.2	–	–	×	×
Lenovo	M7605D	1827C	–	–	×	×
Ricoh	PJ X5300	1.42	1.41	–	√	×
Sharp	SF S201N	1.03	–	–	×	×
TOSHIBA	e-STUDIO2309A	1.3	–	–	×	×
ICSP	YPS 4022NH	2.32	–	–	×	×
AURORA	AD330PDN	2.11	–	–	×	×
Pantum	CP 2500DN	F.22 Rev.A	F.10 Rev.A	–	√	×
Fuji Xerox	DocuPrint M158 ab	2.1	–	–	×	×
Kyocera	FS C5150DN	1.1	–	–	×	×

[a]Roll back from the factory version to the oldest version.
[b]Roll back from the latest version to the oldest version.

significantly higher than the target printer's firmware version. Figure 2 shows version checking mechanism of a update program. However, we could bypass this check by patching the firmware update program.

Partial results of rolling back firmware test are shown in Table 3. 10 of the 18 vendors of network printers can be rolled back. Other printers could not be rolled back, because we couldn't obtain their older firmware. The detailed results are shown in Table 6 in Appendix A.

Exploit Public Vulnerabilities. We collected 115 vulnerabilities to attack network printers.

Vulnerabilities test results are shown in Table 11 in Appendix A. Elevation of privilege attacks, disclosure of information attacks, denial of service attacks and remote code execution attacks have a higher success rate in attack, because most of the vulnerabilities we collected belong to these four types.

3.3 Network Projector

Rolling Back Vectors. Attackers could leverage the following attack vectors to roll back the firmware of the network projector.

- Network rolling vector through web management interface. Attackers could roll back the firmware on the web management interface.
- Network rolling vector through upgrading port. Attackers could roll back the firmware by leveraging the upgrading port.
- Physical rolling vector through the USB. Attackers could roll back the firmware through a USB flash drive.

Roll Back Firmware. In our test, network projectors did not implement version checking mechanism. Attackers could roll back the device by uploading the older firmware to the upgrading port.

Partial results of rolling back firmware test are shown in Table 4. The detailed results are shown in Table 8 in Appendix A. Many vendors' network projectors could not be downgraded because we couldn't collect their firmware. Only a few vendors provide older versions of firmware.

Table 4. Partial results of rolling back firmware test on network projectors.

Vendor	Model	Factory version	Oldest version	Latest version	C2V[a]	L2V[b]
Sony	VPL EW575	1.0	–	–	×	×
LG	PH550G	03.00.08	02.10.01	03.00.08	√	√
ViewSonic	DLP PJD6550LW	2.1	–	–	×	×
InFocus	IN3134a	1.4	–	–	×	×
Casio	XJ FC330XN	1.2	–	–	×	×
Epson	CB X27	1.03	–		×	×
Canon	LV 8320	2.1	–	–	×	×
HITACHI	HCP D767X	1.0	–	–	×	×
Optoma	DLP X316ST	1.1	–	–	×	×
ASUS	P3B	21.1	–	–	×	×
NEC	NP M403X	22.301	–	–	×	×
Sharp	XG MX465A	1.61.2	–	–	×	×
Acer	H6517ST	4.2	–	–	×	×
Ricoh	PJ HD5900	1.005.1	–	–	×	×

[a]Roll back from the factory version to the oldest version.
[b]Roll back from the latest version to the oldest version.

Exploit Public Vulnerabilities. We collected four CVEs in total to test target devices.

Vulnerabilities test results are shown in Table 12 in Appendix A. Network projectors we tested were not affected by vulnerabilities because these projectors' vulnerabilities had not been disclosed for the time being. Rolling attack had no effect on devices that had no public vulnerabilities.

3.4   Server

Rolling Back Vectors. Attackers could leverage the following attack vectors to roll back the firmware of the server.

– Network rolling back vector through web management interface. The server usually offers a web management interface for administrators to manage the server. We found some servers offered option to roll back older firmware in web management interface. An attacker could downgrade the device after logging in through the web management interface.

– Physical rolling back vector through the serial console port. Serial console port [25] is used to update firmware in most servers. Attackers could downgrade BMC firmware through the serial console port.

Roll Back Firmware. Many servers implemented weak rollback prevention.

Table 5. Partial results of rolling back firmware test on servers.

Vendor	Model	Factory version	Oldest version	Latest version	C2V[a]	L2V[b]
HPE	ML150 Gen9 E5-2609v4	2.56	2.00	2.76	√	√
Dell	PowerEdge R420	2.60.60.60	1.57.57	2.63.60.62	√	√
Lenovo	ThinkServer RD450	v4.93.0	v2.19.0	v4.93.0	√	√
Inspur	NF5280M4	4.22.0	4.19.0	4.25.9	√	√
Cisco	UCS C240 M4 Rack Server	4.1	2.0	4.1	√	√
Huawei	RH2288H V3	C527	C202	C712	√	√

[a]Roll back from the factory version to the oldest version.
[b]Roll back from the latest version to the oldest version.

Partial results of rolling back firmware test on servers are shown in Table 5. The detailed results are shown in Table 9 in Appendix A. Many vendors' servers could be rolled back from the factory version or the latest version to the oldest version. Because the older firmware of servers we tested were not removed, and they implemented poor version checking mechanism.

Exploit Public Vulnerabilities. We tested 41 vulnerabilities like CVE-2018-1207 [23] after rolling back the firmware.

Vulnerabilities test results are shown in Table 13 in Appendix A. Elevation of privilege attacks and denial of service attacks were most successful in server attacks, because most of the vulnerabilities we collected belong to these two types of vulnerabilities. Besides, remote code execution attacks, disclosure of information attacks and authentication bypass attacks have also been successfully on several servers. So Rolling Attack could play an important role in the actual attack on servers.

4   Rolling Attack Pentest System

This section describes the framework of Rolling Attack Pentest System and how it works. Framework of Rolling Attack Pentest System is shown as Fig. 3.

The work flow of the system is detailed as follows.

1) Information Collector collects information of the target device and identifies the target's firmware version.
2) Firmware Downloader downloads older versions of firmware from the Firmware Museum according to information collected from Information Collector.

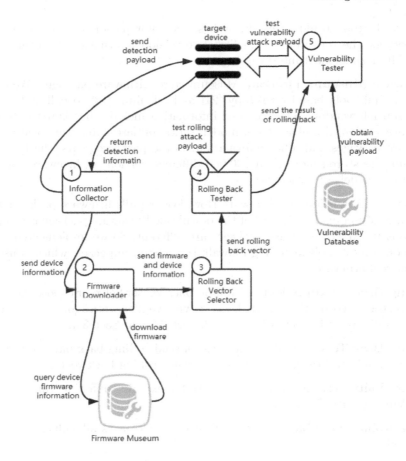

Fig. 3. Framework of Rolling Attack Pentest System.

3) Rolling Back Vector Selector selects all possible vectors to roll back firmware.
4) Rolling Back Tester rolls back firmware through vectors selected from Rolling Back Vector Selector.
5) Vulnerability Tester selects vulnerabilities from the Vulnerability Database based on the results of the Rolling Back Vector Selector. Then Vulnerability Tester test these vulnerabilities.

The user only needs to input the target device's ip or local serial port, and then the system automatically executes the work flow.

The detailed information of each component in the system is as follows:

Information Collector. Information Collector collects various information of the target device. A common method to obtain device information is to use tools like nmap [14] to scan the target device. However, the information obtained by network scanning may not contain firmware version information. In order to solve this problem, we have implemented a tool to obtain firmware version information of different types of devices. For network printers and network projector devices, the tool would access its web service. For personal computer devices and servers, the tool would gain firmware version information from interfaces like BMC management interface.

Firmware Museum. Firmware Museum stores firmware packages. We developed several tools based on scrapy [21] and selenium [18] to collect firmware from multiple vendors. The recorded information includes but is not limited to firmware version, download date, model, series, update date, size, local path of firmware packages and other information. In the past two years, the Firmware Museum has stored more than 200,000 different versions of firmware packages for 99,120 models of device models.

Firmware Downloader. Firmware Downloader pulls firmware packages from Firmware Museum. The format of the downloaded firmware package is complex. Methods to extract firmware packages are different. So we implemented a tool based on several tools including binwalk [11], unzip, unpacker, which is used to extract real firmware.

Rolling Back Vector Selector. Rolling Back Vector Selector choose the rolling back vector based on the target device's type, vendor, series and model, which has been discussed in Sect. 3.1, Sect. 3.2, Sect. 3.3 and Sect. 3.4.

Rolling Back Tester. Rolling Back Tester sends rolling back payload (payload that can roll back firmware) to devices through rolling back vector.

Vulnerability Tester. Vulnerability Tester exploits different vulnerabilities from Vulnerability Database.

Vulnerability Database. Vulnerability Database saves all vulnerabilities we collected.

5   Evaluation

After rolling back test, the number of devices that can eventually be downgraded is shown in Fig. 4.

Product type	From the factory version to the oldest version	From the latest version to the oldest version	Number of devices that could be rolled back	Number of devices we tested
Personal computer	15	15	15	15
Network printer	18	13	19	50
Network projecter	4	4	4	25
Server	14	14	14	14

Fig. 4. Number of devices whose firmware can be rolled back.

50.00% of the total 104 devices could be rolled back.

Almost all personal computers and servers we tested could be rolled back. One reason is that vendors usually provide historical firmware downloads of personal computers and servers. Another reason is that vendors allow users to downgrade for stability.

Nearly half of the network printers we tested could be rolled back, because older firmware for some network printers we tested could not be obtained. So rolling back on network printers we tested was not as effective as personal computers and servers.

Many network projectors we tested could not be rolled back. The reason is that vendors rarely update firmware for network projectors we tested, many of them only had one firmware version.

Based on the rolling back results, we conducted vulnerability tests.

Figure 5 shows that devices were vulnerable to few vulnerabilities before rolling back the firmware.

As shown in Fig. 6, devices suffered more vulnerabilities than before after the firmware is rolled back.

After rolling back the firmware, more devices were affected by vulnerabilities. Among them, the number of vulnerabilities in personal computers and network

Device type	Remote Code Execution	Escalation of Privilege	DoS	Disclosure of Information	Authentication Bypass	XSS	Information Tampering	Total number of CVEs we tested
Personal computer	0	7	5	7	0	0	0	64
Network printer	3	0	5	2	1	0	0	115
Network projecter	0	0	0	0	0	0	0	4
Server	1	2	3	0	2	0	0	41

Fig. 5. Vulnerabilities before rolling back.

Device type	Remote Code Execution	Escalation of Privilege	DoS	Disclosure of Information	Authentication Bypass	XSS	Information Tampering	Total number of CVEs we tested
Personal computer	2	17	8	14	1	0	0	64
Network printer	7	2	15	6	5	1	0	115
Network projecter	0	0	0	0	0	0	0	4
Server	3	7	6	4	4	0	0	41

Fig. 6. Vulnerabilities after rolling back.

printers had increased relatively more, because they frequently update firmware to fix vulnerabilities.

Personal computers and servers we tested were most vulnerable to escalation of privilege attacks. Therefore, rolling back firmware may greatly increase the possibility of attackers gaining access to privileges of these personal computers and servers for which they were not entitled. Network printers we tested were most vulnerable to denial of service attacks. Therefore, rolling back firmware may greatly increase the possibility of attackers blocking access to some network printers we tested. No device was affected by the information tampering attack, because we did not find the firmware affected by this attack. In addition, personal computers suffered the most from information leakage attacks after the rolling back firmware. Network projectors we tested were not vulnerable to vulnerabilities we collected, because no vulnerabilities had been publicly disclosed in the projectors we tested. For devices that were not affected by vulnerabilities before rolling back, rolling back may not affect the number of vulnerabilities on the device. Network projectors were not affected by remote code execution during Rolling Attack because we couldn't find this type of network projectors' public vulnerabilities.

The number of three types of vulnerabilities including escalation of privilege, denial of service and disclosure of information increased after downgrading because most of the firmware we rolled back were affected by these types of public vulnerabilities.

We also compared the ability to exploit vulnerabilities between before and after Rolling Attack, the result is shown in Fig. 7. It is obvious that after these devices were downgraded, they were affected by more vulnerabilities than before. Rolling Attack could make it easy to carry out attacks that cannot be executed previously, such as obtaining leaked information or executing code on the target device. **88.46%** of models of device that had been rolled back were vulnerable to public vulnerabilities.

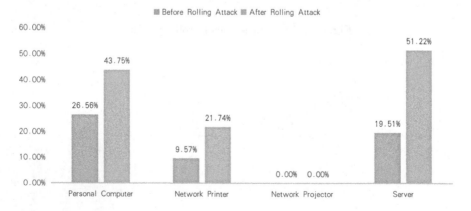

Fig. 7. Percentage of vulnerabilities that can be applied to devices before and after Rolling Attack.

In summary, **44.23%** of the devices we tested were affected by the Rolling Attack. More detailed results are shown in Table 10, Table 11, Table 12 and Table 13 in Appendix A.

6 Related Work

We did some research on studies with similar ideas, which mentioned methods by downgrading the software or firmware. Their ideas were similar to Rolling Attack.

Software. Downgrade attack was used in TLS (Transport Layer Security [33]) attack [24,26]. Recently, this method has been applied to attack in conventional softwares. We found that some APTs (Advanced Persistent Threat [29]) leveraged some methods similar to our Rolling Attack to bypass AVs (Antivirus Software [28]). They installed vulnerable and old signed Windows drivers [1] to bypass some protections against Windows 10 system.

Firmware. Chen et al. [5] downgraded the trustlet (TA) and TrustZone (a system-wide security method suitable for a large number of applications [2]) OS. After that, they exploited device with previous privilege escalation vulnerability. This method is useful for devices with TrustZone enabled.

7 Discussion

In this section we discussed limitations of Rolling Attack and measures to mitigate Rolling Attack.

Here are limitations of Rolling Attack.

- Rolling Attack is less effective on devices with fewer vulnerabilities, such as network projectors, because Rolling Attack rely on historical vulnerabilities.
- Rolling Attack cannot be performed on devices that we can't get historical firmware.
- Device user may be aware of the process of Rolling Attack. In the Rolling Attack process, it is generally necessary to restart the device or related services, which may be noticed by the user.
- Performing Rolling Attack on some devices requires physical access.

Here are ways to mitigate Rolling Attack.

- Forbid downgrading firmware and make sure that the version checking mechanism is implemented correctly in firmware.
- Force the device to update to the latest version automatically.

8 Conclusion

In this paper, we proposed Rolling Attack to attack office automation devices. Using Rolling Attack, attacker could easily leverage public vulnerabilities to attack various office automation devices after rolling back the firmware. Rolling Attack could carry out attacks including authentication bypass, elevation of privilege, denial of service, disclosure of information or remote code execution on office automation devices. For four types of devices we tested, Rolling Attack could be carried out without physical access. We also provided a system called Rolling Attack Pentest System to automate the process of Rolling Attack. Using the system, we tested Rolling Attack on 104 different models of devices in four types. As can be seen from the results, it worked well on four types of devices. Devices that whose firmware can be rolled back account for **50.00%** of the total devices. **88.46%** of devices that have been rolled back are vulnerable to public vulnerabilities. In summary, **44.23%** of the devices we tested were affected by the Rolling Attack.

Appendix A Detailed Test Results of Rolling Attack

Table 6. Detailed results of rolling back firmware test on network printers.

Vendor	Model	Factory version	Oldest version	Latest version	C2V[a]	L2V[b]
HP	OfficeJet Pro 8210	1937C	1709A	1937C	✓	✓
HP	OfficeJet Pro 8710	1828A	1716A	1937A	✓	✓
HP	PageWide Pro 477dw	1937D	1603A	1937D	✓	✓
HP	LaserJet MFP M277dw	20181003	20171003	20191203	✓	✓
HP	LaserJet MFP M226dw	20180718	20161101	20190716	✓	✓
HP	LaserJet Pro M1536dnf	20140630	–	–	×	×
HP	LaserJet MFP M436n	V3.82.01.20	–	–	×	×
Samsung	CLP 680ND	V4.00.02.32	V3.00.17	V4.00.02	✓	✓
Samsung	Laser Multifunction SCX-4650	3.17	3.13	3.23	✓	✓
Samsung	Xpress SL-M2676	V3.07.01.37	–	–	×	×
Samsung	SCX 4821HN	–	–	–	×	×
Samsung	ML 3710ND	–	–	–	×	×
Canon	Pixma TS9020	–	–	–	×	×
Canon	TS3180	1.100	–	–	×	×
Canon	LBP 252dw	1.16	1.16	5.01	×	✓
Canon	MF621Cn	–	–	–	×	×
Canon	2520i	–	–	–	×	×
Canon	MF620C	V03.05	1.15	V03.05	✓	✓
Konica Minolta	PagePro 1550DN	3.17	–	–	×	×
Konica Minolta	PagePro 1390MF	F.31	F.10	F.31	✓	✓
Brother	DCP 7180DN	3.17	3.13	–	✓	×
Brother	HL 3150CDN	302	311	–	✓	×
Brother	MFC 9140CDN	1.10	–	–	×	×
Brother	MFC J6910DW	1.15	–	–	×	×
Epson	WF 3011	F.10	–	–	×	×
Epson	L551 C463A	GM01I7	GM00I6	–	✓	×
Panasonic	KX MB2128CN	–	–	–	×	×
Panasonic	PT UX315C	1.15	–	–	×	×
Panasonic	DP-MB536CN	–	–	–	×	×

(*continued*)

Table 6. (*continued*)

Vendor	Model	Factory version	Oldest version	Latest version	C2V[a]	L2V[b]
OKI	B840	1.2	–	–	×	×
OKI	C711	1.2	–	–	×	×
Lenovo	M7605D	1827C	–	–	×	×
Lenovo	M7615DHA	1827D	1652D	1827D	✓	✓
Lenovo	M7675DXF	1827D	1652D	1827D	✓	✓
Lenovo	iB4180	1.2	–	–	×	×
Ricoh	SP 212SFNw	Ver.1.05	–	–	×	×
Ricoh	PJ X5300	1.42	1.41	–	✓	×
Sharp	SF S201N	1.03	–	–	×	×
TOSHIBA	e-STUDIO2309A	1.3	–	–	×	×
ICSP	YPS 4022NH	2.32	–	–	×	×
AURORA	AD330PDN	2.11	–	–	×	×
Lexmark	MX511de	LW74.SB4.P268	LW74.SB4.P230	–	✓	×
Pantum	P2206NW	20180302	–	–	×	×
Pantum	CP 2500DN	F.22 Rev.A	F.10 Rev.A	–	✓	×
Fuji Xerox	DocuPrint CM228 fw	1.03	–	–	×	×
Fuji Xerox	DocuPrint M158 ab	2.1	–	–	×	×
Fuji Xerox	DocuCentre S2110	2018011405	2017005206	2018011405	✓	✓
Fuji Xerox	Phaser 3435DN	3.01	–	–	×	×
Fuji Xerox	VersaLink C7020	57.50.61	–	–	×	×
Kyocera	FS C5150DN	1.1	–	–	×	×

[a]Roll back from the factory version to the oldest version.
[b]Roll back from the latest version to the oldest version.

Table 7. Detailed results of rolling back firmware test on personal computers.

Vendor	Model	Factory version	Oldest version	Latest version	C2V[a]	L2V[b]
Lenovo	ThinkPad E431	1.16	1.12	1.33	✓	✓
Lenovo	ThinkPad L470	1.68	1.50	1.70	✓	✓
Lenovo	ThinkPad T420	1.51	1.15	1.52	✓	✓
Lenovo	ThinkPad L440	1.81	1.07	1.93	✓	✓
Lenovo	ThinkPad T400	3.22	3.15	3.23	✓	✓
Lenovo	ThinkPad X280	1.36	1.08	1.38	✓	✓
Lenovo	V310 14IKB	2WCN35WW	2WCN35WW	2WCN45WW	✓	✓
ASUS	453UJ	308	305	308	✓	✓
HP	Zhan 86 Pro G2	F.40 Rev.A	F.10 Rev.A	F.40 Rev.A	✓	✓
HP	TowerWorkstation Z240	01.78	01.63	01.78	✓	✓
MSI	B450	7C02v18	7C02v10	7C02v1D	✓	✓
GIGABYTE	G1.Sniper B7	F20	F1	F22f	✓	✓
GIGABYTE	GA-Gaming B8	F7	F4	F8d	✓	✓
GIGABYTE	B365 HD3	F3	F1	F4c	✓	✓
GIGABYTE	B365M POWER	F3	F1	F5A	✓	✓

[a]Roll back from the factory version to the oldest version.
[b]Roll back from the latest version to the oldest version.

Table 8. Detailed results of rolling back firmware test on network projectors.

Vendor	Model	Factory version	Oldest version	Latest version	C2V[a]	L2V[b]
Sony	VPL EW575	1.0	–	–	×	×
Sony	VPL SX226	V2.42	V2.31	v2.42	√	√
Sony	VPL SW235	2.33	–	–	×	×
Sony	VPL DX147	2.41	2.03	2.41	√	√
Sony	VPL CX239	1.0	–	–	×	×
Sony	VPL EX226	1.0	–	–	×	×
LG	PF1500G	04.00.18	03.01.28	04.00.18	√	√
LG	PH550G	03.00.08	02.10.01	03.00.08	√	√
ViewSonic	DLP PJD6550LW	2.1	–	–	×	×
InFocus	IN3134a	1.4	–	–	×	×
Casio	XJ FC330XN	1.2	–	–	×	×
Epson	CB X27	1.03	–	–	×	×
Epson	EB C745WN	1.22	–	–	×	×
Canon	LV X320	23.11	–	–	×	×
Canon	LV 8320	2.1	–	–	×	×
HITACHI	HCP D767X	1.0	–	–	×	×
HITACHI	HCP FW50	1.01	–	–	×	×
HITACHI	HCP A837	1.1	–	–	×	×
Optoma	DLP X316ST	1.1	–	–	×	×
ASUS	P3B	21.1	–	–	×	×
NEC	NP M403X	22.301	–	–	×	×
Sharp	XG MX465A	1.61.2	–	–	×	×
Acer	H6517ST	4.2	–	–	×	×
Ricoh	PJ HD5900	1.005.1	–	–	×	×
Panasonic	PT P3B	22.012.033	–	–	×	×

[a]Roll back from the factory version to the oldest version.
[b]Roll back from the latest version to the oldest version.

Table 9. Detailed results of rolling back firmware test on servers.

Vendor	Model	Factory version	Oldest version	Latest version	C2V[a]	L2V[b]
HPE	ML150 Gen9 E5-2609v4	2.56	2.00	2.76	√	√
Dell	PowerEdge R420	2.60.60.60	1.57.57	2.63.60.62	√	√
Dell	PowerEdge R430	2.60.60.60	2.10.10.10	2.70.70.70	√	√
Dell	PowerEdge T630	2.52.52.52	2.01.00.01	2.70.70.70	√	√
Dell	PowerEdge R730	2.60.60.60	2.01.00.01	2.70.70.70	√	√
Dell	PowerEdge R630	2.52.52.52	2.01.00.01	2.70.70.70	√	√
Lenovo	ThinkServer RD450	v4.93.0	v2.19.0	v4.93.0	√	√
Lenovo	TowerServer TD350	v4.93.0	v3.19.0	v4.93.0	√	√
Lenovo	System x3650 M5	2.61	2.51	2.61	√	√
Sugon	I620 G20	18.100.00.00	17.100.00.00	18.100.00.00	√	√
Sugon	A620r-G	18.100.00.00	17.100.00.00	18.100.00.00	√	√
Inspur	NF5280M4	4.22.0	4.19.0	4.25.9	√	√
Cisco	UCS C240 M4 Rack Server	4.1	2.0	4.1	√	√
Huawei	RH2288H V3	C527	C202	C712	√	√

[a]Roll back from the factory version to the oldest version.
[b]Roll back from the latest version to the oldest version.

Table 10. Vulnerability test results of personal computers after rolling back the firmware.

CVE-ID	Authentication bypass	Elevation of privilege	Denial of service	Disclosure of information	Remote code execution	Attack result
CVE-2002-2059	○					×
CVE-2005-0963		○				×
CVE-2005-4175		○		○		×
CVE-2005-4176		○		○		×
CVE-2008-0211			○			×
CVE-2008-0706		○	○			×
CVE-2008-3894		○		○		×
CVE-2008-3900				○		×
CVE-2008-3902				○		×
CVE-2008-7096		○				×
CVE-2010-0560		○				×
CVE-2012-5218	○					×
CVE-2013-3582		○				×
CVE-2015-2890		○				×
CVE-2015-3692		○				×
CVE-2016-2243		○				×
CVE-2016-8224		○	○			×
CVE-2016-8222			○			×
CVE-2017-2751					○	×
CVE-2017-3197			○			×
CVE-2017-3198					○	×
CVE-2017-3753		○				×

(continued)

Table 10. (*continued*)

CVE-ID	Authentication bypass	Elevation of privilege	Denial of service	Disclosure of information	Remote code execution	Attack result
CVE-2017-3754		○				×
CVE-2017-5700				○		×
CVE-2017-5686				○		×
CVE-2017-5704				○		×
CVE-2017-5715				●		✓
CVE-2017-5721		○				×
CVE-2017-5722		○				×
CVE-2017-5701				○		×
CVE-2017-8083		○				×
CVE-2017-9457				○		×
CVE-2017-5689		●			●	✓
CVE-2018-3652		●				✓
CVE-2018-12201			●			✓
CVE-2018-3627		●	●			✓
CVE-2018-12169	●	●				✓
CVE-2018-12126				●		✓
CVE-2018-12127				●		✓
CVE-2018-12130				●		✓
CVE-2019-11091				●		✓
CVE-2018-9062		●			●	✓
CVE-2018-9069				●		✓
CVE-2019-6156		●				✓
CVE-2019-6171		○				×
CVE-2019-6188		●				✓
CVE-2019-0117				●		✓
CVE-2019-0123		●				✓
CVE-2019-0124		●				✓
CVE-2019-0151		●				✓
CVE-2019-0152		●				✓
CVE-2019-0184				●		✓
CVE-2019-0154			●			✓
CVE-2019-0185				●		✓
CVE-2019-6170		●	●	●		✓
CVE-2019-14607		○				×
CVE-2019-6172		●	●	●		✓
CVE-2019-11135				●		✓
CVE-2019-11136		●	●	●		✓
CVE-2019-11139			●			✓
CVE-2019-11137		●	●	●		✓
CVE-2019-16284		●				✓
CVE-2019-11108		●				✓
CVE-2019-11097		○				×

●: The attack succeeded. ○: The attack failed.

Table 11. Vulnerability test results of printers after rolling back the firmware.

CVE-ID	Authentication bypass	Elevation of privilege	Denial of service	Disclosure of information	Remote code execution	XSS	Information tampering	Attack result
CVE-1999-1061				o				×
CVE-1999-1062				o				×
CVE-1999-1563				o				×
CVE-2000-1062			o					×
CVE-2000-1063			o					×
CVE-2000-1064			o					×
CVE-2000-1065			o					×
CVE-2001-0044		o						×
CVE-2001-0484		o						×
CVE-2001-1134				o	o			×
CVE-2002-1048		o						×
CVE-2002-1055			o					×
CVE-2002-2373					o			×
CVE-2003-0257		o						×
CVE-2003-0697		o	o					×
CVE-2004-2166	o							×
CVE-2004-2439	o							×
CVE-2005-2988				o				×
CVE-2006-0577		o						×
CVE-2006-0788					o			×
CVE-2006-6742			o					×
CVE-2007-4236		o						×
CVE-2007-5764		o						×
CVE-2008-0374		o						×
CVE-2008-2743		o						×
CVE-2008-5385	o							×
CVE-2009-1333							o	×
CVE-2009-2684							o	×
CVE-2010-0101			o					×
CVE-2011-1531				o				×
CVE-2011-1532						o		×
CVE-2011-1533							o	×
CVE-2012-4964		o						×
CVE-2011-4161					o			×
CVE-2012-2017			o					×
CVE-2013-2507							o	×
CVE-2013-2670							o	×
CVE-2013-2671							o	×
CVE-2013-4615			o					×
CVE-2013-4845							o	×
CVE-2013-6032		o						×
CVE-2013-6033		o						×

(continued)

Table 11. (*continued*)

CVE-ID	Authentication bypass	Elevation of privilege	Denial of service	Disclosure of information	Remote code execution	XSS	Information tampering	Attack result
CVE-2013-6193			○					×
CVE-2014-0160				●				✓
CVE-2015-1056						○		×
CVE-2015-5729	○							×
CVE-2016-1896	○							×
CVE-2016-1503			●					✓
CVE-2016-2244				○				×
CVE-2016-3145				○				×
CVE-2017-2741			●		●			✓
CVE-2017-2747				○	○			×
CVE-2018-0688						○		×
CVE-2018-14899						○		×
CVE-2018-14900	○							×
CVE-2018-14903			○					×
CVE-2018-15748	○							×
CVE-2018-17001						○		×
CVE-2018-17309						○		×
CVE-2018-17310						○		×
CVE-2018-17311						○		×
CVE-2018-17312						○		×
CVE-2018-17313						○		×
CVE-2018-17314						○		×
CVE-2018-17315						○		×
CVE-2018-17316						○		×
CVE-2018-19248			○					×
CVE-2018-5924			●		●			✓
CVE-2018-5925			●		●			✓
CVE-2019-6324			○		○			×
CVE-2019-6335			○					×
CVE-2019-10057	●			●				✓
CVE-2019-10058	●			●				✓
CVE-2019-10059				●				✓
CVE-2019-10627			●					✓
CVE-2019-10960			○		○			×
CVE-2019-13165					●			✓
CVE-2019-13166				○				×
CVE-2019-13167			○					×
CVE-2019-13168			○					×
CVE-2019-13169			○					×
CVE-2019-13170			○					×
CVE-2019-13171			○					×

(*continued*)

Table 11. (*continued*)

CVE-ID	Authentication bypass	Elevation of privilege	Denial of service	Disclosure of information	Remote code execution	XSS	Information tampering	Attack result
CVE-2019-13172					o			×
CVE-2019-13192		o		o				×
CVE-2019-13193		o		o				×
CVE-2019-13194		o		o				×
CVE-2019-13195		o		o	o			×
CVE-2019-13196				o				×
CVE-2019-13197		o						×
CVE-2019-13198		o						×
CVE-2019-13199		o						×
CVE-2019-13200				●				✓
CVE-2019-13201			●			●		✓
CVE-2019-13202			●					✓
CVE-2019-13203			●					✓
CVE-2019-13204			●					✓
CVE-2019-13205	●							✓
CVE-2019-13206			●		●			✓
CVE-2019-14300			o		o			×
CVE-2019-14305			●					✓
CVE-2019-14307			o		o			×
CVE-2019-14308			o					×
CVE-2019-16240			●		●			✓
CVE-2019-17184		●						✓
CVE-2019-6323		o						×
CVE-2019-6326					o			×
CVE-2019-6327			o					×
CVE-2019-6337				●				✓
CVE-2019-9930		●		●				✓
CVE-2019-9931			●					✓
CVE-2019-9932			●					✓
CVE-2019-9933			●		●			✓
CVE-2019-9934	●							✓
CVE-2019-9935	●							✓

●: The attack succeeded. o: The attack failed.

Table 12. Vulnerability test results of network projectors after rolling back the firmware.

CVE-ID	Authentication bypass	Disclosure of information	Elevation of privilege	Attack result
CVE-2014-8383	o			×
CVE-2014-8384			o	×
CVE-2017-12860			o	×
CVE-2017-12861			o	×

●: The attack succeeded. o: The attack failed.

Table 13. Vulnerability test results of servers after rolling back the firmware.

CVE-ID	Authentication bypass	Elevation of privilege	Denial of service	Disclosure of information	Remote code execution	XSS	Attack result
CVE-2007-0661			o				×
CVE-2009-0345		o			o		×
CVE-2010-5107			•				√
CVE-2012-4096		o		o			×
CVE-2012-4112					o		×
CVE-2013-3607					o		×
CVE-2013-4782	o						×
CVE-2013-4784				o			×
CVE-2012-4078				o			×
CVE-2012-4074				o			×
CVE-2013-4786				•			√
CVE-2014-3566				•			√
CVE-2014-2532	•						√
CVE-2015-0739	o						×
CVE-2015-4265			•				√
CVE-2016-1542	o	o					×
CVE-2016-2349	o	o					×
CVE-2016-6899			•				√
CVE-2016-6900			•				√
CVE-2017-17323	•						√
CVE-2018-12171		o					×
CVE-2018-1207	•		•		•		√
CVE-2018-1208			•				√
CVE-2018-1209		•					√
CVE-2018-1210		•					√
CVE-2018-1211				•			√
CVE-2018-1243	•				•		√
CVE-2018-1244					•		√
CVE-2018-3682		•					√
CVE-2018-7941		•					√
CVE-2018-7942				•			√
CVE-2018-7949		•					√
CVE-2018-7950		•					√
CVE-2018-7951		•					√
CVE-2018-9086					o		×
CVE-2019-16649	o	o					×
CVE-2019-16650	o	o					×
CVE-2019-5497	o						×
CVE-2019-6159						o	×
CVE-2019-6161	o						×
CVE-2019-6260		o					×

•: The attack succeeded. o: The attack failed.

References

1. 0xrepnz: Abusing signed windows drivers. https://repnz.github.io/posts/abusing-signed-drivers/
2. Arm: Description of trustzone. https://developer.arm.com/ip-products/security-ip/trustzone/. Accessed 4 Apr 2018
3. Bruno: Code check(mate) in SMM. https://www.synacktiv.com/posts/exploit/code-checkmate-in-smm.html
4. Bulygin, Y., Furtak, A., Bazhaniuk, O.: A tale of one software bypass of windows 8 secure boot. Black Hat USA (2013)
5. Chen, Y., Zhang, Y., Wang, Z., Wei, T.: Downgrade attack on trustzone. arXiv preprint arXiv:1707.05082 (2017)
6. Cui, A., Costello, M., Stolfo, S.: When firmware modifications attack: a case study of embedded exploitation (2013)
7. Embleton, S., Sparks, S., Zou, C.C.: SMM rootkit: a new breed of OS independent malware. Secur. Commun. Netw. **6**(12), 1590–1605 (2013)
8. UEFI Forum: Description of UEFI. https://uefi.org/specifications
9. h5ai: Firmware center. https://firmware.center
10. Intel: SMM protection in EDKII Intel. https://uefi.org/sites/default/files/resources/Jiewen%20Yao%20-%20SMM%20Protection%20in%20%20EDKII_Intel.pdf
11. ReFirm Labs: Binwalk description. https://github.com/ReFirmLabs/binwalk
12. Lenovo: Lenovo bios security vulnerabilities description. https://support.lenovo.com/us/en/product_security/ps500279
13. Cauldron Development LLC: Oh brother tools. https://github.com/CauldronDevelopmentLLC/oh-brother
14. Lyon, G.: Nmap introduction. https://nmap.org/
15. Matrosov, A.: UEFI firmware rootkits (2017). https://www.blackhat.com/docs/asia-17/materials/asia-17-Matrosov-The-UEFI-Firmware-Rootkits-Myths-And-Reality.pdf
16. Müller, J., Mladenov, V., Somorovsky, J., Schwenk, J.: PRET firmware updates (2017). http://hacking-printers.net/wiki/index.php/Firmware_updates
17. Müller, J., Mladenov, V., Somorovsky, J., Schwenk, J.: SoK: exploiting network printers. In: 2017 IEEE Symposium on Security and Privacy (SP), pp. 213–230. IEEE (2017)
18. Muthukadan, B.: Selenium description. https://selenium-python.readthedocs.io/
19. Périgaud, F., Gazet, A., Czarny, J.: Subverting your server through its BMC: the HPE iLO4 case. Recon Brussels (2018)
20. Check Point Research: Faxploit: breaking the unthinkable. https://research.checkpoint.com/2018/sending-fax-back-to-the-dark-ages/
21. Scrapy: Scrapy framwork (2020). https://scrapy.org/
22. FoxGlove Security: A sheep in Wolf's clothing - finding RCE in HP's printer fleet (2017). https://foxglovesecurity.com/2017/11/20/a-sheep-in-wolfs-clothing-finding-rce-in-hps-printer-fleet/
23. Kraud Security: CVE-2018-1207. https://github.com/KraudSecurity/Exploits/tree/master/CVE-2018-1207
24. Sheffer, Y., Holz, R., Saint-Andre, P.: Summarizing known attacks on transport layer security (TLS) and datagram TLS (DTLS). RFC 7457 (2015)
25. Sophos: Serial console port. https://community.sophos.com/kb/en-us/123197

26. Teyou, C.C.T., Zhang, P.: Solving downgrade and dos attack due to the four ways handshake vulnerabilities (WIFI). Int. J. Eng. Manag. Res. (IJEMR) **8**(4), 1–10 (2018)
27. Wiki: Office automation (2018). https://en.wikipedia.org/wiki/Office_automation
28. Wikipedia: Antivirus software. https://en.wikipedia.org/wiki/Antivirus_software
29. Wikipedia: APT description. https://en.wikipedia.org/wiki/Advanced_persistent_threat
30. Wikipedia: BMC description. https://en.wikipedia.org/wiki/Intelligent_Platform_Management_Interface
31. Wikipedia: BOOTP description. https://en.wikipedia.org/wiki/Bootstrap_Protocol
32. Wikipedia: Description of BIOS. https://en.wikipedia.org/wiki/BIOS
33. Wikipedia: Transport layer security. https://en.wikipedia.org/wiki/Transport_Layer_Security
34. Zaddach, J., Bruno, L., Francillon, A., Balzarotti, D., et al.: AVATAR: a framework to support dynamic security analysis of embedded systems' firmwares. In: NDSS 2014, pp. 1–16 (2014)
35. Zoomeye: zoomeye (2020). https://www.zoomeye.org/statistics

Improving Key Mismatch Attack
on NewHope with Fewer Queries

Satoshi Okada[1]($\boxtimes$), Yuntao Wang[2], and Tsuyoshi Takagi[1]

[1] Graduate School of Information Science and Technology, The University of Tokyo,
Bunkyo City, Japan
`okada-satoshi323@g.ecc.u-tokyo.ac.jp`, `takagi@mist.i.u-tokyo.ac.jp`
[2] School of Information Science,
Japan Advanced Institute of Science and Technology, Nomi, Japan
`y-wang@jaist.ac.jp`

Abstract. NewHope is a lattice cryptoscheme based on the Ring Learning With Errors (Ring-LWE) problem, and it has received much attention among the candidates of the NIST post-quantum cryptography standardization project. Recently, key mismatch attacks on NewHope have been proposed, where the adversary tries to recover the server's secret key by observing the mismatch of the shared key from chosen queries. At CT-RSA 2019, Bauer et al. first proposed a key mismatch attack on NewHope, and then at ESORICS 2019, Qin et al. proposed an improved version with success probability of 96.9% using about 880,000 queries. In this paper, we further improve their key mismatch attacks on NewHope. First, we reduce the number of queries by adapting the terminating condition to the response from the server using an early abort technique. Next, the success rate of recovering the secret key polynomial is raised by setting a deterministic condition for judging its coefficients. We also improve the method of generating queries. Furthermore, the search range of the secret key in Qin et al.'s attack is extended without increasing the number of queries. As a result, about 73% of queries can be reduced compared with Qin et al.'s method under the success rate of 97%. Moreover, we analyze the trade-off between the number of queries and the success rate. In particular, we show that a lower success rate of 20.9% is available by further reduced queries of 135,000, simultaneously.

Keywords: PQC · Ring-LWE · Key mismatch attack · NewHope

1 Introduction

The current public-key cryptosystems based on the hardness of the factorization problem or the discrete logarithm problem can be broken by quantum computers in polynomial time [17]. For this reason, it is urgent to develop post-quantum cryptography (PQC) which is secure against the threat of quantum computers. PQC is being standardized by the National Institute of Standards and Technology (NIST) [1]. There, lattice-based cryptography is one of the most promising

© Springer Nature Switzerland AG 2020
J. K. Liu and H. Cui (Eds.): ACISP 2020, LNCS 12248, pp. 505–524, 2020.
https://doi.org/10.1007/978-3-030-55304-3_26

categories, and NewHope is one of the lattice-based key exchange candidates selected in the second round of the NIST PQC standardization project. The security of NewHope [2] is based on the difficulty of the underlying Ring-LWE problem [12]. Comparing to the typical LWE problem [15], the Ring-LWE based cryptoschemes enjoy smaller key sizes that benefit from its ring structure. On the other hand, some potential demerits from the ring structure may be maliciously used by attackers, thus more careful cryptanalysis of these cryptoschemes is required.

Nowadays it is common to reuse keys in Internet communications, so as to improve the performance of the protocols. For example, TLS 1.3 [16] adopts the pre-shared key (PSK) mode where the server is allowed to reuse the same secret key and public key in intermittent communication with the clients, in order to reduce the procedure of handshakes. Meanwhile, such protocols may have a risk of leakage of the server's secret key when the adversary has enough chances to send queries to the honest server and get correct responses from it. There is a kind of key mismatch attack on the Ring-LWE based key exchange protocols. As its name implies, the key mismatch attack generally works as follows: an adversary sends chosen ciphertexts to the server, and recovers the server's secret key by observing a match or mismatch of a common key. In particular, there are mainly two key mismatch attacks on NewHope [4,13] which take advantage of the property that the secret key of NewHope is a polynomial constructed with integer coefficients sampled from -8 to 8 in a key-reuse scenario.

The first key mismatch attack on NewHope was proposed by Bauer et al. [4] at CT-RSA 2019, which can recover the secret coefficients belonging to the interval $[-6, 4]$. However, the success rate of recovering coefficients in $[-6, 4]$ was not so high. Bauer et al. also reported that the coefficients belonging to $\{-8, -7, 5, 6, 7, 8\}$ can be recovered by the brute-force attack, nevertheless, the computational complexity is as large as $6^{11} \simeq 2^{39}$ due to the fact that about 11.16 coefficients of 1024 ones are belonging to $\{-8, -7, 5, 6, 7, 8\}$ on average in one secret key.

Furthermore, Qin et al. [13] improved Bauer et al.'s attack at ESORICS 2019 so that the coefficients in $[-6, 4]$ can be successfully recovered with a high rate of 99.22%, and the others in $\{-8, -7, 5, 6, 7, 8\}$ can be recovered with fewer queries than the brute-force attack. As a result, the rate of recovering the secret key correctly achieves 96.88%. However, the attack proposed by Qin et al. requires a large number of 880,000 queries for recovering a secret key, which makes the attack not efficient. Besides, some specific patterns of secret keys can not be recovered successfully in this attack.

1.1   Our Contributions

In this paper, we further improve Qin et al.'s attack to reduce the number of queries, and evaluate its relationship with the success rate of recovering secret keys. First, we introduce an early abort technique to reduce the number of queries. Namely, we set an appropriate query stop condition according to the response (i.e. match or mismatch with the common key) from the server. Then, to raise the success rate of the attack, we propose a deterministic condition when judging the secret polynomial's coefficients; and we improve the method of generating queries sent by the adversary. Moreover, we observe that without increasing the number of queries, the attack of Qin et al. on the secret key coefficients in $[-6, 4]$ can be extended to a wider range of $[-6, 7]$. Since only 0.28 coefficients on average belonging to the remaining set of $\{-8, -7, 8\}$ in one secret key, we decide to perform a brute-force attack. As a result, to achieve almost the same success rate of 97%, the number of queries is reduced to about 230,000 which is 73% less than the cost claimed in Qin et al.'s method. Furthermore, the recovery success rate can be improved to 100.0% experimentally in our method. Simultaneously, by evaluating the relationship between the success rate and the number of queries, we can further reduce the number of queries to 135,000 with 20.9% success rate.

1.2 Related Works

A number of key recovery attacks have been developed to Ring-LWE based cryptography, under the assumption of a key reusing scenario. Generally, they are divided into two types: the signal leakage attacks with exploiting the flaws of the signal function [5,8,11], and the key mismatch attacks taking advantage of constructing the final shared key. In this work, we focus on the latter key mismatch attacks, as we already introduced two previous works of [4,13] above. Besides, in ACISP 2018, Ding et al. [7] proposed a general key mismatch attack model for Ring-LWE based key exchange scheme without using the signal leakage. Recently, there are also some key mismatch attacks on several specific lattice-based cryptographic schemes. For instance, in 2020, Greuet et al. [10] proposed the mismatch attack on LAC which is a Ring-LWE based cryptoscheme but with small key size. In 2019, Qin et al. [14] applied their attack on the Module-LWE based Kyber as well. And Ding et al. [6] analyzed the NTRU cryptoscheme by adapting the key mismatch attack to it. Especially, the mismatch attack using the quantum algorithm was proposed by Băetu et al. [3] in Eurocrypt 2019.

1.3 Roadmap

We recall the NewHope cryptoscheme and its relevant functions in Sect. 2. Then we introduce the previous works of mismatch attacks on NewHope in Sect. 3, including the methods proposed by Bauer et al. [4] and its improvement by Qin et al. [13], respectively. In Sect. 4, we propose our mismatch attack which is evidently improving Qin et al.'s attack. We give our experimental results, and show the trade-off between the number of queries and the success rate in Sect. 5. Finally, we conclude our work in Sect. 6.

2 Preliminaries

In this section, we introduce the algebraic definitions and notations used in NewHope. Next, we show the outline of NewHope's protocol, including several important functions being used in it.

pre-shared key a	
Alice	Bob

$\mathbf{s}_A, \mathbf{e}_A \xleftarrow{\$} \psi_8^n$

$\mathbf{P}_A \leftarrow \mathbf{a}\mathbf{s}_A + \mathbf{e}_A \qquad \xrightarrow{\ \mathbf{P}_A\ } \qquad \mathbf{s}_B, \mathbf{e}_B, \mathbf{e}_B' \xleftarrow{\$} \psi_8^n$

$\mathbf{P}_B \leftarrow \mathbf{a}\mathbf{s}_B + \mathbf{e}_B$

$\nu_B \xleftarrow{\$} \{0,1\}^{256}$

$\nu_B' \leftarrow \mathrm{SHA3\text{-}256}\,(\nu_B)$

$\mathbf{k} \leftarrow \mathrm{Encode}\,(\nu_B')$

$\mathbf{c} \leftarrow \mathbf{P}_A\mathbf{s}_B + \mathbf{e}_B' + \mathbf{k}$

$\mathbf{c}' \leftarrow \mathrm{Decompress}(\overline{\mathbf{c}}) \qquad \xleftarrow{\ (\mathbf{P}_B, \overline{\mathbf{c}})\ } \qquad \overline{\mathbf{c}} \leftarrow \mathrm{Compress}(\mathbf{c})$

$\mathbf{k}' = \mathbf{c}' - \mathbf{P}_B\mathbf{s}_A \qquad\qquad\qquad\quad S_{k_B} \leftarrow \mathrm{SHA3\text{-}256}\,(\nu_B')$

$\nu_A' \leftarrow \mathrm{Decode}\,(\mathbf{k}')$

$S_{k_A} \leftarrow \mathrm{SHA3\text{-}256}\,(\nu_A')$

Fig. 1. NewHope key exchange protocol

Set $\mathbb{Z}_q$ the integer remainder ring modulo q, and $\mathbb{Z}_q[x]$ represents a polynomial ring whose coefficients are sampled from $\mathbb{Z}_q$. We also denote the residue ring of $\mathbb{Z}_q[x]$ modulo $(x^n + 1)$ by $\mathcal{R}_q = \mathbb{Z}_q[x]/(x^n + 1)$. Bold letters such as $\mathbf{P}, \mathbf{s}$ refer to elements in $\mathcal{R}_q$. We also use vector notation for polynomials in this paper, e.g. the vector notation for $\mathbf{a}\left(= \sum_{i=0}^{n-1} a_i x^i\right) \in \mathcal{R}_q$ is $(a_0, a_1, \cdots, a_{n-2}, a_{n-1})$. $\mathbf{a}[i]$ represents the coefficient of x^i in the polynomial, and the corresponding i-th element of the vector as well. For a real number x, $\lfloor x \rfloor$ represents the largest integer no larger than x and $\lceil x \rfloor = \lfloor x + \frac{1}{2} \rfloor$. For the sake of convenience, we set $s = \lfloor q/8 \rfloor$ where q is the integer modulus in NewHope.

We denote by ψ_8 a binomial distribution with a standard deviation of 8, and its element is sampled by calculating $\sum_{i=1}^8 (b_i - b_i')$. Here, b_i and b_i' are sampled from $\{0, 1\}$ uniformly at random. Let ψ_8^n be the polynomial set whose each coefficient is sampled from ψ_8. In the figures and algorithms, the notation $\xleftarrow{\$} \mathcal{D}$ means randomly sampling an element from distribution (or set) $\mathcal{D}$.

Ring-LWE Problem: Let χ be a distribution on $\mathcal{R}_q$. For randomly sampled polynomials $\mathbf{s}, \mathbf{e} \xleftarrow{\$} \chi, \mathbf{a} \xleftarrow{\$} \mathcal{R}_q$, the set of $(\mathbf{a}, \mathbf{b} = \mathbf{a}\mathbf{s} + \mathbf{e} \in \mathcal{R}_q)$ is called as *ring LWE sample*. The *ring learning with errors* (Ring-LWE) problem is to find the secret polynomial $\mathbf{s}$ (and the error $\mathbf{e}$ simultaneously) from a given Ring-LWE sample of $(\mathbf{a}, \mathbf{b})$.

2.1 NewHope Key Exchange Protocol

An outline of the NewHope key exchange protocol is shown in Fig. 1. Here we omit the procedures that are not directly related to the key mismatch attack, such as NTT (Number Theoretic Transform) being used to speed up polynomial multiplication. NewHope aims to securely exchange a shared key between Alice and Bob and it executes the below three steps. Note that the public polynomial **a** is shared in advance, which is sampled from $\mathcal{R}_q$ uniformly at random. The security of NewHope is based on the hardness of the Ring-LWE problem, where χ is the distribution of ψ_8^n.

1. Alice randomly samples a secret key $\mathbf{s}_A$ and an error $\mathbf{e}_A$ from ψ_8^n. Then, she calculates the public key $\mathbf{P}_A = \mathbf{a}\mathbf{s}_A + \mathbf{e}_A$ using the previously shared $\mathbf{a}(\in \mathcal{R}_q)$, and sends $\mathbf{P}_A$ to Bob. From the public key $\mathbf{P}_A$ and the previously shared polynomial $\mathbf{a}$, it is difficult to obtain information about the secret key $\mathbf{s}_A$ thanks to the hardness of Ring-LWE problem.
2. Bob selects $\mathbf{s}_B$, $\mathbf{e}_B$ and $\mathbf{e}'_B$ from ψ_8^n and computes the public key $\mathbf{P}_B = \mathbf{a}\mathbf{s}_B + \mathbf{e}_B$. Then, Bob chooses a 256-bit long bit string ν_B that is the basis of the shared key S_{k_B}, and hashes it by calculating $\nu'_B = \text{SHA3-256}\,(\nu_B)$. Subsequently, he computes $\mathbf{k} = \text{Encode}\,(\nu'_B)$, $\mathbf{c} = \mathbf{P}_A\mathbf{s}_B + \mathbf{e}'_B + \mathbf{k}$, $\overline{\mathbf{c}} = \text{Compress}(\mathbf{c})$ and sends $(\mathbf{P}_B, \overline{\mathbf{c}})$ to Alice. The shared key S_{k_B} is obtained by calculating $S_{k_B} = \text{SHA3-256}\,(\nu'_B)$.
3. When Alice receives $(\mathbf{P}_B, \overline{\mathbf{c}})$, she calculates $\mathbf{k}' = \mathbf{c}' - \mathbf{P}_B\mathbf{s}_A = \mathbf{e}_A\mathbf{s}_B - \mathbf{e}_B\mathbf{s}_A + \mathbf{e}'_B + \mathbf{k}$. Alice can get ν'_A equal to ν'_B with high probability by computing $\text{Decode}\,(\mathbf{k}')$ because the coefficients of $\mathbf{e}_A\mathbf{s}_B - \mathbf{e}_B\mathbf{s}_A + \mathbf{e}'_B$ are small. Then, she also gains a shared key $S_{k_A} = \text{SHA3-256}\,(\nu'_A)$.

In NewHope, $q = 12289$ and $n = 512$ or 1024 are employed. NewHope512 and NewHope1024 refer to the case of $n = 512$ and $n = 1024$, respectively. In the five security levels defined by NIST, NewHope512 is at the lowest level (level 1), and NewHope1024 is at the highest level (level 5) [1]. In this paper, we deal with the higher secure NewHope1024.

2.2 The Functions Used in NewHope

We simply review four functions being used in NewHope (Fig. 1): $\text{Compress}(\mathbf{c})$, $\text{Decompress}(\overline{\mathbf{c}})$, $\text{Encode}(\nu'_B)$, and $\text{Decode}(\mathbf{k}')$.

The Compress function (Algorithm 1) and the Decompress function (Algorithm 2) perform coefficient-wise modulus switching between modulus q and 8. By compressing $\mathbf{c} \in \mathcal{R}_q$, the total size of coefficients becomes smaller; thereby the transmission cost is lower.

The function Encode (Algorithm 3) takes a 256-bit string ν'_B as an input and maps each bit to four coefficients in $\mathbf{k} \in \mathcal{R}_q$: $\mathbf{k}[i]$, $\mathbf{k}[i + 256]$, $\mathbf{k}[i + 512]$, and $\mathbf{k}[i + 768]$ (for $i = 0 \cdots 255$). In contrast, The function Decode (Algorithm 4) restores each bit of $\nu'_A \in \{0, 1\}^{256}$ from four coefficients in $\mathbf{k}' \in \mathcal{R}_q$. Namely, $\nu'_A[i] = 1$ if the summation of the four coefficients is smaller than q, and $\nu'_A[i] = 0$ otherwise.

3   Key Mismatch Attack on NewHope

In this section, we first explain a general model of a key mismatch attack on NewHope. Then we recall the attacks proposed by Bauer et al. [4] and Qin et al. [13], respectively.

Algorithm 1: Compress(c)
Input: $c \in \mathcal{R}_q$
Output: $\overline{c} \in \mathcal{R}_8$
1 **for** $i \leftarrow 0$ **to** 255 **do**
2 $\quad \lfloor \overline{c}[i] \leftarrow \lfloor (c[i] \cdot 8)/q \rceil \quad (\bmod 8)$
3 Return $\overline{c}$

Algorithm 2: Decompress($\overline{c}$)
Input: $\overline{c} \in \mathcal{R}_8$
Output: $c' \in \mathcal{R}_q$
1 **for** $i \leftarrow 0$ **to** 255 **do**
2 $\quad \lfloor c'[i] \leftarrow \lfloor (\overline{c}[i] \cdot q)/8 \rceil$
3 Return c'

Algorithm 3: Encode(ν'_B)
Input: $\nu'_B \in \{0,1\}^{256}$
Output: $k \in \mathcal{R}_q$
1 $k \leftarrow 0$
2 **for** $i \leftarrow 0$ **to** 255 **do**
3 $\quad$ **for** $j \leftarrow 0$ **to** 3 **do**
4 $\quad\quad \lfloor k[i + 256j] \leftarrow 4s \cdot \nu'_B[i]$
5 Return k

Algorithm 4: Decode(k')
Input: $k' \in \mathcal{R}_q$
Output: $\nu'_A \in \{0,1\}^{256}$
1 $\nu'_A \leftarrow 0$
2 **for** $i \leftarrow 0$ **to** 255 **do**
3 $\quad m \leftarrow \sum_{j=0}^{3} |k'[i + 256j] - 4s|$
4 $\quad$ **if** $m < q$ **then**
5 $\quad\quad | \; \nu'_A[i] \leftarrow 1$
$\quad$ **else**
6 $\quad\quad \lfloor \nu'_A[i] \leftarrow 0$
7 Return ν'_A

3.1   The General Model

In the model of the key mismatch attack, we assume that Alice is an honest server and Bob plays the role of an adversary in Fig. 1. An adversary sends a query including $(\mathbf{P}_B, \overline{c}, S_{k_B})$ to the server. Then, the server calculates the shared key S_{k_A} and returns whether S_{k_A} and S_{k_B} match or mismatch. Here, the server is set to reuse the same secret key and honestly respond to any number of queries.

For the sake of convenience, we build an oracle $\mathcal{O}$ (Algorithm 5) to simulate the behavior of the server in this paper. The oracle outputs 1 if $S_{k_A} = S_{k_B}$ and outputs 0 otherwise. Changing the formats of queries sent to the oracle, the adversary can get information about s_A by observing the responses.

3.2   Bauer et al.'s Method

Bauer et al. proposed a method for recovering the coefficients in $[-6, 4]$ of the secret key s_A. To recover the coefficient $s_A[i]$, the adversary forges the following query and send it to the oracle.

$$\begin{cases} \nu'_B = (1, 0, \cdots, 0) \\ \mathbf{P}_B = \dfrac{s}{2} x^{-i'} \quad\quad (i' \equiv i \ (\bmod \ 256)) \\ \overline{c} = \displaystyle\sum_{j=0}^{3} (l_j + 4) \, x^{256j} \quad (l_j \in [-4, 3]) \end{cases}$$

Algorithm 5: Oracle($\mathbf{P}_B, \overline{\mathbf{c}}, S_{k_B}$)

Input: $\mathbf{P}_B, \overline{\mathbf{c}}, S_{k_B}$
Output: 1 or 0

1 $\mathbf{c}' \leftarrow$ Decompress($\overline{\mathbf{c}}$)
2 $\mathbf{k}' \leftarrow \mathbf{c}' - \mathbf{P}_B \mathbf{s}_A$
3 $\nu'_A \leftarrow$ Decode($\mathbf{k}'$)
4 $S_{k_A} \leftarrow$ SHA3-256 (ν'_A)
5 **if** $S_{k_A} = S_{k_B}$ **then**
6 | Return 1
   else
7 | Return 0

In this case, $\mathbf{k}'$ is calculated as follows:

$$\mathbf{k}' = \mathbf{c}' - \mathbf{P}_B \mathbf{s}_A$$

$$= \sum_{j=0}^{3} \left(\text{Decompress}(\overline{\mathbf{c}})[256j] - \frac{s}{2} \mathbf{s}_A[i' + 256j] \right) x^{256j}$$

$$+ \sum_{\substack{k \not\equiv i \\ (\bmod\ 256)}} \left(0 - \frac{s}{2} \mathbf{s}_A[k] \right) x^k. \tag{1}$$

In $\nu'_A (= \text{Decode}(\mathbf{k}'))$, all elements except $\nu'_A[0]$ are calculated from the second term of Eq. (1) and they become 0 with high probability. Therefore, the key mismatch corresponds to the mismatch between $\nu'_B[0](= 1)$ and $\nu'_A[0]$, which depends on selected l_j ($j = 0, 1, 2, 3$). The adversary fixes l_j other than $l_{\lfloor \frac{i}{256} \rfloor}$ to a random value and observes the change of the oracle's output by increasing $l_{\lfloor \frac{i}{256} \rfloor}$ from -4 to 3. If the adversary gets a string of outputs like $1, \cdots, 1, 0, \cdots, 0, 1, \cdots, 1$, he can calculate an estimated value τ of $\mathbf{s}_A[i]$ from the two possible values $\tau_1 < \tau_2$. The oracle's output goes from 1 to 0 at point $l_{\lfloor \frac{i}{256} \rfloor} = \tau_1$ and then from 0 to 1 at point $l_{\lfloor \frac{i}{256} \rfloor} = \tau_2$. Here such a form of outputs is called a favorable case. Please refer to [4] for the details of the attack.

3.3   Qin et al.'s Method

Qin et al. pointed out the low success rate of the attack proposed by Bauer et al. They proposed the following improvements to Bauer et al.'s attack on recovering the coefficients in $[-6, 4]$. In their method, they used the same way to generate the queries as Bauer et al.'s. However, they observed that a form of outputs like $0, \cdots, 0, 1, \cdots, 1, 0, \cdots, 0$ is also a favorable case. Besides, they indicated that Bauer et al.'s attack algorithm is not deterministic. For example, in the case of $\mathbf{s}_A[i] = 2$, the adversary may get a value of the incorrect 1 along with the correct 2. Since the attack algorithm is probabilistic, the more times the attacks are applied, the higher success probability can be achieved. However, the number of queries increases accordingly. To take a balance between the cost and the success rate, Qin et al. decided to collect 50τs for each coefficient and recover the coefficient from the breakdown of them.

Additionally, they proposed a new attack for coefficients in $\{-8, -7, 5, 6, 7, 8\}$. However, this attack is conditional and its success rate is smaller than 11.2%. We analyze the details of their attack and show its drawbacks in Appendix A.

4   Our Improved Method

We propose an improved method to increase the success rate of key recovery and reduce the number of queries. In this section, we first describe the improvements in three parts, and finally introduce the overall attack flow.

4.1   Improvement on the Construction of Queries

We focus on the point that there are some secret key patterns that cannot be recovered in Qin et al.'s and Bauer et al.'s attacks. In their attacks, when recovering the coefficients in $[-6, 4]$, an adversary sets $\nu'_B = (1, 0, \cdots, 0)$. In this case, depending on the pattern of $\mathbf{s}_A$, some elements except for $\nu'_A[0]$ become unexpected value of 1 where $\nu'_A = \text{Decode}(\mathbf{k}')$. Due to this, the oracle keeps returning 0 because $\nu'_A \neq \nu'_B$ regardless of the value of $\nu'_A[0]$. Therefore, a key mismatch attack will never be established.

To solve this problem, we propose a new query construction. In our method, when an adversary wants to recover the coefficient $\mathbf{s}_A[i]$, he directly sets the query like

$$
\begin{cases}
\mathbf{P}_B = \dfrac{s}{2} \\[2ex]
\overline{\mathbf{c}} = \displaystyle\sum_{j=0}^{3} (l_j + 4)\, x^{i'+256j} \qquad (l_j \in [-4, 3],\ i' \equiv i \ (\text{mod } 256)).
\end{cases}
$$

The oracle receives it and calculates

$$
\begin{aligned}
\mathbf{k}' = \mathbf{c}' - \mathbf{P}_B \mathbf{s}_A \\
= \sum_{j=0}^{3} \left(\text{Decompress}(\overline{\mathbf{c}})[256j] - \frac{s}{2}\mathbf{s}_A[i' + 256j] \right) x^{256j} \\
+ \sum_{\substack{k \not\equiv 0 \\ (\text{mod } 256)}} \left(0 - \frac{s}{2}\mathbf{s}_A \right)[k]x^k.
\end{aligned}
\tag{2}
$$

Then, the oracle gets $\nu'_A = (\text{Decode}(\mathbf{k}'))$, where $\nu'_A[i']$ is calculated from the first term of Formula (2) and other elements are from the second term. Here, if ν'_B meets two conditions such as

$$
\begin{cases}
\nu'_B = \text{Decode}(0 - \dfrac{s}{2}\mathbf{s}_A), & (3) \\[2ex]
\nu'_B[i'] = 1, & (4)
\end{cases}
$$

Algorithm 6: Find$-\nu'_B()$

Output: $\nu'_B \in \{0,1\}^{256}$

1 $\mathbf{P}_B \leftarrow \frac{s}{2}, \bar{\mathbf{c}} \leftarrow 0$
2 $\nu'_B \leftarrow (0, \cdots, 0)$
3 $S_{k_B} \leftarrow$ SHA3-256 (ν'_B)
4 **if** $\mathcal{O}(\mathbf{P}_B, \bar{\mathbf{c}}, S_{k_B}) = 1$ **then**
5 $\quad$ Return ν'_B

6 **for** $i \leftarrow 0$ **to** 255 **do**
7 $\quad$ $\nu'_B \leftarrow (0, \cdots, 0)$
8 $\quad$ $\nu'_B[i] \leftarrow 1$
9 $\quad$ $S_{k_B} \leftarrow$ SHA3-256 (ν'_B)
10 $\quad$ **if** $\mathcal{O}(\mathbf{P}_B, \bar{\mathbf{c}}, S_{k_B}) = 1$ **then**
11 $\quad\quad$ Return ν'_B

12 **for** $i \leftarrow 0$ **to** 255 **do**
13 $\quad$ **for** $j \leftarrow i+1$ **to** 255 **do**
14 $\quad\quad$ $\nu'_B \leftarrow (0, \cdots, 0)$
15 $\quad\quad$ $\nu'_B[i] \leftarrow 1, \nu'_B[j] \leftarrow 1$
16 $\quad\quad$ $S_{k_B} \leftarrow$ SHA3-256 (ν'_B)
17 $\quad\quad$ **if** $\mathcal{O}(\mathbf{P}_B, \bar{\mathbf{c}}, S_{k_B}) = 1$ **then**
18 $\quad\quad\quad$ Return ν'_B

19 Terminate the entire program

---

the value returned by the oracle (matching or mismatching between the two shared keys) can be reduced to the value of $\nu'_A[i']$.

In Algorithm 6, we show how to set ν'_B to satisfy the above two conditions. Here we decide to find ν'_B that meets Eq. (3) by the exhaustive search. First, $\mathbf{P}_B$ and $\bar{\mathbf{c}}$ are set as $\mathbf{P}_B = \frac{s}{2}, \bar{\mathbf{c}} = 0$. Then, ν'_B is set to be an 256-bit string in the following orders: (I) all elements are 0, (II) except for one 1, all elements are 0, and (III) except for two 1s, all elements are 0. Simultaneously, the adversary sends a query $(\mathbf{P}_B, \bar{\mathbf{c}}, S_{k_B})$ to the oracle. When the oracle returns 1, this algorithm stops and returns ν'_B. In contrast, if the oracle does not return 1 even after examining all of the above patterns (I)(II)(III), the algorithm can judge that the secret key $\mathbf{s}_A$ cannot be recovered successfully, and the whole program is terminated. The reason why we only deals with three patterns (I)(II)(III) is as follows.

1. The case that ν'_B includes three or more 1s appears with probability of only 0.003% (see Table 1).
2. For the case of ν'_B with three or more 1s, the exhaustive search needs much more queries than Qin et al.'s method. For instance, it takes $_{256}C_3 = 2,763,520$ queries when searching ν'_B with three 1s.

By performing Algorithm 6, ν'_B that satisfies the Eq. (3) is set. Then, when querying the oracle, an adversary has to additionally set $\nu'_B[i'] = 1$ to meet Eq. (4).

Table 1. Distribution of secret key $\mathbf{s}_A$

The number of 1 included in $\texttt{Decode}(0 - \frac{s}{2}\mathbf{s}_A)$	Secret key $\mathbf{s}_A$
0	94.547%
1	5.302%
2	0.148%
3 or more	0.003%

4.2 Extending the Search Range of Secret Key

After setting a proper query, an adversary changes $l_{\lfloor \frac{i}{256} \rfloor}$ from -4 to 3 analogous to Qin et al.'s method. Then, he calculates an estimated value τ of the coefficient $\mathbf{s}_A[i]$ by observing the oracle's outputs. Qin et al. claimed that this attack was valid on coefficients of $\mathbf{s}_A[i]$ in $[-6, 4]$. However, we point out that the attack can be applied to a wider range such as $[-6, 7]$, without any additional queries.

It is clear that the oracle's output is relative to $\nu'_A[i']$ whose value depends on the size of m comparing with the size of q (Algorithm 4). Remark that m is calculated by

$$m = \sum_{j=0}^{3} |\mathbf{k}'[i' + 256j] - 4s|$$

$$\approx \sum_{j=0}^{3} \left| (l_j + 4)\, s - \frac{s}{2}\mathbf{s}_A[i' + 256j] - 4s \right|$$

$$= \sum_{j=0}^{3} \left| l_j - \frac{1}{2}\mathbf{s}_A[i' + 256j] \right| s.$$

Moreover, all l_j $(j \in \{0, 1, 2, 3\}\backslash\{\lfloor \frac{i}{256} \rfloor\})$ are fixed at random values. From these facts, we can conclude that the string of oracle's outputs depends on the change of

$$u = |\mathbf{k}'[i] - 4s|. \tag{5}$$

Meanwhile, there are two kinds of favorable cases such as $0, \cdots, 0, 1, \cdots, 1,$ $0, \cdots, 0$ and $1, \cdots, 1, 0, \cdots, 0, 1, \cdots, 1$. Next, we study the condition of u for meeting favorable cases from the oracle.

We explain the case of $1, \cdots, 1, 0, \cdots, 0, 1, \cdots, 1$ here, and the analysis for the case of $0, \cdots, 0, 1, \cdots, 1, 0, \cdots, 0$ is similar due to symmetry. For example, an adversary wants to recover $\mathbf{s}'_A[i] = -7$. He randomly fixes l_j $(j \in \{0, 1, 2, 3\}\backslash\{\lfloor \frac{i}{256} \rfloor\})$ first. Then, we assume that he gets $v = 6s$ which is fixed by the computation of

$$v = m - u$$

$$= \sum_{i'+256j \neq i} |\mathbf{k}'[i' + 256j] - 4s|.$$

Table 2. The behavior of m and the oracle's output $(s'_A[i] = -7)$

$l_{\lfloor \frac{i}{256} \rfloor}$	-4	-3	-2	-1	0	1	2	3
$u(=m-v)$	$0.5s$	$0.5s$	$1.5s$	$2.5s$	$3.5s+1$	$3.5s$	$2.5s$	$1.5s$
The oracle's output	1	1	1	0	0	0	0	1

In this case, when $l_{\lfloor \frac{i}{256} \rfloor}$ varies, the behavior of m used in Decode function and the oracle's output is shown in Table 2.

We can conclude that if u monotonically increases and then monotonically decreases, the oracle's outputs become $1, \cdots, 1, 0, \cdots, 0, 1, \cdots, 1$. On the contrary, due to the symmetry, if u monotonically decreases and then monotonically increases, the oracle's outputs become $0, \cdots, 0, 1, \cdots, 1, 0, \cdots, 0$.

Furthermore, we show how u changes according to $l_{\lfloor \frac{i}{256} \rfloor}$ for each value of $s_A[i] \in [-8,8]$ in Table 3. As we can see, for each $s_A[i]$, u always monotonically increases and then decreases or monotonically decreases and then increases. Therefore, the estimated value τ of each $s_A[i] \in [-8,8]$ can be obtained theoretically.

Next, we consider how to determine $s_A[i]$ from τs. We invite Qin et al.'s algorithm (Algorithm 7) to calculate τ from the string of oracle's outputs b. Note that the output τ is expanded from -7 to 8, where τ belongs to $[-6, 4]$ in Qin et al.'s paper. We show the relationship between possible τs and $s_A[i]$ in Table 4.

Table 3. The behavior of u (Formula 5) corresponding to parameter $l_{\lfloor \frac{i}{256} \rfloor}$ and $s_A[i]$

$s_A[i]$ \ $l_{\lfloor \frac{i}{256} \rfloor}$	-4	-3	-2	-1	0	1	2	3
-8	0	s	$2s$	$3s$	$4s$	$3s$	$2s$	s
-7	$0.5s$	$0.5s$	$1.5s$	$2.5s$	$3.5s+1$	$3.5s$	$2.5s$	$1.5s$
-6	s	0	s	$2s$	$3s+1$	$4s$	$3s$	$2s$
-5	$1.5s$	$0.5s$	$0.5s$	$1.5s$	$2.5s+1$	$3.5s+1$	$3.5s$	$2.5s$
-4	$2s$	s	0	s	$2s+1$	$3s+1$	$4s$	$3s$
-3	$2.5s$	$1.5s$	$0.5s$	$0.5s$	$1.5s+1$	$2.5s+1$	$3.5s+1$	$3.5s$
-2	$3s$	$2s$	s	0	$s+1$	$2s+1$	$3s+1$	$4s$
-1	$3.5s$	$2.5s$	$1.5s$	$0.5s$	$0.5s+1$	$1.5s+1$	$2.5s+1$	$3.5s+1$
0	$4s$	$3s$	$2s$	s	1	$s+1$	$2s+1$	$3s+1$
1	$3.5s+1$	$3.5s$	$2.5s$	$1.5s$	$0.5s-1$	$0.5s+1$	$1.5s+1$	$2.5s+1$
2	$3s+1$	$4s$	$3s$	$2s$	$s-1$	1	$s+1$	$2s+1$
3	$2.5s+1$	$3.5s+1$	$3.5s$	$2.5s$	$1.5s-1$	$0.5s-1$	$0.5s+1$	$1.5s+1$
4	$2s+1$	$3s+1$	$4s$	$3s$	$2s-1$	$s-1$	1	$s+1$
5	$1.5s+1$	$2.5s+1$	$3.5s+1$	$3.5s$	$2.5s-1$	$1.5s-1$	$0.5s-1$	$0.5s+1$
6	$s+1$	$2s+1$	$3s+1$	$4s$	$3s-1$	$2s-1$	$s-1$	1
7	$0.5s+1$	$1.5s+1$	$2.5s+1$	$3.5s+1$	$3.5s-1$	$2.5s-1$	$1.5s-1$	$0.5s-1$
8	1	$s+1$	$2s+1$	$3s+1$	$4s-1$	$3s-1$	$2s-1$	$s-1$

Table 4. $s_A[i]$ and possible τs, outputs of Algorithm 7

$s_A[i]$	−8	−7		−6		−5		−4		−3		−2		−1		0		1		2		3		4		5		6		7		8
τ	8	8	−7	−7	−6	−6	−5	−5	−4	−4	−3	−3	−2	−2	−1	−1	0	0	1	1	2	2	3	3	4	4	5	5	6	6	7	7	8

Algorithm 7: Find$-\tau(b)$

Input: $b \in \{0,1\}^8$
Output: $\tau \in [-7,8]$ or NULL
1 $\tau, \tau_1, \tau_2 \leftarrow$ NULL
2 **for** $i \leftarrow 0$ **to** 6 **do**
3   **if** $b[i] \neq b[i+1]$ **then**
4   **if** $\tau_1 =$ NULL **then**
5          $\tau_1 \leftarrow i - 4$
6   **else if** $\tau_2 =$ NULL **then**
7          $\tau_2 \leftarrow i - 3$

8 **if** $\tau_1 \neq$ NULL *and* $\tau_2 \neq$ NULL **then**
9     $\tau = \tau_1 + \tau_2$
10   **if** $\tau > 0$ *and* $b[0] = 1$ **then**
11        $\tau = \tau - 8$
12   **else if** $\tau \leq 0$ *and* $b[0] = 1$ **then**
13        $\tau = \tau + 8$

14 Return τ

In particular, three values of $s_A[i] \in \{-8, -7, 8\}$ correspond to $\tau = 8$. Namely, when $\tau = 8$ appears, an adversary has to determine $s_A[i]$ from $\{-8, -7, 8\}$. Thus, we conduct this attack only against $s_A[i] \in [-6, 7]$ in our improved method.

4.3 Early Abort Technique for Terminating Queries

In Qin et al.'s method, 50 τs are collected for each coefficient and $s_A[i]$ is determined from the breakdown of them. For example, if 35 τs out of 50 are 3 and 15 τs are 2, then $s_A[i] = 3$. However, this probabilistic process is inefficient. In our algorithm, we set a deterministic condition for judging $s_A[i]$. As shown in Table 4, two types of τ correspond to unique value of $s_A[i]$ in $[-6, 7]$. Therefore, we can terminate collecting τ when two different types appear. We apply this condition at Step 20 in Algorithm 8.

4.4 Our Proposed Algorithm

We first propose Algorithm 8 to recover the coefficient of s_A in $[-6, 7]$. To launch this attack, an adversary sets $\mathbf{P}_B = \frac{s}{2}$, $\nu'_B =$ Find$-\nu'_B()$, $\nu'_B[i'] = 1$, and $\bar{c} = \sum_{k=0}^{3} (l_k + 4) x^{i' + 256k}$ according to the coefficient $s_A[i' + 256j]$ that he wants to

---

Algorithm 8: Partial−recovery(p)

Input: $p \in \mathbb{N}$

Output: $s'_A \in \mathcal{R}_q$

1 $\mathbf{P}_B \leftarrow \frac{s}{2}$

2 $\nu'_B \leftarrow \text{Find}-\nu'_B()$

3 **for** $i' \leftarrow 0$ **to** 255 **do**

4      $\nu'_B[i'] \leftarrow 1$

5      $S_{k_B} \leftarrow \text{SHA3-256}(\nu'_B)$

6   **for** $j \leftarrow 0$ **to** 3 **do**

7          $count \leftarrow 0$

8          $t, temp \leftarrow \text{NULL}$

9   **while** $count < p$ **do**

10              $(l_0, l_1, l_2, l_3) \xleftarrow{\$} [-4,3]^4$

11              $b \leftarrow []$

12   **for** $l_j \leftarrow -4$ **to** 3 **do**

13                  $\overline{\mathbf{c}} \leftarrow \sum_{k=0}^{3}(l_k + 4)x^{i'+256k}$

14                  $b.\text{append}(\mathcal{O}(\mathbf{P}_B, \overline{\mathbf{c}}, S_{k_B}))$

15              $l \leftarrow \text{Find}-\tau(b)$

16   **if** $t \neq \text{NULL}$ **then**

17                  $count = count + 1$

18   **if** $temp = \text{NULL}$ **then**

19                      $temp \leftarrow t$

20   **else if** $temp \neq t$ **then**

21   break

22   **if** $temp \neq 8$ *and* $t \neq 8$ **then**

23   **if** $temp = t$ **then**

24                  $s'_A[i' + 256j] \leftarrow temp$

            else

25                  $s'_A[i' + 256j] \leftarrow \max(temp, l)$

        else

26              $s'_A[i' + 256j] \leftarrow \text{NULL}$

27 Return s'_A

---

recover. Then, the queries including $(\mathbf{P}_B, \overline{\mathbf{c}}, S_{k_B})$ are sent to the oracle. When $l_{i'}$ varies from -4 to 3, the outputs from the oracle are appended to the array b (Step 14). Then the adversary gets τs from $\text{Find}-\tau(b)$. He keeps sending queries until he gets two different values of τ or he gets same τs for p times. We execute our experiments with different p and analyze the performance of the algorithm. If $\tau = 8$, this algorithm returns NULL without determining the value of the target coefficient (Step 26). Besides, if two different τs are obtained, the larger one is adopted (Step 25), otherwise $s'_A[i' + 256j] = \tau$.

Finally, we propose Algorithm 9 to recover the entire secret key s_A. Taking account of the fact that averagely only 0.28 coefficients in $\{-8, -7, 8\}$ are

---

Algorithm 9: Full−recovery(p)

Input: $p \in \mathbb{N}$

Output: $\mathbf{s}'_A \in \mathcal{R}_q$

1 $\mathbf{s}'_A \leftarrow$ Partial-recovery(p)

2 $\mathbf{s}_B, \mathbf{e}_B, \mathbf{e}'_B \xleftarrow{\$} \psi_8^n$

3 $\mathbf{P}_B \leftarrow \mathbf{a}\mathbf{s}_B + \mathbf{e}_B$

4 $\nu_B \xleftarrow{\$} \{0,1\}^{256}$

5 $\mathbf{k} \leftarrow$ Encode (ν'_B)

6 $\nu'_B \leftarrow$ SHA3-256 (ν_B)

7 $S_{k_B} \leftarrow$ SHA3-256 (ν'_B)

8 $index \leftarrow []$

9 **for** $i \leftarrow 0$ **to** 1024 **do**

10 | **if** $\mathbf{s}'_A[i] =$ NULL **then**

11 | | $index$.append(i)

12 **for** $list \in \{-8, -7, 8\}^{index.\text{length}()}$ **do**

13 | **for** $j \leftarrow 0$ **to** $index.\text{length}() - 1$ **do**

14 | | $\mathbf{s}'_A[index[j]] = list[j]$

15 | $\mathbf{P}_A \leftarrow \mathbf{a}\mathbf{s}'_A$

16 | $\mathbf{c} \leftarrow \mathbf{P}_A \mathbf{s}_B + \mathbf{e}'_B + \mathbf{k}$

17 | $\bar{\mathbf{c}} \leftarrow$ Compress($\mathbf{c}$)

18 | **if** $\mathcal{O}(\mathbf{P}_B, \bar{\mathbf{c}}, S_{k_B}) = 1$ **then**

19 | | break

20 Return $\mathbf{s}'_A$

---

included in one secret key, so we decide to perform an exhaustive search on them. First, by running Partial-recovery(p), an adversary gets $\mathbf{s}'_A$ whose coefficients in $[-6, 7]$ can be recovered. Next, he sets the public key $\mathbf{P}_B$, the secret key $\mathbf{s}_B$, and the error polynomial $\mathbf{e}_B, \mathbf{e}'_B$ in the same way as Bob does in Fig. 1. ν_B is set random bit string, because it has no significant meaning in this exhaustive attack. Simultaneously, S_{k_B} is calculated by hashing ν_B. Finally, he exhaustively substitutes values in $\{-8, -7, 8\}$ for $\mathbf{s}'_A[i]$ where is NULL (Step 14). Originally, $\mathbf{P}_A$ sent from Alice is used when Bob calculates $\bar{\mathbf{c}}$. However, the goal of this attack is to check whether $\mathbf{s}'_A = \mathbf{s}_A$, thus $\mathbf{P}_A = \mathbf{a}\mathbf{s}'_A$ is used (Step 15). The queries generated by the above procedure are sent to the oracle repeatedly and when the oracle outputs 1, this program stops and returns $\mathbf{s}'_A$.

5 Our Experiments

At first, we implement NewHope1024-CPA-KEM [1] with parameters $(n, q) = (1024, 12289)$. Then, we generate 1000 secret keys $\mathbf{s}_A$ randomly. Our goal is to recover $\mathbf{s}_A$ by using our proposed Algorithm 9, where we try different parameters p in the set of $\{5, 10, 12, 15, 20, 30, 50\}$. All the algorithms and oracles are implemented by Python3. Polynomial calculation is implemented using poly1d

Table 5. The success rate and the number of queries when increasing the value of p

The value of p	5	10	12	15	20	30	50
The success rate (%)	0	20.9	52.3	80.7	97.4	100.0	100.0
The number of queris	78,648	135,602	155,610	185,789	233,803	327,659	512,435

of numerical calculation library NumPy. We run the programs on Intel Xeon Sky-lake Gold 6130 with CPUs at 2.1 GHz.

The experimental results are shown in Table 5, where we illustrate the trade-off between the number of required queries and the success rate. In addition, we also represent the data in Fig. 2. It is notable that the attack can achieve 100.0% success rate when $p \geq 30$. Meanwhile, it indicates that decreasing p reduces not only the number of queries but also decreases the success rate. Specifically, if we sacrifice the success rate to 20.9%, we can reduce the number of queries to 135,602.

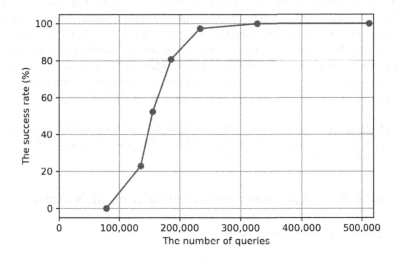

Fig. 2. The relationship between the number of queries and the success rate (each dot from left to right corresponds to the value of $p = 5, 10, \ldots, 50$)

Moreover, a comparison with Qin et al.'s experimental results is summarized in Table 6. In the case of $p = 20$, the success rate is almost the same as that of Qin et al.'s, but the number of queries is reduced by about 73%.

Table 6. Comparison of experimental results of key mismatch attacks

	Qin et al. [13]	Our attack ($p = 20$)
The success rate (%)	96.9	97.4
The number of queries	879,725	**233,803**

6   Conclusion

In this paper, we improved Qin et al.'s key mismatch attack on NewHope, and evaluated the trade-off between the number of queries and the success rate of recovering the secret keys. As a result, the number of required queries can be reduced by about 73% with almost the same success rate as that in Qin et al.'s attack. Moreover, our attack can achieve 100.0% success rate.

The current key mismatch attacks, including ours, Qin et al.'s, and Bauer et al.'s, are feasible under the assumption that the server honestly responses to freely chosen queries and continues to reuse the secret key. For this reason, they are not applicative to the CCA-secure NewHope using Fujisaki-Okamoto transformation [9]. However, considering the aspect of efficiency in practical use, there may be some cases where only CPA-secure NewHope is used without updating the server's secret key for a time. Then it is necessary to take some countermeasures to prevent the leakage of secret information, such as updating keys periodically or setting a detection system to malicious queries.

Acknowledgments. We thank Dr. Atsushi Takayasu for his helpful comments on this work. This work was supported by JSPS KAKENHI Grant Number 19F19378, JST CREST Grant Number JPMJCR14D6, Japan.

Appendix A   An Observation of Qin et al.'s Attack.

A.1   Qin et al.'s Method [13]

Qin et al. analyzed the distribution of the quadruplet ($\mathbf{s}_A[i]$, $\mathbf{s}_A[i + 256]$, $\mathbf{s}_A[i + 512]$, and $\mathbf{s}_A[i + 768]$). They show that with 98.50% probability, there are 3 coefficients in $\{-6, -5, \ldots, 2, 3, 4\}$ and 1 coefficient is in $\{-8, -7, 5, 6, 7, 8\}$ in each quadruplet (Table 4, [13]). In the following, we call this quadruplet Ξ for convenience sake.

Assume that an adversary wants to recover $\mathbf{s}_A[i]$ ($\in \{-8, -7, 5, 6, 7, 8\}$) after he recovered other 3 coefficients, $\mathbf{s}_A[i + 256]$, $\mathbf{s}_A[i + 512]$, and $\mathbf{s}_A[i + 768]$ by their attack for the coefficients in $[-6, 4]$. He sets each polynomials with parameter h_1 as follows:

$$\begin{cases} \mathbf{s}_B, \mathbf{e}'_B = 0 \\ \mathbf{e}_B = h_1 x^{512} \ (h_1 \in \mathbb{Z}_q) \\ \nu'_B = (0, \cdots, 0, 1, 0, \cdots, 0)(\text{only } i\text{-th element is 1}). \end{cases}$$

After receiving the query, the server has

$$\mathbf{k'} = \sum_{j=0}^{3} (4s+1)x^{i+256j} - h_1 x^{512} \mathbf{s}_A$$

$$= \sum_{j=0}^{3} (4s+1)x^{i+256j} - \left(-h_1 \mathbf{s}_A[512] - \cdots - h_1 \mathbf{s}_A[1023]x^{511}\right.$$

$$\left. + h_1 \mathbf{s}_A[0]x^{512} + \cdots + h_1 \mathbf{s}_A[511]x^{1023}\right).$$

Finally, the parameter m used in `Decode` function to calculate $\nu'_A[i]$ is like

$$m = \sum_{j=0}^{3} |\mathbf{k'}[i+256j] - 4s|$$

$$\approx |1 + \mathbf{s}_A[i+512]h_1| + |1 + \mathbf{s}_A[i+768]h_1| + |1 - \mathbf{s}_A[i]h_1| + |1 - \mathbf{s}_A[i+256]h_1|$$

$$\approx \left(|\mathbf{s}_A[i]| + |\mathbf{s}_A[i+256]| + |\mathbf{s}_A[i+512]| + |\mathbf{s}_A[i+768]|\right) h_1.$$

It sets $\nu'_A[i] = 1$ if this $m \geq q$, and $\nu'_A[i] = 0$ otherwise. If $\nu'_A[\ell] = 0(\forall \ell \neq i)$, the oracle's output corresponds to the relationship between m and q. In other words, if h_1 is so small that $m < q$, the oracle keeps returning 1, but only after h_1 becomes large enough such that $m \geq q$, it returns 0. The adversary varies the value of h_1 from 1 to 12289. At the point that the oracle's output changes from 1 to 0, the following equation holds.

$$q \approx \left(|\mathbf{s}_A[i]| + |\mathbf{s}_A[i+256]| + |\mathbf{s}_A[i+512]| + |\mathbf{s}_A[i+768]|\right) h_1$$

At this time, the adversary have

$$|\mathbf{s}_A[i]| + |\mathbf{s}_A[i+256]| + |\mathbf{s}_A[i+512]| + |\mathbf{s}_A[i+768]| \approx \frac{q}{h_1}.$$

He knows 3 coefficients except for $\mathbf{s}_A[i]$ in the quadruplet. Therefore, he can calculate $|\mathbf{s}_A[i]|$ from Eq. A.1. Furthermore he can determine $\mathbf{s}_A[i]$ from the absolute value and the information on the sign of $\mathbf{s}_A[i]$ which is obtained by the attack on the coefficients in $[-6, 4]$.

A.2   The Condition for Qin et al.'s Method

In this subsection, we consider the conditions for the success of Qin et al.'s attack. Hereinafter, we define m_i as m used in `Decode` function to calculate $\nu'_A[i]$. As shown above,

$$m_i = \sum_{j=0}^{3} |\mathbf{k'}[i+256j] - 4s|$$

$$\approx \left(|\mathbf{s}_A[i]| + |\mathbf{s}_A[i+256]| + |\mathbf{s}_A[i+512]| + |\mathbf{s}_A[i+768]|\right) h_1.$$

Meanwhile, for all $\ell \neq i$, we have

$$m_\ell = \sum_{j=0}^{3} |\mathbf{k}'[\ell + 256j] - 4s|$$

$$\approx 16s - (|\mathbf{s}_A[\ell]| + |\mathbf{s}_A[\ell + 256]| + |\mathbf{s}_A[\ell + 512]| + |\mathbf{s}_A[\ell + 768]|) h_1$$

when h_1 is small. In this method, an adversary can calculate $\mathbf{s}_A[i]$ only when $\nu'_A[i]$ changes from 1 to 0 and all other elements of ν'_A keep 0s. Namely, until m_i becomes no smaller than q, m_ℓ ($\forall \ell \neq i$) must be smaller than q. Therefore, in Qin et al.'s attack, the following inequality is required for all ℓ.

$$\sum_{j=0}^{3} |\mathbf{s}_A[i + 256j]| > \sum_{j=0}^{3} |\mathbf{s}_A[\ell + 256j]|. \tag{6}$$

A.3   The Success Rate of Qin et al.'s Method

We show the distribution of the maximum value of $\sum_{j=0}^{3} |\mathbf{s}_A[\ell' + 256j]|$ ($0 \leq \ell' \leq 255$) in Table 7. We can see that $\max_{\ell'}(\sum_{j=0}^{3} |\mathbf{s}_A[\ell' + 256j]|)$ is larger than 12 with (almost) 100% for every $\mathbf{s}_A$. In Table 8, we also show the distribution of Ξ about its summation ($= \sum_{j=0}^{3} |\mathbf{s}_A[i + 256j]|$).

Table 7. The distribution of $\max_{\ell'}(\sum_{j=0}^{3} |\mathbf{s}_A[\ell' + 256j]|)$

$\max_{\ell'}(\sum_{j=0}^{3} |\mathbf{s}_A[\ell' + 256j]|)$	$\mathbf{s}_A$
12	5%
13	25%
14	34%
15	22%
16	10%
17	3%
18	1%

We can estimate the success rate of Qin et al.'s attack by using Inequality (6) and Table 8. For instance, if $\max_{\ell}(\sum_{j=0}^{3} |\mathbf{s}_A[\ell + 256j]|) = 12$, $\mathbf{s}_A[i]$ can be calculated only if $\sum_{j=0}^{3} |\mathbf{s}_A[i + 256j]|$ is 13 or larger. In this case, the success rate of recovering $\mathbf{s}_A[i]$ is 11.2%($= 6.0\% + 3.1\% + 1.3\% + 0.8\%$). We show the relationship between the success rate and the values of $\max_{\ell}(\sum_{j=0}^{3} |\mathbf{s}_A[\ell + 256j]|)$ in Table 9. We can conclude that the success rate of Qin et al.'s method for recovering coefficients in $\{-8, -7, 5, 6, 7, 8\}$ is not so high.

Table 8. The distribution of Ξ about $\sum_{j=0}^{3} |\mathbf{s}_A[i + 256j]|$

$\sum_{j=0}^{3} |\mathbf{s}_A[i + 256j]|$	Ξ
5	0.6%
6	3.4%
7	8.8%
8	14.8%
9	18.3%
10	18.1%
11	14.7%
12	10.1%
13	6.0%
14	3.1%
15	1.3%
16 or larger	0.8%

Table 9. The relationship between $\max_{\ell}(\sum_{j=0}^{3} |\mathbf{s}_A[\ell + 256j]|)$ and the success rate

$\max_{\ell}(\sum_{j=0}^{3} |\mathbf{s}_A[\ell + 256j]|)$	The success rate
12	11.2%
13	6.2%
14	2.1%
15	0.8%

References

1. US Department of Commerce, National Institute of Standards and Technology. Post-Quantum Cryptography (2019). http://csrc.nist.gov/projects/post-quantum-cryptography/
2. Alkim, E., Ducas, L., Pöppelmann, T., Schwabe, P.: Post-quantum key exchange - a new hope. In: Proceedings of the 25th USENIX Security Symposium, USENIX Security 2016, 10–12 August 2016, pp. 327–343 (2016)
3. Băetu, C., Durak, F.B., Huguenin-Dumittan, L., Talayhan, A., Vaudenay, S.: Misuse attacks on post-quantum cryptosystems. In: Ishai, Y., Rijmen, V. (eds.) EUROCRYPT 2019. LNCS, vol. 11477, pp. 747–776. Springer, Cham (2019). https://doi.org/10.1007/978-3-030-17656-3_26
4. Bauer, A., Gilbert, H., Renault, G., Rossi, M.: Assessment of the key-reuse resilience of NewHope. In: Matsui, M. (ed.) CT-RSA 2019. LNCS, vol. 11405, pp. 272–292. Springer, Cham (2019). https://doi.org/10.1007/978-3-030-12612-4_14
5. Ding, J., Alsayigh, S., Saraswathy, R.V., Fluhrer, S.R., Lin, X.: Leakage of signal function with reused keys in RLWE key exchange. In: Proceedings of the IEEE International Conference on Communications, ICC 2017, 21–25 May 2017, pp. 1–6 (2017)

6. Ding, J., Deaton, J., Schmidt, K., Vishakha, Zhang, Z.: A simple and practical key reuse attack on NTRU cryptosystem. IACR Cryptology ePrint Archive, 2020:1022 (2019). http://eprint.iacr.org/2019/1022

7. Ding, J., Fluhrer, S., Rv, S.: Complete attack on RLWE key exchange with reused keys, without signal leakage. In: Susilo, W., Yang, G. (eds.) ACISP 2018. LNCS, vol. 10946, pp. 467–486. Springer, Cham (2018). https://doi.org/10.1007/978-3-319-93638-3_27

8. Fluhrer, S.R.: Cryptanalysis of ring-LWE based key exchange with key share reuse. IACR Cryptology ePrint Archive, 2016:85 (2016). http://eprint.iacr.org/2016/085

9. Fujisaki, E., Okamoto, T.: Secure integration of asymmetric and symmetric encryption schemes. J. Cryptol. **26**(1), 80–101 (2013)

10. Greuet, A., Montoya, S., Renault, G.: Attack on LAC key exchange in misuse situation. IACR Cryptology ePrint Archive, 2020:63 (2020). http://eprint.iacr.org/2020/063

11. Liu, C., Zheng, Z., Zou, G.: Key reuse attack on NewHope key exchange protocol. In: Lee, K. (ed.) ICISC 2018. LNCS, vol. 11396, pp. 163–176. Springer, Cham (2019). https://doi.org/10.1007/978-3-030-12146-4_11

12. Lyubashevsky, V., Peikert, C., Regev, O.: On ideal lattices and learning with errors over rings. In: Gilbert, H. (ed.) EUROCRYPT 2010. LNCS, vol. 6110, pp. 1–23. Springer, Heidelberg (2010). https://doi.org/10.1007/978-3-642-13190-5_1

13. Qin, Y., Cheng, C., Ding, J.: A complete and optimized key mismatch attack on NIST candidate NewHope. In: Sako, K., Schneider, S., Ryan, P.Y.A. (eds.) ESORICS 2019. LNCS, vol. 11736, pp. 504–520. Springer, Cham (2019). https://doi.org/10.1007/978-3-030-29962-0_24

14. Qin, Y., Cheng, C., Ding, J.: An efficient key mismatch attack on the NIST second round candidate Kyber. IACR Cryptology ePrint Archive, 2019:1343 (2019). http://eprint.iacr.org/2019/1343

15. Regev, O.: On lattices, learning with errors, random linear codes, and cryptography. J. ACM **56**(6), 34:1–34:40 (2009)

16. Rescorla, E.: The transport layer security (TLS) protocol version 1.3. Technical report. http://www.rfc-editor.org/info/rfc8446

17. Shor, P.W.: Polynomial-time algorithms for prime factorization and discrete logarithms on a quantum computer. SIAM J. Comput. **26**(5), 1484–1509 (1997)

A Novel Duplication Based Countermeasure to Statistical Ineffective Fault Analysis

Anubhab Baksi[1]([✉]), Vinay B. Y. Kumar[1], Banashri Karmakar[2],
Shivam Bhasin[1], Dhiman Saha[2], and Anupam Chattopadhyay[1]

[1] Nanyang Technological University, Singapore, Singapore
anubhab001@e.ntu.edu.sg, {vinay.kumar,sbhasin,anupam}@ntu.edu.sg
[2] de.ci.phe.red Lab, Department of Electrical Engineering and Computer Science,
Indian Institute of Technology, Bhilai, Raipur, India
{banashrik,dhiman}@iitbhilai.ac.in

Abstract. The Statistical Ineffective Fault Analysis, SIFA, is a recent addition to the family of fault based cryptanalysis techniques. SIFA based attack is shown to be formidable and is able to bypass virtually all the conventional fault attack countermeasures. Reported countermeasures to SIFA incur overheads of the order of at least thrice the unprotected cipher. We propose a novel countermeasure that reduces the overhead (compared to all existing countermeasures) as we rely on a simple duplication based technique. In essence, our countermeasure eliminates the observation that enables the attacker to perform SIFA. The core idea we use here is to choose the encoding for the state bits randomly. In this way, each bit of the state is free from statistical bias, which renders SIFA unusable. Our approach protects against stuck-at faults and also does not rely on any side channel countermeasure. We show the effectiveness of the countermeasure through an open source gate-level fault attack simulation tool. Our approach is probably the simplest and the most cost effective.

Keywords: Fault attack · Countermeasure · SIFA

1 Introduction

Fault Attacks[1] (FAs) have been proven to be a powerful new attack vector targeting devices performing cryptographic operations (both as software and hardware). The rapid growth of low-end devices together with reducing cost and barriers to mounting advanced fault attacks is being recognized as a serious concern. This type of attack requires the attacker to force the device to perform outside its designated condition of operation, thus producing incorrect (*faulty*)

A. Baksi—This work is partially supported by TUM CREATE.
[1] We use the terms 'attack' and 'analysis' interchangeably.

J. K. Liu and H. Cui (Eds.): ACISP 2020, LNCS 12248, pp. 525–542, 2020.
https://doi.org/10.1007/978-3-030-55304-3_27

output from the cipher operation. The attacker can do this by using a multitude of techniques such as shooting optical pulses, overheating, using hardware Trojans etc. This faulty output, or even just the information whether the device actually produced a faulty output, can be used by an attacker, to deduce information on the secret state of the underlying cipher and ultimately the secret key. Fault attacks are shown to be powerful enough to compromise the security of a cipher which is considered secure with respect to theoretical cipher evaluation criteria. It is also shown in the literature that a fault attack can be carried out with cheap equipment, thus making this type of attack a serious concern.

The earliest and probably the most common fault attack model in the symmetric key setting is the *Differential Fault Attack* (DFA) [8]. In a DFA, the device is allowed to run normally (without a fault) once. Next, the attacker injects a fault that effectively toggles a bit (or few bits) in the cipher execution. The difference between the faulty and the non-faulty output lets the attacker learn information on the secret key.

In contrast to DFA, the *Safe Error Attack* (SEA) [20,30,31] makes use of the cases where the fault injection does not change the output from the non-faulty case. One particular case of SEA, known as *Ineffective Fault Attack* (IFA) [11], is of particular interest. In an IFA, the attacker injects a potential disturbance, but the cases where the disturbance does not effectively change the execution of the cipher. In another direction of fault analysis, statistical information of a variable is observed (SFA). The distribution which becomes biased as a result of fault injection can be used [23].

The recently proposed *Statistical Ineffective Fault Attack* (SIFA) [15] combines IFA and SFA. Like IFA, SIFA makes use of the cases where a fault injection does not result in a change in the output. Also, similar to SFA, the statistical distribution of bias of a variable caused by the effect of fault is used to recover the variable.

Another class of attacks, known as the *Side Channel Attacks* (SCAs) [22], is also capable of finding information on the secret key from a device running a cipher. Generally, fault attack countermeasures are not capable of inherently protecting against SCAs, hence a separate protection is commonly needed.

On top of being a direct way to mitigate the security of the ciphers as in [25] and [18], SIFA is also able to bypass duplication based countermeasures. Those duplication based countermeasures have been proposed to counter DFA. Such countermeasures work by implementing two instances of the same cipher execution, which we call the *actual* and the *redundant* computations, following [4]. Assuming a fault can alter at most one of the executions; it is explicitly detected by the *detective* countermeasures, whereas *infective* countermeasures implicitly detect the difference [4]. If a fault injection does not alter the course of non-faulty execution of the cipher, this case is considered as if no fault is injected by the duplication based countermeasures. Since SIFA utilizes the cases where the fault injection does not alter the normal execution of the cipher, those countermeasures cannot (at least in the current form) protect against SIFA.

Very recently, four countermeasures dedicated to protect against SIFA have been proposed in the literature. In one work, Breier et al. [10] use a triplication of the circuit to correct up to 1-bit error. Since at most one bit is assumed to subject to SIFA, the majority of the three will correct the error and hence the attacker will receive the correct (non-faulty) output. In [12], Daemen et al. suggest to use an error detection mechanism based on Toffoli gates which follow the reversible computing paradigm. Any successful fault would result in a garbage output and hence will be detected. Saha et al. in [26] present a combination of masking (which is used as a countermeasure to SCAs) [22, Section 9]) and encoding. In the *impeccable circuits II* [28], an error correction facility is introduced (extending the idea of *impeccable circuits* [1]) to protect against SIFA.

Given this backdrop, our approach neither does any error correction nor any other expensive technique. Instead, we basically use duplication (and comparison) in a way that removes the bias utilized by SIFA. Hence, our countermeasure is by far the simplest and least expensive. While it may be required to implement the cipher almost completely from scratch in other countermeasures (which can be non-trivial), our countermeasure can be easily implemented to protect any symmetric key cipher.

It has been argued [15] that the duplication based countermeasures do not protect against SIFA. Indeed this argument is valid with respect to the countermeasures proposed till date, such as [21]. This argument extends to DFA countermeasures proposed even after SIFA was published, e.g., [6] or [4]. On the other hand, the SIFA countermeasures [10,12,26,28] rely on some form of triplication (including error correcting codes) of the cipher execution possibly with masking. The cost for any such countermeasure is more than thrice the cost of the unprotected cipher. Hence the community seems to accept the norm that it is not possible to have a SIFA countermeasure with cost less than thrice the cost of the basic (unprotected) implementation of the cipher. Our detailed analysis reveals that while triplication can protect against SIFA, a sophisticated version of duplication can also do the same. The idea of our protection stems from the existing duplication based DFA countermeasures [4].

Contribution

We extend the idea of duplication to accommodate randomized encoding to destroy statistical bias (which is exploited by SIFA). This is done by choosing an encoding based on a 1-bit random parameter λ. If $\lambda = 0$, both the actual and redundant computations are done as is, and this is referred to as *actual logic*. When $\lambda = 1$, we encode $\forall x$ bits of the state as $(x \oplus 1)$ for both the actual and the redundant computations, we refer to this as *inverted logic*. In other words, we invert the bits (0 is encoded as 1, and 1 is encoded as 0) when $\lambda = 1$. This removes the statistical bias (since $\lambda \xleftarrow{\$} \{0, 1\}$ and is kept hidden from the attacker), thereby forestalling SIFA. This idea can be used atop the duplication based countermeasures, namely detective and infective ones [4], depending on the security warranted. The proper output from the cipher is given only if there is no difference between the computations of the actual logic and the inverted logic (i.e., the fault is ineffective/no fault is injected). In such a situation, reverse encoding is performed on the actual execution (if $\lambda = 1$), or (if $\lambda = 0$) the output is returned as is. Otherwise (i.e., the fault is effective), necessary steps are taken, such as a random output is produced (detective) or the output is suppressed (infective).

Hence, unlike the existing SIFA countermeasures, our solution does not rely on (any form of) error correction. Instead, it simply blocks the attacker to get information on the statistical bias. The attacker is able to see the cases of ineffective faults in our proposed solution, however, this does not help the attacker to gain any extra information as we explore later on.

The proposed simple and low-cost idea can be applied to any symmetric key cipher with minimal changes to the implementation. We do not claim any inherent SCA protection, though, SCA countermeasures can be applied easily. Our approach also has advantages when put in perspective to existing countermeasures. For example, our approach does not increase side channel leakage, which is the case for [10].

We present further details in Sect. 4 with Fig. 2 shows a visual representation. The security evaluation of it is done by an open-source tool used by the authors of [28], with the PRESENT-80 cipher (similar to [26]) in Sect. 4.3. We subsequently present benchmarking results in Sect. 4.4.

2   Fault Attack Preliminaries

2.1   Differential Fault Attack (DFA)

As mentioned already, DFA is likely the most commonly used FA technique in the symmetric key community. It has been successfully applied against most, if not all, symmetric key ciphers. First it lets the cipher run as it is (without any fault). It then injects faults at some later round of the cipher. Then it uses the difference of the faulty and non-faulty outputs that works as a variant of the *Differential Attack* [7].

2.2   General Countermeasures Against Fault Attacks

In general, the countermeasures against the fault attacks can be classified into three broad categories [4], as we discuss here.

1. To use a specialized device. This device is separate from the cipher design and dedicated for protection against such attack. Examples include a sensor that detects a potential fault [19].
2. To use redundancy. Commonly, this class of countermeasures duplicates (can be fully or partially) the circuit. After this, a recovery procedure (which dictates what to do in case a fault is sensed) takes place. Based on the recovery procedure, two types of countermeasures exist [4]. First, in the detection based countermeasures, the XOR of the non-faulty and faulty is explicitly computed.

If this results in zero, the output from one of the computations (the so-called *actual* computation [4]) is directly made available, otherwise the output is suppressed/a garbage or random output is given. In the second category, the infective countermeasures do not explicitly compute the difference. Instead, such countermeasures implicitly sense the presence of a fault. By using a sophisticated mechanism (*infection* [4]), either the non-faulty output (in case no fault is sensed) or a random output is given (otherwise).

3. To use the communication protocol in such a way that the conditions required for a successful fault to happen with low probability [3,16]. For example, in order to utilize DFA, the inputs to the cipher have to be unchanged; the probability of which can be reduced by using a suitable protocol.

3   Statistical Ineffective Fault Attack (SIFA)

As mentioned earlier, SIFA [15] is a new type of fault attack which combines the concept of ineffective and statistical faults. In SIFA, the attacker exploits the bias (which is caused by the fault injection) of one/more state bits. Unlike DFA, SIFA does not need the non-faulty output, but at the same time requires more fault injections compared to DFA.

Here we present an example of SIFA for better clarity, more information on SIFA can be found in [15]. Suppose a device is more prone to bit reset $(1 \rightarrow 0)$ than bit set $(0 \rightarrow 1)$ due to a fault injection. This can be achieved by, for example, by fixing a particular intensity of the optical fault injection set-up. This results in the bias of bit flip. In other words, the probability that the output will be changed depends on whether the target bit is actually 0 (high probability) or 1 (low probability). This bias where fault does not change the output (i.e., ineffective) can be observed by the attacker statistically. When such a state bit is known, the procedure can be repeated to get information on the other state bits and finally the secret key can be recovered. In one extreme, the probability of bit reset (respectively, 1) can be 1, in which case the fault model is known as stuck-at 0 (respectively, stuck-at 1).

3.1   Duplication Based Countermeasures and Need for Specialization

From the types of fault protection given in Sect. 2.2, the duplication based countermeasures are the closest to cipher design and hence are of particular interest.

As noted earlier, such countermeasures can be classified into detective and infective [4]. The schematic for the two types is shown in Fig. 1. Figure 1(a) shows the detection based or detective countermeasure. Here the XOR difference of the actual computation (C from E_K^1) and the redundant computation (C' from E_K^2), denoted by Δ, is explicitly computed (here P is the input and K is the secret key, both are common to both of the computations). If $\Delta = 0$, then no fault is detected and C is given as output. Otherwise a garbage output (could be random or a predetermined constant) is given or the output is suppressed. Figure 1(b) shows the infection mechanism used in infection based or infective countermeasure. Here the XOR difference Δ of $C \oplus C'$ is computed. However, instead of taking the if–then decision, Δ is implicitly used to compute $\tau_R(\Delta)$ such that $\tau_R(0) = 0$ but $\tau_R(d) = R' \neq 0$ for $d \neq 0$ where R is randomly generated and hence R' is also random (it is possible that $R' = R$). Thereafter $C \oplus \tau_R(\Delta)$ is given as output. Hence, when fault is sensed, Δ is non-zero and the attacker gets a random output. Otherwise (in case of no fault), the actual output C is returned. The XOR difference can be computed at the end of the cipher execution (such as [21]), or after each round (the basic idea is introduced in [17]); depending on which, a further classification of infective countermeasures as discussed in [4].

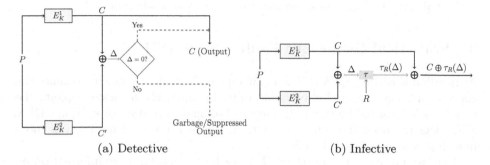

(a) Detective   (b) Infective

Fig. 1. Schematic for detective and infective countermeasures

Both the detective and the infective countermeasures are suitable to protect against DFA, except for one specific type of DFA. This type is named *double fault* [4] and is shown practical in [27]. In this case, both the actual and the redundant computations are injected with the identical faults. As a result, the XOR difference is 0 and the countermeasure in place senses it as a case of no fault. Impeccable circuits [1] attempts to solve the problem by employing different encodings for the two computations and finally with an error detection mechanism. This idea is later extended to a block cipher named CRAFT [6]. Employing such technique can increase the cost (depending on the error detecting code used). For example, protecting against single bit faults at the output has 2.45× overhead for CRAFT [6].

However, it may be noted that none of these duplication based countermeasures is able to protect against SIFA. SIFA only makes use of the cases where the fault injection does not alter the regular flow of the cipher. All the countermeasures, including impeccable circuits/CRAFT, treat such a case as no fault. This underlies the need for specialized countermeasures for SIFA, which is described next.

3.2 Existing SIFA Countermeasures

To the best of our knowledge, four specialized countermeasures aiming at protecting against SIFA have been proposed in the literature. We describe those here for better clarity.

Repetition Code. Breier et al. propose an error correction based on binary repetition code [10] and taking majority. Assuming the fault injection can alter at most one bit, the error correction will fix it back to its original content. Hence, the attacker will not get any information whether the fault has occurred or not. This actually blocks the attacker's ability to mount SIFA.

Masking and Repetition Code. Saha et al. [26] propose a two phase countermeasure. The first type (called, *transform*) is based on masking that aims at protecting faults induced into the state of the cipher. Further, under a stronger attack model where the attacker can inject fault with high precision within the computation of individual sub-operations like SBox, [26] proposes an *encoding* which allows error correction. The countermeasure was tested with a LASER based fault injection experiments and shown to be sound in a practical setting. Depending on the attacker's capability, the overhead limits to just that of a masking or error correction with masking. As an additional benefit, the implemented masking protects the design against side channel attacks as well.

Error Detection Through Toffoli Gate and Masking. Daemen et al. [12] propose an error detection mechanism based on Toffoli gates. This countermeasure acts as a combined SCA and a SIFA that targets at most one bit. The non-linear components are designed using Toffoli gates in such a way that a single bit flip would result in a garbage output. On top, the entire circuit is masked. It may be mentioned that the concept relies on non-standard gates.

Error Correction. Shahmirzadi et al. [28] extend the idea of [1] to incorporate error correction, and verifies with the open-source tool VerFI presented in [2][2]. The error correction is done through an error correcting code as the authors note shortcoming of repetition with majority voting.

From the discussions, a few basic characteristics of the existing SIFA countermeasures can be noted. Except [12], the rest (namely, [10, 26, 28]) depend on some form of error correction, thus making the cost of such countermeasure at least triple of the unprotected cipher. Error correction also suffers from the coverage of the underlying error correcting code being used. The concepts of [12] and [26] require masking, which is a costly operation. The scheme in [12] uses detection, but relies on non-standard Toffoli gates. As elaborated in Sect. 4, our proposed approach relies on simple duplication. Hence, no customized gate such as Toffoli or costly operation such as masking would be required. This makes our proposal the least expensive in the category.

4   Our Proposed Solution

Here we describe our proposed approach in more detail. As mentioned, the basic idea of our approach is to use duplication in such a way that the attacker does not get any useful information.

---

[2] Available at https://github.com/emsec/VerFI.

As we noted in Sect. 3.1, the basic duplication based countermeasures fail to protect against SIFA. Using an error detecting mechanism is said not to have protection against the same [6]. Therefore, we use a novel idea that changes the encoding of the bits to its inversion with probability $\frac{1}{2}$, so that the statistical bias is removed. A basic pictorial and algorithmic descriptions are given in Fig. 2 and Algorithm 1. Figure 2 shows a form of quadruplication, though both the branches for $\lambda = 0$ and $\lambda = 1$ are not taken at the same time.

Here we choose a random bit λ ($\lambda \xleftarrow{\$} \{0, 1\}$). It is regenerated at each invocation and is kept secret from the attacker.

As a part of duplication, we run two instances of the cipher, namely the actual (denoted by E_K^1) and the redundant (denoted by E_K^2) where E denotes the cipher and K is the secret key, and the corresponding outputs are denoted by C and C'. However, depending on λ we either choose the logic as is (if $\lambda = 0$), or the inverted logic where 0 is encoded as 1 and 1 is encoded as 0 (if $\lambda = 1$). So, the input to E, denoted by P is passed as is if $\lambda = 0$; but as its inversion $\overline{P}$ otherwise. The actual and the redundant computations for the inverted logic are denoted respectively by $\overline{E_K^1}$ and $\overline{E_K^2}$, and the corresponding outputs by $\overline{C}$ and $\overline{C'}$.

After this, a recovery mechanism is applied. Here we adopt detection for the purpose of illustration. Instead of detection, infection could be used if the attacker is powerful enough to flip the 1-bit judgement condition, together with another DFA-type fault at the cipher instance (more details in this regard can be found in [4]). We choose detection as DFA protection is not the focus of this work. In some sense, we also refute the claim made in [15].

As a part of the detection mechanism, the XOR difference (Δ for the actual logic and $\overline{\Delta}$ in case of the inverted logic) is computed at the end of the cipher execution. For the actual logic, the output C is given if $\Delta = 0$, otherwise a garbage output is given or the output is suppressed. Similarly, for the inverted logic, if $\overline{\Delta} = 0$ the actual output C is computed by inverting logic of $\overline{C}$ and given, otherwise a garbage output is given/no output is given.

Hence, the encoding of the actual and the redundant computations are same and is determined by the random bit λ. We assume the attacker can target at most one of the computations. Under our countermeasure, the encoding of that computation changes uniformly. More precisely, the probabilities of bit set and bit reset for one particular bit are both equal. As λ is kept secret, the encoding used is not known to the attacker. Suppose, the probability for bit set and that of bit reset for an (unprotected) cipher are p_0 and p_1, respectively. Because of the random encoding, both the probabilities are not $(p_0 + p_1)/2$. This destroys the statistical property utilized by SIFA, thus rendering it useless.

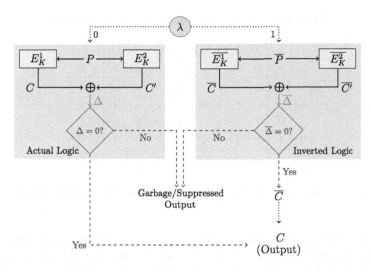

Fig. 2. Schematic for our SIFA protection (with detection mechanism)

Algorithm 1. SIFA Countermeasure (Ours)

Input: $P; K$
Output: C if no fault (SIFA); suppress output, otherwise

1: $\lambda \xleftarrow{\$} \{0,1\}$ ▷ λ is unknown to the attacker
2: **if** $\lambda = 0$ **then**   ▷ Actual logic
3:     $\Delta = E_K^1(P) \oplus E_K^2(P)$
4:     **if** $\Delta = 0$ **then**
5:        **return** $C = E_K^1(P)$

6: **else**   ▷ Inverted logic
7:     Compute $\overline{P}$ from P
8:     $\overline{\Delta} = \overline{E_K^1(\overline{P})} \oplus \overline{E_K^2(\overline{P})}$
9:     **if** $\overline{\Delta} = 0$ **then**
10:       $\overline{C} = \overline{E_K^1(\overline{P})}$
11:       Compute C from $\overline{C}$
12:       **return** C

Security of λ. It may be noted that λ plays a vital role in the overall security of the countermeasure. In this context, we note the following points:

- The attacker can recover λ by SCA, if left unprotected. We believe, protecting λ against SCA will incur minimal overhead as it is only one bit.
- The attacker can inject a bit flip (as in the case for DFA) to λ. However, this will only flip the value of λ but will not affect the security of the countermeasure.
- The attacker can also inject a biased fault. This may lead to biased distribution of λ, and can compromise the security. However, we would like to note that this would result in a second order SIFA. We do not consider this model

Table 1. XOR and AND operations in inverted logic

(a) $\overline{y} = \overline{\text{XOR}}(\overline{x}_0, \overline{x}_1)$						(b) $\overline{y} = \overline{\text{AND}}(\overline{x}_0, \overline{x}_1)$					
x_0	x_1	$\overline{x}_0$	$\overline{x}_1$	y	$\overline{y}$	x_0	x_1	$\overline{x}_0$	$\overline{x}_1$	y	$\overline{y}$
0	0	1	1	0	1	0	0	1	1	0	1
0	1	1	0	1	0	0	1	1	0	0	1
1	0	0	1	1	0	1	0	0	1	0	1
1	1	0	0	0	1	1	1	0	0	1	0

within the scope as it is not yet proposed in the literature, to the best of our knowledge.

Stuck-at Fault Protection. For simplicity, consider stuck-at 0 fault only. Regardless of the attacker's ability, half of the time a particular bit will be encoded 0 and rest half of the time as 1. If the attacker is able to inject a stuck-at 0 fault, then half of the times it will result in changed output (the cases where that bit is encoded as 1) and hence be detected (by detective mechanism). Therefore, such cases are not useful to SIFA (as SIFA only makes use of ineffective faults). Rest half of the time, the attacker will know that the fault injection resulted in a stuck-at fault. However, since it is assumed the attacker does not know whether it is stuck-at 0 or stuck-at 1, such information will not be useful. We thus conclude our proposal can resist against stuck-at based SIFA.

Effect on the Key Schedule. The key schedule algorithm will not change in the inverted logic. Hence, no extra cost/protection would be necessary. The round key addition operations are done by XOR.

4.1 Adopting Inverted Logic to Symmetric Key Ciphers

In order to see how the inverted logic works, first we show the inverted XOR ($\overline{\text{XOR}}$) and inverted AND ($\overline{\text{AND}}$) operations in Table 1. With this, it is now possible to convert an SBox to its inversion.

Now we discuss how to implement any symmetric key cipher in the inverted logic. If the circuit is already described in terms of XOR and AND gates (typical for stream ciphers), implementing it in inverted logic should be straightforward. For a typical block cipher, the circuit is described in terms of a linear layer and non-linear layer (such the SBoxes).

Adopting to Linear Layer. Overall, the linear layer can be classified into three categories – bit permutation as in PRESENT [9], binary non-singular matrix as in MIDORI [5], and non-singular matrix over higher order finite field such as AES. However, at a closer look, all the three categories can be described as binary non-singular matrices. In particular, bit permutation corresponds to binary permutation matrices.

Since bit permutation does not have any impact on the inverted logic implementation, we only consider the case with binary matrices. Suppose, we want implement the matrix $M = (m_{i,j})$ for $i, j = 1 \cdots n$. Considering the system of affine equations, $\boldsymbol{y}^\top = M \boldsymbol{x}^\top$ where $\boldsymbol{y} = (y_1, \ldots y_n)$ and $\boldsymbol{x} = (x_1, \ldots, x_n)$, we can equivalently write, $y_k = m_{k,1} x_1 \oplus m_{k,2} x_2 \oplus \cdots \oplus m_{k,n} x_n$ for each $k = 1 \cdots n$. Since in the inverted logic each variable x_i will be inverted as well as the entire result will inverted, we deduce,

$$\overline{y_k} = \overline{m_{k,1} \overline{x_1} \oplus m_{k,2} \overline{x_2} \oplus \cdots \oplus m_{k,n} \overline{x_n}}$$
$$= m_{k,1} \overline{x_1} \oplus m_{k,2} \overline{x_2} \oplus \cdots \oplus m_{k,n} \overline{x_n} \oplus 1$$
$$= m_{k,1}(x_1 \oplus 1) \oplus m_{k,2}(x_2 \oplus 1) \oplus \cdots \oplus m_{k,n}(x_n \oplus 1) \oplus 1$$
$$= \underbrace{m_{k,1} x_1 \oplus m_{k,2} x_2 \oplus \cdots \oplus m_{k,n} x_n}_{} \oplus \underbrace{m_{k,1} \oplus m_{k,2} \oplus \cdots \oplus m_{k,n}}_{} \oplus 1$$
$$= y_k \oplus (\text{parity of } k^{\text{th}} \text{ row of } M) \oplus 1$$

Hence, converting a binary matrix to its inversion is straightforward. For example, the AES MixColumn is a 32×32 binary matrix. The parity for each of its rows is 1. Therefore, for AES MixColumn, the same source code/hardware description will work for both the original logic and the inverted logic.

Adopting to Non-linear Layer. To begin with, consider the Boolean function, $y = x_1 \oplus x_1 x_2$. The inverted function, $\overline{y}$ is given by $\overline{y} = \overline{\overline{x_1} \oplus \overline{x_1} \overline{x_2}} = (1 \oplus x_1) \oplus (1 \oplus x_1)(1 \oplus x_2) \oplus 1 = x_2 \oplus x_1 x_2 \oplus 1$.

With this example, now consider the PRESENT SBox, C56B90AD3EF84712 [9], which is represented by the following coordinate functions (in ANF):

$$y_0 = x_0 \oplus x_2 \oplus x_1 x_2 \oplus x_3,$$
$$y_1 = x_1 \oplus x_0 x_1 x_2 \oplus x_3 \oplus x_1 x_3 \oplus x_0 x_1 x_3 \oplus x_2 x_3 \oplus x_0 x_2 x_3,$$
$$y_2 = 1 \oplus x_0 x_1 \oplus x_2 \oplus x_3 \oplus x_0 x_3 \oplus x_1 x_3 \oplus x_0 x_1 x_3 \oplus x_0 x_2 x_3,$$
$$y_3 = 1 \oplus x_0 \oplus x_1 \oplus x_1 x_2 \oplus x_0 x_1 x_2 \oplus x_3 \oplus x_0 x_1 x_3 \oplus x_0 x_2 x_3.$$

Now the inverted SBox is given by the coordinate functions (in ANF) by (these are obtained by inverting each variable):

$$y_0 = 1 \oplus x_0 \oplus x_1 \oplus x_1 x_2 \oplus x_3,$$
$$y_1 = x_0 \oplus x_2 \oplus x_1 x_2 \oplus x_0 x_1 x_2 \oplus x_3 \oplus x_0 x_1 x_3 \oplus x_0 x_2 x_3,$$
$$y_2 = 1 \oplus x_1 \oplus x_0 x_2 \oplus x_3 \oplus x_0 x_3 \oplus x_0 x_1 x_3 \oplus x_2 x_3 \oplus x_0 x_2 x_3,$$
$$y_3 = 1 \oplus x_2 \oplus x_0 x_1 x_2 \oplus x_3 \oplus x_1 x_3 \oplus x_0 x_1 x_3 \oplus x_2 x_3 \oplus x_0 x_2 x_3.$$

This leads us to the SBox DE8B701C25F649A3. The Algorithm 2 shows the implementation of PRESENT-80 cipher in the inverted logic (which we call $\overline{\text{PRESENT-80}}$).

Adopting to PRESENT-80. Now both the linear and the non-linear layers are adopted to the inverted logic, we explain how the overall design would be adopted for PRESENT-80. The key schedule, the round key additions (including the final round key addition at the end) and the bit permutation layer would remain unchanged. The state is inverted before and after the encryption function. Also the SBox is changed in $\overline{\text{PRESENT-80}}$ as DE8B701C25F649A3. Figure 3 gives visual representation for PRESENT-80 in both the actual and the inverted logic.

It may be noted that the SBox in the inverted logic is not same as its inverse, in general. For example, the inverse of the PRESENT SBox is 5EF8C12DB463 079A. If an SBox with this property exists, it could be beneficial to reduced cost for a combined encryption and decryption circuits if our countermeasure is adopted. We leave this problem open for future research.

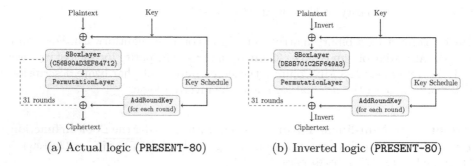

(a) Actual logic (PRESENT-80)   (b) Inverted logic ($\overline{\text{PRESENT-80}}$)

Fig. 3. Overview of PRESENT-80 in actual and inverted logic

Algorithm 2. Convert PRESENT-80 to inverted logic ($\overline{\text{PRESENT-80}}$)

Input: $P; K$
Output: C
1: Run Key Schedule   ▷ No change (from PRESENT-80)
2: Compute $\overline{P}$ ▷ Invert the bits of P
3: $S_t = \overline{P}$ ▷ State is initialized
4: **for** $i \leftarrow 1; i \leq 31; i \leftarrow i + 1$ **do**
5:     $S_t \leftarrow \text{AddRoundKey}_i(S_t)$ ▷ Add the corresponding round key; No change
6:     $S_t \leftarrow \text{SBoxLayer}(S_t)$ ▷ Use SBox DE8B701C25F649A3
7:     $S_t \leftarrow \text{PermutationLayer}(S_t)$ ▷ No change
8: $S_t \leftarrow \text{AddRoundKey}_{32}(S_t)$ ▷ Add the last round key; No change
9: $C \leftarrow \overline{S_t}$ ▷ Ciphertext is the inverted state

---

4.2 Benchmarks

Evaluation of the proposed countermeasure is presented in terms of PRESENT-80 [9] cipher (similar to [26]). Table 2 reports the area overheads of the countermeasure targeting the 45 nm NangateOpenCellLibrary PDK v13 v201012[3] in terms of NAND2 equivalents. Similar to [4], we do not consider the cost for generating randomness.

Table 2. Area overhead of the proposed countermeasure

PRESENT-80 cipher implementation	Gate equivalent (45 nm Technology)		
	Combinational	Non-combinational	Total
Unprotected	1620.00	844.32	2464.32 (1.00×)
Proposed countermeasure	3570.99	2264.66	5835.65 (2.37×)

As for the software benchmark, we note that the inverted implementation can be done with only a little change to the actual cipher implementation. Thus the code size will only be marginally increased. The time taken would also be basically the same as the number of rounds for the cipher is invariant over actual or inverted implementation.

4.3 Evaluation

The evaluation of the proposed countermeasure is done through fault attack simulation on the gate-level netlist of the protected PRESENT-80 cipher, using VerFI [2] (the same tool used in [28])[4]. It may be noted that the FA simulation through VerFI considers much finer level granularity, not just the state bits, thereby conforming to the SIFA-2 model used in [26].

We show in Fig. 4 an evaluation of our countermeasure through the simulation tool VerFI when biased faults are applied at random locations at the 30th round. The data shown in both Fig. 4(a) (unprotected) and Fig. 4(b) (protected by our countermeasure) are collected over a simulation of 120000 runs for PRESENT-80, for the cases where the fault is ineffective (therefore a usual duplication based countermeasure would treat those cases as no fault). When the countermeasure is applied, significant biases (that are caused by the fault) are removed, as seen in Fig. 4(b). Thus, we conclude our countermeasure is capable of removing the statistical bias.

4.4 Comparison with Existing Countermeasures

The hardware cost of protecting the 3×3 SBox χ of XOODOO [13] by the SIFA countermeasures proposed in [10, 12, 26, 28] using two 65 nm technologies, namely UMC (uk65lscllmvbbh_120c25_t) and Faraday (fse0k_d generic_core_ss1p08v125c) are given in Table 3. The authors in [28] use $[7, 4, 3]_2$

---

[3] An open-source research cell library, available at https://www.silvaco.com/products/nangate/FreePDK45_Open_Cell_Library/.

[4] The source code we use can be found at https://github.com/vinayby/VerFI.

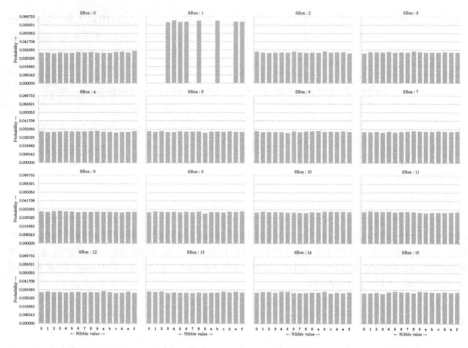

(a) Without countermeasure

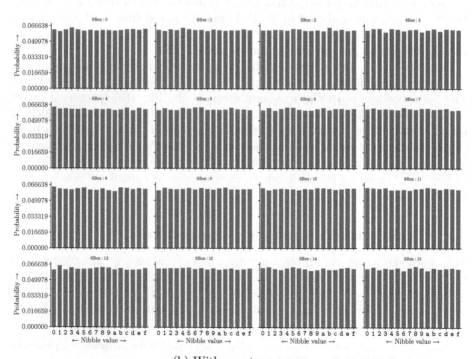

(b) With countermeasure

Fig. 4. Evaluation of our countermeasure through VerFI simulation

and $[11, 4, 5]_2$ codes. Since χ is of three bits, we use a $[6, 3, 3]_2$ code with the generator matrix:

$$\begin{bmatrix} 0 & 1 & 1 & 1 & 0 & 0 \\ 1 & 0 & 1 & 0 & 1 & 0 \\ 1 & 1 & 0 & 0 & 0 & 1 \end{bmatrix}.$$

All in all, we conclude that our solution has the least overhead compared to the rest of the countermeasures. Further, the evaluation is done through gate-level simulation and hence is comparable to SIFA-2 of [26] (which is a stronger SIFA model).

Table 3. Comparison of cost of protecting χ (of XOODOO) by SIFA countermeasures

Design	Gate equivalent				Method
	UMC		Faraday		
χ (unprotected)	14.58	(1.0×)	14.06	(1.0×)	–
Breier et al. [10]	45.14	(3.1×)	42.97	(3.1×)	Error correction
Daemen et al. [12]	No standard cell library exists				Reversible computing
Saha et al. [26]	>45.14	(>3.1×)	>42.97	(>3.1×)	Masking, Error correction
Shahmirzadi et al. [28]	71.53	(4.9×)	68.75	(4.9×)	Error correction
Ours	27.77	(1.9×)	25.78	(1.8×)	Remove bias by duplication

Here we note few other points. The proposal of [12] inherently requires masking (thus also protects against SCA), similar is the case for [26]. From a different angle, only [12] relies on error detection, while the rest rely on some form of error correction (hence the cost is at least tripled). Also, [12] needs Toffoli gates which is not available in the standard gate libraries, to the best of our knowledge. For this reason, we do not provide any benchmark for the protection proposed in [12]. The cost for applying [26] protection is at least that of [10]. In comparison, our proposal simply depends on duplication with randomized bit encoding. It does not require masking or specialized gate, nor it is restricted by the error coverage of the underlying code. In essence, the inverted logic based cipher can be thought of as a cipher (which could also share components with the actual logic based cipher). Also, our countermeasure works at the cipher design level (thus it has an edge when adopting to any symmetric key cipher), whereas other countermeasures work at the implementation level.

4.5   Connection with Side Channel Countermeasures

Our proposal does not have any inherent side channel protection. We mention that side channel countermeasures can be easily adopted as essentially the inverted logic based implementation works like a cipher. Hence, no special technique would be necessary.

As already mentioned, the randomly generated bit λ is needed to be protected from a side channel attacker, aside from the usual protection for the actual and redundant computations. We believe, this would add minimal cost since λ is only of 1-bit.

It is to be mentioned that our proposal does not inherently increase side channel leakage (which happens for [10]). In fact, the basic concept used here is similar to that of the *Masked Dual-Rail Pre-charge Logic* which was proposed as a countermeasure to the side channel attacks in 2005 [24]. However, this method was shown not secure in [14,29].

Since the countermeasure uses two different SBoxes (actual and inverted logic), each SBox can depict minor differences in their side channel leakage (for example, operating in two memory locations may result in distinct time signatures). If such a model is considered within scope, we propose to combine the two SBoxes (say, $n \times n$) to one combined ($n \times 2n$) SBox. For example, the combined SBox in case of PRESENT-80 would be the 4×8 SBox: CD, 5E, 68, BB, 97, 00, A1, DC, 32, E5, FF, 86, 44, 79, 1A, 23. Once this SBox has been fetched from memory, either the most significant n bits or the least significant n bits are obtained by masking the unnecessary part.

One idea to perform SCA is to check if there is any inversion of state at either the beginning or the end (since this operation is done only for the inverted logic). To prevent that, we propose to compute dummy inversion of the state both at the beginning and at the end regardless of the value of λ, but then choose the inverted state only when $\lambda = 1$.

5   Conclusion

In this work, we present a duplication based SIFA countermeasure. The basic idea is to use randomized encoding for the state bits. This removes the statistical bias caused by ineffective faults. Consequently, the attacker cannot mount SIFA. Our countermeasure by far is the least expensive. More precisely, ours is the only one in the category to have the overhead cost of less than thrice that of an unprotected cipher. The verification is done through a gate-level SIFA simulation tool. Our countermeasure, being designed at the cipher design level, is almost readily adoptable to any symmetric key cipher.

In the future scope, one may consider a combined SIFA and SCA countermeasure atop our design. Also, our design does not protect against double fault (Sect. 3.1) since both the actual and redundant computations are using the same encoding. Hence, one may think of extending our work to protect against double fault. Another interesting problem could be to search for an SBox whose inverse (in actual logic) is same as itself in inverted logic.

References

1. Aghaie, A., Moradi, A., Rasoolzadeh, S., Shahmirzadi, A.R., Schellenberg, F., Schneider, T.: Impeccable circuits. Cryptology ePrint Archive, Report 2018/203 (2018). https://eprint.iacr.org/2018/203
2. Arribas, V., Wegener, F., Moradi, A., Nikova, S.: Cryptographic fault diagnosis using VerFI. IACR Cryptology ePrint Archive 2019, 1312 (2019). https://eprint.iacr.org/2019/1312

3. Baksi, A., Bhasin, S., Breier, J., Khairallah, M., Peyrin, T.: Protecting block ciphers against differential fault attacks without re-keying. In: 2018 IEEE International Symposium on Hardware Oriented Security and Trust, HOST 2018, Washington, DC, USA, 30 April–4 May 2018, pp. 191–194 (2018). https://doi.org/10.1109/HST.2018.8383913
4. Baksi, A., Saha, D., Sarkar, S.: To infect or not to infect: a critical analysis of infective countermeasures in fault attacks. IACR Cryptology ePrint Archive 2019, 355 (2019). https://eprint.iacr.org/2019/355
5. Banik, S., et al.: Midori: a block cipher for low energy. In: Iwata, T., Cheon, J.H. (eds.) ASIACRYPT 2015. LNCS, vol. 9453, pp. 411–436. Springer, Heidelberg (2015). https://doi.org/10.1007/978-3-662-48800-3_17
6. Beierle, C., Leander, G., Moradi, A., Rasoolzadeh, S.: Craft: lightweight tweakable block cipher with efficient protection against DFA attacks. IACR Trans. Symmetric Cryptol. **2019**(1), 5–45 (2019). https://tosc.iacr.org/index.php/ToSC/article/view/7396
7. Biham, E., Shamir, A.: Differential cryptanalysis of DES-like cryptosystems. In: Menezes, A.J., Vanstone, S.A. (eds.) CRYPTO 1990. LNCS, vol. 537, pp. 2–21. Springer, Heidelberg (1991). https://doi.org/10.1007/3-540-38424-3_1
8. Biham, E., Shamir, A.: Differential fault analysis of secret key cryptosystems. In: Kaliski, B.S. (ed.) CRYPTO 1997. LNCS, vol. 1294, pp. 513–525. Springer, Heidelberg (1997). https://doi.org/10.1007/BFb0052259
9. Bogdanov, A., et al.: PRESENT: an ultra-lightweight block cipher. In: Paillier, P., Verbauwhede, I. (eds.) CHES 2007. LNCS, vol. 4727, pp. 450–466. Springer, Heidelberg (2007). https://doi.org/10.1007/978-3-540-74735-2_31
10. Breier, J., Khairallah, M., Hou, X., Liu, Y.: A countermeasure against statistical ineffective fault analysis. Cryptology ePrint Archive, Report 2019/515 (2019). https://eprint.iacr.org/2019/515
11. Clavier, C.: Secret external encodings do not prevent transient fault analysis. In: Paillier, P., Verbauwhede, I. (eds.) CHES 2007. LNCS, vol. 4727, pp. 181–194. Springer, Heidelberg (2007). https://doi.org/10.1007/978-3-540-74735-2_13
12. Daemen, J., Dobraunig, C., Eichlseder, M., Gross, H., Mendel, F., Primas, R.: Protecting against statistical ineffective fault attacks. Cryptology ePrint Archive, Report 2019/536 (2019). https://eprint.iacr.org/2019/536
13. Daemen, J., Hoffert, S., Peeters, M., Assche, G.V., Keer, R.V.: Xoodoo cookbook. Cryptology ePrint Archive, Report 2018/767 (2018). https://eprint.iacr.org/2018/767
14. De Mulder, E., Gierlichs, B., Preneel, B., Verbauwhede, I.: Practical DPA attacks on MDPL. In: 2009 First IEEE International Workshop on Information Forensics and Security (WIFS), pp. 191–195, December 2009
15. Dobraunig, C., Eichlseder, M., Korak, T., Mangard, S., Mendel, F., Primas, R.: SIFA: exploiting ineffective fault inductions on symmetric cryptography. IACR Trans. Cryptogr. Hardware Embed. Syst. **2018**(3), 547–572 (2018). https://doi.org/10.13154/tches.v2018.i3.547-572
16. Dobraunig, C., Koeune, F., Mangard, S., Mendel, F., Standaert, F.-X.: Towards fresh and hybrid re-keying schemes with beyond birthday security. In: Homma, N., Medwed, M. (eds.) CARDIS 2015. LNCS, vol. 9514, pp. 225–241. Springer, Cham (2016). https://doi.org/10.1007/978-3-319-31271-2_14
17. Gierlichs, B., Schmidt, J.-M., Tunstall, M.: Infective computation and dummy rounds: fault protection for block ciphers without check-before-output. In: Hevia, A., Neven, G. (eds.) LATINCRYPT 2012. LNCS, vol. 7533, pp. 305–321. Springer, Heidelberg (2012). https://doi.org/10.1007/978-3-642-33481-8_17

18. Gruber, M., Probst, M., Tempelmeier, M.: Statistical ineffective fault analysis of GIMLI. CoRR abs/1911.03212 (2019). http://arxiv.org/abs/1911.03212
19. He, W., Breier, J., Bhasin, S.: Cheap and cheerful: a low-cost digital sensor for detecting laser fault injection attacks. In: Carlet, C., Hasan, M.A., Saraswat, V. (eds.) SPACE 2016. LNCS, vol. 10076, pp. 27–46. Springer, Cham (2016). https://doi.org/10.1007/978-3-319-49445-6_2
20. Joye, M., Jean-Jacques, Q., Sung-Ming, Y., Yung, M.: Observability analysis - detecting when improved cryptosystems fail -. In: Preneel, B. (ed.) CT-RSA 2002. LNCS, vol. 2271, pp. 17–29. Springer, Heidelberg (2002). https://doi.org/10.1007/3-540-45760-7_2
21. Lomné, V., Roche, T., Thillard, A.: On the need of randomness in fault attack countermeasures - application to AES. In: 2012 Workshop on Fault Diagnosis and Tolerance in Cryptography, Leuven, Belgium, 9 September 2012, pp. 85–94 (2012). https://doi.org/10.1109/FDTC.2012.19
22. Mangard, S., Oswald, E., Popp, T.: Power Analysis Attacks - Revealing the Secrets of Smart Cards. Springer, Heidelberg (2007). https://doi.org/10.1007/978-0-387-38162-6
23. Ghalaty, N.F., Yuce, B., Schaumont, P.: Analyzing the efficiency of biased-fault based attacks. Cryptology ePrint Archive, Report 2015/663 (2015). https://eprint.iacr.org/2015/663
24. Popp, T., Mangard, S.: Masked dual-rail pre-charge logic: DPA-resistance without routing constraints. In: Rao, J.R., Sunar, B. (eds.) CHES 2005. LNCS, vol. 3659, pp. 172–186. Springer, Heidelberg (2005). https://doi.org/10.1007/11545262_13
25. Ramezanpour, K., Ampadu, P., Diehl, W.: A statistical fault analysis methodology for the Ascon authenticated cipher. In: IEEE International Symposium on Hardware Oriented Security and Trust, HOST 2019, McLean, VA, USA, 5–10 May 2019, pp. 41–50 (2019). https://doi.org/10.1109/HST.2019.8741029
26. Saha, S., Jap, D., Roy, D.B., Chakraborty, A., Bhasin, S., Mukhopadhyay, D.: A framework to counter statistical ineffective fault analysis of block ciphers using domain transformation and error correction. IEEE Trans. Inf. Forensics Secur. **15**, 1905–1919 (2020). https://doi.org/10.1109/TIFS.2019.2952262
27. Selmke, B., Heyszl, J., Sigl, G.: Attack on a DFA protected AES by simultaneous laser fault injections. In: 2016 Workshop on Fault Diagnosis and Tolerance in Cryptography (FDTC), pp. 36–46, August 2016
28. Shahmirzadi, A.R., Rasoolzadeh, S., Moradi, A.: Impeccable circuits ii. Cryptology ePrint Archive, Report 2019/1369 (2019). https://eprint.iacr.org/2019/1369
29. Suzuki, D., Saeki, M.: Security evaluation of DPA countermeasures using dual-rail pre-charge logic style. In: Goubin, L., Matsui, M. (eds.) CHES 2006. LNCS, vol. 4249, pp. 255–269. Springer, Heidelberg (2006). https://doi.org/10.1007/11894063_21
30. Yen, S., Joye, M.: Checking before output may not be enough against fault-based cryptanalysis. IEEE Trans. Comput. **49**(9), 967–970 (2000). https://doi.org/10.1109/12.869328
31. Sung-Ming, Y., Kim, S., Lim, S., Moon, S.: A countermeasure against one physical cryptanalysis may benefit another attack. In: Kim, K. (ed.) ICISC 2001. LNCS, vol. 2288, pp. 414–427. Springer, Heidelberg (2002). https://doi.org/10.1007/3-540-45861-1_31

Design and Evaluation of Enumeration Attacks on Package Tracking Systems

Hanbin Jang, Woojoong Ji, Simon S. Woo, and Hyoungshick Kim[✉]

Department of Electrical and Computer Engineering, Sungkyunkwan University,
Suwon, Republic of Korea
{hanbin,woojoong,swoo,hyoung}@skku.edu

Abstract. Most shipping companies provide a package tracking system where customers can easily track their package delivery status when the package is being shipped. However, we present a security problem called *enumeration attacks* against package tracking systems in which attackers can collect customers' personal data illegally through the systems. We specifically examine the security of the package tracking websites of the top five popular shipping companies (Korea Post, CJ Logistics, Lotte Logistics, Logen, and Hanjin Shipping) in South Korea and found that enumeration attacks can be easily implemented with package tracking numbers or phone numbers. To show potential risks of enumeration attacks on the package tracking system, we automatically collected package tracking records from those websites through our attack tool. We gathered 1,398,112, 2,614,839, 797,676, 1,590,933, and 163,452 package delivery records from the websites of Korea Post, CJ Logistics, Lotte Logistics, Logen and Hanjin Shipping, respectively, during 6 months. Using those records, we uncover 4,420,214 names, 2,527,205 phone numbers, and 4,467,329 addresses. To prevent such enumeration attacks, we also suggest four practical defense approaches.

Keywords: Package tracking systems · Enumeration attack · Privacy

1 Introduction

Most shipping companies provide a web service to allow people to track their packages and monitor the status of their package information online. A *package tracking number* (PTN) or phone number is popularly used to check and track the real-time package delivery status. That is, if a user enters a valid PTN or his/her phone number, the package tracking website displays the corresponding package status information along with some types of personal information, such as the full or partial name of the sender or the receiver, time-stamps, transit locations, the expected delivery time, etc. Such package tracking systems are widely used in the shipping industry because they are highly usable and convenient for customers to monitor and track their packages without directly logging in to the shipping company's website. As an example, Fig. 1 shows the package tracking website

© Springer Nature Switzerland AG 2020
J. K. Liu and H. Cui (Eds.): ACISP 2020, LNCS 12248, pp. 543–559, 2020.
https://doi.org/10.1007/978-3-030-55304-3_28

provided by UPS (https://www.ups.com). If a user enters a valid PTN into the input text field called 'Track', the website displays not only the details of the package delivery status but also additional personal information (e.g., name, phone number and address) of the sender or the recipient.

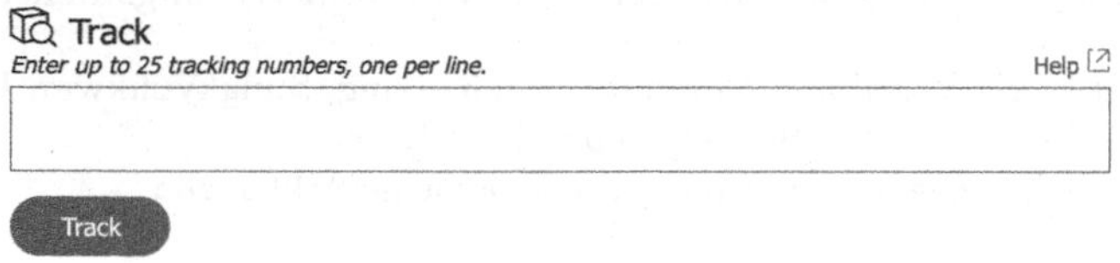

Fig. 1. UPS website for the package tracking service.

However, in most services, we found that explicit user authentication is not required in package tracking websites. We surmise that a package tracking system is generally designed for even non-members of the system to use their services with ease because the sender and/or the recipient can be a non-member of the system who cannot login to the website. At first glance, this package tracking service seems to be a useful feature, because the package tracking status information is only provided to the recipient and/or the sender who know the corresponding PTN or user's phone number. As long as these PTNs or phone numbers are kept confidential among legitimate parties, displaying information can be adequate. However, if those PTNs and phone numbers are guessable, then any 3rd party can also see the displayed information. We are wondering whether this feature can potentially be abused to harvest customers' personal data such as customers' names, phone numbers, and addresses at large scale; those stolen data would be abused or sold for conducting ads or additional cyber criminal activities such as sending spam/phishing messages [13] or creating Sybil accounts [11]. Recently, Woo et al. [15] showed the possibility of *enumeration attacks* with the top three package service providers (FedEx [4], DHL [3], and UPS [5]) in which the enumeration attack is a type of dictionary attack in which an attacker tries each of a list of possible candidate values (in a valid format) to determine the correct secret values (e.g., email addresses, phone numbers, and PTNs) through an online verification tool. However, their work was focused on those three service providers only and did not explain how the existence of these attack vectors is systemically detected and tested. Our work is motivated by extending their research to additional services for generalization and developing a systematic method to analyze the attack vectors related to web enumeration attacks on different websites.

To achieve these goals, we first analyze the main causes of enumeration attacks and then develop a framework to identify attack holes that can be exploited to perform enumeration attacks. As case studies of our framework, we chose the top five most popular shipping companies (Korea Post, CJ Logistics, Lotte Logistics, Logen, and Hanjin Shipping) in South Korea and then analyzed attack vectors of their package tracking websites.

To show the feasibility of enumeration attacks identified by our systematic method, we implemented a tool to automatically collect users' personal data in package tracking services by enumerating a specific range of PTNs or phone numbers. Although we focused on analyzing package tracking systems in South Korea, our attack techniques were not designed to solely work on specific companies or countries. Our framework is generic enough and can be extended to any package tracking systems in the world, which provide web-based status checking information, as shown in Fig. 1. Our contributions are summarized as follows:

- We present a framework to systematically analyze enumeration attacks against package tracking systems. Our research is the first to examine how web enumeration attacks can be tested, exploited, and detected systematically.
- We implemented the automatic enumeration attack generation tool against package tracking systems. Using this tool, we collected more than 4 million package delivery records and identified more than 4 million unique names, 2 million unique phones, and 4 million unique addresses. We clearly show that existing package tracking systems are at a real serious risk of revealing their customers' data.
- We propose four practical defense approaches for package tracking systems such as limiting the number of PTN verification failed attempts, using CAPT-CHAs, generating unpredictable PTNs, and minimizing information leakage from those systems to reduce the chance of enumeration attacks. Our proposed defense approaches would be integrated into the existing systems without incurring significant costs.

2   Design of Enumeration Attacks

In this section, we explain how enumeration attacks can be launched automatically to harvest users' personal data from a target website. In the target website, enumeration attacks can be implemented by sending a sequence of request messages for a specific service in the target website and monitoring the corresponding responses in an automated manner. To generate valid request messages, attackers should follow the data formats and protocols used in the service. Figure 2 shows the overview of the automatic enumeration attack testing framework consisting of four steps. In the following sections, we present the process of each step in detail.

2.1   UI Analysis

Given a web page as an input, the goal of this step is to analyze the web page components and discover all web forms (e.g., `<input type="text">`) that can be potentially exploited to perform enumeration attacks. The identified web forms are passed to the step of "data-flow analysis." We note that hidden fields can be often used to implement enumeration attacks. Therefore, we also need to consider hidden fields as candidate web forms for enumeration attacks.

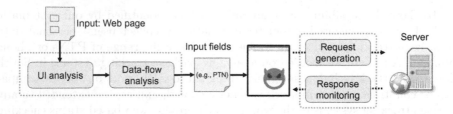

Fig. 2. Overview of the proposed framework for automated enumeration attack testing.

2.2   Data-Flow Analysis

With the web forms delivered from "UI analysis," we narrow down the list of further possible candidate input fields (i.e., web forms) whose values can be enumerated. In practice, it is hard to identify such input fields without any information about input field formats. Therefore, we first collect or generate some initial request message samples and then analyze the format of each input field with those request messages. We can use a heuristic technique to determine whether the values for each input field can be enumerated or countable by checking whether input field values consist of (decimal or hexadecimal) digits only; if an input field value contains characters other than digits, we remove the field from the list of candidate input fields for enumeration attacks because it would be difficult to define a rule to enumerate such input field values in an automated manner.

2.3   Request Generation

Once candidate input fields are determined, the framework computes input field values according to some pre-defined rules to enumerate input field values. Then, a web testing tool generates service request messages containing an input field value and sends it to the target web server.

2.4   Response Monitoring

The final step is to monitor and verify the response from the web server. We can determine whether a service request message (containing enumerated input field values) is correct or not, according to the query response result. The request is successful if the query response is successfully returned; otherwise, it is failed. Next, if successful, the proposed framework extracts the user data from the query result. After finalizing this step, we go back to the step of "request generation." All steps can be repeatedly carried out to harvest a sufficiently large number of user data.

3   Analysis of Services in Package Tracking Systems

To show the feasibility of our framework for performing enumeration attacks in an automated manner, we analyze the services of package tracking systems.

We first aim to investigate the attack surface of package tracking systems, where enumeration attacks can be performed. To achieve this objective, we analyzed the top five most popular Korean package tracking websites (Korea Post, CJ Logistics, Lotte Logistics, Logen and Hanjin Shipping), which can offer several services related package delivery. Table 1 presents the input parameters, which are needed to access each service of package tracking websites.

Table 1. Input parameters needed for each service of package tracking websites.

Company	Checking the status	Changing the drop-off location	Requesting the receipt	Returning the package
Korea Post	PTN	PTN	Authentication code	PTN, Recipient's name
CJ Logistics	PTN	–	–	PTN, Recipient's phone number
Lotte Logistics	PTN	–	–	PTN
Logen	PTN	–	PTN	PTN, Recipient's phone number
Hanjin Shipping	PTN	–	–	–

From Table 1, we can observe that most services can be accessed with PTN and recipient's name or phone number. We aim to exploit those services by enumerating PTNs or phone numbers because they can be enumerated based on our initial PTN structure analysis. Unlike other systems, the receipt requesting service at Korea Post requires an internally generated authentication code (e.g., Hw17WzULnQ9BgnPZmd), which we will explain more in the next section.

In each package tracking website, the following four services are commonly offered: 1) checking the package delivery status, 2) changing the drop-off location, 3) requesting the package delivery receipt, and 4) returning the package to the sender. Figure 3 presents some examples of each service. However, we note that the above four services can be abused to harvest users' information if we fail to protect PTNs or phone numbers from guessing. The detailed description of each service and the types of displayed personal information are provided as follows:

1) Checking the Package Delivery Status. As shown in Figure. 3a, a user can check the expected delivery time and tracking details. We can obtain the following information through the package delivery status checking service: 1) the package delivery status, time, and item; 2) the sender's *masked* name and address; 3) the recipient's *masked* name and address; and 4) the courier's name and phone number. For example, the sender's and recipient's names (e.g., ***soo Kim) can be masked to hide their full names, while the courier's full name is revealed. Table 2 summarizes the detailed package, sender, recipient and courier information provided by each company. Not surprisingly, the degree of information provided through this service slightly varies across different companies.

(a) Checking the status (b) Changing the drop-off location

(c) Requesting the receipt (d) Returning the package

Fig. 3. Four common services in package tracking websites.

Table 2. Information types obtained from the package delivery status checking service.

Company	Package	Sender	Recipient	Courier
Korea Post	Status, Time	Masked name	Masked name	Name, Phone number
CJ Logistics	Status, Time , Item	Masked name	Masked name	Name, Phone number
Lotte Logistics	Status, Time	City	City	Name, Phone number
Logen	Status, Time	Masked name, City	Masked name, City	Name, Phone number
Hanjin Shipping	Status, Time, Item	Masked name	Masked name, City	Name, Phone number

2) Changing the Drop-Off Location. In all services, the package is directly delivered to the recipient's home address by default. However, recipients can often change their final drop-off location. As shown in Fig. 3b, the recipient can choose a drop-off location to security office, unmanned delivery box, front door, or other places.

Although three package service providers (Korea Post, CJ Logistics, and Logen) offer an option to change the drop-off location, CJ Logistics, and Logen do not provide any information through this service. From only Korea Post, we can obtain the following additional information through the drop-off location changing service: 1) the package item (e.g., electronics, books, etc.); and 2) the recipient's name and address.

3) Requesting the Package Delivery Receipt. Senders and recipients can further request the receipt of payment for a proof of the package delivery. Two package service providers (Korea Post and Logen) offer an option to display the receipt of the payment for the package delivery, as shown in Fig. 3c. In particular, we can obtain the following auxiliary information through the receipt requesting service: 1) the package item, 2) the sender's name, phone number and address, and 3) the recipient's name, phone number, and address. Table 3 summarizes the auxiliary information types provided by each company.

Table 3. Information types obtained from the receipt requesting service.

Company	Package	Sender	Recipient
Korea Post	–	Name	Name, Address
CJ Logistics	–	–	–
Lotte Logistics	–	–	–
Logen	Item	Name, Phone number, Address	Name, Phone number, Address
Hanjin Shipping	–	–	–

4) Returning the Package to the Sender. Recipients often want to return the received items to the senders. Therefore all package service providers except Hanjin Shipping offer an option to allow users to return the received item through their website. As shown in Fig. 3d, this service typically displays the sender's and recipient's details such as their names and addresses. We can obtain the following user and package information through the package returning service: (1) the package item, (2) the sender's name, phone number, and address, and (3) the recipient's name, phone number, and address. In Logen, the recipient's name and phone number are masked, while the sender's name and phone number are fully visible in plain text. Table 4 summarizes the auxiliary information types provided by each company.

Table 4. Information types obtained from the package returning service.

Company	Package	Sender	Recipient
Korea Post	Item	Name, Phone number, Address	Name, Phone number, Address
CJ Logistics	Item	Name, Phone number, Address	Name, Phone number, Address
Lotte Logistics	Item	Name, Phone number, Address	-
Logen	Item	Name, Phone number, Address	Masked name, Masked phone number, Masked address
Hanjin Shipping	–	–	–

4   Experimental Results

To show the feasibility of the proposed enumeration attacks presented in Sect. 2, we implemented a tool to perform enumeration attacks in Python 3.7. We also used an open source automated web testing tool, `Selenium` (https://selenium. dev), to modify query cookies and HTTP headers. For testing, we executed this tool on the Ubuntu 16.04 64-bit running on an Intel(R) Core(TM) i5-6500 CPU (with 16 GB RAM), equipped with a 100 MB LAN connection.

If the package tracking record is successfully displayed on a web page while performing enumeration attacks, we can extract specific customer's data from the web page. Interestingly, in some services (e.g., the receipt requesting service at Logen, the drop-off location changing service at Korea Post, and the package returning service at CJ logistics), customers' data is not directly visible in the web page because values are presented in hidden fields in the HTML source file. Therefore, we use Chrome Devtools (https://developers.google.com/web/tools/ chrome-devtools) to extract hidden field values from the source file.

4.1   Enumeration Attacks with PTNs

We first manually collected several initial PTNs used in the four package tracking systems (Korea Post, Lotte Logistics, Logen and Hanjin Shipping) to analyze the underlying structure of valid PTNs for each system. On the other hand, for CJ Logistics, we did not use PTNs because we found that enumeration attacks can be more effectively implemented with phone numbers on package return service – PTNs can additionally be obtained with phone numbers.

We used Naver (https://www.naver.com/), which is the most popular search engine in South Korea, to collect valid PTNs. For the initial PTNs collection, we searched web pages containing specific keywords such as "package tracking number" and then extracted strings in the format of package tracking number from the search results. As a result, we obtained the following number of initial PTNs: 1,518 for Korea Post; 770 for Lotte Logistics; 1,693 for Logen; and 1,366 for Hanjin Shipping. With those initial seed PTNs, we can analyze the valid PTN formats used for each tracking system, and they are summarized in Table 5, where all service providers' PTNs consist of digits only.

Table 5. PTN formats and maximum possible PTN spaces.

Company	PTN format	Example	Max. space
Korea Post	13-digits	1102914267781	10^{13}
CJ Logistics	10- or 12-digits	101835579911	10^{12}
Lotte Logistics	12-digits	101821471776	10^{12}
Logen	11-digits	12796430323	10^{11}
Hanjin Shipping	12-digits	304139498250	10^{12}

Even though it is not feasible to correctly guess a specific PTN having the range of 10–13 digits, enumeration attacks can be practically performed because the goal of enumeration attacks is just to identify any valid PTNs rather than to find a specific PTN. Furthermore, we found that PTNs are not randomly generated. Therefore, we can efficiently find new valid PTNs from existing PTNs. That is, given an initial PTN, we generate a candidate PTN by increasing a certain number and try to search for tracking information with the candidate PTN on the tracking service website. If the package tracking information is successfully returned from the website, the information is crawled and stored in a database; otherwise, we sequentially repeated the searching and crawling step with the next candidate PTN. In Sect. 5, from the collected data, we will show the difference between two consecutive PTNs is very small in practice.

4.2 Enumeration Attacks with Phone Numbers

For CJ Logistics, we specifically implemented a new enumeration attack, which uses phone numbers by analyzing its Android application. Specifically, we focused on designing enumeration attacks exploiting the package returning

```
POST /express.xml/delivery.do?cmd=SAFLISTRCVC HTTP/1.1
Host: mobile.cjlogistics.com
...


—
     "BPARAM": —
         "AUTHTEL1": "010", PGMONTH:0 ,
         "AUTHTEL2": "1234",
         "AUTHTEL3": "5678", PGNUM:1 "
"
```

Fig. 4. Input parameters used to access the customer's service usage history information at CJ Logistics, where a user's phone number (e.g., 010-1234-5678) is divided into AUTH_TEL1, AUTH_TEL2, and AUTH_TEL3.

service, because CJ Logistics' package delivery status checking service only displays customers' masked name instead of their full name (see Table 2).

We found that the CJ Logistics' Android application provides a login option for users' phone numbers. For example, when the login process has been successfully completed with a phone number, the user's service usage history can be accessed for 90 days. Figure 4 shows the example request message to obtain the customer's service usage history information. Therefore, if we modify the B_PARAM field with another valid phone number in Fig. 4, we can easily obtain the corresponding customer's entire 90 of days service usage history information.

In the service usage history information, each transaction record is composed of PTN, masked recipient's name, city, and item information. Therefore, if we have a customer's phone number, we can obtain all those information. In fact, the South Korea's phone number format has 11-digits (e.g., 010-1234-5678) as shown in Fig. 4. At first glance, the theoretically possible space of 11-digits seems sufficiently large to resist against guessing because an attacker would try 10^{11} number of guesses at the worst case. However, phone numbers are not random in practice; the first three digits (i.e., "010") of phone numbers are always the same. Furthermore, in the second part, there are some specific 4-digits that appear more frequently. For example, the 4-digits between 0000 and 1999 are reserved for the Korean government. Therefore the actual phone number space is much smaller than our expectation, making enumeration attacks feasible.

4.3   Summary of Enumeration Attack Results

In Table 6, three possible attack results are presented for each service. Specifically, "Attacked" means when the service can be executed with artificially generated input parameters (e.g., PTN, phone number, and/or name) in a short time (e.g., within a minute), and "Not Attacked" represents when we failed to find a method for enumeration attacks. "Not Applicable" indicates when the service is not provided or there is no personal information provided by the service.

Table 6. Summary of our attack analysis results for the top 5 package delivery providers in South Korea.

Company	Checking the status	Changing the drop-off location	Requesting the receipt	Returning the package
Korea Post	✓	✓	✗	✓
CJ Logistics	✓	—	—	✓
Lotte Logistics	✓	—	—	✓
Logen	✓	—	✓	✓
Hanjin Shipping	✓	—	—	—

✓ Attacked ✗ Not Attacked — Not Applicable

As explained in Sect. 4.1 and 4.2, we can successfully perform enumeration attacks on all the services, requiring PTN alone as input parameter (see Table 1).

At first glance, it does not seem straightforward to implement enumeration attacks on the other four services (the receipt requesting service at Korea Post, the package returning service at Korea Post, the package returning service at CJ Logistics, and the package returning service at Logen), because those services require some other parameters in addition to PTN.

However, for the package returning service at Korea Post, CJ Logistics, and Logen, we can still perform enumeration attacks efficiently. For the package returning service at Korea Post, two input parameters (PTN and the recipient's name) are needed (see Table 1). In this case, we first obtain the recipient's name with a PTN through the drop-off location changing service and perform enumeration attacks on the package returning service with a PTN and the recipient's name. Figure 5 illustrates this process in detail.

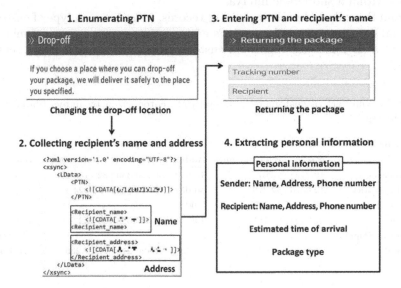

Fig. 5. Process of enumeration attacks on Korea Post: 1) we first perform an enumeration attack with PTNs on the drop-off location changing service; 2) we extract a recipient's name from the search result if a valid PTN is entered; 3) we then execute the package returning service with the obtained PTN and name; and 4) we extract the target personal information from the search result of the package returning service.

Similarly, for the package returning service at Logen, we first obtain the recipient's phone number with a PTN through the receipt requesting service (see Table 3) and perform enumeration attacks on the package returning service with the PTN and the recipient's phone number. For the package returning service at CJ Logistics, we can use phone numbers instead of PTNs for enumeration attacks. As explained in Sect. 4.2, we can obtain PTNs with phone numbers by modifying the parameters to access the user's service usage history at its Android application. In summary, we only failed to perform enumeration attacks on the receipt requesting service at Korea Post because this service requires an internally generated authentication code to access (see Table 1).

5   Analysis of Collected Data

During 6 months (from May 2019 to November 2019), we collected package delivery records as follows: 1,398,112 for Korea Post; 2,614,839 for CJ Logistics; 797,676 for Lotte Logistics; 1,590,933 for Logen; and 163,452 for Hanjin Shipping. We collected at least 700,000 package delivery records from all providers except Hanjin Shipping. Hanjin Shipping blocked the IP addresses used for our experiments. We surmise that Hanjin shipping only used a proper security solution to block the IP addresses used for generating a large volume of suspicious queries within a short time interval.

From the collected package delivery records, we count each type of customers' personal data categorized by sender's and recipient's name, phone number, and address, after removing duplicated customer data. The results are presented in Table 7.

Table 7. Numbers of customers' personal data categorized by name, phone number and address.

Company	Sender			Recipient		
	Name	Phone number	Address	Name	Phone number	Address
Korea Post	19,712	1,207	18,012	1,220,350	822,159	1,212,029
CJ Logistics	128,426	52,329	56,062	1,811,325	724,824	1,734,623
Lotte Logistics	7,268	1,844	5,004	–	–	–
Logen	204,405	92,755	140,847	1,388,539	980,222	1,366,470
Hanjin Shipping	–	–	–	–	–	154,207
Total	359,811	148,135	219,925	4,420,214	2,527,205	4,467,329

Personal Information. As shown in Table 7, the number of senders' data is less than the number of recipients' data because a vast majority of senders are professional sellers or companies, while most recipients are normal customers. Therefore, we note that recipients' personal information appears more attractive to attackers than senders' information. For recipients' data, we collected 4,420,214 names, 2,527,205 phone numbers, 4,467,329 addresses, respectively, in total. Perhaps, such people's personal information could be abused to conduct additional cyber criminal activities such as sophisticated spam/phishing attacks [8,13] and Sybil accounts creation [11], and invade user privacy. For example, we found that some military officers used their military rank as a part of their name (e.g., Captain John Doe). In this situation, their private home address or the location of a military base can be exposed to the public including potential attackers. Furthermore, a celebrity's phone number and/or home address can be potentially revealed by linking his/her publicly known other information (e.g., real name, location of home address). Previous studies demonstrated that the inclusion of more detailed contextual information would increase the success probability of phishing attacks [9].

Fig. 6. Example of targeted SMiShing attacks.

Figure 6 shows a targeted SMiShing attack, which is a type of phishing communication that is sent to a victim's mobile phone through an SMS message. In this example, the personal information (name, PTN, and address) about a victim (John Doe) is added to deceive the victim into believing that this SMS is sent from the original shipping company (CJ Logistics) in order to entice the victim to click the link to the attacker's website.

Predictability of PTN. Furthermore, we examine patterns in a sequence of PTNs to predict PTNs. We specifically measure the difference between two consecutive PTNs ($\Delta PTN(i) = PTN(i+1) - PTN(i)$) where $PTN(i)$ is the ith PTN in the sequence of PTNs. We calculate the cumulative distribution functions (CDF) of $\Delta PTN(i)$ (from 1 to 20) with all the collected PTNs from Korea Post, CJ Logistics, Lotte Logistics, Logen, and Hanjin Shipping tracking systems, respectively.

Figure 7 shows the calculated CDFs for Korea Post, CJ Logistics, Lotte Logistics, Logen, and Hanjin Shipping, respectively, where the X-axis represents the difference between two successive PTNs[1], and the Y-axis represents the cumulative percentage of the number of PTNs with less than or equal to ΔPTN. We can see that in most cases, the gaps between two successive PTNs are smaller than 20, indicating that PTNs can be efficiently enumerated in a sequential manner.

6 Possible Defense Mechanisms

In this section, we suggest three possible defense mechanisms to mitigate the security threats.

---

[1] We denote $\Delta PTN(i)$ for all i in the collected PTNs as ΔPTN.

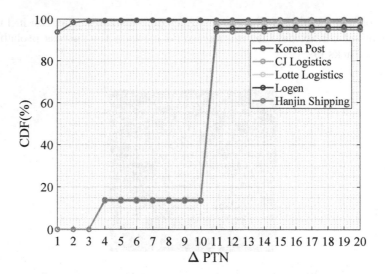

Fig. 7. Cumulative distribution function (CDF) of ΔPTN for Korea Post, CJ Logistics, Lotte Logistics, Logen, and Hanjin Shipping.

Limiting the Number of PTN (or Phone Number) Verification Failed Attempts: Limiting the number of PTN (or phone number) verification failed attempts can be the first line of defense to prevent enumeration attacks because a large number of PTN (or phone number) verification failed attempts are necessarily induced while performing enumeration attacks. In practice, this approach can be implemented by simply counting the number of verification failed attempts from a specific client. Hence, we can apply this policy in package tracking systems with a low deployment cost. The idea of limiting the number of attempts from a specific client (e.g., with an IP address) or imposing a minimum time interval between failed attempts is not new [6]. However, none of the package tracking systems that we tested to limit the number of failed attempts, and seem to be considering enumeration attacks[2]. If we deploy the policy of "maximum failed attempts allowed," attackers would try to change their strategy into more complicated enumeration attack scenarios (e.g., [11]) with multiple hosts and diverse query patterns, leading to the increase in attackers' efforts.

Using CAPTCHA Challenges: Another promising approach is to use CAPTCHA [16] challenges to hinder automated attempts which are necessary to perform enumeration attacks. However, the use of CAPTCHA challenges can incur the usability cost of taking the time to solve CAPTCHA challenges for

---

[2] We believe that Hanjin Shipping would use a DDoS mitigation solution at the network level rather than the policy of "maximum failed attempts allowed" at the web application level because we cannot access the website itself when we queried multiple times within a short time interval.

normal users. Therefore, it seems better to combine this approach with our first recommendation – we can ask users to solve a CAPTCHA problem only when the number of PTN (or phone number) verification failed attempts is greater than the maximum number of failed attempts allowed (e.g., five) or suspicious query patterns are detected.

Generating Unpredictable PTNs: The problem with PTNs is that they are highly predictable and can easily be enumerated[3] (see Fig. 7). Therefore, we need to change the existing structure of PTNs by reserving at least some reasonable number of digits (e.g., 6 digits) in PTNs to represent a random number, which makes PTNs harder to enumerate within a reasonable time. A cryptographically secure pseudo-random number generator (CSPRNG) such as Fortuna [12] can be used to generate random digits in an unpredictable manner.

Minimizing Information Leakage: Current package tracking systems provide unnecessary personal information about sender and recipient in their online website, which can be viewed and harvested by a third party. To address this problem, we suggest that package tracking systems should not provide any personal information (e.g., name, phone number, address, etc.) about the sender (or recipient) with a PTN alone. That is if a user enters a PTN or his/her phone number, package tracking websites can show the only information about package status such as current package location and estimated delivery date, but no user-related personal data. For some situations where senders' or recipients' personal data is needed (e.g., some recipients may want to contact their senders), however, sender's (or recipient's) personal data can be additionally provided only when the recipient (or sender) successfully logs-in into the package tracking website.

7   Ethical Considerations

The main motivation of our experiments is to show the risk of potential enumeration attacks on package delivery service and discuss effective defense mechanisms to mitigate such attacks. Therefore, we only checked service providers' responses for our enumeration attack attempts; however, actual user data were not stored. Furthermore, we queried the websites' tracking services at a very slow rate to minimize adverse impacts on the websites' normal operations. Finally, we reported the discovered design flaws and our recommendations to shipping companies running those services.

8   Related Work

In recent years, the possibility of enumeration attacks has been intensively studied in social network and instant messenger services.

---

[3] We surmise that PTNs may contain some meaningful information (e.g., location and time) about package delivery records because they have a well-formatted structure.

Balduzzi et al. [7] discussed the possibility of enumeration attacks to automatically harvest active email addresses by using Facebook's friend-finder feature. About 10.4 million e-mail addresses were tested and more than 1.2 million user profiles were found to be associated with these addresses. To fix this problem, Facebook employed several defense mechanisms such as detecting suspicious query patterns and using CAPTCHA challenges. More recently, however, Kim et al. [11] showed that an advanced enumeration attack scenario with a few Sybil accounts can evade those defense mechanisms in the real-world situations. Similar problems related to enumeration attacks were also reported in instant messenger services. Schrittwieser et al. [14] presented an enumeration attack to collect 21,095 live phone numbers from WhatsApp within less than 2.5 h. Kim et al. [10] also collected 50,567 users' phone numbers, names, and profile pictures from KakaoTalk (https://www.kakaocorp.com/service/KakaoTalk?lang=en) through enumeration attacks. Gupta et al. [8] demonstrated that the collected phone numbers could potentially be abused to perform sophisticated targeted phishing attacks or a larger phishing campaign. Recently, Woo et al. [15] demonstrated the possibility of *enumeration attacks* with the top three package service providers (FedEx [4], DHL [3], and UPS [5]). However, their work was focused on those three service providers only and did not explain how enumeration attacks can be systematically detected and tested. We extend their study to additional services for generalization, and further develop a framework to systemically analyze the attack vectors related to enumeration attacks on websites.

Many customers are already concerned about shipping companies that have maintained customers' personal data insecurely. For example, personal information of thousands of FedEx customers was exposed [1] because of the insecure cloud storage server. Also, USPS exposed 60 Million user information due to the flaws in its APIs [2].

9   Conclusion

In this work, we examined the possibility of enumeration attacks on existing package tracking systems. We developed effective enumeration attack scenarios for the websites of top shipping companies (Korea Post, CJ Logistics, Lotte Logistics, Logen and Hanjin Shipping) in South Korea. Our experimental results demonstrate that those companies do not fully consider a reasonable level of security practices to protect their customer data. We collected a large number of package delivery records from those companies' websites and finally extracted 4,420,214 names, 2,527,205 phone numbers, and 4,467,329 addresses in total through our enumeration attack implementations in an automated manner. To address this security concern, we suggest four practical defense approaches such as limiting the number of PTN verification fail attempts, using CAPTCHA challenges and generating unpredictable PTNs to prevent enumeration attacks.

Although our analysis and observation are package tracking system-specific, they could offer valuable lessons for other websites that provide services with tracking numbers alone. As part of future work, we plan to implement a generic tool for testing the possibility of enumeration attacks on websites.

Acknowledgement. This work was supported in part by the NRF of Korea (NRF-2019R1C1C1007118), the ITRC Support Program (IITP-2019- 2015-0-00403), and the ICT R&D Programs (No. 2017-0-00545).

References

1. FedEx Data Breach (2018). https://www.informationsecuritybuzz.com/expert-comments/fedex-data-breach/. Accessed 14 Oct 2019
2. USPS Site Exposed Data on 60 Million Users (2018). https://krebsonsecurity.com/2018/11/usps-site-exposed-data-on-60-million-users/. Accessed 14 Oct 2019
3. DHL global (2019). http://www.dhl.com/en.html. Accessed 14 Oct 2019
4. Fedex (2019). https://www.fedex.com. Accessed 14 Oct 2019
5. UPS (2019). https://www.ups.com. Accessed 14 Oct 2019
6. Alsaleh, M., Mannan, M., van Oorschot, P.C.: Revisiting defenses against large-scale online password guessing attacks. IEEE Trans. Dependable Secure Comput. **9**, 128–141 (2012)
7. Balduzzi, M., Platzer, C., Holz, T., Kirda, E., Balzarotti, D., Kruegel, C.: Abusing social networks for automated user profiling. In: Jha, S., Sommer, R., Kreibich, C. (eds.) RAID 2010. LNCS, vol. 6307, pp. 422–441. Springer, Heidelberg (2010). https://doi.org/10.1007/978-3-642-15512-3_22
8. Gupta, S., Gupta, P., Ahamad, M., Kumaraguru, P.: Exploiting phone numbers and cross-application features in targeted mobile attacks. In: Proceedings of the 6th Workshop on Security and Privacy in Smartphones and Mobile Devices (2016)
9. Hong, J.: The state of phishing attacks. Commun. ACM **55**(1), 74–81 (2012)
10. Kim, E., Park, K., Kim, H., Song, J.: Design and analysis of enumeration attacks on finding friends with phone numbers: a case study with kakaotalk. Comput. Secur. **52**, 267–275 (2015)
11. Kim, J., Kim, K., Cho, J., Kim, H., Schrittwieser, S.: Hello, Facebook! here is the stalkers' paradise!: design and analysis of enumeration attack using phone numbers on Facebook. In: Proceedings of the 13th International Conference on Information Security Practice and Experience (2017)
12. McEvoy, R., Curran, J., Cotter, P., Murphy, C.: Fortuna: cryptographically secure pseudo-random number generation in software and hardware (2006)
13. Palmer, D.: Phishing attack: students' personal information stolen in university data breach (2019). https://www.zdnet.com/article/phishing-attack-students-personal-information-stolen-in-university-data-breach/. Accessed 30 Dec 2019
14. Schrittwieser, S., et al.: Guess who's texting you? Evaluating the security of smartphone messaging applications. In: Proceedings of the 19th Annual Symposium on Network and Distributed System Security (2012)
15. Woo, S., Jang, H., Ji, W., Kim, H.: I've got your packages: harvesting customers' delivery order information using package tracking number enumeration attacks. In: Proceedings of The Web Conference (WWW 2020) (2020)
16. von Ahn, L., Blum, M., Hopper, N.J., Langford, J.: CAPTCHA: using hard AI problems for security. In: Biham, E. (ed.) EUROCRYPT 2003. LNCS, vol. 2656, pp. 294–311. Springer, Heidelberg (2003). https://doi.org/10.1007/3-540-39200-9_18

Privacy

JTaint: Finding Privacy-Leakage in Chrome Extensions

Mengfei Xie, Jianming Fu[(⊠)], Jia He, Chenke Luo, and Guojun Peng

MOE Key Laboratory of Aerospace Information Security and Trusted Computing,
School of Cyber Science and Engineering, Wuhan University, Wuhan 430072, China
{mfxie96,jmfu,jiahe97,kernelthread,guojpeng}@whu.edu.cn

Abstract. Extensions are used by many Chrome browser users to enhance browser functions and users' online experience. These extensions run with special permissions, they can read and modify the element of DOM (Document Object Model) in users' web pages. But, excessive permissions and operation behaviors have brought users heavy risks such as the privacy leakage caused by extensions. Dynamic taint analysis techniques are often exploited to discover the privacy leakage, it monitors code execution by modifying the JavaScript interpreter or rewriting the JavaScript source code. However, interpreter-level taint technique needs to overcome the complexity of the interpreter, and there are also many difficulties in designing taint propagation rules for bytecode. And source-level taint technique is undertainted like Jalangi2, which will trigger some exceptions in practice.

To this end, we design JalangiEX based on Jalangi2. JalangiEX fixes problems in Jalangi2 and strips its redundant codes. Besides, JalangiEX also monitors two types of initialization actions and provides taint propagation support for message passing between different pages, which further solves the undertaint problem of Jalangi2. Moreover we implement JTaint, a dynamic taint analysis system that uses JalangiEX to rewrite the extension and monitors the process of taint propagation to discover potential privacy leaks in Chrome extensions. Finally, we use JTaint to analyze 20,000 extensions from Chrome Web Store and observe the data flow of extensions on a special honey page. Fifty-seven malicious extensions are recognized to leak sensitive-privacy information and are still active in the Chrome Web Store.

Keywords: Chrome extension · Privacy-leakage · Taint propagation

1 Introduction

Among Chrome, Firefox, IE, and other browsers, Chrome occupies 60% of the world's users due to its simple, efficient, and secure features. Like other browsers, Chrome also supports extra extensions to enhance browser features and users' experience. People can use extensions to manage tags, collect web page information, and modify network requests.

Chrome extension can freely observe users' behaviors on the page without applying for additional permissions, because these privileges are granted to installed extensions

© Springer Nature Switzerland AG 2020
J. K. Liu and H. Cui (Eds.): ACISP 2020, LNCS 12248, pp. 563–583, 2020.
https://doi.org/10.1007/978-3-030-55304-3_29

by default. Therefore, user identity, browsing behavior, financial transactions, and other information generated by users may be captured by extensions, which will cause information leakage. The Applied Threat Research Team [1] disclosed four malicious extensions in 2018, affecting a total of more than 5 million users. These extensions will proxy victim's network traffic, implement conduct click fraud and search engine optimization. In 2019, Jadali [2] disclosed the privacy leaks of eight malicious extensions such as Hover Zoom in a report that affected a total of more than 4 million people.

There have been many researches on browser extension security, including static analysis [3–7] and dynamic analysis [8–18]. Since static analysis methods tend to be weak in dealing with code obfuscation and runtime information collection, dynamic analysis is increasingly favored by researchers. Extension dynamic analysis mainly focuses on network traffic analysis [8, 9], API call analysis [10–13], and data flow analysis [14–18]. Traffic analysis is a relatively direct way to recognize sensitive-privacy words among browser network traffic, but it is easy to miss privacy leakage due to obfuscation and encryption [8, 12]. API call analysis needs to collect the critical APIs in extension operations, then perform model training and classify them, but its malicious behavior recognition is content-insensitive. Data flow analysis requires more fine-grained tracking of the code execution to analyze the flow of private data.

Dynamic taint analysis is a type of data flow analysis, it is often effective in finding privacy leaks. Information-flow policies can be defined between Chromium entities such as DOM elements and scripts to implement coarse-grained, light-weight taint tracking [15]. A fine-grained, heavy-weight tracking needs to be based on operation instructions, which can be achieved from the perspective of modifying the JavaScript engine (interpreter-level) and rewriting the extension code (code-level).

The interpreter-level solution adds taint propagation code during the execution of the bytecode of the JavaScript interpreter. Mystique [16] modifies the V8 engine of Chrome to perform dynamic taint analysis. It is difficult to support various interpreters, specially interpreter update or patch.

The code-level solution is to rewrite the extension code, that is, to add instrumenting instructions directly to the source code. This solution does not modify the JavaScript interpreter, so it can run in all environments that support the standard JavaScript syntax. ExtensionGuard [17] uses Jalangi2 [19] to rewrite extension codes and inject taint propagation rules. However, Jalangi2 will report an error when processing JavaScript code above the ECMAScript5 standard, since it stops update as early as 2017. Furthermore, ExtensionGuard will miss some sensitive-privacy information in practice due to special data type.

In this paper, we fixed the problems existing in Jalangi2, and broke the limitation of ExtensionGuard to solve the undertaint problem. In summary, our contributions are described as follows.

1. We propose a novel taint analysis technique to handle undertaint in Jalangi2. Using this technique, we provide necessary and additional both taint data type, and taint propagation among message passing.
2. We present JTaint, a dynamic taint analysis framework that builds on our technique to discover abuse privacy-sensitive information. This framework strips unnecessary code in Jalangi2 according to taint analysis and constructs a separate library to

support chrome extension instrumentation. The source code of JTaint is available at https://github.com/whucs303/JTaint.

3. More than 20,000 chrome extensions are investigated within our analysis framework, 57 of which leaked user privacy. In these extensions, obfuscations of taint data are identified and taint propagation models are recognized.

2 Background

Because of its simple interface, fast speed, and extension support, Chrome has become the most popular browser in the world. This section gives the introduction of chrome extension, and the communication mechanism between different pages. Sensitive-privacy information leakage will be discussed.

2.1 Chrome Extension

Chrome extension is a compressed file with a suffix named *crx*, consisting of JavaScript, CSS, HTML, and a manifest file that indicates the permission and running setting of JavaScript files. Chrome extension runs on the browser and calls the Chrome API to implement special functions through JavaScript, such as modifying tabs, intercepting network requests, blocking ads, managing bookmarks and history.

Unlike ordinary JavaScript programs, scripts in the extension run in different environments according to the match patterns declared in the manifest file and have different permissions. There are three types scripts [20]: Background Script, Content Script, and Injected Script.

Background Script. It runs on a separate page and can use all the APIs provided by the Chrome browser for the extension, and manages global states.

Content Script. It is responsible for interacting with the web page viewed by the user, and can read and modify the details of the web page that the user visits.

Injected Script. It is inserted into to the user web page by the content scripts, and can access the JavaScript environment in the page, but cannot use the API provided by Chrome for the extension.

2.2 Message Passing

The extension's three scripts run in separate environments, in Fig. 1. Popup pages, option pages, and background pages belong to the extension's background. They can use the API provided by Chrome to obtain the window object of other pages directly, so no communication is required. There are other message transmissions among the three scripts below.

Injected Script and Content Script share the DOM object of the page, so they can use the communication function provided by the window object to pass messages. The sender uses the *window.postMessage* to send messages, and the receiver uses the

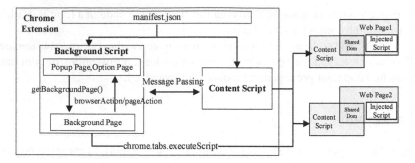

Fig. 1. Relationships of 3 types of scripts

window.addEventListener to set a message listener for receiving. Content Script and Background Script can use the message mechanism provided by Chrome to exchange information, which supports two types: one-time request and long-lived connection. The one-time request uses the *runtime.sendMessage* or *tabs.sendMessage* to send a one-time JSON-serializable message. The receiver initializes a *runtime.onMessage* event listener to handle the message. The long-lived connection uses the *runtime.connect* or *tabs.connect* to create a long connection channel. Each channel returns a *runtime.Port* object after creation and the communicating peers use the *port* object to send or receive data. The Fig. 1 illustrates the relationships among the three scripts.

2.3 Privacy Leakage Threat

Chrome extension uses least privilege, privilege separation, and strong isolation [21] to mitigate the security threats posed by extension. But related researches show that there are still many malicious extensions in the Chrome Web Store. Hulk [10] sorted out some of the typical malicious behaviors, including Ad Manipulation, Affiliate Fraud, Information Theft, OSN Abuse, and so on. Threats caused by extensions will be further extended to other components of Chrome, Dolière's research shows that malicious Web Applications can communicate with extensions to empower themselves [22].

In this paper, we focus on the privacy threats that Chrome extensions pose to users. Chrome provides multiple permissions for extensions, but some of them are quite dangerous. For example, the *clipboardRead* permission can access the data copied and pasted by the user; the *privacy* permission can manage privacy-related settings of the user. Chrome extension has such high permissions that it can get almost all the information generated by the user. However, Chrome only pops up a prompt after the extension is installed or updated to inform the permissions requested by extension, and lacks the mechanism for runtime permission application. Besides, users often lack attention to the security threats of extensions, and can easily ignore the high-risk permissions requested by extension.

Our crawler shows that the Chrome Web Store currently has more than 100,000 extensions. Faced with such a large number of extensions, the review mechanism of the store for extensions seems too loose. Adblock Plus is a well-known ad-blocking extension, but after its release, malicious extensions such as Adblock and uBlock have also been successfully listed in Chrome Web Store [23]. These two extensions engage in cookie stuffing to defraud affiliate marketing programs. In general, due to the loose review mechanism, the high permissions of the extension, and the low-security awareness of some users, Chrome extension has brought considerable privacy threats to users.

3 System Design

In this section, we will first describe the structure of JTaint, and then introduce two improvements of JalangiEX compared to Jalangi2.

3.1 JTaint OverView

JTaint runs instrumented extensions in Chrome and monitors the taint propagation through dynamic taint tracking. The structure of JTaint is shown in Fig. 2.

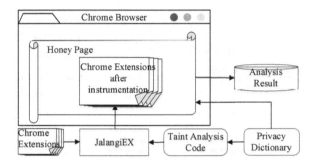

Fig. 2. JTaint design

JTaint first calls JalangiEX to instrument the extension and adds the taint analysis code to it. JTaint then installs the rewritten extension into Chrome and simulates it on the honey page. Finally, JTaint outputs the results of taint propagation. In order to trigger more malicious behaviors, we use the following two schemes:

- We simulate extensions on the honey page specially constructed by the privacy dictionary. We use the NLP technique to expand 43 privacy word seeds into 411 privacy words, and use them as the id of DOM elements to generate the honey page to trigger more privacy-leaking behaviors in the extension.
- We use ChromeDriver to automatically simulate form filling, form submission, and page switching on the honey page to trigger certain event listeners registered by extensions.

In this paper, we only consider privacy-leaking extensions that are not sensitive to URLs, because JTaint only simulates extensions on the honey page. For example, for the extension that steals the sensitive form of pages, JTaint can detect it correctly, but JTaint may not be able to discover the privacy theft of special extension that only runs on predefined sites like Twitter.

3.2 Optimization for Jalangi2

We will discuss problems when applying Jalangi2 to the extension analysis. And then, we will present improvements in these issues, which are integrated into JalangiEX.

Jalangi2 Overview

As the dynamic analysis framework of JavaScript language, Jalangi2 implements instrumentation by rewriting code, to achieve dynamic monitoring of JavaScript code runtime. Jalangi2 first parses the JavaScript code into Abstract Syntax Tree (AST), and then converts 25 types of nodes defined by AST into 30 types of intermediate codes defined by Jalangi2, in the Post-Order Traversal of the nodes. During program execution, intermediate codes will transfer control to the Analysis Function before and after completing the original semantics. Users can customize analysis code in these 29 types of Analysis Functions, to implement dynamic monitoring of JavaScript code runtime. We show this process in Fig. 3.

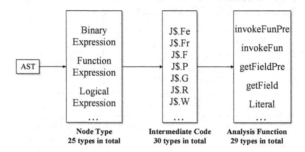

Fig. 3. Jalangi2's process

Striping Redundant Codes of Jalangi2

Jalangi2 is unmaintained at least two years old. In using Jalangi2, we found the following problems:

Problem 1. Jalangi2 reports errors when instrumenting some JavaScript codes. There are two main reasons for these errors. On the one hand, Jalangi2 uses the Acorn library to convert between JavaScript source code and AST. Updating the Acorn library can prevent Jalangi2 from reporting errors when processing syntax defined in the new JavaScript syntax standard. On the other hand, Jalangi2 may break the correct structure of AST when rewriting them, which will cause the modified AST cannot be converted into JavaScript source code. For example, Jalangi2 will report errors when rewriting codes that contain Class syntax. This is because Jalangi2 incorrectly converted the FunctionExpression Node to the CallExpression Node when processing Class syntax, which prevents the AST from being translated into source code.

Problem 2. Code rewritten by Jalangi2 reports errors that do not exist in the original code in execution. This is mainly due to the slight semantic difference between the rewritten code and the original code. For example, Jalangi2 will add a layer of exception catching code outside the instrumented code, which may cause the scope of the variable to change. Besides, Jalangi2 uses *arguments.callee* to get the currently executing function, but this syntax is forbidden in strict mode.

Code rewritten by Jalangi2 is complicated. We tested on 363 JavaScript files and found the volume of the rewitten script increased by an average of 17 times compared to the original script. Complex instrumentation results are the reason why Jalangi2 is prone to the two types of problems. Therefore, JalangiEX strips redundant code that is not needed for dynamic taint analysis in Jalangi2.

According to the taint propagation rule we defined, JalangiEX needs to write analysis codes in 5 types of Analysis Functions to detect the source and sink points and control taint propagation. According to reverse traceback based on the Jalangi2 working process, there are 7 types of Intermediate Codes that call these 5 types of Analysis Functions in execution. Therefore, among the 30 types of Intermediate Codes defined by Jalangi2, the remaining 23 types can be deleted, which will not affect the accuracy of dynamic taint analysis. Similarly, of the 25 Node types rewritten by Jalangi2, only 12 of them need to be rewritten for code monitoring.

Extracting the Library Dependencies from Jalangi2
The execution of instrumented JavaScript code requires the library dependencies provided by Jalangi2, the code length of the library is about 10,000 lines, including the definition of intermediate codes and analysis functions. Starting from the 7 Intermediate Codes and 5 Analysis Functions required for dynamic taint Analysis, we strip the library dependencies to about 1000 lines and add it to the header of the instrumented script. When the script is running, it will first check whether the current environment contains library dependencies and add them if they are missing. Therefore, this solution does not repeatedly introduce library dependencies in the same environment to avoid unnecessary execution overhead. The process is shown in Fig. 4.

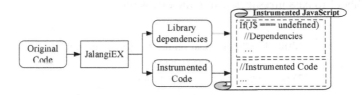

Fig. 4. Build process of instrumental JavaScript.

3.3 Fixing the Undertaint of Jalangi2

Jalangi2 suffers from the undertaint problem when applied to dynamic taint analysis, which is mainly due to the lack of monitoring of certain codes. We will describe two types of undertaints in this section, and JalangiEX's solution.

Monitoring Object and Array
Jalangi2 lacks monitoring of initialization of two basic types, Array and Object, and they play an important role in taint propagation. As shown in Fig. 5(a), because of the lack

of monitoring of the Object initialization process, the variable taintURL cannot spread its taint into the entire object, resulting in the taint propagation being interrupted and the privacy leakage cannot be found.

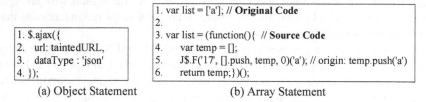

(a) Object Statement   (b) Array Statement

Fig. 5. The statement about array and object respective.

In order to solve this problem, we added the rewrite processing of two types of Node: ArrayExpression and ObjectExpression in JalangiEX. They correspond to the initialization statements of the two basic types of Object and Array, respectively.

Taking ArrayExpression as an example, the statements corresponding to the Array-Expression node before and after rewriting are shown in Fig. 5(b). We decompose the initialization process of array into two parts: initializing an empty array and adding elements to the array. The initialization process of an empty array does not contain any elements, so no monitoring is required. The subsequent process of adding elements to the array is monitored by the intermediate code J\$.F. Thus, the taint status of elements will be spread to the array.

Monitoring Message Passing

According to the introduction of Message Passing [24] by the Chrome Extension Development Guide, extension's three types of scripts can use eight communication functions listed in Table 1 to pass messages within the extension.

Table 1. Communication functions of extension.

Type	Communication function
Send	chrome.runtime.sendMessage
	chrome.tabs.sendMessage
	chrome.runtime.connect
	chrome.tabs.connect
Receive	chrome.runtime.onMessage.addListener
	chrome.runtime.onConnect.addListener
Send	window.sendMessage
Receive	window.addEventListener('message')

The sending function serializes the data to be sent, and the receiver deserializes it. JTaint records taint status in variable's attributes, so it will not be sent with the variable serialized, which will cause undertaint in message passing process. To solve this problem, we use Jalangi2 to hook these eight communication functions, and design the encode and decode functions to wrap messages before and after they are sent. These two functions can record taint status during serialization and parse taint status to the results during deserialization. Messages are packed twice during passing. Take the following code as an example:

chrome.runtime.sendMessage (data, function (response) {});

JTaint hooks the function *sendMessage* before it is called, and encodes the variable *data*. Also, JTaint decodes the variable *response* returned by the peer side.

At the end of this section, we compared Jalangi2 and JalangiEX in Table 2 to clearly show the improvements made by JalangiEX.

Table 2. A comparison between Jalangi2 and JalangiEX.

	Jalangi2	JalangiEX
Number of Node Type	25	12
Number of Intermediate Code	30	7
Number of Analysis Function	29	5
Instrumenting Extension	×	√
Monitoring Object and Array	×	√
Monitoring Message Passing	×	√

4 Define Privacy-Leaking Behavior

In this section, we will define the privacy leakage from three aspects: Source point, Sink point, and taint propagation rules. Source point represents the code segment that obtains privacy-sensitive information; Sink point represents the code segment that exfiltrates privacy-sensitive information; Taint propagation rules define the direction of taint spread between variables.

4.1 Define Source

To detect extensions that abuse their privileges while obtaining users' privacy, JTaint currently considers the following five categories as sink points in its analysis: URL, host, sensitive DOM elements, cookies, and sensitive event listeners. In this section, we will describe each of these sink points and show how to identify them in dynamic taint analysis.

Source Point Description

URL. Jadali [2] divided the privacy data that URLs may leak into six categories in a research report, such as Shared links, PII (personally identifiable information) embedded in URL, and so on. Shared link is the unique, publicly accessible link that users often share with family, friends, and colleagues. Attackers can use these unique links to locate internal resources that are not public on the web. Besides, URL may also contain some sensitive parameters, such as password, authorization strings, token, and PII, these sensitive parameters will be leaked with URLs.

Host. Although host does not contain sensitive parameters except URLs, attackers can roughly infer user's daily habits through host records. In the internal network, attackers can also obtain the IP address of the internal server through host records.

Sensitive DOM Element. Extension may be interested in some sensitive DOM elements on pages. For example, they will look for an input field with the type "password" and steal internal values, or they will gather and exfiltrate sensitive information in form when user clicks to submit the form. We design a honey page to trigger these operations on sensitive DOM elements as much as possible.

Cookie. Cookie is a data that website stores on user's browser in order to identify them and track the session. The leakage of cookie means that attackers can use the user's identity to perform malicious operations on the corresponding website.

Sensitive Event Listeners. JavaScript provides many listeners for monitoring various events related to DOM elements, such as the onclick event triggered after DOM elements are clicked. Attackers can register event listeners for DOM elements to trigger stealing code after users complete element operations. Event listener will point to the DOM element it is bound to after being triggered, so this kind of behavior should be classified as Sensitive DOM element. JTaint pays special attention to two types of keystroke events, keyup and keydown. User can obtain the keycode from the return value after the keystroke event is triggered, instead of from certain DOM elements bound with the event. Therefore, the return value of these two types of events should be marked as tainted.

Feature Code of Source Point

We identify the Source point by examining the feature code associated with the behavior of obtaining sensitive information. Table 6 (Appendix A) lists the correspondence between Source points and feature codes.

There are two types of feature codes corresponding to the behavior of source acquisition: function and object property. Because function objects are unique globally, we embed flags in feature functions to identify them, which can effectively resist the obfuscation of function names. For object attributes, because the memory addresses of different instances are not unique, the addresses of object attributes are also not unique. We can only identify by matching the base class and function name.

4.2 Define Sink

To monitor the exfiltration of privacy-sensitive information, JTaint considers two broad categories of sink points: network transmission and local storage. Either way, we think it is unsafe, because privacy-sensitive information should only be processed locally, and cannot be stored externally, which will lead to the risk of privacy leakage. Table 7 (Appendix A) summarizes the sink points considered by JTaint.

In the way of network transmission, we mainly focus on jQuery, XMLHttpRequest, fetch, and src attribute of DOM element. Extension can use these four methods to access servers in the network through the HTTP protocol. Because different methods have different control capabilities for the HTTP request, the privacy data to be sent may be stored in different locations of the HTTP request such as GET parameters, POST parameters, path, headers, and so on.

In the way of local storage, we mainly focused on two types of feature codes. The first type is two APIs provided by *chrome.storage* [25], which are used to store and retrieve user data. Data stored using the *chrome.storage.sync* function will also be synchronized through the synchronization function of Chrome. The second type is localStorage, which is a type of web storage. The *setItem* function provided by it can also store data locally in user's browser. It should be noted that both types of local storage store data locally in plaintext for a long time. Therefore, it is dangerous to use these two types of local storage to store privacy-sensitive information, which is why we list them as sink points.

4.3 Define Taint Propagation Rules

JTaint adds taint propagation codes to five types of Analysis Functions defined by Jalang-iEX. We show these rules in Table 8 (Appendix A). In taint propagation, we use two levels: taint and partial taint to mark variables. When the subset is tainted, the parent set will be marked as partially taint instead of taint, which can effectively improve the accuracy of taint propagation. For example, the variable *Parent* contains two member variables: *sub1 and sub2*, one is tainted and the other is not, then the variable *Parent* will be marked as partially taint instead of taint. In this way, the variables *Parent.sub2* will not be incorrectly marked as taint when reading it.

5 Evaluation

In order to evaluate the effectiveness of JTaint, we randomly crawled 20,000 extensions from the Chrome Web Store. Except for a few extensions that could not be installed due to the wrong format of the manifest file, through JTaint's batch analysis, we found 57 extensions with privacy disclosure behaviors, including an extension with more than 6 million users and multiple extensions with more than 10,000 users. Our extension was crawled in October 2019. However, in a check on February 15, 2020, we found that there are still 51 extensions that can be downloaded normally in the Chrome Web Store. Based on the large user number of these malicious extensions, it can be speculated that the privacy of many users has been leaked during this period. In this section, we will show the necessity and effectiveness of the work done by JTaint, and then conduct a detailed classification and comparison of these extensions from multiple perspectives. Finally, we detail a typical extension.

5.1 Capabilities of JTaint

In Sect. 3, we introduced three improvements made by JTaint to complete the dynamic taint analysis task of extensions. In this section, we will start from the analysis results of JTaint to confirm the necessity and effectiveness of the three improvements mentioned above.

Simplify the Jalangi2 Instruction Set. We used two JavaScript code dynamic analysis frameworks, Jalangi2 and JalangiEX, to perform instrumentation tests on 390 JavaScript scripts in 57 extensions discovered by JTaint. The result shows that there are 27 scripts reported errors and could not be instrumented during the Jalangi2 rewriting process, some rewritten code also report errors that do not exist in the source code at runtime. However, JalangiEX correctly completed the instrumentation work of all 390 JavaScript scripts, and the code rewritten by JalangiEX did not report the error that does not exist in the source code. The result shows that compared with Jalangi2, JalangiEX can instrument code with a higher success rate, and the rewritten code behaves closer to the source code during execution.

Add New Monitoring Instructions. We analyzed the taint propagation process of 57 extensions discovered by JTaint, and found that 30 of them used the initialization of Object or Array. If we did not add these two types of monitoring instructions in JalangiEX, 30 extensions would be undetectable due to the interruption of taint propagation.

Add Taint Support for Spreading Across Pages. Of the 57 privacy-leaking extensions, nine extensions use communication functions to send the information collected in Content Script to Background Script. JalangiEX provides support for this kind of cross-page taint propagation.

5.2 Source-Based Statistics

We classified the privacy data leaked by 57 extensions according to the five types of Source points defined in Sect. 4.1. The results are shown in Table 3.

Table 3. Extensions' number for privacy types

Source	#Extension
URL	47
Host	20
Sensitive DOM element	4
Sensitive event listener	1
Cookie	0

URL & Host. URL and host are the two types of information most commonly stolen. Except for two extensions that filter out URLs containing keywords such as google, facebook, etc., all other extensions were near real-time, unrestricted collect URL or host, which will leak user's personal account information, Internet habits, and even threaten intranet security according to the description in Sect. 4.1. Besides, blacklist filtering is not safe, which does not indicate what kind of URL extensions want to obtain, so those two extensions may still be stealing URLs or hosts.

Sensitive DOM Elements. We found 4 extensions that steal sensitive DOM elements. After users install them, these four extensions will collect the title of each page. Title is a general expression of the entire page content, and it may also involve the user's personal privacy information. For example, the page title of "Password has been reset to xxx" will leak the user's password, and the page title of "Firewall needs to be re-enabled, all ports are currently open" provides the attacker with opportunity for a cyber attack.

We designed the honey page to discover the theft of sensitive DOM elements. But unfortunately, of the 20,000 extensions we analyzed, JTaint did not find any extensions that stole sensitive DOM elements preset on the honey page. We guess this code only runs on specific URL and DOM structure, but JTaint only simulates the extension on the honey page. Although no complete propagation chain was found from Source to Sink, rich DOM operations still exist on the honey page. We extract the parameter in the DOM selector, then sort the ten most frequently selected privacy words according to the privacy dictionary, as shown in Table 9 (Appendix A). It can be seen that extensions have done many operations on DOM elements containing keywords such as login, background, etc. Among them, there may also be other undetected malicious behaviors.

Sensitive Event Listeners. JTaint discovered an extension that leaks the keycode of keystroke event. It will add a logger script to each page visited by the user. The logger will hook the built-in functions such as *alter* and *open* functions in the page to record the parameter when these functions are called, and then register event listeners such as keyup, focus, mousedown to the page. Keystroke of the user will be monitored as a keyup event and the keycode will be sent to Background Script from Content Script through the message passing. Finally, Background Script will send the keycode to the local server of Oxygen IDE with port 7778. There are two hidden threats in this process. On the one hand, the port is fixed and the data is not encrypted. It is easy to be maliciously monitored by other programs running locally. On the other hand, we cannot know what Oxygen will do with this information. For the above reasons, we believe that users are at risk of privacy leakage when using this extension.

5.3 Sink-Based Statistics

We classify the 57 privacy-leaking extensions based on the two types of Sink points in Sect. 4.2, as shown in Table 4. The XMLHttpRequest in the table corresponds to the *send* and *open* functions in Table 7. The jQuery in the table corresponds to the five functions of jQuery in Table 7.

Overall, of the 57 privacy-leaking extensions, 40 extensions send privacy over network, and the remaining 17 extensions save privacy locally in plaintext format.

Table 4. Extensions' number of different Sink points.

Sink	#Extension
XMLHttpRequest	26
jQuery	10
HTMLElement.src	2
fetch	2
chrome.storage	14
LocalStorage	3

In the way of network transmission, the XMLHttpRequest object and the fetch function are native in JavaScript, which can send network requests in the background asynchronously. If the page contains the jQuery library, the extension can use the Network Request API provided by jQuery. We add five APIs of jQuery as sink points, and finally found 10 extensions that use these functions to leak privacy. We also found two extensions dynamically create iframe tags on each page, and add the URL of the page as the request parameter to the *src* attribute of iframe, which will leak the URL when iframe is loaded.

We extract 40 server addresses from these privacy-leaking extensions, including 3 local server addresses and 37 public network server addresses. In the local server address, the privacy is sent to the three ports 7778, 8888, 56797 in plaintext format, respectively. Of the 37 public server addresses, we confirm that at least 26 of them are owned by the extension developer by comparing the server address with the developer name and extension name. Although some servers that receive privacy are not owned by the extension developer, they only focus on using third-party services to richen functions of their extension. However, privacy-sensitive information is sent to an external server, where there exists the possibility of privacy leakage.

In the way of local storage, 14 extensions use the API provided by Chrome to store privacy, and the other 3 extensions use the API provided by the *window* object to store data. Neither of these APIs should be used to store sensitive data because they save data locally in plaintext format for a long time, which would lead to the risk of leakage.

5.4 Taint Propagation Analysis

In this section, we will show the behavioral characteristics of the taint propagation process from the perspective of the direction of taint propagation and the encoding of the taint data.

Direction of Taint Propagation. In order to monitor all pages visited by users, extensions can take two ways. One way is to write the privacy collection code in Content Script, and set the script to match all URLs in manifest file. In extensions using this way, we observed that sink points are located in Content Script or Background Script, and the latter requires message passing in taint propagation. The second way is to write the privacy collection code in Background Script, and monitor the user's behavior through event listeners provided by APIs such as *chrome.tabs* and *chrome.webRequest*, then trigger malicious code execution in callback functions. We observed that all extensions choose to deliver the taint data to the sink point directly in Background Script. According to the page where the source point and sink point are located and whether there is cross-page propagation of the taint data, we divide the direction of taint propagation into three categories, as shown in Table 5.

Table 5. Extensions' number of three types of taint propagation directions.

Taint propagation direction	#Extension
Background→background	37
Content→content	11
Content→background	9

Encoding of Taint Data. We observed that most extensions encode taint data before delivering it to sink points. URL encoding is the most common way. However, taint data encoded by URL encoding can still be easily identified by humans because characters such as letters and numbers do not change after URL encoding. Besides, we observed that two extensions use Base64 encoding and three extensions use Caesar cipher. These two encoding methods can completely hide the original plaintext features. Even if the user observes this data, it is difficult to recognize that this is sensitive information. Caesar cipher is an ancient offset encoding method. All characters are shifted forward or backward on the ASCII table by a fixed value to generate ciphertext. Of the three extensions we found using Caesar cipher, two extensions shift each character backward by 23, and the other extension shifts each character forward by 10.

5.5 False Positives Analysis

All of the 57 extensions reported by JTaint were all analyzed manually by us and confirmed that there was indeed a privacy leak. Besides, JTaint also reported 16 extensions, which were confirmed as false positives after our manual analysis. We sorted them into two categories. The first type of false positive is due to the overtaint in taint propagation, normal variables are also tainted and reported by JTaint in the sink point. In the second type, although the taint propagation is correct, the leaked data contains only the first three characters of the privacy, or the sensitive-information is used as the host of the requested URL. In general, these extensions did not leak enough sensitive-information or did not send sensitive-information to the attacker's server, so they were excluded during our manual analysis.

5.6 Code Reuse in Chrome Extensions

We noticed that there are two sets (two per group) extensions whose source points, sink points, and taint propagation paths are the same. In a further code comparison, we found that the two sets of extensions are completely the same except for the script name and destination server where the private data is sent, which indicates that code reuse does exist in malicious extensions.

The source code of Chrome extensions is visible to everyone, which can cause two problems. On the one hand, attackers can easily copy a well-known extension and add the privacy collection code, then publish it to the Chrome Web Store. A developer posted the plagiarism of his work on Github [26]. On the other hand, visible extensions' source code also means that malicious codes are easier to be reused. As the sample introduced in this section, we speculate that the developer directly reused other malicious extension code after modifying the server to himself. In short, although code reuse is not the focus of this paper, our results show that code reuse exists in Chrome extensions, and this may be further mined by matching similar code execution paths.

5.7 Case Study

We found an extension on the Chrome Web Store that had 35,001 uses when we detected it. The extension's name is "Unlock Premium Content" and it's ID is bjmcpnogioojilao-halakcjniiaekgcp. According to the introduction of the extension, users who install the extension can access advanced content and features in popular Apps and websites such as Instagram and Twitter for free.

The extension's privacy stealing code runs in Background Script. It first accesses the third-party service to obtain the user's city and country, and then uses *chrome.tabs.query* function to read all pages opened by the user in 15 s cycle periodically and stores the URL in a list. In order to send the collected information, the extension periodically triggers the sending code in 300 s cycle. The sending code will perform Caesar cipher on all information collected during this period and the user's location, and then send them to the domain named www.oinkandstuff.com. Since the domain is consistent with the extension developer's, we can confirm that the information was sent to the server controlled by the developer.

We decode the transmitted data and display them in Fig. 6. It can be clearly seen from the decoded data that the extension stole the user's URL, host, and geographic location information. After we submitted feedback, this extension has now been removed from the Chrome Web Store.

```
{
    "d1":"4b9a35ab-4177-f772-ad1f-e1916c15dc3d",          // Random String
    "d2":"bjmcpnogioojilaohalakcjniiaekgcp",              // ID of the extension
    "d3":"Qingdao",                                        // City
    "d4":"China",                                          // Country
    "d5":"CN",                                             // Country name abbreviation
    "d6":"https://console.cloud.google.com/?hl=zh-cn&pli=1",  // URL visited by the user
    "d7":"console.cloud.google.com",                       // Host of the URL
    "d8":"2020-02-25T11:58:54.907Z",                       // Time
    "d9":"",
    "d10":""
}
```

Fig. 6. Data sent by the sample extension.

6   Related Work

In previous work, static analysis was mainly used to find the abuse of permissions of extensions [3, 4]. Dynamic analysis drives extensions to run in a monitored environment and observes the behavior of extensions. Traffic analysis [8, 9], API call analysis [10–13], data flow analysis [14–18] are three main methods used in dynamic analysis.

Traffic analysis is the most intuitive one of the three methods. BrowseringFog [8] built a network traffic analysis system for the four types of privacy information to detect whether there are keywords corresponding to privacy in the traffic. Ex-ray [9] detects history leakage by comparing the difference of traffic under different browsing history conditions. Although the traffic analysis is easy to implement and does not need to analyze the internal process of code execution, it is powerless once the communication uses more complex or user-defined encryption methods.

Dynamic analysis system based on API call analysis, such as Hulk [10] and WebEval [11], monitors API call logs and network traffic to detect malicious extensions. Hulk detects malicious extensions based on API call features. WebEval uses machine learing model to classify extensions by using developer reputation and other related features. Although analyzing API calls can identify malicious behaviors such as modifying network requests and preventing uninstallation, it is difficult to find extension's privacy leaks. For example, Hulk classifies extensions as "Steals password from form" if extensions look for a form field with the name "password", but it could not determine whether the password field was leaked without data flow analysis.

In order to accurately identify the privacy leakage in the extension, it is necessary to use data flow analysis to track the taint data in extension execution. Sabre [14] and Mystique [16] implement the interpreter-level monitoring of the code by modifying the SpiderMonkey interpreter of the Firefox browser and the V8 interpreter of the Chrome browser, respectively. Compared to the solution of rewriting extension code, modifying the JavaScript interpreter requires more work. It cannot be used across platforms and requires new support to be added as the JavaScript interpreter is updated. For example, the applicability of Mystique is limited to the Chrome platform, and has to use static analysis to assist in the taint propagation because the V8 engine is too complicated. Our solution is independent of the JavaScript engine, and our taint propagation rules are pretty intuitive.

The closest system to our own is ExtensionGuard [17], which uses Jalangi2 to rewrite the extension code and implement the taint propagation of extensions. Unlike ExtensionGuard, we analyze the shortcomings of Jalangi2 for extension analysis, and design JalangiEX to rewrite the extension. We showed the advantages and effectiveness of JalangiEX in the analysis of the test results in Sect. 5. Besides, compared to ExtensionGuard, we performed a batch analysis of extensions in the Chrome Web Store, and finally found multiple actual privacy-leaking extensions.

7 Conclusion

In this paper we presented JTaint, a dynamic taint analysis system to identify privacy leakage of Chrome extensions. JTaint rewrites code by using JalangiEX to monitor the taint propagation process. Compared with Jalangi2, JalangiEX solves the undertaint problem in taint propagation, and strips the redundant codes to reduce the intrusion into host web page. After performing a batch analysis of 20,000 extensions randomly crawled in the Chrome Web Store, we identified 57 privacy-leaking extensions, many of which remain live in the Chrome Web Store, and found code reuse in some extensions, and encoding behavior of sensitive-privacy information. Our finds are helpful to dissect malicious extensions from the store. In the future, we will investigate more extensions from Chrome Web Store and other third-parties chrome extension stores under various sites in Alex rank, and discover more effective features and behaviors for recognizing malicious extensions.

Acknowledgments. We sincerely thank ACISP anonymous reviewers for their valuable feedback. This work was supported in part by the National Natural Science Foundation of China(61972297, U1636107).

Appendix A

Table 6. Feature code for different source.

Source	Feature code
URL	document.url document.referrer location.href location.pathname location.search
Host	location.host location.hostname location.origin
Sensitive DOM element	getElementBy[Id|Name|ClassName|TagName] querySelector querySelectorAll $
Cookie	document.cookie
Sensitive event listener	addEventListener

Table 7. Feature codes for different sink.

Local storage	Network
chrome.storage.local.set	$.ajax
chrome.storage.sync.set	$.get
localStorage.setItem	$.post
	$.getJSON
	$.load
	XMLHttpRequest.send
	XMLHttpRequest.open
	fetch
	HTMLElement.src

Table 8. Taint propagation rules.

Function	Trigger	Base mode	Taint propagation rule
invokeFun	a function call	result = base.func(args)	if isTaint(args) or isTaint(base): addTaint(result)
getField	an object property is accessed	val = base.offset	if isTaint(base) and !isPartTaint(base): addTaint(val)
putField	an object property is written	base.offset = val	if isTaint(val): addPartTaint(base)
Binary	binary operation	result = (left) op (right)	if isTaint(left) or isTaint(right): addTaint(result)
Unary	unary operation	result = op (left)	if isTaint(left): addTaint(result)

Table 9. Top 10 privacy words in dom choice

Top 10 privacy words in dom choice	#Extension
Login	1385
Background	1132
Result	1038
Username	2909
Content	767
Id	591

(*continued*)

Table 9. (*continued*)

Top 10 privacy words in dom choice	#Extension
Name	566
Data	531
Input	524
City	477

References

1. Malicious Chrome Extensions Enable Criminals to Impact Half a Million Users and Global Businesses. https://atr-blog.gigamon.com/2018/01/18/malicious-chrome-extensions-enable-criminals-to-impact-half-a-million-users-and-global-businesses. Accessed 20 Feb 2020
2. DataSpii: The catastrophic data leak via browser extensions. https://securitywithsam.com/2019/07/dataspii-leak-via-browser-extensions/
3. Aravind, V., Sethumadhavan, M.: A framework for analysing the security of chrome extensions. Adv. Comput. Netw. Inf. **2**, 267–272 (2014)
4. Akshay Dev, P.K., Jevitha, K.P.: STRIDE based analysis of the chrome browser extensions API. In: Satapathy, S.C., Bhateja, V., Udgata, S.K., Pattnaik, P.K. (eds.) Proceedings of the 5th International Conference on Frontiers in Intelligent Computing: Theory and Applications. AISC, vol. 516, pp. 169–178. Springer, Singapore (2017). https://doi.org/10.1007/978-981-10-3156-4_17
5. Guha, A., Fredrikson, M., Livshits, B., Swamy, N.: Verified security for browser extensions. In: 2011 IEEE Symposium on Security and Privacy, pp. 115–130. IEEE (2011)
6. Calzavara, S., Bugliesi, M., Crafa, S., Steffinlongo, E.: Fine-grained detection of privilege escalation attacks on browser extensions. In: Vitek, J. (ed.) ESOP 2015. LNCS, vol. 9032, pp. 510–534. Springer, Heidelberg (2015). https://doi.org/10.1007/978-3-662-46669-8_21
7. Starov, O., Laperdrix, P., Kapravelos, A., Nikiforakis, N.: Unnecessarily identifiable: quantifying the fingerprintability of browser extensions due to bloat. In: The World Wide Web Conference, pp. 3244–3250 (2019)
8. Starov, O., Nikiforakis, N.: Extended tracking powers: measuring the privacy diffusion enabled by browser extensions. In: Proceedings of the 26th International Conference on World Wide Web, pp. 1481–1490. ACM (2017)
9. Weissbacher, M., Mariconti, E., Suarez-Tangil, G., Stringhini, G., Robertson, W., Kirda, E.: Ex-ray: detection of history-leaking browser extensions. In: Proceedings of the 33rd Annual Computer Security Applications Conference, pp. 590–602. ACM, New York (2017)
10. Kapravelos, A., Grier, C., Chachra, N., Kruegel, C., Vigna, G., Paxson, V.: Hulk: eliciting malicious behavior in browser extensions. In: 23rd USENIX Security Symposium (USENIX Security 2014), pp. 641–654. USENIX Association, USA (2014)
11. Jagpal, N., et al.: Trends and lessons from three years fighting malicious extensions. In: 24th USENIX Security Symposium (USENIX Security 2015), pp. 579–593. USENIX Association, USA (2015)
12. Zhao, Y., et al.: Large-scale detection of privacy leaks for BAT browsers extensions in China. In: 2019 International Symposium on Theoretical Aspects of Software Engineering (TASE), pp. 57–64. IEEE (2019)
13. Aggarwal, A., Viswanath, B., Zhang, L., Kumar, S., Shah, A., Kumaraguru, P.: I spy with my little eye: analysis and detection of spying browser extensions. In: 2018 IEEE European Symposium on Security and Privacy (EuroS&P), pp. 47–61. IEEE (2018)

14. Dhawan, M., Ganapathy, V.: Analyzing information flow in JavaScript-based browser extensions. In: 2009 Annual Computer Security Applications Conference, pp. 382–391. IEEE (2009)
15. Bauer, L., Cai, S., Jia, L., Passaro, T., Stroucken, M., Tian, Y.: Run-time monitoring and formal analysis of information flows in chromium. In: NDSS, February 2015
16. Chen, Q., Kapravelos, A.: Mystique: uncovering information leakage from browser extensions. In: Proceedings of the 2018 ACM SIGSAC Conference on Computer and Communications Security, pp. 1687–1700. ACM (2018)
17. Chang, W., Chen, S.: ExtensionGuard: towards runtime browser extension information leakage detection. In: 2016 IEEE Conference on Communications and Network Security (CNS), pp. 154–162. IEEE (2016)
18. Chang, W., Chen, S.: Defeat information leakage from browser extensions via data obfuscation. In: Qing, S., Zhou, J., Liu, D. (eds.) ICICS 2013. LNCS, vol. 8233, pp. 33–48. Springer, Cham (2013). https://doi.org/10.1007/978-3-319-02726-5_3
19. Sen, K., Kalasapur, S., Brutch, T., Gibbs, S.: Jalangi: a selective record-replay and dynamic analysis framework for JavaScript. In: Proceedings of the 2013 9th Joint Meeting on Foundations of Software Engineering, pp. 488–498 (2013)
20. Extension Overview. https://developer.chrome.com/extensions/overview. Accessed 20 Feb 2020
21. Liu, L., Zhang, X., Yan, G., Chen, S.: Chrome extensions: threat analysis and countermeasures. In: NDSS (2012)
22. Somé, D.F.: EmPoWeb: empowering web applications with browser extensions. In: 2019 IEEE Symposium on Security and Privacy (SP), pp. 227–245. IEEE, May 2019
23. Fake Ad Blockers. https://adguard.com/en/blog/fake-ad-blockers-part-2.html
24. Message Passing. https://developer.chrome.com/extensions/messaging. Accessed 20 Feb 2020
25. Chrome.storage. https://developer.chrome.com/apps/storage. Accessed 20 Feb 2020
26. Plagiarism Notice. https://github.com/dmtspoint/OpenGG/blob/master/Hall-of-shame.md. Accessed 20 Feb 2020

Unlinkable Updatable Databases and Oblivious Transfer with Access Control

Aditya Damodaran and Alfredo Rial[✉]

SnT, University of Luxembourg, Esch-sur-Alzette, Luxembourg
{aditya.damodaran,alfredo.rial}@uni.lu

Abstract. An oblivious transfer with access control protocol (OTAC) allows us to protect privacy of accesses to a database while enforcing access control policies. Existing OTAC have several shortcomings. First, their design is not modular. Typically, to create an OTAC, an adaptive oblivious transfer protocol (OT) is extended ad-hoc. Consequently, the security of the OT is reanalyzed when proving security of the OTAC, and it is not possible to instantiate the OTAC with any secure OT. Second, existing OTAC do not allow for policy updates. Finally, in practical applications, many messages share the same policy. However, existing OTAC cannot take advantage of that to improve storage efficiency.

We propose an UC-secure OTAC that addresses the aforementioned shortcomings. Our OTAC uses as building blocks the ideal functionalities for OT, for zero-knowledge (ZK) and for an *unlinkable updatable database* (UUD), which we define and construct. UUD is a protocol between an updater $\mathcal{U}$ and multiple readers $\mathcal{R}_k$. $\mathcal{U}$ sets up a database and updates it. $\mathcal{R}_k$ can read the database by computing UC ZK proofs of an entry in the database, without disclosing what entry is read. In our OTAC, UUD is used to store and read the policies.

We construct an UUD based on subvector commitments (SVC). We extend the definition of SVC with update algorithms for commitments and openings, and we provide an UC ZK proof of a subvector. Our efficiency analysis shows that our UUD is practical.

Keywords: Vector commitments · Bilinear maps · Universal composability

1 Introduction

Oblivious transfer with access control protocols [8,15] (OTAC) run between a sender $\mathcal{U}$ and receivers $\mathcal{R}_k$. $\mathcal{U}$ receives as input a tuple $(m_i, \mathsf{ACP}_i)_{\forall i \in [1,N]}$ of messages and their associated access control policies. In a transfer phase, a receiver $\mathcal{R}_k$ chooses an index $i \in [1,N]$ and obtains the message m_i if $\mathcal{R}_k$ satisfies the policy ACP_i. $\mathcal{U}$ does not learn i, whereas $\mathcal{R}_k$ does not learn any information about other messages.

This research is supported by the Luxembourg National Research Fund (FNR) CORE project "Stateful Zero-Knowledge" (Project code: C17/11650748).

J. K. Liu and H. Cui (Eds.): ACISP 2020, LNCS 12248, pp. 584–604, 2020.
https://doi.org/10.1007/978-3-030-55304-3_30

In the following, we only consider OTAC in which the receivers learn all the policies $(\mathsf{ACP}_i)_{\forall i \in [1,N]}$, that are stateless, i.e. fulfilment of a policy by $\mathcal{R}_k$ does not depend on the history of messages received by $\mathcal{R}_k$, and that are adaptive, i.e. there are several transfers and $\mathcal{R}_k$ can choose i after receiving messages in previous transfers. In Sect. 7, we discuss stateful and adaptive OTAC and OTAC with hidden policies. Additionally, we focus on OTAC that provide anonymity and unlinkability, i.e., OTAC where $\mathcal{U}$ cannot link a transfer to a receiver identity $\mathcal{R}_k$ and where transfers to $\mathcal{R}_k$ are unlinkable with respect to each other.

Existing adaptive and stateless OTAC follow a common pattern in their design. In the initialization phase, $\mathcal{U}$ computes N ciphertexts c_i that encrypt m_i. Some OTAC [1,8,21] use a signature that binds ACP_i to c_i, while others [25,28–30] use fuzzy identity-based encryption (IBE) or ciphertext-policy attribute-based encryption (CP-ABE) to encrypt m_i under ACP_i. The receivers obtain $(c_i, \mathsf{ACP}_i)_{\forall i \in [1,N]}$. To prove fulfilment of policies, $\mathcal{R}_k$ proves to an authority that she possesses some attributes and obtains a credential or secret key for her attributes. In the transfer phase, $\mathcal{R}_k$ interacts with $\mathcal{U}$ in such a way that $\mathcal{R}_k$ can decrypt c_i for her choice i only if her certified attributes satisfy ACP_i. Those OTAC have several design shortcomings.

Modularity. Although some OTAC are extensions of adaptive oblivious transfer protocols (OT), they do not use OT as building block. Instead, the OT is modified ad-hoc to create the OTAC, blurring which elements were part of the OT and which ones were added to provide access control. The lack of modularity has two disadvantages. First, when the security of the OTAC is analyzed, the security of the underlying OT needs to be reanalyzed. Second, the OTAC cannot be instantiated with any secure adaptive OT, and consequently, whenever more efficient OT schemes are proposed, the OTAC cannot use them and would need to be redesigned.

Policy Updates. All the existing OTAC do not allow for policy updates, i.e., if a policy ACP_i needs to be updated, the initialization phase needs to be rerun. In practical applications of OTAC (e.g. medical or financial databases), it would be desirable to update policies dynamically throughout the protocol execution without needing to re-encrypt messages. To enable policy updates, we would need to separate the encryptions c_i of m_i from the method used to encode policies ACP_i. As explained above, OTAC use signatures schemes or CP-ABE to bind policies to ciphertexts. It would be possible to separate, e.g., a signature on the policy ACP_i from the encryption c_i of m_i, while still allowing $\mathcal{R}_k$ to prove the association between c_i and ACP_i in the transfer phase. However, a revocation mechanism to revoke the outdated signatures would also need to be implemented, which would decrease efficiency.

Storage cost. All the existing OTAC associate each encryption c_i with a policy ACP_i. However, in practical applications, multiple database records are associated with a single policy. Therefore, if we separate the ciphertexts c_i from the method used to encode policies ACP_i, it would be possible to improve efficiency by associating a policy to multiple ciphertexts.

1.1 Our Contribution

We define and construct an unlinkable updatable database (UUD), a novel building block that may be of independent interest, and we use UUD to construct modularly OTAC that enable dynamic policy updates without the need of a revocation mechanism, and that can associate a policy to multiple messages.

Functionality $\mathcal{F}_{\text{UUD}}$. We use the universal composability (UC) framework [13] and define an ideal functionality $\mathcal{F}_{\text{UUD}}$ in Sect. 3. We define UUD as a task between multiple readers $\mathcal{R}_k$ and an updater $\mathcal{U}$. $\mathcal{U}$ sets a database DB and updates it at any time throughout the protocol execution. DB consists of N entries of the form $[i, v_{i,1}, \ldots, v_{i,L}]$, where i identifies the database entry and $(v_{i,1}, \ldots, v_{i,L})$ are the values stored in that entry. Any $\mathcal{R}_k$ and $\mathcal{U}$ know the content of DB. A reader $\mathcal{R}_k$ can read DB by computing a zero-knowledge (ZK) proof of knowledge of an entry $[i, v_{i,1}, \ldots, v_{i,L}]$. $\mathcal{F}_{\text{UUD}}$ hides from $\mathcal{U}$ which entry was read but ensures that it is not possible to prove that an entry is stored in DB if that is not the case. $\mathcal{F}_{\text{UUD}}$ allows $\mathcal{R}_k$ to remain anonymous and unlinkable when reading DB.

OTAC. In Sect. 6, we propose a functionality $\mathcal{F}_{\text{OTAC}}$. $\mathcal{F}_{\text{OTAC}}$ follows previous OTAC functionalities [8] but introduces two main modifications. First, it splits the initialization interface into two interfaces: otac.init, in which the sender $\mathcal{U}$ receives $(m_i)_{\forall i \in [1,N]}$, and otac.policy, in which $\mathcal{U}$ receives $(\text{ACP}_i)_{\forall i \in [1,N]}$. This enables $\mathcal{U}$ to make policy updates via otac.policy throughout the protocol execution. Second, previous functionalities include an issuance phase where an issuer certifies $\mathcal{R}_k$ attributes. Instead, $\mathcal{F}_{\text{OTAC}}$ leaves more open and flexible how access control is proven. $\mathcal{U}$ sets and updates a relation R_{ACP} that specifies what $\mathcal{R}_k$ must prove to obtain access to messages. Each policy ACP_i is an instance *ins* for R_{ACP} and, in the transfer phase, $\mathcal{R}_k$ must provide a witness *wit* such that $(wit, ins) \in R_{\text{ACP}}$. *wit* could contain, e.g., signatures from an issuer on $\mathcal{R}_k$ attributes, but in general any data required by R_{ACP}.

We also describe a modular construction Π_{OTAC}. In the UC framework, modularity is achieved by describing hybrid protocols. In a hybrid protocol, the building blocks are described by their ideal functionalities, and parties in the real world invoke those ideal functionalities. Π_{OTAC} uses as building block $\mathcal{F}_{\text{OT}}$, and thus Π_{OTAC} can be instantiated by any secure adaptive OT. To implement access control, Π_{OTAC} uses $\mathcal{F}_{\text{UUD}}$ and $\mathcal{F}_{\text{ZK}}^{R_{\text{ACP}'}}$. $\mathcal{U}$ stores $(\text{ACP}_i)_{\forall i \in [1,N]}$ in DB in $\mathcal{F}_{\text{UUD}}$. Each entry $[i, v_{i,1}, \ldots, v_{i,L}]$ stores the index i and the representation $\text{ACP}_i = (v_{i,1}, \ldots, v_{i,L})$ of a policy. In a transfer phase, $\mathcal{R}_k$ uses $\mathcal{F}_{\text{UUD}}$ to read ACP_i for her choice i and then $\mathcal{F}_{\text{ZK}}^{R_{\text{ACP}'}}$ to prove fulfilment of ACP_i. One challenge when defining a hybrid protocol is to ensure that two functionalities receive the same input. For example, in the transfer interface of Π_{OTAC}, we need to ensure that the choice i sent to $\mathcal{F}_{\text{OT}}$ (to obtain m_i) and to $\mathcal{F}_{\text{UUD}}$ (to read ACP_i) are equal. To this end, we use the method in [11], in which functionalities receive committed inputs produced by a functionality $\mathcal{F}_{\text{NIC}}$ for non-interactive commitments.

Our modular design has the following advantages. First, it simplifies the security analysis because security proofs in the hybrid model are simpler and because, by splitting the protocol into smaller building blocks, security analysis of constructions for those building blocks are also simpler. Second, it allows multiple instantiations by replacing each of the functionalities by any protocols that realize them. Third, it allows the study of the UUD task in isolation, which eases the comparison of different constructions for it.

Construction Π_{UUD}. In Sect. 4, we propose a construction Π_{UUD} for $\mathcal{F}_{\text{UUD}}$. Π_{UUD} is based on subvector commitments (SVC) [20], which we extend with a UC ZK proof of knowledge of a subvector. A SVC scheme allows us to compute a commitment *com* to a vector $\mathbf{x} = (\mathbf{x}[1], \dots, \mathbf{x}[N])$. *com* can be opened to a subvector $\mathbf{x}_I = (\mathbf{x}[i_1], \dots, \mathbf{x}[i_n])$, where $I = \{i_1, \dots, i_n\} \subseteq [1, N]$. The size of the opening w_I is independent of N and of $|I|$. SVC were recently proposed as an improvement of vector commitments [14,23], where the size of w_I is independent of N but dependent on $|I|$. We extend the definition of SVC to include algorithms to update commitments and openings when part of the vector is updated.

Π_{UUD} works as follows. $\mathcal{U}$ uses a bulletin board BB to publish the database DB and any $\mathcal{R}_k$ obtains DB from BB. A BB ensures that all readers obtain the same version of DB, which we need to guarantee unlinkability. Both $\mathcal{U}$ and any $\mathcal{R}_k$ map a DB with N entries of the form $[i, v_{i,1}, \dots, v_{i,L}]$ to a vector $\mathbf{x}$ of length $N \times L$ such that $\mathbf{x}[(i-1)L + j] = v_{i,j}$ for all $i \in [1, N]$ and $j \in [1, L]$, and they compute a commitment *com* to $\mathbf{x}$. To update a database entry, $\mathcal{U}$ updates BB, and $\mathcal{U}$ and any $\mathcal{R}_k$ update *com*. Therefore, updates do not need any revocation mechanism. To prove in ZK that an entry $[i, v_{i,1}, \dots, v_{i,L}]$ is in DB, $\mathcal{R}_k$ computes an opening w_I for $I = \{(i-1)L + 1, \dots, (i-1)L + L\}$ and uses it to compute a ZK proof of knowledge of the subvector $(\mathbf{x}[(i-1)L + 1], \dots, \mathbf{x}[(i-1)L + L])$. This proof guarantees that I is the correct set for index i.

We describe an efficient instantiation of Π_{UUD} in Sect. 5 that uses a SVC scheme based on the Cube Diffie-Hellman assumption [20]. In terms of efficiency, the storage cost grows quadratically with the vector length $N \times L$. However, after initializing *com* and the openings w_I to the initial DB, the communication and computation costs of the update and read operations are independent of N. Therefore, our instantiation allows for an OTAC where the database of policies can be updated and read efficiently. We have implemented our instantiation. Our efficiency measurements in Sect. 5 show that it is practical.

We describe a variant of our instantiation where each database entry is $[i_{min}, i_{max}, v_{i,1}, \dots, v_{i,L}]$, where $[i_{min}, i_{max}] \in [1, N]$ is a range of indices. This allows for an OTAC with reduced storage cost. If the messages $(m_{i_{min}}, \dots, m_{i_{max}})$ are associated with a single policy ACP, only one database entry is needed to store ACP. In contrast, previous OTAC that use signatures or CP-ABE need to embed a policy in every ciphertext.

Π_{UUD} can be regarded as an efficient way of implementing a ZK proof for a disjunction of statements. Namely, proving that an entry $[i, v_{i,1}, \dots, v_{i,L}]$ is in DB is equivalent to computing an OR proof where the prover proves that he knows at least one of the entries. The proof in Π_{UUD} is of size independent of N. We compare our construction with related work in Sect. 7.

2   Modular Design and $\mathcal{F}_{\mathrm{NIC}}$

We summarize the UC framework in the full version [18]. An ideal functionality can be invoked by using one or more interfaces. In the notation in [11], the name of a message in an interface consists of three fields separated by dots, e.g., uud.read.ini in $\mathcal{F}_{\mathrm{UUD}}$ in Sect. 3. The first field indicates the name of $\mathcal{F}_{\mathrm{UUD}}$ and is the same for all interfaces. This field is useful for distinguishing between invocations of different functionalities in a hybrid protocol. The second field indicates the kind of action performed by $\mathcal{F}_{\mathrm{UUD}}$ and is the same in all messages that $\mathcal{F}_{\mathrm{UUD}}$ exchanges within the same interface. The third field distinguishes between the messages that belong to the same interface. A message uud.read.ini is the incoming message received by $\mathcal{F}_{\mathrm{UUD}}$, i.e., the message through which the interface is invoked. uud.read.end is the outgoing message sent by $\mathcal{F}_{\mathrm{UUD}}$, i.e., the message that ends the execution of the interface. uud.read.sim is used by $\mathcal{F}_{\mathrm{UUD}}$ to send a message to the simulator $\mathcal{S}$, and uud.read.rep is used to receive a message from $\mathcal{S}$.

In our OTAC, to ensure, when needed, that $\mathcal{F}_{\mathrm{UUD}}$ and other functionalities receive the same input, we use the method in [11]. In [11], a functionality $\mathcal{F}_{\mathrm{NIC}}$ for non-interactive commitments is proposed. $\mathcal{F}_{\mathrm{NIC}}$ consists of four interfaces:

1. Any party $\mathcal{P}_i$ uses the com.setup interface to set up the functionality.
2. Any party $\mathcal{P}_i$ uses the com.commit interface to send a message m and obtain a commitment com and an opening $open$. A commitment com consists of $(com', parcom, \mathsf{COM.Verify})$, where com' is the commitment, $parcom$ are the public parameters, and COM.Verify is the verification algorithm.
3. Any party $\mathcal{P}_i$ uses the com.validate interface to send a commitment com to check that com contains the correct $parcom$ and COM.Verify.
4. Any party $\mathcal{P}_i$ uses the com.verify interface to send $(com, m, open)$ to verify that com is a commitment to m with opening $open$.

$\mathcal{F}_{\mathrm{NIC}}$ can be realized by a perfectly hiding commitment scheme, such as Pedersen commitments [11]. To ensure that a party $\mathcal{P}_i$ sends the same input m to several ideal functionalities, $\mathcal{P}_i$ first uses com.commit to get a commitment com to m with opening $open$. Then $\mathcal{P}_i$ sends $(com, m, open)$ as input to each of the functionalities, and each functionality runs COM.Verify to verify the commitment. Finally, other parties in the protocol receive the commitment com from each of the functionalities and use the com.validate interface to validate com. Then, if com received from all the functionalities is the same, the binding property provided by $\mathcal{F}_{\mathrm{NIC}}$ ensures that all the functionalities received the same input m. Our functionality $\mathcal{F}_{\mathrm{UUD}}$ receives committed inputs as described in [11].

3   Functionality $\mathcal{F}_{\text{UUD}}$

$\mathcal{F}_{\text{UUD}}$ interacts with readers $\mathcal{R}_k$ and an updater $\mathcal{U}$. $\mathcal{F}_{\text{UUD}}$ maintains a database DB. DB consists of N entries of the form $[i, v_{i,1}, \ldots, v_{i,L}]$. $\mathcal{F}_{\text{UUD}}$ has three interfaces uud.update, uud.getdb and uud.read:

1. $\mathcal{U}$ sends the uud.update.ini message on input $(i, v_{i,1}, \ldots, v_{i,L})_{\forall i \in [1,N]}$. For all $i \in [1, N]$, $\mathcal{F}_{\text{UUD}}$ updates DB to contain value $v_{i,j}$ at position $j \in [1, L]$ of entry i. If $v_{i,j} = \bot$, no update at position j of entry i takes place.
2. $\mathcal{R}_k$ sends the uud.getdb.ini message to $\mathcal{F}_{\text{UUD}}$. $\mathcal{F}_{\text{UUD}}$ sends DB to $\mathcal{R}_k$.
3. $\mathcal{R}_k$ sends the uud.read.ini message on input a pseudonym P and a tuple $(i, com_i, open_i, \langle v_{i,j}, com_{i,j}, open_{i,j} \rangle_{\forall j \in [1,L]})$, where $[i, v_{i,1}, \ldots, v_{i,L}]$ is a database entry and $(com_i, open_i)$ and $(com_{i,j}, open_{i,j})_{\forall j \in [1,L]}$ are commitments and openings to i and to the values $(v_{i,1}, \ldots, v_{i,L})$. $\mathcal{F}_{\text{UUD}}$ verifies the commitments and checks that there is an entry $[i, v_{i,1}, \ldots, v_{i,L}]$ in DB. $\mathcal{F}_{\text{UUD}}$ sends $(com_i, \langle com_{i,j} \rangle_{\forall j \in [1,L]})$ to $\mathcal{U}$.

$\mathcal{F}_{\text{UUD}}$ stores counters cr_k for $\mathcal{R}_k$ and a counter cu for $\mathcal{U}$. These counters are used to check that $\mathcal{R}_k$ has the last version of DB. When $\mathcal{U}$ sends an update, cu is incremented. When $\mathcal{R}_k$ receives DB, $\mathcal{F}_{\text{UUD}}$ sets $cr_k \leftarrow cu$. When $\mathcal{R}_k$ reads DB, $\mathcal{F}_{\text{UUD}}$ checks that $cr_k = cu$, which ensures that $\mathcal{R}_k$ and $\mathcal{U}$ have the same DB.

When invoked by $\mathcal{U}$ or $\mathcal{R}_k$, $\mathcal{F}_{\text{UUD}}$ first checks the correctness of the input and aborts if it does not belong to the correct domain. $\mathcal{F}_{\text{UUD}}$ also aborts if an interface is invoked at an incorrect moment in the protocol. For example, $\mathcal{R}_k$ cannot invoke uud.read if uud.update was never invoked.

The session identifier sid has the structure $(\mathcal{U}, sid')$. Including $\mathcal{U}$ in sid ensures that any $\mathcal{U}$ can initiate an instance of $\mathcal{F}_{\text{UUD}}$. $\mathcal{F}_{\text{UUD}}$ implicitly checks that sid in a message equals the one received in the first invocation. Before $\mathcal{F}_{\text{UUD}}$ queries the simulator $\mathcal{S}$, $\mathcal{F}_{\text{UUD}}$ saves its state, which is recovered when receiving a response from $\mathcal{S}$. To match a query to a response, $\mathcal{F}_{\text{UUD}}$ creates a query identifier qid.

Description of $\mathcal{F}_{\text{UUD}}$. $\mathcal{F}_{\text{UUD}}$ is parameterised by a universe of pseudonyms $\mathbb{U}_p$, a universe of values $\mathbb{U}_v$ and by a database size N.

1. On input (uud.update.ini, $sid, (i, v_{i,1}, \ldots, v_{i,L})_{\forall i \in [1,N]})$ from $\mathcal{U}$:
   - Abort if $sid \notin (\mathcal{U}, sid')$.
   - For all $i \in [1, N]$ and $j \in [1, L]$, abort if $v_{i,j} \notin \mathbb{U}_v$.
   - If (sid, DB, cu) is not stored:
     • For all $i \in [1, N]$ and $j \in [1, L]$, abort if $v_{i,j} = \bot$.
     • Set $\text{DB} \leftarrow (i, v_{i,1}, \ldots, v_{i,L})_{\forall i \in [1,N]}$ and $cu \leftarrow 0$ and store (sid, DB, cu).
   - Else:
     • For all $i \in [1, N]$ and $j \in [1, L]$, if $v_{i,j} \neq \bot$, update DB by storing $v_{i,j}$ at position j of entry i.
     • Increment cu and update DB and cu in (sid, DB, cu).

- Create a fresh qid and store qid.
- Send (uud.update.sim, sid, qid, $(i, v_{i,1}, \ldots, v_{i,L})_{\forall i \in [1,N]}$) to $\mathcal{S}$.

S. On input (uud.update.rep, sid, qid) from $\mathcal{S}$:
  - Abort if qid is not stored.
  - Delete qid.
  - Send (uud.update.end, sid) to $\mathcal{U}$.

2. On input (uud.getdb.ini, sid) from $\mathcal{R}_k$:
  - Create a fresh qid and store $(qid, \mathcal{R}_k)$.
  - Send (uud.getdb.sim, sid, qid) to $\mathcal{S}$.

S. On input (uud.getdb.rep, sid, qid) from $\mathcal{S}$:
  - Abort if $(qid', \mathcal{R}_k)$ such that $qid' = qid$ is not stored.
  - If (sid, DB, cu) is not stored, set $\mathsf{DB} \leftarrow \bot$.
  - Else, set $cr_k \leftarrow cu$, store $(\mathcal{R}_k, \mathsf{DB}, cr_k)$ and delete any previous tuple $(\mathcal{R}_k, \mathsf{DB}', cr'_k)$.
  - Delete $(qid, \mathcal{R}_k)$.
  - Send (uud.getdb.end, sid, DB) to $\mathcal{R}_k$.

3. On input (uud.read.ini, sid, P, $(i, com_i, open_i, \langle v_{i,j}, com_{i,j}, open_{i,j} \rangle_{\forall j \in [1,L]})$) from $\mathcal{R}_k$:
  - Abort if $P \notin \mathbb{U}_p$, or if $[i, v_{i,1}, \ldots, v_{i,L}] \notin \mathsf{DB}$, or if $(\mathcal{R}_k, \mathsf{DB}, cr_k)$ is not stored.
  - Parse the commitment com_i as $(com'_i, parcom, \mathsf{COM.Verify})$.
  - Abort if $1 \neq \mathsf{COM.Verify}(parcom, com'_i, i, open_i)$.
  - For all $j \in [1, L]$:
    • Parse the commitment $com_{i,j}$ as $(com'_{i,j}, parcom, \mathsf{COM.Verify})$.
    • Abort if $1 \neq \mathsf{COM.Verify}(parcom, com'_{i,j}, v_{i,j}, open_{i,j})$.
  - Create a fresh qid and store $(qid, P, (com_i, \langle com_{i,j} \rangle_{\forall j \in [1,L]}), cr_k)$.
  - Send (uud.read.sim, sid, qid, $(com_i, \langle com_{i,j} \rangle_{\forall j \in [1,L]})$) to $\mathcal{S}$.

S. On input (uud.read.rep, sid, qid) from $\mathcal{S}$:
  - Abort if $(qid', P, (com_i, \langle com_{i,j} \rangle_{\forall j \in [1,L]}), cr'_k)$ such that $qid' = qid$ is not stored or if $cr'_k \neq cu$, where cu is in (sid, DB, cu).
  - Delete the record $(qid, P, (com_i, \langle com_{i,j} \rangle_{\forall j \in [1,L]}), cr'_k)$.
  - Send (uud.read.end, sid, P, $(com_i, \langle com_{i,j} \rangle_{\forall j \in [1,L]})$) to $\mathcal{U}$.

$\mathcal{F}_{\mathrm{UUD}}$ guarantees anonymity and unlinkability. Namely, $\mathcal{F}_{\mathrm{UUD}}$ reveals to $\mathcal{U}$ a pseudonym P rather than the identifier $\mathcal{R}_k$. $\mathcal{R}_k$ can choose different random pseudonyms so that read operations are unlinkable. $\mathcal{F}_{\mathrm{UUD}}$ also ensures zero-knowledge, i.e. a read operation does not reveal the database entry read to $\mathcal{U}$. Additionally, $\mathcal{F}_{\mathrm{UUD}}$ guarantees unforgeability, i.e. $\mathcal{R}_k$ cannot read an entry if that entry was not stored in DB by $\mathcal{U}$.

It is straightforward to modify the uud.read interface to allow $\mathcal{R}_k$ to read several database entries simultaneously. This variant allows us to reduce communication rounds when $\mathcal{R}_k$ needs to read more than one entry simultaneously. $\mathcal{F}_{\mathrm{UUD}}$ can also be modified to interact with two parties such that both of them can read and update the database, or such that a party reads and updates and the other party receives read and update operations. Π_{UUD} can be easily adapted to realize the variants of $\mathcal{F}_{\mathrm{UUD}}$ discussed here.

4   Construction Π_{UUD}

4.1   Building Blocks

Subvector Commitments. A subvector commitment (SVC) scheme allows us to succinctly compute a commitment *com* to a vector $\mathbf{x} = (\mathbf{x}[1], \ldots, \mathbf{x}[\ell]) \in \mathcal{M}^\ell$. A commitment *com* to $\mathbf{x}$ can be opened to a subvector $\mathbf{x}_I = (\mathbf{x}[i_1], \ldots, \mathbf{x}[i_n])$, where $I = \{i_1, \ldots, i_n\} \subseteq [1, \ell]$ is the set of indices that determine the positions of the committed vector $\mathbf{x}$ that are opened. The size of an opening w_I for $\mathbf{x}_I$ is independent of both the size of I and of the length ℓ of the committed vector. We extend the definition of SVC in [20] with algorithms to update commitments and openings.

SVC.Setup$(1^k, \ell)$. On input the security parameter 1^k and an upper bound ℓ on the size of the vector, generate the parameters *par*, which include a description of the message space $\mathcal{M}$.

SVC.Commit$(par, \mathbf{x})$. On input a vector $\mathbf{x} \in \mathcal{M}^\ell$, output a commitment *com* to $\mathbf{x}$.

SVC.Open$(par, I, \mathbf{x})$. On input a vector $\mathbf{x}$ and a set $I = \{i_1, \ldots, i_n\} \subseteq [1, \ell]$, compute an opening w_I for the subvector $\mathbf{x}_I = (\mathbf{x}[i_1], \ldots, \mathbf{x}[i_n])$.

SVC.Verify$(par, com, \mathbf{x}_I, I, w_I)$. Output 1 if w_I is a valid opening for the set of positions $I = \{i_1, \ldots, i_n\} \subseteq [1, \ell]$ such that $\mathbf{x}_I = (\mathbf{x}[i_1], \ldots, \mathbf{x}[i_n])$, where $\mathbf{x}$ is the vector committed in *com*. Otherwise output 0.

SVC.ComUpd$(par, com, \mathbf{x}, i, x)$. On input a commitment *com* to a vector $\mathbf{x}$, output a commitment *com'* to a vector $\mathbf{x}'$ such that $\mathbf{x}'[i] = x$ and, for all $j \in [1, \ell] \setminus \{i\}$, $\mathbf{x}'[j] = \mathbf{x}[j]$.

SVC.OpenUpd$(par, w_I, \mathbf{x}, I, i, x)$. On input an opening w_I for a set I valid for a commitment to a vector $\mathbf{x}$, output an opening w_I' valid for a commitment to a vector $\mathbf{x}'$ such that $\mathbf{x}'[i] = x$ and, for all $j \in [1, \ell] \setminus \{i\}$, $\mathbf{x}'[j] = \mathbf{x}[j]$.

A SVC scheme must be correct and binding [20]. In the full version [18], we recall those properties and define correctness for the update algorithms. In the full version [18], we also depict $\mathcal{F}_{\mathrm{CRS}}^{\mathrm{CRS.Setup}}$, $\mathcal{F}_{\mathrm{ZK}}^{R}$ and $\mathcal{F}_{\mathrm{RR}}$, which we describe briefly below.

Ideal Functionality $\mathcal{F}_{\mathrm{CRS}}^{\mathrm{CRS.Setup}}$. Π_{UUD} uses the functionality $\mathcal{F}_{\mathrm{CRS}}^{\mathrm{CRS.Setup}}$ for common reference string generation in [13]. $\mathcal{F}_{\mathrm{CRS}}^{\mathrm{CRS.Setup}}$ interacts with any parties $\mathcal{P}$ that obtain the common reference string, and consists of one interface crs.get. A party $\mathcal{P}$ uses the crs.get interface to request and receive the common reference string *crs* from $\mathcal{F}_{\mathrm{CRS}}^{\mathrm{CRS.Setup}}$. In the first invocation, $\mathcal{F}_{\mathrm{CRS}}^{\mathrm{CRS.Setup}}$ generates *crs* by running algorithm CRS.Setup. The simulator $\mathcal{S}$ also receives *crs*.

$\mathcal{F}_{\mathrm{ZK}}^{R}$. Let R be a polynomial time computable binary relation. For tuples $(wit, ins) \in R$ we call *wit* the witness and *ins* the instance. Π_{UUD} uses a functionality $\mathcal{F}_{\mathrm{ZK}}^{R}$ for zero-knowledge. $\mathcal{F}_{\mathrm{ZK}}^{R}$ runs with multiple provers $\mathcal{P}_k$ and a verifier $\mathcal{V}$. $\mathcal{F}_{\mathrm{ZK}}^{R}$ follows the functionality for zero-knowledge in [13], except that a prover $\mathcal{P}_k$ is identified by a pseudonym P towards $\mathcal{V}$. $\mathcal{F}_{\mathrm{ZK}}^{R}$ consists of one interface zk.prove.

$\mathcal{P}_k$ uses zk.prove to send a witness wit, an instance ins and a pseudonym P to $\mathcal{F}_{\mathrm{ZK}}^R$. $\mathcal{F}_{\mathrm{ZK}}^R$ checks whether $(wit, ins) \in R$, and, in that case, sends ins and P to $\mathcal{V}$.

Ideal Functionality $\mathcal{F}_{\mathrm{BB}}$. Π_{UUD} uses the functionality $\mathcal{F}_{\mathrm{BB}}$ for a public bulletin board BB [27]. A BB is used to ensure that all the readers receive the same version of the database, which is needed to provide unlinkability. $\mathcal{F}_{\mathrm{BB}}$ interacts with a writer $\mathcal{W}$ and readers $\mathcal{R}_k$. $\mathcal{W}$ uses the bb.write interface to send a message m to $\mathcal{F}_{\mathrm{BB}}$. $\mathcal{F}_{\mathrm{BB}}$ increments a counter ct of the number of messages stored in BB and appends $[ct, m]$ to BB. $\mathcal{R}_k$ uses the bb.getbb interface on input an index i. If $i \in [1, ct]$, $\mathcal{F}_{\mathrm{BB}}$ takes the message m stored in $[i, m]$ in BB and sends m to $\mathcal{R}_k$.

4.2   Description of Π_{UUD}

In Π_{UUD}, a SVC com is used to commit to the database DB with N entries of the form $[i, v_{i,1}, \ldots, v_{i,L}]$. To this end, com commits to a vector $\mathbf{x}$ of length $N \times L$ such that $\mathbf{x}[(i-1)L+j] = v_{i,j}$ for all $i \in [1, N]$ and $j \in [1, L]$.

In the uud.update interface, $\mathcal{U}$ uses $\mathcal{F}_{\mathrm{BB}}$ to publish the DB and to update it. In the uud.getdb interface, any $\mathcal{R}_k$ retrieves DB and its subsequent updates through $\mathcal{F}_{\mathrm{BB}}$. When DB is published for the first time, $\mathcal{U}$ and $\mathcal{R}_k$ run SVC.Commit to commit to DB. When DB is updated, $\mathcal{U}$ and $\mathcal{R}_k$ update com by using SVC.ComUpd. If $\mathcal{R}_k$ already stores openings w_i, $\mathcal{R}_k$ runs SVC.OpenUpd to update them.

In the uud.read interface, $\mathcal{R}_k$ uses $\mathcal{F}_{\mathrm{ZK}}^R$ to prove that $(com_i, \langle com_{i,j} \rangle_{\forall j \in [1,L]})$ commit to an entry i and values $v_{i,1}, \ldots, v_{i,L}$ such that $\mathbf{x}[(i-1)L+j] = v_{i,j}$ for all $j \in [1, L]$, where $\mathbf{x}$ is the vector committed in com. R requires proving knowledge of an opening w_I for the set $I = \{(i-1)L+1, \ldots, (i-1)L+L\}$ of positions where the values for the database entry i are stored. $\mathcal{R}_k$ runs SVC.Open to compute w_I if it is not stored. R also requires a proof to associate i with I, which we denote by $I = f(i)$, where f is a function that on input i outputs the indices $I = \{(i-1)L+1, \ldots, (i-1)L+L\}$. In Sect. 5, we show a concrete UC ZK proof for R for the SVC scheme in [20].

Description of Π_{UUD}. N denotes the database size and L the size of any entry. The function $f(i) = ((i-1)L+1, \ldots, (i-1)L+L)$ maps $i \in [1, N]$ to a set of indices where the database entry i is stored. The universe of values $\mathbb{U}_v$ is given by the message space of the SVC scheme.

1. On input (uud.update.ini, $sid, (i, v_{i,1}, \ldots, v_{i,L})_{\forall i \in [1,N]}$), $\mathcal{U}$ does the following:
   – If $(sid, par, com, \mathbf{x}, cu)$ is not stored:
     • $\mathcal{U}$ uses crs.get to obtain the parameters par from $\mathcal{F}_{\mathrm{CRS}}^{\mathrm{SVC.Setup}}$. To compute par, $\mathcal{F}_{\mathrm{CRS}}^{\mathrm{SVC.Setup}}$ runs SVC.Setup($1^k, N \times L$).
     • $\mathcal{U}$ initializes a counter $cu \leftarrow 0$ and a vector $\mathbf{x}$ such that $\mathbf{x}[(i-1)L+j] = v_{i,j}$ for all $i \in [1, N]$ and $j \in [1, L]$. $\mathcal{U}$ runs $com \leftarrow$ SVC.Commit($par, \mathbf{x}$) and stores $(sid, par, com, \mathbf{x}, cu)$.

- Else:
  - $\mathcal{U}$ sets $cu' \leftarrow cu + 1$, $\mathbf{x}' \leftarrow \mathbf{x}$ and $com' \leftarrow com$. For all $i \in [1, N]$ and $j \in [1, L]$ such that $v_{i,j} \neq \bot$, $\mathcal{U}$ computes $com' \leftarrow$ SVC.ComUpd$(par, com', \mathbf{x}', (i-1)L+j, v_{i,j})$ and sets $\mathbf{x}'[(i-1)L+j] \leftarrow v_{i,j}$.
  - $\mathcal{U}$ replaces the stored tuple $(sid, par, com, \mathbf{x}, cu)$ by $(sid, par, com', \mathbf{x}', cu')$.
- $\mathcal{U}$ uses the bb.write interface to append $(i, v_{i,1}, \ldots, v_{i,L})_{\forall i \in [1,N]}$ to the bulletin board.
- $\mathcal{U}$ outputs (uud.update.end, sid).
2. On input (uud.getdb.ini, sid), $\mathcal{R}_k$ does the following:
   - If $(sid, par, com, \mathbf{x}, cr_k)$ is not stored, $\mathcal{R}_k$ obtains par from $\mathcal{F}_{\text{CRS}}^{\text{SVC.Setup}}$ and initializes a counter $cr_k \leftarrow 0$.
   - $\mathcal{R}_k$ increments cr_k and uses the bb.getbb interface to read the message $(i, v_{i,1}, \ldots, v_{i,L})_{\forall i \in [1,N]}$ stored at position cr_k in the bulletin board. $\mathcal{R}_k$ continues incrementing the counter and reading the bulletin board until the returned message is $\bot$.
   - $\mathcal{R}_k$ sets a tuple $(i, v_{i,1}, \ldots, v_{i,L})_{\forall i \in [1,N]}$, such that $v_{i,j}$ (for $i \in [1, N]$ and $j \in [1, L]$) is the most recent update for position j of the database entry i received from the bulletin board. If $(sid, par, com, \mathbf{x}, cr_k)$ is not stored, $(i, v_{i,1}, \ldots, v_{i,L})_{\forall i \in [1,N]}$ contains the current database to be used to set $\mathbf{x}$, else it contains the update that needs to be performed on $\mathbf{x}$.
   - For $i = 1$ to N, if (sid, i, w_I) is stored, $\mathcal{R}_k$ sets $\mathbf{x}' \leftarrow \mathbf{x}$ and $w_I' \leftarrow w_I$ and, for all $i \in [1, N]$ and $j \in [1, L]$ such that $v_{i,j} \neq \bot$, $w_I' \leftarrow$ SVC.OpenUpd$(par, w_I', \mathbf{x}', I, (i-1)L+j, v_{i,j})$ and $\mathbf{x}'[(i-1)L+j] = v_{i,j}$. $\mathcal{R}_k$ replaces (sid, i, w_I) by (sid, i, w_I').
   - $\mathcal{R}_k$ performs the same operations as $\mathcal{U}$ to set or update com and $\mathbf{x}$, and stores a tuple $(sid, par, com, \mathbf{x}, cr_k)$.
   - $\mathcal{R}$ outputs (uud.getdb.end, sid, $\mathbf{x}$).
3. On input (uud.read.ini, sid, P, $(i, com_i, open_i, \langle v_{i,j}, com_{i,j}, open_{i,j} \rangle_{\forall j \in [1,L]})$):
   - $\mathcal{R}_k$ parses com_i as $(com_i', parcom, \text{COM.Verify})$.
   - $\mathcal{R}_k$ aborts if $1 \neq \text{COM.Verify}(parcom, com_i', i, open_i)$.
   - For all $j \in [1, L]$:
     - $\mathcal{R}_k$ parses the commitment $com_{i,j}$ as $(com_{i,j}', parcom, \text{COM.Verify})$.
     - $\mathcal{R}_k$ aborts if $1 \neq \text{COM.Verify}(parcom, com_{i,j}', v_{i,j}, open_{i,j})$.
   - $\mathcal{R}_k$ takes the stored tuple $(sid, par, com, \mathbf{x}, cr_k)$ and aborts if, for any $j \in [1, L]$, $\mathbf{x}[(i-1)L+j] \neq v_{i,j}$.
   - If (sid, i, w_I) is not stored, $\mathcal{R}_k$ computes $I \leftarrow f(i)$, executes the algorithm $w_I \leftarrow$ SVC.Open$(par, I, \mathbf{x})$ and stores (sid, i, w_I).
   - $\mathcal{R}_k$ sets the witness $wit \leftarrow (w_I, I, i, open_i, \langle v_{i,j}, open_{i,j} \rangle_{\forall j \in [1,L]})$ and the instance $ins \leftarrow (par, com, parcom, com_i', \langle com_{i,j}' \rangle_{\forall j \in [1,L]}, cr_k)$. $\mathcal{R}_k$ uses zk.prove to send wit, ins and P to $\mathcal{F}_{\text{ZK}}^R$. The relation R is

$$R = \{(wit, ins) :$$
$$1 = \text{COM.Verify}(parcom, com_i', i, open_i) \land$$
$$\langle 1 = \text{COM.Verify}(parcom, com_{i,j}', v_{i,j}, open_{i,j}) \rangle_{\forall j \in [1,L]} \land$$
$$1 = \text{SVC.Verify}(par, com, \langle v_{i,j} \rangle_{\forall j \in [1,L]}, I, w_I) \land I = f(i)\}$$

- $\mathcal{U}$ receives P and $ins = (par', com', parcom, com'_i, \langle com'_{i,j} \rangle_{\forall j \in [1,L]}, cr_k)$ from $\mathcal{F}^R_{\mathrm{ZK}}$.
- $\mathcal{U}$ takes the stored tuple $(sid, par, com, \mathbf{x}, cu)$ and aborts if $cr_k \neq cu$, or if $par' \neq par$, or if $com' \neq com$.
- $\mathcal{U}$ sets $com_i \leftarrow (com'_i, parcom, \mathsf{COM.Verify})$ and $\langle com_{i,j} \leftarrow (com'_{i,j}, parcom, \mathsf{COM.Verify}) \rangle_{\forall j \in [1,L]}$. ($\mathsf{COM.Verify}$ is in the description of R.)
- $\mathcal{U}$ outputs $(\mathsf{uud.read.end}, sid, P, (com_i, \langle com_{i,j} \rangle_{\forall j \in [1,L]}))$.

Theorem 1. Π_{UUD} *securely realizes* $\mathcal{F}_{\mathrm{UUD}}$ *in the* $(\mathcal{F}^{\mathsf{SVC.Setup}}_{\mathrm{CRS}}, \mathcal{F}_{\mathrm{BB}}, \mathcal{F}^R_{\mathrm{ZK}})$-*hybrid model if the SVC scheme is binding.*

When $\mathcal{R}_k$ is corrupt, the binding property of the SVC scheme guarantees that the adversary is not able to open the VC com to a value $v_{i,j}$ if that value was not previously committed by $\mathcal{U}$ at position $(i-1)L+j$. We analyze in detail the security of Π_{UUD} in the full version [18].

5   Instantiation and Efficiency Analysis

Bilinear Maps. Let $\mathbb{G}$, $\tilde{\mathbb{G}}$ and $\mathbb{G}_t$ be groups of prime order p. A map $e : \mathbb{G} \times \tilde{\mathbb{G}} \to \mathbb{G}_t$ must satisfy bilinearity, i.e., $e(g^x, \tilde{g}^y) = e(g, \tilde{g})^{xy}$; non-degeneracy, i.e., for all generators $g \in \mathbb{G}$ and $\tilde{g} \in \tilde{\mathbb{G}}$, $e(g, \tilde{g})$ generates $\mathbb{G}_t$; and efficiency, i.e., there exists an efficient algorithm $\mathcal{G}(1^k)$ that outputs the pairing group setup $grp \leftarrow (p, \mathbb{G}, \tilde{\mathbb{G}}, \mathbb{G}_t, e, g, \tilde{g})$ and an efficient algorithm to compute $e(a, b)$ for any $a \in \mathbb{G}$, $b \in \tilde{\mathbb{G}}$.

Cube Diffie-Hellman (CubeDH) Assumption. Let $(p, \mathbb{G}, \tilde{\mathbb{G}}, \mathbb{G}_t, e, g, \tilde{g}) \leftarrow \mathcal{G}(1^k)$ and $x \leftarrow \mathbb{Z}_p$. Given $(p, \mathbb{G}, \tilde{\mathbb{G}}, \mathbb{G}_t, e, g, \tilde{g}, g^x, \tilde{g}^x)$, for any p.p.t. adversary $\mathcal{A}$, $\Pr[e(g, \tilde{g})^{x^3} \leftarrow \mathcal{A}(p, \mathbb{G}, \tilde{\mathbb{G}}, \mathbb{G}_t, e, g, \tilde{g}, g^x, \tilde{g}^x)] \leq \epsilon(k)$.

SVC Scheme. We use a SVC scheme secure under the CubeDH assumption [20], which we extend with update algorithms for commitments and openings.

$\mathsf{SVC.Setup}(1^k, \ell)$. Generate $(p, \mathbb{G}, \tilde{\mathbb{G}}, \mathbb{G}_t, e, g, \tilde{g}) \leftarrow \mathcal{G}(1^k)$. For all $i \in [1, \ell]$, pick $z_i \leftarrow \mathbb{Z}_p$ and compute $g_i \leftarrow g^{z_i}$ and $\tilde{g}_i \leftarrow \tilde{g}^{z_i}$. For all $i \in [1, \ell]$ and $i' \in [1, \ell]$ such that $i \neq i'$, compute $h_{i,i'} \leftarrow g^{z_i z_{i'}}$. Output $par \leftarrow (p, \mathbb{G}, \tilde{\mathbb{G}}, \mathbb{G}_t, e, g, \tilde{g}, \{g_i, \tilde{g}_i\}_{\forall i \in [1,\ell]}, \{h_{i,i'}\}_{\forall i,i' \in [1,\ell], i \neq i'})$.

$\mathsf{SVC.Commit}(par, \mathbf{x})$. Output $com = \prod_{i=1}^{\ell} g_i^{\mathbf{x}[i]}$.

$\mathsf{SVC.Open}(par, I, \mathbf{x})$. Output $w_I = \prod_{i \in I} \prod_{i' \notin I} h_{i,i'}^{\mathbf{x}[i']}$.

$\mathsf{SVC.Verify}(par, com, \mathbf{x}_I, I, w_I)$. Parse I as $\{i_1, \ldots, i_n\} \subseteq [1, \ell]$ and $\mathbf{x}_I$ as $(\mathbf{x}[i_1], \ldots, \mathbf{x}[i_n])$. Output 1 if

$$e\left(\frac{com}{\prod_{i \in I} g_i^{\mathbf{x}[i]}}, \prod_{i \in I} \tilde{g}_i\right) = e(w_I, \tilde{g})$$

$\mathsf{SVC.ComUpd}(par, com, \mathbf{x}, i, x)$. Output $com' = com \cdot g_i^{x - \mathbf{x}[i]}$.

$\mathsf{SVC.OpenUpd}(par, w_I, \mathbf{x}, I, i, x)$. If $i \in I$, output w_I, else $w'_I = w_I \cdot \prod_{j \in I} h_{j,i}^{x - \mathbf{x}[i]}$.

Commitments. We use Pedersen commitments [24], which we recall in the full version [18].

Signatures. We use the structure-preserving signature (SPS) scheme in [2]. In SPSs, the public key, the messages, and the signatures are group elements in $\mathbb{G}$ and $\tilde{\mathbb{G}}$, and verification must consist purely in the checking of pairing product equations. We employ SPSs to sign group elements, while still supporting efficient ZK proofs of signature possession. In this SPS scheme, a elements in $\mathbb{G}$ and b elements in $\tilde{\mathbb{G}}$ are signed.

KeyGen(grp, a, b). Let $grp \leftarrow (p, \mathbb{G}, \tilde{\mathbb{G}}, \mathbb{G}_t, e, g, \tilde{g})$ be the bilinear map parameters. Pick at random $u_1, \ldots, u_b, v, w_1, \ldots w_a, z \leftarrow \mathbb{Z}_p^*$ and compute $U_i = g^{u_i}$, $i \in [1..b]$, $V = \tilde{g}^v$, $W_i = \tilde{g}^{w_i}$, $i \in [1..a]$ and $Z = \tilde{g}^z$. Return the verification key $pk \leftarrow (grp, U_1, \ldots, U_b, V, W_1, \ldots, W_a, Z)$ and the signing key $sk \leftarrow (pk, u_1, \ldots, u_b, v, w_1, \ldots, w_a, z)$.

Sign($sk, \langle m_1, \ldots, m_{a+b} \rangle$). Pick $r \leftarrow \mathbb{Z}_p^*$, set $R \leftarrow g^r$, $S \leftarrow g^{z-rv} \prod_{i=1}^{a} m_i^{-w_i}$, and $T \leftarrow (\tilde{g} \prod_{i=1}^{b} m_{a+i}^{-u_i})^{1/r}$, and output the signature $s \leftarrow (R, S, T)$.

VfSig($pk, s, \langle m_1, \ldots, m_{a+b} \rangle$). Output 1 if $e(R, V)e(S, \tilde{g}) \prod_{i=1}^{a} e(m_i, W_i) = e(g, Z)$ and $e(R, T) \prod_{i=1}^{b} e(U_i, m_{a+i}) = e(g, \tilde{g})$.

UC ZK Proof. To instantiate $\mathcal{F}_{ZK}^R$, we use the scheme in [12]. In [12], a UC ZK protocol proving knowledge of exponents $(w_1, \ldots, w_n)$ that satisfy the formula $\phi(w_1, \ldots, w_n)$ is described as

$$\rtimes w_1, \ldots, w_n : \phi(w_1, \ldots, w_n) \tag{1}$$

The formula $\phi(w_1, \ldots, w_n)$ consists of conjunctions and disjunctions of "atoms". An atom expresses *group relations*, such as $\prod_{j=1}^{k} g_j^{\mathcal{F}_j} = 1$, where the g_j's are elements of prime order groups and the $\mathcal{F}_j$'s are polynomials in the variables $(w_1, \ldots, w_n)$.

A proof system for (1) can be transformed into a proof system for more expressive statements about secret exponents *sexps* and secret bases *sbases*:

$$\rtimes sexps, sbases : \phi(sexps, bases \cup sbases) \tag{2}$$

The transformation adds an additional base h to the public bases. For each $g_j \in sbases$, the transformation picks a random exponent ρ_j and computes a blinded base $g_j' = g_j h^{\rho_j}$. The transformation adds g_j' to the public bases *bases*, ρ_j to the secret exponents *sexps*, and rewrites $g_j^{\mathcal{F}_j}$ into $g_j'^{\mathcal{F}_j} h^{-\mathcal{F}_j \rho_j}$.

The proof system supports pairing product equations $\prod_{j=1}^{k} e(g_j, \tilde{g}_j)^{\mathcal{F}_j} = 1$ in groups of prime order with a bilinear map e, by treating the target group $\mathbb{G}_t$ as the group of the proof system. The embedding for secret bases is unchanged, except for the case in which both bases in a pairing are secret. In this case, $e(g_j, \tilde{g}_j)^{\mathcal{F}_j}$ must be transformed into $e(g_j', \tilde{g}_j')^{\mathcal{F}_j} e(g_j', \tilde{h})^{-\mathcal{F}_j \tilde{\rho}_j} e(h, \tilde{g}_j')^{-\mathcal{F}_j \rho_j} e(h, \tilde{h})^{\mathcal{F}_j \rho_j \tilde{\rho}_j}$.

UC ZK Proof for Relation R. To instantiate $\mathcal{F}_{ZK}^R$ with the protocol in [12], we need to instantiate R with our chosen SVC and commitment schemes. Then we need to express R following the notation for UC ZK proofs described above.

In R, we need to prove that $I = f(i) = \{(i-1)L+1, \ldots, (i-1)L+L\}$, i.e., we need to prove that the set I of positions opened contains the positions where the database entry i is stored. To prove this statement, the public parameters of the SVC scheme are extended with SPSs that bind g^i with $(g_{(i-1)L+1}, \tilde{g}_{(i-1)L+1}, \ldots, g_{(i-1)L+L}, \tilde{g}_{(i-1)L+L})$, i.e., i is bound with the bases of the positions in I. Given the parameters $par \leftarrow (p, \mathbb{G}, \tilde{\mathbb{G}}, \mathbb{G}_t, e, g, \tilde{g}, \{g_i, \tilde{g}_i\}_{\forall i \in [1,\ell]}, \{h_{i,i'}\}_{\forall i,i' \in [1,\ell], i \neq i'})$, we create the key pair $(sk, pk) \leftarrow \mathsf{KeyGen}(\langle p, \mathbb{G}, \tilde{\mathbb{G}}, \mathbb{G}_t, e, g, \tilde{g}\rangle, L+1, L+1)$ and, for $i \in [1, \ell]$, we compute $s_i \leftarrow \mathsf{Sign}(sk, \langle g_{(i-1)L+1}, \ldots, g_{(i-1)L+L}, g^i, \tilde{g}_{(i-1)L+1}, \ldots, \tilde{g}_{(i-1)L+L}, \tilde{g}^{sid}\rangle)$, where sid is the session identifier. We remark that these signatures do not need to be updated when the database is updated.

Let $(U_1, \ldots, U_{L+1}, V, W_1, \ldots, W_{L+1}, Z)$ be the public key of the signature scheme. Let (R, S, T) be a signature on $(g_{(i-1)L+1}, \ldots, g_{(i-1)L+L}, g^i, \tilde{g}_{(i-1)L+1}, \ldots, \tilde{g}_{(i-1)L+L}, \tilde{g}^{sid})$. Let (g, h) be the parameters of the Pedersen commitment scheme. R involves proofs about secret bases and we use the transformation described above for those proofs. The base h is also used to randomize secret bases in $\mathbb{G}$, and another base $\tilde{h} \leftarrow \tilde{\mathbb{G}}$ is added to randomize bases in $\tilde{\mathbb{G}}$. Following the notation in [12], we describe the proof as follows.

$$\mathbb{Z} i, open_i, \langle v_{i,j}, open_{i,j}, g_{(i-1)L+j}, \tilde{g}_{(i-1)L+j}\rangle_{\forall j \in [1,L]}, w_I, R, S, T :$$

$$com_i' = g^i h^{open_i} \wedge \langle com_{i,j}' = g^{v_{i,j}} h^{open_{i,j}}\rangle_{\forall j \in [1,L]} \wedge \tag{3}$$

$$e(R, V)e(S, \tilde{g})(\prod_{j \in [1,L]} e(g_{(i-1)L+j}, W_j))e(g, W_{L+1})^i e(g, Z)^{-1} = 1 \wedge \tag{4}$$

$$e(R, T)(\prod_{j \in [1,L]} e(U_j, \tilde{g}_{(i-1)L+j}))e(U_{L+1}, \tilde{g}^{sid})e(g, \tilde{g})^{-1} = 1 \wedge \tag{5}$$

$$e\left(\frac{com}{\prod_{j \in [1,L]} g_{(i-1)L+j}^{v_{i,j}}}, \prod_{j \in [1,L]} \tilde{g}_{(i-1)L+j}\right) = e(w_I, \tilde{g}) \tag{6}$$

Equation 3 proves knowledge of the openings of the Pedersen commitments com_i' and $\langle com_{i,j}'\rangle_{\forall j \in [1,L]}$. Equation 4 and Eq. 5 prove knowledge of a signature (R, S, T) on a message $(g_{(i-1)L+1}, \ldots, g_{(i-1)L+L}, g^i, \tilde{g}_{(i-1)L+1}, \ldots, \tilde{g}_{(i-1)L+L}, \tilde{g}^{sid})$. Equation 6 proves that the values $\langle v_{i,j}\rangle_{\forall j \in [1,L]}$ in $\langle com_{i,j}'\rangle_{\forall j \in [1,L]}$ are equal to the values committed in the positions $I = f(i) = \{(i-1)L+1, \ldots, (i-1)L+L\}$ of the vector commitment com. We remark that, in comparison to the relation R in Sect. 4.2, in the witness we replace I by the secret bases $\langle g_{(i-1)L+j}, \tilde{g}_{(i-1)L+j}\rangle_{\forall j \in [1,L]}$, from which I can be derived. Like in R, the positions $j \in [1, L]$ inside the database entry i of the values $v_{i,j}$ committed in $com_{i,j}'$ are revealed to the verifier.

When a range of indices $[i_{min}, i_{max}]$ stores always (i.e., even after database updates) the same tuple $[v_{i,1}, \ldots, v_{i,L}]$, we can improve storage efficiency as follows. We compute signatures on tuples $(g_{(i'-1)L+1}, \ldots, g_{(i'-1)L+L}, g^{i_{min}}, g^{i_{max}}, \tilde{g}_{(i'-1)L+1}, \ldots, \tilde{g}_{(i'-1)L+L}, \tilde{g}^{sid})$ that bind all the indices in $[i_{min}, i_{max}]$ with the bases for the positions where the tuple is stored. (i' is used to denote the position in the SVC where the tuple is stored.) Then, in the UC ZK proof for R, we add a range proof to prove that $i \in [i_{min}, i_{max}]$, where i is committed in com'_i, to prove that we are opening the correct subvector for i.

Efficiency Analysis. We analyze the storage, communication, and computation costs of our instantiation of Π_{UUD}.

Storage Cost. Any $\mathcal{R}_k$ and $\mathcal{U}$ store the common reference string, whose size grows quadratically with N. Throughout the protocol execution, $\mathcal{R}_k$ and $\mathcal{U}$ also store the last update of com and the committed vector. $\mathcal{R}_k$ stores the openings w_I. In conclusion, the storage cost is quadratic in $N \times L$.

Communication Cost. In the uud.update interface, $\mathcal{U}$ sends the tuples $(i, v_{i,1}, \ldots, v_{i,L})_{\forall i \in [1,N]}$, which are retrieved by $\mathcal{R}_k$ in the uud.getdb interface. The communication cost is linear in the number of entries updated, except for the first update in which all entries must be initialized. In the uud.read interface, $\mathcal{R}_k$ sends an instance and a ZK proof to $\mathcal{U}$. The size of the witness and of the instance grows linearly with L but is independent of N. In conclusion, after the first update phase, the communication cost does not depend on N.

Computation Cost. In the uud.update and uud.getdb interfaces, $\mathcal{U}$ and $\mathcal{R}_k$ update com with cost linear in the number t of updates, except for the first update where all the positions are initialized. $\mathcal{R}_k$ also updates the stored openings w_I with cost linear in $t \times L$. In the uud.read interface, if w_I is not stored, $\mathcal{R}_k$ computes it with cost that grows linearly with $N \times L$. However, if w_I is stored, the computation cost of the proof grows linearly with L but is independent of N.

It is possible to defer opening updates to the uud.read interface, so as to only update openings that are actually needed to compute ZK proofs. Thanks to that, the computation cost in the uud.getdb interface is independent of N. In the uud.read interface, if w_I is stored but needs to be updated, the computation cost grows linearly with $t \times L$ but it is independent of N. The only overhead introduced by deferring opening updates is the need to store the tuples $(i, v_{i,1}, \ldots, v_{i,L})_{\forall i \in [1,N]}$.

In summary, after initialization of com and the openings w_I, the communication and computation costs are independent of N, so in terms of communication and computation our instantiation of Π_{UUD} is practical for large databases.

Table 1. Π_{UUD} execution times in seconds

Interface	$N = 50$ $L = 10$	$N = 100$ $L = 5$	$N = 100$ $L = 15$	$N = 150$ $L = 10$	$N = 200$ $L = 5$	$N = 200$ $L = 15$
Setup	61.35	61.37	553.71	554.52	249.61	2205.72
Update	0.0001	0.0002	0.0001	0.0001	0.0002	0.0001
Getdb	0.0004	0.0004	0.0006	0.0004	0.0003	0.0004
Computation of com	0.0371	0.0350	0.1093	0.1035	0.0707	0.2145
One value update of com	1.59e−05	1.59e−05	1.71e−05	1.99e−05	1.69e−05	1.59e−05
Computation of w_I	0.3491	0.1753	1.5659	1.0485	0.3513	3.1330
One value update of w_I	0.0002	0.0001	0.0003	0.0002	0.0001	0.0003
Read proof (1024 bit key)	3.6737	2.1903	4.9621	3.6811	2.1164	5.0268
Read proof (2048 bit key)	16.6220	10.6786	25.2909	16.8730	9.8916	23.4896

Implementation and Efficiency Measurements. We have implemented our instantiation of Π_{UUD} in the Python programming language, using the Charm cryptographic framework [4], on a computer equipped with an Intel Core i5-7300U CPU clocked at 2.60 GHz, and 8 gigabytes of RAM. The BN256 curve was used for the pairing group setup.

To compute UC ZK proofs for $\mathcal{R}_k$, we use the compiler in [12]. The public parameters of the proof system contain a public key of the Paillier encryption scheme, the parameters for a multi-integer commitment scheme, and the specification of a DSA group. (We refer to [12] for a description of how those primitives are used in the compiler.) The cost of a proof depends on the number of elements in the witness and on the number of equations composed by Boolean ANDs. The computation cost for the prover of a Σ-protocol for $\mathcal{R}_k$ involves one evaluation of each of the equations and one multiplication per value in the witness. The compiler in [12] extends a Σ-protocol and requires, additionally, a computation of a multi-integer commitment that commits to the values in the witness, an evaluation of a Paillier encryption for each of the values in the witness, a Σ-protocol to prove that the commitment and the encryptions are correctly generated, and 3 exponentiations in the DSA group. The computation cost for the verifier, as well as the communication cost, also depends on the number of values in the witness, and on the number of equations. Therefore, as the number of values in the witness and the number of equations is independent of N in our proof for relation R, the computation and communication costs of our proof do not depend on N.

Table 1 lists the execution times of the uud.update and uud.getdb interfaces, the computation costs for read proofs, and the costs for computing and updating w_I and com, in our implementation, in seconds. The execution times of the interfaces of the protocol have been evaluated against the size N of the database, and the size of each entry L of the database. In the setup phase, the public parameters of all the building blocks are computed, and the database is set up by computing com. In the second and third rows of Table 1, we depict the execution times for the uud.update and uud.getdb interfaces for the updater $\mathcal{U}$, and a reader $\mathcal{R}_k$ respectively, after the update of a single value in an entry of the database. In the fourth row of Table 1, we show the cost of computing com, and as can be seen from these values, the computation times for com depend on the total number of values $N \times L$ in the database. However, the cost of updating com is very small, and linear in the number t of updates, and this in turn results in small computation costs for the uud.update interface, independent of N. (As required by our applications in Sect. 6, the committed vector that we use consists of small numbers rather than random values in $\mathbb{Z}_p$.) The cost of computation of w_I also depends on the total number of values $N \times L$ in the database, while the cost of updating w_I is linear in $t \times L$, and thus the execution times for the uud.getdb interface (which involves the updates of stored witnesses, in addition to the update of com as in the case of the uud.update interface) are also small.

In the last two rows of Table 1, we show the computation costs for a read proof. These values have been evaluated against varying key lengths for the Paillier encryption scheme used in the proof system in our instantiation of Π_{UUD}. The execution times for the read interface depend greatly upon the security parameters of the Paillier encryption scheme, and increase linearly with the entry size of the database L. However, the execution times are independent of the database size N.

6 Modular Design with $\mathcal{F}_{\mathrm{UUD}}$ and Application to OTAC

First, we show how to describe a protocol modularly by using $\mathcal{F}_{\mathrm{UUD}}$ as building block. As an example, consider the following relation R':

$$R' = \{(wit, ins) :$$
$$[i, v_{i,1}, \dots, v_{i,L}] \in \mathsf{DB} \ \wedge \ 1 = \mathrm{pred}_i(i) \ \wedge \ \langle 1 = \mathrm{pred}_j(v_{i,j}) \rangle_{\forall j \in [1,L]}\}$$

where the witness is $wit = (i, \langle v_{i,j} \rangle_{\forall j \in [1,L]})$ and the instance is $ins = \mathsf{DB}$. pred_i and pred_j represent predicates that i and $\langle v_{i,j} \rangle_{\forall j \in [1,L]}$ must fulfill, e.g., predicates that require i and $\langle v_{i,j} \rangle_{\forall j \in [1,L]}$ to belong to a range or set of values.

We would like to construct a ZK protocol for R' between a prover $\mathcal{P}$ and a verifier $\mathcal{V}$ that uses different functionalities $\mathcal{F}_{\mathrm{ZK}}^{R_i}$ and $\langle \mathcal{F}_{\mathrm{ZK}}^{R_j} \rangle_{\forall j \in [1,L]}$ to prove each of the statements in R'. We show how this protocol is constructed by using $\mathcal{F}_{\mathrm{UUD}}$ and $\mathcal{F}_{\mathrm{NIC}}$ as building blocks.

1. On input DB, $\mathcal{V}$ uses the uud.update interface to send DB to $\mathcal{F}_{\mathrm{UUD}}$.
2. $\mathcal{P}$ uses the uud.getdb interface to retrieve DB.
3. On input $(i, v_{i,1}, \dots, v_{i,L})$ and P, $\mathcal{P}$ checks that $[i, v_{i,1}, \dots, v_{i,L}] \in \mathsf{DB}$.
4. $\mathcal{P}$ runs the com.setup interface of $\mathcal{F}_{\mathrm{NIC}}$. $\mathcal{P}$ uses the com.commit interface of $\mathcal{F}_{\mathrm{NIC}}$ on input i to obtain a commitment com_i with opening $open_i$. Similarly, from $j = 1$ to L, $\mathcal{P}$ obtains from $\mathcal{F}_{\mathrm{NIC}}$ commitments $com_{i,j}$ to $v_{i,j}$ with opening $open_{i,j}$.
5. $\mathcal{P}$ uses the uud.read interface to send the tuple $(P, i, com_i, open_i, \langle v_{i,j}, com_{i,j}, open_{i,j} \rangle_{\forall j \in [1,L]})$ to $\mathcal{F}_{\mathrm{UUD}}$, which sends $(P, com_i, \langle com_{i,j} \rangle_{\forall j \in [1,L]})$ to $\mathcal{V}$.

6. $\mathcal{V}$ runs the com.setup interface of $\mathcal{F}_{\mathrm{NIC}}$. $\mathcal{V}$ uses the com.validate interface of $\mathcal{F}_{\mathrm{NIC}}$ to validate the commitments com_i and $\langle com_{i,j}\rangle_{\forall j\in[1,L]}$. Then $\mathcal{V}$ stores P, com_i and $\langle com_{i,j}\rangle_{\forall j\in[1,L]}$ and sends a message to $\mathcal{P}$ to acknowledge the receipt of the commitments.

7. $\mathcal{P}$ parses the commitment com_i as $(com_i', parcom, \mathsf{COM.Verify})$. $\mathcal{P}$ sets the witness $wit \leftarrow (i, open_i)$ and the instance $ins \leftarrow (parcom, com_i')$. $\mathcal{P}$ uses the zk.prove interface to send wit, ins and P to $\mathcal{F}_{\mathrm{ZK}}^{R_i}$, where R_i is

$$R_i = \{(wit, ins) :$$
$$1 = \mathsf{COM.Verify}(parcom, com_i', i, open_i) \ \wedge \ 1 = \mathrm{pred}_i(i)\}$$

8. $\mathcal{V}$ receives ins from $\mathcal{F}_{\mathrm{ZK}}^{R_i}$. $\mathcal{V}$ checks that pseudonym and the commitment in ins are equal to the stored pseudonym and commitment com_i. If the commitments are equal, the binding property guaranteed by $\mathcal{F}_{\mathrm{NIC}}$ ensures that $\mathcal{F}_{\mathrm{UUD}}$ and $\mathcal{F}_{\mathrm{ZK}}^{R_i}$ received as input the same position i.

9. The last two steps are replicated to prove, for $j = 1$ to L, that $v_{i,j}$ fulfills $1 = \mathrm{pred}_j(v_{i,j})$ by using $\mathcal{F}_{\mathrm{ZK}}^{R_j}$.

Application to OTAC. In the full version [18], we depict our functionality $\mathcal{F}_{\mathrm{OTAC}}$ and our construction Π_{OTAC}. $\mathcal{F}_{\mathrm{OTAC}}$ consists of the following interfaces:

1. The sender $\mathcal{U}$ uses the otac.init interface to send the messages $\langle m_n\rangle_{n=1}^N$.
2. The receiver $\mathcal{R}_k$ uses the otac.retrieve interface to retrieve N.
3. $\mathcal{U}$ uses the otac.policy interface to send (or update) the policies $\langle \mathsf{ACP}_n\rangle_{n=1}^N$ and the relation R_{ACP} to $\mathcal{F}_{\mathrm{OTAC}}$.
4. $\mathcal{R}_k$ uses the otac.getpol interface to obtain $\langle \mathsf{ACP}_n\rangle_{n=1}^N$ and R_{ACP}.
5. $\mathcal{R}_k$ uses the otac.transfer to send a choice i and a witness wit to $\mathcal{F}_{\mathrm{OTAC}}$. If $(wit, \mathsf{ACP}_i) \in R_{\mathsf{ACP}}$, $\mathcal{F}_{\mathrm{OTAC}}$ sends m_i to $\mathcal{R}_k$.

$\mathcal{F}_{\mathrm{OTAC}}$ follows previous OTAC functionalities [8] but introduces two main modifications. First, it splits the initialization interface into two interfaces: otac.init and otac.policy, to enable $\mathcal{U}$ to make policy updates. Second, previous functionalities include an issuance phase where an issuer certifies $\mathcal{R}_k$ attributes, whereas $\mathcal{F}_{\mathrm{OTAC}}$ does not have it. Instead, in the transfer phase of $\mathcal{F}_{\mathrm{OTAC}}$, $\mathcal{R}_k$ must provide a witness wit such that $(wit, \mathsf{ACP}_i) \in R_{\mathsf{ACP}}$. wit could contain, e.g., signatures from an issuer on $\mathcal{R}_k$ attributes, but in general any data required by R_{ACP}.

Π_{OTAC} uses $\mathcal{F}_{\mathrm{OT}}$, $\mathcal{F}_{\mathrm{NIC}}$, $\mathcal{F}_{\mathrm{UUD}}$, $\mathcal{F}_{\mathrm{ZK}}^{R_{\mathsf{ACP}'}}$, $\mathcal{F}_{\mathrm{BB}}$ and a functionality $\mathcal{F}_{\mathrm{NYM}}$ for a secure pseudonymous channel. $\mathcal{F}_{\mathrm{OT}}$ and $\mathcal{F}_{\mathrm{NYM}}$ are depicted in the full version [18]. $\mathcal{F}_{\mathrm{OT}}$ is used to implement the otac.init and otac.retrieve interfaces, as well as to allow $\mathcal{R}_k$ to obtain messages obliviously in the otac.transfer interface. $\mathcal{F}_{\mathrm{OT}}$ receives a committed input to the choice i. It is generally straightforward to adapt existing UC OTs to realize our $\mathcal{F}_{\mathrm{OT}}$ with committed inputs.

To implement access control, Π_{OTAC} uses $\mathcal{F}_{\mathrm{UUD}}$, $\mathcal{F}_{\mathrm{BB}}$ and $\mathcal{F}_{\mathrm{ZK}}^{R_{\mathsf{ACP}'}}$. In the otac.policy interface, $\mathcal{U}$ uses $\mathcal{F}_{\mathrm{UUD}}$ to store the policies, and $\mathcal{U}$ uses $\mathcal{F}_{\mathrm{BB}}$ to store the relation R_{ACP}. In the otac.getpol interface, $\mathcal{R}_k$ retrieves the policies and the relation from $\mathcal{F}_{\mathrm{UUD}}$ and $\mathcal{F}_{\mathrm{BB}}$.

In the otac.transfer interface, $\mathcal{R}_k$ reads the policy $\mathsf{ACP}_i = \langle v_{i,j} \rangle_{\forall j \in [1,L]}$ for her choice i by using $\mathcal{F}_{\mathsf{UUD}}$. To do so, $\mathcal{R}_k$ obtains commitments com_i and $\langle com_{i,j} \rangle_{\forall j \in [1,L]}$ to i and to the values $\langle v_{i,j} \rangle_{\forall j \in [1,L]}$ that represent the policy from $\mathcal{F}_{\mathsf{NIC}}$. $\langle com_{i,j} \rangle_{\forall j \in [1,L]}$ are sent as input to $\mathcal{F}_{\mathsf{ZK}}^{R_{\mathsf{ACP'}}}$ so that $\mathcal{R}_k$ proves fulfilment of the policy. com_i is sent as input to $\mathcal{F}_{\mathsf{OT}}$ to obtain the message m_i.

$R_{\mathsf{ACP'}}$ is a modification of R_{ACP}. In $R_{\mathsf{ACP'}}$, the instance $\mathsf{ACP}_i = \langle v_{i,j} \rangle_{\forall j \in [1,L]}$ of R_{ACP} is replaced by $\langle com_{i,j} \rangle_{\forall j \in [1,L]}$, while the witness is extended to contain $wit' \leftarrow (wit, \langle v_{i,j}, open_{i,j} \rangle_{\forall j \in [1,L]})$. I.e., the instance in $R_{\mathsf{ACP'}}$ contains commitments to the policy rather than the policy itself, which allows $\mathcal{R}_k$ to hide what policy is being used from $\mathcal{U}$.

Π_{OTAC} supports any policies that can be represented by tuples of values. In [21], policies are represented by branching programs. If the ZK proof for a policy committed in $\langle com_{i,j} \rangle_{\forall j \in [1,L]}$ requires $\mathcal{R}_k$ to hide the indices j that are used from the policy, the proof for $\mathcal{F}_{\mathsf{ZK}}^{R_{\mathsf{ACP'}}}$ can follow an approach similar to Π_{UUD} to compute an OR proof. I.e., the values committed in $\langle com_{i,j} \rangle_{\forall j \in [1,L]}$ can be committed in a vector commitment, and then a position of the vector commitment can be opened, without disclosing what position is opened.

Π_{OTAC} uses $\mathcal{F}_{\mathsf{OT}}$ as building block. Thanks to that, it can be instantiated with multiple OT schemes and their security does not need to be reanalyzed. Moreover, $\mathcal{U}$ can update the access control policies at any time without restarting or modifying the OT used as building block, and without using a revocation mechanism to disallow old policies. Additionally, when many messages are associated with the same policy, we can use our optimization in Sect. 5 so that the policies in the database do not need to be replicated.

7 Related Work

Vector Commitments (VC). SVC schemes are an extension of VC schemes [14,23]. While an opening in SVC allows us to open a subset of positions, in VC it allows us to open one position. Our construction could be based on a VC scheme. In that case, the efficiency of the UC ZK proof for the uud.read interface would decrease because we would need to prove knowledge of L openings. However, storage cost would improve because the public parameter size of some VC schemes grows linearly with the vector length. We note that [6,20] propose SVC with short parameters based on hidden order groups, but those constructions are better suited for bit vectors.

Polynomial commitments (PC) allow a committer to commit to a polynomial and open the commitment to an evaluation of the polynomial. PC can be used as vector commitments by committing to a polynomial that interpolates the vector to be committed. The PC construction in [19] has the disadvantage that efficient updates cannot be computed without knowledge of the trapdoor. A further generalization of vector commitments and polynomial commitments are functional commitments [20,22].

OTAC. Our OTAC is adaptive, i.e., $\mathcal{R}_k$ can choose an index i after receiving other messages previously. In [5], an oblivious language-based envelope protocol (OLBE) is proposed based on smooth projective hash functions. OLBE can be viewed as a non-adaptive OTAC.

Our OTAC is stateless, i.e. fulfilment of a policy by $\mathcal{R}_k$ does not depend in the history of messages accessed by $\mathcal{R}_k$. In [15], a stateful OTAC is proposed where policies are defined by a directed graph that determines the possible states of $\mathcal{R}_k$, the transitions between states and the messages that can be accessed at each stage. Price oblivious transfer protocols (POT) [3,9,26] require the user to pay a price for each message. Typically, they involve a prepaid method, where $\mathcal{R}_k$ makes a deposit and later subtracts the prices paid from it without revealing the current funds or the prices paid. Those stateful OTAC where not designed modularly. Recently, a modular POT protocol was proposed [16] based on an updatable database without unlinkability [17]. Our OTAC differs from it in that it provides unlinkability to $\mathcal{R}_k$ and in that it considers more complex policies expressed by tuples of values, while in POT the policy is simply the message price. Additionally, our OTAC can improve storage efficiency when the same policy is applied to several messages.

Our OTAC reveals the policies to $\mathcal{R}_k$. In [7,10], OTAC with hidden policies are proposed. Our approach based on SVC cannot be followed to design modularly OTAC with hidden policies that allow for policy updates.

8   Conclusion and Future Work

We propose an OTAC protocol that can be instantiated with any secure OT scheme, that allows for policy updates and that can reduce storage cost when a policy is associated to a group of messages. As building block, we define and construct an unlinkable updatable database. Our construction based on subvector commitments allows efficient policy updates. As future work, we plan to extend our OTAC protocol to consider stateful policies.

References

1. Abe, M., Camenisch, J., Dubovitskaya, M., Nishimaki, R.: Universally composable adaptive oblivious transfer (with access control) from standard assumptions. In: DIM 2013, Proceedings of the 2013 ACM Workshop on Digital Identity Management, pp. 1–12 (2013)
2. Abe, M., Groth, J., Haralambiev, K., Ohkubo, M.: Optimal structure-preserving signatures in asymmetric bilinear groups. In: Rogaway, P. (ed.) CRYPTO 2011. LNCS, vol. 6841, pp. 649–666. Springer, Heidelberg (2011). https://doi.org/10.1007/978-3-642-22792-9_37
3. Aiello, B., Ishai, Y., Reingold, O.: Priced oblivious transfer: how to sell digital goods. In: Pfitzmann, B. (ed.) EUROCRYPT 2001. LNCS, vol. 2045, pp. 119–135. Springer, Heidelberg (2001). https://doi.org/10.1007/3-540-44987-6_8
4. Akinyele, J.A., et al.: Charm: a framework for rapidly prototyping cryptosystems. J. Cryptogr. Eng. **3**(2), 111–128 (2013)

5. Blazy, O., Chevalier, C., Germouty, P.: Adaptive oblivious transfer and generalization. In: Cheon, J.H., Takagi, T. (eds.) ASIACRYPT 2016. LNCS, vol. 10032, pp. 217–247. Springer, Heidelberg (2016). https://doi.org/10.1007/978-3-662-53890-6_8
6. Boneh, D., Bünz, B., Fisch, B.: Batching techniques for accumulators with applications to IOPs and stateless blockchains. In: Boldyreva, A., Micciancio, D. (eds.) CRYPTO 2019. LNCS, vol. 11692, pp. 561–586. Springer, Cham (2019). https://doi.org/10.1007/978-3-030-26948-7_20
7. Camenisch, J., Dubovitskaya, M., Enderlein, R.R., Neven, G.: Oblivious transfer with hidden access control from attribute-based encryption. In: Visconti, I., De Prisco, R. (eds.) SCN 2012. LNCS, vol. 7485, pp. 559–579. Springer, Heidelberg (2012). https://doi.org/10.1007/978-3-642-32928-9_31
8. Camenisch, J., Dubovitskaya, M., Neven, G.: Oblivious transfer with access control. In: ACM Conference on Computer and Communications Security, CCS 2009, pp. 131–140 (2009)
9. Camenisch, J., Dubovitskaya, M., Neven, G.: Unlinkable priced oblivious transfer with rechargeable wallets. In: Sion, R. (ed.) FC 2010. LNCS, vol. 6052, pp. 66–81. Springer, Heidelberg (2010). https://doi.org/10.1007/978-3-642-14577-3_8
10. Camenisch, J., Dubovitskaya, M., Neven, G., Zaverucha, G.M.: Oblivious transfer with hidden access control policies. In: Catalano, D., Fazio, N., Gennaro, R., Nicolosi, A. (eds.) PKC 2011. LNCS, vol. 6571, pp. 192–209. Springer, Heidelberg (2011). https://doi.org/10.1007/978-3-642-19379-8_12
11. Camenisch, J., Dubovitskaya, M., Rial, A.: UC commitments for modular protocol design and applications to revocation and attribute tokens. In: Robshaw, M., Katz, J. (eds.) CRYPTO 2016. LNCS, vol. 9816, pp. 208–239. Springer, Heidelberg (2016). https://doi.org/10.1007/978-3-662-53015-3_8
12. Camenisch, J., Krenn, S., Shoup, V.: A framework for practical universally composable zero-knowledge protocols. In: Lee, D.H., Wang, X. (eds.) ASIACRYPT 2011. LNCS, vol. 7073, pp. 449–467. Springer, Heidelberg (2011). https://doi.org/10.1007/978-3-642-25385-0_24
13. Canetti, R.: Universally composable security: a new paradigm for cryptographic protocols. In: FOCS 2001, pp. 136–145 (2001)
14. Catalano, D., Fiore, D.: Vector commitments and their applications. In: Kurosawa, K., Hanaoka, G. (eds.) PKC 2013. LNCS, vol. 7778, pp. 55–72. Springer, Heidelberg (2013). https://doi.org/10.1007/978-3-642-36362-7_5
15. Coull, S., Green, M., Hohenberger, S.: Controlling access to an oblivious database using stateful anonymous credentials. In: Jarecki, S., Tsudik, G. (eds.) PKC 2009. LNCS, vol. 5443, pp. 501–520. Springer, Heidelberg (2009). https://doi.org/10.1007/978-3-642-00468-1_28
16. Damodaran, A., Dubovitskaya, M., Rial, A.: UC priced oblivious transfer with purchase statistics and dynamic pricing. In: Hao, F., Ruj, S., Sen Gupta, S. (eds.) INDOCRYPT 2019. LNCS, vol. 11898, pp. 273–296. Springer, Cham (2019). https://doi.org/10.1007/978-3-030-35423-7_14
17. Damodaran, A., Rial, A.: UC updatable databases and applications. In: Nitaj, A., Youssef, A. (eds.) AFRICACRYPT 2020. LNCS, vol. 12174, pp. 66–87. Springer, Cham (2020). https://doi.org/10.1007/978-3-030-51938-4_4
18. Damodaran, A., Rial, A.: Unlinkable updatable databases and oblivious transfer with access control. http://hdl.handle.net/10993/43250
19. Kate, A., Zaverucha, G.M., Goldberg, I.: Constant-size commitments to polynomials and their applications. In: Abe, M. (ed.) ASIACRYPT 2010. LNCS, vol. 6477, pp. 177–194. Springer, Heidelberg (2010). https://doi.org/10.1007/978-3-642-17373-8_11

20. Lai, R.W.F., Malavolta, G.: Subvector commitments with application to succinct arguments. In: Boldyreva, A., Micciancio, D. (eds.) CRYPTO 2019. LNCS, vol. 11692, pp. 530–560. Springer, Cham (2019). https://doi.org/10.1007/978-3-030-26948-7_19

21. Libert, B., Ling, S., Mouhartem, F., Nguyen, K., Wang, H.: Adaptive oblivious transfer with access control from lattice assumptions. In: Takagi, T., Peyrin, T. (eds.) ASIACRYPT 2017. LNCS, vol. 10624, pp. 533–563. Springer, Cham (2017). https://doi.org/10.1007/978-3-319-70694-8_19

22. Libert, B., Ramanna, S.C., Yung, M.: Functional commitment schemes: from polynomial commitments to pairing-based accumulators from simple assumptions. In: ICALP 2016, pp. 30:1–30:14 (2016)

23. Libert, B., Yung, M.: Concise mercurial vector commitments and independent zero-knowledge sets with short proofs. In: Micciancio, D. (ed.) TCC 2010. LNCS, vol. 5978, pp. 499–517. Springer, Heidelberg (2010). https://doi.org/10.1007/978-3-642-11799-2_30

24. Pedersen, T.P.: Non-interactive and information-theoretic secure verifiable secret sharing. In: Feigenbaum, J. (ed.) CRYPTO 1991. LNCS, vol. 576, pp. 129–140. Springer, Heidelberg (1992). https://doi.org/10.1007/3-540-46766-1_9

25. Rial, A.: Blind attribute-based encryption and oblivious transfer with fine-grained access control. Des. Codes Crypt. **81**(2), 179–223 (2015). https://doi.org/10.1007/s10623-015-0134-y

26. Rial, A., Kohlweiss, M., Preneel, B.: Universally composable adaptive priced oblivious transfer. In: Shacham, H., Waters, B. (eds.) Pairing 2009. LNCS, vol. 5671, pp. 231–247. Springer, Heidelberg (2009). https://doi.org/10.1007/978-3-642-03298-1_15

27. Wikström, D.: A universally composable mix-net. In: Naor, M. (ed.) TCC 2004. LNCS, vol. 2951, pp. 317–335. Springer, Heidelberg (2004). https://doi.org/10.1007/978-3-540-24638-1_18

28. Xu, L., Zhang, F.: Oblivious transfer with threshold access control. J. Inf. Sci. Eng. **28**(3), 555–570 (2012)

29. Xu, L., Zhang, F.: Oblivious transfer with complex attribute-based access control. In: Rhee, K.-H., Nyang, D.H. (eds.) ICISC 2010. LNCS, vol. 6829, pp. 370–395. Springer, Heidelberg (2011). https://doi.org/10.1007/978-3-642-24209-0_25

30. Zhang, Y., et al.: Oblivious transfer with access control: realizing disjunction without duplication. In: Joye, M., Miyaji, A., Otsuka, A. (eds.) Pairing 2010. LNCS, vol. 6487, pp. 96–115. Springer, Heidelberg (2010). https://doi.org/10.1007/978-3-642-17455-1_7

Secure and Compact Elliptic Curve LR Scalar Multiplication

Yaoan Jin[1] and Atsuko Miyaji[1,2(✉)]

[1] Graduate School of Engineering, Osaka University, Suita, Japan
jin@cy2sec.comm.eng.osaka-u.ac.jp, miyaji@comm.eng.osaka-u.ac.jp
[2] Japan Advanced Institute of Science and Technology, Nomi, Japan

Abstract. Elliptic curve cryptography (ECC) can ensure an equivalent security with much smaller key sizes. Elliptic curve scalar multiplication (ECSM) is a fundamental computation used in ECC. This paper focuses on ECSM resisting simple power attack and safe error attack of side-channel attack specifically. Elliptic curve complete addition (CA) formulae can achieve secure ECSM algorithms but are inefficient from memory and computational cost perspectives. Another secure ECSM, which uses (extended) affine, is more efficient for both memory and computational costs. However, it scans input scalars from right to left. In this paper, our developed scalar multiplication algorithms also use their extended affine, but scan from left to right (LR). We also prove the security of our LR ECSM algorithms and analyze them both theoretically and experimentally. Our new LR ECSM algorithms can reduce the amount of memory by 37.5% and reduce the computational time by more than 40% compared to Joye's regular 2-ary LR algorithm with CA formulae.

Keywords: Elliptic curve scalar multiplication · Side-channel attack

1 Introduction

Elliptic curve cryptography (ECC) can ensure an equivalent security with much smaller key sizes. Hence, ECC has been implemented in secure Internet-of-Things (IoT) devices [1] and various blockchain applications. Elliptic curve scalar multiplication (ECSM) is a fundamental computation used in ECC. It is therefore important to construct a secure and efficient ECSM. Studies on secure and efficient ECSM algorithms can be divided into two categories. The first direction is to find secure and efficient scalar multiplication algorithms [9–11,13,14]. The second direction is to find secure and efficient coordinates with addition formulae [3,6,7,15,17]. This paper concentrates on resisting simple power attack (SPA) and safe error attack (SEA). SPA makes use of "if statements" and SEA makes use of "dummy statements" to reveal significant bits of input scalars. Thus, secure ECSM algorithms should exclude conditional and dummy statements. Elliptic curve CA formulae [7,15,17] can achieve secure ECSM algorithms but are inefficient in terms of memory and computational costs. Another secure ECSM, which uses (extended) affine, is more efficient for both memory and computational costs [8]. However, it scans input scalars from right to left (RL).

© Springer Nature Switzerland AG 2020
J. K. Liu and H. Cui (Eds.): ACISP 2020, LNCS 12248, pp. 605–618, 2020.
https://doi.org/10.1007/978-3-030-55304-3_31

In this paper, we propose secure and compact left-to-right (LR) ECSM algorithms based on affine coordinates. We improve Joye's LR 2-ary algorithm to exclude exceptional computations of affine formulae and extended affine formulae [8]. We propose secure scalar multiplication algorithms, Algorithm 7 and Algorithm 8 through 2-bit scanning using the affine double and quadruple algorithm (DQ-algorithm) [12]. Subsequently, along with applying the idea of a Montgomery trick [4,12], we revise three affine combination-addition formulae, which reduce the number of inversion computations to one during all computations. We combine Algorithm 7 and Algorithm 8 with affine combination-addition algorithms and modify Algorithm 8 to Algorithm 9 with our affine combination-addition algorithm (Algorithm 6).

For memory, (Algorithm 7) and (Algorithm 7 with Algorithm 2) use the least amount of memory for ten field elements, reducing that of Joye's LR with CA formulae by 37.5% and that of Joye's RL with CA formulae by 47.37%. For computational cost, we evaluate all ECSMs by estimating the number of modulo multiplication (M), modulo square (S), and inversion (I). Modulo multiplication with parameters a and b (m_a and m_b) and modulo addition (A) are omitted. In many cases, such as the National Institute of Standard and Technology (NIST) elliptic curves, we can only omit m_a and A. Then, our ECSMs of (Algorithm 7 with (extended) affine), (Algorithm 7 with (extended) affine and Algorithm 2), and (Algorithm 9 with (extended) affine and Algorithm 6) can be the most efficient during a larger interval of $\frac{I}{M} \leq \frac{26.8-54/\ell}{1+17/\ell}$ (24.93 when bit length $\ell = 256$) compared to Joye's LR with CA formulae. Experiments also show that our new LR ECSM algorithms can reduce the computational time by more than 40% compared to Joye's LR with CA formulae.

The remainder of this paper is organized as follows. Related studies are provided in Sect. 2. Our proposed algorithms are described in Sect. 3. In Sect. 4, we analyze our Algorithms 7–9 with (extended) affine and affine combination-addition algorithms (Algorithms 2, 3, 4, 5 and 6) from the theoretical and experimental perspectives. Finally, we conclude our work in Sect. 5.

2   Related Work

ECSM algorithms consist of two parts: scalar multiplication algorithms and elliptic curve addition formulae. Thus, related studies on secure and efficient ECSM algorithms can be divided into two categories: scalar multiplication algorithms [9–11,13,14] and elliptic curve coordinates with addition formulae [3,7,15,17]. We briefly introduce related studies in this section.

affine addition formula ($P \neq \pm Q$)   affine doubling formula ($2P \neq \mathcal{O}$)

$$x_3 = \left(\frac{y_2 - y_1}{x_2 - x_1} \right)^2 - x_1 - x_2 \qquad\qquad x_3 = \left(\frac{3x_1^2 + a}{2y_1} \right)^2 - 2x_1$$

$$y_3 = \left(\frac{y_2 - y_1}{x_2 - x_1} \right)(x_1 - x_3) - y_1 \qquad\qquad y_3 = \left(\frac{3x_1^2 + a}{2y_1} \right)(x_1 - x_3) - y_1$$

$$\text{(1)} \qquad\qquad\qquad\qquad\qquad\qquad \text{(2)}$$

2.1   Addition Formulae and Exceptional Computations

Let $E(\mathbb{F}_p)$ be a Weierstrass elliptic curve over $\mathbb{F}_p$, $E(\mathbb{F}_p) : y^2 = x^3 + ax + b$, $(a, b \in \mathbb{F}_p)$. Then affine coordinates compute addition and doubling as Eqs. 1 and 2. A point at infinity cannot be represented clearly by the affine coordinates. Thus, $\mathcal{O} + P$, $P + Q = \mathcal{O}$ and $2P = \mathcal{O}$, which cannot be computed correctly by the affine addition formulae, are so-called exceptional computations of affine addition formulae. In addition, $P + P$ becomes an exceptional computation of the affine addition formula. In summary, $\mathcal{O} + P$, $P + Q = \mathcal{O}$ and $P + P$ are exceptional computations of the affine addition formula and $2P = \mathcal{O}$ is the exceptional computation of the affine doubling formula. Similarly, $\mathcal{O} + P$ and $P + P$ are exceptional computations of Jacobian and projective addition formula. To reduce exceptional computations from affine coordinates, extended affine coordinates assign $(0, 0)$ as the point at infinity for elliptic curves without point $(0, 0)$, such as prime order elliptic curves [8]. Using the extended affine addition formulae, $P + Q = \mathcal{O}$ and $2P = \mathcal{O}$ can be computed as $(0, 0)$, which is exactly the point at infinity. Both $\mathcal{O} + P$ and $P + P$ are still exceptional computations of the extended affine addition formula. We use (extended) affine to indicate the mixed use of the original affine addition and the extended affine addition.

The complete addition (CA) formulae of an elliptic curve [15] can be used to compute the addition of any elliptic curve point pair, and thus, can be employed to secure scalar multiplication algorithms without introducing conditional statements to process exceptional computations. However, CA formulae are inefficient in terms of memory and computational costs. In addition, note that they only work for prime order elliptic curves.

Table 1 summarizes the computational cost of the elliptic curve addition formulae, where M, S, I, and A are the computational costs for one field multiplication, square, inversion, and addition, respectively. Further, m_a and m_b are the computational costs for one field multiplication with parameters a and b, respectively. Assuming that $S = 0.8M$, and ignoring the computational costs of m_a, m_b, and A, the computational cost of one elliptic curve addition (ADD) and one elliptic curve doubling (DBL) using the CA formulae is $24M$ in total. Subsequently, the computational cost of the ADD and DBL using affine addition formulae is more efficient than those using the CA formulae, Jacobian addition formulae, or projective addition formulae when $I < 8.8M$, $I < 8M$ or $I < 9.1M$, respectively. If we employ these addition formulae on NIST elliptic curves, where $a = -3$ and the computational cost m_b cannot be ignored, the computational cost of ADD and DBL using the CA formulae is $26.4M$ in total. The computational cost of ADD and DBL using affine addition formulae is more efficient when $I < 10M$.

2.2   Scalar Multiplication Algorithms

SCA has several attack methods to reveal significant bits of input scalars: a simple power analysis (SPA), which makes use of conditional statements applied during an algorithm depending on the data being processed; a differential power

Table 1. Computational cost of elliptic curve addition formulae

Addition formulae	Conditions	ADD $(P + Q)$	DBL $(2P)$	Memory
CA formulae [15]	$2 \nmid \#E(\mathbb{F}_p)$	$12M + 3m_a + 2m_b + 23A$	$12M + 3m_a + 2m_b + 23A$	15
Affine	–	$2M + S + I$	$2M + 2S + I$	5
Extended affine [8]	$(0, 0) \notin E(\mathbb{F}_p)$	$6M + S + I$	$4M + 4S + I$	7
Projective	–	$12M + 2S$	$7M + 5S$	7
Jacobian	–	$11M + 5S$	$M + 8S$	8

analysis (DPA), which uses the correlation between the power consumption and specific key-dependent bits; a timing attack, which uses the relation between the implementation time and the bits of the scalars; and a safe error attack (SEA), which uses dummy statements [2,5]. Therefore, to resist these attacks, we need to eliminate conditional statements in the ECSM for the SPA, the relation between the implementation time and the input scalars for the timing attack, and dummy statements for the SEA. In addition, the power consumption should be changed at each new execution for the DPA. Note that countermeasure to timing attack is taken by padding '0's in front of the input scalars to make certain that almost the same execution time can be easy employed in our algorithms [16]. In this paper, we focus on the SPA and SEA.

Regarding secure ECSM resisting SPA and SEA, three properties, namely, the *generality of k*, *secure generality*, and *executable coordinates* are defined in [8]. In their paper, the authors evaluated secure ECSM focusing on RL scalar multiplication algorithms. We can evaluate Joye's regular 2-ary LR algorithm (Algorithm 1) in the same way as shown in Theorem 1.

Algorithm 1. Joye's regular 2-ary LR algorithm [10]

Input: $P \in E(\mathbb{F}_p)$, $k = \sum_{i=0}^{\ell-1} k_i 2^i$
Output: kP
Uses: A, $R[1]$, $R[2]$
Initialization
1: $R[1] \leftarrow P$, $R[2] \leftarrow 2P$
2: $A \leftarrow (k_{\ell-1} - 1)P$
Main Loop
3: **for** $i = \ell - 2$ to 0 **do**
4:     $A \leftarrow 2A + R[1 + k_i]$
5: **end for**
Final Correction
6: $A \leftarrow A + R[1]$
7: **return** A

Theorem 1. *Joye's regular 2-ary LR algorithm satisfies the generality of k and the secure generality. Coordinates with CA formulae are its executable coordinates. Affine and Jacobian coordinates are not executable coordinates of this algorithm.*

New (two-bit) 2-ary RL scalar multiplication algorithms by improving Joye's regular 2-ary RL algorithm to make (extended) affine be *executable coordinates* for it are proposed in [8]. In fact, Joye's regular 2-ary LR algorithm uses two fewer memories than Joye's regular 2-ary RL algorithm. We would like to employ the same idea to improve Joye's regular LR algorithm to use the (extended) affine as *executable coordinates*.

2.3 Inversion-Reduction Combination-Addition Formulae

We can compute any two or more inversions of the field elements using only a single inversion by applying the Montgomery trick. The computational cost of nI becomes $3(n-1)M + I$, which is more efficient when $I > 3M$. Using this method, Eisentrager et al. proposed an affine doubling and addition algorithm (DA-algorithm), computing $2P+Q$ as $P+Q+P$ with $P(x_1, y_1)$, $Q(x_2, y_2)$ using the following formulae [4]:

$$x_3 = \lambda_1^2 - x_1 - x_2, y_3 = \lambda_1(x_1 - x_3) - y_1, \lambda_1 = \left(\frac{y_2 - y_1}{x_2 - x_1} \right) \tag{3}$$

$$x_4 = (\lambda_2 - \lambda_1)(\lambda_2 + \lambda_1) + x_2, y_4 = \lambda_2(x_1 - x_4) - y_1, \lambda_2 = -\lambda_1 - \frac{2y_1}{x_3 - x_1} \tag{4}$$

DA-algorithm computes an inversion of $(x_2 - x_1)^3(x_3 - x_1) = (x_2 - x_1)(y_2 - y_1)^2 - (2x_1 + x_2)(x_2 - x_1)^3$ first and then computes inversions of $(x_2 - x_1)$ and $(x_3 - x_1)$. The result (x_4, y_4) can be computed without computing (x_3, y_3) completely. The computational cost is $9M + 2S + I$.

Le and Nguyen proposed an affine double and quadruple algorithm (DQ-algorithm) [12]. Their algorithm can compute both $2P$ and $4P$ simultaneously with only one inversion computation. The computational cost is $8M + 8S + I$. Its memory use is improved to 11 field elements, as described in [8].

3   Secure and Efficient LR-ECSM Algorithms

Algorithm 1 satisfies the *generality of k* and the *secure generality*, and uses two fewer memories than Joye's regular 2-ary RL algorithm. The affine addition formulae save memory and are efficient depending on the ratio of inversion and multiplication costs but are not the *executive coordinates* of Algorithm 1. In the case of Joye's regular 2-ary RL algorithm, accelerated version with (extended) affine is proposed in [8]. However, the authors failed to apply them to Algorithm 1. With the advantages of Algorithm 1 and affine coordinates, in this section, we describe the improvement of Algorithm 1 to adapt (extended) affine.

First, we revise affine combination-addition formulae using the Montgomery trick, which are used in our new LR ECSM to enhance the efficiency. We then propose our new LR scalar multiplication algorithms with (extended) affine and prove their security.

3.1 Affine Combination-Addition Formulae

In this section, using the Montgomery trick, we revise several affine combination-addition formulae, which are used in our LR ECSM Algorithms 7, 8 and 9. Table 2 shows our affine combination-addition formulae together with the previous formulae. When using the Montgomery trick to reduce the inversion cost, inverses needed to be computed depend on each other. Thus, it is not straightforward to apply the Montgomery trick. First, we improve DQ-algorithm [8, 12] to optimize the use of memory as ten field elements in Algorithm 3, which saves one memory from [8].

Algorithm 2. DA-algorithm

Memory: $4+3=7$ field elements.

Computational cost: $9M + 2S + I$.

Input: $P = (x_1, y_1)$, $Q = (x_2, y_2)$
Output: $2P + Q$
1: $y_2 = y_2 - y_1$, $t_0 = y_2^2$, $t_1 = 2x_1 + x_2$
2: $x_2 = x_2 - x_1$, $t_2 = x_2^2$, $t_1 = t_1 t_2$
3: $t_0 = t_0 - t_1$, $t_1 = t_0 x_2$, $t_1 = t_1^{-1}$
4: $t_0 = t_0 t_1 y_2$, $t_1 = -2t_1 x_2 t_2 y_1 - t_0$, $t_2 = t_1 + t_0$
5: $t_0 = t_1 - t_0$, $t_0 = t_0 t_2 + x_2 + x_1$, $x_2 = x_2 + x_1$
6: $x_1 = (x_1 - t_0)t_1 - y_1$, $y_2 = y_2 + y_1$, $y_1 = x_1$, $x_1 = t_0$
7: **return** (x_1, y_1)

Algorithm 3. DQ-algorithm

Memory: $6+4=10$ field elements.

Computational cost: $8M + 8S + I$.

Input: $P(x_1, y_1)$
Output: $2P, 4P$
1: $t_0 = x_1^2$, $t_1 = 2y_1^2$, $t_2 = t_1^2$
2: $t_1 = 3((t_1 + x_1)^2 - t_0 - t_2)$, $t_0 = 3t_0 + a$, $t_3 = t_0^2$
3: $t_1 = (t_1 - t_3)t_0$, $t_2 = 2t_2$, $t_1 = t_1 - t_2$
4: $t_3 = 2t_1 y_1$, $t_3 = t_3^{-1}$, $t_0 = t_0 t_1 t_3$
5: $x_2 = t_0^2 - 2x_1$, $y_2 = (x_1 - x_2)t_0 - y_1$, $t_3 = t_2 t_3$
6: $t_0 = (3x_2^2 + a)t_3$, $x_3 = t_0^2 - 2x_2$, $y_3 = (x_2 - x_3)t_0 - y_2$
7: **return** $(x_2, y_2), (x_3, y_3)$

Algorithm 4. Double-add

Memory: $4+4=8$ field elements.

Computational cost: $9M + 5S + I$.

Input: $P = (x_1, y_1)$, $Q = (x_2, y_2)$
Output: $2P + Q$
1: $t_0 = (2y_1)^2$, $x_2 = x_2 + 2x_1$, $t_1 = -t_0 x_2$
2: $x_2 = x_2 - 2x_1$, $t_2 = 3x_1^2 + a$, $t_3 = t_2^2$
3: $t_1 = t_1 + t_3$, $t_3 = 2t_3 y_1$, $t_3 = (t_3)^{-1}$
4: $t_2 = t_2 t_3 t_1$, $t_3 = 2t_3 y_1 t_0$, $t_1 = t_2^2 - 2x_1$
5: $t_0 = (x_1 - t_1)t_2 - y_1$, $t_0 = (t_0 - y_2)t_3$
6: $x_1 = t_0^2 - x_2 - t_1$, $y_1 = (x_2 - x_1)t_0 - y_2$
7: **return** (x_1, y_1)

Algorithm 5. Two-Continuous Adds

Memory: $6+4=10$ field elements.

Computational cost: $9M + 4S + I$.

Input: $P = (x_1, y_1)$, $Q = (x_2, y_2)$, $R = (x_3, y_3)$
Output: $P + Q + R$
1: $y_2 = y_2 - y_1$, $t_0 = y_2^2$, $t_1 = x_2 - x_1$
2: $t_2 = t_1^2$, $t_3 = x_1 + x_2 + x_3$, $t_3 = t_0 - t_3 t_2$
3: $t_0 = t_1 t_3$, $t_0 = (t_0)^{-1}$, $y_2 = y_2 t_0 t_3$
4: $t_3 = y_2^2 - x_1 - x_2$, $x_2 = (x_1 - t_3)y_2 - y_1 - y_3$, $t_0 = t_0 t_1 t_2 x_2$, $x_2 = t_0^2 - x_3 - t_3$
5: $y_2 = (x_3 - x_2)t_0 - y_3$
6: **return** (x_2, y_2)

DA, the computation of $2P + Q$, is a basic computation formulae in the main loop of Algorithm 1. DA-algorithm is not described in detail, and it is thus unclear how much memory is required [4]. We specify the DA-algorithm to optimize the use of memory as seven field elements in Algorithm 2. DA-algorithm in [4] has exceptional inputs of $P + Q = \mathcal{O}$ and $P = Q$, where P and Q have the same x-coordinate.

If an exceptional input $P + Q = \mathcal{O}$ or $P = Q$ is computed using Algorithm 2, $-P$ is its output. That's $DA(P, Q) \to -P$, where $P + Q = \mathcal{O}$ or $P = Q$. If we make use of Algorithm 2 twice with exceptional input $P + Q = \mathcal{O}$ (for example $P = (x, y)$ and $Q = -P = (x, -y)$), then Algorithm 2 outputs $P \leftarrow DA(P, Q) = -P$ first, whereas $2P + Q = P$. Next, input the updated P and the original Q into the algorithm again, then Algorithm 2 outputs $P \leftarrow DA(-P, Q) = P$. Thus, Algorithm 2 outputs $DA(DA(P, Q), Q)$, where $P + Q = \mathcal{O}$, correctly. This is why we can not directly use Algorithm 2 in our Algorithm 7. In Algorithms 2 and 3, inversions are computed in the same way as in the extended affine formulae [8], which means an inversion of zero is computed as zero.

Algorithm 6. Quadruple-Add
Memory: 4+6=10 field elements.
Computational cost: $18M + 14S + I$.

Input: $P(x_1, y_1)$, $Q(x_2, y_2)$
Output: $4P + Q$
1: $t_0 = x_1^2$, $t_1 = 2y_1^2$, $t_2 = t_1^2$, $t_3 = (t_1 + x_1)^2 - t_0 - t_2$, $t_0 = 3t_0 + a$, $t_4 = t_0^2$, $t_4 = t_4 - 2t_3$
2: $t_3 = t_3 - t_4$, $t_3 = t_0 t_3$, $t_3 = t_3 - 2t_2$, $t_1 = 2t_1 x_2 + 2t_4$, $t_5 = t_3^2$, $t_1 = 4t_1 t_5$, $t_5 = 4t_2 a$
3: $t_4 = 3t_4^2$, $t_4 = t_4 + t_5$, $t_4 = t_4^2$, $t_4 = t_4 - t_1$, $t_5 = 2t_3 t_4 y_1$, $t_5 = (t_5)^{-1}$, $t_1 = 2t_2 t_4 t_5$
4: $t_5 = t_3 t_5$, $t_0 = t_0 t_4 t_5$, $t_2 = t_2^2$, $t_5 = 32 t_2 t_5 y_1$, $t_2 = t_0^2 - 2x_1$, $x_1 = (x_1 - t_2)t_0 - y_1$
5: $y_1 = 3t_2^2 + a$, $t_1 = t_1 y_1$, $y_1 = t_1^2 - 2t_2$, $t_2 = (t_2 - y_1)t_1 - x_1$, $x_1 = 4x_1^2$, $t_5 = t_5 x_1$
6: $t_2 = t_2 - y_2$, $t_2 = t_2 t_5$, $x_1 = t_2^2 - x_2 - y_1$, $y_1 = (x_2 - x_1)t_2 - y_2$
7: **return** (x_1, y_1)

Table 2. Comparison of affine combination-addition algorithms

Affine combination-addition algorithms	Ordinary	Computational cost	Memory
DA-algorithm Algorithm 2 $(2P + Q)$ [4]	$4M + 3S + 2I$	$9M + 2S + I$	7
DQ-algorithm Algorithm 3 $(2P, 4P)$ [12]	$4M + 4S + 2I$	$8M + 8S + I$	10
Double-Add Algorithm 4 $(2P + Q)$	$4M + 3S + 2I$	$9M + 5S + I$	8
Two-Continuous Adds Algorithm 5 $(P + Q + R)$	$4M + 2S + 2I$	$9M + 4S + I$	10
Quadruple-Add Algorithm 6 $(4P + Q)$	$6M + 5S + 3I$	$18M + 14S + I$	10

Our double-add algorithm (Algorithm 4) computes $2P$ followed by $2P + Q$ instead of first computing $P + Q$, and then $(P + Q) + P$ in Algorithm 2. Algorithm 4 can correctly compute $2P + Q$ if $2P \neq \mathcal{O}$, $2P \neq Q$, $2P + Q \neq \mathcal{O}$ and $Q \neq \mathcal{O}$. Note that Algorithm 4 can compute $2P + Q$ correctly even when $P + Q = \mathcal{O}$ or $P = Q$, which cannot be computed correctly by Algorithm 2. Algorithm 4 can be used in Algorithm 7 without exceptional inputs. The memory usage is eight field elements and the computational cost is $9M + 5S + I$. Next, Algorithm 5 combines two continuous affine additions into a single unit, which can compute $P + Q + R$ correctly if $P + Q \neq \mathcal{O}$, $P + Q + R \neq \mathcal{O}$, $P \neq Q$, $P + Q \neq R$ and $P, Q, R \neq \mathcal{O}$, used in Algorithm 8. The memory usage is ten field elements and the computational cost is $9M + 4S + I$. Finally, our affine quadruple and addition algorithm (Algorithm 6) combines the computations in the main loop of our extended new two-bit 2-ary LR algorithm (Algorithm 9), $4P + Q$. In general, to obtain $4P + Q$, we need to compute $P \leftarrow 2P$, $P \leftarrow 2P$, and $P \leftarrow P + Q$, which cost $3I$. Algorithm 6 can compute $4P + Q$ correctly if $4P + Q \neq \mathcal{O}$, $4P \neq Q$ and $P, 2P, 4P, Q \neq \mathcal{O}$. The memory usage is ten field elements and the computational cost is $18M + 14S + I$.

3.2 Secure and Efficient LR Scalar Multiplication

We improve Algorithm 1 to a new 2-ary LR algorithm (Algorithm 7) and a new two-bit 2-ary LR algorithm (Algorithm 8). We then combine Algorithms 7 and 8 with affine combination-addition algorithms to reduce the inversion computations.

Algorithm 8 uses two-bit scanning, which is different from Algorithm 7. Algorithm 8 adjusts the length of the input scalars k including the sign bit to be even by padding '0's after the sign bit of input scalars[1]. Therefore, two-bit scanning can operate well for both even and odd lengths of input scalars k.

Algorithm 7. New 2-ary LR	**Algorithm 8.** New two-bit 2-ary LR
Input: $P \in E(\mathbb{F}_p)$, $k \in [-\frac{N}{2}, \frac{N}{2}]$, $k = (-1)^{k_\ell} \sum_{i=0}^{\ell-1} k_i 2^i$, sign bit $k_\ell \in \{0,1\}$	**Input:** $P \in E(\mathbb{F}_p)$, $k \in [-\frac{N}{2}, \frac{N}{2}]$, $k = (-1)^{k_\ell} \sum_{i=0}^{\ell-1} k_i 2^i$, sign bit $k_\ell \in \{0,1\}$
Output: kP	**Output:** kP
Uses: A, and R[0], R[1]	**Uses:** A and R[0], R[1], R[2], R[3]
Initialization	**Initialization**
1: $A \leftarrow 2P$	1: $R[1] \leftarrow -P$, $\{R[0], R[2]\} \leftarrow DQ(R[1])$
2: $R[0] \leftarrow -2P$	2: $R[3] \leftarrow R[0]$, $A \leftarrow -R[0]$
3: $R[1] \leftarrow -P$	**Main loop**
Main loop	3: **for** $i = \ell - 1$ to 1 **do**
4: **for** $i = \ell - 1$ to 1 **do**	4: $A \leftarrow DQ(A)[1] = 4A$
5: $\quad A \leftarrow 2A + R[k_i]$	5: $\quad A \leftarrow A + R[k_i + 2] + R[k_{i-1}]$, $i = i - 2$
6: **end for**	6: **end for**
Final correction	**Final correction**
7: $A \leftarrow 2A + R[0]$	7: $A \leftarrow 2A + R[0]$
8: $A \leftarrow A + R[k_0]$	8: $A \leftarrow A + R[k_0]$
9: $A \leftarrow (-1)^{k_\ell} \times A$	9: $A \leftarrow (-1)^{k_\ell} \times A$
10: **return** A	10: **return** A

Both Algorithms 7 and 8 assume that $k \in \mathbb{Z}/N\mathbb{Z}$ is in $k \in [-\frac{N}{2}, \frac{N}{2}]$, which ensures that our algorithms exclude exceptional computations as shown in Theorem 2. Then, k is represented by $k = (-1)^{k_\ell} \sum_{i=0}^{\ell-1} k_i 2^i$ ($k_i \in \{0,1\}$), where $k_\ell \in \{0,1\}$ is the sign bit and $0 \leq |k| \leq \frac{N}{2}$. Algorithms 7 and 8 consist of three parts: initialization, a main loop, and a final correction. Compared with Algorithm 1, we change the initialization of $R[.]$ and A to avoid the exceptional initialization of $A \leftarrow \mathcal{O}$ when $k_{\ell-1} = 1$ and the exceptional computations of $2\mathcal{O} + P$, $2\mathcal{O} + 2P$, and $-2P + 2P$ in the main loop. Our initializations of $R[.]$ and A cause $4P$, or $3P$, to be added to the final result when $k_0 = 0$, or $k_0 = 1$, respectively. We correct this in Steps 7 and 8 of the final correction of Algorithm 7 and Algorithm 8, and thus, avoid the exceptional computation, $A \leftarrow A + R[1]$, in the original final correction of Algorithm 1. Remark that the extended affine is used only once in Step 8 of Algorithm 7 and Algorithm 8. Actually, the extended

---

[1] The sign bit is '0' at the beginning of k when k is positive, or '1' at the beginning of k when k is negative.

affine is only necessary for $k = 0$. If $k = 0$ is excluded from the input, then only the original affine can work well.

As for further reduction of inversion computations, Algorithms 2 or 4 can be applied in Steps 5 and 7 of Algorithm 7, respectively. Although Algorithm 2 cannot be directly employed in Algorithm 7 when $k_{\ell-1} = 0$, twice use of of Algorithm 2 to exceptional inputs $A + R[k_i] = \mathcal{O}$ outputs a correct result $A \leftarrow 2P$. Thus, in Algorithm 7, using Algorithm 2, we can make sure it can compute correctly by adjusting the number of '0's from $k_{\ell-1}$ until the first bit '1' on the left to be even, by padding '0's after the sign bit of k. Algorithm 3 is applied in Step 4 of Algorithm 8. Algorithm 5 is applied in Step 5 of Algorithm 8.

Our Algorithms 7 and 8 satisfy the *generality of* k as well as the *secure generality*, and the affine coordinates are *executable coordinates* for them. Algorithms 7 and 8 have no conditional or dummy statements. (Extended) affine and affine combination-addition algorithms can be employed without introducing conditional statements, which will be given in the final paper. Thus, Algorithms 7 and 8 with (extended) affine and affine combination-addition are secure ECSM algorithms.

Algorithm 9. Extended New two-bit 2-ary LR algorithm

Input: $P \in E(\mathbb{F}_p)$
$\quad k \in [-\frac{N}{2}, \frac{N}{2}]$, $k = (-1)^{k_\ell} \sum_{i=0}^{\ell-1} k_i 2^i$, sign bit $k_\ell \in \{0, 1\}$
Output: kP
Uses: A and R[0], R[1], R[2], R[3]
Initialization
1: $\{R[2], A\} \leftarrow DQ(P)$, $R[1] \leftarrow -(R[2] + P)$, $R[0] \leftarrow -(R[2] + A)$
2: $R[3] = P \leftarrow -(P + A)$, $R[2] \leftarrow -R[2]$
Main loop
3: **for** $i = \ell - 1$ to 1 **do**
4: $\quad A \leftarrow QA(A, R[2k_i + k_{i-1}])$ (Algorithm 6), $i = i - 2$
5: **end for**
Final correction
6: $R[1] \leftarrow R[1] - R[2]$, $R[0] \leftarrow R[3] - R[1]$
7: $A \leftarrow 2A + R[0]$, $A \leftarrow A + R[k_0]$, $A \leftarrow (-1)^{k_\ell} \times A$
8: **return** A

Theorem 2. *Let $E(\mathbb{F}_p)$ be an elliptic curve without two-torsion points. Let $P \in E(\mathbb{F}_p)$, $P \neq \mathcal{O}$ be an elliptic curve point, whose order is $N > 4$. Then, Algorithms 7 and 8 using (extended) affine and affine combination-addition formulae can compute kP correctly without exceptional computations for any input $k \in [-\frac{N}{2}, \frac{N}{2}]$.*

Algorithm 7 combined with Algorithm 2 (or Algorithm 4) can reduce the inversions from two-times to one-time in the main loop. By contrast, Algorithm 8 computes two inversions in the main loop. To reduce inversions to one-time in the main loop of Algorithm 8, we propose an extended new two-bit 2-ary LR algorithm (Algorithm 9), where our Quadruple-Add algorithm (Algorithm 6) is used in the main loop of Algorithm 9.

In Algorithm 9, we initialize $R[0] = -6P$, $R[1] = -5P$, $R[2] = -4P$, $R[3] = -3P$, $A = 2P$, which can be computed without exceptional computations if $N > 6$. Because of initialization, the condition of $N > 4$ is changed to $N > 6$. We compute $R[0]$ and $R[1]$ back to $-2P$ and $-P$ in Step 6 of Algorithm 9 to what they were in Algorithm 8 to make sure the remaining part of the final correction of Algorithm 9 can be computed correctly. Algorithm 9 has the *generality of k* and the *secure generality* and avoids all exceptional computations of the affine formulae when $k \in [-\frac{N}{2}, \frac{N}{2}]$, similar to Algorithm 8. The proof of Theorems 2 can be easy extended to Algorithm 9.

4   Efficiency and Memory Analysis

4.1   Theoretical Analysis

Table 3. Computational cost and memory cost analysis

	Computational cost	Memory
Joye's RL + CA [10,15]	$(\ell + 1)(24M + 6m_a + 4m_b + 46A)$	19
2-ary RL + (extended) affine [8]	$(6.4\ell + 16)M + (2\ell + 4)I$	12
two-bit 2-ary RL + (extended) affine [8]	$(10\ell + 23.2)M + (\frac{3\ell+9}{2})I$	15
Algorithm 1 + CA [10,15]	$\ell(24M + 6m_a + 4m_b + 46A)$	16
Algorithm 7 + (extended) affine	$(6.4\ell + 10.4)M + (2\ell + 2)I$	10
Algorithm 7 + (extended) affine + Algorithm 2	$(10.6\ell + 10.4)M + (\ell + 2)I$	10
Algorithm 7 + (extended) affine + Algorithm 4	$(13\ell + 10.4)M + (\ell + 2)I$	11
Algorithm 8 + (extended) affine	$(10\ell + 17.6)M + (\frac{3\ell+5}{2})I$	13
Algorithm 8 + (extended) affine + Algorithm 5	$(13.3\ell + 18.5)M + (\ell + 2)I$	13
Algorithm 9 + (extended) affine + Algorithm 6	$(14.6\ell + 27)M + (\frac{\ell+17}{2})I$	17

Table 4. The most efficient algorithm with the conditions of $r = \frac{I}{M}$ ($m_a = m_b = A = 0$, ℓ is bit length of k)

Algorithm	Condition	Memory
Algorithm 7 + (extended) affine	$r < 4.2$	10
Algorithm 7 + (extended) affine + Algorithm 2	$4.2 \leq r \leq \frac{8+33.2/\ell}{1-13/\ell}$	10
Algorithm 9 + (extended) affine + Algorithm 6	$\frac{8+33.2/\ell}{1-13/\ell} \leq r \leq \frac{18.8-54/\ell}{1+17/\ell}$	17
Algorithm 1 + CA [10,15]	$r > \frac{18.8-54/\ell}{1+17/\ell}$	16

We analyzed the computational and memory costs of Algorithms 7–9 with (extended) affine and affine combination-addition algorithms in comparison with

Table 5. NIST elliptic curves($y^2 = x^3 - 3x + c$)

P-224	c = 18958286285566660800040866854449392641550468096867932107578723467256
P-256	c = 41058363725152142129326129780047268409114441015993725554835256314039467401291
P-384	c = 27580193559597058778490118403890480930569058563615685214287073019886892413098608651362607648837451077654397612305

the Algorithm 1 with CA formulae, Joye's regular 2-ary RL algorithm with CA formulae, and two RL algorithms [8], the results of which are shown in Table 3.

The memory cost considers the number of $\mathbb{F}_p$ elements, including the memory used in the scalar multiplication algorithms. For the computational cost, we evaluated all algorithms by estimating the number of modulo multiplications (M), modulo squaring (S), multiplications with parameters a and b (m_a and m_b), additions (A), and inversions (I). We assume that $S = 0.8M$, and that ℓ is the length of the input scalar k. Let us describe the ratio of inversion cost to the multiplication cost by r, i.e., $I = rM$.

The total computational cost of Algorithm 1 with CA formulae is $24\ell M$, and that of Joye's RL with CA formulae is $(\ell + 1)24M$, if we ignore the computational costs of m_a, m_b, and A. Therefore, Algorithm 1 with CA formulae is more efficient than Joye's regular 2-ary RL algorithm with CA formulae and uses less memory. Both the memory and computational costs of Algorithm 7 with Algorithm 2 are less than those of Algorithm 7 with Algorithm 4. However, as stated earlier, Algorithm 2 can be applied to Algorithm 7 only when the number of '0's between the sign bit and the first bit '1' on the left is even. Packaging all computations of the main loop as a single computation unit reduces the inversion computations, and we can see that Algorithm 9 with (extended) affine and Algorithm 6 has a computational cost of $(14.6\ell + 27)M + (\frac{\ell+17}{2})I$, which is the best when $\frac{8+33.2/\ell}{1-13/\ell} \leq r \leq \frac{18.8-54/\ell}{1+17/\ell}$. Therefore, if the ratio r is approximately 11, then Algorithm 9 with (extended) affine and Algorithm 6 is the most efficient approach. Its memory usage is costly but less than that of Joye's RL with CA formulae. Table 4 shows the most efficient ECSM algorithm with the ratio $r = \frac{I}{M}$. Note that the conditions do not change according to the size of the scalar ℓ. In numerous cases, such as the NIST elliptic curves in Table 5, we can only assume that $m_a = A = 0$. The interval of r where our algorithms are more efficient is larger.

Regarding the memory cost, Algorithm 7 uses the least amount of memory of ten field elements, which reduces that of Algorithm 1 with CA formulae by 37.5%.

4.2 Experimental Analysis

We implemented all algorithms listed in Table 3 on NIST P-224, P-256, and P-384. Table 5 shows their comparison. We randomly generated 2×10^5 test scalars during the interval of $[-\frac{N}{2}, \frac{N}{2}]$, where N is the order of point P used to measure the average scalar multiplication time of the algorithms. The experimental platform uses C programming language with GUN MP 6.1.2, which is a multiple precision arithmetic library, and Intel (R) Core (TM) i7-8650U CPU @ 1.90 GHz 2.11 GHz personal computer with 16.0 GB RAM 64-bit; the operating system is Windows 10. We turn off Intel turbo boost, which is Intel's technique that automatically raises certain of its processors' operating frequency, and thus performance, when demanding tasks are running to make sure our computer works at 2.11 GHz.

Table 6. Average computation time for one scalar multiplication (milliseconds)

	P-224	P-256	P-384	Memory
Joye's RL + CA [10,15]	4.02373	4.593395	7.68237	19
2-ary RL + (extended) affine [8]	2.87742	3.552715	7.733155	12
Two-bit 2-ary RL [8] + (extended) affine	2.56329	3.049545	6.113945	15
Algorithm 1 + CA [10,15]	3.945075	4.591625	7.7481	16
Algorithm 7 + (extended) affine	2.8306	3.804565	7.6338	10
Algorithm 7 + (extended) affine + Algorithm 2	2.15022	2.554765	4.695785	10
Algorithm 7 + (extended) affine + Algorithm 4	2.408305	2.962435	6.042845	11
Algorithm 8 + (extended) affine	2.53023	3.259545	6.23321	13
Algorithm 8 + (extended) affine + Algorithm 5	2.40751	2.698705	5.55319	13
Algorithm 9 + (extended) affine + Algorithm 6	1.904045	2.684335	4.92462	17

Table 7. Time of fundamental computations of GUN MP (milliseconds)

	M	S	I	$\frac{I}{M}$
224 bits	0.00138518	0.00129926	0.00486555	4.08232
256 bits	0.00130389	0.00129878	0.00548586	4.56714
384 bits	0.0014351	0.00141946	0.00766026	6.22689

Table 6 shows the average scalar multiplication time. Table 6 shows that Algorithm 7 with Algorithm 2 is the most efficient for NIST P-256 and P-384, which reduces the computation time of Joye's RL with CA by 46.56% for P-224, 44.38% for P-256, and 38.88% for P-384, and the computation time of Algorithm 1 with CA by 45.5% for P-224, 44.36% for P-256, and 39.39% for P-384, and the computation time of two-bit 2-ary RL [8] by 16.11% for P-224, 16.22% for P-256, and 23.2% for P-384. Algorithm 7 with Algorithm 2 uses the least amount of memory of ten field elements. Algorithm 9 with (extended) affine and Algorithm 6 is the most efficient for NIST P-224.

As we previously discussed, the efficiency of our algorithms depends on the ratio $r = \frac{I}{M}$. Algorithm 7 with (extended) affine and Algorithm 2 is the most efficient when applied to P-256 and P-384 during our experiments. The ratio $r = \frac{I}{M}$ in the GUN MP library is 4.56714 and 6.22689, respectively, as shown in Table 7. These implementation results reflect the theoretic analysis in Table 4.

Algorithm 9 with (extended) affine and Algorithm 6 is the most efficient when applied to P-224, where the ratio $\frac{I}{M}$ is 4.08232. By contrast, Algorithm 7 with (extended) affine is the most efficient, as indicated in Table 4. For the implementation time, both function calls and the number of loops in an algorithm cost time according to the compiler. Algorithm 9 has much fewer function calls and loops than the other algorithms, which may save time.

5 Conclusion

We improved the affine combination-addition formulae of double-add (DA), double-quadruple (DQ), two-adds (TA), and quadruple-add (QA) in terms of the memory or computational cost. We also proposed three new secure LR scalar multiplication Algorithms 7, 8 and 9, and we proved that our new LR ECSM algorithms satisfy the *generality of k* and the *secure generality*; in addition, they can exclude exceptional computations of $\mathcal{O} + P$, $P + Q = \mathcal{O}$, and $P + P$, which means the affine coordinates are *executable coordinates* for them.

We analyzed our LR scalar multiplication algorithms with (extended) affine and affine combination-addition formulae from the theoretical perspective. In many cases, such as with NIST elliptic curves, we can only omit the computational cost of m_a and A. In this case, our algorithms of Algorithm 7 with (extended) affine, Algorithm 7 with (extended) affine and Algorithm 2, and Algorithm 9 with (extended) affine and Algorithm 6 are the most efficient when $\frac{I}{M} \leq \frac{26.8-54/\ell}{1+17/\ell}$ (24.93 at $\ell = 256$) compared to Algorithm 1 with CA formulae.

We also analyzed the algorithms from an experimental perspective. Algorithm 7 with (extended) affine and Algorithm 2 achieves a high efficiency. Algorithm 7 with (extended) affine and Algorithm 2 uses the least memory of ten field elements, which reduces the memory requirements of Algorithm 1 with CA formulae by 37.5%.

Acknowledgements. This work is partially supported by CREST (JPMJCR1404) at Japan Science and Technology Agency, enPiT (Education Network for Practical Information Technologies) at MEXT, and Innovation Platform for Society 5.0 at MEXT.

References

1. Afreen, R., Mehrotra, S.: A review on elliptic curve cryptography for embedded systems. arXiv preprint arXiv:1107.3631 (2011)
2. Ciet, M., Joye, M.: (Virtually) free randomization techniques for elliptic curve cryptography. In: Qing, S., Gollmann, D., Zhou, J. (eds.) ICICS 2003. LNCS, vol. 2836, pp. 348–359. Springer, Heidelberg (2003). https://doi.org/10.1007/978-3-540-39927-8_32
3. Cohen, H., Miyaji, A., Ono, T.: Efficient elliptic curve exponentiation using mixed coordinates. In: Ohta, K., Pei, D. (eds.) ASIACRYPT 1998. LNCS, vol. 1514, pp. 51–65. Springer, Heidelberg (1998). https://doi.org/10.1007/3-540-49649-1_6

4. Eisenträger, K., Lauter, K., Montgomery, P.L.: Fast elliptic curve arithmetic and improved weil pairing evaluation. In: Joye, M. (ed.) CT-RSA 2003. LNCS, vol. 2612, pp. 343–354. Springer, Heidelberg (2003). https://doi.org/10.1007/3-540-36563-X_24

5. Fouque, P.-A., Guilley, S., Murdica, C., Naccache, D.: Safe-errors on SPA protected implementations with the atomicity technique. In: Ryan, P.Y.A., Naccache, D., Quisquater, J.-J. (eds.) The New Codebreakers. LNCS, vol. 9100, pp. 479–493. Springer, Heidelberg (2016). https://doi.org/10.1007/978-3-662-49301-4_30

6. Goundar, R.R., Joye, M., Miyaji, A., Rivain, M., Venelli, A.: Scalar multiplication on weierstraß elliptic curves from Co-Z arithmetic. J. Cryptogr. Eng. 1(2), 161 (2011)

7. Izu, T., Takagi, T.: A fast parallel elliptic curve multiplication resistant against side channel attacks. In: Naccache, D., Paillier, P. (eds.) PKC 2002. LNCS, vol. 2274, pp. 280–296. Springer, Heidelberg (2002). https://doi.org/10.1007/3-540-45664-3_20

8. Jin, Y., Miyaji, A.: Secure and compact elliptic curve cryptosystems. In: Jang-Jaccard, J., Guo, F. (eds.) ACISP 2019. LNCS, vol. 11547, pp. 639–650. Springer, Cham (2019). https://doi.org/10.1007/978-3-030-21548-4_36

9. Joye, M.: Highly regular right-to-left algorithms for scalar multiplication. In: Paillier, P., Verbauwhede, I. (eds.) CHES 2007. LNCS, vol. 4727, pp. 135–147. Springer, Heidelberg (2007). https://doi.org/10.1007/978-3-540-74735-2_10

10. Joye, M.: Highly regular m-ary powering ladrs. In: Jacobson, M.J., Rijmen, V., Safavi-Naini, R. (eds.) SAC 2009. LNCS, vol. 5867, pp. 350–363. Springer, Heidelberg (2009). https://doi.org/10.1007/978-3-642-05445-7_22

11. Joye, M., Yen, S.-M.: The montgomery powering ladder. In: Kaliski, B.S., Koç, K., Paar, C. (eds.) CHES 2002. LNCS, vol. 2523, pp. 291–302. Springer, Heidelberg (2003). https://doi.org/10.1007/3-540-36400-5_22

12. Le, D.P., Nguyen, B.P.: Fast point quadrupling on elliptic curves. In: Proceedings of the Third Symposium on Information and Communication Technology, pp. 218–222. ACM (2012)

13. Mamiya, H., Miyaji, A., Morimoto, H.: Efficient countermeasures against RPA, DPA, and SPA. In: Joye, M., Quisquater, J.-J. (eds.) CHES 2004. LNCS, vol. 3156, pp. 343–356. Springer, Heidelberg (2004). https://doi.org/10.1007/978-3-540-28632-5_25

14. Miyaji, A., Mo, Y.: How to enhance the security on the least significant bit. In: Pieprzyk, J., Sadeghi, A.-R., Manulis, M. (eds.) CANS 2012. LNCS, vol. 7712, pp. 263–279. Springer, Heidelberg (2012). https://doi.org/10.1007/978-3-642-35404-5_20

15. Renes, J., Costello, C., Batina, L.: Complete addition formulas for prime order elliptic curves. In: Fischlin, M., Coron, J.-S. (eds.) EUROCRYPT 2016. LNCS, vol. 9665, pp. 403–428. Springer, Heidelberg (2016). https://doi.org/10.1007/978-3-662-49890-3_16

16. Susella, R., Montrasio, S.: A compact and exception-free ladder for all short weierstrass elliptic curves. In: Lemke-Rust, K., Tunstall, M. (eds.) CARDIS 2016. LNCS, vol. 10146, pp. 156–173. Springer, Cham (2017). https://doi.org/10.1007/978-3-319-54669-8_10

17. Wronski, M.: Faster point scalar multiplication on short weierstrass elliptic curves over FP using twisted hessian curves over FP2. J. Telecommun. Inf. Technol. (2016)

Short Papers

User Identity Linkage Across Social Networks via Community Preserving Network Embedding

Xiaoyu Guo[1], Yan Liu[1(✉)], Lian Liu[2], Guangsheng Zhang[2], Jing Chen[1], and Yuan Zhao[1]

[1] State Key Laboratory of Mathematical Engineering and Advanced Computing, Zhengzhou 450001, China
guoxy_ieu@outlook.com, ms_liuyan@aliyun.com, jingchen1101@yeah.net, zhao18703973381@163.com
[2] Investigation Technology Center PLCMC, Beijing 100000, China
donick@163.com, zhanggstide@163.com

Abstract. User Identity Linkage (UIL) across social networks refers to the recognition of the accounts belonging to the same individual among multiple social network platforms. Most existing network structure-based methods focus on extracting local structural proximity from the local context of nodes, but the inherent community structure of the social network is largely ignored. In this paper, with an awareness of labeled anchor nodes as supervised information, we propose a novel community structure-based algorithm for UIL, called CUIL. Firstly, inspired by the network embedding, CUIL considers both proximity structure and community structure of the social network simultaneously to capture the structural information conveyed by the original network as much as possible when learning the feature vectors of nodes in social networks. Given a set of labeled anchor nodes, CUIL then applies the back-propagation neural network to learn a stable cross-network mapping function for identities linkage. Experiments conducted on the real-world dataset show that CUIL outperforms the state-of-the-art network structure-based methods in terms of linking precision even with only a few labeled anchor nodes. CUIL is also shown to be efficient with low vector dimensionality and a small number of training iterations.

Keywords: User Identity Linkage · Community structure · Network embedding · Social network analysis

1 Introduction

Different social networks provide different types of services, people usually join multiple social networks simultaneously according to their needs of work or life [1]. Each user often has multiple separate accounts in different social networks. However, these accounts belonging to the same user are mostly isolated without any connection or correspondence to each other.

The typical aim of User Identity Linkage (UIL) is to detect that users from different social platforms are actually one and the same individual [2]. It is a crucial prerequisite

J. K. Liu and H. Cui (Eds.): ACISP 2020, LNCS 12248, pp. 621–630, 2020.
https://doi.org/10.1007/978-3-030-55304-3_32

for many interesting inter-network applications, such as friend recommendation across platforms, user behavior prediction, information dissemination across networks, etc.

Early research uses the public attributes and statistical features of users to solve the UIL problem [3, 4], such as username, user's hobbies, language patterns, etc. However, there is a lot of false information in the user's public attributes and user's statistics in different social networks are unbalanced. The correctness and richness of user's public attributes cannot be guaranteed.

Compared with user's attributes, the relationships between users are reliable and rich, and can also be directly used to solve the UIL problem. Therefore, the methods based on network structure are receiving more and more attention. Most of the existing methods [5–8] extract the local structural proximity from the context of nodes and focus on the microscopic structure of network. However, some typical properties of social network are ignored, such as community structure, etc.

Community structure is one of the most prominent features of social networks. A user primarily interacts with a part of the social network. Users in the same community are closely connected, but the connections among users from different communities are relatively sparse [9]. If a pair of friends connects closely to each other on Twitter and they exist in the same community because of common hobbies, then they should be closely connected and in the same community on Foursquare or Facebook.

In this paper, we introduce the community structure into user identity linkage across social networks and propose a novel model via community preserving network embedding, called CUIL. The contributions of this paper are as follows:

- CUIL applies network embedding and community structure to UIL problem simultaneously to retain the proximity structure and community structure to the vector representations of nodes; and learns a nonlinear mapping function between two networks through the BP neural network to achieve a unified model for UIL.
- We perform several experiments on a real-world dataset. The results show that CUIL can significantly improve the accuracy of user identity linkage compared to the state-of-the-art methods, e.g., up to 45% for *top-1* and more than 60% for *top-5* in terms of linking precision.

2 Preliminaries

2.1 Terminology Definition

We consider a set of social networks as $G^1, G^2, \ldots, G^n$, each of which is represented as an undirected and unweighted graph. Let $G = (V, E)$ represent the network, where V is the set of nodes, each representing a user, and E is the set of edges, each representing the relationship between two users.

In this paper, we take two social networks as an example, which are treated as source network, $G^s = (V^s, E^s)$, and target network, $G^t = (V^t, E^t)$ respectively. For ease of description, we have the following definitions.

Definition 1 (Anchor Link). *Link (v_i^s, v_k^t) is an anchor link between G^s and G^t iff. $(v_i^s \in V^s) \wedge (v_k^t \in V^t) \wedge (v_i^s$ and v_k^t are accounts owned by the same user in G^s and G^t respectively).*

Definition 2 (Anchor Users). *Users who are involved in two social networks simultaneously are defined as the anchor users (nodes) while the other users are non-anchor users (nodes).*

2.2 Problem Definition

Based on the definitions of the above terms, we formally define the problem of user identity linkage across social networks. The UIL problem is to determine whether a pair of accounts, (v_i^s, v_k^t), $v_i^s \in V^s$, $v_k^t \in V^t$, corresponds to the same real natural person, which can be formally defined as:

$$\Phi_V\left(v_i^s, v_k^t\right) = \begin{cases} 1 & v_i^s = v_k^t, \\ 0 & otherwise. \end{cases} \tag{1}$$

where $\Phi_V\left(v_i^s, v_k^t\right) = 1$ means v_i^s and v_k^t belong to the same individual.

3   CUIL: The Proposed Model

As shown in Fig. 1, CUIL consists of three main components: Cross Network Extension, Network Embedding, and BP Neural Network-based Mapping Learning, which will be introduced in detail later.

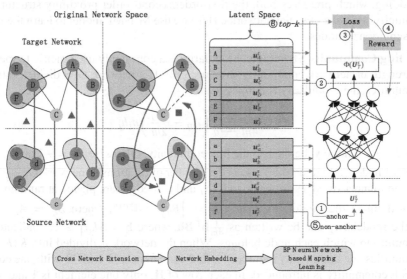

Fig. 1. The framework of CUIL. In the process of mapping learning, the training process is as ①–④, and the testing process is as ⑤⑥.

3.1 Cross Network Extension

For a real-world social network dataset, some edges that exist in practice may be unobserved, as they have not been explicitly built or failed to be crawled. These missing edges can lead to unreliable representations when embedding networks into latent vector spaces. In order to solve this problem, we apply *Cross Network Extension* to extend the source network and target network respectively according to the observed anchor links.

Usually, if two anchor nodes in the source network are connected, then their counterparts in the target network should also be connected [10]. Based on such an observation, we can perform *Cross Network Extension* by the following strategy. Given two social networks G^s, G^t, and a set of anchor links T, the extended network $\widetilde{G^s} = \left(\widetilde{V^s}, \widetilde{E^s}\right)$ can be described as:

$$\widetilde{V^s} = V^s \tag{2}$$

$$\widetilde{E^s} = E^s \cup \left\{ \left(v_i^s, v_j^s\right) : (v_i^s, v_k^t) \in T, (v_j^s, v_l^t) \in T, (v_k^t, v_l^t) \in E^t \right\} \tag{3}$$

Similarly, the target network G^t is extended into $\widetilde{G^t}$.

3.2 Network Embedding

The first-order and second-order proximity describe social networks from the microscopic level, while the community structure constrains the network representation from a mesoscopic perspective. M-NMF [11] integrates the community structure into network embedding, which preserves both the first-order/second-order proximity structure and community structure of social networks. Here we use M-NMF model to learn the vector representation of nodes.

Modeling Community Structure. Modularity is a commonly used metric to measure the strength of network community structure [12]. If a network G is divided into two communities, the modularity is defined as:

$$Q = \frac{1}{4m} \sum_{ij} \left(A_{ij} - \frac{k_i k_j}{2m} \right) h_i h_j \tag{4}$$

where $h_i = 1$ if node v_i belongs to the first community, otherwise, $h_i = -1$ and k_i is the degree of node v_i. And m $= \frac{1}{2} \sum_i k_i$ is the number of relations in network G, $\frac{k_i k_j}{2m}$ is the expected number of edges between nodes v_i and v_j if edges are placed at random.

By defining the modularity matrix $\mathbf{B} = \left[B_{ij}\right] \in \mathbb{R}^{n*n}$, where $B_{ij} = A_{ij} - \frac{k_i k_j}{2m}$, then the modularity can be written as $\frac{1}{4m} \mathbf{h}^T \mathbf{B} \mathbf{h}$, where $\mathbf{h} = \left[h_{ij}\right] \in \mathbb{R}^n$ indicates the community to which each node belongs. When the network is divided into $K(K > 2)$ communities, the community membership indicator matrix $\mathbf{H} \in \mathbb{R}^{n*K}$ with one column for each community is introduced. In each row of $\mathbf{H}$, only one element is 1 and all the others are 0, so we have the constraint $tr\left(\mathbf{H}^T \mathbf{H}\right) = n$. Finally, we have:

$$Q = tr\left(\mathbf{H}^T \mathbf{B} \mathbf{H}\right), \quad s.t. \quad tr\left(\mathbf{H}^T \mathbf{H}\right) = n \tag{5}$$

where $tr(\mathbf{X})$ is the trace of matrix $\mathbf{X}$.

Modeling Proximity Structure. Modeling proximity structure mainly uses the first-order and second-order proximity. The first-order proximity indicates the similarity between two nodes connected directly and it is a direct expression of network structure. But in social networks, two nodes that have no direct connection do not mean there is no similarity. Therefore, in order to make full use of the proximity structure of social networks, the abundant second-order proximity is used to compensate for the sparse problem of first-order proximity.

The first-order proximity $\mathbf{S}^{(1)}$ is characterized by the adjacency matrix, then it can be defined as:

$$\mathbf{S}^{(1)} = [S_{ij}^{(1)}] \in \mathbb{R}^{n*n}, \ s.t. \ S_{ij}^{(1)} = A_{ij} = 0 \ or \ 1 \tag{6}$$

Let $N_i = \left(S_{i1}^{(1)}, \ldots, S_{in}^{(1)}\right)$, the i-th row of $\mathbf{S}^{(1)}$, be the first-order proximity between node v_i and other nodes. The second-order proximity $\mathbf{S}^{(2)}$ of a pair of nodes is the similarity between their neighborhood structures, which can be described as:

$$\mathbf{S}^{(2)} = [S_{ij}^{(2)}] \in \mathbb{R}^{n*n}, \ s.t. \ S_{ij}^{(2)} = \frac{N_i * N_j}{\|N_i\| \|N_j\|} \in [0, 1] \tag{7}$$

Let similarity matrix $\mathbf{S} = \mathbf{S}^{(1)} + \eta \mathbf{S}^{(2)}$ to combine the first-order and second-order proximity together, where $\eta > 0$ is the weight of the second-order proximity. Using $\mathbf{U} \in \mathbb{R}^{n*d}$ to represent the node vector space, d is the dimensionality of representation, and introducing a nonnegative basis matrix $\mathbf{M} \in \mathbb{R}^{n*d}$, the objective function is described as:

$$\min \left\| \mathbf{S} - \mathbf{M}\mathbf{U}^T \right\|_F^2 \ s.t. \ \mathbf{M} \geq 0, \ \mathbf{U} \geq 0 \tag{8}$$

The United Network Embedding Model. In order to integrate the proximity structure and community structure in a unified framework, the community representation matrix $\mathbf{C} \in \mathbb{R}^{K*d}$ is introduced, where the r-th row $\mathbf{C}_r$ corresponding to the community r. If node v_i belongs to community r, formulated as $\mathbf{U}_i \mathbf{C}_r$, then the representation of v_i should be highly similar to that community r. As the community indicator matrix $\mathbf{H}$ offers a guide for all the nodes, $\mathbf{U}\mathbf{C}^T$ is expected to be as closely consistent as possible with $\mathbf{H}$. Then the overall objective function is described as:

$$\underset{\mathbf{M},\mathbf{U},\mathbf{H},\mathbf{C}}{\text{Min}} \ \|\mathbf{S} - \mathbf{M}\mathbf{U}^T\|_F^2 + \alpha \|\mathbf{H} - \mathbf{U}\mathbf{C}^T\|_F^2 - \beta tr\left(\mathbf{H}^T \mathbf{B} \mathbf{H}\right),$$

$$s.t. \ \mathbf{M} \geq 0, \mathbf{U} \geq 0, \mathbf{H} \geq 0, \mathbf{C} \geq 0, tr\left(\mathbf{H}^T \mathbf{B} \mathbf{H}\right) = n, \alpha > 0, \beta > 0 \tag{9}$$

3.3 BP Neural Network-Based Mapping Learning

After obtaining the latent vector space of each social network, CUIL applies the BP neural network (BPNN) to learn the mapping function Φ from G^s to G^t. Given any pair of anchor nodes (v_i^s, v_k^t) and their vector representations $(\boldsymbol{u}_i^s, \boldsymbol{u}_k^t)$, we firstly use the mapping function $\Phi(\boldsymbol{u}_i^s)$ map node vector $\boldsymbol{u}_i^s$ to another vector space, and then minimize the distance between $\Phi(\boldsymbol{u}_i^s)$ and $\boldsymbol{u}_k^t$. In this paper, the *Cosine Distance* is selected and the loss function can be formally described as:

$$\ell(\boldsymbol{u}_i^s, \boldsymbol{u}_k^t) = 1 - \cos(\Phi(\boldsymbol{u}_i^s), \boldsymbol{u}_k^t) \tag{10}$$

The set of known anchor links is T, and the sub-vector spaces composed of anchor nodes are $\mathbf{U}_T^s \in \mathbb{R}^{|T| \times d}$ and $\mathbf{U}_T^t \in \mathbb{R}^{|T| \times d}$ respectively. Then the objective function of the mapping learning can be formally described as:

$$\ell(\mathbf{U}_T^s, \mathbf{U}_T^t) = \arg \min_{\mathbf{W}, \mathbf{b}}(1 - \cos(\Phi(\mathbf{U}_T^s), \mathbf{U}_T^t); \mathbf{W}, \mathbf{b}) \tag{11}$$

where $\mathbf{W}$ and $\mathbf{b}$ are the weight parameters and bias parameters obtained by the back-propagation algorithm respectively. We minimize the loss function by stochastic gradient descent algorithm using the known anchor links as supervised information.

Construct the *top - k* for non-anchor nodes. For a non-anchor node v_x^s in the source network, firstly we input its vector representation $\boldsymbol{u}_x^s$ into the BPNN model trained above and get the mapping vector $\Phi(\boldsymbol{u}_x^s)$, like ⑤ in Fig. 1. Then we find k nodes that are most similar to the mapping vector $\Phi(\boldsymbol{u}_x^s)$ from the target network to form the *top - k* of node v_x^s, like ⑥ in Fig. 1.

4   Experiments

4.1   Datasets, Baselines and Parameter Setup, and Evaluation Metrics

Datasets. The real-world dataset is provided by [7], which contains two social networks, Twitter and Foursquare. Table 1 summarizes the statistics of this dataset.

Table 1. Statistics of twitter-foursquare dataset.

Networks	#Users	#Relations	#Anchor users
Twitter	5120	164919	1609
Foursquare	5313	76792	

Baselines and Parameter Setup. The model we proposed in this paper is based on network structure, so we compare CUIL with several structure-based methods for UIL.

- **PALE:** Predicting Anchor Links via Embedding [6] employs network embedding to capture the major and specific structural regularities and further learns a stable cross-network mapping for predicting anchor links.
- **IONE:** Input Output Network Embedding [7] tries to model followers/followees as different context vectors. With hard/soft constraints of anchor users, IONE learns a unified vector space by preserving second-order structural proximity.

- **DeepLink:** A Deep Learning Approach for User Identity Linkage [8] samples networks by random walks and learns to encode network nodes into vector representations to capture the local and global network structures. Finally, a deep neural network model is trained through the dual learning to realize user identity linkage.
- **PUIL:** Proximity Structure-based User Identity Linkage (PUIL) is based only on the proximity structure while without considering community structure.

Parameter Setup. The baselines are implemented according to the original papers. For CUIL (PUIL), we employ a four-layer neural network (2 hidden layers) to capture the non-linear mapping function between the source and target networks: $500\,d$ (first hidden layer), $800\,d$ (second hidden layer) and $300\,d$ (input and output layer). The learning rate for training is 0.001, and the batch size is set to 16.

Evaluation Metrics. Inspired by *the Success at rank k* proposed in [13], we use *Precision@k(P@k)* as the evaluation metric of user identity linkage.

$$P@k = \sum_i^n \mathbb{1}_i\{success@k\}/n \tag{12}$$

where n is the number of testing anchor nodes and $\mathbb{1}_i\{success@k\}$ measures whether the counterpart of v_i^s exists in $top\text{-}k(k \leq n)$.

4.2 Experiments

We firstly evaluate the influence of the parameters on the performance of algorithms, such as the training iteration i, the percentage r of anchor nodes used for training, and the vector dimensionality d. We set the basic experimental environment as: r is 0.8, i is 1 million, and d is 800. We change one parameter at a time while keeping the other two parameters constant.

As can be seen from Fig. 2(a), there is no overfitting problem for CUIL compared to IONE. By comparison, CUIL can not only get better results, but also reach the convergence faster.

The percentage r of anchor nodes used for training is an important parameter. As shown in Fig. 2(b), with the increase of training ratio r from 0.1 to 0.9, the performance of CUIL is always superior to other baselines. CUIL performs excellently even though the training ratio r is only 0.1 or 0.2.

The impact of the vector dimensionality d on the results is shown in Fig. 2(c). IONE, DeepLink, and CUIL all perform well on low-dimensional vector spaces. When the dimensionality is below 100, DeepLink performs best. But when the dimensionality reaches up to 200, the performance of CUIL is significantly better than other methods.

Finally, we conduct experiments for each method with the most appropriate parameters: the training ratio r is 0.8 and the vector dimensionality d is 300. The training iteration i is 3 hundred thousand for CUIL (PUIL) and PALE, 1 million for DeepLink, and 6 million for IONE. And we randomly select 6 different k values between 0 and 30 to compare the performance of different algorithms, as illustrated in Table 2. In order to compare and analyze the results intuitively, we show the results in a line chart, as shown in Fig. 2(d).

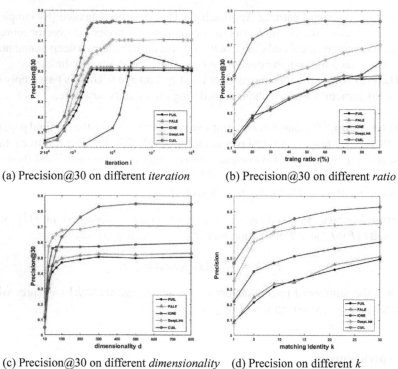

(a) Precision@30 on different *iteration*   (b) Precision@30 on different *ratio*

(c) Precision@30 on different *dimensionality*   (d) Precision on different *k*

Fig. 2. Result analysis on twitter-foursquare dataset.

Table 2. Comparisons of user identity linkage on twitter-foursquare dataset.

P@k	Precision					
	P@1	P@5	P@9	P@13	P@21	P@30
PALE	0.0906	0.2848	0.3625	0.3981	0.4628	0.5178
PUIL	0.0874	0.2136	0.3139	0.3592	0.4272	0.4984
IONE	0.2201	0.4142	0.4692	0.5113	0.5631	0.6052
DeepLink	0.3526	0.6019	0.6667	0.6926	0.7120	0.7249
CUIL	**0.4660**	**0.6634**	**0.7023**	**0.7540**	**0.8091**	**0.8317**

4.3 Discussions

With the experiments on the twitter-foursquare dataset, we have the following discussions:

- Through horizontal comparisons, CUIL proposed in this paper outperforms PALE, IONE, and DeepLink, even the $P@1$ can reach more than 45%. And through longitudinal comparisons, CUIL performs better than PUIL which only uses the proximity structure.
- The percentage of anchor nodes used for training greatly affects the performance of all algorithms, while CUIL achieves much better than other baselines even with only a few labeled anchor nodes. It is well known that the number of known anchor nodes is very limited and difficult to obtain. Therefore, our method is more advantageous in the practical applications.
- When the dimensionality reaches up to 200, the performance of CUIL has a significant improvement. With the rapid development of computing power and the continuous optimization of machine learning algorithms, the vector dimensionality is no longer a hard problem that restricts the performance of algorithm. In order to get better results, it is acceptable that the vector dimensionality reaches 200 or more for CUIL.

5 Conclusion

In this paper, we studied the problem of user identity linkage across social networks and proposed a novel community structure-based method, called CUIL. Many previous studies extracted the proximity structure of social networks from the local content of nodes while ignoring the important community structure. Therefore, we introduced the community structure and network embedding to UIL problem simultaneously. CUIL applied the embedding method, which preserves the microscopic proximity structure and the mesoscopic community structure, to map the original social network space into the vector space. Then based on the labeled anchor nodes, CUIL employed BP neural network to learn a stable mapping across different social networks. We conducted extensive experiments on the real-world dataset and the results showed that CUIL achieved superior performance over the state-of-the-art baseline methods that are based on the network structure.

Acknowledgements. This work was supported by the National Natural Science Foundation of China (U1636219, 61602508, 61772549, U1736214, 61572052, U1804263, 61872448) and Plan for Scientific Innovation Talent of Henan Province (No. 2018JR0018).

References

1. Zhang, J., Yu, P., Zhou, Z.: Meta-path based multi-network collective link prediction. In: The 20th International Conference on Knowledge Discovery and Data, pp. 1286–1295. ACM (2014)
2. Shu, K., Wang, S., Tang, J., Zafarani, R., Liu, H.: User identity linkage across online social networks: a review. In: SIGKDD Explorations Newsletter, pp. 5–17. ACM (2017)
3. Liu, J., Zhang, F., Song, X., Song, Y., Lin, C., Hon, H.: What's in a name? An unsupervised approach to link users across communities. In: The 6th International Conference on Web Search Data Mining, pp. 495–504. ACM (2013)

4. Zafarani, R., Liu, H.: Connecting users across social media sites: a behavioral-modeling approach. In: The 19th ACM SIGKDD International Conference on Knowledge Discovery and Data Mining, pp. 41–49. ACM (2013)
5. Wang, C., Zhao, Z., Wang, Y., Qin, D., Luo, X., Qin, T.: DeepMatching: a structural seed identification framework for social network alignment. In: The 38th International Conference on Distributed Computing Systems, pp. 600–610. IEEE (2018)
6. Man, T., Shen, H., Liu, S., Jin, X., Cheng, X.: Predict anchor links across social networks via an embedding approach. In: The 25th International Joint Conference on Artificial Intelligence, pp. 1823–1829. IJCAI (2016)
7. Liu, L., Cheung, W., Li, X., Liao, L.: Aligning users across social networks using network embedding. In: The 25th International Joint Conference on Artificial Intelligence, pp. 1774–1780. IJCAI (2016)
8. Zhou, F., Liu, L., Zhang, K., Trajcevski, G., Wu J., Zhong, T.: DeepLink: a deep learning approach for user identity linkage. In: INFOCOM, pp. 1313–1321. IEEE (2018)
9. Girvan, M., Newman, M.: Community structure in social and biological networks. Proc. Natl. Acad. Sci. U.S.A. **99**(12), 7821–7826 (2002)
10. Bayati, M., Gerritsen, M., Gleich, D., Saberi, A., Wang, Y.: Algorithms for large, sparse network alignment problems. In: ICDM, pp. 705–710. IEEE (2009)
11. Wang, X., Cui, P., Wang, J., Pei, J., Zhu, W., Yang, S.: Community preserving network embedding. In: The 31st AAAI, pp. 203–209. AAAI (2017)
12. Newman, M.: Modularity and community structure in networks. Proc. Natl. Acad. Sci. **103**(23), 8577–8582 (2006)
13. Iofciu, T., Fankhauser, P., Abel, F., Bischoff, K.: Identifying users across social tagging systems. In: 5th International AAAI Conference on Weblogs and Social Media, pp. 522–525. ACM (2011)

Improvement of Attribute-Based Encryption Using Blakley Secret Sharing

Zhe Xia[1,2], Bo Yang[3(✉)], Yanwei Zhou[3], Mingwu Zhang[4], and Yi Mu[5]

[1] School of Computer Science, Wuhan University of Technology, Wuhan, China
xiazhe@whut.edu.cn
[2] Guizhou Key Laboratory of Public Big Data, Guizhou University, Guiyang, China
[3] School of Computer Science, Shaanxi Normal University, Xi'an, China
{byang,zyw}@snnu.edu.cn
[4] School of Computer Science and Information Security,
Guilin University of Electronic Technology, Guilin, China
csmwzhang@gmail.com
[5] Fujian Provincial Key Laboratory of Network Security and Cryptology,
College of Mathematics and Informatics, Fujian Normal University, Fuzhou, China
ymu.ieee@gmail.com

Abstract. Attribute-based encryption (ABE) enables fine-grained access control of encrypted data. This technique has been carefully scrutinised by the research community for over a decade, and it has wide theoretical interests as well as practical potentials. Thus, any efficiency improvement of it is highly desirable but non-trivial. In this paper, we demonstrate that the computational costs in ABE can be slightly reduced using Blakley secret sharing. The main reason that contributes to this improvement is a unique feature enjoyed by Blakley secret sharing, i.e. it is more efficient to handle (n, n)-threshold secret sharing compared with Shamir secret sharing. Due to the space limitation, we only describe how to improve key-policy attribute-based encryption (KP-ABE), but our method is very general and it can be used to improve some of its variants similarly, e.g. cipher-policy attribute-based encryption (CP-ABE). This work may also inspire further investigations on Blakley secret sharing, both applying this unique feature to other cryptographic primitives and exploring more undiscovered features.

1 Introduction

Encryption guarantees that certain information is never disclosed to unauthorised entities. Among the existing encryption schemes, attribute-based encryption (ABE) [4,9] is a prominent example[1]. A user can decrypt a ciphertext if the

---

[1] In this paper, we focus our attentions on key-policy attribute-based encryption (KP-ABE) with a tree-access structure [9], in which the ciphertexts are labelled with sets of attributes and the private keys are associated with tree-access structures, but our proposed method can be applied with some of its variants similarly, e.g. ciphertext-policy attribute-based encryption (CP-ABE) [4].

© Springer Nature Switzerland AG 2020
J. K. Liu and H. Cui (Eds.): ACISP 2020, LNCS 12248, pp. 631–641, 2020.
https://doi.org/10.1007/978-3-030-55304-3_33

attributes associated with the ciphertext satisfy the private key's access structure. In other words, a ciphertext can be decrypted using a given key if and only if the ciphertext contains an assignment of attributes to the nodes of the tree such that the tree-access structure can be satisfied. Because any linear access structure can be represented as a tree consisting of threshold gates [3], ABE is very useful to achieve fine-grained access control of encrypted data.

Nowadays, ABE has not only attracted theoretical interests in the academia but also found various applications in practice [11,12]. Thus, efficiency improvements for this technique are desirable if they can be found. In this paper, we demonstrate that the computational costs in ABE can be slightly reduced if Shamir secret sharing [14] was replaced by Blakley secret sharing [5], thanks to a unique feature enjoyed by the latter that is not widely known by the research community yet.

1.1 Related Works

In general, the design of ABE can be considered as the combination of IBE and secret sharing.

The concept of IBE was first conceived by Shamir in the mid-1980s [15]. However, the practical scheme was not found until 2001 [6]. Different from the traditional public key encryption schemes that are relying on the public key infrastructure (PKI), the public key in IBE can be expressed as an arbitrary string associated with the identity. Hence, the entity's public key is naturally bound with its identity. The benefit is that to encrypt a message for a certain receiver, there is no need to obtain this receiver's public key certificate.

Secret sharing enhances both confidentiality and availability of sensitive information by distributing the secret across a number of locations so that either to learn the secret or destroy it, the adversary has to compromise multiple of these locations instead of a single one. The existing (t, n)-threshold secret sharing schemes can be classified into three main categories: based on polynomial interpolation [14], based on hyperplane geometry [5], and based on the Chinese Remainder Theorem [1,13]. The first two categories are called Shamir secret sharing and Blakley secret sharing, respectively. Although they appear to be different in the mathematical structures, these two techniques are closely related. Kothari [10] has shown that both of them are linear secret sharing schemes and the former is a special case of the latter. In previous works, researchers have paid very unequal attentions to them. Shamir secret sharing has been widely used to design various cryptographic primitives, but Blakley's one has attracted almost no attention. For example, the existing ABE schemes with tree-access structure [4,9] are all designed using Shamir secret sharing.

In this paper, we describe an attractive feature of Blakley secret sharing and demonstrate its applications in constructing more efficient ABE schemes.

1.2 Our Contributions

The contributions of this paper can be summarised as follows:

- We describe a unique feature of Blakley secret sharing that is not widely known by the research community yet, i.e. it is as efficient as Shamir secret sharing in (t, n)-threshold secret sharing where $t < n$, but it is more efficient than Shamir secret sharing to handle (n, n)-threshold secret sharing.
- We demonstrate how the above feature of Blakley secret sharing can be used to improve the ABE scheme in [9]. In our proposed scheme, Shamir secret sharing is replaced by Blakley secret sharing. If the tree-access structure within a user's private key satisfies some condition, i.e. it contains at least one node with (n, n)-threshold gate, this user can decrypt all ciphertexts that she has the ability to decrypt in a more efficient way.

1.3 Organisation of the Paper

The following of this paper is organised as follows. In Sect. 2, we compare Blakley secret sharing with Shamir secret sharing and describe a unique feature enjoyed by the former. In Sect. 3, we introduce the models and definitions for ABE. Our improvement of ABE is presented in Sect. 4. Finally, we discuss and conclude in Sect. 5.

2 Blakley Secret Sharing

In Blakley secret sharing [5], the secret is encoded as some coordinate of a random point P in the t dimensional space. Each of the n parties is given an independent t-dimensional hyperplane in the space passing through P. When t parties work together, they can solve a system of equations to retrieve the secret, but less than t parties are unable to learn any information of the secret. Blakley secret sharing works as follows:

- **Initialisation phase.** To share a secret $s = a_1$, the dealer $\mathcal{D}$ selects $t - 1$ random values $\{a_2, a_3, \ldots, a_t\}$. Then, $\mathcal{D}$ generates an $n \times t$ matrix M and broadcasts it. It is required that all the rows in M are independent, e.g. this ensures that any t rows of M will form a $t \times t$ invertible matrix M_S.
- **Share generation phase.** $\mathcal{D}$ computes the shares $s_i = b_{i,1}a_1 + b_{i,2}a_2 + \cdots + b_{i,t}a_t$ for $i = 1, 2, \ldots, n$, where $b_{i,j}$ is the (i, j)-th entry of M, and sends these shares to the corresponding parties through some private channels.
- **Secret reconstruction phase.** If any subset containing at least t parties reveal their shares, the secret s can be reconstructed. Without loss of generality, suppose the vector of shares $\bar{s} = [s_{i_1}, s_{i_2}, \ldots, s_{i_t}]$ is revealed. Then, the vector $\bar{a} = [a_1, a_2, \ldots, a_t]$ can be computed as $\bar{a}^T = \mathsf{M}_S^{-1} \cdot \bar{s}^T$, where $\bar{a}^T$ denotes the transpose of $\bar{a}$ and M_S^{-1} denotes the inverse of M_S. Note that to recover the secret $s = a_1$, only the first row of M_S^{-1} needs to be computed[2].

---

[2] When j parties participate in the secret reconstruction phase where $j > t$, the sub-matrix M_S of M is not a square matrix. In this case, we can use the equation $\bar{a}^T = (\mathsf{M}_S^T \cdot \mathsf{M}_S)^{-1} \cdot \mathsf{M}_S^T \cdot \bar{s}^T$ to compute $\bar{a}^T$. Similarly, to recover the secret $s = a_1$, only the first row of $(\mathsf{M}_S^T \cdot \mathsf{M}_S)^{-1} \cdot \mathsf{M}_S^T$ needs to be computed.

Shamir secret sharing can be considered as a special case of Blakley secret sharing by initialising M using the Vandermonde matrix, and it enjoys some attractive features: 1) only n different values are required to represent the entire matrix M; 2) it automatically guarantees that all the rows in M are independent; 3) with the knowledge of t shares, one can interpolate any other share without recovering the secret. These features are very useful, making Shamir secret sharing popular in the literature. But since Blakley secret sharing is a more general case, we may also use some other special matrix to initialise M. As long as all the rows in M are independent, such an initialisation may provide some other unique features not enjoyed by Shamir secret sharing.

One such special matrix we have found is the Hadamard matrix, which satisfies the following property: every two rows in a Hadamard matrix are perpendicular to each other. Let H be a Hadamard matrix of order n. The transpose of H is closely related to its inverse as: $H \times H^T = n \cdot I_n$, where H^T denotes the transpose of H and I_n denotes the $n \times n$ identity matrix. Recall that to recover the secret in Blakley secret sharing, the most computationally expensive task is to invert the matrix M_S. Therefore, when M is initialised using the Hadamard matrix, such a computation is almost for free, i.e. we can simply perform the required computations using the transpose of H and then divide the final result by the value n. However, since the Hadamard matrix is always a square matrix, this efficiency improvement only works for (n, n)-threshold secret sharing[3]. In other words, when dealing with (n, n)-threshold secret sharing, the computational complexity of the secret reconstruction phase in Shamir secret sharing is $O(n^2)$, but it can be reduced to $O(n)$ in Blakley secret sharing.

In this paper, we use Blakley secret sharing as follows: when handling (t, n)-threshold secret sharing where $t < n$, M is initialised using the Vandermonde matrix, and when handling (n, n)-threshold secret sharing, M is initialised using the Hadamard matrix. Therefore, we can be benefited from both the attractive features of Shamir secret sharing and the unique feature of Blakley secret sharing introduced above. In the following sections, we demonstrate how this idea helps to reduce the computational costs in ABE.

3 Models and Definitions

3.1 Notations

In the rest of this paper, we assume that all participants are probabilistic polynomial time (PPT) algorithms with respect to the security parameter λ. We use standard notations for probabilistic algorithms and experiments. For example, if A is a probabilistic algorithm, then $A(x_1, x_2, \ldots)$ is denoted as the result of running A on inputs x_1, x_2, etc. We denote $y \leftarrow A(x_1, x_2, \ldots)$ as the experiment

---

[3] A restriction of the Hadamard matrix is that its order has to be the power of 2, and this may cause some inconvenience in practice. To address this issue, we can either add some dummy entities to make the total number of entities as the power of 2, or we can use the Weighing matrix instead that has similar properties.

of assigning y as $A(x_1, x_2, \ldots)$. If S is a finite set, then we denote $x \overset{R}{\leftarrow} S$ as the operation of picking an element uniformly from S. A function $\epsilon(\cdot) : \mathbb{N} \to \mathbb{R}^+$ is called negligible if for all $c > 0$, there exists a k_0 such that $\epsilon(k) < 1/k^c$ for all $k > k_0$.

3.2 Some Definitions

Bilinear Map. Let $\mathbb{G}_1$ and $\mathbb{G}_2$ be two multiplicative cyclic groups with order p for some large prime p. Let g be a generator of $\mathbb{G}_1$ and $\hat{e}$ be a bilinear map $\hat{e} : \mathbb{G}_1 \times \mathbb{G}_1 \to \mathbb{G}_2$ defined between these two groups. An admissible bilinear map $\hat{e}$ should satisfy the following properties:

- *Bilinear:* $\hat{e} : \mathbb{G}_1 \times \mathbb{G}_1 \to \mathbb{G}_2$ is said to be bilinear if $\hat{e}(u^a, v^b) = \hat{e}(u, v)^{ab}$ for all $u, v \in \mathbb{G}_1$ and $a, b \in \mathbb{Z}_p$.
- *Non-degenerate:* the bilinear map $\hat{e}$ does not send all pairs in $\mathbb{G}_1 \times \mathbb{G}_1$ to the identity in $\mathbb{G}_2$, i.e. $\hat{e}(g, g) \neq 1$.
- *Computable:* there exists an efficient algorithm to compute $\hat{e}(P, Q)$ for all $P, Q \in \mathbb{G}_1$.

Access Structure [2]. Let $\{P_1, P_2, \ldots, P_n\}$ denotes a set of parties. A collection $\mathbb{A} \subseteq 2^{\{P_1, P_2, \ldots, P_n\}}$ is monotone if $\forall B, C$: if $B \in \mathbb{A}$ and $B \subset C$, then $C \in \mathbb{A}$. A access structure (resp. monotone access structure) is a collection (resp. monotone collection) $\mathbb{A}$ of non-empty subset of $\{P_1, P_2, \ldots, P_n\}$, i.e. $\mathbb{A} \subseteq 2^{\{P_1, P_2, \ldots, P_n\}} \setminus \{\emptyset\}$. The sets in $\mathbb{A}$ are called the *authorised sets*, and the sets not in $\mathbb{A}$ are called the *unauthorised sets*. In this paper, we focus our attentions on monotone access structures.

3.3 Security Model for KP-ABE

The KP-ABE scheme consists of four randomised algorithms: Setup, KeyGen, Enc, Dec.

- The Setup algorithm takes as input the security parameter λ, and it outputs the public parameters PK and a master key MK.
- The key generation algorithm KeyGen takes as input an identity associated with the access structure $\mathbb{A}$, the master key MK and the public parameters PK. It outputs the decryption key D.
- The encryption algorithm Enc takes as input a message M, a set of attributes γ and the public parameters PK. It outputs the ciphertext E.
- The decryption algorithm Dec takes as input the ciphertext E that was encrypted under the set of attributes γ, the decryption key D associated with the access structure $\mathbb{A}$ and the public parameters PK. It outputs the message M if $\gamma \in \mathbb{A}$, or $\perp$ otherwise.

The following security game played between the adversary and the challenger is used to model the semantic security of KP-ABE in the selective-ID model[4]:

---

[4] Note that our proposed scheme is only proved to be CPA-secure in the selective-ID model. One can adapt the FO transformation [8] or the CHK transformation [7] to modify it into a scheme with CCA-security.

- **Init:** The adversary declares the set of attributes γ that she wishes to be challenged upon.
- **Setup:** The challenger takes the security parameter λ and runs the Setup algorithm. The adversary is given the public parameter PK, but not the master key MK.
- **Phase 1:** The adversary can issue many queries for private keys associated with access structures $\mathbb{A}_j$. If $\gamma \notin \mathbb{A}_j$, the challenger runs the KeyGen algorithm and forwards its output to the adversary. Otherwise, the challenger does not respond to the query.
- **Challenge:** The adversary submits two messages M_0, M_1 with equal length. The challenger flips a coin $b \xleftarrow{R} \{0,1\}$ and uses the Enc algorithm to encrypt the message M_b with the set of attributes γ. This ciphertext is sent to the adversary.
- **Phase 2:** The adversary continues querying for private keys as in Phase 1.
- **Guess:** The adversary outputs a guess b' of b.

The advantage of the adversary $\mathcal{A}$ in this game is defined as:

$$\mathsf{Adv}_{\mathcal{A}} = |\Pr[b = b'] - 1/2|$$

Definition 1 (Semantic security for KP-ABE). *A KP-ABE scheme is said to be semantically secure against chosen plaintext attacks in the selective-ID model if no PPT adversary $\mathcal{A}$ has a non-negligible advantage against the challenger in the above security game.*

3.4   Security Assumptions

Definition 2 (Decisional Bilinear Diffie-Hellman (BDH) assumption). *Given two multiplicative cyclic groups $\mathbb{G}_1, \mathbb{G}_2$ with order p, a generator g of $\mathbb{G}_1$, and an admissible bilinear map $\hat{e} : \mathbb{G}_1 \times \mathbb{G}_1 \to \mathbb{G}_2$. Select $a \xleftarrow{R} \mathbb{Z}_p$, $b \xleftarrow{R} \mathbb{Z}_p$, $c \xleftarrow{R} \mathbb{Z}_p$ and $z \xleftarrow{R} \mathbb{Z}_p$. The decisional BDH assumption implies that there exists a negligible function $\epsilon(\cdot)$ such that for all PPT adversaries $\mathcal{A}_{BDH}$, we have:*

$$|\Pr[\mathcal{A}_{BDH}(g^a, g^b, g^c, \hat{e}(g,g)^{abc}) = 1] - \Pr[\mathcal{A}_{BDH}(g^a, g^b, g^c, \hat{e}(g,g)^z) = 1]| < \epsilon(\lambda)$$

4   Our Proposed KP-ABE Scheme

4.1   Our Motivations

In KP-ABE schemes with a tree-access structure, the ciphertexts are labelled with a set of attributes, and the private keys are associated with the tree-access structure. Each interior node of the tree is a threshold gate and the leave nodes are associated with attributes. These threshold gates can be classified into two types: (t, n)-threshold ones where $t < n$, and (n, n)-threshold ones. Therefore, Blakley secret sharing with the Vandermonde matrix can be used for the first type of gates and Blakley secret sharing with the Hadamard matrix can be used for the other gates. This allows us to enjoy both the attractive features of Shamir secret sharing scheme and the unique feature of Blakley secret sharing scheme. For example, if the access tree associated with a certain user's private key contains at least one (n, n)-threshold gate, this user could decrypt the ciphertexts quicker. The more (n, n)-threshold gates contained in a user's private key, the more computational advantages can be enjoyed by this user in the decryption process. Note that in real-world applications, it is quite possible that a subset of the users' private keys would satisfy this condition.

4.2   Our Proposed Scheme

Denote T as a tree representing an access structure, and every interior node of T is associated with a threshold gate. For a node x, num_x is denoted as the number of its children and k_x is denoted as its threshold value satisfying $0 < k_x \leq num_x$.

The function $parent(x)$ is defined as the parent node of x in T, and the function $att(x)$ denotes the attribute associated with the leaf node x in T. The children of the node x are numbered, and the function $index(x)$ records this number associated with the node x. Implicitly, it is assumed that r is the root node of T. Denote T_x as a sub-tree of T rooted at the node x. If a set of attributes γ satisfies the access tree T_x, it is denoted as $T_x(\gamma) = 1$. Otherwise, it is denoted as $T_x(\gamma) = 0$. The value $T_x(\gamma)$ is evaluated recursively from the bottom of the tree to the top. The leaf node x is first evaluated, and $T_x(\gamma)$ returns 1 if only if $att(x) \in \gamma$. If x is an interior node, evaluate $T_{x'}(\gamma)$ for all the children x' of x. $T_x(\gamma)$ will return 1 if and only if at least k_x children return 1.

Let $\mathbb{G}_1$ and $\mathbb{G}_2$ be multiplicative cyclic groups of prime order p, where $|p|$ is some polynomial of the security parameter λ. Let g be a generator of $\mathbb{G}_1$ and $\hat{e} : \mathbb{G}_1 \times \mathbb{G}_1 \rightarrow \mathbb{G}_2$ be an admissible bilinear map. Moreover, we denote the Vandermonde matrix as M with $b_{i,j}$ as its (i, j)-th entry, and M_S as a square sub-matrix of M. The first row of M_S^{-1} is denoted as a vector $\mathcal{L}$, where $\mathcal{L}_i$ is the i-th value of $\mathcal{L}$. Similarly, we denote the Hadamard matrix as H with $h_{i,j}$ as its (i, j)-th entry. The first row of H^{-1} is denoted as a vector $\mathcal{L}'$, where $\mathcal{L}'_i$ is the i-th value of $\mathcal{L}'$. Our proposed KP-ABE scheme works as follows:

- **Setup.** Define the universe U of all possible attributes. Choose $t_1, \ldots, t_{|U|} \xleftarrow{R} \mathbb{Z}_p$ and $y \xleftarrow{R} \mathbb{Z}_p$. The public parameters PK are $T_1 = g^{t_1}, \ldots, T_{|U|} = g^{t_{|U|}}, Y = \hat{e}(g, g)^y$, and the master key MK is $t_1, \ldots, t_{|U|}, y$.
- **KeyGen.** This algorithm will output a private key with access structure T that allows the user to decrypt any message encrypted with a set of attributes γ if and only if $T(\gamma) = 1$. It works recursively from the top of the tree to the bottom. For every interior node x in the tree T, if $k_x < num_x$, choose a random point $\mathsf{P}_x = [a_1, a_2, \ldots, a_{k_x}]$ in the k_x-dimensional space with the first coordinate $a_1 = parent(x)(index(x))$ and all other coordinates are randomly chosen in $\mathbb{Z}_p$. Denote $s_i = b_{i,1}a_1 + b_{i,2}a_2 + \cdots + a_{i,k_x}a_{k_x}$. Each child node of x is assigned one of these s_i values. If $k_x = num_x$, choose a random point $\mathsf{P}'_x = [a'_1, a'_2, \ldots, a'_{num_x}]$ in the num_x-dimensional space with the first coordinate $a'_1 = parent(x)(index(x))$ and all other coordinates are randomly

chosen in $\mathbb{Z}_p$. Denote $s_i' = h_{i,1}a_1' + h_{i,2}a_2' + \cdots + h_{i,num_x}a_{num_x}'$. Each child node of x is assigned one of these s_i' values. For every leaf node x, compute $D_x = g^{\frac{parent(x)(index(x))}{t_i}}$ where $i = att(x)$. The private key D consists of these D_x components and it is sent to the user.

- **Enc.** To encrypt a message $M \in \mathbb{G}_2$ with a set of attributes γ, choose a random value $s \in \mathbb{Z}_p$ and the ciphertext is:

$$E = (\gamma, E' = MY^s, \{E_i = T_i^{\,s}\}_{i \in \gamma})$$

- **Dec.** This algorithm is performed recursively from the bottom of the tree to its top. Define an algorithm DecryptNode that takes as input the ciphertext E, the private key D and a node x in T, it outputs a group element of $\mathbb{G}_2$ or $\perp$. If the node x is a leaf node and $i = att(x) \in \gamma$, we have

$$\mathsf{DecryptNode}(E, D, x) = \hat{e}(D_x, E_i) = \hat{e}(g^{\frac{parent(x)(index(x))}{t_i}}, g^{st_i})$$
$$= \hat{e}(g, g)^{s \cdot parent(x)(index(x))}$$

If $i \notin \gamma$, DecryptNode simply outputs $\perp$. For the interior nodes, the algorithm DecryptNode(E, D, x) proceeds as follows. For all nodes z that are children of x, it calls DecryptNode(E, D, z) and stores the output as F_z. Let S_x be the set of child nodes z such that $F_z \neq \perp$. Then, there are several different cases:

- If $num_x = k_x = |S_x|$, x is a node with (num_x, num_x)-threshold gate and S_x satisfies the node x. In this case, the algorithm DecryptNode(E, D, x) computes:

$$F_x = \prod_{z=1}^{num_x} F_z^{\mathcal{L}'_z}$$
$$= \prod_{z=1}^{num_x} (\hat{e}(g, g)^{s \cdot parent(z)(index(z))})^{\mathcal{L}'_z}$$
$$= \prod_{z=1}^{num_x} \hat{e}(g, g)^{s \cdot s_z' \cdot \mathcal{L}'_z}$$
$$= \hat{e}(g, g)^{s \cdot parent(x)(index(x))}$$

Note that this computation contributes to some efficiency improvement, because the value L_z' can be computed quicker than its counterpart L_z that has been used in the existing ABE schemes with tree-access structure.

- If $num_x = k_x > |S_x|$, x is a node with (num_x, num_x)-threshold gate but S_x does not satisfy the node x. In this case, the algorithm DecryptNode(E, D, x) simply outputs $\perp$.

- If $k_x < num_x$ and $k_x \leq |S_x|$, x is a node with (k_x, num_x)-threshold gate and S_x satisfies the node x. In this case, the DecryptNode(E, D, x) algorithm computes:

$$F_x = \prod_{z \in S_x} F_z^{\mathcal{L}_z}$$

$$= \prod_{z \in S_x} (\hat{e}(g,g)^{s \cdot parent(z)(index(z))})^{\mathcal{L}_z}$$

$$= \prod_{z \in S_x} \hat{e}(g,g)^{s \cdot s_z \cdot \mathcal{L}_z}$$

$$= \hat{e}(g,g)^{s \cdot parent(x)(index(x))}$$

- If $k_x < num_x$ and $k_x > |S_x|$, x is a node with (k_x, num_x)-threshold gate but S_x does not satisfy the node x. In this case, the DecryptNode(E, D, x) algorithm simply outputs $\bot$.

To decrypt a ciphertext E, the Dec algorithm calls the DecryptNode algorithm on the root r of the tree T. Hence, we have DecryptNode$(E, D, r) = \hat{e}(g,g)^{ys} = Y^s$ if and only if the attributes associated with the ciphertext satisfy the tree T. Moreover, the message M can be recovered by dividing E' by Y^s.

4.3   Security Analysis

Theorem 1. *If the decisional BDH assumption holds, our proposed KP-ABE scheme satisfies the semantic security in the selective-ID model.*

Proof (Sketch.) Due to the space limitation, we only provide a sketch of the proof. The complete proof is very similar as in [9] which is done via a security reduction: if there exists a PPT adversary $\mathcal{A}$ who can break our proposed KP-ABE scheme in the selective-ID model with non-negligible probability, another PPT adversary $\mathcal{B}$ can be constructed using $\mathcal{A}$ as a sub-routine that breaks the decisional BDH assumption with non-negligible probability. $\mathcal{B}$ plays another security game with the challenger, trying to distinguish between the values $\hat{e}(g,g)^{abc}$ and $\hat{e}(g,g)^z$. $\mathcal{B}$ simulates the KP-ABE environment for $\mathcal{A}$, answering the private key queries in Phase 1 and 2, and then use $\mathcal{A}$'s guess to generate its answer to the challenger. All the steps of the security game are exactly the same as in [9], except that $\mathcal{B}$ may answer $\mathcal{A}$'s private key queries slightly different in Phase 1 and 2. In our proposed scheme, the (n, n)-threshold gate is instantiated using the Hadamard matrix instead of the Vandermonde matrix. Suppose $\mathcal{A}$ makes a request for the secret key associated with an access structure T' such that $T'(\gamma) = 0$. And without loss of generality, suppose T' contains a node x with the (num_x, num_x)-threshold gate. Depending on the value of $T'_x(\gamma)$, the simulation needs to consider two different cases. If $T'_x(\gamma) = 1$, $\mathcal{B}$ randomly selects $\lambda_x \in \mathbb{Z}_p$ and sets the first coordinate of the random point P' as $a'_1 = \lambda_x$. Then, $\mathcal{B}$ fixed the point P' by setting the random points for every child node x' of x such that $parent(x')(index(x')) = s'_{index(x')}$. If $T'_x(\gamma) = 0$, $\mathcal{B}$ first chooses a random value $\lambda_x \in \mathbb{Z}_p$ and computes $g^{\lambda_x} \in \mathbb{G}_1$. $\mathcal{B}$ then sets the first coordinate of the random point P' as $a_1' = \lambda_x$. Within x's child nodes, suppose d_x of them are satisfied, then $\mathcal{B}$ can fix them similarly. For the unsatisfied children nodes, $\mathcal{B}$ uses random values to define them. The requirement is that the collection of x's children nodes is consistent with the element $g^{\lambda_x} \in \mathbb{G}_1$. In this way, $\mathcal{B}$ can simulate all private key components for the access structure T', and the distribution of these components are identical to that of the original scheme.

4.4 Efficiency Analysis

Compared with the KP-ABE scheme in [9], if the access tree contains at least one node with (n, n)-threshold gate, our proposed scheme could enjoy some computational advantages in the Dec algorithm. This is because the (n, n)-threshold gate can be processed quicker using Blakley secret sharing with the Hadamard matrix. The computational costs in the Enc algorithm and the storage requirements are exactly the same as in [9]. For example, in both schemes, the cost in Enc is linear with the number of attributes for encryption in γ, the number of elements that compose a user's private key is linear with the number of nodes in the access tree, and the number of elements in the ciphertext is linear with the number of attributes for encryption in γ.

5   Conclusion

In this paper, we described a unique feature enjoyed in Blakley secret sharing, i.e. it is more efficient to handle (n, n)-threshold secret sharing. We have used this feature to improve a KP-ABE scheme, reducing its computational costs in the decryption process. Note that our method is very general and it can be used to improve some of its variants in a similar way, e.g. CP-ABE.

This paper also made it clear that both the attractive features in Shamir secret sharing and the unique feature in Blakley secret sharing are brought by the specific matrix employed. Therefore, it would be useful if we could find more special matrices with appealing properties. This not only increases the capabilities of Blakley secret sharing, but also has the potentials to contribute to various cryptographic primitives (e.g. threshold cryptosystems, secure multiparty computations, etc.) since secret sharing is a fundamental building block in cryptography.

Acknowledgement. This work was partially supported by the National Natural Science Foundation of China (Grant No. 61572303, 61772326, 61822202, 61672010, 61872087) and Guizhou Key Laboratory of Public Big Data (Grant No. 2019BDK-FJJ005). We are very grateful to the anonymous reviewers for their valuable comments on the paper.

References

1. Asmuth, C., Bloom, J.: A modular approach to key safeguarding. IEEE Trans. Inf. Theory **29**(2), 208–210 (1983)
2. Beimel, A.: Secure schemes for secret sharing and key distribution. Technion-Israel Institute of Technology, Faculty of Computer Science (1996)
3. Benaloh, J., Leichter, J.: Generalized secret sharing and monotone functions. In: Goldwasser, S. (ed.) CRYPTO 1988. LNCS, vol. 403, pp. 27–35. Springer, New York (1990). https://doi.org/10.1007/0-387-34799-2_3
4. Bethencourt, J., Sahai, A., Waters, B.: Ciphertext-policy attribute-based encryption. In: 2007 IEEE Symposium on Security and Privacy (SP 2007), pp. 321–334. IEEE (2007)
5. Blakley, G.R., et al.: Safeguarding cryptographic keys. In: Proceedings of the National Computer Conference, vol. 48 (1979)
6. Boneh, D., Franklin, M.: Identity-based encryption from the weil pairing. In: Kilian, J. (ed.) CRYPTO 2001. LNCS, vol. 2139, pp. 213–229. Springer, Heidelberg (2001). https://doi.org/10.1007/3-540-44647-8_13
7. Canetti, R., Halevi, S., Katz, J.: Chosen-ciphertext security from identity-based encryption. In: Cachin, C., Camenisch, J.L. (eds.) EUROCRYPT 2004. LNCS, vol. 3027, pp. 207–222. Springer, Heidelberg (2004). https://doi.org/10.1007/978-3-540-24676-3_13
8. Fujisaki, E., Okamoto, T.: Secure integration of asymmetric and symmetric encryption schemes. In: Wiener, M. (ed.) CRYPTO 1999. LNCS, vol. 1666, pp. 537–554. Springer, Heidelberg (1999). https://doi.org/10.1007/3-540-48405-1_34
9. Goyal, V., Pandey, O., Sahai, A., Waters, B.: Attribute-based encryption for fine-grained access control of encrypted data. In: Proceedings of the 13th ACM Conference on Computer and Communications Security, pp. 89–98. ACM (2006)
10. Kothari, S.C.: Generalized linear threshold scheme. In: Blakley, G.R., Chaum, D. (eds.) CRYPTO 1984. LNCS, vol. 196, pp. 231–241. Springer, Heidelberg (1985). https://doi.org/10.1007/3-540-39568-7_19
11. Li, J., Huang, X., Li, J., Chen, X., Xiang, Y.: Securely outsourcing attribute-based encryption with checkability. IEEE Trans. Parallel Distrib. Syst. **25**(8), 2201–2210 (2013)
12. Li, M., Shucheng, Y., Zheng, Y., Ren, K., Lou, W.: Scalable and secure sharing of personal health records in cloud computing using attribute-based encryption. IEEE Trans. Parallel Distrib. Syst. **24**(1), 131–143 (2012)
13. Mignotte, M.: How to share a secret. In: Beth, T. (ed.) EUROCRYPT 1982. LNCS, vol. 149, pp. 371–375. Springer, Heidelberg (1983). https://doi.org/10.1007/3-540-39466-4_27
14. Shamir, A.: How to share a secret. Commun. ACM **22**(11), 612–613 (1979)
15. Shamir, A.: Identity-based cryptosystems and signature schemes. In: Blakley, G.R., Chaum, D. (eds.) CRYPTO 1984. LNCS, vol. 196, pp. 47–53. Springer, Heidelberg (1985). https://doi.org/10.1007/3-540-39568-7_5

Recovering CRT-RSA Secret Keys from Noisy Square-and-Multiply Sequences in the Sliding Window Method

Kento Oonishi[1](✉) and Noboru Kunihiro[2]

[1] The University of Tokyo, Tokyo, Japan
kento_oonishi@mist.i.u-tokyo.ac.jp
[2] University of Tsukuba, Tsukuba, Japan
kunihiro@cs.tsukuba.ac.jp

Abstract. We discuss side-channel attacks on CRT-RSA encryption or signature scheme (the RSA scheme with the Chinese remainder theorem) implemented via the sliding window method. The sliding window method calculates exponentiations through repeated squaring and multiplication. These square-and-multiply sequences can be obtained by side-channel attacks, and there is the risk of recovering CRT-RSA secret keys from these sequences. Especially, in CHES 2017, it is proved that we can recover secret keys from the correct square-and-multiply sequences in polynomial time when the window size w is less than 4. However, there are errors in the obtained sequences. Oonishi and Kunihiro proposed a method for recovering secret keys from noisy sequences when $w = 1$. Although this work only addresses the case with $w = 1$, it should be possible to recover secret keys for larger values of w. In this paper, we propose a new method for recovering secret keys from noisy sequences in the sliding window method. Moreover, we clarify the amount of errors for which our method works.

Keywords: Side-channel attacks · Sliding window method · CRT-RSA scheme · Secret key recovery · Error correction

1 Introduction

1.1 Background

In this study, we evaluate the risk of side-channel attacks [8] on CRT-RSA [11] (RSA [15] with the Chinese remainder theorem) encryption or signature scheme, which is widely used in public-key cryptosystems. Side-channel attacks extract unrevealed information by observing such as running time [8], power consumption [10], electromagnetic signals [4], or cache access [1,7,14,17].

In the CRT-RSA scheme, there are various kinds of side-channel attacks, especially on exponentiations in decryption [1,4,7,17]. The most common attacks are the extraction of square-and-multiply sequences. First attacks are applied

© Springer Nature Switzerland AG 2020
J. K. Liu and H. Cui (Eds.): ACISP 2020, LNCS 12248, pp. 642–652, 2020.
https://doi.org/10.1007/978-3-030-55304-3_34

to a binary method [10]. These attacks distinguish squaring from multiplication and calculate the exponent immediately, because the exponent and the sequences have a one-to-one correspondence.

However, we cannot determine the exponent immediately from the square-and-multiply sequences in the fixed or sliding window methods, because there are many candidates for each multiplication. Walter addressed this problem by proposing the Big Mac attack [16]. This attack obtains what we multiply in each multiplication, and we can therefore recover the exponent immediately. There are many studies following this strategy [4,7,14,17], and they have discussed how to obtain the multipliers correctly and efficiently.

Unlike the Big Mac Attack, [1] proposed a method for recovering CRT-RSA secret keys d_p and d_q without the multipliers, based on the Heninger–Shacham method [5]. Moreover, it has been proved that this method calculates secret keys in polynomial time when the window size w satisfies $w \le 4$. This method needs less side-channel information and is more reasonable than Big Mac Attack.

However, in practice, [1] fails at recovering secret keys because there are errors in the retrieved square-and-multiply sequences. Experiments in [1] showed that errors occur at an average rate of 0.011 in square-and-multiply sequences. [1] recover these errors via majority voting on 20 square-and-multiply sequences, but there is no guarantee that obtaining 20 square-and-multiply sequences is possible. Therefore, we must consider the security of the CRT-RSA encryption scheme based on one square-and-multiply sequence with errors.

To solve this problem, [13] considered recovering secret keys from square-and-multiply sequences with errors for $w = 1$. Moreover, it has been proved that this method can recover secret keys in polynomial time when there are errors whose rate is less than 0.058 in the obtained square-and-multiply sequences.

However, there is a gap between [1] and [13]. Naturally, it may be possible to recover secret keys in polynomial time from square-and-multiply sequences with errors when $w \le 4$. Thus, we tackle the following two questions:

1. How do we recover secret keys from square-and-multiply sequences with errors?
2. How many errors are tolerable when we recover secret keys?

1.2   Our Contribution

In this paper, by answering these two questions, we discuss recovering CRT-RSA secret keys from square-and-multiply sequences with errors in sliding window method. First, we propose a method for recovering secret keys from square-and-multiply sequences with errors. This is the answer to the first question. Our method is an extension of [13], and thus covers more general cases than it does.

Second, we analyze our method theoretically. This is the answer to the second question. We assume that a squaring flips into a multiplication with probability δ, and a multiplication flips into a squaring with probability δ. We show that our method can recover secret keys when the error rate δ is less than the values in Table 1. There are no ranges of error rate δ for which our method can recover secret keys when $w \geq 5$. Table 1 shows that our method can recover keys from sequences with a higher error rate, namely 0.108 for $w = 1$, compared with the maximum error rate of 0.058 reported in [13].

Finally, we perform numerical experiments using the proposed method. We first perform numerical experiments with various error rate δ values in square-and-multiply sequences. Through these experiments, our method recovers secret keys when δ takes the values given in Table 1. Moreover, our method succeed in $w \leq 4$ at the real error $\delta = 0.011$ as shown in [1]. Therefore, our method recovers secret keys from actual side-channel information in the sliding window method.

Table 1. Tolerable error rate of our method

w	1	2	3	4
Tolerable error rate	0.108	0.067	0.034	0.008

2   Preliminary

In this section, we introduce the CRT-RSA scheme [11] and the left-to-right sliding window method. Moreover, we introduce previous methods for calculating CRT-RSA secret keys from square-and-multiply sequences.

2.1   CRT-RSA Scheme

The CRT-RSA encryption or signature scheme is a faster scheme than the standard RSA scheme [15] because it uses the Chinese remainder theorem (CRT). The CRT-RSA scheme has public keys (N, e) and secret keys (p, q, d, d_p, d_q, q_p). We choose two $n/2$-bit distinct prime numbers p and q, and we choose a small public key e that is prime to $(p - 1)(q - 1)$. Then, we calculate the remain values as $N = pq$, d satisfying $ed \equiv 1 \bmod (p - 1)(q - 1)$, $d_p := d \bmod p - 1$, $d_q := d \bmod q - 1$, and $q_p := q^{-1} \bmod p$.

Now, we explain the CRT-RSA encryption and signature schemes. In the standard RSA scheme, we calculate two exponentiations, $x^e \bmod N$ using public key e and $x^d \bmod N$ using secret keys d. The former exponentiation is used in encryption or verifying the signatures, and the latter exponentiation is used in decryption or generating signatures. In CRT-RSA scheme, instead of calculating $x^d \bmod N$, we calculate two modular exponentiations, $x^{d_p} \bmod p$ and $x^{d_q} \bmod q$, and apply CRT to these two values. This calculation is about four times faster in the CRT-RSA scheme than in the standard RSA scheme.

2.2   Left-to-Right Sliding Window Method

In sliding window method, we precompute the value of c^i for odd i values satisfying $1 \leq i \leq 2^w - 1$ before we calculate an exponentiation. After that, we calculate exponentiations by reading bits from the MSB side to the LSB side. If we read **0**, we conduct a squaring (**S**) once. If we read **1**, we read more $(w - 1)$-bits and conduct squaring (**S**) w times and multiplication (**M**) once in each w-bits. More detail, we find the longest bit-string with the LSB is 1. Next, we set t as the length of bit-string is t and a as the decimalize this bit-string. Then, we square (**S**) t times, multiply (**M**) by a once, and square (**S**) $w - t$ times.

In the sliding window method, an exponentiation can be calculated with less multiplication for a larger w, whereas the number of squaring operations does not change. Therefore, when a larger w is used, exponentiations can be calculated faster. However, to multiply the bits simultaneously, we must store multiple candidate values of c^i in memory, which grows exponentially large with w. Thus, when using the sliding window method, parameter w is set considering this trade-off between implementation time and memory. The value of w used in current applications is 4 or 5.

2.3   Extracting Side-Channel Information from the CRT-RSA Scheme

As mentioned in the previous subsection, we calculate exponentiations through repeated squaring (**S**) and multiplication (**M**) in the sliding window method. [1] proposed a method for recovering secret keys when they obtain the correct square-and-multiply sequences. However, their experiments show that, in practice, there are errors in the obtained square-and-multiply sequences.

In this study, we assume similarly as in [13] that a squaring flips into a multiplication with probability δ, and a multiplication flips into a squaring with probability δ. In this way, we evaluate the number of errors that are tolerable when recovering CRT-RSA secret keys.

2.4   Previous Methods for Recovering CRT-RSA Secret Keys from Square-and-Multiply Sequences

At first, we explain Heninger–Shacham method [5], which is a method for constructing a candidate tree of CRT-RSA secret keys. It uses parameters $(k_p, k_q) \in \mathbb{Z}^2$ satisfying $ed_p = 1 + k_p(p - 1)$ and $ed_q = 1 + k_q(q - 1)$. There are at most $e - 1$ candidate values of (k_p, k_q), and these are calculated by [7,17]. Moreover, we define $\tau(x)$ as $\max_{m \in \mathbb{Z}} 2^m | x$, and $x[i - 1]$ as the i-th bit from LSB side of x.

At each depth of the secret key candidate tree, we have partial information of p, q, d_p, and d_q, defined as p', q', d'_p, and d'_q. At the i-th depth, p' and q' have $(i + 1)$-bits, d'_p has $(i + 1 + \tau(k_p))$-bits, and d'_q has $(i + 1 + \tau(k_q))$-bits. At the root, we set p' and q' as 1, and we calculate d'_p and d'_q using $ed'_p \equiv 1 \bmod 2^{\tau(k_p)+1}$, and $ed_q' \equiv 1 \bmod 2^{\tau(k_q)+1}$. After that, we calculate the bits of p, q, d_p, and d_q using the following equations:

$$p[i] + q[i] \equiv (N - p'q')\,[i],$$
$$d_p[i + \tau(k_p)] + p[i] \equiv (k_p\,(p' - 1) + 1 - ed_p')\,[i + \tau(k_p)],$$
$$d_q[i + \tau(k_q)] + q[i] \equiv (k_q\,(q' - 1) + 1 - ed_q')\,[i + \tau(k_q)].$$

We recover bits to $(n/2 - 1)$-th depth. Then, there is always one correct leaf out of $2^{n/2}$ candidates, which grows exponentially with n. Thus, to search for the correct secret keys efficiently, [1,13] use square-and-multiply sequences.

In [1], we recover secret keys from the correct square-and-multiply sequences. At first, we search the start position of bits generating square-and-multiply sequences correctly. When we recover these bits, we convert the calculated bits into a square-and-multiply sequence, and we discard a leaf if there are mismatches with the given sequence. In theory, we recover secret keys in polynomial time in n when the window size w satisfies $w \leq 4$. This analysis is based on transition matrix on a square-and-multiply sequence proposed in [2]. It should be noted that their method is improved by [12], but this is also based on the correctness of square-and-multiply sequences.

In [13], we recover secret keys from the square-and-multiply sequences with errors in $w = 1$. First, we calculate t bits of d_p and d_q. Second, we convert these bits into square-and-multiply sequences each in d_p and d_q. Then, the square-and-multiply sequences obtained from $2t$ new bits and the given sequences are compared, and the disagreement rate is calculated. After that, the leaves whose disagreement rate is larger than Y are discarded. In theory, we recover secret keys in polynomial time in n when the error rate δ satisfies $\delta \leq 0.058$.

3   Our Proposed Method

3.1   Our Key Recovery Method

Our method adopts a branch-and-bound strategy based on the Heninger–Shacham method [5]. First, we calculate each bit in p, q, d_p, and d_q. Second, we calculate the distance between the given sequences and the calculated sequences. Finally, we prune the leaves whose rank is higher than L, similar to [9]. The difference between our method and [9] is that our method calculates distance based on square-and-multiply sequences.

From now on, we define distance D. First, we define $D_{p,t}$ as the disagreement rate between the given sequences and the calculated sequences generated from the t LSBs of d_p. Similarly, we define $D_{q,t}$ using d_q instead of d_p. Then,

$$D := \max\left(\min_{0 \leq j \leq w-1} D_{p,i+\tau(k_p)+1-j},\ \min_{0 \leq j \leq w-1} D_{q,i+\tau(k_q)+1-j}\right).$$

We now show an example with $w = 3$ in Table 2. Consider the situation that the square-and-multiply sequence of d_p is given as **SMSSMMS** and the square-and-multiply sequence of d_q is given as **SSMSMSM**. Moreover, we calculate 5

LSBs of d_p as **10110** and 5 LSBs of d_q as **01101**. After we convert bits to a square-and-multiply sequence, we calculate the disagreement rate by comparing from the final operations for both sequences. Then, the value of D is 0.25.

Table 2. Example of calculating distance D when $w = 3$

	j	0	1	2
d_p	Bits	**10110**	**0110**	**110**
	Calculated sequence	SSSMSMS	SSSMS	SSMS
	Given sequence	SMSSMMS	SSMMS	SMMS
	Disagreement rate	$3/7 = 0.429$	$1/5 = 0.2$	$1/4 = 0.25$
	$\min_t D_{p,t}$		0.2	
d_q	Bits	**01101**	**1101**	**101**
	Calculated sequence	SSSMSSM	SSMSSM	SSSM
	Given sequence	SSMSMSM	SMSMSM	SMSM
	Disagreement rate	$3/7 = 0.429$	$3/6 = 0.5$	$1/4 = 0.25$
	$\min_t D_{q,t}$			0.25
D	0.25			

3.2 Analysis of the Proposed Method

We will now analyze our method. The main result is given as Theorem 1.

Theorem 1. We set Y_w as Table 1 for each $w \leq 4$. Moreover, we assume that the error rate δ satisfies $\delta < Y_w$. If we store L leaves at each level of the candidate tree of the CRT-RSA secret keys, our method will correctly recover n-bit CRT-RSA secret keys in $\max\left(O\left(n^2 L\right), O\left(nL \log L\right)\right)$ time with probability

$$1 - \left(\frac{w^2 2^{2w - 2\alpha_\varepsilon - 4}}{1 - 2^{-2\alpha_\varepsilon}} \frac{n}{L} + \frac{2\exp\left(2(w-1)\varepsilon^2\right)}{1 - \exp\left(-2\varepsilon^2\right)} L^{-2\varepsilon^2 \log e} \right)$$

for some positive real numbers ε and α_ε.

In Theorem 1, the failure probability converges to 0 when $L \to \infty$. The value of L for which our method runs in polynomial time in n is given in Corollary 1.

Corollary 1. Let $L = n^{1+\gamma}$ $(\gamma > 0)$ in our proposed method. Then, as $n \to \infty$, the success probability of our method converges to 1, and the time complexity is given as $O\left(n^{3+\gamma} \log n\right)$, which is polynomial time in n.

Now, we focus on the evaluation of success probability. The analysis of time complexity is given as the full version. To evaluate success probability, we adopt new assumptions similar to [3]. The major difference is that we consider errors to analyze our proposed method.

1. The given square-and-multiply sequences are generated from random bits.
2. The calculated bits of d_p and d_q from incorrect leaves are independent.
3. When $(i + \tau(k_p) + 1)$ LSBs of d_p' are the same and the next bit is different with d_p, $\Pr\left[D_{p,t+\tau(k_p)+1} \leq Y\right] \leq 2^{-(t-i)H}$ with some constant $H \in [0,1]$. This is satisfied similarly in d_q.

Our analysis is divided into two parts, obtaining the condition of δ and Y satisfying $H > 1/2$, and evaluating the failure probability in a similar as [9]. When $H > 1/2$, the number of leaves satisfying $D \leq Y$ is constant, then the success probability is $1 - O(n/L)$. Now, we deal the first part by proving Lemma 1. We give the sketch proof, and the detailed proof is given in the full version.

Lemma 1. Let the value of Y_w be as in Table 1 and the value of δ be $\delta < Y_w$ for $w \leq 4$. We define x_t as the randomly chosen t bits and define C_{x_t} as the square-and-multiply sequence generated from x_t. Moreover, we define O as the given square-and-multiply sequence, which is generated from random bits and has an added error rate of δ. We define $d_{C_{x_t},O}$ as the disagreement rate between C_{x_t} and the corresponding operations in O. Then, some positive real values ε and α_ε exist such that $\Pr\left[d_{C_{x_t},O} \leq \delta + \varepsilon\right] = 2^{-t(1/2+\alpha_\varepsilon)}$.

Proof. First, we evaluate the probability P_Y of the calculated sequence having a disagreement rate less than Y when compared with O. We define random variable l_{x_t} as the length of C_{x_t}. Then, we define $O_{l_{x_t}}$ as the corresponding operations in O. We also define random variable e_{x_t} as the number of errors found between $O_{l_{x_t}}$ and C_{x_t}. Moreover, we define random variable Z_{x_t} as $Z_{x_t} = l_{x_t}Y - e_{x_t}$. Then, P_Y is less than $\inf\limits_{s>0} E\left[\exp\left(sZ_{x_t}\right)\right]$.

Now, we can write $E\left[\exp\left(sZ_{x_t}\right)\right]$ as $\boldsymbol{v}M_s^t\left[11\ldots1\right]^T$, where $\boldsymbol{v}$ is some constant-valued vector, and T means the transpose. We define J_s as the Jordan form of M_s. Then, a regular matrix Q exists such that $M_s = QJ_sQ^{-1}$. Therefore,

$$E\left[\exp\left(sZ_{x_t}\right)\right] = \boldsymbol{v}M_s^t\left[11\ldots1\right]^T = (\boldsymbol{v}Q)\,J_s^t\left(Q^{-1}\left[11\ldots1\right]^T\right).$$

Now, we define λ_{M_s} as the largest absolute value of the eigenvalues of M_s. Then, we have $\inf\limits_{s>0} E\left[\exp\left(sZ_{x_t}\right)\right] \sim \left(\inf\limits_{s>0}\lambda_{M_s}\right)^t$, and this means $P_Y \leq \left(\inf\limits_{s>0}\lambda_{M_s}\right)^t$.

Next, we calculate the value of λ_{M_s} numerically using Matlab, because we cannot calculate the value of λ_{M_s} analytically. First, we generate matrix M_s by setting the values of δ, Y, and s. From this matrix M_s, we calculate $H_s = -\log\lambda_{M_s}$. The value of H_s is given as in Table 3. For larger δ, we cannot find any s satisfying $H_s > 1/2$.

We now prove Lemma 1. If $\delta < Y_w$ and $Y = \delta$, there is an s such that $H_s > 1/2$, as shown in Table 3. Moreover, because $E\left[\exp\left(sZ_{x_t}\right)\right]$ is a continuous function of Y, there are some positive real-valued ε and α_ε such that $P_{\delta+\varepsilon} \leq 2^{-t(1/2+\alpha_\varepsilon)}$. This proves Lemma 1 . $\qquad\square$

Table 3. Values of H_s

w	1	2	3	4
$\delta = Y$	0.108	0.067	0.034	0.008
s	1.7	1.9	2.1	3.1
H_s	0.5001	0.5008	0.5002	0.5026

We now give brief evaluation of the failure probability of the proposed method using Lemma 1. First, we evaluate P_t, which is the probability that a leaf containing correct information is discarded at the t-th depth of the candidate tree of the CRT-RSA secret keys. The number of leaves generated is 2^t at the t-th depth. Then, we define X_1 as a leaf containing correct information, and we define the other leaves as X_i $(2 \leq i \leq 2^t)$. Moreover, we define C_i as the distance of X_i from the given square-and-multiply sequences. Now, similar as [9],

$P_t \leq \dfrac{1}{L} \displaystyle\sum_{i=2}^{2^t} \Pr\left[C_i \leq \delta + \varepsilon\right] + \Pr\left[C_1 \geq \delta + \varepsilon\right]$. By using Lemma 1, the first term

is upper bounded by $\dfrac{w^2 2^{2w - 2\alpha_\varepsilon - 3}}{L\left(1 - 2^{-2\alpha_\varepsilon}\right)}$ with some positive real value $\alpha_\varepsilon > 0$. More-

over, by using Hoeffding's theorem [6], the second term is upper bounded by $2\exp\left(-2(t - w + 1)\varepsilon^2\right)$. Pruning is conducted on $(\lfloor \log L \rfloor + 1) \leq t \leq n/2$. Thus,

$$P = \sum_{t=\lfloor \log L \rfloor + 1}^{n/2} P_t \leq \frac{w^2 2^{2w - 2\alpha_\varepsilon - 4}}{1 - 2^{-2\alpha_\varepsilon}} \frac{n}{L} + \frac{2\exp\left(2(w - 1)\varepsilon^2\right)}{1 - \exp\left(-2\varepsilon^2\right)} L^{-2\varepsilon^2 \log e}.$$

In conclusion, we prove the failure probability in Theorem 1.

4 Numerical Experiments

In this section, we show the results of numerical experiments conducted on the proposed method. We conducted these numerical experiments using NTL library 11.3.2 on C++. Moreover, we assumed that we know the values of k_p and k_q, and the actual time may be 2^{15} times as long as these experimental results.

We ran the proposed method on 1024-bit and 2048-bit CRT-RSA, corresponding to $n = 1024$ and 2048, respectively. For each n, we set parameters (w, δ, L). For $n = 1024$, we set $L = 2^{10}$ based on Corollary 1. Similarly, for $n = 2048$, we set $L = 2^{11}$. Moreover, we set (w, δ). For each (n, w, δ, L), we generated 100 secret keys and measured the success rate and average implementation times for each successful trial. The results are given in Tables 4, 5, 6 and 7.

From these results, it can be seen that we can almost always recover CRT-RSA secret keys when δ is less than that shown in Table 1. Moreover, we can even recover a few secret keys when δ is slightly more than that shown in Table 1. Therefore, our theoretical analysis matches these experimental results. However, when $w = 4$, our method recovered 29% of the secret keys for $n = 1024$ and 9%

Table 4. Experimental results for $w = 1$

	δ	0	0.02	0.04	0.06	0.08	0.09	0.1	0.11	0.12	0.13
$n = L = 1024$	Success rate (%)	100	99	88	59	31	19	7	3	1	0
	Time (s)		8.76	9.73	8.11	8.63	9.24	10.7	9.13	15.4	10.8	–
$n = L = 2048$	Success rate (%)	100	100	77	35	10	6	0			
	Time (s)		49.7	49.8	53.2	54.2	54.0	66.8	–			

Table 5. Experimental results for $w = 2$

	δ	0	0.02	0.04	0.06	0.07	0.08	0.09
$n = L = 1024$	Success rate (%)	100	89	45	16	6	1	0
	Time (s)		10.9	11.2	10.1	9.85	18.5	8.06	–
$n = L = 2048$	Success rate (%)	100	73	26	2	1	0	
	Time (s)		58.8	61.6	55.3	62.8	46.3	–	

Table 6. Experimental results for $w = 3$

	δ	0	0.01	0.02	0.03	0.035	0.04	0.045	0.05
$n = L = 1024$	Success rate (%)	100	84	42	23	15	7	7	0
	Time (s)		9.23	9.10	10.0	9.54	19.1	13.0	17.8	–
$n = L = 2048$	Success rate (%)	100	61	25	3	1	1	0	
	Time (s)		62.6	59.4	60.5	57.8	55.9	54.6	–	

Table 7. Experimental results for $w = 4$

	δ	0	0.005	0.01	0.015	0.02	0.025	0.03	0.035
$n = L = 1024$	Success rate (%)	100	58	29	7	5	1	2	0
	Time (s)		11.5	11.3	11.8	9.92	15.6	8.11	8.10	–
$n = L = 2048$	Success rate (%)	100	41	9	1	1	0		
	Time (s)		71.2	66.0	54.2	55.4	58.5	–		

for $n = 2048$ when $\delta = 0.01$, although the theoretical bound is $\delta = 0.008$. This is because we just evaluated the lower bound of the success probability.

Next, we consider the actual errors $\delta = 0.011$ reported in [1]. From Tables 4, 5 and 6, our method can recover many secret keys when $w \leq 3$. When $w = 4$ and $\delta = 0.011$, we conducted an additional experiment, and our method recovered 18% of the secret keys for $n = L = 1024$ and 5% for $n = L = 2048$. Thus, our method recovered secret keys for $w \leq 4$.

5 Conclusion

In this paper, we discuss how to recover CRT-RSA secret keys from square-and-multiply sequences with errors in the sliding window method. First, we proposed a method for recovering secret keys from square-and-multiply sequences with errors. Second, we analyzed our method theoretically, and calculated the upper bounds of the error rates δ in the square-and-multiply sequences, as in Table 1. Finally, we performed numerical experiments using the proposed method.

Acknowledgements. The first author is supported by a JSPS Fellowship for Young Scientists. This research was partially supported by JSPS Grant-in-Aid for JSPS Fellows 20J11754 and JST CREST Grant Number JPMJCR14D6, Japan.

References

1. Bernstein, D.J., et al.: Sliding right into disaster: left-to-right sliding windows leak. In: Fischer, W., Homma, N. (eds.) CHES 2017. LNCS, vol. 10529, pp. 555–576. Springer, Cham (2017). https://doi.org/10.1007/978-3-319-66787-4_27
2. Breitner, J., Skorski, M.: Analytic formulas for renyi entropy of hidden Markov models. eprint arXiv: 1709.09699 (2017)
3. Breitner, J.: More on sliding right. IACR eprint: 2018.1163 (2018)
4. Genkin, D., Pachmanov, L., Pipman, I., Tromer, E.: Stealing keys from PCs using a radio: cheap electromagnetic attacks on windowed exponentiation. In: Güneysu, T., Handschuh, H. (eds.) CHES 2015. LNCS, vol. 9293, pp. 207–228. Springer, Heidelberg (2015). https://doi.org/10.1007/978-3-662-48324-4_11
5. Heninger, N., Shacham, H.: Reconstructing RSA private keys from random key bits. In: Halevi, S. (ed.) CRYPTO 2009. LNCS, vol. 5677, pp. 1–17. Springer, Heidelberg (2009). https://doi.org/10.1007/978-3-642-03356-8_1
6. Hoeffding, W.: Probability inequalities for sums of bounded random variables. J. Am. Stat. Assoc. **58**, 13–30 (1963). https://doi.org/10.1080/01621459.1963.10500830
7. İnci, M.S., Gulmezoglu, B., Irazoqui, G., Eisenbarth, T., Sunar, B.: Cache attacks enable bulk key recovery on the cloud. In: Gierlichs, B., Poschmann, A.Y. (eds.) CHES 2016. LNCS, vol. 9813, pp. 368–388. Springer, Heidelberg (2016). https://doi.org/10.1007/978-3-662-53140-2_18
8. Kocher, P.C.: Timing attacks on implementations of Diffie-Hellman, RSA, DSS, and other systems. In: Koblitz, N. (ed.) CRYPTO 1996. LNCS, vol. 1109, pp. 104–113. Springer, Heidelberg (1996). https://doi.org/10.1007/3-540-68697-5_9
9. Kunihiro, N., Honda, J.: RSA meets DPA: recovering RSA secret keys from noisy analog data. In: Batina, L., Robshaw, M. (eds.) CHES 2014. LNCS, vol. 8731, pp. 261–278. Springer, Heidelberg (2014). https://doi.org/10.1007/978-3-662-44709-3_15
10. Messerges, T.S., Dabbish, E.A., Sloan, R.H.: Power analysis attacks of modular exponentiation in smartcards. In: Koç, Ç.K., Paar, C. (eds.) CHES 1999. LNCS, vol. 1717, pp. 144–157. Springer, Heidelberg (1999). https://doi.org/10.1007/3-540-48059-5_14
11. Moriarty, K., Kaliski, B., Jonsson, J., Rusch, A.: PKCS #1: RSA cryptography specifications version 2.2 (2016). https://tools.ietf.org/html/rfc8017

12. Oonishi, K., Huang, X., Kunihiro, N.: Improved CRT-RSA secret key recovery method from sliding window leakage. In: Seo, J.H. (ed.) ICISC 2019. LNCS, vol. 11975, pp. 278–296. Springer, Cham (2020). https://doi.org/10.1007/978-3-030-40921-0_17

13. Oonishi, K., Kunihiro, N.: Attacking noisy secret CRT-RSA exponents in binary method. In: Lee, K. (ed.) ICISC 2018. LNCS, vol. 11396, pp. 37–54. Springer, Cham (2019). https://doi.org/10.1007/978-3-030-12146-4_3

14. Percival, C.: Cache missing for fun and profit (2005). http://www.daemonology.net/papers/htt.pdf

15. Rivest, R.L., Shamir, A., Adleman, L.: A method for obtaining digital signatures and public-key cryptosystems. Commun. ACM **21**, 120–126 (1978). https://doi.org/10.1145/359340.359342

16. Walter, C.D.: Sliding windows succumbs to big mac attack. In: Koç, Ç.K., Naccache, D., Paar, C. (eds.) CHES 2001. LNCS, vol. 2162, pp. 286–299. Springer, Heidelberg (2001). https://doi.org/10.1007/3-540-44709-1_24

17. Yarom, Y., Genkin, D., Heninger, N.: CacheBleed: a timing attack on OpenSSL constant time RSA. In: Gierlichs, B., Poschmann, A.Y. (eds.) CHES 2016. LNCS, vol. 9813, pp. 346–367. Springer, Heidelberg (2016). https://doi.org/10.1007/978-3-662-53140-2_17

Security Analysis on Tangle-Based Blockchain Through Simulation

Bozhi Wang[1,3], Qin Wang[2,3](✉), Shiping Chen[3], and Yang Xiang[2]

[1] University of New South Wales, Sydney, Australia
bozhi.wang@student.unsw.edu.au
[2] Swinburne University of Technology, Hawthorn, Australia
{qinwang,yixang}@swin.edu.au
[3] CSIRO Data 61, Sydney, Australia
Shiping.Chen@data61.csiro.au

Abstract. Tangle provides an enlightening paradigm for DAG-based structures. We build a simple but flexible simulation network for Tangle by identifying its features. Based on that, we construct three types of attack strategies via defining basic actions and behaviours. We further evaluate these attacks in multi-dimensions with 12 sets of experiments, followed by comprehensive discussions. The results show the trend under different strategies and configurations. Our work provides an educational example for both attack and defense towards Tangle-based blockchains.

Keywords: Tangle · DAG · Blockchain · Attack · IOTA

1 Introduction

Directed Acyclic Graph (DAG) is designed to improve the scalability and performance of traditional blockchains. Tangle structure, proposed by IOTA [8], is one of the leading DAG-based projects. Tangle has properties of *high throughput*: transactions can be attached to the network from different directions and verified by previous transactions in parallel without serious congestion; *high performance*: newly arrived transactions are confirmed by the previous two transactions via a tiny Proof of Work (PoW) mechanism, where the computer consumption can be ignored when compared to traditional PoW; *low cost*: no transaction fees are charged to fit for situations such as IoT and edge computing.

However, Tangle structure confronts potential threats on the fork of subgraphs due to the multi-directional expansive network [9]. Specifically, Tangle achieves delayed confirmation and partial consistency in multiple directions, instead of an instant confirmation such as BFT-style consensus [3]. The gap between delayed confirmation and instant confirmation leaves a blank of uncertainty and reversibility for attackers [5]. Existing chains are also threatened

---

B. Wang and Q. Wang—These authors contributed equally to the work.

J. K. Liu and H. Cui (Eds.): ACISP 2020, LNCS 12248, pp. 653–663, 2020.
https://doi.org/10.1007/978-3-030-55304-3_35

by miners who own insurmountable computing power to send massive transactions. Newly issued transactions are unpredictably attached to different subgraphs without global reconciliation. As a result, no leading subgraph is formed to maintain stability. The forks will frequently happen and the system confronts the risk of parasite chain attack and double-spending attack [1]. In this paper, we aim to provide analyses on such risks by establishing three types of attacks through a simluation network. Detailed contributions are summarized as follows.

- **Simulation of Tangle:** We rebuild a simulation network with identified features of Tangle to provide an experimental environment in Sect. 2.
- **Construction of attack strategy:** We define three actions as the basic benchmarks to construct our attack strategies in Sect. 3 and Sect. 4.
- **Evaluations/Discussions of attacks:** We provide evaluations and discussions on constructed attack strategies by multiple metrics in Sect. 5.

Related Work. Rather than focusing on the consensus at block level, DAG prioritizes consensus at transaction level. Tangle, inheriting advantages from transaction-based structures, is suitable for micro-services. The properties and applications of Tangle are explicitly described in [6,8,9]. Further improvements of Tangle [1,2,4] are also proposed to strengthen the potential weakness.

2 Structure of Tangle Simulation

In this section, we identify key features of IOTA for the Tangle simulation.

Feature of Data Structure. Transactions are the smallest component serving for basic operations and metadata storage in IOTA, but a complete cycle of event like token transferring relies on a data structure called *bundle*. Bundle is a top-level construction used to link related transactions in one group. The bundle itself cannot be broadcast, instead, a collection of individual transactions are broadcast. Since bundle is a virtual entity where all steps are executed through transactions, we employ a transaction model (UTXO) to simplify the bundle.

Feature of Topology. Tangle bases on DAG where the vertex represents *transaction* and the edge represents *verification relationship*. It integrates the processes of generating transaction and making consensus into one step. Once newly generated transactions, *a.k.a* tips, are attached to Tangle, the consensus is simultaneously launched. Tips are loosely organized by the rule – each tip verifies two parent transactions. Our simulation follows this rule without modifications.

Feature of Tip Selection. Tip selection represents selection strategies of newly generated transactions. Three mechanisms are provided in [8]. No matter which mechanisms is adopted, the selection processes can be regarded as a variant of random algorithm. We captures three influential factors including cumulative weight, level difference, and operation time as our simulated parameters.

3   Construction of Attack Strategies

In this section, we provide three main attack strategies: Parasite Attack (PS), Double Spending Attack (DS) and Hybrid Attack (HB). Each strategy represents a family of concrete attacks that inherit the same foundations.

Layer0: Unit Action. The smallest unit actions at the bottom layer (*layer0*) is to describe the behaviours a node may select. Specifically, we list three actions: *Action A* - it represents whether a tip is: *valid* $[A_1]$ or *invalid* $[A_2]$. *Action B* - it represents whether a tip is attach to parent tips: by the random selection mechanism $[B_1]$ or by selecting transactions issued by the same nodes/entities $[B_2]$. Here we call B_2 as selfish selection. *Action C* - it represents whether a tip is selected from the valid pool $[C_1]$ or invalid pool $[C_2]$. Each unit action is determined by two possible choices and we denote this process as a *binary selection* for simplicity. The combination of unit actions make up an atomic behaviour in *layer1*. The *selfish* selection means a tip and a parent transaction is issued by the node with a same identity (honest/malicious). Note that, all actions and behaviours are mainly focused on the malicious nodes since the honest nodes can only conduct honest behaviours. Here, we summarise the possible selections.

Action A	Action B	Action C
Valid Tx $[A_1]$	Random Selection $[B_1]$	Valid Pool $[C_1]$
Invalid Tx $[A_2]$	Selfish Selection $[B_2]$	Invalid Pool $[C_2]$

Layer1: Atomic Behaviour. *Layer1* is a collective set of behaviours made up by different combinations of unit actions. The behavior is used to present how to generate a transaction at the initial stage. The behaviour is atomic for the construction of attack strategies and is closely related to the category of attack types. Every single behaviour covers unit actions A, B, and C, and we employ the binary selection 1 and 0 to distinguish their combinations, where 1 to represents the element in $\{A_1, B_1, C_1\}$, and 0 is $\{A_2, B_2, C_2\}$.

There are 8 possible *atomic behaviours*, which is used to describe how a malicious node executes transactions. Take 101 - (A_1, B_2, C_1) as an example, it means the behaviour that: *A malicious node generates a valid transaction, being selfishly attached to parent tips from a valid pool*. These behaviors are feasible in the simulation without logic error, denoted as Y. On the contrary, the behaviors 100 is infeasible, since there is no invalid transaction in the network if malicious nodes only send valid transactions. And the behaviors 000 is infeasible, neither, since for a malicious node, selfishly attaching process from an invalid pool is equal to the random selection from an invalid pool, so that 000 is equal to 010. Therefore, only 6 of them are feasible with the index from a to f, respectively.

Layer2: Combined Attack Strategy. Based on the behaviors in *layer1*, we construct attack strategies in *layer2*. We categorize three types including Parasite Attack (PS), Double Spending Attacks (DS) and Hybrid Attacks (HB).

Binary selection	Action combination	Feasibility	Index
111	(A_1, B_1, C_1)	Y	a
110	(A_1, B_1, C_2)	Y	b
101	(A_1, B_2, C_1)	Y	c
100	(A_1, B_2, C_2)	N	–
011	(A_2, B_1, C_1)	Y	d
010	(A_2, B_1, C_2)	Y	e
001	(A_2, B_2, C_1)	Y	f
000	(A_2, B_2, C_2)	N	–

The parasite attack means an attacker secretly creates a sub-Tangle with a high weight for the profit. It may reverse the main Tangle when newly generated transactions are loosely distributed. Double spending attack splits Tangle into two branches so that s/he can spend a coin multiple times.

We define PS and DS are pure attacks without mutual overlaps, and HB represents attacks covering overlapped behaviors such as f. We also define the decision principle Φ on how to categorize attack types by a four-stage process: *Stage1* - Confusion behavior; *Stage2* - Send the invalid Tx; *Stage3* - Verify the invalid Tx; *Stage4* - Overlapped behaviour. In *Stage1*, the confusion behavior means a malicious node pretends to act as an honest node, such as a: *A malicious node sends a valid transaction, being randomly attached to parent tips from a valid pool.* We cannot distinguish whether the transaction is issued by an honest or malicious node. *Stage2* represents a malicious node sends invalid transactions, and related behaviors in *layer2* are (d, e, f). *Stage3* refers to the parent tip selection, and related behaviors are (b, e). *Stage4* provides overlapped behaviors including (c, f). Putting them together, a general decision principle Φ is $\boxed{\Phi : (a, -) \mid (d, e, f, -) \mid (b, e, -) \mid (c, f, -)}$.

Alternatively, based on Φ, we provide concrete decision principles for PS, DS, and HB, which are denoted as $\Phi[\text{PS}]$, $\Phi[\text{DS}]$ and $\Phi[\text{HB}]$, respectively. The key principle of PS is to selfishly select the parent transactions, while the key of DS is to send/verify invalid transactions. But there are several overlapped behaviors and some logic errors. Therefore, we provide specified decision principles separately listed as $\{\Phi \mid \Phi[\text{PS}], \Phi[\text{DS}], \Phi[\text{HB}]\}$. Then, we back to the reason why the behavior f is an overlapped behavior. f means: *A malicious node sends an invalid transaction, being selfishly attached to the parent tips from the valid pool.* f selfishly selects its parent tips, satisfying $\Phi[\text{PS}]$. Meanwhile, f sends an invalid transaction to the network, satisfying $\Phi[\text{DS}]$. Thus, f is an overlapped behavior applied in hybrid attacks ($\Phi[\text{HB}]$). We summarise attack strategies as follows.

Attack types	Decision principle	Feasible behavior	Attack strategies
	(a, -) | (d, e, f, -) | (b, e, -) | (c,f,-)		
PS	(a, -) | - | - | (c)	c, f	c, ac (2)
DS	(a,-) | (d, e) | (b,e) | -	b, d, e, f	e,ae,bd,de,abd, ade,bde,abde (7)
HB	(a, -) | (d, e, f) | (b, e) | (c, f)	f	ce, bf, ef, cef, bcf, bef, bce, def, cde, bdf, bcd, aef, acef, abf, abcf, ace, abef, abce, adef, acde, abdf, abcd (22)

4 Implementation

Parameters and Notations. There are two types of parameters. The first are binary parameters such as (A_1, A_2) used for the construction of attacks. The second are parameters such as operating time, number of total transactions, *etc*, which are used for adjusting configurations. Related continuous variables are: total transactions T, honest transaction H, invalid Transaction F, interval between two tips D, height of block h, simulation operating time $\mathcal{T}$, level difference $\mathcal{L}$ and cumulative weight $\mathcal{W}$. Specifically, *Level Difference $\mathcal{L}$:* level represents transactions that are identified with the same height. Level Difference is the distance of the heights between current tips and the selected parent transactions. *Cumulative Weight $\mathcal{W}$:* it is the sum of unit weights from attached transactions. The unit weight $w[i]$ randomly varies from 1 to 4 to avoid the fraud, and w_c is current weight. p is the tip selection probability. *Operation Time $\mathcal{T}$:* it represents the executed time of a transaction since it was generated. A transaction will be discarded when times out. Besides, derived parameters include: strategy space $\mathbb{S}$, total transactions $ratio(\mathcal{F}) = F/T$ and ratio between different behaviors in one strategy $ratio(\mathcal{B}) = x : y : z$, where xyz is depended on initial settings.

Key Principles. The growth of a DAG relies on increasingly attached transactions. Previous transactions get weighted through *cumulative weight ($\mathcal{W}$)*. Two aspects are considered: the configurations of unit weights and the methods to select parent tips. The unit weight of a single transaction randomly varies from 1 to 4 to provide a better simulation for the real scenario. The parent selection takes key metrics into consideration, containing cumulative weight, operation time, level difference. Then, we provide two principles limit the size of network:

Tip selection decides how tips choose parent transactions, and *Invalid transaction decision* shows how a transaction is discarded.

Definition 1 (Mechanism For Tip Selection).

$$p = 3 \times |15 - \mathcal{W}_i| + \frac{100}{5^{\mathcal{L}}} - 1.5^{\frac{\mathcal{T}}{60}} \quad (p \geq 0)$$
$$where, \quad w[1] = w_c \quad (\mathcal{L} = 1)$$
$$w[i] = 0.8w[i-1] \quad (\mathcal{L} = 2 - 6)$$
$$= 0.9w[i-1] \quad (\mathcal{L} = 7 - 16)$$
$$= 0.01w[1] \quad (\mathcal{L} = 17 - 29)$$
$$\mathcal{W}_i = \mathcal{W}_{i-1} + w[i], \quad i \in \mathcal{L}$$

We observe that the selection probability p is mainly influenced by three factors: $\mathcal{L}$, $\mathcal{W}$ and $\mathcal{T}$. $\mathcal{L}$ varies inversely with p, which means a tip tends to be impossibly selected as the level difference increases. $\mathcal{W}$ is an iterative algorithm within three intervals according to $\mathcal{L}$. The equation at different intervals has a different decay rate. The tips need to be smoothly decayed with a small level difference (meaning near to the latest transaction) while be sharply decayed at a high difference. $\mathcal{T}$ is used to prevent tips from being suspended for a long time.

Definition 2 (Decision For Invalid Transaction). *A tip is discarded, $Tx = \perp$, when triggering the condition:* $\{Tx = \perp \mid \underline{\mathcal{L} > 30} \mid\mid \mathcal{W} < 30 \cap \underline{\mathcal{T} > 1000\,s}\}$.

We obtain that a tip will be decided as invalid when exceeding thresholds either on the specified level difference (30) or on the operation time (1000 s). Our simulations and evaluations only consider valid transactions.

Implementation Logic. Our implementation is based on a Tangle simulation and constructed attack strategies. The main logic of our implementation includes: receiving transactions from peer nodes, generating/sending new transactions, and launching the attack strategies. Due to the page limitation, the logic with source codes could be found in: https://github.com/BozhiWang/Tangle-based-Blockchain-attack-simulation.

Implementation Goals. We provide four goals to evaluate attack strategies under different configurations. *Goal I* aims to test the influence of different attacks strategies (mainly hybrid attacks), namely (S). *Goal II* is going to test the influence of different ratios of combined behaviours, namely Ratio($\mathcal{B}$). *Goal III* is to test the influence of total nodes. *Goal IV* is focused on the selfish strategy combine by ac. Detailed settings are presented at Table 1 in Appendix A.

5 Evaluation and Discussion

Based on Goals, the simulations provide different types of results. In this section, we firstly give the specified inputs and outputs, and then show the trends of different testing sets. Detailed data and other outputs are presented in Appendix B.

Analysis on Result I. In Simulation I, we provide totally eight attack strategies $\{S \mid bd, be, ac, abe, ade, abd, e, abcd, abdf\}$, the corresponding Ratio($\mathcal{B}$) of each strategy, and three Ratio($\mathcal{F}$) = $\{\mathcal{F} \mid 10\%\}$ as the input parameters. The outputs contain confirmed invalid transactions, confirm time, abandoned invalid transactions and abandoned valid transactions. From *Result I* in Fig. 1(a), we can find the trend caused by different factors. (1) For the same strategies, no matter how they are made up, such as *ade e* and *abcd*, the confirmed invalid transactions are increasing along with the number of malicious nodes in a positive correlation. The confirm time varies in a range of 200–800 s. The abandoned transactions significantly increase with the number of malicious nodes. (2) For the different hybrid strategies, Ratio($\mathcal{F}$) has different influences on them. Several strategies are sensitive to the changes like *abe, be*. (3) The abandoned invalid transactions and valid transactions increase at the same time along with changes on Ratio($\mathcal{F}$) where malicious nodes have a significant influence.

Analysis on Result II. In Simulation II, we set strategies $\{S \mid abe, ade, abd\}$, Ratio($\mathcal{F}$) = $\{\mathcal{F} \mid 10\%, 20\%, 30\%\}$, and Ratio($\mathcal{B}$) = $\{\mathcal{B} \mid 811, 622, 433, 631, 613\}$ as the input parameters. The outputs are ratios between invalid transactions and total transactions. From *Result II* in Fig. 1(b), we find that (1) For the Ratio($\mathcal{F}$) in the same strategies such as *ade*, invalid transactions significantly increases along with nodes. The trend is determinate for such situations. (2) For different strategies, Ratio($\mathcal{F}$) has different influences on them. *ade* varies monotonously with the ratio, while the other two have a peak value at a certain ratio. (3) The attack is sensitive to some behaviors such as *b*. Invalid transactions in strategies containing *b* (*abe, abd*) are significantly that without *b*.

Analysis on Result III. In Simulation III, we set three attack strategies $\{S \mid abe, adeabd\}$ with initial Ratio($\mathcal{B}$) = $\{\mathcal{B} \mid 622\}$. There are three Ratio($\mathcal{F}$) = $\{\mathcal{F} \mid 10\%, 20\%, 30\%\}$ and four sets of total nodes $\{Tx \mid 20, 50, 100, 200\}$ as the input parameters. The outputs are the ratio between confirmed invalid transactions and total transactions. From *Result III* in Fig. 1(c), we find (1) For the same strategy, such as *ade*, the trend of ratio is relatively stable under different Ratio($\mathcal{F}$). (2) The ratio maintains stable when the Ratio($\mathcal{B}$) increases. This also means the ratio of invalid with total transactions varies slightly with the malicious nodes. The number of malicious nodes has little influence on the ratio. (3) For different combinations, strategies like *ade* are sensitive to variations than others like *abe, abd*. The results show a significant difference in these strategies.

Analysis on Result IV. In Simulation IV, the first test initializes 100 nodes with Ratio($\mathcal{F}$) = $\{\mathcal{F} \mid 10\%\}$ and Ratio($\mathcal{B}$) = $\{\mathcal{B} \mid 91, 82, 73, 64, 55, 46\}$. The second sets Ratio($\mathcal{F}$) = $\{\mathcal{F} \mid 10\%, 20\%, 30\%\}$, Ratio($\mathcal{B}$) = $\{\mathcal{B} \mid 82\}$ and $\{T \mid 20, 50, 100, 200\}$. The third test initializes 100 total nodes, Ratio($\mathcal{F}$) = $\{\mathcal{F} \mid 10\%, 20\%, 30\%\}$ and Ratio($\{\mathcal{B} \mid 91, 82, 73, 64, 55, 46\}$) as input parameters. The outputs are the ratio between valid transactions and total transactions. From *Result IV* in Fig. 1(d), we find (1) valid transactions maintain relatively stable under different Ratio($\mathcal{B}$). (2) The ratio is stable whenever Ratio($\mathcal{F}$) increases or total nodes increase. This means the ratio of valid with total transactions vary slightly with malicious nodes and the number of malicious nodes has slight impact. (3) The changes of Ratio($\mathcal{B}$) and Ratio($\mathcal{F}$) have slight influences on results. The results show that selfish results are only related to selfish behaviors and independent of their combination/strategy. Tangle maintains stable under selfish behaviors.

Discussions on Our Simulations. We answer the questions listed below.

Myth 1. Are Tangle-Based Blockchains Important in DAG Systems? DAG systems aim to improve the scalability via parallel processing. Tangle is a pioneer to inspire numerous open-sourced projects. DAG projects based on blocks such as Conflux [7] partially change the original concept of scalability, since transactions need to be eventually sequenced in a uniform order. At present, Tangle maximally inherits the concept of DAG, where security analyses on it are educational.

Myth 2. Does the Simulation Benefit for a Real Scenario? The simulation captures key features of real Tangle-based projects. Although a simulation cannot completely reflect real situations in large network due to the design limitation, it still provides an intuitive way to quantitatively analyze the properties and security under different strategies or configurations. The results demonstrate several vulnerabilities in different scenarios, which would be a benefit for future design.

Myth 3. What the Main Factors of the Attack Effects? The attacks (DS, PS, HB) are sensitive to Ratio($\mathcal{B}$), and the methods on how to make up a strategy have significant impact on attacks. To prevent such effects, factors need to be carefully considered including binary actions, ratio of behaviors, ratio of malicious nodes, and strategies. However, the effect of a selfish behavior is limited in a specified range. The effect appears when a strategy contains one or more selfish behaviors.

Myth 4. What do We Learned from the Simulation? This provide us several enlightening points. (1) Tangle can maintain stability in case of selfish behaviors no matter how it made up or how many selfish nodes exist. (2) Increasing malicious nodes will significantly increase the absolute number of transactions instead of probability since successful attacks (the ratio of {Confirmed Invalid Tx}/{Total Invalid Tx}) maintains stable under different Ratio($\mathcal{F}$). (3) Tangle structure is sensitive to binary actions in *Layer0*. Actions are deterministic for a final success.

Limitations and Future Work. The complicated testing goals and experimental results may confuse readers. However, this paper mainly explains how to analyze a fresh new blockchain structure by building up a simulation model and progressively establishing on-top attack strategies. The comprehensive experiments are tested in multi-dimensions, where various aspects could be further studied. Detailed analyses on the single attack are not provided due to the limitation of pages, such as whether 51% is enough for parasite attacks. Therefore, we will continue diving into more specific attacks in the future.

Conclusion. Tangle is a promising structure in current DAGs. However, the performance gain brings potential security risks. In this paper, we construct three

Table 1. Configurations on goals (Appendix A)

Total Node	Ratio(F)	S (HB)	Ratio(B)	Total Node	Ratio(F)	S (HB)	Ratio(B)	Total Node	Ratio(F)	S (HB)	Ratio(B)
	Set 1				Set 2				Set 3		
100	20%	bd	5:5	100	20%	ade	4:3:3	100	20%	e	4:2:2:2
100	20%	be	5:5	100	20%	abe	4:3:3	100	20%	abcd	4:2:2:2
100	20%	-	-	100	20%	abd	4:3:3	100	20%	abdf	4:2:2:2

Total Node	Ratio(F)	S (PS/DS)	Ratio(B)	Total Node	Ratio(F)	S (PS/DS)	Ratio(B)	Total Node	Ratio(F)	S (PS/DS)	Ratio(B)
	Set 4				Set 5				Set 6		
100	10%	*[a]	8:1:1	100	20%	*	8:1:1	100	30%	*	8:1:1
100	10%	*	6:2:2	100	20%	*	6:2:2	100	30%	*	6:2:2
100	10%	*	4:3:3	100	20%	*	4:3:3	100	30%	*	4:3:3
100	10%	*	6:3:1	100	20%	*	6:3:1	100	30%	*	6:3:1
100	10%	*	6:1:3	100	20%	*	6:1:3	100	30%	*	6:1:3

Total Node	F	S	Ratio(F)	Total Node	F	S	Ratio(F)	Total Node	F	S	Ratio(F)
	Set 7				Set 8				Set 9		
20	2	*	10%	20	4	*	20%	20	6	*	30%
50	5	*	10%	50	10	*	20%	50	15	*	30%
100	10	*	10%	100	10	*	20%	100	30	*	30%
200	20	*	10%	200	40	*	20%	200	60	*	30%

Total Node	Ratio(F)	S	Ratio(B)	Total Node	Ratio(B)	Ratio(F)	Total Node	Ratio(B)	Ratio(F)
	Set 10				Set 11			Set 12	
100	10%	ac	9:1	20	8:2	10%, 20%, 30%	100	9:1	10%, 20%, 30%
100	10%	ac	8:2	50	8:2	10%, 20%, 30%	100	8:2	10%, 20%, 30%
100	10%	ac	7:3	100	8:2	10%, 20%, 30%	100	7:3	10%, 20%, 30%
100	10%	ac	6:4	200	8:2	10%, 20%, 30%	100	6:4	10%, 20%, 30%
100	10%	ac	5:5	-	-	10%, 20%, 30%	100	5:5	10%, 20%, 30%
100	10%	ac	4:6	-	-	10%, 20%, 30%	100	4:6	10%, 20%, 30%

[a] "*" represents the strategies of ade/abe/abd

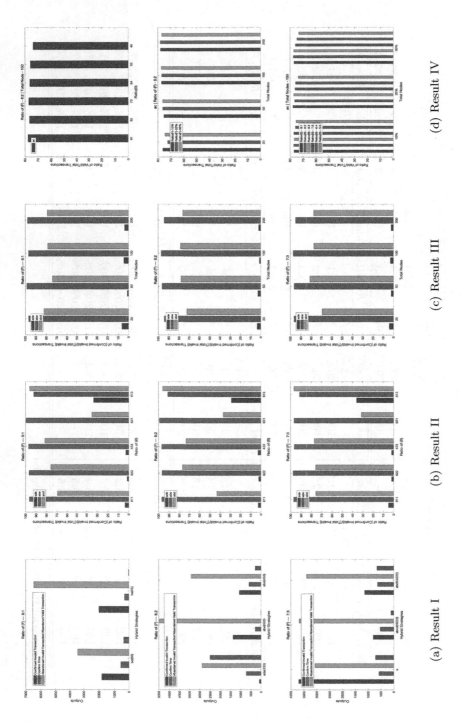

Fig. 1. Testing results for attack strategies (Appendix B)

(a) Result I   (b) Result II   (c) Result III   (d) Result IV

types of attacks with evaluations. To achieve that, we abstract main components of Tangle to rebuild a simple network for the simulation. Then, we informally define three smallest actions to build up attack strategies layer by layer. Finally, we provide analyses and discussions on different attacks in multiple dimensions. Our study provide a complete cycle of analysis through the simulation.

References

1. Acharya, A., et al.: CellTree: a new paradigm for distributed data repositories (2019)
2. Bu, G., Gürcan, Ö., Potop-Butucaru, M.: G-IOTA: fair and confidence aware tangle. In: IEEE INFOCOM WKSHPS, pp. 644–649. IEEE (2019)
3. Castro, M., et al.: Practical Byzantine fault tolerance. In: OSDI, pp. 173–186 (1999)
4. Ferraro, P., King, C., Shorten, R.: IOTA-based directed acyclic graphs without orphans. arXiv preprint arXiv:1901.07302 (2018)
5. Gervais, A., et al.: On the security and performance of proof of work blockchains. In: ACM SIGSAC CCS, pp. 3–16 (2016)
6. Kusmierz, B.: The first glance at the simulation of the tangle: discrete model (2017). http://iota.org
7. Li, C., Li, P., Zhou, D., Xu, W., Long, F., Yao, A.: Scaling nakamoto consensus to thousands of transactions per second. arXiv preprint arXiv:1805.03870 (2018)
8. Popov, S.: The tangle (2016). http://iota.org
9. Popov, S., et al.: Equilibria in the tangle. arXiv preprint arXiv:1712.05385 (2017)

Tightly Secure Chameleon Hash Functions in the Multi-user Setting and Their Applications

Xiangyu Liu[1,2], Shengli Liu[1,2,3(✉)], and Dawu Gu[1]

[1] Department of Computer Science and Engineering, Shanghai Jiao Tong University, Shanghai 200240, China
{xiangyu_liu,slliu,dwgu}@sjtu.edu.cn
[2] State Key Laboratory of Cryptology, P.O. Box 5159, Beijing 100878, China
[3] Westone Cryptologic Research Center, Beijing 100070, China

Abstract. We define the security notion of strong collision resistance for chameleon hash functions in the multi-user setting (S-MU-CR security). We also present three specific constructions CHF_{dl}, CHF_{rsa} and CHF_{fac} of chameleon hash functions, and prove their tight S-MU-CR security based on the discrete logarithm, RSA and factoring assumptions, respectively. In applications, we show that tightly S-MU-CR secure chameleon hash functions can lift a signature scheme from (weak) unforgeability to strong unforgeability with a tight security reduction in the multi-user setting.

Keywords: Chameleon hash functions · Tight security · Multi-user setting · Signatures

1 Introduction

Chameleon hash function (CHF) has been studied for decades since it was first introduced by Krawczyk and Rabin [11]. Informally, CHF is a special hash function indexed by a hash key, which is associated with a trapdoor. On the one hand, it has the property of collision resistance, i.e., it is hard to find a collision given the hash key only. On the other hand, one can easily find collisions with the help of the trapdoor. Over the years, various constructions of CHF were proposed [4,7,13], and they found wide applications in signatures (SIG) [6,11–13].

Tight Security. Generally, the collision resistance of CHF is proved by security reduction. That is, once an adversary finds a collision for CHF with probability ϵ, then another algorithm can be built to make use of the collision, and solve some well-known hard problem with success probability ϵ/L. The parameter L is called the security loss factor. If L is a constant, the security reduction is tight. And if L is a polynomial of security parameter λ, the security reduction is loose. With a loose security reduction, the deployments of CHF (and other primitives) have to be equipped with a larger security parameter to compensate the loss

© Springer Nature Switzerland AG 2020
J. K. Liu and H. Cui (Eds.): ACISP 2020, LNCS 12248, pp. 664–673, 2020.
https://doi.org/10.1007/978-3-030-55304-3_36

factor L. This yields larger elements and slower computations. For instance, if $L \approx 2^{30}$, there will be a great efficiency loss.

Most constructions of CHF consider single user setting only. In the era of IoT, cryptographic primitives are deployed in systems of multi-users. Hence, it is important for us to consider tight security of CHF in the multi-user setting. With hybrid argument, collision resistance of CHF in single user setting implies collision resistance in the multi-user setting, but with a security loss factor $L = \mu$, where μ is the number of users. In consideration of wide applications of CHF, it is desirable for us to exploit tight collision resistance for CHF.

Related Works. In [11], Krawczyk and Rabin gave two constructions of chameleon hash functions. One is a generic construction from "claw-free" trapdoor permutations [8], and is implemented based on the factoring assumption. The other is based on the discrete logarithm (DL) assumption. Later, numerous constructions of CHFs are proposed in [1,2,7,13], to name a few.

In [4], Bellare and Ristov proved that CHFs and Sigma protocols are equivalent. Due to this equivalence, many new chameleon hash functions CHF_{fs}, CHF_{ms}, CHF_{oka}, CHF_{hs} are obtained from well-studied Sigma protocols. Meanwhile, some variants of CHFs came up in needs of different applications, like identity-based CHF [1], key-exposure free CHF [2], etc.

CHFs have found numerous applications in different types of signatures. The first application of CHF is chameleon signatures [11], which provide non-transferability. In [13], Shamir and Tauman gave a generic construction from (traditional) signature to online/offline signature with the help of CHF. Consequently many proxy signatures are constructed based on CHF [6,12]. Meanwhile, CHF can also be used to strengthen a (weakly) unforgeable signature to a strong unforgeable one [5,14].

Most of these constructions consider single user setting only. Though they also work in the multi-user setting, but the price is a great security loss factor μ. As far as we know, there is no research considering tight security of CHF in the multi-user setting, and that is exactly the focus of this paper.

Tight Strong Multi-user Collision Resistance of CIIF. We define the security notion of strong multi-user collision resistance (S-MU-CR) for CHFs. In the multi-user setting, each user has its own hash key/trapdoor pair, and each hash key determines a specific chameleon hash function. Informally, S-MU-CR security means that after seeing all the hash keys, the adversary cannot find a collision under a specific hash key of its choice.

Over the years, there are lots of proposals of CHFs, which are tightly secure in single user setting. For example, the chameleon hash function CHF_{claw} from the claw-free permutations [11], CHF_{st} from the factoring assumption by Shamir and Tauman [13], CHF_{rsa-n} from the RSA$[n, n]$ assumption [2], CHF_{vsh} from the very smooth hash [7], CHF_{ms} from the Micali-Shamir protocol [4], etc. We believe that it is hard for these CHFs to achieve tight S-MU-CR security. Let us take CHF_{st} as an example. Each user has trapdoor (p_i, q_i) and hash key $N_i = p_i q_i$. In the security reduction, the factoring problem instance N is embedded into a specific

$N_j := N$. However, the adversary chooses N_j as its target with probability $1/\mu$. As a result, the security loss factor is at least μ.

Nevertheless, we identify some CHFs, like CHF_{dl} [11], CHF_{rsa} [1] and CHF_{fac} [4], and prove their tight S-MU-CR security based on the DL, RSA and factoring assumptions, respectively. Intuitively, the DL problem and RSA problem are random self-reducible. For example, given one DL instance (g, g^x), we can create multiple instances (g, g^{x+b_i}), so that the DL problem can be embedded into hash keys of all users. As for CHF_{fac}, we embed the factoring problem instance into the public parameter, which is shared by all users. In this way, no matter which target hash key is chosen by the adversary, the collision can be used to solve the hard problem. That is why tight S-MU-CR security can be achieved.

Applications of Tightly S-MU-CR Secure CHF to Signatures. By using our tightly secure CHFs, we can extend the GBSW transform [14] to the multi-user setting, which lifts a SIG from (weak) unforgeability (MU-EUF-CMA) to strong unforgeability (S-MU-EUF-CMA) with a tight security reduction. Furthermore, we can cope with corruptions through the "double-key" mechanism [3], and get a tightly S-MU-EUF-CMA^{Corr} secure SIG, see Fig. 1.

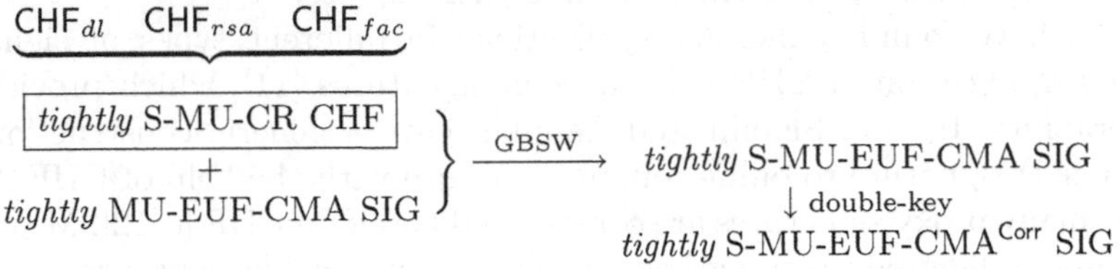

Fig. 1. Applications of tightly S-MU-CR secure CHF to signatures.

Our Contribution

1. We define the security notion of *strong multi-user collision resistance (S-MU-CR)* for chameleon hash functions (CHF). Then we present three constructions (CHF_{dl}, CHF_{rsa} and CHF_{fac}) of CHF and prove their tight S-MU-CR security based on the discrete logarithm, RSA and factoring assumptions, respectively.
2. We extend the generic GBSW transform to the multi-user setting, resulting in tightly S-MU-EUF-CMA secure signature schemes.

2   Preliminaries

Let $\lambda \in \mathbb{N}$ denote the security parameter. For $\mu \in \mathbb{N}$, define $[\mu] := \{1, 2, ..., \mu\}$. Denote by $x := y$ the operation of assigning y to x. Denote by $x \xleftarrow{\$} \mathcal{X}$ the operation of sampling x uniformly at random from a set $\mathcal{X}$. For an algorithm $\mathcal{A}$, denote by $y \leftarrow \mathcal{A}(x)$, the operation of running $\mathcal{A}$ with input x and assigning the output to y. "PPT" is short for probabilistic polynomial-time.

Definition 1 (Chameleon Hash Family). *A chameleon hash family (CHF) consists of four algorithms, namely* CHF = (Setup, KGen, Eval, TdColl).

- Setup(1^λ) *takes as input the security parameter* 1^λ, *and outputs public parameter* pp, *which determines the key space* $\mathcal{HK} \times \mathcal{TD}$, *input domains* $\mathcal{M} \times \mathcal{R}$, *and range* $\mathcal{Y}$. *Here* pp *is an implicit input of* Eval *and* TdColl.
- KGen(pp) *takes as input* pp, *and outputs a hash key* $hk \in \mathcal{HK}$ *along with a trapdoor* $td \in \mathcal{TD}$. *Here* hk *determines a specific chameleon hash function* $H_{hk}(\cdot, \cdot)$ *in the chameleon hash family* $\mathsf{H} = \{H_{hk}(\cdot, \cdot)\}_{hk \in \mathcal{HK}}$.
- Eval(hk, m, r) *takes as input* hk, $m \in \mathcal{M}$ *and* $r \in \mathcal{R}$, *and outputs the hash value* $h = H_{hk}(m, r)$.
- TdColl(td, m_1, r_1, m_2) *takes as input* td, (m_1, r_1), *and another message* m_2, *and outputs* r_2 *such that* $H_{hk}(m_1, r_1) = H_{hk}(m_2, r_2)$.

CHF *is strongly secure if it has the following two properties.*

Strong Collision Resistance (S-CR). *For any PPT adversary* $\mathcal{A}$, *the advantage* $\mathsf{Adv}^{\text{s-cr}}_{\mathsf{CHF},\mathcal{A}}(\lambda)$ *is negligible, where* $\mathsf{Adv}^{\text{s-cr}}_{\mathsf{CHF},\mathcal{A}}(\lambda) :=$

$$\Pr\left[\begin{array}{l} \mathsf{pp} \leftarrow \mathsf{Setup}(1^\lambda); (hk, td) \leftarrow \mathsf{KGen}(\mathsf{pp}); \\ (m_1, r_1, m_2, r_2) \leftarrow \mathcal{A}(\mathsf{pp}, hk) \end{array} : \begin{array}{l} H_{hk}(m_1, r_1) = H_{hk}(m_2, r_2) \\ \wedge (m_1, r_1) \neq (m_2, r_2) \end{array}\right].$$

Random Trapdoor Collision (RTC). *For* $\forall\, hk, td, m_1, m_2$, *if* r_1 *is distributed uniformly over* $\mathcal{R}$, *then* $r_2 := \mathsf{TdColl}(td, m_1, r_1, m_2)$ *enjoys a uniform distribution over* $\mathcal{R}$.

Now we extend the S-CR security of CHF to the multi-user setting.

Definition 2. *A chameleon hash family* CHF *is strongly secure in the multi-user setting if it has RTC property and strong multi-user collision resistance.*

Strong Multi-User Collision Resistance (S-MU-CR). *For any PPT adversary* $\mathcal{A}$, *the advantage* $\mathsf{Adv}^{\text{s-mu-cr}}_{\mathsf{CHF},\mu,\mathcal{A}}(\lambda)$ *is negligible, where* $\mathsf{Adv}^{\text{s-mu-cr}}_{\mathsf{CHF},\mu,\mathcal{A}}(\lambda) :=$

$$\Pr\left[\begin{array}{l} \mathsf{pp} \leftarrow \mathsf{Setup}(1^\lambda); (hk_i, td_i) \leftarrow \mathsf{KGen}(\mathsf{pp}) \text{ for } i \in [\mu]; \\ (i^*, m_1, r_1, m_2, r_2) \leftarrow \mathcal{A}(\mathsf{pp}, \{hk_i\}_{i \in [\mu]}) \end{array} : \begin{array}{l} H_{hk_{i*}}(m_1, r_1) = H_{hk_{i*}}(m_2, r_2) \\ \wedge (m_1, r_1) \neq (m_2, r_2) \end{array}\right].$$

3 Tightly Secure Chameleon Hash Functions in the Multi-user Setting

3.1 Chameleon Hash Family Based on the DL Assumption

Let GGen be a group generation algorithm that outputs a cyclic group $\mathbb{G}$ of prime order q with generator g. In formula, $\mathcal{G} := (\mathbb{G}, q, g) \leftarrow \mathsf{GGen}(1^\lambda)$.

Definition 3 (The DL Assumption). *The discrete logarithm (DL) assumption states that for any PPT adversary* $\mathcal{A}$, $\mathsf{Adv}^{\text{dl}}_{\mathbb{G},\mathcal{A}}(\lambda)$ *is negligible, where*

$$\mathsf{Adv}^{\text{dl}}_{\mathbb{G},\mathcal{A}}(\lambda) := \Pr[(\mathbb{G}, q, g) \leftarrow \mathsf{GGen}(1^\lambda); x \xleftarrow{\$} \mathbb{Z}_q : \mathcal{A}(\mathbb{G}, q, g, g^x) = x].$$

Setup(1^λ):	Eval(hk, m, r):
$(\mathbb{G}, q, g) \leftarrow \mathsf{GGen}(1^\lambda)$ Return $\mathsf{pp} := (\mathbb{G}, q, g, \mathcal{M} := \mathbb{Z}_q, \mathcal{R} := \mathbb{Z}_q, \mathcal{Y} := \mathbb{G})$	Return $h := hk^m \cdot g^r$
KGen(pp):	TdColl(td, m_1, r_1, m_2):
$x \xleftarrow{\$} \mathbb{Z}_q; X := g^x$ Return $(hk := X, td := x)$	$r_2 := td \cdot (m_1 - m_2) + r_1 \mod q$ Return r_2

Fig. 2. Construction of CHF$_{dl}$.

The construction of CHF$_{dl}$[1] [11] is shown in Fig. 2.

Theorem 1. *CHF$_{dl}$ has tight strong security in the multi-user setting based on the DL assumption. More precisely, for any PPT adversary $\mathcal{A}$ with advantage* $\mathsf{Adv}^{\mathsf{s\text{-}mu\text{-}cr}}_{\mathsf{CHF}_{dl},\mu,\mathcal{A}}(\lambda)$*, there exists a PPT algorithm $\mathcal{B}$ such that* $\mathsf{Adv}^{\mathsf{s\text{-}mu\text{-}cr}}_{\mathsf{CHF}_{dl},\mu,\mathcal{A}}(\lambda) \leq \mathsf{Adv}^{\mathsf{dl}}_{\mathbb{G},\mathcal{B}}(\lambda)$.

Proof. It is easy to prove the RTC property. For any $td = x$, $r_1 \in \mathbb{Z}_q$, $m_1, m_2 \in \mathbb{Z}_q$, we have $r_2 := x \cdot (m_1 - m_2) + r_1$. Hence, if r_1 is independently chosen from $\mathbb{Z}_q$ uniformly at random, then r_2 is uniform over $\mathbb{Z}_q$ as well.

Next we construct a PPT algorithm $\mathcal{B}$ and prove $\mathsf{Adv}^{\mathsf{s\text{-}mu\text{-}cr}}_{\mathsf{CHF}_{dl},\mu,\mathcal{A}}(\lambda) \leq \mathsf{Adv}^{\mathsf{dl}}_{\mathbb{G},\mathcal{B}}(\lambda)$. $\mathcal{B}$ gets a group description $\mathcal{G} = (\mathbb{G}, q, g)$ along with a challenge $(g, X = g^x)$ from its DL challenger. $\mathcal{B}$ directly sets $\mathsf{pp} := (\mathbb{G}, q, g, \mathcal{M}, \mathcal{R}, \mathcal{Y})$ with $\mathcal{M} := \mathbb{Z}_q$, $\mathcal{R} := \mathbb{Z}_q$, $\mathcal{Y} := \mathbb{G}$. For $i \in [\mu]$, $\mathcal{B}$ samples $b_i \xleftarrow{\$} \mathbb{Z}_q$, and sets $hk_i := X \cdot g^{b_i}$. In this way, $\mathcal{B}$ implicitly sets $td_i := x_i := x + b_i$. Then $\mathcal{B}$ sends pp and $\{hk_i\}_{i \in [\mu]}$ to $\mathcal{A}$. Finally $\mathcal{A}$ outputs $(i^*, m_1, r_1, m_2, r_2)$. If $m_1 \neq m_2$, $\mathcal{B}$ outputs $(r_2 - r_1)/(m_1 - m_2) - b_{i^*}$ as its answer to the DL problem.

If $\mathcal{A}$ successfully finds a collision, then $g^{x_{i^*} m_1 + r_1} = g^{x_{i^*} m_2 + r_2}$ and $(m_1, r_1) \neq (m_2, r_2)$. We must have $m_1 \neq m_2$ (otherwise $r_1 = r_2$) and $x_{i^*} = (r_2 - r_1)/(m_1 - m_2)$. As a result, $x := x_{i^*} - b_{i^*}$ is the correct answer to the DL problem. $\square$

3.2 Chameleon Hash Family Based on the RSA Assumption

Let RSAGen be an algorithm that outputs an RSA tuple (N, p, q, e, d), where p, q are safe primes of bit-length $\lambda/2$, $N = pq$ and $ed \equiv 1 \mod \varphi(N)$. In formula, $(N, p, q, e, d) \leftarrow \mathsf{RSAGen}(1^\lambda)$. Here we limit that e is a prime and $e > 2^{L(\lambda)}$, where $L(\cdot)$ is the challenge length function associated with RSAGen.

Definition 4 (The RSA Assumption). *The RSA assumption states that for any PPT adversary $\mathcal{A}$, $\mathsf{Adv}^{\mathsf{rsa}}_{N,e,\mathcal{A}}(\lambda)$ is negligible, where*

$$\mathsf{Adv}^{\mathsf{rsa}}_{N,e,\mathcal{A}}(\lambda) := \Pr[(N, p, q, e, d) \leftarrow \mathsf{RSAGen}(1^\lambda); x \xleftarrow{\$} \mathbb{Z}_N^* : \mathcal{A}(N, e, x^e) = x].$$

The construction of CHF$_{rsa}$ [1,4] is shown in Fig. 3.

---

[1] Here we compute the hash value with $h = X^m \cdot g^r$ instead of $h = g^m \cdot X^r$ as in [11].

Setup(1^λ):	Eval(hk, m, r):
$(N, p, q, e, d) \leftarrow \mathsf{RSAGen}(1^\lambda)$; $\ell := L(\lambda)$	$h := hk^m \cdot r^e \mod N$
Return pp $:= (N, e, \mathcal{M} := \{0,1\}^\ell, \mathcal{R} := \mathbb{Z}_N^*, \mathcal{Y} := \mathbb{Z}_N^*)$	Return h
KGen(pp):	TdColl(td, m_1, r_1, m_2):
$x \xleftarrow{\$} \mathbb{Z}_N^*$; $X := x^e \mod N$	$r_2 := td^{m_1 - m_2} \cdot r_1 \mod N$
Return ($hk := X, td := x$)	Return r_2

Fig. 3. Construction of CHF_{rsa}.

Theorem 2. CHF_{rsa} *has tight strong security in the multi-user setting based on the RSA assumption. More precisely, for any PPT adversary $\mathcal{A}$ with advantage* $\mathsf{Adv}^{\mathsf{s\text{-}mu\text{-}cr}}_{\mathsf{CHF}_{rsa}, \mu, \mathcal{A}}(\lambda)$, *there exists a PPT algorithm $\mathcal{B}$ such that* $\mathsf{Adv}^{\mathsf{s\text{-}mu\text{-}cr}}_{\mathsf{CHF}_{rsa}, \mu, \mathcal{A}}(\lambda) \leq$ $\mathsf{Adv}^{\mathsf{rsa}}_{N, e, \mathcal{B}}(\lambda)$.

Proof. Recall that $\mathbb{Z}_N^*$ is a multiplicative group. For any fixed $td - x$ and $m_1, m_2 \in \{0,1\}^\ell$, if r_1 is uniform over $\mathbb{Z}_N^*$, then $r_2 := x^{m_1 - m_2} \cdot r_1$ is also uniform. This gives the RTC property of CHF_{rsa}.

Next we construct a PPT algorithm $\mathcal{B}$ and prove $\mathsf{Adv}^{\mathsf{s\text{-}mu\text{-}cr}}_{\mathsf{CHF}_{rsa}, \mu, \mathcal{A}}(\lambda) \leq$ $\mathsf{Adv}^{\mathsf{rsa}}_{N, e, \mathcal{B}}(\lambda)$. $\mathcal{B}$ gets (N, e) and $X = x^e$ from its challenger, where $x \xleftarrow{\$} \mathbb{Z}_N^*$. The public parameter is set as pp $:= (N, e, \mathcal{M}, \mathcal{R}, \mathcal{Y})$ with $\mathcal{M} := \{0,1\}^\ell, \mathcal{R} :=$ $\mathbb{Z}_N^*, \mathcal{Y} := \mathbb{Z}_N^*$. For $i \in [\mu]$, $\mathcal{B}$ samples $b_i \xleftarrow{\$} \mathbb{Z}_N^*$ and sets $hk_i := X_i = X \cdot b_i^e$. In this way, $\mathcal{B}$ implicitly sets $td_i := x_i := x \cdot b_i$. Then $\mathcal{B}$ sends pp and $\{hk_i\}_{i \in [\mu]}$ to $\mathcal{A}$. Finally $\mathcal{A}$ outputs $(i^*, m_1, r_1, m_2, r_2)$, and $\mathcal{B}$ outputs $(r_2/r_1)^\beta \cdot X_{i^*}^\alpha \cdot b_{i^*}^{-1}$ as its answer to the RSA problem, where $\alpha e + \beta(m_1 - m_2) = 1$.

Suppose $\mathcal{A}$ successfully finds a collision. That is, $H_{X_{i^*}}(m_1, r_1) = H_{X_{i^*}}(m_2, r_2)$, so $(x_{i^*}^{m_1} \cdot r_1)^e = (x_{i^*}^{m_2} \cdot r_2)^e$. Note that $f_e : x \mapsto x^e$ is a bijection over $\mathbb{Z}_N^*$. Hence $x_{i^*}^{m_1} \cdot r_1 = x_{i^*}^{m_2} \cdot r_2$, equivalently $x_{i^*}^{m_1 - m_2} = r_2/r_1$. We must have $m_1 \neq m_2$, otherwise $r_1 = r_2$ and $\mathcal{A}$ fails. Let α, β be two integers s.t. $\alpha e + \beta(m_1 - m_2) = 1$ (α and β can always be found since e is a prime and $e > 2^{L(\lambda)}$), then $x_{i^*} = (r_2/r_1)^\beta \cdot X_{i^*}^\alpha$. And $x := x_{i^*}/b_{i^*}$ is the correct answer to the RSA problem. $\qquad \square$

3.3 Chameleon Hash Family Based on the Factoring Assumption

Let FacGen be an algorithm that outputs (N, p, q), where p, q are safe primes of bit-length $\lambda/2$ and $N = pq$. In formula, $(N, p, q) \leftarrow \mathsf{FacGen}(1^\lambda)$.

Definition 5 (The Factoring Assumption). *The factoring assumption states that for any PPT adversary $\mathcal{A}$, $\mathsf{Adv}^{\mathsf{fac}}_{N, \mathcal{A}}(\lambda)$ is negligible, where*

$$\mathsf{Adv}^{\mathsf{fac}}_{N, \mathcal{A}}(\lambda) := \Pr[(N, p, q) \leftarrow \mathsf{FacGen}(1^\lambda) : \mathcal{A}(N) = p \ \vee \ \mathcal{A}(N) = q].$$

Define $\mathbb{Z}_N^+ := \mathbb{Z}_N^* \cap \{1, ..., N/2\}$. For $m \in \{0,1\}^\ell$, denote by m_k the k-th bit of m. The construction of CHF_{fac} [4] is shown in Fig. 4.

Setup(1^λ):	Eval(hk, m, r):
$(N, p, q) \leftarrow \mathsf{FacGen}(1^\lambda); \ell := \mathsf{poly}(\lambda)$	Parse $hk = (u_1, ..., u_\ell)$
Return $\mathsf{pp} := (N, \mathcal{M} := \{0,1\}^\ell, \mathcal{R} := \mathbb{Z}_N^+, \mathcal{Y} := \mathbb{QR}_N)$	Return $h := \prod_{k=1}^\ell u_k^{m_k} \cdot r^2 \mod N$
KGen(pp):	TdColl(td, m_1, r_1, m_2):
For $k \in [\ell]$:	Parse $td = (s_1, ..., s_\ell)$
$\quad s_k \xleftarrow{\$} \mathbb{Z}_N^*; u_k := s_k^2 \mod N$	$r_2 := \prod_{k=1}^\ell s_k^{m_{1,k} - m_{2,k}} \cdot r_1$
Return $(hk := (u_1, ..., u_\ell), td := (s_1, ..., s_\ell))$	Return $r_2 := \min\{r_2, N - r_2\}$

Fig. 4. Construction of CHF_{fac}.

Theorem 3. CHF_{fac} *has tight strong security in the multi-user setting based on the factoring assumption. More precisely, for any PPT adversary $\mathcal{A}$ with advantage $\mathsf{Adv}^{\mathsf{s\text{-}mu\text{-}cr}}_{\mathsf{CHF}_{fac}, \mu, \mathcal{A}}(\lambda)$, there exists a PPT algorithm $\mathcal{B}$ such that $\mathsf{Adv}^{\mathsf{s\text{-}mu\text{-}cr}}_{\mathsf{CHF}_{fac}, \mu, \mathcal{A}}(\lambda) \leq 2\mathsf{Adv}^{\mathsf{fac}}_{N, \mathcal{B}}(\lambda)$.*

Proof. For the proof of RTC property, consider fixed values of $td = (s_1, ..., s_\ell)$, $m_1, m_2 \in \{0,1\}^\ell$. We have $r_2 := \min\{\tau \cdot r_1, N - \tau \cdot r_1\}$, where $\tau = \prod_{k=1}^\ell s_k^{m_{1,k} - m_{2,k}}$ is some fixed value in $\mathbb{Z}_N^*$. For $r_1, r_1' \in \mathbb{Z}_N^+$ with $r_1 \neq r_1'$, neither $\tau \cdot r_1 \equiv \tau \cdot r_1'$ nor $\tau(r_1 + r_1') \equiv 0 \mod N$, i.e., no two distinct inputs correspond to the same output. Hence the function $f_\tau(r_1) := \min\{\tau \cdot r_1, N - \tau \cdot r_1\}$ is an injection (hence bijection) over $\mathbb{Z}_N^+$, and $r_2 := f_\tau(r_1)$ is uniformly random as long as r_1 is.

Next we construct a PPT algorithm $\mathcal{B}$ and prove $\mathsf{Adv}^{\mathsf{s\text{-}mu\text{-}cr}}_{\mathsf{CHF}_{fac}, \mu, \mathcal{A}}(\lambda) \leq 2\mathsf{Adv}^{\mathsf{fac}}_{N, \mathcal{B}}(\lambda)$. $\mathcal{B}$ gets N from its own challenger. The public parameter is set as $\mathsf{pp} := (N, \mathcal{M}, \mathcal{R}, \mathcal{Y})$ with $\mathcal{M} := \{0,1\}^\ell, \mathcal{R} := \mathbb{Z}_N^+, \mathcal{Y} := \mathbb{QR}_N$. For $i \in [\mu], k \in [\ell]$, $\mathcal{B}$ samples $s_{i,k} \xleftarrow{\$} \mathbb{Z}_N^*$ and sets $u_{i,k} := s_{i,k}^2$. In this way, $hk_i = (u_{i,1}, ..., u_{i,\ell})$ and $td_i = (s_{i,1}, ..., s_{i,\ell})$. Then $\mathcal{B}$ sends pp and $\{hk_i\}_{i \in [\mu]}$ to $\mathcal{A}$.

If $\mathcal{A}$ finds a collision with output $(i^*, m_1, r_1, m_2, r_2)$, then

$$\prod_{k=1}^\ell (u_{i^*, k})^{m_{1,k}} \cdot r_1^2 = \prod_{k=1}^\ell (u_{i^*, k})^{m_{2,k}} \cdot r_2^2. \tag{1}$$

Case 1. $m_1 = m_2$ but $r_1 \neq r_2$.

In this case, Eq. (1) implies $r_1^2 \equiv r_2^2 \mod N$, i.e., $(r_1 + r_2)(r_1 - r_2) \equiv 0 \mod N$. Note that $r_1, r_2 \in \mathbb{Z}_N^+$ and $r_1 \neq r_2$. Thus, $\mathcal{B}$ can always find a factor of N by outputting $\gcd(r_1 + r_2, N)$.

Case 2. $m_1 \neq m_2$. Then there must exist $z \in [\ell]$ such that $m_{1,z} \neq m_{2,z}$. We can rewrite Eq. (1) as

$$(u_{i^*, z})^{m_{1,z} - m_{2,z}} = \prod_{k \neq z} (u_{i^*, k})^{m_{2,k} - m_{1,k}} \cdot (r_2 / r_1)^2. \tag{2}$$

$$\iff \left((s_{i^*, z})^{m_{1,z} - m_{2,z}} \right)^2 = \left(\prod_{k \neq z} (s_{i^*, k})^{m_{2,k} - m_{1,k}} \cdot (r_2 / r_1) \right)^2. \tag{3}$$

We denote the right part of Eq.(3) by Δ^2. Note that $m_{1,z} - m_{2,z} = \pm 1$.

- If $m_{1,z} - m_{2,z} = 1$, then Eq. (3) is simplified to $(s_{i^*,z})^2 = \Delta^2$, and $\mathcal{B}$ outputs $\gcd(s_{i^*,z} + \Delta, N)$.
- If $m_{1,z} - m_{2,z} = -1$, then Eq. (3) is simplified to $(s_{i^*,z}^{-1})^2 = \Delta^2$, and $\mathcal{B}$ outputs $\gcd(s_{i^*,z}^{-1} + \Delta, N)$.

Recall that $s_{i^*,z}$ is chosen randomly in $\mathbb{Z}_N^*$, and the only information $\mathcal{A}$ gets is $u_{i^*,z} = (s_{i^*,z})^2$. Thus, $s_{i^*,z} \notin \{\Delta, N - \Delta\}$ with probability $1/2$, or $s_{i^*,z}^{-1} \notin \{\Delta, N - \Delta\}$ with probability $1/2$. In either case, $\mathcal{B}$ successfully factors N with probability $1/2$. $\qquad\square$

Remark 1. CHF_{dl}, CHF_{rsa} and CHF_{fac} are originally proposed in [1,4,11], but their collision resistance security are proved in the single user setting.

Remark 2. For a chameleon hash family H, we can extend the message space from $\mathcal{M}$ to bit strings of any polynomial length by applying a traditional collision resistant hash function to the message first [11].

4 Generic Transform for Signatures from MU-EUF-CMA Security to S-MU-EUF-CMA Security

Due to space limitation, we assume familiarity with the syntax and standard security notions for signature (SIG) schemes, and leave them in the full version.

In [14], Steinfeld, Pieprzyk and Wang proposed a generic transform (the GBSW transform), which can invert an EUF-CMA secure SIG to a S-EUF-CMA secure SIG. The GBSW transform is (security) tightness preserving, but limited only in single user setting. By using our strongly secure CHFs, we are able to extend the GBSW transform to the multi-user setting, which strengthens SIG from weak unforgeability (MU-EUF-CMA) to strong unforgeability (S-MU-EUF-CMA) and enjoys a tight security reduction.

The GBSW Transform [14]. Let $\mathsf{S} = (\mathsf{S.Setup}, \mathsf{S.KGen}, \mathsf{S.Sign}, \mathsf{S.Ver})$ be a SIG with EUF-CMA security, and Γ, H be two CHFs with strong security (i.e., S-CR security and RTC property). Define $\mathsf{S_{GBSW}}$ as follows.

1. $\mathsf{S_{GBSW}.Setup}(1^\lambda)$. Invoke $\mathsf{pp_S} \leftarrow \mathsf{S.Setup}(1^\lambda)$, $\mathsf{pp_F} \leftarrow \mathsf{F.Setup}(1^\lambda)$, $\mathsf{pp_H} \leftarrow \mathsf{H.Setup}(1^\lambda)$, and return $\mathsf{pp_{S_{GBSW}}} := (\mathsf{pp_S}, \mathsf{pp_F}, \mathsf{pp_H})$.
2. $\mathsf{S_{GBSW}.KGen}(\mathsf{pp_{S_{GBSW}}})$. Invoke $(vk, sk) \leftarrow \mathsf{S.KGen}(\mathsf{pp_S})$, $(hk_\mathsf{F}, td_\mathsf{F}) \leftarrow \mathsf{F.KGen}(\mathsf{pp_F})$, $(hk_\mathsf{H}, td_\mathsf{H}) \leftarrow \mathsf{H.KGen}(\mathsf{pp_H})$, compute $vk_{\mathsf{S_{GBSW}}} := (vk, hk_\mathsf{F}, hk_\mathsf{H})$, $sk_{\mathsf{S_{GBSW}}} := (sk, td_\mathsf{H}, hk_\mathsf{F}, hk_\mathsf{H})$, and return $(vk_{\mathsf{S_{GBSW}}}, sk_{\mathsf{S_{GBSW}}})$.
3. $\mathsf{S_{GBSW}.Sign}(sk_{\mathsf{S_{GBSW}}}, m)$.
   (a) Choose random r', s;
   (b) Choose random m', σ', and compute $h := H_{hk_\mathsf{H}}(m'||\sigma', r')$;
   (c) Compute $\bar{m} := F_{hk_\mathsf{F}}(h, s)$ and $\sigma \leftarrow \mathsf{S.Sign}(sk, \bar{m})$;
   (d) Invoke $r \leftarrow \mathsf{H.TdColl}(td_\mathsf{H}, m'||\sigma', r', m||\sigma)$, return $\sigma_{\mathsf{S_{GBSW}}} := (\sigma, r, s)$.
4. $\mathsf{S_{GBSW}.Ver}(vk_{\mathsf{S_{GBSW}}}, m, \sigma_{\mathsf{S_{GBSW}}})$.
   (a) Compute $h := H_{hk_\mathsf{H}}(m||\sigma, r)$, $\bar{m} := F_{hk_\mathsf{F}}(h, s)$;
   (b) Return $\mathsf{S.Ver}(vk, \bar{m}, \sigma)$.

The Extended GBSW Transform. The transform is similar to the GBSW transform, except that the building block S is replaced with a SIG with MU-EUF-CMA security[2], and F, H are replaced with CHFs with S-MU-CR security and RTC property.

Theorem 4. *If* F *and* H *are strongly secure in the multi-user setting,* S *is MU-EUF-CMA secure, then the extended GBSW transform results in a S-MU-EUF-CMA secure signature scheme* S_{GBSW}. *More precisely, for any PPT adversary* $\mathcal{A}$ *with advantage* $\mathsf{Adv}^{\text{s-mu-euf-cma}}_{S_{GBSW},\mu,\mathcal{A}}(\lambda)$, *there exist PPT adversaries* $\mathcal{B}_S, \mathcal{B}_F$ *and* $\mathcal{B}_H$, *such that* $\mathsf{Adv}^{\text{s-mu-euf-cma}}_{S_{GBSW},\mu,\mathcal{A}}(\lambda) \leq \mathsf{Adv}^{\text{mu-euf-cma}}_{S,\mu,\mathcal{B}_S}(\lambda) + \mathsf{Adv}^{\text{s-mu-cr}}_{F,\mu,\mathcal{B}_F}(\lambda) + \mathsf{Adv}^{\text{s-mu-cr}}_{H,\mu,\mathcal{B}_H}(\lambda)$.

Note that the underlying building blocks are tightly secure. On the one hand, the reduction algorithm can answer signing queries with the help of trapdoors of H&F and signing keys of S. On the other hand, once the adversary generates a valid forgery message-signature pair under i^*, then either it forges a signature for a new message under i^*, or it finds a collision of H or F w.r.t. hk_H or hk_F. That is why our extended GBSW transform can achieve tight security in the multi-user setting. We refer the reader to the full version for the details.

Extension to SIG Against Adaptive Corruptions. The adversary may corrupt some users and get their signing keys in some applications, and the security is formalized by the notion MU-EUF-CMA^{Corr} security [3]. Similarly, we also have S-MU-EUF-CMA^{Corr} security for SIG. Note that we have S-MU-EUF-CMA secure SIGs, then we can use the "double-key" mechanism [3,9] to cope with corruptions and get a S-MU-EUF-CMA^{Corr} secure SIG (as shown in Fig. 1). See the full version for details.

Acknowledgments. This work is supported by National Natural Science Foundation of China (61925207, 61672346, U1636217), Guangdong Major Project of Basic and Applied Basic Research (2019B030302008), and Major Project of the Ministry of Industry and Information Technology of China (2018-36).

References

1. Ateniese, G., de Medeiros, B.: Identity-based chameleon hash and applications. In: Juels, A. (ed.) FC 2004. LNCS, vol. 3110, pp. 164–180. Springer, Heidelberg (2004). https://doi.org/10.1007/978-3-540-27809-2_19
2. Ateniese, G., de Medeiros, B.: On the key exposure problem in chameleon hashes. In: Blundo, C., Cimato, S. (eds.) SCN 2004. LNCS, vol. 3352, pp. 165–179. Springer, Heidelberg (2005). https://doi.org/10.1007/978-3-540-30598-9_12
3. Bader, C., Hofheinz, D., Jager, T., Kiltz, E., Li, Y.: Tightly-secure authenticated key exchange. In: Dodis, Y., Nielsen, J.B. (eds.) TCC 2015. LNCS, vol. 9014, pp. 629–658. Springer, Heidelberg (2015). https://doi.org/10.1007/978-3-662-46494-6_26
4. Bellare, M., Ristov, T.: A characterization of chameleon hash functions and new, efficient designs. J. Cryptol. **27**(4), 799–823 (2014). https://doi.org/10.1007/s00145-013-9155-8

---

[2] Tightly MU-EUF-CMA secure SIG schemes can be found in [10,15,16].

5. Boneh, D., Shen, E., Waters, B.: Strongly unforgeable signatures based on computational Diffie-Hellman. In: Yung, M., Dodis, Y., Kiayias, A., Malkin, T. (eds.) PKC 2006. LNCS, vol. 3958, pp. 229–240. Springer, Heidelberg (2006). https://doi.org/10.1007/11745853_15

6. Chandrasekhar, S., Chakrabarti, S., Singhal, M., Calvert, K.L.: Efficient proxy signatures based on trapdoor hash functions. IET Inf. Secur. **4**(4), 322–332 (2010). https://doi.org/10.1049/iet-ifs.2009.0204

7. Contini, S., Lenstra, A.K., Steinfeld, R.: VSH, an efficient and provable collision-resistant hash function. In: Vaudenay, S. (ed.) EUROCRYPT 2006. LNCS, vol. 4004, pp. 165–182. Springer, Heidelberg (2006). https://doi.org/10.1007/11761679_11

8. Damgård, I.B.: Collision free hash functions and public key signature schemes. In: Chaum, D., Price, W.L. (eds.) EUROCRYPT 1987. LNCS, vol. 304, pp. 203–216. Springer, Heidelberg (1988). https://doi.org/10.1007/3-540-39118-5_19

9. Gjøsteen, K., Jager, T.: Practical and tightly-secure digital signatures and authenticated key exchange. In: Shacham, H., Boldyreva, A. (eds.) CRYPTO 2018. LNCS, vol. 10992, pp. 95–125. Springer, Cham (2018). https://doi.org/10.1007/978-3-319-96881-0_4

10. Hofheinz, D., Jager, T.: Tightly secure signatures and public-key encryption. Des. Codes Crypt. **80**(1), 29–61 (2015). https://doi.org/10.1007/s10623-015-0062-x

11. Krawczyk, H., Rabin, T.: Chameleon hashing and signatures. IACR Cryptology ePrint Archive 1998, 10 (1998). http://eprint.iacr.org/1998/010

12. Mehta, M., Harn, L.: Efficient one-time proxy signatures. IEE Proc. - Commun. **152**(2), 129–133 (2005)

13. Shamir, A., Tauman, Y.: Improved online/offline signature schemes. In: Kilian, J. (ed.) CRYPTO 2001. LNCS, vol. 2139, pp. 355–367. Springer, Heidelberg (2001). https://doi.org/10.1007/3-540-44647-8_21

14. Steinfeld, R., Pieprzyk, J., Wang, H.: How to strengthen any weakly unforgeable signature into a strongly unforgeable signature. In: Abe, M. (ed.) CT-RSA 2007. LNCS, vol. 4377, pp. 357–371. Springer, Heidelberg (2006). https://doi.org/10.1007/11967668_23

15. Zhang, X., Liu, S., Gu, D., Liu, J.K.: A generic construction of tightly secure signatures in the multi-user setting. Theor. Comput. Sci. **775**, 32–52 (2019). https://doi.org/10.1016/j.tcs.2018.12.012

16. Zhang, X., Liu, S., Pan, J., Gu, D.: Tightly secure signature schemes from the LWE and subset sum assumptions. Theor. Comput. Sci. **795**, 326–344 (2019). https://doi.org/10.1016/j.tcs.2019.07.015

Author Index

Printed in the United States
By Bookmasters